Global Visual and Material Culture
Beginnings to 1800

OCAD University
LBST 1B04

Taken from:
Art History, Fourth Edition
by Marilyn Stokstad and Michael W. Cothren

Graphic Design History: A Critical Guide, Second Edition
by Johanna Drucker and Emily McVarish

Compiled and Edited by
Keith Bresnahan, Bonnie Devine, and Ryan Whyte
Plus Eric Nay and Kathryn Shailer

Pearson Learning Solutions, 501 Boylston Street, Suite 900, Boston, MA 02116
A Pearson Education Company
www.pearsoned.com

Printed in Canada

1 2 3 4 5 6 7 8 9 10 V0YA 17 16 15 14 13 12

000200010271671990

CG/JG

ISBN 10: 1-256-84805-0
ISBN 13: 978-1-256-84805-9

Copyright Acknowledgments

BRIEF CONTENTS

CONTENTS vi • PEARSON CHOICES AND RESOURCES xi • ACKNOWLEDGMENTS AND GRATITUDE xii •
USE NOTES xiv • STARTER KIT xv

1 INTRODUCTION: GLOBAL BEGINNINGS
   (HUNTER-GATHERER SOCIETIES) 1

2 BEGINNINGS OF SETTLED COMMUNITIES:
   AGRICULTURE, WRITING, RELIGION 64

3 EGYPT, GREECE, AND ROME 149

4 SCULPTURE: FROM ABSTRACTION TO
   NATURALISM, SACRED TO SECULAR 251

5 ISLAM, BYZANTIUM, ANCIENT NEAR EAST
   MONOTHEISM: RELIGIONS OF THE BOOK 304

6 CATHEDRALS AND CRUSADES: EUROPE AND
   ITS NEIGHBORS IN THE MIDDLE AGES 403

7 EMPIRES IN ASIA: FROM MONGOLS
   TO MUGHALS 451

8 THE AMERICAS 484

9 TECHNIQUE, TEXTILES, AND TEXT 529

10 HIGH ART IN EUROPE 575

11 REVOLUTIONS IN PRINTING 653

INDEX 698

CONTENTS

PEARSON CHOICES AND RESOURCES xi • ACKNOWLEDGMENTS AND GRATITUDE xii • USE NOTES xiv • STARTER KIT xv

1 INTRODUCTION: GLOBAL BEGINNINGS (HUNTER-GATHERER SOCIETIES) 1

THOUGHT PIECE 1
WHAT IS ART? 2
WHAT IS ART HISTORY? 4
 Assessing Physical Properties 4
 Analyzing Formal Structure 7
 Identifying Subject Matter 8

PREHISTORIC ART 10
THE STONE AGE 11
THE PALEOLITHIC PERIOD 11
 Shelter or Architecture? 13
 Artifacts or Works of Art? 14
 Cave Painting 17
 Cave Sculptures 21
THE NEOLITHIC PERIOD 22
 Architecture 22
 Sculpture and Ceramics 29
NEW METALLURGY, ENDURING STONE 31
 The Bronze Age 31
 Rock Carvings 32

EARLY AFRICAN ART 36
THE LURE OF ANCIENT AFRICA 37
AFRICA—THE CRADLE OF ART AND CIVILIZATION 37
AFRICAN ROCK ART 37
 Saharan Rock Art 38
SUB-SAHARAN CIVILIZATIONS 39
 Nok 40

ART OF PACIFIC CULTURES 43
THE PEOPLING OF THE PACIFIC 44
AUSTRALIA 45
MELANESIA 46
 New Guinea 47
 New Ireland 49
 New Britain 50
MICRONESIA 50
POLYNESIA 52
 Marquesas Islands 53
 Hawaii 56
 Monumental Moai on Rapa Nui 57
 Samoa 58
ADDITIONAL READINGS 59

BOXES
■ ART AND ITS CONTEXTS
Art and Architecture 3
The Power of Naming 15
Intentional House Burning 29
The Myth of "Primitive" Art 39
Southern African Rock Art 41

■ THE OBJECT SPEAKS
Prehistoric Woman and Man 33
Te-Hau-ki-Turanga 54
■ A CLOSER LOOK
Visual Elements of Pictorial Expression Line, Light, Form, and Color. 5
A House in Çatalhöyük 24
■ ELEMENTS OF ARCHITECTURE
Early Construction Methods 25
■ TECHNIQUE
Prehistoric Wall Painting 19
Pottery and Ceramics 31
■ RECOVERING THE PAST
How Early Art is Dated 21

2 BEGINNINGS OF SETTLED COMMUNITIES: AGRICULTURE, WRITING, RELIGION 64

THOUGHT PIECE 64
ART OF THE ANCIENT NEAR EAST 68
THE FERTILE CRESCENT AND MESOPOTAMIA 69
 Sumer 69
 Akkad 74
 Ur and Lagash 77
 Babylon 78

ART OF SOUTH AND SOUTHEAST ASIA BEFORE 1200 81
THE INDIAN SUBCONTINENT 82
INDUS CIVILIZATION 82
THE VEDIC PERIOD 85
THE MAURYA PERIOD 85
THE PERIOD OF THE SHUNGAS AND EARLY ANDHRAS 88
 Stupas 88
 Buddhist Rock-Cut Halls 92
THE KUSHAN AND LATER ANDHRA PERIODS 92
 The Gandhara Style 93
 The Mathura Style 93
 The Southeast Indian Style 95
THE MIDDLE KINGDOM 96
NEOLITHIC CULTURES 96
 Painted Pottery Cultures 96
 Liangzhu Culture 96
BRONZE AGE CHINA 98
 Shang Dynasty 98
 Zhou Dynasty 99
THE CHINESE EMPIRE: QIN DYNASTY 102
HAN DYNASTY 102
 Philosophy and Art 103
 Architecture 105

PREHISTORIC JAPAN 106
Jomon Period 106
Yayoi Period 106
Kofun Period 106

ASUKA PERIOD 109
Horyuji 110

NARA PERIOD 111

ART OF THE AMERICAS BEFORE 1300 115

THE NEW WORLD 116

MESOAMERICA 116
The Olmec 116
Teotihuacan 119
The Maya 122

CENTRAL AMERICA 128

SOUTH AMERICA: THE CENTRAL ANDES 129
Chavin de Huantar 129
The Paracas and Nazca Cultures 130
The Moche Culture 131

FROM PREHISTORY TO EARLY WRITING, 35,000–500 BCE 135

MARK-MAKING 135

PREHISTORY 135

PROTO-WRITING 136

EARLY WRITING 137

THE SPREAD OF WRITING AS IDEA AND SCRIPT 139

THE ALPHABET 140

CONCLUSION 141
Tools of the Trade 146

ADDITIONAL READINGS 147

BOXES

■ ART AND ITS CONTEXTS
Art as Spoils of War—Protection or Theft? 73
The Code of Hammurabi 79
Buddhism 87
Hinduism 88
Mudras 94
Chinese Characters 101
Daoism 104
Writing, Language, and Culture 107
Buddhist Symbols 112
Maya Writing 123
The Cosmic Ballgame 127

■ THE OBJECT SPEAKS
A Lyre from a Royal Tomb in Ur 75

■ A CLOSER LOOK
Rubbing of a Stone Relief 105
Maya Stela 125

■ ELEMENTS OF ARCHITECTURE
Stupas and Temples 91

■ TECHNIQUE
Cuneiform Writing 71
Piece-mold Casting 99
Andean Textiles 132

CHAPTER

3

EGYPT, GREECE,
AND ROME **149**

THOUGHT PIECE 149

ART OF ANCIENT EGYPT 151

THE GIFT OF THE NILE 152

EARLY DYNASTIC EGYPT, C. 2950–2575 BCE 152
The God-Kings 152
Artistic Conventions 153
Funerary Architecture 155

THE OLD KINGDOM, C. 2575–2150 BCE 157
The Great Pyramids at Giza 157
Sculpture 161
Pictorial Relief in Tombs 163

THE MIDDLE KINGDOM, C. 1975–C. 1640 BCE 164
Portraits of Senusret III 164
Rock-cut Tombs 164
Funerary Stelae 165
Town Planning 166

THE NEW KINGDOM, C. 1539–1075 BCE 166
The Great Temple Complexes 167
Hatshepsut 169
The Tomb of Ramose 171
Akhenaten and the Art of the Amarna Period 172
The Return to Tradition: Tutankhamun and Ramses II 174
The Books of the Dead 178

THE THIRD INTERMEDIATE PERIOD, C. 1075–715 BCE 180

LATE EGYPTIAN ART, C. 715–332 BCE 181

ART OF ANCIENT GREECE 183

THE EMERGENCE OF GREEK CIVILIZATION 184
Historical Background 184
Religious Beliefs and Sacred Places 184

GREEK ART C. 900–C. 600 BCE 184
The Geometric Period 184
The Orientalizing Period 187

THE ARCHAIC PERIOD, C. 600–480 BCE 189
The Sanctuary at Delphi 189
Temples 190
Ceramic Painting 196

THE HIGH CLASSICAL PERIOD, C. 450–400 BCE 196
The Acropolis 197
The Parthenon 198
The Temple of Athena Nike 204
The Athenian Agora 204
City Plans 204
Stele Sculpture 206
The Julio-Claudians 207
Roman Cities and the Roman Home 207
Wall Painting 210
The Flavians 216
Imperial Architecture 219
Imperial Portraits 227
Constantine the Great 229
Roman Art after Constantine 231

CLASSICAL LITERACY 700 BCE–400 CE 238

VARIATIONS OF LITERACY AND THE ALPHABET 238

THE FUNCTION OF GRAPHIC CODES 241

MODELS OF WRITING: GESTURAL AND CONSTRUCTED 245

WRITING AT THE END OF THE CLASSICAL AGE 247

CONCLUSION 248

BOXES

■ ART AND ITS CONTEXTS
Egyptian Symbols 153
Greek and Roman Deities 186
Who Owns the Art? The Elgin Marbles and the
   Euphronios Krater 203
Women at a Fountain House 205

■ THE OBJECT SPEAKS
The Temples of Ramses II at Abu Simbel 176

■ A CLOSER LOOK
The Palette of Narmer 154

■ ELEMENTS OF ARCHITECTURE
Mastaba to Pyramid 157
The Greek Orders 192

Roman Vaulting   217
Concrete   224

■ **TECHNIQUE**
Preserving the Dead   158
Egyptian Pictorial Relief   167
Glassmaking   175
Color in Greek Sculpture   195
"The Canon of Polykleitos"   202

■ **RECOVERING THE PAST**
The Rosetta Stone   179
The Mildenhall Treasure   233

CHAPTER 4
SCULPTURE: FROM ABSTRACTION TO NATURALISM, SACRED TO SECULAR   251

THOUGHT PIECE   251
THE FOURTH THROUGH SEVENTH CENTURIES   252
Buddhist Sculpture   252
Painting   252
The Early Northern Temple   254
Monumental Narrative Reliefs   255
The Early Southern Temple   258
THE EIGHTH THROUGH THE FOURTEENTH CENTURIES   258
The Monumental Northern Temple   259
The Monumental Southern Temple   263
The Bhakti Movement in Art   264
ART OF SOUTHEAST ASIA   265
Free-standing Sculpture   270
Marble Sculpture   273
Bronze Sculpture   274
Sculpture   277
The Art of the Goldsmith   280
Sculpture   280
THE ROMANS   288
Origins of Rome   288
Roman Religion   289
THE REPUBLIC, 509–27 BCE   289
Portrait Sculpture   289
Roman Temples   293
THE EARLY EMPIRE, 27 BCE–96 CE   294
Art in the Age of Augustus   294
Imperial Portraits   296
THE LATE EMPIRE, THIRD AND FOURTH CENTURIES CE   299
The Severan Dynasty   299
The Soldier Emperors   301

BOXES

■ **ART AND ITS CONTEXTS**
Meaning and Ritual in Hindu Temples and Images   256
Classic and Classical   274
The Celts   282
Roman Writers on Art   289
Roman Portraiture   290

■ **THE OBJECT SPEAKS**
Shiva Nataraja of the Chola Dynasty   260

■ **A CLOSER LOOK**
"Descent of the Ganges" Relief   259
Sarcophagus with the Indian Triumph of Dionysus   303

■ **ELEMENTS OF ARCHITECTURE**
The Roman Arch   292

■ **TECHNIQUE**
Roman Mosaics   298

CHAPTER 5
ISLAM, BYZANTIUM, ANCIENT NEAR EAST MONOTHEISM: RELIGIONS OF THE BOOK   304

THOUGHT PIECE   304
THE HITTITES OF ANATOLIA   305
ASSYRIA   305
Kalhu   305
Dur Sharrukin   307
Nineveh   309
NEO-BABYLONIA   309
PERSIA   310
JEWISH, EARLY CHRISTIAN, AND BYZANTINE ART   315
JEWS, CHRISTIANS, AND MUSLIMS   316
Early Jewish Art   316
Early Christian Art   320
IMPERIAL CHRISTIAN ARCHITECTURE AND ART   324
Architecture   324
Sculpture   327
Ravenna   328
EARLY BYZANTINE ART   331
The Golden Age of Justinian   331
Objects of Veneration and Devotion   340
Icons and Iconoclasm   342
MIDDLE BYZANTINE ART   344
Architecture and Mosaics   345
Objects of Veneration and Devotion   350
LATE BYZANTINE ART   352
Constantinople: The Chora Church   352
Moscow: Rublyov   357
ISLAMIC ART   359
ISLAM AND EARLY ISLAMIC SOCIETY   360
ART AND ARCHITECTURE THROUGH THE FOURTEENTH CENTURY   363
Early Architecture   363
THE LATER PERIOD   368
Architecture of the Mediterranean   369
Architecture of the East   373
Portable Arts   374
The Arts of the Book   377
Manuscript Painting   378
ART AND ARCHITECTURE OF THE THREE EMPIRES   380
The Ottoman Empire   380
The Safavid Dynasty   383
Mughal Dynasty   386
THE MODERN ERA   387
ADDITIONAL READINGS   388

BOXES

■ **ART AND ITS CONTEXTS**
Narrative and Iconic   322
The Life of Jesus   329
Naming Christian Churches: Designation + Dedication + Location   337
Scroll and Codex   341
Iconoclasm   344
The Five Pillars of Islam   365

■ **THE OBJECT SPEAKS**
The Funerary Chapel of Theodore Metochites   354
The Great Mosque of Cordoba   366

■ **A CLOSER LOOK**
Enemies Crossing the Euphrates to Escape Assyrian Archers   307
The Mosaic Floor of the Beth Alpha Synagogue   319
A Mamluk Glass Oil Lamp   371

■ **ELEMENTS OF ARCHITECTURE**
Longitudinal-Plan and Central-Plan Churches   326
Pendentives and Squinches   334
Arches   369

■ **TECHNIQUE**
Textiles   309
Ornament   362
Carpet Making   384

■ **RECOVERING THE PAST**
Dura-Europos   321

CHAPTER 6
CATHEDRALS AND CRUSADES: EUROPE AND ITS NEIGHBORS IN THE MIDDLE AGES   403

THOUGHT PIECE   403

THE EARLY MIDDLE AGES   404

THE ART OF THE "BARBARIANS" IN EUROPE   405
The Merovingians   405
The Norse   407
The Celts and Anglo-Saxons in Britain   407

ROMANESQUE ART   409

EUROPE IN THE ROMANESQUE PERIOD   410
Political and Economic Life   410
The Church   410

ROMANESQUE ART   411

ARCHITECTURE   412
"First Romanesque"   413
Pilgrimage Churches   413
Cluny   416
The Cistercians   419
Regional Styles in Romanesque Architecture   420
Secular Architecture: Dover Castle, England   428

ARCHITECTURAL SCULPTURE   429
Wiligelmo at the Cathedral of Modena   430
The Priory Church of Saint-Pierre at Moissac   430
The Church of Saint-Lazare at Autun   433

SCULPTURE IN WOOD AND BRONZE   436
Christ on the Cross (Majestat Batlló)   436
Mary as the Throne of Wisdom   436
Tomb of Rudolf of Swabia   437
Renier of Huy   438

TEXTILES AND BOOKS   438
Chronicling History   439
Sacred Books   442

ADDITIONAL READINGS   446

BOXES

■ **ART AND ITS CONTEXTS**
Defining the Middle Ages   405
The Pilgrim's Journey   414
Relics and Reliquaries   418
St. Bernard and Theophilus: The Monastic Controversy over
the Visual Arts   420
The Paintings of San Climent in Taull: Mozarabic Meets
Byzantine   424
Hildegard of Bingen   443

■ **THE OBJECT SPEAKS**
The Bayeux Embroidery   440

■ **A CLOSER LOOK**
The Last Judgment Tympanum at Autun   434

■ **ELEMENTS OF ARCHITECTURE**
The Romanesque Church Portal   429

■ **RECOVERING THE PAST**
Sutton Hoo   408

CHAPTER 7
EMPIRES IN ASIA: FROM MONGOLS TO MUGHALS   451

THOUGHT PIECE   451
Vietnamese Ceramics   452
Indonesian Traditions   452

MUGHAL PERIOD   452
Mughal Architecture   453
Mughal Painting   455
Rajput Painting   458

INDIA'S ENGAGEMENT WITH THE WEST   460
British Colonial Period   460
The Modern Period   461

THE MONGOL INVASIONS   464

YUAN DYNASTY   465

MING DYNASTY   467
Court and Professional Painting   468
Decorative Arts   470
Architecture and City Planning   471
The Literati Aesthetic   472

QING DYNASTY   476
Orthodox Painting   477
Individualist Painting   477

THE MODERN PERIOD   478

ARTS OF KOREA: THE JOSEON DYNASTY TO
THE MODERN ERA   479
Joseon Ceramics   479
Joseon Painting   480
Modern Korea   482

BOXES

■ **ART AND ITS CONTEXTS**
Foundations of Chinese Culture   465
Marco Polo   466

■ **THE OBJECT SPEAKS**
Luxury Arts   456
Poet on a Mountaintop   474

■ **A CLOSER LOOK**
Private Audience Hall, Fatehpur Sikri   454
Spring Dawn in the Han Palace   470

■ **TECHNIQUE**
Indian Painting on Paper   458
Formats of Chinese Painting   469
The Secret of Porcelain   471

CHAPTER 8
THE AMERICAS   484

THOUGHT PIECE   484

ART OF THE AMERICAS AFTER 1300   485

THE AZTEC EMPIRE   486
Tenochtitlan   486
Sculpture   487
Featherwork   488
Manuscripts   489

THE INCA EMPIRE   489
Cuzco   491
Machu Picchu   491
Textiles   492
Metalwork   493
The Aftermath of the Spanish Conquest   493

NORTH AMERICA   493
The Eastern Woodlands   494
The Great Plains   496
The Northwest Coast   499
The Southwest   502

ADDITIONAL READINGS   505

BOXES

■   ART AND ITS CONTEXTS
Navajo Night Chant   504

■ THE OBJECT SPEAKS
Hamatsa Masks   500

■ A CLOSER LOOK
Calendar Stone   490

■ ELEMENTS OF ARCHITECTURE
Inca Masonry   492

■ TECHNIQUE
Basketry   495

CHAPTER **9** TECHNIQUE, TEXTILES, AND TEXT   **529**

THOUGHT PIECE   529
Manuscript Illumination   530
Metalwork and Ivory   530

ENGLAND   533
Embroidery: Opus Anglicanum   533

ADDITIONAL READINGS   536

BOXES

■ ART AND ITS CONTEXTS
The Black Death   531

■ THE OBJECT SPEAKS
An Ivory Chest with Scenes of Romance   534

■ A CLOSER LOOK
The Hours of Jeanne d'Évreux   532
A Goldsmith in His Shop   536

CHAPTER **10** HIGH ART IN EUROPE   **575**

THOUGHT PIECE   575

RENAISSANCE ART IN FIFTEENTH-CENTURY ITALY   577
HUMANISM AND THE ITALIAN RENAISSANCE   578
FLORENCE   578
Architecture   579
Sculpture   586
Painting   593
Painting in Florence after Masaccio   596

SIXTEENTH-CENTURY ART IN ITALY   601
EUROPE IN THE SIXTEENTH CENTURY   602
ITALY IN THE EARLY SIXTEENTH CENTURY: THE HIGH
    RENAISSANCE   602
Three Great Artists of the Early Sixteenth Century   603
ART AND THE COUNTER-REFORMATION   616
Art and Architecture in Rome and the Vatican   616

SIXTEENTH-CENTURY ART IN NORTHERN EUROPE AND
THE IBERIAN PENINSULA   621
THE REFORMATION AND THE ARTS   622
GERMANY   623
Sculpture   623
Painting   625

SEVENTEENTH-CENTURY ART IN EUROPE   632
"BAROQUE"   633
ITALY   633
Architecture and Sculpture in Rome   633
Painting   639
France   647
Architecture and its Decoration at Versailles   649

BOXES
■ ART AND ITS CONTEXTS
The Competition Reliefs   585
The Vitruvian Man   607
Science and the Changing Worldview   648
Academies and Academy Exhibitions   652

■ THE OBJECT SPEAKS
The Foundling Hospital   582
Caravaggio in the Contarelli Chapel   644

■ A CLOSER LOOK
The School of Athens   610

■ TECHNIQUE
Renaissance Perspective   592
German Metalwork: A Collaborative Venture   624

CHAPTER **11** REVOLUTIONS IN PRINTING   **653**

THOUGHT PIECE   653
THE GRAPHIC ARTS   653
Single Sheets   653
Printed Books   654

ADDITIONAL READINGS   656

INDEX   698

Ordering Options

Art History is offered in a variety of formats to suit any course need, whether your survey is Western, global, comprehensive or concise, online or on the ground. Please contact your local representative for ordering details or visit www.pearsonhighered.com/art. In addition to this combined hardcover edition, *Art History* may be ordered in the following formats:

Volume I, Chapters 1–17 (ISBN: 978-0-205-74420-6)
Volume II, Chapters 17–32 (ISBN: 978-0-205-74421-3)

Art History **Portable Edition** has all of the same content as the comprehensive text in six slim volumes. Available in value-package combinations (Books 1, 2, 4, and 6) to suit **Western-focused survey** courses or available individually for period or region specific courses.
Book 1: Ancient Art, Chapters 1–6
Book 2: Medieval Art, Chapters 7, 8, 14–17
Book 3: A View of the World: Part One, Chapters 8–13
Book 4: Fourteenth to Seventeenth Century Art, Chapters 17–22
Book 5: A View of the World: Part Two, Chapters 23–28
Book 6: Eighteenth to Twenty-first Century Art, Chapters 29–32

Books À La Carte Give your students flexibility and savings with the new Books à la Carte edition of *Art History*. This edition features exactly the same content as the traditional textbook in a convenient three-hole-punched, loose-leaf version—allowing students to take only what they need to class. The Books à la Carte edition costs less than a used text—which helps students save about 35% over the cost of a new book.
Volume I, Books à la Carte Edition, 4/e
(ISBN: 978-0-205-79557-4)
Volume II, Books à la Carte Edition, 4/e
(ISBN: 978-0-205-79558-1)

 **CourseSmart Textbooks Online** is an exciting new choice for students looking to save money. As an alternative to purchasing the print textbook, students can subscribe to the same content online and save up to 50% off the suggested list price of the print text. For more information, or to subscribe to the CourseSmart eTextbook, visit www.coursesmart.com.

Combined Volume (ISBN: 978-0-205-80032-2)
Volume I (ISBN: 978-0-205-00189-7)
Volume II (ISBN: 978-0-205-00190-3)

Digital Resources

 **www.myartslab.com** This dynamic website provides a wealth of resources geared to meet the diverse teaching and learning needs of today's instructors and students. Keyed specifically to the chapters of *Art History*, Fourth Edition, MyArtsLab's many tools will encourage students to experience and interact with works of art. Here are some of the key features:

- A complete **Pearson e-Text** of the book, enriched with multi-media, including: a unique human scale figure by all works of fine art, an audio version of the text read by the author, primary source documents, video demonstrations, and much more. Students can highlight, make notes and bookmark pages.
- 360 degree **Architectural Panoramas** for most of the major monuments in the book help students understand buildings from the inside and out.
- **Closer Look Tours** These interactive walkthroughs offer an in-depth look at key works of art, enabling the student to zoom in to see detail they could not otherwise see on the printed page or even in person. Enhanced with expert audio, they help students understand the meaning and message behind the work of art.
- A **Gradebook** that reports progress of students and the class as a whole.
- Instructors can also download the Instructor's Manual & Test Item File, PowerPoint questions for Classroom Response Systems, and obtain the PearsonMyTest assessment generation program.
- **MyArtsLab with e-Text** is available for no additional cost when packaged with any version of *Art History*, 4/e; it is also available standalone for less than the cost of a used text, and it is also available without e-Text for an even lower price.

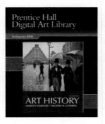 **The Prentice Hall Digital Art Library** Instructors who adopt *Art History* are eligible to receive this unparalleled resource containing all of the images in *Art History* at the highest resolution (over 300 dpi) and pixellation possible for optimal projection and easy download. This resource features over 1,600 illustrations in jpeg and in PowerPoint, an instant download function for easy import into any presentation software, along with a unique zoom and "Save Detail" feature. (ISBN: 978-0-205-80037-7)

ACKNOWLEDGMENTS AND GRATITUDE

Art History, which was first published in 1995 by Harry N. Abrams, Inc. and Prentice Hall, Inc., continues to rely, each time it is revised, on the work of many colleagues and friends who contributed to the original texts and subsequent editions. Their work is reflected here, and we extend to them our enduring gratitude.

In preparing this fourth edition, we worked closely with two gifted and dedicated editors at Pearson/Prentice Hall, Sarah Touborg and Helen Ronan, whose almost daily support in so many ways was at the center of our work and created the foundation of what we have done. At Pearson, Barbara Cappuccio, Marlene Gassler, Melissa Feimer, Cory Skidds, Brian Mackey, David Nitti, and Carla Worner also supported us in our work. For the design we thank Kathy Mrozek and John Christiana. At Laurence King Publishing, Melissa Danny, Sophie Page, Kara Hattersley-Smith, Julia Ruxton and Simon Walsh oversaw the production of this new edition. We are very grateful for the editing of Cynthia Ward, Margaret Manos, and Robert Shore. For layout design we thank Nick Newton and for photo research we thank Emma Brown. Much appreciation also goes to Brandy Dawson, Director of Marketing, and Kate Stewart Mitchell, Marketing Manager, as well as the entire Social Sciences and Arts team at Pearson.

From Marilyn Stokstad:

The fourth edition of *Art History* represents the cumulative efforts of a distinguished group of scholars and educators. The work done by Stephen Addiss, Chutsing Li, Marylin M. Rhie, and Christopher D. Roy for the original edition has been updated and expanded by David Binkley and Patricia Darish (Africa), Claudia Brown and Robert Mowry (China and Korea), Patricia Graham (Japan), and Rick Asher (South and Southeast Asia). Joy Sperling has reworked the modern material previously contributed by Patrick Frank, David Cateforis and Bradford R. Collins. Dede Ruggles (Islamic), Claudia Brittenham (Americas), and Carol Ivory (Pacific Cultures) also have contributed to the fourth edition.

In addition, I want to thank University of Kansas colleagues Sally Cornelison, Susan Craig, Susan Earle, Charles Eldredge, Kris Ercums, Valija Evalds, Sherry Fowler, Stephen Goddard, Saralyn Reece Hardy, Marsha Haufler, Marni Kessler, Amy McNair, John Pulz, Linda Stone Ferrier, and John Younger for their help and advice. My thanks also to my friends Katherine Giele and Katherine Stannard, David and Nancy Dinneen, William Crowe, David Bergeron, Geraldo de Sousa, and the entire Clement family for their sympathy and encouragement. Of course, my very special thanks go to my sister, Karen Leider, and my niece, Anna Leider.

From Michael Cothren:

Words are barely adequate to express my gratitude to Marilyn Stokstad for welcoming me with such trust, enthusiasm, and warmth into the collaborative adventure of revising this book. Working alongside her—and our extraordinary editors Sarah Touborg and Helen Ronan—has been delightful and rewarding, enriching and challenging. I look forward to continuing the partnership.

My work was greatly facilitated by two extraordinary research assistants, Fletcher Coleman and Andrew Finegold, who found materials and offered opinions just when I needed them. I also have been supported by a host of colleagues at Swarthmore College. Generations of students challenged me to hone my pedagogical skills and steady my focus on what is at stake in telling the history of art. My colleagues in the Art Department—especially Stacy Bomento, June Cianfrana, Randall Exon, Constance Cain Hungerford, Janine Mileaf, Patricia Reilly, and Tomoko Sakomura—have answered all sorts of questions, shared innumerable insights on works in their areas of expertise, and offered unending encouragement and support. I am so lucky to work with them. In Classics, Gil Rose and William Turpin generously shared their expertise in Latin.

Many art historians have provided assistance, often at a moment's notice, and I am especially grateful to Betina Bergman, Claudia Brown, Brigitte Buettner, Madeline Caviness, Cheri Falkenstien-Doyle, Ed Gyllenhaal, Julie Hochstrasser, Penny Jolly, Alison Kettering, Benton Kidd, Ann Kuttner, Cary Liu, Elizabeth Marlowe, Thomas Morton, Mary Shepard, David Simon, Donna Sadler, Jeffrey Chipps Smith, and Mark Tucker.

I was fortunate to have the support of many friends. John Brendler, David Eldridge, Tricia Kramer, Stephen Lehmann, Mary Marissen, Bianca O'Keefe, and Bruce and Carolyn Stephens, patiently listened and truly relished my enjoyment of this work.

My mother and my late father, Mildred and Wat Cothren believed in me and made significant sacrifices to support my education from pre-school to graduate school. My extraordinary daughters Emma and Nora are a constant inspiration. I am so grateful for their delight in my passion for art's history, and for their dedication to keeping me from taking myself too seriously. My deepest gratitude is reserved for Susan Lowry, my wife and soul-mate, who brings joy to every facet of my life. She was not only patient and supportive during the long distraction of my work on this book; she provided help in so very many ways. The greatest accomplishment of my life in art history occurred on the day I met her at Columbia in 1973.

If the arts are ultimately an expression of human faith and integrity as well as human thought and creativity, then writing and producing books that introduce new viewers to the wonders of art's history, and to the courage and visions of the artists and art historians that stand behind it—remains a noble undertaking. We feel honored to be a part of such a worthy project.

Marilyn Stokstad
Lawrence, KS

Michael W. Cothren
Swarthmore, PA

Winter 2010

In Gratitude:

As its predecessors did, this Fourth Edition of *Art History* benefited from the reflections and assessments of a distinguished team of scholars and educators. The authors and Pearson are grateful to the following academic reviewers for their numerous insights and suggestions for improvement:

Craig Adcock, University of Iowa
Kimberly Allen-Kattus, Northern Kentucky University
Susan Jane Baker, University of Houston
Stephen Caffey, Texas A & M University
Charlotte Lowry Collins, Southeastern Louisiana University
Cindy B. Damschroder, University of Cincinnati
Rachael Z. DeLue, Princeton University
Anne Derbes, Hood College
Caroline Downing, State University of New York at Potsdam
Suzanne Eberle, Kendall College of Art & Design of Ferris State University
April Eisman, Iowa State University
Allen Farber, State University of New York at Oneonta
Richard Gay, University of North Carolina - Pembroke
Regina Gee, Montana State University
Mimi Hellman, Skidmore College
Julie Hochstrasser, University of Iowa
Evelyn Kain, Ripon College
Nancy Kelker, Middle Tennessee State University
Patricia Kennedy, Ocean County College
Jennie Klein, Ohio University
Katie Kresser, Seattle Pacific University
Cynthia Kristan-Graham, Auburn University
Barbara Platten Lash, Northern Virginia Community College
Elisa C. Mandell, California State University, Fullerton
Elizabeth C. Mansfield, New York University
Pamela Margerm, Kean University
Elizabeth Marlowe, Colgate University
Marguerite Mayhall, Kean University
Katherine A. McIver, University of Alabama at Birmingham
Janine Mileaf, Swarthmore College
Johanna D. Movassat, San Jose State University
Jacqueline Marie Musacchio, Wellesley College
Lynn Ostling, Santa Rosa Junior College
Ariel Plotek, Clemson University
Patricia V. Podzorski, University of Memphis
Margaret Richardson, George Mason University
James Rubin, Stony Brook University
Donna Sandrock, Santa Ana College
Michael Schwartz, Augusta State University
Joshua A. Shannon, University of Maryland
Karen Shelby, Baruch College
Susan Sidlauskas, Rutgers University
Royce W. Smith, Wichita State University
Jeffrey Chipps Smith, University of Texas - Austin
Stephen Smithers, Indiana State University
Laurie Sylwester, Columbia College (Sonora)
Carolyn Tate, Texas Tech University
Rita Tekippe, University of West Georgia
Amelia Trevelyan, University of North Carolina at Pembroke
Julie Tysver, Greenville Technical College
Jeryn Woodard, University of Houston

This edition has continued to benefit from the assistance and advice of scores of other teachers and scholars who generously answered questions, gave recommendations on organization and priorities, and provided specialized critiques during the course of work on previous editions.

We are grateful for the detailed critiques that the following readers across the country who were of invaluable assistance during work on the third edition:

Charles M. Adelman, University of Northern Iowa; Fred C. Albertson, University of Memphis; Frances Altvater, College of William and Mary; Michael Amy, Rochester Institute of Technology; Jennifer L. Ball, Brooklyn College, CUNY; Samantha Baskind, Cleveland State University; Tracey Boswell, Johnson County Community College; Jane H. Brown, University of Arkansas at Little Rock; Roger J. Crum, University of Dayton; Brian A. Curran, Penn State University; Michael T. Davis,

Mount Holyoke College; Juilee Decker, Georgetown College; Laurinda Dixon, Syracuse University; Laura Dufresne, Winthrop University; Dan Ewing, Barry University; Arne Flaten, Coastal Carolina University; John Garton, Cleveland Institute of Art; Rosi Gilday, University of Wisconsin, Oshkosh; Eunice D. Howe, University of Southern California; Phillip Jacks, George Washington University; William R. Levin, Centre College; Susan Libby, Rollins College; Henry Luttikhuizen, Calvin College; Lynn Mackenzie, College of DuPage; Dennis McNamara, Triton College; Gustav Medicus, Kent State University; Lynn Metcalf, St. Cloud State University; Jo-Ann Morgan, Coastal Carolina University; Beth A. Mulvaney, Meredith College; Dorothy Munger, Delaware Community College; Bonnie Noble, University of North Carolina at Charlotte; Leisha O'Quinn, Oklahoma State University; Willow Partington, Hudson Valley Community College; Martin Patrick, Illinois State University; Albert Reischuck, Kent State University; Jeffrey Ruda, University of California, Davis; Diane Scillia, Kent State University; Stephanie Smith, Youngstown State University; Janet Snyder, West Virginia University; James Terry, Stephens College; Michael Tinkler, Hobart and William Smith Colleges; Reid Wood, Lorain County Community College. Our thanks also to additional expert readers including: Susan Cahan, Yale University; David Craven, University of New Mexico; Marian Feldman, University of California, Berkeley; Dorothy Johnson, University of Iowa; Genevra Kornbluth, University of Maryland; Patricia Mainardi, City University of New York; Clemente Marconi, Columbia University; Tod Marder, Rutgers University; Mary Miller, Yale University; Elizabeth Penton, Durham Technical Community College; Catherine B. Scallen, Case Western University; Kim Shelton, University of California, Berkeley.

Many people reviewed the original edition of *Art History* and have continued to assist with its revision. Every chapter was read by one or more specialists. For work on the original book and assistance with subsequent editions my thanks go to: Barbara Abou-el-Haj, SUNY Binghamton; Roger Aiken, Creighton University; Molly Aitken; Anthony Alofsin, University of Texas, Austin; Christiane Andersson, Bucknell University; Kathryn Arnold; Julie Aronson, Cincinnati Art Museum; Michael Auerbach, Vanderbilt University; Larry Beck; Evelyn Bell, San Jose State University; Janetta Rebold Benton, Pace University; Janet Berlo, University of Rochester; Sarah Blick, Kenyon College; Jonathan Bloom, Boston College; Suzaan Boettger; Judith Bookbinder, Boston College; Marta Braun, Ryerson University; Elizabeth Broun, Smithsonian American Art Museum; Glen R. Brown, Kansas State University; Maria Elena Buszek, Kansas City Art Institute; Robert G. Calkins; Annmarie Weyl Carr; April Clagget, Keene State College; William W. Clark, Queens College, CUNY; John Clarke, University of Texas, Austin; Jaqueline Clipsham; Ralph T. Coe; Robert Cohon, The Nelson-Atkins Museum of Art; Alessandra Comini; James D'Emilio, University of South Florida; Walter Denny, University of Massachusetts, Amherst; Jerrilyn Dodds, City College, CUNY; Lois Drewer, Index of Christian Art; Joseph Dye, Virginia Museum of Art; James Farmer, Virginia Commonwealth University; Grace Flam, Salt Lake City Community College; Mary D. Garrard; Paula Gerson, Florida State University; Walter S. Gibson; Dorothy Glass; Oleg Grabar; Randall Griffey, Amherst College; Cynthia Hahn, Florida State University; Sharon Hill, Virginia Commonwealth University; John Hoopes, University of Kansas; Reinhild Janzen, Washburn University; Wendy Kindred, University of Maine at Fort Kent; Alan T. Kohl, Minneapolis College of Art; Ruth Kolarik, Colorado College; Carol H. Krinsky, New York University; Aileen Laing, Sweet Briar College; Janet LeBlanc, Clemson University; Charles Little, The Metropolitan Museum of Art; Laureen Reu Liu, McHenry County College; Loretta Lorance; Brian Madigan, Wayne State University; Janice Mann, Bucknell University; Judith Mann, St. Louis Art Museum; Richard Mann, San Francisco State University; James Martin,; Elizabeth Parker McLachlan; Tamara Mikailova, St. Petersburg, Russia, and Macalester College; Anta Montet-White; Anne E. Morganstern, Ohio State University; Winslow Myers, Bancroft School; Lawrence Nees, University of Delaware; Amy Ogata, Cleveland Institute of Art; Judith Oliver, Colgate University; Edward Olszewski, Case Western Reserve University; Sara Jane Pearman; John G. Pedley, University of Michigan; Michael Plante, Tulane University; Eloise Quiñones-Keber, Baruch College and the Graduate Center, CUNY; Virginia Raguin, College of the Holy Cross; Nancy H. Ramage, Ithaca College; Ann M. Roberts, Lake Forest College; Lisa Robertson, The Cleveland Museum of Art; Barry Rubin; Charles Sack, Parsons, Kansas; Jan Schall, The Nelson-Atkins Museum of Art; Tom Shaw, Kean College; Pamela Sheingorn, Baruch College, CUNY; Raechell Smith, Kansas City Art Institute; Lauren Soth; Anne R. Stanton, University of Missouri, Columbia; Michael Stoughton; Thomas Sullivan, OSB, Benedictine College (Conception Abbey); Pamela Trimpe, University of Iowa; Richard Turnbull, Fashion Institute of Technology; Elizabeth Valdez del Alamo, Montclair State College; Lisa Vergara; Monica Visoná, University of Kentucky; Roger Ward, Norton Museum of Art; Mark Weil, St. Louis; David Wilkins; Marcilene Wittmer, University of Miami.

The various features of this book reinforce each other, helping the reader to become comfortable with terminology and concepts that are specific to art history.

Starter Kit and Introduction   The Starter Kit is a highly concise primer of basic concepts and tools. The Introduction explores the way they are used to come to an understanding of the history of art.

Captions   There are two kinds of captions in this book: short and long. Short captions identify information specific to the work of art or architecture illustrated:

> artist (when known)
> title or descriptive name of work date
> original location (if moved to a museum or other site)
> material or materials a work is made of
> size (height before width) in feet and inches, with meters
>   and centimeters in parentheses
> present location

The order of these elements varies, depending on the type of work illustrated. Dimensions are not given for architecture, for most wall paintings, or for most architectural sculpture. Some captions have one or more lines of small print below the identification section of the caption that gives museum or collection information. This is rarely required reading; its inclusion is often a requirement for gaining permission to reproduce the work.

Longer, discursive captions contain information that complements the narrative of the main text.

Definitions of Terms   You will encounter the basic terms of art history in three places:

> **In the Text**, where words appearing in boldface type are defined, or glossed, at their first use. Some terms are boldfaced and explained more than once, especially those that experience shows are hard to remember.

> **In Boxed Features**, on technique and other subjects, where labeled drawings and diagrams visually reinforce the use of terms.

Maps   At the beginning of each chapter you will find a map with all the places mentioned in the chapter.

Boxes   Special material that complements, enhances, explains, or extends the narrative text is set off in six types of tinted boxes.

Art and its Contexts and The Object Speaks boxes expand on selected works or issues related to the text. A Closer Look boxes use leader-line captions to focus attention on specific aspects of important works. Elements of Architecture boxes clarify specifically architectural features, often explaining engineering principles or building technology. Technique boxes outline the techniques and processes by which certain types of art are created. Recovering the Past boxes highlight the work of archaeologists who uncover and conservators who assure the preservation and clear presentation of art.

Learn About It   Placed at the beginning of each chapter, this feature captures in bulleted form the key learning objectives, or outcomes, of the chapter. They point to what will have been accomplished upon its completion.

Think About It   These critical thinking questions appear at the end of each chapter and help students assess their mastery of the learning objectives (Learn About It) by asking them to think through and apply what they have learned.

MyArtsLab prompts   These notations are found throughout the chapter and are keyed to MyArtsLab resources that enrich and reinforce student learning.

Dates, Abbreviations, and Other Conventions   This book uses the designations BCE and CE, abbreviations for "Before the Common Era" and "Common Era," instead of BC ("Before Christ") and AD ("Anno Domini," "the year of our Lord"). The first century BCE is the period from 99 BCE to 1 BCE; the first century CE is from the year 1 CE to 99 CE. Similarly, the second century CE is the period from 199 BCE to 100 BCE; the second century CE extends from 100 CE to 199 CE.

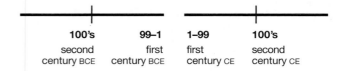

100's	**99–1**	**1–99**	**100's**
second	first	first	second
century BCE	century BCE	century CE	century CE

Circa ("about") is used with approximate dates, spelled out in the text and abbreviated to "c." in the captions. This indicates that an exact date is not yet verified.

An illustration is called a "figure," or "fig." Thus, figure 6–7 is the seventh numbered illustration in Chapter 6, and fig. Intro-3 is the third figure in the Introduction. There are two types of figures: photographs of artworks or of models, and line drawings. Drawings are used when a work cannot be photographed or when a diagram or simple drawing is the clearest way to illustrate an object or a place.

When introducing artists, we use the words *active* and *documented* with dates, in addition to "b." (for "born") and "d." (for "died"). "Active" means that an artist worked during the years given. "Documented" means that documents link the person to that date.

Accents are used for words in French, German, Italian, and Spanish only. With few exceptions, names of cultural institutions in Western European countries are given in the form used in that country.

Titles of Works of Art   It was only over the last 500 years that paintings and works of sculpture created in Europe and North America were given formal titles, either by the artist or by critics and art historians. Such formal titles are printed in italics. In other traditions and cultures, a single title is not important or even recognized.

In this book we use formal descriptive titles of artworks where titles are not established. If a work is best known by its non-English title, such as Manet's *Le Déjeuner sur l'Herbe (The Luncheon on the Grass)*, the original language precedes the translation.

Art history focuses on the visual arts—painting, drawing, sculpture, prints, photography, ceramics, metalwork, architecture, and more. This Starter Kit contains basic information and addresses concepts that underlie and support the study of art history. It provides a quick reference guide to the vocabulary used to classify and describe art objects. Understanding these terms is indispensable because you will encounter them again and again in reading, talking, and writing about art.

Let us begin with the basic properties of art. A work of art is a material object having both form and content. It is often described and categorized according to its *style* and *medium*.

FORM

Referring to purely visual aspects of art and architecture, the term *form* encompasses qualities of *line, shape, color, light, texture, space, mass, volume,* and *composition.* These qualities are known as *formal elements.* When art historians use the term *formal,* they mean "relating to form."

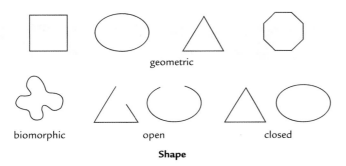

geometric

biomorphic   open   closed

Shape

Line and **shape** are attributes of form. Line is an element—usually drawn or painted—the length of which is so much greater than the width that we perceive it as having only length. Line can be actual, as when the line is visible, or it can be implied, as when the movement of the viewer's eyes over the surface of a work follows a path determined by the artist. Shape, on the other hand, is the two-dimensional, or flat, area defined by the borders of an enclosing *outline* or *contour.* Shape can be *geometric, biomorphic* (suggesting living things; sometimes called *organic*), *closed,* or *open.* The *outline* or *contour* of a three-dimensional object can also be perceived as line.

Color has several attributes. These include *hue, value,* and *saturation.*

Hue is what we think of when we hear the word *color,* and the terms are interchangeable. We perceive hues as the result of differing wavelengths of electromagnetic energy. The visible spectrum, which can be seen in a rainbow, runs from red through violet. When the ends of the spectrum are connected through the hue red-violet, the result may be diagrammed as a color wheel. The primary hues (numbered 1) are red, yellow, and blue. They are known as primaries because all other colors are made by combining these hues. Orange, green, and violet result from the mixture of two primaries and are known as secondary hues (numbered 2). Intermediate hues, or tertiaries (numbered 3), result from the mixture of a primary and a secondary. Complementary colors are the two colors directly opposite one another on the color

wheel, such as red and green. Red, orange, and yellow are regarded as warm colors and appear to advance toward us. Blue, green, and violet, which seem to recede, are called cool colors. Black and white are not considered colors but neutrals; in terms of light, black is understood as the absence of color and white as the mixture of all colors.

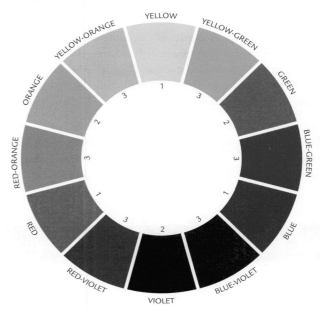

Value is the relative degree of lightness or darkness of a given color and is created by the amount of light reflected from an object's surface. A dark green has a deeper value than a light green, for example. In black-and-white reproductions of colored objects, you see only value, and some artworks—for example, a drawing made with black ink—possess only value, not hue or saturation.

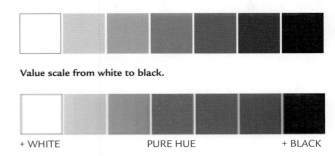

Value scale from white to black.

+ WHITE   PURE HUE   + BLACK

Value variation in red.

Saturation, also sometimes referred to as *intensity,* is a color's quality of brightness or dullness. A color described as highly saturated looks vivid and pure; a hue of low saturation may or look a little muddy or greyed.

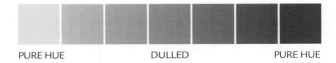

PURE HUE   DULLED   PURE HUE

Intensity scale from bright to dull.

Texture, another attribute of form, is the tactile (or touch-perceived) quality of a surface. It is described by words such as *smooth*, *polished*, *rough*, *prickly*, *grainy*, or *oily*. Texture takes two forms: the texture of the actual surface of the work of art and the implied (illusionistically described) surface of objects represented in the work of art.

Space is what contains forms. It may be actual and three-dimensional, as it is with sculpture and architecture, or it may be fictional, represented illusionistically in two dimensions, as when artists represent recession into the distance on a flat surface—such as a wall or a canvas--by using various systems of perspective.

Mass and volume are properties of three-dimensional things. Mass is solid matter—whether sculpture or architecture—that takes up space. Volume is enclosed or defined space, and may be either solid or hollow. Like space, mass and volume may be illusionistically represented on a two-dimensional surface, such as in a painting or a photograph.

Composition is the organization, or arrangement, of forms in a work of art. Shapes and colors may be repeated or varied, balanced symmetrically or asymmetrically; they may be stable or dynamic. The possibilities are nearly endless and artistic choice depends both on the time and place where the work was created as well as the objectives of individual artists. Pictorial depth (spatial recession) is a specialized aspect of composition in which the three-dimensional world is represented on a flat surface, or *picture plane*. The area "behind" the picture plane is called the *picture space* and conventionally contains three "zones": *foreground*, *middle ground*, and *background*.

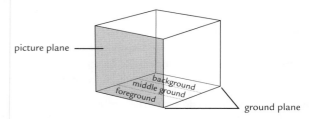

Various techniques for conveying a sense of pictorial depth have been devised by artists in different cultures and at different times. A number of them are diagrammed here. In some European art, the use of various systems of *perspective* has sought to create highly convincing illusions of recession into space. At other times and in other cultures, indications of recession are actually suppressed or avoided to emphasize surface rather than space.

TECHNIQUE | Pictorial devices for depicting recession in space

overlapping

In overlapping, partially covered elements are meant to be seen as located behind those covering them.

diminution

In diminution of scale, successively smaller elements are perceived as being progressively farther away than the largest ones.

vertical perspective

Vertical perspective stacks elements, with the higher ones intended to be perceived as deeper in space.

atmospheric perspective

Through atmospheric perspective, objects in the far distance (often in bluish-gray hues) have less clarity than nearer objects. The sky becomes paler as it approaches the horizon.

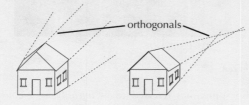

divergent perspective   **intuitive perspective**

In divergent or reverse perspective, forms widen slightly and imaginary lines called orthogonals diverge as they recede in space.

Intuitive perspective takes the opposite approach from divergent perspective. Forms become narrower and orthogonals converge the farther they are from the viewer, approximating the optical experience of spatial recession.

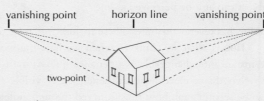

linear perspective

Linear perspective (also called scientific, mathematical, one-point and Renaissance perspective) is a rationalization or standardization of intuitive perspective that was developed in fifteenth-century Italy. It uses mathematical formulas to construct images in which all elements are shaped by, or arranged along, orthogonals that converge in one or more vanishing points on a horizon line.

CONTENT

Content includes *subject matter*, but not all works of art have subject matter. Many buildings, paintings, sculptures, and other art objects include no recognizable references to things in nature nor to any story or historical situation, focusing instead on lines, colors, masses, volumes, and other formal elements. However, all works of art—even those without recognizable subject matter—have content, or meaning, insofar as they seek to communicate ideas, convey feelings, or affirm the beliefs and values of their makers, their patrons, and usually the people who originally viewed or used them.

Content may derive from the social, political, religious, and economic *contexts* in which a work was created, the *intention* of the artist, and the *reception* of the work by beholders (the audience). Art historians, applying different methods of *interpretation*, often arrive at different conclusions regarding the content of a work of art, and single works of art can contain more than one meaning because they are occasionally directed at more than one audience.

The study of subject matter is called *iconography* (literally, "the writing of images") and includes the identification of *symbols*—images that take on meaning through association, resemblance, or convention.

STYLE

Expressed very broadly, *style* is the combination of form and composition that makes a work distinctive. *Stylistic analysis* is one of art history's most developed practices, because it is how art historians recognize the work of an individual artist or the characteristic manner of groups of artists working in a particular time or place. Some of the most commonly used terms to discuss *artistic styles* include *period style*, *regional style*, *representational style*, *abstract style*, *linear style*, and *painterly style*.

Period style refers to the common traits detectable in works of art and architecture from a particular historical era. It is good practice not to use the words "style" and "period" interchangeably. Style is the sum of many influences and characteristics, including the period of its creation. An example of proper usage is "an American house from the Colonial period built in the Georgian style."

Regional style refers to stylistic traits that persist in a geographic region. An art historian whose specialty is medieval art can recognize Spanish style through many successive medieval periods and can distinguish individual objects created in medieval Spain from other medieval objects that were created in, for example, Italy.

Representational styles are those that describe the appearance of recognizable subject matter in ways that make it seem lifelike.

> **Realism** and **Naturalism** are terms that some people used interchangeably to characterize artists' attempts to represent the observable world in a manner that appears to describe its visual appearance accurately. When capitalized, Realism refers to a specific period style discussed in Chapter 5 of Volume 2.

> **Idealization** strives to create images of physical perfection according to the prevailing values or tastes of a culture. The artist may work in a representational style and idealize it to capture an underlying value or expressive effect.

> **Illusionism** refers to a highly detailed style that seeks to create a convincing illusion of physical reality by describing its visual appearance meticulously.

Abstract styles depart from mimicking lifelike appearance to capture the essence of a form. An abstract artist may work from nature or from a memory image of nature's forms and colors, which are simplified, stylized, perfected, distorted, elaborated, or otherwise transformed to achieve a desired expressive effect.

> **Nonrepresentational (or Nonobjective) Art** is a term often used for works of art that do not aim to produce recognizable natural imagery.

> **Expressionism** refers to styles in which the artist exaggerates aspects of form to draw out the beholder's subjective response or to project the artist's own subjective feelings.

Linear describes both styles and techniques. In linear styles artists use line as the primary means of definition. But linear paintings can also incorporate *modeling*—creating an illusion of three-dimensional substance through shading, usually executed so that brushstrokes nearly disappear.

Painterly describes a style of representation in which vigorous, evident brushstrokes dominate, and outlines, shadows, and highlights are brushed in freely.

MEDIUM AND TECHNIQUE

Medium (plural, *media*) refers to the material or materials from which a work of art is made. Today, literally anything can be used to make a work of art, including not only traditional materials like paint, ink, and stone, but also rubbish, food, and the earth itself.

Technique is the process that transforms media into a work of art. Various techniques are explained throughout this book in Technique boxes. Two-dimensional media and techniques include painting, drawing, prints, and photography. Three-dimensional media and techniques are sculpture (for example, using stone, wood, clay or cast metal), architecture, and many small-scale arts (such as jewelry, containers, or vessels) in media such as ceramics, metal, or wood.

Painting includes wall painting and fresco, illumination (the decoration of books with paintings), panel painting (painting on wood panels), painting on canvas, and handscroll and hanging scroll painting. The paint in these examples is pigment mixed with a liquid vehicle, or binder. Some art historians also consider pictorial media such as mosaic and stained glass—where the pigment is arranged in solid form—as a type of painting.

Graphic arts are those that involve the application of lines and strokes to a two-dimensional surface or support, most often paper. Drawing is a graphic art, as are the various forms of printmaking. Drawings may be sketches (quick visual notes, often made in preparation for larger drawings or paintings); studies (more carefully drawn analyses of details or entire compositions); cartoons (full-scale drawings made in preparation for work in another medium, such as fresco, stained glass, or tapestry); or complete artworks in themselves. Drawings can be made with ink, charcoal, crayon, or pencil. Prints, unlike drawings, are made in multiple copies. The various forms of printmaking include woodcut, the intaglio processes (engraving, etching, drypoint), and lithography.

Photography (literally, "light writing") is a medium that involves the rendering of optical images on light-sensitive surfaces. Photographic images are typically recorded by a camera.

Sculpture is three-dimensional art that is *carved*, *modeled*, *cast*, or *assembled*. Carved sculpture is subtractive in the sense that the image is created by taking away material. Wood, stone, and ivory are common materials used to create carved sculptures. Modeled sculpture is considered additive, meaning that the object is built up from a material, such as clay, that is soft enough to be molded and shaped. Metal sculpture is usually cast or is assembled by welding or a similar means of permanent joining.

Sculpture is either free-standing (that is, surrounded by space) or in pictorial relief. Relief sculpture projects from the background surface of the same piece of material. High-relief sculpture projects far from its background; low-relief sculpture is only slightly raised; and sunken relief, found mainly in ancient Egyptian art, is carved into the surface, with the highest part of the relief being the flat surface.

Ephemeral arts include processions, ceremonies, or ritual dances (often with décor, costumes, or masks); performance art; earthworks; cinema and video art; and some forms of digital or computer art. All impose a temporal limitation—the artwork is viewable for a finite period of time and then disappears forever, is in a constant state of change, or must be replayed to be experienced again.

Architecture creates enclosures for human activity or habitation. It is three-dimensional, highly spatial, functional, and closely bound with developments in technology and materials. Since it is difficult to capture in a photograph, several types of schematic drawings are commonly used to enable the visualization of a building:

  Plans depict a structure's masses and voids, presenting a view from above of the building's footprint or as if it had been sliced horizontally at about waist height.

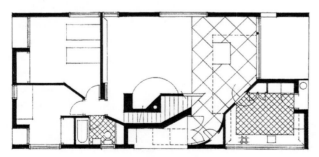

Plan: Philadelphia, Vanna Venturi House

Sections reveal the interior of a building as if it had been cut vertically from top to bottom.

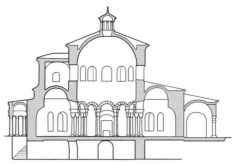

Section: Rome, Sta. Costanza

Isometric Drawings show buildings from oblique angles either seen from above ("bird's-eye view") to reveal their basic three-dimensional forms (often cut away so we can peek inside) or from below ("worm's-eye view") to represent the arrangement of interior spaces and the upward projection of structural elements.

Isometric cutaway from above: Ravenna, San Vitale

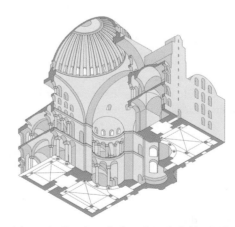

Isometric projection from below: Istanbul, Hagia Sophia

INTRODUCTION: GLOBAL BEGINNINGS (HUNTER-GATHERER SOCIETIES)

THOUGHT PIECE

Brave Buffalo [Sioux: Tatan ka-ohi tika] stated that about two years after his dream of the elk he had a dream of a wolf. This dream came to him as he was hunting alone. He had been wandering for several days in search of game when he met a pack of wolves. They formed a circle around him, and as they stood looking at him he noticed that their nostrils and paws were painted red. They came toward him, whereupon he grew dizzy. When they reached him, he was unconscious. They stood around him until he regained his senses; then they moved on, telling him to follow them. They led the way to a wolf den on top of a high hill.

While he was there, more wolves came out of the hole, painted like the others. The wolves have always been wanderers, not knowing where they would find food. They knew he had been hunting and had had much difficulty in finding game, and they wanted to help him. They said there was a certain herb which, if dried, would enable him to catch all kinds of snakes. He was told to dry this herb, and put it on the ground where the snakes are wont to come. He did so and caught a live rattlesnake. The wolves told him to carry this live snake when giving the demonstration of his wolf dream. Instead of the mask of elk hide which he wore in his former demonstration, he used a similar mask of wolf skin, wearing practically the entire hide and carry-

ing in his hand a bent stick somewhat resembling a bow, which was painted red. Brave Buffalo stated that he carried this and the snake in the same hand, the snake coiling itself around the bow. He held the snake close to its head during the demonstration and let it go after the demonstration was closed. The wolves told him that when he was making this demonstration a live owl would alight on his back. Brave Buffalo said that this actually happened. After this dream and its demonstration he "prayed to the wolves" when he wanted to locate game, and they always told him where to secure it.

—Frances Densmore, in *Teton Sioux Music,* Bulletin 61 of *The Smithsonian Institution Bureau of American Ethnology* (Washington, D.C.: Government Printing Office, 1918), p. 179.

THINGS TO CONSIDER

- How do we frame history?
- What are the different ways in which we can read works of art/visual culture?
- How is "art" a historically determined/limited category?
- What can the origins of mark-making and figurative sculpture tell us about the different purposes of "art" or visual-material culture?

1.1 Consider the criteria used to identify and characterize those cultural artifacts that are labeled as "art."

1.2 Survey the methods used by art historians to analyze works of art and interpret their meaning within their original cultural contexts.

1.3 Explore the methods and objectives of visual analysis.

1.4 Assess the way art historians identify conventional subject matter and symbols in a process called iconography.

1.5 Trace the process of art-historical interpretation in a case study.

HEAR MORE: Listen to an audio file of your chapter **www.myartslab.com**

1–1 • Mark Rothko
NO. 3/NO. 13 (MAGENTA, BLACK AND GREEN ON ORANGE)
1949. Oil on canvas, 7′1⅜″ × 5′5″ (2.165 × 1.648 m).
Museum of Modern Art, New York.

To view this image, please go to page xxvi of the *Art History*, Fourth Edition by Marilyn Stokstad ebook.

WHAT IS ART?

Artists, critics, art historians, and the general public all grapple with this thorny question. The *Random House Dictionary* defines "art" as "the quality, production, expression, or realm of what is beautiful, or of more than ordinary significance." Others have characterized "art" as something human-made that combines creative imagination and technical skill and satisfies an innate desire for order and harmony—perhaps a human hunger for the beautiful. This seems relatively straightforward until we start to look at modern and contemporary art, where there has been a heated and extended debate concerning "What is Art?" The focus is often far from questions of transcendent beauty, ordered design, or technical skill, and centers instead on the meaning of a work for an elite target audience or the attempt to pose challenging questions or unsettle deep-seated cultural ideas.

The works of art discussed in this book represent a privileged subset of artifacts produced by past and present cultures. They were usually meant to be preserved, and they are currently considered worthy of conservation and display. The determination of which artifacts are exceptional—which are works of art—evolves through the actions, opinions, and selections of artists, patrons, governments, collectors, archaeologists, museums, art historians, and others. Labeling objects as art is usually meant to signal that they transcended or now transcend in some profound way their practical function, often embodying cherished cultural ideas or foundational values. Sometimes it can mean they are considered beautiful, well designed, and made with loving care, but this is not always the case, especially in the twentieth and twenty-first centuries when the complex notion of what is art has little to do with the idea of beauty. Some critics and historians argue that works of art are tendentious embodiments of power and privilege, hardly sublime expressions of beauty or truth. After all, art can be unsettling as well as soothing, challenging as well as reassuring, whether made in the present or surviving from the past.

Increasingly we are realizing that our judgments about what constitutes art—as well as what constitutes beauty—are conditioned by our own education and experience. Whether acquired at home, in classrooms, in museums, at the movies, or on the internet, our responses to art are learned behaviors, influenced by class, gender, race, geography, and economic status as well as education. Even art historians find that their definitions of what constitutes art—and what constitutes artistic quality—evolve with additional research and understanding. Exploring works by twentieth-century painter Mark Rothko and nineteenth-century quiltmakers Martha Knowles and Henrietta Thomas demonstrates how definitions of art and artistic value are subject to change over time.

Rothko's painting, **MAGENTA, BLACK AND GREEN ON ORANGE** (FIG. 1–1), is a well-known example of the sort of abstract painting that was considered the epitome of artistic sophistication by the mid-twentieth-century New York art establishment. It was created by an artist who meant it to be a work of art. It was acquired by the Museum of Modern Art in New York, and its position on the walls of that museum is a sure sign that it was accepted as such by a powerful cultural institution. However, beyond the context of the American artists, dealers, critics, and collectors who made up Rothko's art world, such paintings were often received with skepticism. They were seen by many as incomprehensible—lacking both technical skill and recognizable subject matter, two criteria that were part of the general public's definition of art at the time. Abstract paintings soon inspired a popular retort: "That's not art; my child could do it!" Interestingly enough, Rothko saw in the childlike character of his own paintings one of the qualities that made them works of art. Children, he said, "put forms, figures, and views into pictorial arrangements, employing out of necessity most of the rules of optical perspective and geometry but without the knowledge that they are employing them." He characterized his own art as childlike, as "an attempt to recapture the freshness and naiveté of childish vision." In part because they are carefully crafted by an established artist who provided these kinds of intellectual justifications for their character and appearance, Rothko's abstract paintings are broadly considered works of art and are treasured possessions of major museums across the globe.

Art and Architecture

This book contains much more than paintings and textiles. Within these pages you will also encounter sculpture, vessels, books, jewelry, tombs, chairs, photographs, architecture, and more. But as with Rothko's *Magenta, Black, and Green on Orange* (SEE FIG. 1–1) and Knowles and Thomas's *My Sweet Sister Emma* (SEE FIG. 1–2), criteria have been used to determine which works are selected for inclusion in this book. Architecture presents an interesting case.

Buildings meet functional human needs by enclosing human habitation or activity. Many works of architecture, however, are considered "exceptional" because they transcend functional demands by manifesting distinguished architectural design or because they embody in important ways the values and goals of the culture that built them. Such buildings are usually produced by architects influenced, like painters, by great works and traditions from the past. In some cases they harmonize with, or react to, their natural or urban surroundings. For such reasons, they are discussed in books on the history of art.

Typical of such buildings is the church of Nôtre-Dame-du-Haut in Ronchamp, France, designed and constructed between 1950 and 1955 by Swiss architect Charles-Edouard Jeanneret, better known by his pseudonym, Le Corbusier. This building is the product of a significant historical moment, rich in global cultural meaning. A pilgrimage church on this site had been destroyed during World War II, and the creation here of a new church symbolized the end of a devastating war, embodying hopes for a brighter global future. Le Corbusier's design—drawing on sources that ranged from Algerian mosques to imperial Roman villas, from crab shells to airplane wings—is sculptural as well as architectural. It soars at the crest of a hill toward the sky but at the same time seems solidly anchored in the earth. And its coordination with the curves of the natural landscape complement the creation of an outdoor setting for religious ceremonies (to the right in the figure) to supplement the church interior that Le Corbusier characterized as a "container for intense concentration." In fact, this building is so renowned today as a monument of modern architecture, that the bus-loads of pilgrims who arrive at the site are mainly architects and devotees of architectural history.

> To view this image, please go to page xxviii of the *Art History*, Fourth Edition by Marilyn Stokstad ebook.

Le Corbusier **NÔTRE-DAME-DU-HAUT**
1950–1955. Ronchamp, France.

Works of art, however, do not always have to be created by individuals who perceive themselves as artists. Nor are all works produced for an art market surrounded by critics and collectors ready to explain, exhibit, and disperse them, ideally to prestigious museums. Such is the case with this quilt **(FIG. 1–2)**, made by Martha Knowles and Henrietta Thomas a century before Rothko's

painting. Their work is similarly composed of blocks of color, and like Rothko, they produced their visual effect by arranging these flat chromatic shapes carefully and regularly on a rectangular field. But this quilt was not meant to hang on the wall of an art museum. It is the social product of a friendship, intended as an intimate gift, presented to a loved one for use in her home. An inscription on

To view this image, please go to page xxvii of the *Art History*, Fourth Edition by Marilyn Stokstad ebook.

1-2 • Martha Knowles and Henrietta Thomas
MY SWEET SISTER EMMA
1843. Cotton quilt, 8′11″ × 9′1″ (2.72 × 2.77 m). International Quilt Studies Center, University of Nebraska, Lincoln, Nebraska.

the quilt itself makes this clear—"From M. A. Knowles to her Sweet Sister Emma, 1843." Thousands of such friendship quilts were made by women during the middle years of the nineteenth century for use on beds, either to provide warmth or as a covering spread. Whereas quilts were sometimes displayed to a broad and enthusiastic audience of producers and admirers at competitions held at state and county fairs, they were not collected by art museums or revered by artists until relatively recently.

In 1971, at the Whitney Museum in New York—an establishment bastion of the art world in which Rothko moved and worked—art historians Jonathan Holstein and Gail van der Hoof mounted an exhibition entitled "Abstract Design in American Quilts," demonstrating the artistic affiliation we have already noted in comparing the way Knowles and Thomas, like Rothko, create abstract patterns with fields of color. Quilts were later accepted—or should the word be "appropriated?"—as works of art and hung on the walls of a New York art museum because of their visual similarities with the avant-garde, abstract works of art created by establishment, New York artists.

Art historian Patricia Mainardi took the case for quilts one significant step further in a pioneering article of 1973 published in *The Feminist Art Journal*. Entitled, "Quilts: The Great American Art," her argument was rooted not only in the aesthetic affinity of quilts with the esteemed work of contemporary abstract painters, but also in a political conviction that the definition of art had to be broadened. What was at stake here was historical veracity. Mainardi began, "Women have always made art. But for most women, the arts highest valued by male society have been closed to them for just that reason. They have put their creativity instead into the needlework arts, which exist in fantastic variety wherever there are women, and which in fact are a universal female art, transcending race, class, and national borders." She argued for the inclusion of quilts within the history of art to give deserved attention to the work of women artists who had been excluded from discussion because they created textiles and because they worked outside the male-dominated professional structures of the art world—because they were women. Quilts now hang as works of art on the walls of museums and appear with regularity in books that survey the history of art.

As these two examples demonstrate, definitions of art are rooted in cultural systems of value that are subject to change. And as they change, the list of works considered by art historians is periodically revised. Determining what to study is a persistent part of the art historian's task.

WHAT IS ART HISTORY?

There are many ways to study or appreciate works of art. Art history represents one specific approach, with its own goals and its own methods of assessment and interpretation. Simply put, art historians seek to understand the meaning of art from the past within its original cultural contexts, both from the point of view of its producers—artists, architects, and patrons—as well as from the point of view of its consumers—those who formed its original audience. Coming to an understanding of the cultural meaning of a work of art requires detailed and patient investigation on many levels, especially with art that was produced long ago and in societies distinct from our own. This is a scholarly rather than an intuitive exercise. In art history, the work of art is seen as an embodiment of the values, goals, and aspirations of its time and place of origin. It is a part of culture.

Art historians use a variety of theoretical perspectives and a host of interpretive strategies to come to an understanding of works of art within their cultural contexts. But as a place to begin, the work of art historians can be divided into four types of investigation:

1. assessment of physical properties,
2. analysis of visual or formal structure,
3. identification of subject matter or conventional symbolism, and
4. integration within cultural context.

ASSESSING PHYSICAL PROPERTIES

Of the methods used by art historians to study works of art, this is the most objective, but it requires close access to the work itself. Physical properties include shape, size, materials, and technique. For instance, many pictures are rectangular (e.g., SEE FIG. 1–1), but some are round (see page 6, FIG. C). Paintings as large as Rothko's require us to stand back if we want to take in the whole image, whereas some paintings (see page 5, FIG. A) are so small that we are drawn up close to examine their detail. Rothko's painting and Knowles and Thomas's quilt are both rectangles of similar size, but they are distinguished by the materials from which they are made—oil paint on canvas versus cotton fabric joined by stitching. In art history books, most physical properties can only be

Visual Elements of Pictorial Expression › Line, Light, Form, and Color.

To view this image, please go to page xxx of the *Art History*, Fourth Edition by Marilyn Stokstad ebook.

LINE

A. *Carpet Page* **from the Lindisfarne Gospels**
From Lindisfarne, England.
c. 715–720. Ink and tempera on vellum, 13⅜ × 9⁷⁄₁₆″ (34 × 24 cm). British Library, London. Cotton MS Nero D.IV fol. 26v

To view this image, please go to page xxx of the *Art History*, Fourth Edition by Marilyn Stokstad ebook.

Every element in this complicated painting is sharply outlined by abrupt barriers between light and dark or between one color and another; there are no gradual or shaded transitions. Since the picture was created in part with pen and ink, the linearity is a logical feature of medium and technique. And although line itself is a "flattening" or two-dimensionalizing element in pictures, a complex and consistent system of overlapping gives the linear animal forms a sense of shallow but carefully worked-out three-dimensional relationships to one another.

LIGHT

B. Georges de la Tour *The Education of the Virgin*
c. 1650. Oil on canvas, 33 × 39½″ (83.8 × 100.4 cm). The Frick Collection, New York.

The source of illumination is a candle depicted within the painting. The young girl's upraised right hand shields its flame, allowing the artist to demonstrate his virtuosity in painting the translucency of human flesh.

Since the candle's flame is partially concealed, its luminous intensity is not allowed to distract from those aspects of the painting most brilliantly illuminated by it—the face of the girl and the book she is reading.

To view this image, please go to page xxx of the *Art History*, Fourth Edition by Marilyn Stokstad ebook.

FORM

C. Michelangelo *The Holy Family (Doni Tondo)*
c. 1503. Oil and tempera on panel, diameter 3′11¼″ (1.2 m). Galleria degli Uffizi, Florence.

To view this image, please go to page xxxi of the *Art History*, Fourth Edition by Marilyn Stokstad ebook.

The complex overlapping of their highly three-dimensionalized bodies conveys the somewhat contorted spatial positioning and relationship of these three figures.

Through the use of modeling or shading—a gradual transition from lights to darks—Michelangelo imitates the way solid forms are illuminated from a single light source—the side closest to the light source is bright while the other side is cast in shadow—and gives a sense of three-dimensional form to his figures.

The actual three-dimensional projection of the sculpted heads in medallions around the frame—designed for this painting by Michelangelo himself—heightens the effect of fictive three-dimensionality in the figures painted on its flat surface.

In a technique called **foreshortening**, the carefully calculated angle of the Virgin's elbow makes it seem to project out toward the viewer.

To view this image, please go to page xxxi of the *Art History*, Fourth Edition by Marilyn Stokstad ebook.

COLOR

D. Junayd *Humay and Humayun*, **from a manuscript of the** *Divan* **of Kwaju Kirmani**
Made in Baghdad, Iraq. 1396. Color, ink, and gold on paper, 12⅝ × 9⁷⁄₁₆″ (32 × 24 cm). British Library, London. MS Add. 18113, fol. 31r

To view this image, please go to page xxxi of the *Art History*, Fourth Edition by Marilyn Stokstad ebook.

Junayd chose to flood every aspect of his painting with light, as if everything in it were illuminated from all sides at once. As a result, the emphasis here is on jewel-like color. The vibrant tonalities and dazzling detail of the dreamy landscape are not only more important than the simulation of three-dimensional forms distributed within a consistently described space; they actually upstage the human drama taking place against a patterned, tipped-up ground in the lower third of the picture.

understood from descriptions in captions, but when we are in the presence of the work of art itself, size and shape may be the first thing we notice. To fully understand medium and technique, however, it may be necessary to employ methods of scientific analysis or documentary research to elucidate the practices of artists at the time when and place where the work was created.

ANALYZING FORMAL STRUCTURE

Art historians explore the visual character that artists bring to their works—using the materials and the techniques chosen to create them—in a process called **formal analysis**. On the most basic level, it is divided into two parts:

- assessing the individual visual elements or formal vocabulary that constitute pictorial or sculptural communication, and
- discovering the overall arrangement, organization, or structure of an image, a design system that art historians often refer to as **composition**.

THE ELEMENTS OF VISUAL EXPRESSION. Artists control and vary the visual character of works of art to give their subjects and ideas meaning and expression, vibrancy and persuasion, challenge or delight (see "A Closer Look," pages 5–6). For example, the motifs, objects, figures, and environments within paintings can be sharply defined by line (SEE FIGS. 1–2 and 1–3), or they can be suggested by a sketchier definition (SEE FIGS. 1–1 and 1–4). Painters can simulate the appearance of three-dimensional form through **modeling** or shading (SEE FIG. 1–3 and page 6, FIG. C), that is by describing the way light from a single source will highlight one side of a solid while leaving the other side in shadow. Alternatively, artists can avoid any strong sense of three-dimensionality by emphasizing patterns on a surface rather than forms in space (SEE FIG. 1–1 and page 5, FIG. A). In addition to revealing the solid substance of forms through modeling, dramatic lighting can guide viewers to specific areas of a picture (see page 5, FIG. B), or it can be lavished on every aspect of a picture to reveal all its detail and highlight the vibrancy of its color (see page 6, FIG. D). Color itself can be muted or intensified, depending on the mood artists want to create or the tastes and expectations of their audiences.

Thus artists communicate with their viewers by making choices in the way they use and emphasize the elements of visual expression, and art historical analysis seeks to reveal how artists' decisions bring meaning to a work of art. For example in two paintings of women with children (SEE FIGS. 1–3 and 1–4), Raphael and Renoir work with the same visual elements of line, form, light, and color in the creation of their images, but they employ these shared elements to differing expressive ends. Raphael concentrates on line to clearly differentiate each element of his picture as a separate form. Careful modeling describes these outlined forms as substantial solids surrounded by space. This gives his subjects a sense of clarity, stability, and grandeur. Renoir, on the other hand, foregrounds the flickering of light and the play of color as he downplays the sense of three-dimensionality in individual forms. This gives his image a more ephemeral, casual sense. Art historians pay close attention to such variations in the use of visual elements—the building blocks of artistic expression—and use visual analysis to characterize the expressive effect of a particular work, a particular artist, or a general period defined by place and date.

To view this image, please go to page xxxii of the *Art History*, Fourth Edition by Marilyn Stokstad ebook.

COMPOSITION. When art historians analyze composition, they focus not on the individual elements of visual expression but on the overall arrangement and organizing design or structure of a work of art. In Raphael's **MADONNA OF THE GOLDFINCH** (FIG. **1–3**), for example, the group of figures has been arranged in a triangular shape and placed at the center of the picture. Raphael emphasized this central weighting by opening the clouds to reveal a patch of blue in the middle of the sky, and by flanking the figural group with lace-like trees. Since the Madonna is at the

1–3 • Raphael MADONNA OF THE GOLDFINCH (MADONNA DEL CARDELLINO)
1506. Oil on panel, 42 × 29½″ (106.7 × 74.9 cm). Galleria degli Uffizi, Florence.

The vibrant colors of this important work were revealed in the course of a careful, ten-year restoration, completed only in 2008.

1-4 •
Auguste Renoir
**MME. CHARPENTIER
AND HER CHILDREN**
1878. Oil on canvas,
60½ × 74⅞" (153.7 × 190.2
cm). Metropolitan Museum
of Art, New York.

To view this image, please go to page xxxiii of the *Art History*, Fourth Edition by Marilyn Stokstad ebook.

center and since the two boys are divided between the two sides of the triangular shape, roughly—though not precisely—equidistant from the center of the painting, this is a bilaterally symmetrical composition: on either side of an implied vertical line at the center of the picture, there are equivalent forms on left and right, matched and balanced in a mirrored correspondence. Art historians refer to such an implied line—around which the elements of a picture are organized—as an **axis**. Raphael's painting has not only a vertical, but also a horizontal axis, indicated by a line of demarcation between light and dark—as well as between degrees of color saturation—in the terrain of the landscape. The belt of the Madonna's dress is aligned with this horizontal axis, and this correspondence, taken with the coordination of her head with the blue patch in the sky, relates her to the order of the natural world in which she sits, lending a sense of stability, order, and balance to the picture as a whole.

The main axis in Renoir's painting of **MME. CHARPENTIER AND HER CHILDREN (FIG. 1–4)** is neither vertical nor horizontal, but diagonal, running from the upper right to the lower left corner of the painting. All major elements of the composition are aligned along this axis—dog, children, mother, and the table and chair that represent the most complex and detailed aspect of the setting. The upper left and lower right corners of the painting balance each other on either side of the diagonal axis as relatively simple fields of neutral tone, setting off and framing the main subjects between them. The resulting arrangement is not bilaterally symmetrical, but blatantly asymmetrical, with the large figural mass pushed into the left side of the picture. And unlike Raphael's composition, where the spatial relationship of the figures and their environment is mapped by the measured placement of elements that become increasingly smaller in scale and fuzzier in definition as they recede into the background, the relationship of Renoir's figures to their spatial environment is less

clearly defined as they recede into the background along the dramatic diagonal axis. Nothing distracts us from the bold informality of this family gathering.

Both Raphael and Renoir arrange their figures carefully and purposefully, but they follow distinctive compositional systems that communicate different notions of the way these figures interact with each other and the world around them. Art historians pay special attention to how pictures are arranged because composition is one of the principal ways artists charge their paintings with expressive meaning.

IDENTIFYING SUBJECT MATTER

Art historians have traditionally sought subject matter and meaning in works of art with a system of analysis that was outlined by Irwin Panofsky (1892–1968), an influential German scholar who was expelled from his academic position by the Nazis in 1933 and spent the rest of his career of research and teaching in the United States. Panofsky proposed that when we seek to understand the subject of a work of art, we derive meaning initially in two ways:

- First we perceive what he called "natural subject matter" by recognizing forms and situations that we know from our own experience.
- Then we use what he called "**iconography**" to identify the conventional meanings associated with forms and figures as bearers of narrative or symbolic content, often specific to a particular time and place.

Some paintings, like Rothko's abstractions, do not contain subjects drawn from the world around us, from stories, or from conventional symbolism, but Panofsky's scheme remains a standard method of investigating meaning in works of art that present narrative subjects, portray specific people or places, or embody cultural values with iconic imagery or allegory.

To view this image, please go to page xlii of the *Art History*, Fourth Edition by Marilyn Stokstad ebook.

1-5 • SPOTTED HORSES AND HUMAN HANDS   Pech-Merle Cave. Dordogne, France.
Horses 25,000–24,000 BCE; hands c. 15,000 BCE. Paint on limestone, individual horses over 5′ (1.5 m) in length.

PREHISTORIC ART

Two horses are positioned back to back on the wall of a chamber within the Pech-Merle Cave, located in France's Dordogne region; one of the horses is shown in the detail at left (FIG. 1–5). The head of the horse follows the natural shape of the rock. Black dots surround areas of both horses and cover their bodies. At a later date, a large fish (58 inches long and almost impossible to see) was painted in red on top of them. Yet the painters left more than images of animals, fish, and geometric shapes; they left their own handprints in various places around the animals. These images, and many others hidden in chambers at the ends of long, narrow passages within the cave, connect us to an almost unimaginably ancient world of 25,000 BCE.

Prehistory includes all of human existence before the emergence of writing, though long before that defining moment people were carving objects, painting images, and creating shelters and other structures. Thirty thousand years ago our ancestors were not making "works of art" and there were no "artists" as we understand the term today. They were flaking, chipping, and polishing flints into spear points, knives, and scrapers, not into sculptures, however pleasing these artifacts are to the eye and to the touch. Wall paintings, too, must have seemed vitally important to their makers in terms of everyday survival.

For art historians, archaeologists, and anthropologists, prehistoric art provides a significant clue—along with fossils, pollen, and artifacts—to understanding early human life and culture. Although specialists continue to discover more about when and how these works were created, they may never be able to tell us why they were made. In fact, there may be no single meaning or use for any one image on a cave wall; cave art probably meant different things to the different people who saw it, depending on their age, experience, and specific needs and desires. The sculpture, paintings, and structures that survive are only a tiny fraction of what must have been created over a very long time span. The conclusions and interpretations drawn from them are only hypotheses, making prehistoric art one of the most speculative, but exciting, areas of art history.

LEARN ABOUT IT

1.6 Examine the origins of art in the prehistoric past.

1.7 Discover the location and motifs of Paleolithic cave art and assess the range of scholarly interpretations for them.

1.8 Investigate the early use of architecture in domestic and sacred contexts, including megalithic monuments such as Stonehenge.

1.9 Explore the use and meaning of human figurines in the Paleolithic and Neolithic periods.

1.10 Trace the emergence of pottery making and metalworking and examine the earliest works made of fired clay and hammered gold.

HEAR MORE: Listen to an audio file of your chapter www.myartslab.com

THE STONE AGE

How and when modern humans evolved is the subject of ongoing debate, but anthropologists now agree that the species called *homo sapiens* appeared about 400,000 years ago, and that the subspecies to which we belong, *homo sapiens sapiens* (usually referred to as modern humans), evolved as early as 120,000 years ago. Based on archaeological evidence, it is now clear that modern humans spread from Africa across Asia, into Europe, and finally to Australia and the Americas. This vast movement of people took place between 100,000 and 35,000 years ago.

Scholars began the systematic study of prehistory only about 200 years ago. Nineteenth-century archaeologists, struck by the wealth of stone tools, weapons, and figures found at ancient sites, named the whole period of early human development the Stone Age. Today, researchers divide the Stone Age into the Paleolithic (from the Greek *paleo-*, "old," and *lithos*, "stone") and the Neolithic (from the Greek *neo-*, "new") periods. The Paleolithic period is divided into three phases reflecting the relative position of objects found in the layers of excavation: Lower (the oldest), Middle, and Upper (the most recent). In some places archaeologists can identify a transitional, or Mesolithic (from the Greek *meso-*, "middle") period.

To view this image, please go to page 2 of the *Art History*, Fourth Edition by Marilyn Stokstad ebook.

1–6 • RAINBOW SERPENT ROCK
Western Arnhem Land, Australia. Appearing in Australia as early as 6000 BCE, images of the Rainbow Serpent play a role in rituals and legends of the creation of human beings, the generation of rains, storms, and floods, and the reproductive power of nature and people.

The dates for the transition from Paleolithic to Neolithic vary with geography and with local environmental and social circumstances. For some of the places discussed in this chapter, such as Western Europe, the Neolithic way of living did not emerge until 3000 BCE; in others, such as the Near East, it appeared as early as 8000 BCE. Archaeologists mark time in so many years ago, or BP ("before present"). However, to ensure consistent style throughout the book, which reflects the usage of art historians, this chapter uses BCE (before the Common Era) and CE (the Common Era) to mark time.

Much is yet to be discovered about prehistoric art. In Australia, some of the world's very oldest images have been dated to between 50,000 and 40,000 years ago, and the tradition of transient communities who marked the land in complex, yet stunningly beautiful ways continues into historical time. In western Arnhem land **(FIG. 1–6)**, rock art images of the Rainbow Serpent have their origins in prehistory, and were perhaps first created during times of substantial changes in the environment. Africa, as well, is home to ancient rock art in both its northern and southern regions. In all cases, archaeologists associate the arrival of modern humans in these regions with the advent of image making.

Indeed, it is the cognitive capability to create and recognize symbols and imagery that sets us as modern humans apart from all of our predecessors and from all of our contemporary animal relatives. We are defined as a species by our abilities to make and understand art. This chapter focuses primarily on the rich traditions of prehistoric European art from the Paleolithic and Neolithic periods and into the Bronze Age **(MAP 1–1)**. Later chapters consider the prehistoric art of other continents and cultures, such as the Americas (Chapter 8), and sub-Saharan Africa.

THE PALEOLITHIC PERIOD

Researchers found that human beings made tools long before they made what today we call "art." Art, in the sense of image making, is the hallmark of the Upper Paleolithic period and the emergence of our subspecies, *homo sapiens sapiens*. Representational images are seen in the archaeological record beginning about 38,000 BCE in Australia, Africa, and Europe. Before that time, during the Lower Paleolithic period in Africa, early humans made tools by flaking and chipping (knapping) flint pebbles into blades and scrapers with sharp edges. Dating to 2.5 million years ago, the earliest objects made by our human ancestors were simple stone tools, some with sharp edges, that were used to cut animal skin and meat and bash open bones to access marrow, and also to cut wood and soft plant materials. These first tools have been found at sites such as Olduvai Gorge in Tanzania. Although not art, they are important as they document a critical development in our evolution: humans' ability to transform the world around them into specific tools and objects that could be used to complete a task.

MAP 1–1 • PREHISTORIC EUROPE

As the Ice Age glaciers receded, Paleolithic, Neolithic, Bronze Age, and Iron Age settlements increased from south to north.

By 1.65 million years ago, significant changes in our ancestors' cognitive abilities and manual dexterity can be seen in sophisticated stone tools, such as the teardrop-shaped hand-axes (**FIG. 1–7**) that have been found at sites across Eurasia. These extraordinary objects, symmetrical in form and produced by a complex multistep process, were long thought of as nothing more than tools (or perhaps even as weapons), but the most recent analysis suggests that they had a social function as well. Some sites (as at Olorgesailie in Kenya) contain hundreds of hand-axes, far more than would have been needed in functional terms, suggesting that they served to announce an individual's skills, status, and standing in his or her community. Although these ancient hand-axes are clearly not art in the representational sense, it is important to see them in terms of performance and process, concepts that though central to modern Western art also have deep prehistoric roots.

Evolutionary changes took place over time and by 400,000 years ago, during the late Middle Paleolithic period, a *homo sapiens*

subspecies called Neanderthal inhabited Europe. Its members used a wider range of stone tools and may have carefully buried their dead with funerary offerings. Neanderthals survived for thousands of years and overlapped with modern humans, though the two groups did not interbreed. *Homo sapiens sapiens*, who had evolved and spread out of Africa some 300,000 years after the Neanderthals, eventually replaced them, probably between 38,000 and 33,000 BCE.

The critical abilities that set modern humans apart from all of their predecessors were cognitive ones; indeed the fact that *homo sapiens sapiens*, as a species, outlasted Neanderthals was because they had the mental capacity to solve problems of human survival. The new cognitive abilities included improvements in recognizing and benefiting from variations in the natural environment, and in managing social networking and alliance making (skills that enabled organized hunting). The most important new ability, however, was the capacity to think symbolically: to create

To view this image, please go to page 4 of the *Art History*, Fourth Edition by Marilyn Stokstad ebook.

1–7 • PALEOLITHIC HAND-AXE
From Isimila Korongo, Tanzania. 60,000 years ago. Stone, height 10″ (25.4 cm).

To view this image, please go to page 4 of the *Art History*, Fourth Edition by Marilyn Stokstad ebook.

1–8 • DECORATED OCHER
From Blombos Cave. Southern Cape coast, South Africa. 77,000 years ago.

representational analogies between one person, animal, or object, and another, and to recognize and remember those analogies. This cognitive development marks the evolutionary origin of art.

The world's earliest pieces of art come from South Africa: two 77,000-year-old, engraved blocks of red ocher (probably used as crayons) found in the Blombos Cave **(FIG. 1–8)**. Both the blocks are engraved in an identical way with cross-hatched lines on their sides. Archaeologists argue that the similarity of the engraved patterns means these two pieces were intentionally made and decorated following a common pattern. Thousands of fragments of ocher have been discovered at Blombos and there is little doubt that people were using it to draw patterns and images, the remains of which have long since disappeared. Although it is impossible to prove, it is highly likely that the ocher was used to decorate peoples' bodies as well as to color objects such as tools or shell ornaments. Indeed, in an earlier layer on the same site, archaeologists uncovered more than 36 shells, each of which had been perforated so that it could be hung from a string or thong, or attached to clothing or a person's hair; these shells would have been used to decorate the body. An ostrich eggshell bead came from the same site and would have served the same purpose. The importance of the Blombos finds cannot be overstated: Here we have our early ancestors, probably modern humans but possibly even their predecessors, using the earth's raw materials to decorate themselves with jewelry (with the shells) and body art (with the ocher).

SHELTER OR ARCHITECTURE?

The term architecture has been applied to the enclosure of spaces with at least some aesthetic intent. Some people object to its use in connection with prehistoric improvisations, but building even a simple shelter requires a degree of imagination and planning deserving of the name "architecture." In the Upper Paleolithic period, humans in some regions used great ingenuity to build shelters that were far from simple. In woodlands, evidence of floors indicates that circular or oval huts of light branches and hides were built. These measured as much as 15–20 feet in diameter. (Modern tents to accommodate six people vary from 10- by 11-foot ovals to 14- by 7-foot rooms.)

In the treeless grasslands of Upper Paleolithic Russia and Ukraine, builders created settlements of up to ten houses using the bones of the now extinct woolly mammoth, whose long, curving tusks made excellent roof supports and arched door openings **(FIG. 1–9)**. This bone framework was probably covered with animal hides and turf. Most activities centered around the inside fire pit, or hearth, where food was prepared and tools were fashioned. Larger houses might have had more than one hearth and spaces were set aside for

To view this image, please go to page 5 of the *Art History*, Fourth Edition by Marilyn Stokstad ebook.

1-9 • RECONSTRUCTION DRAWING OF MAMMOTH-BONE HOUSES
Ukraine. c. 16,000–10,000 BCE.

To view this image, please go to page 5 of the *Art History*, Fourth Edition by Marilyn Stokstad ebook.

specific uses—working stone, making clothing, sleeping, and dumping refuse. Inside the largest dwelling on a site in Mezhirich, Ukraine, archaeologists found 15 small hearths that still contained ashes and charred bones left by the last occupants. Some people also colored their floors with powdered ocher in shades that ranged from yellow to red to brown. These Upper Paleolithic structures are important because of their early date: The widespread appearance of durable architecture concentrated in village communities did not occur until the beginning of the Neolithic period in the Near East and southeastern Europe.

ARTIFACTS OR WORKS OF ART?

As early as 30,000 BCE small figures, or figurines, of people and animals made of bone, ivory, stone, and clay appeared in Europe and Asia. Today we interpret such self-contained, three-dimensional pieces as examples of **sculpture in the round**. Prehistoric carvers also produced relief sculpture in stone, bone, and ivory. In **relief sculpture**, the surrounding material is carved away, forming a background that sets off the projecting figure.

THE LION-HUMAN. An early and puzzling example of a sculpture in the round is a human figure—probably male—with a feline head **(FIG. 1–10)**, made about 30,000–26,000 BCE. Archaeologists excavating at Hohlenstein-Stadel, Germany, found broken pieces of ivory (from a mammoth tusk) that they realized were parts of an entire figure. Nearly a foot tall, this remarkable statue surpasses most early figurines in size and complexity. Instead of copying what he or she saw in nature, the carver created a unique creature, part human and part beast. Was the figure intended to represent a person wearing a ritual lion mask? Or has the man taken on the

1-10 • LION-HUMAN
From Hohlenstein-Stadel, Germany. c. 30,000–26,000 BCE. Mammoth ivory, height 11⅝″ (29.6 cm). Ulmer Museum, Ulm, Germany.

The Power of Naming

Words are only symbols for ideas, and it is no coincidence that the origins of language and of art are often linked in our evolutionary development. But the very words we invent—or our ancestors invented—reveal a certain view of the world and can shape our thinking. Today, we exert the power of naming when we select a name for a baby or call a friend by a nickname. Our ideas about art can also be affected by names, even the ones used for captions in a book. Before the twentieth century, artists usually did not name, or title, their works. Names were eventually supplied by the works' owners or by art historians writing about them, and thus often express the cultural prejudices of the labelers or of the times in which they lived.

An excellent example of such distortion is the names given to the hundreds of small prehistoric statues of women that have been found. Earlier scholars called them by the Roman name Venus. For example,

the sculpture in FIGURE 1–11 was once called the *Venus of Willendorf* after the place where it was found. Using the name of the Roman goddess of love and beauty sent a message that this figure was associated with religious belief, that it represented an ideal of womanhood, and that it was one of a long line of images of "classical" feminine beauty. In a short time, most similar works of sculpture from the Upper Paleolithic period came to be known as Venus figures. The name was repeated so often that even experts began to assume that the statues had to be fertility figures and Mother Goddesses, although there is no proof that this was so.

Our ability to understand and interpret works of art creatively is easily compromised by distracting labels. Calling a prehistoric figure a woman instead of Venus encourages us to think about the sculpture in new and different ways.

To view this image, please go to page 6 of the *Art History*, Fourth Edition by Marilyn Stokstad ebook.

1–11 • WOMAN FROM WILLENDORF
From Austria. c. 24,000 BCE. Limestone, height 4⅜″ (11 cm).
Naturhistorisches Museum, Vienna.

appearance of an animal? Archaeologists now think that the people who lived at this time held very different ideas (from our twenty-first-century ones) about what it meant to be a human and how humans were distinct from animals; it is quite possible that they thought of animals and humans as parts of one common group of beings who shared the world. What is absolutely clear is that the Lion-Human shows highly complex thinking and creative imagination: the uniquely human ability to conceive and represent a creature never seen in nature.

FEMALE FIGURES. While a number of figurines representing men have been found recently, most human figures from the Upper Paleolithic period are female. The most famous of these, the **WOMAN FROM WILLENDORF (FIG. 1–11)**, from Austria, dates from about 24,000 BCE (see "The Power of Naming," above). Carved from limestone and originally colored with red ocher, the statuette's swelling, rounded forms make it seem much larger than its actual 4⅜-inch height. The sculptor exaggerated the figure's female attributes by giving it pendulous breasts, a big belly with a deep navel (a natural indentation in the stone), wide hips, dimpled knees and buttocks, and solid thighs. By carving a woman with a well-nourished body, the artist may have been expressing health and fertility, which could ensure the ability to produce strong children, thus guaranteeing the survival of the clan.

The most recent analysis of the Paleolithic female sculptures has replaced the traditional fertility interpretation with more nuanced understandings of how and why the human figure is represented in this way, and who may have had these kinds of objects made. According to archaeologist Clive Gamble, these little sculptures were subtle forms of nonverbal communication among

To view this image, please go to page 7 of the *Art History*, Fourth Edition by Marilyn Stokstad ebook.

1–12 • WOMAN FROM DOLNÍ VEŠTONICE
From Moravia, Czech Republic. 23,000 BCE. Fired clay, 4¼ × 1⁷⁄₁₀″ (11 × 4.3 cm). Moravske Museum, Brno, Czech Republic.

these objects further still. The site of Dolní Veštonice is important because it marks a very early date (23,000 BCE) for humans to use fire to make durable objects out of mixtures of water and soil. What makes the figures from this site and those from other sites in the region (Pavlov and Předmosti) unusual is their method of manufacture. By mixing the soil with water—to a very particular recipe—and then placing the wet figures in a hot kiln to bake, the makers were not intending to create durable, well-fired statues. On the contrary, the recipe used and the firing procedure followed tell us that the intention was to make the figures explode in the kilns before the firing process was complete, and before a "successful" figure could be produced. Indeed, the finds at these sites support this interpretation: There are very few complete figures, but numerous fragments that bear the traces of explosions at high temperatures. The Dolní Veštonice fragments are records of performance and process art in their rawest and earliest forms.

Another remarkable female image, discovered in the Grotte du Pape in Brassempouy, France, is the tiny ivory head known as the **WOMAN FROM BRASSEMPOUY (FIG. 1–13)**. Though the finders did not record its archaeological context, recent studies prove it

small isolated groups of Paleolithic people spread out across vast regions. Gamble noted the tremendous (and unusual) similarity in the shapes of figures, even those found in widely distant parts of Europe. He suggested that when groups of Paleolithic hunter-gatherers did occasionally meet up and interact, the female statues may have been among several signature objects that signaled whether a group was friendly and acceptable for interaction and, probably, for mating. As symbols, these figures would have provided reassurance of shared values about the body, and their size would have demanded engagement at a close personal level. It is not a coincidence, then, that the largest production of these types of Paleolithic figurine occurred during a period when climatic conditions were at their worst and the need for interaction and alliance building would have been at its greatest.

More provocative is art historian Leroy McDermott's suggestion that the body-shape of the female figures tell us a great deal about who made them. Noticing the bulbous shape of the figures and the fact that many do not have clearly defined feet, McDermott argued that the perspective was that of a pregnant woman looking down at her own body. McDermott 's theory that the figures were sculpted by pregnant women and were depictions of their own bodies offers an intriguing vision of women as artists, in control of how they were represented.

Another figure, found in the Czech Republic, the **WOMAN FROM DOLNÍ VEŠTONICE (FIG. 1–12)**, takes our understanding of

To view this image, please go to page 7 of the *Art History*, Fourth Edition by Marilyn Stokstad ebook.

1–13 • WOMAN FROM BRASSEMPOUY
From Grotte du Pape, Brassempouy, Landes, France. Probably c. 30,000 BCE. Ivory, height 1¼″ (3.6 cm). Musée des Antiquités Nationales, Saint-Germain-en-Laye, France.

to be authentic and date it as early as 30,000 BCE. The carver captured the essence of a head, or what psychologists call the **memory image**—those generalized elements that reside in our standard memory of a human head. An egg shape rests atop a long neck, a wide nose and strongly defined browline suggest deep-set eyes, and an engraved square patterning may be hair or a headdress. The image is an abstraction (what has come to be known as **abstract** art): the reduction of shapes and appearances to basic yet recognizable forms that are not intended to be exact replications of nature. The result in this case looks uncannily modern to the contemporary viewer. Today, when such a piece is isolated in a museum case or as a book illustration we enjoy it as an aesthetic object, but we lose its original cultural context.

CAVE PAINTING

Art in Europe entered a rich and sophisticated phase after 30,000 BCE, when images were painted on the walls of caves in central and southern France and northern Spain. No one knew of the existence of prehistoric cave paintings until one day in 1879, when a young girl, exploring with her father in Altamira in northern Spain, crawled through a small opening in the ground and found herself in a chamber whose ceiling was covered with painted animals (SEE FIG. 1–17). Her father, a lawyer and amateur archaeologist, searched the rest of the cave, told authorities about the remarkable find, and published his discovery the following year. Few people believed that these amazing works could have been made by "primitive" people, and the scientific community declared the paintings a hoax. They were accepted as authentic only in 1902, after many other cave paintings, drawings, and engravings had been discovered at other places in northern Spain and in France.

THE MEANING OF CAVE PAINTINGS.   What caused people to paint such dramatic imagery on the walls of caves? The idea that human beings have an inherent desire to decorate themselves and their surroundings—that an aesthetic sense is somehow innate to the human species—found ready acceptance in the nineteenth century. Many believed that people create art for the sheer love of beauty. Scientists now agree that human beings have an aesthetic impulse, but the effort required to accomplish the great cave paintings suggests their creators were motivated by more than simple pleasure (see "Prehistoric Wall Painting," page 19). Since the discovery at Altamira, anthropologists and art historians have devised several hypotheses to explain the existence of cave art. Like the search for the meaning of prehistoric female figurines, these explanations depend on the cultural views of those who advance them.

In the early twentieth century it was believed that art has a social function and that aesthetics are culturally relative. It was proposed that the cave paintings might be products both of rites to strengthen clan bonds and of ceremonies to enhance the fertility of animals used for food. In 1903, French archaeologist Salomon Reinach suggested that cave paintings were expressions of sympathetic magic (the idea, for instance, that a picture of a reclining bison would ensure that hunters found their prey asleep). Abbé Henri Breuil took these ideas further and concluded that caves were used as places of worship and were the settings for initiation rites. In the second half of the twentieth century, scholars rejected these ideas and based their interpretations on rigorous scientific methods and current social theory. André Leroi-Gourhan and Annette Laming-Emperaire, for example, dismissed the sympathetic magic theory because statistical analysis of debris from human settlements revealed that the animals used most frequently for food were not the ones traditionally portrayed in caves.

Researchers continue to discover new cave images and to correct earlier errors of fact or interpretation. A study of the Altamira Cave in the 1980s led anthropologist Leslie G. Freeman to conclude that the artists had faithfully represented a herd of bison during the mating season. Instead of being dead, asleep, or disabled—as earlier observers had thought—the animals were dust-wallowing, common behavior during the mating season. Similar thinking has led to a more recent interpretation of cave art by archaeologist Steve Mithen. In his detailed study of the motifs of the art and its placement within caves, Mithen argued that hoofprints, patterns of animal feces, and hide colorings were recorded and used as a text to teach novice hunters within a group about the seasonal appearance and behavior of the animals they hunted. The fact that so much cave art is hidden deep in almost inaccessible parts of caves (indeed, the fact that it is placed within caves at all), suggested to Mithen that this knowledge was intended for a privileged group and that certain individuals or groups were excluded from acquiring that knowledge.

South African rock-art expert David Lewis-Williams suggests a different interpretation. Using a deep comparative knowledge of art made by hunter-gatherer communities that are still in existence, Lewis-Williams has argued that Upper Paleolithic cave art is best understood in terms of shamanism: the belief that certain people (shamans) can travel outside of their bodies in order to mediate between the worlds of the living and the spirits. Traveling under the ground as a spirit, particularly within caves, or conceptually within the stone walls of the cave, Upper Paleolithic shamans would have participated in ceremonies that involved hallucinations. Images conceived during this trancelike state would likely combine recognizable (the animals) and abstract (the non-representational) symbols. In addition, Lewis-Williams interprets the stenciled human handprints found on the cave walls alongside the other marks as traces of the nonshaman participants in the ritual reaching towards and connecting with the shaman spirits traveling within the rock.

Although hypotheses that seek to explain cave art have changed and evolved over time, there has always been agreement that decorated caves must have had a special meaning because people returned to them time after time over many generations, in some cases over thousands of years. Perhaps Upper Paleolithic cave art was the product of rituals intended to gain the favor of the supernatural. Perhaps because much of the art was made deep inside the caves and nearly inaccessible, its significance may have had less to do with the finished painting than with the very act of creation. Artifacts and footprints (such as those found at Chauvet, below, and Le Tuc d'Audoubert, FIG. 1–18) suggest that the subterranean galleries, which were far from living quarters, had a religious or magical function. Perhaps the experience of exploring the cave may have been significant to the image-makers. Musical instruments, such as bone flutes, have been found in the caves, implying that even acoustical properties may have had a role to play.

CHAUVET.   The earliest known site of prehistoric cave paintings, discovered in December 1994, is the Chauvet Cave (called after one of the persons who found it) near Vallon-Pont-d'Arc in south-eastern France—a tantalizing trove of hundreds of paintings (FIG. 1–14). The most dramatic of the images depict grazing, running, or resting animals, including wild horses, bison, mammoths, bears, panthers, owls, deer, aurochs, woolly rhinoceroses, and wild goats (or ibex). Also included are occasional humans, both male and female, many handprints, and hundreds of geometric markings such as grids, circles, and dots. Footprints in the Chauvet Cave, left in soft clay by a child, go to a "room" containing bear skulls. The charcoal used to draw the rhinos has been radiocarbon-dated to 32,410 +/− 720 years before the present.

LASCAUX.   The best-known cave paintings are those found in 1940 at Lascaux, in the Dordogne region of southern France (FIG. 1–15 and SEE FIG. 1–16). They have been dated to about 15,000 BCE. Opened to the public after World War II, the prehistoric "museum" at Lascaux soon became one of the most popular tourist sites in France. Too popular, because the visitors brought heat, humidity, exhaled carbon dioxide, and other contaminants. The cave was closed to the public in 1963 so that conservators could battle an aggressive fungus. Eventually they won, but instead of reopening the site authorities created a facsimile of it. Visitors at what is called Lascaux II may now view copies of the paintings without harming the precious originals.

The scenes they view are truly remarkable. The Lascaux painters depicted cows, bulls, horses, and deer along the natural ledges of the rock, where the smooth white limestone of the ceiling and upper wall meets a rougher surface below. They also utilized the curving wall to suggest space. Lascaux has about 600 paintings and 1,500 engravings. Ibex, a bear, engraved felines, and a woolly rhinoceros have also been found. The animals appear singly, in rows, face to face, tail to tail, and even painted on top of one another. Their most characteristic features have been emphasized. Horns, eyes, and hooves are shown as seen from the front, yet heads and bodies are rendered in profile in a system known as **composite pose**. Even when their poses are exaggerated or

To view this image, please go to page 9 of the *Art History*, Fourth Edition by Marilyn Stokstad ebook.

1-14 • WALL PAINTING WITH HORSES, RHINOCEROSES, AND AUROCHS
Chauvet Cave. Vallon-Pont-d'Arc, Ardèche Gorge, France. c. 32,000–30,000 BCE. Paint on limestone.

SEE MORE: View a video about cave painting **www.myartslab.com**

In a dark cave, working by the light of an animal-fat lamp, an artist chews a piece of charcoal to dilute it with saliva and water. Then he blows out the mixture on the surface of a wall, using his hand as a stencil. The drawing demonstrates how cave archaeologist Michel Lorblanchet and his assistant used the step-by-step process of the original makers of a cave painting at Pech-Merle (SEE FIG. 1–5) in France created a complex design of spotted horses.

By turning himself into a human spray can, Lorblanchet can produce clear lines on the rough stone surface much more easily than he could with a brush. To create the line of a horse's back, with its clean upper edge and blurry lower one, he blows pigment below his hand. To capture its angular rump, he places his hand vertically against the wall, holding it slightly curved. To produce the sharpest lines, such as those of the upper hind leg and tail, he places his hands side by side and blows between them. To create the forelegs and the hair on the horses' bellies, he fingerpaints. A hole punched in a piece of leather serves as a stencil for the horses' spots. It takes Lorblanchet only 32 hours to reproduce the Pech-Merle painting of spotted horses, his speed suggesting that a single artist created the

original (perhaps with the help of an assistant to mix pigments and tend the lamp).

Homo sapiens sapiens artists used three painting techniques: the spraying demonstrated by Lorblanchet, drawing with fingers or blocks of ocher, and daubing with a paintbrush made of hair or moss. In some places in prehistoric caves three stages of image creation can be seen: engraved lines using flakes of flint, followed by a color wash of ocher and manganese, and a final engraving to emphasize shapes and details.

distorted, the animals are full of life and energy, and the accuracy in the drawing of their silhouettes, or outlines, is remarkable.

Painters worked not only in large caverns, but also far back in the smallest chambers and recesses, many of which are almost inaccessible today. Small stone lamps found in such caves—over 100 lamps have been found at Lascaux—indicate that the artists worked in flickering light from burning animal fat (SEE FIG. 1–19). (Although 1 pound of fat would burn for 24 hours and produce no

To view this image, please go to page 10 of the *Art History*, Fourth Edition by Marilyn Stokstad ebook.

1-15 • HALL OF BULLS
Lascaux Cave. Dordogne, France. c. 15,000 BCE. Paint on limestone, length of largest auroch (bull) 18′ (5.50 m).

To view this image, please go to page 11 of the *Art History*, Fourth Edition by Marilyn Stokstad ebook.

1–16 • BIRD-HEADED MAN WITH BISON
Shaft scene in Lascaux Cave. c. 15,000 BCE. Paint on limestone, length approx. 9′ (2.75 m).

ALTAMIRA. The cave paintings at Altamira, near Santander in the Cantabrian Mountains in Spain—the first to be discovered and attributed to the Upper Paleolithic period—have been recently dated to about 12,500 BCE (see "How Early Art is Dated," page 21). The Altamira artists created sculptural effects by painting over and around natural irregularities in the cave walls and ceilings. To produce the herd of bison on the ceiling of the main cavern **(FIG. 1–17)**, they used rich, red and brown ocher to paint the large areas of the animals' shoulders, backs, and flanks, then sharpened the contours of the rocks and added the details of the legs, tails, heads, and horns in black and brown. They mixed yellow and brown from iron-based ocher to make the red tones, and they derived black from manganese or charcoal.

soot, the light would not have been as strong as that created by a candle.)

One scene at Lascaux was discovered in a remote setting on a wall at the bottom of a 16-foot shaft that contained a stone lamp and spears. The scene is unusual because it is the only painting in the cave complex that seems to tell a story **(FIG. 1–16)**, and it is stylistically different from the other paintings at Lascaux. A figure who could be a hunter, greatly simplified in form but recognizably male and with the head of a bird or wearing a bird's-head mask, appears to be lying on the ground. A great bison looms above him. Below him lie a staff, or baton, and a spear-thrower (*atlatl*)—a device that allowed hunters to throw farther and with greater force—the outer end of which has been carved in the shape of a bird. The long, diagonal line slanting across the bison's hindquarters may be a spear. The bison has been disemboweled and will soon die. To the left of the cleft in the wall a woolly rhinoceros seems to run off. Why did the artist portray the man as only a sticklike figure when the bison was rendered with such accurate detail? Does the painting illustrate a story or a myth regarding the death of a hero? Is it a record of an actual event? The painting may also depict the vision of a shaman.

To view this image, please go to page 11 of the *Art History*, Fourth Edition by Marilyn Stokstad ebook.

1–17 • BISON
Ceiling of a cave at Altamira, Spain. c. 12,500 BCE. Paint on limestone, length approx. 8′3″ (2.5 m).

Since the first discoveries at Altamira, archaeologists have developed increasingly sophisticated ways of dating cave paintings and other objects. Today, they primarily use two approaches to determine an artifact's age. **Relative dating** relies on the chronological relationships among objects in a single excavation or among several sites. If archaeologists have determined, for example, that pottery types A, B, and C follow each other chronologically at one site, they can apply that knowledge to another site. Even if type B is the only pottery present, it can still be assigned a relative date. **Absolute dating** aims to determine a precise span of calendar years in which an artifact was created.

The most accurate method of absolute dating is **radiometric dating**, which measures the degree to which radioactive materials have disintegrated over time. Used for dating organic (plant or animal) materials—including some pigments used in cave paintings—one radiometric method measures a carbon isotope called radiocarbon, or carbon-14, which is constantly replenished in a living organism. When an organism dies, it stops absorbing carbon-14 and starts to lose its store of the isotope at a predictable rate. Under the right circumstances, the amount of carbon-14 remaining in organic material can tell us how long ago an organism died.

This method has serious drawbacks for dating works of art. Using carbon-14 dating on a carved antler or wood sculpture shows only when the animal died or when the tree was cut down, not when the artist created the work using those materials. Also, some part of the object must be destroyed in order to conduct this kind of test—something that is never a desirable procedure to conduct on a work of art. For this reason, researchers frequently test organic materials found in the same context as the work of art rather than in the work itself.

Radiocarbon dating is most accurate for materials no more than 30,000 to 40,000 years old. **Potassium-argon dating**, which measures the decay of a radioactive potassium isotope into a stable isotope of argon, an inert gas, is most reliable with materials more than a million years old. Two newer techniques have been used since the mid 1980s. **Thermo-luminescence dating** measures the irradiation of the crystal structure of a material subjected to fire, such as pottery, and the soil in which it is found, determined by the luminescence produced when a sample is heated. **Electron spin resonance** techniques involve using a magnetic field and microwave irradiation to date a material such as tooth enamel and the soil surrounding it.

Recent experiments have helped to date cave paintings with increasing precision. Radiocarbon analysis has determined, for example, that the animal images at Lascaux are 17,000 years old—to be more precise, 17,070 years plus or minus 130 years.

CAVE SCULPTURES

Caves were sometimes adorned with relief sculpture as well as paintings. At Altamira, an artist simply heightened the resemblance of a natural projecting rock to a similar and familiar animal form. Other reliefs were created by **modeling**, or shaping, the damp clay of the cave's floor. An excellent example of such work in clay (dating to 13,000 BCE) is preserved at Le Tuc d'Audoubert, south of the Dordogne region of France. Here the sculptor created two bison leaning against a ridge of rock (**FIG. 1–18**). Although the beasts are modeled in very high relief (they extend well forward from the background), they display the same conventions as in earlier painted ones, with emphasis on the broad masses of the meat-bearing flanks and shoulders. To make the animals even more lifelike, their creator engraved short parallel lines below their necks to represent their shaggy coats. Numerous small footprints found in the clay floor of this cave suggest that important group rites took place here.

An aesthetic sense and the ability to express it in a variety of ways are among the characteristics unique to *homo sapiens sapiens*. Lamps found in caves provide an example of objects that were both functional and aesthetically pleasing. Some were carved in simple abstract shapes; others were adorned with engraved images, like one found at La Mouthe, France (**FIG. 1–19**). The maker decorated its underside with an

To view this image, please go to page 12 of the *Art History*, Fourth Edition by Marilyn Stokstad ebook.

1–18 • BISON
Le Tuc d'Audoubert, France. c. 13,000 BCE. Unbaked clay, length 25″ (63.5 cm) and 24″ (60.9 cm).

To view this image, please go to page 13 of the *Art History*, Fourth Edition by Marilyn Stokstad ebook.

1–19 • LAMP WITH IBEX DESIGN
From La Mouthe Cave. Dordogne, France. c. 15,000–13,000 BCE. Engraved stone. Musée des Antiquités Nationales, Saint-Germain-en-Laye, France.

ibex. The animal's distinctive head is shown in profile, its sweeping horns reflecting the curved outline of the lamp itself. Objects such as this were made by people whose survival depended upon their skill at hunting animals and gathering wild grains and other edible plants. But a change was already under way that would completely alter human existence.

THE NEOLITHIC PERIOD

Today, advances in technology, medicine, transportation, and electronic communication change human experience in a generation. Many thousands of years ago, change took place much more slowly. In the tenth millennium BCE the world had already entered the present interglacial period, and our modern climate was taking shape. The world was warming up, and this affected the distribution, density, and stability of plant and animal life and

To view this image, please go to page 13 of the *Art History*, Fourth Edition by Marilyn Stokstad ebook.

marine and aquatic resources. However, the Ice Age ended so gradually and unevenly among regions that people could not have known what was happening.

One of the fundamental changes that took place in our prehistoric past was in the relationship people had with their environment. After millennia of established interactions between people and wild plants and animals (ranging from opportunistic foraging to well-scheduled gathering and collecting), people gradually started to exert increasing control over the land and its resources. Seen from the modern perspective, this change in economy (archaeologists use "economy" to refer to the ways people gather or produce food) seems abrupt and complete. Different communities adopted and adapted new sets of technologies, skills, and plant and animal species that allowed them to produce food: This is the origin of plant and animal domestication. Wheat and barley were cultivated; sheep, goats, cattle, and pigs were bred. This new economy appeared at different rates and to varying degrees of completeness in different parts of the Near East and Europe, and no community relied exclusively on the cultivation of plants or on breeding animals. Instead they balanced hunting, gathering, farming, and animal breeding in order to maintain a steady food supply.

ARCHITECTURE

At the same time as these new food technologies and species appeared, people began to establish stronger, more lasting connections to particular parts of the landscape. The beginnings of architecture in Europe are marked by people building their social environments by constructing simple but durable structures made of clay, mud, dung, and straw interwoven among wooden posts. While some of these buildings were simple huts, used for no more than a season at a time, others were much more substantial, with foundations made of stone, set into trenches, and supporting walls of large timbers. Some buildings were constructed from simple bricks made of clay, mud, and straw given shape by a rectangular mold and then dried in the sun. Regardless of the technique used, the result was the same: people developed a new attachment to the land, and with settlement came a new kind of social life.

At the site of Lepenski Vir, on the Serbian banks of the Danube River, rows of trapezoidal buildings made of wooden posts, branches, mud, and clay (but with stone foundations and stone-faced hearths) face the river from which the inhabitants took large river fish (FIG. 1–20). Although this site dates to between 6300–5500 BCE, there is little evidence for the domesticated plants and animals one might expect at this time and in association with architecture. Archaeologists found human burials under the floors of these structures as well as in the spaces

1–20 • RECONSTRUCTION OF LEPENSKI VIR HOUSE/SHRINE
Serbia. 6000 BCE.

To view this image, please go to page 14 of the *Art History*, Fourth Edition by Marilyn Stokstad ebook.

1–21 • HUMAN-FISH SCULPTURE
Lepenski Vir, Serbia. c. 6300–5500 BCE.

between individual buildings. In some houses extraordinary art was found, made of carefully pecked and shaped river boulders (**FIG. 1–21**). Some of the boulders appear to represent human forms. Others are more similar to fish. A few seem to consist of mixtures of human and fish features. Here we have a site with a confusing combination of architecture with a nondomesticated economy, very unusual art, and many burials. Archaeologists interpret sites like Lepenski Vir as temporary habitations where people carried out special rites and activities linked to death and to the natural and wild worlds. Art played a part in these.

In some places early architecture was dramatic and long-lasting, with the repeated building of house upon house in successive architectural generations (sometimes over 1,000 years or more) resulting in the gradual rise of great mounds of villages referred to as tells or mound settlements. A particularly spectacular example is Çatalhöyük (Chatal Huyuk) in the Konya Plain in central Turkey where the first traces of a village date to 7400 BCE in the early Neolithic. The oldest part of the site consists of many, densely clustered houses separated by areas of rubbish. They were made of rectangular mud bricks held together with mortar; walls, floors, and ceilings were covered with plaster and lime-based paint and were frequently replastered and repainted (see "A Closer Look" on the next page). The site was large and was home to as many as 3,000 people at any one time. Beyond the early date of the site and its size and population, the settlement at Çatalhöyük is important to art history for two reasons: the picture it provides of the use of early architecture and the sensational art that has been found within its buildings.

It is often assumed by archaeologists and anthropologists that the decision to create buildings such as the houses at Neolithic sites was based on a universal need for shelter from the elements. However, as

hinted at by the special nature of the activities at Lepenski Vir, recent work at Çatalhöyük shows clearly that while structures did provide shelter, early houses had much more significant functions for the communities of people who lived in them. For the Neolithic people of Çatalhöyük, their houses were the key component of their world-view. Most importantly, they became an emblem of the spirit and history of a community. The building of house upon house created a historical continuity that outlasted any human lifetime; indeed, some house rebuilding sequences lasted many hundreds of years. The seasonal replastering and repainting of walls and floors added to the long-term continuity of the buildings as history-makers. In fact, Ian Hodder, the current director of excavations at Çatalhöyük, and his colleagues call some of them "history houses" and have found no evidence to suggest that they were shrines or temples as earlier interpreters had mistakenly concluded.

The dead were buried under the floors of many of the buildings, so the site connected the community's past, present, and future. While there were no burials in some houses, a few contained between 30 and 60 bodies (the average is about six per house), and one had 62 burials, many of people who had lived their lives in other parts of the village. Periodically, perhaps to mark special community events and ceremonies, people dug down into the floors of their houses and removed the heads of the long-deceased, then buried the skulls in new graves under the floors. Skulls were also placed in the foundations of new houses as they were built (and rebuilt) and in other special deposits around the settlement. In one extraordinary burial, a deceased woman holds in her arms a man's skull that had been plastered and painted (perhaps it, too, had been removed from an earlier underfloor grave).

The houses of Çatalhöyük were powerful places not only because of the (literal) depths of their histories, but also because of the extraordinary art that decorated their interiors. Painted on the walls of some of the houses are violent and wild scenes. In some, humans are represented without heads as if they had been decapitated. Vultures or other birds of prey appear huge next to them. The narrative scenes are of dangerous interactions between people and animals. In one painting, a huge, horned wild animal (probably a deer) is surrounded by small humans who are jumping or running; one of them is pulling on something sticking out of the deer's mouth, perhaps its tongue. There is great reference to men and maleness: some of the human figures are bearded and the deer has an erect penis. The site's excavators see this painting as a depiction of a dangerous game or ritual of baiting and taunting a wild animal. In other paintings, people hunt or tease boars or bulls. Conservation of the wall paintings is highly complex and many of the most dramatic examples were excavated before modern preservation techniques existed, and thus we must rely on the archaeologist's narrative descriptions or quick field sketches.

Other representations of wild animals are modeled in relief on the interior walls, the most frequent are the heads and horns of bulls. In some houses, people placed boar tusks, vulture skulls, and fox and weasel teeth under the floors; in at least one case, they dug

A House in Çatalhöyük ➤ Çatalhöyük, Turkey. 7400–6200 BCE.

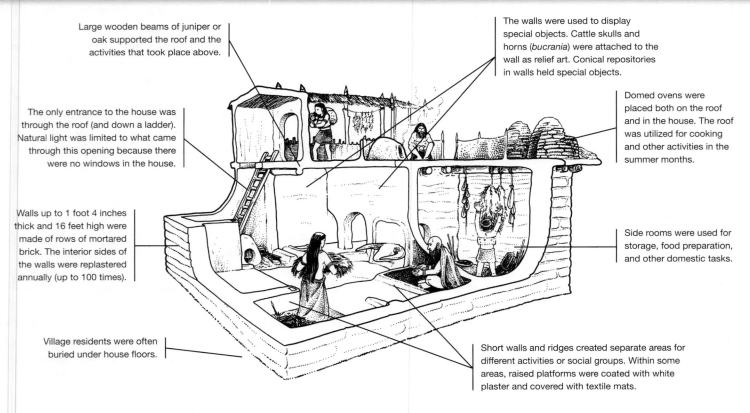

Large wooden beams of juniper or oak supported the roof and the activities that took place above.

The walls were used to display special objects. Cattle skulls and horns (*bucrania*) were attached to the wall as relief art. Conical repositories in walls held special objects.

The only entrance to the house was through the roof (and down a ladder). Natural light was limited to what came through this opening because there were no windows in the house.

Domed ovens were placed both on the roof and in the house. The roof was utilized for cooking and other activities in the summer months.

Walls up to 1 foot 4 inches thick and 16 feet high were made of rows of mortared brick. The interior sides of the walls were replastered annually (up to 100 times).

Side rooms were used for storage, food preparation, and other domestic tasks.

Village residents were often buried under house floors.

Short walls and ridges created separate areas for different activities or social groups. Within some areas, raised platforms were coated with white plaster and covered with textile mats.

SEE MORE: View the Closer Look feature for the House in Çatalhöyük **www.myartslab.com**

---

into previous house generations to retrieve the plastered and painted heads of bulls.

The importance of sites such as Lepenski Vir and Çatalhöyük is that they have forced archaeologists to think in new ways about the role of architecture and art in prehistoric communities (see "Intentional House Burning," page 29). Critically, the mixture of shelter, architecture, art, spirit, ritual, and ceremony at these and many other Neolithic sites makes us realize that we cannot easily distinguish between "domestic" and "sacred" architecture. This point re-emerges from the recent work at Stonehenge in England (see page 27). In addition, the clear and repeated emphasis on death, violence, wild animals, and male body parts at Çatalhöyük has replaced previous interpretations that the Neolithic worldview was one in which representations of the female body, human fertility, and cults of the Mother Goddess were all-powerful.

Most early architectural sites in the Neolithic were not as visually sensational as Çatalhöyük. At the site of Sesklo in northern Greece, dated to 6500 BCE, people built stone-based, long-lasting structures (**FIG. 1–22**) in one part of a village and less substantial

To view this image, please go to page 15 of the *Art History*, Fourth Edition by Marilyn Stokstad ebook.

1–22 • SESKLO STONE FOUNDATION HOUSE
Sesklo, Greece. 6500 BCE.

Of all the methods for spanning space, **post-and-lintel construction** is the simplest. At its most basic, two uprights (posts) support a horizontal element (**lintel**). There are countless variations, from the wood structures, dolmens, and other underground burial chambers of prehistory, to Egyptian and Greek stone construction, to medieval timber-frame buildings, and even to cast-iron and steel construction. Its limitation as a space spanner is the degree of tensile strength of the lintel material: the more flexible, the greater the span possible. Another early method for creating openings in walls and covering space is **corbeling**, in which rows or layers of stone are laid with the end of each row projecting beyond the row beneath, progressing until opposing layers almost meet and can then be capped with a stone that rests across the tops of both layers.

1. Post and lintel

2. Cross section of post-and-lintel underground burial chamber

3. Cross section of corbeled underground burial chamber

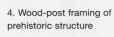
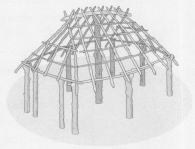

4. Wood-post framing of prehistoric structure

5. Granite post-and-lintel construction, Valley Temple of Khafre, Giza, Egypt, c. 2500 BCE

SEE MORE: View a simulation of post-and-lintel construction **www.myartslab.com**

mud, clay, and wood buildings in another part. The stone-based buildings may have had a special function within the community (whether ritual, crafts-based, or political is difficult to determine) as they were rebuilt again and again over a long period of time so that the part of the village where they were located "grew" vertically into a mound or tell. Some buildings had easily recognizable functions, such as a place for making ceramic vessels. The distinction between the area of the longer-lasting, often rebuilt buildings and the more temporary structures is clear in the style of architecture as well as in the quality of artifacts found (finer, decorated pottery is more abundant in the former).

In different parts of Europe, people created architecture in different ways, as the crowded buildings of Çatalhöyük differed from the structures at Sesklo, and as these differed from the trapezoidal huts at Lepenski Vir. To the northwest in Germany and central Europe, villages of this period typically consisted of three or four long timber buildings, each up to 150 feet long, housing 45 to 50 people. The structures were rectangular, with a row of posts down the center supporting a **ridgepole**, a long horizontal beam

1-23 • NEOLITHIC BUILDING METHODS
Thessaly, Greece. 6000 BCE.

To view this image, please go to page 16 of the *Art History*, Fourth Edition by Marilyn Stokstad ebook.

To view this image, please go to page 17 of the *Art History*, Fourth Edition by Marilyn Stokstad ebook.

1-24 • TOMB INTERIOR WITH CORBELING AND ENGRAVED STONES
Newgrange, Ireland. c. 3000–2500 BCE.

societies in which powerful religious or political leaders dictated their design and inspired (and coerced) large numbers of people to contribute their labor to such engineering projects. Skilled "engineers" devised methods for shaping, transporting, and aligning the stones. Other interpreters argue that these massive monuments are clear evidence for equally shared collaboration within and between groups, with people working together on a common project, the successful completion of which fueled social cohesion in the absence of a powerful individual.

Many of these megalithic structures are associated with death. Most recent interpretations stress the role of death and burial as fundamental, public performances in which individual and group identity, cohesion, and dispute were played out. In this reasoning, death and its rituals are viewed as theater, with the deceased as well as grave goods perceived as props, the monument as a stage, the celebrants and mourners as actors, and the entire event proceeding in terms of an (unwritten) script with narrative and plot.

Elaborate megalithic tombs first appeared in the Neolithic period. Some were built for single burials; others consisted of multiple burial chambers. The simplest type of megalithic tomb was the **dolmen**, built on the post-and-lintel principle (see examples 1 and 2 in "Early Construction Methods," page 25). The tomb chamber was formed of huge upright stones supporting one or more tablelike rocks, or capstones. The structure was then mounded over with smaller rocks and dirt to form a **cairn** or artificial hill. A more imposing structure was the **passage grave**, which was entered by one or more narrow, stone-lined passageways into a large room at the center.

At Newgrange, in Ireland, the mound of an elaborate passage grave (**FIG. 1–24**) originally stood 44 feet tall and measured about 280 feet in diameter. The mound was built of sod and river pebbles and was set off by a circle of engraved standing stones around its perimeter. Its passageway, 62 feet long and lined with standing stones, leads into a three-part chamber with a corbel **vault** (an arched structure that spans an interior space) rising to a height of 19 feet (see example 3 in "Early Construction Methods," page 25). Some of the stones are engraved with linear designs, mainly rings, spirals, and diamond shapes. These patterns may have been marked out using strings or compasses, then carved by

against which the slanting roof poles were braced (see example 4 in "Early Construction Methods," opposite). The walls were probably made of what is known as **wattle and daub**, branches woven in a basketlike pattern, then covered with mud or clay (**FIG. 1–23**). They were probably roofed with **thatch**, plant material such as reeds or straw tied over a framework of poles. These houses also included large granaries, or storage spaces for the harvest; some buildings contain sections for animals and for people. Around 4000 BCE, Neolithic settlers began to locate their communities at defensible sites—near rivers, on plateaus, or in swamps. For additional protection, they also frequently surrounded them with wooden walls, earth embankments, and ditches.

CEREMONIAL AND TOMB ARCHITECTURE.   In western and northern Europe, people erected megaliths to build ceremonial structures and tombs. In some cases, they had to transport these great stones over long distances. The monuments thus created are examples of what is known as **megalithic architecture**, the descriptive term derived from the Greek words for "large" (*mega-*) and "stone" (*lithos*).

Archaeologists disagree about the types of society that created these monuments. Some believe they reflect complex, stratified

1-25 • STONEHENGE
Salisbury Plain, Wiltshire,
England. c. 2900–1500 BCE.

EXPLORE MORE:
Click the Google
Earth link for
Stonehenge
www.myartslab.com

To view this image, please go to page 18 of the *Art History*, Fourth Edition by Marilyn Stokstad ebook.

1-26 • PLAN OF STONEHENGE AND ITS SURROUNDING SETTLEMENTS

To view this image, please go to page 18 of the *Art History*, Fourth Edition by Marilyn Stokstad ebook.

the particularities of perception by the eye), and that we should understand them in terms of the neuropsychological effect they would have had on people visiting the tomb. These effects may have included hallucinations. Archaeologists argue that key entoptic motifs were positioned at entrances and other important thresholds inside the tomb, and that they played important roles in ritual or political ceremonies that centered around death, burial, and the commemoration and visitation of the deceased by the living.

STONEHENGE. Of all the megalithic monuments in Europe, the one that has stirred the imagination of the public most strongly is **STONEHENGE**, on Salisbury Plain in southern England **(FIGS. 1–25, 1–26)**. A **henge** is a circle of stones or posts, often surrounded by a ditch with built-up embankments. Laying out such circles with accuracy would have posed no particular

picking at the rock surface with tools made of antlers. Recent detailed analysis of the art engraved on passage graves like Newgrange, but also at Knowth in Ireland, suggest that the images are entoptic (meaning that their significance and function relate to

problem. Architects likely relied on the human compass, a simple but effective surveying method that persisted well into modern times. All that is required is a length of cord either cut or knotted to mark the desired radius of the circle. A person holding one end of the cord is stationed in the center; a co-worker, holding the other end and keeping the cord taut, steps off the circle's circumference. By the time of Stonehenge's construction, cords and ropes were readily available.

Stonehenge is not the largest such circle from the Neolithic period, but it is one of the most complex, with eight different phases of construction and activity starting in the Neolithic in 3000 BCE, and stretching over a millennium and a half through the Bronze Age. The site started as a cemetery of cremation burials marked by a circle of bluestones. Through numerous sequences of alterations and rebuildings, it continued to function as a place of the dead. Between 2900 and 2600 BCE, the bluestones were rearranged into an arc. Around 2500 BCE, a circle of sarsen stones was used to create the famous appearance of the site—sarsen is a gray sandstone—and the bluestones were rearranged within the sarsens. The center of the site was now dominated by a horseshoe-shaped arrangement of five sandstone trilithons, or pairs of upright stones topped by lintels. The one at the middle stood considerably taller than the rest, rising to a height of 24 feet, and its lintel was more than 15 feet long and 3 feet thick. This group was surrounded by the so-called sarsen circle, a ring of sandstone uprights weighing up to 26 tons each and averaging 13 feet 6 inches tall. This circle, 106 feet in diameter, was capped by a continuous lintel. The uprights were tapered slightly toward the top, and the gently curved lintel sections were secured by **mortise-and-tenon** joints, that is, joints made by a conical projection at the top of each upright that fits like a peg into a hole in the lintel. Over the next thousand years people continued to alter the arrangement of the bluestones and continued to make cremation burials in pits at the site.

The differences in the types of stone used in the different phases of construction are significant. The use of bluestone in the early phases (and maintained and rearranged through the sequence) is particularly important. Unlike the sarsen stone, bluestone was not locally available and would have been transported over 150 miles from the west, where it had been quarried in the mountains of west Wales. The means of transporting the bluestones such distances remains a source of great debate. Some argue that they were floated around the coast on great barges; others hold that they were brought over land on wooden rollers. Regardless of the means of transport, the use of this distant material tells us that the people who first transformed the Stonehenge landscape into a ceremonial one probably also had their ancestral origins in the west. By bringing the bluestones and using them in the early Stonehenge cemetery, these migrants made a powerful connection with their homelands.

Through the ages, many theories have been advanced to explain Stonehenge. In the Middle Ages, people thought that Merlin, the magician of the King Arthur legend, had built it. Later, the site was erroneously associated with the rituals of the Celtic druids (priests). Because its orientation is related to the movement of the sun, some people have argued that it may have been an observatory or that it had special importance as a calendar for regulating early agricultural schedules. Today none of these ideas is supported by archaeologists and the current evidence.

It is now believed that Stonehenge was the site of ceremonies linked to death and burial. This theory has been constructed from evidence that looks not only at the stone circles but also at the nearby sites dating from the periods when Stonehenge was in use. A new generation of archaeologists, led by Mike Parker Pearson, has pioneered this contextual approach to the puzzle of Stonehenge (SEE FIG. 1–26).

The settlements built near Stonehenge follow circular layouts, connecting them in plan to the ceremonial site (**FIG. 1–27**). Unlike the more famous monument, however, these habitations were built

To view this image, please go to page 19 of the *Art History*, Fourth Edition by Marilyn Stokstad ebook.

1-27 • RECONSTRUCTION DRAWING OF DURRINGTON WALLS
The settlement at Durrington Walls, near Stonehenge in southern England, 2600 BCE.

Intentional House Burning

While much research has focused on the origins and technology of the earliest architecture as at Çatalhöyük, Lepenski Vir, and other sites, some of the most exciting new work has come from studies of how Neolithic houses were destroyed. Excavations of settlements dating to the end of the Neolithic in eastern and central Europe commonly reveal a level of ash and other evidence for great fires that burned down houses at these sites. The common interpretation had been that invaders, coming on horseback from Ukraine and Russia, had attacked these villages and burned the settlements.

In one of the most innovative recent studies, Mira Stevanović and Ruth Tringham exploited the methods of modern forensic science and meticulously reconstructed the patterns of Neolithic house conflagrations. The results proved that the fires were not part of village-wide destructions, but were individual events of firings, confined to particular houses. Most significantly, they showed that each fire had been deliberately set. In fact, in order to get the fires to consume the houses completely, buildings had been stuffed with combustibles before they were set alight. Repeated tests by experimental archaeologists have supported these conclusions. Each intentional, house-destroying fire was part of a ritual killing of the house and a rupture of the historical and social entity that the house had represented for the community. Critically, even in their destruction, prehistoric architecture played important and complex roles within the ways that individuals and community created (and destroyed) social identities and continuities.

of wood, in particular large posts and tree trunks. A mile from Stonehenge is one of these sites, Durrington Walls, which was a large settlement (almost 1,500 feet across) surrounded by a ditch. Inside the site are a number of circles made not from stone but from wood; there are also many circular houses also made with wooden posts. The rubbish left behind at this and similar sites has given archaeologists insights into the inhabitants. Chemical analysis of animal bone debris, for example, indicates that the animals consumed came from great distances before they were slaughtered, and therefore that the people who stayed here had come from regions very far from the site.

Significantly, both Stonehenge and Durrington Walls are connected to the Avon River by banked avenues. These connected the worlds of the living (the wood settlement) with the world of the dead (the stone circle). Neolithic people would have moved between these worlds as they walked the avenues, sometimes bringing the deceased to be buried or cremated, other times approaching the stone circle for ceremonies and rituals dedicated to the memories of the deceased and the very ancient ancestors. The meaning of Stonehenge therefore rests within an understanding of the larger landscape that contained not only other ritual sites but also the places of the living.

SCULPTURE AND CERAMICS

In addition to domestic and ceremonial architecture and a food-producing economy, the other critical component of the Neolithic way of life was the ability to make ceramic vessels (see "Pottery and Ceramics," page 31). This "pot revolution" marked a shift from a complete reliance on skin, textile, and wooden containers to the use of pots made by firing clay. Pottery provided a new medium of extraordinary potential for shaping and decorating durable objects. Ceramic technology emerged independently, at different times, across the globe, with the earliest examples being produced by the Jomon culture of hunter-gatherers in Japan in 12,000 BCE (**FIG. 1–28**). It is extremely difficult to determine with certainty why pottery was first invented or why subsequent cultures adopted it. The idea that pottery would only emerge out of farming settlements is confounded by the example of the Jomon. Rather, it seems that

To view this image, please go to page 20 of the *Art History*, Fourth Edition by Marilyn Stokstad ebook.

1-28 • EARLY POTTERY: FROM JAPAN'S JOMON CULTURE
12,000 BCE.

To view this image, please go to page 21 of the *Art History*, Fourth Edition by Marilyn Stokstad ebook.

1-29 • EARLY POTTERY: FRANCHTHI CAVE, GREECE
6500 BCE.

pits: one assemblage consisted of 12 busts and 13 full figures; in the other were two full figures, two fragmental busts, and three figures which had two heads. The figures, each about 3 feet tall, are disturbing to look at (at least from a modern perspective): the eyes, made with cowrie shells painted with bitumen (a natural asphalt) to represent pupils and the edges of the eyes, are open and make the figures appear lifelike. Nostrils are clearly defined, but the mouths are tight-lipped. Clothes and other features were painted on the bodies. Though without arms, the legs and feet (with toes) are clearly modeled with plaster. The impression is of living, breathing individuals who are not able (or willing) to speak.

there was no one set of social, economic, or environmental circumstances that led to the invention of ceramics.

It is likely that the technology for producing ceramics evolved in stages. Archaeologist Karen Vitelli's detailed studies of the early Neolithic site at Franchthi Cave, Greece, have shown that pottery making at this site started with an experimental stage during which nonspecialist potters produced a small number of pots. These early pots were used in ceremonies, especially those where medicinal or narcotic plants were consumed (**FIG. 1–29**). Only later did specialist potters share manufacturing recipes to produce enough pots for standard activities such as cooking and eating. It is probable that a similar pattern occurred in other early potting communities.

In addition to firing clay to make pots, cups, pitchers, and large storage containers, Neolithic people made thousands of miniature figures of humans (see "Prehistoric Woman and Man," page 33). While it was once thought that these figurines refer to fertility cults and matriarchal societies, archaeologists now agree that they had many different functions (as toys, portraits, votives). More importantly, specialists have shown that there are great degrees of similarity in figurine shape and decoration within each distinct cultural region. This degree of similarity, and the huge numbers of figurines that would have been in circulation at any one (Neolithic) place and time, have convinced experts that the critical significance of these objects is that they mark the emergence of the human body as the core location of the human identity. Thus, the central role the body has played in the politics, philosophy and art of historical and modern times began in 6000 BCE with Neolithic figurines.

Prehistoric figures of the human form were most numerous and diverse in the Neolithic of central and eastern Europe. In Jordan in the Near East, at the site of 'Ain Ghazal, archaeologist Gary Rollefson found 32 extraordinary **HUMAN FIGURES (FIG. 1–30)**. Dated to 6500 BCE and constructed by covering bundled-twig figures with layers of plaster, the statues were found in two

To view this image, please go to page 21 of the *Art History*, Fourth Edition by Marilyn Stokstad ebook.

1-30 • HUMAN FIGURE
From 'Ain Ghazal, Jordan. 6500 BCE. Fired lime plaster with cowrie shell, bitumen, and paint, height approx. 35″ (90 cm). National Museum, Amman, Jordan.

The terms pottery and ceramics may be used interchangeably—and often are. Because it covers all baked-clay wares, **ceramics** is technically a more inclusive term than pottery. Pottery includes all baked-clay wares except **porcelain**, which is the most refined product of ceramic technology.

Pottery vessels can be formed in several ways. It is possible, though difficult, to raise up the sides from a ball of raw clay. Another method is to coil long rolls of soft, raw clay, stack them on top of each other to form a container, and then smooth them by hand. A third possibility is to simply press the clay over an existing form, a dried gourd for example. By about 4000 BCE, Egyptian potters had developed the potter's wheel, a round, spinning platform on which a lump of clay is placed and then formed with the fingers, making it relatively simple to produce a uniformly shaped vessel in a very short time. The potter's wheel appeared in the ancient Near East about 3250 BCE and in China about 3000 BCE.

After a pot is formed, it is allowed to dry completely before it is fired. Special ovens for firing pottery, called **kilns**, have been discovered at prehistoric sites in Europe dating from as early as 26,000 BCE (as at Dolní Věstonice). For proper firing, the temperature must be maintained at a relatively uniform level. Raw clay becomes porous pottery when heated to at least 500° Centigrade. It then holds its shape permanently and will not disintegrate in water. Fired at 800° Centigrade, pottery is technically known as **earthenware**. When subjected to temperatures between 1,200° and 1,400° Centigrade, certain stone elements in the clay vitrify, or become glassy, and the result is a stronger type of ceramic called **stoneware**.

Pottery is relatively fragile, and new vessels were constantly in demand to replace broken ones, so fragments of low-fired ceramics—fired at the hearth, rather than the higher temperature kiln—are the most common artifacts found in excavations of prehistoric settlements. Pottery fragments, or **potsherds**, serve as a major key in dating sites and reconstructing human living and trading patterns.

Scholars have looked for clues about the function of these figures. The people who lived on the site built and rebuilt houses, replastered walls, and buried their dead under house floors—they even dug down through the floors to retrieve the skulls of long-deceased relatives—just like the inhabitants of Çatalhöyük. They used the same plaster to coat the walls of their houses that they used to make the figures. The site also contains buildings that may have served special, potentially ceremonial functions, and it has been suggested that the figures are linked to these rites. In addition to the figures' lifelike appearance, the similarity between the burial of bodies under house floors and the burial of the plaster figures in pits is striking. At the same time, however, there are differences in the burials: the figures are buried in groups while the humans are not; the figures are buried in pits and not in houses; the figures' eyes are open, as if they are alive and awake. At this point in the research it is difficult to get any closer to a clear understanding of how they were used and what they meant to the people of 'Ain Ghazal.

NEW METALLURGY, ENDURING STONE

The technology of metallurgy is closely allied to that of ceramics. Although Neolithic culture persisted in northern Europe until about 2000 BCE (and indeed all of its key contributions to human evolution—farming, architecture, and pottery—continue through present times), the age of metals made its appearance in much of Europe about 3000 BCE. In central and southern Europe, and in the Aegean region, copper, gold, and tin had been mined, worked, and traded even earlier. Smelted and cast copper beads and ornaments dated to 4000 BCE have been discovered in Poland.

Metals were first used for ornamentation. Toward the end of the Neolithic, people shaped simple beads by cold-hammering malachite, a green-colored carbonate mineral that can be found on the surface of the ground in many regions. Gold was also one of the first metals to be used in prehistory; it was used to make jewelry (ear, lip, and nose rings) or ornament clothing (appliqués sewn into fabric).

Over time, the objects made from copper and gold became more complicated and technologies of extraction (the mining of copper in Bulgaria) and of metalworking (casting copper) improved. Some of the most sensational (and earliest) gold and copper objects from prehistory were discovered by Ivan Ivanov in the late Neolithic cemetery at Varna on Bulgaria's Black Sea coast. While the cemetery consisted of several hundred burials of men, women and children, a few special burials contained gold and copper artifacts (**FIGS. 1–31, 1–32**). Objects such as gold-covered scepters, bracelets, beads, armrings, lip-plugs, and copper axes and chisels mark out the graves of a few adult males. In a very few of these graves no skeleton was present: The body was represented by a clay mask richly decorated with gold adornments (SEE FIG. 1–31) and the grave contained extraordinary concentrations of metal and special marine-shell ornaments. As in other prehistoric contexts, death and its attendant ceremonies were the focus for large and visually expressive displays of status and authority.

THE BRONZE AGE

The period that followed the introduction of metalworking is commonly called the Bronze Age. Although copper is relatively abundant in central Europe and in Spain, objects fashioned from it are too soft to be functional and therefore usually have a ceremonial or metaphoric use and value. However, bronze—an **alloy**, or mixture, of tin and copper—is a stronger, harder substance with a wide variety of uses.

The introduction of bronze, especially for weapons such as daggers and short swords, changed the peoples of Europe in fundamental ways. Where copper ore was widely available across Europe, either as surface outcrops or to be mined, the tin that was required to make bronze had a much more limited natural distribution and often required extraction by mining. Power bases shifted within communities as the resources needed to make bronze were not widely available to all. Trade and intergroup contacts across the continent and into the Near East increased, and bronze objects circulated as prized goods.

ROCK CARVINGS

Bronze Age artistry is not limited to metalworking; indeed, some of the most exciting imagery of the period is found in the rock art of northern Europe. For a thousand years starting around 1500 BCE people scratched outlines of a design, then pecked and ground the surface of exposed rock faces using stone hammers and sometimes grains of sand as an abrasive. The Swedish region of northern Bohuslän is especially rich in rock carvings dating to this period; archaeologists have recorded over 40,000 individual images from more than 1,500 sites. The range of motifs is wide, including boats, animals (bulls, elk, horses, and a few snakes, birds, and fish), people (mostly sexless, some with horned helmets, but also men with erect penises), wheeled vehicles and ploughs (and unassociated

To view this image, please go to page 23 of the *Art History*, Fourth Edition by Marilyn Stokstad ebook.

1–31 • GOLD FACE MASK
From Tomb 3, Varna I, Bulgaria. Neolithic, 3800 BCE. Terra cotta and gold. Archaeological Museum, Plovdiv, Bulgaria.

To view this image, please go to page 23 of the *Art History*, Fourth Edition by Marilyn Stokstad ebook.

1–32 • GOLD SCEPTERS
From Varna, Bulgaria. 3800 BCE. National Museum of History, Sofia, Bulgaria.

Prehistoric Woman and Man

For all we know, the person who created these figurines at around 4500 BCE had nothing particular in mind—people had been modeling clay figures in southeastern Europe for a long time. Perhaps a woman who was making cooking and storage pots out of clay amused herself by fashioning images of the people she saw around her. But because these figures were found in a grave in Cernavodă, Romania, they suggest to us an otherworldly message.

The woman, spread-hipped and big-bellied, sits directly on the ground, expressive of the mundane world. She exudes stability and fecundity. Her ample hips and thighs seem to ensure the continuity of her family. But in a lively, even elegant, gesture, she joins her hands coquettishly on one raised knee, curls up her toes, and tilts her head upward. Though earthbound, is she a spiritual figure communing with heaven? Her upwardly tilted head could suggest that she is watching the smoke rising from the hearth, or worrying about holes in the roof, or admiring hanging containers of laboriously gathered drying berries, or gazing adoringly at her partner. The man is rather slim, with massive legs and shoulders. He rests his head on his hands in a brooding, pensive pose, evoking thoughtfulness, even weariness or sorrow.

We can interpret the Cernavodă woman and man in many ways, but we cannot know what they meant to their makers or owners. Depending on how they are displayed, we spin out different stories about them. When set facing each other, side by side as they are in the photograph, we tend to see them as a couple—a woman and man in a relationship. In fact, we do not know whether the artist conceived of them in this way, or even made them at the same time. For all their visual eloquence, their secrets remain hidden from us.

To view this image, please go to page 24 of the *Art History*, Fourth Edition by Marilyn Stokstad ebook.

To view this image, please go to page 24 of the *Art History*, Fourth Edition by Marilyn Stokstad ebook.

FIGURES OF A WOMAN AND A MAN
From Cernavodă, Romania. c. 4500 BCE. Ceramic, height 4½″ (11.5 cm). National Historical Museum, Bucharest.

To view this image, please go to page 25 of the *Art History*, Fourth Edition by Marilyn Stokstad ebook.

1–33 • ROCK ART: BOAT AND SEA BATTLE
Fossum, northern Bohuslän, Sweden. Bronze Age. c. 1500–500 BCE.

disks, circles, and wheels), and weapons (swords, shields, and helmets). Within this range, however, the majority of images are boats **(FIG. 1–33)**, not just in Sweden but across northern Europe. Interestingly, the boat images are unlike the boats that archaeologists have excavated. The rock-engraved images do not have masts nor are they the dugouts or log boats that are known from this period. Instead they represent boats made from wooden planks or with animal skins.

What is the meaning of these boat images? It is generally agreed that the location of the majority of the rock art (near current or past shorelines) is the critical clue to their meaning. Archaeologist Richard Bradley suggests that rock art connects sky, earth, and sea, perhaps reflecting the community's view of the three-part nature of the universe. Others suggest that the art is intentionally located between water and earth to mark a boundary between the living and the spirit worlds. In this view, the character of the rock (permanent and grounded deep in the earth) provided a means of communication and connection between distinct worlds.

For people of the prehistoric era, representational and abstract art had a symbolic importance that matched the labor required to paint in the deep recesses of caves, move enormous stones great distances, or create elaborately ornamented masks. This art and architecture connected the worlds of the living and the spirits, established social power hierarchies, and helped people learn and remember critical information about the natural world. It was not art for art's sake, but it was one of the fundamental elements of our development as a human species.

THINK ABOUT IT

1.6 Discuss the likely origins of art in its earliest days in the prehistoric past. What needs are the visual arts believed to have first fulfilled in human culture?

1.7 What are the common motifs found in cave paintings such as those at Lascaux and Altamira? Summarize the current theories about their original purpose.

1.8 Explain how Stonehenge was likely created and discuss its probable purpose, according to present interpretations.

1.9 Discuss what the use and meaning of figurines such as the Paleolithic *Woman from Willendorf* (SEE FIG. 1–11) and Neolithic *Figures of a Woman and a Man* (see "Prehistoric Woman and Man," page 33) might have been and contrast the forms of the two directly.

1.10 How did the emergence of ceramics and metallurgy transform art making in the Neolithic era? Select and analyze a work discussed in the chapter that was made in one of these new media and discuss the unique properties of the medium.

PRACTICE MORE: Compose answers to these questions, get flashcards for images and terms, and review chapter material with quizzes
www.myartslab.com

To view this image, please go to page 402 of the *Art History*, Fourth Edition by Marilyn Stokstad ebook.

1–34 • CROWNED HEAD OF A KING   Ife, Yoruba. 12th–15th century CE.
Zinc brass, height 9⁷⁄₁₆″ (24 cm). Museum of Ife Antiquities, Ife, Nigeria.

EARLY AFRICAN ART

The Yoruba people of southwestern Nigeria regard the city of Ife (also known as Ile-Ife) as the "navel of the world," the site of creation, the place where Ife's first ruler—the *oni* Oduduwa—came down from heaven to create earth and then to populate it. By the eleventh century CE, Ife was a lively metropolis. Today, every Yoruba city claims "descent" from Ife.

Ife was, and remains, the sacred city of the Yoruba people. A tradition of naturalistic sculpture began there about 1050 CE and flourished for some four centuries. Although the ancestral line of the Ife *oni* (king) has continued unbroken, knowledge of the precise purpose of these works has been lost.

A cast-bronze head (FIG. 1–34) shows the extraordinary artistry of ancient Ife. The modeling of the flesh is remarkably sensitive, especially the subtle transitions around the nose and mouth. The lips are full and delicate, and the eyes are strikingly similar in shape to those of some modern Yoruba. The face is covered with thin, parallel **scarification** patterns (decorations made by scarring). The head was cast of zinc brass using the lost-wax method.

The head was cast with a crown; its size and delicate features suggest it may represent a female *oni*. Although its precise use is not known, similar life-size heads have large holes in the neck, suggesting they may have been attached to wooden figures. Mannequins with naturalistic facial features have been documented at memorial services for deceased individuals among contemporary Yoruba peoples. The Ife mannequin was probably dressed in the *oni*'s robes; the head probably bore his crown. The head could also have been used to display a crown during annual purification and renewal rites.

There is debate as to whether the Ife heads are true portraits. Their realism gives an impression that they could be. The heads, however, all seem to represent individuals of the same age and embody a similar concept of physical perfection, suggesting they are idealized images representing both physical beauty and moral character. Idealized images of titled individuals are a common feature of sub-Saharan African sculpture, as they are among many cultures throughout the world.

The superb naturalism of Ife sculpture contradicted everything Europeans thought they knew about African art. The German scholar, Leo Frobenius, who "discovered" Ife sculpture in 1910 suggested that it was created not by Africans but by survivors from the legendary lost island of Atlantis. Later, there was speculation that influence from ancient Greece or Renaissance Europe must have reached Ife. Scientific study, however, finally put such prejudiced ideas to rest.

LEARN ABOUT IT

1.11 Identify and summarize the key roles that the visual arts play in sub-Saharan Africa.

1.12 Explore how African arts mediate and support communication between the temporal and the supernatural worlds of various spirit forces.

1.13 Specify how African visual arts are only fully realized in their context of use.

1.14 Contrast the role of African arts related to leadership as compared to the role of leadership arts in Western cultural traditions.

HEAR MORE: Listen to an audio file of your chapter **www.myartslab.com**

THE LURE OF ANCIENT AFRICA

"I descended [the Nile] with three hundred asses laden with incense, ebony, grain, panthers, ivory, and every good product." Thus the Egyptian envoy Harkhuf described his return from Nubia, the African land to the south of Egypt, in 2300 BCE. The riches of Africa attracted merchants and envoys in ancient times, and trade brought the continent in contact with the rest of the world. Egyptian relations with the rest of the African continent continued through the Hellenistic era and beyond. Phoenicians and Greeks founded dozens of settlements along the Mediterranean coast of North Africa between 1000 and 300 BCE to extend trade routes across the Sahara to the peoples of Lake Chad and the bend of the Niger River (MAP 1–2). When the Romans took control of North Africa, they continued this lucrative trans-Saharan trade. In the seventh and eighth centuries CE, the expanding empire of Islam swept across North Africa, and thereafter Islamic merchants were regular visitors to Bilad al-Sudan (the Land of the Blacks—sub-Saharan Africa). Islamic scholars chronicled the great West African empires of Ghana, Mali, and Songhay, and West African gold financed the flowering of Islamic culture.

East Africa, meanwhile, had been drawn since at least the beginning of the Common Era into the maritime trade that ringed the Indian Ocean and extended east to Indonesia and the South China Sea. Arab, Indian, and Persian ships plied the coastline. A new language, Swahili, evolved from centuries of contact between Arabic-speaking merchants and Bantu-speaking Africans, and great port cities such as Kilwa, Mombasa, and Mogadishu arose.

In the fifteenth century, Europeans ventured by ship into the Atlantic Ocean and down the coast of Africa. Finally rediscovering the continent firsthand, they were often astonished by what they found (see "The Myth of 'Primitive' Art," page 39). "Dear King My Brother," wrote a fifteenth-century Portuguese king to his new trading partner, the king of Benin in west Africa. The Portuguese king's respect was well founded—Benin was vastly more powerful and wealthier than the small European country that had just stumbled upon it.

Africa was home to one of the world's earliest great civilizations, that of ancient Egypt, and as we will see in Chapter 3, Egypt and the rest of North Africa contributed prominently to the development of Islamic art and culture. This chapter examines the artistic legacy of the rest of ancient Africa.

AFRICA—THE CRADLE OF ART AND CIVILIZATION

During the twentieth century, the sculpture of traditional African societies—wood carvings of astonishing formal inventiveness and power—found admirers the world over. While avidly collected, these works were much misunderstood. For the past 75 years, art historians and cultural anthropologists have studied African art firsthand, which has added to our overall understanding of art making in many African cultures. However, except for a few isolated examples (such as in Nigeria and Mali), the historical depth of our understanding is still limited by the continuing lack of systematic archaeological research. Our understanding of traditions that are more than 100 years old is especially hampered by the fact that most African art was made from wood, which decays rapidly in sub-Saharan Africa. Consequently, few examples of African masks and sculpture remain from before the nineteenth century, and for the most part it is necessary to rely on contemporary traditions and oral histories to help extrapolate backward in time to determine what may have been the types, styles, and meaning of art made in the past. Nevertheless, the few ancient African artworks we have in such durable materials as terra cotta, stone, and bronze, and from an extensive record in rock art that has been preserved in sheltered places, bear eloquent witness to the skill of ancient African artists and the splendor of the civilizations in which they worked.

Twentieth-century archaeology has made it popular to speak of Africa as the cradle of human civilization. Certainly the earliest evidence for our human ancestors comes from southern Africa (see "Southern African Rock Art," page 41). Now evidence of the initial stirrings of artistic activity also comes from the southern tip of Africa. Recently, quantities of ocher pigment thought to have been used for ceremonial or decorative purposes, and perforated shells thought to have been fashioned into beads and worn as personal adornment, have been found in Blombos Cave on the Indian Ocean coast of South Africa, dating to approximately 77,000 years ago. Also discovered together with these were two small, ocher blocks that had been smoothed and then decorated with geometric arrays of carved lines (SEE FIG. 1–8 for an illustration of the decorated ocher). These incised abstract patterns predate any other findings of ancient art by more than 30,000 years, and they suggest a far earlier development of modern human behavior than had been previously recognized.

The earliest known figurative art works from the African continent are animal figures dating to about 25,000 BCE, painted in red and black pigment on flat stones found in a cave designated as Apollo 11, located in the desert mountains of Namibia. These figures are comparable to the better-known European cave drawings such as those from the Chauvet Cave (c. 32,000–30,000 BCE) and Lascaux Cave (c. 15,000–13,000 BCE).

AFRICAN ROCK ART

Like the Paleolithic inhabitants of Europe, early Africans painted and inscribed images on the walls of caves and rock shelters. Rock art is found throughout the African continent in places where the environment has been conducive to preservation—areas ranging from small, isolated shelters to great cavernous formations. Distinct geographic zones of rock art can be identified broadly encompassing the northern, central, southern, and eastern regions of the continent. These rock paintings and engravings range in

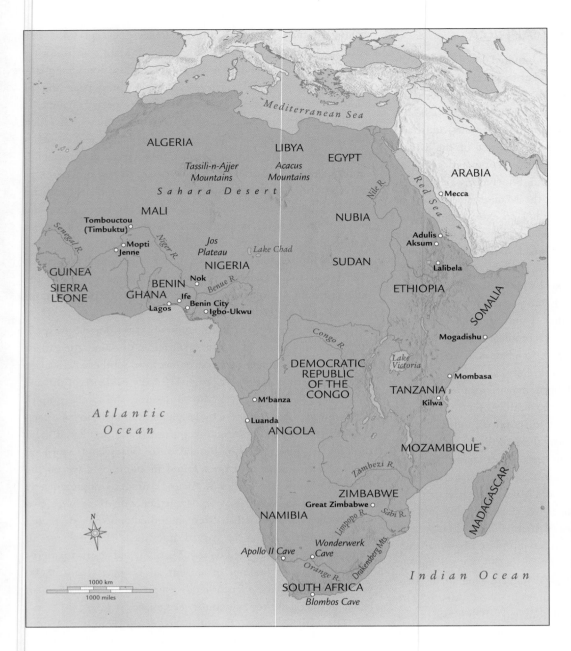

MAP 1-2 • ANCIENT AFRICA

Nearly 5,000 miles from north to south, Africa is the second-largest continent and was the home of some of the earliest and most advanced cultures of the ancient world.

form from highly abstract geometric designs to abstract and naturalistic representations of human and animal forms, including hunting scenes, scenes of domestic life, and costumed figures that appear to be dancing. The long record of rock art, extending over thousands of years in numerous places, charts dramatic environmental and social change in the deserts of Africa. Images depicting human subjects are also important evidence that the African artistic traditions of body decoration, mask-making and performance spring from ancient African roots.

SAHARAN ROCK ART

The mountains of the central Sahara—principally the Tassili-n-Ajjer range in the south of present-day Algeria and the Acacus Mountains in present-day Libya—contain images that span a period of thousands of years. They record not only the artistic and

cultural development of the peoples who lived in the region, but also the transformation of the Sahara from a fertile grassland to the vast desert we know today.

The earliest images of Saharan rock art are thought to date from at least 8000 BCE, during the transition into a geological period known as the Makalian Wet Phase. At that time the Sahara was a grassy plain, perhaps much like the game-park reserves of modern east Africa. Vivid images of hippopotamus, elephant, giraffe, antelope, and other animals incised on rock surfaces attest to the abundant wildlife that roamed the region.

A variety of scenes found on rock walls in both southern Algeria and Libya depict men and women dancing or performing various ceremonial activities. The artists who created these works paid close attention to details of clothing, body decoration, and headdresses; in some examples the figures are depicted wearing

The Myth of "Primitive" Art

The word "primitive" was once used by Western art historians to categorize the art of Africa, the art of the Pacific islands, and the indigenous art of the Americas. The term itself means "early" or "first of its kind," but its use was meant to imply that these cultures were crude, simple, backward, and stuck in an early stage of development.

This attitude was accepted by Christian missionaries and explorers, who often described the peoples among whom they worked as "heathen," "barbaric," "ignorant," "tribal," "primitive," and other terms rooted in racism and colonialism. Such usages were extended to these peoples' creations, and "primitive art" became the conventional label for their cultural products.

Criteria that have been used to label a people "primitive" include the use of so-called Stone Age technology, the absence of written histories, and the failure to build great cities. Based on these criteria, however, the accomplishments of the peoples of Africa, to take just one example, contradict such prejudiced condescension: Africans south of the Sahara have smelted and forged iron since at least 500 BCE. Africans in many areas made and used high-quality steel for weapons and tools. Many African peoples have recorded their histories in Arabic since at least the tenth century CE. The first European visitors to Africa admired the style and sophistication of urban centers such as

Benin and Luanda, to name only two of the continent's great cities. Clearly, neither the cultures of ancient Africa nor the artworks they produced were "primitive" at all.

Until quite recently, Westerners tended to see Africa as a single country and not as an immense continent of vastly diverse cultures. Moreover, they perceived artists working in Africa as craftworkers bound to styles and images dictated by village elders and producing art that was anonymous and interchangeable. Over the past several decades, however, these misconceptions have crumbled. Art historians and anthropologists have now identified numerous African cultures and artists and compiled catalogs of their work. For example, the well-known Yoruba artist Olowe of Ise was commissioned by rulers throughout the Yoruba region in the early twentieth century to create prestige objects such as palace veranda posts and palace doors or *tour-de-force* carvings such as magnificent lidded bowls supported by kneeling figures. Certainly we will never know the names of the vast majority of African artists of the past, just as we do not know the names of the sculptors responsible for the portrait busts of ancient Rome or the monumental reliefs of the Hindu temples of South Asia. But, as elsewhere, the greatest artists in Africa were famous and sought after, while innumerable others labored honorably and not at all anonymously.

---

masks that cover their faces. It is suggested that they are engaged in rituals intended to ensure adequate rainfall or success in hunting, or to honor their dead. These images, produced in a variety of styles, document the development of the complex ceremonial and ritual lives of the people who created them **(FIG. 1–35)**.

By 4000 BCE the climate had become more arid, and hunting had given way to herding as the primary life-sustaining activity of the Sahara's inhabitants. Among the most beautiful and complex examples of Saharan rock art created in this period are scenes of sheep, goats, and cattle and of the daily lives of the people who tended them. Some scenes found at Tassili-n-Ajjer date from late in the herding period, about 5000–2000 BCE, and illustrate men and women gathered in front of round, thatched houses. As the men tend cattle, the women prepare a meal and care for children. Some scenes attempt to create a sense of depth and distance with overlapping forms, and the placement of near figures lower and distant figures higher in the picture plane.

By 2500–2000 BCE the Sahara was drying and the great game had disappeared, but other animals were introduced that appear in the rock art. The horse was brought from Egypt by about 1500 BCE and is seen regularly in rock art over the ensuing millennia. The fifth-century BCE Greek historian Herodotus described a chariot-driving people called the Garamante, whose kingdom corresponds roughly to present-day Libya. Rock-art images of horse-drawn

chariots bear out his account. Around 600 BCE the camel was introduced into the region from the east, and images of camels were painted on and incised into the rock.

The drying of the Sahara coincided with the rise of Egyptian civilization along the Nile Valley to the east. Similarities can be noted between Egyptian and Saharan motifs, among them images of rams with what appear to be disks between their horns. These similarities have been interpreted as evidence of Egyptian influence on the less-developed regions of the Sahara. Yet in light of the great age of Saharan rock art, it seems just as plausible that the influence flowed the other way, carried by people who had migrated into the Nile Valley when the grasslands of the Sahara disappeared.

SUB-SAHARAN CIVILIZATIONS

Saharan peoples presumably migrated southward as well, into the Sudan, the broad belt of grassland that stretches across Africa south of the Sahara Desert. They brought with them knowledge of settled agriculture and animal husbandry. The earliest evidence of settled agriculture in the Sudan dates from about 3000 BCE. Toward the middle of the first millennium BCE, at the same time that iron technology was being developed elsewhere in Africa, knowledge of ironworking spread across the Sudan as well,

To view this image, please go to page 407 of the *Art History*, Fourth Edition by Marilyn Stokstad ebook.

1-35 • DANCERS IN CEREMONIAL ATTIRE
Section of rock-wall painting, Tassili-n-Ajjer, Algeria. c. 5000–2000 BCE.

Nok sculpture was discovered in modern times by tin miners digging in alluvial deposits on the Jos plateau north of the confluence of the Niger and Benue rivers. Presumably, floods from centuries past had removed the sculptures from their original contexts, dragged and rolled them along, and then deposited them, scratched and broken, often leaving only the heads from what must have been complete human figures. Following archaeological convention, the name of a nearby village, Nok, was given to the culture that created these works. Nok-style works of sculpture have since been found in numerous sites over a wide area.

The Nok head shown (FIG. 1–36), slightly larger than life-size, probably formed part of a complete figure. The triangular or D-shaped eyes are characteristic of Nok style and appear also on sculptures of animals. Holes in the pupils, nostrils, and mouth allowed air to pass freely as the figure was fired. Each of the large buns of its elaborate hairstyle is pierced with a hole that may have held ornamental feathers. Other Nok figures were created displaying beaded necklaces,

enabling its inhabitants to create more effective weapons and farming tools. In the wake of these developments, larger and more complex societies emerged, especially in the fertile basins of Lake Chad in the central Sudan and the Niger and Senegal rivers to the west.

NOK

Some of the earliest evidence of iron technology in sub-Saharan Africa comes from the so-called Nok culture, which arose in the western Sudan, in present-day Nigeria, as early as 500 BCE. The Nok people were farmers who grew grain and oil-bearing seeds, but they were also smelters with the technology for refining ore. Slag and the remains of furnaces have been discovered, along with clay nozzles from the bellows used to fan the fires. The Nok people created the earliest known sculpture of sub-Saharan Africa, producing accomplished terra-cotta figures of human and animal subjects between about 500 BCE and 200 CE.

To view this image, please go to page 407 of the *Art History*, Fourth Edition by Marilyn Stokstad ebook.

1-36 • HEAD
From Nok. c. 500 BCE–200 CE. Terra cotta, height 14³⁄₁₆″ (36 cm). National Museum, Lagos, Nigeria.

Southern African Rock Art

Rock painting and engraving from sites in southern Africa differ in terms of style and age from those discussed for the Sahara region. Some works of art predate those found in the Sahara, while others continued to be produced into the modern era. Early works include an engraved fragment found in dateable debris in Wonderwerk Cave, South Africa, which dates back to 10,000 years ago. Painted stone flakes found at a site in Zimbabwe suggest dates between 13,000 and 8000 BCE.

Numerous examples of rock painting are also found in South Africa in the region of the Drakensberg Mountains. Almost 600 sites have been located in rock shelters and caves, with approximately 35,000 individual images catalogued. It is believed the paintings were produced, beginning approximately 2,400 years ago, by the predecessors of San peoples who still reside in the region. Ethnographic research among the San and related peoples in southern Africa suggest possible interpretations for some of the paintings. For example, rock paintings depicting groups of dancing figures may relate to certain forms of San rituals that are still performed today to heal individuals or to cleanse communities. These may have been created by San ritual specialists or shamans to record their curing dances or trance experiences of the spirit world. San rock artists continued to create rock paintings into the late nineteenth century. These latter works depict the arrival of Afrikaner pioneers in the region as well as British soldiers brandishing guns used to hunt eland.

To view this image, please go to page 408 of the *Art History*, Fourth Edition by Marilyn Stokstad ebook.

SECTION OF SAN ROCK-WALL PAINTING San peoples, n.d. Drakensberg Mountains, South Africa. Pigment and eland blood on rock.

armlets, bracelets, anklets, and other prestige ornaments. Nok sculpture may represent ordinary people dressed for special occasions or it may portray people of high status, thus reflecting social stratification in this early farming culture. In either case, the sculpture provides evidence of considerable technical accomplishment, which has led to speculation that Nok culture was built on the achievements of an earlier culture still to be discovered.

To view this image, please go to page 858 of the *Art History*, Fourth Edition by Marilyn Stokstad ebook.

1–37 • THE BARUNGA STATEMENT   Various artists from Arnhem Land and central Australia. 1988.
Ochers on composition board with collage of printed text on paper, 48 × 47¼″ (122 × 120 cm). Parliament House Art Collection, Parliament House, Canberra.

ART OF PACIFIC CULTURES

In 1788, when Captain James Cook arrived in Australia, at least 300,000 Indigenous Australians, whose ancestors had arrived 50,000 years earlier, and who spoke over 250 languages, were living there. For 40,000 years these Aboriginal Australians had been creating rock art—the oldest continuous culture in the world. Nevertheless, Cook claimed Australia for Britain as a *terra nullius*, a land that belonged to no one. Within a few decades, European diseases had killed 50 percent of Indigenous Australians. Colonization and the advent of missionaries would change their lives forever.

Two hundred years later, Indigenous Australians presented what is now known as THE BARUNGA STATEMENT (FIG. 1–37) to the then prime minister Bob Hawke. It was inspired by the Yirrkala Bark Petitions, which 25 years earlier had gained national attention when indigenous land rights claims were presented to the government on traditional bark paintings from Arnhem Land in the Northern Territory. The Barunga Statement placed its call for broader Aboriginal rights in text on paper collaged onto composition board decorated with two different styles of indigenous painting: one from Arnhem Land (on the left; SEE ALSO FIG. 1–9) and the other from Australia's central desert area (on the right). Painted in natural ochers, the cross hatching (*rarrk*) and zigzag patterns from the north contrast with the more fluid curved lines and dots that fill the central desert painting. In both, the artists use symbols to retell stories about the adventures of ancestral beings while dazzling the eye.

In 1992, the Australian High Court rejected Cook's *terra nullius* argument and granted land rights to Indigenous Australians. When no treaty between the national government and Indigenous Australians followed, Galarrwuy Yunupingu, an indigenous leader, asked for the Barunga Statement back so that he could bury it. Today, however, it still hangs in Parliament and the struggle for full rights for Indigenous Australians continues.

Throughout the Pacific, indigenous cultures have been impacted by contact with the West, though to different degrees. In New Zealand, for example, the Treaty of Waitangi (1840) recognized Maori ownership of land and gave Maori the rights of British subjects, establishing a different political dynamic. Nonetheless, numerous issues remain there, as in other parts of the region. Pacific islanders today use the arts to express and preserve their own rich and distinctive cultural identities.

LEARN ABOUT IT

1.15 Recognize how the availability of raw materials affects artistic choices and styles throughout the Pacific.

1.16 Investigate ways that ancestor rituals influence the art in different Pacific cultures.

1.17 Examine the role the human body plays as a subject in Pacific art.

1.18 Compare the differences between ephemeral and enduring materials in different societies across the Pacific.

1.19 Assess the impact of Western contact on art in the Pacific.

HEAR MORE: Listen to an audio file of your chapter **www.myartslab.com**

THE PEOPLING OF THE PACIFIC

On a map with the Pacific Ocean as its center, only the peripheries of the great landmasses of Asia and the Americas appear. Nearly one-third of the earth's surface is taken up by this vast expanse. Europeans arriving in Oceania in the late eighteenth and early nineteenth centuries noted four distinct but connected cultural-geographic areas: Australia, Melanesia, Micronesia, and Polynesia (MAP 1–3). Australia includes the continent, as well as the island of Tasmania to the southeast. Melanesia ("black islands," a reference to the dark skin color of its inhabitants) includes New Guinea and the string of islands that extend eastward from it as far as Fiji and New Caledonia. Micronesia ("small islands"), to the north of Melanesia, is a region of small islands and coral atolls. Polynesia ("many islands") is scattered over a huge, triangular region defined by New Zealand in the south, Rapa Nui (Easter Island) in the east, and the Hawaiian Islands to the north. The last region on earth to be inhabited by humans, Polynesia covers some 7.7 million square miles, of which fewer than 130,000 square miles are dry land—and most of that is New Zealand. With the exception of temperate New Zealand, with its marked seasons and snowcapped mountains, Oceania is in the tropics, that is, between the tropic of Cancer in the north and the tropic of Capricorn to the south.

Australia, Tasmania, and New Guinea formed a single continent during the last Ice Age, which began some 2.5 million years ago. About 50,000 years ago, when the sea level was some 330 feet lower than it is today, people moved to this continent from Southeast Asia, making at least part of the journey over open water.

Some 27,000 years ago humans were settled on the large islands north and east of New Guinea as far south as San Cristobal, but they ventured no farther for another 25,000 years. By about 4000 BCE—possibly as early as 7000 BCE—the people of Melanesia were raising pigs and cultivating taro, a plant with edible rootstocks. As the glaciers melted, the sea level rose, flooding low-lying coastal land. By around 4000 BCE a 70-mile-wide waterway, now called the Torres Strait, separated New Guinea from Australia, whose indigenous people continued their hunting and gathering way of life into the twentieth century.

The settling of the rest of the islands of Melanesia and the westernmost islands of Polynesia—Samoa and Tonga—coincided with the spread of the Lapita culture, named for a site in New Caledonia. The Lapita people were Austronesian speakers who probably migrated from Taiwan to Melanesia about 6,000 years ago. They spread throughout the islands of Melanesia beginning around 1500 BCE. They were farmers and fisherfolk who cultivated taro and yams, and brought with them dogs, pigs, and chickens, animals that these colonizers needed for food. They also carried with them the distinctive ceramics whose remnants today enable us to trace the extent of their travels. Lapita potters produced dishes, platters, bowls, and jars. Sometimes they covered their wares with a red slip, and they often decorated them with bands of incised and stamped patterns—dots, lines, and hatching—that may also have been used to decorate bark cloth and for tattooing. Most of the decoration was geometric, but some was figurative. The human face that appears in the example in FIGURE 1–38 is among the earliest representations of a human being, one of the most important subjects in Oceanic art. The Lapita people were skilled shipbuilders and navigators and engaged in inter-island trade. Over time the Lapita culture lost its widespread cohesion and evolved into various local forms. Its end is generally dated to the early centuries of the Common Era.

Polynesian culture emerged in the eastern Lapita region on the islands forming Tonga and Samoa. Just prior to the beginning of the first millennium CE, daring Polynesian seafarers, probably in double-hulled sailing canoes, began settling the scattered islands of Far Oceania and eastern Micronesia. Voyaging over open water, sometimes for thousands of miles, they reached Hawaii and Rapa Nui after about 500 CE and settled New Zealand around 800/900–1200 CE.

While this history of migrations across Melanesia to Polynesia and Micronesia allowed for cross-cultural borrowings, there are distinctions between these areas and within the regions as well. The islands that make up Micronesia, Melanesia, and Polynesia include both low-lying coral atolls and the tall tops of volcanic mountains that rise from the ocean floor. Raw materials available to residents of these islands vary greatly, and islander art and architecture utilize these materials in different ways. The soil of volcanic islands can be very rich and thus can support densely populated settlements with a local diversity of plants and animals. On the other hand, coral atolls do not generally have very good soil and thus cannot support

To view this image, please go to page 860 of the *Art History*, Fourth Edition by Marilyn Stokstad ebook.

1–38 • FRAGMENTS OF A LARGE LAPITA JAR
Venumbo Reef, Santa Cruz Island, Solomon Islands. c. 1200–1100 BCE. Clay, height of human face motif approx. 1½″ (4 cm).

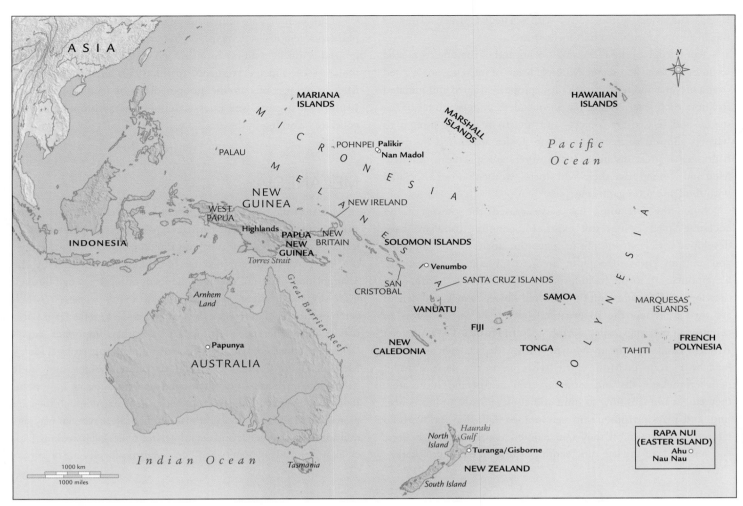

MAP 1-3 • PACIFIC CULTURAL-GEOGRAPHIC REGIONS

The Pacific cultures are found in four vast areas: Australia, Melanesia, Micronesia, and Polynesia.

large populations. In a like manner, volcanic islands can provide good stone for tools and building (as at Nan Madol, SEE FIG. 1–46), while coral is sharp but not particularly hard, and the strongest tools on a coral atoll are often those made from giant clam shells. Generally, the diversity of both plants and animals decreases from west to east among the Pacific islands.

The arts of this vast and diverse region display an enormous variety that is closely linked to each community's ritual and religious life. In this context, the visual arts were often just one strand in a rich weave that also included music, dance, and oral literature.

AUSTRALIA

The hunter-gatherers of Australia were closely attuned to the environments in which they lived until European settlers disrupted their way of life. Their only modification of the landscape was regular controlled burning of the underbrush, which encouraged new plant life and attracted animals. Their intimate knowledge of plants, animals, and water sources enabled them to survive and thrive in a wide range of challenging environments.

Indigenous Australian life is intimately connected with the concept of the Dreamtime, or the Dreaming. Not to be confused with our notions of sleep and dreams, the Dreaming refers to the period before humans existed. (The term, a translation from Arrente, one of the more than 250 languages spoken in Australia when Europeans arrived, was first used in the late nineteenth century to try to understand the indigenous worldview.) According to this complex belief system, the world began as a flat, featureless place. Ancestral Spirit Beings emerged from the earth or arrived from the sea, taking many different forms. The Spirit Beings had many adventures, and in crossing the continent they created all of its physical features: mountains, sand hills, creeks, and water holes. They also brought about the existence of animals, plants, and humans and created the ceremonies and sacred objects needed to ensure that they themselves were remembered, a system sometimes referred to as Aboriginal Laws. The Spirit Beings eventually returned to the earth or became literally one of its features. Thus, they are identified with specific places, which are honored as sacred sites. Indigenous Australians who practice this traditional religion believe that they are descended from the Spirit

Beings and associate themselves with particular places related to the ancestors' stories and transformations.

Knowledge of the Dreaming stories, and of the objects related to them, is sacred and secret. Multiple levels of meaning are learned over a lifetime and restricted to those properly trained and initiated to know each level. As a result, an outsider's understanding of the stories and related art (objects and motifs) is strictly limited to what is allowed to be public. Some stories are shared by many tribes across great distances, while others are specific to an area. Men and women have their own stories, women's often associated with food and food gathering.

Since the Dreaming has never ceased, the power of the ancestral Spirit Beings still exists. Indigenous Australians have developed a rich artistic life to relive the stories of the ancestors and transmit knowledge about them to subsequent generations. Ceremonial art forms include paintings on rock and bark, sand drawings, and ground sculptures. Sacred objects, songs, and dances are used to renew the supernatural powers of the ancestors in ceremonial meetings, called corroborees. In **FIGURE 1–39**, Western Arnhem Land artist Jimmy Midjaw Midjaw depicts such a meeting held by a group of Mimi, spirits who live in the narrow spaces between rocks by day and come out at night. Specific to this area, they taught humans how to hunt and cook animals, and to dance, sing, and play instruments in ceremonies. Tall, thin, human-like figures, often in motion, they were painted in ancient rock shelters, and since at least the late nineteenth century, on eucalyptus bark.

Bark paintings are found throughout northern Australia, where numerous regional styles exist. In Western Arnhem Land, the background is usually a monochromatic red ocher wash, with figures in white, black, and red pigments. In the 1950s and 1960s, Midjaw Midjaw was part of a prolific group of artists on Minjilang (Croker Island) that became well known through the anthropologists and collectors working in the area.

MELANESIA

In Melanesia the people usually rely at least partially on agriculture, and as a result they live in permanent settlements, many of which feature spaces set aside for ritual use. Position and status in society are not inherited or determined by birth, but are achieved by the accumulation of wealth (often in the form of pigs), prestige through leadership, and, often, participation in men's societies. Much ceremony is related to rituals associated with these societies, such as initiation into different levels or grades. Other important rituals facilitate relationships with the deceased and with supernatural forces. Melanesian art is often bold and dazzling. Masking and body decoration, often as part of ceremonial performances, are important, though often ephemeral, aspects of Melanesian art. Although men are prominent in the sculptural and masking traditions, women play significant roles as audience and are known for their skill in making bark cloth, woven baskets, pottery, and other aesthetically pleasing objects.

To view this image, please go to page 862 of the *Art History*, Fourth Edition by Marilyn Stokstad ebook.

1-39 • Jimmy Midjaw Midjaw THREE DANCERS AND TWO MUSICIANS: CORROBOREE OF MIMI, SPIRITS OF THE ROCKS
Minjilang (Croker Island), West Arnhem Land, Australia. Mid 20th century. Natural pigments on eucalyptus bark, 23 × 35″ (59 × 89 cm). Musée du Quai Branly, Paris, France. MNAO 64.9.103

NEW GUINEA

New Guinea, the largest island in the Pacific (and, at 1,500 miles long and 1,000 miles wide, the second-largest island in the world), is today divided between two countries. Its eastern half is part of the modern nation of Papua New Guinea; the western half is West Papua, a province of present-day Indonesia. Located near the equator and with mountains that rise to 16,000 feet, the island inhabitants utilize a variety of environments, from coastal mangrove marshes to grasslands, from dense rainforests to swampy river valleys. The population is equally diverse, with coastal fishermen, riverine hunters, slash-and-burn agriculturalists, and more stable farmers in the highlands. Between New Guinea itself and the smaller neighboring islands more than 700 languages have been identified.

THE *KORAMBO* OR CEREMONIAL HOUSE OF THE ABELAM OF PAPUA NEW GUINEA.

The Abelam, who live in the foothills of the mountains on the north side of the Sepik River in Papua New Guinea, raise pigs and cultivate yams, taro, bananas, and sago palms. In traditional Abelam society, people live in extended families or clans in hamlets. Wealth among the Abelam is measured in pigs, but men gain status from participation in a yam cult that has a central place in Abelam society. The yams that are the focus of this cult—some of which reach an extraordinary 12 feet in length—are associated with clan ancestors and the potency of their growers. Village leaders renew their relationship with the forces of nature that yams represent during the Long Yam Festival, which is held at harvest time and involves processions, masked figures, singing, and the ritual exchange of the finest yams.

An Abelam hamlet includes sleeping houses, cooking houses, storehouses for yams, a central space for rituals, and a ceremonial or spirit house, the **korambo** (*haus tambaran* in Pidgin). In this ceremonial structure reserved for the men of the village, the objects associated with the yam cult and with clan identity are kept hidden from women and uninitiated boys. Men of the clan gather in the *korambo* to organize rituals, especially initiation rites, and conduct community business. The prestige of a hamlet is linked to the quality of its *korambo* and the size of its yams. Constructed on a frame of poles and rafters and roofed with split cane and thatch, *korambo* are built with a triangular floor plan, the side walls meeting at the back of the building. The elaborately decorated façade consists of three parts, beginning at the bottom: a woven mat, a painted and carved wooden lintel, and painted sago bark panels **(FIG. 1–40)**. In this example, built about 1961, red, white, and black faces of spirits (*nggwal*) appear on the façade's bark panels, and the figure at the top is said to represent a female flying witch. This last figure is associated with the feminine power of the house itself. The projecting pole at the top of the *korambo* is the only male element of the architecture, and is said to be the penis of the house. The small door at the lower right is a female element, a womb; entering and exiting the house is the symbolic equivalent to death and rebirth. The Abelam believe the paint itself has magical qualities. Regular, ritual repainting revitalizes the images and ensures their continued potency.

Every stage in the construction of a *korambo* is accompanied by ceremonies, which are held in the early morning while women and boys are still asleep. The completion of the façade of a house is celebrated with a ceremony called *mindja*, which includes all-night dancing, and which may continue for six months, until the roof is completely thatched. Women participate in these inaugural ceremonies and are allowed to enter the new house, which afterward is ritually cleansed and closed to them.

To view this image, please go to page 863 of the *Art History*, Fourth Edition by Marilyn Stokstad ebook.

1–40 • EXTERIOR OF *KORAMBO* (*HAUS TAMBARAN*)
Kinbangwa village, Sepik River, Papua New Guinea. Abelam, 20th century.

BILUM—CONTEMPORARY NET BAGS OF HIGHLAND NEW GUINEA.

Women's arts in Papua New Guinea tend to be less spectacular and more subtle than men's, but are nonetheless significant. Both functionally and symbolically, they contribute to a balance between male and female roles in society. **Bilum**, for example, are netted bags made mainly by women throughout the central

To view this image, please go to page 864 of the *Art History*, Fourth Edition by Marilyn Stokstad ebook.

1–41 • WOMEN WEARING NET BAGS (*BILUM*)
Wahgi valley, Western Highlands Province, Papua New Guinea. 1990.

highlands of New Guinea **(FIG. 1–41)**. Looped from a single long thread spun on the thigh, *bilum* are very strong and, as loosely woven work bags, are used to carry items from vegetables to beer. The bones of a deceased man may be stored in a special *bilum* in a village's men's house (which is similar in function to the Abelam *korambo* in FIGURE 1–40), while his widow wears his personal bag as a sign of mourning. Women wear decorative *bilum*, into which marsupial fur is often incorporated, as adornment, exchange them as gifts, and use them to carry babies.

Bilum are rich metaphorical symbols. Among the women of the Wahgi tribe, who live in the Wahgi valley of the central highlands, seen in FIGURE 1–41, the term *bilum* may be used as a synonym for womb and bride, and they are also associated with ideas of female attractiveness; depending on how they are worn, they can indicate whether a girl is eligible for marriage.

In the past, *bilum* were made from natural fibers, most commonly the inner bark of a ficus plant. Today, while the technique for making them remains unchanged, a wide array of colorful, contemporary fibers, including nylon and acrylic yarn, are used, and new designs incorporating complicated patterns and words are constantly appearing. *Bilum* are now made by women throughout Papua New Guinea, not just in the highlands. They are sold commercially in markets and towns, and have become one of the country's national symbols.

SPIRIT POLES OF THE ASMAT OF WEST PAPUA.   The Asmat, who live along rivers in the coastal swamp forests on the southwest coast, were known in the past as warriors and headhunters (head-hunting was generally believed to maintain balance between hostile groups). In their culture, they identified trees with human beings, their fruit with human heads. Fruit-eating birds were thus the equivalent of headhunters, and were often represented in war and mortuary arts, along with the praying mantis, whose female bites off the head of the male during mating. In the past, the Asmat believed that death was always caused by an enemy, either by direct killing or through magic, and that it required revenge, usually in the form of taking an enemy's head, to appease the spirit of the person who had died.

Believing that the spirit of the dead person remained in the village, the Asmat erected elaborately sculpted memorial poles

(FIG. 1–42), known as *bisj* (pronounced bish), which embodied the spirits of the ancestors and paid tribute to them. *Bisj* poles are generally carved from mangrove trees, although some in a museum in Leiden recently have been found to be from the wild nutmeg. The felling of a tree is a ritual act in which a group of men attack the tree as if it were an enemy. The figures on the poles represent the dead individuals who are to be avenged; small figures represent dead children. The bent pose of the figures associates them with the praying mantis. The large, lacy phalluses emerging from the figures at the top of the poles are carved from the projecting roots of the tree and symbolize male fertility, while the surface decoration suggests body ornamentation. The *bisj* were placed in front of special houses belonging to the village's men's society. The poles faced the river to ensure that the spirits of the dead would travel to the realm of the ancestors (*safan*), which lay beyond the sea. The *bisj* pole also served symbolically as the dugout canoe that would take the spirit of the deceased down the river to *safan*.

By carving *bisj* poles (usually for several deceased at the same time) and organizing a *bisj* feast, relatives publicly indicated their responsibility to avenge their dead in a headhunting raid. As part of the ceremonies, mock battles were held, the men boasting of their bravery, the women cheering them on. After the ceremonies, the poles were left in the swamp to deteriorate and transfer their supernatural power back to nature. Today, Asmat continue to carve *bisj* poles and use them in funerary ceremonies, although they stopped headhunting in the 1970s. Poles are also made to sell to outsiders.

NEW IRELAND

MALAGAN DISPLAY OF NEW IRELAND.   New Ireland is one of the large eastern islands of the nation of Papua New Guinea. The northern people on the island still practice a complex set of death and commemorative rites known as *malagan* (pronounced malang-gan), which could take place as much as two years after a person's death. In the past, clan leaders rose to prominence primarily through *malagan* ceremonies that honored their wives' recently deceased family members. The greater the *malagan* ceremony, the greater prominence the clan leader had achieved.

To view this image, please go to page 865 of the *Art History*, Fourth Edition by Marilyn Stokstad ebook.

1–42 • ASMAT ANCESTRAL SPIRIT POLES (*BISJ*)
Buepis village, Fajit River, West Papua Province, Indonesia. c. 1960. Wood, paint, palm leaves, and fiber, height approx. 18′ (5.48 m).

Malagan also included rites to initiate young men and women into adulthood. After several months' training in seclusion in a ritual enclosure, they were presented to the public and carved and painted figures were given to them. The combined funerary and initiation ceremonies included feasts, masked dances, and the creation of a special house to display elaborately carved and painted sculptures **(FIG. 1–43)** that honored the dead. The display house illustrated, which dates to the early 1930s, is more than 14 feet wide and 12 deceased individuals are being honored. The carvings are large (the first on the left is nearly 6 feet in height) and take the form of horizontal friezes, standing figures, and poles containing several figures. They are visually complex, with tensions created between solid and pierced void, and between the two-dimensional painted patterns on three-dimensional sculptural forms. Kept secret until the final phase of the ceremonies, their unveiling was the climax of the festivities. After the ceremonies they were no longer considered ritually "active" and were destroyed or, since the late nineteenth century, sold to outsiders. *Malagan* figures are still being carved and ceremonies are held today.

NEW BRITAIN

TUBUAN MASK OF NEW BRITAIN. In the Papua New Guinea province of New Britain, which includes the Duke of York Islands, Tubuan masks represent the Tolai male secret society. This has different levels or grades of increasing knowledge and power, and wields both spiritual and social control, especially during the three months of ceremonies known as the "Time of the Tubuan."

Though initiation to the society is the main purpose of the ceremonies, the men of the village, who have achieved power through the accumulation of wealth, and in the past through bravery in war, use this period to call up the spirits represented by the masks, who have the authority to settle disputes, stop fights, punish lawbreakers, and force the payment of debts. Political power and authority are underscored and enhanced by their appearance, and in the past they had the power of life and death.

The masks represent both female and male spirits, though all the masks are danced by men. Local stories say women originally owned the masks and that they were stolen from them by men. The **TUBUAN MASK (FIG. 1–44)** represents the Mother, who gives birth to her children, the Duk Duk masks, which represent the new initiates into the society. With the appearance, first of the Mother masks, then of the Duk Duk masks, the initiates return to the village from the bush, where they have undergone intensive preparation to enter the society. The Tubuan mask has a distinctive, tall conical shape and prominent eyes formed by concentric white circles. The green leaf skirt is a very sacred part of the mask, which is made from painted bark cloth, various fibers, and feathers: Black feathers on top indicate a more powerful spirit than white feathers.

MICRONESIA

The majority of Micronesia's islands are small, low-lying coral atolls, but in the western region several are volcanic in origin. The eastern islands are more closely related culturally to Polynesia,

To view this image, please go to page 866 of the *Art History*, Fourth Edition by Marilyn Stokstad ebook.

1-43 • *MALAGAN DISPLAY*
Medina village, New Ireland, Papua New Guinea. c. 1930. Height 82⅝" (210 cm), width 137¾" (350 cm).
Museum für Völkerkunde, Basel, Switzerland.

while those in the west show connections to Melanesia, especially in the men's houses found on Palau and Yap. The atolls—circular coral reefs surrounding lagoons where islands once stood—have a limited range of materials for creating objects of any kind. Micronesians are known especially for their navigational skills and their fine canoes. They also create textiles from banana and coconut fibers, bowls from turtle shells, and abstract human figures from wood, which is scarce. As in other parts of the Pacific, tattooing and the performative arts remain central to life.

WAPEPE NAVIGATION CHART.   Sailors from the Marshall Islands relied on celestial navigation (navigating by the sun and moon and stars) as well as a detailed understanding of the ocean currents and trade winds to travel from one island to another. To teach navigation to younger generations, elders traditionally used stick charts (*wapepe* or *mattang*)—maps that showed land, but also the path from one island to the next, the water a sailor would cross during his voyage.

In common use until the 1950s, the stick chart (**FIG. 1–45**) was a schematic diagram of the prevailing ocean currents and the characteristic wave patterns encountered between islands. The currents are represented by sticks held together by coconut fibers; the shells mark islands on the route. The arrangement of sticks around a shell indicates a zone of distinctive waves shaped by the effect of an island deflecting the prevailing wind. Such refracted waves enable a

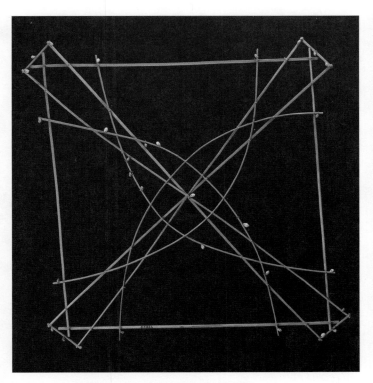

1–45 • *WAPEPE* NAVIGATION CHART
Marshall Islands. 19th century. Sticks, coconut fiber, shells, 29½ × 29½″ (75 × 75 cm). Peabody Essex Museum, Salem.

navigator to sense the proximity of land without being able to see it, and to discern the least difficult course for making landfall. Although the *wapepe* is primarily functional, its combination of clarity, simplicity, and abstraction has an aesthetic impact.

NAN MADOL.   The basalt cliffs of the island of Pohnpei provided the building material for one of the largest and most remarkable stone architectural complexes in Oceania. Nan Madol, on its southeast coast, consists of 92 artificial islands set within a network of canals covering about 170 acres (**MAP 1–4**). Seawalls and break-waters 15 feet high and 35 feet thick protect the area from the ocean. When it was populated, openings in the breakwaters gave canoes access to the ocean and allowed seawater to flow in and out with the tides, flushing clean the canals. While other similar complexes have been identified in Micronesia, Nan Madol is the largest and most impressive, reflecting the importance of the kings who ruled from the site. The artificial islands and the buildings atop them were built between the early thirteenth and seventeenth centuries, until the dynasty's political decline. The site had been abandoned by the time Europeans discovered it in the nineteenth century.

Nan Madol was an administrative and ceremonial center as well as, at one time, a home for as many as 1,000 people. The powerful kings drew upon this labor force to construct a monumental city. Both the buildings and the underlying islands are built of massive pieces of stone set in alternating layers of log-shaped stones and boulders of prismatic basalt. The largest of the

To view this image, please go to page 867 of the *Art History*, Fourth Edition by Marilyn Stokstad ebook.

1–44 • TUBUAN MASK BEING DANCED
Tolai people, Duke of York Islands, New Britain, Papua New Guinea. c. 1990. Cloth, paint, fiber, feathers.

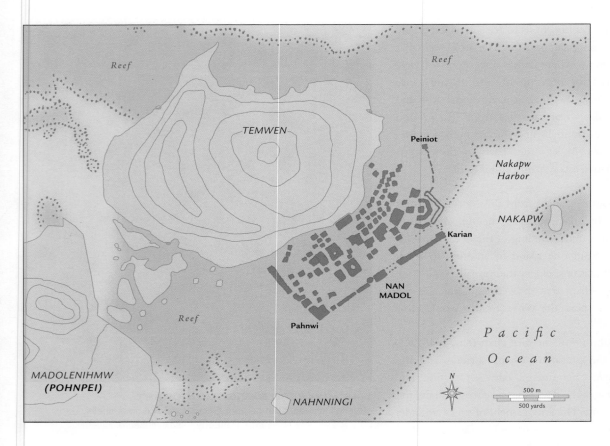

artificial islets is more than 100 yards long, and one basalt corner-stone alone is estimated to weigh about 50 tons. The stone logs were split from the cliffs by alternately heating the stone and dousing it with water. Most of the islands are oriented northeast–southwest, receiving the benefit of the cooling prevailing winds.

The royal mortuary compound, which once dominated the southeast side of Nan Madol **(FIG. 1–46)**, has walls rising in subtle upward and outward curves to a height of 25 feet. To achieve the sweeping, rising lines, the builders increased the number of stones in the header courses (those with the ends of the stones laid facing out along the wall) relative to the stretcher courses (those with the lengths of the stones laid parallel to the wall) as they came to the corners and entryways. The plan of the structure consists simply of progressively higher rectangles within rectangles—the outer walls leading by steps up to interior walls that lead up to a central courtyard with a small, cubical tomb.

POLYNESIA

The settlers of the far-flung islands of Polynesia developed distinctive cultural traditions but also retained linguistic and cultural affinities that reflect their common origin. Traditional Polynesian

To view this image, please go to page 868 of the *Art History*, Fourth Edition by Marilyn Stokstad ebook.

1–46 • ROYAL MORTUARY COMPOUND, NAN MADOL
Pohnpei, Federated States of Micronesia. Basalt blocks,
wall height up to 25′ (7.62 m).

society was generally far more stratified than Melanesian society: A person's genealogy, tracing his or her descent from an ancestral god, determined his or her place in society. First-born children of the hereditary elite were considered the most sacred because they inherited more spiritual power (*mana*) at their birth. *Mana* could be gained through leadership, courage, or skill or lost due to failure in warfare. It was protected by strict laws of conduct called *tapu*, a word that came into the English language as taboo.

All of the arts in Polynesia were sacred, and their creation was a sacred act: Master artists were also ritual specialists. Objects were crafted from a variety of materials, some of which, like jadite in New Zealand, were considered spiritually powerful. Some objects were useful ones, such as canoes, fishhooks, and weapons; others indicated the status and rank of the society's elite. The objects had their own *mana* that could increase or decrease depending on how successful they were in performing their functions. Their quality and beauty were important: Objects were made to endure and many were handed down as heirlooms from generation to generation. In addition, the human body itself was the canvas for the art of tattoo (*tatau* in several Polynesian languages).

Polynesian religions included many levels of gods, from creator gods and semidivine hero-gods (such as Maui, who appears in the stories of many of the Polynesian cultures) to natural forces, but the most important were one's ancestors, who became gods at their death. They remained influential in daily life, so needed to be honored and placated, and their help was sought for important projects and in times of trouble. Throughout much of Polynesia, figures in human form, often generically called *tiki*, were carved in stone, wood, and in some places, such as the Marquesas Islands, human bone. These statues represented the ancestors and were often placed on sacred ritual sites attended by ritual specialists (SEE FIG. 1–49) or, as in New Zealand, incorporated into meeting houses (see "Te-Hau-ki-Turanga," pages 54–55).

MARQUESAS ISLANDS

TATTOO IN THE MARQUESAS ISLANDS. The art of tattoo was widespread and ancient in Oceania. Tattoo chisels made of bone have been found in Lapita sites. They are quite similar to the tools used to create the decorated Lapita pottery, suggesting some symbolic connection between the marking of the pottery and of human skin. The Polynesians, descendants of the Lapita people, brought tattooing with them as they migrated throughout the Pacific. As they became isolated from each other over time, distinctive styles evolved: Spirals became a hallmark of the Maori facial tattoo (*moko*), and rows of triangles became prominent in Hawaiian designs.

The people of the Marquesas Islands, an archipelago about 900 miles northeast of Tahiti, were the most extensively tattooed of all Polynesians. The process of tattooing involves shedding blood, the most *tapu* (sacred), substance in Polynesia. In the Marquesas, the process for a young man of high social rank began around age 18; by age 30 he would be fully tattooed. Because of the sacredness

and prestige of the process, some men continued to be tattooed until their skin was completely covered and the designs disappeared. Marquesan women were also tattooed, usually on the hands, ankles, lips, and behind the ears.

The process was painful and expensive. Though women could be tattooed with little ceremony in their own homes, in the case of both high-ranking men and women, special houses were built for the occasion. The master tattooer and his assistants had to be fed and paid. At the end of the session a special feast was held to display the new tattoos. Each design had a name and a meaning: Tattooing was done to mark passages in people's lives and their social positions, and to commemorate special events or accomplishments. Some tattoos denoted particular men's societies or eating groups. Especially for men, tattoos showed their courage and were essential to their sexual attractiveness to women.

Tattooing was forbidden in the nineteenth century by French colonial administrators and Catholic missionaries, and died out in the Marquesas. Beginning in the 1970s, tattooing underwent a resurgence throughout the Pacific and in 1980 **TEVE TUPUHIA** became the first Marquesan in modern times to be fully tattooed **(FIG. 1–47)**. He went to Samoa, the only place in Polynesia where the traditional art form continued, to be tattooed by master

To view this image, please go to page 869 of the *Art History*, Fourth Edition by Marilyn Stokstad ebook.

1-47 • TEVE TUPUHIA
Marquesan man tattooed in 1980 by Samoan Lese li'o.

Te-Hau-ki-Turanga

New Zealand was settled sometime after 800 CE by intrepid seafaring Polynesians now known as the Maori. As part of the process of adapting their Polynesian culture to the temperate New Zealand environment, they began to build wooden-frame homes, the largest of which, the chief's house, evolved after Western contact into the meeting house (*whare nui*). The meeting house stands on an open plaza (*marae*) a sacred place where a Maori tribe (*iwi*) or subtribe (*hapu*) still today greets visitors, discusses important issues, and mourns the dead. In it, tribal history and genealogy are recorded and preserved. Carved by the master carver Raharuhi Rukupo in the early 1840s, Te-Hau-ki-Turanga is the oldest existing, fully decorated meeting house in New Zealand (FIG. A). Built by Rukupo as a memorial to his elder brother, its name refers to the region of New Zealand where it was made—Turanga, today Gisborne, on the northeast coast of North Island—and can be translated as the Breezes of Turanga.

In this area of New Zealand, the meeting house symbolizes the tribe's founding ancestor, for whom it is often named. The ridgepole is the backbone, the rafters are the ribs, and the slanting **bargeboards**—the boards attached to the projecting end of the gable—are the outstretched enfolding arms. The face appears in the gable mask. Relief figures of ancestors cover the support poles, wall planks, and the lower ends of the rafters. The ancestors, in effect, support the house. They were thought to take an active interest in community affairs and to participate in the discussions held in the meeting house. Rukupo, an important political and religious leader as well as a master carver, included an unusual naturalistic portrait of himself among them.

Painted curvilinear patterns (**kowhaiwhai**) decorate the rafters in red and black on a white background. The **koru** pattern, a curling stalk with a bulb at the end that resembles the young tree fern, dominates the design system. Lattice panels

To view this image, please go to page 870 of the *Art History*, Fourth Edition by Marilyn Stokstad ebook.

A. Raharuhi Rukupo, master carver **TE-HAU-KI-TURANGA (MAORI MEETING HOUSE)**
Gisborne/Turanga, New Zealand; built and owned by the Rongowhakaata people of Turanga. 1842–1843, restored in 1935.
Wood, shell, grass, flax, and pigments. Museum of New Zealand/Te Papa Tongarewa, Wellington. Neg. B18358

To view this image, please go to page 871 of the *Art History*, Fourth Edition by Marilyn Stokstad ebook.

(**tukutuku**) made by women fill the spaces between the wall planks. Because ritual prohibitions, or taboos, prevented women from entering the meeting house, they worked from the outside and wove the panels from the back. They created the black, white, and orange patterns from grass, flax, and flat slats. Each pattern has a symbolic meaning: chevrons represent the teeth of the sea monster Taniwha; steps represent the stairs of heaven climbed by the hero-god Tawhaki; and diamonds represent the flounder.

When Captain Cook arrived in New Zealand in the second half of the eighteenth century, each tribe and geographical region had its own style. A storehouse doorway from the Ngati Paoa tribe (FIG. B), who lived in the Hauraki Gulf area to the west of Turanga, dates to this period of time (or earlier) and shows the soft, shallow surface carving resulting from the use of stone tools. In comparison, a house panel (**poupou**) from

Te-Hau-ki-Turanga, carved with steel tools, is much more fully three-dimensional, with the deeply cut, very precisely detailed surface carving characteristic of that time.

As is typical throughout Polynesia (SEE FIG. 1–49), the figures face frontally and have large heads with open eyes. Their hands are placed on the stomach and their tongues stick out in defiance from their figure-eight-shaped mouths. The Hauraki Gulf figure represents a male ancestor, while the Te-Hau-ki-Turanga figure (FIG. C) is a female ancestor nursing a child. Both have a small figure, representing their descendants, between their legs.

Considered a national treasure by the Maori, this meeting house was restored in 1935 by Maori artists who knew the old, traditional methods; it is now preserved at the Museum of New Zealand/Te Papa Tongarewa in Wellington and considered *taonga* (cultural treasure).

B. CARVED FIGURE FROM STOREHOUSE DOORWAY
Ngäti Päoa, Hauraki Gulf, New Zealand. 1500–1800. Wood, height 33⅞″ (86 cm). Museum of New Zealand/Te Papa Tongarewa, Wellington.

C. POUPOU
(panel) from Te-Hau-ki-Turanga. Wood and red pigment, height 4′7″ (140 cm). Museum of New Zealand/Te Papa Tongarewa, Wellington.

To view this image, please go to page 871 of the *Art History*, Fourth Edition by Marilyn Stokstad ebook.

Front

To view this image, please go to page 871 of the *Art History*, Fourth Edition by Marilyn Stokstad ebook.

Interior side wall

Parts of the meeting house

To view this image, please go to page 871 of the *Art History*, Fourth Edition by Marilyn Stokstad ebook.

Interior rear wall

To view this image, please go to page 871 of the *Art History*, Fourth Edition by Marilyn Stokstad ebook.

SEE MORE: View a simulation explaining the construction of the meeting house **www.myartslab.com**

To view this image, please go to page 872 of the *Art History*, Fourth Edition by Marilyn Stokstad ebook.

1–48 • FEATHER CLOAK, KNOWN AS THE KEARNY CLOAK
Hawaii. c. 1843. Red, yellow, and black feathers, olona cordage, and netting, length 55¾″ (143 cm). Bishop Museum, Honolulu.

King Kamehameha III (r. 1825–1854) presented this cloak to Commodore Lawrence Kearny, commander of the frigate USS *Constellation*.

Samoan artist Lese I'io. The process took six weeks and cost $35,000. Teve based his tattoo designs on drawings made by George Langsdorff, a German naturalist who visited the Marquesas in 1804 as part of a Russian scientific expedition. Today, Marquesan-style tattoo designs are seen throughout French Polynesia.

HAWAII

FEATHER CLOAK FROM HAWAII.   The Hawaiian islanders had one of the most highly stratified of all Polynesian societies, with valleys and whole islands ruled by high chiefs. Soon after contact with the West, the entire archipelago was unified for the first time under the rule of Kamehameha I (r. 1810–1819), who assumed the title of king in the European manner.

Among the members of the Hawaiian elite, feathered capes and cloaks were emblems of their high social status. The most valuable were full-length and made with thousands of red and yellow feathers. A full-length cloak, like the one in **FIGURE 1–48**, was reserved for the highest ranks of the elite men. It was called an *'ahu 'ula* ("red cloak"); the color red is associated with high status and rank throughout Polynesia. Often given as gifts to important visitors to Hawaii, this particular cloak was presented in 1843 to Commodore Lawrence Kearny, commander of the USS *Constellation*, by King Kamehameha III (r. 1825–1854).

Draped over the wearer's shoulders, such a cloak creates a sensuously textured and colored abstract design, which in this example joins to create matching patterns of paired crescents on front and back. The cloak's foundation consisted of coconut fiber netting onto which bundles of feathers were tied. The feathers were part of an annual tribute paid to the king by his subjects. The red, and especially the yellow feathers, were highly prized and came from several species of birds including the *i'iwi, apapane, 'o'o,* and *mamo* (which is now extinct). In some cases, each bird yielded only seven or eight feathers, making the collecting of feathers very labor-intensive and increasing the value of the cloaks.

The cloaks were so closely associated with the spiritual power (*mana*) of the elite person that they could be made only by specialists trained in both the complicated technique of manufacture and the rituals attending their fabrication. Surrounded by protective objects, they created the cloak while reciting the chief's genealogy and imbuing it with the power of his ancestors. As a result, the cloaks were seen as protective of the wearer, while also proclaiming his elite status, and political and economic power.

Feathers were used for decorating not just cloaks, but also helmets, capes, blankets, and garlands (*leis*), all of which conferred status and prestige. The annual tribute paid to the king by his subjects included feathers, and tall feather pompons (*kahili*) mounted on long slender sticks were symbols of royalty. Even the effigies of gods that Hawaiian warriors carried into battle were made of light, basketlike structures covered with feathers.

MONUMENTAL MOAI ON RAPA NUI

Rapa Nui (Easter Island) is the most isolated inhabited locale in Oceania, some 2,300 miles west of the coast of South America and 1,200 miles from Pitcairn Island, the nearest Polynesian outpost. Three volcanoes, one at each corner, make up the small triangular island. Originally known to its native inhabitants as Te Pito o te Henúa (Navel of the World) and now known as Rapa Nui, it was named Easter Island by Captain Jacob Roggeveen, the Dutch explorer who first landed there on Easter Sunday in 1722. Rapa Nui became part of Chile in 1888.

MONUMENTAL MOAI. Rapa Nui is the site of Polynesia's most impressive stone sculpture. Though many imaginative theories have been posited regarding the origins of its statues, from space aliens to Native Americans, they are most definitely part of an established Polynesian tradition. Sacred religious sites (*marae*) with stone altar platforms (*ahu*) are common throughout Polynesia. On Rapa Nui, most of the *ahu* are near the coast, parallel to the shore. About 900 CE, the islanders began to erect stone figures on the *ahu*, perhaps as memorials to deceased chiefs. Nearly 1,000 of the figures, called **moai**, have been found on the island, including some 400 unfinished ones in the quarry at Rano Raraku where they were being carved. The statues themselves are made from tufa, a yellowish-brown volcanic stone. On their heads, *pukao* (topknots of hair) were rendered in red scoria. When the statues were in place, the insertion of white coral and stone "opened" the eyes. In 1978 several figures on Ahu Nau Nau **(FIG. 1–49)** were restored to their original condition. They are about 36 feet tall, but *moai* range in size from much smaller to a 65-foot statue that is still in the quarry. Like other Polynesian statues, the figures here face frontally. Their large heads have deep-set eyes under a prominent brow ridge; a long, concave, pointed nose; a small mouth with pursed lips; and an angular chin. The extremely elongated earlobes have parallel engraved lines that suggest ear ornaments. The figures have schematically indicated breastbones and pectorals, and small arms with hands pressed close to the sides. Their bodies emerge from the site at just below waist level, so they have no legs.

The islanders stopped erecting *moai* around 1500 and entered a period of warfare among themselves, apparently because overpopulation was straining the island's available resources. Most of the *moai* were knocked down and destroyed during this period, which marked the emergence of a new religious focus on what is usually termed the bird–man cult. The island's indigenous population, which may at one time have consisted of as many as 10,000 people, was

To view this image, please go to page 873 of the *Art History*, Fourth Edition by Marilyn Stokstad ebook.

1-49 • *MOAI* ANCESTOR FIGURES
Ahu Nau Nau, Rapa Nui (Easter Island). c. ?1000–1500 CE, restored 1978. Volcanic stone (tufa), average height approx. 36′ (11 m).

SEE MORE: View the podcast on the *Moai* Ancestor Figures
www.myartslab.com

nearly eradicated in 1877 when Peruvian slave traders precipitated an epidemic of smallpox and tuberculosis that left only 110 inhabitants alive. Today, a vibrant population of some 4,000 people is known especially for its energetic and athletic dance performances.

SAMOA

TAPA (SIAPO) IN SAMOA. As they migrated across the Pacific, Polynesians brought with them the production of bark cloth. Known by various names throughout the Pacific, most commonly as **tapa**, in Samoa it is called **siapo**. Bark cloth is usually made by women, although sometimes men help to obtain the bark or decorate the completed cloth. In Samoa, *siapo* is made by stripping the inner bark from branches of the paper mulberry tree, although banyan and breadfruit are sometimes used in other archipelagoes. The bark is beaten with a wooden mallet, then folded over and beaten again, to various degrees of softness. Larger pieces can be made by building up the cloth in a process of felting or using natural pastes as glue. The heavy wooden mallets used for beating the cloth are often incised with complex patterns, which leave impressions like watermarks in the cloth, viewable when the cloth is held up to the light.

Plain and decorated *tapa* of various thicknesses and qualities was used throughout Polynesia for clothing, sails, mats, and ceremonial purposes, including wrapping the dead. *Tapa* was also used to wrap wooden or wicker frames to make human effigies in the Marquesas and Rapa Nui, serving a purpose we still do not completely understand. In western Polynesia (Samoa and Tonga) very large pieces, 7–10 feet across and hundreds of feet long, were traditionally given in ceremonial exchanges of valuables and as gifts. Along with fine mats, *siapo* is still sometimes given as gifts on important ceremonial occasions.

A widespread use of *tapa* was for clothing. For example, Samoan men and women wore large pieces of *siapo* as wraparound skirts (*lavalava*). Special chiefs, called talking chiefs, who spoke on behalf of the highest-ranking chief in the village council, wore special *tapa* skirts called *siapo vala* **(FIG. 1–50)**.

Distinctive design styles for *tapa* cloth evolved across the Pacific, even when the material used was essentially the same from one island to the next. It could be dyed bright yellow with turmeric or brown with dyes made from nuts. It could also be exposed to smoke to turn it black or darker brown. Today, contemporary fabric paint is often used. Decorative designs were made through a variety of means from freehand painting to impressing on the coloring with tiny bamboo stamps, or using stencils, as is done in Fiji. This Samoan *siapo vala* has designs that are produced by first placing the cloth over a wooden design tablet, an **upeti**, and then rubbing pigment over the cloth to pick up the carved pattern. The second stage is to overpaint this lighter rubbed pattern by hand. The result is a boldly patterned, symmetrical design.

To view this image, please go to page 874 of the *Art History*, Fourth Edition by Marilyn Stokstad ebook.

1–50 • TAPA (SIAPO VALA)
Samoa. 20th century. 58⅝ × 57″ (149 × 145 cm).
Auckland Museum, New Zealand. AM 46892

ADDITIONAL READINGS

IMAGES, POWER, AND POLITICS

Every day, we engage in practices of looking to make sense of the world. To those of us who are blind or have low vision, seeing and visuality are no less important than they are to those of us who are sighted, because the everyday world is so strongly organized around visual and spatial cues that take seeing for granted. Looking is a social practice, whether we do it by choice or compliance. Through looking, and through touching and hearing as means of navigating space organized around the sense of sight, we negotiate our social relationships and meanings.

Like other practices, looking involves relationships of power. To willfully look or not is to exercise choice and compliance and to influence whether and how others look. To be made to look, to try to get someone else to look at you or at something you want to be noticed, or to engage in an exchange of looks entails a play of power. Looking can be easy or difficult, pleasurable or unpleasant, harmless or dangerous. Conscious and unconscious aspects of looking intersect. We engage in practices of looking to communicate, to influence, and to be influenced. Even when we choose not to look, or when we look away, these are activities that have meaning within the economy of looking.

We live in cultures that are increasingly permeated by visual images with a variety of purposes and intended effects. These images can produce in us a wide array of emotions and responses. We invest the visual artifacts and images we create and encounter on a daily basis with significant power—for instance, the power to conjure an absent person, the power to calm or incite to action, the power to persuade or mystify, the power to remember. A single image can serve a multitude of purposes, appear in a range of settings, and mean different things to different people.

This image of women and schoolchildren looking at a murder scene in the street dramatically draws our attention to practices of looking. The photograph was taken by Weegee, a self-taught photographer of the mid-twentieth century whose real name was Arthur Fellig. The name *Weegee* is a play on the board game called Ouija, because he showed up at crime scenes so quickly that it was joked he must have supernatural psychic powers. He was known for his hard-core depictions of crime and violence in the streets of New York. Weegee listened to a police radio he kept in his car in order to arrive at crime scenes quickly, then, while onlookers watched, he would develop the photographs he took in the trunk of his car, which was set up as a portable darkroom.

"A woman relative cried . . . but neighborhood dead-end kids enjoyed the show when a small-time racketeer was shot and killed," states the caption accompanying this image, titled "The First Murder," in Weegee's 1945 publication *Naked New York*. On the facing page is displayed a photograph of what the children saw: the dead body of a gangster. In *The First Murder*, Weegee calls attention to both the act of looking at the forbidden scene and the capacity of the still camera to capture heightened fleeting emotion. The children are gawking at the murder scene with morbid fascination, ignoring the bawling relative. As viewers, we look with equal fascination on the scene, catching the children in the act of

1–51 • Weegee (Arthur Felig), THE FIRST MURDER, before 1945
Courtesy of J. Paul Getty Trust Publications. Copyright © by the International Center for Photography.

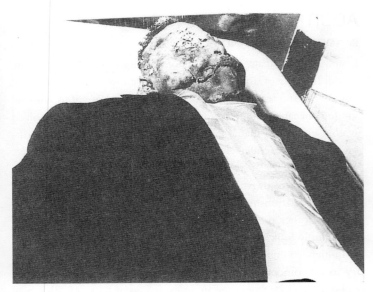

1-53 • Photograph of Emmett Till's brutalized body in his casket, 1955
Courtesy of the Chicago Defender.

1-52 • Weegee working in the trunk of his Chevrolet, 1942
Courtesy of Intstitue of Contemporary Photography/Getty Images, Inc.

looking, their eyes wide with shock and wonder. We also witness the woman crying. Her eyes are closed, as if to shut out the sight of her dead relative. Near her another woman, the only other adult in the photograph, lowers her eyes, averting her look in the face of something awful. This is an adult practice that serves as a counterpoint to the children's bold first look at murder to which the title draws our attention.

The role of images in providing views of violence, and of voyeurism and fascination with violence, is countered by a history of using images to expose the devastating aspects of violence. One particularly graphic historical example of this use of images was the wide circulation of an image of Emmett Till, a boy who was murdered during the beginning of the civil rights movement in the United States. Till, a 14-year-old young black man from Chicago, was visiting relatives in a small Mississippi town in August 1955. In the context of the strict codes of Jim Crow segregation, he allegedly whistled at a white woman. In retaliation for this act, he was kidnapped by white men, tortured (his eye gouged out), beaten, and shot through the head, then thrown into the Tallahatchie River with a gin mill tied to his neck with barbed wire. Till's mother, recognizing the power of visual evidence, insisted on holding an open-casket funeral. She allowed his corpse to be photographed so everyone could see the gruesome evidence

of violence exacted upon her son. The highly publicized funeral, which brought 50,000 mourners, and the graphic photograph of Till's brutalized body (**FIG. 1–53**), which was published in *Jet* magazine, were major catalysts of the nascent civil rights movement. This image showed in shockingly graphic detail the violence that was enacted on a young black man for allegedly whistling at a white woman. It represented the violent oppression of blacks in the time period. In this image, the power of the photograph to provide evidence of violence and injustice is coupled with the photograph's power to shock and horrify.

REPRESENTATION

Representation refers to the use of language and images to create meaning about the world around us. We use words to understand, describe, and define the world as we see it, and we also use images this way. This process takes place through systems such as language that are structured according to rules and conventions. A language has a set of rules about how to express and interpret meaning. So do the systems of representation used in painting, drawing, photography, cinema, television, and digital media. Although these systems of representation are not languages, they are in some ways *like* language systems and therefore can be analyzed through methods borrowed from linguistics and semiotics.

Throughout history, debates about representation have considered whether representations reflect the world as it is, mirroring it back to us through mimesis or imitation, or whether we construct the world and its meaning through representations. In this book, we argue that we make meaning of the material world through understanding objects and entities in their specific cultural contexts. This process of understanding the meaning of things in context takes place in part through our use of written, gestural,

spoken, or drawn representations. The material world has meaning and can be "seen" by us only through representations. The world is not simply reflected back to us through representations that stand in for things by copying their appearance. We construct the meaning of things through the process of representing them. Although the concept of mimesis has a long history, today it is no longer accepted that representations are mere copies of things as they are or as the person who created them believes they ought to be.

The distinction between the idea of reflection, or mimesis, and representation as a construction of the material world can be difficult to make. The still life, for instance, has been a favored genre of artists for many centuries. One might surmise that the still life is motivated by the desire to reflect, rather than make meaning of, material objects as they appear in the world. In this still life, painted in 1765 by French painter Henri-Horace Roland de la Porte, an array of food and drink is carefully arranged on a table and painted with attention to each minute detail. The objects, such as the fruit, the bowl and cup, and the wooden tabletop, are rendered with close attention to light and detail. They seem so lifelike that one imagines one could touch them. Yet, is this image simply a reflection of this particular scene, rendered with skill by the artist? Is it simply a mimetic copy of a scene, painted for the sake of showing us what was there? Roland de la Porte was a student of Jean-Batiste-Siméone Chardin, a French painter who was fascinated with the style of the seventeenth-century Dutch painters, who developed techniques of pictorial realism more than a century before the advent of photography. The seventeenth- and eighteenth-century still life ranged from paintings that were straightforwardly representational to those that were deeply symbolic. This painting includes many symbols of rustic peasant life. It invokes a way of living even without the presence of human figures. Elements such as food and drink convey philosophical as well as symbolic meanings, such as the transience of earthly life through the ephemeral materiality of basic, humble foods. The fresh fruits and wildflowers evoke earthy

flavors and aromas. The crumbs of cheese and the half-filled carafe conjure the presence of someone who has eaten this simple meal.

In 2003, artist Marion Peck produced this painting, *Still Life with Dralas*, in the style of the Roland de la Porte still life. *Drala* is a term used in Buddhism to refer to energy in matter and the universe. Peck, a contemporary pop surrealist painter, interprets Roland de la Porte's still life to contain a kind of anthropomorphic energy in the rendering of the fruit and the dishes and glassware, which she brings to life with comic little faces. The painting holds an abundance of looks. Each tiny grape contains an eyeball. The conventions of painting used in the eighteenth-century work are understood to convey realism according to the terms of that era. In Peck's contemporary painting, the genre of the still life is subject to a kind of reflexive interpretation that humorously animates and makes literal its meanings, emphasizing possible metaphysical values contained in the original painting's symbolism. Here, we want to note that that these paintings produce meanings through the ways that they are composed and rendered, and not just in the choices of objects depicted.

We learn the rules and conventions of the systems of representation within a given culture. Many artists have attempted to defy those conventions, to break the rules of various systems of representation, and to push the boundaries of definitions of representation. This painting, by the Belgian Surrealist artist René Magritte, comments on the process of representation. Entitled *The Treachery of Images* (1928–1929), the painting depicts a pipe with

the line in French, "This is not a pipe." One could argue, on the one hand, that Magritte is making a joke, that of course it is an image of a pipe that he has created. However, he is also pointing to the relationship between words and things, as this is not a pipe itself but rather the representation of a pipe; it is a painting rather than the material object itself. Magritte produced a series of paintings and drawings on this theme, including *The Two Mysteries* (1966), a painting in which a pipe is rendered ambiguously as floating in space either behind, in front of, or just above a painting of a pipe, with the same witty subscript, propped on an easel. Here, we have two pipes—or rather, two drawings of the same pipe—or a painting of a pipe and a painting of a painting of a pipe and a subscript identifying it. French philosopher Michel Foucault elaborated on Magritte's ideas by exploring these images' implied commentary about the relationship between words and things and the complex relationship between the drawing, the paintings, their words, and their referent (the pipe). One could not pick up and smoke this pipe. So Magritte can be seen to be pointing out something so obvious as to render the written message absurd. He highlights the very act of labeling as something we should think about, drawing our attention to the word "pipe" and the limits of its function in representing the object, as well as the limits of the drawing in representing the pipe. Magritte asks us to consider how labels and images produce meaning yet cannot fully invoke the experience of the object. Negations, Foucault explains, multiply, and the layers of representation pile on one another to the point of incoherence. As we stop to examine the process of representation in this series by Magritte, we can see how the most banal and everyday, sensible uses of representation can so

easily fall apart, can be simply silly. In many of his other visual works, Magritte demonstrated that between words and objects one may create new relations and meanings through juxtaposition and changing contexts.

Magritte's painting is famous. Many artists have played off of it. The cartoon artist Scott McCloud, in his book *Understanding Comics,* uses Magritte's *Treachery of Images* to explain the concept of representation in the vocabulary of comics, noting that the reproduction of the painting in his book is a printed copy of a drawing of a painting of a pipe, and following this with a hilarious series of pictograms of icons such as the American flag, a stop sign, and a smiley face, all drawn with disclaimers attached (this is not America, this is not law, this is not a face). The digital theorist Talan

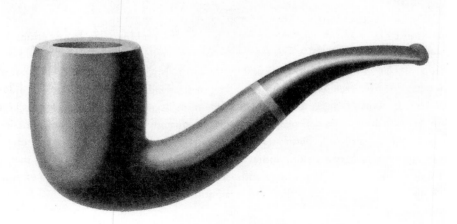

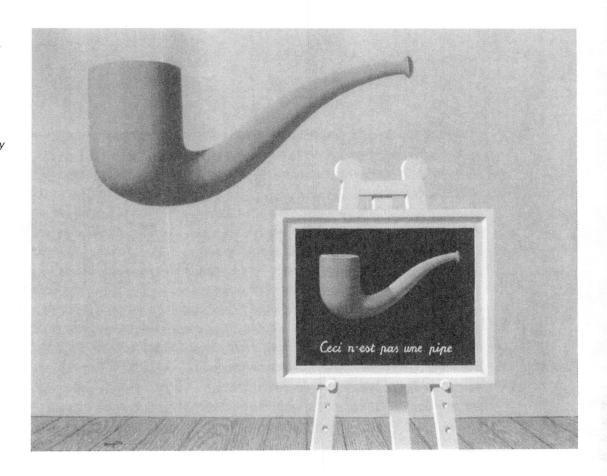

Memmott, in a work of digital media called *The Brotherhood of the Bent Billiard,* offers a "hypermediated art historical fiction" about Magritte's *Treachery* and the generations of textual and visual interpretations it spawned. Book One of *The Brotherhood* traces the development of the pipe as an emblem from its first appearance in a painting of 1926 to the famous works reproduced here. In Memmott's piece, Magritte's image play with meaning and representation is the impetus for the production of a reauthored narrative of Magritte that is an opportunity for considering meaning and representation in the era of digital imaging. Memmott describes his work as a "narrative hack" of the complex system of allegories and symbols built up over Magritte's career, referred to as his "symbolic calculus." As these examples all make clear, today we are surrounded by images that play with representation, unmasking our initial assumptions and inviting us to experience layers of meanings beyond the obvious or the apparent real or true meaning.

CHAPTER 2

BEGINNINGS OF SETTLED COMMUNITIES: AGRICULTURE, WRITING, RELIGION

THOUGHT PIECE

THE COMING OF ENKIDU

GILGAMESH went abroad in the world, but he met with none who could withstand his arms till he came to Uruk. But the men of Uruk muttered in their houses, 'Gilgamesh sounds the tocsin for his amusement, his arrogance has no bounds by day or night. No son is left with his father, for Gilgamesh takes them all, even the children; yet the king should be a shepherd to his people. His lust leaves no virgin to her lover, neither the warrior's daughter nor the wife of the noble; yet this is the shepherd of the city, wise, comely, and resolute.'

The gods heard their lament, the gods of heaven cried to the Lord of Uruk, to Anu the god of Uruk: 'A goddess made him, strong as a savage bull, none can withstand his arms. No son is left with his father, for Gilgamesh takes them all; and is this the king, the shepherd of his people? His lust leaves no virgin to her lover, neither the warrior's daughter nor the wife of the noble.' When Anu had heard their lamentation the gods cried to Aruru, the goddess of creation, 'You made him, O Aruru, now create his equal; let it be as like him as his own reflection, his second self, stormy heart for stormy heart. Let them contend together and leave Uruk in quiet.'

So the goddess conceived an image in her mind, and it was of the stuff of Anu of the firmament. She dipped her hands in water and pinched off clay, she let it fall in the wilderness, and noble Enkidu was created. There was virtue in him of the god of war, of Ninurta himself. His body was rough, he had long hair like a woman's; it waved like the hair of Nisaba, the goddess of corn. His body was covered with matted hair like Samuqan's, the god of cattle. He was innocent of mankind; he knew nothing of the cultivated land.

Enkidu ate grass in the hills with the gazelle and lurked with wild beasts at the water-holes; he had joy of the water with the herds of wild game. But there was a trapper who met him one day face to face at the drinking-hole, for the wild game had

entered his territory. On three days he met him face to face, and the trapper was frozen with fear. He went back to his house with the game that he had caught, and he was dumb, benumbed with terror. His face was altered like that of one who has made a long journey. With awe in his heart he spoke to his father: 'Father, there is a man, unlike any other, who comes down from the hills. He is the strongest in the world, he is like an immortal from heaven. He ranges over the hills with wild beasts and eats grass; he ranges through your land and comes down to the wells. I am afraid and dare not go near him. He fills in the pits which I dig and tears up my traps set for the game; he helps the beasts to escape and now they slip through my fingers.'

His father opened his mouth and said to the trapper, 'My son, in Uruk lives Gilgamesh; no one has ever prevailed against him, he is strong as a star from heaven. Go to Uruk, find Gilgamesh, extol the strength of this wild man. Ask him to give you a harlot, a wanton from the temple of love; return with her, and let her woman's power overpower this man. When next he comes down to drink at the wells she will be there, stripped naked; and when he sees her beckoning he will embrace her, and then the wild beasts will reject him.'

So the trapper set out on his journey to Uruk and addressed himself to Gilgamesh saying, 'A man unlike any other is roaming now in the pastures; he is as strong as a star from heaven and I am afraid to approach him. He helps the wild game to escape; he fills in my pits and pulls up my traps.' Gilgamesh said, 'Trapper, go back, take with you a harlot, a child of pleasure. At the drinking-hole she will strip, and when he sees her beckoning he will embrace her and the game of the wilderness will surely reject him.'

Now the trapper returned, taking the harlot with him. After a three days' journey they came to the drinking-hole, and there they sat down; the harlot and the trapper sat facing one another and waited for the game to come. For the first day and for the second day the two sat waiting, but on the third day the herds came; they came down to drink and Enkidu was with them. The small wild creatures of the plains were glad of the water, and Enkidu with them, who ate grass with the gazelle and was born in the hills; and she saw him, the savage man, come from far-off in the hills. The trapper spoke to her: 'There he is. Now, woman, make your breasts bare, have no shame, do not delay but welcome his love. Let him see you naked, let him possess your body. When he comes near uncover yourself and lie with him; teach him, the savage man, your woman's art, for when he murmurs love to you the wild beasts that shared his life in the hills will reject him.'

She was not ashamed to take him, she made herself naked and welcomed his eagerness; as he lay on her murmuring love she taught him the woman's art. For six days and seven nights they lay together, for Enkidu had forgotten his home in the hills; but when he was satisfied he went back to the wild beasts. Then, when the gazelle saw him, they bolted away; when the wild creatures saw him they fled. Enkidu would have followed, but his body was bound as though with a cord, his knees gave way when he started to run, his swiftness was gone. And now the wild creatures had all fled away; Enkidu was grown weak, for wisdom was in him, and the thoughts of a man were in his heart. So he returned and sat down at the woman's feet, and listened intently to what she said. 'You are wise, Enkidu, and now you have become like a god. Why do you want to run wild with the beasts in the hills? Come with me. I will take you to strong-walled Uruk, to the blessed temple of Ishtar and of Anu, of love and of heaven: there Gilgamesh lives, who is very strong, and like a wild bull he lords it over men.'

When she had spoken Enkidu was pleased; he longed for a comrade, for one who would understand his heart. 'Come, woman, and take me to that holy temple, to the house of Anu and of Ishtar, and to the place where Gilgamesh lords it over the people. I will challenge him boldly, I will cry out aloud in Uruk, "I am the strongest here, I have come to change the old order, I am he who was born in the hills, I am he who is strongest of all." '

She said, 'Let us go, and let him see your face. I know very well where Gilgamesh is in great Uruk. O Enkidu, there all the people are dressed in their gorgeous robes, every day is holiday, the young men and the girls are wonderful to see. How sweet they smell! All the great ones are roused from their beds. O Enkidu, you who love life, I will show you Gilgamesh, a man of many moods; you shall look at him well in his radiant manhood. His body is perfect in strength and maturity; he never rests by night or day. He is stronger than you, so leave your boasting. Shamash the glorious sun has given favours to Gilgamesh, and Anu of the heavens, and Enlil, and Ea the wise has given him deep understanding. I tell you, even before you have left the wilderness, Gilgamesh will know in his dreams that you are coming.'

Now Gilgamesh got up to tell his dream to his mother, Ninsun, one of the wise gods. 'Mother, last night I had a dream. I was full of joy, the young heroes were round me and I walked through the night under the stars of the firmament, and one, a meteor of the stuff of Anu, fell down from heaven. I tried to lift it

but it proved too heavy. All the people of Uruk came round to see it, the common people jostled and the nobles thronged to kiss its feet; and to me its attraction was like the love of woman. They helped me, I braced my forehead and I raised it with thongs and brought it to you, and you yourself pronounced it my brother.'

Then Ninsun, who is well-beloved and wise, said to Gilgamesh, 'This star of heaven which descended like a meteor from the sky; which you tried to lift, but found too heavy, when you tried to move it it would not budge, and so you brought it to my feet; I made it for you, a goad and spur, and you were drawn as though to a woman. This is the strong comrade, the one who brings help to his friend in his need. He is the strongest of wild creatures, the stuff of Anu; born in the grass-lands and the wild hills reared him; when you see him you will be glad; you will love him as a woman and he will never forsake you. This is the meaning of the dream.'

Gilgamesh said, 'Mother, I dreamed a second dream. In the streets of strong-walled Uruk there lay an axe; the shape of it was strange and the people thronged round. I saw it and was glad. I bent down, deeply drawn towards it; I loved it like a woman and wore it at my side.' Ninsun answered, 'That axe, which you saw, which drew you so powerfully like love of a woman, that is the comrade whom I give you, and he will come in his strength like one of the host of heaven. He is the brave companion who rescues his friend in necessity.' Gilgamesh said to his mother, 'A friend, a counsellor has come to me from Enlil, and now I shall befriend and counsel him.' So Gilgamesh told his dreams; and the harlot retold them to Enkidu.

And now she said to Enkidu, 'When I look at you you have become like a god. Why do you yearn to run wild again with the beasts in the hills? Get up from the ground, the bed of a shepherd.' He listened to her words with care. It was good advice that she gave. She divided her clothing in two and with the one half she clothed him and with the other herself; and holding his hand she led him like a child to the sheepfolds, into the shepherds' tents. There all the shepherds crowded round to see him, they put down bread in front of him, but Enkidu could only suck the milk of wild animals. He fumbled and gaped, at a loss what to do or how he should eat the bread and drink the strong wine. Then the woman said, 'Enkidu, eat bread, it is the staff of life; drink the wine, it is the custom of the land.' So he ate till he was full and drank strong wine, seven goblets. He became merry, his heart exulted and his face shone. He rubbed down the matted hair of his body and anointed himself with oil. Enkidu had become a man; but when he had put on man's clothing he appeared like a bridegroom. He took arms to hunt the lion so that the shepherds could rest at night. He caught wolves and lions and the herdsmen lay down in peace; for Enkidu was their watchman, that strong man who had no rival.

He was merry living with the shepherds, till one day lifting his eyes he saw a man approaching. He said to the harlot, 'Woman, fetch that man here. Why has he come? I wish to know his name.'

She went and called the man saying, 'Sir, where are you going on this weary journey?' The man answered, saying to Enkidu, 'Gilgamesh has gone into the marriage-house and shut out the people. He does strange things in Uruk, the city of great streets. At the roll of the drum work begins for the men, and work for the women. Gilgamesh the king is about to celebrate marriage with the Queen of Love, and he still demands to be first with the bride, the king to be first and the husband to follow, for that was ordained by the gods from his birth, from the time the umbilical cord was cut. But now the drums roll for the choice of the bride and the city groans.' At these words Enkidu turned white in the face. 'I will go to the place where Gilgamesh lords it over the people, I will challenge him boldly, and I will cry aloud in Uruk, "I have come to change the old order, for I am the strongest here." '

Now Enkidu strode in front and the woman followed behind. He entered Uruk, that great market, and all the folk thronged round him where he stood in the street in strong-walled Uruk. The people jostled; speaking of him they said, 'He is the spit of Gilgamesh.' 'He is shorter.' 'He is bigger of bone.' 'This is the one who was reared on the milk of wild beasts. His is the greatest strength.' The men rejoiced: 'Now Gilgamesh has met his match. This great one, this hero whose beauty is like a god, he is a match even for Gilgamesh.'

In Uruk the bridal bed was made, fit for the goddess of love. The bride waited for the bridegroom, but in the night Gilgamesh got up and came to the house. Then Enkidu stepped out, he stood in the street and blocked the way. Mighty Gilgamesh came on and Enkidu met him at the gate. He put out his foot and prevented Gilgamesh from entering the house, so they grappled, holding each other like bulls. They broke the doorposts and the walls shook, they snorted like bulls locked together. They shattered the doorposts and the walls shook. Gilgamesh bent his knee with his foot planted on the ground and with a turn Enkidu was thrown. Then immediately his fury died. When Enkidu was thrown he said to Gilgamesh, 'There is not another like you in the world. Ninsun, who is as strong as a wild ox in the byre, she was the mother who bore you, and now you are raised above all men, and Enlil has given you the kingship, for your strength surpasses the strength of men.' So Enkidu and Gilgamesh embraced and their friendship was sealed.

—*Epic of Gilgamesh* (Penguin classics 2003), Tablet I: The Coming of Enkidu, pp. 62–69.

THINGS TO CONSIDER

- What impact did the shift from hunter-gatherer to agrarian communities have on visual culture?
- How are writing, architecture, and religion linked to agriculture?
- What can the emergence of institutionalized religion tell us about the relationship between religion and the arts?

To view this image, please go to page 26 of the *Art History*, Fourth Edition by Marilyn Stokstad ebook.

2–1 • STELE OF NARAM-SIN
Sippar. Found at Susa.
Naram-Sin r. 2254–2218 BCE. Limestone,
height 6′6″ (1.98 m).
Musée du Louvre, Paris.

ART OF THE ANCIENT NEAR EAST

In public works such as this stone **stele** (upright stone slab), the artists of Mesopotamia developed a sophisticated symbolic visual language—a kind of conceptual art—that both celebrated and communicated the political stratification that gave order and security to their world. Akkadian ruler Naram-Sin (ruled 2254–2218 BCE) is pictured proudly here (FIG. 2–1). His preeminence is signaled directly by size: he is by far the largest person in this scene of military triumph, conforming to an artistic practice we call **hieratic scale**, where relative size indicates relative importance. He is also elevated well above the other figures, boldly silhouetted against blank ground, striding toward a stylized peak that recalls his own shape, increasing his own sense of grandeur by association. He clasps a veritable arsenal of weaponry—spear, battle axe, bow and arrow—and the grand helmet that crowns his head sprouts horns, an attribute heretofore reserved for gods, here claiming divinity for this earthly ruler. Art historian Irene Winter has gone even further, pointing to the eroticized pose and presentation of Naram-Sin, to the conspicuous display of a well-formed male body. In ancient Mesopotamian culture, male potency and vigor were directly related to political power and dominance. Like the horns of his helmet, toned, muscular bodies were most frequently associated with gods. Thus every aspect of the representation of this ruler speaks to his religious and political authority as leader of the state.

This stele is more than an emblem of Naram-Sin's divine right to rule, however. It also tells the story of one of his important military victories. The ruler stands above a crowded scene enacted by smaller figures. Those to the left, dressed and posed in a fashion similar to their ruler, represent his army, marching in diagonal bands up the hillside into battle. The artist has included identifiable native trees along the mountain pathway to heighten the sense that this portrays an actual event rather than a generic battle scene. Before Naram-Sin, both along the right side of the stele and smashed under his forward striding leg, are representations of the enemy, in this case the Lullubi people from eastern Mesopotamia (modern Iran). One diminutive adversary has taken a fatal spear to the neck, while companions behind and below him beg for mercy.

Perhaps this ancient art, which combines symbols with stories, looks naïve or crude in relation to our own artistic standards, but we should avoid allowing such modern value judgments to block our appreciation of the artistic accomplishments of the ancient Near East—or, indeed, the art of any era or culture. For these ancient works of art maintain the power to communicate with us forcefully and directly, even across over four millennia of historical distance.

LEARN ABOUT IT

2.1 Explore the development of visual narrative conventions to tell stories of gods, heroes, and rulers in the sculpted reliefs of the ancient Near East.

2.2 Discover how artists of the ancient Near East used colorful and precious materials to create dazzling effects in art and architecture.

2.3 Survey the various ways rulers in the ancient Near East expressed their power in portraits, historical narrative, and great palace complexes.

2.4 Appreciate the distinctive form of architecture that evolved for worship.

HEAR MORE: Listen to an audio file of your chapter **www.myartslab.com**

THE FERTILE CRESCENT AND MESOPOTAMIA

Well before farming communities appeared in Europe, people in Asia Minor and the ancient Near East domesticated grains. This first occurred in an area known today as the Fertile Crescent (MAP 2–1). A little later, in the sixth or fifth millennium BCE, agriculture developed in the alluvial plains between the Tigris and Euphrates rivers, which the Greeks called *Mesopotamia*, meaning the "land between the rivers," now in present-day Iraq. Because of problems with periodic flooding as well as drought, there was a need for large-scale systems to control the water supply. Meeting this need may have contributed to the development of the first cities.

Between 4000 and 3000 BCE, a major cultural shift seems to have taken place. Agricultural villages evolved into cities simultaneously and independently in both northern and southern Mesopotamia. These prosperous cities joined with their surrounding territories to create what are known as city-states, each with its own gods and government. Social hierarchies—rulers and workers—emerged with the development of specialized skills beyond those needed for agricultural work. To grain mills and ovens were added brick and pottery kilns and textile and metal workshops. With extra goods and even modest affluence came increased trade and contact with other cultures.

Builders and artists labored to construct huge temples and government buildings. Organized religion played an important role, and the people who controlled rituals and the sacred sites eventually became priests. The people of the ancient Near East worshiped numerous gods and goddesses. Each city had a special protective deity, and people believed the fate of the city depended on the power of that deity. (The names of comparable deities varied over time and place—for example, Inanna, the Sumerian goddess of fertility, love, and war, was equivalent to the Babylonians' Ishtar.) Large architectural complexes—clusters of religious, administrative, and service buildings—developed in each city as centers of ritual and worship and also of government.

Although the stone-free alluvial plain of southern Mesopotamia was prone to floods and droughts, it was a fertile bed for agriculture and successive, interlinked societies. But its wealth and agricultural resources, as well as its few natural defenses, made Mesopotamia vulnerable to political upheaval. Over the centuries, the balance of power shifted between north and south and between local powers and outside invaders. First the Sumerians controlled the south, filling their independent city-states with the fruits of new technology, literacy, and impressive art and architecture. Then they were eclipsed by the Akkadians, their neighbors to the north. When invaders from farther north in turn conquered the Akkadians, the Sumerians regained power locally. During this period the city-states of Ur and Lagash thrived under strong leaders. The Amorites were next to dominate the south. Under them and their king, Hammurabi, a new, unified society arose with its capital in the city of Babylon.

SUMER

The cities and city-states that developed along the rivers of southern Mesopotamia between about 3500 and 2340 BCE are known collectively as Sumer. The Sumerians, who had migrated from the north but whose origins are otherwise obscure, are credited with important "firsts." They may have invented the wagon wheel and the plow. But perhaps their greatest contribution to later civilizations was the invention in about 3100 BCE of a form of writing on clay tablets.

WRITING. Sumerians pressed **cuneiform** ("wedge-shaped") symbols into clay tablets with a **stylus**, a pointed writing instrument, to keep business records (see "Cuneiform Writing," page 71). Thousands of surviving Sumerian tablets have allowed scholars to trace the gradual evolution of writing and arithmetic, another tool of commerce, as well as an organized system of justice. The world's first literary epic also has its origins in Sumer, although the fullest surviving version of this tale is written in Akkadian, the language of Sumer's neighbors to the north. The *Epic of Gilgamesh* records the adventures of a legendary Sumerian king of Uruk and his companion Enkidu. When Enkidu dies, a despondent King Gilgamesh sets out to find the secret of eternal life from the only man and woman who had survived a great flood sent by the gods to destroy the world, because the gods had granted them immortality. Gilgamesh ultimately accepts his own mortality, abandons his quest, and returns to Uruk, recognizing the majestic city as his lasting accomplishment.

THE ZIGGURAT. The Sumerians' most impressive surviving archaeological remains are their **ziggurats**, huge stepped structures with a temple or shrine on top. The first ziggurats may have developed from the practice of repeated rebuilding at a sacred site, with rubble from one structure serving as the foundation for the next. Elevating the buildings also protected the shrines from flooding.

Whatever the origin of their design, ziggurats towering above the flat plain proclaimed the wealth, prestige, and stability of a city's rulers and glorified its gods. Ziggurats functioned symbolically too, as lofty bridges between the earth and the heavens—a meeting place for humans and their gods. They were given names such as "House of the Mountain" and "Bond between Heaven and Earth."

URUK. Two large temple complexes in the 1,000-acre city at Uruk (present-day Warka, Iraq) mark the first independent Sumerian city-state. One was dedicated to Inanna, the goddess of love and war, while the other complex belonged to the sky god Anu. The temple platform of Anu, built up in stages over the centuries, ultimately rose to a height of about 40 feet. Around 3100 BCE, a whitewashed brick temple that modern archaeologists refer to as the White Temple was erected on top of the platform (FIG. 2–2). This now-ruined structure was a simple rectangle with an off-center doorway that led into a large chamber containing an altar, and smaller spaces opened to each side.

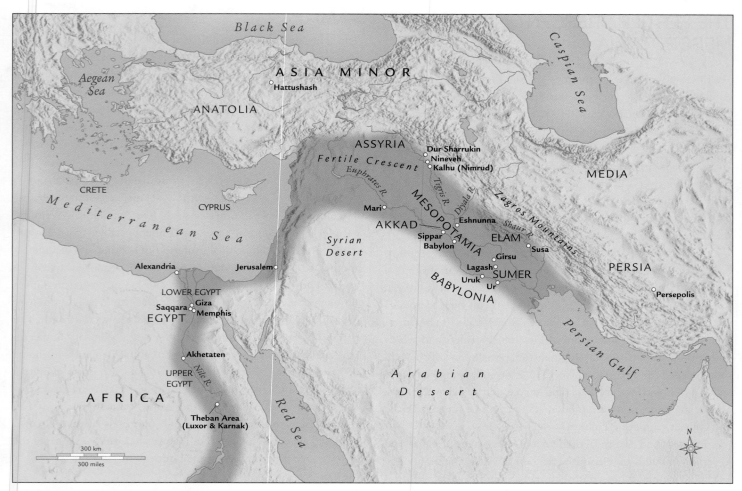

MAP 2–1 • THE ANCIENT NEAR EAST

The green areas represent fertile land that would support early agriculture, notably the area between the Tigris and Euphrates rivers and the strips of land on either side of the Nile in Egypt.

Anu District of Uruk

To view this image, please go to page 29 of the *Art History*, Fourth Edition by Marilyn Stokstad ebook.

To view this image, please go to page 29 of the *Art History*, Fourth Edition by Marilyn Stokstad ebook.

2-2 • RUINS AND PLAN OF THE ANU ZIGGURAT AND WHITE TEMPLE
Uruk (present-day Warka, Iraq). c. 3300–3000 BCE.

Many ancient Near Eastern cities still lie undiscovered. In most cases an archaeological site in a region is signaled by a large mound—known locally as a *tell*, *tepe*, or *huyuk*—that represents the accumulated debris of generations of human habitation. When properly excavated, such mounds yield evidence about the people who inhabited the site.

EXPLORE MORE: View a simulation about the White Temple **www.myartslab.com**

TECHNIQUE | Cuneiform Writing

Sumerians invented writing around 3100 BCE, apparently as an accounting system for goods traded at Uruk. The symbols were pictographs, simple pictures cut into moist clay slabs with a pointed tool. Between 2900 and 2400 BCE, the symbols evolved from pictures into phonograms—representations of syllable sounds—thus becoming a writing system as we know it. During the same centuries, scribes adopted a stylus, or writing tool, with one triangular end and one pointed end that could be pressed easily and rapidly into a wet clay tablet to produce cuneiform writing.

These drawings demonstrate the shift from pictographs to cuneiform. The c. 3100 BCE drawing of a bowl (which means "bread" or "food") was reduced to a four-stroke sign by about 2400 BCE, and by about 700 BCE to a highly abstract arrangement of vertical marks. By combining the pictographs and, later, cuneiform signs, writers created composite signs; for example, a combination of the signs for "head" and "food" meant "to eat."

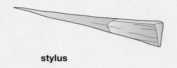

stylus

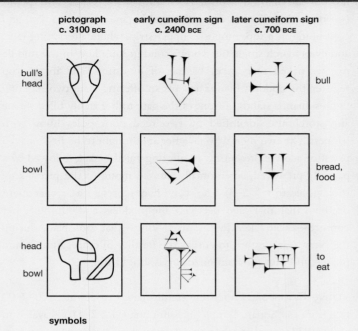

symbols

Statues of gods and donors were placed in Sumerian temples. A striking life-size marble face from Uruk (see "Art as Spoils of War," page 73) may represent a goddess. It could have been attached to a wooden head on a full-size wooden body. Now stripped of its original paint, wig, and the **inlay** set in for brows and eyes, it appears as a stark white mask. Shells may have been used for the whites of the eyes and lapis lazuli for the pupils, and the hair may have been gold.

A tall vessel of carved alabaster (a fine, white stone) found near the temple complex of Inanna at Uruk **(FIG. 2–3)** shows how early Mesopotamian sculptors told stories in stone with great clarity and economy. The visual narrative here is organized into three **registers**, or horizontal bands, and the story condensed to its essential

To view this image, please go to page 30 of the *Art History*, Fourth Edition by Marilyn Stokstad ebook.

2-3 • CARVED VESSEL
From Uruk (present-day Warka, Iraq). c. 3300–3000 BCE. Alabaster, height 36″ (91 cm). Iraq Museum, Baghdad.

elements. The lowest register shows in a lower strip the sources of life in the natural world, beginning with water and plants (variously identified as date palm and barley, wheat and flax) and continuing in a superimposed upper strip, where alternating rams and ewes march single file along a solid ground line. In the middle register naked men carry baskets of foodstuffs, and in the top register, the goddess Inanna accepts an offering from two standing figures. Inanna stands in front of the gate to her richly filled shrine and storehouse, identified by two reed door poles hung with banners. The two men who face her are thought to be first a naked priest or acolyte presenting an offering-filled basket, followed by a partially preserved, ceremonially dressed figure of the priest-king (not visible in FIG. 2–3). The scene may represent a re-enactment of the ritual marriage between the goddess and Dumuzi, her consort—a role taken by the priest-king—that took place during the New Year's festival to ensure the fertility of crops, animals, and people, and thus the continued survival of Uruk.

VOTIVE FIGURES.   Limestone statues dated to about 2900–2600 BCE from the Square Temple in Eshnunna (FIG. 2–4), excavated in 1932–1933, reveal another aspect of Sumerian religious art. These **votive figures** of men and women—images dedicated to the gods—are directly related to an ancient Near Eastern devotional practice in which individual worshipers could set up images of themselves in a shrine before a larger, more elaborate image of a god. A simple inscription might identify the figure as "One who offers prayers." Longer inscriptions might recount in detail all the

things the donor had accomplished in the god's honor. Each sculpture served as a stand-in for the donor, locked in eye-contact with the god, caught perpetually in the act of worship.

The sculptors of these votive statues followed conventions that were important in Sumerian art. Figures are represented with stylized faces and bodies, dressed in clothing that emphasizes pure cylindrical shapes. They stand solemnly, hands clasped in respect, perhaps a posture expected in devotional contexts. The bold, glaring eyes may be related to statements in contemporary Sumerian texts that advise worshipers to approach their gods with an attentive gaze. As with the face of the woman from Uruk, arched brows were inlaid with dark shell, stone, or bitumen that once emphasized the huge, staring eyes. The male figures, bare-chested and dressed in what appear to be sheepskin skirts, are stocky and muscular, with heavy legs, large feet, big shoulders, and cylindrical bodies. The female figures are as massive as the men. Their long sheepskin skirts reveal sturdy legs and feet.

Sumerian artisans worked in various precious metals, and in bronze, often combining them with other materials. Many of these creations were decorated with—or were in the shape of—animals or composite animal-human-bird creatures. A superb example of their skill is a lyre—a kind of harp—from the city of Ur (present-day Muqaiyir, Iraq), to the south of Uruk. This combines wood, gold, lapis lazuli, and shell (see "A Lyre from a Royal Tomb in Ur," pages 75–76). Projecting from the base is a wood-sculpted head of a bearded bull overlaid with gold, intensely lifelike despite the decoratively patterned blue beard created from the semiprecious

To view this image, please go to page 31 of the *Art History*, Fourth Edition by Marilyn Stokstad ebook.

2-4 • VOTIVE FIGURES
From the Square Temple, Eshnunna (present-day Tell Asmar, Iraq). c. 2900–2600 BCE. Limestone, alabaster, and gypsum, height of largest figure approx. 30″ (76.3 cm). Oriental Institute of the University of Chicago.

Art as Spoils of War—Protection or Theft?

Art has always been a casualty in times of social unrest. One of the most recent examples is the looting of the unguarded Iraq National Museum after the fall of Baghdad to U.S.-led coalition forces in April 2003. Among the many thousands of treasures that were stolen is a precious marble head of a woman from Warka, over 5,000 years old. Fortunately it was later recovered, but not without significant damage. Also looted was a carved Sumerian vessel (FIG. 2–3), eventually returned to the museum two months later, shattered into 14 pieces. The museum itself managed to reopen in 2009, but thousands of its antiquities are still missing.

Some of the most bitter resentment spawned by war has involved the taking by the victors of art objects that held great value for the conquered population. Two historically priceless objects unearthed in Elamite Susa, for example—the Akkadian Stele of Naram-Sin (SEE FIG. 2–1) and the Babylonian Stele of Hammurabi (see page 79)—were not Elamite at all, but Mesopotamian. Both had been brought there as military trophies by an Elamite king, who added an inscription to the Stele of Naram-Sin explaining that he had merely "protected" it. Uncovered in Susa during excavations organized by French archaeologist Jacques de Morgan, both works were taken back to Paris at the turn of the twentieth century and are now displayed in the Louvre. Museums around the world contain such works, either snatched by invading armies or acquired as a result of conquest.

The Rosetta Stone, the key to deciphering Egyptian hieroglyphs, was discovered in Egypt by French troops in 1799, fell into British hands when they forced the French from Egypt, and ultimately ended up in the British Museum in London. In the early nineteenth century, the Briton Lord Elgin purchased and removed classical Greek sculpture from the Parthenon in Athens with the permission of the Ottoman authorities who governed Greece at the time. Although his actions may indeed have protected these treasures from neglect and damage in later wars, they have remained installed in the British Museum, despite continuing protests from Greece. Many German collections include works that were similarly "protected" at the end of World War II and are surfacing now. In the United States, Native Americans are increasingly vocal in their demands that artifacts and human remains collected by anthropologists and archaeologists be returned to them.

"To the victor," it is said, "belong the spoils." But passionate and continuous debate surrounds the question of whether this notion remains valid in our own time, especially in the case of revered cultural artifacts.

To view this image, please go to page 32 of the *Art History*, Fourth Edition by Marilyn Stokstad ebook.

FACE OF A WOMAN, KNOWN AS THE WARKA HEAD
Displayed by Iraqi authorities on its recovery in 2003 by the Iraq Museum in Baghdad. The head is from Uruk (present-day Warka, Iraq). c. 3300–3000 BCE. Marble, height approx. 8″ (20.3 cm).

---

gem stone, lapis lazuli. Since lapis lazuli had to be imported from Afghanistan, the work documents widespread trade in the region at this time.

CYLINDER SEALS. About the time written records appeared, Sumerians developed seals for identifying documents and establishing property ownership. By 3300–3100 BCE, record keepers redesigned the stamp seal as a cylinder. Rolled across documents on clay tablets or over the soft clay applied to a closure

that needed sealing—a jar lid, the knot securing a bundle, or the door to a room—the cylinders left a raised mirror image of the design incised (cut) into their surface. Such sealing attested to the authenticity or accuracy of a text or assured that no unauthorized person could gain access to a room or container. Sumerian **cylinder seals**, usually less than 2 inches high, were generally made of a hard stone so that the tiny but elaborate incised scenes would not wear away during repeated use. Individuals often acquired seals as signs of status or on appointment to a high

To view this image, please go to page 33 of the *Art History*, Fourth Edition by Marilyn Stokstad ebook.

2-5 • CYLINDER SEAL AND ITS MODERN IMPRESSION
Tomb of Queen Puabi (PG 800), Ur (present-day Muqaiyir, Iraq).
c. 2600–2500 BCE. Lapis lazuli, height 1⁹⁄₁₆″ (4 cm), diameter ²⁵⁄₃₂″ (2 cm). University of Pennsylvania Museum of Archaeology and Anthropology, Philadelphia.

administrative position, and the seals were buried with them, along with other important possessions.

The lapis lazuli **CYLINDER SEAL** in **FIG. 2–5** is one of over 400 that were found in excavations of the royal burials at Ur. It comes from the tomb of a royal woman known as Puabi, and was found leaning against the right arm of her body. The modern clay impression of its incised design shows two registers of a convivial banquet at which all the guests are women, with fringed skirts and long hair gathered up in buns behind their necks. Two seated women in the upper register raise their glasses, accompanied by standing servants, one of whom, at far left, holds a fan. The single seated figure in the lower register sits in front of a table piled with food, while a figure behind her offers a cup of drink, presumably drawn from the jar she carries in her other hand, reminiscent of the container held by the lion on the lyre plaque (see page 76, FIG. C). Musical entertainment is provided by four women, standing to the far right.

AKKAD

During the Sumerian period, a people known as the Akkadians had settled north of Uruk. They adopted Sumerian culture, but unlike the Sumerians, the Akkadians spoke a Semitic language (the same family of languages that includes Arabic and Hebrew). Under the powerful military and political figure Sargon I (ruled c. 2332–2279 BCE), they conquered most of Mesopotamia. For more than half a century, Sargon, "King of the Four Quarters of the World," ruled this empire from his capital at Akkad, the actual site of which is yet to be discovered.

HEAD OF A RULER. Few artifacts can be identified with Akkad, making a life-size bronze head—found in the northern city of Nineveh (present-day Kuyunjik, Iraq) and thought to date from the time of Sargon—especially precious **(FIG. 2–6)**. It is the earliest major work of hollow-cast copper sculpture known in the ancient Near East.

The facial features and hairstyle probably reflect a generalized ideal rather than the appearance of a specific individual, although

To view this image, please go to page 33 of the *Art History*, Fourth Edition by Marilyn Stokstad ebook.

2-6 • HEAD OF A MAN (KNOWN AS AKKADIAN RULER)
From Nineveh (present-day Kuyunjik, Iraq). c. 2300–2200 BCE. Copper alloy, height 14³⁄₈″ (36.5 cm). Iraq Museum, Baghdad.

A Lyre from a Royal Tomb in Ur

Sir Leonard Woolley's excavations at Ur during the 1920s initially garnered international attention because of the association of this ancient Mesopotamian city with the biblical patriarch Abraham. It was not long, however, before the exciting discoveries themselves moved to center stage, especially 16 royal burials that yielded spectacular objects crafted of gold and lurid evidence of the human sacrifices associated with Sumerian royal burial practices, when retainers were seemingly buried with the rulers they served.

Woolley's work at Ur was a joint venture of the University of Pennsylvania Museum in Philadelphia and the British Museum in London, and in conformance with Iraq's Antiquities Law of 1922, the uncovered artifacts were divided between the sponsoring institutions and Iraq itself. Although Woolley worked with a large team of laborers and assistants over 12 seasons of digging at Ur, he and his wife Katherine reserved for themselves the painstakingly delicate process of uncovering the most important finds. Woolley's own account of work within one tomb outlines the practice—"Most of the workmen were sent away … so that the final work with knives and brushes could be done by my wife and myself in comparative peace. For ten days the two of us spent most of the time from sunrise to sunset lying on our tummies brushing and blowing and threading beads in their order as they lay…. You might suppose that to find three-score women all richly bedecked with jewelry could be a very thrilling experience, and so it is, in retrospect, but I'm afraid that at the moment one is much more conscious of the toil than of the thrill" (quoted in Zettler and Horne, p. 31).

One of the most spectacular discoveries in the royal burials at Ur was an elaborate lyre, which rested over the body of the woman who had presumably played it during the funeral ceremony for the royal figure buried nearby. Like nine other lyres Woolley found at Ur, the wooden sound box of this one had long since deteriorated and disappeared, but an exquisitely crafted bull's head finial of gold and lapis lazuli survived, along with a plaque of carved shell inlaid with bitumen, depicting at the top a heroic image of a man interlocked with and in control of two bulls, and below them three scenes of animals personifying the activities of humans. On one register, a seated donkey plucks the strings of a bull lyre—similar to the instrument on which this set of images originally appeared—stabilized by a standing bear, while a fox accompanies him with a rattle. On the register above, upright animals bring food and drink for a feast. A hyena to the left—assuming the role of a butcher with a knife in his belt—carries a table piled high with meat. A lion follows, toting a large jar and pouring vessel.

The top and bottom registers are particularly intriguing in relation to the *Epic of Gilgamesh*, a 3,000-line poem that is Sumer's great contribution to world literature. Rich in descriptions of heroic feats and fabulous creatures, Gilgamesh's story probes the question of immortality and expresses the heroic aim to understand hostile surroundings and to find meaning in human existence. Gilgamesh encounters scorpion-men, like the one pictured in the lowest register, and it is easy to see the hero himself in the commanding but unprotected bearded figure centered in the top register, naked except for a wide belt, masterfully controlling in his grasp the two powerfully rearing human-headed bulls that flank him. Because the poem was first written down 700 years after this harp was created, this plaque may document a very long oral tradition.

On another level, because we know lyres were used in funeral rites, this imagery may

To view this image, please go to page 34 of the *Art History*, Fourth Edition by Marilyn Stokstad ebook.

A. KATHERINE AND LEONARD WOOLLEY (ABOVE) EXCAVATING AT UR IN 1937, BESIDE TWO ARCHAEOLOGICAL ASSISTANTS IN ONE OF THE ROYAL BURIALS
Archives of the University of Pennsylvania Museum, Philadelphia.

depict a heroic image of the deceased in the top register, and a funeral banquet in the realm of the dead at the bottom. The animals shown are the traditional guardians of the gateway through which the deceased had first to pass. Cuneiform tablets preserve songs of mourning, perhaps chanted by priests accompanied by lyres at funerals. One begins, "Oh, lady, the harp of mourning is placed on the ground," a particularly poignant statement considering that the lyres of Ur may have been buried on top of the sacrificed bodies of the women who originally played them.

To view this image, please go to page 35 of the *Art History*, Fourth Edition by Marilyn Stokstad ebook.

To view this image, please go to page 35 of the *Art History*, Fourth Edition by Marilyn Stokstad ebook.

B. THE GREAT LYRE WITH BULL'S HEAD
Royal Tomb (PG 789), Ur (present-day Muqaiyir, Iraq). c. 2600–2500 BCE. Wood with gold, silver, lapis lazuli, bitumen, and shell, reassembled in modern wood support; height of head 14″ (35.6 cm); height of front panel 13″ (33 cm); maximum length of lyre 55½″ (140 cm); height of upright back arm 46½″ (117 cm). University of Pennsylvania Museum of Archaeology and Anthropology, Philadelphia.

C. FRONT PANEL, THE SOUND BOX OF THE GREAT LYRE
Ur (present-day Muqaiyir, Iraq). Wood with shell inlaid in bitumen, height 12¼ × 4½″ (31.1 × 11 cm). University of Pennsylvania Museum of Archaeology and Anthropology, Philadelphia.

the sculpture was once identified as Sargon himself. The enormous curling beard and elaborately braided hair (circling the head and ending in a knot at the back) indicate both royalty and ideal male appearance. The deliberate damage to the left side of the face and eye suggests that the head was symbolically mutilated to destroy its power. Specifically, the ears and the inlaid eyes appear to have been removed to deprive the head of its ability to hear and see.

THE STELE OF NARAM-SIN.

The concept of imperial authority was literally carved in stone by Sargon's grandson Naram-Sin (SEE FIG. 2–1). This 6½-foot-high stele memorializes one of his military victories, and is one of the first works of art created to celebrate a specific achievement of an individual ruler. The inscription states that the stele commemorates the king's victory over the Lullubi people of the Zagros Mountains. Watched over by three solar deities (symbolized by the rayed suns at the top of the stele) and wearing a horned helmet-crown—heretofore associated only with gods—the hieratically scaled king stands proudly above his soldiers and his fallen foes, boldly silhouetted against the sky next to the smooth surface of a mountain. Even the shape of the stone slab is used as an active part of the composition. Its tapering top perfectly accommodates the carved mountain within it, and Naram-Sin is posed to reflect the profile of both.

UR AND LAGASH

The Akkadian Empire fell around 2180 BCE to the Guti, a mountain people from the northeast. For a brief time, the Guti controlled most of the Mesopotamian plain, but ultimately Sumerian people regained control of the region and expelled the Guti in 2112 BCE, under the leadership of King Urnammu of Ur. He reintroduced the Sumerian language and sponsored magnificent building campaigns, notably a ziggurat dedicated to the moon god Nanna, also called Sin (FIG. 2–7). Although located on the site of an earlier temple, this imposing mud-brick structure was not the accidental result of successive rebuilding. Its base is a rectangle 205 by 141 feet, with three sets of stairs converging at an imposing entrance gate atop the first of what were three platforms. Each platform's walls slope outward from top to base, probably to prevent rainwater from forming puddles and eroding the mud-brick pavement below. The first two levels of the ziggurat and their retaining walls are recent reconstructions.

One large Sumerian city-state remained independent throughout this period: Lagash, whose capital was Girsu (present-day Telloh, Iraq), on the Tigris River. Gudea, the ruler, built and restored many temples, and within them, following a venerable Mesopotamian tradition, he placed votive statues representing himself as governor and embodiment of just rule. The statues are made of diorite, a very hard stone, and the difficulty of carving it may have prompted sculptors to use compact, simplified forms for the portraits. Or perhaps it was the desire for powerful, stylized images that prompted the choice of this imported stone for this series of statues. Twenty of them survive, making Gudea a familiar figure in the study of ancient Near Eastern art.

Images of Gudea present him as a strong, peaceful, pious ruler worthy of divine favor (FIG. 2–8). Whether he is shown sitting or standing, he wears a long garment, which provides ample, smooth space for long cuneiform inscriptions. In this imposing statue, only 2½ feet tall, his right shoulder is bare, and he wears a cap with a wide brim carved with a pattern to represent fleece. He holds a vessel in front of him, from which life-giving water flows in two streams, each filled with leaping fish. The text on his garment states that he dedicated himself, the statue, and its temple to the goddess Geshtinanna, the divine poet and interpreter of dreams. The sculptor has emphasized the power centers of the human body: the eyes, head, and smoothly muscled chest and arms. Gudea's face is youthful and serene, and his eyes—oversized and

To view this image, please go to page 36 of the *Art History*, Fourth Edition by Marilyn Stokstad ebook.

2-7 • NANNA ZIGGURAT
Ur (present-day Muqaiyir, Iraq). c. 2100–2050 BCE.

wide open—perpetually confront the gaze of the deity with intense concentration.

BABYLON

For more than 300 years, periods of political turmoil alternated with periods of stable government in Mesopotamia, until the Amorites (a Semitic-speaking people from the Syrian Desert, to the west) reunited the region under Hammurabi (ruled 1792–1750 BCE). Hammurabi's capital city was Babylon and his subjects were called Babylonians. Among Hammurabi's achievements was a written legal code that detailed the laws of his realm and the penalties for breaking them (see "The Code of Hammurabi," page 79).

To view this image, please go to page 37 of the *Art History*, Fourth Edition by Marilyn Stokstad ebook.

2-8 • VOTIVE STATUE OF GUDEA
Girsu (present-day Telloh, Iraq). c. 2090 BCE. Diorite, height 29″ (73.7 cm). Musée du Louvre, Paris.

EXPLORE MORE: Gain insight from a primary source related to the statue of Gudea **www.myartslab.com**

The Code of Hammurabi

Babylonian ruler Hammurabi's systematic codification of his people's rights, duties, and punishments for wrongdoing was engraved on a black diorite slab known as the Stele of Hammurabi. This imposing artifact, therefore, is both a work of art that depicts a legendary event and a precious historical document that records a conversation about justice between god and man.

At the top of the stele, we see Hammurabi standing in an attitude of prayer before Shamash, the sun god and god of justice. Rays rise from Shamash's shoulders as he sits, crowned by a conical horned cap, on a backless throne, holding additional symbols of his power—the measuring rod and the rope circle. Shamash gives the law to the king, his intermediary, and the codes of justice flow forth underneath them in horizontal bands of exquisitely engraved cuneiform signs. The idea of god-given laws engraved on stone tablets has a long tradition in the ancient Near East: Moses, the lawgiver of Israel, received two stone tablets containing the Ten Commandments from God on Mount Sinai (Exodus 32:19).

A prologue on the front of the stele lists the temples Hammurabi has restored, and an epilogue on the back glorifies him as a peacemaker, but most of the stele "publishes" the laws themselves, guaranteeing uniform treatment of people throughout his kingdom. Within the inscription, Hammurabi declares that he intends "to cause justice to prevail in the land and to destroy the wicked and the evil, that the strong might not oppress the weak nor the weak the strong." Most of the 300 or so entries that follow deal with commercial and property matters. Only 68 relate to domestic problems, and a mere 20 deal with physical assault.

Punishments are based on the wealth, class, and gender of the parties—the rights of the wealthy are favored over the poor, citizens over slaves, men over women. Most famous are instances when punishments are specifically tailored to fit crimes—an eye for an eye, a tooth for a tooth, a broken bone for a broken bone. The death penalty is decreed for crimes such as stealing from a temple or palace, helping a slave to escape, or insubordination in the army. Trial by water and fire could also be imposed, as when an adulterous woman and her lover were to be thrown into the water; if they did not drown, they were deemed innocent. Although some of the punishments may seem excessive today, Hammurabi was breaking new ground by regulating laws and punishments rather than leaving them to the whims of rulers or officials.

To view this image, please go to page 38 of the *Art History*, Fourth Edition by Marilyn Stokstad ebook.

STELE OF HAMMURABI
Susa (present-day Shush, Iran). c. 1792–1750 BCE. Diorite, height of stele approx. 7′ (2.13 m); height of relief 28″ (71.1 cm). Musée du Louvre, Paris.

EXPLORE MORE: Gain insight from a primary source related to the Code of Hammurabi **www.myartslab.com**

To view this image, please go to page 290 of the *Art History*, Fourth Edition by Marilyn Stokstad ebook.

2-9 • ASHOKAN PILLAR
Lauriya Nandangarh, Bihar, India. Maurya period, c. 246 BCE.

ART OF SOUTH AND SOUTHEAST ASIA BEFORE 1200

According to legend, the ruler Ashoka (r. 273–232 BCE) was stunned by grief and remorse as he looked across the battlefield. As was the custom of his dynasty, he had gone to war, expanding his empire until he had conquered many of the kingdoms that had comprised the Indian subcontinent. Now, about 265 BCE, after the final battle in his conquest of the northern kingdoms, he was suddenly—unexpectedly—shocked by the horror of the suffering he had caused. In the traditional account, it is said that only one form on the battlefield moved: The stooped figure of a Buddhist monk slowly making his way through the carnage. Watching this spectral figure, Ashoka abruptly turned the moment of triumph into one of renunciation. Decrying violence and warfare, he vowed to become a *chakravartin* ("world-conquering ruler"), not through the force of arms but through spreading the teachings of the Buddha and establishing Buddhism as the major religion of his realm.

Although there is no proof that Ashoka himself converted to Buddhism, he erected and dedicated monuments to the Buddha throughout his empire—shrines, monasteries, and the columns commonly called **Ashokan pillars (FIG. 2–9)**. With missionary ardor, he dispatched delegates throughout the Indian subcontinent and to countries as distant as Syria, Egypt, and Greece. In his impassioned propagation of Buddhism, perhaps as a means of securing his enormous empire, Ashoka stimulated an intensely rich period of art.

Despite the emissaries he sent and his widespread placement of inscriptions on the face of large rocks, his pillars are few in number and quite concentrated in location. Only eight can be attributed to Ashoka's time by the inscriptions they bear, although several other pillars are commonly assigned to this period. Most were placed at the site of Buddhist monasteries along a route leading from Punjab in the northwest to Ashoka's capital, Pataliputra, in the northeast. One pillar some distance from this route, at Sanchi, suggests that others, perhaps not yet discovered, may have been placed along a more southerly path.

Not only are the pillars the first sculptural remains in India after a hiatus of some 1,600 years, but their inscriptions are the first preserved Indian writing that we can read and interpret. The script, known as Brahmi, was deciphered in 1837 by James Prinsep, a brilliant amateur scholar who served the East India Company as assay master of the Calcutta mint. He discovered that the inscriptions were written in Prakrit, a language closely related to classical Sanskrit, and that they set down laws of righteous behavior for the monks and nuns resident in the monasteries where the pillars were erected, as well as for passing travelers. Like so many aspects of Indian art, these pillars raise intriguing questions that have yet to be answered, most notably: How could such pillars be made in the absence of any known precedent?

LEARN ABOUT IT

2.5 Recognize the characteristic differences between a Hindu temple and a Buddhist stupa.

2.6 Appreciate the diffusion of religion in Southeast Asia.

2.7 Understand the correlation between religious worldviews and architectural form.

2.8 Assess the variety of ways in which storytelling can be accomplished in pictorial art.

2.9 Identify the distinguishing features of a Buddha image.

HEAR MORE: Listen to an audio file of your chapter **www.myartslab.com**

THE INDIAN SUBCONTINENT

The South Asian subcontinent, or Indian subcontinent, as it is commonly called, is a peninsular region that includes the present-day countries of India, Afghanistan, Pakistan, Nepal, Bhutan, Bangladesh, and Sri Lanka (MAP 2–2). From the beginning, these areas have been home to societies whose cultures are closely linked and which have maintained remarkable continuity over time. (South Asia is distinct from Southeast Asia, which includes Brunei, Myanmar, Cambodia, East Timor, Indonesia, Laos, Malaysia, the Philippines, Singapore, Thailand, and Vietnam.) Although the modern Republic of India is about a third the size of the United States, South Asia as a whole is about two-thirds its size. A low mountain range, the Vindhya Hills, acts as a natural division that separates north India from south India. On the northern border rises the protective barrier of the Himalayas, the world's highest mountains. To the northwest are other mountains through whose passes came invasions and immigrations that profoundly affected the civilization of the subcontinent. Over these passes, too, wound the major trade routes that linked the Indian subcontinent by land to the rest of Asia and to Europe. Surrounded on its remaining sides by oceans since ancient times, the subcontinent has also been connected to the world by maritime trade, and during much of the period under discussion here it formed part of a coastal trading network that extended from eastern Africa to China.

Differences in language, climate, and terrain within India have fostered distinct regional and cultural characteristics and artistic traditions. However, despite such diversity, several overarching traits tend to unite Indian art. Most evident is a distinctive sense of beauty, with voluptuous forms and a profusion of ornament, texture, and color. Visual abundance is considered auspicious, and it reflects a belief in the generosity and favor of the gods. Another characteristic is the pervasive symbolism that enriches all Indian arts with intellectual and emotional layers. Third, and perhaps most important, is an emphasis on capturing the vibrant quality of a world seen as infused with the dynamics of the divine. Gods and humans, ideas and abstractions, are given tactile, sensuous forms, radiant with inner spirit.

INDUS CIVILIZATION

The earliest civilization of South Asia was nurtured in the lower reaches of the Indus River, in present-day Pakistan and in northwestern India. Known as the Indus or Harappan civilization (after Harappa, the first-discovered site), it flourished from approximately 2600 to 1900 BCE, or during roughly the same time as the Old Kingdom period of Egypt, the Minoan civilization of the Aegean, and the dynasties of Ur and Babylon in Mesopotamia. Indeed, it is considered, along with Egypt and Mesopotamia, to be one of the world's earliest urban river-valley civilizations.

It was the chance discovery in the late nineteenth century of some small seals, such as those in FIGURE 2–10, that provided the

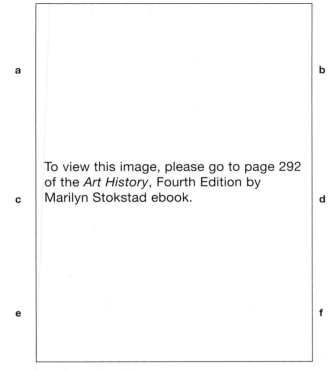

2-10 • SEAL IMPRESSIONS
a., d. horned animal; b. buffalo; c. sacrificial rite to a goddess (?); e. yogi; f. three-headed animal. Indus Valley civilization, c. 2500–1500 BCE. Steatite, each seal approx. 1¼ × 1¼″ (3.2 × 3.2 cm).

The more than 2,000 small seals and impressions that have been found offer an intriguing window on the Indus Valley civilization. Usually carved from steatite stone, the seals were coated with alkali and then fired to produce a lustrous, white surface. A perforated knob on the back of each may have been for suspending them. The most popular subjects are animals, most commonly a one-horned bovine standing before an altarlike object (a, d). Animals on Indus Valley seals are often portrayed with remarkable naturalism, their taut, well-modeled surfaces implying their underlying skeletons. The function of the seals remains enigmatic, and the script that is so prominent in the impressions has yet to be deciphered.

first clue that an ancient civilization had existed in this region. The seals appeared to be related to, but not the same as, seals known from ancient Mesopotamia (SEE FIG. 2–5). Excavations begun in the 1920s and continuing into the present subsequently uncovered a number of major urban areas at points along the lower Indus River, including Harappa, Mohenjo-Daro, and Chanhu-Daro.

MOHENJO-DARO. The ancient cities of the Indus Valley resemble each other in design and construction, suggesting a coherent culture. At Mohenjo-Daro, the best preserved of the sites, archaeologists discovered an elevated citadel area about 50 feet high, presumably containing important government structures, surrounded by a wall. Among the buildings is a remarkable water tank, a large watertight pool that may have been a public bath but could also have had a ritual use (FIG. 2–11). Stretching out below the elevated area was the city, arranged in a gridlike plan with wide avenues and narrow side streets. Its houses, often two stories high, were generally built

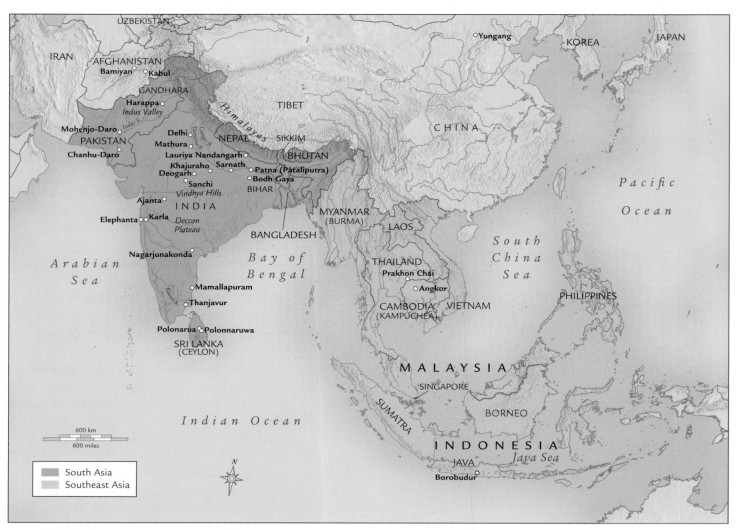

MAP 2-2 • SOUTH AND SOUTHEAST ASIA

The borders of India are created by natural features, with the Himalayas to the north and the Indian Ocean on the remaining borders. Nearly all the rivers in the region flow east–west and are an important conduit for trade and new ideas.

To view this image, please go to page 293 of the *Art History*, Fourth Edition by Marilyn Stokstad ebook.

2-11 • LARGE WATER TANK, MOHENJO-DARO

Indus Valley civilization (Harappan), c. 2600–1900 BCE.

Possibly a public or ritual bathing area.

around a central courtyard. Like other Indus Valley cities, Mohenjo-Daro was constructed of fired brick, in contrast to the less durable sun-dried brick used in other cultures of the time. The city included a network of covered drainage systems that channeled away waste and rainwater. Clearly the technical and engineering skills of this civilization were highly advanced. At its peak, about 2500 to 2000 BCE, Mohenjo-Daro was approximately 6–7 square miles in size and had a population of about 20,000–50,000.

INDUS VALLEY SEALS.   Although our knowledge of the Indus civilization is limited by the fact that we cannot read its writing, motifs on seals as well as the few artworks that have been discovered strongly suggest continuities with later South Asian cultures. The seal in FIGURE 2–10e, for example, depicts a man in the meditative posture associated in Indian culture with a yogi, one who seeks mental and physical purification and self-control, usually for spiritual purposes. In FIGURE 2–10c, the persons with elaborate headgear in a row or procession observe a figure standing in a tree—possibly a goddess—and a kneeling worshiper. This scene may offer some insight into the religious or ritual customs of Indus people, whose deities may have been ancient prototypes of later Indian gods and goddesses.

Numerous terra-cotta figurines and a few stone and bronze statuettes have been found at Indus sites. They reveal a confident maturity of artistic conception and technique. The terra cottas resemble Mesopotamian art in their motifs and rather abstract rendering. On the other hand, the stone figures foreshadow the later Indian artistic tradition in their sensuous naturalism.

"PRIEST-KING" FROM MOHENJO-DARO.   The identity of the male torso in FIGURE 2–12, sometimes called the "priest-king," is uncertain, suggesting a structure of society—where priests functioned as kings—for which we have no evidence at all. Several features of this figure, including a low forehead, a broad nose, thick lips, and long slit eyes, are seen on other works from Mohenjo-Daro. The man's garment is patterned with a **trefoil** (three-lobed) motif. The depressions of the trefoil pattern were originally filled with red paint, and the eyes were inlaid with colored shell or stone. A narrow band with a circular ornament encircles the upper arm and the head. It falls in back into two long strands and may be an indication of rank. Certainly, with its formal pose and simplified, geometric form, the statue conveys a commanding human presence.

NUDE TORSO FROM HARAPPA.   Although its date is disputed by some, a nude male torso found at Harappa is an example of a contrasting naturalistic style **(FIG. 2–13)** of ancient Indus origins. Less than 4 inches tall, it is one of the most extraordinary portrayals of the human form to survive from any early civilization. In contrast to the more athletic male ideal developed much later in ancient Greece, this sculpture emphasizes the soft texture of the human body and the subtle nuances of muscular form. The abdomen is relaxed in the manner of a yogi able to control his breath. With these characteristics the Harappa torso forecasts the essential aesthetic attributes of later Indian sculpture.

The reasons for the demise of this flourishing civilization are not yet understood. All we know is

To view this image, please go to page 294 of the *Art History*, Fourth Edition by Marilyn Stokstad ebook.

2-12 • TORSO OF A "PRIEST-KING"
From Mohenjo-Daro. Indus Valley civilization, c. 2600–1900 BCE. Steatite, height 6⅞″ (17.5 cm). National Museum of Pakistan, Karachi.

To view this image, please go to page 295 of the *Art History*, Fourth Edition by Marilyn Stokstad ebook.

2-13 • TORSO

From Harappa. Indus Valley civilization, c. 2600–1900 BCE. Red sandstone, height 3¾″ (9.5 cm). National Museum, New Delhi.

that between 2000 and 1750—possibly because of climate change, a series of natural disasters, and invasions—the cities of the Indus civilization declined, and predominantly rural societies evolved.

THE VEDIC PERIOD

About 2000 BCE nomadic shepherds, the Aryans, entered India from central Asia and the Russian steppes. Gradually they supplanted the indigenous populations and introduced the horse and chariot, the Sanskrit language, a hierarchical social order, and religious practices that centered on the propitiation of gods through fire sacrifice. Their sacred writings known as the Vedas, gave the period its name. The earliest Veda consists of hymns to various Aryan gods including the divine king Indra. The importance of the fire sacrifice, overseen by a powerful priesthood—the Brahmins—and religiously sanctioned social classes, persisted through the Vedic period. At some point, the class structure became hereditary and immutable, with lasting consequences for Indian society.

During the latter part of this period, from about 800 BCE, the Upanishads were composed. These metaphysical texts examine the meanings of the earlier, more cryptic Vedic hymns. They focus on the relationship between the individual soul, or *atman*, and the universal soul, or Brahman, as well as on other concepts central to subsequent Indian philosophy. One is the assertion that the material world is illusory and that only Brahman is real and eternal. Another holds that our existence is cyclical and that beings are caught in *samsara*, a relentless cycle of birth, life, death, and rebirth. Believers aspire to attain liberation from *samsara* and to unite the individual *atman* with the eternal, universal Brahman.

The latter portion of the Vedic period also saw the flowering of India's epic literature, written in the melodious and complex Sanskrit language. By around 400 BCE, the 18-volume *Mahabharata*, the longest epic in world literature, and the *Ramayana*, the most popular and enduring religious epic in India and Southeast Asia, were taking shape. These texts, the cornerstones of Indian literature, relate histories of gods and humans that bring the philosophical ideas of the Vedas to a more accessible and popular level.

In this stimulating religious, philosophical, and literary climate numerous religious communities arose. The most influential teachers of these times were Shakyamuni Buddha and Mahavira. The Buddha, or "enlightened one," lived and taught in India around 500 BCE; his teachings form the basis of the Buddhist religion (see "Buddhism," page 87). Mahavira (c. 599–527 BCE), regarded as the last of 24 highly purified superbeings called pathfinders *(tirthankaras)*, was the founder of the Jain religion. Both Shakyamuni Buddha and Mahavira espoused some basic Upanishadic tenets, such as the cyclical nature of existence and the need for liberation from the material world. However, they rejected the authority of the Vedas, and with it the legitimacy of the fire sacrifice and the hereditary class structure of Vedic society, with its powerful, exclusive priesthood. In contrast, Buddhism and Jainism were open to all, regardless of social position.

Buddhism became a vigorous force in South Asia and provided the impetus for much of the major surviving art created between the third century BCE and the fifth century CE. The Vedic tradition, meanwhile, continued to evolve, emerging later as Hinduism, a loose term that encompasses the many religious forms that resulted from the mingling of Vedic culture with indigenous beliefs (see "Hinduism," page 88).

THE MAURYA PERIOD

After about 700 BCE, cities again began to reappear on the subcontinent, especially in the north, where numerous kingdoms arose. For most of its subsequent history, India was a shifting mosaic of regional kingdoms. From time to time, however, a particularly powerful dynasty formed an empire. The first of these was the Maurya dynasty (c. 322–185 BCE), which extended its rule over all but the southernmost portion of the subcontinent.

To view this image, please go to page 296 of the *Art History*, Fourth Edition by Marilyn Stokstad ebook.

2–14 • FEMALE FIGURE HOLDING A FLY-WHISK

From Didarganj, Patna, Bihar, India. Probably Maurya period, c. 250 BCE. Polished sandstone, height 5'4¼" (1.63 m). Patna Museum, Patna.

Commonly identified as a *yakshi*, this sculpture has become one of the most famous works of Indian art. Holding a fly-whisk in her raised right hand, the figure wears only a long shawl and a skirtlike cloth. The cloth rests low on her hips, held in place by a girdle. Subtly sculpted parallel creases indicate that it is gathered closely about her legs. The ends, drawn back up over the girdle, cascade down to her feet in a broad, central loop of flowing folds ending in a zigzag of hems. Draped low over her back, the shawl passes through the crook of her arm and then flows to the ground. (The missing left side of the shawl probably mirrored this motion.) The figure's jewelry is prominent. A double strand of pearls hangs between her breasts, its shape echoing and emphasizing the voluptuous curves of her body. Another strand of pearls encircles her neck. She wears a simple tiara, plug earrings, and rows of bangles. The nubbled tubes about her ankles probably represent anklets made of beaten gold. Her hair is bound behind in a large bun, and a small bun sits on her forehead. This hairstyle appears again in Indian sculpture of the later Kushan period (c. second century CE).

FEMALE FIGURE FROM DIDARGANJ. The art of the Maurya period reflects an age of heroes. At this time emerged the ideal of upholding *dharma*, the divinely ordained moral law believed to keep the universe from falling into chaos. This heroic ideal seems fully embodied in a life-size statue found at Didarganj, near the Maurya capital of Pataliputra **(FIG. 2–14)**. The statue, dated by most scholars to the Maurya period, probably represents a **yakshi**, a spirit associated with the productive forces of nature. With its large breasts and pelvis, the figure embodies the association of female beauty with procreative abundance, bounty, and auspiciousness—qualities that in turn reflect the generosity of the gods and the workings of *dharma* in the world.

Sculpted from fine-grained sandstone, the statue conveys the *yakshi*'s authority through the frontal rigor of her pose, the massive volumes of her form, and the strong, linear patterning of her

To view this image, please go to page 296 of the *Art History*, Fourth Edition by Marilyn Stokstad ebook.

2–15 • LION CAPITAL

From Ashokan pillar at Sarnath, Uttar Pradesh, India. Maurya period, c. 250 BCE. Polished sandstone, height 7' (2.13 m). Archaeological Museum, Sarnath.

Buddhism

The Buddhist religion developed from the teachings of Shakyamuni Buddha, who lived from about 563 to 483 BCE in the present-day regions of Nepal and northern India. At his birth, it is believed, seers foretold that the infant prince, named Siddhartha Gautama, would become either a *chakravartin* ("world-conquering ruler") or a *buddha* ("fully enlightened being"). Hoping for a ruler like himself, Siddhartha's father tried to surround his son with pleasure and shield him from pain. Yet the prince was eventually exposed to the sufferings of old age, sickness, and death—the inevitable fate of all mortal beings. Deeply troubled by the human condition, Siddhartha at age 29 left the palace, his family, and his inheritance to live as an ascetic in the wilderness. After six years of meditation, he attained complete enlightenment at a site in India now called Bodh Gaya.

Following his enlightenment, the Buddha ("Enlightened One") gave his first teaching in the Deer Park at Sarnath. Here he expounded the Four Noble Truths that are the foundation of Buddhism: (1) life is suffering; (2) this suffering has a cause, which is ignorance; (3) this ignorance can be overcome and extinguished; (4) the way to overcome this ignorance is by following the eightfold path of right view, right resolve, right speech, right action, right livelihood, right effort, right mindfulness, and right concentration. After the Buddha's death at age 80, his many disciples developed his teachings and established the world's oldest monastic institutions.

A buddha is not a god but rather one who sees the ultimate nature of the world and is therefore no longer subject to *samsara*, the cycle of birth, death, and rebirth that otherwise holds us in its grip, whether we are born into the world of the gods, humans, animals, demons, tortured spirits, or hellish beings.

The early form of Buddhism, known as Theravada or Hinayana, stresses self-cultivation for the purpose of attaining *nirvana*, which is the extinction of *samsara* for oneself. Theravada Buddhism has continued mainly in Sri Lanka and Southeast Asia. Within 500 years of the Buddha's death, another form of Buddhism, known as Mahayana, became popular mainly in northern India; it eventually flourished in China, Korea, Japan, and in Tibet (as Vajrayana). Compassion for all beings is the foundation of Mahayana Buddhism, whose goal is not *nirvana* for oneself but buddhahood (enlightenment) for every being throughout the universe. Mahayana Buddhism recognizes buddhas other than Shakyamuni from the past, present, and future. One such is Maitreya, the next buddha to appear on earth. Another is Amitabha Buddha, the Buddha of Infinite Light and Infinite Life (that is, incorporating all space and time), who dwells in a paradise known as the Western Pure Land. Amitabha Buddha became particularly popular in east Asia. Mahayana Buddhism also developed the category of **bodhisattvas** ("those whose essence is wisdom"), saintly beings who are on the brink of achieving buddhahood but have vowed to help others achieve buddhahood before crossing over themselves. In art, bodhisattvas and buddhas are most clearly distinguished by their clothing and adornments: bodhisattvas wear the princely garb of India, while buddhas wear monks' robes.

EXPLORE MORE: Gain insight from a primary source of words spoken by the Buddha **www.myartslab.com**

---

ornaments and dress. Alleviating and counterbalancing this hierarchical formality are her soft, youthful face, the precise definition of prominent features such as the stomach muscles, and the polished sheen of her exposed flesh. This lustrous polish is a special feature of Maurya sculpture.

THE RISE OF BUDDHISM.   During the reign of the third Maurya emperor Ashoka (ruled c. 273–232 BCE), Buddhism was expanded from a religion largely localized in the Maurya heartland, a region known as Magadha, to one extending across the entire empire. Among the monuments he erected were monolithic pillars set up primarily at the sites of Buddhist monasteries.

Pillars may have been used as flag-bearing standards in India since earliest times. Thus the creators of the pillars erected during Ashoka's reign may have adapted this already ancient form to the symbolism of Indian creation myths and the new religion of Buddhism. The fully developed Ashokan pillar—a slightly tapered sandstone shaft that usually rested on a stone foundation slab sunk more than 10 feet into the ground—rose to a height of around 50 feet (SEE FIG. 2–9). On it were carved inscriptions relating to rules of *dharma* that ideal kings were enjoined to uphold, and that many later Buddhists interpreted as also referring to Buddhist teachings or exhorting the Buddhist community to unity. At the top, carved from a separate block of sandstone, an elaborate capital bore animal sculpture. Both shaft and capital were given the characteristic Maurya polish. Scholars believe that the pillars symbolized the **axis mundi** ("axis of the world"), joining earth with the cosmos. It represented the vital link between the human and celestial realms, and through it the cosmic order was impressed onto the terrestrial.

LION CAPITAL FROM SARNATH.   The capital in **FIGURE 2–15** originally crowned the pillar erected at Sarnath in north central India, the site of the Buddha's first sermon. The lowest portion represents the down-turned petals of a lotus blossom. Because the lotus flower emerges from murky waters without any mud sticking to its petals, it symbolizes the presence of divine purity in the imperfect world. Above the lotus is an **abacus** (the slab forming the top of a capital) embellished with low-relief carvings

Hinduism

Hinduism is not one religion but many related beliefs and innumerable sects. It results from the mingling of Vedic beliefs with indigenous, local beliefs and practices. All three major Hindu sects draw upon the texts of the Vedas, which are believed to be sacred revelations set down about 1200–800 BCE. The gods lie outside the finite world, but they can appear in visible form to believers. Each Hindu sect takes its particular deity as supreme. By worshiping gods with rituals, meditation, and intense love, individuals may be reborn into increasingly higher positions until they escape the cycle of life, death, and rebirth, which is called *samsara*. The most popular deities are Vishnu, Shiva, and the Great Goddess, Devi. Deities are revealed and depicted in multiple aspects.

Vishnu: Vishnu is a benevolent god who works for the order and well-being of the world. He is often represented lying in a trance or asleep on the Cosmic Waters, where he dreams the world into existence. His symbols are the wheel and a conch shell, the mace and lotus. He usually has four arms and wears a crown and lavish jewelry. He rides a man-bird, Garuda. Vishnu appears in ten different incarnations, including Rama and Krishna, who have their own sects. Rama embodies virtue, and, assisted by the monkey king, he fights the demon Ravana. As Krishna, Vishnu is a supremely beautiful, blue-skinned youth who lives with the cowherds, loves the maiden Radha, and battles the demon Kansa.

Shiva: Shiva is both creative and destructive, light and dark, male and female. His symbol is the *linga*, an upright phallus, which is represented as a low pillar. As an expression of his power and creative energy, he is often represented as Lord of the Dance, dancing the Cosmic Dance, the endless cycle of death and rebirth,

destruction and creation. He dances within a ring of fire, his four hands holding fire, a drum, and gesturing to the worshipers. Shiva's animal vehicle is the bull. His consort is Parvati; their sons are the elephant-headed Ganesha, the overcomer of obstacles, and Karttikeya, often associated with war.

Devi: Devi, the Great Goddess, controls material riches and fertility. She has forms indicative of beauty, wealth, and auspiciousness, but also forms of wrath, pestilence, and power. As the embodiment of cosmic energy, she provides the vital force to all the male gods. Her symbol is an abstract depiction of female genitals, often associated with the *linga* of Shiva. When armed and riding a lion (as the goddess Durga), she personifies righteous fury. As the goddess Lakshmi, she is the goddess of wealth and beauty. She is often represented by the basic geometric forms: squares, circles, triangles.

Brahma: Brahma, who once had his own cult, embodies spiritual wisdom. His four heads symbolize the four cosmic cycles, four earthly directions, and four classes of society: priests (brahmins), warriors, merchants, and laborers.

There are countless other deities, but central to Hindu practice are *puja* (forms of worship) and *darshan* (beholding a deity), generally performed to obtain a deity's favor and in the hope that this favor will lead to liberation from *samsara*. Because desire for the fruits of our actions traps us, the ideal is to consider all earthly endeavors as sacrificial offerings to a god. Pleased with our devotion, he or she may grant us an eternal state of pure being, pure consciousness, and pure bliss.

---

of wheels, called in Sanskrit *chakra*s, alternating with four different animals: lion, horse, bull, and elephant. The animals may symbolize the four great rivers of the world, which are mentioned in Indian creation myths. Standing on this abacus are four back-to-back lions. Facing the four cardinal directions, the lions may be emblematic of the universal nature of Buddhism and the universal currency of Ashoka's law inscribed on the pillar. Their roar might be compared with the speech of the Buddha that spreads far and wide. The lions may also refer to the Buddha himself, who is known as "the lion of the Shakya clan" (the clan into which the Buddha was born as prince). The lions originally supported a great wheel, now lost. A universal Buddhist symbol, the wheel refers to Buddhist teaching, for with his sermon at Sarnath the Buddha "set the wheel of the law [*dharma*] in motion." The wheel is also a symbol of the *chakravartin*, the ideal universal monarch, and so refers to Ashoka as well as the Buddha.

Their formal, heraldic pose imbues the lions with something of the monumental quality evident in the statue of the *yakshi* of the same period. We also find the same strong patterning of realistic

elements: Veins and tendons stand out on the legs; the claws are large and powerful; the mane is richly textured; and the jaws have a loose and fluttering edge.

THE PERIOD OF THE SHUNGAS AND EARLY ANDHRAS

With the demise of the Maurya Empire, India returned to rule by regional dynasties. Between the second century BCE and the early first century CE, two of the most important of these dynasties were the Shunga dynasty (185–72 BCE) in central India and the Andhra dynasty (72 BCE–third century CE) who initially ruled in central India and after the first century in the south. During this period, some of the most magnificent early Buddhist structures were created.

STUPAS

Religious monuments called **stupas**, solid mounds enclosing a reliquary, are fundamental to Buddhism (see "Stupas and Temples," page 91). A stupa may be small and plain or large and elaborate. Its

To view this image, please go to page 299 of the *Art History*, Fourth Edition by Marilyn Stokstad ebook.

2–16 • GREAT STUPA, SANCHI
Madhya Pradesh, India. Founded 3rd century BCE, enlarged c. 150–50 BCE.

SEE MORE: View a video about the Great Stupa, Sanchi **www.myartslab.com**

form may vary from region to region, but its symbolic meaning remains virtually the same, and its plan is a carefully calculated **mandala**, or diagram of the cosmos as it is envisioned in Buddhism. Stupas are open to all for private worship.

The first stupas were constructed to house the Buddha's remains after his cremation. According to tradition, the relics were divided into eight portions and placed in eight **reliquaries**. Each reliquary was then encased in its own burial mound, called a stupa. Since the early stupas held actual remains of the Buddha, they were venerated as his body and, by extension, his enlightenment and attainment of *nirvana* (liberation from rebirth). The method of veneration was, and still is, to circumambulate, or walk around, the stupa in a clockwise direction. In the mid third century BCE, King Ashoka is said to have opened the original eight stupas and divided their relics among many more stupas, probably including the Great Stupa at Sanchi.

THE GREAT STUPA AT SANCHI. Probably no early Buddhist structure is more famous than the **GREAT STUPA** at Sanchi in central India **(FIG. 2–16)**. In its original form probably dating to

the time of Ashoka, the Great Stupa was part of a large monastery complex crowning a hill. During the mid second century BCE, it was enlarged to its present size, and the surrounding stone railing was constructed. About 100 years later, elaborately carved stone gateways were added to the railing.

The Great Stupa at Sanchi is a representative of the early central Indian type. Its solid, hemispherical dome was built up from rubble and dirt, faced with dressed stone, then covered with a shining white plaster made from lime and powdered seashells. The dome—echoing the arc of the sky—sits on a raised base. Around the perimeter is a walkway enclosed by a railing; an elevated walkway is approached by a staircase on the south side. As is often true in religious architecture, the railing provides a physical and symbolic boundary between an inner, sacred area and the outer, profane world. On top of the dome, another stone railing, square in shape, defines the abode of the gods atop the cosmic mountain. It encloses the top of a mast bearing three stone disks, or "umbrellas," of decreasing size. These disks have been interpreted in various ways. They may correspond to the "Three Jewels of Buddhism"—the Buddha, the Law, and the Monastic

inscription, also on the south gateway, specifies a gift during the reign of King Satakarni of the Andhra dynasty, providing the first-century BCE date for the gateways. The only elements of the Great Stupa at Sanchi to be ornamented with sculpture, the gateways rise to a height of 35 feet. Their square posts and horizontal members are carved with symbols and scenes drawn mostly from the Buddha's life and the **jataka tales**, stories of the Buddha's past lives. A relief from the east gateway is illustrated in **FIGURE 2–17**. Typical of Indian narrative relief of the second and first centuries BCE, the scenes are organized not in a time sequence, but according to where they take place. Thus, at the top of this relief is a scene of Queen Maya's dream anticipating the birth of the Buddha, while below is a scene showing the Buddha's father in a chariot, riding out to greet his return, and at the bottom the Buddha, symbolized by a plank, levitates above the crowd gathered to witness the gift of a garden for the Buddha and his followers. All three of these scenes take place at Kapilavastu, the city of his birth.

To view this image, please go to page 300 of the *Art History*, Fourth Edition by Marilyn Stokstad ebook.

2-17 • RELIEF FROM EAST GATEWAY OF THE GREAT STUPA, SANCHI
Early Andhra period, mid 1st century BCE. Stone.

This relief illustrates the birth of the Buddha at the top and the return of the Buddha to the city of his birth in the panels below.

Order—and they may also refer to the Buddhist concept of the three realms of existence: desire, form, and formlessness. The mast itself symbolizes an *axis mundi*, connecting the Cosmic Waters below the earth with the celestial realm above it and anchoring everything in its proper place.

A 10-foot-tall stone railing demarcates a circumambulatory path at ground level. Carved with octagonal uprights and lens-shaped crossbars, it probably simulates the wooden railings of the time. This design pervaded early Indian art, appearing in relief sculpture and as architectural ornament. Four stone gateways, or **toranas**, punctuate the railing. Aligned with the four cardinal directions, the gateways symbolize the Buddhist cosmos. An inscription on the south gateway indicates that it was provided by ivory carvers from the nearby town of Vidisha, while another

To view this image, please go to page 300 of the *Art History*, Fourth Edition by Marilyn Stokstad ebook.

2-18 • *YAKSHI* BRACKET FIGURE
East *torana* of the Great Stupa at Sanchi. Stone, height approx. 60″ (152.4 cm).

Buddhist architecture in South Asia consists mainly of stupas and temples, often at monastic complexes containing **viharas** (monks' cells and common areas). These monuments may be either structural—built up from the ground—or rock-cut—hewn out of a mountainside. Stupas derive from burial mounds and contain relics beneath a solid, dome-shaped core. A major stupa is surrounded by a railing that creates a sacred path for ritual circumambulation at ground level. This railing is punctuated by gateways, called **toranas** in Sanskrit, aligned with the cardinal points. The stupa sits on a round or square terrace; stairs lead to an upper circumambulatory path around the platform's edge. On top of the stupa's dome a railing defines a square, from the center of which rises a mast supporting tiers of disk-shaped "umbrellas."

Hindu architecture in South Asia consists mainly of temples, either structural or rock-cut, executed in a number of styles and dedicated to diverse deities. The two general Hindu temple types are the northern and southern styles prevalent in northern India and southern India respectively. Within these broad categories is great stylistic diversity, though all are raised on plinths and dominated by their superstructures. In north India, the term **shikhara** is used to refer to the entire superstructure, while in the south it refers only to the finial, that is, the uppermost member of the superstructure. North Indian *shikhara*s are crowned by **amalakas**. Inside, a series of **mandapas** (halls) leads to an inner sanctuary, the **garbhagriha**, which contains a sacred image. An *axis mundi* is imagined to run vertically up from the Cosmic Waters below the earth, through the *garbhagriha*'s image, and out through the top of the tower.

Jain architecture consists mainly of structural and rock-cut monasteries and temples that have much in common with their Buddhist and Hindu counterparts. Buddhist, Hindu, and Jain temples may share a site, as may the structures of still other religions.

To view this image, please go to page 301 of the *Art History*, Fourth Edition by Marilyn Stokstad ebook.

SEE MORE: View a simulation of stupas and temples **www.myartslab.com**

The capitals above the posts consist of four back-to-back elephants on the north and east gates, dwarfs on the west gate, and lions on the south gate. The capitals in turn support a three-tiered superstructure in which posts and crossbars are elaborately carved with still more symbols and scenes, and studded with free-standing sculptures depicting such subjects as *yakshi*s and *yaksha*s, riders on real and mythical animals, and the Buddhist wheel. As in other early Buddhist art before the late first century BCE, the Buddha himself is not shown in human form. Instead, he is represented by symbols such as his footprints, an empty "enlightenment" seat, or a plank.

Forming a bracket between each capital and the lowest cross-bar is a sculpture of a *yakshi* (**FIG. 2–18**). These *yakshi*s are some of the finest female figures in Indian art, and they make an instructive comparison with the *yakshi* of the Maurya period (SEE FIG. 2–14).

The earlier figure was distinguished by a formal, somewhat rigid pose, an emphasis on realistic details, and a clear distinction between clothed and nude parts of the body. In contrast, the Sanchi *yakshi* leans daringly into space with casual abandon, supported by one leg as the other charmingly crosses behind. Her thin, diaphanous garment is noticeable only by its hems, and so she appears almost nude, which emphasizes her form. The band pulling gently at her abdomen accentuates the suppleness of her flesh. The swelling, arching curves of her body evoke this deity's procreative and bountiful essence. As the personification of the waters, she is the source of life. Here she symbolizes the sap of the tree, which flowers at her touch.

The profusion of designs, symbols, scenes, and figures carved on all sides of the gateways to the Great Stupa not only relates the history and lore of Buddhism, but also represents the teeming life of the world and the gods.

BUDDHIST ROCK-CUT HALLS

From ancient times, caves have been considered hallowed places in India, for they were frequently the abode of holy men and ascetics. Around the second century BCE, cavelike sanctuaries were hewn out of the stone plateaus in the region of south central India known as the Deccan. Made for the use of Buddhist monks, the sanctuaries were carved from top to bottom like great pieces of sculpture, with all details completely finished in stone. To enter one of these remarkable halls is to feel transported to an otherworldly, sacred space. The atmosphere created by the dark recess and the echo that magnifies the smallest sound combine to promote a state of heightened awareness.

THE CHAITYA HALL AT KARLE.   The monastic community made two types of rock-cut halls. One was the **vihara**, used for the monks' living quarters, and the other was the **chaitya** ("sanctuary"), which usually enshrined a stupa. A *chaitya* hall at Karle, dating from the first century BCE to the first century CE, is one of the largest and most fully developed examples of these early Buddhist works (**FIG. 2–19**). At the entrance, columns once supported a balcony, in front of which a pair of Ashokan-type

To view this image, please go to page 302 of the *Art History*, Fourth Edition by Marilyn Stokstad ebook.

2-19 • *CHAITYA* HALL, KARLE
Maharashtra, India. 1st century BCE–1st century CE.

pillars stood. The walls of the vestibule are carved in relief with rows of small balcony railings and arched windows, simulating the façade of a great multi-storied palace. At the base of the side walls, enormous statues of elephants seem to be supporting the entire structure on their backs. Dominating the upper portion of the main façade is a large horseshoe-shaped opening, which provides the hall's main source of light. The window was originally fitted with a carved wood screen, some of which remains, that filtered the light streaming inside.

Three entrances pierce the main façade. Flanking the entrances are sculpted panels of **mithuna** couples, amorous male and female figures that evoke the harmony and fertility of life and suggest the devotion with which the worshiper should confront the Buddha represented by the stupa inside. The interior hall, 123 feet long, has a 46-foot-high ceiling carved in the form of a barrel vault ornamented with arching wooden ribs. Both the interior and exterior of the hall were once brightly painted. Pillars demarcate a pathway for circumambulation around the stupa in the apse at the far end.

The side aisles are separated from the main aisle by closely spaced columns whose bases resemble a large pot set on a stepped pyramid of planks. From this potlike form rises a massive octagonal shaft. Crowning the shaft, a bell-shaped lotus capital supports an inverted pyramid of planks, which serves in turn as a platform for sculpture. The statues depict pairs of kneeling elephants, each bearing a *mithuna* couple. These figures, the only sculpture within this austere hall, may represent the nobility coming to pay homage at the temple. The pillars around the apse are plain, and the stupa is simple. A railing motif ornaments the base; the dome was once topped with wooden "umbrella" disks, only one of which remains. As with nearly everything in the cave, the stupa is carved from the cliff's rock. Like the stupa at Sanchi, the sculptural decoration is restricted to the entranceway. This stupa, however, could not contain the Buddha's relics because it is solid rock; likely it was worshiped as if it did.

THE KUSHAN AND LATER ANDHRA PERIODS

Around the first century CE, the regions of present-day Afghanistan, Pakistan, and north India came under the control of the Kushans, originally a nomadic people forced out of northwest China by the Han. Exact dates are uncertain, but they ruled from the first to the third century CE. The beginning of the long reign of their most illustrious king, Kanishka, is variously dated from 78 to 143 CE.

Buddhism during this period underwent a profound evolution that resulted in the form known as Mahayana, or Great Vehicle (see "Buddhism," page 87). This vital new movement, which was to sweep most of northern India and eastern Asia, probably inspired the first depictions of the Buddha himself in art. (Previously, as in the Great Stupa at Sanchi, the Buddha had been indicated solely by symbols.) Distinctive styles arose in the Gandhara region in the northwest (present-day Pakistan and Afghanistan) and in the famous religious center of Mathura in central India. Both of these areas were ruled by the Kushans. About the same time, a third style evolved in southeast India under the Andhra dynasty, whose rule continued in this region through the third century CE.

To view this image, please go to page 303 of the *Art History*, Fourth Edition by Marilyn Stokstad ebook.

2-20 • STANDING BUDDHA
From Gandhara, Pakistan. Kushan period, c. 2nd–3rd century CE. Schist, height 7′6″ (2.28 m). Lahore Museum, Lahore.

While all three styles are quite distinct, they shared a basic visual language, or iconography, in which the Buddha is readily recognized by certain characteristics. He wears a monk's robe, a long length of cloth draped over the left shoulder and around the body. The Buddha is said to have had 32 major distinguishing marks, called **lakshanas**, some of which are reflected in the iconography (see "Buddhist Symbols," page 112). These include a golden-colored body, long arms that reached to his knees, the impression of a wheel (*chakra*) on the palms of his hands and the soles of his feet, and the **urna**—a tuft of white hair between his eyebrows. Because he had been a prince in his youth and had worn the customary heavy earrings, his earlobes are usually shown elongated. The top of his head is said to have had a protuberance called an **ushnisha**, which in images often resembles a bun or top-knot and symbolizes his enlightenment.

THE GANDHARA STYLE

Gandhara art combines elements of Hellenistic, Persian, and Indian styles. A typical image from Gandhara portrays the Buddha as a superhuman figure, more powerful and heroic than an ordinary human (**FIG. 2–20**). Although it is difficult to determine the dates of Gandhara images, this over-life-size Buddha may date to the fully developed stage of the Gandhara style, possibly around the third century CE. It is carved from schist, a fine-grained dark stone. The Buddha's body, revealed through the folds of the garment, is broad and massive, with heavy shoulders and limbs and a well-defined torso. His left knee bends gently, suggesting a slightly relaxed posture.

The treatment of the robe is especially characteristic of the Gandhara manner. Tight, riblike folds alternate with delicate creases, setting up a clear, rhythmic pattern of heavy and shallow lines. On the upper part of the figure, the folds break asymmetrically along the left arm; on the lower part, they drape in a symmetric U shape. The strong tension of the folds suggests life and power within the image. This complex fold pattern resembles the treatment of togas on certain Roman statues, and it exerted a strong influence on portrayals of the Buddha in central and east Asia. The Gandhara region's relations with the Hellenistic world may have led to this strongly Western style in its art. Pockets of Hellenistic culture had thrived in neighboring Bactria (present-day northern Afghanistan and southern Uzbekistan) since the fourth century BCE, when the Greeks under Alexander the Great reached the borders of India. Also, Gandhara's position near the east–west trade routes appears to have stimulated contact with Roman culture in the Near East during the early centuries of the first millennium CE.

THE MATHURA STYLE

The second major style of Buddhist art in the Kushan period—that found at Mathura—was not allied with the Hellenistic-Roman tradition. Instead, the Mathura style evolved from representations of *yaksha*s, the indigenous male nature deities. Images produced at

Mudras

Mudras (the Sanskrit word for "signs") are ancient symbolic hand gestures that are regarded as physical expressions of different states of being. In Buddhist art, they function iconographically. *Mudras* are also used during meditation to release these energies. The following are the most common *mudras* in Asian art.

Dharmachakra Mudra

The gesture of teaching, setting the *chakra* (wheel) of the *dharma* (law or doctrine) in motion. Hands are at chest level.

Dhyana Mudra

A gesture of meditation and balance, symbolizing the path toward enlightenment. Hands are in the lap, the lower representing *maya*, the physical world of illusion, the upper representing *nirvana*, enlightenment and release from the world.

Vitarka Mudra

This variant of *dharmachakra mudra* stands for intellectual debate. The right and/or left hand is held at shoulder level with thumb and forefinger touching.

Abhaya Mudra

The gesture of reassurance, blessing, and protection, this *mudra* means "have no fear." The right hand is at shoulder level, palm outward.

Bhumisparsha Mudra

This gesture calls upon the earth to witness Shakyamuni Buddha's enlightenment at Bodh Gaya. A seated figure's right hand reaches toward the ground, palm inward.

Varada Mudra

The gesture of charity, symbolizing the fulfillment of all wishes. Alone, this *mudra* is made with the right hand; but when combined with *abhaya mudra* in standing Buddha figures (as is most common), the left hand is shown in *varada mudra*.

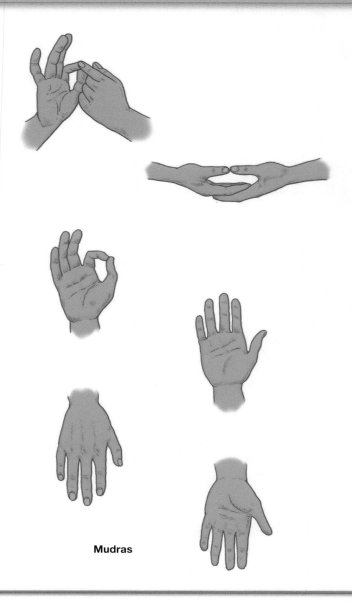

Mudras

Mathura during the early days of the Kushan period may be the first representations of the Buddha to appear in art.

The stele in **FIGURE 2–21** is one of the finest of the early Mathura images. The sculptors worked in a distinctive red sandstone flecked with cream-colored spots. Carved in **high relief** (forms projecting strongly from the background), it depicts a seated Buddha with two attendants. The Buddha sits in a yogic posture on a pedestal supported by lions. His right hand is raised in a symbolic gesture meaning "have no fear." Images of the Buddha rely on a repertoire of such gestures, called **mudras**, to communicate certain ideas, such as teaching, meditation, or the attaining of enlightenment (see "Mudras," above). The Buddha's *urna*, his *ushnisha*, and the impressions of wheels on his palms and soles are

all clearly visible in this figure. Behind his head is a large, circular halo; the scallop points of its border represent radiating light. Behind the halo are branches of the pipal tree, the tree under which the Buddha was seated when he achieved enlightenment. Two celestial beings hover above.

As in Gandhara sculptures, the Mathura work gives a powerful impression of the Buddha. Yet this Buddha's riveting outward gaze and alert posture impart a more intense, concentrated energy. The robe is pulled tightly over the body, allowing the fleshy form to be seen as almost nude. Where the pleats of the robe appear, such as over the left arm and fanning out between the legs, they are depicted abstractly through compact parallel formations of ridges with an incised line in the center of each ridge. This characteristic

Mathura tendency to abstraction also appears in the face, whose features take on geometric shapes, as in the rounded forms of the widely opened eyes. Nevertheless, the torso with its subtle and soft modeling is strongly naturalistic.

THE SOUTHEAST INDIAN STYLE

Events from the Buddha's life were popular subjects in the reliefs decorating stupas and Buddhist temples. One example from Nagarjunakonda depicts a scene when he was Prince Siddhartha, before his renunciation of his princely status and his subsequent quest for enlightenment (**FIG. 2–22**). Carved in low relief, the panel reveals a scene of pleasure around a pool of water. Gathered around Siddhartha, the largest figure and the only male, are some of the palace women. One holds his foot, entreating him to come into the water; another sits with legs drawn up on the nearby rock; others lean over his shoulder or fix their hair; one comes into the scene with a box of jewels on her head. The panel is framed by decorated columns, crouching lions, and amorous *mithuna* couples. (One of these couples is visible at the right of the illustration.) The scene is skillfully orchestrated to revolve around the prince as the main focus of all eyes. Typical of the southeast Indian style, the figures are slighter than those of Gandhara and Mathura. They are sinuous and mobile, even while at rest. The rhythmic nuances of the limbs and varied postures not only create interest in the activity of each individual but also engender a light and joyous effect.

During the first to third century CE, each of the three major styles of Buddhist art developed its own distinct idiom for expressing the complex imagery of Buddhism and depicting the image of the Buddha. The production of art in Gandhara and the region around Nagarjunakonda declined over the ensuing centuries. However, the artists of central India continued to work productively, and from them came the next major development in Indian Buddhist art.

To view this image, please go to page 305 of the *Art History*, Fourth Edition by Marilyn Stokstad ebook.

2-21 • BUDDHA AND ATTENDANTS
From Katra Keshavdev, Mathura, Madhya Pradesh, India. Kushan period, c. late 1st–early 2nd century CE. Red sandstone, height 27¼″ (69.2 cm). Government Museum, Mathura.

To view this image, please go to page 305 of the *Art History*, Fourth Edition by Marilyn Stokstad ebook.

2-22 • SIDDHARTHA IN THE PALACE
Detail of a relief from Nagarjunakonda, Andhra Pradesh, India. Later Andhra period, c. 3rd century CE. Limestone. National Museum, New Delhi.

EXPLORE MORE: Gain insight from a primary source about the life of the Buddha
www.myartslab.com

THE MIDDLE KINGDOM

Among the cultures of the world, China is distinguished by its long, uninterrupted development, now traced back some 8,000 years. From Qin, pronounced "chin," comes our name for the country that the Chinese call the Middle Kingdom, the country in the center of the world. Present-day China occupies a large landmass in the center of Asia, covering an area slightly larger than the continental United States. Within its borders lives one-fifth of the human race.

The historical and cultural heart of China is the land watered by its three great rivers, the Yellow, the Yangzi, and the Xi (MAP 2–3). The Qinling Mountains divide Inner China into north and south, regions with strikingly different climates, cultures, and historical fates. In the south, the Yangzi River flows through lush green hills to the fertile plains of the delta. Along the southern coastline, rich with natural harbors, arose China's port cities, the focus of a vast maritime trading network. The Yellow River, nicknamed "China's Sorrow" because of its disastrous floods, winds through the north. The north country is a dry land of steppe and desert, hot in the summer and lashed by cold winds in the winter. Over its vast and vulnerable frontier have come the nomadic invaders that are a recurring theme in Chinese history, but caravans and emissaries from Central Asia, India, Persia, and, eventually, Europe also crossed this border.

NEOLITHIC CULTURES

Early archaeological evidence had led scholars to believe that agriculture, the cornerstone technology of the Neolithic period, made its way to China from the ancient Near East. More recent findings, however, suggest that agriculture based on rice and millet arose independently in east Asia before 5000 BCE and that knowledge of Near Eastern grains followed some 2,000 years later. One of the clearest archaeological signs of Neolithic culture in China is evidence of the vigorous emergence of towns and cities. At Jiangzhai, near modern Xi'an, for example, the foundations of more than 100 dwellings have been discovered surrounding the remains of a community center, a cemetery, and a kiln. Dated to about 4000 BCE, the ruins point to the existence of a highly developed early society. Elsewhere in China, the foundations of the earliest known palace have been uncovered and dated to about 2000 BCE.

PAINTED POTTERY CULTURES

In China, as in other places, distinctive forms of Neolithic pottery identify different cultures. One of the most interesting objects thus far recovered is a shallow red bowl with a turned-out rim (FIG. 2–23). Found in the village of Banpo near the Yellow River, it was crafted sometime between 5000 and 4000 BCE. The bowl is an artifact of the Yangshao culture, one of the most important of the so-called Painted Pottery cultures of Neolithic China. Although the potter's wheel had not yet been developed, the bowl is perfectly round and its surfaces are highly polished, bearing witness

To view this image, please go to page 326 of the *Art History*, Fourth Edition by Marilyn Stokstad ebook.

2-23 • BOWL
From Banpo, near Xi'an, Shaanxi. Neolithic period, Yangshao culture, 5000–4000 BCE. Painted pottery, height 7″ (17.8 cm). Banpo Museum.

to a distinctly advanced technology. The decorations are especially intriguing. The marks on the rim may be evidence of the beginnings of writing in China, which was fully developed by the time the first definitive examples appear during the second millennium BCE, in the later Bronze Age.

Inside the bowl, a pair of stylized fish suggests that fishing was an important activity for the villagers. The image between the two fish represents a human face with four more fish, one on each side. Although there is no certain interpretation of the image, it may be a depiction of an ancestral figure who could assure an abundant catch, for the worship of ancestors and nature spirits was a fundamental element of later Chinese beliefs.

LIANGZHU CULTURE

Banpo lies near the great bend in the Yellow River, in the area traditionally regarded as the cradle of Chinese civilization, but archaeological finds have revealed that Neolithic cultures arose over a far broader area. Recent excavations in sites more than 800 miles away, near Hangzhou Bay, in the southeastern coastal region, have turned up human and animal images—often masks or faces—more than 5,000 years old (FIG. 2–24). Large, round eyes, a flat nose, and a rectangular mouth protrude slightly from the background pattern of wirelike lines. Above the forehead, a second, smaller face grimaces from under a huge headdress. The upper face may be human, perhaps riding the animal figure below. The image is one of eight that were carved in low relief on the outside of a large jade **cong**, an object resembling a cylindrical tube encased in

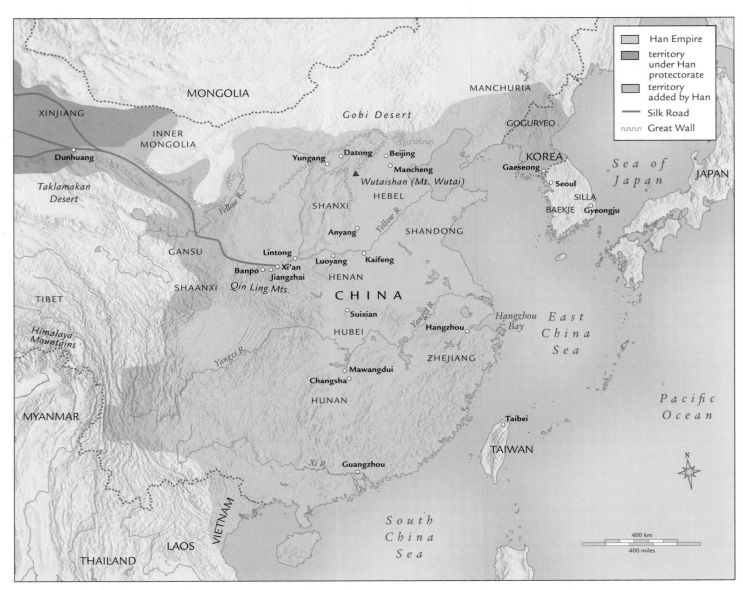

MAP 2-3 • CHINA AND KOREA

The map shows the borders of contemporary China and Korea. Bright-colored areas indicate the extent of China's Han dynasty (206 BCE–221 CE).

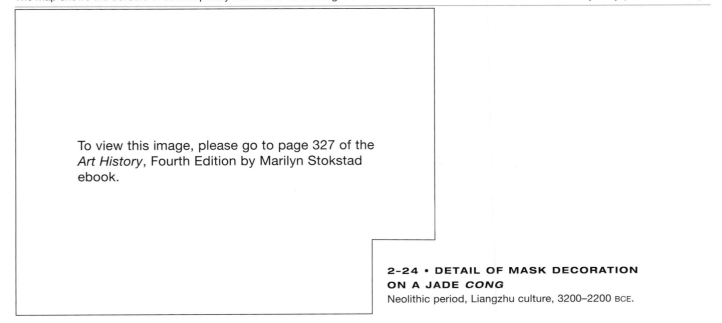

To view this image, please go to page 327 of the *Art History*, Fourth Edition by Marilyn Stokstad ebook.

2-24 • DETAIL OF MASK DECORATION ON A JADE *CONG*

Neolithic period, Liangzhu culture, 3200–2200 BCE.

To view this image, please go to page 328 of the *Art History*, Fourth Edition by Marilyn Stokstad ebook.

2-25 • CONG
Neolithic period, Liangzhu culture, 3200–2200 BCE. Jade, height 1⅞ × width 2⅝" (5 × 6.6 cm). Shanghai Museum.

The *cong* is one of the most prevalent and mysterious of early Chinese jade shapes. Originating in the Neolithic period, it continued to play a prominent role in burials through the Shang and Zhou dynasties. Many experts believe the *cong* was connected with the practice of contacting the spirit world. They suggest that the circle symbolized heaven; the square, earth; and the hollow, the axis connecting these two realms.

a rectangular block. Another *cong* **(FIG. 2–25)** also from Liangzhu bears a beautiful finish and similar delineated mask motifs. These were found near the remains of persons buried with what appear to be sets of numerous jade objects.

The intricacy of the carving shows the technical sophistication of this jade-working culture, named the Liangzhu, which seems to have emerged around 3300 BCE. Jade, a stone cherished by the Chinese throughout their history, is extremely hard and is difficult to carve. Liangzhu artists must have used sand as an abrasive to slowly grind the stone down; modern artisans marvel at how they produced such fine work.

The meaning of the masklike image in FIGURE 2–24 is open to interpretation. Its combination of human and animal features seems to show how the ancient Chinese imagined supernatural beings, either deities or dead ancestors. Similar masks later formed the primary decorative motif of Bronze Age ritual objects. Still later, Chinese historians began referring to the ancient mask motif as **taotie**, but the motif's original meaning had already been lost. The jade carving here seems to be a forerunner of this most central and mysterious image.

BRONZE AGE CHINA

China entered its Bronze Age in the second millennium BCE. As with agriculture, scholars at first theorized that the technology had been imported from the Near East. Archaeological evidence now makes clear, however, that bronze casting using the **piece-mold casting** technique arose independently in China, where it attained an unparalleled level of excellence (see "Piece-Mold Casting," opposite).

SHANG DYNASTY

Traditional Chinese histories tell of three Bronze Age dynasties: the Xia, the Shang, and the Zhou. Experts at one time tended to dismiss the Xia and Shang as legendary, but twentieth-century archaeological discoveries fully established the historical existence of the Shang (c. 1700–1100 BCE) and point strongly to the historical existence of the Xia as well.

Shang kings ruled from a succession of capitals in the Yellow River Valley, where archaeologists have found walled cities, palaces, and vast royal tombs. Their state was surrounded by numerous other states—some rivals, others clients—and their culture spread widely. Society seems to have been highly stratified, with a ruling group that had the bronze technology needed to make weapons. They maintained their authority in part by claiming power as intermediaries between the supernatural and human realms. The chief Shang deity, Shangdi, may have been a sort of "Great Ancestor." It is thought that nature and fertility spirits were also honored, and that regular sacrifices were thought necessary to keep the spirits of dead ancestors vital so that they might help the living.

Shang priests communicated with the supernatural world through oracle bones. An animal bone or piece of tortoiseshell was inscribed with a question and heated until it cracked, then the crack was interpreted as an answer. Oracle bones, many of which have been recovered and deciphered, contain the earliest known form of Chinese writing, a script fully recognizable as the ancestor of the system still in use today (see "Chinese Characters," page 101).

RITUAL BRONZES.   Shang tombs reveal a warrior culture of great splendor and violence. Many humans and animals were sacrificed to accompany the deceased. In one tomb, for example, chariots were found with the skeletons of their horses and drivers; in another, dozens of human skeletons lined the approaches to the central burial chamber. The tombs contain hundreds of jade, ivory, and lacquer objects, gold and silver ornaments, and bronze vessels. The enormous scale of Shang burials illustrates the great wealth of the civilization and the power of a ruling class able to consign such great quantities of treasure to the earth, and also suggests this culture's reverence for the dead.

Bronze vessels are the most admired and studied of Shang artifacts. Like oracle bones and jade objects, they were connected with ritual practices, serving as containers for offerings of food and wine. A basic repertoire of about 30 shapes evolved. Some shapes derive from earlier pottery forms, while others seem to reproduce wooden containers. Still others are highly sculptural and take the form of fantastic composite animals.

One functional shape, the **fang ding**, a rectangular vessel with four legs, was used for food offerings. Early examples (see "Piece-Mold Casting," opposite) featured decoration of raised bosses and mask-like (*taotie*) motifs in horizontal registers on the sides and the legs. A late Shang example, one of hundreds of vessels recovered from the royal tombs near the last of the Shang capitals, Yin

The early piece-mold technique for bronze casting is different from the lost-wax process developed in the ancient Mediterranean and Near East. Although we do not know the exact steps ancient Chinese artists followed, we can deduce the general procedure for casting a vessel.

First, a model of the bronze-to-be was made of clay and dried. Then, to create a mold, damp clay was pressed onto the model; after the clay mold dried, it was cut away in pieces, which were keyed for later reassembly and then fired. The original model itself was shaved down to serve as the core for the mold. After this, the pieces of the mold were reassembled around the core and held in place by bronze spacers, which locked the core in position and ensured an even casting space around the core. The reassembled mold was then

covered with another layer of clay, and a sprue, or pouring duct, was cut into the clay to receive the molten metal. A riser duct may also have been cut to allow the hot gases to escape. Molten bronze was then poured into the mold. When the metal cooled, the mold was broken apart to reveal a bronze copy of the original clay model. Finely cast relief decoration could be worked into the model or carved into the sectional molds, or both. Finally, the vessel could be burnished—a long process that involved scouring the surface with increasingly fine abrasives.

The vessel shown here is a *fang ding*. A *ding* is a ceremonial cooking vessel used in Shang rituals and buried in Shang tombs. The Zhou people also made, used, and buried *ding* vessels.

To view this image, please go to page 329 of the *Art History*, Fourth Edition by Marilyn Stokstad ebook.

To view this image, please go to page 329 of the *Art History*, Fourth Edition by Marilyn Stokstad ebook.

Sectional clay molds for casting bronze vessels. This sketch is based on a vessel in the Zhengzhou Institute of Cultural Relics and Archaeology.

(present-day Anyang), is extraordinary for its size. Weighing nearly 2,000 pounds, it is the largest Shang *ding* vessel thus far recovered. In typical Shang style, its surface is decorated with a complex array of images based on animal forms, including *taotie* masks, confronting horned animals (dragons?) and composite beaked animals (birds?). A ritual pouring vessel, called a *guang* (FIG. 2–26), shows a highly sculptural rendition of animal forms. The pouring spout and cover are modeled as the head and body of a tiger, while the rear portion of the vessel and cover is conceived as an owl. Overall geometric decoration combines with suggestive zoomorphic forms. Such images seem to be related to the hunting life of the Shang, but their deeper significance is unknown. Sometimes strange, sometimes fearsome, Shang creatures seem always to have a sense of mystery, evoking the Shang attitude toward the supernatural world.

ZHOU DYNASTY

Around 1100 BCE, the Shang were conquered by the Zhou from western China. During the Zhou dynasty (1100–221 BCE) a feudal society developed, with nobles related to the king ruling over numerous small states. (Zhou nobility are customarily ranked in English by such titles as duke and marquis.) The supreme deity became known as Tian, or Heaven, and the king ruled as the Son of Heaven. Later Chinese ruling dynasties continued to follow the belief that imperial rule emanated from a mandate from Heaven.

The first 300 years of this longest-lasting Chinese dynasty were generally stable and peaceful. In 771 BCE, however, the Zhou suffered defeat in the west at the hands of a nomadic tribe. Although they quickly established a new capital to the east, their authority had been crippled, and the later Eastern Zhou period was a troubled one. States grew increasingly independent, giving

To view this image, please go to page 330 of the *Art History*, Fourth Edition by Marilyn Stokstad ebook.

2–26 • COVERED RITUAL WINE-POURING VESSEL (*GUANG*) WITH TIGER AND OWL DÉCOR

Shang dynasty, 13th century BCE. Cast bronze, height with cover 9¾″ (25 cm), width including handle 12⅜″ (31.5 cm). Arthur M. Sackler Museum, Harvard Art Museum, Cambridge, Massachusetts.
Bequest of Grenville L. Winthrop 1943.52.103

the Zhou kings merely nominal allegiance. Smaller states were swallowed up by their larger neighbors. During the time historians call the Spring and Autumn period (722–481 BCE), 10 or 12 states, later reduced to seven, emerged as powers. During the ensuing Warring States period (481–221 BCE) intrigue, treachery, and increasingly ruthless warfare became routine.

Against this background of social turmoil, China's great philosophers arose—such thinkers as Confucius, Laozi, and Mozi. Traditional histories speak of China's "one hundred schools" of philosophy, indicating a shift of focus from the supernatural to the human world. Nevertheless, elaborate burials on an even larger scale than before reflected the continuation of traditional beliefs.

BRONZE BELLS. Ritual bronze objects continued to play an important role during the Zhou dynasty, and new forms developed. One of the most spectacular recent discoveries is a carillon of 65 bronze components, mostly bells arranged in a formation 25 feet long (FIG. 2–27), found in the tomb of Marquis Yi of the state of Zeng. Each bell is precisely calibrated to sound two tones—one when struck at the center, another when struck at a corner. The bells are arranged in scale patterns in a variety of registers, and several musicians would have moved around the carillon, striking the bells in the appointed order.

Music may well have played a part in rituals for communicating with the supernatural, for the *taotie* typically appears on the front and back of each bell. The image is now much more intricate and stylized, partly in response to the refinement available with the lost-wax casting process, which had replaced the older piece-mold technique. On the coffin of the marquis are painted guardian warriors with half-human, half-animal attributes. The marquis, who died in 433 BCE, must have considered music important, for among the more than 15,000 objects recovered from his tomb were many musical instruments. Zeng was one of the smallest and shortest-lived states of the Eastern Zhou, but the contents of this tomb, in quantity and quality, attest to the high level of its culture.

Chinese Characters

Each word in Chinese is represented by its own unique symbol, called a character. Some characters originated as **pictographs**, images that mean what they depict. Writing reforms over the centuries have often disguised the resemblance, but if we place modern characters next to their ancestors, the picture comes back into focus:

	water	horse	moon	child	tree	mountain
Ancient	〣	馬	𦥑	𭕄	朮	屾
Modern	水	馬	月	千	木	山

Other characters are **ideographs**, pictures that represent abstract concepts or ideas:

sun	+	moon	=	bright
日		月		明

woman	+	child	=	good
女		千		好

Most characters were formed by combining a radical, which gives the field of meaning, with a phonetic, which originally hinted at pronunciation. For example, words that have to do with water have the character for "water" 水 abbreviated to three strokes 氵 as their radical. Thus "to bathe," 沐 pronounced *mu*, consists of the water radical and the phonetic 木, which by itself means "tree" and is also pronounced *mu*. Here are other "water" characters. Notice that the connection to water is not always literal.

river	sea	weep	pure, clear	extinguish, destroy
河	海	泣	清	滅

These phonetic borrowings took place centuries ago. Many words have shifted in pronunciation, and for this and other reasons there is no way to tell how a character is pronounced or what it means just by looking at it. While at first this may seem like a disadvantage, in the case of Chinese it is advantageous. Spoken Chinese has many dialects. Some are so far apart in sound as to be virtually different languages. But while speakers of different dialects cannot understand each other, they can still communicate through writing, for no matter how they say a word, they write it with the same character. Writing has thus played an important role in maintaining the unity of Chinese civilization through the centuries.

To view this image, please go to page 331 of the *Art History*, Fourth Edition by Marilyn Stokstad ebook.

2-27 • SET OF BELLS
From the tomb of Marquis Yi of Zeng, Suixian, Hubei. Zhou dynasty, 433 BCE. Bronze, with bronze and timber frame, frame height 9′ (2.74 m), length 25′ (7.62 m). Hubei Provincial Museum, Wuhan.

THE CHINESE EMPIRE: QIN DYNASTY

Toward the middle of the third century BCE, the state of Qin launched military campaigns that led to its triumph over the other states by 221 BCE. For the first time in its history, China was united under a single ruler. This first emperor of Qin, Shihuangdi, a man of exceptional ability, power, and ruthlessness, was fearful of both assassination and rebellion. Throughout his life, he sought ways to attain immortality. Even before uniting China, he began his own mausoleum at Lintong, in Shaanxi Province. This project continued throughout his life and after his death, until rebellion abruptly ended the dynasty in 206 BCE. Since that time, the mound over the mausoleum has always been visible, but not until an accidental discovery in 1974 was its army of terra-cotta soldiers and horses even imagined. Modeled from clay and then fired, the figures claim a prominent place in the great tradition of Chinese ceramic art. Individualized faces and meticulously rendered uniforms and armor demonstrate the sculptors' skill. Literary sources suggest that the tomb itself, which has not yet been opened, reproduces the world as it was known to the Qin, with stars overhead and rivers and mountains below. Thus did the tomb's architects try literally to ensure that the underworld—the world of souls and spirits—would match the human world.

Qin rule was harsh and repressive. Laws were based on a totalitarian philosophy called legalism, and all other philosophies were banned, their scholars executed, and their books burned. Yet the Qin also established the mechanisms of centralized bureaucracy that molded China both politically and culturally into a single entity. Under the Qin, the country was divided into provinces and prefectures, the writing system and coinage were standardized, roads were built to link different parts of the country with the capital, and battlements on the northern frontier were connected to form the Great Wall. To the present day, China's rulers have followed the administrative framework first laid down by the Qin.

HAN DYNASTY

The commander who overthrew the Qin became the next emperor and founded the Han dynasty (206 BCE–220 CE). During this period the Chinese enjoyed peace, prosperity, and stability. Borders were extended and secured, and Chinese control over strategic stretches of Central Asia led to the opening of the Silk Road, a land route that linked China by trade all the way to Rome. One of the precious goods traded, along with spices, was silk, which had been cultivated and woven in China since at least the third millennium BCE. From as early as the third century BCE, Chinese silk cloth was treasured in Greece and Rome.

PAINTED BANNER FROM CHANGSHA.   The early Han dynasty marks the twilight of China's so-called mythocentric age, when people believed in a close relationship between the human and supernatural

To view this image, please go to page 332 of the *Art History*, Fourth Edition by Marilyn Stokstad ebook.

2-28 • PAINTED BANNER
From the tomb of the Marquess of Dai, Mawangdui, Changsha, Hunan. Han dynasty, c. 160 BCE. Colors on silk, height 6'8½" (2.05 m). Hunan Provincial Museum.

worlds. The most elaborate and most intact painting that survives from this time is a T-shaped silk banner, which summarizes this early worldview (FIG. 2–28). Found in the tomb of a noblewoman on the outskirts of present-day Changsha, the banner dates from the second century BCE and is painted with scenes representing three levels of the universe: heaven, earth, and underworld. The pictorial motifs include a portrait of the deceased.

The heavenly realm is shown at the top, in the crossbar of the T. In the upper-right corner is the sun, inhabited by a mythical crow; in the upper left, a mythical toad stands on a crescent moon. Between them is a primordial deity shown as a man with a long serpent's tail—a Han image of the Great Ancestor. Dragons and other celestial creatures swarm below.

A gate guarded by two seated figures stands where the horizontal of heaven meets the banner's long, vertical stem. Two intertwined dragons loop through a circular jade piece known as a **bi**, itself usually a symbol of heaven, dividing this vertical segment into two areas. The portion above the *bi* represents the earthly realm. Here, the deceased woman and three attendants stand on a platform while two kneeling figures offer gifts. The portion beneath the *bi* represents the underworld. Silk draperies and a stone chime hanging from the *bi* form a canopy for the platform below. Like the bronze bells we saw earlier, stone chimes were ceremonial instruments dating from Zhou times. On the platform, ritual bronze vessels contain food and wine for the deceased, just as they did in Shang tombs. The squat, muscular man holding up the platform stands in turn on a pair of fish whose bodies form another *bi*. The fish and the other strange creatures in this section are inhabitants of the underworld.

PHILOSOPHY AND ART

The Han dynasty marked the beginning of a new age. During this dynasty, the philosophical ideals of Daoism and Confucianism, formulated during the troubled times of the Eastern Zhou, became central to Chinese thought. Their influence since then has been continuous and fundamental.

DAOISM AND NATURE. Daoism emphasizes the close relationship between humans and nature. It is concerned with bringing the individual life into harmony with the Dao, or the Way, of the universe (see "Daoism," page 104). For some a secular, philosophical path, Daoism on a popular level developed into an organized religion, absorbing many traditional folk practices and the search for immortality.

Immortality was as intriguing to Han rulers as it had been to the first emperor of Qin. Daoist adepts experimented with diet, physical exercise, and other techniques in the belief that immortal life could be achieved on earth. Popular Daoist legend told of the Land of Immortals in the Eastern Sea, depicted on a bronze **INCENSE BURNER** from the tomb of Prince Liu Sheng, who died in 113 BCE **(FIG. 2–29)**. Around the bowl, gold inlay outlines the stylized waves of the sea. Above them rises the mountainous island, busy with birds, animals, and the immortals themselves, all cast in bronze with highlights of inlaid gold. Technically, this exquisite piece represents the ultimate development of the long tradition of bronze casting in China.

To view this image, please go to page 333 of the *Art History*, Fourth Edition by Marilyn Stokstad ebook.

2-29 • INCENSE BURNER
From the tomb of Prince Liu Sheng, Mancheng, Hebei. Han dynasty, 113 BCE. Bronze with gold inlay, height 10½″ (26 cm). Hebei Provincial Museum, Shijiazhuang.

CONFUCIANISM AND THE STATE. In contrast to the metaphysical focus of Daoism, Confucianism is concerned with the human world, and its goal is the attainment of equity. To this end, it proposes a system of ethics based on reverence for ancestors and the correct relationships among people. Beginning with self-discipline in the individual, Confucianism teaches how to rectify relationships within the family, and then, in ever-widening circles, with friends and others, all the way up to the level of the emperor and the state.

Emphasis on social order and respect for authority made Confucianism especially attractive to Han rulers, who were eager to distance themselves from the disastrous legalism of the Qin. The Han emperor Wudi (r. 141–87 BCE) made Confucianism the official imperial philosophy, and it remained the state ideology of China for more than 2,000 years, until the end of imperial rule in the twentieth century. Once institutionalized, Confucianism took on so many rituals that it too eventually assumed the form and force of a religion. Han philosophers contributed to this process by

Daoism

Daoism is an outlook on life that brings together many ancient ideas regarding humankind and the universe. Its primary text, a slim volume called the *Daodejing* (*The Way and Its Power*), is ascribed to the Chinese philosopher Laozi, who is said to have been a contemporary of Confucius (551–479 BCE). Later, a philosopher named Zhuangzi (369–286 BCE) took up many of the same ideas in a book that is known simply by his name: *Zhuangzi*. Together the two texts formed a body of ideas that crystallized into a school of thought during the Han period.

A *dao* is a way or path. The Dao is the Ultimate Way, the Way of the universe. The Way cannot be named or described, but it can be hinted at. It is like water. Nothing is more flexible and yielding, yet water can wear down the hardest stone. Water flows downward, seeking the lowest ground. Similarly, a Daoist sage seeks a quiet life, humble and hidden, unconcerned with worldly success. The Way is great precisely because it is small. The Way may be nothing, yet nothing turns out to be essential.

To recover the Way, we must unlearn. We must return to a state of nature. To follow the Way, we must practice *wu wei* (nondoing). "Strive for nonstriving," advises the *Daodejing*.

All our attempts at asserting ourselves, at making things happen, are like swimming against a current and are thus ultimately futile, even harmful. If we let the current carry us, however, we will travel far. Similarly, a life that follows the Way will be a life of pure effectiveness, accomplishing much with little effort.

It is often said that the Chinese are Confucians in public and Daoists in private, and the two approaches do seem to balance each other. Confucianism is a rational political philosophy that emphasizes propriety, deference, duty, and self-discipline. Daoism is an intuitive philosophy that emphasizes individualism, nonconformity, and a return to nature. If a Confucian education molded scholars outwardly into responsible, ethical officials, Daoism provided some breathing room for the artist and poet inside.

---

infusing Confucianism with traditional Chinese cosmology. They emphasized the Zhou idea, taken up by Confucius, that the emperor ruled by the mandate of Heaven. Heaven itself was reconceived more abstractly as the moral force underlying the universe. Thus the moral system of Confucian society became a reflection of universal order.

Confucian subjects turn up frequently in Han art. Among the most famous examples are the reliefs from the Wu family shrines built in 151 CE in Jiaxiang. Carved and engraved in low relief on stone slabs, the scenes were meant to teach Confucian themes such as respect for the emperor, filial piety, and wifely devotion. Daoist motifs also appear, as do figures from traditional myths and legends. Such mixed iconography is characteristic of Han art (see "A Closer Look," opposite).

When compared with the Han-dynasty banner (SEE FIG. 2–28), this late Han relief clearly shows the change that took place in the Chinese worldview in the span of 300 years. The banner places equal emphasis on heaven, earth, and the underworld; human beings are dwarfed by a great swarming of supernatural creatures and divine beings. In the relief in the Wu shrine, the focus is clearly on the human realm. The composition conveys the importance of the emperor as the holder of the

To view this image, please go to page 334 of the *Art History*, Fourth Edition by Marilyn Stokstad ebook.

2-30 • TOMB MODEL OF A HOUSE
Eastern Han dynasty, 1st–mid 2nd century CE. Painted earthenware, 52 × 33½ × 27" (132.1 × 85.1 × 68.6 cm). The Nelson-Atkins Museum of Art, Kansas City, Missouri. Purchase, Nelson Trust (33-521)

Rubbing of a Stone Relief ›

Detail from a rubbing of a stone relief in the Wu family shrine (Wuliangci). Jiaxiang, Shandong. Han dynasty, 151 CE. 27½ × 66½″ (70 × 169 cm).

Birds and small figures, possibly alluding to mythical creatures or immortals.

Women—and an empress?—receiving visitors on the upper floor.

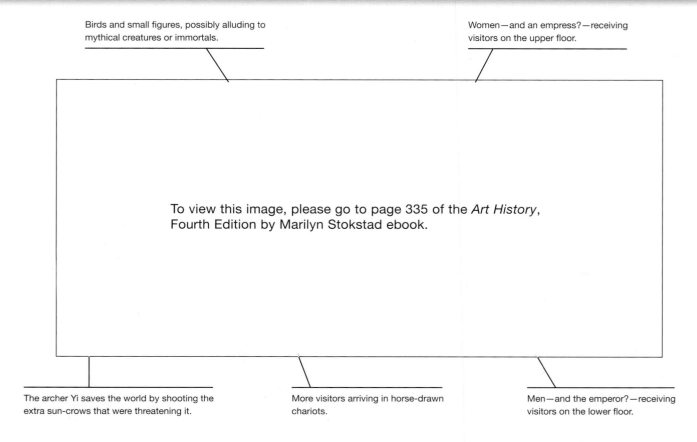

To view this image, please go to page 335 of the *Art History*, Fourth Edition by Marilyn Stokstad ebook.

The archer Yi saves the world by shooting the extra sun-crows that were threatening it.

More visitors arriving in horse-drawn chariots.

Men—and the emperor?—receiving visitors on the lower floor.

mandate of Heaven and illustrates fundamental Confucian themes of social order and decorum.

ARCHITECTURE

Contemporary literary sources are eloquent on the wonders of the Han capital. Unfortunately, nothing of Han architecture remains except ceramic models. One model of a house found in a tomb, where it was provided for the dead to use in the afterlife, represents a Han dwelling (FIG. 2–30). Its four stories are crowned with a watchtower and face a small walled courtyard. Pigs and oxen probably occupied the ground floor, while the family lived in the upper stories.

Aside from the multi-level construction, the most interesting feature of the house is the **bracketing** system (architectural elements projecting from the wall) that supports the rather broad eaves of its tiled roofs. Bracketing became a standard element of east Asian architecture, not only in private homes but more typically in palaces and temples. Another interesting aspect of the model is the elaborate painting on the exterior walls. Much of the painting is purely decorative, though some of it illustrates structural features such as posts and lintels. Still other images evoke the world outdoors, for example, the trees flanking the gateway with crows perched in their branches. Literary sources describe the walls of Han palaces as decorated with paint and lacquer, and also inlaid with precious metals and stones.

PREHISTORIC JAPAN

Human habitation in Japan dates to around 30,000 years ago (**MAP 2–4**). Sometime after 15,000 years ago Paleolithic peoples gave way to Neolithic hunter-gatherers, who gradually developed the ability to make and use ceramics. Recent scientific dating methods have shown that some works of Japanese pottery date to earlier than 10,000 BCE, making them the oldest now known.

JOMON PERIOD

The early potters lived during the Jomon period (c. 11,000–400 BCE), named for the patterns on much of the pottery they produced. They made functional earthenware vessels, probably originally imitating reed baskets, by building them up with coils of clay, then firing them in bonfires at relatively low temperatures. They also created small humanoid figures known as **dogu**, which were probably effigies that manifested a kind of sympathetic magic. Around 5000 BCE agriculture emerged with the planting and harvesting of beans and gourds.

YAYOI PERIOD

During the succeeding Yayoi era (c. 400 BCE–300 CE), the introduction of rice cultivation by immigrants from Korea helped transform Japan into an agricultural nation. As it did elsewhere in the world, this shift to agriculture brought larger permanent settlements, class structure with the division of labor into agricultural and nonagricultural tasks, more hierarchical forms of social organization, and a more centralized government. Korean settlers also brought metal technology. Bronze was used to create weapons as well as ceremonial objects such as bells. Iron metallurgy developed later in this period, eventually replacing stone tools in everyday life.

KOFUN PERIOD

Centralized government developed further during the ensuing Kofun ("old tombs") period (c. 300–552 CE), named for the large royal tombs that were built then. With the emergence of a more complex social order, the veneration of leaders grew into the beginnings of an imperial system. Still in existence today in Japan, this system eventually explained that the emperor (or, very rarely, empress) descended directly from Shinto deities. When an emperor died, chamber tombs were constructed following Korean examples. Various grave goods were placed inside the tomb chambers, including large amounts of pottery, presumably to pacify the spirits of the dead and to serve them in their next life. As part of a general cultural transfer from China through Korea, fifth-century potters in Japan gained knowledge of finishing techniques and improved kilns, and began to produce high-fired ceramic ware.

The Japanese government has never allowed the major sacred tombs to be excavated, but much is known about the mortuary practices of Kofun-era Japan. Some of the huge tombs of the fifth and sixth centuries were constructed in a shape resembling a large

MAP 2-4 • JAPAN

Melting glaciers at the end of the Ice Age in Japan 15,000 years ago raised the sea level and formed the four main islands of Japan: Hokkaido, Honshu, Shikoku, and Kyushu.

keyhole and surrounded by moats dug to protect the sacred precincts. Tomb sites might extend over more than 400 acres, with artificial hills built over the tombs themselves. On the top of the hills were placed ceramic works of sculpture called **haniwa**.

HANIWA.   The first *haniwa* were simple cylinders that may have held jars with ceremonial offerings. By the fifth century, these cylinders came to be made in the shapes of ceremonial objects, houses, and boats. Gradually, living creatures were added to the repertoire of *haniwa* subjects, including birds, deer, dogs, monkeys, cows, and horses. By the sixth century, **HANIWA** in human shapes were crafted, including males and females of various types, professions, and classes (**FIG. 2–31**).

Haniwa illustrate several enduring characteristics of Japanese aesthetic taste. Unlike Chinese tomb ceramics, which were often

Writing, Language, and Culture

Chinese culture enjoyed great prestige in east Asia. Written Chinese served as an international language of scholarship and cultivation, much as Latin did in medieval Europe. Educated Koreans, for example, wrote almost exclusively in Chinese until the fifteenth century. In Japan, Chinese continued to be used for certain kinds of writing, such as Buddhist *sutra*s, philosophical and legal texts, and Chinese poetry (by Japanese writers), into the nineteenth century.

When it came to writing their own language, the Japanese initially borrowed Chinese characters, or *kanji*. Differences between the Chinese and Japanese languages made this system extremely unwieldy, so during the ninth century they developed two syllabaries, or *kana*, from simplified Chinese characters. (A syllabary is a system of lettering in which each symbol stands for a syllable.) *Katakana*, consisting of angular symbols, was developed to aid pronunciation of Chinese Buddhist texts and now is generally used for foreign words. *Hiragana*, comprised of graceful, cursive symbols, was the written language the Japanese first used to write native poetry and prose. Eventually it came to be used to represent only the grammatical portions of the written Japanese language in conjunction with Chinese characters that convey meaning. Japanese written in *hiragana* was once called "women's hand" because its rounded forms looked feminine. During the Heian period *hiragana* were used to create a large body of literature, written either by women or sometimes for women by men.

A charming poem originated in Heian times to teach the new writing system. In two stanzas of four lines each, it uses almost all of the syllable sounds of spoken Japanese and thus almost every *kana* symbol. It was memorized as we would recite our ABCs. The first stanza translates as:

> Although flowers glow with color
> They are quickly fallen,
> And who in this world of ours
> Is free from change?
> (Translation by Earl Miner)

Like Chinese, Japanese is written in columns from top to bottom and across the page from right to left. (Following this logic, Chinese and Japanese narrative paintings also read from right to left.) Below is the stanza written three ways. At the right, it appears in *katakana* glossed with the original phonetic value of each symbol. (Modern pronunciation has shifted slightly.) In the center, the stanza appears in flowing *hiragana*. To the left is the mixture of *kanji* and *hiragana* that eventually became standard.

kanji hiragana mixed   *hiragana*   *katakana*

To view this image, please go to page 357 of the *Art History*, Fourth Edition by Marilyn Stokstad ebook.

To view this image, please go to page 358 of the *Art History*, Fourth Edition by Marilyn Stokstad ebook.

2–31 • *HANIWA*
Kyoto. Kofun period, 6th century CE. Earthenware, height 27" (68.5 cm). Collection of the Tokyo National Museum. Important Cultural Property.

There have been many theories as to the function of *haniwa*. The figures seem to have served as some kind of link between the world of the dead, over which they were placed, and the world of the living, from which they could be viewed. This figure has been identified as a seated female shaman, wearing a robe, belt, and necklace and carrying a mirror at her waist. In early Japan, shamans acted as agents between the natural and the supernatural worlds, just as *haniwa* figures were links between the living and the dead.

glazed, *haniwa* were left with their clay bodies unglazed. Nor do *haniwa* show a preoccupation with technical skill seen in Chinese ceramics. Instead, their makers explored the expressive potentials of simple and bold form. *Haniwa* are never perfectly symmetrical; their slightly off-center eye slits, irregular cylindrical bodies, and unequal arms impart the idiosyncrasy of life and individuality.

SHINTO. As described at the outset of this chapter, Shinto is Japan's indigenous religious belief system. It encompasses a variety of ritual practices that center around family, village, and national devotion to *kami* (Shinto deities). The term Shinto was not coined until after the arrival of Buddhism in the sixth century CE, and as *kami* worship was influenced by and incorporated into Buddhism it became more systematized, with shrines, a hierarchy of deities, and more strictly regulated ceremonies.

THE ISE SHRINE. One of the great Shinto monuments is the Grand Shrine of Ise, on the coast southwest of Tokyo (FIG. 2–32), where the main deity worshiped is the sun goddess Amaterasu-o-mi-*kami*, the legendary progenitor of Japan's imperial family. Japan's earliest written historical texts recorded by the imperial

court in the eighth century state that the Ise Shrine dates to the first century CE. Although we do not know for certain if this is true, it is known that it has been ritually rebuilt, alternately on two adjoining sites at 20-year intervals with few breaks since the year 690, a time when the imperial family was solidifying its hegemony. Its most recent rebuilding took place in 1993, by carpenters who train for the task from childhood. After the *kami* is ceremonially escorted to the freshly copied shrine, the old shrine is dismantled. Thus—like Japanese culture itself—this exquisite shrine is both ancient and constantly renewed. In this sense it embodies one of the most important characteristics of Shinto faith—ritual purification—derived from respect for the cycle of the seasons in which pure new life emerges in springtime and gives way to death in winter, yet is reborn again in the following year.

Although Ise is visited by millions of pilgrims each year, only members of the imperial family and a few Shinto priests are allowed within the enclosure that surrounds its inner shrine. Although detailed documents on its appearance date back to the tenth century, shrine authorities never allowed photographers access to its inner compound until 1953, when the iconic photograph of it reproduced in FIGURE 2–32 was taken by a photographer officially

To view this image, please go to page 359 of the *Art History*, Fourth Edition by Marilyn Stokstad ebook.

2-32 • MAIN HALL, INNER SHRINE, ISE
Mie Prefecture. Last rebuilt 1993. Photograph by Watanabe Yoshio (1907–2000), 1953. National Treasure.

SEE MORE: View a video about the re-building of the Ise Shrine
www.myartslab.com

engaged by a quasi-governmental cultural relations agency. The reluctance of shrine officials to permit photography even then may stem from beliefs that such intimate pictures would violate the privacy of the shrine's most sacred spaces.

The Ise Shrine has many aspects that are typical of Shinto architecture, including wooden piles raising the building off the ground, a thatched roof held in place by horizontal logs, the use of unpainted cypress wood, and the overall feeling of natural simplicity rather than overwhelming size or elaborate decoration. The building's shape is indebted to raised granaries used by the Yayoi people, which are known from drawings on bronze artifacts of the Yayoi period. The sensitive use of wood and thatch in the Ise Shrine suggests an early origin for the Japanese appreciation of natural materials that persists to the present day.

ASUKA PERIOD

During the Asuka period's single century (552–645 CE), new forms of philosophy, medicine, music, food, clothing, agriculture, city planning, religion, visual art, and architecture entered Japan from Korea and China at an astonishing pace. Most significant among these were the Buddhist religion, a centralized governmental

structure, and a system of writing. Each was adopted and gradually modified to suit Japanese conditions, and each has had an enduring legacy.

Buddhism reached Japan in Mahayana form, with its many buddhas and bodhisattvas (see "Buddhism," page 87). After being accepted by the imperial family, it was soon adopted as a state religion. Buddhism represented not only different gods from Shinto but an entirely new concept of religion. Worship of Buddhist deities took place inside worship halls of temples situated in close proximity to imperial cities. The temples looked like nothing constructed in Japan before, with Chinese-influenced buildings housing anthropomorphic Buddhist icons possessing an elaborate iconography (see "Buddhist Symbols," page 112). At that time, *kami* were not portrayed in human form. Yet Buddhism attracted followers because it offered a rich cosmology with profound teachings of meditation and enlightenment, and the protective powers of its deities enabled the ruling elites to justify their own power, through association with Buddhism. They called upon Buddhist deities to nurture and protect the populace over whom they ruled. Many highly developed aspects of continental Asian art accompanied the new religion, including new methods of painting and sculpture.

2-33 • AERIAL VIEW OF HORYUJI COMPOUND
Pagoda to the west (left), golden hall (*kondo*) to the east (right). Nara Prefecture. Asuka period, 7th century CE. UNESCO World Heritage Site, National Treasure.

To view this image, please go to page 360 of the *Art History*, Fourth Edition by Marilyn Stokstad ebook.

HORYUJI

The most significant surviving early Japanese temple is Horyuji, located on Japan's central plains not far from Nara. The temple was founded in 607 by Prince Shotoku (574–622), who ruled Japan as a regent and became the most influential early proponent of Buddhism. Rebuilt after a fire in 670, Horyuji is the oldest wooden temple in the world. It is so famous that visitors are often surprised at its modest size. Yet its just proportions and human scale, together with the artistic treasures it contains, make Horyuji an enduringly beautiful monument to Buddhist faith in early Japan.

The main compound of Horyuji consists of a rectangular courtyard surrounded by covered corridors, one of which contains a gateway. Within the compound are only two buildings, the **kondo** (golden hall), and a five-story pagoda. Within a simple asymmetrical layout, the large *kondo* perfectly balances the tall, slender pagoda (**FIG. 2–33**). The *kondo* is filled with Buddhist images and is used for worship and ceremonies. The pagoda serves as a reliquary and is not entered. Other monastery buildings lie outside the main compound, including an outer gate, a lecture hall, a repository for sacred texts, a belfry, and dormitories for monks.

Among the many treasures still preserved in Horyuji is a shrine decorated with paintings in lacquer. It is known as the Tamamushi Shrine after the *tamamushi* beetle, whose iridescent wings were originally affixed to the shrine to make it glitter, much

To view this image, please go to page 360 of the *Art History*, Fourth Edition by Marilyn Stokstad ebook.

2-34 • HUNGRY TIGRESS JATAKA
Panel of the Tamamushi Shrine, Horyuji. Asuka period, c. 650 CE. Lacquer on wood, height of shrine 7'7½" (2.33 m). Horyuji Treasure House, Nara. National Treasure.

To view this image, please go to page 361 of the *Art History*, Fourth Edition by Marilyn Stokstad ebook.

2-35 • Tori Busshi BUDDHA SHAKA AND ATTENDANT BODHISATTVAS IN THE HORYUJI *KONDO*
Asuka period, c. 623 CE. Gilt bronze, height of seated figure 34½″ (87.5 cm). Horyuji, Nara. National Treasure.

like mother-of-pearl. Its architectural form replicates an ancient palace-form building type that predates Horyuji itself.

HUNGRY TIGRESS JATAKA. Paintings on the sides of the Tamamushi Shrine are among the few two-dimensional works of art to survive from the Asuka period. Most celebrated among them are two that illustrate Jataka tales, stories about former lives of the Buddha. One depicts the future Buddha nobly sacrificing his life in order to feed his body to a starving tigress and her cubs (FIG. 2–34). The tigers are at first too weak to eat him, so he must jump off a cliff to break open his flesh. The anonymous artist has created a full narrative within a single frame. The graceful form of the Buddha appears three times, harmonized by the curves of the rocky cliff and tall sprigs of bamboo. First, he hangs his shirt on a tree, then he dives downward onto the rocks, and finally starving animals devour his body. The elegantly slender renditions of the figure and the somewhat abstract treatment of the cliff, trees,

and bamboo represent an international Buddhist style that was transmitted to Japan via China and Korea. These illustrations of Jataka tales helped popularize Buddhism in Japan.

SHAKA TRIAD. Another example of the international style of early Buddhist art at Horyuji is the sculpture called the Shaka Triad, traditionally identified as being made by Tori Busshi (FIG. 2–35). (Shaka is the Japanese name for Shakyamuni, the historical Buddha.) Tori Busshi (Busshi means Buddhist image-maker) may have been a descendant of Korean craftsmen who emigrated to Japan as part of an influx of Buddhists and artisans from Korea. The Shaka Triad reflects the strong influence of Chinese art of the Northern Wei dynasty. The frontal pose, the outsized face and hands, and the linear treatment of the drapery all suggest that the maker of this statue was well aware of earlier continental models, while the fine bronze casting of the figures shows his advanced technical skill. The Shaka Triad and the Tamamushi Shrine reveal the importance of Buddhist imagery to the transmission of the faith.

NARA PERIOD

The Nara period (645–794) is named for Japan's first permanent imperial capital, founded in 710. Previously, an emperor's death was thought to taint his entire capital city, so for reasons of purification (and perhaps also of politics), his successor usually selected a new site. As the government adopted ever more complex aspects of the Chinese political system, necessitating construction of huge administrative complexes, it abandoned this custom in the eighth century when Nara was founded. During this period, divisions of the imperial bureaucracy grew exponentially and hastened the swelling of the city's population to perhaps 200,000 people.

One result of the strong central authority was the construction in Nara of magnificent Buddhist temples and Shinto shrines that dwarfed those built previously. The expansive park in the center of Nara today is the site of the largest and most important of these, including the Shinto Kasuga Shrine. The grandest of the Buddhist temples in Nara Park is Todaiji, which Emperor Shomu (r. 724–749) conceived as the headquarters of a vast network of branch temples throughout the nation. He had it constructed because of his deep faith in Buddhism. Todaiji served as both a state-supported central monastic training center and as the setting for public religious ceremonies. The most spectacular of these took place in 752 and celebrated the consecration of the main Buddhist statue of the temple in a traditional "eye-opening" ceremony, in its newly constructed Great Buddha Hall (*Daibutsuden*). The statue, a giant gilt bronze image of the Buddha Birushana (Vairochana in Sanskrit), was inspired by the Chinese tradition of erecting monumental stone Buddhist statues in cave-temples.

The ceremony, which took place in the vast courtyard in front of the Great Buddha Hall, was presided over by an illustrious

Buddhist Symbols

A few of the most important Buddhist symbols, which have myriad variations, are described here in their most generalized forms.

Lotus flower: Usually shown as a white waterlily, the lotus (Sanskrit, *padma*) symbolizes spiritual purity, the wholeness of creation, and cosmic harmony. The flower's stem is an *axis mundi* ("axis of the world").

Lotus throne: Buddhas are frequently shown seated on an open lotus, either single or double, a representation of *nirvana*.

Chakra: An ancient sun symbol, the *chakra* (wheel) symbolizes both the various states of existence (the Wheel of Life) and the Buddhist doctrine (the Wheel of the Law). A *chakra*'s exact meaning depends on how many spokes it has (SEE FIG. 2–15).

Marks of a buddha: A buddha is distinguished by 32 physical attributes (*lakshanas*). Among them are a bulge on top of the head (*ushnisha*), a tuft of hair between the eyebrows (*urna*), elongated earlobes, and 1,000-spoked *chakras* on the soles of the feet.

Mandala: *Mandalas* are diagrams of cosmic realms, representing order and meaning within the spiritual universe. They may be simple or complex, three- or two-dimensional, and in a wide array of forms— such as an Indian stupa (SEE FIG. 2–16) or a Womb World *mandala*, an early Japanese type.

To view this image, please go to page 362 of the *Art History*, Fourth Edition by Marilyn Stokstad ebook.

Indian monk and included *sutra* chanting by over 10,000 Japanese Buddhist monks and sacred performances by 4,000 court musicians and dancers. Vast numbers of Japanese courtiers and emissaries from the Asian continent comprised the audience. Numerous ritual objects used in the ceremony came from exotic Asian and Near Eastern lands. The resulting cosmopolitan atmosphere reflected the position Nara then held as the eastern terminus of the Central Asian Silk Road.

Many of these treasures have been preserved in the Shosoin Imperial Repository at Todaiji, which today contains some 9,000

To view this image, please go to page 363 of the *Art History*,
Fourth Edition by Marilyn Stokstad ebook.

**2-36 • FIVE-STRINGED LUTE (*BIWA*) WITH DESIGN OF A
CENTRAL ASIAN MAN PLAYING A *BIWA* ATOP A CAMEL**
Chinese. Tang dynasty, 8th century CE. Red sandalwood and chestnut inlaid with
mother-of-pearl, amber, and tortoiseshell. Length 42½″ (108.1 cm), width 12″
(30.9 cm), depth 3½″ (9 cm). Shosoin, Todaiji, Nara.

objects. The Shosoin came into being in the year 756, when Emperor Shomu died and his widow donated some 600 of his possessions to the temple, including a number of objects used during the Great Buddha's consecration ceremony. Many years later, objects used in Buddhist rituals and previously stored elsewhere at Todaiji were added to these. The objects formerly owned by Emperor Shomu consisted mainly of his personal possessions, such as documents, furniture, musical instruments, games, clothing, medicine, weapons, food and beverage vessels of metal, glass, and lacquer, and some Buddhist ritual objects. Some of these were made in Japan while others were clearly not and came from as far away as China, India, Iran, Greece, Rome, and Egypt. They reflect the vast international trade network that existed at this early date.

One of the items Emperor Shomu's widow donated in 756 is a magnificently crafted five-stringed lute (*biwa*) made of lacquered red sandalwood and chestnut, and inlaid with mother-of-pearl, amber, and tortoiseshell. Its plectrum guard features a design of a man of central Asian origin (apparent from his clothing and physical features) sitting atop a camel and playing a lute **(FIG. 2–36)**. This instrument is the only existing example of an ancient five-stringed lute. Its form was invented in India and transmitted to China and Japan via the Silk Road. The Shosoin piece is generally identified as Chinese. However, as with many of the objects preserved in the Shosoin, the location of its manufacture is not absolutely certain. While it was most likely crafted in China and imported to Japan for use in the consecration ceremony (researchers have recently conclusively determined that it was indeed played), it is also plausible that Chinese (or Japanese) craftsmen made it in Japan using imported materials. Its meticulous workmanship reveals the high level of crafts production that artists of this era achieved. Such consummate skill has been a hallmark of Japanese crafts since then.

Influenced by Emperor Shomu, the Buddhist faith permeated all aspects of court society of the Nara period. Indeed, in 749 Shomu abdicated the throne to retire as a monk. His daughter, who succeeded him as empress, was also a devout Buddhist and wanted to cede her throne to a Buddhist monk. This dismayed her advisors and prompted them to move the capital city away from Nara, where they felt Buddhist influence had become overpowering, and establish a new one, Kyoto, within whose bounds, at first, only a few Buddhist temples would be allowed. The move of the capital to Kyoto marked the end of the Nara period.

To view this image, please go to page 376 of the *Art History*, Fourth Edition by Marilyn Stokstad ebook.

2-37 • OFFERING 4, LA VENTA Mexico. Olmec culture, c. 900–400 BCE. Jade, greenstone, and sandstone, height of figures 6¼–7″ (16–18 cm). Museo Nacional de Antropología, Mexico City.

ART OF THE AMERICAS BEFORE 1300

The scene hints at a story in progress. Fifteen figures of precious greenstone converge on a single figure made of a baser, more porous stone. The tall oblong stones (**celts**) in the background evoke an architectural space, perhaps a location within the Olmec center of La Venta, where this tableau was created sometime between 900 and 400 BCE. The figures have the slouching bodies, elongated heads, almond-shaped eyes, and downturned mouths characteristic of Olmec art. Holes for earrings and the simple lines of the bodies suggest that these sculptures may originally have been dressed and adorned with perishable materials. The poses of the figures, with their knees slightly bent and their arms flexed at their sides, lend a sense of arrested movement to this enigmatic scene. Is it a council? a trial? an initiation? Are the greenstone figures marching in front of the reddish granite figure as he reviews them, or moving to confront him? With no texts to explain the scene, the specific tale it narrates may never be known, but it is clear that this offering commemorates an important event.

And it was remembered. This tableau **(FIG. 2–37)** was set up in the earth and buried underneath a plaza at La Venta, one of a number of offerings of works of art and precious materials beneath the surface of the city. Colored sand and floors covered the offerings, each colored floor signifying a successive renovation of the plaza. Over a century after these sculptures were buried, a hole was dug directly over the offering and it was viewed once more. Pieces of the later floors fell into the hole, but the figures themselves were not disturbed. After this, the scene was buried once again. The precision of this later excavation suggests that the exact location of the tableau was remembered. The archaeological record makes clear that this work of art, although hidden, still exerted tremendous power.

This extraordinary find demonstrates the importance of scientific archaeological excavations for understanding ancient art. Had these objects been torn out of the ground by looters and sold piecemeal on the black market, we would never have known how Olmec sculptures were used to create narrative installations or imagined that buried art could be remembered for so long. Instead, this discovery provides a context for isolated greenstone figures that have been found throughout Mesoamerica (modern Mexico, Guatemala, and Honduras). It provides evidence that these sculptures were made by the Olmec, Mesoamerica's first great civilization, and suggests that these objects, scattered today, might have once been assembled in meaningful ways like the offering at La Venta.

LEARN ABOUT IT

2.10 Recognize how differences in environmental conditions affected the artistic output of Mesoamerica, South America, and North America.

2.11 Explore how the role or function of an object is critical to understanding its meaning in ancient American visual arts.

2.12 Compare and contrast the use of urban planning in ancient American cultures.

2.13 Examine how Maya writing functions, and how it relates to Maya images.

HEAR MORE: Listen to an audio file of your chapter **www.myartslab.com**

THE NEW WORLD

In recent years the question of the original settlement of the Americas has become an area of debate. The traditional view has been that human beings arrived in North and South America from Asia during the last Ice Age, when glaciers trapped enough of the world's water to lower the level of the oceans and expose a land bridge across the Bering Strait. Although most of present-day Alaska and Canada was covered by glaciers at that time, an ice-free corridor along the Pacific coast would have provided access from Asia to the south and east. Thus, this theory holds that sometime before 12,000 years ago, perhaps as early as 20,000 to 30,000 years ago, Paleolithic hunter-gatherers emerged through this corridor and began to spread out into two vast, uninhabited continents. This view is now challenged by the early dates of some new archaeological finds and by evidence suggesting the possibility of early connections with Europe as well, perhaps along the Arctic coast of the North Atlantic. In any event, by between 10,000 and 12,000 years ago, bands of hunters roamed throughout the Americas, and after the ice had retreated, the peoples of the Western Hemisphere were essentially cut off from the rest of the world until they were overrun by European invaders, beginning at the end of the fifteenth century CE.

In this isolation the peoples of the Americas experienced cultural transformations similar to those seen elsewhere around the world following the end of the Paleolithic era. In most regions they developed an agricultural way of life. A trio of native plants—corn, beans, and squash—was especially important, but people also cultivated potatoes, tobacco, cacao, tomatoes, and avocados. New World peoples also domesticated many animals: dogs, turkeys, guinea pigs, llamas, and their camelid cousins—alpacas, guanacos, and vicuñas.

As elsewhere, the shift to agriculture in the Americas was accompanied by population growth and, in some places, the rise of hierarchical societies, the appearance of ceremonial centers and towns with monumental architecture, and the development of sculpture, ceramics, and other arts. The people of Mesoamerica—the region that extends from central Mexico well into Central America—developed writing, astronomy, a complex and accurate calendar, and a sophisticated system of mathematics. Central and South American peoples had advanced metallurgy and produced exquisite gold, silver, and copper objects. The metalworkers of the Andes, the mountain range along the western coast of South America, began to produce metal jewelry, weapons, and agricultural implements in the first millennium CE, and people elsewhere in the Americas made tools, weapons, and art from other materials such as bone, ivory, stone, wood, and, where it was available, obsidian, a volcanic glass capable of a cutting edge 500 times finer than surgical steel. Basketry and weaving became major art forms. In the American Southwest, Native American people built multi-storied, apartmentlike village and cliff dwellings, as well as elaborate irrigation systems with canals. Evidence of weaving in the American Southwest dates to about 7400 BCE.

Extraordinary artistic traditions flourished in many regions in the Americas before 1300 CE. This chapter explores the accomplishments of some of the cultures in five of those areas: Mesoamerica, Central America, the central Andes of South America, the Southeastern Woodlands and great river valleys of North America, and the North American Southwest.

MESOAMERICA

Ancient Mesoamerica encompasses the area from north of the Valley of Mexico (the location of Mexico City) to present-day Belize, Honduras, and western Nicaragua in Central America (MAP 2–5). The region is one of great contrasts, ranging from tropical rainforest to semiarid mountains. The civilizations that arose in Mesoamerica varied, but they were linked by cultural similarities and trade. Among their shared features were a ballgame with religious and political significance (see "The Cosmic Ballgame," page 127), aspects of monumental building construction, and a complex system of multiple calendars including a 260-day divinatory cycle and a 365-day ritual and agricultural cycle. Many Mesoamerican societies were sharply divided into elite and commoner classes.

The transition to farming began in Mesoamerica between 7000 and 6000 BCE, and by 3000 to 2000 BCE settled villages were widespread. Customarily the region's subsequent history is divided into three broad periods: Formative or Preclassic (1500 BCE–250 CE), Classic (250–900 CE), and Postclassic (900–1521 CE). This chronology derives primarily from the archaeology of the Maya—the people of Guatemala, southern Mexico, and the Yucatan Peninsula—with the Classic period bracketing the era during which the Maya erected dated stone monuments. The term reflects the view of early scholars that the Classic period was a kind of golden age. Although this view is no longer current—and the periods are only roughly applicable to other cultures of Mesoamerica—the terminology has endured.

THE OLMEC

The first major Mesoamerican art style, that of the Olmec, emerged during the Formative/Preclassic period, beginning around 1500 BCE. Many of the key elements of Mesoamerican art, including monumental stone sculpture commemorating individual rulers, finely carved jades, elegant ceramics, and architectural elements such as pyramids, plazas, and ballcourts, were first developed by the Olmec. In the fertile, swampy coastal areas of the present-day Mexican states of Veracruz and Tabasco, the Olmec raised massive earth mounds on which they constructed ceremonial centers. These centers probably housed an elite group of rulers and priests supported by a larger population of farmers who lived in villages of pole-and-thatch houses. The presence at Olmec sites of goods such as obsidian, iron ore, and jade that are not found in the Gulf of Mexico region but come from throughout Mesoamerica indicates that the Olmec participated in extensive long-distance trade. They went to especially great lengths

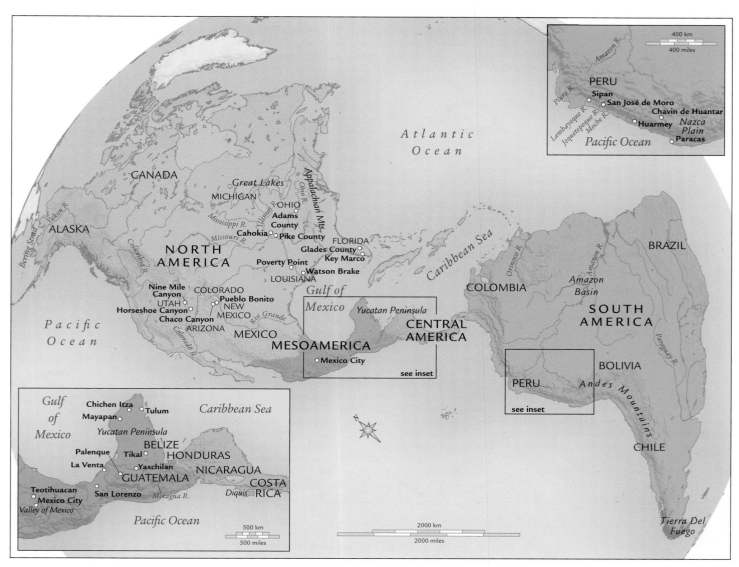

MAP 2-5 • THE AMERICAS BEFORE 1300

People moved across North America, then southward through Central America until they reached the Tierra del Fuego region of South America.

to acquire jade, which was one of the most precious materials in ancient Mesoamerica.

The earliest Olmec ceremonial center (c. 1200–900 BCE), at San Lorenzo, was built atop a giant earthwork, nearly three-quarters of a mile long, with an elaborate stone drainage system running throughout the mound. Other architectural features included a palace with basalt columns, a possible ballcourt, and a stone-carving workshop. Another center, at La Venta, thriving from about 900 to 400 BCE, was built on high ground between rivers. Its most prominent feature, an earth mound known as the Great Pyramid, still rises to a height of over 100 feet (FIG. 2–38). The pyramid stands at the south end of a large, open plaza arranged on a north–south axis and defined by long, low earth mounds. Many of the physical features of La Venta—including the symmetrical arrangement of earth mounds, platforms, and central open spaces along an axis that was probably determined by

astronomical observations—are characteristic of later monumental and ceremonial architecture throughout Mesoamerica. What was buried beneath the surface of La Venta—massive stone mosaics, layers of colored clay, and greenstone figures like those in FIGURE 2–37, discussed at the beginning of the chapter—may have been as important as what was visible on the surface.

The Olmec produced an abundance of monumental basalt sculpture, including **COLOSSAL HEADS** (FIG. 2–39), altars, and seated figures. The huge basalt blocks for the large works of sculpture were quarried at distant sites and transported to San Lorenzo, La Venta, and other centers. Colossal heads ranged in height from 5 to 12 feet and weighed from 5 to more than 20 tons. The heads portray adult males wearing close-fitting caps with chin straps and large, round earspools (cylindrical earrings that pierce the earlobe). The fleshy faces have almond-shaped eyes, flat broad noses, thick protruding lips, and downturned mouths. Each face is different, suggesting that

To view this image, please go to page 380 of the *Art History*,
Fourth Edition by Marilyn Stokstad ebook.

**2-38 • GREAT PYRAMID
AND PLAZA, LA VENTA**
Mexico. Olmec culture,
c. 900–400 BCE. Pyramid height
approx. 100′ (30 m).

To view this image, please go to page 380
of the *Art History*, Fourth Edition by
Marilyn Stokstad ebook.

they may represent specific individuals. Ten colossal heads were found at San Lorenzo. Many had been mutilated and buried by about 900 BCE, when the site went into decline. At La Venta, 102 basalt monuments have been found, including four more colossal heads, massive thrones or altars, tall stone **stelae**, and other kinds of figural sculpture. The colossal heads and the subjects depicted on other monumental sculpture suggest that the Olmec elite were interested in commemorating rulers and historic events.

In addition to these heavy basalt monuments, Olmec artists also made smaller, more portable jade and ceramic objects (SEE FIG. 2–37). Jade, available only from the Motagua River valley in present-day Guatemala, was prized for its brilliant blue-green color and the smooth, shiny surfaces it could achieve with careful polishing. Jade is one of the hardest materials in Mesoamerica, and with only stone tools available, Olmec craftsmen used jade tools and powdered jade dust as an abrasive to carve and polish these sculptures. Other figurines were made out of softer and more malleable greenstones, like serpentine, which occur in many parts of Mesoamerica. Olmec ceramics, including decorated vessels and

2-39 • COLOSSAL HEAD, SAN LORENZO
Mexico. Olmec culture, c. 1200–900 BCE. Basalt, height 7′5″ (2.26 m).

2-40 • CEREMONIAL CENTER OF THE CITY OF TEOTIHUACAN

Mexico. Teotihuacan culture, c. 100–650 CE. View from the southeast. The Pyramid of the Sun is in the foreground, and the Pyramid of the Moon is visible in the distance. The Avenue of the Dead, the north–south axis of the city, which connects the two pyramids, continues for over a mile.

SEE MORE: View a simulation about the Ceremonial Center of Teotihuacan
www.myartslab.com

remarkably lifelike clay babies, also appear to have been prized far beyond the Olmec heartland. Olmec greenstone and ceramic objects have been found throughout Mesoamerica, evidence of the extensive reach and influence of Olmec art and culture.

By 200 CE, forests and swamps had begun to reclaim Olmec sites, but Olmec civilization had spread widely throughout Mesoamerica and was to have an enduring influence on its successors. As the Olmec centers of the Gulf Coast faded, the great Classic period centers in the Maya region and Teotihuacan area in the Valley of Mexico were beginning their ascendancy.

TEOTIHUACAN

Located some 30 miles northeast of present-day Mexico City, the city of Teotihuacan experienced a period of rapid growth early in the first millennium CE. By 200 CE, it had emerged as Mesoamerica's first truly urban settlement, a significant center of commerce and manufacturing. At its height, between 300 and 650, Teotihuacan covered nearly nine square miles and had a population of at least 125,000, making it the largest city in the Americas and one of the largest in the world at that time (**FIG. 2–40**). Its residents lived in walled "apartment compounds," and the entire city was organized on a grid (**FIG. 2–41**), its orientation chosen both for its calendrical significance and to respond to the surrounding landscape.

Although Teotihuacan declined in power after 650, it was never forgotten. Centuries later, it remained a legendary pilgrimage center. The much later Aztec people (c. 1300–1525) revered the site, believing it to be the place where the gods created the sun and the moon. In fact, Teotihuacan, a word indicating a place of divinity, is the Aztec name for the city. The names we use for its principal monuments are also Aztec names. We do not know what

2-41 • PLAN OF THE CEREMONIAL CENTER OF TEOTIHUACAN

2-42 • PYRAMID OF THE FEATHERED SERPENT

The Ciudadela, Teotihuacan, Mexico. Teotihuacan culture, c. 200 CE.

To view this image, please go to page 382 of the *Art History*, Fourth Edition by Marilyn Stokstad ebook.

the original inhabitants of Teotihuacan called these buildings or what they called their own city.

The center of the city is bisected by a broad thoroughfare laid out on a north–south axis, extending for more than a mile and in places as much as 150 feet wide, which the Aztecs called the Avenue of the Dead. At the center of the Teotihuacan grid, a series of canals forced the San Juan River to run perpendicular to the avenue. At the north end of this central axis stands the Pyramid of the Moon, facing a large plaza flanked by smaller, symmetrically placed platforms. It seems to echo the shape of the mountain behind it, and as one walks towards the pyramid, it looms above, eclipsing the mountain completely. The Pyramid of the Moon was enlarged several times, as were many Mesoamerican pyramids; each enlargement completely enclosed the previous structure and was accompanied by rich sacrificial offerings.

The largest of Teotihuacan's architectural monuments, the Pyramid of the Sun, located just to the east of the Avenue of the Dead, is slightly over 200 feet high and measures about 720 feet on each side at its base, similar in size to, but not as tall as, the largest Egyptian pyramid at Giza. It is built over a multi-chambered cave

with a spring that may have been the original focus of worship at the site and its source of prestige. The pyramid rises in a series of sloping steps to a flat platform, where a small temple once stood. A monumental stone stairway led from level to level up the side of the pyramid to the temple platform. The exterior was faced with stone, which was then stuccoed and painted.

At the southern end of the ceremonial center, and at the heart of the city, is the Ciudadela (Spanish for a fortified city center), a vast sunken plaza surrounded by temple platforms. One of the city's principal religious and political centers, the plaza could accommodate an assembly of more than 60,000 people. Early in Teotihuacan's history, its focal point was the **PYRAMID OF THE FEATHERED SERPENT (FIG. 2–42)**. This seven-tiered structure exhibits the *talud-tablero* (slope-and-panel) construction that is a hallmark of the Teotihuacan architectural style. The *talud* (sloping base) of each platform supports a *tablero* (entablature), that rises vertically and is surrounded by a frame.

Archaeological excavations of the temple's early phase have revealed undulating feathered serpents floating in a watery space punctuated by reliefs of aquatic shells. Their flat, angular, abstract

To view this image, please go to page 383 of the *Art History*,
Fourth Edition by Marilyn Stokstad ebook.

2-43 • BLOODLETTING RITUAL
Fragment of a fresco from Teotihuacan, Mexico. Teotihuacan culture, c. 550–650 CE. Pigment on lime plaster,
32¼ × 45¼" (82 × 116.1 cm). The Cleveland Museum of Art. Purchase from the J. H. Wade Fund (63.252)

The maguey plant supplied the people of Teotihuacan with food, with fiber for making clothing, rope, and paper, and
with the precious drink pulque. As this painting indicates, priestly officials used its spikes in rituals to draw their own
blood as a sacrifice.

style, typical of Teotihuacan art, is in marked contrast to the curvilinear forms of Olmec art. While the bodies of the feathered serpents are rendered in low relief, three-dimensional fanged serpent heads emerge from aureoles of stylized feathers. In the vertical *tablero* sections, each serpent carries on its body a squarish headdress with a protruding upper jaw, huge, round eyes originally inlaid with obsidian, and a pair of round goggles on its forehead between the eyes. These mosaic headdresses seem to represent an aspect of the Teotihuacan Storm God associated with warfare—other works of art at Teotihuacan and elsewhere in Mesoamerica show armed warriors wearing the same headdress. Inside the pyramid, this militaristic message was reinforced by the burials of dozens of sacrificial victims, some of them wearing necklaces made of human maxillae and jawbones (or shell imitations thereof), their arms tied behind their backs. In the fourth century, the elaborate sculptural façade of the Pyramid of the Feathered Serpent was concealed behind a plainer *talud-tablero* structure tacked onto the front of the pyramid.

The residential sections of Teotihuacan fanned out from the city's center. The large and spacious palaces of the elite, with as many as 45 rooms and seven patios, stood nearest the ceremonial center. Artisans, foreign traders, and peasants lived farther away, in more crowded compounds, all aligned to the Teotihuacan grid. Palaces and more humble homes alike were rectangular one-story structures with high walls and suites of rooms arranged around open courtyards. Walls were plastered and covered with paintings.

Teotihuacan's artists worked in a fresco technique, applying pigments directly on damp lime plaster. Once the paint was applied, the walls were polished to give a smooth, shiny, and durable surface. The style, like that of the sculpture, was flat, angular, and abstract, often featuring processions of similarly dressed figures, rows of mythological animals, or other kinds of repeating images. Teotihuacan painters worked in several different coloristic modes, including a bright polychrome and a more restricted palette emphasizing tones of red. A detached fragment of a wall painting, now in the Cleveland Museum of Art, depicts a **BLOODLETTING RITUAL** in which an elaborately dressed man enriches and revitalizes the earth with his own blood **(FIG. 2–43)**. The man's large animal headdress, decorated with precious feathers from the quetzal bird, indicates his high rank. He stands between rectangular plots of earth or bundles of grass pierced with bloody maguey spines (used in bloodletting), and he scatters seeds or drops of blood from his right hand, as indicated by the stream of conventionalized symbols for blood, seeds, and flowers falling from his hand. The sound scroll emerging from his open mouth symbolizes his ritual chant. The visual weight accorded the headdress and the sound scroll suggests that the man's priestly office and chanted words were essential elements of the ceremony. Such bloodletting rituals were widespread in Mesoamerica.

Teotihuacan was a wealthy and cosmopolitan city, home to people from all over Mesoamerica. One reason for its wealth was its control of a source of high-quality obsidian. Goods made at Teotihuacan, including obsidian tools and pottery, were distributed widely throughout Mesoamerica in exchange for luxury items such as the brilliant green feathers of the quetzal bird. Yet not all interactions between Teotihuacan and other Mesoamerican centers were peaceful—the threat of Teotihuacan military force, so clearly expressed at the Pyramid of the Feathered Serpent, was always present.

Sometime in the early seventh century disaster struck Teotihuacan. The ceremonial center was sacked and burned, and the city went into a permanent decline. Nevertheless, its influence continued as other centers throughout Mesoamerica, as far south as the highlands of Guatemala, borrowed and transformed its imagery over the next several centuries.

THE MAYA

The ancient Maya are noted for a number of achievements. In densely populated cities they built imposing pyramids, temples, palaces, and administrative structures. They developed the most advanced hieroglyphic writing in Mesoamerica and perfected a sophisticated version of the Mesoamerican calendrical system (see "Maya Writing," opposite). Using these, they recorded the accomplishments of their rulers on sculpture, ceramic vessels, wall paintings, and in books. They studied astronomy and the natural cycles of plants and animals, and used sophisticated mathematical concepts such as zero and place value.

An increasingly detailed picture of the Maya has been emerging from recent archaeological research and from advances in deciphering their writing. That picture shows a society divided into competing city-states, each with a hereditary ruler and an elite class of nobles and priests supported by a large group of farmer-commoners. Rulers established their legitimacy, maintained links with their divine ancestors, commemorated important calendrical dates, and sustained the gods through elaborate rituals, including ballgames, bloodletting ceremonies, and human sacrifice. Rulers commemorated such events and their military exploits on carved stelae. A complex pantheon of deities presided over the Maya universe.

To view this image, please go to page 384 of the *Art History*, Fourth Edition by Marilyn Stokstad ebook.

2-44 • BASE OF NORTH ACROPOLIS (LEFT) AND TEMPLE I
Tikal, Guatemala. Maya culture. North Acropolis, 4th century BCE–5th century CE; Temple I (Tomb of Ruler A), c. 734 CE.

Maya Writing

Maya writing is **logosyllabic**—it consists of ideographs or logographs that represent entire words as well as a set of symbols that stand for the sound of each syllable in the Maya language. Thus, a word like *balam* (jaguar) could be written in many different ways: with the logograph "BALAM," a picture of the head of a jaguar (top right); with three syllables, "ba-la-ma," for the sounds of the word *balam* (bottom right); or a combination of the two systems—the logograph "BALAM" complemented with one or more phonetic syllables, to make it clear which logograph was represented (to avoid the possibility of confusing this logograph with the symbol for *hix*, another kind of feline, for example) (middle right). The combination of these two systems allowed Maya scribes extraordinary flexibility, and some calligraphers seem to have delighted in finding as many different ways as possible to write the same word. Many Maya logographs remained very pictorial, like the glyph for jaguar illustrated here, which meant that Maya writing was never too distant from other kinds of image making. In fact, the same word, *ts'ib*, signified both writing and painting in the Classic Mayan language.

With major advances in the decipherment of Maya hieroglyphic writing—beginning in the 1950s and continuing to this day—it has become clear that the inscriptions on Maya architecture and stelae appear almost entirely devoted to historical events. They record the dates of royal marriages, births of heirs, alliances between cities, and great military victories, and they tie these events to astronomical events and propitious dates in the Maya calendar. We know that the Maya also wrote books, but only four of these fragile manuscripts—called codices—have survived, all of them from the Postclassic period.

To view this image, please go to page 385 of the *Art History*, Fourth Edition by Marilyn Stokstad ebook.

Maya civilization emerged during the late Preclassic period (400 BCE–250 CE), reached its peak in the southern lowlands of Mexico and Guatemala during the Classic period (250–900 CE), and shifted to the northern Yucatan Peninsula during the Postclassic period (900–1521 CE). Throughout this time, the Maya had strong ties with other regions of Mesoamerica: They inherited many ideas and technologies from the Olmec, had trade and military interactions with Teotihuacan, and, centuries later, were in contact with the Aztec Empire.

TIKAL. The monumental buildings of Maya cities were masterly examples of the use of architecture for public display. Tikal (in present-day Guatemala) was one of the largest Maya cities, with a population of as many as 70,000 at its height. Like other Maya cities—yet unlike Teotihuacan, with its grid plan—Tikal conformed to the uneven terrain of the rainforest. Plazas, pyramid-temples, ballcourts, and other structures stood on high ground connected by wide elevated roads, or causeways.

Tikal was settled in the Late Preclassic period, in the fourth century BCE, and continued to flourish through the Early Classic period. The kings of Tikal were buried in funerary pyramids in the North Acropolis, visible on the left in **FIGURE 2–44**, which was separated by a wide plaza from the royal palace to the south.

Tikal suffered a major upheaval in 378 CE, recorded in texts from the city and surrounding centers, when the arrival of strangers from Teotihuacan precipitated the death of Tikal's king and the installation of a new ruler with ties to Central Mexico. Art from this period shows strong Teotihuacan influence in ceramic and architectural forms, though both were soon adapted to suit local Maya aesthetics. The city enjoyed a period of wealth and regional dominance until a military defeat led to a century of decline.

In the eighth century CE, the city of Tikal again flourished during the reign of Jasaw Chan K'awiil (nicknamed Ruler A before his name could be fully read, r. 682–734), who initiated an ambitious construction program and commissioned many stelae decorated with his own portrait. One of these, Stela 16, was dedicated on the period-ending date of 9.14.0.0.0 in the Maya calendar (December 5, 711; see "A Closer Look," page 125). His portrait fills nearly the entire space of this nearly 6-foot-tall stone. He stands with his head in profile, his body frontal, and his legs splayed out with the heels together. His elaborate costume—embellished with quetzal feathers, jade, and other precious materials—almost completely conceals his body. Ruler A's program culminated in the construction of Temple I (SEE FIG. 2–44), a tall pyramid that faces a companion pyramid, Temple II, across a large central plaza. Containing Ruler A's tomb in the limestone bedrock

To view this image, please go to page 386 of the *Art History*,
Fourth Edition by Marilyn Stokstad ebook.

2–45 • PALACE (FOREGROUND) AND TEMPLE OF THE INSCRIPTIONS
Palenque, Mexico. Maya culture. Palace, 5th–8th century CE; Temple of the Inscriptions
(Tomb of Pakal the Great), c. 683 CE.

below, Temple I rises above the forest canopy to a height of more than 140 feet. Its base has nine layers, probably reflecting the belief that the underworld had nine levels. Priests climbed the steep stone staircase on the exterior to the temple on top, which consists of two narrow, parallel rooms covered with a steep roof supported by corbel vaults. The crest that rises over the roof of the temple, known as a **roof comb**, was originally covered with brightly painted sculpture. Ritual performances on the narrow platform at the top of the pyramid would have been visible throughout the plaza. Inspired by Ruler A's building program, later kings of Tikal also built tall funerary pyramids that still tower above the rainforest canopy.

PALENQUE. The small city-state of Palenque (in the present-day Mexican state of Chiapas) rose to prominence later than Tikal, during the Classic period. Hieroglyphic inscriptions record the beginning of its royal dynasty in 431 CE, but the city had only limited regional importance until the ascension of a powerful ruler, K'inich Janahb Pakal (*pakal* is Mayan for "shield"), who ruled from 615 to 683. Known as Pakal the Great, he and his sons, who succeeded him, commissioned most of the structures visible at Palenque today. As at Tikal, urban planning responds to the

landscape. Perched on a ridge over 300 feet above the swampy lowland plains, the buildings of Palenque are terraced into the mountains with a series of aqueducts channeling rivers through the urban core. The center of the city houses the palace, the Temple of the Inscriptions, and other temples (**FIG. 2–45**). Still other temples, elite palaces, and a ballcourt surround this central group.

The palace was an administrative center as well as a royal residence. At its core was the throne room of Pakal the Great, a spacious structure whose stone roof imitated the thatched roofs of more humble dwellings. Over time, the palace grew into a complex series of buildings organized around four courtyards, where the private business of the court was transacted. From the outside, the palace presented an inviting façade of wide staircases and open colonnades decorated with stucco sculptures, but access to the interior spaces was tightly limited.

Next to the palace stands the Temple of the Inscriptions, Pakal the Great's funerary pyramid. Rising 75 feet above the plaza, it has nine levels like Temple I at Tikal (SEE FIG. 2–44). The shrine on the summit consists of a portico with five entrances and a vaulted inner chamber originally surmounted by a tall roof comb. Its façade still retains much of its stucco sculpture. The inscriptions that give the

A CLOSER LOOK

Maya Stela ▸ Stela 16
Tikal, Guatemala. Maya culture, 711 CE.

The text in this cartouche records the dedication date for this stela, 6 Ahaw 13 Muwaan (9.14.0.0.0, or December 5, 711 CE), an important period-ending date that was celebrated throughout the Maya region.

Ruler A's face peers out from all his finery. He wears large jade earspools and a long bar or nose ornament reaches out in front of his face.

Pectoral necklaces, made of jade and bone, lie above a collar of round jade beads. Jade and feathers were among the most precious materials in ancient Mesoamerica, so this costume is a stunning display of wealth.

The text in these two cartouches names Jasaw Chan K'awiil (Ruler A) as Holy Lord of Tikal and lists other of his titles.

Elaborate feathered headdress decorated with a skull mask, perhaps representing a deity that Ruler A impersonated in the dedication ceremony for this monument. Note how some of the plumes break the borders of the stela.

This feathered backrack, like the feathered headdress, may have been made out of quetzal feathers or other precious tropical plumes. These brightly colored, iridescent feathers would have shimmered as Ruler A moved.

In his hands Ruler A holds a ceremonial bar of rulership, the traditional emblem of authority of Maya kings.

Ruler A also wears a belt decorated with three jade masks, one shown frontally at the center and two shown in profile at the hips. Jade masks like these have been found at several Maya sites.

To view this image, please go to page 387 of the *Art History*, Fourth Edition by Marilyn Stokstad ebook.

SEE MORE: View the Closer Look feature for the Maya Stela **www.myartslab.com**

building its name consist of three large panels of text that line the back wall of the outer chamber at the top of the temple, linking Pakal's accomplishments to the mythical history of the city. A corbel-vaulted stairway beneath the summit shrine zigzags down 80 feet to a small subterranean chamber that contained the undisturbed tomb of Pakal, which was discovered in the 1950s.

Pakal the Great lay in a monolithic carved sarcophagus that represented him balanced between the underworld and the earth.

To view this image, please go to page 388 of the *Art History*, Fourth Edition by Marilyn Stokstad ebook.

2-46 • PORTRAIT OF PAKAL THE GREAT
From Pakal's tomb, Temple of the Inscriptions, Palenque, Mexico. Maya culture, mid 7th century CE. Stucco and red paint, height 16⅞″ (43 cm). Museo Nacional de Antropología, Mexico City.

His ancestors, carved on the sides of the sarcophagus, witness his death and apotheosis. The stucco portrait of Pakal found with his sarcophagus shows him as a young man wearing a diadem of jade and flowers **(FIG. 2–46)**. His features—sloping forehead and elongated skull (babies' heads were bound to produce this shape), large curved nose (enhanced by an ornamental bridge), full lips, and open mouth—are characteristic of the Maya ideal of beauty, that of the youthful Maize God whose stepped and upswept hairstyle this portrait adopts. His long, narrow face and jaw are individual characteristics. Traces of pigment indicate that this portrait, like much Maya sculpture, was colorfully painted.

SCULPTURE FOR LADY XOK.   Elite men and women, rather than gods, were the usual subjects of Maya sculpture, and most works show rulers performing religious rituals in elaborate costumes and headdresses. Although they excelled at three-dimensional clay and stucco sculpture (SEE FIG. 2–46), the Maya favored low relief for carving stelae and buildings. One outstanding example is a carved

lintel from a temple in the city of Yaxchilan, dedicated in 726 by Lady Xok, the principal wife and queen of the ruler nicknamed "Shield Jaguar the Great." In this retrospective image of a rite conducted when Shield Jaguar became the ruler of Yaxchilan in 681, Lady Xok conjures up a serpent vision that spews forth a warrior in Teotihuacan costume who aims his spear at the kneeling queen **(FIG. 2–47)**. The relief is unusually high, giving the sculptor ample opportunity to display a virtuoso carving technique, for example, in Lady Xok's garments and jewelry. The lintels were originally brightly painted as well. The calm idealized face of the queen recalls the portrait of Pakal the Great. That the queen commissioned her depictions on the lintels of this temple is an indication of her importance at court, and of the power that elite Maya women could attain.

To view this image, please go to page 388 of the *Art History*, Fourth Edition by Marilyn Stokstad ebook.

2-47 • LADY XOK'S VISION (ACCESSION CEREMONY)
Lintel 25 of a temple (Structure 23), Yaxchilan, Mexico. Maya culture. Dedicated in 726 CE. Limestone, 46½ × 29⅛″ (118 × 74 cm). British Museum. Acquired by the British Museum in 1883

The Cosmic Ballgame

The ritual ballgame was one of the defining characteristics of Mesoamerican society. It was generally played on a long, rectangular court with a large, solid, heavy rubber ball. Using their elbows, knees, or hips—but not their hands—heavily padded players directed the ball toward a goal or marker. The rules, size and shape of the court, the number of players on a team, and the nature of the goal varied. The largest surviving ballcourt at Chichen Itza was about the size of a modern football field. Large stone rings set in the walls of the court about 25 feet above the field served as goals.

The game was a common subject in Mesoamerican art (SEE FIG. 2–48). Players, complete with equipment, appear as ceramic figurines and on stone sculptures and painted vases. The game may have had religious and political significance: It features in creation stories, and was sometimes associated with warfare. Captive warriors might have been made to play the game, and players might have been sacrificed when the stakes were high.

PAINTING. Artists had high status in Maya society: Vase painters and scribes were sometimes members of the ruling elite, perhaps even members of the royal family. Some of our most vivid impressions of Maya courtly life and painting style come from cylindrical vessels. The example illustrated in FIGURE 2–48 shows four lords playing the ballgame, the architectural space of the ballcourt suggested by a few horizontal lines (see "The Cosmic Ballgame," above). The men wear elaborate headdresses and padded protective gear to protect them from the heavy rubber ball. The painter has chosen a moment of arrested movement: One player kneels to hit the ball—or has just hit it—while the others gesture and lean toward him. The roll-out photograph here shows the entire scene, but a person holding the vase would have to turn the vessel to see what was happening. The text running around the rim of the vase is a standard dedicatory inscription, naming it as a vessel for drinking chocolate, and tests of residues inside such vases have confirmed this use. Without sugar or milk, Maya chocolate was a very different drink from the one we are used to, a frothy and bitter beverage consumed on courtly and ritual occasions.

To view this image, please go to page 389 of the *Art History*, Fourth Edition by Marilyn Stokstad ebook.

2-48 • CYLINDRICAL VESSEL WITH BALLGAME SCENE
(Roll-out photograph) Maya culture, 600–800 CE. Painted ceramic, diameter 6⅜″ (15.9 cm), height 8⅛″ (20.5 cm).
Dallas Museum of Art. 1983.148. Gift of Mr. and Mrs. Raymond Nasher

EXPLORE MORE: Gain insight from a primary source on the Maya civilization **www.myartslab.com**

POSTCLASSIC PERIOD. After warfare and environmental crisis led to the abandonment of the lowland Maya city-states around 800, the focus of Maya civilization shifted north to the Yucatan Peninsula. One of the principal cities of the Postclassic period was Chichen Itza, which means "at the mouth of the well of the Itza," and may refer to the deep *cenote* (sinkhole) at the site that was sacred to the Maya. The city flourished from the ninth to the thirteenth century, and at its height covered about 6 square miles.

One of Chichen Itza's most conspicuous structures is a massive nine-level pyramid in the center of a large plaza, nicknamed El Castillo ("the castle" in Spanish) **(FIG. 2–49)**. A stairway on each side of the radial pyramid leads to a square temple on the summit. At the spring and fall equinoxes, the setting sun casts undulating shadows on the stairway, forming bodies for the serpent heads carved at the base of the north balustrades, pointing towards the Sacred Cenote. Many prominent features of Chichen Itza are markedly different from earlier Maya sites and hint at ties to Central Mexico, including long, colonnaded halls and inventive columns in the form of inverted, descending serpents. Brilliantly colored relief sculpture and painting covered the buildings of Chichen Itza. Many of the surviving works show narrative scenes that emphasize military conquests. Sculpture at Chichen Itza, including the serpent columns and balustrades, and the half-reclining figures known as **chacmools**, has the sturdy forms, proportions, and angularity of architecture, rather than the curving subtlety of Classic Maya sculpture. The *chacmools* may represent fallen warriors and were used to receive sacrificial offerings.

After Chichen Itza's decline, Mayapan, in the center of the Yucatan Peninsula, became the principal Maya center. But by the time the Spanish arrived in the early sixteenth century, Mayapan, too, had declined (destroyed in the mid fifteenth century), and smaller cities like Tulum, located on the Caribbean coast, were all that remained. The Maya people and much of their culture would survive the devastation of the conquest, adapting to the imposition of Hispanic customs and beliefs. Many Maya continue to speak their own languages, to venerate traditional sacred places, and to follow traditional ways.

CENTRAL AMERICA

Unlike their neighbors in Mesoamerica, who lived in complex hierarchical societies, the people of Central America lived in extended family groups, in towns led by chiefs. A notable example of these small chiefdoms was the Diquis culture (located in present-day Costa Rica), which lasted from about 700 to 1500 CE. The Diquis occupied fortified villages and seem to have engaged in constant warfare with one another. Although they did not produce monumental architecture or sculpture, they created fine featherwork, ceramics, textiles, and objects of gold and jade.

Metallurgy and the use of gold and copper-gold alloys were widespread in Central America. The technique of lost-wax casting probably first appeared in present-day Colombia between 500 and 300 BCE. From there it spread north to the Diquis. A small, exquisite pendant **(FIG. 2–50)** illustrates the style and technique of Diquis goldwork. The pendant depicts a male figure wearing bracelets, anklets, and a belt with a snake-headed penis sheath. He plays a drum while holding the tail of a snake in his teeth and its head in his left hand. The wavy forms with serpent heads emerging from his scalp suggest an elaborate headdress, and the creatures emerging from his legs suggest some kind of reptile costume. The inverted triangles on the headdress probably represent birds' tails.

In Diquis mythology, serpents and crocodiles inhabited a lower world, humans and birds a higher one. Diquis art depicts animals and insects as fierce and dangerous. Perhaps the man in the pendant is a shaman transforming himself into a composite serpent-bird or performing a ritual snake dance surrounded by serpents or crocodiles. The scrolls on the sides of his head may represent the shaman's power to hear and understand the speech of

To view this image, please go to page 390 of the *Art History*, Fourth Edition by Marilyn Stokstad ebook.

2-49 • PYRAMID ("EL CASTILLO") WITH CHACMOOL IN FOREGROUND
Chichen Itza, Yucatan, Mexico. Maya culture, 9th–12th century CE. Library, Getty Research Institute, Los Angeles.

From the top of the Temple of the Warriors, where a reclining *chacmool* sculpture graces the platform, there is a clear view of the radial pyramid nicknamed "El Castillo."

To view this image, please go to page 391 of the *Art History*, Fourth Edition by Marilyn Stokstad ebook.

2-50 • SHAMAN WITH DRUM AND SNAKE
Costa Rica. Diquis culture, c. 13–16th century CE. Gold, 4¼ × 3¼"
(10.8 × 8.2 cm). Museos del Banco Central de Costa Rica, San José,
Costa Rica.

animals. Whatever its specific meaning, the pendant evokes a ritual of mediation between earthly and cosmic powers involving music, dance, and costume.

Whether gold figures of this kind were protective amulets or signs of high status, they were certainly more than personal adornment. Shamans and warriors wore gold to inspire fear, perhaps because gold was thought to capture the energy and power of the sun. This energy was also thought to allow shamans to leave their bodies and travel into cosmic realms.

SOUTH AMERICA: THE CENTRAL ANDES

Like Mesoamerica, the central Andes of South America—primarily present-day Peru and Bolivia—saw the development of complex hierarchical societies with rich and varied artistic traditions. The area is one of dramatic contrasts. The narrow coastal plain, bordered by the Pacific Ocean on the west and the abruptly soaring Andes mountains on the east, is one of the driest deserts in the world. Life here depends on the rich marine resources of the Pacific Ocean and the rivers that descend from the Andes, forming a series of valley oases. The Andes themselves are a region of lofty

snowcapped peaks, high grasslands, steep slopes, and deep, fertile river valleys. The high grasslands are home to the Andean camelids that have served for thousands of years as beasts of burden and a source of wool and meat. The lush eastern slopes of the Andes descend to the tropical rainforest of the Amazon basin.

In contrast to developments in other parts of the world, Andean peoples developed monumental architecture and textiles long before ceramics and intensive agriculture, usually the two hallmarks of early civilization. Thus, the earliest period of monumental architecture, beginning around 3000 BCE, is called the Preceramic period. On the coast, sites with ceremonial mounds and plazas were located near the sea, while in the highlands early centers consisted of multi-roomed stone-walled structures with sunken central fire pits for burning ritual offerings. In the second millennium BCE (the Initial Period), as agriculture became more important both in the highlands and on the coast, the scale and pace of construction increased dramatically. Communities in the coastal valleys built massive U-shaped ceremonial complexes, while highland religious centers focused on sunken circular courtyards. By adding to these constructions bit by bit over generations, and using older constructions as the nucleus of new buildings, relatively small communities could generate mountain-size pyramids.

CHAVIN DE HUANTAR

Located on a trade route between the coast and the Amazon basin, the highland site of Chavin de Huantar was an important religious center between 900 and 200 BCE, home to an art style that spread through much of the Andes. In Andean chronology, this era is known as the Early Horizon, the first of three so-called Horizon periods. The period was one of artistic and technical innovation in ceramics, metallurgy, and textiles.

The architecture of Chavin synthesizes coastal and highland traditions, combining the U-shaped pyramid typical of the coast with a sunken circular plaza lined with carved reliefs, a form common in the highlands. The often fantastical animals that adorn Chavin sculpture have features of jaguars, hawks, caimans, and other tropical Amazonian beasts.

Within the U-shaped Old Temple at Chavin is a mazelike system of narrow galleries, at the very center of which lies a sculpture called the Lanzón **(FIG. 2–51)**. Wrapped around a 15-foot-tall blade-shaped stone with a narrow projection at the top—a form that may echo the shape of traditional Andean planting sticks—this complex carving depicts a powerful creature with a humanoid body, clawed hands and feet, and enormous fangs. Its eyebrows and strands of hair terminate in snakes—a kind of composite and transformational imagery shared by many Chavin images. The image is bilaterally symmetrical, except that the creature has one hand raised and the other lowered. Compact frontality, flat relief, curvilinear design, and the combination of human, animal, bird, and reptile parts characterize this early art.

It has been suggested that the Lanzón was an oracle (a chamber directly above the statue would allow priests' disembodied voices to

bodies of the dead. Some bodies were wrapped in as many as 200 pieces of cloth.

Weaving is of great antiquity in the central Andes and continues to be among the most prized arts in the region (see "Andean Textiles," page 132). Fine textiles were a source of prestige and wealth. The designs on Paracas textiles include repeated embroidered figures of warriors, dancers, and composite creatures such as bird-people (FIG. 2–52). Embroiderers used tiny overlapping stitches to create colorful, curvilinear patterns, sometimes using as many as 22 different colors within a single figure, but only one simple stitch. The effect of the clashing and contrasting colors and tumbling figures is dazzling.

NAZCA. The Nazca culture, which dominated portions of the south coast of Peru from about the year 0 to 700 CE, overlapped the Paracas culture to the north. Nazca artisans wove fine fabrics, and also produced multicolored pottery with painted and modeled images reminiscent of those on Paracas textiles.

The Nazca are best known for their colossal earthworks, or **geoglyphs**, which dwarf even the most ambitious twentieth-century environmental sculpture. On great stretches of desert they literally drew in the earth. By removing dark, oxidized stones, they exposed the light underlying stones. In this way they created gigantic images—including a hummingbird with a beak 120 feet long (FIG. 2–53), a killer whale, a monkey, a spider, a duck, and other birds—similar to those with which they decorated their pottery. They also made abstract patterns and groups of straight, parallel lines that extend for up to 12 miles. The purpose and meaning of the glyphs remain a mystery, but the "lines" of stone are wide enough to have been ceremonial pathways.

To view this image, please go to page 392 of the *Art History*, Fourth Edition by Marilyn Stokstad ebook.

2-51 • LANZÓN, CHAVIN DE HUANTAR
Peru. Chavin culture, c. 900 BCE. Height, 15′ (4.5 m). Granite.

filter into the chamber below), which would explain why people from all over the Andes made pilgrimages to Chavin, bringing exotic goods to the highland site and spreading its art style throughout the Andean region as they returned home.

THE PARACAS AND NAZCA CULTURES

While Chavin de Huantar was flourishing as a highland center whose art was enormously influential throughout the Andes, different valleys on the Pacific coast developed distinctive art styles and cultures.

PARACAS. The Paracas culture of the Peruvian south coast flourished from about 600 BCE to 200 CE, overlapping the Chavin period. It is best known for its stunning textiles, which were found in cemeteries as wrappings, in many layers, around the

To view this image, please go to page 392 of the *Art History*, Fourth Edition by Marilyn Stokstad ebook.

2-52 • MANTLE WITH BIRD IMPERSONATORS
Paracas Peninsula, Peru. Paracas culture, c. 200 BCE–200 CE. Camelid fiber, plain weave with stem-stitch embroidery (detail), approx. 40″ × 7′11″ (1.01 × 2.41 m). Museum of Fine Arts, Boston. Denman Waldo Ross Collection (16.34a)

THE MOCHE CULTURE

The Moche culture dominated the north coast of Peru from the Piura Valley to the Huarmey Valley—a distance of some 370 miles—between about 100 and 700 CE. Moche lords ruled each valley in this region from a ceremonial-administrative center. The largest of these, in the Moche Valley (from which the culture takes its name), contained the so-called Huaca del Sol (Pyramid of the Sun) and Huaca de la Luna (Pyramid of the Moon), both built of **adobe** brick (sun-baked blocks of clay mixed with straw). The Huaca del Sol, one of the largest ancient structures in South America, was originally 1,100 feet long by 500 feet wide, rising in a series of terraces to a height of 59 feet. Much of this pyramid was destroyed in the seventeenth century, when a Spanish mining company diverted a river through it to wash out the gold contained in its many burials. Recent excavations at the Huaca de la Luna have revealed brightly painted reliefs of deities, captives, and warriors, remade during successive renovations of the pyramid. This site had been thought to be the capital of the entire Moche realm, but evidence is accumulating that indicates that the Moche maintained a decentralized social network.

The Moche were exceptional potters and metalsmiths. Vessels were made in the shape of naturalistically modeled human beings, animals, and architectural structures. They developed ceramic molds, which allowed them to mass-produce some forms. They also created realistic **PORTRAIT VESSELS (FIG. 2–54)** and recorded mythological narratives and ritual scenes in intricate fine-line painting. Similar scenes were painted on the walls of temples and

To view this image, please go to page 393 of the *Art History*, Fourth Edition by Marilyn Stokstad ebook.

2-54 • MOCHE PORTRAIT VESSEL
Moche culture, Peru. c. 100–700 CE. Clay, height 11" (28 cm). Ethnologisches Museum, Staatliche Museen zu Berlin.

This is one of several portrait vessels, made from the same mold, that seems to show a particular individual.

To view this image, please go to page 393 of the *Art History*, Fourth Edition by Marilyn Stokstad ebook.

2-53 • EARTH DRAWING (GEOGLYPH) OF A HUMMINGBIRD, NAZCA PLAIN
Southwest Peru. Nazca culture, c. 0–700 CE. Length approx. 450' (137 m); wingspan approx. 220' (60.9 m).

Textiles were one of the most important forms of art and technology in Andean society. Specialized fabrics were developed for everything from ritual burial shrouds and shamans' costumes to rope bridges and knotted cords for record keeping. Clothing indicated ethnic group and social status and was customized for certain functions, the most rarefied being royal ceremonial garments made for specific occasions and worn only once. The creation of textiles, among the most technically complex cloths ever made, consumed a major portion of ancient Andean societies' resources.

Andean textile artists used two principal materials: cotton and camelid fiber. (Camelid fiber—llama, alpaca, guanaco, or vicuña hair—is the Andean equivalent of wool.) Cotton grows on the coast, while llamas, alpacas, and other camelids thrive in the highlands. The presence of cotton fibers in the highlands and camelid fibers on the coast demonstrates trade between the two regions from very early times. The production of textiles was an important factor in the domestication of both plants (cotton) and animals (llamas).

The earliest Peruvian textiles were made by twining, knotting, wrapping, braiding, and looping fibers. Those techniques continued to be used even after the invention of weaving looms in the early second millennium BCE. Most Andean textiles were woven on a simple, portable backstrap loom in which the undyed cotton warp (the lengthwise threads) was looped and stretched between two bars. One bar was tied to a stationary object and the other strapped to the waist of the weaver. The weaver controlled the tension of the warp threads by leaning back and forth while threading a shuttle from side to side to insert the weft (crosswise threads). Changing the arrangement of the warp threads between each passage of the weft created a stable interlace of warp and weft: a textile.

Andean artists used a variety of different techniques to decorate their textiles, creating special effects that were prized for their labor-intensiveness and difficulty of manufacture as well as their beauty. In tapestry weaving, a technique especially suited to representational textiles, the weft does not run the full width of the fabric; each colored section is woven as an independent unit. Embroidery with needle and thread on an already woven textile allows even greater freedom from the rigid warp-and-weft structure of the loom, allowing the artist to create curvilinear forms with thousands of tiny stitches. As even more complex techniques developed, the

production of a single textile might involve a dozen processes requiring highly skilled workers. Dyeing technology, too, was an advanced art form in the ancient Andes, with some textiles containing dozens of colors.

Because of their complexity, deciphering how these textiles were made can be a challenge, and scholars rely on contemporary Andean weavers—inheritors of this tradition—for guidance. Now, as then, fiber and textile arts are primarily in the hands of women.

To view this image, please go to page 394 of the *Art History*, Fourth Edition by Marilyn Stokstad ebook.

MANTLE WITH BIRD IMPERSONATORS (DETAIL)
From the Paracas Peninsula, Peru. Paracas culture, c. 200 BCE–200 CE. Camelid fiber, plain weave with stem-stitch embroidery. Museum of Fine Arts, Boston. Denman Waldo Ross Collection (16.34a)

administrative buildings. Moche metalsmiths, the most sophisticated in the central Andes, developed several innovative metal alloys.

THE TOMB OF THE WARRIOR PRIEST. A central theme in Moche iconography is the sacrifice ceremony, in which prisoners captured in battle are sacrificed and several elaborately dressed figures then drink their blood. Archaeologists have labeled the principal figure in the ceremony as the Warrior Priest and other important figures as the Bird Priest and the Priestess. The recent discovery of a number of spectacularly rich Moche tombs indicates that the

sacrifice ceremony was an actual Moche ritual and that Moche lords and ladies assumed the roles of the principal figures. The occupant of a tomb at Sipán, in the Lambayeque Valley on the northwest coast, was buried with the regalia of the Warrior Priest. In tombs at the site of San José de Moro, just south of Sipán, several women were buried with the regalia of the Priestess.

Among the riches accompanying the Warrior Priest at Sipán was a pair of exquisite gold-and-turquoise **EARSPOOLS**, each of which depicts three Moche warriors (**FIG. 2–55**). The central figure bursts into three dimensions, while his companions are shown in profile, in a flat inlay technique. All three are adorned

To view this image, please go to page 395 of the *Art History*, Fourth Edition by Marilyn Stokstad ebook.

with tiny gold-and-turquoise earspools, simpler versions of the object they themselves adorn. They wear gold-and-turquoise headdresses topped with delicate sheets of gold that resemble the crescent-shaped knives used in sacrifices. The central figure has a crescent-shaped nose ornament and carries a removable gold club and shield. A necklace of owl's-head beads strung with gold thread hangs around his shoulders; similar objects have been found in other tombs at Sipán. These earspools illustrate some of the most notable features of Moche art: its capacity for naturalism and its close attention to detail.

2-55 • EARSPOOL
Sipán, Peru. Moche culture, c. 300 CE. Gold, turquoise, quartz, and shell, diameter approx. 3″ (9.4 cm). Bruning Archaeological Museum, Lambayeque, Peru.

To view this image, please go to page 2 of the *Graphic Design History*,
Second Edition by Johanna Drucker and Emily McVarish ebook.

2-56 • STENCILED HAND, PECH MERLE, FRANCE, 23,000–18,000 BCE
The urge to make marks is a fundamental human impulse. Creating external symbols gives back an image of the self while leaving a sign in the world. The stenciled hand shown here is thousands of years old, but similar signs can be found throughout history. Graphic design arises from the relation between that basic impulse and the system of communication that connects individuals within a culture. The impulse toward personal expression and compliance with convention are the twin engines of all graphic design.

- From its beginnings, **graphic** communication has depended not only on workable tools and production processes but also on **visual** principles and the design of **symbolic forms** (**signs** and images) that can be recognized according to the conventions and beliefs of a community.

- The design of **proto-writing** systems introduced the first stable codes for graphic **representation** of things and quantities by signs and tokens.

- The meaningful organization of graphic signs depended on compositional principles, such as juxtaposition, sequence, **hierarchy**, and direction, that followed systematic rules.

- The impulse to design symbolic forms suggests that humans do not simply use signs to record their needs and activities but place great value on the representation of *ideas*.

- Literate culture developed when a social group agreed on conventions for the representation of **language** by a **visual code**. The effects of writing as a form of social control and power spring from this consensus.

Cro-Magnon culture in Europe laid the foundations for graphic **communication** in cave paintings and other designs around 35,000 BCE. Prehistoric artists shared a visual vocabulary, indicating that they worked within a system of socially recognized **conventions**. They organized their surfaces to support **figure** and **ground** distinctions and used forms consistently for their **symbolic value** as signs. This systematic use of signs is the basis of communication. On these foundations, proto-writing took shape in tokens and seals after about 10,000 BCE. By 3000 BCE, more specialized tools for carving, inscribing, and marking were developed and used on material supports of varying durability, such as clay, stone, papyrus, skin, bone, wax, metal, and wood. But the design of writing as a stable **code** to represent language depended on more than tools and media. It required the conceptual linkage of visual signs to a linguistic system. The shapes of the first **glyphs**, **letters**, and signs are related to present-day **alphabetic** and **character**-based **scripts**. Our writing still uses versions of some of the earliest written **symbols** ever invented. Writing changed the power of language by aligning it with the administration of culture through economic, political, religious, and other social activities. Writing conveyed laws and constraints that could be enforced by symbolic rather than physical force. The uses and effects of written language distinguish **literate** from **oral** cultures. Oral communication is ephemeral and takes place in real-time circumstances that rely on presence. **Inscriptions** and textual records can reach contexts that are remote in time and space from their author or moment of origin (**FIG. 2–56**).

MARK-MAKING

Mark-making is the most basic form of graphic expression and design. Drawing a line in the sand or making a handprint on a wall is a direct sign of individual identity. Such imprints have a curious existence: a mark that is a sign of the self is also always *other* than the self. Once made, **marks** exist independently of their makers. A line makes a division, whether in physical space as a boundary or in an intellectual zone to define a category. Differentiating between marked and unmarked things is a conceptual act of enormous significance. We might even suggest that the idea of **difference** forms the basis of human knowledge, and that the making of a mark is the primary way of inscribing such difference. On this simple principle of differentiation, we can structure the complicated oppositions of I/you, this/that, self/other, and subject/object, which form our understanding of the world. Marks are not only different from each other but also distinct from the ground on which they are made and from the **intervals** that separate them. We take these notions for granted and rarely pause to consider the conceptual leap required for their development (**FIG. 2–57**).

PREHISTORY

The terms Paleolithic, Mesolithic, and Neolithic describe states of cultural complexity, not chronological periods, and occur at different moments in different parts of the world. In Western Europe, by about 35,000 BCE, Paleolithic (Stone Age) sculptures and cave paintings exhibit the high level of craft that characterizes Cro-Magnon art. **Artifacts** of this period can be considered the origin of graphic design insofar as they present clear evidence of conscious decisions about form. They often feature decorative images and marks. Their striking shapes, styles, and imagery carry information about social and ritual practices and have thus been the focus of **anthropological** study. These artifacts have much to tell us about the **technological** and cultural

2-57 • PAINTED STONES, MAS-D'AZIL, FRANCE, 10,000 BCE

These are some of the earliest remains of systematic mark-making. The careful graphic execution and regular repetition of marks indicate deliberate intention. Though too few in number to represent a language, they may have been conventionalized representations of things. The stick-figure form is referred to as the "hallelujah man" because it appears to be a person with arms raised in jubilation. This sign, like the other simple forms on these rocks, is common to many so-called "primitive" systems of marks. Even when they develop independently, human scripts often share formal characteristics. This does not suggest that a "**universal**" code underlies all writing but rather, pragmatically, that simple lines and shapes can be combined in a certain number of fairly predictable ways.

conditions that produced them. They show us that human beings could imagine a shape and purpose for an object independent of their embodiment in a specific thing. These people had ideas about form-giving and an abstract model in mind to guide tool-making (**FIG. 2–58**).

Cro-Magnon painters approached their subjects realistically. Dating from 15,000–10,000 BCE, renderings of bison, deer, and other game in the cave art of Altamira, Spain, and Lascaux, France are still recognizable. But the graphic qualities of these images go beyond **likeness**. The **composition**, elegance of line, care in pro-

duction, and considerations of scale, color, and pattern in these paintings display a considerable investment in the quality of their visual design. These artists did not simply use raw materials lifted from the campfire but mixed their **pigments** deliberately. Evidence of advanced material preparation implies a pause between conception and execution that allows for critical reflection upon the act of making. This gap between thinking and making is crucial to all forms of design. As for the meaning of cave art, it has traditionally been interpreted as a form of sympathetic hunting magic. More recent theories suggest that these graphic forms are the symbolic expression of a worldview rather than simply an attempt to gain power over the uncertain forces of nature. The realization that prehistoric graphic signs embody values and express beliefs places them on a continuum that includes contemporary design (**FIG. 2–59**).

> Prehistoric graphic signs embody values and express beliefs.

PROTO-WRITING

The Mesolithic period (or Middle Stone Age)—about 10,000–7000 BCE—is characterized by the development of agriculture, leading to the rise of cities and civic organization in the ancient Middle East. It is also marked by a huge leap in graphic communication: the appearance of proto-writing. This development is linked to changes in the social organization of human settlements, such as the appearance of city structures within clearly defined boundaries (the walls in the ancient city of Jericho were 13 feet high by 8000 BCE). The invention of proto-writing coincides with the successful cultivation of hard grains (capable of being stored without rotting) at the beginning of the Neolithic period (or New Stone Age)—about 8000–4000 BCE—in the ancient Mesopotamian region. When more of this grain could be grown in a season than was needed for immediate or local use, accounting systems became necessary to help monitor its ownership, distribution, and storage. For the first time, these systems relied on symbols designed to signify numerical values and specific objects in the world. After about 8000 BCE, the numeric

2-58 • CARVED SPEAR THROWER, MAS-D'AZIL, FRANCE, 16,000-9000 BCE

Carved tools and other decorated artifacts have been found among human settlements dating back to the Upper Paleolithic period (the last phase of the Old Stone Age), about 40,000–10,000 BCE, although humans first made crude tools as early as 2.6 million years ago. Design clearly mattered in the crafting of these objects. Considerable effort went into shaping and decorating them. The care taken suggests that the object's symbolic purpose was as important as its effectiveness in propelling a spear. The ability to create meaningful patterns and attach symbolic value to forms is a distinctly human characteristic. Other animals may produce exquisitely shaped or highly organized nests, dances, or songs, but no other animal makes recognizable **effigies** or adds decoration to its tools or environment.

To view this image, please go to page 5 of the *Graphic Design History*, Second Edition by Johanna Drucker and Emily McVarish ebook.

2-59 • CAVE PAINTING, ALTAMIRA, SPAIN, 16,000-9000 BCE

When the cave paintings at Altamira, Spain, were discovered in the late 1870s, they created a sensation. Far from being primitive expressions by unskilled artists, these paintings were sophisticated at every level of conception and execution. Because they were recognized as finely made, they challenged concepts of progress in art. The figures are clear and distinct, and the ground on which they appear is a well-prepared and organized surface. These paintings are not only powerful **aesthetic** expressions, they also document a long history. Successive waves of climate change, for example, were recorded in cave art. Images of reindeer, painted on earlier layers, were replaced by those of ibexes and other animals as the ice sheets receded in later millennia. Although drawn from memory, the images are naturalistic. What is remarkable, however, is how much similarity exists among cave paintings. This striking fact shows that a distinct set of visual conventions had been established for producing artworks. Although it would be a stretch to call the world of prehistoric cave painters a **design community**, rules governing what was formally possible and acceptable were followed by these artists. The artists did not simply invent visual solutions at random in response to circumstances or impulses. They produced highly organized works of art, designed according to formal and cultural conventions. This social basis for form arguably marks the beginning of graphic communication.

To view this image, please go to page 6 of the *Graphic Design History*, Second Edition by Johanna Drucker and Emily McVarish ebook.

2-60 • CLAY TOKENS, SUSA, IRAN, FOURTH MILLENNIUM BCE

These regularly shaped objects served as a form of notation for business transactions. Their shapes each corresponded to a different category of agricultural product. The marks on their surfaces were highly schematic and used for detailed accounting. When these tokens were pressed into wet clay, their imprints were part of a graphic system in which relative size, shape, orientation, and groupings were all significant. These tokens demonstrate the emergence of a set of sophisticated graphic principles. The spatial organization of the surface and the elaboration of rules governing the use of visual signs are evidence of graphic refinement. This notation system is still not considered "writing" because that term designates the representation of language, and these tokens are basically accounting receipts or tallies.

and **pictographic** signs of this proto-writing were used on tokens and clay tablets to mark ownership and quantities of goods. Proto-writing systems made use of fundamental **graphic principles** to order the shape, size, placement, and sequence of signs. Accounting tokens were designed to make impressions in clay. These impressions were precursors to the wedge-shaped signs of **cuneiform**, probably the oldest system of actual writing (**FIG. 2–60**).

EARLY WRITING

Graphic **media** entered a new era when writing proper evolved in ancient Mesopotamia around 3200 BCE, in the so-called Fertile Crescent that lies between the Tigris and Euphrates rivers. Fully developed writing has the capacity to represent language in a stable system of signs, and cuneiform is the first known example of such a system. Egyptian writing may have been a simultaneous development, or it may have evolved, in part, as an imitation of cuneiform scripts. In China, writing emerged after 1500 BCE, apparently independently, although some debate suggests cultural influences from Europe to Asia. Glyphic writing originated in Mesoamerican cultures around 900 BCE, in advance of contact with Europeans, and has its own graphic rules (**FIGS. 2–61A** and **2–61B**).

Cuneiform was first used to represent ancient Sumerian, one of a handful of languages that have never been deciphered. The

> Fully developed writing has the capacity to represent language.

number of cuneiform signs suggests that they represented words in a **logographic** script. Signs recovered from sites like the city of Uruk in ancient Sumeria indicate pictographic origins, but these Sumerian **pictograms** soon became schematized so that they could be drawn in a few quick strokes of the stylus on a soft tablet. Writing and sign-making were directly related to administrative tasks and the social structures that enable civil societies. For instance, by 3000 BCE, the state bureaucracy of Uruk had ten different numerical systems in use, each associated with a specialized sphere of activity. Writing codified law, and its enforcement came to supplement (and sometimes replace) violence as an instrument of power (**FIG. 2–62**).

2-62 • CLAY TABLET WITH CUNEIFORM, IRAQ, 3000 BCE (ABOVE)
The signs on this clay tablet are considered an early form of cuneiform writing. Made with many small strokes, the signs seem to be drawings of particular things. The pictorial origins of cuneiform can be traced in these and other artifacts. These signs are considered writing because they can be related to the sounds in the Sumerian language. The visual structure of cuneiform tablets is well ordered. The surface is usually divided into columns and/or rows, either by visible or implied lines. The size and spacing of the marks are regular, and their rhythm has a momentum that carries the eye forward. The marks are grouped according to a system which, visually, is as elaborate a code for language as speech is verbally. Graphic organization aids the signs' production of meaning.

2-61A • CHINESE WRITING, SECOND MILLENNIUM BCE TO THE PRESENT
The transformation of Chinese characters from their pictorial origins to schematic signs happened with relative rapidity. Chinese characters most frequently represent either words or sounds, or some combination of the two. No writing system that required a sign for every word would be practical. The adaptation of characters for Japanese, Korean, and other languages demonstrates the versatility of Chinese script.

To view this image, please go to page 6 of the *Graphic Design History*, Second Edition by Johanna Drucker and Emily McVarish ebook.

2-61B • DRESDEN CODEX, YUCATAN, 1200–1250 CE (RIGHT)
Mesoamerican writing, both Mayan and Aztec, appears to have been an independent invention and has a uniquely graphic feature: it uses spatial organization in a meaningful way, arranging different elements of language such as prefixes and suffixes so that they are legible according to their placement around a central glyph. Mayan glyphs take advantage of visual structure in a manner very different from that of alphabetic sequence or cuneiform and **hieroglyphic** organizations. These glyphs can be very elaborate, with additional graphic elements known as **attributes** spreading over a large area. Although the earliest existing artifacts of Mayan writing date to only about 200–300 CE, some scholars believe that the system evolved from earlier practices. In the sixteenth century, European conquerors destroyed the majority of Mayan and Aztec codices and written documents, making recovery of this history almost impossible.

To view this image, please go to page 7 of the *Graphic Design History*, Second Edition by Johanna Drucker and Emily McVarish ebook.

Cuneiform script spread through the ancient Near East and was used extensively across various cultures and languages for diplomatic purposes in the third and second millennia BCE. The popularity of cuneiform reached its peak in about 1400 BCE, when its diplomatic use extended throughout a region that included present-day Iraq, Turkey, Syria, Egypt, Palestine, Lebanon, and Israel. Cuneiform signs were used by language groups from Indo-European, Afro-Asiatic, and other families. The adoption of a **writing system** developed for one language by another is a pattern that is repeated many times in the history of scripts **(FIG. 2–63)**.

THE SPREAD OF WRITING AS IDEA AND SCRIPT

The *idea* of writing that developed with cuneiform may have been as influential as the actual script. Both spread to other areas in the ancient Near East. A host of scripts developed throughout the ancient Near and Middle East in the second millennium BCE, varying in form from hybrids of cuneiform and pictographic scripts to advanced **schematic** sign systems. But only a few sustained widespread use. The oldest artifacts containing Egyptian hieroglyphics—from the Greek words *hiero* ("sacred") and *glyph* ("carving")—show them almost fully developed. Many of their standard shapes were already set by the time they were adopted in 3200–3100 BCE. Little **archeological** evidence exists for dating Egyptian hieroglyphs any earlier **(FIG. 2–64)**.

Connections between the Egyptian writing system and those of the ancient Near East are debated. Some evidence of cultural influence can be found along the trade routes that passed through Syria. In any case, hieroglyphics did not spread. Both hieroglyphics and cuneiform fell out of use, although for different reasons. Hieroglyphics were banned when Christianity became the state religion in Egypt in the fourth century CE, while cuneiform was displaced by the more efficient alphabetic system beginning in the second millennium BCE **(FIG. 2–65)**.

To view this image, please go to page 8 of the *Graphic Design History*, Second Edition by Johanna Drucker and Emily McVarish ebook.

2-63 • DEVELOPMENT OF CUNEIFORM, 3100–600 BCE
The need for efficiency in writing systems propelled simplification from pictorial to schematic signs. A stylus in wet clay made some marks more easily than others, and the orientation as well as the shape and combination of these marks changed as writing became stabilized. Sumerian **linear** and cuneiform marks from about 2400 BCE were adopted by successive peoples in the same geographic regions: Akkadians, Babylonians, and Assyrians each used cuneiform for their own distinct language. Not only was cuneiform graphically efficient, but also it represented an enormous conceptual advancement: it was a fully developed, adaptable written code for language.

2-64 • HIEROGLYPHICS, LINTEL FROM THE REIGN OF SESOSTRIS III, EGYPT, 1887–1850 BCE

An underlying grid organizes these signs into quadrants according to a principle of graphic efficiency rather than grammar. Hieroglyphics were meaningful as representations of words and syllables, but their direction and groupings were also significant. Signs in proximity were read as a unit. Note that a graphic system constrains the size of these signs. Objects that are very unlike in scale are allotted the same unitary area in conformance with a distinct design principle. Although figurative in their appearance, hieroglyphics could represent words (**logograms**), sounds (**phonograms**), or categories (**determinatives**). Determinatives, or classifiers, were used to clarify the meaning of sign combinations. For instance, one combination of signs means "to be stable," unless it is accompanied by the image of a sparrow, the sign for evil, in which case it is read as "to be bad."

To view this image, please go to page 9 of the *Graphic Design History*, Second Edition by Johanna Drucker and Emily McVarish ebook.

2-65 • HIERATIC AND DEMOTIC SCRIPTS, 2900–100 BCE

The evolution of a **hieratic** script from hieroglyphic forms provided a far more efficient system that could be written quickly with a brush and ink. **Demotic** script represented an even more schematic, informal writing form used for daily occasions. The more elaborate pictorial forms of hieroglyphics were used for formal, official purposes. After the Greek conquest of Egypt around 332 BCE, by Alexander the Great, hieroglyphics took on their arcane and esoteric associations. The priestly caste introduced a deliberate obscurity into the use of hieroglyphics as a way of resisting Greek influence.

To view this image, please go to page 9 of the *Graphic Design History*, Second Edition by Johanna Drucker and Emily McVarish ebook.

THE ALPHABET

The letters used in the type on this page first appeared in a limited, schematic system in the cosmopolitan Canaanite culture that flourished in the Sinai region 4,000 years ago. This system consisted of about twenty signs and combined the simplified forms of the Egyptian hieratic script with principles of sound representation that were the basis of cuneiform **syllabaries**. The efficiency and flexibility of the early alphabet represented an advance over both of these precedents. The order of the letters seems to have been fixed almost from the outset. Archaeological remains reveal that this sequence was used as a guide for assembling architectural elements in the building of temples (**FIG. 2–66**).

The alphabet was a remarkable invention. The letters were assigned names as an aid to memory and use. A word beginning with a given letter was often used as that letter's name. According to this **acrophonic** principle, the early *a* was called *aleph* (from the Hebrew word for "ox"), and *b* was *beth* (from the Hebrew word for "house"). The letters' shapes were not necessarily derived from an ox and a house, but their schematic forms resembled these objects enough to make taking their names work as a memory device. No myth is more persistent than that of the pictorial origin of the alphabet. Actually, the schematic and arbitrary nature of alphabetic signs was partly responsible for their efficiency and rapid spread. Easily drawn, alphabetic letters could be combined to represent the sounds of many languages. When disseminated by Phoenician

Many different scripts developed in the ancient Near East. All of these scripts are directly related to the earliest formation of the alphabet. This chart shows some of the stages through which the alphabet passed. New developments did not always replace earlier ones. Some changes occurred as the alphabet spread through various geographical and cultural locations. Others occurred over time, or in response to cultural influences and technical constraints imposed by the availability of materials.

To view this image, please go to page 10 of the *Graphic Design History*, Second Edition by Johanna Drucker and Emily McVarish ebook.

traders who sailed throughout the Mediterranean region, the alphabet gained a foothold among Etruscan and Greek people who spoke quite different tongues. The alphabet also spread into northern Africa, throughout the Middle East, into India, and beyond **(FIGS. 2–67A** and **2.67B)**.

The alphabet's development, spread, and longevity are proof of its viability as a system of writing. Some variations of the **alphabetic script**, such as those found in Arabic and Indonesian writing, look so different from our letters that it is difficult to see their connection. Yet the order, number, and even names of the letters indicate the common origin of these scripts. Myths and misconceptions continue to surround the history of writing. Many scholars place the beginnings of **literacy** at the time of the Greek alphabet's consolidation of vowel **notation**. Yet the list of cultural accomplishments and written texts that predate the advent of the Greek alphabet is a long one. On this list are the ancient Near Eastern tale of Gilgamesh with its legend of the flood; the Babylonian law code of Hammurabi; the developed philosophical systems of India and Asia; successes of astronomy, navigation, cartography; civic structures and administration; and advanced arts of poetry **(FIG. 2–68)**.

CONCLUSION

The cultural impact of writing was so far-reaching that it was considered by many societies to have been a divine gift. Its invention seemed beyond the skills of any mere mortal. The creation of writing was attributed to the tracks of birds, the constellations in the heavens, the Indian god Ganesh, the Egyptian deity Thoth, and the tablets Moses brought down from Mount Sinai. The Greeks attributed responsibility to Prometheus, who, according to legend, stole writing from the gods along with fire, thereby incurring eternal

punishment. Theoretical distinctions between oral and literate cultures stress the power of written documents to **codify** law, produce historical records, **objectify** experience, and facilitate rational, logical processes. Oral cultures, by contrast, rely on reinforcing memory by means of repetition or rhythmic pattern and tend to see language as a form of action (naming, telling, performing) associated with events in the present. In literate cultures, a record has its own existence, independent of its original context. The authority of the written word derives, in part, from this ability to circulate independently. The permanence of a written record lends its autonomy a power that is almost mythic **(FIG. 2–69)**.

To view this image, please go to page 11 of the *Graphic Design History*, Second Edition by Johanna Drucker and Emily McVarish ebook.

2-67A • ORIGINS AND DEVELOPMENT OF ALPHABETIC SCRIPTS, 3500 BCE–900 CE
The incredible variety of forms into which alphabets have evolved creates the illusion of a proliferation of different scripts. In fact, most of the alphabets of the world are derived from a single source whose sequence and basic forms provided a foundation for scripts in Africa, the Near East, Asia, Europe, and the Americas. Chinese characters are the other successful script form and, like the alphabet, were adopted and modified for use across a remarkable number of languages.

To view this image, please go to page 12 of the *Graphic Design History*, Second Edition by Johanna Drucker and Emily McVarish ebook.

2-67B • FUNERARY STELE, GREECE, 459 BCE

The regular, simplified shapes of Greek lettering on this funerary stele fill space in a stable and ordered way that seems to indicate the influence of geometry on design. But the most important Greek contribution to the alphabet was the addition of signs to represent vowels around 700 BCE. The new letters can be seen throughout this inscription. In early alphabetic scripts, vowel sounds were indicated by small dots or points (later known by the term *matres lectionis*—or "aids for reading"). The Greeks' Indo-European language depended more heavily on vowels to clarify the meaning of words than did the Semitic language spoken by the alphabet's inventors, hence their addition.

2-68 • HAMMURABI'S CODE, IRAQ, EIGHTEENTH CENTURY BCE

This stele is inscribed with a detailed code of law, governing behavior in daily Babylonian life. Hammurabi's code is the oldest existing written document of laws. It consists of several hundred laws, concerning all aspects of life: conspiracy, marriage, rape, slavery, property, damages for negligence, and so on. The code provides a great deal of information about gender roles. It shows that women were in business in Babylonia and had certain rights with respect to adultery and childbearing. The image depicts Hammurabi receiving the gift of law from Shamash, the god of justice.

To view this image, please go to page 12 of the *Graphic Design History*, Second Edition by Johanna Drucker and Emily McVarish ebook.

To view this image, please go to page 13 of the *Graphic Design History*, Second Edition by Johanna Drucker and Emily McVarish ebook.

2-69 • RUNES, CA. 600 CE

Runes were a version of the alphabet invented by Germanic and Scandinavian people in the early centuries of the Common Era. The *futhark* alphabet is one of the earliest of such rune writing systems and consists of only twenty-four characters. Although runes are frequently associated with mysterious cults and ritual practices, they are really just another modification of the alphabet whose forms were determined largely by the tools and materials of wood and stone inscription. Runes are somewhat different in form than Latin letters, and each has a distinctive name. The significance attributed to these names fostered the use of runes as signs with magical properties, not just as a practical means for expressing language.

From Prehistory to Early Writing, 35,000–500 BCE

2 billion years ago	Protozoan life forms
300 million years ago	Life on land, amphibians and reptiles
65–55 million years ago	**Paleocene epoch: warm, tropical, proto-primates like lemurs**
40 million years ago	Proto-monkeys
25–5 million years ago	**Miocene epoch: beginning of human evolution as distinctive branch**
4 million years ago	Australopithecus, early hominid
2–1.5 million years ago	Advanced australopithecus and proto-human use of tools
1.8 million–10,000 years ago	**Pleistocene epoch: Homo erectus**
700,000 years ago	Erectines (upright hominids) throughout Africa and Asia
220,000–30,000 years ago	Neanderthals, a separate species, coexist with modern humans
150,000 years ago	Homo sapiens sapiens develops and begins displacing Neanderthals
	Evidence of language through tools and social organization
100,000 years ago	Migration of Homo sapiens into Middle East, then India, East Asia, Australia
40,000 years ago	Migration to Europe (Stone Age people, Cro-Magnon culture)
34,000 years ago	First cave art
19,000 years ago	Warming trends: migration to North America over Bering Strait
12,000–6,000 years ago	**Mesolithic period**
12,000 years ago	End of glaciation, earliest settlements in Americas
9000–8500 BCE	Major cities developing in Levant, including Jericho
8000 BCE	Limited navigation of Mediterranean
8000–6000 BCE	Fired clay pottery and clay tokens for agricultural economy
6000–3500 BCE	**Neolithic period in Middle East**
6000–5000 BCE	Cultivation of hard grains, irrigation, early civic bureaucracy in Sumer
5000 BCE	Saharan region dry, population migrates toward Nile valley
4000–2000 BCE	**Neolithic culture in Europe**
4000s BCE	Ancient Egyptian culture begins
3700–2700 BCE	Clay tokens enclosed in envelopes
3200 BCE	Primitive sailboats in Egypt
3100 BCE	Cuneiform script used as a syllabary by Sumerians
	Hieroglyphics make their first appearance in Egypt
3000 BCE	Yams, coffee, watermelon, gourds cultivated in West Africa
	Narmer Palette; coherent sentences and stable hieroglyphics in Egypt
2800 BCE	Egyptian lunar calendar established with twenty-eight-day cycle
2800 BCE	Rice cultivated in China
2800–1500 BCE	Stonehenge built in stages
2650–2000 BCE	*Legend of Gilgamesh* composed (with flood narrative)
2600–1800 BCE	Indus Valley script and culture flourish and disappear
2575–2465 BCE	Great pyramids and Sphinx constructed at Giza
2500–2300 BCE	Biblical flood
2300–1400 BCE	Minoan civilization in Crete
2000–1500 BCE	Age of patriarchs Abraham, Isaac, and Jacob
1800 BCE	Early Bronze Age in China

1750 BCE	Signs of zodiac invented in Babylonia
1700 BCE	Canaanites and proto-alphabet
1700–1400 BCE	Palace at Knossos built
1600 BCE	Hittites adopt cuneiform for Indo-European language
	Volcano erupts on island of Santorini (legendary Atlantis)
1500 BCE	Iron perfected by Hittites
	Earliest remaining Egyptian *Book of the Dead*
	Earliest Olmec culture in Mesoamerica
	Hindu religion brought by nomads to India
1447 BCE	Exodus of Jews from Egypt begins
1400 BCE	Cuneiform peaks as diplomatic script in Near East
1325 BCE	Death of King Tutankhamun
1300 BCE	Shang dynasty in China, earliest oracle writing
1100 BCE	Phoenicians adopt, modify, and spread Canaanite alphabet
1100–1000 BCE	Etruscans settle in southern Italy
1000 BCE	Mayan culture begins in Mesoamerica
900s BCE	Phoenician traders from Syrian coast go as far as Spain
900 BCE	*I Ching*, oldest Chinese classical text composed
650 BCE	Phoenicians circumnavigate Africa
	Assurbanipal's library contains 22,000 tablets
600 BCE	Hanging gardens of Babylon built by Nebuchadnezzar II
582–500 BCE	Life of Pythagoras, Greek mathematician
580–500 BCE	Life of Lao Tzu, founder of Taoism
531 BCE	Enlightenment of Siddhartha (Buddha)

TOOLS OF THE TRADE

Pigments (animal, vegetable, mineral)

Ash and charcoal

Water

Spittle (medium)

Hands

Mouth (spray)

Flint burins

Bone tools

Metal blades for knives and chisels

Primitive stencils

Frayed twigs and notched sticks

Animal skin and leather

Knotted cords

Surfaces of stone, marble, clay, wood, papyrus, wax

Animal fat, candles, oil lamps

Ink from soot, water, gum arabic

Reed, wood, and bone styluses

Hair and reed brushes

Limestone flakes as surface

Cloth

Carved seals

Lead

Gold

Glass (after 2500 BCE)

Candles

Oil lamps (nut and olive oils, fats)

ADDITIONAL READINGS

THE THREE JEWELS

The recitation of the formula 'I go for refuge to the Buddha. I go for refuge to the dharma. *I go for refuge to the* sangha' *(recited three times) is the most fundamental Buddhist practice, the Buddhist correlate to the confession of faith. The practice of taking refuge is said to derive from the days following the Buddha's enlightenment. He had remained in the vicinity of the Bodhi tree meditating for seven weeks, without eating. A deity informed two passing merchants that a nearby* yogin *had recently achieved buddhahood and suggested that they pay their respects. They offered him his first meal as a buddha (some honey cakes), which he received in a bowl provided for him by the four gods of the cardinal directions. They then bowed down before him and said, 'We take refuge in the Buddha and in the* dharma.' *(Because the Buddha did not yet have any disciples, there was no* sangha.) *The Buddha presented them with a lock of his hair and his fingernails and instructed them to enshrine them in a* stūpa.

The refuge formula itself was prescribed by the Buddha shortly thereafter. After the conversion of his five old friends, all of whom became arhats, *the Buddha taught the* dharma *to the wealthy merchant's son Yasa and fifty-four of his friends. They also became monks and* arhats, *bringing to sixty the number of enlightened disciples. The Buddha then sent them out to teach, explaining that a monk could admit a layman into the monkhood if he shaved his hair and beard, donned a yellow robe, bowed at the monk's feet, and then, sitting on his heels with joined palms, said three times, 'I go for refuge to the Buddha. I go for refuge to the* dharma. *I go for refuge to the* sangha.' *(This method of ordination was later replaced.)*

The Buddha, the dharma, *and the* sangha *are called the three jewels* (triratna), *because they are rare and of great value. Given the centrality of the refuge formula as the point of entry into the practice of Buddhism and as the sign that distinguishes the Buddhist from the followers of other teachers, it is unsurprising that these three terms, their definition, their relation to each other and the significance of their order received extensive commentary, which often made clever use of true and false cognates, of which Buddhist scholars are so fond. The word* dharma *is derived from the Sanskrit root* √dhṛ, *meaning 'to hold'. It is explained, then, that the* dharma *is that which upholds those who follow the path and holds them back from falling into suffering. Exactly what the* dharma *is is much discussed, with some holding that the true* dharma *is only* nirvāna, *others saying that it includes both* nirvāna *and the path to it. Others speak of the verbal* dharma, *the spoken explication of the path, and the realized* dharma, *the manifestation of those teachings in one's mind. The constitution of the* sangha *is also considered. Although the term is used loosely to include the community of Buddhists, in the refuge formula it is used more exclusively to include those who have achieved at least the first level of the path and are destined to achieve* nirvāna. *The Buddha is mentioned first because he is the teacher of refuge; the* dharma *is mentioned next because it is the actual refuge; the* sangha *is mentioned third because it is they who help others to find that refuge.*

The three jewels are also explained in terms of similes, as in the selection that follows. It is drawn from a text called Paramatthajotikā *('Illustrator of the Ultimate Meaning'), traditionally ascribed to the great scholar monk Buddhaghosa (fourth to fifth century* CE), *commenting on the refuge formula as it appears in a Pali text called the* Khuddakapāṭha *('Minor Readings').*

The Buddha is like the full moon; the *dharma* taught by him is like the shedding of the moon's effulgence; and the *sangha* is like the world inspired with happiness by the effulgence of the full moon. The Buddha is like the rising sun; the *dharma* as already stated is like the web of his rays; and the *sangha* is like the world rid by him of darkness. The Buddha is like a man who burns a jungle; the *dharma*, which burns up the jungle of defilements, is like the fire which burns the jungle; and the *sangha*, which has become a field of merit since its defilements have been burnt up, is like the piece of ground which has become a field [for sowing] since its jungle has been burnt up. The Buddha is like the great rain-cloud; the *dharma* is like a downpour of rain; and the *sangha*, in which the dust of defilement has been laid, is like the countryside in which the dust has been laid by the fall of rain. The Buddha is like a good trainer [of thoroughbreds]; the true *dharma* is like the means for the disciplining of thoroughbred horses; and the *sangha* is like a mass of well-disciplined thoroughbreds. The Buddha is like a dart-extractor because he removes all darts of [wrong] views; the *dharma* is like the means for removing the darts; and the *sangha*, from whom the darts of [wrong] views have been removed, is like people from whom darts have been removed. Or else the Buddha is like a lancet-user because he dissects away the cataract of delusion; the *dharma* is like the means for dissecting the cataract away; and the *sangha*, whose eye of knowledge is cleared by the dissecting away of the cataract of delusion, is like people whose eyes are cleared with the dissecting away of the cataract. Or else the Buddha is like a clever physician because he is able to cure the sickness consisting in defilement by underlying tendencies; the *dharma* is like a rightly applied medicine; and the *sangha*, whose underlying tendencies to the sickness of defilement are quite cured, is like people whose sickness is quite cured by the application of the medicine. Or else the Buddha is like a good guide; the *dharma* is like a good path to a land of safety; and the *sangha* is like [people] who enter upon the path and reach the land of safety. The Buddha is like a good pilot; the *dharma* is like a ship; and the *sangha* is like people who have succeeded in reaching the farther shore. The Buddha is like the Himalaya Mountain; the *dharma* is like the healing herbs that are given their being by that mountain; and the *sangha* is like people free from ailment owing to the use of the healing herbs. The Buddha is like a bestower of riches; the *dharma* is like the riches; and the *sangha*, which has rightly obtained the noble one's riches, is like people who have obtained riches in the way hoped for. The Buddha is like one who shows a hidden treasure-store; the *dharma* is like the hidden-treasure store; and the *sangha* is like people who have found the hidden treasure-store. Furthermore, the Buddha is like a steadfast man who gives protection from fear; the *dharma* is the protection from fear; and the *sangha*, which has found complete protection from fear, is like people who have found protection from fear. The Buddha is like a consoler; the *dharma* is like a consolation; and the *sangha* is like people consoled. The Buddha is like a good friend; the *dharma* is like helpful advice; and the *sangha* is like people who have reached all their aims through following the helpful advice. The Buddha is like a mine of riches; the *dharma* is like the vein of riches; and the *sangha* is like people who exploit the vein of riches. The Buddha is like one who bathes a prince; the *dharma* is like the water for washing the head; and the *sangha*, which has been well bathed in the water of the true *dharma*, is like a company of well-bathed princes. The Buddha is like the maker of an ornament; the *dharma* is like the ornament; and the *sangha*, which is adorned with the true *dharma*, is like a party of kings' sons wearing ornaments. The Buddha is like a sandalwood tree; the *dharma* is like the scent given

its being by that [tree]; and the *sangha*, whose fever has been quelled by the true *dharma*, is like people whose fever has been quelled by the use of sandalwood. The Buddha is like the bestower of an inheritance; the true *dharma* is like the inheritance; and the *sangha*, which is heir to the heritage consisting of the true *dharma*, is like a company of children who are heirs to the inheritance. The Buddha is like an opened lotus flower; the *dharma* is like the honey being given its being by that [flower]; and the *sangha* is like a swarm of bees making use of that [honey].

From 'The Three Refuges (Saraṇattayaṃ)', in *The Minor Readings* (*Khuddakapāṭha*), trans. Bhikkhu Ñāṇamoli, Pali Text Society Translation Series, No. 32 (London: Luzac & Company, Ltd, 1960), pp. 14–16.

EGYPT, GREECE, AND ROME

THOUGHT PIECE

BOOK OF THE DEAD

Plate XX.

Vignette: Osiris and Isis in a sepulchral shrine.

Text [Chapter XV.]: (1) A HYMN OF PRAISE TO RĀ WHEN HE RISETH IN THE EASTERN PART OF THE HEAVEN. They who are in (2) his train rejoice, and lo! Osiris Ani in triumph saith: "Hail, thou Disk, thou lord of rays, who risest (3) in the horizon day by day. Shine thou with thy beams of light upon the face of Osiris Ani, who is victorious : for he singeth hymns of praise unto thee at (4) dawn, and he maketh thee to set at eventide with words of adoration. May the soul of Osiris Ani, the triumphant one, come forth with (5) thee from heaven, may he go forth in the *mātet* boat, may he come into port in the *sektet* boat, may he cleave his path among the (6) never resting stars in the heavens."

Osiris Ani, being at peace and in triumph, adoreth his lord, the lord of (7) eternity, saying: "Homage to thee, O Horus of the two horizons, who art Kheperà, the self-created ; when thou risest on the horizon and (8) sheddest thy beams of light upon the lands of the North and South thou art beautiful, yea beautiful, and all the gods rejoice when they behold thee, (9) the King of heaven. The goddess Nebt-Unnet is stablished upon thy head ; her portions of the south and of the north are upon thy brow (10) ; she taketh her place before thee. The god Thoth is stablished in the bows of thy boat to destroy utterly all thy foes. (11) Those who dwell in the underworld come forth to meet thee, bowing in homage as they come towards thee, and to behold [thy] beautiful (12) Image. And I have come before thee that I may be with thee to behold thy Disk every day. May I not be shut in the tomb, may I not be turned back (13), may the limbs of my body be made new again when I view thy beauties, even as do all thy favoured ones, (14) because I am one of those who worshipped thee whilst they lived upon earth. May I come in unto the land of eternity, may I come even (15) unto the everlasting land, for behold, O my lord, this hast thou ordained for me."

THINGS TO CONSIDER

* How does monumental architecture reflect the aspirations of a society?
* What can memorials and temples tell us about a culture's understanding both of divinities and human lives?

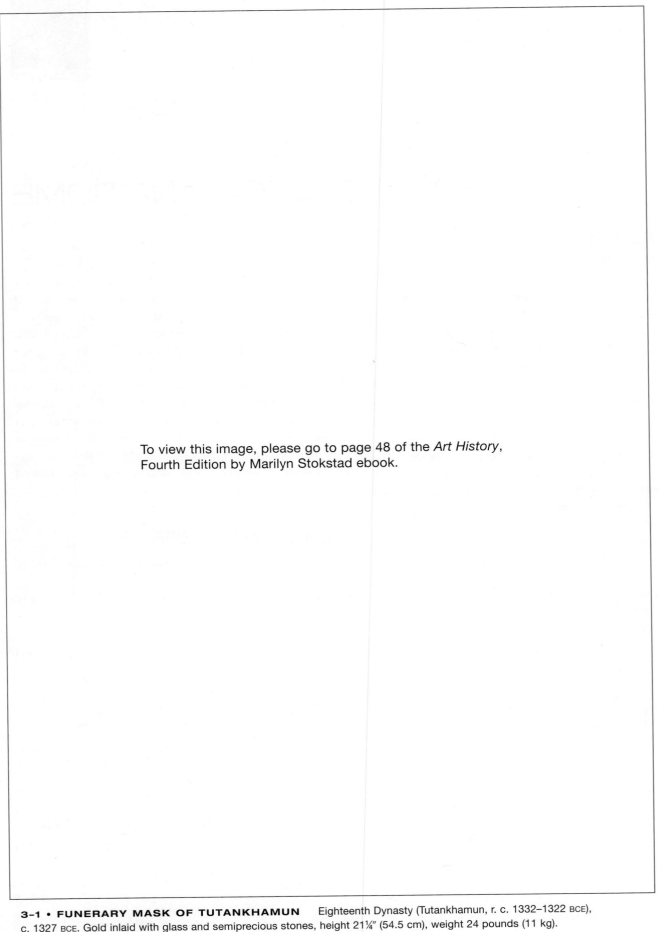

To view this image, please go to page 48 of the *Art History*,
Fourth Edition by Marilyn Stokstad ebook.

3-1 • FUNERARY MASK OF TUTANKHAMUN Eighteenth Dynasty (Tutankhamun, r. c. 1332–1322 BCE), c. 1327 BCE. Gold inlaid with glass and semiprecious stones, height 21¼″ (54.5 cm), weight 24 pounds (11 kg). Egyptian Museum, Cairo. JE 60672

ART OF ANCIENT EGYPT

On February 16, 1923, *The Times* of London cabled the *New York Times* with dramatic news of a discovery: "This has been, perhaps, the most extraordinary day in the whole history of Egyptian excavation…. The entrance today was made into the sealed chamber of [Tutankhamun's] tomb … and yet another door opened beyond that. No eyes have seen the King, but to practical certainty we know that he lies there close at hand in all his original state, undisturbed." And indeed he did. A collar of dried flowers and beads covered the chest, and a linen shroud was draped around the head. A gold **FUNERARY MASK** (**FIG. 3–1**) had been placed over the head and shoulders of his mummified body, which was enclosed in three nested coffins, the innermost made of gold (SEE FIG. 3–29, and page 175). The coffins were placed in a yellow quartzite **sarcophagus** (a stone coffin) that was itself encased within gilt wooden shrines nested inside one another.

The discoverer of this treasure, the English archaeologist Howard Carter, had worked in Egypt for more than 20 years before he undertook a last expedition, sponsored by the wealthy British amateur Egyptologist Lord Carnarvon. Carter was convinced that the tomb of Tutankhamun, one of the last Eighteenth-Dynasty royal burial places still unidentified, lay hidden in the Valley of the Kings. After 15 years of digging, on November 4, 1922, he unearthed the entrance to Tutankhamun's tomb and found unbelievable treasures in the antechamber: jewelry, textiles, gold-covered furniture, a carved and inlaid throne, four gold chariots. In February 1923, Carter pierced the wall separating the anteroom from the actual burial chamber and found the greatest treasure of all, Tutankhamun himself.

Since ancient times, tombs have tempted looters; more recently, they also have attracted archaeologists and historians. The first large-scale "archaeological" expedition in history landed in Egypt with the armies of Napoleon in 1798. The French commander must have realized that he would find great wonders there, for he took French scholars with him to study ancient sites. The military adventure ended in failure, but the scholars eventually published richly illustrated volumes of their findings, unleashing a craze for all things Egyptian that has not dimmed since. In 1976, the first blockbuster museum exhibition was born when treasures from the tomb of Tutankhamun began a tour of the United States and attracted over 8 million visitors. Most recently, in 2006, Otto Schaden excavated a tomb containing seven coffins in the Valley of the Kings, the first tomb to be found there since Tutankhamun's in 1922.

LEARN ABOUT IT

3.1 Explore the pictorial conventions for representing the human figure in ancient Egyptian art, established early on and maintained for millennia.

3.2 Trace the evolution of royal portrait styles from the Old Kingdom through the New Kingdom and assess the differences between depictions of royalty and ordinary people.

3.3 Analyze how religious beliefs were reflected in the funerary art and architecture of ancient Egypt.

3.4 Appreciate the complexity of construction and decoration brought to New Kingdom temple architecture rooted in the same post-and-lintel architectural tradition that had been used since the Old Kingdom.

HEAR MORE: Listen to an audio file of your chapter **www.myartslab.com**

THE GIFT OF THE NILE

The Greek traveler and historian Herodotus, writing in the fifth century BCE, remarked, "Egypt is the gift of the Nile." This great river, the longest in the world, winds northward from equatorial Africa and flows through Egypt in a relatively straight line to the Mediterranean (MAP 3–1). There it forms a broad delta before emptying into the sea. Before it was dammed in 1970 by the Aswan High Dam, the lower (northern) Nile, swollen with the runoff of heavy seasonal rains in the south, overflowed its banks for several months each year. Every time the floodwaters receded, they left behind a new layer of rich silt, making the valley and delta a continually fertile and attractive habitat.

By about 8000 BCE, the valley's inhabitants had become relatively sedentary, living off the abundant fish, game, and wild plants. Not until about 5000 BCE did they adopt the agricultural village life associated with Neolithic culture (see Chapter 1). At that time, the climate of north Africa grew increasingly dry. To ensure adequate resources for agriculture, the farmers along the Nile began to manage flood waters in a system called basin irrigation.

The Predynastic period, from roughly 5000 to 2950 BCE, was a time of significant social and political transition that preceded the unification of Egypt under a single ruler. (After unification, Egypt was ruled by a series of family dynasties and is therefore characterized as "dynastic.") Rudimentary federations emerged and began conquering and absorbing weaker communities. By about 3500 BCE, there were several larger states, or chiefdoms, in the lower Nile Valley and a centralized form of leadership had emerged. Rulers were expected to protect their subjects, not only from outside aggression, but also from natural catastrophes such as droughts and insect plagues.

The surviving art of the Predynastic period consists chiefly of ceramic figurines, decorated pottery, and reliefs carved on stone plaques and pieces of ivory. A few examples of wall painting—lively scenes filled with small figures of people and animals—were found in a tomb at Hierakonpolis, in Upper Egypt, a Predynastic town of mud-brick houses that was once home to as many as 10,000 people.

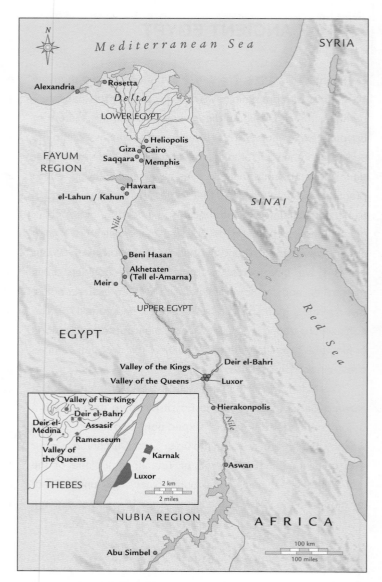

MAP 3–1 • ANCIENT EGYPT

Upper Egypt is below Lower Egypt on this map because the designations "upper" and "lower" refer to the directional flow of the Nile, not to our conventions for south and north in drawing maps. The two kingdoms were united c. 3000 BCE, just before the Early Dynastic period.

EARLY DYNASTIC EGYPT, C. 2950–2575 BCE

Around 3000 BCE, Egypt became a consolidated state. According to legend, the country had previously evolved into two major kingdoms—the Two Lands—Upper Egypt in the south (upstream on the Nile) and Lower Egypt in the north. But a powerful ruler from Upper Egypt conquered Lower Egypt and unified the two kingdoms. In the art of the subsequent Early Dynastic period we see the development of ideas about kingship and the cosmic order. Since the works of art and architecture that survive from ancient Egypt come mainly from tombs and temples—the majority of which were located in secure places and built with the most

durable materials—most of what we now know about the ancient art of Egypt is rooted in religious beliefs and practices.

THE GOD-KINGS

The Greek historian Herodotus thought the Egyptians were the most religious people he had ever encountered. In their world-view, the movements of heavenly bodies, the workings of gods, and the humblest of human activities were all believed to be part of a balanced and harmonious grand design. Death was to be feared only by those who lived in such a way as to disrupt that harmony. Upright souls could be confident that their spirits would live on eternally.

Egyptian Symbols

Four crowns symbolize kingship: the tall, club-like white crown of Upper Egypt (sometimes adorned with two plumes); the flat or scooped red cap with projecting spiral of Lower Egypt; the double crown representing unified Egypt; and, in the New Kingdom, the blue oval crown, which evolved from a war helmet.

A striped gold and blue linen head cloth, known as the **nemes headdress**, having the cobra and vulture at the center front, was commonly used as royal headgear. The upright form of the cobra, known as the *uraeus*, represents the goddess Wadjet of Lower Egypt

and is often included in king's crowns as well (SEE FIG. 3–1). The queen's crown included the feathered skin of the vulture goddess Nekhbet of Upper Egypt.

The god Horus, king of the earth and a force for good, is represented as a falcon or falcon-headed man. His eyes symbolize the sun and moon; the solar eye is called the *wedjat*. The looped cross, called the **ankh**, is symbolic of everlasting life. The **scarab** beetle (*khepri*, meaning "he who created himself") was associated with creation, resurrection, and the rising sun.

To view this image, please go to page 51 of the *Art History*, Fourth Edition by Marilyn Stokstad ebook.

By the Early Dynastic period, Egypt's kings were revered as gods in human form. A royal jubilee, the *heb sed* or *sed* festival, held in the thirtieth year of the living king's reign, renewed and re-affirmed his divine power, and when they died, kings rejoined their father, the sun god Ra, and rode with him in the solar boat as it made its daily journey across the sky.

In order to please the gods and ensure their continuing goodwill toward the state, kings built splendid temples and provided priests to maintain them. The priests saw to it that statues of the gods, placed deep in the innermost rooms of the temples, were never without fresh food and clothing. Egyptian gods and goddesses were depicted in various forms, some as human beings, others as animals, and still others as humans with animal heads. For example, Osiris, the overseer of the realm of the dead, regularly appears in human form wrapped in linen as a mummy. His son, the sky god Horus, is usually depicted as a falcon or falcon-headed man (see "Egyptian Symbols," above).

Over the course of ancient Egyptian history, Amun (chief god of Thebes, represented as blue and wearing a plumed crown), Ra (of Heliopolis), and Ptah (of Memphis) became the primary national gods. Other gods and their manifestations included Thoth (ibis), god of writing, science, and law; Ma'at (feather), goddess of truth, order, and justice; Anubis (jackal), god of embalming and cemeteries; and Bastet (cat), daughter of Ra.

ARTISTIC CONVENTIONS

Conventions in art are established ways of representing things, widely accepted by artists and patrons at a particular time and place. Egyptian artists followed a set of fairly strict conventions, often based on conceptual principles rather than on the observation of the natural world with an eye to rendering it in lifelike fashion. Eventually a system of mathematical formulas was developed to determine design and proportions (see "Egyptian Pictorial Relief," page 167). The underlying conventions that govern ancient Egyptian art

The Palette of Narmer ▸

Hierakonpolis. Early Dynastic period, c. 2950 BCE.
Green schist, height 25″ (64 cm). Egyptian Museum, Cairo. JE 32169 = CG 14716

A sandal-bearer, named by hieroglyphic inscription, accompanies the king, standing on his own ground line. His presence emphasizes the fact that the king, being barefoot, is standing on sacred ground, performing sacred acts. The same individual, likewise labeled, follows Narmer on the other side of the palette.

Phonetic **hieroglyphs** at the center top of each side of the palette name the king: a horizontal fish (*nar*) above a vertical chisel (*mer*). A depiction of the royal palace—seen simultaneously from above, as a groundplan, and frontally, as a **façade** (front wall of a building)—surrounds Narmer's name to signify that he is king.

Narmer wears the Red Crown of Lower Egypt on this side of the palette and is identified by the hieroglyph label next to his head, as well by as his larger size in relation to the other figures (hieratic scale).

Two rows of decapitated enemies, their heads neatly tucked between their feet, are inspected by the royal procession.

To view this image, please go to page 52 of the *Art History*, Fourth Edition by Marilyn Stokstad ebook.

Narmer is attacking a figure of comparable size who is also identified by a hieroglyphic label, indicating that he is an enemy of real importance, likely the ruler of Lower Egypt.

Next to the heads of these two defeated enemies are, on the left, an aerial depiction of a fortified city, and on the right, a gazelle trap, perhaps emblems of Narmer's control over both city and countryside.

A bull—symbolizing the might of the king, who is shown wearing a bull's tail on both sides of the palette—strikes down another enemy in front of a fortified city, seen both from above and in elevation.

Palettes were tablets with circular depressions on one side, in which eye makeup was ground and prepared. Although this example was undoubtedly ceremonial rather than functional, a mixing saucer is framed by the elongated, intertwined necks of lions, perhaps signifying the union of Upper and Lower Egypt.

SEE MORE: View the Closer Look feature for the Palette of Narmer www.myartslab.com

appear early, however, and are maintained, with subtle but significant variations, over almost three millennia of its history.

THE NARMER PALETTE. This historically and artistically significant work of art (see "A Closer Look," opposite) dates from the Early Dynastic period and was found in the temple of Horus. It is commonly interpreted as representing the unification of Egypt and the beginning of the country's growth as a powerful nation-state. It employs many of the representational conventions that would dominate in royal Egyptian art from this point on.

On the reverse side of the palette, as in the Stele of Naram-Sin (SEE FIG. 2–1), hieratic scale signals the importance of Narmer by showing him overwhelmingly larger than the other human figures around him. He is also boldly silhouetted against a blank ground, just like Naram-Sin, distancing details of setting and story so they will not distract from his preeminence. He wears the white crown of Upper Egypt while striking the enemy who kneels before him with a mace. Above this foe, the god Horus—depicted as a falcon with a human hand—holds a rope tied around the neck of a man whose head is attached to a block sprouting stylized papyrus, a plant that grew in profusion along the Nile and symbolized Lower Egypt. This combination of symbols made the central message clear: Narmer, as ruler of Upper Egypt, is in firm control of Lower Egypt.

Many of the figures on the palette are shown in composite poses, so that each part of the body is portrayed from its most characteristic viewpoint. Heads are shown in profile, to capture most clearly the nose, forehead, and chin, while eyes are rendered frontally, from their most recognizable and expressive viewpoint. Hips, legs, and feet are drawn in profile, and the figure is usually striding, to reveal both legs. The torso, however, is fully frontal. This artistic convention for representing the human figure as a conceptualized composite of multiple viewpoints was to be followed for millennia in Egypt when depicting royalty and other dignitaries. Persons of lesser social rank engaged in active tasks (compare the figure of Narmer with those of his standard bearers) tend to be represented in ways that seem to us more lifelike.

FUNERARY ARCHITECTURE

Ancient Egyptians believed that an essential part of every human personality is its life force, or soul, called the *ka*, which lived on after the death of the body, forever engaged in the activities it had enjoyed in its former existence. But the *ka* needed a body to live in, either the mummified body of the deceased or, as a substitute, a sculpted likeness in the form of a statue. The Egyptians developed elaborate funerary practices to ensure that their deceased moved safely and effectively into the afterlife.

It was especially important to provide a comfortable home for the *ka* of a departed king, so that even in the afterlife he would continue to ensure the well-being of Egypt. Egyptians preserved the bodies of the royal dead with care and placed them in burial chambers filled with sculpted body substitutes and all the supplies and furnishings the *ka* might require throughout eternity (see "Preserving the Dead," page 158).

MASTABA AND NECROPOLIS. In Early Dynastic Egypt, the most common tomb structure—used by the upper level of society, the king's family and relatives—was the **mastaba**, a flat-topped, one-story building with slanted walls erected above an underground burial chamber (see "Mastaba to Pyramid," page 157). Mastabas were at first constructed of mud brick, but toward the end of the Third Dynasty (c. 2650–2575 BCE), many incorporated cut stone, at least as an exterior facing.

In its simplest form, the mastaba contained a **serdab**, a small, sealed room housing the *ka* statue of the deceased, and a chapel designed to receive mourning relatives and offerings. A vertical shaft dropped from the top of the mastaba down to the actual burial chamber, where the remains of the deceased reposed in a coffin—at times placed within a larger stone sarcophagus—surrounded by appropriate grave goods. This chamber was sealed off after interment. Mastabas might have numerous underground burial chambers to accommodate whole families, and mastaba burial remained the standard for Egyptian elites for centuries.

Mastabas tended to be grouped together in a **necropolis**—literally, a "city of the dead"—at the edge of the desert on the west bank of the Nile, for the land of the dead was believed to be in the direction of the setting sun. Two of the most extensive of these early necropolises are at Saqqara and Giza, just outside modern Cairo.

DJOSER'S COMPLEX AT SAQQARA. For his tomb complex at Saqqara, the Third-Dynasty King Djoser (c. 2650–2631 BCE) commissioned the earliest known monumental architecture in Egypt (FIG. 3–2). The designer of the complex was Imhotep, who served as Djoser's prime minister. Imhotep is the first architect in history to be identified; his name is inscribed together with Djoser's on the base of a statue of the king found near the Step Pyramid.

It appears that Imhotep first planned Djoser's tomb as a single-story mastaba, only later deciding to enlarge upon the concept. The final structure is a step pyramid formed by six mastaba-like elements of decreasing size stacked on top of each other (FIG. 3–3). Although the step pyramid resembles the ziggurats of Mesopotamia, it differs in both meaning (signifying a stairway to the sun god Ra) and purpose (protecting a tomb). A 92-foot shaft descended from the original mastaba enclosed within the pyramid. A descending corridor at the base of the step pyramid provided an entrance from outside to a granite-lined burial vault.

The adjacent funerary temple, where priests performed rituals before placing the king's mummified body in its tomb, was used for continuing worship of the dead king. In the form of his *ka* statue, Djoser intended to observe these devotions through two peepholes in the wall between the serdab and the funerary chapel. To the east of the pyramid, buildings filled with debris represent actual structures in which the spirit of the dead king could continue to observe the *sed* rituals that had ensured his long reign.

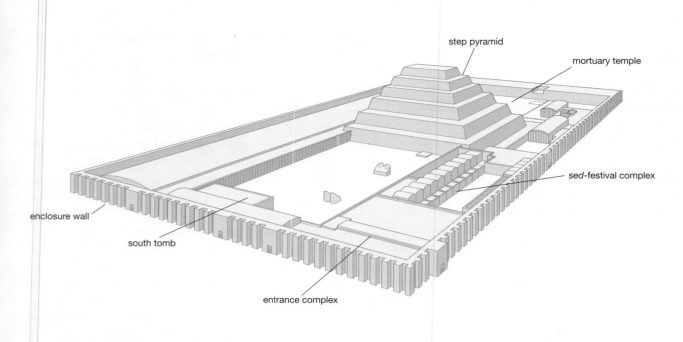

step pyramid

mortuary temple

sed-festival complex

enclosure wall

south tomb

entrance complex

3-2 • RECONSTRUCTION DRAWING OF DJOSER'S FUNERARY COMPLEX, SAQQARA

Third Dynasty, c. 2630–2575 BCE. Situated on a level terrace, this huge commemorative complex—some 1,800′ (544 m) long by 900′ (277 m) wide—was designed as a replica in stone of the wood, brick, and reed buildings used in rituals associated with kingship. Inside the wall, the step pyramid dominated the complex.

To view this image, please go to page 54 of the *Art History*, Fourth Edition by Marilyn Stokstad ebook.

3-3 • THE STEP PYRAMID AND SHAM BUILDINGS, FUNERARY COMPLEX OF DJOSER, SAQQARA

Limestone, height of pyramid 204′ (62 m).

EXPLORE MORE: Click the Google Earth link for the Pyramid of Djoser **www.myartslab.com**

As the gateway to the afterlife for Egyptian kings and members of the royal court, the Egyptian burial structure began as a low, solid, rectangular mastaba with an external niche that served as the focus of offerings. Later mastabas had either an internal serdab (the room where the *ka* statue was placed) and chapel (as in the drawing) or an attached chapel and serdab (not shown). Eventually, mastaba forms of decreasing size were stacked over an underground burial chamber to form the step pyramid. The culmination of this development is the pyramid, in which the actual burial site may be within the pyramid—not below ground—with false chambers, false doors, and confusing passageways to foil potential tomb robbers.

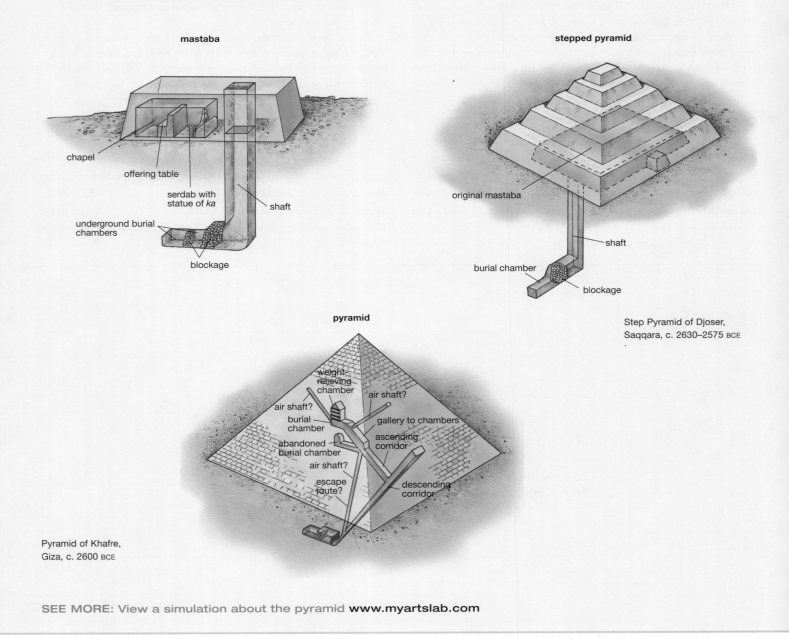

mastaba

chapel
offering table
serdab with statue of *ka*
shaft
underground burial chambers
blockage

stepped pyramid

original mastaba
shaft
burial chamber
blockage

Step Pyramid of Djoser, Saqqara, c. 2630–2575 BCE

pyramid

weight relieving chamber
air shaft?
air shaft?
burial chamber
gallery to chambers
abandoned burial chamber
ascending corridor
air shaft?
escape route?
descending corridor

Pyramid of Khafre, Giza, c. 2600 BCE

SEE MORE: View a simulation about the pyramid **www.myartslab.com**

THE OLD KINGDOM, C. 2575–2150 BCE

The Old Kingdom was a time of social and political stability, despite increasingly common military excursions to defend the borders. The growing wealth of ruling families of the period is reflected in the enormous and elaborate tomb complexes they commissioned for themselves. Kings were not the only patrons of the arts, however. Upper-level government officials also could afford tombs decorated with elaborate carvings.

THE GREAT PYRAMIDS AT GIZA

The architectural form most closely identified with Egypt is the true pyramid with a square base and four sloping triangular faces,

Egyptians developed mummification techniques to ensure that the *ka*, soul or life force, could live on in the body in the afterlife. No recipes for preserving the dead have been found, but the basic process seems clear enough from images found in tombs, the descriptions of later Greek writers such as Herodotus and Plutarch, scientific analysis of mummies, and modern experiments.

By the time of the New Kingdom, the routine was roughly as follows: The body was taken to a mortuary, a special structure used exclusively for embalming. Under the supervision of a priest, workers removed the brains, generally through the nose, and emptied the body cavity—except for the heart—through an incision in the left side. They then covered the body with dry natron, a naturally occurring salt, and placed it on a sloping surface to allow liquids to drain. This preservative caused the skin to blacken, so workers often used paint or powdered makeup to restore some color, using red ocher for a man, yellow ocher for a woman. They then packed the body cavity with clean linen soaked in various herbs and ointments, provided by the family of the deceased. The major organs were wrapped in separate packets and stored in special containers called **canopic jars**, to be placed in the tomb chamber.

Workers next wound the trunk and each of the limbs separately with cloth strips, before wrapping the whole body in additional layers of cloth to produce the familiar mummy shape. The workers often inserted charms and other smaller objects among the wrappings.

first erected in the Fourth Dynasty (2575–2450 BCE). The angled sides may have been meant to represent the slanting rays of the sun, for inscriptions on the walls of pyramid tombs built in the Fifth and Sixth Dynasties tell of deceased kings climbing up the rays to join the sun god Ra.

Although not the first pyramids, the most famous are the three great pyramid tombs at Giza (**FIGS. 3–4, 3–5**). These were built by three successive Fourth-Dynasty kings: Khufu (r. c. 2551–2528 BCE), Khafre (r. 2520–2494 BCE), and Menkaure (r. c. 2490–2472 BCE). The oldest and largest pyramid at Giza is that of Khufu, which

To view this image, please go to page 56 of the *Art History*, Fourth Edition by Marilyn Stokstad ebook.

3-4 • GREAT PYRAMIDS, GIZA
Fourth Dynasty (c. 2575–2450 BCE). Erected by (from the left) Menkaure, Khafre, and Khufu. Limestone and granite, height of pyramid of Khufu, 450′ (137 m).

EXPLORE MORE: Click the Google Earth link for the Pyramids of Giza www.myartslab.com

To view this image, please go to page 57 of the *Art History*, Fourth Edition by Marilyn Stokstad ebook.

3–5 • MODEL OF THE GIZA PLATEAU
From left to right: the temples and pyramids of Menkaure, Khafre, and Khufu.

covers 13 acres at its base. It was originally finished with a thick veneer of polished limestone that lifted its apex to almost 481 feet, some 30 feet above the present summit. The pyramid of Khafre is slightly smaller than Khufu's, and Menkaure's is considerably smaller.

The site was carefully planned to follow the sun's east–west path. Next to each of the pyramids was a funerary temple connected by a causeway—an elevated and enclosed pathway or corridor—to a valley temple on the bank of the Nile (SEE FIG. 3–5). When a king died, his body was embalmed and ferried west across the Nile from the royal palace to his valley temple, where it was received with elaborate ceremonies. It was then carried up the causeway to his funerary temple and placed in its chapel, where family members presented offerings of food and drink, and priests performed rites in which the deceased's spirit consumed a meal. These rites were to be performed at the chapel in perpetuity. Finally, the body was entombed in a vault deep within the pyramid, at the end of a long, narrow, and steeply rising passageway. This tomb chamber was sealed off after the burial with a 50-ton stone block. To further protect the king from intruders, three false passageways obscured the location of the tomb.

CONSTRUCTING THE PYRAMIDS. Building a pyramid was a formidable undertaking. A large workers' burial ground discovered at Giza attests to the huge labor force that had to be assembled, housed, and fed. Most of the cut stone blocks—each weighing an average of 2.5 tons—used in building the Giza complex were quarried either on the site or nearby. Teams of workers transported them by sheer muscle power, employing small logs as rollers or pouring water on mud to create a slippery surface over which they could drag the blocks on sleds.

Scholars and engineers have various theories about how the pyramids were raised. Some ideas have been tested in computerized projections and a few models on a small but representative scale have been constructed. The most efficient means of getting the stones into position might have been to build a temporary, gently sloping ramp around the body of the pyramid as it grew higher. The ramp could then be dismantled as the stones were smoothed out or slabs of veneer were laid.

The designers who oversaw the building of such massive structures were capable of the most sophisticated mathematical calculations. They oriented the pyramids to the points of the compass and may have incorporated other symbolic astronomical calculations as well. There was no room for trial and error. The huge foundation layer had to be absolutely level and the angle of each of the slanting sides had to remain constant so that the stones would meet precisely in the center at the top.

3-6 • GREAT SPHINX, FUNERARY COMPLEX OF KHAFRE

Giza. Old Kingdom, c. 2520–2494 BCE. Sandstone, height approx. 65′ (19.8 m).

EXPLORE MORE: Click the Google Earth link for The Great Sphinx **www.myartslab.com**

To view this image, please go to page 58 of the *Art History*, Fourth Edition by Marilyn Stokstad ebook.

KHAFRE'S COMPLEX. Khafre's funerary complex is the best preserved. Its pyramid is the only one of the three to have maintained some of its veneer facing at the top. But the complex is most famous for the Great Sphinx that sits just behind Khafre's valley temple. This colossal portrait of the king—65 feet tall—combines his head with the long body of a crouching lion, seemingly merging notions of human intelligence with animal strength **(FIG. 3–6)**.

In the adjacent valley temple, massive blocks of red granite form walls and piers supporting a flat roof **(FIG. 3–7)**. (See "Early Construction Methods," page 25.) A **clerestory** (a row of tall, narrow windows in the upper walls, not visible in the figure), lets in light that reflects off the polished Egyptian alabaster floor. Within the temple were a series of over-life-size statues, portraying **KHAFRE** as an enthroned king **(FIG. 3–8)**. The falcon god Horus perches on the back of the throne, protectively enfolding the king's head with his wings. Lions—symbols of regal authority—form the throne's legs, and the intertwined lotus and papyrus plants beneath the seat symbolize the king's power over Upper (lotus) and Lower (papyrus) Egypt.

Khafre wears the traditional royal costume—a short, pleated kilt, a linen headdress, and a false beard symbolic of royalty. He exudes a strong sense of dignity, calm, and above all permanence. In his right hand, he holds a cylinder, probably a rolled piece of cloth. His arms are pressed tightly within the contours of his body, which is firmly anchored in the confines of the stone block from which it was carved. The statue was created from an unusual stone, a type of

To view this image, please go to page 58 of the *Art History*, Fourth Edition by Marilyn Stokstad ebook.

3-7 • VALLEY TEMPLE OF KHAFRE
Giza, Old Kingdom, c. 2520–2494 BCE. Limestone and red granite.

3-8 • KHAFRE
Giza, valley temple of
Khafre. Fourth Dynasty,
c. 2520–2494 BCE.
Diorite-gabbro gneiss,
height 5'6⅛" (1.68 m).
Egyptian Museum, Cairo.
(JE 10062 = CG 14)

To view this image, please go to page 59 of the *Art History*, Fourth Edition by Marilyn Stokstad ebook.

gneiss (related to diorite), imported from Nubia, that produces a rare optical effect. When illuminated by sunlight entering through the temple's clerestory, it glows a deep blue, the celestial color of Horus, filling the space with a blue radiance.

SCULPTURE

As the surviving statues of Khafre's valley temple demonstrate, Egyptian sculptors were adept at creating lifelike three-dimensional figures that also express a feeling of strength and permanence consistent with the unusually hard stones from which they were carved.

MENKAURE AND A QUEEN.   Dignity, calm, and permanence also characterize a sleek double portrait of Khafre's heir King Menkaure and a queen, probably Khamerernebty II, discovered in Menkaure's valley temple **(FIG. 3–9)**. The couple's separate figures, close in size, are joined by the stone from which they emerge, forming a single unit. They are further united by the queen's symbolic gesture of embrace. Her right hand comes from behind to clasp his torso, and her left hand rests gently, if stiffly, over his upper arm.

The king—depicted in accordance with Egyptian ideals as an athletic, youthful figure, nude to the waist and wearing the royal kilt and headcloth—stands in a conventional, balanced pose, striding with the left foot forward, his arms straight at his sides, and his fists clenched over cylindrical objects. His equally youthful queen, taking a smaller step forward, echoes his striding pose. Her sheer, close-fitting garment reveals the soft curves of her gently swelling body, a foil for the tight muscularity of the king. The time-consuming task of polishing this double statue was never completed, suggesting that the work may have been undertaken only a few years before Menkaure's death in about 2472 BCE. Traces of red paint remain on the king's face, ears, and neck (male figures were traditionally painted red), as do traces of black on the queen's hair.

To view this image, please go to page 59 of the *Art History*, Fourth Edition by Marilyn Stokstad ebook.

3-9 • MENKAURE AND A QUEEN
Perhaps his wife Khamerernebty II, from Giza. Fourth Dynasty, 2490–2472 BCE. Graywacke with traces of red and black paint, height 54½" (142.3 cm). Museum of Fine Arts, Boston.
(11.1738) Harvard University–MFA Expedition

SEATED SCRIBE. Old Kingdom sculptors also produced statues of less prominent people, rendered in a more relaxed, lifelike fashion. A more lively and less formal mode is employed in the statue of a **SEATED SCRIBE** from early in the Fifth Dynasty (**FIG. 3–10**)—with round head, alert expression, and cap of close-cropped hair—that was discovered near the tomb of a government official named Kai. It could be a portrait of Kai himself. The irregular contours of his engaging face project a sense of individual likeness and human presence.

The scribe's sedentary vocation has made his sagging body slightly flabby, his condition advertising a life free from hard physical labor. An ancient Egyptian inscription emphasizes this point: "Become a scribe so that your limbs remain smooth and your hands soft and you can wear white and walk like a man of standing whom [even] courtiers will greet" (cited in Strouhal, p. 216). This scribe sits holding a papyrus scroll partially unrolled on his lap, his right hand clasping a now-lost reed brush used in writing. The alert expression on his face reveals more than a lively intelligence. Because the pupils are slightly off-center in the irises, the eyes give the illusion of being in motion, as if they were seeking contact, and the reflective quality of the polished crystal inlay reproduces with eerie fidelity the contrast between the moist surface of eyes and the surrounding soft flesh in a living human face.

To view this image, please go to page 60 of the *Art History*, Fourth Edition by Marilyn Stokstad ebook.

3–11 • BUTCHER
Perhaps from the tomb of the official Ni-kau-inpu and his wife Hemet-re, Giza? Fifth Dynasty, c. 2450–2325 BCE. Painted limestone (knife restored), height 14⅝″ (37 cm). Oriental Institute of the University of Chicago. (10626)

Although statues such as this have been assumed to represent the deceased's servants, it has recently been proposed that instead they depict relatives and friends of the deceased in the role of servants, allowing these loved ones to accompany the deceased into the next life.

To view this image, please go to page 60 of the *Art History*, Fourth Edition by Marilyn Stokstad ebook.

3–10 • SEATED SCRIBE
Found near the tomb of Kai, Saqqara. Fifth Dynasty, c. 2450–2325 BCE. Painted limestone with inlaid eyes of rock crystal, calcite, and magnesite mounted in copper, height 21″ (53 cm). Musée du Louvre, Paris. (N 2290 = E 3023)

High-ranking scribes could hope to be appointed to one of several "houses of life," where they would copy, compile, study, and repair valuable sacred and scientific texts.

STATUETTES OF SERVANTS. Even more lifelike than the scribe were smaller figures of servants at work that were made for inclusion in Old Kingdom tombs so that the deceased could be provided for in the next world. Poses are neither formal nor reflective, but rooted directly in the labor these figures were expected to perform throughout eternity. A painted limestone statuette from the Fifth Dynasty (**FIG. 3–11**) captures a butcher, raised up on the balls of his feet to bend down and lean forward, poised, knife in hand, over the throat of an ox that he has just slaughtered. Having accomplished his work, he looks up to acknowledge us, an action that only enhances his sense of lifelike presence. The emphasis on involved poses and engagement with the viewer may have been an attempt to underscore the ability of such figures to perform their assigned tasks, or perhaps it was meant to indicate their lower social status by showing them involved in physical labor. Both may be signified here. The contrast between the detached stylization of upper-class figures and the engaging lifelikeness of laborers can be seen in Old Kingdom pictorial relief works as well.

To view this image, please go to page 61 of the *Art History*, Fourth Edition by Marilyn Stokstad ebook.

3-12 • TI WATCHING A HIPPOPOTAMUS HUNT
Tomb of Ti, Saqqara. Fifth Dynasty, c. 2450–2325 BCE. Painted limestone relief, height approx. 45″ (114.3 cm).

PICTORIAL RELIEF IN TOMBS

To provide the *ka* with the most pleasant possible living quarters for eternity, wealthy families often had the interior walls and ceilings of their tombs decorated with paintings and reliefs. This decoration carried religious meaning, but it could also evoke the deceased's everyday life or depict ceremonial events that proclaimed the deceased's importance. Tombs therefore provide a wealth of information about ancient Egyptian culture.

THE TOMB OF TI. On the walls of the large mastaba of a wealthy Fifth Dynasty government official named Ti, a painted relief shows him watching a hippopotamus hunt—an official duty of royal courtiers (FIG. 3–12). It was believed that Seth, the god of chaos, disguised himself as a hippo. Hippos were also destructive since they wandered into fields, damaging crops. Tomb depictions of such hunts therefore proclaimed the valor of the deceased and the triumph of good over evil, or at least order over destructiveness.

The artists who created this picture in painted limestone relief used a number of established Egyptian representational conventions. The river is conceived as if seen from above, rendered as a band of parallel wavy lines below the boats. The creatures in this river, however—fish, a crocodile, and hippopotami—are shown in profile for easy identification. The shallow boats carrying Ti and his men by skimming along the surface of the water are shown straight on in relation to the viewers' vantage point, and the papyrus stalks that choke the marshy edges of the river are disciplined into a regular pattern of projecting, linear, parallel, vertical forms that highlight the contrastingly crisp and smooth contour of Ti's stylized body. At the top of the papyrus grove, however, this patterning relaxes while enthusiastic animals of prey—perhaps foxes—stalk birds among the leaves and flowers. The hieratically scaled and sleekly stylized figure of Ti, rendered in the conventional composite pose, looms over all. In a separate boat ahead of him, the actual hunters, being of lesser rank and engaged in more strenuous activities, are rendered in a more lifelike and lively fashion than their master. They are captured at the charged moment of closing in on the hunted prey, spears positioned at the ready, legs extended for the critical lunge forward.

THE MIDDLE KINGDOM, c. 1975–c. 1640 BCE

The collapse of the Old Kingdom, with its long succession of powerful kings, was followed by roughly 150 years of political turmoil, fragmentation, and warfare traditionally referred to as the First Intermediate period (c. 2125–1975 BCE). About 2010 BCE, a series of kings named Mentuhotep (Eleventh Dynasty, c. 2010–c. 1938 BCE) gained power in Thebes, and the country was reunited under Nebhepetre Mentuhotep, who reasserted royal power and founded the Middle Kingdom.

The Middle Kingdom was another high point in Egyptian history. Arts and writing flourished in the Twelfth Dynasty (1938–1756 BCE), while reflecting a burgeoning awareness of the political upheaval from which the country had just emerged. Using a strengthened military, Middle Kingdom rulers expanded and patrolled the borders, especially in lower Nubia, south of present-day Aswan (SEE MAP 3–1, page 50). By the Thirteenth Dynasty (c. 1755–1630 BCE), however, central control by the government was weakened by a series of short-lived kings and an influx of foreigners, especially in the Delta.

PORTRAITS OF SENUSRET III

Some royal portraits from the Middle Kingdom appear to express an unexpected awareness of the hardship and fragility of human existence. Statues of Senusret III, a king of the Twelfth Dynasty, who ruled from c. 1836 to 1818 BCE, reflects this new sensibility. Old Kingdom rulers such as Khafre (SEE FIG. 3–8) gaze into eternity confident and serene, toned and unflinching, whereas the portrait of **SENUSRET III** seems to capture a monarch preoccupied and emotionally drained **(FIG. 3–13)**. Creases line his sagging cheeks, his eyes are sunken, his eyelids droop, his forehead is flexed, and his jaw is sternly set—a bold image of a resolute ruler, tested but unbowed.

Senusret was a dynamic king and successful general who led four military expeditions into Nubia, overhauled the Egyptian central administration, and was effective in regaining control over the country's increasingly independent nobles. To modern viewers, his portrait raises questions of interpretation. Are we looking at the face of a man wise in the ways of the world but lonely, saddened, and burdened by the weight of his responsibilities? Or are we looking at a reassuring statement that in spite of troubled times—that have clearly left their mark on the face of the ruler himself—royal rule endures in Egypt? Given what we know about Egyptian history at this time, it is difficult to be sure.

ROCK-CUT TOMBS

During the Eleventh and Twelfth Dynasties, members of the nobility and high-level officials commissioned tombs hollowed out of the face of a cliff. A typical rock-cut tomb included an entrance **portico** (projecting porch), a main hall, and a shrine with a burial chamber under the offering chapel. The chambers of these tombs, as well as their ornamental columns, lintels, false doors, and niches, were all carved into the solid rock. An impressive necropolis was created in the cliffs at **BENI HASAN** on the east bank of the Nile **(FIG. 3–14)**. Painted scenes cover the interior walls of many tombs. Among the best preserved are those in the Twelfth Dynasty tomb

To view this image, please go to page 62 of the *Art History*, Fourth Edition by Marilyn Stokstad ebook.

3-13 • HEAD OF SENUSRET III
Twelfth Dynasty, c. 1836–1818 BCE. Yellow quartzite, height 17¾ × 13½ × 17″ (45.1 × 34.3 × 43.2 cm). The Nelson-Atkins Museum of Art, Kansas City, Missouri. Purchase: Nelson Trust (62-11)

To view this image, please go to page 62 of the *Art History*, Fourth Edition by Marilyn Stokstad ebook.

3-14 • ROCK-CUT TOMBS, BENI HASAN
Twelfth Dynasty (1938–1756 BCE). At the left is the entrance to the tomb of a provincial governor and the commander-in-chief Amenemhat.

from their perches within the trees **(FIG. 3–15)**. One man reaches for a fig to add to the ordered stack in his basket, while his companion carefully arranges the harvest in a larger box for transport. Like the energetic hunters on the much earlier painted relief in the Tomb of Ti (SEE FIG. 3–12), the upper torsos of these farm workers take a more lifelike profile posture, deviating from the strict frontality of the royal composite pose.

FUNERARY STELAE

Only the wealthiest and noblest of ancient Egyptians could afford elaborately decorated mastabas or rock-cut tombs. Prosperous people, however, could still commission funerary stelae depicting themselves, their family, and offerings of food. These personal monuments—meant to preserve the memory of the deceased and inspire the living to make offerings to them—contain compelling works of ancient Egyptian pictorial art. An unfinished stele made for the tomb of the **SCULPTOR USERWER (FIG. 3–16)** presents three levels of decoration: one large upper block with five bands of hieroglyphs, beneath which are two registers with figures, each identified by inscription.

To view this image, please go to page 63 of the *Art History*, Fourth Edition by Marilyn Stokstad ebook.

3-15 • PICKING FIGS
Wall painting from the tomb of Khnumhotep, Beni Hasan. Twelfth Dynasty, c. 1890 BCE. Tempera facsimile by Nina de Garis.

of local noble Khnumhotep, some of which portray vivid vignettes of farm work on his estates. In one painting two men harvest figs, rushing to compete with three baboons who relish the ripe fruit

To view this image, please go to page 63 of the *Art History*, Fourth Edition by Marilyn Stokstad ebook.

3-16 • STELE OF THE SCULPTOR USERWER
Twelfth Dynasty, c. 1850 BCE. Limestone, red and black ink, 20½ × 19″ (52 cm × 48 cm). British Museum London. (EA 579)

The text is addressed to the living, imploring them to make offerings to Userwer: "O living ones who are on the earth who pass by this tomb, as your deities love and favor you, may you say: 'A thousand of bread and beer, a thousand of cattle and birds, a thousand of alabaster [vessels] and clothes, a thousand of offerings and provisions that go forth before Osiris.'" (Robins, p. 103)

At left, on the register immediately below this inscription, Userwer sits before a table piled with offerings of food. Behind him is his wife Satdepetnetjer, and facing him on the other side of the offering table is Satameni, a standing woman also identified as his wife. Userwer could have had more than one wife, but one of these women might also be a deceased first wife of the sculptor. At the other side of the stele on this same register but facing in the opposite direction sits another couple before another table heaped with food. They are identified as Userwer's parents, and the figure on the other side of their offering table is his son, Sneferuweser. In the lowest register are representations of other family members (probably Userwer's children) and his grandparents.

One of the most striking features of the lowest register of this stele is its unfinished state. The two leftmost figures were left uncarved, but the stone surface still maintains the preparatory ink drawing meant to guide the sculptor, preserving striking evidence of a system of canonical figure proportions that was established in the Middle Kingdom (see "Egyptian Pictorial Relief," opposite). The unfinished state of this stele has led to the suggestion that Userwer might have been in the process of carving it for himself when his sudden death left it incomplete.

A more modest stele for a man named **AMENEMHAT** was brought to completion as a vibrantly painted relief (**FIG. 3–17**). Underneath an inscription, inviting food offerings for the deceased Amenemhat, is a portrait of his family. Amenemhat sits on a lion-legged bench between his wife Iyi and their son Antef, embraced by both. Next to the trio is an offering table, heaped with meat, topped with onions, and sheltering two loaves of bread standing under the table on the floor. On the far right is Anenemhat and Iyi's daughter, Hapy, completing this touching tableau of family unity, presumably projected into their life after death. The painter of this relief follows an established Egyptian convention of differentiating gender by skin tonality, dark red-brown for men and lighter yellow-ocher for women.

TOWN PLANNING

Although Egyptians used durable materials in the construction of tombs, they built their own dwellings with simple mud bricks, which have either disintegrated over time or been carried away for fertilizer by farmers. Only the foundations of these dwellings now remain.

Archaeologists have unearthed the remains of Kahun, a town built by Senusret II (ruled c. 1842–1837 BCE) for the many officials, priests, and workers who built and maintained his pyramid complex. Parallel streets were laid out on a **grid**, forming rectangular blocks divided into lots for homes and other buildings.

3-17 • STELE OF AMENEMHAT
Assasif. Late Eleventh Dynasty. c. 2000 BCE. Painted limestone, 11 × 15″ (30 × 50 cm). Egyptian Museum, Cairo. (JE 45626)

The houses of priests, court officials, and their families were large and comfortable, with private living quarters and public rooms grouped around central courtyards. The largest had as many as 70 rooms spread out over half an acre. Workers and their families made do with small, five-room row-houses built back to back along narrow streets.

A New Kingdom workers' village, discovered at Deir el-Medina on the west bank of the Nile near the Valley of the Kings, has provided us with detailed information about the lives of the people who created the royal tombs. Workers lived together here under the rule of the king's chief minister. During a ten-day week, they worked for eight days and had two days off, and also participated in many religious festivals. They lived a good life with their families, were given clothing, sandals, grain, and firewood by the king, and had permission to raise livestock and birds and to tend a garden. The residents had a council, and the many written records that survive suggest a literate and litigious society that required many scribes. Because the men were away for most of the week working on the tombs, women had a prominent role in the town.

THE NEW KINGDOM, c. 1539–1075 BCE

During the Second Intermediate period (1630–1520 BCE)—another turbulent interruption in the succession of dynasties ruling a unified country—an eastern Mediterranean people called the Hyksos invaded Egypt's northernmost regions. Finally, the kings of the Eighteenth Dynasty (c. 1539–1292 BCE) regained control of the entire Nile region, extending from Nubia in the south to the Mediterranean Sea in the north, and restored political and economic strength. Roughly a century later, one of the same dynasty's most dynamic kings, Thutmose III (r. 1479–1425 BCE), extended Egypt's influence along the eastern Mediterranean coast as far as the region of present-day Syria. His accomplishment was the result of 15 or more military campaigns and his own skill at diplomacy. The heartland of ancient Egypt was now surrounded by a buffer of empire.

Painting usually relies on color and line for its effect, while relief sculpture usually depends on the play of light and shadow alone, but in Egypt, relief sculpture was also painted (SEE FIG. 3–17). The walls and closely spaced columns of Egyptian tombs and temples were almost completely covered with colorful scenes and hieroglyphic texts. Until the Eighteenth Dynasty (c. 1539–1292 BCE), the only colors used were black, white, red, yellow, blue, and green. Modeling might be indicated by overpainting lines in a contrasting color, although the sense of three-dimensionality was conveyed primarily by the carved forms and incised inscriptions underneath the paint. The crisp outlines created by such carving assured the primacy of line in Egyptian pictorial relief.

With very few exceptions, figures, scenes, and texts were composed in bands, or registers. The scenes were first laid out with inked lines, using a squared grid to guide the designer in proportioning the human figures. The sculptor who executed the carving followed these drawings, and it may have been another person who smoothed the carved surfaces of the relief and eventually covered them with paint.

The lower left corner of the unfinished Twelfth-Dynasty stele of Userwer shown here still maintains its preliminary underdrawings. In some figures there are also the tentative beginnings of the relief carving. The figures are delineated with black ink and the grid lines are rendered in red. Every body part had its designated place on the grid. For example, figures are designed 18 squares tall, measuring from the soles of their feet to their hairline; the tops of their knees conform with the sixth square up from the ground-line. Their shoulders align with the top of square 16 and are six squares wide. Slight deviations exist within this structured design format, but this **canon of proportions** represents an ideal system that was standard in pictorial relief throughout the Middle Kingdom.

To view this image, please go to page 65 of the *Art History*, Fourth Edition by Marilyn Stokstad ebook.

DETAIL OF THE STELE OF THE SCULPTOR USERWER IN FIG. 3-16.

Thutmose III was the first ruler to refer to himself as "pharaoh," a term that literally meant "great house." Egyptians used it in the same way that Americans say "the White House" to mean the current U.S. president and his staff. The successors of Thutmose III continued to call themselves pharaohs, and the term ultimately found its way into the Hebrew Bible—and modern usage—as the title for the kings of Egypt.

THE GREAT TEMPLE COMPLEXES

At the height of the New Kingdom, rulers undertook extensive building programs along the entire length of the Nile. Their palaces, forts, and administrative centers disappeared long ago, but remnants of temples and tombs of this great age have endured. Thebes was Egypt's religious center throughout most of the New Kingdom, and worship of the Theban triad of deities—Amun, his wife Mut, and their son Khons—had spread throughout the country. Temples to these and other gods were a major focus of royal patronage, as were tombs and temples erected to glorify the kings themselves.

THE NEW KINGDOM TEMPLE PLAN. As the home of the god, an Egyptian temple originally took the form of a house—a simple, rectangular, flat-roofed building preceded by a courtyard and gateway. The builders of the New Kingdom enlarged and multiplied these elements. The gateway became a massive **pylon** with tapering walls; the semipublic courtyard was surrounded by columns (a **peristyle** court); the temple itself included an outer **hypostyle hall** (a vast hall filled with columns) and an inner offering hall and sanctuary. The design was symmetrical and axial—that is, all of its separate elements are symmetrically arranged along a dominant center line, creating a processional path from the outside straight into the sanctuary. The rooms became smaller, darker, and more exclusive as they neared the sanctuary, where the cult image of the god was housed. Only the pharaoh and the priests entered these inner rooms.

Two temple districts consecrated primarily to the worship of Amun, Mut, and Khons arose near Thebes—a huge complex at Karnak to the north and, joined to it by an avenue of sphinxes, a more compact temple at Luxor to the south.

KARNAK.   Karnak was a longstanding sacred site, where temples were built and rebuilt for over 1,500 years. During the nearly 500 years of the New Kingdom, successive kings renovated and expanded the complex of the **GREAT TEMPLE OF AMUN** until it covered about 60 acres, an area as large as a dozen football fields (FIG. 3–18).

Access to the heart of the temple, a sanctuary containing the statue of Amun, was from the west (on the left side of the reconstruction drawing) through a principal courtyard, a hypostyle hall, and a number of smaller halls and courts. Pylons set off each of these separate elements. Between the reigns of Thutmose I (Eighteenth Dynasty, r. c. 1493–1482 BCE), and Ramses II (Nineteenth Dynasty, r. c. 1279–1213 BCE), this area of the complex underwent a great deal of construction and renewal. The greater part of the pylons leading to the sanctuary and the halls and courts behind them were renovated or newly built and embellished with colorful pictorial wall reliefs. A sacred lake was also added to the south of the complex, where the king and priests might undergo ritual purification before entering the temple. Thutmose III erected a court and festival temple to his own glory behind the sanctuary of Amun. His great-grandson Amenhotep III (r. 1390–1353 BCE) placed a large stone statue of the god Khepri, the scarab (beetle) symbolic of the rising sun, rebirth, and everlasting life, next to the sacred lake.

In the sanctuary of Amun, priests washed the god's statue every morning and clothed it in a new garment. Because the god was thought to derive nourishment from the spirit of food, his statue was provided with tempting meals twice a day, which the priests then removed and ate themselves. Ordinary people entered the temple precinct only as far as the forecourts of the hypostyle halls, where they found themselves surrounded by inscriptions and images of kings and the god on columns and walls. During religious festivals, they lined the waterways, along which statues of the gods were carried in ceremonial boats, and were permitted to submit petitions to the priests for requests they wished the gods to grant.

To view this image, please go to page 66 of the *Art History*, Fourth Edition by Marilyn Stokstad ebook.

3–18 • RECONSTRUCTION DRAWING OF THE GREAT TEMPLE OF AMUN AT KARNAK
New Kingdom, c. 1579–1075 BCE.

To view this image, please go to page 67 of the *Art History*, Fourth Edition by Marilyn Stokstad ebook.

3–19 • RECONSTRUCTION DRAWING OF THE HYPOSTYLE HALL, GREAT TEMPLE OF AMUN AT KARNAK
Nineteenth Dynasty (c. 1292–1190 BCE).

THE GREAT HALL AT KARNAK. One of the most prominent features of the complex at Karnak is the enormous hypostyle hall set between two pylons at the end of the main forecourt. Erected in the reigns of the Nineteenth-Dynasty rulers Sety I (r. c. 1290–1279 BCE) and his son Ramses II (r. c. 1279–1213 BCE), and called the "Temple of the Spirit of Sety, Beloved of Ptah in the House of Amun," it may have been used for royal coronation ceremonies. Ramses II referred to it as "the place where the common people extol the name of his majesty." The hall was 340 feet wide and 170 feet long. Its 134 closely spaced columns supported a roof of flat stones, the center section of which rose some 30 feet higher than the broad sides **(FIGS. 3–19, 3–20)**. The columns supporting this higher part of the roof are 69 feet tall and 12 feet in diameter, with massive papyrus capitals. On each side, smaller columns with bud capitals seem to march off forever into the darkness. In each of the side walls of the higher center section, a long row of window openings created a clerestory. These openings were filled with stone grillwork, so they cannot have provided much light, but they did permit a cooling flow of air through the hall. Despite the dimness of the interior, artists covered nearly every inch of the columns, walls, and cross-beams with painted pictorial reliefs and inscriptions.

HATSHEPSUT

Across the Nile from Karnak and Luxor lay Deir el-Bahri and the Valleys of the Kings and Queens. These valleys on the west bank of the Nile held the royal necropolis, including the tomb of the pharaoh Hatshepsut. The dynamic Hatshepsut (Eighteenth Dynasty, r. c. 1473–1458 BCE) is a notable figure in a period otherwise dominated by male warrior-kings. Besides Hatshepsut, very few women ruled Egypt—they included the little-known Sobekneferu, Tausret, and much later, the well-known Cleopatra VII.

To view this image, please go to page 67 of the *Art History*, Fourth Edition by Marilyn Stokstad ebook.

3–20 • COLUMNS WITH PAPYRIFORM AND BUD CAPITALS, HYPOSTYLE HALL, GREAT TEMPLE OF AMUN AT KARNAK

EXPLORE MORE: Click the Google Earth link for the Hypostyle Hall of Amun-Ra **www.myartslab.com**

To view this image, please go to page 68 of the *Art History*, Fourth Edition by Marilyn Stokstad ebook.

3-21 • HATSHEPSUT KNEELING
Deir el-Bahri. Eighteenth Dynasty, c. 1473–1458 BCE. Red granite, height 8′6″ (2.59 m). Metropolitan Museum of Art, New York.

The daughter of Thutmose I, Hatshepsut married her half-brother, who then reigned for 14 years as Thutmose II. When he died in c. 1473, she became regent for his underage son—Thutmose III—born to one of his concubines. Within a few years, Hatshepsut had herself declared "king" by the priests of Amun, a maneuver that made her co-ruler with Thutmose III for 20 years. There was no artistic formula for a female pharaoh in Egyptian art, yet Hatshepsut had to be portrayed in her new role. What happened reveals something fundamentally important about the art of ancient Egypt. She was represented as a male king (**FIG. 3–21**), wearing a kilt and linen headdress, occasionally even a king's false beard. The formula for portraying kings was not adapted to suit one individual; she was adapted to conform to convention. There could hardly be a more powerful manifestation of the premium on tradition in Egyptian royal art.

At the height of the New Kingdom, rulers undertook extensive personal building programs, and Hatshepsut is responsible for one of the most spectacular: her funerary temple located at Deir el-Bahri, about a mile away from her actual tomb in the Valley of the Kings (**FIG. 3–22**). This imposing complex was designed for funeral rites and commemorative ceremonies and is much larger and more prominent than the tomb itself, reversing the scale relationship we saw in the Old Kingdom pyramid complexes.

Magnificently sited and sensitively reflecting the natural three-part layering in the rise of the landscape—from flat desert, through a sloping hillside, to the crescendo of sheer stone cliffs—Hatshepsut's temple was constructed on an axial plan (**FIG. 3–23**). A causeway lined with sphinxes once ran from a valley temple on the Nile to the huge open space of the first court, where rare myrrh trees were planted in the temple's garden terraces. From there, visitors ascended a long, straight ramp to a second court where shrines to Anubis and Hathor occupy the ends of the columned porticos. On the temple's uppermost court, colossal royal statues fronted another **colonnade**

To view this image, please go to page 68 of the *Art History*, Fourth Edition by Marilyn Stokstad ebook.

3-22 • FUNERARY TEMPLE OF HATSHEPSUT, DEIR EL-BAHRI
Eighteenth Dynasty, c. 1473–1458 BCE. (At the far left, ramp and base of the funerary temple of Mentuhotep III. Eleventh Dynasty, r. c. 2009–1997 BCE.)

To view this image, please go to page 69 of the *Art History*, Fourth Edition by Marilyn Stokstad ebook.

3-23 • SCHEMATIC DRAWING OF THE FUNERARY TEMPLE OF HATSHEPSUT
Deir el-Bahri.

(a row of columns supporting a lintel or a series of arches), and behind this lay a large hypostyle hall with chapels dedicated to Hatshepsut, her father, and the gods Amun and Ra-Horakhty— a powerful form of the sun god Ra combined with Horus. Centered in the hall's back wall was the entrance to the innermost sanctuary, a small chamber cut deep into the cliff.

THE TOMB OF RAMOSE

The traditional art of pictorial relief, employing a representational system that had dominated Egyptian figural art since the time of Narmer, reached a high degree of aesthetic refinement and technical sophistication during the Eighteenth-Dynasty reign of Amenhotep III (r. c. 1390–1353 BCE), especially in the reliefs carved for the unfinished tomb of Ramose near Thebes (FIG. 3–24).

As mayor of Thebes and vizier (principal royal advisor or minister) to both Amenhotep III and Amenhotep IV (r. 1353–c. 1336 BCE), Ramose was second only to the pharaoh in power and prestige. Soon after his ascent to political prominence, he began construction of an elaborate tomb comprised of four rooms, including an imposing hypostyle hall 82 feet wide. Walls were covered with paintings or with shallow pictorial relief carvings, celebrating the accomplishments, affiliations, and lineage of Ramose and his wife Merytptah, or visualizing the funeral rites that would take place after their death. But the tomb was not used by Ramose. Work on it ceased in the fourth year of Amenhotep IV's reign, when, renamed Akhenaten, he relocated the court from Thebes to the new city of Akhetaten. Presumably Ramose moved with the court to the new capital, but neither his name nor a new tomb has been discovered there.

To view this image, please go to page 69 of the *Art History*, Fourth Edition by Marilyn Stokstad ebook.

3-24 • RAMOSE'S BROTHER MAY AND HIS WIFE WERENER
Tomb of Ramose, Thebes. Eighteenth Dynasty, c. 1375–1365 BCE.

The tomb was abandoned in various stages of completion. The reliefs were never painted, and some walls preserve only the preliminary sketches that would have guided sculptors. But the works that were executed are among the most sophisticated relief carvings in the history of art. On one wall, Ramose and his wife Merytptah appear, hosting a banquet for their family. All are portrayed at the same moment of youthful perfection, even though they represent two successive generations. Sophisticated carvers lavished their considerable technical virtuosity on the portrayal of these untroubled and majestic couples, creating clear textural differentiation of skin, hair, clothes, and jewelry. The easy elegance of linear fluidity is not easy to obtain in this medium, and the convincing sense of three-dimensionality in forms and their placement is managed within an extraordinarily shallow depth of relief. In the detail of Ramose's brother May and sister-in-law Werener in FIG. 3–24, the traditional ancient Egyptian marital embrace (SEE FIGS. 3–9, 3–17) takes on a new tenderness, recalling—especially within the eternal stillness of a tomb—the words of a New Kingdom love poem:

> While unhurried days come and go,
> Let us turn to each other in quiet affection,
> Walk in peace to the edge of old age.
> And I shall be with you each unhurried day,
> A woman given her one wish: to see
> For a lifetime the face of her lord. (Foster, p. 18)

The conceptual conventions of Egyptian pharaonic art are rendered in these carvings with such warmth and refinement that they become almost believable. Our rational awareness of their artificiality is momentarily eclipsed by their sheer beauty. But within this refined world of stable convention, something very jarring took place during the reign of Amenhotep III's successor, Amenhotep IV.

AKHENATEN AND THE ART OF THE AMARNA PERIOD

Amenhotep IV was surely the most unusual ruler in the history of ancient Egypt. During his 17-year reign (c. 1353–1336 BCE), he radically transformed the political, spiritual, and cultural life of the country. He founded a new religion honoring a single supreme god, the life-giving sun deity Aten (represented by the sun's disk), and changed his own name in about 1348 BCE to Akhenaten ("One Who Is Effective on Behalf of Aten"). Abandoning Thebes, the capital of Egypt since the beginning of his dynasty and a city firmly in the grip of the priests of Amun, Akhenaten built a new capital much farther north, calling it Akhetaten ("Horizon of the Aten"). Using the modern name for this site, Tell el-Amarna, historians refer to Akhenaten's reign as the Amarna period.

THE NEW AMARNA STYLE. Akhenaten's reign not only saw the creation of a new capital and the rise of a new religious focus; it also led to radical changes in royal artistic conventions. In portraits

To view this image, please go to page 70 of the *Art History*, Fourth Edition by Marilyn Stokstad ebook.

3-25 • COLOSSAL FIGURE OF AKHENATEN
From the temple known as the Gempaaten, built early in Akhenaten's reign just southeast of the Temple of Karnak. Sandstone with traces of polychromy, height of remaining portion about 13′ (4 m). Egyptian Museum, Cairo. (JE 49528)

EXPLORE MORE: Gain insight from a primary source related to the Colossal Figure of Akhenaten www.myartslab.com

of the king, artists subjected his representation to startling stylizations, even physical distortions. This new royal figure style can be seen in a colossal statue of Akhenaten, about 16 feet tall, created for a new temple to the Aten that he built near the temple complex of Karnak, openly challenging the state gods (FIG. 3–25). This portrait was placed in one of the porticos of a huge courtyard (c. 426 by 394 feet), oriented to the movement of the sun.

The sculpture's strange, softly swelling forms suggest androgyny. The sagging stomach and inflated thighs contrast with spindly arms, protruding clavicles, and an attenuated neck, on which sits a strikingly stylized head. Facial features are exaggerated, often distorted. Slit-like eyes turn slightly downward, and the bulbous, sensuous lips are flanked by dimples that evoke the expression of ephemeral human emotion. Such stark deviations from convention are disquieting, especially since Akhenaten holds the flail and shepherd's crook, traditional symbols of the pharoah's super-human sovereignty.

The new Amarna style characterizes not only official royal portraits, but also pictorial relief sculpture portraying the family life of Akhenaten and Queen Nefertiti. In one panel the king and queen sit on cushioned stools playing with their nude daughters (FIG. 3–26), whose elongated shaved heads conform to the newly minted figure type. The royal couple receive the blessings of the Aten, whose rays end in hands that penetrate the open pavilion to offer ankhs before their nostrils, giving them the "breath of life." The king holds one child and lovingly pats her head, while she pulls herself forward to kiss him. The youngest of the three perches on Nefertiti's shoulder, trying to attract her mother's attention by stroking her cheek, while the oldest sits on the queen's lap, tugging at her mother's hand and pointing to her father. What a striking contrast with the relief from Ramose's tomb! Rather than composed serenity, this artist has conveyed the fidgety behavior of children and the loving involvement of their parents in a manner not even hinted at in earlier royal portraiture.

To view this image, please go to page 71 of the *Art History*, Fourth Edition by Marilyn Stokstad ebook.

3-26 • AKHENATEN AND HIS FAMILY
Akhetaten (present-day Tell el-Amarna). Eighteenth Dynasty, c. 1353–1336 BCE. Painted limestone relief, 12¼ × 15¼" (31.1 × 38.7 cm). Staatliche Museen zu Berlin, Preussischer Kulturbesitz, Ägyptisches Museum. (14145)

Egyptian relief sculptors often employed the **sunken relief** technique seen here. In ordinary reliefs, the background is carved back so that the figures project out from the finished surface. In sunken relief, the original flat surface of the stone is reserved as background, and the outlines of the figures are deeply incised, permitting the development of three-dimensional forms within them.

EXPLORE MORE: Gain insight from a primary source about Akhenaten **www.myartslab.com**

THE PORTRAIT OF TIY. Akhenaten's goals were actively supported not only by Nefertiti but also by his mother, **QUEEN TIY (FIG. 3–27)**. She had been the chief wife of the king's father, Amenhotep III, and had played a significant role in affairs of state during his reign. Queen Tiy's personality seems to emerge from a miniature portrait head that reveals the exquisite bone structure of her dark-skinned face, with its arched brows, uptilted eyes, and slightly pouting lips. Originally, this portrait included a funerary silver headdress covered with gold cobras and gold jewelry. But after her son came to power and established his new religion, the portrait was altered. A brown cap covered with blue glass beads was placed over the original headdress.

THE HEAD OF NEFERTITI. The famous head of **NEFERTITI (FIG. 3–28)** was discovered in the studio of the sculptor Thutmose and may have served as a model for full-length sculptures or paintings of the queen. The proportions of Nefertiti's refined, regular features, long neck, and heavy-lidded eyes appear almost too ideal to be human, but are eerily consistent with standards of beauty in our own culture. Part of the appeal of this portrait bust, aside from its stunning beauty, may be the artist's dramatic use of color. The hues of the blue headdress and its striped band are repeated in the rich red, blue, green, and gold of the jeweled necklace. The queen's brows, eyelids, cheeks, and lips are heightened with color, as they no doubt were heightened with cosmetics in real life. Whether or not Nefertiti's beauty is exaggerated, phrases used by her subjects when referring to her—"Beautiful of Face," "Mistress

To view this image, please go to page 72 of the *Art History*, Fourth Edition by Marilyn Stokstad ebook.

3-28 • NEFERTITI
Akhetaten (modern Tell el-Amarna). Eighteenth Dynasty, c. 1353–1336 BCE. Painted limestone, height 20″ (51 cm). Staatliche Museen zu Berlin, Preussischer Kulturbesitz, Ägyptisches Museum. (21300)

of Happiness," "Great of Love," or "Endowed with Favors"—tend to support the artist's vision.

GLASS. Glassmaking could only be practiced by artists working for the king, and Akhenaten's new capital had its own glassmaking workshops (see "Glassmaking," opposite). A bottle produced there and meant to hold scented oil was fashioned in the shape of a fish that has been identified as a bolti, a species that carries its eggs in its mouth and spits out its offspring when they hatch. The bolti was a common symbol for birth and regeneration, complementing the self-generation that Akhenaten attributed to the sun disk Aten.

THE RETURN TO TRADITION: TUTANKHAMUN AND RAMSES II

Akhenaten's new religion and revolutionary reconception of pharaonic art outlived him by only a few years. The priesthood of Amun quickly regained its former power, and his son Tutankhaten (Eighteenth Dynasty, r. c. 1332–1322 BCE) returned to traditional religious beliefs, changing his name to Tutankhamun—"Living Image of Amun"—and moving his court back to Thebes. He died young and was buried in the Valley of the Kings.

To view this image, please go to page 72 of the *Art History*, Fourth Edition by Marilyn Stokstad ebook.

3-27 • QUEEN TIY
Kom Medinet el-Ghurab (near el-Lahun). Eighteenth Dynasty, c. 1352 BCE. Wood (perhaps yew and acacia), ebony, glass, silver, gold, lapis lazuli, cloth, clay, and wax, height 3¾″ (9.4 cm). Staatliche Museen zu Berlin, Preussischer Kulturbesitz, Ägyptisches Museum. (21834)

No one knows precisely when or where the technique of glassmaking first developed, but the basics of the process are quite clear. Heating a mixture of sand, lime, and sodium carbonate or sodium sulfate to a very high temperature produces glass. The addition of minerals can make the glass transparent, translucent, or opaque, as well as create a vast range of colors.

The first objects to be made entirely of glass in Egypt were produced with the technique known as core-formed glass. A lump of sandy clay molded into the desired shape was wrapped in strips of cloth, then skewered on a fireproof rod. It was then briefly dipped into a pot of molten glass. When the resulting coating of glass had cooled, the clay core was removed through the opening left by the skewer. To decorate the vessel, glassmakers frequently heated thin rods of colored glass and fused them on and flattened them against the surface in strips. In the fish-shaped bottle shown here—an example of core-formed glass from the New Kingdom's Amarna period—the body was created from glass tinted with cobalt, and the surface was then decorated with small rods of white and orange glass, achieving the wavy pattern that resembles fish scales by dragging a pointed tool along the surface. Then two slices of a rod of spiraled black and white glass were fused to the surface to create its eyes.

To view this image, please go to page 73 of the *Art History*, Fourth Edition by Marilyn Stokstad ebook.

FISH-SHAPED PERFUME BOTTLE
Akhetaten (present-day Tell el-Amarna). Eighteenth Dynasty, reign of Akhenaten, c. 1353–1336 BCE. Core formed glass, length 5¾″ (14.5 cm). British Museum, London. (EA 55193)

TUTANKHAMUN'S TOMB. The sealed inner chamber of Tutankhamun's tomb was never plundered, and when it was found in 1922 its incredible riches were just as they had been left since his interment. His mummified body, crowned with a spectacular mask preserving his royal likeness (SEE FIG. 3–1), lay inside three nested coffins that identified him with Osiris, the god of the dead. The innermost coffin, in the shape of a mummy, is the richest of the three (**FIG. 3–29**). Made of over 240 pounds (110.4 kg) of gold, its surface is decorated with colored glass and semiprecious gemstones, as well as finely incised linear designs and hieroglyphic inscriptions. The king holds a crook and a flail, symbols that were associated with Osiris and had become a traditional part of the royal regalia. A *nemes* headcloth with projecting cobra and vulture covers his head, and a blue braided beard is attached to his chin. Nekhbet and Wadjet, vulture and cobra goddesses of Upper and Lower Egypt, spread their wings across his body. The king's features as reproduced on the coffin and masks are those of a very young man, and the unusually full lips, thin-bridged nose, and pierced earlobes suggest the continuing vitality of some Amarna stylizations.

To view this image, please go to page 73 of the *Art History*, Fourth Edition by Marilyn Stokstad ebook.

3-29 • INNER COFFIN OF TUTANKHAMUN'S SARCOPHAGUS
Tomb of Tutankhamun, Valley of the Kings. Eighteenth Dynasty, c. 1332–1322 BCE. Gold inlaid with glass and semiprecious stones, height 6′7⅞″ (1.85 m), weight nearly 243 pounds (110.4 kg). Egyptian Museum, Cairo. (JE 60671)

SEE MORE: View a video about Tutankhamen **www.myartslab.com**

The Temples of Ramses II at Abu Simbel

Many art objects speak to us subtly, through their enduring beauty or mysterious complexity. Monuments such as Ramses II's temples at Abu Simbel speak to us more directly across the ages with a sense of raw power born of sheer scale. This king-god of Egypt, ruler of a vast empire, a virile wonder who fathered nearly a hundred children, is self-described in an inscription he had carved into an obelisk (now standing in the heart of Paris): "Son of Ra: Ramses-Meryamun ['Beloved of Amun']. As long as the skies exist, your monuments shall exist, your name shall exist, firm as the skies."

Abu Simbel was an auspicious site for Ramses II's great temples. It is north of the second cataract of the Nile, in Nubia, the ancient land of Kush, which Ramses ruled and which was the source of his gold, ivory, and exotic animal skins. The monuments are carved directly into the living rock of the sacred hills. The larger temple is dedicated to Ramses and the Egyptian gods Amun, Ra-Horakhty, and Ptah. The dominant feature is a row of four colossal seated statues of the king himself, 65 feet high, flanked by relatively small statues of family members, including his principal wife Nefertari. Inside the temple, eight 23-foot statues of the god Osiris with the face of the god-king Ramses further proclaim his divinity. The corridor they form leads to seated figures of Ptah, Amun, Ramses II, and Ra. The corridor was oriented in such a way that twice a year the first rays of the rising sun shot through its entire depth to illuminate statues of the king and the three gods placed against the back wall.

About 500 feet away, Ramses ordered a smaller temple to be carved into a mountain sacred to Hathor, goddess of fertility, love, joy, and music, and to be dedicated to Hathor and to Nefertari. The two temples were oriented so that their axes crossed in the middle of the Nile, suggesting that they may have been associated with the annual life-giving flood.

Ironically, rising water nearly destroyed them both. Half-buried in the sand over the ages, the temples were only rediscovered early in the nineteenth century. But in the 1960s, construction of the Aswan High Dam flooded the Abu Simbel site. An international

To view this image, please go to page 74 of the *Art History*, Fourth Edition by Marilyn Stokstad ebook.

TEMPLE OF RAMSES II
Abu Simbel. Nineteenth Dynasty, c. 1279–1213 BCE.

team of experts mobilized to find a way to safeguard Ramses II's temples, deciding in 1963 to cut them out of the rock in blocks and re-erect them on higher ground, secure from the rising waters of Lake Nasser. The projected cost of $32 million was financed by UNESCO, with Egypt and the United States each pledging contributions of $12 million. Work began in 1964 and was completed in 1968. Because of such international cooperation and a combination of modern technology and patient, hard labor, Ramses II's temples were saved from sure destruction so they can continue to speak to future generations.

To view this image, please go to page 75 of the *Art History*, Fourth Edition by Marilyn Stokstad ebook.

To view this image, please go to page 75 of the *Art History*, Fourth Edition by Marilyn Stokstad ebook.

SCHEMATIC DRAWING OF THE TEMPLE OF RAMSES II Abu Simbel.

EXPLORE MORE: Click the Google Earth link for the Temple of Ramses II at Abu Simbel **www.myartslab.com**

RAMSES II AND ABU SIMBEL. By Egyptian standards Tutankhamun was a rather minor king. Ramses II, on the other hand, was both powerful and long-lived. Under Ramses II (Nineteenth Dynasty, r. c. 1279–1213 BCE), Egypt was a mighty empire. Ramses was a bold leader and an effective political strategist. Although he did not win every battle, he was an effective master of royal propaganda, able to turn military defeats into glorious victories. He also triumphed diplomatically by securing a peace agreement with the Hittites, a rival power centered in Anatolia that had tried to expand to the west and south at Egypt's expense. Ramses twice reaffirmed that agreement by marrying Hittite princesses.

In the course of a long and prosperous reign, Ramses II initiated building projects on a scale rivaling the Old Kingdom Pyramids at Giza. Today, the most awe-inspiring of his many architectural monuments are found at Karnak and Luxor, and at Abu Simbel in Egypt's southernmost region (see "The Temples of Ramses II at Abu Simbel," pages 176–177). At Abu Simbel, Ramses ordered two large temples to be carved into natural rock, one for himself and the other for his principal wife, Nefertari.

The temples at Abu Simbel were not funerary monuments. Ramses' and Nefertari's tombs are in the Valleys of the Kings and Queens. The walls of Nefertari's tomb are covered with exquisite paintings. In one mural, Nefertari offers jars of perfumed ointment to the goddess Isis (**FIG. 3–30**). The queen wears the vulture-skin headdress and jeweled collar indicating her royal position, and a long, semitransparent white linen gown. Isis, seated on her throne behind a table heaped with offerings, holds a long scepter in her left hand, the ankh in her right. She wears a headdress surmounted by the horns of Hathor framing a sun disk, clear indications of her divinity.

The artists responsible for decorating the tomb diverged very subtly but distinctively from earlier stylistic conventions. The outline drawing and use of pure colors within the lines reflect traditional practices, but quite new is the slight modeling of the body forms by small changes of hue to enhance the appearance of three-dimensionality. The skin color of these women is much darker than that conventionally used for females in earlier periods, and lightly brushed-in shading emphasizes their eyes and lips.

THE BOOKS OF THE DEAD

By the time of the New Kingdom, the Egyptians had come to believe that only a person free from wrongdoing could enjoy an afterlife. The dead were thought to undergo a last judgment consisting of two tests presided over by Osiris, the god of the underworld, and supervised by the jackal-headed god of embalming and cemeteries, Anubis. After the deceased were questioned about their behavior in life, their hearts—which the Egyptians believed to

To view this image, please go to page 76 of the *Art History*, Fourth Edition by Marilyn Stokstad ebook.

3-30 • QUEEN NEFERTARI MAKING AN OFFERING TO ISIS
Wall painting in the tomb of Nefertari, Valley of the Queens. Nineteenth Dynasty, 1290–1224 BCE.

After centuries of foreign rule, beginning with the arrival of the Greeks in 332 BCE, the ancient Egyptian language gradually died out. Modern scholars were only able to recover this long-forgotten language through a fragment of a stone stele, dated 196 BCE. Known today as the Rosetta Stone—for the area of the Delta where one of Napoleon's officers discovered it in 1799—it contains a decree issued by the priests at Memphis honoring Ptolemy V (r. c. 205–180 BCE) carved in hieroglyphs, **demotic** (a simplified, cursive form of hieroglyphs), and Greek.

Even with the juxtaposed Greek translation, the two Egyptian texts remained incomprehensible until 1818, when Thomas Young, an English physician interested in ancient Egypt, linked some of the hieroglyphs to specific names in the Greek version. A short time later, French scholar Jean-François Champollion located the names Ptolemy and Cleopatra in both of the Egyptian scripts. With the phonetic symbols for P, T, O, and L in demotic, he was able to build up an "alphabet" of hieroglyphs, and by 1822 he had deciphered the two Egyptian texts.

To view this image, please go to page 77 of the *Art History*, Fourth Edition by Marilyn Stokstad ebook.

ROSETTA STONE
196 BCE. British Museum, London.

p   t   o   l   m   y   s

Hieroglyphic signs for the letters P, T, O, and L, which were Champollion's clues to deciphering the Rosetta Stone.

be the seat of the soul—were weighed on a scale against an ostrich feather, the symbol of Ma'at, goddess of truth, order, and justice.

Family members commissioned papyrus scrolls containing magical texts or spells, which the embalmers sometimes placed among the wrappings of the mummified bodies. Early collectors of Egyptian artifacts referred to such scrolls, often beautifully illustrated, as "Books of the Dead." A scene in one that was created for a man named Hunefer (Nineteenth Dynasty) shows three successive stages in his induction into the afterlife (**FIG. 3–31**). At the left, Anubis leads him by the hand to the spot where he will

To view this image, please go to page 77 of the *Art History*, Fourth Edition by Marilyn Stokstad ebook.

3-31 • JUDGMENT OF HUNEFER BEFORE OSIRIS
Illustration from a Book of the Dead. Nineteenth Dynasty, c. 1285 BCE. Painted papyrus, height 15⅝" (39.8 cm). British Museum, London. (EA 9901)

weigh his heart against the "feather of Truth." Ma'at herself appears atop the balancing arm of the scales wearing the feather as a headdress. To the right of the scales, Ammit, the dreaded "Eater of the Dead"—part crocodile, part lion, and part hippopotamus—watches eagerly for a sign from the ibis-headed god Thoth, who prepares to record the result of the weighing

But the "Eater" goes hungry. Hunefer passes the test, and Horus, on the right, presents him to the enthroned Osiris, who floats on a lake of natron (see "Preserving the Dead," page 158). Behind the throne, the goddesses Nephthys and Isis support the god's left arm, while in front of him Horus's four sons, each entrusted with the care of one of the deceased's vital organs, stand atop a huge lotus blossom rising up out of the lake. In the top register, Hunefer, finally accepted into the afterlife, kneels before 14 gods of the underworld.

THE THIRD INTERMEDIATE PERIOD, C. 1075–715 BCE

After the end of the New Kingdom, Egypt was ruled by a series of new dynasties, whose leaders continued the traditional patterns of royal patronage and pushed figural conventions in new and interesting directions. One of the most extraordinary, and certainly one of the largest, surviving examples of ancient Egyptian bronze sculpture dates from this period (FIG. 3–32). An inscription on the base identifies the subject as Karomama, divine consort of Amun and member of a community of virgin priestesses selected from the pharaoh's family or retinue who were dedicated to him. Karomama herself was the granddaughter of king Osorkan I (Twenty-First Dynasty, r. c. 985–978 BCE). These priestesses amassed great power, held property, and maintained their own court, often passing on their position to one of their nieces. The *sistra* (ritual rattles) that Karomama once carried in her hands would have immediately identified her as a priestess rather than a princess.

The main body of this statue was cast in bronze and subsequently covered with a thin sheathing of bronze, which was then exquisitely engraved with patterns inlaid with gold, silver, and electrum (a natural alloy of gold and silver). Much of the inlay has disappeared, but we can still make out the elaborately incised drawing of the bird wings that surround Karomama and accentuate the fullness of her figure, conceived to embody a new female ideal. Her slender limbs, ample hips, and more prominent breasts contrast with the uniformly slender female figures of the late New Kingdom (SEE FIG. 3–30).

To view this image, please go to page 78 of the *Art History*, Fourth Edition by Marilyn Stokstad ebook.

3-32 • KAROMAMA
Third Intermediate period, Twenty-Second Dynasty, c. 945–715 BCE. Bronze inlaid with gold, silver, electrum, glass, and copper, height 23½" (59.5 cm). Musée du Louvre, Paris.

3-33 • MUMMY WRAPPING OF A YOUNG BOY
Hawara. Roman period, c. 100–120 CE. Linen wrappings with gilded
stucco buttons and inserted portrait in encaustic on wood, height of
mummy 53⅜″ (133 cm), portrait 9½ × 6½″ (24 × 16.5 cm).
British Museum, London. (EA 13595)

LATE EGYPTIAN ART, C. 715–332 BCE

The Late period in Egypt saw the country and its art in the hands
and service of foreigners. Nubians, Persians, Macedonians, Greeks,
and Romans were all attracted to Egypt's riches and seduced by its
art. The Nubians conquered Egypt and re-established capitals at
Memphis and Thebes (712–657 BCE).

In 332 BCE the Macedonian Greeks led by Alexander the
Great conquered Egypt, and after Alexander's death in 323 BCE, his
generals divided up his empire. Ptolemy, a Greek, took Egypt,
declaring himself king in 305 BCE. The Ptolemaic dynasty ended
with the death of Cleopatra VII (r. 51–30 BCE), when the Romans
succeeded as Egypt's rulers and made it the breadbasket of Rome.

Not surprisingly, works from this period combine the
conventions of Greco-Roman and Egyptian art. For example, the
tradition of mummifying the dead continued well into Egypt's
Roman period. Thousands of mummies and hundreds of mummy
portraits from that time have been found in the Fayum region of
Lower Egypt. The mummy becomes a "soft sculpture" with a
Roman-style portrait **(FIG. 3–33)** painted on a wood panel in
encaustic (hot, colored wax), inserted over the face. Although
great staring eyes invariably dominate the images—as they had in
the funerary mask of Tutankhamun—these artists have seemingly
recorded individual features of the deceased. Such Fayum portraits
link Egyptian art with ancient Roman art.

THINK ABOUT IT

3.1 Discuss how the distinctive pictorial conventions for
representing the human figure in ancient Egypt are used in the
Palette of Narmer ("Closer Look," page 154) and the Tomb of
Ramose (fig. 3–24).

3.2 Explain how depictions of royalty differ from those of ordinary
people in ancient Egyptian art. Then compare and contrast
Egyptian royal portraits from two different periods, making
sure to explain the distinctive traits that characterize each.

3.3 Summarize the religious beliefs of ancient Egypt with regard
to the afterlife, and explain how their beliefs inspired specific
traditions in art and architecture.

3.4 Select a New Kingdom temple in this chapter that best
represents the complexity of construction and decoration that
New Kingdom builders brought to this traditional form of
ancient Egyptian architecture. Support your choice with a
discussion of its structural and decorative features.

PRACTICE MORE: Compose answers to these
questions, get flashcards for images and terms,
and review chapter material with quizzes
www.myartslab.com

To view this image, please go to page 100 of the *Art History*, Fourth Edition by Marilyn Stokstad ebook.

3–34 • Exekias (potter and painter) AJAX AND ACHILLES PLAYING A GAME
c. 540–530 BCE. Black-figure painting on a ceramic amphora, height of amphora 2′ (61 cm). Vatican Museums, Rome.

SEE MORE: View a video about the process of ceramics **www.myartslab.com**

ART OF ANCIENT GREECE

This elegantly contoured **amphora** was conceived and created to be more than the all-purpose storage jar signaled by its shape, substance, and size (FIG. 3–34). A strip around the belly of its bulging form was reserved by Exekias—the mid-sixth-century BCE Athenian artist who signed it proudly as both potter and painter—for the presentation of a narrative episode from the Trojan War, one of the signal stories of the ancient Greeks' mythical conception of their past. Two heroic warriors, Achilles and Ajax, sit across from each other, supporting themselves on their spears as they lean in toward the block between them that serves as a makeshift board for their game of dice. Ajax, to the right, calls out "three"—the spoken word written out diagonally on the surface as if issuing from his mouth. Achilles counters with "four," the winning number, his victory presaged by the visual prominence of the boldly silhouetted helmet perched on his head. (Ajax's headgear has been set casually aside on his shield, leaning behind him.) Ancient Greek viewers, however, would have perceived the tragic irony of Achilles' victory. When these two warriors returned from this playful diversion into the serious contest of battle, Achilles would be killed. Soon afterwards, the grieving Ajax would take his own life in despair.

The poignant narrative encounter portrayed on this amphora is also a masterful compositional design. Crisscrossing diagonals and compressed overlapping of spears, bodies, and table describe spatial complexity as well as surface pattern. The varying textures of hair, armor and clothing are dazzlingly evoked by the alternation between expanses of unarticulated surface and the finely incised lines of dense pattern. Careful contours convey a sense of three-dimensional human form. And the arrangement coordinates with the very shape of the vessel itself, its curving outline matched by the warriors' bending backs, the line of its handles continued in the tilt of the leaning shields.

There is no hint here of gods or kings. Focus rests on the private diversions of heroic warriors as well as on the identity and personal style of the artist who portrayed them. Supremely self-aware and self-confident, the ancient Greeks developed a concept of human supremacy and responsibility that required a new visual expression. Their art was centered in the material world, but it also conformed to strict ideals of beauty and mathematical concepts of design, paralleling the Greek philosophers' search for the human values of truth, virtue, and harmony, qualities that imbue both subject and style in this celebrated work.

LEARN ABOUT IT

3.5 Trace the emergence of a distinctive style and approach to art and architecture during the early centuries of Greek civilization.

3.6 Compare and contrast the black-figure and red-figure techniques of ceramic painting.

3.7 Assess the differences between the three order systems used in temple architecture.

3.8 Explore the nature and meaning of the High Classical style in ancient Greek art.

3.9 Discover the ways Hellenistic sculptors departed from the norms of High Classicism.

HEAR MORE: Listen to an audio file of your chapter **www.myartslab.com**

THE EMERGENCE OF GREEK CIVILIZATION

Ancient Greece was a mountainous land of spectacular natural beauty. Olive trees and grapevines grew on the steep hillsides, producing oil and wine, but there was little good farmland. In towns, skilled artisans produced metal and ceramic wares to trade abroad for grain and raw materials. Greek merchant ships carried pots, olive oil, and bronzes from Athens, Corinth, and Aegina around the Mediterranean Sea, extending the Greek cultural orbit from mainland Greece south to the Peloponnee, north to Macedonia, and east to the Aegean islands and the coast of Asia Minor (MAP 3–2). Greek colonies in Italy, Sicily, and Asia Minor rapidly became powerful independent commercial and cultural centers themselves, but they remained tied to the homeland by common language, heritage, religion, and art.

Within a remarkably brief time, Greek artists developed focused and distinctive ideals of human beauty and architectural design that continue to exert a profound influence today. From about 900 BCE until about 100 BCE, they concentrated on a new, rather narrow range of subjects and produced an impressive body of work with focused stylistic aspirations in a variety of media. Greek artists were restless. They continually sought to change and improve existing artistic trends and fashions, effecting striking stylistic change over the course of a few centuries. This is in stark contrast to the situation we discovered in ancient Egypt, where a desire for permanence and continuity maintained stable artistic conventions for nearly 3,000 years.

HISTORICAL BACKGROUND

In the ninth and eighth centuries BCE, long after Mycenaean dominance in the Aegean had come to an end, the Greeks began to form independently governed city-states. Each city-state was an autonomous region with a city—Athens, Corinth, Sparta—as its political, economic, religious, and cultural center. Each had its own form of government and economy, and each managed its own domestic and foreign affairs. The power of these city-states initially depended at least as much on their manufacturing and commercial skills as on their military might.

Among the emerging city-states, Corinth, located on major land and sea trade routes, was one of the oldest and most powerful. By the sixth century BCE, Athens rose to commercial and cultural preeminence. Soon it had also established a representative government in which every community had its own assembly and magistrates. All citizens participated in the assembly and all had an equal right to own private property, to exercise freedom of speech, to vote and hold public office, and to serve in the army or navy. Citizenship, however, was open only to Athenian men. The census of 309 BCE in Athens listed 21,000 citizens, 10,000 foreign residents, and 400,000 others—that is, women, children, and slaves.

RELIGIOUS BELIEFS AND SACRED PLACES

According to ancient Greek legend, the creation of the world involved a battle between the earth gods, called Titans, and the sky gods. The victors were the sky gods, whose home was believed to be atop Mount Olympos in the northeast corner of the Greek mainland. The Greeks saw their gods as immortal and endowed with supernatural powers, but more than peoples of the ancient Near East and the Egyptians, they also visualized them in human form and attributed to them human weaknesses and emotions. Among the most important deities were the supreme god and goddess, Zeus and Hera, and their offspring (see "Greek and Roman Deities," page 186).

Many sites throughout Greece, called **sanctuaries**, were thought to be sacred to one or more gods. The earliest sanctuaries included outdoor altars or shrines and a sacred natural element such as a tree, a rock, or a spring. As more buildings were added, a sanctuary might become a palatial home for the gods, with one or more temples, several treasuries for storing valuable offerings, various monuments and statues, housing for priests and visitors, an outdoor dance floor or permanent theater for ritual performances and literary competitions, and a stadium for athletic events. The Sanctuary of Zeus near Olympia, in the western Peloponnese, housed an extensive athletic facility with training rooms and arenas for track-and-field events. It was here that athletic competitions, prototypes of today's Olympic Games, were held.

Greek sanctuaries (SEE FIGS. 3–38, 3–39) are quite different from the religious complexes of the ancient Egyptians. Egyptian builders dramatized the power of gods or god-rulers by organizing their temples along straight, processional ways. The Greeks, in contrast, treated each building and monument as an independent element to be integrated with the natural features of the site, in an irregular arrangement that emphasized the exterior of each building as a discrete sculptural form on display.

GREEK ART c. 900–c. 600 BCE

Around the mid eleventh century BCE, a new culture began to form on the Greek mainland. Athens began to develop as a major center of ceramic production, creating both sculpture and vessels decorated with organized abstract designs. In this Geometric period, the Greeks, as we now call them, were beginning to create their own architectural forms and were trading actively with their neighbors to the east. By c. 700 BCE, in a phase called the Orientalizing period, they began to incorporate exotic foreign motifs into their native art.

THE GEOMETRIC PERIOD

What we call the Geometric period flourished in Greece between 900 and 700 BCE, especially in the decoration of ceramic vessels with linear motifs, such as spirals, diamonds, and cross-hatching.

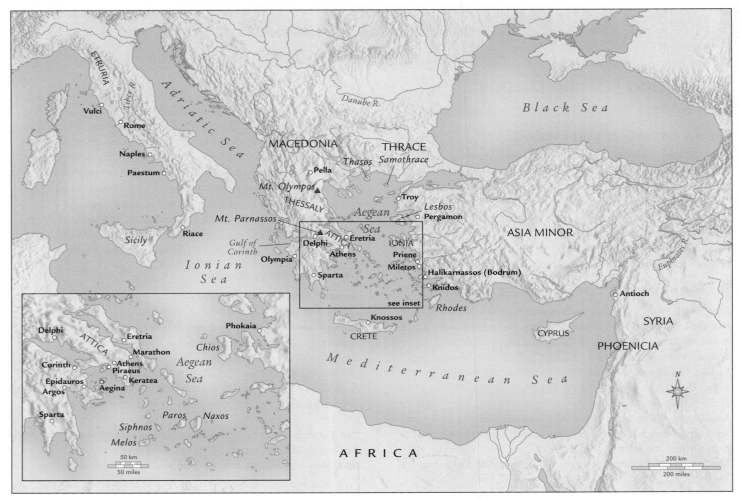

MAP 3-2 • ANCIENT GREECE

The cultural heartland of ancient Greece consisted of the Greek mainland, the islands of the Aegean, and the west coast of Asian Minor, but colonies on the Italic peninsula and the island of Sicily extended Greek cultural influence further west into the Mediterranean.

This abstract vocabulary is strikingly different from the stylized plants, birds, and sea creatures that had characterized Minoan pots.

Large funerary vessels were developed at this time for use as grave markers, many of which have been uncovered at the ancient cemetery of Athens just outside the Dipylon Gate, once the main western entrance into the city. The krater illustrated here (**FIG. 3–35**) provides a detailed pictorial record of funerary rituals—including the relatively new Greek practice of cremation—associated with the important person whose death is commemorated by this work. On the top register, the body of the deceased is depicted laying on its side atop a funeral bier, about to be cremated. Male and

To view this image, please go to page 103 of the *Art History*, Fourth Edition by Marilyn Stokstad ebook.

3-35 • FUNERARY KRATER

From the Dipylon Cemetery, Athens. c. 750–700 BCE. Attributed to the Hirschfeld Workshop. Ceramic, height 42⅝″ (108 cm). Metropolitan Museum of Art, New York. Rogers Fund, 1914 (14.130.14)

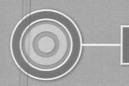

Greek and Roman Deities

(The Roman form of the name is given after the Greek name.)

THE FIVE CHILDREN OF EARTH AND SKY

Zeus (Jupiter), supreme Olympian deity. Mature, bearded man, often holding scepter or lightning bolt; sometimes represented as an eagle.
Hera (Juno), goddess of marriage. Sister/wife of Zeus. Mature woman; cow and peacock are sacred to her.
Hestia (Vesta), goddess of the hearth. Sister of Zeus. Her sacred flame burned in communal hearths.
Poseidon (Neptune), god of the sea. Holds a three-pronged spear.
Hades (Pluto), god of the underworld, the dead, and wealth.

THE SEVEN SKY GODS, OFFSPRING OF THE FIRST FIVE

Ares (Mars), god of war. Son of Zeus and Hera.
Hephaistos (Vulcan), god of the forge, fire, and metal handicrafts. Son of Hera (in some myths, also of Zeus); husband of Aphrodite.
Apollo (Phoebus), god of the sun, light, truth, music, archery, and healing. Sometimes identified with Helios (the Sun), who rides a chariot across the daytime sky. Son of Zeus and Leto (a descendant of Earth); brother of Artemis.
Artemis (Diana), goddess of the hunt, wild animals, and the moon. Sometimes identified with Selene (the Moon), who rides a chariot or oxcart across the night sky. Daughter of Zeus and Leto; sister of Apollo. Carries bow and arrows and is accompanied by hunting dogs.

Athena (Minerva), goddess of wisdom, war, victory, and the city. Also goddess of handcrafts and other artistic skills. Daughter of Zeus; sprang fully grown from his head. Wears helmet and carries shield and spear.
Aphrodite (Venus), goddess of love. Daughter of Zeus and the water nymph Dione; alternatively, born of sea foam; wife of Hephaistos.
Hermes (Mercury), messenger of the gods, god of fertility and luck, guide of the dead to the underworld, and god of thieves and commerce. Son of Zeus and Maia, the daughter of Atlas, a Titan who supports the sky on his shoulders. Wears winged sandals and hat; carries caduceus, a wand with two snakes entwined around it.

OTHER IMPORTANT DEITIES

Demeter (Ceres), goddess of grain and agriculture. Daughter of Kronos and Rhea, sister of Zeus and Hera.
Persephone (Proserpina), goddess of fertility and queen of the underworld. Wife of Hades; daughter of Demeter.
Dionysos (Bacchus), god of wine, the grape harvest, and inspiration. His female followers are called **maenads** (Bacchantes).
Eros (Cupid), god of love. In some myths, the son of Aphrodite. Shown as an infant or young boy, sometimes winged, carrying bow and arrows.
Pan (Faunus), protector of shepherds, god of the wilderness and of music. Half-man, half-goat, he carries panpipes.
Nike (Victory), goddess of victory. Often shown winged and flying.

---

female figures stand on each side of the body, their arms raised and both hands placed on top of their heads in a gesture of anguish, as if these mourners were literally tearing their hair out with grief. In the register underneath, horse-drawn chariots and footsoldiers, who look like walking shields with tiny antlike heads and muscular legs, move in solemn procession.

The geometric shapes used to represent human figures on this pot—triangles for torsos; more triangles for the heads in profile; round dots for eyes; long, thin rectangles for arms; tiny waists; and long legs with bulging thigh and calf muscles—are what has given the Geometric style its name. Figures are shown in either full-frontal or full-profile views that emphasize flat patterns and crisp outlines. Any sense of the illusion of three-dimensional forms occupying real space has been avoided. But the artist has captured a deep sense of human loss by exploiting the stylized solemnity and strong rhythmic accents of the carefully arranged elements.

Egyptian funerary art reflected the strong belief that the dead, in the afterlife, could continue to engage in activities they enjoyed while alive. For the Greeks, the deceased entered a place of mystery and obscurity that living humans could not define

precisely, and their funerary art, in contrast, focused on the emotional reactions of the survivors. The scene of human mourning on this pot contains no supernatural beings, nor any identifiable reference to an afterlife, only poignant evocations of the sentiments and rituals of those left behind on earth.

Greek artists of the Geometric period also produced figurines of wood, ivory, clay, and cast bronze. These small statues of humans and animals are similar in appearance to those painted on pots. A tiny bronze of this type **(FIG. 3–36)**, depicting a **MAN AND CENTAUR**—a mythical creature, part man and part horse—dates to about the same time as the funerary krater. Although there were wise and good centaurs in Greek lore, this work takes up the theme of battling man and centaur, prominent throughout the history of Greek art (SEE FIG. 3–54). The two figures confront each other after the man—perhaps Herakles—has stabbed the centaur; the spearhead is visible on the centaur's left side. Like the painter of the contemporary funerary krater, the sculptor here has distilled the body parts of the figures to elemental geometric shapes, arranging them in a composition of solid forms and open, or negative, spaces that makes the piece pleasing from multiple

3-36 • MAN AND CENTAUR
Perhaps from Olympia. c. 750 BCE. Bronze, height 4⁵⁄₁₆″ (11.1 cm).
Metropolitan Museum of Art, New York. Gift of J. Pierpont Morgan, 1917
(17.190.2072)

swans—stride in horizontal bands against a light background with stylized flower forms called **rosettes** filling the spaces around them. An example of the **black-figure** technique, dark shapes define the silhouettes of the animals against a background of very pale buff, the natural color of the Corinthian clay. The artist incised fine details inside the silhouetted shapes with a sharp tool and added touches of white and red slip to enliven the design.

viewpoints. Most such sculptures have been found in sanctuaries, suggesting that they may have served as votive offerings to the gods.

THE ORIENTALIZING PERIOD

By the seventh century BCE, painters in major pottery centers in Greece had moved away from the dense linear decoration of the Geometric style. They now created more open compositions built around large motifs that included real and imaginary animals, abstract plant forms, and human figures. The source of these motifs can be traced to the arts of the Near East, Asia Minor, and Egypt. Greek painters did not simply copy the work of Eastern artists, however. Instead, they drew on work in a variety of media—including sculpture, metalwork, and textiles—to invent an entirely new approach to painting vessels.

The Orientalizing style (c. 700–600 BCE) began in Corinth, a port city where luxury wares from the Near East and Egypt inspired artists. The new style is evident in a Corinthian **olpe**, or wide-mouthed pitcher, dating to about 650–625 BCE **(FIG. 3–37)**. Silhouetted creatures—lions, panthers, goats, deer, bulls, boars, and

3-37 • OLPE (PITCHER)
Corinth. c. 650–625 BCE. Ceramic with black-figure decoration, height 12⁷⁄₈″ (32.8 cm). J. Paul Getty Museum, Malibu.

To view this image, please go to page 106 of the *Art History*,
Fourth Edition by Marilyn Stokstad ebook.

3-38 • SANCTUARY OF APOLLO, DELPHI
6th–3rd century BCE. View of archaeological site from the air.

**3-39 • RECONSTRUC-
TION DRAWING OF THE
SANCTUARY OF APOLLO,
DELPHI**

To view this image, please go to page 106 of the *Art History*,
Fourth Edition by Marilyn Stokstad ebook.

THE ARCHAIC PERIOD, c. 600–480 BCE

The Archaic period does not deserve its name. "Archaic" means "antiquated" or "old-fashioned," even "primitive," and the term was chosen by art historians who wanted to stress what they perceived as a contrast between the undeveloped art of this time and the subsequent Classical period, once thought to be the most admirable and highly developed phase of Greek art. But the "Archaic" period was a time of great new achievement in Greece. In literature, Sappho wrote her inspired poetry on the island of Lesbos, while on another island the legendary storyteller, Aesop, crafted his animal fables. Artists and architects shared in the growing prosperity as city councils and wealthy individuals sponsored the creation of extraordinary sculpture and fine ceramics and commissioned elaborate civic and religious buildings in cities and sanctuaries.

THE SANCTUARY AT DELPHI

According to Greek myth, Zeus was said to have released two eagles from opposite ends of the earth and they met exactly at the rugged mountain site of Apollo's sanctuary (**FIG. 3–38**). From very early times, the sanctuary at Delphi was renowned as an oracle, a place where the god Apollo was believed to communicate with humans by means of cryptic messages delivered through a human intermediary, or medium (the Pythia). The Greeks and their leaders routinely sought advice at oracles, and attributed many twists of fate to misinterpretations of the Pythia's statements. Even foreign rulers journeyed to request help at Delphi.

Delphi was the site of the Pythian Games which, like the Olympian Games, attracted participants from all over Greece. The principal events were the athletic contests and the music, dance, and poetry competitions in honor of Apollo. As at Olympia, hundreds of statues dedicated to the victors of the competitions, as well as mythological figures, filled the sanctuary grounds. The sanctuary of Apollo was significantly developed during the Archaic period and included the main temple, performance and athletic areas, treasuries, and other buildings and monuments, which made full use of limited space on the hillside (**FIG. 3–39**).

After visitors climbed the steep path up the lower slopes of Mount Parnassos, they entered the sanctuary by a ceremonial gate in the southeast corner. From there they zigzagged up the Sacred Way, so named because it was the route of religious processions during festivals. Moving past the numerous treasuries and memorials built by the city-states, they arrived at the long colonnade of the Temple of Apollo, rebuilt in c. 530 BCE on the site of an earlier temple. Below the temple was a **stoa**, a columned pavilion open on three sides, built by the people of Athens. There visitors rested, talked, or watched ceremonial dancing. At the top of the sanctuary hill was a stadium area for athletic contests.

TREASURY OF THE SIPHNIANS. Sanctuaries also included treasuries built by the citizens of Greek city-states to house and protect their offerings. The small but luxurious **TREASURY OF THE SIPHNIANS (FIG. 3–40)** was built in the sanctuary of Apollo at Delphi by the residents of the island of Siphnos near the Cyclades, between about 530 and 525 BCE. It survives today only in fragments housed in the museum at Delphi. Instead of columns, the builders used two stately **caryatids**—columns carved in the form of clothed women with their finely pleated, flowing garments, raised on **pedestals** and balancing elaborately carved

To view this image, please go to page 107 of the *Art History*, Fourth Edition by Marilyn Stokstad ebook.

3-40 • RECONSTRUCTION DRAWING OF THE TREASURY OF THE SIPHNIANS
Sanctuary of Apollo, Delphi. c. 530–525 BCE.

This small treasury building at Delphi was originally elegant and richly ornamented. The figure sculpture and decorative moldings were once painted in strong colors, mainly dark blue, bright red, and white, with touches of yellow to resemble gold.

To view this image, please go to page 108 of the *Art History*,
Fourth Edition by Marilyn Stokstad ebook.

3-41 • BATTLE BETWEEN THE GODS AND THE GIANTS (TITANS)
Fragments of the north frieze of the Treasury of the Siphnians, from the Sanctuary of Apollo, Delphi.
c. 530–525 BCE. Marble, height 26″ (66 cm). Archaeological Museum, Delphi.

capitals on their heads. The capitals support a tall **entablature** conforming to the **Ionic order**, which features a plain, or three-panel, **architrave** and a continuous carved **frieze**, set off by richly carved moldings (see "The Greek Orders," page 192).

Both the continuous frieze and the **pediments** of the Siphnian Treasury were originally filled with relief sculpture. A surviving section of the frieze from the building's north side, which shows a scene from the legendary **BATTLE BETWEEN THE GODS AND THE GIANTS (TITANS)**, is notable for its complex representation of space **(FIG. 3–41)**. To give a sense of three-dimensional recession, the sculptors placed some figures behind others, overlapping as many as three of them and varying the depth of the relief to allow viewers to grasp their placement within space. Originally such sculptures were painted with bright color that enhanced the lifelike effect.

TEMPLES

For centuries ancient Greeks had worshiped at sanctuaries where an outdoor altar stood near a temple that sheltered a statue of a god. As Greek temples grew steadily in size and complexity, stone and marble replaced the earlier mud-brick and wood construction. A number of standardized plans evolved, ranging from simple, one-room structures with columned **porches** (covered, open space in front of an entrance) to buildings with double porches (front and back), surrounded entirely by columns. Builders also experimented with the design of temple **elevations**—the arrangement, proportions, and appearance of the columns and the lintels, which now grew into elaborate entablatures. Two elevation designs emerged during the Archaic period: the **Doric order** and the Ionic order. The **Corinthian order**, a variant of the Ionic order, would develop later (see "The Greek Orders," page 192).

A particularly well-preserved Archaic temple, built around 550 BCE, still stands at the former Greek colony of Poseidonia (Roman Paestum) about 50 miles south of the modern city of Naples, Italy **(FIG. 3–42)**. Dedicated to Hera, the wife of Zeus, it is known today as Hera I to distinguish it from a second, adjacent temple to Hera built about a century later. The builders used the Doric order. A row of columns called the **peristyle** surrounded the main room, the **cella**. The columns of Hera I are especially robust—only about four times as high as their maximum diameter—and topped with a widely flaring capital and a broad, blocky **abacus**, creating an impression of great stability and permanence. As the column shafts rise, they swell in the middle and contract again toward the top, a refinement known as **entasis**. This adjustment gives a sense of energy and lift. Hera I has an uneven number of columns—nine—across the short ends of the peristyle, with a column instead of a space at the center of the two ends. The entrance to the **pronaos** (enclosed vestibule) has three columns in antis (between flanking wall piers), and a row of columns runs down the center of the wide cella to help support the ceiling and roof. The unusual two-aisle, two-door arrangement leading to the small room at the end of the cella proper suggests that the temple had two presiding deities: either Hera and Poseidon (patron of the city), or Hera and Zeus, or perhaps Hera in her two manifestations (as warrior and protector of the city and as mother and protector of children).

THE TEMPLE OF APHAIA ON AEGINA. A fully developed and somewhat sleeker Doric temple—part of a sanctuary dedicated to a local goddess named Aphaia—was built on the island of Aegina at the turn of the fifth century BCE **(FIG. 3–43)**. Spectacularly sited on the top of a hill overlooking the sea, the temple is reasonably well-preserved, in spite of the loss of pediments, roof, and sections

To view this image, please go to page 109 of the *Art History*, Fourth Edition by Marilyn Stokstad ebook.

To view this image, please go to page 109 of the *Art History*, Fourth Edition by Marilyn Stokstad ebook.

3-42 • PLAN AND EXTERIOR VIEW OF TEMPLE OF HERA I, POSEIDONIA (ROMAN PAESTUM)
Italy. c. 550–540 BCE.

EXPLORE MORE: Click the Google Earth link for The Temple of Hera I **www.myartslab.com**

To view this image, please go to page 109 of the *Art History*, Fourth Edition by Marilyn Stokstad ebook.

3-43 • TEMPLE OF APHAIA, AEGINA
c. 500 BCE. View from the east. Column height about 17′ (5.18 m).

Each of the three Classical Greek architectural **orders**—Doric, Ionic, and Corinthian—constitutes a system of interdependent parts whose proportions are based on mathematical ratios. No element of an order could be changed without producing a corresponding change in other elements.

The basic components are the **column** and the **entablature**, which function as post and lintel in the structural system. All three types of columns have a **shaft** and a **capital**; Ionic and Corinthian also have a **base**. The shafts are formed of stacked round sections, or **drums**, which are joined inside by metal pegs. In Greek temple architecture, columns stand on the **stylobate**, the "floor" of the temple, which rests on top of a set of steps that form the temple's base, known as the **stereobate**.

In the **Doric order**, shafts sit directly on the stylobate, without a base. They are **fluted**, or channeled, with sharp edges. The height of the substantial columns ranges from five-and-a-half to seven times the diameter of the base. A **necking** at the top of the shaft provides a transition to the capital itself, composed of the rounded **echinus**, and the tabletlike **abacus**. The entablature includes the **architrave**, the distinctive frieze of alternating **triglyphs** and **metopes**, and the **cornice**, the topmost, projecting horizontal element. The roofline may have decorative waterspouts and terminal decorative elements called **acroteria**.

The **Ionic order** has more elongated proportions than the Doric, the height of a column being about nine times the diameter of its base. The flutes on the columns are deeper and are separated by flat surfaces called **fillets**. The capital has a distinctive spiral scrolled **volute**; the entablature has a three-panel architrave, continuous sculptured or decorated frieze, and richer decorative moldings.

The **Corinthian order**, a variant of the Ionic order originally developed by the Greeks for use in interiors, was eventually used on temple exteriors as well. Its elaborate capitals are sheathed with stylized **acanthus** leaves that rise from a convex band called the **astragal**.

To view this image, please go to page 110 of the *Art History*, Fourth Edition by Marilyn Stokstad ebook.

SEE MORE: View a simulation of the Greek architectural orders **www.myartslab.com**

To view this image, please go to page 111 of the *Art History*, Fourth Edition by Marilyn Stokstad ebook.

3–44 • RECONSTRUCTION DRAWING OF THE TEMPLE OF APHAIA, AEGINA c. 500 BCE.

To view this image, please go to page 111 of the *Art History*, Fourth Edition by Marilyn Stokstad ebook.

3–45 • PLAN OF COMPLEX, TEMPLE OF APHAIA, AEGINA c. 500 BCE.

of its colonnade. Enough evidence remains to form a reliable reconstruction of its original appearance (FIG. 3–44). The plan combines six columns on the façades with 12 on the sides, and the cella—whose roof was supported by superimposed colonnades—could be entered from porches on both short sides. The slight swelling of the columns (entasis) seen at Poseidonia is evident here as well, and the outside triglyphs are pushed to the ends of frieze, out of alignment with the column underneath them, to avoid the awkwardness of a half metope (rectangular panel with a relief or painting) at the corner.

Like most Greek temples, this building was neither isolated nor situated in open space, but set in relation to an outside altar where religious ceremonies were focused. By enclosing the temple within a walled precinct, the designer could control the viewer's initial experience of the temple. As the viewer entered the sacred space through a gatehouse—the Propylaia—the temple would be seen at an oblique angle (FIG. 3–45). Unlike ancient Egyptian temples, where long processional approaches led visitors directly to the flat entrance façade of a building, the Greek architect revealed from the outset the full shape of a closed, compact, sculptural mass, inviting viewers not to enter seeking something within, but rather to walk around the exterior, exploring the rich sculptural embellishment on pediments and frieze. Cult ceremonies, after all, took place outside the temples.

Modern viewers, however, will not find exterior sculpture at Aegina. Nothing remains from the metopes, and substantial surviving portions of the two pediments were purchased in the early nineteenth century by the future Ludwig I of Bavaria and are now exhibited in Munich. They are precious documents in the development of Greek architectural sculpture. The triangular pediments in Greek temples created challenging compositional problems for sculptors intent on fitting figures into the tapering spaces at the outside corners, since the scale of figures could not change, only their poses. The earlier, west pediment of Aegina (FIG. 3–46), dated about 500–490 BCE, represents a creative solution that became a design standard, appearing with variations throughout the fifth century BCE. The subject of the pediment, rendered in fully three-dimensional figures, is the participation of local warriors in the military expedition against Troy. Fallen warriors fill the angles at both ends of the pediment base, while others crouch and lunge, rising in height toward an image of Athena as warrior

To view this image, please go to page 112 of the *Art History*,
Fourth Edition by Marilyn Stokstad ebook.

3–46 • WEST PEDIMENT OF THE TEMPLE OF APHAIA, AEGINA
c. 500–490 BCE. Width about 49′ (15 m). Surviving fragments as assembled in the Staatliche Antikensammlungen und
Glyptothek, Munich (early restorations removed).

To view this image, please go to page 112 of the *Art History*,
Fourth Edition by Marilyn Stokstad ebook.

3–47 • DYING WARRIOR
From the right corner of the west pediment of the Temple of Aphaia, Aegina. c. 500–490 BCE. Marble, length 5′6″
(1.68 m). Staatliche Antikensammlungen und Glyptothek, Munich.

To view this image, please go to page 112 of the *Art History*,
Fourth Edition by Marilyn Stokstad ebook.

3–48 • DYING WARRIOR
From the left corner of the east pediment of the Temple of Aphaia, Aegina. c. 490–480 BCE. Marble, length 6′
(1.83 m). Staatliche Antikensammlungen und Glyptothek, Munich.

For many modern viewers, it comes as a real surprise, even a shock, that the stone sculptures of ancient Greece did not always have stark white, pure marble surfaces, comparable in appearance to—and consistent in taste with—the more recent, but still classicizing sculptures of Michelangelo or Canova. But they were originally painted with brilliant colors. A close examination of Greek sculpture and architecture has long revealed evidence of polychromy, even to the unaided eye, but our understanding of the original appearance of these works has been greatly enhanced recently. Since the 1980s, German scholar Vinzenz Brinkmann has used extensive visual and scientific analysis to evaluate the traces of painting that remain on ancient Greek sculpture, employing tools such as ultraviolet and x-ray fluorescence, microscopy, and pigment analysis. Based on this research, he and his colleague Ulrike Koch-Brinkmann have fashioned reconstructions that allow us to imagine the exuberant effect these works would have had when they were new.

Illustrated here is their painted reconstruction of a kneeling archer from about 500 BCE that once formed part of the west pediment of the Temple of Aphaia at Aegina. To begin with they have replaced features of the sculpture—ringlet hair extensions, a bow, a quiver, and arrows—probably made of bronze or lead and attached to the stone after it was carved, using the holes still evident in the current state of the figure's hip and head. Most stunning, however, is the diamond-shaped patterns that were painted on his leggings and sleeves, using pigments derived from malachite, azurite, arsenic, cinnabar and charcoal. And the surfaces of such figures were not simply colored in. Artists created a sophisticated integration of three-dimensional form, color, and design. The patterning applied to this archer's leggings actually changes in size and shape in relation to the body beneath it, stretching out on expansive thighs and constricting on tapering ankles. Ancient authors indicate that sculpture was painted to make figures more lifelike, and these recent reconstructions certainly back them up.

To view this image, please go to page 113 of the *Art History*, Fourth Edition by Marilyn Stokstad ebook.

A. Vinzenz Brinkmann and Ulrike Koch-Brinkmann
RECONSTRUCTION OF ARCHER
From the west pediment of the Temple of Aphaia, Aegina. 2004 CE. Staatliche Antikensammlungen und Glyptothek, Munich.

To view this image, please go to page 113 of the *Art History*, Fourth Edition by Marilyn Stokstad ebook.

B. ARCHER ("PARIS")
From the west pediment of the Temple of Aphaia, Aegina. c. 500–490 BCE. Marble. Staatliche Antikensammlungen und Glyptothek, Munich.

goddess—who can fill the elevated pointed space at the center peak since she is allowed to be represented larger (hieratic scale) than the humans who flank her.

Among the best-preserved fragments from the west pediment is the **DYING WARRIOR** from the far right corner **(FIG. 3–47)**. This tragic but noble figure struggles to rise up, supported on bent leg and elbow, in order to extract an arrow from his chest, even though his death seems certain. This figure originally would have been painted and fitted with authentic bronze accessories, heightening the sense of reality (see "Color in Greek Sculpture," above).

A similar figure appeared on the east pediment, created a decade or so after its counterpart on the west **(FIG. 3–48)**. The sculptor of

this dying warrior also exploited the difficult framework of the pediment corner, only here, instead of an uplifted frontal form in profile, we see a twisted body capable of turning in space. The figure is more precariously balanced on his shield, clearly about to collapse. There is an increased sense of softness in the portrayal of human flesh and a greater sophistication in tailoring bodily posture not only to the tapering shape of the pediment, but also to the expression of the warrior's own emotional involvement in the agony and vulnerability of his predicament, which in turn inspires a sense of pathos or empathy in the viewer. Over the course of a decade, the sculptors of Aegina allow us to trace the transition from Archaic toward Early Classical art.

3–49 • Douris A YOUTH POURING WINE INTO THE KYLIX OF A COMPANION
Red-figure decoration on a kylix. c. 480 BCE. Ceramic, height 12¾″ (32.4 cm). The Soprintendenza Speciale per i Beni Archeologici di Napoli e Pompei.

CERAMIC PAINTING

Greek potters and painters continued to work with the red-figure technique throughout the fifth century BCE, refining their ability to create supple, rounded figures, posed in ever more complicated and dynamic compositions. One of the most prolific Early Classical artists was Douris, whose signature appears on over 40 surviving pots, decorated with scenes from everyday life as well as from mythology.

But Douris was also capable of more lyrical compositions, as seen in the painting he placed within a kylix (**FIG. 3–49**), similar in shape to those used as props by the satyrs on the psykter. This **tondo** (circular painting) was an intimate picture. It became visible only to the user of the cup when he tilted up the kylix to drink from it; otherwise, sitting on a table, the painting would have been obscured by the dark wine pool within it. A languidly posed and elegantly draped youth stands behind an altar pouring wine from an **oinochoe** (wine jug) into the kylix of a more dignified, bearded older man. Euphronios' tentative essay in foreshortening Sarpedon's bent leg on his krater blossoms in the work of Douris to become full-scale formal projection as the graceful youth on this kylix bends his arm from the background to project his frontal oinochoe over the laterally held kylix of his seated companion.

For the well-educated reveler using this cup at a symposium, there were several possible readings for the scene he was observing. This could be the legendary Athenian king Kekrops, who appears, identified by inscription, in the scene Douris painted on the underside of the kylix. Also on the bottom of the cup are Zeus and the young Trojan prince Ganymede, whom the supreme god abducted to Olympus to serve as his cup-bearer. Or, since the symposia themselves were the site of amorous conquests between older and younger men, the user of this cup might have found his own situation mirrored in what he was observing while he drank.

THE HIGH CLASSICAL PERIOD, c. 450–400 BCE

The "High" Classical period of Greek art lasted only a half-century, 450 to 400 BCE. The use of the word "high" to qualify the art of this time reflects the value judgments of art historians who have considered this period a pinnacle of artistic refinement, producing works that set a standard of unsurpassed excellence. Some have even referred to this half-century as Greece's "Golden Age," although these decades were also marked by turmoil and destruction. Without a common enemy, Sparta and Athens turned on each other in a series of conflicts known as the Peloponnesian War. Sparta dominated the Peloponnese peninsula and much of the rest of mainland Greece, while Athens controlled the Aegean and became the wealthy and influential center of a maritime empire. Today we remember Athens more for its cultural and intellectual brilliance and its experiments with democratic government, which reached its zenith in the fifth century BCE under the charismatic leader Perikles (c. 495–429 BCE), than for the imperialistic tendencies of its considerable commercial power.

Except for a few brief interludes, Perikles dominated Athenian politics and culture from 462 BCE until his death in 429 BCE.

Although comedy writers of the time sometimes mocked him, calling him "Zeus" and "The Olympian" because of his haughty personality, he was a dynamic, charismatic political and military leader. He was also a great patron of the arts, supporting the use of Athenian wealth for the adornment of the city, and encouraging artists to promote a public image of peace, prosperity, and power. Perikles said of his city and its accomplishments: "Future generations will marvel at us, as the present age marvels at us now." It was a prophecy he himself helped fulfill.

THE ACROPOLIS

Athens originated as a Neolithic **acropolis**, or "part of the city on top of a hill" (*akro* means "high" and *polis* means "city") that later served as a fortress and sanctuary. As the city grew, the Acropolis became the religious and ceremonial center devoted primarily to the goddess Athena, the city's patron and protector.

After Persian troops destroyed the Acropolis in 480 BCE, the Athenians vowed to keep it in ruins as a memorial, but Perikles convinced them to rebuild it, arguing that this project honored the

To view this image, please go to page 129 of the *Art History*, Fourth Edition by Marilyn Stokstad ebook.

3-50 • MODEL/RECONSTRUCTION OF THE ACROPOLIS, ATHENS
c. 447–432 BCE.

EXPLORE MORE: Click the Google Earth link for the Acropolis **www.myartslab.com**

To view this image, please go to page 130 of the *Art History*, Fourth Edition by Marilyn Stokstad ebook.

3-51 • RECREATION OF PHEIDIAS' HUGE GOLD AND IVORY FIGURE
Royal Ontario Museum, Toronto.

gods, especially Athena, who had helped the Greeks defeat the Persians. Perikles intended to create a visual expression of Athenian values and civic pride that would bolster the city's status as the capital of the empire he was instrumental in building. He placed his close friend Pheidias, a renowned sculptor, in charge of the rebuilding and assembled under him the most talented artists in Athens.

The cost and labor involved in this undertaking were staggering. Large quantities of gold, ivory, and exotic woods had to be imported. Some 22,000 tons of marble had to be transported 10 miles from mountain quarries to city workshops. Perikles was severely criticized by his political opponents for this extravagance, but it never cost him popular support. In fact, many working-class Athenians—laborers, carpenters, masons, sculptors, and the farmers and merchants who kept them supplied and fed—benefited from his expenditures.

Work on the **ACROPOLIS** continued after Perikles' death and was completed by the end of the fifth century BCE **(FIG. 3–50)**. Visitors to the Acropolis in 400 BCE would have climbed a steep ramp on the west side of the hill (in the foreground of FIG. 3–50) to the sanctuary entrance, perhaps pausing to admire the small temple dedicated to Athena Nike (Athena as goddess of victory in war), poised on a projection of rock above the ramp. After passing

through an impressive porticoed gatehouse called the Propylaia, they would have seen a huge bronze figure of Athena Promachos (the Defender), designed and executed by Pheidias between about 465 and 455 BCE. Sailors entering the Athenian port of Piraeus, about 10 miles away, could see the sun reflected off her helmet and spear tip. Behind this statue was a walled precinct that enclosed the Erechtheion, a temple dedicated to several deities.

Religious buildings and votive statues filled the hilltop. On the right stood the largest building on the Acropolis—the Parthenon, a temple dedicated to Athena Parthenos (the Virgin). Visitors approached the temple from its northwest corner, seeing both its short and long side, instantly grasping the imposing size of this building, isolated like a work of sculpture elevated on a pedestal. With permission from the priests, they could have climbed the east steps to look into the cella, where they would have seen Pheidias' colossal gold and ivory statue of Athena—outfitted in armor and holding a shield in one hand and a winged Nike (Victory) in the other—which was installed in the temple and dedicated 438 BCE **(FIG. 3–51)**.

THE PARTHENON

Sometime around 490 BCE, Athenians had begun work on a temple to Athena Parthenos that was still unfinished when the Persians sacked the Acropolis a decade later. In 447 BCE Perikles commissioned the architects Kallikrates and Iktinos to design a larger temple using the existing foundation and stone elements. The finest white marble was used throughout—even on the roof, in place of the more usual terra-cotta tiles **(FIG. 3–52)**. The planning and execution of the Parthenon (dedicated in 438 BCE) required extraordinary mathematical and mechanical skills and would have been impossible without a large contingent of distinguished architects and builders, as well as talented sculptors and painters. The result is as much a testament to the administrative skills as to the artistic vision of Pheidias, who supervised the entire project.

One key to the Parthenon's sense of harmony and balance is an attention to proportions—especially the ratio of 4:9, expressing the relationship of breadth to length and also the relationship of column diameter to space between columns. Also important are subtle refinements of design, deviations from absolute regularity to create a harmonious effect when the building was actually viewed. For example, since long, straight horizontal lines seem to sag when seen from a distance, base and entablature curve slightly upward to correct this optical distortion. The columns have a subtle swelling (entasis) and tilt inward slightly from bottom to top; the corners are strengthened visually by reducing the space between columns at those points. These subtle refinements in the arrangement of seemingly regular elements give the Parthenon a buoyant organic appearance and assure that it will not look like a heavy, lifeless stone box. The significance of their achievement was clear to its builders—Iktinos even wrote a book on the proportions of this masterpiece.

The sculptural decoration of the Parthenon reflects Pheidias' unifying aesthetic vision. At the same time, it conveys a number of political and ideological themes: the triumph of the democratic Greek city-states over imperial Persia, the preeminence of Athens thanks to the favor of Athena, and the triumph of an enlightened Greek civilization over despotism and barbarism.

THE PEDIMENTS.   As with most temples, sculpture in the round filled both pediments of the Parthenon, set on the deep shelf of the cornice and secured to the wall with metal pins. Unfortunately, much has been damaged or lost over the centuries (also see "Who Owns the Art?" page 203). Using the locations of the pinholes and weathering marks on the cornice, scholars have been able to determine the placement of surviving statues and infer the poses of missing ones. The west pediment sculpture, facing the entrance to the Acropolis, illustrated the contest Athena won over the sea god

To view this image, please go to page 131 of the *Art History*, Fourth Edition by Marilyn Stokstad ebook.

3-52 • Kallikrates and Iktinos **VIEW AND PLAN OF THE PARTHENON, ACROPOLIS**
Athens. 447–432 BCE. Photograph: view from the northwest. Pantelic marble.

EXPLORE MORE: Click the Google Earth link for The Parthenon **www.myartslab.com**

To view this image, please go to page 131 of the *Art History*, Fourth Edition by Marilyn Stokstad ebook.

To view this image, please go to page 132 of the *Art History*,
Fourth Edition by Marilyn Stokstad ebook.

3-53 • PHOTOGRAPHIC MOCK-UP OF THE EAST PEDIMENT OF THE PARTHENON (USING PHOTOGRAPHS OF THE EXTANT MARBLE SCULPTURE)
c. 447–432 BCE. The gap in the center represents the space that would have been occupied by the missing sculpture. The pediment is over 90 feet (27.45 m) long; the central space of about 40 feet (12.2 m) is missing.

Poseidon for rule over the Athenians. The east pediment figures, above the entrance to the cella, illustrated the birth of Athena, fully grown and clad in armor, from the brow of her father, Zeus.

The statues from the east pediment are the best preserved of the two groups **(FIG. 3–53)**. Flanking the missing central figures—probably Zeus seated on a throne with the newborn adult Athena standing at his side—were groups of three goddesses followed by single reclining male figures. In the left corner was the sun god Helios in his horse-drawn chariot rising from the sea, while at the right the moon goddess Selene descends in her chariot to the sea, the head of her tired horse hanging over the cornice. The reclining male nude, who fits so easily into the left pediment, has been identified as either Herakles with his lion's skin or Dionysos (god of wine) lying on a panther skin. His easy pose conforms to the slope of the pediment without a hint of awkwardness. The two seated women may be the earth and grain goddesses Demeter and Persephone. The running female figure just to the left of center is Iris, messenger of the gods, already spreading the news of Athena's birth.

The three female figures on the right side, two sitting upright and one reclining, are probably Hestia (a sister of Zeus and the goddess of the hearth), Dione (one of Zeus's many consorts), and her daughter, Aphrodite. These monumental interlocked figures seem to be awakening from a deep sleep. The sculptor, whether Pheidias or someone working in his style, expertly rendered

To view this image, please go to page 132 of the *Art History*,
Fourth Edition by Marilyn Stokstad ebook.

3-54 • LAPITH FIGHTING A CENTAUR
Metope relief from the Doric frieze on the south side of the Parthenon. c. 447–432 BCE. Marble, height 56″ (1.42 m). British Museum, London.

the female form beneath the fall of draperies, which both cover and reveal their bodies. The clinging fabric also creates circular patterns rippling with a life of their own and uniting the three figures into a single mass.

THE DORIC FRIEZE. The all-marble Parthenon had two sculptured friezes, one above the outer peristyle and another atop the cella wall inside. The Doric frieze on the exterior had 92 metope reliefs depicting legendary battles, symbolized by combat between two representative figures: a centaur against a Lapith (a legendary people of pre-Hellenic times); a god against a Titan; a Greek against a Trojan; a Greek against an Amazon (members of the mythical tribe of female warriors sometimes said to be the daughters of the war god Ares). Each of these mythic struggles represented for the Greeks the triumph of reason over unbridled animal passion.

Among the best-preserved metope reliefs are several depicting the battle between Lapiths and centaurs from the south side of the Parthenon. The panel shown here **(FIG. 3–54)** presents a pause within the fluid struggle, a timeless image standing for an extended historical episode. Forms are reduced to their most characteristic essentials, and so dramatic is the chiasmic (X-shaped) composition that we easily accept its visual contradictions. The Lapith is caught at an instant of total equilibrium. What could be a grueling tug-of-war between a man and a man-beast has been transformed into an athletic ballet, choreographed to show off the Lapith warrior's flexed muscles and graceful movements against the implausible backdrop of his carefully draped cloak.

THE PROCESSIONAL FRIEZE. Enclosed within the Parthenon's Doric peristyle, a continuous, 525-foot-long Ionic frieze ran along the exterior wall of the cella. The subject is a procession celebrating the festival that took place in Athens every four years, when the women of the city wove a new wool *peplos* and carried it to the Acropolis to clothe an ancient wooden cult statue of Athena.

In Pheidias' portrayal of this major event, the figures—skilled riders managing powerful steeds, for example **(FIG. 3–55)**, or graceful but physically sturdy young walkers **(FIG. 3–56)**—seem to be representative types, ideal inhabitants of a successful city-state.

3-55 • HORSEMEN
Detail of the Procession, from the Ionic frieze on the north side of the Parthenon. c. 447–432 BCE. Marble, height 41¾" (106 cm). British Museum, London.

Just as Greek architects defined and followed a set of standards for ideal temple design, Greek sculptors sought an ideal for representing the human body. Studying actual human beings closely and selecting those human attributes they considered most desirable, such as regular facial features, smooth skin, and particular body proportions, sculptors combined them into a single ideal of physical perfection.

The best-known theorist of the High Classical period was the sculptor Polykleitos of Argos. About 450 BCE, balancing careful observation with generalizing idealization, he developed a set of rules for constructing what he considered the ideal human figure, which he set down in a treatise called "The Canon" (*kanon* is Greek for "measure," "rule," or "law"). To illustrate his theory, Polykleitos created a larger-than-lifesize bronze statue of a standing man carrying a spear—perhaps the hero Achilles. Neither the treatise nor the original statue has survived, but both were widely discussed in the writings of his contemporaries, and later Roman artists made marble copies of the *Spear Bearer* (*Doryphoros*). By studying these copies, scholars have tried to determine the set of measurements that defined ideal human proportions in Polykleitos' canon.

The canon included a system of ratios between a basic unit and the length of various body parts. Some studies suggest that this basic unit may have been the length of the figure's index finger or the width of its hand across the knuckles; others suggest that it was the height of the head from chin to hairline. The canon also included guidelines for *symmetria* ("commensurability"), by which Polykleitos meant the relationship of body parts to one another. In the *Spear Bearer*, he explored not only proportions, but also the relationships between weight-bearing and relaxed legs and arms in a perfectly balanced figure. The balancing of tense or supporting with relaxed or at ease elements in a figure is referred to as contrapposto.

The Roman marble copy of the *Spear Bearer* illustrated here shows a male athlete, perfectly balanced, with the whole weight of the upper body supported over the straight (engaged) right leg. The left leg is bent at the knee, with the left foot poised on the ball of the foot, suggesting preceding and succeeding movement. The pattern of tension and relaxation is reversed in the arrangement of the arms, with the right relaxed on the engaged side, and the left bent to support the weight of the (missing) spear. This dynamically balanced body pose—characteristic of High Classical standing figure sculpture—evolved out of the pose of the *Kritios Boy* of a generation earlier. The tilt of the *Spear Bearer*'s hipline is a little more pronounced to accommodate the raising of the left foot onto its ball, and the head is turned toward the same side as the engaged leg.

To view this image, please go to page 134 of the *Art History*, Fourth Edition by Marilyn Stokstad ebook.

Polykleitos **SPEAR BEARER (DORYPHOROS)**
Roman copy after the original bronze of c. 450–440 BCE. Marble, height 6'11" (2.12 m); tree trunk and brace strut are Roman additions. National Archeological Museum, Naples.

The underlying message of the frieze as a whole is that the Athenians are a healthy, vigorous people, united in a democratic civic body looked upon with favor by the gods. The people are inseparable from and symbolic of the city itself.

As with the metope relief of the *Lapith Fighting a Centaur* (SEE FIG. 3–54), viewers of the processional frieze easily accept its disproportions, spatial compression and incongruities, and such implausible compositional features as men and women standing as tall as rearing horses. Carefully planned rhythmic variations—indicating changes in the speed of the participants in the procession as it winds around the walls—contribute to the effectiveness of the frieze. Horses plunge ahead at full gallop; women proceed with a slow, stately step; parade marshals pause to look back at the progress of those behind them; and human-looking deities rest on conveniently placed benches as they await the arrival of the marchers.

In executing the frieze, the sculptors took into account the

Who Owns the Art? The Elgin Marbles and the *Euphronios Krater*

At the beginning of the nineteenth century, Thomas Bruce, the British earl of Elgin and ambassador to Constantinople, acquired much of the surviving sculpture from the Parthenon, which was at that time being used for military purposes. He shipped it back to London in 1801 to decorate a lavish mansion for himself and his wife; but by the time he returned to England, his wife had left him and the ancient treasures were at the center of a financial dispute and had to be sold. Referred to as the Elgin Marbles, most of the sculpture is now in the British Museum, including all the elements seen in FIGURE 3–53. The Greek government has tried unsuccessfully to have the Elgin Marbles returned.

Recently, another Greek treasure has been in the news. In 1972, a krater, painted by Euphronios and depicting the death of the warrior Sarpedon during the Trojan War, had been purchased by the Metropolitan Museum of Art in New York. Museum officials were told that it had come from a private collection, and it became the centerpiece of the museum's galleries of Greek vessels. But in 1995, Italian and Swiss investigators raided a warehouse in Geneva, Switzerland, where they found documents showing that the krater had been stolen from an Etruscan tomb near Rome. The Italian government demanded its return. The controversy was only resolved in 2006. The krater, along with other objects known to have been stolen from other Italian sites, were returned, and the Metropolitan Museum will display pieces "of equal beauty" under long-term loan agreements with Italy.

spectators' low viewpoint and the dim lighting inside the peristyle. They carved the top of the frieze band in higher relief than the lower part, thus tilting the figures out to catch the reflected light from the pavement, permitting a clearer reading of the action. The subtleties in the sculpture may not have been as evident to Athenians in the fifth century BCE as they are now, because the frieze, seen at the top of a high wall and between columns, was originally completely painted. Figures in red and ocher, accented with glittering gold and real metal details, were set against a contrasting background of dark blue.

To view this image, please go to page 135 of the *Art History*, Fourth Edition by Marilyn Stokstad ebook.

3-56 • MARSHALS AND YOUNG WOMEN
Detail of the procession, from the Ionic frieze on the east side of the Parthenon. c. 447–432 BCE. Marble, height 3′6″ (1.08 m). Musée du Louvre, Paris.

To view this image, please go to page 138 of the *Art History*, Fourth Edition by Marilyn Stokstad ebook.

3-57 • NIKE (VICTORY) ADJUSTING HER SANDAL
Fragment of relief decoration from the parapet (now destroyed), Temple of Athena Nike, Acropolis, Athens. Last quarter of the 5th century (perhaps 410–405) BCE. Marble, height 3′6″ (1.06 m). Acropolis Museum, Athens.

THE TEMPLE OF ATHENA NIKE

Between 410 and 405 BCE, this temple was surrounded by a **parapet** or low wall, faced with sculptured panels depicting Athena presiding over the preparation of a celebration by winged Nikes (victory figures). The parapet no longer exists, but some panels have survived, including the greatly admired **NIKE (VICTORY) ADJUSTING HER SANDAL (FIG. 3–57)**. The figure bends forward gracefully, allowing her *chiton* to slip off one shoulder. Her large overlapping wings effectively balance her unstable pose. Unlike the decorative swirls of heavy fabric covering the Parthenon goddesses, or the weighty, pleated robes of the Erechtheion caryatids, the textile covering this Nike appears delicate and light, clinging to her body like wet silk, one of the most discreetly erotic images in ancient art.

THE ATHENIAN AGORA

In Athens, as in most cities of ancient Greece, commercial, civic, and social life revolved around the marketplace, or **agora**. The Athenian Agora, at the foot of the Acropolis, began as an open space where farmers and artisans displayed their wares. Over time, public and private structures were erected on both sides of the Panathenaic Way, a ceremonial road used during an important festival in honor of Athena **(FIG. 3–58)**. A stone drainage system was installed to prevent flooding, and a large fountain house was built to provide water for surrounding homes, administrative buildings, and shops (see "Women at a Fountain House," opposite). By 400 BCE, the Agora contained several religious and administrative structures and even a small racetrack. The Agora also had the city mint, its military headquarters, and two buildings devoted to court business.

In design, the stoa, a distinctively Greek structure found nearly everywhere people gathered, ranged from a simple roof held up by columns to a substantial, sometimes architecturally impressive, building with two stories and shops along one side. Stoas offered protection from the sun and rain, and provided a place for strolling and talking business, politics, or philosophy. While city business could be, and often was, conducted in the stoas, agora districts also came to include buildings with specific administrative functions.

In the Athenian Agora, the 500-member *boule*, or council, met in a building called the *bouleuterion*. This structure, built before 450 BCE but probably after the Persian destruction of Athens in 480 BCE, was laid out on a simple rectangular plan with a vestibule and large meeting room. Near the end of the fifth century BCE, a new *bouleuterion* was constructed to the west of the old one. This too had a rectangular plan. The interior, however, may have had permanent tiered seating arranged in an ascending semicircle around a ground-level **podium**, or raised platform.

Nearby was a small, round building with six columns supporting a conical roof, a type of structure known as a **tholos**. Built about 465 BCE, this tholos was the meeting place of the 50-member executive committee of the boule. The committee members dined there at the city's expense, and a few of them always spent the night there in order to be available for any pressing business that might arise.

Private houses surrounded the Agora. Compared with the often grand public buildings, houses of the fifth century BCE in Athens were rarely more than simple rectangular structures of stucco-faced mud brick with wooden posts and lintels supporting roofs of terra-cotta tiles. Rooms were small and included a dayroom in which women could sew, weave, and do other chores, a dining room with couches for reclining around a table, a kitchen, bedrooms, and occasionally an indoor bathroom. Where space was not at a premium, houses sometimes opened onto small courtyards or porches.

CITY PLANS

In older Greek cities such as Athens, buildings and streets developed in conformance to the needs of their inhabitants and the requirements of the terrain. As early as the eighth century BCE, however, builders in some western Greek settlements began to use

Women at a Fountain House

The Archaic period ceramic artist known as the Priam Painter has given us an insight into Greek city life in the agora by painting a Greek fountain house in use on a black-figure **hydria** (water jug). Since most women in ancient Greece were confined to their homes, their daily trip to the communal well or fountain house was an important event. At a fountain house, in the shade of a Doric-columned porch, three women fill hydriae just like the one on which they are painted. A fourth balances her empty jug on her head as she waits, while a fifth woman, without a jug, seems to be waving a greeting to someone. The building is designed like a stoa, open on one side, but having animal-head spigots on three walls. The Doric columns support a Doric entablature with an architrave above the colonnade and a colorful frieze—here black-and-white blocks replace carved metopes. The circular **palmettes** (fan-shaped petal designs) framing the main scenes suggest a rich and colorful civic center.

Priam Painter WOMEN AT A FOUNTAIN HOUSE
520–510 BCE. Black-figure decoration on a hydria. Ceramic, height of hydria 20⅞″ (53 cm). Museum of Fine Arts, Boston. William Francis Warden Fund (61.195)

To view this image, please go to page 139 of the *Art History*, Fourth Edition by Marilyn Stokstad ebook.

To view this image, please go to page 139 of the *Art History*, Fourth Edition by Marilyn Stokstad ebook.

3-58 • RECONSTRUCTION DRAWING OF THE AGORA (MARKETPLACE)
Athens. c. 400 BCE.

a mathematical concept of urban development based on the **orthogonal** (or **grid**) **plan**. New cities or rebuilt sections of old cities were laid out on straight, evenly spaced parallel streets that intersected at right angles to create rectangular blocks. These blocks were then subdivided into identical building plots.

During the Classical period, Hippodamos of Miletos, a major urban planner of the fifth century BCE, held views on the reasoned perfectibility of urban design akin to those of the Athenian philosophers (such as Socrates) and artists (such as Polykleitos). He believed the ideal city should be limited to 10,000 citizens divided into three classes—artists, farmers, and soldiers—and three zones—sacred, public, and private. The basic Hippodamian plot was a square 600 feet on each side, divided into quarters. Each quarter was subdivided into six rectangular building plots measuring 100 by 150 feet on a side, a scheme still widely used in American and European cities and suburbs.

Orthogonal plans obviously work best when laid out on relatively flat land. But the Greeks applied orthogonal planning even in less hospitable terrain, such as that of the Ionian city of Priene, which lies on a rugged hillside in Asia Minor. In this case, the city's planners made no attempt to accommodate their grid to the irregular mountainside, meaning that some streets are in fact stairs.

STELE SCULPTURE

Upright stone slabs called **stelae** (singular, stele) were used in Greek cemeteries as gravestones, carved in low relief with an image (actual or allegorical) of the person(s) to be remembered. Instead of the proud warriors or athletes used in the Archaic period, however, Classical stelae place figures in personal or domestic contexts that often feature women and children. A touching mid-fifth-century BCE example found on the island of Paros portrays a sweet young girl, seemingly bidding farewell to her pet birds, one of which she kisses on the beak (**FIG. 3–59**). She wears a loose *peplos*, which parts at the side to disclose the tender flesh underneath and clings elsewhere over her body to reveal its three-dimensional form. The extraordinary carving recalls the contemporary reliefs of the Parthenon frieze, and like them, this stele would have been painted with color to provide details such as the straps of the girl's sandals or the feathers on her beloved birds.

Another, somewhat later, stele commemorates the relationship between a couple, identified by name across an upper frieze resting on two Doric pilaster. The husband Ktesilaos stands casually with crossed legs and joined hands, gazing at his wife Theano, who sits before him on a bench, pulling at her gauzy wrap with her right hand in a gesture that is often associated with Greek brides. Presumably this was a tombstone for a joint grave, since both names are inscribed on it, but we do not know which of the two might have died first, leaving behind a mate to mourn and memorialize by commissioning this stele. The air of introspective melancholy here, as well as the softness and delicacy of both flesh and fabric, seem to point forward, out of the High Classical period and into the increased sense of narrative and delicacy that was to characterize the fourth century BCE.

To view this image, please go to page 140 of the *Art History*, Fourth Edition by Marilyn Stokstad ebook.

3-59 • GRAVE STELE OF A LITTLE GIRL
c. 450–440 BCE. Marble, height 31½″ (80 cm). Metropolitan Museum of Art, New York.

THE JULIO-CLAUDIANS

After his death in 14 CE, Augustus was deified by decree of the Roman Senate. Augustus's successor was his stepson Tiberius (r. 14–37 CE), and in acknowledgment of the lineage of both—Augustus from Julius Caesar and Tiberius from his father, Tiberius Claudius Nero, Livia's first husband—the dynasty is known as the Julio-Claudian (14–68 CE). It ended with the death of Nero in 68 CE.

Exquisite skill characterizes the arts of the first century CE. A large onyx **cameo** (a gemstone carved in low relief) known as the **GEMMA AUGUSTEA** glorifies Augustus as triumphant over **barbarians** (a label for foreigners that the Romans adopted from the Greeks) and as the deified emperor (**FIG. 3–60**). The emperor, crowned with a victor's wreath, sits at the center right of the upper register. He has assumed the pose and identity of Jupiter, the king of the gods; an eagle, sacred to Jupiter, stands at his feet. Sitting next to him is a personification of Rome that seems to have Livia's features. The sea goat in the roundel between them may represent Capricorn, the emperor's zodiac sign.

Tiberius, as the adopted son of Augustus, steps out of a chariot at far left, returning victorious from the German front and prepared to assume the imperial throne as Augustus's chosen heir. Below this realm of godlike rulers, Roman soldiers are raising a post or standard on which armor captured from the defeated enemy is displayed as a trophy. The cowering, shackled barbarians on the bottom right wait to be tied to it. The artist of the *Gemma Augustea* brilliantly combines idealized, heroic figures based on Classical Greek art with recognizable Roman portraits, the dramatic action of Hellenistic art with Roman attention to descriptive detail and historical specificity.

ROMAN CITIES AND THE ROMAN HOME

In good times and bad, individual Romans—like people everywhere at any time—tried to live a decent or even comfortable life with adequate shelter, food, and clothing. The Romans loved to have contact with the natural world. The middle classes enjoyed their gardens, wealthy city dwellers maintained rural estates, and Roman emperors had country villas that were both functioning farms and places of recreation. Wealthy Romans even brought nature indoors by commissioning artists to paint landscapes on the interior walls of their homes. Through the efforts of the modern archaeologists who have excavated them, Roman cities and towns, houses, apartments, and country villas still evoke for us the ancient Roman way of life with amazing clarity.

ROMAN CITIES. Roman architects who designed new cities or who expanded and rebuilt existing ones based the urban plan on the layout of Roman army camps. Like Etruscan towns, they were laid out in a grid with two bisecting main streets crossed at right angles to divide the layout into quarters. The **forum** and other public buildings were located at this intersection, where the commander's headquarters was placed in a military camp.

Much of the housing in a Roman city consisted of brick apartment blocks called *insulae*. These apartment buildings had internal courtyards, multiple floors joined by narrow staircases, and occasionally overhanging balconies. City dwellers—then as now—were social creatures who spent much of their lives in public markets, squares, theaters, baths, and neighborhood bars. The city dweller returned to the *insulae* to sleep, perhaps to eat. Even women enjoyed a public life outside the home—a marked contrast to the circumscribed lives of Greek women.

The affluent southern Italian city of Pompeii, a thriving center of between 10,000 and 20,000 inhabitants, gives a vivid picture of Roman city life. In 79 CE Mount Vesuvius erupted, burying the city under more than 20 feet of volcanic ash and preserving it until its rediscovery and excavation, beginning in the eighteenth century (**FIGS. 3–61, 3–62**). Temples and government buildings surrounded a main square, or forum; shops and houses lined

To view this image, please go to page 178 of the *Art History*, Fourth Edition by Marilyn Stokstad ebook.

3-60 • GEMMA AUGUSTEA
Early 1st century CE. Onyx, 7½ × 9″ (19 × 23 cm). Kunsthistorisches Museum, Vienna.

3-61 • AERIAL VIEW OF THE RUINS OF POMPEII
Destroyed 79 CE.

SEE MORE: See a video about Pompeii
www.myartslab.com

To view this image, please go to page 179 of the *Art History*, Fourth Edition by Marilyn Stokstad ebook.

To view this image, please go to page 179 of the *Art History*, Fourth Edition by Marilyn Stokstad ebook.

3-62 • RECONSTRUCTION DRAWING OF POMPEII

3-63 • PLAN AND RECONSTRUCTION DRAWING, HOUSE OF THE SILVER WEDDING
Pompeii. 1st century CE.

mostly straight, paved streets; and a protective wall enclosed the heart of the city. The forum was the center of civic life in Roman cities, as the agora was in Greek cities. Business was conducted in its basilicas and porticos, religious duties performed in its temples, and speeches delivered in its open square. For recreation, people went to the nearby baths or to events in the theater or amphitheater.

ROMAN HOUSES. City dwellers lived in houses, and even gracious private residences with gardens often had shops in front of them facing the street. The Romans emphasized the interior rather than the exterior in their domestic architecture.

A Roman house usually consisted of small rooms laid out around one or two open courts, the atrium and the peristyle (**FIG. 3–63**). People entered the house through a vestibule and stepped into the atrium, a large space with a pool or cistern for catching rainwater. The peristyle was a planted courtyard, further into the house, enclosed by columns. Off the peristyle was the formal reception room or office called the tablinum, and here the head of the household conferred with clients. Portrait busts of the family's ancestors might be displayed in the tablinum or in the atrium. The private areas—such as the family dining and sitting rooms, as well as bedrooms (cubicula)—and service areas—such as the kitchen and servants' quarters—could be arranged around the peristyle or the atrium. In Pompeii, where the mild southern climate permitted gardens to flourish year-round, the peristyle was often turned into an outdoor living room with painted walls, fountains, and

3-64 • PERISTYLE GARDEN, HOUSE OF THE VETTII
Pompeii. Rebuilt 62–79 CE.

sculpture, as in the mid first-century CE remodeling of the second-century BCE **HOUSE OF THE VETTII** (FIG. 3–64). Since Roman houses were designed in relation to a long axis that runs from the entrance straight through the atrium and into the peristyle, visitors were greeted at the door of the house with a deep vista, showcasing the lavish residence of their host and its beautifully designed and planted gardens extending into the distance.

Little was known about these gardens until archaeologist Wilhelmina Jashemski began the excavation of the peristyle in the House of G. Polybius in Pompeii in 1973. Earlier archaeologists had usually ignored, or unwittingly destroyed, evidence of gardens, but Jashemski developed a new way to find and analyze the layout and the plants cultivated in them. Workers first removed layers of debris and volcanic material to expose the level of the soil as it was before the eruption in 79 CE. They then collected samples of pollen, seeds, and other organic material and carefully injected plaster into underground root cavities. When the surrounding earth was removed, the roots, now in plaster, enabled botanists to

identify the types of plants and trees cultivated in the garden and to estimate their size.

The garden in the house of Polybius was surrounded on three sides by a portico, which protected a large cistern on one side that supplied the house and garden with water. Young lemon trees in pots lined the fourth side of the garden, and nail holes in the wall above the pots indicated that the trees had been espaliered—pruned and trained to grow flat against a support—a practice still in use today. Fig, cherry, and pear trees filled the garden space, and traces of a fruit-picking ladder, wide at the bottom and narrow at the top to fit among the branches, was found on the site.

An aqueduct built during the reign of Augustus eliminated Pompeii's dependence on wells and rainwater basins and allowed residents to add pools, fountains, and flowering plants that needed heavy watering to their gardens. In contrast to earlier, unordered plantings, formal gardens with low, clipped borders and plantings of ivy, ornamental boxwood, laurel, myrtle, acanthus, and rosemary—all mentioned by writers of the time—became fashionable. There is also evidence of topiary work, the clipping of shrubs and hedges into fanciful shapes. Sculpture and purely decorative fountains became popular. The peristyle garden of the House of the Vettii, for example, had more than a dozen fountain statues jetting water into marble basins (SEE FIG. 3–64). In the most elegant peristyles, mosaic decorations covered the floors, walls, and even the fountains.

WALL PAINTING

The interior walls of Roman houses were plain, smooth plaster surfaces with few architectural moldings or projections. On these invitingly blank fields, artists painted decorations. Some used mosaic, but most employed pigment suspended in a water-based solution of lime and soap, sometimes with a little wax. After such paintings were finished, they were polished with a special metal, glass, or stone burnisher and then buffed with a cloth. Many fine wall paintings have come to light through excavations, first in Pompeii and other communities surrounding Mount Vesuvius, near Naples, and more recently in and around Rome.

HOUSE OF THE VETTII. Some of the finest surviving Roman wall paintings are found in the Pompeian House of the Vettii, whose peristyle garden we have already explored (SEE FIG. 3–64). The house was built in conformity to the axial house plan—with entrance leading through atrium to peristyle garden (FIG. 3–65)—by two brothers, wealthy freed slaves A. Vettius Conviva

To view this image, please go to page 181 of the *Art History*, Fourth Edition by Marilyn Stokstad ebook.

3-65 • PLAN, HOUSE OF THE VETTII
Pompeii. Rebuilt 62–79 CE.

3-66 • WALL PAINTING IN THE "IXION ROOM," HOUSE OF THE VETTII
Pompeii. Rebuilt 62–79 CE.

and A. Vettius Restitutus. Between its damage during an earthquake in 62 CE and the eruption of Vesuvius in 79 CE, the walls of the house were repainted, and this spectacular decoration was uncovered in a splendid state of preservation during excavations at the end of the nineteenth century.

A complex combination of painted fantasies fills the walls of a reception room off the peristyle garden (**FIG. 3–66**). At the base of the walls is a lavish frieze of simulated colored-marble revetment, imitating the actual stone veneers that are found in some Roman residences. Above this "marble" **dado** are broad areas of pure red or white, onto which are painted pictures resembling framed panel paintings, swags of floral garlands or unframed figural vignettes. The framed picture here illustrates a Greek mythological scene from the story of Ixion, who was bound by Zeus to a spinning wheel in punishment for attempting to seduce Hera. Between these pictorial fields, and along a long strip above them that runs around the entire room, are fantastic architectural vistas with multicolored columns and undulating entablatures that recede into fictive space through the use of fanciful linear perspective. The fact that this fictive architecture is occupied here and there by volumetric figures only enhances the sense of three-dimensional spatial definition. On the broad red fields covering the walls of another room of this house, energetic cupids play at industrious human pursuits such as pharmacy, goldsmithing, and making perfume (**FIG. 3–67**).

3-67 • CUPIDS MAKING PERFUME, WALL PAINTING IN THE HOUSE OF THE VETTII
Pompeii. Rebuilt 62–79 CE.

VILLA OF THE MYSTERIES. The eruption of Vesuvius in 79 CE preserved not only the houses along the city streets within Pompeii, but also the so-called **VILLA OF THE MYSTERIES** just outside the city walls **(FIG. 3–68)**. Villas were the country houses of wealthy Romans, and their plans, though resembling town houses, were often more expansive and irregular. At the Villa of the Mysteries, for example, the entrance leads through the peristyle to the atrium, a reversal of the standard progression. Within this suburban villa a series of elaborate figural murals **(FIG. 3–69)** seem to portray the initiation rites of a mystery religion, probably the

3-68 • PLAN, VILLA OF THE MYSTERIES
Pompeii, early 2nd century BCE.
1 entrance foyer
2 peristyle
3 atrium
4 pool (water basin)
5 tablinum (office, official reception room)
6 room with paintings of mysteries
7 terrace
8 bedroom

To view this image, please go to page 183 of the *Art History*, Fourth Edition by Marilyn Stokstad ebook.

3-69 • INITIATION RITES OF THE CULT OF BACCHUS (?), VILLA OF THE MYSTERIES
Pompeii. Wall painting. c. 60–50 BCE.

To view this image, please go to page 183 of the *Art History*, Fourth Edition by Marilyn Stokstad ebook.

To view this image, please go to page 184 of the *Art History*, Fourth Edition by Marilyn Stokstad ebook.

cult of Bacchus, which were often performed in private homes as well as in special buildings or temples. Perhaps this room in this villa was a shrine or meeting place for such a cult to this god of vegetation, fertility, and wine. Bacchus (or Dionysus) was one of the most important deities in Pompeii.

The entirely painted architectural setting consists of a simulated marble dado (similar to that which we saw in the House of the Vettii) and, around the top of the wall, an elegant frieze supported by pilaster strips. The figural scenes take place on a shallow "stage" along the top of the dado, with a background of a brilliant, deep red—now known as Pompeian red—that, as we have already seen, was very popular with Roman painters. The tableau unfolds around the entire room, perhaps depicting a succession of events that culminate in the acceptance of an initiate into the cult.

VILLA AT BOSCOREALE. The walls of a room from another villa, this one at Boscoreale, farther removed from Pompeii, open onto a fantastic urban panorama (**FIG. 3–70**). Surfaces seem to dissolve behind an inner frame of columns and lintels, opening onto a maze of complicated architectural forms, like the painted scenic backdrops of a stage. Indeed, the theater may have inspired this kind of decoration, as the theatrical masks hanging from the lintels seem to suggest. By using a kind of **intuitive perspective**, the artists have created a general impression of real space. In intuitive perspective, the architectural details follow diagonal lines that the eye interprets as parallel lines receding into the distance, and objects meant to be perceived as far away from the surface plane of the wall are shown gradually smaller and smaller than those intended to appear in the foreground.

ROMAN REALISM IN DETAILS: STILL LIFES AND PORTRAITS. In addition to city views and figural tableaux, other subjects that appeared in Roman art included delicately painted landscapes, exquisitely rendered **still lifes** (compositions of inanimate objects), and portraits. A still-life panel from Herculaneum, a community in the vicinity of Mount Vesuvius near Pompeii, depicts everyday domestic objects—still-green peaches just picked from the tree and a glass jar half-filled with water (**FIG. 3–71**). The items have been carefully arranged on two stepped shelves to give the composition clarity and balance. A strong, clear light floods the picture from left to right, casting shadows, picking up highlights, and enhancing the illusion of solid objects in real space.

Among the paintings discovered on the walls of Pompeian houses, few are as arresting as a double portrait of a young husband and wife (**FIG. 3–72**), who look out from their simulated spatial world through the wall into the viewers' space within the room. The swarthy, wispy-bearded man addresses us with a direct stare, holding a scroll in his left hand, a conventional attribute of educational achievement seen frequently in Roman portraits. Though his wife overlaps him to stake her claim to the

To view this image, please go to page 185 of the *Art History*, Fourth Edition by Marilyn Stokstad ebook.

3-71 • STILL LIFE, HOUSE OF THE STAGS (CERVI)
Herculaneum. Detail of a wall painting. Before 79 CE. Approx. 1′2″ × 1′1½″ (35.5 × 31.7 cm). Museo Archeologico Nazionale, Naples.

To view this image, please go to page 185 of the *Art History*, Fourth Edition by Marilyn Stokstad ebook.

3-72 • PORTRAIT OF A MARRIED COUPLE
Wall painting from Pompeii. Mid 1st century CE. Height 25½″ (64.8 cm). Museo Archeologico Nazionale, Naples.

To view this image, please go to page 186 of the *Art History*, Fourth Edition by Marilyn Stokstad ebook.

3-73 • THE ARCH OF TITUS

Rome. c. 81 CE (restored 1822–1824). Concrete and white marble, height 50′ (15 m).

The dedication inscribed across the tall attic story above the arch opening reads: "The Senate and the Roman people to the Deified Titus Vespasian Augustus, son of the Deified Vespasian." The perfectly sized and spaced Roman capital letters meant to be read from a distance and cut with sharp terminals (serifs) to catch the light established a standard that calligraphers and font designers still follow.

SEE MORE: Click the Google Earth link for the Arch of Titus **www.myartslab.com**

foreground, her gaze out at us is less direct. She also holds fashionable attributes of literacy—the stylus she elevates in front of her chin and the folding writing tablet on which she would have used the stylus to inscribe words into a wax infill. This picture is comparable to a modern studio portrait photograph—perhaps a wedding picture—with its careful lighting and retouching, conventional poses and accoutrements. But the attention to physiognomic detail—note the differences in the spacing of their eyes and the shapes of their noses, ears, and lips—makes it quite clear that we are in the presence of actual human likenesses.

THE FLAVIANS

The Julio-Claudian dynasty ended with the suicide of Nero in 68 CE, which led to a brief period of civil war. Eventually an astute general, Vespasian, seized control of the government in 69 CE, founding a new dynasty known as the Flavians. The new line of emperors were practical military men who inspired confidence and ruled for the rest of the first century. They restored the imperial finances and stabilized the frontiers. They also replaced the Julio-Claudian fashion for classicizing imperial portraiture with a return to the ideal of time-worn faces, enhancing the effects of old age.

THE ARCH OF TITUS. Among the most impressive surviving official commissions from the Flavian dynasty is a distinctive Roman structure: the triumphal arch. Part architecture, part sculpture, the free-standing arch commemorates a triumph, or formal victory celebration, during which a victorious general or emperor paraded through Rome with his troops, captives, and booty. When Domitian assumed the throne in 81 CE, for example, he immediately commissioned a triumphal arch to honor the capture of Jerusalem in 70 CE by his brother and deified predecessor, Titus (**FIG. 3–73**). The **ARCH OF TITUS**, constructed of concrete and faced with marble, is essentially a free-standing gateway whose passage is covered by a barrel vault. The arch served as a giant base, 50 feet tall, for a lost bronze statue of the emperor in a four-horse chariot, a typical triumphal symbol. Applied to the faces of the arch are columns in the **Composite order** supporting an entablature. The inscription on the uppermost, or attic, story declares that the Senate and the Roman people erected the monument to honor Titus.

Titus' capture of Jerusalem ended a fierce campaign to crush a revolt of the Jews in Palestine. The Romans sacked and destroyed the Second Temple in Jerusalem, carried off its sacred treasures, then displayed them in a triumphal procession in Rome (**FIG. 3–74**). A relief on the inside walls of the arch, capturing the drama of the occasion, depicts Titus' soldiers flaunting this booty as they carry it through the streets of Rome. The soldiers are headed toward the right and through an arch, turned obliquely to project into the viewers' own space, thus allowing living spectators a sense

To view this image, please go to page 187 of the *Art History*, Fourth Edition by Marilyn Stokstad ebook.

3-74 • SPOILS FROM THE TEMPLE OF SOLOMON
Relief in the passageway of the Arch of Titus. Marble, height 6′8″ (2.03 m).

The Romans became experts in devising methods of covering large, open architectural spaces with concrete and masonry, using barrel vaults, groin vaults, or domes.

A **barrel vault** is constructed in the same manner as the round arch. In a sense, it is a series of connected arches extended in sequence along a line. The outward pressure exerted by the curving sides of the barrel vault requires buttressing within or outside the supporting walls.

When two barrel-vaulted spaces intersect each other at the same level, the result is a **groin vault**. Both the weight and outward thrust of the groin vault are concentrated on four corner piers; only the piers require buttressing, so the walls on all four sides can be opened. The Romans used the groin vault to construct some of their grandest interior spaces.

A third type of vault brought to technical perfection by the Romans is the **dome**. The rim of the dome is supported on a circular wall, as in the Pantheon (SEE FIGS. 3–85, 3–86, 3–88). This wall is called a drum when it is raised on top of a main structure. Sometimes a circular opening, called an **oculus**, is left at the top.

buttress

buttress

barrel vault

pier

pier

space included in bay

pier

groin vault

SEE MORE: View a simulation of the groin vault **www.myartslab.com**

of the press of a boisterous, disorderly crowd. They might expect at any moment to hear soldiers and onlookers shouting and chanting.

The mood of the procession depicted in this relief contrasts with the relaxed but formal solemnity of the procession portrayed on the Ara Pacis. Like the sculptors of the Ara Pacis, the sculptors of the Arch of Titus showed the spatial relationships among figures, varying the depth of the relief by rendering nearer elements in higher relief than those more distant. A menorah, or seven-branched lampholder, from the Temple of Jerusalem, dominates the scene; the sculptors rendered it as if seen from the low point of view of a spectator at the event.

THE FLAVIAN AMPHITHEATER.   Romans were huge sports fans, and the Flavian emperors catered to their tastes by building splendid facilities. Construction of the **FLAVIAN AMPHITHEATER**, Rome's greatest arena **(FIG. 3–75)**, began under Vespasian in 70 CE and was completed under Titus, who dedicated it in 80 CE. The Flavian Amphitheater came to be known as the "Colosseum," because a gigantic statue of Nero called the *Colossus* stood next to it. "Colosseum" is a most appropriate description of this enormous entertainment center. Its outer wall stands 159 feet high. It is an oval, measuring 615 by 510 feet, with a floor 280 by 175 feet. This floor was laid over a foundation of service rooms and tunnels that provided an area for the athletes, performers, animals, and equipment. The floor was covered

by sand, *arena* in Latin, hence the English term "arena" for a building of this type.

Roman audiences watched a variety of athletic events, blood sports, and spectacles, including animal hunts, fights to the death

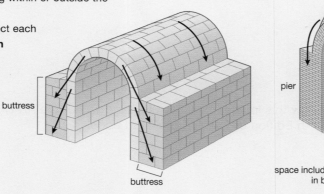

To view this image, please go to page 188 of the *Art History*, Fourth Edition by Marilyn Stokstad ebook.

3-75 • RECONSTRUCTION DRAWING OF THE FLAVIAN AMPHITHEATER (COLOSSEUM)
Rome. 70–80 CE.

SEE MORE: View a video about the Flavian Amphitheater (Colosseum) **www.myartslab.com**

To view this image, please go to page 189 of the *Art History*, Fourth Edition by Marilyn Stokstad ebook.

3–76 • FLAVIAN AMPHITHEATER, OUTER WALL
Rome. 70–80 CE.

between gladiators or between gladiators and wild animals, performances of trained animals and acrobats, and even mock sea battles, for which the arena would be flooded. The opening performances in 80 CE lasted 100 days, during which time it was claimed that 9,000 wild animals and 2,000 gladiators died for the amusement of the spectators.

The amphitheater is a remarkable piece of planning, with easy access, perfect sight lines for everyone, and effective crowd control. Stadiums today are still based on this efficient plan. Some 50,000 spectators could move easily through the 76 entrance doors to the three levels of seats and the standing area at the top. Each spectator had an uninterrupted view of the events below. Each level of seats was laid over barrel-vaulted access corridors and entrance tunnels (SEE FIG. 3–75). The intersection of the barrel-vaulted entrance tunnels and the ring corridors created groin vaults (see "Roman Vaulting," page 217). The walls on the top level of the arena supported a huge awning that could shade the seating areas. Sailors, who had experience in handling ropes, pulleys, and large expanses of canvas, worked the apparatus that extended the awning.

The curving, outer wall of the Colosseum consists of three levels of arcades surmounted by a wall-like attic (top) story. Each arch is framed by engaged columns. Entablature-like friezes mark the divisions between levels (FIG. 3–76). Each level also uses a different architectural order, increasing in complexity from bottom to top: the plain Tuscan order on the ground level, Ionic on the second level, Corinthian on the third, and Corinthian pilasters on the fourth. The attic story is broken by small, square windows, which originally alternated with gilded-bronze shield-shaped ornaments called **cartouches**, supported on brackets that are still in place.

All these elements are purely decorative. The addition of post-and-lintel decoration to arched structures was an Etruscan innovation. The systematic use of the orders in a logical succession from sturdy Tuscan to lighter Ionic to decorative Corinthian follows a tradition inherited from Hellenistic architecture. This orderly, dignified, and visually satisfying way of organizing the façades of large buildings is still popular. Unfortunately, much of the Colosseum was dismantled in the Middle Ages as a source of marble, metal fittings, and materials for buildings such as churches.

IMPERIAL ARCHITECTURE

The Romans believed their rule extended to the ends of the Western world, but the city of Rome remained the nerve center of the empire. During his long and peaceful reign, Augustus had paved the city's old Republican Forum, restored its temples and basilicas, and followed Julius Caesar's example by building an Imperial Forum. These projects marked the beginning of a continuing effort to transform the capital itself into a magnificent monument to imperial rule. While Augustus' claim of having turned Rome into a city of marble is exaggerated, he certainly began the process of creating a monumental civic center. Such grand structures as the Imperial Forums, the Colosseum, the Circus Maximus (a track for chariot races), the Pantheon, and aqueducts stood amid the temples, baths, warehouses, and homes in the city center as expressions of successive emperors' beneficence and their desire to leave their mark on, and preserve their memory in, the capital.

THE FORUM OF TRAJAN. A model of Rome's city center makes apparent the dense building plan (**FIG. 3–77**). The last and largest Imperial Forum was built by Trajan about 110–113 CE and finished under Hadrian about 117 CE on a large piece of property next to the earlier forums of Augustus and Julius Caesar (**FIG. 3–78**). For this major undertaking, Trajan chose a Greek architect, Apollodorus of Damascus, who was experienced as a military engineer. A straight, central axis leads from the Forum of Augustus through a triple-arched gate surmounted by a bronze chariot group into a large, colonnaded square with a statue of Trajan on horseback at its center. Closing off the courtyard at the north end was the **BASILICA ULPIA** (**FIG. 3–79**), dedicated in c. 112 CE, and named for the family to which Trajan belonged.

A **basilica** was a large, rectangular building with an extensive interior space, adaptable for a variety of administrative governmental functions. The Basilica Ulpia was a court of law, but other

To view this image, please go to page 192 of the *Art History*, Fourth Edition by Marilyn Stokstad ebook.

3–77 • MODEL OF IMPERIAL ROME
c. 324 CE.

basilicas served as imperial audience chambers, army drill halls, and schools. The Basilica Ulpia was a particularly grand interior space, 385 feet long (not including the apses) and 182 feet wide. A large central area (the **nave**) was flanked by double colonnaded aisles surmounted by open galleries or by a clerestory, an upper nave wall with windows. The timber truss roof had a span of about 80 feet. The two **apses**, rounded extensions at each end of the building, provided imposing settings for judges when the court was in session.

To view this image, please go to page 192 of the *Art History*, Fourth Edition by Marilyn Stokstad ebook.

3-78 • PLAN OF TRAJAN'S FORUM AND MARKET
c. 110–113 CE.

3-79 • RESTORED PERSPECTIVE VIEW OF THE CENTRAL HALL, BASILICA ULPIA
Rome. c. 112 CE. Drawn by Gilbert Gorski. Trajan's architect was Apollodorus of Damascus.

The building may have had clerestory windows instead of the gallery shown in this drawing. The Column of Trajan can be seen at the right.

To view this image, please go to page 193 of the *Art History*, Fourth Edition by Marilyn Stokstad ebook.

3-80 • RECONSTRUCTION OF TRAJAN'S MARKET
Rome. 100–112 CE.

3-81 • MAIN HALL, TRAJAN'S MARKET
Rome. 100–112 CE.

During the site preparation for Trajan's forum, part of a commercial district had to be razed and excavated. To make up for the loss, Trajan ordered the construction of a handsome public market (**FIGS. 3–80, 3–81**). The market, comparable in size to a large modern shopping mall, had more than 150 individual shops on several levels and included a large groin-vaulted main hall. In compliance with a building code that was put into effect after a disastrous fire in 64 CE, the market, like most Roman buildings of the time, was constructed of concrete (see "Concrete," page 224) faced with brick, with only occasional detailing in stone and wood.

Behind the Basilica Ulpia stood twin libraries built to house the emperor's collections of Latin and Greek manuscripts. These buildings flanked an open court, the location of the great spiral column that became Trajan's tomb when Hadrian placed a golden urn containing his predecessor's ashes in its base. The column commemorated Trajan's victory over the Dacians and was erected either c. 113 CE, at about the same time as the Basilica Ulpia, or by Hadrian after Trajan's death in 117 CE.

THE COLUMN OF TRAJAN. The relief decoration on the **COLUMN OF TRAJAN** spirals upward in a band that would stretch almost 625 feet if laid out straight. Like a giant, unfurled version of the scrolls housed in the libraries next to it, the column presents a continuous pictorial narrative of the Dacian campaigns of 102–103 and 105–106 CE (**FIG. 3–82**). The remarkable sculpture includes more than 2,500 individual figures linked by landscape and architecture, and punctuated by the recurring figure of Trajan. The narrative band slowly expands from about 3 feet in height at the bottom, near the viewer, to 4 feet at the top of the column, where it is farther from view. The natural and architectural elements in the scenes have been kept small so the important figures can occupy as much space as possible.

The scene at the beginning of the spiral, at the bottom of the column, shows Trajan's army crossing the Danube River on a pontoon bridge as the first Dacian campaign of 101 CE is launched **(FIG. 3–83)**. Soldiers construct battlefield headquarters in Dacia from which the men on the frontiers will receive orders, food, and weapons. In this spectacular piece of imperial ideology or propaganda, Trajan is portrayed as a strong, stable, and efficient commander of a well-run army, and his barbarian enemies are shown as worthy opponents of Rome.

THE PANTHEON.   Perhaps the most remarkable ancient building surviving in Rome—and one of the marvels of world architecture in any age—is a temple to the Olympian gods called the **PANTHEON** (literally, "all the gods") **(FIG. 3–84)**. Although this magnificent monument was designed and constructed entirely during the reign of the emperor Hadrian, the long inscription on the architrave states that it was built by "Marcus Agrippa, son of Lucius, who was consul three times." Agrippa, the son-in-law and valued advisor of Augustus, was responsible for building on this site in 27–25 BCE. After a fire in 80 CE, Domitian built a new temple, which Hadrian then replaced in 118–128 CE with the Pantheon. Hadrian, who clearly had a strong sense of history, placed Agrippa's name on the façade in a grand gesture to the memory of the illustrious consul.

The current setting of the temple gives little suggestion of its original appearance. Centuries of dirt and street construction hide its podium and stairs. Attachment holes in the pediment indicate the placement of bronze sculpture, perhaps an eagle within a wreath, the imperial Jupiter. Today we can see the sides of the rotunda flanking the entrance porch, but when the Pantheon was constructed, the façade of this porch—resembling the façades of typical, rectangular temples—was literally all viewers could see of the building. Since their approach was controlled by an enclosed courtyard (SEE FIG. 3–78), the actual circular shape of the Pantheon was concealed. Viewers were therefore surprised to pass through

To view this image, please go to page 194 of the *Art History*, Fourth Edition by Marilyn Stokstad ebook.

3-82 • COLUMN OF TRAJAN

Rome. 113–116 or after 117 CE. Marble, overall height with base 125′ (38 m), column alone 97′8″ (29.77 m); length of relief 625′ (190.5 m).

The height of the column may have recorded the depth of the excavation required to build the Forum of Trajan. The column had been topped by a gilded bronze statue of Trajan that was replaced in 1588 CE with the statue of St. Peter seen today.

SEE MORE: Click the Google Earth link for the Column of Trajan www.myartslab.com

To view this image, please go to page 195 of the *Art History*,
Fourth Edition by Marilyn Stokstad ebook.

3-83 • ROMANS CROSSING THE DANUBE AND BUILDING A FORT
Detail of the lowest part of the Column of Trajan. 113–116 CE, or after 117 CE. Marble, height of the
spiral band approx. 36″ (91 cm).

The Romans were pragmatic builders, and their practicality extended from recognizing and exploiting undeveloped potential in construction methods and physical materials to organizing large-scale building works. Their exploitation of the arch and the vault is typical of their adapt-and-improve approach (see "Roman Vaulting," page 217). But their innovative use of concrete, beginning in the first century BCE, was a technological breakthrough of the greatest importance in the history of architecture.

In contrast to stone—which was expensive and difficult to quarry and transport—the components of concrete were cheap, relatively light, and easily transported. Building stone structures required highly skilled masons, but a large, semiskilled workforce directed by a few experienced supervisors could construct brick-faced concrete buildings.

Roman concrete consisted of powdered lime, a volcanic sand called pozzolana, and various types of rubble, such as small rocks and broken pottery. Mixing these materials in water caused a chemical reaction that blended them, and they hardened as they dried into a strong, solid mass. At first, concrete was used mainly for poured foundations, but with technical advances it became indispensable for the construction of walls, arches, and vaults for ever-larger buildings,

such as the Flavian Amphitheater (SEE FIG. 3–75) and the Markets of Trajan (SEE FIG. 3–81). In the earliest concrete wall construction, workers filled a framework of rough stones with concrete. Soon they developed a technique known as opus reticulatum, in which the framework is a diagonal web of smallish bricks set in a cross pattern. Concrete-based construction freed the Romans from the limits of right-angle forms and comparatively short spans. With this new freedom, Roman builders pushed the established limits of architecture, creating some very large and highly original spaces by pouring concrete over wooden frameworks to mold it into complex curving shapes.

Concrete's one weakness was that it absorbed moisture and would eventually deteriorate if unprotected, so builders covered exposed surfaces with a veneer, or facing, of finer materials—such as marble, stone, stucco, or painted plaster—to protect it. An essential difference between Greek and Roman architecture is that Greek builders reveal the building material itself and accept the design limitations of post-and-lintel construction, whereas Roman buildings expose only an externally applied surface covering. The sophisticated structural underpinnings that allow huge spaces molded by three-dimensional curves are set behind them, hidden from view.

SEE MORE: View a simulation of the Roman use of concrete **www.myartslab.com**

---

the rectilinear and restricted aisles of the portico and the huge main door to encounter the gaping space of the giant **rotunda** (circular room) surmounted by a huge, bowl-shaped dome, 143 feet in diameter and 143 feet from the floor at its summit **(FIGS. 3–85, 3–86)**. Even without the controlled courtyard approach, encountering this glorious space today is still an overwhelming experience—for many of us, one that is repeated even on successive visits to the rotunda.

Standing at the center of this hemispherical temple **(FIG. 3–87)**, the visitor feels isolated from the outside world and intensely aware of the shape and tangibility of the space itself. Our eyes are drawn upward over the patterns made by the sunken panels, or **coffers**, in the dome's ceiling to the light entering the 29-foot-wide **oculus**, or central opening, which illuminates a brilliant circle against the surface of the dome. This disk of light moves around this microcosm throughout the day like a sun. Clouds can be seen traveling across the opening on some days; on others, rain falls through and then drains off through conduits planned by the original engineer. Occasionally a bird flies in. This open, luminous space gives the feeling that one could rise

To view this image, please go to page 196 of the *Art History*, Fourth Edition by Marilyn Stokstad ebook.

3-84 • PANTHEON
Rome. c. 118–128 CE.

Today a huge fountain dominates the square in front of the Pantheon. Built in 1578 by Giacomo della Porta, it now supports an Egyptian obelisk placed there in 1711 by Pope Clement XI.

To view this image, please go to page 197 of the *Art History*, Fourth Edition by Marilyn Stokstad ebook.

3-85 • RECONSTRUCTION DRAWING OF THE PANTHEON

To view this image, please go to page 197 of the *Art History*, Fourth Edition by Marilyn Stokstad ebook.

3-86 • PLAN OF THE PANTHEON

buoyantly upward and escape the spherical hollow of the building to commune with the cosmos.

The simple shape of the Pantheon's dome belies its sophisticated design and engineering (SEE FIG. 3–85). Marble veneer and two tiers of richly colored architectural detail conceal the internal brick arches and concrete structure of the 20-foot-thick walls of the rotunda. More than half of the original decoration—a wealth of columns, pilasters, and entablatures—survives. The simple repetition of square against circle, established on a large scale by juxtaposing the rectilinear portico against the circular rotunda, is found throughout the building's ornamentation. The wall is punctuated by seven **exedrae** (niches)—rectangular alternating with semicircular—that originally held statues of gods. The square, boxlike coffers inside the dome, which help lighten the weight of the masonry, may once have contained gilded bronze rosettes or stars suggesting the heavens. In 609 CE, Pope Boniface IV dedicated the Pantheon as the Christian church of St. Mary of the Martyrs, thus ensuring its survival through the Middle Ages and down to our day.

HADRIAN'S VILLA AT TIVOLI. To imagine Roman life at its most luxurious, one must go to Tivoli, a little more than 20 miles from Rome. **HADRIAN'S VILLA**, or country residence, was not a single building but an architectural complex of many buildings, lakes, and

To view this image, please go to page 198 of the *Art History*, Fourth Edition by Marilyn Stokstad ebook.

3-87 • DOME OF THE PANTHEON
With light from the oculus on its coffered ceiling. 125–128 CE.
Brick, concrete, marble veneer, diameter of dome 143′ (43.5 m).

SEE MORE: View a panorama of the Pantheon
www.myartslab.com

gardens spread over half a square mile **(FIG. 3–88)**. Each section had its own inner logic, and each took advantage of natural land formations and attractive views. Hadrian instructed his architects to re-create his favorite places throughout the empire. In his splendid villa, he could pretend to enjoy the Athenian Grove of Academe, the Painted Stoa from the Athenian Agora, and buildings of the Ptolemaic capital of Alexandria, Egypt.

Landscapes with pools, fountains, and gardens turned the villa into a place of sensuous delight. An area with a long reflecting pool, called the Canal, was framed by a colonnade with alternating semicircular and straight entablatures **(FIG. 3–89)**. It led to an outdoor dining room with concrete couches facing the pool. Copies of famous Greek statues, and sometimes even the originals, filled the spaces between the columns. So great was Hadrian's love of Greek sculpture that he even had the caryatids of the Erechtheion replicated for his pleasure palace.

The individual buildings were not large, but they were extremely complex and imaginatively designed. Roman builders and engineers exploited fully the flexibility offered by concrete vaulted construction. Walls and floors had veneers of marble and travertine or of exquisite mosaics and paintings. A panel from one of the floor mosaics **(FIG. 3–90)** demonstrates the extraordinary artistry of Hadrian's mosaicists. In a rocky landscape with only a few bits of greenery, a desperate male centaur raises a large boulder over his head to crush a tiger that has attacked and severely wounded a female centaur. Two other felines apparently took part in the attack—the white leopard on the rocks to the left and the dead lion at the feet of the male centaur. The artist rendered the figures with three-dimensional shading, foreshortening, and a great sensitivity to a range of figure types, including human torsos and powerful animals in a variety of poses.

IMPERIAL PORTRAITS

Imperial portraits were objects of propaganda. Marcus Aurelius, like Hadrian, was a successful military commander who was equally proud of his intellectual attainments. In a lucky error—or

To view this image, please go to page 199 of the *Art History*, Fourth Edition by Marilyn Stokstad ebook.

3-88 • PLAN OF HADRIAN'S VILLA
Tivoli. c. 125–135 CE.

To view this image, please go to page 200 of the *Art History*,
Fourth Edition by Marilyn Stokstad ebook.

3-89 • THE CANAL (REFLECTING POOL), HADRIAN'S VILLA
Tivoli. c. 125–135 CE.

To view this image, please go to page 200 of the *Art History*,
Fourth Edition by Marilyn Stokstad ebook.

3-90 • BATTLE OF CENTAURS AND WILD BEASTS FROM HADRIAN'S VILLA
Tivoli. c. 125 CE. Mosaic, 23 × 36″ (58.4 × 91.4 cm). Staatliche Museen zu Berlin, Preussischer Kulturbesitz,
Antikensammlung, Berlin.

This floor mosaic may be a copy of a much-admired painting of a fight between centaurs and wild animals done by
the late 5th-century BCE Greek artist Zeuxis.

twist of fortune—a gilded-bronze equestrian statue of the emperor, dressed as a military commander in a tunic and short, heavy cloak (FIG. 3–91), came mistakenly to be revered during the Middle Ages as a statue of Constantine, the first Christian emperor, and consequently the sculpture escaped being melted down. The raised foreleg of his horse once trampled a crouching barbarian.

Marcus Aurelius' head, with its thick, curly hair and full beard (a fashion that was begun by Hadrian), resembles the traditional "philosopher" portraits from the Greek world. The emperor wears no armor and carries no weapons; like Egyptian kings, he conquers effortlessly by divine will. And like his illustrious predecessor Augustus, he reaches out to those around him in a rhetorical gesture of address. It is difficult to create an equestrian portrait in which the rider stands out as the dominant figure without making the horse look too small. The sculptor of this statue found a balance acceptable to viewers of the time and, in doing so, created a model for later artists.

CONSTANTINE THE GREAT

In 305 CE, Diocletian abdicated and forced his fellow Augustus, Maximian, to do so too. The orderly succession he had planned for failed to occur, and a struggle for position and advantage followed almost immediately. Two main contenders appeared in the Western Empire: Maximian's son Maxentius, and Constantine, son of Tetrarch Constantius Chlorus. Constantine emerged victorious in 312, defeating Maxentius at the Battle of the Milvian Bridge at the entrance to Rome.

According to Christian tradition, Constantine had a vision the night before the battle in which he saw a flaming cross in the sky and heard these words: "In this sign you shall conquer." The next morning he ordered that his army's shields and standards be inscribed with the monogram XP (the Greek letters *chi* and *rho*, standing for *Christos*). The victorious Constantine then showed his gratitude by ending the persecution of Christians and recognizing Christianity as a lawful religion. He may have been influenced in that decision by his mother, Helena, a devout Christian—later canonized. Whatever his motivation, in 313 CE, together with Licinius, who ruled the Eastern Empire, Constantine issued the Edict of Milan, a model of religious toleration.

To view this image, please go to page 201 of the *Art History*, Fourth Edition by Marilyn Stokstad ebook.

3-91 • EQUESTRIAN STATUE OF MARCUS AURELIUS

c. 176 CE. Bronze, originally gilded, height of statue 11′6″ (3.5 m). Museo Capitolino, Rome.

Between 1187 and 1538, this statue stood in the piazza fronting the palace and church of St. John Lateran in Rome. In January 1538, Pope Paul III had it moved to the Capitoline Hill, and Michelangelo made it the centerpiece of his newly redesigned Capitoline Piazza. After being removed from its base for cleaning and restoration in recent times, it was taken inside the Capitoline Museum to protect it from air pollution, and a copy has replaced it in the piazza.

The Edict granted freedom to all religious groups, not just Christians. Constantine, however, remained the Pontifex Maximus of Rome's state religion and also reaffirmed his devotion to the military's favorite god, Mithras, and to the Invincible Sun, Sol Invictus, a manifestation of Helios Apollo, the sun god. In 324 CE, Constantine defeated Licinius, his last rival, and ruled as sole emperor until his death in 337. He made the port city of Byzantium the new capital of the Roman Empire after his last visit to Rome in 325, and renamed the city after himself—Constantinople (present-day Istanbul, in Turkey). Rome, which had already ceased to be the seat of government in the West, further declined in importance.

THE ARCH OF CONSTANTINE. In Rome, next to the Colosseum, the Senate erected a triumphal arch to commemorate Constantine's victory over Maxentius (FIG. 3–92), a huge, triple arch that dwarfs the nearby Arch of Titus (SEE FIG. 3–73). Its three barrel-vaulted passageways are flanked by columns on high pedestals and surmounted by a large attic story with elaborate sculptural decoration and a laudatory inscription: "To the Emperor Constantine from the Senate and the Roman People. Since through divine inspiration and great wisdom he has delivered the state from the tyrant and his party by his army and noble arms, [we] dedicate this arch, decorated with triumphal insignia." The "triumphal insignia" were in part appropriated from earlier monuments made for Constantine's illustrious predecessors—Trajan, Hadrian, and Marcus Aurelius. The reused items visually transferred the old Roman virtues of strength, courage, and piety associated with these earlier exemplary emperors to Constantine himself. New reliefs were made for the arch to recount the story of Constantine's victory and to symbolize his own power and generosity. They run in strips underneath the reused Hadrianic tondi (a tondo is a circular composition) (FIG. 3–93).

Although the new Constantinian reliefs reflect the long-standing Roman predilection for depicting important events with recognizable detail, they nevertheless represent a significant change in style, approach, and subject matter (see lower figural frieze in FIG. 3–93). In this scene of Constantine addressing the Roman people in the Roman Forum, the Constantinian reliefs are easily distinguished from the reused Hadrianic tondi mounted just above them because of the faithfulness of the new reliefs to the avant-garde tetrarchic style we have already encountered in portraiture. The forceful, blocky, mostly frontal figures are compressed into the foreground plane. The participants to the sides, below the enthroned Constantine (his head is missing), almost congeal into a uniformly patterned mass that isolates the new emperor and connects him visually with the seated statues of his illustrious predecessors flanking him on the dais. This two-dimensional, hierarchical approach with its emphasis on authority and power rather than on individualized outward form is far

removed from the classicizing illusionism of earlier imperial reliefs. It is one of the Roman styles that will be adopted by the emerging Christian Church.

THE BASILICA NOVA. Constantine's rival Maxentius, who controlled Rome throughout his short reign (r. 306–312), ordered the repair of older buildings there and had new ones built. His most impressive undertaking was a huge new basilica, just southeast of the Imperial Forums, called the **BASILICA NOVA**, or New Basilica. Now known as the Basilica of Maxentius and Constantine, this was the last important imperial government building erected in Rome. Like all basilicas, it functioned as an administrative center and provided a magnificent setting for the emperor when he appeared as supreme judge.

Earlier basilicas, such as Trajan's Basilica Ulpia (SEE FIG. 3–79), had been columnar halls, but Maxentius ordered his engineers to create the kind of large, unbroken, vaulted space found in public baths. The central hall was covered with groin vaults, and the side aisles were covered with lower barrel vaults that acted as buttresses, or projecting supports, for the central vault and allowed generous window openings in the clerestory areas over the side walls.

Three of these brick-and-concrete barrel vaults still loom over the streets of present-day Rome (FIG. 3–94). The basilica originally measured 300 by 215 feet and the vaults of the central nave rose to a height of 114 feet. A groin-vaulted porch extended across the short side and sheltered a triple entrance to the central hall. At the opposite end of the long axis of the hall was an apse of the same width, which acted as a focal point for the building (FIGS. 3–95, 3–96). The directional focus along a central axis from entrance to apse was adopted by Christians for use in churches.

Constantine, seeking to impress the people of Rome with visible symbols of his authority, put his own stamp on projects Maxentius had started, including this one. He may have changed the orientation of the Basilica Nova by adding an imposing new entrance in the center of the long side facing the Via Sacra and a giant apse facing it across the three aisles. He also commissioned a colossal, 30-foot statue of himself to be placed inside within an apse (FIG. 3–97). Sculptors used white marble for the head, chest, arms, and legs, and sheets of bronze for the drapery, all supported on a wooden frame. This statue became a permanent stand-in for the emperor, representing him whenever the conduct of business legally required his presence. The head combines features of traditional Roman portraiture with some of the abstract qualities evident in images of the tetrarchs. The defining characteristics of Constantine's face—his heavy jaw, hooked nose, and jutting chin—have been incorporated into a stylized, symmetrical pattern in which other features, such as his eyes, eyebrows, and hair, have been simplified into repeated geometric arcs. The result is a work that projects imperial power and dignity with no hint of human frailty or imperfection.

To view this image, please go to page 209 of the *Art History*,
Fourth Edition by Marilyn Stokstad ebook.

3-92 • ARCH OF CONSTANTINE
Rome. 312–315 CE (dedicated July 25, 315).

This massive, triple-arched monument to Emperor Constantine's victory over Maxentius in 312 CE is a wonder of recycled sculpture. On the attic story, flanking the inscription over the central arch, are relief panels taken from a monument celebrating the victory of Marcus Aurelius over the Germans in 174 CE. On the attached piers framing these panels are large statues of prisoners made to celebrate Trajan's victory over the Dacians in the early second century CE. On the inner walls of the central arch and on the attic of the short sides (neither seen here) are reliefs also commemorating Trajan's conquest of Dacia. Over each of the side arches is a pair of large tondi taken from a monument to Hadrian (SEE FIG. 3–94). The rest of the decoration is early fourth century, contemporary with the arch.

SEE MORE: Click the Google Earth link for the Arch of Constantine **www.myartslab.com**

ROMAN ART AFTER CONSTANTINE

Although Constantine was baptized only on his deathbed in 337, Christianity had become the official religion of the empire by the end of the fourth century, and non-Christians had become targets of persecution. This religious shift, however, did not diminish Roman interest in the artistic traditions of their pagan Classical past. A large silver **PLATTER** dating from the mid-fourth century CE **(FIG. 3–98)** proves that artists working for Christian patrons continued to use themes involving Bacchus, allowing them the opportunity to create elaborate figural compositions displaying the nude or lightly draped human body in complex, dynamic poses. The platter was found in a cache of silver tableware near Mildenhall, England, and although most of the objects are also decorated with pagan imagery, three of the spoons are engraved with Christian sym-

To view this image, please go to page 210 of the *Art History*, Fourth Edition by Marilyn Stokstad ebook.

3-93 • HADRIAN/CONSTANTINE HUNTING BOAR AND SACRIFICING TO APOLLO; CONSTANTINE ADDRESSING THE ROMAN PEOPLE IN THE ROMAN FORUM
Tondi made for a monument to Hadrian and reused on the Arch of Constantine. c. 130–138 CE.
Marble, diameter 40″ (102 cm). Frieze by Constantinian sculptors 312–315 CE.

The two tondi (circular compositions) were originally part of a lost monument erected by the emperor Hadrian (r. 117–138 CE). The boar hunt demonstrates his courage and physical prowess, and his sacrificial offering to Apollo shows his piety and gratitude to the gods for their support. The classicizing heads, form-enhancing drapery, and graceful poses of the figures betray a debt to the style of Late Classical Greek art. In the fourth century CE, Constantine appropriated these tondi, had Hadrian's head recarved with his own or his father's features, and incorporated them into his own triumphal arch (SEE FIG. 3–93) so that the power and piety of this predecessor could reflect on him and his reign. In a strip of relief underneath the tondi, sculptors from his own time portrayed a ceremony performed by Constantine during his celebration of the victory over his rival, Maxentius, at the Battle of the Milvian Bridge (312 CE). Rather than the Hellenizing mode popular during Hadrian's reign, the Constantinian sculptors employ the blocky and abstract stylizations that became fashionable during the tetrarchy.

bols. The original owner of the hoard was likely to have been a wealthy Roman Christian, living in the provinces. Such opulent items were often hidden or buried to protect them from theft and looting, a sign of the breakdown of the Roman peace, especially in provincial areas (see "The Mildenhall Treasure," opposite).

The Bacchic revelers on this platter whirl, leap, and sway in a dance to the piping of satyrs around a circular central medallion. In the centerpiece, the head of the sea god Oceanus is ringed by nude females frolicking in the waves with fantastic sea creatures. In the outer circle, the figure of Bacchus is the one stable element. With a bunch of grapes in his right hand, a krater at his feet, and one foot on the haunches of his panther, he listens to a male follower begging for another drink. Only a few figures away, the pitifully drunken hero Hercules has lost his lion-skin mantle and collapsed in a stupor into the supporting arms of two satyrs. The detail, clarity, and liveliness of this platter reflect the work of a virtuoso artist. Deeply engraved lines emphasize the contours of the subtly modeled bodies, echoing the technique of **undercutting** used to add depth to figures in stone and marble reliefs and suggesting a connection between silver-working and relief sculpture.

In 1942, a farmer plowing a field outside the town of Mildenhall in Suffolk, England, located near the site of an ancient Roman villa, accidentally discovered one of the greatest archaeological finds of the twentieth century. In total he unearthed 34 pieces of Roman silver dating from the fourth century CE. The find was not made public until four years later, since the farmer and his associates claimed they were unaware of how valuable it was, both materially and historically. When word of the discovery leaked out, however, the silver was confiscated by the government to determine if it was a "Treasure Trove"—gold or silver objects that have been intentionally hidden (rather than, for example, included in a burial) and that by law belong not to the finder, but to the Crown. The silver found at Mildenhall was deemed a "Treasure Trove" and is now one of the great glories of the British Museum in London.

This is the official story of the discovery at Mildenhall. But there are those who do not believe it. None of the silver in the hoard showed any sign of having been dented by a plough, and some believe that the quality and style of the objects are inconsistent with a provincial Roman context, especially so far in the hinterlands in England. Could the treasure have been looted from Italy during World War II, brought back to England (Mildenhall is not far from an American airfield), and buried to set up a staged discovery? The farmer who discovered the hoard and his associates, some argue, changed their story several times over the course of its history. Most scholars do believe the official story—that the silver was buried quickly for safekeeping by wealthy provincial Romans in Britain who felt threatened by a possible invasion or attack, and was forgotten (perhaps its owners were killed in the expected turmoil) until its accidental discovery in 1942. But when the history of art is founded on undocumented archaeological finds, there is usually room for doubt.

To view this image, please go to page 211 of the *Art History*, Fourth Edition by Marilyn Stokstad ebook.

3-94 • BASILICA OF MAXENTIUS AND CONSTANTINE (BASILICA NOVA)
Rome. 306–313 CE.

SEE MORE: Click the Google Earth link for the Basilica of Maxentius and Constantine www.myartslab.com

To view this image, please go to page 212 of the *Art History*, Fourth Edition by Marilyn Stokstad ebook.

3–95 • FLOOR PLAN OF THE BASILICA OF MAXENTIUS AND CONSTANTINE (BASILICA NOVA)

To view this image, please go to page 212 of the *Art History*, Fourth Edition by Marilyn Stokstad ebook.

3–96 • RECONSTRUCTION OF THE BASILICA OF MAXENTIUS AND CONSTANTINE (BASILICA NOVA)

Not all Romans, however, converted to Christianity. Among the champions of paganism were the Roman patricians Quintus Aurelius Symmachus and Virius Nicomachus Flavianus. A famous ivory diptych **(FIG. 3–99)** attests to the close relationship between their families, perhaps through marriage, as well as to their firmly held beliefs. A **diptych** was a pair of panels attached with hinges, not unlike the modest object held by the woman in FIG. 3–72, but in this case made of a very precious material and carved with reliefs on the exterior sides. On the interior of a diptych there were shallow, traylike recessions filled with wax, into which messages could be written with a stylus and sent with a servant as a letter to a friend or acquaintance, who could then smooth out the wax surface, incise a reply with his or her own stylus, and send the diptych back to its owner with the servant. Here one family's name is inscribed at the top of each panel. On the panel inscribed "Symmachorum" (illustrated here), a stately, elegantly attired priestess burns incense at a beautifully decorated altar. On her head is a wreath of ivy, sacred to Bacchus. She is assisted by a small child, and

3-97 • CONSTANTINE THE GREAT

Basilica of Maxentius and Constantine, Rome. 325–326 CE. Marble, height of head 8′6″ (2.6 m). Palazzo dei Conservatori, Rome.

To view this image, please go to page 213 of the *Art History*, Fourth Edition by Marilyn Stokstad ebook.

3-98 • PLATTER
From Mildenhall, England. Mid 4th century CE. Silver, diameter approx. 24″ (61 cm). British Museum, London.

the event takes place out of doors under an oak tree, sacred to Jupiter. Like the silversmiths, Roman ivory carvers of the fourth century CE were highly skillful, and their work was widely admired. For conservative patrons like the Nicomachus and Symmachus families, they imitated the Augustan style effortlessly. The exquisite rendering of the drapery and foliage recalls the reliefs of the Ara Pacis.

Classical subject matter remained attractive to artists and patrons throughout the late Roman period. Even such great Christian thinkers as the fourth-century CE bishop Gregory of Nazianzus (a saint and Father of the Orthodox Church) spoke out in support of the right of the people to appreciate and enjoy their Classical heritage, so long as they were not seduced by it to return to pagan practices. As a result, stories of the ancient gods and heroes entered the secular realm as lively, visually delightful, even erotic decorative elements. As Roman authority gave way to local rule by powerful barbarian tribes in much of the West, many people continued to appreciate Classical learning and to treasure Greek and Roman art. In the East, Classical traditions and styles were cultivated to become an enduring element of Byzantine art.

To view this image, please go to page 215 of the *Art History*, Fourth Edition by Marilyn Stokstad ebook.

3-99 • PRIESTESS OF BACCHUS (?)
Right panel of the diptych of Symmachus and Nicomachus.
c. 390–401 CE. Ivory, 11¾ × 4¾″ (29.9 × 12 cm).
Victoria & Albert Museum, London.

3.5 Compare the scenes celebrating the vitality of human life on the walls of Etruscan tombs with the scenes portrayed on the walls of the Egyptian tombs.

3.6 Explain how the Roman interest in portraits grew out of early funeral rituals.

3.7 Describe three themes that are found in the murals of Roman houses in Pompeii, using specific examples from this chapter. Why do you think these themes were chosen for the decoration of homes?

3.8 Identify two key structural advances made by Roman builders and discuss their use in one large civic building in this chapter.

3.9 Discuss how Roman emperors used portraiture as imperial propaganda.

PRACTICE MORE: Compose answers to these questions, get flashcards for images and terms, and review chapter material with quizzes
www.myartslab.com

CLASSICAL LITERACY 700 BCE–400 CE

- In the Classical period, graphic design became a component of literacy. Design literacy suggests the existence of a common cultural understanding of the meaning of the visual forms, as well as the materials and contexts, of graphic information.

- In Classical culture, the functions of written language were encoded in distinct graphic forms:

    Informal communication between individuals was expressed in the ephemeral form of handwritten script, often on impermanent materials.

    Conventional communication regarding professional, personal, or public business relied on standard codes and consistent, legible letterforms written on **papyrus**, **parchment**, or wax.

    Commemorative writing used permanent materials, such as stone or clay, to inscribe acts of official memory or tribute in formal scripts and highly visible public spaces that signified importance.

- **Performative** discourse—containing statements that enacted events, laws, or decrees—was marked by ritual or ceremonial warrants, seals, official signs, and sites that conferred authority.

- The distinction between spoken and written language became more elaborate, as writing came to be considered not merely a transcription of speech but a communication system with its own formal properties.

- The design of letters was defined in two very different ways: as a sequence of expressive gestures and as a set of ideal shapes or constructed models to be copied.

- Access to writing did not map precisely onto class or gender divisions, but the shift from oral to literate culture introduced new means of representing and administering power.

In the Classical period, literacy took on new graphic and cultural dimensions. When the alphabet arrived in ancient Greece and Italy around 700 BCE, earlier writing systems had fallen out of use, but their legacy had established the value of written communication in many areas of public and private life. Within the city-states of Greece and the extensive, multicultural empire of Rome, reading entailed more than the recognition of letters and words. A text's physical and social setting were taken into account, and its graphic and material codes were interpreted. Classical Greek and Roman cultures used writing for individual expression, communication, commemorative acts of public record, and decrees or commands. These functions were distinguished graphically by letterforms and styles, and physically by the contexts in which messages were located. Formal properties signaled to a reader important information about the relative authority of their source and the intended effect of their message even before texts were read. Urban and cosmopolitan, Classical societies were attuned to such graphic nuances. Degrees of literacy marked social distinctions and shaped networks of political power. In this cultural context, two very different approaches to the design of letters were established: one based on gestures and expressive forms and the other based on ideal **models** and **constructed forms.** These two approaches would continue to diverge in subsequent centuries. Basic principles of visual literacy in the production and reception of graphic forms were encoded in the Classical period in enduring and thus familiar ways (**FIG. 3–100**).

VARIATIONS OF LITERACY AND THE ALPHABET

Variants of the alphabet were used in Greece and southern Italy in the Classical period. With the exception of early indigenous writing in Crete, all were derived from scripts in the ancient Near East and dispersed by Phoenicians along their trade routes throughout the Mediterranean. By the eighth century BCE, this alphabet had taken hold among the Greeks, as well as the Etruscans (who populated southern Italy before the Romans). In Greece, the new writing system was linked to democracy insofar as literacy was a requirement for citizenship and its rights. But whether the unique properties of Greek writing *caused* the advent of this form of government or merely participated in its institutions is an open question (**FIGS. 3–101A** and **3–101B**).

The oldest Greek inscriptions used letters that were very close in shape to their Phoenician sources. These scripts had only **majuscules** (uppercase letters). Lowercase versions of the letters (**minuscules**) came later. The format of early Classical

To view this image, please go to page 16 of the *Graphic Design History*, Second Edition by Johanna Drucker and Emily McVarish ebook.

3-100 • INSCRIPTION FROM A DIPYLON VASE, 730-720 BCE
This early Greek inscription almost seems to have been scratched into the neck of the vase as an afterthought. It says, "Who now of all dancers most delicately performs, may he accept this." Expressive in character, the line feels spontaneously emotional, as if a celebratory mood had moved its author to this act of writing. The letters are crudely made but regular enough to be readable. Their sticklike forms have sharp angles and few curves. The writing reads from right to left, as in Phoenician texts, and the letters lie on their sides—another feature of the older or "parent" alphabet that gave rise to both Greek and Latin scripts.

inscriptions was varied, as was the orientation of writing. Conventions for basic elements of graphic presentation, such as reading direction and word spacing, were not yet fixed. The distinctive style of arrangement known as *boustrophedon* (literally, "as the ox ploughs") had precedents in Egyptian hieroglyphics. By the sixth and fifth centuries BCE, a clean, **monoline** script with little variation in weight became typical of Greek Classical letterform design. This writing was very evenly spaced and aligned, and the letters were regular in size and proportion (**FIG. 3–102**).

Greek and early Latin alphabets were soon modified. Like dialects of a spoken language, scripts developed local variations. Many of these variants are referred to by their geographical location. Thus, Eastern, Western, and Chalcidian scripts derive their names from parts of Greece. Other forms of the alphabet, such as the Etruscan and Roman, came from Italy. In spite of their differences, remarkable consistency united these alphabets, and many innovations were shared among them—a sign of close communication among peoples of the region. Their variations were a cultural equivalent to individual handwriting. The alphabet was the same in sequence and number of letters, but each local

> Rules for reading direction and word spacing were not yet fixed.

3-101A • GORTYNA INSCRIPTION, 638 BCE, AND 3-101B SITE OF THE INSCRIPTION
This inscription is nearly 8 feet high and twelve columns wide and was found in the wall of a public theater in Crete. The text follows the early **boustrophedon** format: each line changes direction, winding first right to left, then left to right. The orientation of the letters switches as well, so that the letters in alternate lines are reversed. Like many early **monumental** texts, this inscription defines the state's ability to regulate the affairs of its citizens. As a permanent display of statutes, it presents a clear example of civic communication that encodes state power in a public image. The laws concern domestic issues: "the status of slaves, the rights of widows, heirs at law, children born after divorce, the adoption of children, property rights, and many other laws relating to domestic and family relations." The text was unearthed in 1881 near the ancient city of Gortyna. Known in antiquity as the "well-walled" city, Gortyna was associated with the legendary King Minos and his labyrinth. Although the inscription's letters exhibit the developed shape of Classical Greek, it contains only one (upsilon) of the five vowels that Greek incorporated.

To view this image, please go to page 18 of the *Graphic Design History*, Second Edition by Johanna Drucker and Emily McVarish ebook.

To view this image, please go to page 18 of the *Graphic Design History*, Second Edition by Johanna Drucker and Emily McVarish ebook.

To view this image, please go to page 19 of the *Graphic Design History*, Second Edition by Johanna Drucker and Emily McVarish ebook.

3-102 • DECREE ON A MARBLE STELE DESCRIBING PROCEDURES FOR TRIBUTE, 426 BCE

This formal inscription outlines procedures to be followed in case of a dispute over the payment of tribute money to the city of Athens. As a prescription of behavior, it communicates the power of one city-state over the populace of another. The letters are carefully arranged with both vertical and horizontal columns maintained in a style known as **stoichedon** ("files"). The military procession evoked by this term and the strict graphic organization it describes seem well suited to the imposition of rule among warring city-states. The letters are written from left to right, a practice that became standard in Western scripts. For right-handed writers, this direction allows the text to be visible as it is written, not obscured by the writing hand. In wet media, it prevents smearing.

graphic version had different shapes and proportions. The Ionic script became the official Greek alphabet in 403 BCE, but such decrees had as much to do with the consolidation of political power as they did with the value of one design over another. Military conquests took the Roman alphabet into new territories as an instrument of imperial administration and cultural domination **(FIGS. 3–103A** and **3–103B)**.

The most significant modification made by the Greeks to the alphabet was the addition of five letters to denote vowels. These were derived from Phoenician signs for consonants. Vowels provided considerable flexibility in adapting the script to a wide range of tongues. Because of its efficiency, the Greek alphabet may have been easier to learn than its precedents in the Near East. But the increase in literacy in Greece and Rome was also related to changes in educational patterns and assumptions about the place of writing in politics and the business of everyday life. Precise details about literacy rates among Classical populations are difficult to determine, but certainly reading and writing were no longer limited to a small class of **scribes**. Literacy among men was higher than among women, and many more people could read than write, but a large portion of the population could compose a personal message or conduct daily affairs in writing. In fourth century Athens, schools were established, including the famous gymnasium (school) where Plato taught in a park called Akademeia. **Rhetorical** skills essential to Greek politics were taught in these schools and so were the values on which the social networks of power rested. Literacy training inculcated pupils with cultural norms and social codes even as it passed on the poetry of Homer and the heroic tradition **(FIG. 3–104)**.

In their graphic evolution, Greek and Latin alphabets followed independent paths, and the distinctions that emerged in the seventh and sixth centuries BCE remain characteristic of them today. Both, however, adopted the convention of writing from left to right, with letters consistently oriented in that direction. Roman letterforms were marked by a blocklike geometrical regularity. The tilting diagonals and angular points of earlier scripts were regulated and codified as even curves and upright lines that expressed stasis

To view this image, please go to page 20 of the *Graphic Design History*, Second Edition by Johanna Drucker and Emily McVarish ebook.

To view this image, please go to page 20 of the *Graphic Design History*, Second Edition by Johanna Drucker and Emily McVarish ebook.

3-103A • IONIC INSCRIPTION, LATE FIFTH CENTURY BCE, AND 3-104B ABU SIMBEL, SITE OF THE INSCRIPTION

This commemorative Ionic Greek inscription was carved into one of the monumental statues of Ramses II at the temple of Abu Simbel on the west bank of the Nile in Egypt. The Egyptian monument had been built about 1000 bce, and this Greek text records the travels of a certain King Psamatichos to its site. The inscription's two authors are identified as Archon and Pelegnos, Greek mercenary soldiers traveling with the king. They describe their journey up the Nile and include the name of their Egyptian guide. One of the oldest Greek inscriptions, this graffiti was scraped into a knee of the giant limestone figure, which was half-buried in desert sand. Contrast this script with that of the Temple of Minerva at Priene (Fig. 3–106).

3-104 • BOY WRITING, FIFTH CENTURY BCE
The boy in this elegant painting is posed with a stylus and tablet on his lap. Along with papyrus and parchment, these were the most common writing materials. The tablet could be warmed and smoothed over for repeated use. Writing was a higher-order skill than reading, but literacy in Classical Greece was not limited to a single social group. By the fourth century, state-funded public education existed in Athens and other Greek city-states. Although full citizenship, which required literacy, was restricted to free, native-born, property-owning men, enough slaves and women were literate to allow reading and writing to be an integral part of daily life. No evidence exists of girls going to school, and most likely they were taught at home, but they were not prohibited by their gender from learning to read and write. Outstanding figures, such as the poet Sappho (sixth century bce) and the philosopher/playwright Hipparchia (300 bce), provide evidence of women's participation in the intellectual life of Classical Greece.

3-105 • CHART OF GREEK AND ROMAN LETTERS.
Variations in the number and forms of letters that constitute each script are vividly apparent here. These representations have been simplified, but they show the evolution of reading direction and the basic shapes and orientation of letters in the independent developments of Greek and Italian alphabets. Direction became standardized—not only from letter to letter but also within the component parts of letters. Crossbars and "arms" became horizontal and vertical. Diagonal strokes and curves were regularized. The distinctive features of each letter within its alphabet became graphically marked and aesthetically considered. The regularity of monumental carving in the Classical period came to conform to concepts of order and harmony. Efficiency and effectiveness were not the only governing principles in the design of letters or texts. After all, the early Latin script would have sufficed in practical terms.

and solidity rather than movement. Regimentation and administrative organization were basic features of Roman society, too. Extrapolating from the graphic qualities of a script to characterize a culture can be a risky proposition, but it is safe to say that the graphic stability of Roman letterforms conveyed an image of solid state power and authority (**FIG. 3–105**).

THE FUNCTION OF GRAPHIC CODES

Writing had served many purposes in Egyptian, Babylonian, and Canaanite cultures of the ancient Near East. Legal and literary texts, business records and accounts, official decrees and documents, maps, ritual prayers, and expressive graffiti had all been developed. Long before the alphabet was imported to Greece and Italy, writing included a range of social *functions* and a set of visual *forms*. The relations between specialized functions and particular forms were embodied in the design of letters, their material production, and physical contexts. Chisels, broad brushes, pens, and styluses each had characteristic formal effects. Surfaces were also varied, and marble, papyrus, wax, and pottery each posed specific challenges. But material conditions alone did not determine the style of scripts. The forms and material contexts of writing reflected the occasions and functions for which inscriptions were made. Scale, placement, visibility, and attention to workmanship all contributed to the way a visual communication was received. Formal inscriptions had appeared on temples and monuments throughout the ancient Near East, but in Classical culture, the types and locations of inscriptions multiplied. Tombs, commemorative

3-106 • INSCRIPTION FROM THE TEMPLE OF MINERVA AT PRIENE, THIRD CENTURY BCE

This aesthetically sophisticated script features **serifs** and is carved in elegant proportion and perfect alignment. As with all scripts of antiquity, the regularity of the letterforms results from their designer and carver's skill rather than mechanical repetition. The inscription is formal and monumental, concerned with public matters and conflicts between the people of Priene and their neighbors. In communicating a claim to ownership of the region, its highly regular shape communicates solemnity.

To view this image, please go to page 22 of the *Graphic Design History*, Second Edition by Johanna Drucker and Emily McVarish ebook.

3-107 • TETRADRACHMA FROM KYMAEA, SECOND CENTURY BCE

This coin bears the name of the provincial governor and the state. These recognizable names and the standardized forms of their inscription ensure the value of the currency. As one of the earliest forms of mass-produced graphic media, coins have a unique symbolic identity. They both embody value and represent it abstractly. Coinage, like language, can be used to represent other things, but it also has a value in its own right. Its effective use depends upon a social system in which the terms of exchange are agreed upon by all users. Currency involves an act of collective faith grounded in social conventions, even when the rare materials of the coinage have an apparently intrinsic value. Identification of a coin's source links its relative value to the ruler and city-state in which it is issued. But as coins circulate, they also promote the image and power of that state in any realm in which the money is accepted as valid.

plaques, milestones, and markers assume literacy, and from their remains we can deduce that it was widespread.

Tablets and **scrolls** remained the basic portable media, while stone carving indicated site-specific, official text. The invention of the bound book, enabled by the flexibility of parchment, was an economical and convenient innovation that appeared in the second to fourth centuries CE. But for hundreds of years, the scroll remained the preferred format for literary texts, whereas bound books were more likely to be used for notes. Booksellers employed copyists and effectively published texts. Literary and historical works, although copied by hand, circulated widely among the Classical Greek and Roman populations (**FIG. 3–106**).

We can artificially distinguish between the way writing looks and what it says, but specific lettering styles and materials have their own rhetorical force. Stylistic inflection often reinforces unstated assumptions about the function of a text—who it is for and what it is meant to do. Graphic and material codes distin-

To view this image, please go to page 22 of the *Graphic Design History*, Second Edition by Johanna Drucker and Emily McVarish ebook.

guished broad categories of written language from each other in the Classical period. When writing functioned as a form of personal expression in a letter or graffiti, it usually took the form of a **cursive** script that was **gestural** and informal. Such letters were made with a pen or brush on papyrus, or scratched into a wall, wax tablet, or other readily available material support. **Ostraca**—bits of discarded pottery—often served as scratch paper. These materials may have simply been convenient, whereas others carried explicit symbolic value. *Defixiones* were magic spells written on small sheets of lead that were rolled up and buried to preserve their power. Inscriptions on publicly circulated coins carried the authority of their stated value, backed by their weight in a given metal (**FIG. 3–107**).

> Graphic and material codes distinguished broad categories of written language from each other in the Classical period.

Acts of communication in the Classical period ran the gamut from informal correspondences to more structured and elaborate lists of rules, laws, or contracts. Agreements between city-states or admonitions to citizens were carved with care into walls or tablets and meant to have a permanent presence and carry authority. When an inscription voiced the omnipotence of the state or ruler, a script's measured character reinforced the sense that its text was law. A text that was closely tied to an official site could aspire to enduring significance but might also draw meaning from its geographical or architectural position. Milestones are an interesting instance of writing that defines and derives value from its place in the landscape. These markers also provide evidence of the spread of political power and cultural influence along roads used for commercial and military purposes. A traveler did not need to read Latin to feel the symbolic impact of Roman authority embodied in such stones (**FIG. 3–108**).

Commemorative statements on funeral steles, tributes celebrating victory, and inscriptions marking other civic occasions took on considerable gravity when carved in the most elegant of majuscules. A variety of writing styles existed in Greek and Roman cultures, ranging from highly ordered Greek letters aligned with the regularity of soldiers in formation to Roman majuscules arranged in unbroken lines on a marble surface and carved large enough to be visible from across an open forum. Language at this scale claims public space, naming and marking it with a reference that places citizens in relation to the authority of the state. Scale inscribes social hierarchy as well, distinguishing the relative importance of events and persons within a shared environment. More ephemeral forms of communication rarely formalized their script to so fine a degree (**FIG. 3–109**).

3-108 • LAPIS NIGER, MID-SIXTH CENTURY BCE

One of the oldest Latin inscriptions found in Rome is carved into a milestone. The text describes the correct way to observe rites at the altar next to which it was found. But curiously, the writing is on four sides and cannot be read in any systematic way or all at once from any angle. The text seems ceremonial, as if its significance depended more on its presence than on its ability to communicate. The inscription is a set of instructions relevant to the site, not a set of laws or general principles being communicated to a broad public by a ruler or conqueror. After the Romans conquered the Etruscans at Cumae in 281 BCE, vestiges of the earlier culture remained. Of their script's twenty-six letters, the Romans took twenty-one into their original alphabet and then added some of their own.

To view this image, please go to page 23 of the *Graphic Design History*, Second Edition by Johanna Drucker and Emily McVarish ebook.

Writing in the Classical period could have the power of a command or decree. Such acts of writing remained a feature of civic life throughout the Middle Ages and into the **Renaissance**. Read aloud, a posted notice by a ruling official could enact a law or prohibition. Vestiges of these acts remain today. Performative documents can prescribe behavior or set limits and terms of responsibility in contractual matters. Performative uses of writing depend upon an assumption of explicit authority. Someone is "speaking" to someone else according to a power vested in their person or office. Performativity can be materially enacted, as in the case of wax seals on vellum or parchment documents. The seal is a sign of security that performs a protective and evidential function. If it is broken, trust has been violated, even if the text inside remains unaltered. The ability to show or record change is one of the ways in which the material context of a graphic text participates in its signification. Monumental claims for permanence are perhaps the most basic form of the material inscription of authority **(FIG. 3–110)**.

Graphic communication took shape in the Classical period in ways that directly connect to the present day. Basic design decisions about the way something looked as a function of what it communicated were everywhere apparent in the Classical world, and we still use the square majuscules of the Romans for commemorative inscriptions. No explicit manuals or rule books existed that set out

the conditions for using one type of script or another, just as no such definitive typographic guide exists now. Rather, these conventions come to be understood and followed by consensus among a cultural community and the designers or scribes who work within its tacit codes. Roman scribes were employed by the state and divided into clearly defined professional classes. In general, their role was to compose or copy a written text or to transcribe speech. They even used shorthand (invented by Tiro, the slave of Cicero, to record his master's speeches in the Roman forum). Literary language and vernacular speech were distinct, and formal composition was governed by

> As the social character of written language came to be inscribed in its design, conventions were communicated by example.

3-109 • RUSTIC BRUSHWORK, BEFORE 79 CE

This **rustic** brushwork was found on a wall at Pompeii, an ancient Italian city that was buried in ash when Vesuvius erupted. This vigorous style of majuscule was used to advertise gladiatorial events, wares for sale, and upcoming elections. A combination of tabloid, billboard, and flyer, this sort of inscription communicates with great efficacy. Its messages are timely and ephemeral, and the swift execution of the script signals the freshness of the information. Latin rustic script provided models for writing on papyrus and inscriptions in marble, which preserved the energetic character of brush forms.

To view this image, please go to page 24 of the *Graphic Design History*, Second Edition by Johanna Drucker and Emily McVarish ebook.

3-110 • RUSTIC LETTERS, 194 CE

Rustic letters carved in marble inscribe a military tribute to the Roman Emperor Septimius Severus. Such praise constitutes a performative use of language because it enacts the celebration of the emperor rather than simply describing it. This inscription demonstrates that models of letterforms, rather than just material constraints, govern graphic expression. Carving letters in stone with a chisel is a multiple-stage process and involves conceptual forethought and design decisions. Here, the first line is in formal majuscules and contains an address to the "Imperial Caesar." Next, the writing switches to the message. The decision to use one form of lettering to show respect and another to compress the substance of the tribute indicates that these choices carry meaning. Rustic majuscules and formal capitals are both brush-based in their design, and nothing about their shape is natural to the medium of stone carving. Rather, the idea of a letterform—a rustic majuscule—was at work in the series of decisions that led to execution of this carving.

3-112 • FUNERAL STONE WITH IMAGE OF A TEN-YEAR-OLD GIRL, FIRST CENTURY BCE

Roman culture was highly literate. Streets were filled with signage of all kinds from the most ephemeral advertisements to monumental inscriptions. Wax tablets were used to educate young scholars, and both men and women were frequently depicted reading them. Tombstones and **sarcophagi** often portrayed the deceased with a wax tablet or pair of wax tablets hinged to protect their soft surface. The public life of language was rich and varied in Rome and other Latin cities.

strict rules. But writing tasks were further specialized according to the media they involved. Stone carvers had the task of designing appropriate styles for each inscription, and their work took distance, sight lines, and scale into account. Preliminary designs were often sketched by an **ordinator** who provided the outlines the carver would follow. Such specialization suggests a well-developed professional culture. Urban environments were particularly important sites for the management of communication and the formation of social values **(FIG. 3–111)**.

As the social character of written language came to be inscribed in its design, conventions were communicated and understood by example. If Classical readers could register the graphic difference between a formal script and an informal script, then the visual distinction could be given a value that was understood as part of its message. Graphic codes operated within a social context as well as a physical one. In the stratified, hierarchical societies of Greece and Rome, propertied and nonpropertied, patrician and plebian classes were delineated. This social organization found formal expression in the physical structure of urban space and the orders of architecture. Funeral monuments carved in stone marked the graves of persons of status. Literary works circulated in scrolls and tablets before books gained favor. Daily business exchanges depended on ink, on clay scraps or bits of papyrus, and on wax-covered or painted wood tablets. Writing was abundant, but scarce materials, such as precious metals, had intrinsic as well as symbolic value. All of these features of production, placement, and format were legible within a Classical society. The legacy of this design literacy is very much with us. It guides our reading and writing of visual forms, and our perception and use of their material contexts **(FIG. 3–112)**.

3-111 • BATH ADVERTISEMENT, EARLY CE

Formal lettering was chosen for this marble inscription advertising a Roman bath and its various waters and services. A commercial purpose shaped this work, and liberties in the rendering of each letter were taken with an eye toward the energized harmony of the whole. Each line features different sizes and varying proportions, but they all belong to the same script family. Creating consistency within variety is a design challenge, and the skill with which this inscription's maker preserved the specific character of the lettering demonstrates mastery of the carver's art. A logic of display governs the visual bid for attention in this 2,000-year-old commercial design.

To view this image, please go to page 26 of the *Graphic Design History*, Second Edition by Johanna Drucker and Emily McVarish ebook.

To view this image, please go to page 26 of the *Graphic Design History*, Second Edition by Johanna Drucker and Emily McVarish ebook.

3-114 • ROMAN CURSIVE, 166 CE (BELOW)
By contrast, this cursive indicates far more gestural efficiency. One can almost see the movement of the scribe's hand over the papyrus surface, a swiftly running stream of strokes. Although the scribe obviously holds an "image" of the letters in mind, his practiced hand outstrips the considered construction associated with drawing or carving more elaborate letterforms.

MODELS OF WRITING: GESTURAL AND CONSTRUCTED

The use of models for lettering was essential to the development of a culture of literacy. Without them, shared signs and conventions for their use could not have become stable. Scribes relied upon models they could copy, as they trained their hands to render shapes. Such knowledge quickly became somatic (bodily), and gestural patterns of production became habitual. Two fundamentally distinct approaches to the design of letters developed in the Classical period, and they may be defined as gestural, cursive forms and intellectually constructed forms **(FIG. 3–113)**.

Cursives are rapidly produced, handwritten versions of the alphabet that are gestural in nature. Often produced under time constraints or for ephemeral purposes, cursives are written immediately and reflect the mood and skill of their author. Although cursives are based on convention, they are executed in a series of physical movements that are as corporeal as dance steps. Cursive scripts were rarely used for any monumental or official documents, and their design often had the idiosyncratic quality of handwriting. The purpose of cursives was to produce texts that were legible and efficient, rather than to create aesthetic forms **(FIG. 3–114)**.

Constructed letters followed a more labored sequence of design stages and sought to achieve formal beauty through principles of proportion and harmony. Constructed letters could be made in any material, but, in monumental inscriptions, they had the effect of conferring gravity upon a text. Preparation for such designs involved laying out the inscription or document as a whole and paying careful attention to the form of each letter. Because its production involved multiple steps, a carved letterform might have its origins in the shapes made by a brush used to sketch it on a marble surface, even if the ultimate use of a chisel somewhat modified the design. Constructed letters may have been based on a system of proportion that was calculated as a division of a grid. But as they were carved their makers took liberties, softening the precise forms through the touch of the hand and a corrective eye. The grace and liveliness of the greatest of Classical letterforms belie any strict adherence to a mathematical design. Instead, they show the sophistication of designers who subtly transformed the idealized images of letters that served as their models **(FIGS. 3–115A** and **3–115B)**.

Whether constructed or cursive, letter designs are always based on internalized models and shaped by the training their designers receive. Samples of writing in the Classical age existed in public places, but, in the gymnasium, students were also given examples to copy. Only one visual model existed for each letter: the one we call the majuscule, or capital. The shape of the letterforms was basically the same in cursives and constructed forms, but the production methods and aesthetic goals were different. The development of the first variants of majuscules, known as **uncial** and **half-uncial** scripts, came later—in the third and fourth centuries CE—and were much more common in book formats than in monumental inscriptions. The development of these graphic variations of writing would signal a major cultural change as the Classical period came to an end **(FIG. 3–116)**.

To view this image, please go to page 27 of the *Graphic Design History*, Second Edition by Johanna Drucker and Emily McVarish ebook.

To view this image, please go to page 27 of the *Graphic Design History*, Second Edition by Johanna Drucker and Emily McVarish ebook.

3–115A • TRAJAN'S COLUMN, DETAIL, 114 CE, AND 3–115B TRAJAN'S COLUMN

The formal capitals inscribed on the base of Trajan's column have long been considered the pinnacle of Roman letter design. Copied and studied by artists and designers over the centuries, the letters are remarkable for their combination of consistency and variety, as well as for the harmony of their nonmechanical proportions. These letters were not constructed by use of a compass or ruler, and yet their effect on the eye is one of profound order and geometrical regularity. These majuscules were based on designs first made with a flat brush. Their layout was the work of an ordinator, who may or may not have been the same person as the carver. The incised chisel work makes a deep V-shape in the stone's surface. By turning the chisel at the end of the stroke, a serif is appended. The differences between thick and thin strokes in the letters are vestiges of the brush stage of their design: thicker downstrokes and thinner upstrokes characterize calligraphy. These designs have been translated into carved forms with enormous care, and the constructed nature of the script through this multistage process never interferes with the confident reinterpretation of each letter as it is sensitively executed. The text commemorates Trajan's victories over the Dacians, and its monumental significance is strengthened by the treatment and scale of the letters. The power of the emperor and state of Rome become aligned with the grandeur of the script, which, not surprisingly, has served as a model for many nations in circumstances that call for an air of seriousness.

3-116 • INKWELL FROM A TOMB IN CAERE, SHOWING AN EARLY ETRUSCAN ABECEDARY, LATE SEVENTH CENTURY BCE

3-116 • INKWELL FROM A TOMB IN CAERE, SHOWING AN EARLY ETRUSCAN ABECEDARY, LATE SEVENTH CENTURY BCE

The earliest inscriptions in Latin were actually made by Etruscans, using letters very close to the Phoenician originals. This alphabet was inscribed on an inkwell, no doubt to keep models of the letters before the eyes of a scribe—a device as convenient as the letters on a modern keyboard. This early instance of Latin lettering displays the same gestural (or **ductal**) approach as was common in early Greek lettering. The models offer instructions for making the letters as a series of strokes rather than simply providing forms to copy or modify.

WRITING AT THE END OF THE CLASSICAL AGE

The sack of Rome in 410 CE by northern invaders marked the end of the Classical period. By then, the identification of Greek and Latin letterforms with the Eastern and Western branches of the Holy Roman Empire had begun to charge their use with a new political meaning. One form of the *A* was so strongly associated with the Eastern Church that its mere appearance seemed to flaunt a claim for the power of Byzantium. During the first centuries of the Common Era, Classical literacy became increasingly absorbed into Church institutions and practices. Early Christians had been marginal in Roman society, and their inscriptions demonstrated a lower level of literacy than those of the dominant culture. But the Church would soon change this situation dramatically. By the fourth century, monastic orders became the main institutions for the production and preservation of knowledge in Western culture (**FIG. 3–117**).

To view this image, please go to page 29 of the *Graphic Design History*, Second Edition by Johanna Drucker and Emily McVarish ebook.

To view this image, please go to page 28 of the *Graphic Design History*, Second Edition by Johanna Drucker and Emily McVarish ebook.

3-117 • CHRISTIAN INSCRIPTION, FOURTH CENTURY CE

The lettering on this inscription from a Christian catacomb has a distinctive aesthetic but lacks the formal control of monumental Roman scripts. A passionate energy is palpable, but this is not the work of a skilled designer or carver. Variation in the length of lines, fit of letters, and shape of individual characters indicates more ad hoc accommodation than forethought. Such qualities characterized the tombstones of Christians who were less educated and tended to exist outside the ruling class of Roman society—a fact that would have been communicated to contemporaries by the very look of this inscription.

To view this image, please go to page 29 of the *Graphic Design History*, Second Edition by Johanna Drucker and Emily McVarish ebook.

3-118 • FILOCALUS, FOURTH CENTURY CE

This inscription was created by a known calligrapher, Filocalus, at San Calisto in Rome. He was a Christian whose hand and style were recognized, and these letterforms are attributed to him as his own invention. The overall quality of the script, its robust roundness and delicate, decoratively curled serifs, anticipate book hands. But such elaborate carving would soon diminish, as the Church replaced the Roman Empire as the major force in Western culture. This broad cultural shift was marked by changes not only in the form but also in the location of scripts. Books, not buildings, would provide the main site of writing in the next centuries. The sack of Rome coincided with the rise of the **codex**—the familiar bound form of the book—and thus marked a turning point from Classical to Medieval literacy, with all of the consequences for design that this transition entailed.

CONCLUSION

In Classical antiquity, writing was conspicuous in public spaces and was used for many personal and commercial purposes. Rome in the early centuries of the Common Era had a lively culture of graphic signage. But sites and contexts were about to change. The development of graphic conventions in the Medieval period had more to do with pages and inked script styles than monumental inscriptions. Direct lines of transmission connected Classical letterforms and visual codes with Medieval and modern usage. But scripts and the instruments of their circulation and use were soon to be altered by the cultural ascendancy of a recently arrived format: the bound book **(FIG. 3–118)**.

Classical Literacy 700 BCE–400 CE

800–700 BCE	Eighteen-letter Phoenician alphabet introduced to Greece and Italy
776 BCE	First Olympic Games
753 BCE	Rome founded
750 BCE	Homer composes *Odyssey*
700 BCE	Marsiliana tablet's script with Phoenician roots in Etruscan lands
700–600 BCE	Aramean alphabet consolidated in Syria
600 BCE	Latin alphabet emerges from Greek root
	Praeneste fibula's early Latin inscription, "Manius made me for Numasius"
586 BCE	Temple in Jerusalem destroyed
544 BCE	First public library founded in Athens
536 BCE	Second Temple begun in Jerusalem
522 BCE	Confucius edits sacred Chinese books
516 BCE	Second Temple in Jerusalem finished
509 BCE	Roman republic founded
508 BCE	Beginning of Athenian democracy
478 BCE	Esther becomes queen of Persia
474 BCE	Etruscans conquered at Cumae
442 BCE	Parthenon built
440 BCE	Democritus proposes existence of the atom
431–404 BCE	Peloponnesian War with Sparta
427–347 BCE	Life of Plato, Greek philosopher
406 BCE	Soldiers in Rome first paid
400 BCE	Catapult invented
	Mahabharata, Indian legends, composed
	Panini's grammar of Sanskrit written
399 BCE	Greek philosopher Socrates drinks hemlock
395–330 BCE	Life of Praxiteles, Greek realist sculptor
384–322 BCE	Life of Aristotle, Greek philospher
356 BCE	Birth of Alexander the Great
332 BCE	Alexander conquers Egypt; Hellenistic period begins in Greece
	Egyptian demotic script used for Greek language (later makes Rosetta stone decipherable)
320–275 BCE	Life of Euclid, Greek mathematician
312 BCE	Aqua Appia, first Roman aqueduct; Via Appia, 350-mile-long road
300–280 BCE	Money first coined in Rome
284 BCE	Library at Alexandria founded, eventually contains over 500,000 volumes
273–232 BCE	Asoka rules great Mauryan empire in India
270 BCE	Mechanical water clocks in Rome
250 BCE	Letter *G* made by "bearding" a *C*
	Archimedes makes a mechanical globe
221 BCE	Great Wall of China begun (eventually 1,200 miles long)
213 BCE	Chin Tain Shihuangti, Emperor of China, orders all books destroyed
200 BCE	Ox-powered irrigation

196 BCE	Rosetta stone inscribed
174 BCE	Paved streets in Rome
106 BCE	Birth of Cicero, Roman orator
70 BCE	Birth of Virgil, Roman poet
63 BCE	Tiro, Cicero's slave, invents shorthand
51 BCE	Cleopatra becomes Queen of Egypt
50 BCE	Glass blowing with metal pipes in Rome
44 BCE	Julius Caesar killed
27 BCE–14 CE	Augustus Caesar and Golden Age of Rome
20 BCE	Vitruvius's *On Architecture*
1 BCE	Ovid's *Metamorphosis*
0	World population 25 million
	Strabo's *Geography* composed
25 CE	Claudius writes *How to Win at Dice*, first gambling theory text
32 CE	John the Baptist beheaded
37 CE	Christmas celebrated for first time
48 CE	Census: 7 million citizens in Rome, more than 20 million in Empire
52–96 CE	New Testament written
54–68 CE	Nero, tyrannical and decadent emperor, rules Rome
61 CE	Roman legions defeat Queen Boadicea in Britain
70 CE	Jerusalem destroyed by Roman army, led by Titus
79 CE	Eruption of Vesuvius destroys Pompeii
84 CE	Britain recognized as an island after Romans circumnavigate
100–600 CE	City of Teotihuacan flourishes in Mesoamerica
105 CE	Paper originates in China
178 CE	Christian missionaries in Britain
200s CE	Parchment invented
300s CE	Silk Route brings trade from China to Rome
	Codex Augusteus: early appearance of bound book
	First paragraphing and punctuation
320–650 CE	Golden Age in India, Gupta Empire
324 CE	Emperor Constantine unites Europe, declares himself Christian
387 CE	Rome sacked by Gauls
400 CE	Saint Jerome edits and translates Gospels
410 CE	Rome sacked by Visigoths

TOOLS OF THE TRADE

Powdered pigments

Ink from soot, gum, oil

Turpentine

Double blade ruling pens

Quill pens from feathers

Bronze pens imitating quills

Metal and bone styluses

Tied hair and frayed reed brushes

Sharpened reeds

Stencils

Pounces for blotting

Rulers

Straightedges

Protractors

Bronze calipers

Proportional dividers

Compasses

Chisels

Cross-bladed scissors (100 CE)

Stone

Lead

Chalk

Wood panels with painted surfaces

Wax tablets

Parchment from animal skins

Paper (China only)

Scrolls

Hinged tablets with leather thongs

Codex books (100–300 CE)

Candles

Oil lamps

Pottery lamps

SCULPTURE: FROM ABSTRACTION TO NATURALISM, SACRED TO SECULAR

THOUGHT PIECE

You should take no action unwillingly, selfishly, uncritically, or with conflicting motives. Do not dress up your thoughts in smart finery: do not be a gabbler or a meddler. Further, let the god that is within you be the champion of the being you are—a male, mature in years, a statesman, a Roman, a ruler: one who has taken his post like a soldier waiting for the Retreat from life to sound, and ready to depart, past the need for any loyal oath or human witness. And see that you keep a cheerful demeanour, and retain your independence of outside help and the peace which others can give. Your duty is to stand straight—not held straight.

If you discover in human life something better than justice, truth, self-control, courage—in short, something better than the self-sufficiency of your own mind which keeps you acting in accord with true reason and accepts your inheritance of fate in all outside your choice: if, as I say, you can see something better than this, then turn to it with all your heart and enjoy this prime good you have found. But if nothing is shown to be better than the very god that is seated in you, which has brought all your own impulses under its control, which scrutinizes your thoughts, which has withdrawn itself, as Socrates used to say, from all inducements of the senses, which has subordinated itself to the gods and takes care for men—if you find all else by comparison with this small and paltry, then give no room to any-thing else: once turned and inclined to any alternative, you will struggle thereafter to restore the primacy of that good which is yours and yours alone. Because it is not right that the rational and social good should be rivalled by anything of a different order, for example the praise of the many, or power, or wealth, or the enjoyment of pleasure. All these things may seem to suit for a little while, but they can suddenly take control and carry you away. So you, I repeat, must simply and freely choose the better and hold to it. 'But better is what benefits.' If to your benefit as a rational being, adopt it: but if simply to your benefit as an animal, reject it, and stick to your judgement without fanfare. Only make sure that your scrutiny is sound.

—Marcus Aurelius, *Meditations* (Penguin, 2006), Book 3, paragraphs 5–6, pp. 18–19.

THINGS TO CONSIDER

- What can abstraction and naturalism tell us about the intentions of art? What is the value of naturalism? Can it be understood as a question of cultural values?
- In what ways does secular portrait sculpture reflect the Roman conception of the individual?
- How can the body ideals of South Asian, Greek and Roman sculpture help us understand 'beauty' as a shifting ground of culture?

SCULPTURE ON THE INDIAN SUBCONTINENT

THE FOURTH THROUGH SEVENTH CENTURIES

The Guptas, who founded a dynasty in the eastern region of central India known as Magadha, expanded their territories during the fourth century CE to form an empire that encompassed northern and much of central India. Although Gupta power ended in 550, the influence of Gupta culture was felt long after that.

The period of the Guptas and their contemporaries is renowned for the flourishing artistic and literary culture that brought forth some of India's most widely admired sculpture and painting. While Buddhism continued to be a major religion, the earliest surviving Hindu temples also date from this time.

BUDDHIST SCULPTURE

Two distinctive styles of Gupta Buddhist sculpture prevailed during the second and third quarters of the fifth century and dominated in northern India: one was based at Mathura, the major center of north Indian sculpture during the Kushan period, and the other at Sarnath, whose style is reflected in Buddhist sculpture over much of northern India.

The **STANDING BUDDHA** in **FIGURE 4–1** embodies the fully developed Sarnath Gupta style. Carved from fine-grained sandstone, the figure stands in a mildly relaxed pose, the body clearly visible through a clinging robe. This plain robe, portrayed with none of the creases and folds so prominent in the Kushan period images, is distinctive of the Sarnath style. Its effect is to concentrate attention on the form of the body, which emerges in high relief. The body is graceful and slight, with broad shoulders and a well-proportioned torso. Only a few lines of the garment at the neck, waist, and hems interrupt the purity of its subtly shaped surfaces; the face, smooth and ovoid, has the same refined elegance. The downcast eyes suggest otherworldly introspection, yet the gentle, open posture maintains a human link. Behind the head are the remains of a large, circular halo. Carved in concentric circles of pearls and foliage, the ornate halo contrasted with the plain surfaces of the figure. Details also may have been indicated by paint.

At the site of Bamiyan, about 155 miles northwest of Kabul, Afghanistan, were two enormous Buddhas carved from the rock of a cliff, one some 115 feet in height **(FIG. 4–2)**, the other about 165 feet. They were seen by a Chinese pilgrim who came to Bamiyan in the fifth century, so they clearly date before his visit, probably to the early fifth century. Pilgrims could walk within the cliff up a staircase on the right side of the smaller figure that ended at the Buddha's shoulder. There they could look into the vault of the niche and see a painted image of the sun god, suggesting a metaphoric pilgrimage to the heavens. They then could circumambulate the figure at the level of the head and return to ground level on a staircase on the

To view this image, please go to page 306 of the *Art History*, Fourth Edition by Marilyn Stokstad ebook.

4–1 • STANDING BUDDHA
From Sarnath, Uttar Pradesh, India. Gupta period, 474 CE. Chunar sandstone, height 6'4" (1.93 m). Archaeological Museum, Sarnath.

figure's left side. These huge figures likely served as the model for those at rock-cut sanctuaries in China, for example, at Yungang. Despite the historical and religious importance of these figures, and ignoring the pleas of world leaders, the Taliban demolished the Bamiyan Buddhas in 2001.

PAINTING

The Gupta aesthetic also found expression in painting, though in a region of India just beyond the Gupta realm. Some of the finest surviving works are murals from the Buddhist rock-cut halls of Ajanta, in the western Deccan region of India **(FIG. 4–3)**. Under a ruling house known as the Vakataka dynasty, many caves were carved around 475 CE, including Cave I, a large *vihara* hall with monks' chambers around the sides and a Buddha shrine chamber in the back. The walls of the central court were covered with murals painted in mineral pigments on a prepared plaster surface. Some of these paintings depict episodes from the Buddha's past lives. Flanking the entrance to the shrine chamber are two large **bodhisattvas**, one of which is seen in FIGURE 4–3.

To view this image, please go to page 307 of the *Art History*, Fourth Edition by Marilyn Stokstad ebook.

4-2 • STANDING BUDDHA
Bamiyan, Afghanistan. c. 5th century CE.

Bodhisattvas are enlightened beings who postpone *nirvana* and buddhahood to help others achieve enlightenment. They are distinguished from Buddhas in art by their princely garments. The bodhisattva here is lavishly adorned with delicate ornaments. He wears a bejeweled crown, large earrings, a pearl necklace, armbands, and bracelets. A striped cloth covers his lower body. The graceful bending posture and serene gaze impart a sympathetic attitude. His spiritual power is suggested by his large size in comparison to the surrounding figures, and his identity as the compassionate bodhisattva Avalokiteshvara is indicated by the lotus flower he holds in his right hand.

The naturalistic style balances outline and softly graded color tones. Outline drawing, always a major ingredient of Indian painting, clearly defines shapes; tonal gradations impart the illusion of three-dimensional form, with lighter tones used for protruding parts such as the nose, brows, shoulders, and chest muscles. Together with the details of the jewels, these highlighted areas resonate against the subdued tonality of the figure. Sophisticated, realistic detail is balanced by the languorous human form. In no other known examples of Indian painting do bodhisattvas appear so graciously divine yet, so palpably human. This particular synthesis is evident also in the Sarnath statue (SEE FIG. 4–1), which shares much in common as well with the sculpture of Ajanta.

Although Buddhism had flourished in India during the fifth century, some of the most important Buddhist monasteries, attracting pilgrims from as far away as China, prospered especially after the Gupta period. Hindu temples, generally small and relatively simple structures during the fifth century, subsequently became increasingly complex and elaborately adorned with sculptured images.

To view this image, please go to page 307 of the *Art History*, Fourth Edition by Marilyn Stokstad ebook.

4-3 • BODHISATTVA
Detail of a wall painting in Cave I, Ajanta, Maharashtra, India. Vakataka dynasty, c. 475 CE.

To view this image, please go to page 308 of the *Art History*,
Fourth Edition by Marilyn Stokstad ebook.

4-4 • VISHNU TEMPLE, DEOGARH
Uttar Pradesh, India. Gupta dynasty, c. 530 CE.

THE EARLY NORTHERN TEMPLE

The Hindu temple developed many different forms throughout India, but it can be classified broadly into two types: northern and southern. The northern type is chiefly distinguished by a superstructure called a **shikhara** (see "Stupas and Temples," page 91). The *shikhara* rises as a solid mass above the flat stone ceiling and windowless walls of the sanctum, or **garbhagriha**, which houses an image of the temple's deity. As it rises, it curves inward in a mathematically determined ratio. (In geometric terms, the *shikhara* is a paraboloid.) Crowning the top is a circular, cushion-like element called an **amalaka**, a fruit. From the *amalaka*, a **finial** (a knoblike decoration at the top point of a spire) takes the eye to a point where the earthly world is thought to join the cosmic world. An imaginary *axis mundi* penetrates the entire temple, running from the point of the finial, through the exact center of the *amalaka* and *shikhara*, down through the center of the *garbhagriha* and its image, finally passing through the base of the temple and into the earth below. In this way the temple becomes a conduit between the celestial realms and the earth. This theme, familiar from Ashokan pillars and Buddhist stupas, is carried out with elaborate exactitude in Hindu temples, and it is one of the most important elements underlying their form and function (see "Meaning and Ritual in Hindu Temples and Images," page 256).

TEMPLE OF VISHNU AT DEOGARH. One of the earliest northern-style temples is the temple of Vishnu at Deogarh in north central India, which dates from around 530 CE **(FIG. 4–4)**. Much of the *shikhara* has crumbled away, so we cannot determine its original shape with precision. Nevertheless, it was clearly a massive, solid structure built of large cut stones. It would have given the impression of a mountain, which is one of several metaphoric meanings of a Hindu temple. This early temple has only one chamber, the *garbhagriha*, which corresponds to the center of a sacred diagram called a *mandala* on which the entire temple site is patterned. As the deity's residence, the *garbhagriha* is likened to a sacred cavern within the "cosmic mountain" of the temple.

Large panels sculpted in relief with images of Vishnu appear as "windows" on the temple's exterior. These elaborately framed panels do not function literally to let light *into* the temple; they function symbolically to let the light of the deity *out* of the temple to be seen by those outside.

One panel depicts Vishnu lying on the Cosmic Waters at the beginning of creation **(FIG. 4–5)**. He sleeps on the serpent of infinity, Ananta, whose body coils endlessly into space. Stirred by his female aspect (*shakti*, or female energy), personified here by the goddess Lakshmi, seen holding his foot, Vishnu dreams the universe into existence. From his navel springs a lotus (shown in this relief behind Vishnu), and the unfolding of space-time begins.

frieze below personify Vishnu's four attributes. They stand ready to fight the appearance of evil, represented at the left of the frieze by two demons who threaten to kill Brahma and jeopardize all creation.

The birth of the universe and the appearance of evil are thus portrayed here in three clearly organized registers. Typical of Indian religious and artistic expression, these momentous events are set before our eyes not in terms of abstract symbols, but as a drama acted out by gods in super-human form.

MONUMENTAL NARRATIVE RELIEFS

The Hindu god Shiva exhibits a wide range of aspects or forms, both gentle and wild: He is the Great Yogi who dwells for vast periods of time in meditation in the Himalayas; he is also the husband par excellence who makes love to the goddess Parvati for eons at a time; he is the Slayer of Demons; and he is the Cosmic Dancer who dances the destruction and re-creation of the world.

TEMPLE OF SHIVA AT ELEPHANTA. Many of these forms of Shiva appear in the monumental relief panels adorning the cave-temple of Shiva carved in the mid sixth century on the island of Elephanta off the coast of Mumbai in western India. The cave-temple is complex in layout and conception, perhaps to reflect the nature of Shiva. While most temples have one entrance, this temple offers three—one facing north, one east, and one west. The interior, impressive in its size and grandeur, is designed along two main axes, one running north–south, the other

To view this image, please go to page 309 of the *Art History*, Fourth Edition by Marilyn Stokstad ebook.

4–5 • VISHNU ON THE COSMIC WATERS
Relief panel in the Vishnu Temple, Deogarh. c. 530 CE. Stone, height approx. 5′ (1.5 m).

SEE MORE: View a video about the process of sculpting in relief
www.myartslab.com

The first being to be created is Brahma (not to be confused with Brahman), who appears here as the central, four-headed figure in the row of gods portrayed above the reclining Vishnu. Brahma turns himself into the universe of space and time by thinking, "May I become Many."

The sculptor has depicted Vishnu as a large, resplendent figure with four arms. His size and his multiple arms denote his omni-potence. He is lightly garbed but richly ornamented. The ideal of the Gupta style is evident in the smooth, perfected shape of the body and in the lavishly detailed jewelry, including Vishnu's characteristic cylindrical crown. The four figures on the right in the

east–west. The three entrances provide the only source of light, and the resulting cross and backlighting effects add to the sense of the cave as a place of mysterious, almost confusing complexity.

Along the east–west axis, large pillars cut from the rock appear to support the low ceiling and its beams, although, as with all architectural elements in a cave-temple, they are not structural **(FIG. 4–6)**. The pillars form orderly rows, but the rows are hard to discern within the framework of the cave shape, which is neither square nor longitudinal, but formed of overlapping *mandalas* that create a symmetric yet irregular space. The pillars are an important aesthetic component of the cave. Each has an

Meaning and Ritual in Hindu Temples and Images

The Hindu temple is one of the most complex and meaningful architectural forms in Asian art. Age-old symbols and ritual functions are embedded not only in a structure's many parts, but also in the process of construction itself. Patron, priest, and architect worked as a team to ensure the sanctity of the structure from start to finish. No artist or artisan was more highly revered in ancient Indian society than the architect, who could oversee the construction of an abode in which a deity would dwell.

For a god to take up residence, however, everything had to be done properly in exacting detail. By the end of the first millennium, the necessary procedures had been recorded in texts called the *Silpa Shastra*. First, an auspicious site was chosen; a site near water was especially favored, for water makes the earth fruitful. Next, the ground was prepared in an elaborate process that took several years: Spirits already inhabiting the site were invited to leave; the ground was planted and harvested through two seasons; then cows—sacred beasts since the Indus civilization—were pastured there to lend their potency to the site. When construction began, each phase was accompanied by ritual to ensure its purity and sanctity.

All Hindu temples are built on a plan known as a ***mandala***, a schematic design of a sacred realm or space—specifically, Vastupurusha *mandala*, the *mandala* of the Cosmic Man, the primordial progenitor of the human species. His body, fallen on earth, is imagined as superimposed on the *mandala* design; together, they form the base on which the temple rises. The Vastupurusha *mandala* always takes the form of a square subdivided into a number of equal squares (usually 64) surrounding a central square. The central square represents Brahman, the primordial, unmanifest Formless One. This square corresponds to the temple's sanctum, the windowless *garbhagriha* ("womb chamber"). The nature of Brahman is clear, pure light; that we perceive the *garbhagriha* as dark is considered a testament to our deluded nature. The surrounding squares belong to lesser deities, while the outermost compartments hold protector gods. These compartments are usually represented by the enclosing wall of a temple compound.

The *garbhagriha* houses the temple's main image—most commonly a stone, bronze, or wood statue of Vishnu, Shiva, or Devi. In the case of Shiva, the image is often symbolic rather than anthropomorphic. To ensure perfection, the proportions of the image follow a set canon, and rituals surround its making. When the image is completed, a priest recites *mantras* (mystic syllables), that bring the deity into the image. The belief that a deity is literally present is not taken lightly. Even in India today, any image "under worship"—whether it be in a temple or a field, an ancient work or a modern piece—will be respected and not taken from the people who worship it.

A Hindu temple is a place for individual devotion, not congregational worship. It is the place where a devotee can make offerings to one or more deities and be in the presence of the god who is embodied in the image in the *garbhagriha*. Worship generally consists of prayers and offerings such as food and flowers or water and oil for the image, but it can also be much more elaborate, including dancing and ritual sacrifices.

---

unadorned, square base rising to nearly half its total height. Above is a circular column, which has a curved contour and a billowing "cushion" capital. Both column and capital are delicately fluted, adding a surprising refinement to these otherwise sturdy forms. The focus of the east–west axis is a square **linga shrine**, shown here at the center of illustration 4–6. Each of its four entrances is flanked by a pair of colossal standing guardian figures. In the center of the shrine is the *linga*, the phallic symbol of Shiva. The *linga* represents the presence of Shiva as the unmanifest Formless One, or Brahman. It symbolizes both his erotic nature and his aspect as the Great Yogi who controls his seed. The *linga* is synonymous with Shiva and is seen in nearly every Shiva temple and shrine.

The focus of the north–south axis, in contrast, is a relief on the south wall with a huge bust of Shiva representing his Sadashiva, or **ETERNAL SHIVA**, aspect **(FIG. 4–7)**. Three heads are shown resting upon the broad shoulders of the upper body, but five heads are implied: the fourth behind and the fifth, never depicted, on top. The heads summarize Shiva's fivefold nature as creator (back), protector (left), destroyer (right), obscurer (front), and releaser (top). The head in the front depicts Shiva deep in introspection. The massiveness of the broad head, the large eyes barely delineated, and the mouth with its heavy lower lip suggest the god's serious depths. Lordly and majestic, he easily supports his huge crown, intricately carved with designs and jewels, and the matted, piled-up hair of a yogi. On his left shoulder, his protector nature is depicted as female, with curled hair and a pearl-festooned crown. On his right shoulder, his wrathful, destroyer nature wears a fierce expression, and snakes encircle his neck.

Like the relief panels at the temple to Vishnu in Deogarh (SEE FIG. 4–5), the reliefs at Elephanta are early examples of the Hindu monumental narrative tradition. Measuring 11 feet in height, they are set in recessed niches. The panels portray the range of Shiva's powers and some of his different aspects, presented in the context of narratives that help devotees understand his nature. Taken as a whole, the reliefs represent the manifestation of Shiva in our world. Indian artists often convey the many aspects or essential nature of a deity through multiple heads or arms—which they

To view this image, please go to page 311 of the *Art History*, Fourth Edition by Marilyn Stokstad ebook.

4-6 • CAVE-TEMPLE OF SHIVA, ELEPHANTA
Maharashtra, India. Post-Gupta period, mid 6th century CE. View along the east–west axis to the *linga* shrine.

do with such convincing naturalism that we readily accept the additions. Here, for example, the artist has united three heads onto a single body so skillfully that we still relate to the statue as an essentially human presence.

"DESCENT OF THE GANGES" RELIEF AT MAMALLAPURAM. An enormous relief at Mamallapuram, near Chennai, in southeastern India, depicts the penance of a king, Bhagiratha, who sought to save his people from drought by subjecting himself to terrible austerities. In response, the god Shiva sent the Ganges River, represented by the natural cleft in the rock, to earth, thereby ending the drought (see "A Closer Look," page 259). Bhagiratha is shown standing in frigid waters while staring directly at the sun through his parted fingers, standing for interminable periods on

To view this image, please go to page 311 of the *Art History*, Fourth Edition by Marilyn Stokstad ebook.

4-7 • ETERNAL SHIVA
Rock-cut relief in the cave-temple of Shiva, Elephanta. Mid 6th century CE. Height approx. 11′ (3.4 m).

one foot, and in deep prayer before a temple. In the upper left part of the relief, Shiva, shown four-armed, appears before Bhagiratha to grant his wish. Elsewhere in the relief, animal families are depicted, generally in mutually protective roles.

This richly carved relief was executed under the Pallava dynasty, which flourished in southeastern India from the seventh to ninth century CE. It very likely serves as a visual allegory for the benevolent king, who protects his people, perhaps specifically by providing canals to control water, a notion reinforced by the relief carved in a cave-temple on the same boulder, to the left of the Descent relief. It shows the god Krishna protecting his people from a deluge by raising a mountain to serve as a sort of natural umbrella. Themes relating to water are particularly appropriate to Mamallapuram, situated on the Bay of Bengal and possibly serving as a port for the Pallavas.

THE EARLY SOUTHERN TEMPLE

The coastal city of Mamallapuram was also a major temple site under the Pallavas. Along the shore are many large granite boulders and cliffs, and from these the Pallava-period stonecutters carved entire temples as well as reliefs such as the one discussed in "A Closer Look," opposite. Among the most interesting of these rock-cut temples is a group known as the Five Rathas, which preserve diverse early architectural styles that probably reflect the forms of contemporary wood or brick structures that have long since disappeared.

DHARMARAJA RATHA AT MAMALLAPURAM. One of this group, called today the Dharmaraja Ratha, epitomizes the early southern-style temple (**FIG. 4–8**). Although strikingly different in appearance from the northern style, it uses the same symbolism to link the heavens and earth and it, too, is based on a *mandala*. The temple, square in plan, remains unfinished, and the *garbhagriha* usually found inside was never hollowed out, suggesting that, like cave-temples, Dharmaraja Ratha was executed from the top downward. On the lower portion, only the columns and niches have been carved. The use of a single deity in each niche forecasts the main trend in temple sculpture in the centuries ahead: The tradition of narrative reliefs declined, and the stories they told became concentrated in statues of individual deities, which conjure up entire mythological episodes through characteristic poses and a few symbolic objects.

Southern- and northern-style temples are most clearly distinguished by their superstructures. The Dharmaraja Ratha does not culminate in the paraboloid of the northern *shikhara* but in a pyramidal tower. Each story of the superstructure is articulated by a cornice and carries a row of miniature shrines. Both shrines and cornices are decorated with a window motif from which faces peer. The shrines not only demarcate each story, but also provide loftiness for this palace intended to enshrine a god. Crowning the superstructure is a dome-shaped octagonal capstone quite different from the *amalaka* of the northern style.

During the centuries that followed, both northern- and southern-style temples developed into complex, monumental forms, but their basic structure and symbolism remained the same as those we have seen in these simple, early examples at Deogarh and Mamallapuram.

THE EIGHTH THROUGH THE FOURTEENTH CENTURIES

During the eighth through the fourteenth centuries, regional styles developed in the realms of the dynasties ruling kingdoms that were generally smaller than the Maurya and Kushan empires. Some dynasties were relatively long-lived, such as the Pallavas and Cholas in the south and the Palas in the northeast. Although Buddhism remained strong in a few areas—notably under the Palas—it generally declined, while the Hindu gods Vishnu, Shiva, and the Great Goddess (mainly Durga) grew increasingly popular. Monarchs rivaled each other in the building of temples to their favored deity, and many complicated and subtle variations of the Hindu temple emerged with astounding rapidity in different regions. By around 1000 the Hindu temple reached unparalleled heights of grandeur and engineering.

To view this image, please go to page 312 of the *Art History*, Fourth Edition by Marilyn Stokstad ebook.

4–8 • DHARMARAJA RATHA, MAMALLAPURAM
Tamil Nadu, India. Pallava period, c. mid 7th century CE.

"Descent of the Ganges" Relief >

Rock-cut relief, Mamallapuram, Tamil Nadu, India.
Pallava period, c. mid 7th century CE. Granite, height approx. 20′ (6 m).

Unfinished cave. Beyond it, on the same rock formation, is the Krishna Cave.

Unfinished portion of the relief suggesting work from the top downward, as at other Mamallapuram monuments.

Shiva offering boon to Bhagiratha.

Bhagiratha meditating in front of a temple.

To view this image, please go to page 313 of the *Art History*, Fourth Edition by Marilyn Stokstad ebook.

Bhagiratha gazing directly at the sun.

A cat imitating the penance of Bhagiratha, a whimsical touch by the artist.

A family of elephants, the bull elephant in front protecting his young elephant, probably a metaphor for the king's protection of his people.

SEE MORE: View the Closer Look feature for the "Descent of the Ganges" relief at Mamallapuram
www.myartslab.com

THE MONUMENTAL NORTHERN TEMPLE

The Kandariya Mahadeva, a temple dedicated to Shiva at Khajuraho, in central India, was probably built by a ruler of the Chandella dynasty in the late tenth or early eleventh century (FIG. 4–9). Khajuraho was the capital and main temple site for the Chandellas, who constructed more than 80 temples there, about 25 of which are well preserved. The Kandariya Mahadeva Temple is in the northern style, with a curvilinear *shikhara* rising over its *garbhagriha*. Larger, more extensively ornamented, and expanded through the addition of halls on the front and porches to the sides and back, the temple seems at first glance to have little in common with its precursor at Deogarh (SEE FIG. 4–4). Actually, however, the basic elements and their symbolism remain unchanged.

Shiva Nataraja of the Chola Dynasty

Perhaps no sculpture is more representative of Hinduism than the statues of Shiva Nataraja, or Dancing Shiva, a form perfected by sculptors under the royal patronage of the south Indian Chola dynasty in the late tenth to eleventh century. (For the architecture and painting of the period, SEE FIGS. 4–11, 4–12.) The dance of Shiva is a dance of cosmic proportions, signifying the universe's cycle of death and rebirth; it is also a dance for each individual, signifying the liberation of the believer through Shiva's compassion. In the iconography of the Nataraja, this sculpture shows Shiva with four arms dancing on the prostrate body of Apasmara, a dwarf figure who symbolizes "becoming" and whom Shiva controls. Shiva's extended left hand holds a ball of fire; a circle of fire rings the god. The fire is emblematic of the destruction of *samsara* and the physical universe as well as the destruction of *maya* (illusion) and our ego-centered perceptions. Shiva's back right hand holds a drum; its beat represents the irrevocable rhythms of creation and destruction, birth and death. His front right arm gestures the "have no fear" *mudra* (see "Mudras," page 94). The front left arm, gracefully stretched across his body with the hand pointing to his raised foot, signifies the promise of liberation.

The artist has rendered the complex pose with great clarity. The central axis, which aligns the nose, navel, and insole of the weight-bearing foot, maintains the figure's equilibrium while the remaining limbs asymmetrically extend far to each side. Shiva wears a short loincloth, a ribbon tied above his waist, and delicately tooled ornaments. The scant clothing reveals his perfected form with its broad shoulders tapering to a supple waist. The jewelry is restrained and the detail does not detract from the beauty of the body.

The deity does not appear self-absorbed and introspective as he did in the Eternal Shiva relief at Elephanta (SEE FIG. 4–7). He turns to face the viewer, appearing lordly and aloof yet fully aware of his benevolent role as he generously displays himself for the devotee. Like the Sarnath Gupta Buddha (SEE FIG. 4–1), the Chola Shiva Nataraja presents a characteristically Indian synthesis of the godly and the human, this time expressing the *bhakti* belief in the importance of an intimate relationship with a lordly god through whose compassion one is saved. The earlier Hindu emphasis on ritual and the depiction of the heroic feats of the gods is subsumed into the all-encompassing, humanizing factor of grace.

The fervent religious devotion of the *bhakti* movement was fueled by the sublime writings of a series of poet-saints who lived in the south of India. One of them, Appar, who lived from the late sixth to mid seventh century CE, wrote this vision of the Shiva Nataraja. The ash the poem refers to is one of many symbols associated with the deity.

In penance for having lopped off one of the five heads of Brahma, the first created being, Shiva smeared his body with ashes and went about as a beggar.

> If you could see
> the arch of his brow,
> the budding smile
> on lips red as the kovvai fruit,
> cool matted hair,
> the milk-white ash on coral skin,
> and the sweet golden foot
> raised up in dance,
> then even human birth on this wide earth
> would become a thing worth having.

(Translated by Indira Vishvanathan Peterson)

To view this image, please go to page 314 of the *Art History*, Fourth Edition by Marilyn Stokstad ebook.

SHIVA NATARAJA
From Thanjavur, Tamil Nadu. Chola dynasty, 12th century CE. Bronze, height 32″ (81.25 cm). National Museum of India, New Delhi.

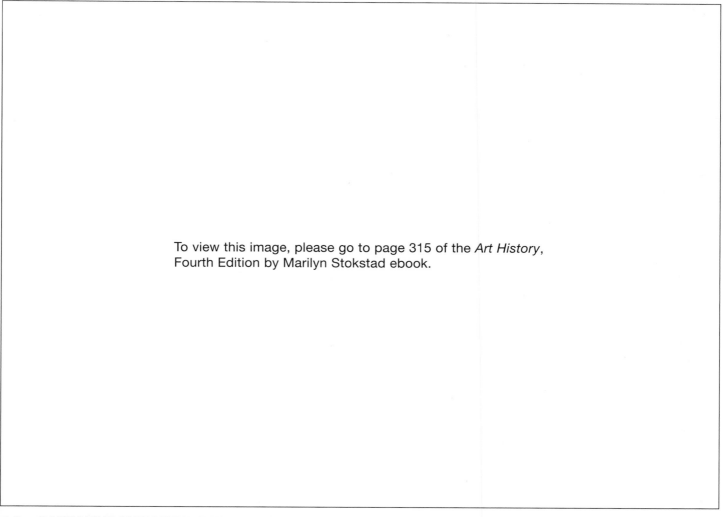

To view this image, please go to page 315 of the *Art History*, Fourth Edition by Marilyn Stokstad ebook.

4-9 • KANDARIYA MAHADEVA TEMPLE, KHAJURAHO
Madhya Pradesh, India. Chandella dynasty, c. 1000 CE.

As at Deogarh, the temple rests on a stone terrace that sets off a sacred space from the mundane world. A steep flight of stairs at the front (to the right in the illustration) leads to a series of three halls, called **mandapas** (distinguished on the outside by pyramidal roofs), preceding the *garbhagriha*. The *mandapa*s serve as spaces for ritual, such as dances performed for the deity, and for the presentation of offerings. The temple is built of stone blocks using only post-and-lintel construction. Because vault and arch techniques are not used, the interior spaces are not large.

The exterior has a strong sculptural presence, its massiveness suggesting a "cosmic mountain" composed of ornately carved stone. The *shikhara* rises more than 100 feet over the *garbhagriha* and is crowned by a small *amalaka*. The *shikhara* is bolstered by the many smaller *shikhara* motifs bundled around it. This decorative scheme adds a complex richness to the surface, but it also obscures the shape of the main *shikhara*, which is slender, with a swift and impetuous upward movement. The roofs of the *mandapa*s contribute to the impression of rapid ascent by growing progressively taller as they near the *shikhara*.

Despite its apparent complexity, the temple has a clear structure and unified composition. The towers of the superstructure are separated from the lower portion by strong horizontal moldings and by the open spaces over the *mandapa*s and porches. The **moldings** (shaped or sculpted strips) and rows of sculpture adorning the lower part of the temple create a horizontal emphasis that stabilizes the vertical thrust of the superstructure. Three rows of sculpture—some 600 figures—are integrated into the exterior walls. Approximately 3 feet tall and carved in high relief, the sculptures depict gods and goddesses, as well as figures in erotic postures. They are thought to express Shiva's divine bliss, the manifestation of his presence within, and the transformation of one into many.

In addition to its horizontal emphasis, the lower portion of the temple is characterized by a verticality that is created by protruding and receding elements. Their visual impact is similar to that of engaged columns and buttresses, and they account for much of the rich texture of the exterior. The porches, two on each side and one in the back, contribute to the complexity by outwardly expanding the ground plan, yet their bases also

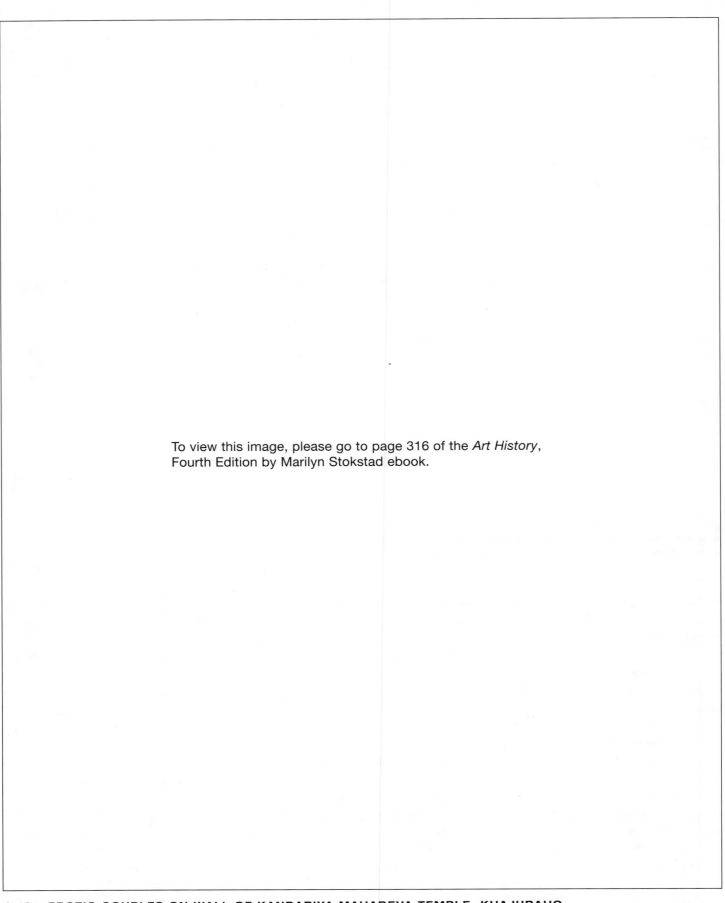

To view this image, please go to page 316 of the *Art History*, Fourth Edition by Marilyn Stokstad ebook.

4–10 • EROTIC COUPLES ON WALL OF KANDARIYA MAHADEVA TEMPLE, KHAJURAHO
Height of sculptures approx. 3′3″ (1 m).

reinforce the sweeping vertical movements that unify the entire structure.

The Khajuraho temples are especially well known for their numerous erotic sculptures such as those illustrated in **FIGURE 4–10**. These carvings are not placed haphazardly, but rather in a single vertical line at the juncture of the walls enclosing the *garbhagriha* and the last *mandapa*. Their significance is uncertain; perhaps they derive from the amorous couples that adorn temple doorways leading to the *garbhagriha*. Such couples are found on some early temples such as the Deogarh temple as well as on Buddhist rock-cut sanctuaries such as the one at Karle, serving as reminders that devotion to god resembles the passion of love.

THE MONUMENTAL SOUTHERN TEMPLE

The Cholas, who succeeded the Pallavas in the mid ninth century, founded a dynasty that governed most of the far south well into the late thirteenth century. The Chola dynasty reached its peak during the reign of Rajaraja I (r. 985–1014). As an expression of gratitude for his many victories in battle, Rajaraja built the Rajarajeshvara Temple to Shiva in his capital, Thanjavur (formerly known as Tanjore). The name Rajarajeshvara means the temple of Rajaraja's Lord, that is, Shiva. Commonly called the Brihadeshvara (the temple of the Great Lord), this temple is a remarkable achievement of the southern style of Hindu architecture **(FIG. 4–11)**. It stands within a huge, walled compound near the banks of the Kaveri River. Although smaller shrines dot the compound, the Rajarajeshvara dominates the area.

Clarity of design, a formal balance of parts, and refined décor contribute to the Rajarajeshvara's majesty. Rising to an astonishing height of 216 feet, this temple was probably the tallest structure in India in its time. Like the contemporaneous Kandariya Mahadeva Temple at Khajuraho, the Rajarajeshvara has a longitudinal axis and greatly expanded dimensions, especially with regard to its superstructure. Typical of the southern style, the *mandapa* at the front of the Rajarajeshvara has a flat roof, as opposed to the pyramidal roofs of the northern style. The walls of the sanctum rise for two

To view this image, please go to page 317 of the *Art History*, Fourth Edition by Marilyn Stokstad ebook.

4-11 • RAJARAJESHVARA TEMPLE OF SHIVA, THANJAVUR
Tamil Nadu, India. Chola Dynasty, 1003–1010 CE.

stories, with each story emphatically articulated by a large cornice. The exterior walls are ornamented with niches, each of which holds a single statue, usually depicting a form of Shiva. The clear, regular, and wide spacing of the niches imparts a calm balance and formality to the lower portion of the temple, in marked contrast to the irregular, concave-convex rhythms of the northern style.

The superstructure of the Rajarajeshvara is a four-sided, hollow pyramid that rises for 13 stories. Each story is decorated with miniature shrines, window motifs, and robust dwarf figures who seem to be holding up the next story. Because these sculptural elements are not large in the overall scale of the superstructure, they appear well integrated into the surface and do not obscure the thrusting shape. This is quite different from the effect of the small

shikhara motifs on the superstructure of the Kandariya Mahadeva Temple (SEE FIG. 4–9). Notice also that in the earlier southern style, as embodied in the Dharmaraja Ratha (SEE FIG. 4–8), the shrines on the temple superstructure were much larger in proportion to the whole and thus each appeared to be nearly as prominent as the superstructure's overall shape.

Because the Rajarajeshvara superstructure is not obscured by its decorative motifs, it forcefully ascends skyward. At the top is an octagonal dome-shaped capstone similar to the one that crowned the earlier southern-style temple. This huge capstone is exactly the same size as the *garbhagriha* housed 13 stories directly below. It thus evokes the shrine a final time before the eye ascends to the point separating the worldly from the cosmic sphere above.

To view this image, please go to page 318 of the *Art History*, Fourth Edition by Marilyn Stokstad ebook.

4-12 • RAJARAJA I AND HIS TEACHER
Detail of a wall painting in the Rajarajeshvara Temple to Shiva. Chola dynasty, c. 1010 CE.

THE BHAKTI MOVEMENT IN ART

Throughout this period, two major religious movements were developing that affected Hindu practice and its art: the Tantric, or Esoteric, and the *bhakti*, or devotional. Although both movements evolved throughout India, the influence of Tantric sects appeared during this period primarily in the art of the north, while the *bhakti* movements found artistic expression in the south as well as the north.

The *bhakti* devotional movement was based on ideas expressed in ancient texts, especially the *Bhagavad-Gita*. *Bhakti* revolves around the ideal relationship between humans and deities. According to *bhakti*, it is the gods who create *maya* (illusion), in which we are all trapped. They also reveal truth to those who truly love them and whose minds are open to them. Rather than focusing on ritual and the performance of *dharma* according to the Vedas, *bhakti* stresses an intimate, personal, and loving relation with the god, and complete devotion and surrender to the deity. Inspired and influenced by *bhakti*, Indian artists produced some of South Asia's most interesting works, among them the few remaining mural paintings and the famous bronze works of sculpture (see "Shiva Nataraja of the Chola Dynasty," page 260).

WALLPAINTING AT RAJARAJESHVARA TEMPLE. Rajaraja's building of the Rajarajeshvara was in part a reflection of the fervent Shiva *bhakti* movement which had reached its peak by that time. The corridors of the circumambulatory passages around the *garbhagriha* were originally adorned with wall paintings. Overpainted later, they were only recently rediscovered. One painting apparently depicts the ruler Rajaraja himself, not as a warrior or majestic king on his throne, but as a simple mendicant humbly standing behind his religious teacher (FIG. 4–12). With his white beard and dark skin, the aged teacher contrasts with the youthful, bronze-skinned king. The position of the two suggests that the king treats the saintly teacher, who in the devotee's or *bhakta*'s view is equated with god, with intimacy and respect. Both figures allude to their devotion to Shiva by holding a small flower as an offering, and both emulate Shiva in their appearance by wearing their hair in the "ascetic locks" of Shiva in his Great Yogi aspect.

The portrayal does not represent individuals so much as a contrast of types: the old and the youthful, the teacher and the devotee, the saint and the king—the highest religious and worldly models, respectively—united as followers of Shiva. Line is the essence of the painting. With strength and grace, the even, skillfully executed line defines the boldly simple forms and features. With less shading and fewer details, these figures are flattened, more linear versions of those in the earlier paintings at Ajanta (SEE FIG. 4–3). A cool, sedate calm infuses the monumental figures, but the power of line also invigorates them with a sense of strength and inner life.

The *bhakti* movement spread during the ensuing centuries into northern India. However, during this period a new religious culture penetrated the subcontinent: Turkic peoples, Persians, and Afghans had been crossing the northwest passes into India since the tenth century, bringing with them Islam and its artistic tradition. New religious forms eventually evolved from Islam's long and complex interaction with the peoples of the subcontinent, and so too arose uniquely Indian forms of Islamic art, adding yet another dimension to India's artistic heritage.

ART OF SOUTHEAST ASIA

Trade and cultural exchange, notably by the sea routes linking China and India, brought Buddhism, Hinduism, and other aspects of India's civilization to the various regions of Southeast Asia and the Asian archipelago. Although Theravada Buddhism (see "Buddhism," page 87) had the most lasting impact in the region, other trends in Buddhism, including Mahayana and esoteric (tantric) traditions, also played a role. Elements of Hinduism, including its epic literature, were also adopted.

THAILAND—PRAKHON CHAI STYLE. Even the earliest major flowering of Buddhist art in eighth- and ninth-century Southeast Asia was characterized by distinctly local interpretations of the inheritance from India. For example, a strikingly beautiful style of Buddhist sculpture in Thailand, one with distinct iconographic elements, has been identified based on the 1964 discovery of a hoard of images in an underground burial chamber in the vicinity of Prakhon Chai, Buriram Province, near the present-day border with Cambodia. Distinguished by exquisite craftsmanship and a charming naturalism, enhanced by inlaid materials for the eyes, a standing figure of the bodhisattva Maitreya (FIG. 4–13) exemplifies the lithe and youthful proportions typical of the Prakhon Chai style. The iconography departs from the princely interpretation of

To view this image, please go to page 319 of the *Art History*, Fourth Edition by Marilyn Stokstad ebook.

4-13 • BUDDHA MAITREYA
From Buriram Province, Thailand. 8th century CE. Copper alloy with inlaid black glass eyes, 38″ (96.5 cm). Asia Society, New York. Mr. and Mrs. John D. Rockefeller 3rd Collection, 1979.063

the Buddha, presenting instead ascetic elements—abbreviated clothing and a loose arrangement of long hair. The esoteric (tantric) associations of these features are further emphasized by the multiple forearms, an element that was highly developed in Hindu sculpture and which came to be common in Esoteric Buddhist art.

To view this image, please go to page 320 of the *Art History*, Fourth Edition by Marilyn Stokstad ebook.

4-14 • BUDDHA SHAKYAMUNI
From Thailand. Mon Dvaravati period, 9th century CE. Sandstone. Norton Simon Museum, Los Angeles.

THAILAND—DVARAVATI STYLE.   The Dvaravati kingdom, of Mon people, flourished in central Thailand from at least the sixth to the eleventh century. This kingdom embraced Theravada Buddhism and produced some of the earliest Buddhist images in Southeast Asia, perhaps based on Gupta-period Indian models. During the later centuries, Dvaravati sculptors restated elements of the Gupta style (SEE FIG. 4–1), and introduced Mon characteristics into classical forms inherited from India (FIG. 4–14).

To view this image, please go to page 320 of the *Art History*, Fourth Edition by Marilyn Stokstad ebook.

4-15 • PLAN OF BOROBUDUR

JAVA—BOROBUDUR.   The most monumental of Buddhist sites in Southeast Asia is **BOROBUDUR (FIGS. 4–15, 4–16)** in central Java, an island of Indonesia. Built about 800 CE and rising more than 100 feet from ground level, this stepped pyramid of volcanic-stone blocks is surmounted by a large stupa, itself ringed by 72 smaller openwork stupas. Probably commissioned to celebrate the Buddhist merit of the Shailendra dynasty rulers, the monument expresses a complex range of Mahayana symbolism, incorporating earthly and cosmic realms. Jataka tales and scenes from the Buddha's life are elaborately narrated in the reliefs of the lower galleries (FIG. 4–17), and more than 500 sculptures of transcendental buddhas on the balustrades and upper terraces complete the monument, conceived as a *mandala* in three dimensions.

CAMBODIA—ANGKOR VAT.   In Cambodia, Khmer kings ruled at Angkor for more than 400 years, from the ninth to the thirteenth century. Among the state temples, Buddhist as well as Hindu, they built **ANGKOR VAT (FIG. 4–18)**, the crowning achievement of Khmer architecture. Angkor had already been the site of royal capitals of the Khmer, who had for centuries vested temporal as well as spiritual authority in their kings, long before King Suryavarman II (r. 1113–1150) began to build the royal complex known today as Angkor Vat. Dedicated to the worship of Vishnu, the vast array of structures is both a temple and a symbolic cosmic mountain. The complex incorporates a stepped pyramid with five towers set within four enclosures of increasing perimeter. Suryavarman's predecessors had associated themselves with Hindu and Buddhist deities at Angkor by building sacred structures. His

To view this image, please go to page 321 of the *Art History*, Fourth Edition by Marilyn Stokstad ebook.

4-16 • BOROBUDUR
Central Java, Indonesia. c. 800 CE.

SEE MORE: View a video about Borobudur **www.myartslab.com**

To view this image, please go to page 321 of the *Art History*, Fourth Edition by Marilyn Stokstad ebook.

4-17 • MAYA RIDING TO LUMBINI
Detail of a narrative relief sculpture, Borobudur.

To view this image, please go to page 322 of the *Art History*,
Fourth Edition by Marilyn Stokstad ebook.

4–18 • ANGKOR VAT
Angkor, Cambodia. 12th century CE.

SEE MORE: View a video about Angkor Vat **www.myartslab.com**

To view this image, please go to page 322 of the *Art History*,
Fourth Edition by Marilyn Stokstad ebook.

4–19 • VISHNU CHURNING THE OCEAN OF MILK
Detail of relief sculpture, Angkor Vat.

To view this image, please go to page 323 of the *Art History*, Fourth Edition by Marilyn Stokstad ebook.

4-20 • PARINIRVANA OF THE BUDDHA
Gal Vihara, near Polonnaruwa, Sri Lanka. 11th–12th century CE. Stone.

construction pairs him with Vishnu to affirm his royal status as well as his ultimate destiny of union with the Hindu god. Low-relief sculptures illustrate scenes from the *Ramayana*, the *Mahabharata*, and other Hindu texts (**FIG. 4–19**), and also depict Suryavarman with his armies.

SRI LANKA.   Often considered a link to Southeast Asia, the island of Sri Lanka is so close to India's southeastern coast that Ashoka's son is said to have brought Buddhism there within his father's lifetime. Sri Lanka played a major role in the strengthening of Theravada traditions, especially by preserving scriptures and relics, and it became a focal point for the Theravada Buddhist world. Sri Lankan sculptors further refined Indian styles and iconography in colossal Buddhist sculptures. The rock-cut Parinirvana of the Buddha at Gal Vihara (**FIG. 4–20**) is one of three colossal Buddhas at the site. This serene and dignified image restates one of the early themes of Buddhist art, that of the Buddha's final transcendence, with a sophistication of modeling and proportion that updates and localizes the classical Buddhist tradition.

THINK ABOUT IT

4.1   Describe the typical form of Indian temples. Contrast the stupa and the temple directly, paying attention to specific building features, such as the superstructure.

4.2   Angkor Vat in Cambodia draws both religious and architectural influence from the Indian subcontinent. Explain what the Khmer architects in Cambodia took from India, with reference to specific religious architectural forms borrowed.

4.3   How does architecture in India and Southeast Asia express a view of the world, even the cosmos?

4.4   Select one architectural work from the chapter, and explain how either Buddhist or Hindu stories are told through its decoration.

4.5   What are some distinguishing features of representations of Buddha?

PRACTICE MORE: Compose answers to these questions, get flashcards for images and terms, and review chapter material with quizzes **www.myartslab.com**

FREE-STANDING SCULPTURE IN GREECE

In addition to statues designed for temple exteriors, sculptors of the Archaic period created a new type of large, free-standing statue made of wood, **terra cotta** (clay fired over low heat, sometimes unglazed), limestone, or white marble from the islands of Paros and Naxos. These free-standing figures were brightly painted and sometimes bore inscriptions indicating that individual men or women had commissioned them for a commemorative purpose. They have been found marking graves and in sanctuaries, where they lined the sacred way from the entrance to the main temple.

A female statue of this type is called a **kore** (plural, *korai*), Greek for "young woman," and a male statue is called a **kouros** (plural, *kouroi*), Greek for "young man." Archaic *korai*, always clothed, probably represented deities, priestesses, and nymphs, young female immortals who served as attendants to gods. *Kouroi*, nearly always nude, have been variously identified as gods, warriors, and victorious athletes. Because the Greeks associated young, athletic males with fertility and family continuity, the *kouroi* figures may have symbolized ancestors.

METROPOLITAN KOUROS. A *kouros* dated about 600 BCE **(FIG. 4–21)** recalls the pose and proportions of Egyptian sculpture. As with Egyptian figures such as the statue of Menkaure, this young Greek stands rigidly upright, arms at his sides, fists clenched, and one leg slightly in front of the other. However, the Greek artist has cut away all stone from around the body to make the human form free-standing. Archaic *kouroi* are also much less lifelike than their Egyptian forebears. Anatomy is delineated with linear ridges and grooves that form regular, symmetrical patterns. The head is ovoid and schematized, and the wiglike hair evenly knotted into tufts and tied back with a narrow ribbon. The eyes are relatively large and wide open, and the mouth forms a conventional closed-lip expression known as the **Archaic smile**. In Egyptian sculpture, male figures usually wore clothing associated with their status, such as the head-dresses, necklaces, and kilts that identified them as kings. The total nudity of the Greek *kouroi* is unusual in ancient Mediterranean cultures, but it is acceptable—even valued—in the case of young men. Not so with women.

BERLIN KORE. Early Archaic *korai* are as severe and stylized as the male figures. The **BERLIN KORE**, found in a cemetery at Keratea and dated about 570–560 BCE, stands more than 6 feet tall **(FIG. 4–22)**. The erect, immobile pose and full-bodied figure—accentuated by a crown and thick-soled clogs—seem appropriate to a goddess, although the statue may represent a priestess or an attendant. The thick robe and tasseled cloak over her shoulders fall in regularly spaced, symmetrically disposed, parallel folds like the

To view this image, please go to page 114 of the *Art History*, Fourth Edition by Marilyn Stokstad ebook.

4-21 • METROPOLITAN KOUROS
Attica. c. 600 BCE. Marble, height 6′ (1.84 m). Metropolitan Museum of Art, New York. Fletcher Fund, 1932 (32.11.1)

fluting on a Greek column. This drapery masks her body but mimics its curving contours. Traces of red—perhaps the red clay used to make thin sheets of gold adhere—indicate that the robe was once painted or gilded. The figure holds a pomegranate in her right hand, a symbol of Persephone, who was abducted by Hades, the god of the underworld, and whose annual return brought the springtime.

ANAVYSOS KOUROS.   The powerful, rounded, athletic body of a *kouros* from Anavysos, dated about 530 BCE, documents the increasing interest of artists and their patrons in a more lifelike rendering of the human figure (FIG. 4–23). The pose, wiglike hair, and Archaic smile echo the earlier style, but the massive torso and limbs have carefully rendered, bulging muscularity, suggesting heroic strength. The statue, a grave monument to a fallen war hero, has been associated with a base inscribed: "Stop and grieve at the tomb of the dead Kroisos, slain by wild Ares [god of war] in the front rank of battle." However, there is no evidence that the figure was meant to preserve the likeness of Kroisos or anyone else. He is a symbolic type, not a specific individual.

"PEPLOS" KORE.   The kore in FIG. 4–24 is dated about the same time as the *Anavysos Kouros*. Like the *kouros*, she has rounded body forms, but unlike him, she is clothed. She has the same motionless, vertical pose of the *Berlin Kore* (SEE FIG. 4–22), but her bare arms and head convey a sense of soft flesh covering a real bone structure, and her smile and hair are considerably less stylized. The original painted colors on both body and clothing must have made her seem even more lifelike, and she also once wore a metal crown and jewelry.

The name we use for this figure is based on an assessment of her clothing as a young girl's **peplos**—a draped rectangle of cloth pinned at the shoulders and belted to give a bloused effect—but it has recently been argued that this *kore* is actually wearing a sheath-like garment, originally painted with a frieze of animals, identifying her not as a young girl but a goddess, perhaps Athena or Artemis. Her missing left forearm—which was made of a separate piece of marble fitted into the still-visible socket—would have extended forward horizontally, and may have held an attribute that provided the key to her identity.

To view this image, please go to page 115 of the *Art History*, Fourth Edition by Marilyn Stokstad ebook.

4-22 • BERLIN KORE
Cemetery at Keratea, near Athens. c. 570–560 BCE. Marble with remnants of red paint, height 6′3″ (1.9 m). Staatliche Museen zu Berlin, Antikensammlung, Preussischer Kulturbesitz, Berlin.

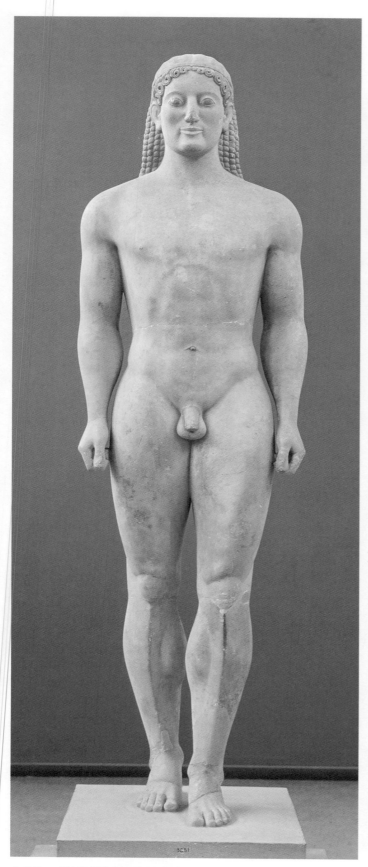

4-23 • ANAVYSOS KOUROS
Cemetery at Anavysos, near Athens. c. 530 BCE. Marble with remnants of paint, height 6′4″ (1.93 m). National Archaeological Museum, Athens.

4-24 • "PEPLOS" KORE
Acropolis, Athens. c. 530 BCE. Marble, height 4′ (1.21 m). Acropolis Museum, Athens.

MARBLE SCULPTURE

In the remarkably short time of only a few generations, Greek sculptors had moved far from the stiff frontality of the Archaic *kouroi* to more relaxed, lifelike figures such as the so-called **KRITIOS BOY** of about 480 BCE **(FIG. 4–25)**. The softly rounded body forms, broad facial features, and calm expression—there is not even a trace of an Archaic smile—give the figure an air of self-confident seriousness. He strikes an easy pose quite unlike the rigid bearing of Archaic *kouroi*. His weight rests on his left, engaged leg, while his right, relaxed leg bends slightly at the knee, and a noticeable curve in his spine counters the slight shifting of his hips and a subtle drop of one of his shoulders. We see here the beginnings of **contrapposto**, the convention of presenting standing figures with opposing alternations of tension and relaxation around a central axis that will dominate Classical art. The slight turn of the head invites the spectator to follow his gaze and move around the figure, admiring the small marble statue from every angle.

To view this image, please go to page 121 of the *Art History*, Fourth Edition by Marilyn Stokstad ebook.

To view this image, please go to page 121 of the *Art History*, Fourth Edition by Marilyn Stokstad ebook.

4-25 • KRITIOS BOY
From Acropolis, Athens.
c. 480 BCE. Marble, height
3′10″ (1.17 m). Acropolis
Museum, Athens.

The damaged figure, excavated from the debris on the Athenian Acropolis, was thought by its finders to be by the Greek sculptor Kritios, whose work they knew only from Roman copies.

Classic and Classical

Our words "classic" and "classical" come from the Latin word *classis*, referring to the division of people into classes based on wealth. Consequently, "classic" has come to mean "first class," "the highest rank," "the standard of excellence." Greek artists in the fifth century BCE sought to create ideal images based on strict mathematical proportions. Since Roman artists were inspired by the Greeks, art historians often use the term Classical to refer to the culture of ancient Greece and Rome. By extension, the word may also mean "in the style of ancient Greece and Rome," whenever or wherever that style is used. In the most general usage, a "classic" is something—perhaps a literary work, an automobile, a film, even a soft drink—thought to be of lasting quality and universal esteem.

BRONZE SCULPTURE

The development of the technique of modeling and hollow-casting bronze in the lost-wax process gave Greek sculptors the potential to create more complex action poses with outstretched arms and legs. These were very difficult to create in marble, since unbalanced figures might topple over and extended appendages might break off due to their pendulous weight. Bronze figures were easier to balance, and the metal's greater tensile strength made complicated poses and gestures technically possible.

The painted underside of an Athenian **kylix** (broad, flat drinking cup) illustrates work in a late Archaic foundry for casting life-size figures **(FIG. 4–26)**, providing clear evidence that the Greeks were creating large bronze statues in active poses as early as the first decades of the fifth century BCE. The walls of the workshop are filled with hanging tools and other foundry paraphernalia including several sketches—a horse, human heads, and human figures in different poses. One worker, wearing what looks like a modern-day construction helmet, squats to tend the

To view this image, please go to page 124 of the *Art History*, Fourth Edition by Marilyn Stokstad ebook.

4–26 • Foundry Painter A BRONZE FOUNDRY
Red-figure decoration on a kylix from Vulci, Italy. 490–480 BCE. Ceramic, diameter of kylix 12″ (31 cm). Staatliche Museen zu Berlin, Preussischer Kulturbesitz, Antikensammlung, Berlin.

The Foundry Painter has masterfully organized this workshop scene within the flaring space that extends upward from the foot of the vessel and along its curving underside up to the lip, thereby using a circle as the groundline for his composition.

To view this image, please go to page 125 of the *Art History,* Fourth Edition by Marilyn Stokstad ebook.

4-27 • CHARIOTEER
From the Sanctuary of Apollo, Delphi. c. 470 BCE. Bronze, copper (lips and lashes), silver (hand), onyx (eyes), height 5′11″ (1.8 m). Archaeological Museum, Delphi.

The setting of a work of art affects the impression it makes. Today, the *Charioteer* is exhibited on a low base in the peaceful surroundings of a museum, isolated from other works and spotlighted for close examination. Its effect would have been very different in its original outdoor location, standing in a horse-drawn chariot atop a tall monument. Viewers in ancient times, tired from the steep climb to the sanctuary and jostled by crowds of fellow pilgrims, could have absorbed only its overall effect, not the fine details of the face, robe, and body visible to today's viewers.

furnace on the left, perhaps aided by an assistant who peeks from behind. The man in the center, perhaps the supervisor, leans on a staff, while a third worker assembles a leaping figure that is braced against a molded support. The unattached head lies between his feet.

THE CHARIOTEER. A spectacular and rare life-size bronze, the **CHARIOTEER** (FIG. 4–27), cast about 470 BCE, documents the skills of Early Classical bronze-casters. It was found in the sanctuary of Apollo at Delphi, together with fragments of a bronze chariot and horses, all buried after an earthquake in 373 BCE. (The earthquake may have saved them from the fate of most ancient bronzes, which were melted down so the material could be recycled and made into a new work.) According to its inscription, the sculptural group commemorated a victory by a driver in the Pythian Games of 478 or 474 BCE.

The face of this handsome youth is highly idealized, but it almost seems to preserve the likeness of a specific individual, calling to mind the report of the Roman historian and naturalist Pliny the Elder that three-time winners in Greek competitions had their features memorialized in stone. The charioteer's head turns slightly to one side, his intense, focused expression enhanced by glittering, onyx eyes and fine copper eyelashes. He stands at attention, sheathed in a long robe with folds falling naturally under their own weight, varying in width and depth, yet seemingly capable of swaying and rippling with the charioteer's movement. The feet, with their closely observed toes, toenails, and swelled veins over the instep, are so realistic that they seem to have been cast from molds made from the feet of a living person.

THE RIACE WARRIORS. The sea as well as the earth has protected ancient bronzes from recycling. As recently as 1972, divers recovered a pair of heavily corroded, larger-than-life-size bronze figures from the seabed off the coast of Riace, Italy. Known as the *Riace Warriors,* they date to about 460–450 BCE. Just what sent them to the bottom is not known, but conservators have restored them to their original condition.

The **WARRIOR** in FIG. 4–28 reveals a striking balance between the idealized smoothness of "perfected" anatomy conforming to Early Classical standards and the reproduction of details observed from nature, such as the swelling veins in the backs of the hands. Contrapposto is even more evident here than in the *Kritios Boy,* and the toned musculature suggests a youthfulness inconsistent with the maturity of the heavy beard and almost haggard face. The lifelike quality of this bronze is further heightened by inserted eyeballs of bone and colored glass, copper inlays on lips and nipples, silver plating on the teeth that show between parted lips, and attached eyelashes and eyebrows of separately cast strands of bronze. This accommodation of the intense study of the human figure to an idealism that belies the irregularity of nature will be continued by artists in the "High" Classical period.

To view this image, please go to page 126 of the *Art History*, Fourth Edition by Marilyn Stokstad ebook.

To view this image, please go to page 126 of the *Art History*, Fourth Edition by Marilyn Stokstad ebook.

4-28 • WARRIOR

Found in the sea off Riace, Italy. c. 460–450 BCE. Bronze with bone and glass eyes, silver teeth, and copper lips and nipples, height 6'9" (2.05 m). National Archeological Museum, Reggio Calabria, Italy.

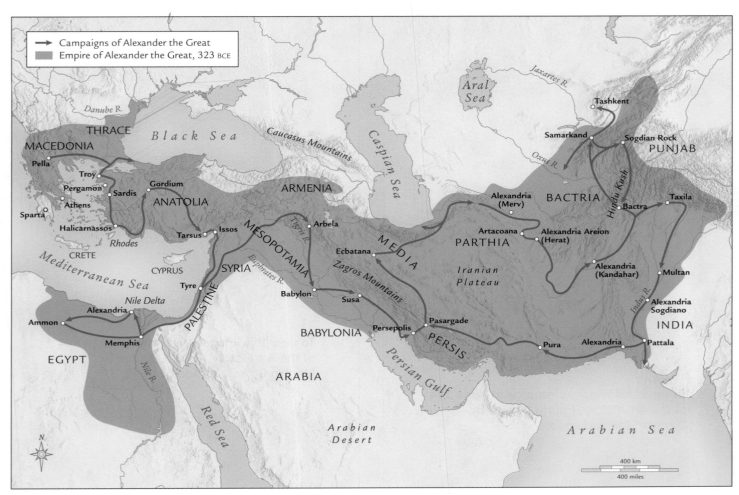

MAP 4–1 HELLENISTIC GREECE

Alexander the Great created a Greek empire that extended from the Greek mainland and Egypt across Asia Minor and as far east as India.

Throughout the fifth century BCE, sculptors accepted and worked within standards established by Pheidias and Polykleitos at mid century for the ideal proportions and idealized forms of the human figure. But fourth-century BCE artists began to challenge and modify those standards. On mainland Greece, in particular, a new canon of proportions emerged for male figures—now eight or more "heads" tall rather than the six-and-a-half or seven-head height of earlier works. The calm, noble detachment characteristic of High Classical figures gave way to more sensitively rendered images of men and women with expressions of wistful introspection, dreaminess, even fleeting anxiety or lightheartedness. This period also saw the earliest depictions of fully nude women in major works of art.

PRAXITELES.   According to the Greek traveler Pausanias, writing in the second century CE, the Late Classical sculptor Praxiteles (active in Athens from about 370 to 335 BCE or later) carved a "Hermes of stone who carries the infant Dionysos" for the Temple of Hera at Olympia. In 1875, just such a statue depicting the messenger god Hermes teasing the baby Dionysos with a bunch of grapes was discovered in the ruins of this temple (FIG. 4–29).

Initially accepted as an original work of Praxiteles because of its high quality, recent studies hold that it is probably a very good Roman or Hellenistic copy.

The sculpture highlights the differences between the fourth- and fifth-century BCE Classical styles. Hermes has a smaller head and a more sensual and sinuous body than Polykleitos' *Spear Bearer*. His off-balance, S-curving pose, requires him to lean on a post—a clear contrast with the balanced posture of Polykleitos' work. Praxiteles also created a sensuous play of contrasting textures over the figure's surface, juxtaposing the gleam of smooth flesh with crumpled draperies and rough locks of hair. Praxiteles humanizes his subject with a hint of narrative—two gods, one a loving adult and the other a playful child, caught in a moment of absorbed companionship.

Around 350 BCE, Praxiteles created a daring statue of Aphrodite for the city of Knidos in Asia Minor. Although artists of the fifth century BCE had begun to hint boldly at the naked female body beneath tissue-thin drapery, as in *Nike Adjusting her Sandal*, this Aphrodite was apparently the first statue by a well-known Greek sculptor to depict a fully nude woman, and it set a new standard

To view this image, please go to page 144
of the *Art History*, Fourth Edition by
Marilyn Stokstad ebook.

To view this image, please go to page 144
of the *Art History*, Fourth Edition by
Marilyn Stokstad ebook.

4-30 • Praxiteles **APHRODITE OF KNIDOS**
Composite of two similar Roman copies after the original marble of
c. 350 BCE. Marble, height 6'8" (2.04 m). Vatican Museums, Museo Pio
Clementino, Gabinetto delle Maschere, Rome.

The head of this figure is from one Roman copy, the body from another.
Seventeenth- and eighteenth-century CE restorers added the nose, the
neck, the right forearm and hand, most of the left arm, and the feet and
parts of the legs. This kind of restoration would rarely be undertaken
today, but it was frequently done and considered quite acceptable in
the past, when archaeologists were trying to put together a body of
work documenting the appearances of lost Greek statues.

EXPLORE MORE: Gain insight from a primary source
related to Praxiteles' *Aphrodite of Knidos*
www.myartslab.com

4-29 • Praxiteles or his followers **HERMES AND
THE INFANT DIONYSOS**
Probably a Hellenistic or Roman copy after a Late Classical
4th-century BCE original. Marble, with remnants of red paint on
the lips and hair, height 7'1" (2.15 m). Archaeological Museum,
Olympia.

(FIG. 4–30). Although nudity among athletic young men was admired in Greek society, nudity among women was seen as a sign of low character. The eventual wide acceptance of female nudes in large statuary may be related to the gradual merging of the Greeks' concept of their goddess Aphrodite with some of the characteristics of the Phoenician goddess Astarte (the Babylonian Ishtar), who was nearly always shown nude in Near Eastern art.

In the version of Praxiteles' statue seen here (actually a composite of two Roman copies), the goddess is preparing to take a bath, with a water jug and her discarded clothing at her side. Her hand is caught in a gesture of modesty that only calls attention to her nudity. The bracelet on her upper left arm has a similar effect. Her strong and well-toned body leans forward slightly, with one projecting knee in a seductive pose that emphasizes the swelling forms of her thighs and abdomen. According to an old legend, the sculpture was so realistic that Aphrodite herself journeyed to Knidos to see it and cried out in shock, "Where did Praxiteles see me naked?" The Knidians were so proud of their Aphrodite that they placed it in an open shrine where people could view it from every side. Hellenistic and Roman copies probably numbered in the hundreds, and nearly 50 survive in various collections today.

LYSIPPOS.   Compared to Praxiteles, more details of Lysippos' life are known, and, although none of his original works has survived, there are many copies of the sculpture he produced between c. 350 and 310 BCE. He claimed to be entirely self-taught and asserted that "nature" was his only model, but he must have received some technical training in the vicinity of his home, near Corinth. He expressed great admiration for Polykleitos, but his own figures reflect a different ideal and different proportions. For his famous portrayal of a man scraping himself (**APOXYOMENOS**), known today only from Roman copies (FIG. 4–31), he chose a typical Classical subject, a nude male athlete. But instead of a figure actively engaged in his sport, striding, or standing at ease, Lysippos depicted a young man after his workout, methodically removing oil and dirt from his body with a scraping tool called a *strigil*.

The *Man Scraping Himself*, tall and slender with a relatively small head, makes a telling comparison with Polykleitos' *Spear Bearer*. Not only does it reflect a different canon of proportions, but the legs are in a wider stance to counterbalance the outstretched arms, and there is a pronounced curve to his posture. The *Spear Bearer* is contained within fairly simple, compact contours and oriented toward a center front viewer. In contrast, the arms of the *Man Scraping Himself* break free into the surrounding space, inviting the viewer to move around the statue to absorb its full aspect. Roman authors, who may have been describing the bronze original rather than a marble copy, remarked on the subtle modeling of the statue's elongated body and the spatial extension of its pose.

Lysippos was widely admired for monumental bronze statues of Herakles (Hercules) and Zeus. Neither survives, but his statue of the weary Herakles, leaning on his club (resting after the last of

To view this image, please go to page 145 of the *Art History*, Fourth Edition by Marilyn Stokstad ebook.

4-31 • Lysippos **MAN SCRAPING HIMSELF (APOXYOMENOS)**
Roman copy after the original bronze of c. 350–325 BCE. Marble, height 6′9″ (2.06 m). Vatican Museums, Museo Pio Clementino, Gabinetto dell'Apoxyomenos, Rome.

with an upraised arm holding a scepter, the same way he posed Zeus. Based on description and later copies, we know Lysippos idealized the ruler as a ruggedly handsome, heavy-featured young man with a large Adam's apple and short, tousled hair. According to the Roman historian Plutarch, Lysippos presented Alexander in a meditative pose, "with his face turned upward toward the sky, just as Alexander himself was accustomed to gaze, turning his neck gently to one side" (Pollitt, p. 20). Perhaps he was caught contemplating grave decisions, waiting to receive divine advice.

THE ART OF THE GOLDSMITH

The detailed, small-scale work of Greek goldsmiths followed the same stylistic trends and achieved the same high standards of technique and execution characterizing other arts. A specialty of Greek goldsmiths was the design of earrings in the form of tiny works of sculpture. They were often placed on the ears of marble statues of goddesses, but they adorned the ears of living women as well. Earrings dated about 330—300 BCE depict the youth Ganymede caught in the grasp of an eagle (Zeus), a surprising subject for a decorative item (this is a scene of abduction) and a technical *tour-de-force*. Slightly more than 2 inches high, they were hollow-cast using the lost-wax process, no doubt to make them light on the ear. Despite their small size, the earrings convey some of the drama of their subject, evoking swift movement through space.

SCULPTURE

Hellenistic sculptors produced an enormous variety of work in a wide range of materials, techniques, and styles. The period was marked by two broad and conflicting trends. One (sometimes called anti-Classical) abandoned Classical strictures and experimented freely with new forms and subjects. The other trend emulated earlier Classical models; sculptors selected aspects of favored works of the fourth century BCE and incorporated them into their own work. The radical anti-Classical style was especially strong in Pergamon and other eastern centers of Greek culture.

PERGAMON. Pergamon—capital of a breakaway state within the Seleucid realm established in the early third century BCE—quickly became a leading center of the arts and the hub of an experimental sculptural style that had far-reaching influence throughout the Hellenistic period. This radical style characterizes a monument commemorating the victory in 230 BCE of Attalos I (ruled 241–197 BCE) over the Gauls, a Celtic people (see "The Celts," page 282). The monument extols the dignity and heroism of the defeated enemies and, by extension, the power and virtue of the Pergamenes.

The bronze figures of Gauls mounted on the pedestal of this monument are known today only from Roman copies in marble. One captures the slow demise of a wounded Celtic soldier-trumpeter (FIG. 4–33), whose lime-spiked hair, mustache, and twisted neck ring or **torc** (reputedly the only thing the Gauls wore

To view this image, please go to page 146 of the *Art History*, Fourth Edition by Marilyn Stokstad ebook.

4–32 • Lysippos THE WEARY HERAKLES (FARNESE HERCULES)
A Roman copy by Glykon of the 4th-century BCE bronze original. Marble, height 10′6″ (3.17 m). National Archeological Museum, Naples.

his Twelve Labors) and holding the apples of the Hesperides, is known from an early third-century CE Roman copy, signed by the Athenian sculptor Glykon (FIG. 4–32). The Romans greatly admired Lysippos' heroic figure, and the marble copy was made for the Baths of Caracalla. In the Renaissance the sculpture was part of the Farnese collection in Rome, where it stood in the courtyard of the family's palace and was studied by artists from all over Europe. It has since been dubbed the *Farnese Hercules*.

When Lysippos was summoned to create a portrait of Alexander the Great, he portrayed Alexander as a full-length standing figure

into battle) identify him as a **barbarian** (a label the ancient Greeks used for all foreigners, whom they considered uncivilized). But the sculpture also depicts his dignity and heroism in defeat, inspiring in viewers both admiration and pity for this fallen warrior. Fatally injured, he struggles to rise, but the slight bowing of his supporting right arm and his unseeing, downcast gaze indicate that he is on the point of death. This kind of deliberate attempt to elicit a specific emotional response in the viewer is known as **expressionism**, and it was to become a characteristic of Hellenistic art.

Pliny the Elder described a work like the *Dying Gallic Trumpeter*, attributing it to an artist named Epigonos. Recent research indicates that Epigonos probably knew the early fifth-century BCE sculpture of the Temple of Aphaia at Aegina, which included the *Dying Warriors*, and could have had it in mind when he created his own works.

The sculptural style and approach seen in the monument to the defeated Gauls became more pronounced and dramatic in later works, culminating in the sculptured frieze wrapped around the base of a Great Altar on a mountainside at Pergamon **(FIG. 4–34)**.

Now reconstructed inside a Berlin museum, the original altar was enclosed within a single-story Ionic colonnade raised on a high podium reached by a monumental staircase 68 feet wide and nearly 30 feet deep. The over-7-feet high sculptural frieze, probably executed during the reign of Eumenes II (197–159 BCE), depicts the battle between the gods and the giants (Titans), a mythical struggle that the Greeks saw as a metaphor for their conflicts with outsiders, all of whom they labeled barbarians. In this case it evokes the Pergamenes' victory over the Gauls.

The Greek gods fight here not only with giants, but also with monsters with snakes for legs emerging from the bowels of the earth. In this detail **(FIG. 4–35)**, the goddess Athena at the left has grabbed the hair of a winged male monster and forced him to his knees. Inscriptions along the base of the sculpture identify him as Alkyoneos, a son of the earth goddess Ge. Ge rises from the ground on the right in fear as she reaches toward Athena, pleading for her son's life. At the far right, a winged Nike rushes to crown Athena with a victor's wreath.

The figures in the Pergamon frieze not only fill the space

To view this image, please go to page 151 of the *Art History*, Fourth Edition by Marilyn Stokstad ebook.

4-33 • Epigonos (?) DYING GALLIC TRUMPETER
Roman copy after the original bronze of c. 220 BCE. Marble, height, 36½″ (93 cm). Capitoline Museum, Rome.

The marble sculpture was found in Julius Caesar's garden in Rome. The bronze original was part of a victory monument made for the Sanctuary of Athena in Pergamon. Pliny wrote that Epigonos "surpassed others with his Trumpeter."

The Celts

During the first millennium BCE, Celtic peoples inhabited most of central and western Europe. The Celtic Gauls portrayed in the Hellenistic Pergamene victory monument (SEE FIG. 4–33) moved into Asia Minor from Thrace during the third century BCE. The ancient Greeks referred to these neighbors, like all outsiders, as barbarians. Pushed out by migrating people, attacked and defeated by challenged kingdoms like that at Pergamon, and then finally by the Roman armies of Julius Caesar, ultimately the Celts were pushed into the northwesternmost parts of the continent—Ireland, Cornwall, and Brittany. Their wooden sculpture and dwellings and their colorful woven textiles have disintegrated, but spectacular funerary goods such as jewelry, weapons, and tableware have survived.

This golden torc, dating sometime between the third and first centuries BCE, was excavated in 1866 from a Celtic tomb in northern France, but it is strikingly similar to the neck ring worn by the noble dying trumpeter illustrated in FIG. 4–33. Torcs were worn by noblemen and were sometimes awarded to warriors for heroic performance in combat. Like all Celtic jewelry, the decorative design of this work consists not of natural forms but of completely abstract ornament, in this case created by the careful twisting and wrapping of strands of pure gold, resolved securely by the definitive bulges of two knobs. In Celtic hands, pattern becomes an integral part of the object itself, not an applied decoration. In stark contrast to the culture of the ancient Greeks, where the human figure was at the heart of all artistic development, here it is abstract, non-representational form and its continual refinement that is the central artistic preoccupation.

To view this image, please go to page 152 of the *Art History*, Fourth Edition by Marilyn Stokstad ebook.

TORC
Found at Soucy, France. Celtic Gaul, 3rd–1st century BCE. Gold, height 5″ × length 5⅝″ (12.7 × 14.5 cm). Musée Nationale du Moyen-Âge, Paris.

along the base of the altar, they also break out of their architectural boundaries and invade the spectators' space, crawling out onto the steps that visitors climbed on their way to the altar. Many consider this theatrical and complex interaction of space and form to be a benchmark of the Hellenistic style, just as they consider the balanced restraint of the Parthenon sculpture to be the epitome of the High Classical style. Where fifth-century BCE artists sought horizontal and vertical equilibrium and control, the Pergamene artists sought to balance opposing forces in three-dimensional space along dynamic diagonals. Classical preference for smooth, evenly illuminated surfaces has been replaced by dramatic contrasts of light and shade playing over complex forms carved with deeply undercut high relief. The composure and stability admired in the Classical style have given way to extreme expressions of pain, stress, wild anger, fear, and despair. Whereas the Classical artist asked only for an intellectual commitment, the Hellenistic artist demanded that the viewer also empathize.

To view this image, please go to page 153 of the *Art History*, Fourth Edition by Marilyn Stokstad ebook.

4-34 • RECONSTRUCTED WEST FRONT OF THE ALTAR FROM PERGAMON (IN MODERN TURKEY)
c. 175–150 BCE. Marble, height of figure 7′7″ (2.3 m). Staatliche Museen zu Berlin, Pergamonmuseum, Preussischer Kulturbesitz, Berlin.

To view this image, please go to page 153 of the *Art History*, Fourth Edition by Marilyn Stokstad ebook.

4-35 • ATHENA ATTACKING THE GIANTS
Detail of the frieze from the east front of the altar from Pergamon. c. 175–150 BCE. Marble, frieze height 7′7″ (2.3 m). Staatliche Museen zu Berlin, Antikensammlung, Pergamonmuseum, Berlin.

THE LAOCOÖN. Pergamene artists may have inspired the work of Hagesandros, Polydoros, and Athenodoros, three sculptors on the island of Rhodes named by Pliny the Elder as the creators of the famed **LAOCOÖN AND HIS SONS** (**FIG. 4–36**). This work has been assumed by many art historians to be the original version from the second century BCE, although others argue that it is a brilliant copy commissioned by an admiring Roman patron in the first century CE.

This complex sculptural composition illustrates an episode from the Trojan War when the priest Laocoön warned the Trojans not to bring within their walls the giant wooden horse left behind by the Greeks. The gods who supported the Greeks retaliated by sending serpents from the sea to destroy Laocoön and his sons as they walked along the shore. The struggling figures, anguished faces, intricate diagonal movements, and skillful unification of diverse forces in a complex composition all suggest a strong relationship between Rhodian and Pergamene sculptors. Although sculpted in the round, the Laocoön was composed to be seen frontally and from close range, and the three figures resemble the relief sculpture on the altar from Pergamon.

THE NIKE OF SAMOTHRACE. This winged figure of Victory (**FIG. 4–37**) is even more theatrical than the Laocoön. In its original setting—in a hillside niche high above the Sanctuary of the Great gods at Samothrace, perhaps drenched with spray from a fountain—

To view this image, please go to page 154 of the *Art History*, Fourth Edition by Marilyn Stokstad ebook.

4-36 • Hagesandros, Polydoros, and Athenodoros of Rhodes **LAOCOÖN AND HIS SONS**
Probably the original of 1st century BCE or a Roman copy of the 1st century CE. Marble, height 8′ (2.44 m). Musei Vaticani, Museo Pio Clementino, Cortile Ottagono, Rome.

To view this image, please go to page 155 of the *Art History*, Fourth Edition by Marilyn Stokstad ebook.

4-37 • NIKE (VICTORY) OF SAMOTHRACE
Sanctuary of the Great Gods, Samothrace. c. 180 BCE (?). Marble, height 8′1″ (2.45 m). Musée du Louvre, Paris.

The wind-whipped costume and raised wings of this Victory indicate that she has just alighted on the prow of the stone ship that formed the original base of the statue. The work probably commemorated an important naval victory, perhaps the Rhodian triumph over the Seleucid king Antiochus III in 190 BCE. The Nike (lacking its head and arms) and a fragment of its stone ship base were discovered in the ruins of the Sanctuary of the Great Gods by a French explorer in 1863 (additional fragments were discovered later). Soon after, the sculpture entered the collection of the Louvre Museum in Paris.

OLD WOMAN. The Hellenistic world was varied and multicultural, and some artists turned from generalizing idealism to an attempt to portray the world as they saw it. Patrons were fascinated by representations of people from every level of society, of unusual physical types as well as of ordinary individuals. This aged woman, on her way to the agora with three chickens and a basket of vegetables, may seem an unlikely subject for sculpture (**FIG. 4–38**). Despite the bunched and untidy disposition of her dress, it appears to be of an elegant design and made of fine fabric, and her hair is not in total disarray. These characteristics, along with the woman's sagging lower jaw, unfocused stare, and lack of concern for her exposed breasts, have led some to speculate that she represents an aging, dissolute follower of the wine god Dionysos on her way to make an offering. Whether an elderly peasant or a Dionysian celebrant, the woman is the antithesis of the Nike of Samothrace. Yet in formal terms, both sculptures stretch out assertively into the space around them, both demand an emotional response from the viewer, and both display technical virtuosity in the rendering of forms and textures.

APHRODITE OF MELOS. Not all Hellenistic artists followed the descriptive and expressionist tendencies of the artists of Pergamon and Rhodes. Some turned to the past, creating an eclectic style by reexamining and borrowing elements from earlier Classical styles and combining them in new ways. Many looked back to Praxiteles and Lysippos for their models. This was the case with the sculptor of the *Aphrodite* (better known as the **VENUS DE MILO**) (**FIG. 4–39**) found on the island of Melos by French excavators in the early nineteenth century. The dreamy gaze recalls Praxiteles' work (SEE FIG. 4–30), and the figure has the heavier proportions of High Classical sculpture, but the twisting stance and the strong projection of the knee are typical of Hellenistic art, as is the rich three-dimensionality of the drapery. The juxtaposition of soft flesh and crisp drapery, seemingly in the process of slipping off the figure, adds a note of erotic tension.

To view this image, please go to page 156 of the *Art History*, Fourth Edition by Marilyn Stokstad ebook.

4–38 • OLD WOMAN
Roman copy, 1st century CE. Marble, height 49½″ (1.25 m). Metropolitan Museum of Art, New York. Rogers Fund, 1909 (09.39)

this huge goddess must have reminded visitors of the god in Greek plays who descends from heaven to determine the outcome of the drama. The forward momentum of the Nike's heavy body is balanced by the powerful backward thrust of her enormous wings. The large, open movements of the figure, the strong contrasts of light and dark on the deeply sculpted forms, and the contrasting textures of feathers, fabric, and skin, typify the finest Hellenistic art.

By the end of the first century BCE, the influence of Greek painting, sculpture, and architecture had spread to the artistic communities of the emerging Roman empire. Roman patrons and artists maintained their enthusiasm for Greek art into Early Christian and Byzantine times. Indeed, so strong was the urge to emulate the work of great Greek artists that, as we have seen throughout this chapter, much of our knowledge of Greek achievements comes from Roman replicas of Greek artworks and descriptions of Greek art by Roman writers.

4-39 • APHRODITE OF MELOS (ALSO CALLED VENUS DE MILO)

c. 150–100 BCE. Marble, height 6′8″ (2.04 m). Musée du Louvre, Paris.

The original appearance of this famous statue's missing arms has been much debated. When it was dug up in a field in 1820, some broken pieces (now lost) found with it indicated that the figure was holding out an apple in its right hand. Many judged these fragments to be part of a later restoration, not part of the original statue. Another theory is that Aphrodite was admiring herself in the highly polished shield of the war god Ares, an image that was popular in the 2nd century BCE. This theoretical "restoration" would explain the pronounced S-curve of the pose and the otherwise unnatural forward projection of the knee.

To view this image, please go to page 157 of the *Art History*, Fourth Edition by Marilyn Stokstad ebook.

THINK ABOUT IT

4.6 Discuss the emergence of a characteristically Greek approach to the representation of the male nude by comparing the *Anavysos Kouros* (FIG. 4–23) and the *Kritios Boy* (FIG. 4–25). What has changed and what remains constant?

4.7 How do the technical possibilities and limitations of black-figure and red-figure techniques affect the representation of the human form on ceramic vessels?

4.8 Distinguish the attributes of the three architectural orders of ancient Greece.

4.9 What ideals are embodied in the term "High Classicism" and what are the value judgments that underlie this art-historical category? Select one sculpture and one building discussed in the chapter, and explain why these works are regarded as High Classical.

4.10 In what ways do the Hellenistic sculptures of the *Dying Gallic Trumpeter* (FIG. 4–33) and *The Great Altar from Pergamon* (FIG. 4–35) depart from the norms of Classicism?

PRACTICE MORE: Compose answers to these questions, get flashcards for images and terms, and review chapter material with quizzes www.myartslab.com

4-40 • HEAD OF A MAN (TRADITIONALLY KNOWN AS "BRUTUS")

c. 300 BCE. Bronze, eyes of painted ivory, height 12½″ (31.8 cm). Palazzo dei Conservatori, Rome.

THE ROMANS

At the same time that the Etruscan civilization was flourishing, the Latin-speaking inhabitants of Rome began to develop into a formidable power. For a time, kings of Etruscan lineage ruled them, but in 509 BCE the Romans overthrew them and formed a republic centered in Rome. The Etruscans themselves were absorbed by the Roman Republic at the end of the third century BCE, by which time Rome had steadily expanded its territory in many directions. The Romans unified what is now Italy and, after defeating their rival, the North African city-state of Carthage, they established an empire that encompassed the entire Mediterranean region.

At its greatest extent, in the early second century CE, the Roman Empire reached from the Euphrates River, in southwest Asia, to Scotland. It ringed the Mediterranean Sea—*mare nostrum*, or "our sea," the Romans called it. Those who were conquered by the Romans gradually assimilated Roman legal, administrative, and cultural structures that endured for some five centuries—and in the eastern Mediterranean until the fifteenth century CE—and left a lasting mark on the civilizations that emerged in Europe.

ORIGINS OF ROME

The Romans saw themselves as descendents of heroic ancestors. Two popular legends told the story of Rome's founding. One focused on Romulus and Remus, twin sons of the god Mars and a mortal woman, who were abandoned on the banks of the Tiber River and discovered by a she-wolf, who nursed them as her own pups. When they reached adulthood, the twins built a city near the place of their rescue. The other story of Rome's founding is part of Virgil's *Aeneid*, where the poet claims the Roman people to be descendants of Aeneas, a Trojan who was the mortal son of Venus. Aeneas and some companions escaped from Troy and made their way to the Italian peninsula. Their sons were the Romans, the people who in fulfillment of a promise by Jupiter to Venus were destined to rule the world.

Archaeologists and historians present a more mundane picture of Rome's origins. In Neolithic times, people settled in permanent villages on the plains of Latium, south of the Tiber River, and on the Palatine, one of the seven hills that would eventually become the city of Rome. By the sixth century BCE, these modest towns had become a major transportation hub and trading center.

Roman Writers on Art

Only one book devoted specifically to architecture and the arts survives from antiquity. All our other written sources consist of digressions and insertions in works on other subjects. That one book, the Ten Books on Architecture by Vitruvius (c. 80–c. 15 BCE), however, is invaluable. Written for Augustus in the first century BCE, it is a practical handbook for builders that discusses such things as laying out cities, siting buildings, and using the Greek architectural orders. Vitruvius argued for appropriateness and rationality in architecture, and he also made significant contributions to art theory, including studies on proportion.

Pliny the Elder (c. 23–79 CE) wrote a vast encyclopedia of "facts, histories, and observations" known as *Naturalis Historia* (*The Natural History*) that often included discussions of art and architecture. Pliny occasionally used works of art to make his points—for example, citing sculpture within his essays on stone and metals. Pliny's scientific turn of mind led to his death, for he was overcome while observing the eruption of Mount Vesuvius that buried Pompeii. His nephew, Pliny the Younger (c. 61–113 CE), a voluminous letter writer, added to our knowledge of Roman domestic architecture with his meticulous descriptions of villas and gardens.

Valuable bits of information can also be found in books by travelers and historians. Pausanias, a second-century CE Greek traveler, wrote descriptions that are basic sources on Greek art and artists. Flavius Josephus (c. 37–100 CE), a historian of the Flavians, wrote in his Jewish Wars a description of the triumph of Titus that includes the treasures looted from the Temple of Solomon in Jerusalem.

EXPLORE MORE: Gain insight from primary sources by Roman writers **www.myartslab.com**

ROMAN RELIGION

The Romans assimilated Greek gods, myths, religious beliefs and practices into their state religion. They also deified their emperors. Worship of ancient gods mingled with homage to past rulers, and oaths of allegiance to the living ruler made the official religion a political duty. Religious worship became increasingly ritualized, perfunctory, and distant from the everyday life of most people.

Many Romans adopted the so-called mystery religions of the people they had conquered. Worship of Isis and Osiris from Egypt, Cybele (the Great Mother) from Anatolia, the hero-god Mithras from Persia, and the single, all-powerful God of Judaism and Christianity from Palestine challenged the Roman establishment. These unauthorized religions flourished alongside the state religion, with its Olympian deities and deified emperors, despite occasional government efforts to suppress them.

THE REPUBLIC, 509–27 BCE

Early Rome was governed by kings and an advisory body of leading citizens called the Senate. The population was divided into two classes: a wealthy and powerful upper class, the patricians, and a lower class, the plebeians. In 509 BCE, Romans overthrew the last Etruscan king and established the Roman Republic as an oligarchy, a government by the aristocrats that would last about 450 years.

As a result of its stable form of government, and especially of its encouragement of military conquest, by 275 BCE Rome controlled the entire Italian peninsula. By 146 BCE, Rome had defeated its great rival, Carthage, on the north coast of Africa, and taken control of the western Mediterranean. By the mid second century BCE, Rome had taken Macedonia and Greece, and by 44 BCE, it had conquered most of Gaul (present-day France) as well as the eastern Mediterranean. Egypt remained independent until Octavian defeated Mark Antony and Cleopatra at the Battle of Actium in 31 BCE.

During the Republic, Roman art was rooted in its Etruscan heritage, but territorial expansion brought wider exposure to the arts of other cultures. Like the Etruscans, the Romans admired Greek art. As Horace wrote (*Epistulae* II, 1): "Captive Greece conquered her savage conquerors and brought the arts to rustic Latium." The Romans used Greek designs and Greek orders in their architecture, imported Greek art, and employed Greek artists. In 146 BCE, for example, they stripped the Greek city of Corinth of its art treasures and shipped them back to Rome.

PORTRAIT SCULPTURE

Portrait sculptors of the Republican period sought to create lifelike images based on careful observation of their subjects, objectives that were related to the Romans' veneration of their ancestors and the making and public display of death masks of deceased relatives (see "Roman Portraiture," page 290).

Perhaps growing out of this early tradition of maintaining images of ancestors as death masks, a new Roman artistic ideal emerged during the Republican period in relation to portrait

Roman Portraiture

The strong emphasis on portraiture in Roman art may stem from the early practice of creating likenesses—in some cases actual wax death masks—of revered figures and distinguished ancestors for display on public occasions, most notably funerals. Contemporary historians have left colorful evocations of this distinctively Roman custom. Polybius, a Greek exiled to Rome in the middle of the second century BCE, wrote home with the following description:

> … after the interment [of the illustrious man] and the performance of the usual ceremonies, they place the image of the departed in the most conspicuous position in the house, enclosed in a wooden shrine. This image is a mask reproducing with remarkable fidelity both the features and the complexion of the deceased. On the occasion of public sacrifices, they display these images, and decorate them with much care, and when any distinguished member of the family dies they take them to the funeral, putting them on men who seem to bear the closest resemblance to the original in stature and carriage…. There could not easily be a more ennobling spectacle for a young man who aspires to fame and virtue. For who would not be inspired by the sight of the images of men renowned for their excellence, all together and as if alive and breathing?… By this means, by the constant renewal of the good report of brave men, the celebrity of those who performed noble deeds is rendered immortal, while at the same time the fame of those who did good services to their country becomes known to the people and a heritage for future generations. (The Histories, VII, 53, 54, trans. W. R. Paton, Loeb Library ed.)

Growing out of this heritage, Roman Republican portraiture is frequently associated with the notion of **verism**—an interest in the faithful reproduction of the immediate visual and tactile appearance of subjects. Since we find in these portrait busts the same sorts of individualizing physiognomic features that allow us to differentiate among the people we know in our own world, it is easy to assume that they are exact likenesses of their subjects as they appeared during their lifetime. Of course, this is impossible to verify, but our strong desire to believe it must realize the intentions of the artists who made these portraits and the patrons for whom they were made.

A life-size marble statue of a Roman patrician shown here, dating from the period of the Emperor Augustus, reflects the practices documented much earlier by Polybius and links the man portrayed with a revered tradition and its laudatory associations. The large marble format emulates a Greek notion of sculpture, and its use here signals not only this man's wealth but also his sophisticated artistic tastes, characteristics he shared with the emperor himself. His toga, however, is not Greek but indigenous and signifies his respectability as a Roman citizen of some standing. The busts of ancestors that he holds in his hands document his distinguished lineage in the privileged upper class—laws regulated which members of society could own such collections—and the statue as a whole proclaims his adherence to the family tradition by having his own portrait created.

To view this image, please go to page 170 of the *Art History*, Fourth Edition by Marilyn Stokstad ebook.

PATRICIAN CARRYING PORTRAIT BUSTS OF TWO ANCESTORS (BARBERINI TOGATUS)
End of 1st century BCE or beginning of 1st century CE.
Marble, height 5′5″ (1.65 m). Palazzo de Conservatori, Rome.

The head of this standing figure, though ancient Roman in origin, is a later replacement and not original to this statue. The separation of head and body in this work is understandable since in many instances the bodies of full-length portraits were produced in advance, waiting in the sculptor's workshop for a patron to commission a head with his or her own likeness that could be attached to it. Presumably the busts carried by this patrician were likewise only blocked out until they could be carved with the faces of the commissioner's ancestors. These faces share a striking family resemblance, and the stylistic difference reproduced in the two distinct bust formats reveals that these men lived in successive generations. They could be the father and grandfather of the man who carries them.

4–41 • PORTRAIT HEAD OF AN ELDER
c. 80 BCE. Marble, life size. Metropolitan
Museum of Art, New York.

4–42 • AULUS METELLUS (THE ORATOR)
Found near Perugia. c. 80 BCE. Bronze, height 5′11″ (1.8 m).
Museo Archeològico Nazionale, Florence.

sculpture, an ideal quite different from the one we encountered in Greek Classicism. Instead of generalizing a human face, smoothed of its imperfections and caught in a moment of detached abstraction, this new Roman idealization emphasized—rather than suppressed—the hallmarks of advanced age and the distinguishing aspects of individual likenesses. This mode is most prominent in bust portraits of Roman patricians **(FIG. 4–41)**, whose time-worn faces embody the wisdom and experience that come with old age. Frequently we take these portraits of wrinkled elders at face value, as highly realistic and faithful descriptions of actual human beings—contrasting Roman realism with Greek idealism—but there is good reason to think that these portraits actually conform to a particularly Roman type of idealization that underscores the effects of aging on the human face.

THE ORATOR. The life-size bronze portrait of **AULUS METELLUS**—the Roman official's name is inscribed on the hem of his garment in Etruscan letters **(FIG. 4–42)**—dates to about 80 BCE. The statue, known from early times as *The Orator*, depicts a man addressing a gathering, his arm outstretched and slightly raised, a pose expressive of rhetorical persuasiveness. The orator wears sturdy laced leather boots and a folded and draped toga, the characteristic garment of a Roman senator. According to Pliny the Elder, large statues like this were often placed atop columns as memorials. It could also have been mounted on an inscribed base in a public space by officials grateful for Aulus' benefactions on behalf of their city.

The round arch was not an Etruscan or Roman invention, but the Etruscans and Romans were the first to make widespread use of it—both as an effective structural idea and an elegant design motif.

Round arches displace most of their weight, or downward **thrust** (see arrows on diagram), along their curving sides, transmitting that weight to adjacent supporting uprights (door or window jambs, columns, or piers). From there, the thrust goes to, and is supported by, the ground. To create an arch, brick or cut stones are formed into a curve by fitting together wedge-shaped pieces, called **voussoirs**, until they meet and are locked together at the top center by the final piece, called the **keystone**. These voussoirs exert an outward as well as a downward thrust, so arches may require added support, called **buttressing**, from adjacent masonry elements.

Until the keystone is in place and the mortar between the bricks or stones dries, an arch is held in place by wooden scaffolding called **centering**. The points from which the curves of the arch rise, called **springings**, are often reinforced by masonry imposts. The wall areas adjacent to the curves of the arch are **spandrels**. In a succession of arches, called an **arcade**, the space encompassed by each arch and its supports is called a **bay**.

A stunning example of the early Roman use of the round arch is a bridge known as the Pont du Gard, part of an aqueduct located near Nîmes, in southern France. An ample water supply was essential for a city, and the Roman invention to supply this water was the aqueduct, built with arcades—a linear series of arches. This aqueduct brought water from springs 30 miles to the north using a simple gravity flow, and it provided 100 gallons a day for every person in Nîmes. Each arch buttresses its neighbors and the huge arcade ends solidly in the hillsides. The structure conveys the balance, proportions, and rhythmic harmony of a great work of art, and although it harmonizes with its natural setting, it also makes a powerful statement about Rome's ability to control nature in order to provide for its cities. Both structure and function are marks of Roman civilization.

PONT DU GARD
Nîmes, France. Late 1st century BCE. Height above river 160′ (49 m), width of road bed on lower arcade 20′ (6 m).

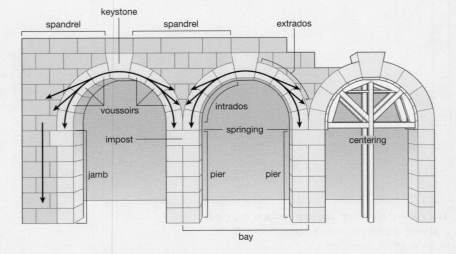

To view this image, please go to page 172 of the *Art History*, Fourth Edition by Marilyn Stokstad ebook.

THE DENARIUS OF JULIUS CAESAR. The propaganda value of portraits was not lost on Roman leaders. In 44 BCE, Julius Caesar issued a denarius (a widely circulated coin) bearing his portrait **(FIG. 4–43)** conforming to the Roman ideal of advanced age. He was the first Roman leader to place his own image on a coin, initiating a practice that would be adopted by his successors, but at the time when this coin was minted, it smacked of the sort of megalomaniacal behavior that would ultimately lead to his assassination. Perhaps it is for this reason that Caesar underscores his age, and thus his old-fashioned respectability, in this portrait, which reads as a mark of his traditionalism as a senator. But the inscription placed around his head—CAESAR DICT PERPETUE, or "Caesar, dictator forever"—certainly contradicts the ideal embodied in the portrait.

ROMAN TEMPLES

Architecture during the Roman Republic reflected both Etruscan and Greek practices. Like the Etruscans, the Romans built urban temples in commercial centers as well as in special sanctuaries. An early example is a small rectangular temple standing on a raised platform, or podium, beside the Tiber River in Rome **(FIG. 4–44)**, probably from the second century BCE and perhaps dedicated to Portunus, the god of harbors and ports. This temple uses the Etruscan system of a rectangular cella and a front porch at one end reached by a broad, inviting flight of steps, but the Roman architects have adopted the Greek Ionic order, with full columns on the porch and half-columns **engaged** (set into the wall) around

To view this image, please go to page 173 of the *Art History*, Fourth Edition by Marilyn Stokstad ebook.

4-43 • DENARIUS WITH PORTRAIT OF JULIUS CAESAR
44 BCE. Silver, diameter approximately ¾" (1.9 cm).
American Numismatic Society, New York.

the exterior walls of the cella **(FIG. 4–45)** and a continuous frieze in the entablature. The overall effect resembles a Greek temple, but there are two major differences. First, Roman architects liberated the form of the column from its post-and-lintel structural roots and engaged it onto the surface of the wall as a decorative feature. Second, while a Greek temple encourages viewers to walk around

To view this image, please go to page 173 of the *Art History*, Fourth Edition by Marilyn Stokstad ebook.

4-44 • TEMPLE, PERHAPS DEDICATED TO PORTUNUS
Forum Boarium (Cattle Market), Rome. Late 2nd century BCE.

To view this image, please go to page 173 of the *Art History*, Fourth Edition by Marilyn Stokstad ebook.

4-45 • PLAN OF TEMPLE
Forum Boarium (Cattle Market), Rome.

SEE MORE: Click the Google Earth link for the Temple of Portunus
www.myartslab.com

the building and explore its uniformly articulated sculptural mass, Roman temples are defined in relation to interior spaces, which visitors are invited to enter through one opening along the longitudinal axis of a symmetrical plan.

By the first century BCE, nearly a million people lived in Rome, which had evolved into the capital of a formidable commercial and political power with a growing overseas empire. As long as Republican Rome was essentially a large city-state, its form of government—an oligarchy under the control of a Senate— remained feasible. But as the empire around it grew larger and larger, a government of competing senators and military commanders could not enforce taxation and maintain order in what was becoming a vast and complicated territorial expanse. As governance of the Republic began to fail, power became concentrated in fewer and fewer leaders, until it was ruled by one man, an emperor, rather than by the Senate.

THE EARLY EMPIRE, 27 BCE–96 CE

The first Roman emperor was born Octavian in 63 BCE. When he was only 18 years old, his brilliant great-uncle, Julius Caesar, adopted him as son and heir, recognizing in him qualities that would make him a worthy successor. Shortly after Julius Caesar refused the Senate's offer of the imperial crown, early in 44 BCE, he was murdered by a group of conspirators, and the 19-year-old Octavian stepped up. Over the next 17 spectacular years, as general, politician, statesman, and public-relations genius, Octavian vanquished warring internal factions and brought peace to fractious provinces. By 27 BCE, the Senate had conferred on him the title of Augustus (meaning "exalted," "sacred"). Assisted by his astute and pragmatic second wife, Livia, Augustus led the state and the empire for 45 years. He established efficient rule and laid the foundation for an extended period of stability, domestic peace, and economic prosperity known as the *Pax Romana* ("Roman Peace"), which lasted over 200 years (27 BCE to 180 CE). In 12 CE, two years before his death, he was given the title Pontifex Maximus ("High Priest"), becoming the empire's highest religious official as well as its political leader.

Conquering and maintaining a vast empire required not only the inspired leadership and tactics of Augustus, but also careful planning, massive logistical support, and great administrative skill. Some of Rome's most enduring contributions to Western civilization reflect these qualities—its system of law, its governmental and administrative structures, and its sophisticated civil engineering and architecture.

To facilitate the development and administration of the empire, as well as to make city life comfortable and attractive to its citizens, the Roman state undertook building programs of unprecedented scale and complexity, mandating the construction of central administrative and legal centers (forums and basilicas), recreational facilities (racetracks, stadiums), temples, markets, theaters, public baths, aqueducts, middle-class housing, and even entire new towns. To accomplish these tasks without sacrificing

beauty, efficiency, and human well-being, Roman builders and architects developed rational plans using easily worked but durable materials and highly sophisticated engineering methods.

To move their armies about efficiently, to speed communications between Rome and the farthest reaches of the empire, and to promote commerce, the Romans built a vast and complex network of roads and bridges. Many modern European highways still follow the lines laid down by Roman engineers, some Roman bridges are still in use, and Roman-era foundations underlie the streets of many cities.

ART IN THE AGE OF AUGUSTUS

Roman artists of the Augustan age created a new style—a new Roman form of idealism that, though still grounded in the appearance of the everyday world, is heavily influenced by a revival of Greek Classical ideals. They enriched the art of portraiture in both official images and representations of private individuals, they recorded contemporary historical events on public monuments, and they contributed unabashedly to Roman imperial propaganda.

AUGUSTUS OF PRIMAPORTA.   In the sculpture known as **AUGUSTUS OF PRIMAPORTA (FIG. 4–46)**—because it was discovered in Livia's villa at Primaporta, near Rome—we see the emperor as he wanted to be seen and remembered. This work demonstrates the creative combination of earlier sculptural traditions that is a hallmark of Augustan art. In its idealization of a specific ruler and his prowess, the sculpture also illustrates the way Roman emperors would continue to use portraiture for propaganda.

The sculptor of this larger-than-life marble statue adapted the standard pose of a Roman orator (SEE FIG. 4–42) by melding it with the contrapposto and canonical proportions developed by the Greek High Classical sculptor Polykleitos, as exemplified by his *Spear Bearer*. Like the heroic Greek figure, Augustus' portrait captures him in the physical prime of youth, far removed from the image of advanced age idealized in the coin portrait of Julius Caesar. Although Augustus lived to age 70, in his portraits he is always a vigorous ruler, eternally young. But like Caesar, and unlike the *Spear Bearer*, Augustus' face is rendered with the kind of details that make this portrait an easily recognizable likeness.

To this combination of Greek and Roman traditions, the sculptor of the *Augustus of Primaporta* added mythological and historical imagery that exalts Augustus' family and celebrates his accomplishments. Cupid, son of the goddess Venus, rides a dolphin next to the emperor's right leg, a reference to the claim of the emperor's family, the Julians, to descent from the goddess Venus through her human son Aeneas. Augustus' anatomically conceived cuirass (torso armor) is also covered with figural imagery. Mid-torso is a scene representing Augustus' 20 BCE diplomatic victory over the Parthians; a Parthian (on the right) returns a Roman military standard to a figure variously identified as a Roman soldier or the goddess Roma. Looming above this scene at the top of the cuirass is a celestial deity who holds an arched canopy, implying that the peace signified by the scene below has cosmic implications. The personification of the earth at the bottom of the cuirass holds an overflowing cornucopia, representing the prosperity that peace brings.

Another Augustan monument that synthesizes Roman traditions and Greek Classical influence to express the peace and prosperity that Augustus brought to Rome is the **ARA PACIS AUGUSTAE**. The processional friezes on the exterior sides of the enclosure wall clearly reflect Classical Greek works like the Ionic frieze of the Parthenon (SEE FIG. 3–56), with their three-dimensional figures wrapped in revealing draperies that also create patterns of rippling folds. But unlike the Greek sculptors who created an unspecific, and thus timeless, procession for the Parthenon, the Roman sculptors of the Ara Pacis depicted actual individuals participating in a specific event at a known time. The Classical style may evoke the general notion of a Golden Age, but the historical references and identifiable figures in the Ara Pacis procession associate that Golden Age specifically with Augustus and his dynasty.

To view this image, please go to page 175 of the *Art History*, Fourth Edition by Marilyn Stokstad ebook.

4-46 • AUGUSTUS OF PRIMAPORTA
Early 1st century CE. Perhaps a copy of a bronze statue of c. 20 BCE. Marble, originally colored, height 6′8″ (2.03 m). Musei Vaticani, Braccio Nuovo, Rome.

To view this image, please go to page 190
of the *Art History*, Fourth Edition by
Marilyn Stokstad ebook.

To view this image, please go to page 190
of the *Art History*, Fourth Edition by
Marilyn Stokstad ebook.

4-47 • YOUNG FLAVIAN WOMAN
c. 90 CE. Marble, height 25″ (65.5 cm). Museo Capitolino, Rome.

PORTRAIT SCULPTURE. Roman patrons continued to expect recognizable likenesses in their portraits, but this did not preclude idealization. A portrait sculpture of a **YOUNG FLAVIAN WOMAN (FIG. 4-47)** is idealized in a manner similar to the *Augustus of Primaporta* (SEE FIG. 4-46). Her well-observed, recognizable features—a strong nose and jaw, heavy brows, deep-set eyes, and a long neck—contrast with the smoothly rendered flesh and soft, sensual lips. Her hair is piled high in an extraordinary mass of ringlets following the latest court fashion. Executing the head required skillful chiseling and **drillwork**, a technique for rapidly cutting deep grooves with straight sides, as was done here to render the holes in the center of the curls. The overall effect, especially from a distance, is quite life-like. The play of natural light over the more subtly sculpted marble surfaces simulates the textures of real skin and hair.

IMPERIAL PORTRAITS

Imperial portraits were objects of propaganda. Marcus Aurelius, like Hadrian, was a successful military commander who was equally proud of his intellectual attainments. In a lucky error—or twist of fortune—a gilded-bronze equestrian statue of the emperor, dressed as a military commander in a tunic and short, heavy cloak **(FIG. 4-48)**, came mistakenly to be revered during the Middle Ages as a statue of Constantine, the first Christian emperor, and consequently the sculpture escaped being melted down. The raised foreleg of his horse once trampled a crouching barbarian.

Marcus Aurelius' head, with its thick, curly hair and full beard (a fashion that was begun by Hadrian), resembles the traditional "philosopher" portraits from the Greek world. The emperor wears no armor and carries no weapons; like Egyptian kings, he conquers effortlessly by divine will. And like his illustrious predecessor Augustus, he reaches out to those around him in a rhetorical gesture of address. It is difficult to create an equestrian portrait in which the rider stands out as the dominant figure without making the horse look too small. The sculptor of this statue found a balance acceptable to viewers of the time and, in doing so, created a model for later artists.

Marcus Aurelius was succeeded as emperor by his son Commodus, a man without political skill, administrative competence, or intellectual distinction. During his unfortunate reign (180–192 CE), he devoted himself to luxury and frivolous pursuits. He claimed at various times to be the reincarnation of Hercules and the incarnation of the god Jupiter. When he proposed to assume the consulship dressed and armed as a gladiator, his associates, including his mistress, arranged to have him strangled in his bath by a wrestling partner. Commodus did, however, sponsor some of the finest artists of the day. In a spectacular marble bust, the emperor poses as **HERCULES (FIG. 4–49)**, adorned with references to the hero's legendary labors: Hercules' club, the skin and head of the Nemean lion, and the golden apples from the Garden of the Hesperides. Commodus' likeness emphasizes his family resemblance to his more illustrious and powerful father (SEE FIG. 4–48), but it also captures his vanity, through the grand pretensions of his costume and the Classical associations of his body type. The sculptor's sensitive modeling and expert drillwork exploit the play of light and shadow on the figure to bring out the textures of the hair, beard, facial features, and drapery, and to capture the illusion of life and movement.

FUNERARY SCULPTURE. During the second and third centuries, a shift from cremation to inhumation created a growing demand for sarcophagi in which to bury the bodies of the deceased. Wealthy Romans commissioned thousands of massive and elaborate marble sarcophagi, encrusted with sculptural relief, created in large production workshops throughout the Roman empire.

In 1885, nine particularly impressive sarcophagi were discovered in private underground burial chambers built for use by a powerful, aristocratic Roman family—the Calpurnii Pisones. One of these sarcophagi, from c. 190 CE, portrays the **INDIAN TRIUMPH OF DIONYSUS** (see "A Closer Look," page 303). This is a popular

To view this image, please go to page 201 of the *Art History*, Fourth Edition by Marilyn Stokstad ebook.

4-48 • EQUESTRIAN STATUE OF MARCUS AURELIUS

c. 176 CE. Bronze, originally gilded, height of statue 11′6″ (3.5 m). Museo Capitolino, Rome.

Between 1187 and 1538, this statue stood in the piazza fronting the palace and church of St. John Lateran in Rome. In January 1538, Pope Paul III had it moved to the Capitoline Hill, and Michelangelo made it the centerpiece of his newly redesigned Capitoline Piazza. After being removed from its base for cleaning and restoration in recent times, it was taken inside the Capitoline Museum to protect it from air pollution, and a copy has replaced it in the piazza.

Mosaics were used widely in Hellenistic times and became enormously popular for decorating homes in the Roman period. Mosaic designs were created with pebbles, or with small, regularly shaped pieces of colored stone and marble, called tesserae. The stones were pressed into a kind of soft cement called grout. When the stones were firmly set, the spaces between them were also filled with grout. After the surface dried, it was cleaned and polished. Since the natural stones produced only a narrow range of colors, glass tesserae were also used to extend the palette as early as the third century BCE.

Mosaic production was made more efficient by the use of **emblemata** (the plural of emblema, "central design"). These small, intricate mosaic compositions were created in the artist's workshop in square or rectangular trays. They could be made in advance, carried to a work site, and inserted into a floor decorated with an easily produced geometric pattern.

Some skilled mosaicists even copied well-known paintings, often by famous Greek artists. Employing a technique in which very small tesserae, in a wide range of colors, were laid down in irregular, curving lines, they effectively imitated painted brushstrokes. One example is The Unswept Floor. Herakleitos, a second-century CE Greek mosaicist living in Rome, made this copy of an original work by the renowned second-century BCE artist Sosos. Pliny the Elder, in his Natural History, mentions a mosaic of an unswept floor and another of doves that Sosos made in Pergamon.

A dining room would be a logical location for a floor mosaic of this theme, with table scraps re-created in meticulous detail, even to the shadows they cast, and a mouse foraging among them. The guests reclining on their banquet couches would certainly be amused by the pictures on the floor, but they could also have shown off their knowledge of the notable Greek precedents for the mosaic beneath their feet.

To view this image, please go to page 202 of the *Art History*, Fourth Edition by Marilyn Stokstad ebook.

THE UNSWEPT FLOOR
Mosaic variant of a 2nd-century BCE painting by Sosos of Pergamon. 2nd century CE. Signed by Herakleitos.
Musei Vaticani, Museo Gregoriano Profano, Rome.

To view this image, please go to page 203 of the *Art History*, Fourth Edition by Marilyn Stokstad ebook.

4-49 • COMMODUS AS HERCULES
Esquiline Hill, Rome. c. 191–192 CE. Marble, height 46½″ (118 cm). Palazzo dei Conservatori, Rome.

THE LATE EMPIRE, THIRD AND FOURTH CENTURIES CE

The comfortable life suggested by the wall paintings in Roman houses and villas was, within a century, to be challenged by hard times. The reign of Commodus marked the beginning of a period of political and economic decline. Barbarian groups had already begun moving into the empire in the time of Marcus Aurelius. Now they pressed on Rome's frontiers. Many crossed the borders and settled within them, disrupting provincial governments. As perceived threats spread throughout the empire, imperial rule became increasingly authoritarian. Eventually the army controlled the government, and the Imperial Guards set up and deposed rulers almost at will, often selecting candidates from among poorly educated, power-hungry provincial leaders in their own ranks.

THE SEVERAN DYNASTY

Despite the pressures brought by political and economic change, the arts continued to flourish under the Severan emperors (193–235 CE) who succeeded Commodus. Septimius Severus (r. 193–211 CE), who was born in Africa, and his Syrian wife, Julia Domna, restored public buildings, commissioned official portraits, and revitalized the old cattle market in Rome into a well-planned center of bustling commerce. Their sons, Geta and Caracalla, succeeded Septimius Severus as co-emperors in 211 CE, but Caracalla murdered Geta in 212 CE and then ruled alone until he in turn was murdered in 217 CE.

PORTRAITS OF CARACALLA. The Emperor Caracalla appears in his portraits as a fierce and courageous ruler, capable of confronting Rome's enemies and safeguarding the security of the Roman Empire. In the example shown here **(FIG. 4–50)**, the sculptor has enhanced the intensity of the emperor's expression by producing strong contrasts of light and dark with careful chiseling and drillwork. Even the marble eyes have been drilled and engraved to catch the light in a way that makes them dominate his expression. The contrast between this style and that of the portraits of Augustus is a telling reflection of the changing character of imperial rule. Augustus envisioned himself as the suave initiator of a Golden Age of peace and prosperity; Caracalla presents himself as a no-nonsense ruler of iron-fisted determination, with a militaristic, close-cropped haircut and a glare of fierce intensity.

THE BATHS OF CARACALLA. The year before his death in 211 CE, Septimius Severus had begun a popular public-works project: the construction of magnificent new public baths on the southeast side of Rome as a new recreational and educational center. Caracalla completed and inaugurated the baths in 216–217 CE, today known by his name. The impressive brick and concrete structure was hidden under a sheath of colorful marble and mosaic. The builders used soaring groin and barrel vaults, which allow the

theme in late second-century CE sarcophagi, but here the carved relief is of especially high quality—complex but highly legible at the same time. The mythological composition owes a debt to imperial ceremony. Dionysus, at far left in a chariot, receives from a personification of Victory standing behind him a laurel crown, identical to the headdress worn by Roman emperors during triumphal processions. Also derived from state ceremony is the display of booty and captives carried by the elephants at the center of the composition. But religion, rather than statecraft, is the real theme here. The set of sarcophagi to which this belongs indicates that the family who commissioned them adhered to a mystery cult of Dionysus that focused on themes of decay and renewal, death and rebirth. The triumph of the deceased over death is the central message here, not one particular episode in the life of Dionysus himself.

maximum space with the fewest possible supports. The groin vaults also made possible large windows in every bay. Windows were important, since the baths depended on natural light and could only be open during daylight hours.

The **BATHS OF CARACALLA** (FIGS. 4–51, 4–52) were laid out on a strictly symmetrical plan. The bathing facilities were grouped in the center of the main building to make efficient use of the below-ground furnaces that heated them and to allow bathers to move comfortably from hot to cold pools and then finish with

To view this image, please go to page 204 of the *Art History*, Fourth Edition by Marilyn Stokstad ebook.

4-50 • CARACALLA
Early 3rd century CE. Marble, height 14½" (36.2 cm). Metropolitan Museum of Art, New York. Samuel D. Lee Fund, 1940 (40.11.1A)

To view this image, please go to page 205 of the *Art History*, Fourth Edition by Marilyn Stokstad ebook.

4-52 • PLAN OF THE BATHS OF CARACALLA

To view this image, please go to page 205 of the *Art History*, Fourth Edition by Marilyn Stokstad ebook.

4-51 • BATHS OF CARACALLA
Rome. c. 211–217 CE.

SEE MORE: Click the Google Earth link for the Baths of Caracalla
www.myartslab.com

a swim. Many other facilities—exercise rooms, shops, latrines, and dressing rooms—were housed on each side of the bathing block. The bath buildings alone covered 5 acres. The entire complex, which included gardens, a stadium, libraries, a painting gallery, auditoriums, and huge water reservoirs, covered an area of 50 acres.

THE SOLDIER EMPERORS

Following the assassination of the last Severan emperor by one of his military commanders in 235 CE, Rome was plunged into a period of anarchy that lasted for 50 years. A series of soldier emperors attempted to rule the empire, but real order was only restored by Diocletian (r. 284–305 CE), also a military commander. This brilliant politician and general reversed the empire's declining fortunes, but he also began an increasingly autocratic form of rule, and the social structure of the empire became increasingly rigid.

To divide up the task of defending and administering the Roman world and to assure an orderly succession, in 286 CE Diocletian divided the empire in two parts. According to his plan, with the title of "Augustus" he would rule in the East, while another Augustus, Maximian, would rule in the West. Then, in 293 CE, he devised a form of government called a **tetrarchy**, or "rule of four," in which each Augustus designated a subordinate and heir, who held the title of "Caesar." And the Roman Empire, now divided into four quadrants, would be ruled by four individuals.

TETRARCHIC PORTRAITURE. Diocletian's political restructuring is paralleled by the introduction of a radically new, hard style of geometricized abstraction, especially notable in portraits of the tetrarchs themselves. A powerful bust of a tetrarch, startlingly alert with searing eyes **(FIG. 4–53)**, embodies this stylistic shift toward the antithesis of the suave Classicism seen in the portrait of Commodus as Hercules (SEE FIG. 4–49). There is no clear sense of likeness. Who this individual is seems to be less significant than the powerful position he holds. Some art historians have interpreted this change in style as a conscious embodiment of Diocletian's new concept of government, while others have pointed to parallels with the provincial art of Diocletian's Dalmatian homeland or with the Neoplatonic aesthetics of idealized abstraction promoted by Plotinus, a third-century CE philosopher who was widely read in the late Roman world. In any event, these riveting works represent not a degeneration of the Classical tradition but its conscious replacement by a different aesthetic viewpoint—militaristic, severe, and abstract rather than suave, slick, and classicizing.

This new mode is famously represented by an actual sculptural group of **THE TETRARCHS (FIG. 4–54)**. The four figures are nearly

To view this image, please go to page 205 of the *Art History*, Fourth Edition by Marilyn Stokstad ebook.

4-53 • PORTRAIT OF A TETRARCH (GALERIUS?)
Early 4th century CE. Porphyry, 2′5½″ (65 cm). Egyptian Museum, Cairo.

identical, except that the senior Augusti have beards while their juniors, the Caesars, are clean-shaven. Dressed in military garb and clasping swords at their sides, they embrace each other in a show of imperial unity, proclaiming an alliance rooted in strength and vigilance. As a piece of propaganda and a summary of the state of affairs at the time, it is unsurpassed.

The sculpture is made of porphyry, an extremely hard, purple stone from Egypt that was reserved for imperial use (SEE FIG. 4–38). The most striking features of the tetrarchs—the simplification of natural forms to geometric shapes, flexibility with human proportions, and the emphasis on a message or idea—appear often in Roman art by the end of the third century. This particular sculpture may have been made in Egypt and moved to Constantinople after 330 CE. Christian crusaders who looted Constantinople in 1204 CE took the statue to Venice and installed it at the Cathedral of St. Mark, where it is today.

To view this image, please go to page 207 of the *Art History*, Fourth Edition by Marilyn Stokstad ebook.

4-54 • THE TETRARCHS
c. 300 CE. Porphyry, height of figures 51″ (129 cm). Brought from Constantinople in 1204, installed at the corner of the façade of the Cathedral of St. Mark, Venice.

Sarcophagus with the Indian Triumph of Dionysus

c. 190 CE. Marble, 47½ × 92½ × 35¹³⁄₁₆″ (120.7 × 234.9 × 90.96 cm).
Walters Art Museum, Baltimore.

Semele, mortal mother of the god Dionysus, gives birth prematurely and then dies. Once grown, Dionysus would travel to the underworld and bring his mother to paradise. Semele's death therefore suggests the promise of eternal life through her son.

These hooked sticks are identical to the ankusha still used by mahouts (elephant drivers) in India today.

As part of their worship, followers of Dionysiac mystery religions re-created the triumphant return of the god from India by parading in the streets after dark. A dancing maenad beats her tambourine here, suggesting the sounds and movements that would accompany such ritual re-enactments.

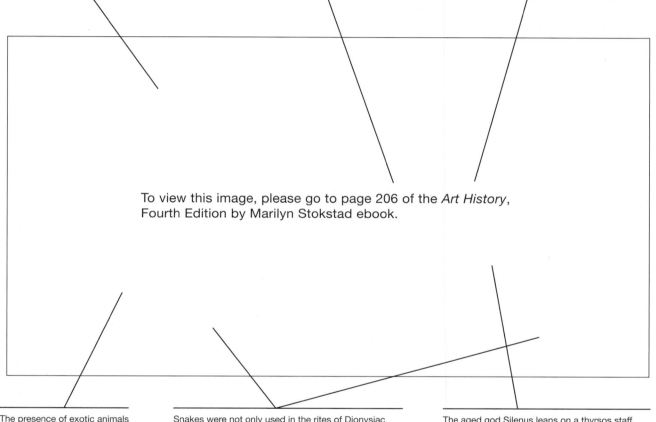

To view this image, please go to page 206 of the *Art History*, Fourth Edition by Marilyn Stokstad ebook.

The presence of exotic animals such as elephants, a lion, a giraffe, and panthers, identifies this scene as Dionysus' triumphant return from India.

Snakes were not only used in the rites of Dionysiac mystery religions; they were powerful symbols of rebirth and phallic fertility, making them especially appropriate in the context of a sarcophagus. Three snakes appear along the groundline of the sculptural frieze.

The aged god Silenus leans on a thyrsos staff, composed of a giant fennel wound with ivy and topped with a pinecone, symbolizing fertility. Dionysus, with whom such staffs were associated, also carries one here as his triumphal scepter.

SEE MORE: View the Closer Look feature for the Sarcophagus with the Indian Triumph of Dionysus
www.myartslab.com

ISLAM, BYZANTIUM, ANCIENT NEAR EAST MONOTHEISM: RELIGIONS OF THE BOOK

THOUGHT PIECE

JOHN 1:1–14
THE WORD BECAME FLESH

[1]In the beginning was the Word, and the Word was with God, and the Word was God. [2]He was with God in the beginning.

[3]Through him all things were made; without him nothing was made that has been made. [4]In him was life, and that life was the light of men. [5]The light shines in the darkness, but the darkness has not understood[b] it.

[6]There came a man who was sent from God; his name was John. [7]He came as a witness to testify concerning that light, so that through him all men might believe. [8]He himself was not the light; he came only as a witness to the light. [9]The true light that gives light to every man was coming into the world.[c]

[10]He was in the world, and though the world was made through him, the world did not recognize him. [11]He came to that which was his own, but his own did not receive him. [12]Yet to all who received him, to those who believed in his name, he gave the right to become children of God— [13]children born not of natural descent,[d] nor of human decision or a husband's will, but born of God.

[14]The Word became flesh and lived for a while among us. We have seen his glory, the glory of the one and only Son,[e] who came from the Father, full of grace and truth.

—*New Testament:* John 1: 1–14

[b]5 Or *overcome*
[c]9 Or *This was the true light that gives light to every man who comes into the world*
[d]13 Greek *of bloods*
[e]14 Or *the Only Begotten*

THE COW
IN THE NAME OF GOD, THE COMPASSIONATE, THE MERCIFUL

ALIF *lām mīm*. This Book is not to be doubted. It is a guide for the righteous, who believe in the unseen and are steadfast in prayer; who give in alms[1] from what We gave them; who believe in what has been revealed to you[2] and what was revealed before you, and have absolute faith in the life to come. These are rightly guided by their Lord; these shall surely triumph.

As for the unbelievers, it is the same whether or not you forewarn them; they will not have faith. God has set a seal upon their hearts and ears; their sight is dimmed and grievous punishment awaits them.

—*Koran,* Surah 2, "The Cow"

[1]Or 'give to the cause'.
[2]Muhammad.

THINGS TO CONSIDER

- What is the significance of the book/scroll/codex form in monotheistic religions?
- What effect did the ban on graven images have on the visual culture of Judaism, Christianity, and Islam?

THE HITTITES OF ANATOLIA

Outside of Mesopotamia, other cultures developed and flourished in the ancient Near East. Anatolia (present-day Turkey) was home to several independent cultures that had resisted Mesopotamian domination, but the Hittites—whose founders had moved into the mountains and plateaus of central Anatolia from the east—were the most powerful among them.

The Hittites established their capital at Hattusha (near present-day Boghazkoy, Turkey) about 1600 BCE, and the city thrived until its destruction about 1200 BCE. Through trade and conquest, the Hittites created an empire that stretched along the coast of the Mediterranean Sea in the area of present-day Syria and Lebanon, bringing them into conflict with the Egyptian Empire, which was expanding into the same region (see Chapter 3). The Hittites also made incursions into Mesopotamia, and their influence was felt throughout the region.

The Hittites may have been the first people to work in iron, which they used for war chariot fittings, weapons, chisels, and hammers for sculptors and masons. They are noted for the artistry of their fine metalwork and for their imposing palace citadels with double walls and fortified gateways, that survive today only in the ruins of archaeological sites. One of the most monumental of these sites consists of the foundations and base walls of the Hittite stronghold at Hattusha, which date to about 1400–1300 BCE. The lower walls were constructed of stone supplied from local quarries, and the upper walls, stairways, and walkways were finished in brick.

The blocks of stone used to frame doorways at Hattusha were decorated in high relief with a variety of guardian figures—some of them 7 feet tall. Some were half-human–half-animal creatures; others were more naturalistically rendered animals like the lions at the **LION GATE (FIG. 5–1)**. Carved from the building stones and consistent with the colossal scale of the wall itself, the lions seem to emerge from the gigantic boulders that form the gate. Despite extreme weathering, the lions have endured over the millennia and still possess a sense of both vigor and permanence.

ASSYRIA

After centuries of struggle among Sumer, Akkad, and Lagash in southern Mesopotamia, a people called the Assyrians rose to dominance in northern Mesopotamia. They began to extend their power by about 1400 BCE, and after about 1000 BCE started to conquer neighboring regions. By the end of the ninth century BCE, the Assyrians controlled most of Mesopotamia, and by the early seventh century BCE they had extended their influence as far west as Egypt. Soon afterward they succumbed to internal weakness and external enemies, and by 600 BCE their empire had collapsed.

Assyrian rulers built huge palaces atop high platforms inside the different fortified cities that served at one time or another as Assyrian capitals. They decorated these palaces with shallow stone reliefs of battle and hunting scenes, of Assyrian victories including presentations of tribute to the king, and of religious imagery.

KALHU

During his reign (883–859 BCE), Assurnasirpal II established his capital at Kalhu (present-day Nimrud, Iraq), on the east bank of the Tigris River, and undertook an ambitious building program. His architects fortified the city with mud-brick walls 5 miles long and 42 feet high, and his engineers constructed a canal that irrigated fields and provided water for the expanded population of the city. According to an inscription commemorating the event, Assurnasirpal gave a banquet for 69,574 people to celebrate the dedication of the new capital in 863 BCE.

To view this image, please go to page 39 of the *Art History*, Fourth Edition by Marilyn Stokstad ebook.

5-1 • LION GATE
Hattusha (near present-day Boghazkoy, Turkey). c. 1400 BCE. Limestone.

To view this image, please go to page 40 of the *Art History*,
Fourth Edition by Marilyn Stokstad ebook.

5-2 • ASSURNASIRPAL II KILLING LIONS

Palace complex of Assurnasirpal II, Kalhu (present-day Nimrud, Iraq). c. 875–860 BCE.
Alabaster, height approx. 39″ (99.1 cm). British Museum, London.

Most of the buildings in Kalhu were made from mud bricks, but limestone and alabaster—more impressive and durable—were used to veneer walls with architectural decoration. Colossal guardian figures flanked the major **portals** (grand entrances, often decorated), and panels covered the walls with scenes in **low relief** (sculpted relief with figures that project only slightly from a recessed background) of the king participating in religious rituals, war campaigns, and hunting expeditions.

THE LION HUNT.   In a vivid lion-hunting scene (FIG. 5–2), Assurnasirpal II stands in a chariot pulled by galloping horses and draws his bow against an attacking lion, advancing from the rear with arrows already protruding from its body. Another expiring beast collapses on the ground under the horses. This was probably a ceremonial hunt, in which the king, protected by men with swords and shields, rode back and forth killing animals as they were released one by one into an enclosed area. The immediacy of this image marks a shift in Mesopotamian art, away from a sense of timeless solemnity, and toward a more dramatic, even emotional, involvement with the event portrayed.

ENEMIES CROSSING THE EUPHRATES TO ESCAPE ASSYRIAN ARCHERS.   In another palace relief, the scene shifts from royal

To view this image, please go to page 40 of the *Art History*,
Fourth Edition by Marilyn Stokstad ebook.

5-3 • RECONSTRUCTION DRAWING OF THE CITADEL AND PALACE COMPLEX OF SARGON II

Dur Sharrukin (present-day Khorsabad, Iraq). c. 721–706 BCE. Courtesy the Oriental Institute of the University of Chicago.

Enemies Crossing the Euphrates to Escape Assyrian Archers

Palace complex of Assurnasirpal II, Kalhu (present-day Nimrud, Iraq). c. 875–860 BCE. Alabaster, height approx. 39″ (99.1 cm). British Museum, London.

These Assyrian archers are outfitted in typical fashion, with protective boots, short "kilts," pointed helmets, and swords, as well as bows and quivers of arrows. Their smaller scale conveys a sense of depth and spatial positioning in this relief, reinforced by the size and placement of the trees.

The detailed landscape setting documents the swirling water of the river, its rocky banks, and the airy environment of the trees, one of which is clearly described as a palm.

The oblique line of the river bank and the overlapping of the swimmers convey a sense of depth receding from the picture plane into pictorial space.

If this is the ruler of the enemy citadel, he seems shocked into powerlessness by the Assyrian invasion. Note the contrast between his lax weapon and those deployed by the archers of the Assyrian vanguard.

To view this image, please go to page 41 of the *Art History*, Fourth Edition by Marilyn Stokstad ebook.

The long robes of the three enemy swimmers signal their high status. They are not ordinary foot soldiers.

The two lower swimmers were clearly taken by surprise. Already engaged in their watery retreat, they are still blowing through "tubes" to inflate their flotation devices, made from sewn animal skins.

This beardless swimmer is probably a eunuch, many of whom served as high officials in ancient Near Eastern courts.

Two figures react to the bleak fate of their arrow-riddled comrades attempting to swim to safety by raising their hands in despair.

SEE MORE: View the Closer Look feature for Enemies Crossing the Euphrates to Escape Assyrian Archers
www.myartslab.com

ceremony to the heat of battle set within a detailed landscape (see "A Closer Look," above). Three of the Assyrian's enemies—two using flotation devices made of inflated animal skins—swim across a raging river, retreating from a vanguard of Assyrian archers who kneel at its banks to launch their assault. The scene evokes a specific event from 878 BCE described in the annals of Assurnasirpal. As the Assyrian king overtook the army of an enemy leader named Kudurru near the modern town of Anu, both leader and soldiers escaped into the Euphrates River in an attempt to save their lives.

DUR SHARRUKIN

Sargon II (ruled 721–706 BCE) built a new Assyrian capital at Dur Sharrukin (present-day Khorsabad, Iraq). On the northwest side of the capital, a walled citadel, or fortress, straddled the city wall (**FIG. 5–3**). Within the citadel, Sargon's **palace complex** (the group of buildings where the ruler governed and resided) stood on a raised, fortified platform about 40 feet high and demonstrates the use of art as political propaganda.

Guarded by two towers, the palace complex was accessible only by a wide ramp leading up from an open square, around

To view this image, please go to page 42 of the *Art History*,
Fourth Edition by Marilyn Stokstad ebook.

5-4 • GUARDIAN FIGURES AT GATE A OF THE CITADEL OF SARGON II DURING ITS EXCAVATION
Dur Sharrukin (present-day Khorsabad, Iraq). c. 721–706 BCE.

which the residences of important government and religious officials were clustered. Beyond the ramp was the main courtyard, with service buildings on the right and temples on the left. The heart of the palace, protected by a reinforced wall with only two small, off-center doors, lay past the main courtyard. Within the inner compound was a second courtyard lined with narrative relief panels showing tribute bearers. Visitors would have waited to see the king in this courtyard that functioned as an audience hall; once granted access to the royal throne room, they would have passed

through a stone gate flanked, like the other gates of citadel and palace **(FIG. 5–4)**, by colossal guardian figures. These guardian figures, known as **lamassus**, combined the bearded head of a man, the powerful body of a lion or bull, the wings of an eagle, and the horned headdress of a god.

In an open space between the palace complex and temple complex at Dur Sharrukin rose a ziggurat declaring the might of Assyria's kings and symbolizing their claim to empire. It probably had seven levels, each about 18 feet high and painted a different

To view this image, please go to page 42 of the *Art History*,
Fourth Edition by Marilyn Stokstad ebook.

5-5 • ASSURBANIPAL AND HIS QUEEN IN THE GARDEN
The Palace at Nineveh (present-day Kuyunjik, Iraq). c. 647 BCE. Alabaster, height approx. 21″ (53.3 cm).
British Museum, London.

TECHNIQUE | Textiles

Textiles were usually a woman's art although men, as shepherds and farmers, often produced the raw materials (wool, flax, and other fibers). And as traveling merchants, men sold or bartered the extra fabrics not needed by the family. Early Assyrian cuneiform tablets preserve correspondence between merchants traveling by caravan and their wives. These astute businesswomen ran the production end of the business back home and often complained to their husbands about late payments and changed orders.

The woman shown spinning in the fragment from Susa is an imposing figure, wearing an elegant hairstyle, many ornaments, and a garment with a patterned border. She sits barefoot and cross-legged on a lion-footed stool covered with sheepskin, spinning thread with a large spindle. A servant stands behind the woman, fanning her, while a fish and six round objects (perhaps fruit) lie on an offering stand in front of her.

The production of textiles is complex. First, fibers gathered from plants (such as flax for linen cloth or hemp for rope) or from animals (wool from sheep, goats, and camels or hair from humans and horses) are cleaned, combed, and sorted. Only then can the fibers be twisted and drawn out under tension—that is, spun—into the long, strong, flexible thread needed for textiles. Weaving is done on a loom. Warp threads are laid out at right angles to weft threads, which are passed over and under the warp. In the earliest vertical looms, warp threads hung from a beam, their tension created either by wrapping them around a lower beam (a tapestry loom) or by tying them to heavy stones. Although weaving was usually a home industry, in palaces and temples slave women staffed large shops, and specialized as spinners, warpers, weavers, and finishers.

Early fiber artists depended on the natural colors of their materials and on natural dyes from the earth, plants, and animals. They combined color and techniques to create a great variety of fiber arts: Egyptians seem to have preferred white linen, elaborately folded and pleated, for their garments. The Minoans of Crete created multicolored patterned fabrics with fancy borders. Greeks excelled in the art of pictorial tapestries. The people of the ancient Near East used woven and dyed patterns and also developed knotted pile (the so-called Persian carpet) and felt (a cloth made of fibers bound by heat and pressure, not by spinning, weaving, or knitting).

To view this image, please go to page 43 of the *Art History*, Fourth Edition by Marilyn Stokstad ebook.

WOMAN SPINNING
Susa (present-day Shush, Iran). c. 8th–7th century BCE. Bitumen compound, 3⅝ × 5⅛″ (9.2 × 13 cm). Musée du Louvre, Paris.

---

color (SEE FIG. 5–3). The four levels still remaining were once white, black, blue, and red. Instead of separate flights of stairs between the levels, a single, squared-off spiral ramp rose continuously along the exterior from the base.

NINEVEH

Assurbanipal (ruled 669–c. 627 BCE), king of the Assyrians three generations after Sargon II, maintained his capital at Nineveh. Like that of Assurnasirpal II two centuries earlier, his palace was decorated with alabaster panels carved with pictorial narratives in low relief. Most show Assurbanipal and his subjects in battle or hunting, but there are occasional scenes of palace life.

An unusually peaceful example shows the king and queen relaxing in a pleasure garden (FIG. 5–5). The king reclines on a couch, and the queen sits in a chair at his feet, while a musician at far left plays diverting music. Three servants arrive from the left with trays of food, while others wave whisks to protect the royal couple from insects. The king has taken off his rich necklace and hung it on his couch, and he has laid aside his weapons—sword, bow, and quiver of arrows—on the table behind him, but this apparently tranquil domestic scene is actually a victory celebration. A grisly trophy, the severed head of his vanquished enemy, hangs upside down from a tree at the far left.

NEO-BABYLONIA

At the end of the seventh century BCE, Assyria was invaded by the Medes, a people from western Iran who were allied with the Babylonians and the Scythians, a nomadic people from northern Asia (present-day Russia and Ukraine). In 612 BCE, the Medes' army captured Nineveh. When the dust had settled, Assyria was no more and the Neo-Babylonians—so named because they recaptured the splendor that had marked Babylon 12 centuries earlier under Hammurabi—controlled a region that stretched from modern Turkey to northern Arabia and from Mesopotamia to the Mediterranean Sea.

The most famous Neo-Babylonian ruler was Nebuchadnezzar II (ruled 605–562 BCE), notorious today for his suppression of the Jews, as recorded in the book of Daniel in the Hebrew Bible, where he may have been confused with the final Neo-Babylonian ruler, Nabonidus. A great patron of architecture, Nebuchadnezzar II built temples dedicated to the Babylonian gods throughout his realm, and transformed Babylon—the cultural, political, and economic hub of his empire—into one of the most splendid cities of its day. Babylon straddled the Euphrates River, its two sections joined by a bridge.

The older, eastern sector of Babylon was traversed by the Processional Way, the route taken by religious processions honoring the city's patron god, Marduk **(FIG. 5–6)**. This street, paved with large stone slabs set in a bed of bitumen, was up to 66 feet wide at some points. It ran from the Euphrates bridge, through the temple district and palaces, and finally through the Ishtar Gate, the ceremonial entrance to the city. The Ishtar Gate's four **crenellated** towers (crenellations are notched walls for military defense) symbolized Babylonian power **(FIG. 5–7)**. Beyond the Ishtar Gate, walls on either side of the route—like the gate itself—were faced with dark blue glazed bricks. The glazed bricks consisted of a film of colored glass placed over the surface of the bricks and fired, a process used since about 1600 BCE. Against that blue background, specially molded turquoise, blue, and gold-colored bricks formed images of striding lions, symbols of the goddess Ishtar as well as the dragons that were associated with Marduk.

PERSIA

In the sixth century BCE, the Persians, a formerly nomadic, Indo-European-speaking people, began to seize power in Mesopotamia. From the region of Parsa, or Persis (present-day Fars, Iran), they established a vast empire. The rulers of this new empire traced their ancestry to a semilegendary Persian king named Achaemenes, and consequently they are known as the Achaemenids.

The dramatic expansion of the Achaemenids began in 559 BCE with the ascension of a remarkable leader, Cyrus II the Great (ruled 559–530 BCE). By the time of his death, the Persian Empire included Babylonia, Media (which stretched across present-day northern Iran through Anatolia), and some of the Aegean islands far to the west. Only the Greeks stood fast against them. When

To view this image, please go to page 44 of the *Art History*, Fourth Edition by Marilyn Stokstad ebook.

5-6 • RECONSTRUCTION DRAWING OF BABYLON IN THE 6TH CENTURY BCE
Courtesy the Oriental Institute of the University of Chicago.

The palace of Nebuchadnezzar II, with its famous Hanging Gardens, can be seen just behind and to the right of the Ishtar Gate, west of the Processional Way. The Marduk Ziggurat looms in the far distance on the east bank of the Euphrates.

To view this image, please go to page 45 of the *Art History*, Fourth Edition by Marilyn Stokstad ebook.

5–7 • ISHTAR GATE AND THRONE ROOM WALL
Reconstructed in a Berlin museum, originally from Babylon (present-day Iraq). c. 575 BCE. Glazed brick, height of gate originally 40′ (12.2 m) with towers rising 100′ (30.5 m). Vorderasiatisches Museum, Staatliche Museen zu Berlin, Preussischer Kulturbesitz.

The Ishtar Gate is decorated with tiers of dragons (with the head and body of a snake, the forelegs of a lion, and the hind legs of a bird of prey) that were sacred to Marduk, and with bulls with blue horns and tails that were associated with Adad, the storm god. Now reconstructed inside a Berlin Museum, it is installed next to a panel from the throne room in Nebuchadnezzar's nearby palace, in which lions walk beneath stylized palm trees.

Darius I (ruled 521–486 BCE) took the throne, he could proclaim: "I am Darius, great King, King of Kings, King of countries, King of this earth."

An able administrator, Darius organized the Persian lands into 20 tribute-paying areas under Persian governors. He often left local rulers in place beneath the governors. This practice, along with a tolerance for diverse native customs and religions, won the Persians the loyalty of many of their subjects. Like many powerful rulers, Darius created palaces and citadels as visible symbols of his authority. He made Susa his first capital and commissioned a 32-acre administrative compound to be built there.

In about 515 BCE, Darius began construction of Parsa, a new capital in the Persian homeland, today known by its Greek name:

Persepolis. It is one of the best-preserved and most impressive ancient sites in the Near East **(FIG. 5–8)**. Darius imported materials, workers, and artists from all over his empire. He even ordered work to be executed in Egypt and transported to his capital. The result was a new multicultural style of art that combined many different traditions—Persian, Mede, Mesopotamian, Egyptian, and Greek.

In Assyrian fashion, the imperial complex at Persepolis was set on a raised platform, 40 feet high and measuring 1,500 by 900 feet, accessible only from a single approach made of wide, shallow steps that could be ascended on horseback. Like Egyptian and Greek cities, it was laid out on a rectangular grid. Darius lived to see the completion only of a treasury, the Apadana (audience hall), and a very small palace for himself. The **APADANA**, set above the rest of the

To view this image, please go to page 46 of the *Art History*, Fourth Edition by Marilyn Stokstad ebook.

5–8 • AIR VIEW OF THE CEREMONIAL COMPLEX, PERSEPOLIS
Iran. 518–c. 460 BCE.

SEE MORE: View a video about Persepolis **www.myartslab.com**

To view this image, please go to page 46 of the *Art History*, Fourth Edition by Marilyn Stokstad ebook.

5–9 • APADANA (AUDIENCE HALL) OF DARIUS AND XERXES
Ceremonial Complex, Persepolis, Iran. 518–c. 460 BCE.

To view this image, please go to page 47 of the *Art History*,
Fourth Edition by Marilyn Stokstad ebook.

5-10 • DARIUS AND XERXES RECEIVING TRIBUTE
Detail of a relief from the stairway leading to the Apadana (ceremonial complex), Persepolis, Iran. 491–486 BCE.
Limestone, height 8′4″ (2.54 m). Courtesy the Oriental Institute of the University of Chicago.

SEE MORE: View a video about the process of sculpting in relief www.myartslab.com

complex on a second terrace **(FIG. 5–9)**, had open porches on three sides and a square hall large enough to hold several thousand people. Darius's son Xerxes I (ruled 485–465 BCE) added a sprawling palace complex for himself, enlarged the treasury building, and began a vast new public reception space, the Hall of 100 Columns.

The central stair of Darius's Apadana displays reliefs of animal combat, tiered ranks of royal guards (the "10,000 Immortals"), and delegations of tribute bearers. Here, lions attack bulls at each side of the Persian generals. Such animal combats (a theme found throughout the Near East) emphasize the ferocity of the leaders and their men. Ranks of warriors cover the walls with repeated patterns and seem ready to defend the palace. The elegant drawing, balanced composition, and sleek modeling of figures reflect the Persians' knowledge of Greek art and perhaps the use of Greek artists. Other reliefs throughout Persepolis depict displays of allegiance or economic prosperity. In one example, once the centerpiece, Darius holds an audience while his son and heir, Xerxes, listens from behind the throne **(FIG. 5–10)**. Such panels would have looked quite different when they were freshly painted in bright colors, with metal objects such as Darius's crown and necklace covered in **gold leaf** (sheets of hammered gold).

At its height, the Persian Empire extended from Africa to India. From Persepolis, Darius in 490 BCE and Xerxes in 480 BCE sent their armies west to conquer Greece, but mainland Greeks successfully resisted the armies of the Achaemenids, preventing them from advancing into Europe. Indeed, it was a Greek who ultimately put an end to their empire. In 334 BCE, Alexander the Great of Macedonia (d. 323 BCE) crossed into Anatolia and swept through Mesopotamia, defeating Darius III and nearly destroying Persepolis in 330 BCE. Although the Achaemenid Empire was at an end, Persia eventually revived, and the Persian style in art continued to influence Greek artists (see Chapter 3) and ultimately became one of the foundations of Islamic art.

THINK ABOUT IT

5.1 Discuss the development of relief sculpture in the ancient Near East. Choose two specific examples, one from the Sumerian period and one from the Assyrian period, and explain how symbols and stories are combined to express ideas that were important to these two cultures.

5.2 Discuss how precious materials are used in "The Great Lyre with bull's head." What are some likely motivations for employing these materials in this work?

5.3 Select two rulers discussed in this chapter and explain how each preserved his legacy through commissioned works of art and/or architecture.

5.4 What are the distinctive features of the Sumerian ziggurat and what led to its development?

PRACTICE MORE: Compose answers to these questions, get flashcards for images and terms, and review chapter material with quizzes www.myartslab.com

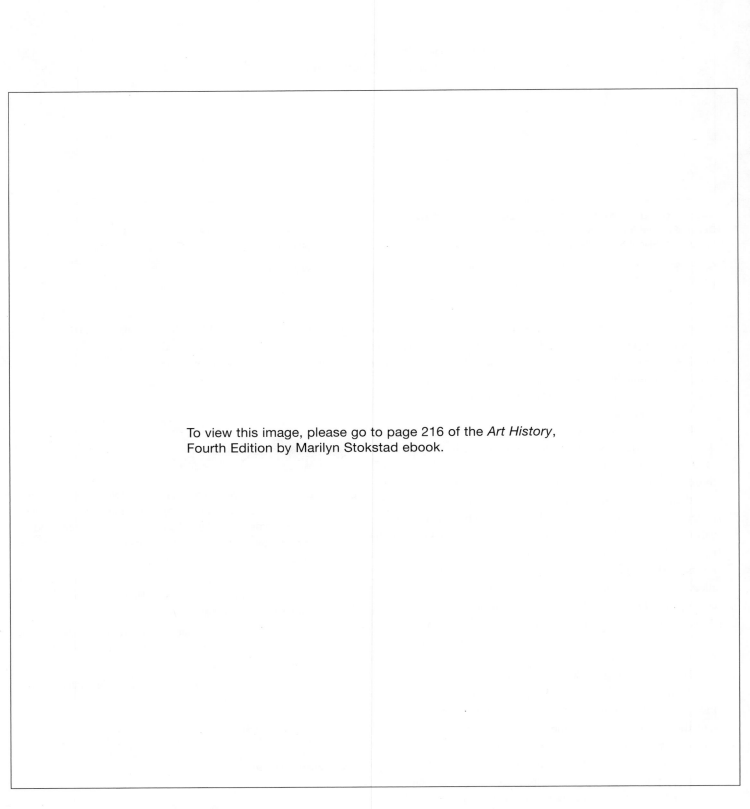

To view this image, please go to page 216 of the *Art History*, Fourth Edition by Marilyn Stokstad ebook.

5–11 • DAVID BATTLING GOLIATH   One of the "David Plates," made in Constantinople. 629–630 CE. Silver, diameter 19⅞" (49.4 cm). Metropolitan Museum of Art, New York.

JEWISH, EARLY CHRISTIAN, AND BYZANTINE ART

The robust figures on this huge silver plate (FIG. 5–11) enact three signature episodes in the youthful hero David's combat with the Philistine giant Goliath (I Samuel 17:41–51). In the upper register, David—easily identified not only by his youth but also by the prominent halo as the "good guy" in all three scenes—and Goliath challenge each other on either side of a seated Classical personification of the stream that will be the source of the stones David will use in the ensuing battle. The confrontation itself appears in the middle, in a broad figural frieze whose size signals its primary importance. Goliath is most notable here for his superior armaments—helmet, spear, sword, and an enormous protective shield. At the bottom, David, stones and slingshot flung behind him, consummates his victory by severing the head of his defeated foe, whose imposing weapons and armor are scattered uselessly behind him.

It may be surprising to see a Judeo–Christian subject portrayed in a style that was developed for the exploits of Classical heroes, but this mixture of traditions is typical of the eclecticism characterizing the visual arts as the Christianized Roman world became the Byzantine Empire. Patrons saw no conflict between the artistic principles of the pagan past and the Christian teaching undergirding their imperial present. To them, this Jewish subject, created for a Christian patron in a pagan style, would have attracted notice only because of its sumptuousness and its artistic virtuosity.

This was one of nine "David Plates" unearthed in Cyprus in 1902. Control stamps—guaranteeing the purity of the material, much like the stamps of "sterling" that appear on silver today—date them to the reign of the Byzantine emperor Heraclius (r. 613–641 CE). Displayed in the home of their owners, they were visual proclamations of wealth, but also of education and refined taste, just like collections of art and antiques in our own day. A constellation of iconographic and historical factors allows us to uncover a subtler message, however. For the original owners, the single combat of David and Goliath might have recalled a situation involving their own emperor and enemies.

The reign of Heraclius was marked by war with the Sassanian Persians. A decisive moment in the final campaign of 628–629 CE occurred when Heraclius himself stepped forward for single combat with the Persian general Razatis, and the emperor prevailed, presaging Byzantine victory. Some contemporaries referred to Heraclius as a new David. Is it possible that the set of David Plates was produced for the emperor to offer as a diplomatic gift to one of his aristocratic allies, who subsequently took them to Cyprus? Perhaps the owners later buried them for safekeeping—like the early silver platter from Mildenhall (SEE FIG. 3–98)—where they awaited discovery at the beginning of the twentieth century.

LEARN ABOUT IT

5.5 Investigate how aspects of Jewish and Early Christian art developed from the artistic traditions of the Roman world.

5.6 Interpret how Early Christian and Byzantine artists used narrative and iconic imagery to convey the foundations of the Christian faith for those already initiated into the life of the Church.

5.7 Analyze the connection between form and function in buildings created for worship.

5.8 Assess the central role of images in the devotional practices of the Byzantine world and explore the reasons for and impact of the brief interlude of iconoclasm.

5.9 Trace the growing Byzantine interest in conveying human emotions and representing human situations when visualizing sacred stories.

HEAR MORE: Listen to an audio file of your chapter **www.myartslab.com**

JEWS, CHRISTIANS, AND MUSLIMS

Three religions that arose in the Near East dominate the spiritual life of the Western world today: Judaism, Christianity, and Islam. All three are monotheistic—believing that the same God of Abraham created and rules the universe, and hears the prayers of the faithful. Jews believe that God made a covenant, or pact, with their ancestors, the Hebrews, and that they are God's chosen people. They await the coming of a savior, the Messiah, "the anointed one." Christians believe that Jesus of Nazareth was that Messiah (the name Christ is derived from the Greek term meaning "Messiah"). They believe that, in Jesus, God took human form, preached among men and women, suffered execution, then rose from the dead and ascended to heaven after establishing the Christian Church under the leadership of the apostles (his closest disciples). Muslims, while accepting the Hebrew prophets and Jesus as divinely inspired, believe Muhammad to be the last and greatest prophet of God (Allah), the Messenger of God through whom Islam was revealed some six centuries after Jesus' lifetime.

All three are "religions of the book," that is, they have written records of God's will and words: the Hebrew Bible; the Christian Bible, which includes the Hebrew Bible as its Old Testament as well as the Christian New Testament; and the Muslim Qur'an, believed to be the Word of God as revealed in Arabic directly to Muhammad through the archangel Gabriel.

Both Judaism and Christianity existed within the Roman Empire, along with various other religions devoted to the worship of many gods. The variety of religious buildings excavated in present-day Syria at the abandoned Roman outpost of Dura-Europos (see "Dura-Europos," page 321) represents the cosmopolitan religious character of Roman society in the second and third centuries. The settlement—destroyed in 256 CE—included a Jewish house-synagogue, a Christian house-church, shrines to the Persian cults of Mithras and Zoroaster, and temples to Greek and Roman gods, including Zeus and Artemis.

EARLY JEWISH ART

The Jewish people trace their origin to a Semitic people called the Hebrews, who lived in the land of Canaan. Canaan, known from the second century CE by the Roman name Palestine, was located along the eastern edge of the Mediterranean Sea (MAP 5–1). According to the Torah, the first five books of the Hebrew Bible, God promised the patriarch Abraham that Canaan would be a homeland for the Jewish people (Genesis 17:8), a belief that remains important for some Jews to this day.

Jewish settlement of Canaan probably began sometime in the second millennium BCE. According to Exodus, the second book of the Torah, the prophet Moses led the Hebrews out of slavery in Egypt to the promised land of Canaan. At one crucial point during the journey, Moses climbed alone to the top of Mount Sinai, where God gave him the Ten Commandments, the cornerstone of Jewish law. The commandments, inscribed on tablets, were kept in a gold-covered wooden box, the Ark of the Covenant.

Jewish law forbade the worship of idols, a prohibition that often made the representational arts—especially sculpture in the round—suspect. Nevertheless, artists working for Jewish patrons depicted both symbolic and narrative Jewish subjects, and they looked to both Near Eastern and Classical Greek and Roman art for inspiration.

THE FIRST TEMPLE IN JERUSALEM.   In the tenth century BCE, the Jewish king Solomon built a temple in Jerusalem to house the Ark of the Covenant. According to the Hebrew Bible (2 Chronicles 2–7),

To view this image, please go to page 218 of the *Art History*, Fourth Edition by Marilyn Stokstad ebook.

5-12 • MENORAHS AND ARK OF THE COVENANT
Wall painting in a Jewish catacomb, Villa Torlonia, Rome. 3rd century. 3'11" × 5'9" (1.19 × 1.8 m).

The menorah form probably derives from the ancient Near Eastern Tree of Life, symbolizing for the Jewish people both the end of exile and the paradise to come.

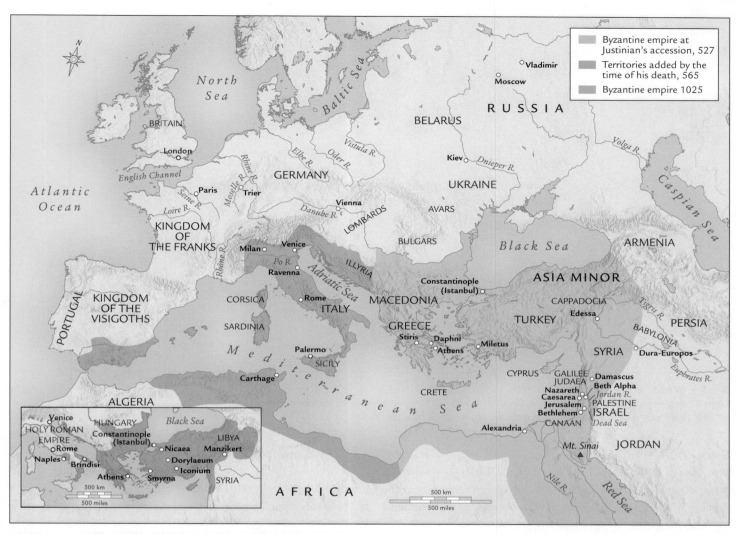

MAP 5–1 • THE LATE ROMAN AND BYZANTINE WORLD

The eastern shores of the Mediterranean, birthplace of Judaism and Christianity, were the focal point of the Byzantine Empire. It expanded further west under the Emperor Justinian, though by 1025 CE it had contracted again to the east.

he sent to nearby Phoenicia for cedar, cypress, and sandalwood, and for a superb construction supervisor. Later known as the First Temple, it was the spiritual center of Jewish life. Biblical texts describe courtyards, two bronze **pillars** (large, free-standing architectural forms), an entrance hall, a main hall, and the Holy of Holies, the innermost chamber that housed the Ark and its guardian cherubim, or attendant angels.

In 586 BCE, the Babylonians, under King Nebuchadnezzar II, conquered Jerusalem. They destroyed the Temple, exiled the Jews, and carried off the Ark of the Covenant. When Cyrus the Great of Persia conquered Babylonia in 539 BCE, he permitted the Jews to return to their homeland (Ezra 1:1–4) and rebuild the Temple, which became known as the Second Temple. When Canaan became part of the Roman Empire, Herod the Great (king of Judaea, 37–34 BCE) restored the Second Temple. In 70 CE, Roman forces led by the general and future emperor Titus

destroyed and looted the Second Temple and all of Jerusalem, a campaign the Romans commemorated on the Arch of Titus (SEE FIG. 3–74). The site of the Second Temple, the Temple Mount, is also an Islamic holy site, the Haram al-Sharif, and is now occupied by the shrine called the Dome of the Rock (SEE FIGS. 5–56, 5–57, 5–58).

JEWISH CATACOMB ART IN ROME. Most of the earliest surviving examples of Jewish art date from the Hellenistic and Roman periods. Six Jewish **catacombs** (underground cemeteries), discovered on the outskirts of Rome and in use from the first to fourth centuries CE, display wall paintings with Jewish themes. In one example, from the third century CE, two **menorahs** (seven-branched lamps), flank the long-lost **ARK OF THE COVENANT (FIG. 5–12)**. The continuing representation of the menorah, one of the precious objects looted from the Second Temple, kept the memory of the lost Jewish treasures alive.

To view this image, please go to page 220 of the *Art History*,
Fourth Edition by Marilyn Stokstad ebook.

5-13 • WALL WITH TORAH NICHE
From a house-synagogue, Dura-Europos, Syria. 244–245 CE. Tempera on plaster, section approx.
40′ (12.19 m) long. Reconstructed in the National Museum, Damascus, Syria.

SYNAGOGUES.   Judaism has long emphasized religious learning. Jews gather in synagogues for study of the Torah—considered a form of worship. A synagogue can be any large room where the Torah scrolls are kept and read; it was also the site of communal social gatherings. Some synagogues were located in private homes or in buildings originally constructed like homes. The first Dura-Europos synagogue consisted of an assembly hall, a separate alcove for women, and a courtyard. After a remodeling of the building, completed in 244–245 CE, men and women shared the hall,

and residential rooms were added. Two architectural features distinguished the assembly hall: a bench along its walls and a niche for the Torah scrolls **(FIG. 5–13)**.

Scenes from Jewish history and the story of Moses, as recorded in Exodus, unfold in a continuous visual narrative around the room, employing the Roman tradition of epic historical presentation (SEE FIG. 3–84). In the scene of **THE CROSSING OF THE RED SEA (FIG. 5–14)**, Moses appears twice to signal sequential moments in the dramatic narrative. To the left he leans toward the army of Pharaoh

To view this image, please go to page 220 of the *Art History*,
Fourth Edition by Marilyn Stokstad ebook.

5-14 • THE CROSSING OF THE RED SEA
Detail of a wall painting from a house-synagogue, Dura-Europos, Syria. 244–245 CE. National Museum, Damascus.

The Mosaic Floor of the Beth Alpha Synagogue

by Marianos and Hanina. Ritual Objects, Celestial Diagram, and Sacrifice of Isaac. Galilee, Israel. 6th century CE.

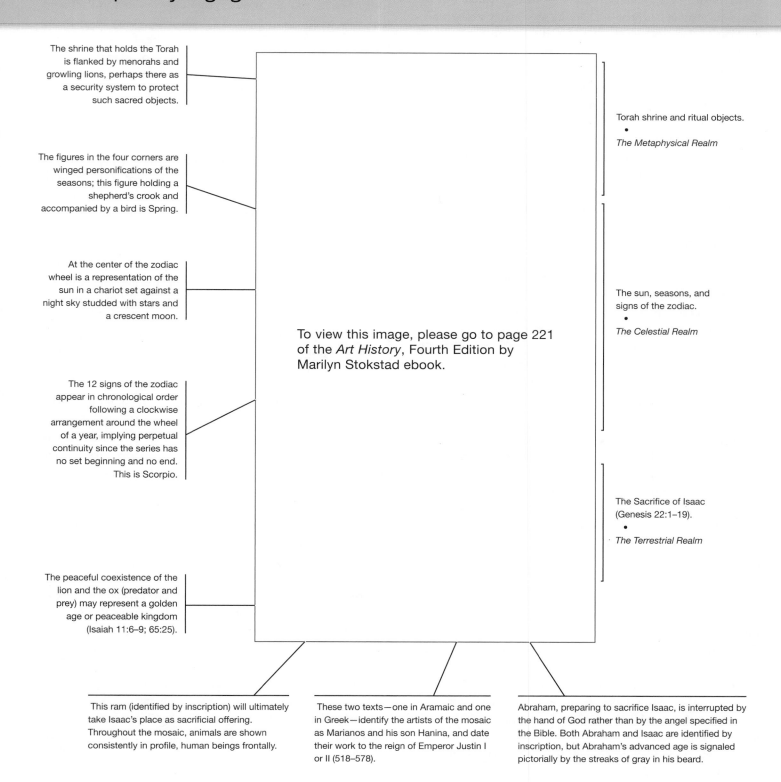

The shrine that holds the Torah is flanked by menorahs and growling lions, perhaps there as a security system to protect such sacred objects.

The figures in the four corners are winged personifications of the seasons; this figure holding a shepherd's crook and accompanied by a bird is Spring.

At the center of the zodiac wheel is a representation of the sun in a chariot set against a night sky studded with stars and a crescent moon.

The 12 signs of the zodiac appear in chronological order following a clockwise arrangement around the wheel of a year, implying perpetual continuity since the series has no set beginning and no end. This is Scorpio.

The peaceful coexistence of the lion and the ox (predator and prey) may represent a golden age or peaceable kingdom (Isaiah 11:6–9; 65:25).

To view this image, please go to page 221 of the *Art History*, Fourth Edition by Marilyn Stokstad ebook.

Torah shrine and ritual objects.
*
The Metaphysical Realm

The sun, seasons, and signs of the zodiac.
*
The Celestial Realm

The Sacrifice of Isaac (Genesis 22:1–19).
*
The Terrestrial Realm

This ram (identified by inscription) will ultimately take Isaac's place as sacrificial offering. Throughout the mosaic, animals are shown consistently in profile, human beings frontally.

These two texts—one in Aramaic and one in Greek—identify the artists of the mosaic as Marianos and his son Hanina, and date their work to the reign of Emperor Justin I or II (518–578).

Abraham, preparing to sacrifice Isaac, is interrupted by the hand of God rather than by the angel specified in the Bible. Both Abraham and Isaac are identified by inscription, but Abraham's advanced age is signaled pictorially by the streaks of gray in his beard.

SEE MORE: View the Closer Look feature for the Mosaic Floor of the Beth Alpha Synagogue **www.myartslab.com**

marching along the path that had been created for the Hebrews by God's miraculous parting of the waters, but at the right, wielding his authoritative staff, he returns the waters over the Egyptian soldiers to prevent them from pursuing his followers. Over both scenes hovers a large hand, representing God's presence in both miracles—the parting and the unparting—using a symbol that will also be frequent in Christian art. Hieratic scale makes it clear who is the hero in this two-part narrative, but the clue to his identity is provided only by the context of the story, which observers would have already known.

In addition to house-synagogues, Jews built meeting places designed on the model of the ancient Roman basilica. A typical basilica synagogue had a central nave; an aisle on both sides, separated from the nave by a line of columns; a semicircular apse with Torah shrine in the wall facing Jerusalem; and perhaps an atrium and porch, or **narthex** (vestibule). The small, fifth-century CE synagogue at Beth Alpha—discovered between the Gilboa mountains and the River Jordan by farmers in 1928—fits well into this pattern, with a three-nave interior, vestibule, and courtyard. Like some other very grand synagogues, it also has a mosaic floor, in this case a later addition from the sixth century. Most of the floor decoration is geometric in design, but in the central nave there are three complex panels full of figural compositions and symbols (see "A Closer Look," page 319) created using 21 separate colors of stone and glass tesserae. The images of ritual objects, a celestial diagram of the zodiac, and a scene of Abraham's near-sacrifice of Isaac, bordered by strips of foliate and geometric ornament, draw on both Classical and Near Eastern pictorial traditions.

EARLY CHRISTIAN ART

Christians believe in one God manifest in three persons—the Trinity of Creator-Father (God), Son (Jesus Christ), and Holy Spirit—and that Jesus was the Son of God by a human mother, the Virgin Mary. At the age of 30, Jesus gathered a group of followers, male and female; he performed miracles of healing and preached love of God and neighbor, the sanctity of social justice, the forgiveness of sins, and the promise of life after death. Christian belief holds that, after his ministry on Earth, Jesus was executed by crucifixion, and after three days rose from the dead.

THE CHRISTIAN BIBLE. The Christian Bible is divided into two parts: the Old Testament (the Hebrew Bible) and the New Testament. The life and teachings of Jesus of Nazareth were recorded between about 70 and 100 CE in New Testament Gospels attributed to the four evangelists (from the Greek *evangelion*, meaning "good news"): Matthew, Mark, Luke, and John. The order was set by St. Jerome, an early Church Father who made a translation of the books from Greek into Latin.

In addition to the four Gospels, the New Testament includes the Acts of the Apostles and the Epistles, 21 letters of advice and encouragement written to Christian communities in Greece, Asia Minor, and other parts of the Roman Empire. The final book is Revelation (Apocalypse), a series of enigmatic visions and prophecies concerning the eventual triumph of God at the end of the world, written about 95 CE.

THE EARLY CHURCH. Jesus limited his ministry primarily to Jews; it was his apostles, as well as later followers such as Paul, who took his teachings to gentiles (non-Jews). Despite sporadic persecutions, Christianity persisted and spread throughout the Roman Empire. The government formally recognized the religion in 313, and Christianity grew rapidly during the fourth century. As well-educated, upper-class Romans joined the Christian Church, they established an increasingly elaborate organizational structure along with ever-more complicated rituals and doctrine.

Christian communities became organized by geographic units, called dioceses, along the lines of Roman provincial governments. Senior church officials called bishops served as governors of dioceses made up of smaller units, parishes, headed by priests. A bishop's church is a **cathedral**, a word derived from the Latin *cathedra*, which means "chair" but took on the meaning of "bishop's throne."

Communal Christian worship focused on the central "mystery," or miracle, of the Incarnation of God in Jesus Christ and the promise of salvation. At its core was the ritual consumption of bread and wine, identified as the Body and Blood of Christ, which Jesus had inaugurated at the Last Supper, a Passover seder meal with his disciples just before his crucifixion. Around these acts developed an elaborate religious ceremony, or liturgy, called the **Eucharist** (also known as Holy Communion or the Mass).

The earliest Christians gathered to worship in private apartments or houses, or in buildings constructed after domestic models such as the third-century church-house excavated at Dura-Europos (see "Dura-Europos," opposite). As their rites became more ritualized and complicated, however, Christians developed special buildings—churches and baptisteries—as well as specialized ritual equipment. They also began to use art to visualize their most important stories and ideas (see "Narrative and Iconic," page 322). The earliest surviving Christian art dates to the early third century and derives its styles and its imagery from Jewish and Roman visual traditions. In this process, known as **syncretism**, artists assimilate images from other traditions and give them new meanings. The borrowings can be unconscious or quite deliberate. For example, **orant** figures—worshipers with arms outstretched in prayer—can be pagan, Jewish, or Christian, depending on the context in which they occur. Perhaps the best-known syncretic image is the Good Shepherd. In pagan art, he was Apollo, or Hermes the shepherd, or Orpheus among the animals, or a personification of philanthropy. For Early Christians, he became the Good Shepherd of the Psalms (Psalm 23) and the Gospels (Matthew 18:12–14, John 10:11–16). Such images, therefore, do not have a stable meaning, but are associated with the meaning(s) that a particular viewer brings to them. They remind rather than instruct.

Our understanding of buildings used for worship by third-century Jews and Christians was greatly enhanced—even revolutionized—by the spectacular discoveries made in the 1930s while excavating the Roman military garrison and border town of Dura-Europos (in modern Syria). In 256, threatened by the Parthians attacking from the east, residents of Dura built a huge earthwork mound around their town in an attempt to protect themselves from the invading armies. In the process—since they were located on the city's margins right against its defensive stone wall—the houses used by Jews and Christians as places of worship were buried under the earthwork perimeter. In spite of this enhanced fortification, the Parthians conquered Dura-Europos. But since the victors never unearthed the submerged margins of the city, an intact Jewish house-synagogue and Christian house-church remained underground awaiting the explorations of modern archaeologists.

We have already seen the extensive strip narratives flanking the Torah shrine in the house-synagogue (SEE FIG. 5–13). The discovery of this expansive pictorial decoration contradicted a long-held scholarly belief that Jews of this period avoided figural decoration of any sort, in conformity to Mosaic law (Exodus 20:4). And a few blocks down the street that ran along the city wall, a typical Roman house built around a central courtyard held another surprise. Only a discreet red cross above the door distinguished it from the other houses on its block, but the arrangement of the interior clearly documents its use as a Christian place of worship. A large assembly hall that could seat 60–70 people sits on one side of the courtyard, and across from it is a smaller but extensively decorated room with a water tank set aside for baptism, the central rite of Christian initiation (FIG. A). Along the walls were scenes from Christ's miracles and a monumental portrayal of women visiting his tomb about to discover his resurrection (below). Above the baptismal basin is a **lunette** (semicircular wall section) featuring the Good Shepherd with his flock, but also including at lower left diminutive figures of Adam and Eve covering themselves in shame after their sinful disobedience (FIG. B). Even this early in Christian art, sacred spaces were decorated with pictures proclaiming the theological meaning of the rituals they housed. In this painting, Adam and Eve's fall from grace is juxtaposed with a larger image of the Good Shepherd (representing Jesus) who came to Earth to care for and guide his sheep (Christian believers) toward redemption and eternal life—a message that was especially appropriate juxtaposed with the rite of Christian baptism, which signaled the converts' passage from sin to salvation.

To view this image, please go to page 223 of the *Art History*, Fourth Edition by Marilyn Stokstad ebook.

A. MODEL OF WALLS AND BAPTISMAL FONT
Baptistery of a Christian house-church, Dura-Europos, Syria. Before 256. Fresco. Yale University Art Gallery, New Haven, Connecticut.

To view this image, please go to page 223 of the *Art History*, Fourth Edition by Marilyn Stokstad ebook.

B. THE GOOD SHEPHERD WITH ADAM AND EVE AFTER THE FALL
Detail of lunette painting above.

Narrative and Iconic

In this Roman catacomb painting (scene at left), Peter, like Moses before him, strikes a rock and water flows from it. Imprisoned in Rome after the arrest of Jesus, Peter converted his fellow prisoners and jailers to Christianity, but he needed water with which to baptize them. Miraculously a spring gushed forth at the touch of his staff.

In the star-studded heavens painted on the vault of this chamber floats the face of Christ, flanked by the first and last letters of the Greek alphabet, alpha and omega. Here Christ takes on the guise not of the youthful teacher or miracle-worker seen so often in Early Christian art, but of a Greek philosopher, with long beard and hair. The halo of light around his head indicates his importance and his divinity, a symbol appropriated from the conventions of Roman imperial art, where haloes often appear around the heads of emperors.

These two catacomb paintings represent two major directions of Christian art—the narrative and the iconic. The **narrative image**

recounts an event drawn from St. Peter's life—striking the rock for water—which in turn evokes the establishment of the Church as well as the essential Christian rite of baptism. The **iconic image**—Christ's face flanked by alpha and omega—offers a tangible expression of an intangible concept. The letters signify the beginning and end of time, and, combined with the image of Christ, symbolically represent not a story, but an idea—the everlasting dominion of the heavenly Christ.

Throughout the history of Christian art these two tendencies will be apparent—the narrative urge to tell a good story, whose moral or theological implications often have instructional or theological value, and the desire to create iconic images that symbolize the core concepts and values of the developing religious tradition. In both cases, the works of art take on meaning only in relation to viewers' stored knowledge of Christian stories and beliefs.

To view this image, please go to page 224 of the *Art History*, Fourth Edition by Marilyn Stokstad ebook.

CUBICULUM OF LEONIS, CATACOMB OF COMMODILLA
Near Rome. Late 4th century.

In the niche seen on the right, two early Roman Christian martyrs, Felix (d. 274) and Adauctus (d. 303) flank a youthful, beardless Jesus, who holds a book emphasizing his role as teacher. By including Peter and Roman martyrs in the chamber's decoration, the early Christians, who dug this catacomb as a place to bury their dead, emphasized the importance of their city in Christian history.

CATACOMB PAINTINGS.   Christians, like Jews, used catacombs for burials and funeral ceremonies, not as places of worship. In the Christian Catacomb of Commodilla, dating from the fourth century, long rectangular niches in the walls, called *loculi*, each held two or three bodies. Affluent families created small rooms, or **cubicula** (singular, *cubiculum*), off the main passages to house sarcophagi (see "Narrative and Iconic," above). The *cubicula* were

hewn out of tufa, soft volcanic rock, then plastered and painted with imagery related to their owners' religious beliefs. The finest Early Christian catacomb paintings resemble murals in houses such as those preserved at Rome and Pompeii.

One fourth-century Roman catacomb contained remains, or relics, of SS. Peter and Marcellinus, two third-century Christians martyred for their faith. Here, the ceiling of a *cubiculum* is

To view this image, please go to page 225 of the *Art History*,
Fourth Edition by Marilyn Stokstad ebook.

5-15 • THE GOOD SHEPHERD, ORANTS, AND THE STORY OF JONAH
Painted ceiling of the Catacomb of SS. Peter and Marcellinus, Rome. Late 3rd–early 4th century.

partitioned by a central **medallion**, or round compartment, and four **lunettes**, semicircular framed by arches **(FIG. 5–15)**. At the center is a Good Shepherd, whose pose has roots in Classical sculpture. In its new context, the image was a reminder of Jesus' promise "I am the good shepherd. A good shepherd lays down his life for the sheep" (John 10:11).

The semicircular compartments surrounding the Good Shepherd tell the story of Jonah and the sea monster from the Hebrew Bible (Jonah 1–2), in which God caused Jonah to be thrown overboard, swallowed by the monster, and released, repentant and unscathed, three days later. Christians reinterpreted this story as a parable of Christ's death and resurrection—and hence of the everlasting life awaiting true believers—and it was a popular subject in Christian catacombs. On the left, Jonah is thrown from the boat; on the right, the monster spits him up; and at the center, Jonah reclines in the shade of a vine, a symbol of paradise. Orant figures stand between the lunettes, presumably images of the faithful Christians who were buried here.

SCULPTURE. Early Christian sculpture before the fourth century is even rarer than painting. What survives is mainly sarcophagi and small statues and reliefs. A remarkable set of small marble figures, discovered in the 1960s and probably made in third-century Asia Minor, features a gracious **GOOD SHEPHERD** **(FIG. 5–16)**. Because it was found with sculptures depicting Jonah—as we have already seen, a popular Early Christian theme—it is probably from a Christian home.

5-16 • THE GOOD SHEPHERD
Eastern Mediterranean, probably Anatolia (Turkey). Second half of the 3rd century. Marble, height 19¾″ (50.2 cm), width 16″ (15.9 cm). Cleveland Museum of Art. John L. Severance Fund, 1965.241

To view this image, please go to page 225 of the *Art History*, Fourth Edition by Marilyn Stokstad ebook.

IMPERIAL CHRISTIAN ARCHITECTURE AND ART

When Constantine issued the Edict of Milan in 313, granting all people in the Roman Empire freedom to worship whatever god they wished, Christianity and Christian art and architecture entered a new phase. Sophisticated philosophical and ethical systems developed, incorporating many ideas from Greek and Roman pagan thought. Church scholars edited and commented on the Bible, and the papal secretary who would become St. Jerome (c. 347–420) undertook a new translation from Hebrew and Greek versions into Latin, the language of the Western Church. The so-called Vulgate (from the same root as the word "vulgar," the Latin *vulgaris*, meaning "common" or "popular") became the official version of the Bible.

ARCHITECTURE

The developing Christian community had special architectural needs. Greek temples had served as the house and treasury of the gods, forming a backdrop for ceremonies that took place at altars in the open air. In Christianity, an entire community gathered inside a building to worship. Christians also needed places or buildings for activities such as the initiation of new members, private prayer, and burials. From the age of Constantine, pagan basilicas provided the model for congregational churches, and tombs provided a model for baptisteries and martyrs' shrines (see "Longitudinal-Plan and Central-Plan Churches," page 326).

OLD ST. PETER'S CHURCH.   Constantine also ordered the construction of a large new basilica to mark the place where Christians believed St. Peter was buried (see "Longitudinal-Plan and Central-Plan Churches," page 326, FIG. A). Our knowledge of what is now called Old St. Peter's (it was destroyed and replaced

To view this image, please go to page 226 of the *Art History*, Fourth Edition by Marilyn Stokstad ebook.

5–17 • Jacopo Grimaldi INTERIOR OF OLD ST. PETER'S
1619 copy of an earlier drawing. Vatican Library, Rome. MS Barberini Lat. 2733, fols. 104v–105r

EXPLORE MORE: Gain insight from a primary source related to Old St. Peter's www.myartslab.com

by a new building in the sixteenth century) is based on written descriptions, drawings made before and while it was being dismantled (FIG. 5–17), the study of other churches inspired by it, and modern archaeological excavations at the site.

Old St. Peter's included architectural elements in an arrangement that has characterized Christian basilica churches ever since. A narthex across the width of the building provided a place for people who had not yet been baptized. Five doorways—a large, central portal into the nave and two portals on each side—gave access to the church. Columns supporting an entablature lined the nave, forming what is called a nave colonnade. Running parallel to the nave colonnade on each side was another row of columns that

To view this image, please go to page 226 of the *Art History*, Fourth Edition by Marilyn Stokstad ebook.

5–18 • CHURCH OF SANTA SABINA
Rome. Exterior view from the southeast. c. 422–432.

SEE MORE: Click the Google Earth link for Santa Sabina www.myartslab.com

To view this image, please go to page 227 of the *Art History*, Fourth Edition by Marilyn Stokstad ebook.

5–19 • INTERIOR, CHURCH OF SANTA SABINA
Rome. View from the south aisle near the sanctuary toward the entrance. c. 422–432.

created double side aisles; these columns supported round arches rather than an entablature. The roofs of both nave and aisles were supported by wooden rafters. Sarcophagi and tombs lined the side aisles. At the apse end of the nave, Constantine's architects added an innovative transept—a perpendicular hall crossing in front of the apse. This area provided additional space for the large number of clergy serving the church, and it also accommodated pilgrims visiting the tomb of St. Peter. Old St. Peter's could hold at least 14,000 worshipers, and it remained the largest church in Christendom until the eleventh century.

SANTA SABINA. Old St. Peter's is gone, but the church of Santa Sabina in Rome, constructed by Bishop Peter of Illyria (a region in the Balkan peninsula) a century later, between about 422 and 432, appears much as it did in the fifth century (**FIGS. 5–18, 5–19**). The basic elements of the Early Christian basilica church are clearly visible here, inside and out: a nave lit by clerestory windows, flanked by single side aisles, and ending in a rounded apse.

Santa Sabina's exterior is simple brickwork. In contrast, the church's interior displays a wealth of marble veneer and 24 fluted marble columns with Corinthian capitals reused from a second-century pagan building. (Material reused from earlier buildings is known as *spolia*, Latin for "spoils.") The columns support round arches, creating a nave arcade, in contrast to the straight rather than arching nave colonnade in Old St. Peter's. The spandrels—above the columns and between the arches—are inlaid with marble images of the chalice (wine cup) and paten (bread plate)—essential equipment for the Eucharistic rite that took place at the altar. In such basilicas, the blind wall between the arcade and the clerestory

typically had paintings or mosaics with biblical scenes, but here the decoration of the upper walls is lost.

SANTA COSTANZA. Central-plan Roman buildings, with vertical (rather than longitudinal) axes, served as models for Christian tombs, martyrs' churches, and baptisteries (see "Longitudinal-Plan and Central-Plan Churches," page 326). One of the earliest surviving central-plan Christian buildings is the mausoleum of Constantina, daughter of Constantine. Her tomb was built outside the walls of Rome just before 350 (**FIG. 5–20**), and it was consecrated as a church

5–20 • CHURCH OF SANTA COSTANZA
Rome. c. 350. View from ambulatory into rotunda.

The forms of Early Christian buildings were based on two Roman prototypes: rectangular basilicas (SEE FIGS. 3–79, 3–96) and circular or squared structures—including rotundas like the Pantheon (SEE FIGS. 3–84, 3–85). As in the basilica of Old St. Peter's in Rome (FIG. A), **longitudinal-plan** churches are characterized by a forecourt, the atrium, leading to an entrance porch, the **narthex**, which spans one of the building's short ends. Doorways—known collectively as the church's portals—lead from the narthex into a long, congregational area called a nave. Rows of columns separate the high-ceilinged nave from one or two lower **aisles** on either side. The nave can be lit by windows along its upper level just under the ceiling, called a **clerestory**, that rises above the side aisles' roofs. At the opposite end of the nave from the narthex is a semicircular projection, the **apse**. The apse functions as the building's focal point where the altar, raised on a platform, is located. Sometimes there is also a **transept**, a wing that

crosses the nave in front of the apse, making the building T-shape. When additional space (a liturgical choir) comes between the transept and the apse, the plan is known as a Latin cross.

Central-plan buildings were first used by Christians, like their pagan Roman forebears, as tombs. Central planning was also employed for baptisteries (where Christians "died"—giving up their old life—and were reborn as believers), and churches dedicated to martyrs (e.g. San Vitale, SEE FIG. 5–30), often built directly over their tombs. Like basilicas, central-plan churches can have an atrium, a narthex, and an apse. But instead of the longitudinal axis of basilican churches, which draws worshipers forward along a line from the entrance toward the apse, central-plan buildings, such as the Mausoleum of Constantina—rededicated in 1256 as the church of Santa Costanza (FIG. B)—have a more vertical axis, from the center up through the dome, which may have functioned as a symbolic "vault of heaven."

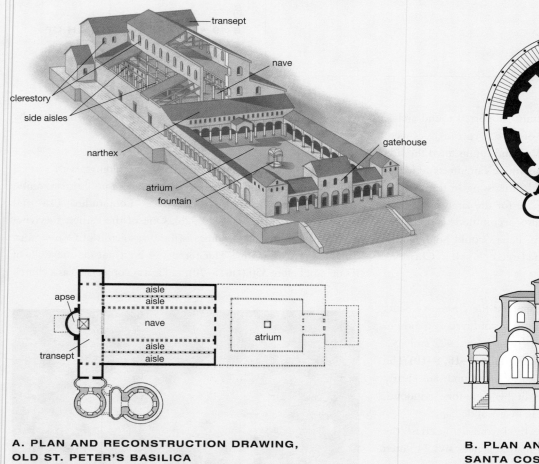

A. PLAN AND RECONSTRUCTION DRAWING, OLD ST. PETER'S BASILICA
Rome. c. 320–327; atrium added in later 4th century.
Approx. 394' (120 m) long and 210' (64 m) wide.

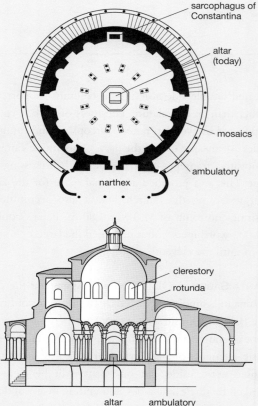

B. PLAN AND SECTION, CHURCH OF SANTA COSTANZA
Rome. c. 350.

in 1256, dedicated to Santa Costanza (the Italian form of Constantina, who was sanctified after her death). The building is a tall rotunda with an encircling barrel-vaulted passageway called an **ambulatory**. Paired columns with Composite capitals and richly molded

entablature blocks support the arcade and dome. Originally, the interior was entirely sheathed in mosaics and veneers of fine marble.

Mosaics still surviving in the ambulatory vault recall the syncretic images in the catacombs. In one section, for example, a

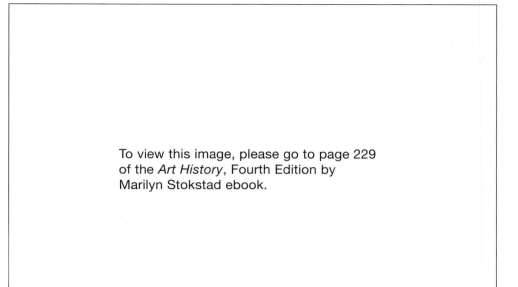

5-21 • HARVESTING OF GRAPES
Ambulatory vault, church of Santa Costanza, Rome. c. 350. Mosaic.

bust portrait of Constantina at the crest of the vault is surrounded by a tangle of grapevines filled with **putti**—naked cherubs, derived from pagan art—who vie with the birds to harvest the grapes **(FIG.**

To view this image, please go to page 229 of the *Art History*, Fourth Edition by Marilyn Stokstad ebook.

5-22 • SARCOPHAGUS OF CONSTANTINA
c. 350. Porphyry, height 7′5″ (2.26 m). Musei Vaticani, Vatican, Rome.

5–21). Along the bottom edges on each side, other *putti* drive wagonloads of grapes toward pavilions housing large vats in which more *putti* trample the grapes into juice for the making of wine. The technique, subject, and style are Roman and traditionally associated with Bacchus and his cult, but the meaning here is new. In a Christian context, the wine references the Eucharist and the trampling of grapes to transform them into wine becomes an image of death and resurrection. Constantina's pagan husband, however, may have appreciated the double allusion.

SCULPTURE

In sculpture, as in architecture, Christians adapted Roman forms for their own needs, especially monumental stone sarcophagi. For instance, within her mausoleum, Constantina (d. 354) was buried within a spectacularly huge porphyry sarcophagus **(FIG. 5–22)** that was installed across from the entrance on the other side of the ambulatory in a rectangular niche (visible on the plan on page 326, FIG. B; an in-place replica peeks over the altar in FIG. 5–20). The motifs are familiar. The same theme of *putti* making wine that we saw highlighted in the mosaics of the ambulatory vaults appears here as well, focused within areas framed by a huge, undulating grapevine, whose subsidiary shoots curl above and below over the flat sides of the box. Striding along its

5-23 • SARCOPHAGUS OF JUNIUS BASSUS Grottoes of St. Peter, Vatican, Rome. c. 359. Marble, 4 × 8′ (1.2 × 2.4 m).

To view this image, please go to page 230 of the *Art History*, Fourth Edition by Marilyn Stokstad ebook.

base, peacocks symbolize eternal life in paradise, while a lone sheep could represent a member of Jesus' flock, presumably Constantina herself.

The contemporary marble **SARCOPHAGUS OF JUNIUS BASSUS (FIG. 5–23)** is packed with elaborate figural scenes like the second-century CE Dionysiac Sarcophagus, only here they are separated into two registers, where columns, entablatures, and gables divide the space into fields for individual scenes. Junius Bassus was a Roman official who, as the inscription here tells us, was "newly baptized" and died on August 25, 359, at the age of 42.

In the center of both registers is a triumphant Christ. Above, he appears as a Roman emperor, distributing legal authority in the form of scrolls to flanking figures of SS. Peter and Paul, and resting his feet on the head of Coelus, the pagan god of the heavens, here representing the cosmos to identify Christ as Cosmocrator (ruler of the cosmos). In the bottom register, the earthly Jesus makes his triumphal entry into Jerusalem, like a Roman emperor entering a conquered city. Jesus, however, rides on a humble ass rather than a powerful steed.

Even in the earliest Christian art, such as that in catacomb paintings and here on the *Sarcophagus of Junius Bassus*, artists employed episodes from the Hebrew Bible allegorically since Christians saw them as prefigurations of important events in the New Testament. At the top left, Abraham passes the test of faith and need not sacrifice his son Isaac. Christians saw in this story an allegory that foreshadowed God's sacrifice of his own son, Jesus, which culminates not in Jesus' death, but his resurrection. Under the triangular gable, second from the end at bottom right, the

Hebrew Bible story of Daniel saved by God from the lions prefigures Christ's emergence alive from his tomb. At bottom far left, God tests the faith of Job, who provides a model for the sufferings of Christian martyrs. Next to Job, Adam and Eve have sinned to set in motion the entire Christian redemption story. Lured by the serpent, they have eaten the forbidden fruit and, conscious of their nakedness, are trying to hide their genitals with leaves.

On the upper right side, spread over two compartments, Jesus appears before Pontius Pilate, who is about to wash his hands, symbolizing that he denies responsibility for Jesus' death. Jesus' position here, held captive between two soldiers, recalls (and perhaps could also be read as) his arrest in Gethsemane, especially since the composition of this panel is reflected in the arrests of the apostles Peter (top, second frame from the left) and Paul (bottom, far right).

RAVENNA

As Rome's political importance dwindled, that of the northern Italian city of Ravenna grew. In 395, Emperor Theodosius I split the Roman Empire into Eastern and Western divisions, each ruled by one of his sons. Heading the West, Honorius (r. 395–423) first established his capital at Milan, but in 402, to escape the siege of Germanic settlers, he moved his government to Ravenna on the east coast. Its naval base, Classis (present-day Classe), had been important since the early days of the empire. In addition to military security, Ravenna offered direct access by sea to Constantinople. When Italy fell in 476 to the Ostrogoths, Ravenna became one of their headquarters, but the beauty and richness of Early Christian buildings can still be experienced there in a remarkable group of well-preserved fifth- and sixth-century buildings.

The Life of Jesus

Episodes from the life of Jesus as recounted in the Gospels form the principal subject matter of Christian visual art. What follows is a list of main events in his life with parenthetical references citing their location in the Gospel texts.

INCARNATION AND CHILDHOOD OF JESUS

The Annunciation: The archangel Gabriel informs the Virgin Mary that God has chosen her to bear his Son. A dove often represents the **Incarnation**, her miraculous conception of Jesus through the Holy Spirit. (Lk 1:26–28)

The Visitation: The pregnant Mary visits her older cousin Elizabeth, pregnant with the future St. John the Baptist. (Lk 1:29–45)

The Nativity: Jesus is born in Bethlehem. The Holy Family—Jesus, Mary, and her husband, Joseph—is usually portrayed in a stable, or, in Byzantine art, a cave. (Lk 2:4–7)

Annunciation to and Adoration of the Shepherds: Angels announce Jesus's birth to shepherds, who hurry to Bethlehem to honor him. (Lk 2:8–20)

Adoration of the Magi: Wise men from the east follow a bright star to Bethlehem to honor Jesus as king of the Jews, presenting him with precious gifts. Eventually these Magi became identified as three kings, often differentiated through facial type as young, middle-aged, and old. (Mat 2:1–12)

Presentation in the Temple: Mary and Joseph bring the Infant Jesus to the Temple in Jerusalem, where he is presented to the high priest. (Lk 2:25–35)

Massacre of the Innocents and Flight into Egypt: An angel warns Joseph that King Herod—to eliminate the threat of a newborn rival king—plans to murder all male babies in Bethlehem. The Holy Family flees to Egypt. (Mat 2:13–16)

JESUS' MINISTRY

The Baptism: At age 30, Jesus is baptized by John the Baptist in the River Jordan. The Holy Spirit appears in the form of a dove and a heavenly voice proclaims Jesus as God's Son. (Mat 3:13–17, Mk 1:9–11, Lk 3:21–22)

Marriage at Cana: At his mother's request Jesus turns water into wine at a wedding feast, his first public miracle. (Jn 2:1–10)

Miracles of Healing: Throughout the Gospels, Jesus performs miracles of healing the blind, possessed (mentally ill), paralytic, and lepers; he also resurrects the dead.

Calling of Levi/Matthew: Jesus calls to Levi, a tax collector, "Follow me." Levi complies, becoming the disciple Matthew. (Mat 9:9, Mk 2:14)

Raising of Lazarus: Jesus brings his friend Lazarus back to life four days after his death. (Jn 11:1–44)

The Transfiguration: Jesus reveals his divinity in a dazzling vision on Mount Tabor as his closest disciples—Peter, James, and John—look on. (Mat 17:1–5, Mk 9:2–6, Lk 9:28–35)

Tribute Money: Challenged to pay the temple tax, Jesus sends Peter to catch a fish, which turns out to have the required coin in its mouth. (Mat 17:24–27, Lk 20:20–25)

JESUS' PASSION, DEATH, AND RESURRECTION

Entry into Jerusalem: Jesus, riding an ass and accompanied by his disciples, enters Jerusalem, while crowds honor him, spreading clothes and palm fronds in his path. (Mat 21:1–11, Mk 11:1–11, Lk 19:30–44, Jn 12:12–15)

The Last Supper: During the Jewish Passover seder, Jesus reveals his impending death to his disciples. Instructing them to drink wine (his blood) and eat bread (his body) in remembrance of him, he lays the foundation for the Christian Eucharist (Mass). (Mat 26:26–30, Mk 14:22–25, Lk 22:14–20)

Jesus Washing the Disciples' Feet: At the Last Supper, Jesus washes the disciples' feet, modeling humility. (Jn 13:4–12)

The Agony in the Garden: In the Garden of Gethsemane on the Mount of Olives, Jesus struggles between his human fear of pain and death and his divine strength to overcome them. The apostles sleep nearby, oblivious. (Lk 22:40–45)

Betrayal (the Arrest): Judas Iscariot (a disciple) has accepted a bribe to indicate Jesus to an armed band of his enemies by kissing him. (Mat 26:46–49, Mk 14:43–46, Lk 22:47–48, Jn 18:3–5)

Jesus before Pilate: Jesus is taken to Pontius Pilate, Roman governor of Judaea, and charged with treason for calling himself king of the Jews. Pilate proposes freeing Jesus but is shouted down by the mob, which demands Jesus be crucified. (Mat 27:11–25, Mk 15:4–14, Lk 23:1–24, Jn 18:28–40)

The Crucifixion: Jesus is executed on a cross, often shown between two crucified criminals and accompanied by the Virgin Mary, John the Evangelist, Mary Magdalen, and other followers at the foot of the cross; Roman soldiers sometimes torment Jesus—one extending a sponge on a pole with vinegar instead of water for him to drink, another stabbing him in the side with a spear. A skull can identify the execution ground as **Golgotha**, "the place of the skull." (Mat 27:35–50, Mk 15:23–37, Lk 23:38–49, Jn 19:18–30)

Descent from the Cross (the Deposition): Jesus' followers take his body down from the cross. (Mat 27:55–59, Mk 15:40–46, Lk 23:50–56, Jn 19:38–40)

The Lamentation/Pietà and Entombment: Jesus' sorrowful followers gather around his body to mourn and then place his body in a tomb. An image of the grieving Virgin alone with Jesus across her lap is known as a **pietà** (from Latin *pietas*, "pity"). (Mat 27:60–61, Jn 19:41–42)

The Resurrection/Holy Women at the Tomb: Three days after his entombment, Christ rises from the dead, and his female followers—usually including Mary Magdalen—discover his empty tomb. An angel announces Christ's resurrection. (Mat 28, Mk 16, Lk 24:1–35, Jn 20)

Descent into Limbo (Harrowing of Hell or Anastasis): The resurrected Jesus descends into limbo, or hell, to free deserving predecessors, among them Adam, Eve, David, and Moses. (Not in the Gospels)

Noli Me Tangere ("Do Not Touch Me"): Christ appears to Mary Magdalen as she weeps at his tomb. When she reaches out to him, he warns her not to touch him. (Lk 24:34–53, Jn 20:11–31)

The Ascension: Christ ascends to heaven from the Mount of Olives, disappearing in a cloud, while his mother and apostles watch. (Acts 1)

To view this image, please go to page 232 of the *Art History*, Fourth Edition by Marilyn Stokstad ebook.

5-24 • ORATORY OF GALLA PLACIDIA
Ravenna. c. 425–426.

SEE MORE: Click the Google Earth link for the Oratory of Galla Placidia **www.myartslab.com**

THE ORATORY OF GALLA PLACIDIA.   One of the earliest surviving Christian structures in Ravenna is an **oratory** (small chapel), attached about 425–426 to the narthex of the church of the imperial palace **(FIG. 5–24)**. It is named after Honorius' remarkable half-sister, Galla Placidia—daughter of the Western Roman emperor, wife of a Gothic king, and mother of Emperor Valentinian. As regent for her son after 425, she ruled the West until about 440. The oratory came to be called the Mausoleum of Galla Placidia because she and her family were once believed to be buried there.

This small building is **cruciform**, or cross-shape. A barrel vault covers each of its arms, and a pendentive dome—a dome continuous with its pendentives—covers the square space at the center (see "Pendentives and Squinches," page 334). The interior of the chapel contrasts markedly with the unadorned exterior, a transition seemingly designed to simulate the passage from the real world into the supernatural realm **(FIG. 5–25)**. The worshiper looking from the western entrance across to the eastern bay of the chapel sees brilliant mosaics in the vaults and panels of veined marble sheathing the walls below. Bands of luxuriant floral designs and geometric patterns cover the arches and barrel vaults. The upper walls of the central space are filled with the figures of standing

To view this image, please go to page 232 of the *Art History*, Fourth Edition by Marilyn Stokstad ebook.

5-25 • ORATORY OF GALLA PLACIDIA
Ravenna. View from entrance, barrel-vaulted arms housing sarchophagi, lunette mosaic of the martyrdom of St. Lawrence. c. 425–426.

SEE MORE: View a panorama of the interior of the Oratory of Galla Placidia **www.myartslab.com**

To view this image, please go to page 233 of the *Art History*,
Fourth Edition by Marilyn Stokstad ebook.

5-26 • THE GOOD SHEPHERD
Lunette over the entrance, Oratory of Galla Placidia.
c. 425–426. Mosaic.

apostles, gesturing like orators. Doves flanking a small fountain between the apostles symbolize eternal life in heaven.

In the lunette at the end of the barrel vault opposite the entrance, a mosaic depicts the third-century St. Lawrence, to whom the building may have been dedicated. The triumphant martyr carries a cross over his shoulder like a trophy and gestures toward the fire-engulfed metal grill on which he was literally roasted in martyrdom. At the left stands a tall cabinet containing the Gospels, signifying the faith for which he gave his life. Opposite St. Lawrence, in a lunette over the entrance portal, is a mosaic of **THE GOOD SHEPHERD (FIG. 5–26)**. A comparison of this version with a fourth-century depiction of the same subject (SEE FIG. 5–15) reveals significant changes in content and design.

Jesus is no longer a boy in a simple tunic, but an adult emperor wearing purple and gold royal robes, his imperial majesty signaled by the golden halo surrounding his head and by a long golden staff that ends in a cross instead of a shepherd's crook. At the time this mosaic was made, Christianity had been the official state religion for 45 years, and nearly a century had past since the last official persecution of Christians. The artists and patrons of this mosaic chose to assert the glory of Jesus Christ in mosaic, the richest known medium of wall decoration, in an imperial image still imbued with pagan spirit but now signaling the triumph of a new faith.

EARLY BYZANTINE ART

Byzantine art can be thought of broadly as the art of Constantinople (whose ancient name, before Constantine renamed it after himself, was Byzantium) and the regions under its influence. In this chapter, we focus on Byzantine art's three "golden ages." The Early Byzantine period, most closely associated with the reign of Emperor Justinian I (527–565), began in the fifth century and ended in 726, at the onset of the iconoclast controversy that led to the destruction of religious images. The Middle Byzantine period began in 843, when Empress Theodora (c. 810–867) reinstated the veneration of icons. It lasted until 1204, when Christian crusaders from the west occupied Constantinople. The Late Byzantine period began with the restoration of Byzantine rule in 1261 and ended with the empire's fall to the Ottoman Turks in 1453, at which point Russia succeeded Constantinople as the "Third Rome" and the center of the Eastern Orthodox Church. Late Byzantine art continued to flourish into the eighteenth century in Ukraine, Russia, and much of southeastern Europe.

THE GOLDEN AGE OF JUSTINIAN

During the fifth and sixth centuries, while invasions and religious controversy wracked the Italian peninsula, the Eastern Empire prospered. Byzantium became the "New Rome." Constantine had chosen the site of his new capital city well. Constantinople lay at the crossroads of the overland trade routes between Asia and Europe and the sea route connecting the Black Sea and the Mediterranean. It was during the sixth century under Emperor Justinian I and his wife, Theodora, that Byzantine political power, wealth, and culture were at their peak. Imperial forces held northern Africa, Sicily, much of Italy, and part of Spain. Ravenna became the Eastern Empire's administrative capital in the west, and Rome remained under nominal Byzantine control until the eighth century.

5-27 • Anthemius of Tralles and Isidorus of Miletus
CHURCH OF HAGIA SOPHIA
Istanbul. 532–537. View from the southwest.

The body of the original church is now surrounded by later
additions, including the minarets built after 1453 by the
Ottoman Turks. Today the building is a museum.

SEE MORE: Click the Google Earth link for Hagia
Sophia www.myartslab.com

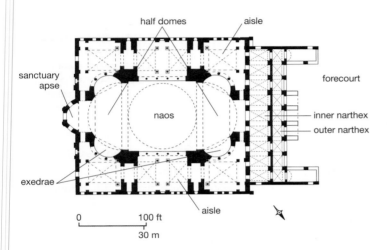

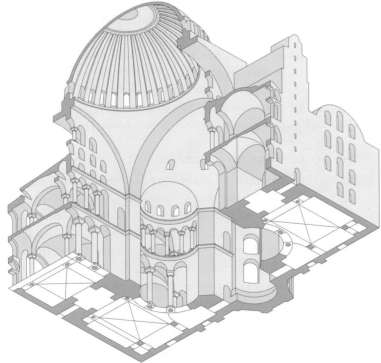

5-28 • **PLAN AND ISOMETRIC DRAWING OF THE
CHURCH OF HAGIA SOPHIA**

HAGIA SOPHIA. In Constantinople, Justinian and Theodora
embarked on a spectacular campaign of building and renovation,
but little now remains of their architectural projects or of the old
imperial capital itself. The church of Hagia Sophia, meaning "Holy
Wisdom," is a spectacular exception **(FIG. 5–27)**. It replaced a
fourth-century church destroyed when crowds, spurred on by Justinian's foes during the devastating urban Nika Revolt in 532, set
the old church on fire and cornered the emperor within his palace.
Empress Theodora, a brilliant, politically shrewd woman, is said to
have goaded Justinian, who was plotting an escape, not to flee the
city, saying "Purple makes a fine shroud"—meaning that she would
rather remain and die an empress (purple was the royal color) than
retreat and preserve her life. Taking up her words as a battle cry, Justinian led the imperial forces in crushing the rebels and restoring
order, reputedly slaughtering 30,000 of his subjects in the process.

To design a new church that embodied imperial power and
Christian glory, Justinian chose two scholar-theoreticians,
Anthemius of Tralles and Isidorus of Miletus. Anthemius was a specialist in geometry and optics, and Isidorus a specialist in physics
who had also studied vaulting. They developed an audacious and
awe-inspiring design, executed by builders who had refined their
masonry techniques building the towers and domed rooms that
were part of the city's defenses. So when Justinian ordered the construction of domed churches, and especially Hagia Sophia, master
masons with a trained and experienced workforce stood ready
to give permanent form to his architects' dreams.

The new Hagia Sophia was not constructed by the
miraculous intervention of angels, as was rumored, but by
mortal builders in only five years (532–537). Procopius of
Caesarea, who chronicled Justinian's reign, claimed poetically
that Hagia Sophia's gigantic dome seemed to hang suspended
on a "golden chain from heaven." Legend has it that Justinian
himself, aware that architecture can be a potent symbol of
earthly power, compared his accomplishment with that of the
legendary builder of the First Temple in Jerusalem, saying
"Solomon, I have outdone you."

Hagia Sophia is an innovative hybrid of longitudinal and
central architectural planning **(FIG. 5–28)**. The building is clearly
dominated by the hovering form of its gigantic dome **(FIG. 5–29)**.
But flanking **conches**—semidomes—extend the central space
into a longitudinal nave that expands outward from the central
dome to connect with the narthex on one end and the halfdome
of the sanctuary apse on the other. This processional core, called

To view this image, please go to page 235 of the *Art History*, Fourth Edition by Marilyn Stokstad ebook.

5-29 • INTERIOR OF THE CHURCH OF HAGIA SOPHIA

EXPLORE MORE: Gain insight from a primary source related to Hagia Sophia **www.myartslab.com**

Pendentives and squinches are two methods of supporting a round dome or its drum over a square space. **Pendentives** are concave, spherical triangles between arches that rise upward and inward to form a circular opening on which a dome rests. **Squinches** are diagonal lintels placed across the upper corner of the wall and supported by an arch or a series of corbeled arches that give it a nichelike shape. Because squinches create an octagon, which is close in shape to a circle, they provide a solid base around the perimeter of a dome, usually elevated on a drum (a circular wall), whereas pendentives project the dome slightly inside the square space it covers, making it seem to float. Byzantine builders preferred pendentives (as at Hagia Sophia, SEE FIG. 5–29), but elaborate, squinch-supported domes became a hallmark of Islamic architecture.

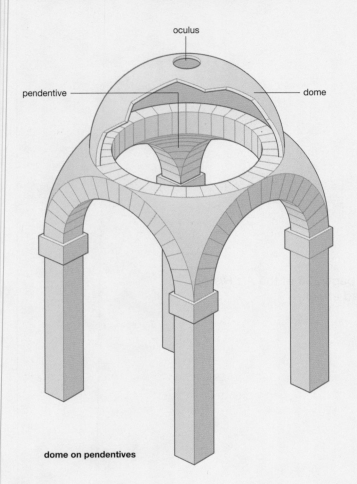

dome on pendentives

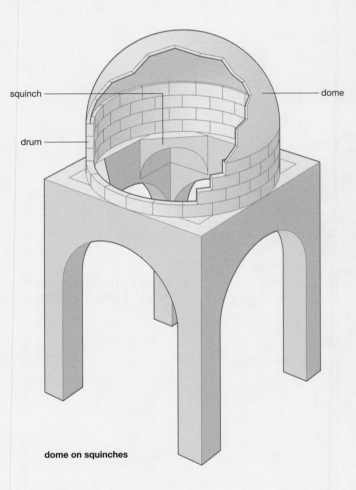

dome on squinches

SEE MORE: View a simulation of pendentives and squinches www.myartslab.com

the **naos** in Byzantine architecture, is flanked by side aisles and **galleries** above them overlooking the naos.

Since its idiosyncratic mixture of basilica and rotunda precludes a ring of masonry underneath the dome to provide support around its circumference (as in the Pantheon, SEE FIGS. 3–84, 3–85), the main dome of Hagia Sophia rests instead on four **pendentives** (triangular curving vault sections) that connect the base of the dome with the huge supporting piers at the four corners of the square area beneath it (see "Pendentives and Squinches," above). And since these piers are essentially submerged back into the darkness of the aisles, rather than expressed within the main space itself (SEE FIG. 5–28), the dome seems to float

mysteriously over a void. The miraculous, weightless effect was reinforced by the light-reflecting gold mosaic that covered the surfaces of dome and pendentives alike, as well as the band of 40 windows that perforate the base of the dome right where it meets its support. This daring move challenges architectural logic by seeming to weaken the integrity of the masonry at the very place where it needs to be strong, but the windows created the circle of light that helps the dome appear to hover, and a reinforcement of buttressing on the exterior made the solution sound as well as shimmering. The origin of the dome on pendentives is obscure, but its large-scale use at Hagia Sophia was totally unprecedented and represents one of the boldest experiments in the history of architecture. It was to become the preferred method of supporting domes in Byzantine architecture.

The architects and builders of Hagia Sophia clearly stretched building materials to their physical limits, denying the physicality of the building in order to emphasize its spirituality. In fact, when the first dome fell in 558, it did so because a pier and pendentive shifted and because the dome was too shallow and exerted too much outward force at its base, not because the windows weakened the support. Confident of their revised technical methods, the architects designed a steeper dome that raised the summit 20 feet higher. They also added exterior buttressing. Although repairs had to be made in 869, 989, and 1346, the church has since withstood numerous earthquakes.

The liturgy used in Hagia Sophia in the sixth century has been lost, but it presumably resembled the rites described in detail for the church in the Middle Byzantine period. The celebration of the Mass took place behind a screen—at Hagia Sophia a crimson curtain embroidered in gold, in later churches an iconostasis, a wall hung with devotional paintings called **icons** (from the Greek *eikon*, meaning "image"). The emperor was the only layperson permitted to enter the sanctuary; men stood in the aisles and women in the galleries. Processions of clergy moved in a circular path from the sanctuary into the nave and back five or six times during the ritual. The focus of the congregation was on the iconostasis and the dome rather than the altar and apse. This upward focus reflects the interests of Byzantine philosophers, who viewed meditation as a way to rise from the material world to a spiritual state. Worshipers standing on the church floor must have felt just such a spiritual uplift as they gazed at the mosaics of saints, angels, and, in the golden central dome, heaven itself.

SAN VITALE. In 540, Byzantine forces captured Ravenna from the Arian Christian Ostrogoths who had themselves taken it from the Romans in 476. Much of our knowledge of the art of this turbulent period comes from the well-preserved monuments at Ravenna. In 526, Ecclesius, bishop of Ravenna, commissioned two new churches, one for the city and one for its port, Classis. Construction began on a central-plan church, a **martyrium** (church built over the grave of a martyr) dedicated to the fourth-century Roman martyr St. Vitalis (Vitale in Italian) in the 520s, but it was not finished until after Justinian had conquered Ravenna and established it as the administrative capital of Byzantine Italy (**FIG. 5–30**).

The design of San Vitale is basically a central-domed octagon surrounded by eight radiating exedrae (wall niches), surrounded in turn by an ambulatory and gallery, all covered by vaults. A rectangular sanctuary and semicircular apse project from one of the sides of the octagon, and circular rooms flank the apse. A separate oval narthex, set off-axis, joined church and palace and also led to cylindrical stair towers that gave access to the second-floor gallery.

The floor plan of San Vitale only hints at the effect of the complex, interpenetrating interior spaces of the church, an effect that was enhanced by the offset narthex, with its double sets of doors leading into the church. People entering from the right saw only arched openings, whereas those entering from the left approached on an axis with the sanctuary, which they saw straight

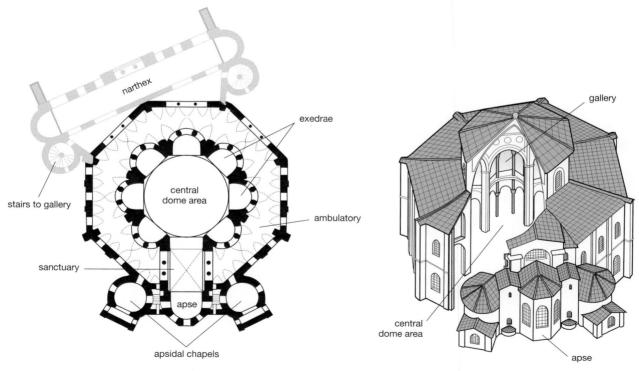

5-30 • PLAN AND CUTAWAY DRAWING, CHURCH OF SAN VITALE
Ravenna. Under construction from c. 520; consecrated 547; mosaics, c. 546–548.

To view this image, please go to page 238 of the *Art History*,
Fourth Edition by Marilyn Stokstad ebook.

5-31 • CHURCH OF SAN VITALE
Ravenna. View into the sanctuary toward the northeast. Consecrated 547.

SEE MORE: View a panorama of San Vitale **www.myartslab.com**

Naming Christian Churches: Designation + Dedication + Location

Christian churches are identified by a three-part descriptive title combining (1) designation (or type), with (2) dedication (usually to a saint), and finally (3) geographic location, cited in that order.

DESIGNATION: There are various types of churches, fulfilling a variety of liturgical and administrative objectives, and the identification of a specific church often begins with an indication of its function within the system. For example, an **abbey church** is the place of worship within a monastery or convent; a **pilgrimage church** is a site that attracts visitors wishing to venerate **relics** (material remains or objects associated with a saint) as well as attend services. A cathedral is a bishop's primary church (the word derives from the Latin *cathedra*, meaning chair, since the chair or throne of a bishop is contained within his cathedral). A bishop's domain is called a diocese, and there can be only one church in the diocese designated as its bishop's cathedral, but the diocese is full of **parish churches** where local residents attend regular services.

DEDICATION: Christian churches are always dedicated to a saint or a sacred concept, for example St. Peter's Basilica or the Church of Hagia Sophia ("Holy Wisdom"). In short-hand identification, when we omit the church designation at the beginning, we always add an apostrophe and an *s* to the saint's name, as when using "St. Peter's" to refer to the Vatican Basilica of St. Peter in Rome

LOCATION: The final piece of information that clearly pinpoints the specific church referred to in a title is its geographic location, as in the Church of San Vitale in Ravenna or the Cathedral of Notre-Dame (French for "Our Lady," referring to the Virgin Mary) in Paris. "Notre-Dame" alone usually refers to this Parisian cathedral, in spite of the fact that many contemporary cathedrals elsewhere (e.g. at Chartres and Reims) were also dedicated to "Notre-Dame." Similarly, "St. Peter's" usually means the Vatican church of the pope in Rome.

---

ahead of them. The dome rests on eight large piers that frame the exedrae and the sanctuary. The undulating, two-story exedrae open through superimposed arcades into the outer aisles on the ground floor and into galleries on the second floor. They push out the circular central space and create an airy, floating sensation,

reinforced by the liberal use of veined marble veneer and colored glass and gold mosaics in the surface decoration. The structure seems to dissolve into shimmering light and color.

In the halfdome of the sanctuary apse **(FIGS. 5–31, 5–32)**, an image of **CHRIST ENTHRONED** is flanked by St. Vitalis and Bishop Ecclesius. The other sanctuary images relate to its use for the celebration of the Eucharist. The lunette on the north wall shows an altar table set for a meal that Abraham offers to three holy visitors, and next to it a portrayal of his near-sacrifice of Isaac. In the spandrels and other framed wall spaces appear prophets and evangelists, and the program is bristling with symbolic references to Jesus, but the focus of the sanctuary program is the courtly tableau in the semidome of the apse.

A youthful, classicizing Christ appears on axis, dressed in imperial purple and enthroned on a cosmic orb in paradise, the setting indicated by the four rivers that flow from the ground underneath him. Two winged angels flank him, like imperial bodyguards or attendants. In his left hand Christ holds a scroll with seven seals that he will open at his Second Coming at the end of time, proclaiming his authority not only over this age, but over the age to come. He extends his right hand to offer a crown of martyrdom to a figure on his right (our left) labeled as St. Vitalis, the saint to whom this church is dedicated. On

> To view this image, please go to page 239 of the *Art History*, Fourth Edition by Marilyn Stokstad ebook.

5-32 • CHRIST ENTHRONED, FLANKED BY ANGELS, ST. VITALIS AND BISHOP ECCLESIUS
Church of San Vitale, Ravenna. Consecrated 547. Mosaic.

5–33 • EMPEROR JUSTINIAN AND HIS ATTENDANTS, NORTH WALL OF THE APSE

Church of San Vitale, Ravenna. Consecrated 547. Mosaic, 8′8″ × 12′ (2.64 × 3.65 m).

As head of state, the haloed Justinian wears a huge jeweled crown and a purple cloak; he carries a large golden paten (plate for Eucharistic bread) that he is donating to San Vitale for the celebration of the Eucharist. Bishop Maximianus at his left holds a jeweled cross and another churchman holds a jewel-covered book. Government officials stand at Justinian's right, followed by barbarian mercenary soldiers, one of whom wears a neck torc, another a Classical cameo cloak clasp.

5–34 • EMPRESS THEODORA AND HER ATTENDANTS, SOUTH WALL OF THE APSE

Church of San Vitale, Ravenna. Consecrated 547. Mosaic 8′8″ × 12′ (2.64 × 3.65 m).

Theodora and her ladies wear the rich textiles and jewelry of the Byzantine court. Both men and women are dressed in linen or silk tunics and cloaks. The men's cloaks are fastened on the right shoulder with a fibula (brooch) and are decorated with a rectangular embroidered panel (tablion). Women wore a second full, long-sleeved garment over their tunics and a large rectangular shawl. Like Justinian, Theodora has a halo and wears imperial purple. Her elaborate jewelry includes a wide collar of embroidered and jeweled cloth. A crown, hung with long strands of pearls (thought to protect the wearer from disease), frames her face.

the other side is the only un-nimbed figure in the tableau, labeled as Bishop Ecclesius, the founder of San Vitale, who holds forward a model of the church itself, offering it to Christ. The artist has imagined a scene of courtly protocol in paradise, where Christ, as emperor, gives a gift to, and receives a gift from, visiting luminaries.

Further visitors appear in separate, flanking rectangular compositions, along the curving wall of the apse underneath the scene in the semidome—Justinian and Theodora and their retinues (the former can be seen in FIG. 5–31). The royal couple did not attend the dedication ceremonies for the church of San Vitale, conducted by Archbishop Maximianus in 547. They may never actually have set foot in Ravenna, but these two large mosaic panels that face each other across its sanctuary picture their presence here in perpetuity. Justinian (FIG. 5–33), on the north wall, carries a large golden paten that will be used to hold the Eucharistic Host and stands next to Maximianus, who holds a golden, jewel-encrusted cross. The priestly celebrants at the right carry the Gospels, encased in a golden, jeweled book cover, symbolizing the coming of the Word, and a censer containing burning incense to purify the altar prior to the Eucharist.

On the south wall, Theodora, standing beneath a fluted shell canopy and singled out by a golden halo and elaborate crown, carries a huge golden chalice studded with jewels (FIG. 5–34). The rulers present these gifts as precious offerings to Christ—emulating most immediately Bishop Ecclesius, who offers a model of the church to Christ in the apse, but also the three Magi who brought valuable gifts to the infant Jesus, depicted in "embroidery" at the bottom of Theodora's purple cloak. In fact, the paten and chalice offered by the royal couple will be used by this church to offer Eucharistic bread and wine to the local Christian community during the liturgy. In this way the entire program of mosaic decoration revolves around themes of offering, extended into the theme of the Eucharist itself.

Theodora's group stands beside a fountain, presumably at the entrance to the women's gallery. The open doorway and curtain are Classical space-creating devices, but here the mosaicists have deliberately avoided allowing their illusionistic power to overwhelm their ability also to create flat surface patterns. Notice, too, that the figures cast no shadows, and, though modeled, their outlines as silhouetted shapes are more prominent than their sense of three-dimensionality. Still, especially in Justinian's panel, a complex and carefully controlled system of overlapping allows us to see these figures clearly and logically situated within a shallow space, moving in a stately procession from left to right toward the entrance to the church and the beginning of the liturgy. So the scenes portrayed in these mosaic paintings are both flattened and three-dimensional, abstract and representational, patterned and individualized. Like Justinian and Theodora, their images are both there and not there at the same time.

SANT'APOLLINARE IN CLASSE. At the same time that he was building the church of San Vitale, Bishop Ecclesius ordered a basilica church in the port of Classis dedicated to St. Apollinaris (Sant'Apollinare), the first bishop of Ravenna. The apse mosaic (FIG. 5–35) is a symbolic depiction of the Transfiguration (Matthew 17:1–5)—Jesus' revelation of his divinity. A narrative episode from the life of Christ has been transformed into an iconic embodiment of its underlying idea. One man and 15 sheep stand in a stylized, verdant landscape below a jeweled cross with the face of Christ at its center. The hand of God and the figures of Moses and Elijah from the Hebrew Bible

To view this image, please go to page 241 of the *Art History*, Fourth Edition by Marilyn Stokstad ebook.

5-35 • THE TRANSFIGURATION OF CHRIST WITH SANT'APOLLINARE, FIRST BISHOP OF RAVENNA
Church of Sant'Apollinare in Classe. Consecrated 549. Mosaics: apse, 6th century; wall above apse, 7th and 9th centuries; side panels, 7th century.

appear in the heavens to authenticate the divinity of Christ. The apostles Peter, James, and John, who witness the event, are represented here by the three sheep with raised heads. Below the cross, Bishop Apollinaris raises his hands in an orant posture of prayer, flanked by 12 lambs who seem to represent the apostles.

This highly complicated work of symbolic narrative, like the mosaics of San Vitale, must have been aimed at a sophisticated population, prepared to appreciate its theological speculations and diagrammatic outlines of Christian doctrine. At this moment in its history, the Church is directing its message to an inside audience of faithful believers, who encounter its visualization within churches in their own community. Such an art could not have been conceived to educate an uninitiated public; rather it was developed to celebrate the values that hold Christian society together by representing them in a refined and urbane visual language.

OBJECTS OF VENERATION AND DEVOTION

The court workshops of Constantinople excelled in the production of luxurious, small-scale works in gold, ivory, and textiles. The Byzantine elite also sponsored vital **scriptoria** (writing centers for **scribes**—professional document writers) for the production of **manuscripts** (handwritten books).

THE ARCHANGEL MICHAEL DIPTYCH. Commemorative ivory diptychs—two carved panels hinged together—originated with Roman politicians elected to the post of consul. New consuls would send notices of their election to friends and colleagues by inscribing them in wax that filled a recessed rectangular area on the inner sides of a pair of ivory panels carved with elaborate decoration on the reverse. Christians adapted the practice for religious use, inscribing a diptych with the names of people to be remembered with prayers during the liturgy.

This large panel depicting the **ARCHANGEL MICHAEL**—the largest surviving Byzantine ivory—was half of such a diptych **(FIG. 5–36)**. In his classicizing beauty, imposing physical presence, and elegant architectural setting, the archangel is comparable to the (supposed) priestess of Bacchus in the fourth-century pagan Symmachus diptych panel (SEE FIG. 3–99). His relationship to the architectural space and the frame around him, however, is more complex. His heels rest on the top step of a stair that clearly lies behind the columns and pedestals, but the rest of his body projects in front of them—since it overlaps the architectural setting—creating a striking tension between this celestial figure and his terrestrial backdrop.

The angel is outfitted here as a divine messenger, holding a staff of authority in his left hand and a sphere symbolizing worldly power in his right. Within the arch is a similar cross-topped orb, framed by a wreath bound by a ribbon with long, rippling extensions, that is set against the background of a scallop shell. The lost half of this diptych would have completed the Greek inscription across the top, which reads: "Receive these gifts, and having learned the cause…." Perhaps the other panel contained a

To view this image, please go to page 242 of the *Art History*, Fourth Edition by Marilyn Stokstad ebook.

5-36 • ARCHANGEL MICHAEL
Panel of a diptych, probably from the court workshop at Constantinople. Early 6th century. Ivory, 17 × 15½″ (43.3 × 14 cm). British Museum, London.

Scroll and Codex

Since people began to write some 5,000 years ago, they have kept records on a variety of materials, including clay or wax tablets, pieces of broken pottery, papyrus, animal skins, and paper. Books have taken two forms: scroll and codex.

Scribes made **scrolls** from sheets of papyrus glued end to end or from thin sheets of cleaned, scraped, and trimmed sheepskin or calfskin, a material known as **parchment** or, when softer and lighter, **vellum**. Each end of the scroll was attached to a rod; the reader slowly unfurled the scroll from one rod to the other. Scrolls could be written to be read either horizontally or vertically.

At the end of the first century CE, the more practical and manageable **codex** (plural, codices)—sheets bound together like the modern book—replaced the scroll as the primary form of recording

texts. The basic unit of the codex was the eight-leaf quire, made by folding a large sheet of parchment twice, cutting the edges free, then sewing the sheets together up the center. Heavy covers kept the sheets of a codex flat. The thickness and weight of parchment and vellum made it impractical to produce a very large manuscript, such as an entire Bible, in a single volume. As a result, individual sections were made into separate books.

Until the invention of printing in the fifteenth century, all books were **manuscripts**—that is, they were written by hand. Manuscripts often included illustrations, called **miniatures** (from *minium*, the Latin word for a reddish lead pigment). Manuscripts decorated with gold and colors were said to be illuminated.

---

portrait of the emperor—many think he would be Justinian—or of another high official who presented the panels as a gift to an important colleague, acquaintance, or family member. Nonetheless, the emphasis here is on the powerful celestial messenger who does not need to obey the laws of earthly scale or human perspective.

THE VIENNA GENESIS.   Byzantine manuscripts were often made with very costly materials. For example, sheets of purple-dyed **vellum** (a fine writing surface made from calfskin) and gold and silver inks were used to produce a codex now known as the Vienna Genesis. It was probably made in Syria or Palestine, and the purple vellum indicates that it may have been created for an imperial patron (costly purple dye, made from the secretions of murex mollusks, was usually restricted to imperial use). The Vienna Genesis is written in Greek and illustrated with pictures that appear below the text at the bottom of the pages.

The story of **REBECCA AT THE WELL (FIG. 5–37)** (Genesis 24) appears here in a single composition, but the painter—clinging to the continuous narrative tradition that had characterized the illustration of scrolls—combines events that take place at different times in the story within a single narrative space. Rebecca, the heroine, appears at the left walking away from the walled city of Nahor with a large jug on her shoulder, going to fetch water. A colonnaded road leads toward a spring, personified by a reclining pagan water nymph who holds a flowing jar. In the foreground, Rebecca appears again. Her jug now full, she encounters a thirsty camel driver and offers him water to drink. Since he is Abraham's servant, Eliezer, in search of a bride for Abraham's son Isaac, Rebecca's generosity results in her marriage to Isaac. The lifelike poses and rounded, full-bodied figures of this narrative scene

To view this image, please go to page 243 of the *Art History*, Fourth Edition by Marilyn Stokstad ebook.

5-37 • REBECCA AT THE WELL
Page from a codex featuring the book of Genesis (known as the Vienna Genesis). Syria or Palestine. Early 6th century. Tempera, gold, and silver paint on purple-dyed vellum, 13½ × 9⅞″ (33.7 × 25 cm). Österreichische Nationalbibliothek, Vienna.

To view this image, please go to page 244 of the *Art History*, Fourth Edition by Marilyn Stokstad ebook.

5-38 • DAVID BATTLING GOLIATH
Detail of silver plate in FIG. 5–11. Made in Constantinople, 629–630. Metropolitan Museum of Art, New York.

conform to the conventions of traditional Roman painting. The sumptuous purple of the background and the glittering metallic letters of the text situate the book within the world of the privileged and powerful in Byzantine society.

LUXURY WORKS IN SILVER. The imperial court at Constantinople had a monopoly on the production of some luxury goods, especially those made of precious metals. It seems to have been the origin of a spectacular set of nine silver plates portraying events in the early life of the biblical King David, including the plate that we examined at the beginning of the chapter (SEE FIG. 5–11).

The plates would have been made by hammering a large silver ingot (the plate in FIG. 5–11 weighs 12 pounds 10 ounces) into a round shape and raising on it the rough semblance of the human figures and their environment. With finer chisels, silversmiths then refined these shapes, and at the end of their work, they punched ornamental motifs and incised fine details. The careful modeling,

lifelike postures, and intricate engraving characterizing the detail reproduced in FIG. 5–38 document the highly refined artistry and stunning technical virtuosity of these cosmopolitan artists at the imperial court who still practiced a classicizing art that can be traced back to the traditions of ancient Greece.

ICONS AND ICONOCLASM

Christians in the Byzantine world prayed to Christ, Mary, and the saints while looking at images of them on independent painted panels known as icons. Church doctrine toward the veneration of icons was ambivalent. Christianity, like Judaism and Islam, has always been uneasy with the power of religious images. But key figures of the Eastern Church, such as Basil the Great of Cappadocia (c. 329–379) and John of Damascus (c. 675–749), distinguished between idolatry—the worship of images—and the veneration of an idea or holy person depicted in a work of art. Icons were thus accepted as aids to meditation and prayer, as intermediaries between worshipers and the holy personages they depicted. Honor showed to the image was believed to transfer directly to its spiritual prototype. Icons were often displayed in Byzantine churches on a screen separating the congregation from the sanctuary called the **iconostasis**.

Surviving early icons are rare, but a few precious examples were preserved in the Monastery of St. Catherine on Mount Sinai, among them the **VIRGIN AND CHILD WITH SAINTS AND ANGELS** (FIG. 5–39). As Theotokos (Greek for "bearer of God"), Jesus' earthly mother was viewed as the powerful, ever-forgiving intercessor, appealing to her divine son for mercy on behalf of repentant worshipers. She was also called the Seat of Wisdom, and many images of the Virgin and Child, like this one, show her holding Jesus on her lap in a way that suggests that she represents the throne of Solomon. Virgin and Child are flanked here by Christian warrior-saints Theodore (left) and George (right)—both legendary figures said to have slain dragons, representing the triumph of the Church over the "evil serpent" of paganism. Angels behind them twist upward to look heavenward. The artist has painted the Christ Child, the Virgin, and the angels in an illusionistic Roman manner that renders them lifelike and three-dimensional in appearance. But the warrior-saints are more stylized. The artist barely hints at bodily form beneath the richly patterned textiles of their cloaks, and their tense faces are frozen in frontal stares of gripping intensity.

In the eighth century, the veneration of icons sparked a major controversy in the Eastern Church, and in 726 Emperor Leo III launched a campaign of **iconoclasm** ("image breaking"), banning the use of icons in Christian worship and ordering the destruction of devotional pictures (see "Iconoclasm," page 344). Only a few early icons survived in isolated places like Mount Sinai, which was no longer a part of the Byzantine Empire at this time. But the iconoclasm did not last. In 843, Empress Theodora, widow of Theophilus, last of the iconoclastic emperors, reversed her husband's policy, and icons would play an increasingly important role as the history of Byzantine art developed.

To view this image, please go to page 245 of the *Art History*, Fourth Edition by Marilyn Stokstad ebook.

5-39 • VIRGIN AND CHILD WITH SAINTS AND ANGELS
Icon. Second half of the 6th century. Encaustic on wood, 27 × 18⅞″ (69 × 48 cm). Monastery of St. Catherine, Mount Sinai, Egypt.

EXPLORE MORE: Gain insight from a primary source about painting icons **www.myartslab.com**

Iconoclasm

Iconoclasm (literally "image breaking," from the Greek words *eikon* for "image" and *klao* meaning "break" or "destroy") is the prohibition and destruction of works of visual art, usually because they are considered inappropriate in religious contexts.

During the eighth century, mounting discomfort with the place of icons in Christian devotion grew into a major controversy in the Byzantine world and, in 726, Emperor Leo III (r. 717–741) imposed iconoclasm, initiating the systematic destruction of images of saints and sacred stories on icons and in churches, as well as the persecution of those who made them and defended their use. His successor, Constantine V (r. 741–775), enforced these policies and practices with even greater fervor. Iconoclasm endured as imperial policy until 843, when the widowed Empress Theodora reversed her husband Theophilus' policy and reinstated the central place of images in Byzantine devotional practice.

A number of explanations have been proposed for this interlude of Byzantine iconoclasm. Some church leaders feared that the use of images in worship could lead to idolatry or at least distract worshipers from their spiritual exercises. Specifically there were questions surrounding the relationship between images and the Eucharist, the latter considered by iconoclasts as sufficient representation of the presence of Christ in the church. But there was also anxiety in Byzantium about the weakening state of the empire, especially in relation to the advances of Arab armies into Byzantine territory. It was easy to pin these hard times on God's displeasure with the idolatrous use of images. Coincidentally, Leo III's success fighting the Arabs could be interpreted as divine sanction of his iconoclastic position, and its very adoption might appease the iconoclastic Islamic enemy itself. Finally, since the production and promotion of icons was centered in monasteries—at that time rivaling the state in strength and wealth—attacking the use of images might check their growing power. Perhaps all these factors played a part, but at the triumph of the **iconophiles** (literally "lovers of images") in 843, the place of images in worship was again secure: Icons proclaimed Christ as God incarnate and facilitated Christian worship by acting as intermediaries between humans and saints. Those who had suppressed icons became heretics.

But iconoclasm is not restricted to Byzantine history. It reappears from time to time throughout the history of art. Protestant reformers in sixteenth-century Europe adopted what they saw as the iconoclastic position of the Hebrew Bible (Exodus 20:4), and many works of Catholic art were destroyed by zealous reformers and their followers.

Even more recently, in 2001, the Taliban rulers of Afghanistan dynamited two gigantic fifth-century CE statues of the Buddha carved into the rock cliffs of the Bamiyan Valley, specifically because they believed such "idols" violated Islamic law.

To view this image, please go to page 246 of the *Art History*, Fourth Edition by Marilyn Stokstad ebook.

CRUCIFIXION AND ICONOCLASTS
From the Chludov Psalter. Mid 9th century. Tempera on vellum, 7¾ × 6″ (19.5 × 15 cm). State Historical Museum, Moscow. MS D.29, fol. 67v

This page and its illustration of Psalm 21—made soon after the end of the iconoclastic controversy in 843—records the iconophiles' harsh judgment of the iconoclasts. Painted in the margin at the right, a scene of the Crucifixion shows a soldier tormenting Christ with a vinegar-soaked sponge. In a striking visual parallel, two named iconoclasts—identified by inscription—in the adjacent picture along the bottom margin employ a whitewash-soaked sponge to obliterate an icon portrait of Christ, thus linking their actions with those who had crucified him.

MIDDLE BYZANTINE ART

After the defeat of the iconoclasts, Byzantine art flourished once again, beginning in 867 under the leadership of an imperial dynasty from Macedonia. This support for the arts continued until Christian crusaders from the west, setting out on a holy war against Islam, diverted their efforts to conquering the wealthy Christian Byzantine Empire. The western crusaders who took Constantinople in 1204 looted the capital and set up a Latin dynasty of rulers to replace the Byzantine emperors.

Early Byzantine civilization had been centered in lands along

5-40 • MONASTERY CHURCHES AT HOSIOS LOUKAS
Greece. View from the east: Katholikon (left), early 11th century, and church of the Theotokos, late 10th century.

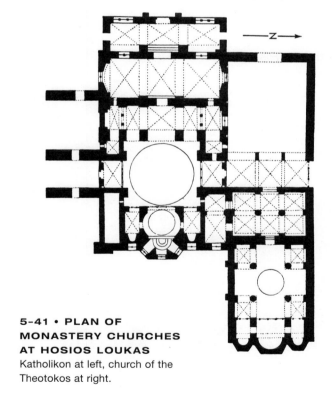

5-41 • PLAN OF MONASTERY CHURCHES AT HOSIOS LOUKAS
Katholikon at left, church of the Theotokos at right.

Under the Macedonian dynasty (867–1056) initiated by Basil I, the empire prospered and enjoyed a cultural rebirth. Middle Byzantine art and architecture, visually powerful and stylistically coherent, reflect the strongly spiritual focus of the period's autocratic, wealthy leadership. From the mid eleventh century, however, other powers entered Byzantine territory. The empire stabilized temporarily under the Comnenian dynasty (1081–1185), extending the Middle Byzantine period well into the time of the western Middle Ages.

ARCHITECTURE AND MOSAICS

Comparatively few Middle Byzantine churches in Constantinople have survived intact, but many central-plan domed churches, favored by Byzantine architects, survive in Greece to the southwest and Ukraine to the northeast, and are reflected in Venice within the Western medieval world. These structures reveal the Byzantine taste for a multiplicity of geometric forms, verticality, and rich decorative effects both inside and out.

HOSIOS LOUKAS. Although an outpost, Greece still lay within the Byzantine Empire, and the eleventh-century Katholikon of the Monastery of Hosios Loukas, built a few miles from the village of Stiris, Greece, is an excellent example of Middle Byzantine architecture. It stands next to the earlier church of the Theotokos (FIGS. 5–40, 5–41, 5–42). The church has a compact central plan with a dome, supported on squinches, rising over an octagonal core (see "Pendentives and Squinches," page 334). On the exterior, the rising forms of apses, walls, and roofs disguise the vaulting roofs of the interior. The Greek builders created a decorative effect

the rim of the Mediterranean Sea that had been within the Roman Empire. During the Middle Byzantine period, Constantinople's scope was reduced to present-day Turkey and other areas by the Black Sea, as well as the Balkan peninsula, including Greece, and southern Italy. The influence of Byzantine culture also extended into Russia and Ukraine, and to Venice, Constantinople's trading partner in northeastern Italy, at the head of the Adriatic Sea.

To view this image, please go to page 248 of the *Art History*, Fourth Edition by Marilyn Stokstad ebook.

5-42 • CENTRAL DOMED SPACE AND APSE (THE NAOS), KATHOLIKON
Monastery of Hosios Loukas. Near Stiris, Greece. Early 11th century and later.

on the exterior, alternating stones with bricks set both vertically and horizontally and using diagonally set bricks to form saw-toothed moldings. Inside the churches, the high central space carries the eyes of worshipers upward into the main dome, which soars above a ring of tall arched openings.

Unlike Hagia Sophia, with its clear, sweeping geometric forms, the Katholikon has a complex variety of forms, including domes, groin vaults, barrel vaults, pendentives, and squinches, all built on a relatively small scale. The barrel vaults and tall sanctuary apse with flanking rooms further complicate the space. Single, double, and triple windows create intricate and unusual patterns of light that illuminated a mosaic of Christ Pantokrator (now lost) in the center of the main dome. The secondary, sanctuary dome is decorated with a mosaic of the Lamb of God surrounded by the Twelve Apostles at Pentecost, and the apse semi-dome has a mosaic of the Virgin and Child Enthroned. Biblical scenes (the Nativity appears on the squinch visible in FIG. 5–42) and figures of saints fill the interior with brilliant color and dramatic images. As at Hagia Sophia, the lower walls are faced with a multicolored stone veneer. An iconostasis separates the congregation from the sanctuary.

SANTA SOPHIA IN KIEV.   During the ninth century, the rulers of Kievan Rus—Ukraine, Belarus, and Russia—adopted Orthodox Christianity and Byzantine culture. These lands had been settled by eastern Slavs in the fifth and sixth centuries, but later were ruled by Scandinavian Vikings who had sailed down the rivers from the Baltic to the Black Sea. In Constantinople, the Byzantine emperor hired the Vikings as his personal bodyguards, and Viking traders established a headquarters in the upper Volga region and in the city of Kiev, which became the capital of the area under their control.

The first Christian member of the Kievan ruling family was Princess Olga (c. 890–969), who was baptized in Constantinople by the patriarch himself, with the Byzantine emperor as her godfather. Her grandson Grand Prince Vladimir (r. 980–1015) established Orthodox Christianity as the state religion in 988. Vladimir sealed the pact with the Byzantines by accepting baptism and marrying Anna, the sister of the powerful Emperor Basil II (r. 976–1025).

Vladimir's son Grand Prince Yaroslav (r. 1036–1054) founded the **CATHEDRAL OF SANTA SOPHIA** in Kiev **(FIG. 5–43)**. The church originally had a typical Byzantine multiple-domed cross design, but the building was expanded with double side aisles, leading to five apses. It culminated in a large central dome surrounded by 12 smaller domes. The small domes were said to stand for the 12 apostles gathered around the central dome, representing Christ Pantokrator, ruler of the universe. The central domed space of the crossing focuses attention on the nave and the main apse. Nonetheless, the many individual bays create a complicated and compartmentalized interior. The walls glow with lavish decoration: Mosaics glitter from the central dome, the apse, and the arches of the crossing. The remaining surfaces are frescoed with scenes from the lives of Christ, the Virgin, the apostles Peter and Paul, and the archangels.

The Kievan mosaics established a standard system of iconography used in Russian Orthodox churches. The Pantokrator fills the curving surface at the crest of the main dome (not visible above the window-pierced drum in FIG. 5–43). At a lower level, the apostles stand between the windows of the drum, with the four

To view this image, please go to page 249 of the *Art History*, Fourth Edition by Marilyn Stokstad ebook.

5-43 • INTERIOR, CATHEDRAL OF SANTA SOPHIA
Kiev. 1037–1046. Apse mosaics: Orant Virgin and Communion of the Apostles.

To view this image, please go to page 250 of the *Art History*, Fourth Edition by Marilyn Stokstad ebook.

To view this image, please go to page 250 of the *Art History*, Fourth Edition by Marilyn Stokstad ebook.

evangelists occupying the pendentives. An orant figure of the Virgin Mary seems to float in a golden heaven on the semidome and upper wall of the apse. In the mosaic on the wall below the Virgin is the Communion of the Apostles. Christ appears not once, but twice, in this scene, offering the Eucharistic bread and wine to the apostles, six on each side of the altar. With such extravagant use of costly mosaic, Prince Yaroslav made a powerful political declaration of his own power and wealth—and that of the Kievan Church as well.

CHURCH OF THE DORMITION AT DAPHNI. The refined mosaicists who worked at the church of the Dormition at Daphni, near Athens, conceived their compositions in relation to an intellectual ideal. They eliminated all "unnecessary" detail to focus on the essential elements of a narrative scene, conveying its mood and message in a moving but elegant style. The main dome of this church has maintained its riveting image of the Pantokrator, centered at the crest of the dome like a seal of divine sanction and surveillance (FIG. 5–44). This imposing figure manages to be elegant and awesome at the same time. Christ blesses or addresses the assembled congregation with one hand, while the slender, attenuated fingers of the other spread to clutch a massive book securely. In the squinches of the corner piers are four signal episodes from his life: Annunciation, Nativity, Baptism, and Transfiguration.

A mosaic of the **CRUCIFIXION** from the lower part of the church (FIG. 5–45) exemplifies the focus on emotional appeal to individuals that characterizes late eleventh-century Byzantine art. The figures inhabit an otherworldly space, a golden universe anchored to the material world by a few flowers, which suggest the promise of new life. A nearly nude Jesus is shown with bowed head and gently sagging body, his eyes closed in death. The witnesses have been reduced to two isolated mourning figures, Mary and the young apostle John, to whom Jesus had just entrusted the care of his mother. The elegant cut of the contours and the eloquent restraint of the gestures only intensify the emotional power of the

5-45 • CRUCIFIXION
Church of the Dormition, Daphni, Greece. East wall of the north arm. Late 11th century. Mosaic.

image. The nobility and suffering of these figures was meant to move worshipers toward a deeper involvement with their own meditation and worship.

This depiction of the Crucifixion has symbolic as well as emotional power. The mound of rocks and the skull at the bottom of the cross represent Golgotha, the "place of the skull," the hill outside ancient Jerusalem where Adam was thought to be buried and where the Crucifixion was said to have taken place. The faithful saw Jesus Christ as the new Adam, whose sacrifice on the cross saved humanity from the sins brought into the world by Adam and Eve. The arc of blood and water springing from Jesus' side refers to Eucharistic and baptismal rites. As Paul wrote in his First Letter to the Corinthians: "For just as in Adam all die, so too in Christ shall all be brought to life" (1 Corinthians 15:22). The timelessness and simplicity of this image were meant to aid the Christian worshiper seeking to achieve a mystical union with the divine through prayer and meditation, both intellectually and emotionally.

THE CATHEDRAL OF ST. MARK IN VENICE.   The northeastern Italian city of Venice, set on the Adriatic at the crossroads of Europe and Asia Minor, was a major center of Byzantine art in Italy. Venice had been subject to Byzantine rule in the sixth and seventh centuries, and up to the tenth century, the city's ruler, the doge ("duke" in Venetian dialect), had to be ratified by the Byzantine emperor. At the end of the tenth century, Constantinople granted Venice a special trade status that allowed its merchants to control much of the commerce between east and west, and the city grew enormously wealthy.

Venetian architects looked to Byzantine domed churches for inspiration in 1063, when the doge commissioned a church to replace the palace chapel that had housed the relics of St. Mark the Apostle since they were brought to Venice from Alexandria in 828/29 (FIG. 5–46). The Cathedral of St. Mark has a Greek-cross plan, each square unit of which is covered by a dome, that is, five great domes in all, separated by barrel vaults and supported by pendentives. Unlike Hagia Sophia in Constantinople, where the space seems to flow from the narthex up into the dome and through the nave to the apse, St. Mark's domed compartments produce a complex space in which each dome maintains its own separate vertical axis. As we have seen elsewhere, marble veneer covers the lower walls, and golden mosaics glimmer above on the vaults, pendentives, and domes. The dome visible in FIG. 5–46 depicts Pentecost, the descent of the Holy Spirit on the apostles. A view of the exterior of St. Mark's as it would have appeared in early modern times can be seen in a painting by the fifteenth-century Venetian artist Gentile Bellini.

To view this image, please go to page 251 of the *Art History*, Fourth Edition by Marilyn Stokstad ebook.

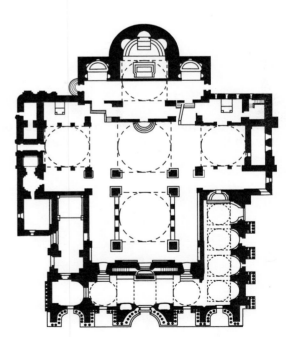

5-46 • INTERIOR AND PLAN OF THE CATHEDRAL OF ST. MARK
Venice. Begun 1063. View looking toward apse.

This church is the third one built on the site. It was both the palace chapel of the doge and the burial place for the bones of the patron of Venice, St. Mark. The church was consecrated as a cathedral in 1807. Mosaics have been reworked continually to the present day.

OBJECTS OF VENERATION AND DEVOTION

As in the Early Byzantine period, artists of great talent and high aesthetic sensibility produced small luxury items for members of the court as well as for the Church. Many of these items were commissioned by rulers and secular and Church functionaries as official gifts for one another. They had to be portable, sturdy, and exquisitely refined. These works often combined exceptional beauty and technical virtuosity with religious meaning. Icons, ivory carving, gold and enamel work, and fine books were especially prized.

THE VIRGIN OF VLADIMIR. The revered icon of Mary and Jesus known as the VIRGIN OF VLADIMIR (FIG. 5–47) was probably created in Constantinople but brought to Kiev. This distinctively humanized image suggests the growing desire for a more immediate and personal religion that we have already seen in the Crucifixion mosaic at Daphni, dating from about the same period. This exquisite icon employs an established iconographic type, known as the "Virgin of Compassion," showing Mary and the Christ Child pressing their cheeks together and gazing at each other with tender affection. It was widely believed that St. Luke had been the first to paint such a portrait of the Virgin and Child as they appeared to him in a vision.

Almost from its creation, the *Virgin of Vladimir* was thought to protect the people of the city where it resided. It arrived in Kiev sometime between 1131 and 1136 and was taken to the city of Suzdal and then to Vladimir in 1155. In 1480, it was moved to the Cathedral of the Dormition in the Moscow Kremlin. Today, even in a museum, it inspires prayer.

THE HARBAVILLE TRIPTYCH. Dating from the mid eleventh century, the small devotional ivory known as the HARBAVILLE TRIPTYCH features a tableau of Christ flanked by Mary and St. John the Baptist, a group known as the "Deësis" (FIG. 5–48). Deësis means "entreaty" in Greek, and here Mary and John intercede, presumably for the owner of this work, pleading with Christ for forgiveness and salvation. The emergence of the Deësis as an important theme is in keeping with an increasing personalization in Byzantine religious art. St. Peter stands directly under Christ, gesturing upward toward him. Inscriptions identify SS. James, John, Paul, and Andrew. The figures in the outer panels are military saints and martyrs. All these figures stand in a neutral space given definition only by the small bases under their feet, effectively removing them from the physical world. They are, however, fully realized human forms with rounded shoulders, thighs, and knees that suggest physical substance beneath their linear, decorative drapery.

THE PARIS PSALTER. The painters of luxuriously illustrated manuscripts matched the combination of intense religious expression, aristocratic elegance, and a heightened appreciation of rich decoration that we have experienced in monumental architectural painting.

To view this image, please go to page 252 of the *Art History*, Fourth Edition by Marilyn Stokstad ebook.

5–47 • VIRGIN OF VLADIMIR
Icon, probably from Constantinople. Faces, 11th–12th century; the figures have been retouched. Tempera on panel, height approx. 31″ (78 cm). Tretyakov Gallery, Moscow.

5-48 • HARBAVILLE TRIPTYCH
Mid 11th century. Ivory, closed 11 × 9½″ (28 × 24.1 cm); open 11 × 19″ (28 × 48.2 cm). Musée du Louvre, Paris.

The luxurious Paris Psalter (named after its current library location), with 14 full-page paintings, was created for a Byzantine aristocrat during the second half of the tenth century. According to ancient tradition, the author of the Psalms was Israel's King David, who as a young shepherd and musician had saved the people of God by killing the giant Goliath (SEE FIG. 5–11). In Christian times, the Psalms were often extracted from the Bible and copied into a separate book called a **psalter**, used by wealthy Christians for private prayer and meditation.

The painters who worked on the Paris Psalter framed their scenes on full pages without text. The first of these depicts a seated David playing his harp **(FIG. 5–49)**. The monumental, idealized figures occupy a spacious landscape filled with lush foliage, a meandering stream, and a distant city. The image seems to have been transported directly from an ancient Roman wall painting. The ribbon-tied memorial column is a convention in Greek and Roman funerary art and, in the ancient manner, the illustrator has personified abstract ideas and landscape features: Melody, a female figure, leans casually on David's shoulder, while another woman, perhaps the nymph Echo, peeks out from behind the column. The swarthy reclining youth in

5-49 • DAVID THE PSALMIST
Page from the Paris Psalter. Second half of 10th century. Paint and gold on vellum, sheet size 14 × 10½″ (35.6 × 26 cm). Bibliothèque Nationale, Paris.

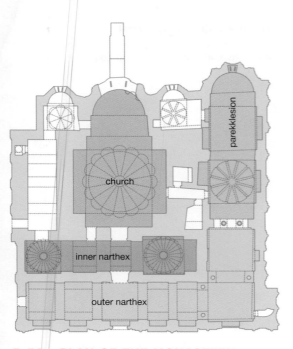

5-50 • PLAN OF THE MONASTERY CHURCH OF CHRIST IN CHORA
Constantinople. (Present-day Kariye Müzesi, Istanbul, Turkey.) 1077–1081, c. 1310–1321.

To view this image, please go to page 254 of the *Art History*, Fourth Edition by Marilyn Stokstad ebook.

5-51 • MOSAICS IN THE VAULTING OF THE INNER NARTHEX
Church of Christ in Chora, Constantinople. (Present-day Kariye Müzesi, Istanbul, Turkey.) c. 1315–1321.

the lower foreground is a personification of Mount Bethlehem, as we learn from his inscription. The image of the dog watching over the sheep and goats while his master strums the harp suggests the Classical subject of Orpheus charming wild animals with music. The subtle modeling of forms, the integration of the figures into a three-dimensional space, and the use of atmospheric perspective all enhance the Classical flavor of the painting, in yet another example of the enduring vitality of pagan artistic traditions at the Christian court in Constantinople.

LATE BYZANTINE ART

The third great age of Byzantine art began in 1261, after the Byzantines expelled the Christian crusaders who had occupied Constantinople for nearly 60 years. Although the empire had been weakened and its realm decreased to small areas of the Balkans and Greece, its arts underwent a resurgence known as the Palaeologue Renaissance after the dynasty of emperors who ruled from Constantinople. The patronage of emperors, wealthy courtiers, and the Church stimulated renewed church building as well as the production of icons, books, and precious objects.

CONSTANTINOPLE: THE CHORA CHURCH

In Constantinople, many existing churches were renovated, redecorated, and expanded during the Palaeologue Renaissance. Among these is the church of the Monastery of Christ in Chora. The expansion of this church was one of several projects that Theodore Metochites (1270–1332), a humanist poet and scientist, and the administrator of the Imperial Treasury at Constantinople, sponsored between c. 1315 and 1321. He added a two-story annex

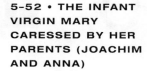

To view this image, please go to page 255 of the *Art History*, Fourth Edition by Marilyn Stokstad ebook.

5–52 • THE INFANT VIRGIN MARY CARESSED BY HER PARENTS (JOACHIM AND ANNA)
Inner narthex, church of Christ in Chora, Constantinople. (Present-day Kariye Müzesi, Istanbul, Turkey.) c. 1315–1321. Mosaic.

The Greek inscription placed over the family group identifies this scene as the fondling of the Theotokos (bearer of God).

on the north side, two narthexes on the west, and a parekklesion (side chapel) used as a funerary chapel on the south **(FIG. 5–50)**. These structures contain the most impressive interior decorations remaining in Constantinople from the Late Byzantine period, rivaling in splendor and technical sophistication the works of the age of Justinian, but on a more intimate scale. The walls and vaults of the parekklesion are covered with frescos (see "The Funerary Chapel of Theodore Metochites," pages 354–355), and the vaults of the narthexes are encrusted with mosaics.

In the new narthexes of the Chora church, above an expanse of traditional marble revetment on the lower walls, mosaics cover every surface—the domical groin vaults, the wall lunettes, even the undersides of arches—with narrative scenes and their ornamental framework **(FIG. 5–51)**. The small-scale figures of these mosaics seem to dance with relentless enthusiasm through the narrative episodes they enact from the lives of Christ and his mother. Unlike the stripped-down narrative scenes of Daphni (SEE FIG. 5–45), here the artists have lavished special attention on the settings, composing their stories against backdrops of architectural fantasies and stylized plants. The architecture of the background is presented in an innovative system of perspective, charting its three-dimensionality not in relation to a point of convergence in the background—as will be the case in the linear, one-point perspective of fifteenth-century Florentine art—but projecting

forward in relationship to a point in the foreground, thereby drawing attention to the figural scenes themselves.

The Chora mosaics build on the growing Byzantine interest in the expression of emotions within religious narrative, but they broach a level of human tenderness that surpasses anything we have seen in Byzantine art thus far. The artists invite viewers to see the participants in these venerable sacred stories as human beings just like themselves, only wealthier and holier. For example, an entire narrative field in one vault is devoted to a scene where the infant Mary is cuddled between her adoring parents, Joachim and Anna **(FIG. 5–52**; part of the scene is visible lit up in FIG. 5–51). Servants on either side of the family look on with gestures and expressions of admiration and approval, perhaps modeling the response that is expected from viewers within the narthex itself. The human interaction even extends to details, such as the nuzzling of Mary's head into the beard of her father as she leans back to look into his eyes, and her tentative reach toward her mother's face at the same time. In another scene, the young Jesus rides on the shoulders of Joseph, in a pose still familiar to fathers and children in our own time. The informality and believability that these anecdotal details bring to this sacred narrative recalls developments as far away as Italy, where at this same time Giotto and Duccio were using similar devices to bring their stories to life.

The Funerary Chapel of Theodore Metochites

Theodore Metochites (1270–1332) was one of the most fascinating personalities of the Late Byzantine world. Son of a disgraced intellectual cleric—condemned and exiled for championing the union of the Roman and Byzantine Churches—Metochites became a powerful intellectual figure in Constantinople. As a poet, philosopher, and astronomer who wrote scores of convoluted commentaries in an intentionally cultivated, arcane, and mannered literary style, he ridiculed a rival for his prose style of "excess clarity." In 1290, Emperor Andronicus II Palaeologus (r. 1282–1328) called Metochites to court service, where the prolific young scholar became an influential senior statesman, ascending to the highest levels of the government and amassing power and wealth second only to that of the emperor himself. Metochites' political and financial status fell when the emperor was overthrown by his grandson in 1328. Stripped of his wealth and sent into exile, he was allowed to return to the capital two years later, retiring to house arrest at the Chora monastery, where he died and was buried in 1332.

It is his association with this monastery that has become Theodore Metochites' greatest claim to enduring fame. Beginning in about 1315, at the peak of his power and wealth, he funded an expansion and restoration of the church of Christ in Chora

(meaning "in the country"), part of an influential monastery on the outskirts of Constantinople. The mosaic decoration he commissioned for the church's expansive narthexes (SEE FIGS. 5–51, 5–52) may be the most sumptuous product of his beneficence, but the project probably revolved around a funerary chapel (or parekklesion) that he built adjacent to the main church (FIG. B), potentially motivated by a desire to create a location for his own funeral and tomb.

The extensive and highly integrative program of frescos covering every square inch of the walls and vaults of this jewel-box space focuses on funerary themes and expectations of salvation and its rewards. Above a dado of imitation marble stand a frieze of 34 stately saints ready to fulfill their roles as intercessors for the faithful. Above them, on the side walls of the main space, are stories from the Hebrew Bible interpreted as prefigurations of the Virgin Mary's own intercessory powers. A portrayal of Jacob's ladder (Genesis 28:11–19), for example, evokes her position between heaven and earth as a bridge from death to life. In the pendentives of the dome over the main space (two of which are seen in the foreground) sit famous Byzantine hymn writers, with quotations from their work. These carefully chosen passages highlight texts associated with funerals, including one

that references the story of Jacob's ladder.

The climax of the decorative program, however, is the powerful rendering of the Anastasis that occupies the halfdome of the apse (FIG. A). In this popular Byzantine representation of the Resurrection—drawn not from the Bible but from the apocryphal Gospel of Nicodemus—Jesus demonstrates his powers of salvation by descending into hell after his death on the cross to save his righteous Hebrew forebears from Satan's grasp. Here a boldly striding Christ—brilliantly outfitted in a pure white that makes him shine to prominence within the fresco program—lunges to rescue Adam and Eve from their tombs, pulling them upward with such force that they seem to float airborne under the spell of his power. Satan lies tied into a useless bundle at his feet, and patriarchs, kings, and prophets to either side look on in admiration, perhaps waiting for their own turn to be rescued. During a funeral in this chapel, the head of the deceased would have been directed toward this engrossing tableau, closed eyes facing upward toward a painting of the Last Judgment, strategically positioned on the vault over the bier. In 1332, this was the location of Metochites' own dead body since this parekklesion was indeed the site of his funeral. He was buried in one of the niche tombs cut into the walls of the chapel itself.

To view this image, please go to page 256 of the *Art History*, Fourth Edition by Marilyn Stokstad ebook.

A. ANASTASIS
Apse of the funerary chapel, church of the Monastery of Christ in Chora. Fresco. Getty Research Library, Los Angeles. Wim Swaan Photograph Collection, 96.P.21

To view this image, please go to page 257 of the *Art History*,
Fourth Edition by Marilyn Stokstad ebook.

B. FUNERARY CHAPEL (PAREKKLESION), CHURCH OF THE MONASTERY OF CHRIST IN CHORA
Constantinople. (Present-day Kariye Müzesi, Istanbul, Turkey.) c. 1310–1321.

To view this image, please go to page 258 of the *Art History*,
Fourth Edition by Marilyn Stokstad ebook.

5-53 • Andrey Rublyov **THE OLD TESTAMENT TRINITY (THREE ANGELS VISITING ABRAHAM)**
Icon. c. 1410–1425. Tempera on panel, 55½ × 44½" (141 × 113 cm).

MOSCOW: RUBLYOV

In the fifteenth and sixteenth centuries, architecture of the Late Byzantine style flourished outside the borders of the empire in regions that had adopted Eastern Orthodox Christianity. After Constantinople's fall to the Ottoman Turks in 1453, leadership of the Orthodox Church shifted to Russia, whose rulers declared Moscow to be the "Third Rome" and themselves the heirs of Caesar (the tsar).

The practice of venerating icons continued—perhaps even intensified—in Russia, where regional schools of icon painting flourished, fostering the work of remarkable artists. A magnificent icon from this time is **THE OLD TESTAMENT TRINITY (THREE ANGELS VISITING ABRAHAM)**, a large panel created sometime between about 1410 and 1425 by the renowned artist-monk Andrey Rublyov **(FIG. 5–53)**. It was commissioned in honor of Abbot Sergius of the Trinity-Sergius Monastery, near Moscow. The theme is the Trinity, always a challenge for artists. One late medieval solution was to show three identical divine individuals—here three angels—to suggest the idea of the Trinity. Rublyov's composition was inspired by a story in the Hebrew Bible of the patriarch Abraham and his wife Sarah, who entertained three strangers who were in fact God represented by three divine beings in human form (Genesis 18). Tiny images of Abraham and Sarah's home and the oak of Mamre can be seen above the angels. On the table, the food the couple offered to the strangers becomes a chalice on an altarlike table.

Rublyov's icon clearly illustrates how Late Byzantine artists relied on mathematical conventions to create ideal figures, as did the ancient Greeks, giving their works remarkable consistency. But unlike the Greeks, who based their formulas on close observation of nature, Byzantine artists invented an ideal geometry to evoke a spiritual realm and conformed their representations of human forms and features to it. Here, as is often the case, the circle—most apparent in the haloes—forms the basic underlying structure for the composition. Despite the formulaic approach, talented artists like Rublyov created a personal, expressive style working within it. Rublyov relied on typical Byzantine conventions—salient contours, elongation of the body, and a focus on a limited number of figures—to capture the sense of the spiritual in his work, yet he distinguished his art by imbuing it with a sweet, poetic ambience. In this master's hands, the Byzantine style took on a graceful and eloquent new life.

The Byzantine tradition would continue in the art of the Eastern Orthodox Church and is carried on to this day in Greek and Russian icon painting. In Constantinople, however, the three golden ages of Byzantine art—and the empire itself—came to an end in 1453. When the forces of the Ottoman sultan Mehmed II overran the capital, the Eastern Empire became part of the Islamic world. But the Turkish conquerors were so impressed with the splendor of the Byzantine art and architecture in the capital that they adopted its traditions and melded them with their own rich aesthetic heritage into a new, and now Islamic, artistic efflorescence.

THINK ABOUT IT

5.5 Discuss the Roman foundations of Early Christian sculpture, focusing your answer on the *Sarcophagus of Junius Bassus* (FIG. 5–23).

5.6 Distinguish the "iconic" from the "narrative" in Early Christian and Byzantine art, locating one example of each in this chapter. How are these two traditions used by the Church and its members?

5.7 Distinguish the identifying features of basilicas and central-plan churches, and discuss how the forms of these early churches were geared toward specific types of Christian worship and devotional practice.

5.8 How were images used in Byzantine worship? Why were images suppressed during Iconoclasm?

5.9 Compare and contrast the mosaics of San Vitale in Ravenna with those in the Chora church in Constantinople. Consider, in particular, how figures are represented, what kinds of stories are told, and in what way.

PRACTICE MORE: Compose answers to these questions, get flashcards for images and terms, and review chapter material with quizzes
www.myartslab.com

To view this image, please go to page 260 of the *Art History*, Fourth Edition by Marilyn Stokstad ebook.

5-54 • Yahya Ibn al-Wasiti **THE *MAQAMAT* OF AL-HARIRI**   From Baghdad, Iraq. 1237. Paper.
Bibliothèque Nationale, Paris. (Arabic MS. 5847, f. 18v)

ISLAMIC ART

The *Maqamat* ("Assemblies"), by al-Hariri (1054–1122), belongs to a popular literary genre of cautionary tales dating from the tenth century. The manuscript's vividly detailed scenes provide windows into ordinary Muslim life, here prayer in the congregational **mosque**, a religious and social institution central to Islam. Al-Hariri's stories revolve around a silver-tongued scoundrel named Abu Zayd, whose cunning inevitably triumphs over other people's naivety. His adventures take place in a world of colorful settings—desert camps, ships, pilgrim caravans, apothecary shops, mosques, gardens, libraries, cemeteries, and courts of law. Humans activate the scenes, pointing fingers, arguing, riding horses, stirring pots, and strumming musical instruments. These comic stories of trickery and theft would seem perfectly suited for illustration, but of the hundreds of surviving manuscript copies, only 13 have pictures.

This illustration (**FIG. 5–54**) shows a mosque with the congregation gathered to hear a sermon preached by the deceitful Abu Zayd, who plans to steal the alms collected from the congregation. The men sit directly on the ground, as is customary in mosques (and traditional dwellings). They look generally forward, but the listener in the front row tilts his chin upward to focus his gaze directly upon the speaker. He is framed and centered by the arch of the niche (**mihrab**) on the rear wall, his white turban contrasting noticeably with the darker background. To the extent that he represents any specific individual, he seems to stand in for the manuscript's reader who, perusing the illustrations of these captivating stories, pauses and perhaps projects himself or herself into the scene.

The columns of the arcades have ornamental capitals from which spring half-round arches. Glass mosque lamps filled with oil hang from the center of each arch. All the figures wear turbans and flowing, loose-sleeved robes with epigraphic borders (*tiraz*) embroidered in gold.

The sermon is delivered from a pulpit (**minbar**) of steps with an arched opening at the lowest level. This *minbar* and the arcades that form the backdrop to the scene and define the mosque's interior are unnaturally reduced in scale. The painter has manipulated the sizes so as to fit the maximum amount of detail into the scene, sacrificing natural space in order to make the painting more communicative. Likewise, although in an actual mosque the *minbar* would share the same wall as the niche in the center, here they have been separated to keep the niche from being hidden by the *minbar*. There is little modeling to represent volume: Instead depth of field is suggested by the overlapping of forms.

LEARN ABOUT IT

5.10 Discover Islamic art's eclecticism and embrace of other cultures.

5.11 Compare and contrast the variety of art and architecture in the disparate areas of the Islamic world.

5.12 Interpret art as a reflection of both religion and secular society.

5.13 Explore the use of ornament and inscription in Islamic art.

5.14 Recognize the role of trade routes and political ties in the creation of Islamic artistic unity.

HEAR MORE: Listen to an audio file of your chapter **www.myartslab.com**

ISLAM AND EARLY ISLAMIC SOCIETY

Islam arose in seventh-century Arabia, a land of desert oases with no cities of great size, sparsely inhabited by tribal nomads. Yet, under the leadership of its founder, the Prophet Muhammad (c. 570–632 CE), and his successors, Islam spread rapidly throughout northern Africa, southern and eastern Europe, and much of Asia, gaining territory and converts with astonishing speed. Because Islam encompassed geographical areas with a variety of long-established cultural traditions, and because it admitted diverse peoples among its converts, it absorbed and combined many different techniques and ideas about art and architecture. The result was a remarkable eclecticism and artistic sophistication.

In the desert outside of Mecca in 610, Muhammad received revelations that led him to found the religion called Islam ("submission to God's will"), whose adherents are Muslims ("those who have submitted to God"). Many powerful Meccans were hostile to the message of the young visionary, and in 622 he and his companions were forced to flee to Medina. There Muhammad built a house that became a gathering place for the converted and thus the first Islamic mosque. Muslims date their history as beginning with this *hijira* ("emigration").

In 630, Muhammad returned to Mecca with an army of 10,000, routed his enemies, and established the city as the spiritual capital of Islam. After his triumph, he went to the Kaaba **(FIG. 5–55)**, a cubical, textile-draped shrine said to have been built for God by Ibrahim (Abraham) and Isma'il (Ishmael) and long the focus of pilgrimage and polytheistic worship. He emptied the shrine, repudiating its accumulated pagan idols, while preserving the enigmatic cubical structure itself and dedicating it to God.

The Kaaba is the symbolic center of the Islamic world, the place to which all Muslim prayer is directed and the ultimate destination of Islam's obligatory pilgrimage, the *hajj*. Each year, huge numbers of Muslims from all over the world travel to Mecca to circumambulate the Kaaba during the month of pilgrimage. The exchange of ideas that occurs during the intermingling of these diverse groups of pilgrims has contributed to Islam's cultural eclecticism.

Muhammad's act of emptying the Kaaba of its pagan idols instituted the fundamental concept of **aniconism** (avoidance of

To view this image, please go to page 262 of the *Art History*, Fourth Edition by Marilyn Stokstad ebook.

5-55 • THE KAABA, MECCA

The Kaaba represents the center of the Islamic world. Its cubical form is draped with a black textile that is embroidered with a few Qur'anic verses in gold.

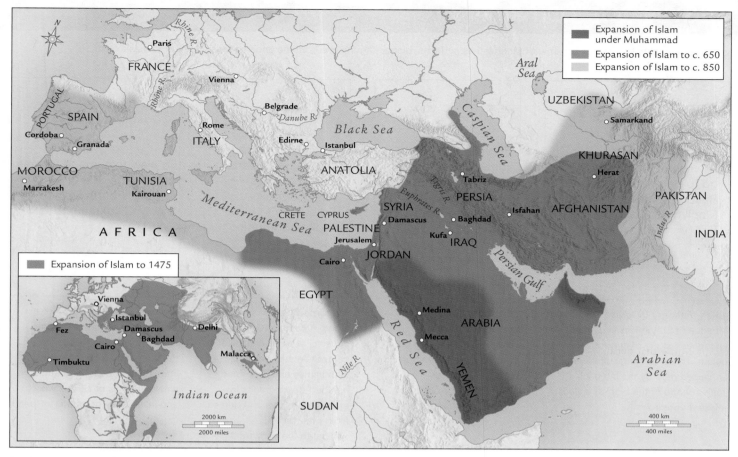

MAP 5-2 • THE ISLAMIC WORLD

Within 200 years after 622 CE, the Islamic world expanded from Mecca to India in the east, and to Morocco and Spain in the west.

figural imagery) in Islamic art. Following his example, the Muslim faith discourages the representation of figures in religious contexts (although such images abound in palaces and illustrated manuscripts). Instead, Islamic artists elaborated a rich vocabulary of nonfigural ornament, including complex geometric designs and scrolling vines sometimes known as **arabesques**. Islamic art revels in surface decoration, in manipulating line, color, and especially pattern, often highlighting the interplay of pure abstraction, organic form, and script.

According to tradition, the Qur'an assumed its final form during the time of the third caliph (successor to the Prophet), Uthman (r. 644–56). As the language of the Qur'an, the Arabic language and script have been a powerful unifying force within Islam. From the eighth through the eleventh centuries, it was the universal language among scholars in the Islamic world and in some Christian lands as well. Inscriptions frequently ornament works of art, sometimes written clearly to provide a readable message, but in other cases written as complex patterns simply to delight the eye.

The Prophet was succeeded by a series of caliphs. The accession of Ali as the fourth caliph (r. 656–61) provoked a power struggle that led to his assassination and resulted in enduring divisions within Islam. Followers of Ali, known as Shi'ites (referring

to the party or *shi'a* of Ali), regard him alone as the Prophet's rightful successor. Sunni Muslims, in contrast, recognize all of the first four caliphs as "rightly guided." Ali was succeeded by his rival Muawiya (r. 661–80), a close relative of Uthman and the founder of the first Muslim dynasty, the Umayyad dynasty (661–750).

Islam expanded dramatically. In just two decades, seemingly unstoppable Muslim armies conquered the Sasanian Persian Empire, Egypt, and the Byzantine provinces of Syria and Palestine. By the early eighth century, under the Umayyads, they had reached India, conquered northern Africa and Spain, and penetrated France before being turned back (MAP 5–2). In these newly conquered lands, the treatment of Christians and Jews who did not convert to Islam was not consistent, but in general, as "People of the Book"—followers of a monotheistic religion based on a revealed scripture—they enjoyed a protected status. However, they were also subject to a special tax and restrictions on dress and employment.

Muslims participate in congregational worship at a mosque (*masjid*, "place of prostration"). The Prophet Muhammad himself lived simply and instructed his followers in prayer at his house, now known as the Mosque of the Prophet, where he resided in Medina. This was a square enclosure that framed a large courtyard with rooms along the east wall where he and his family lived. Along the

Islamic art delights in complex ornament that sheathes surfaces, distracting the eye from the underlying structure or physical form.

To view this image, please go to page 264 of the *Art History*, Fourth Edition by Marilyn Stokstad ebook.

To view this image, please go to page 264 of the *Art History*, Fourth Edition by Marilyn Stokstad ebook.

To view this image, please go to page 264 of the *Art History*, Fourth Edition by Marilyn Stokstad ebook.

To view this image, please go to page 264 of the *Art History*, Fourth Edition by Marilyn Stokstad ebook.

ablaq masonry (*Madrasa*-Mausoleum-Mosque of Sultan Hasan, Cairo) juxtaposes stone of contrasting colors. The ornamental effect is enhanced here by the interlocking jigsaw shape of the blocks, called **joggled voussoirs**.

cut tile (Shah-i Zinda, Samarkand), made up of dozens of individually cut ceramic tile pieces fitted precisely together, emphasizes the clarity of the colored shapes.

muqarnas (Court of the Lions, Alhambra, Granada) consists of small nichelike components, usually stacked in multiples as successive, nonload-bearing units in arches, cornices, and domes, hiding the transition from the vertical to the horizontal plane.

wooden strapwork (Kutubiya *Minbar*, Marrakesh) assembles finely cut wooden pieces to create the appearance of geometrically interlacing ribbons, often framing smaller panels of carved wood and inlaid ivory or mother-of-pearl (shell).

To view this image, please go to page 264 of the *Art History*, Fourth Edition by Marilyn Stokstad ebook.

To view this image, please go to page 264 of the *Art History*, Fourth Edition by Marilyn Stokstad ebook.

To view this image, please go to page 264 of the *Art History*, Fourth Edition by Marilyn Stokstad ebook.

mosaic (Dome of the Rock, Jerusalem) is comprised of thousands of small glass or glazed ceramic tesserae set on a plaster ground. The luminous white circular shapes are mother-of-pearl.

water (Court of the Myrtles, Alhambra, Granada) is a fluid architectural element that reflects surrounding architecture, adds visual dynamism and sound, and, running in channels between halls, unites disparate spaces.

chini khana (Ali Qapu Pavilion, Isfahan)—literally "china cabinet"—is a panel of niches, sometimes providing actual shelving, but used here for its contrast of material and void which reverses the typical figure-ground relationship.

south wall, a thatched portico supported by palm-tree trunks sheltered both the faithful as they prayed and Muhammad as he spoke from a low platform. This simple arrangement inspired the design of later mosques. Lacking an architectural focus such as an altar, nave, or dome, the space of this prototypical **hypostyle** (multicolumned) mosque reflected the founding spirit of Islam in which the faithful pray as equals directly to God, led by an imam, but without the intermediary of a priesthood.

ART AND ARCHITECTURE THROUGH THE FOURTEENTH CENTURY

The caliphs of the Umayyad dynasty (661–750) ruled from Damascus in Syria, and throughout the Islamic Empire they built mosques and palaces that projected the authority of the new rulers and reflected the growing acceptance of Islam. In 750 the Abbasid clan replaced the Umayyads in a coup d'état, ruling as caliphs until 1258 from Baghdad, in Iraq, in the grand manner of the ancient Persian emperors. Their long and cosmopolitan reign saw achievements in medicine, mathematics, the natural sciences, philosophy, literature, music, and art. They were generally tolerant of the ethnically diverse populations in the territories they subjugated, and they admired the past achievements of Roman civilization and the living traditions of Byzantium, Persia, India, and China, freely borrowing artistic techniques and styles from all of them.

In the tenth century, the Islamic world split into separate kingdoms ruled by independent caliphs. In addition to the Abbasids of Iraq, there was a Fatimid Shi'ite caliph ruling Tunisia and Egypt, and a descendant of the Umayyads ruling Spain and Portugal (together then known as al-Andalus). The Islamic world did not reunite under the myriad dynasties who thereafter ruled from northern Africa to Asia, but the loss to unity was a gain to artistic diversity.

EARLY ARCHITECTURE

While Mecca and Medina remained the holiest Muslim cities, the political center shifted to the Syrian city of Damascus in 656. In the eastern Mediterranean, inspired by Roman and Byzantine architecture, the early Muslims became enthusiastic builders of shrines, mosques, and palaces. Although tombs were officially discouraged in Islam, they proliferated from the eleventh century onward, in part due to funerary practices imported from the Turkic northeast, and in part due to the rise of Shi'ism with its emphasis on genealogy and particularly ancestry through Muhammad's daughter, Fatima.

THE DOME OF THE ROCK. The Dome of the Rock is the first great monument of Islamic art. Built in Jerusalem, it is the third most holy site in Islam. In the center of the city rises the Haram al-Sharif ("Noble Sanctuary") (FIG. 5–56), a rocky outcrop from which Muslims believe Muhammad ascended to the presence of God on the "Night Journey" described in the Qur'an. It is the site of the First and Second Jewish Temples, and Jews and Christians variously associate it with Solomon, the site of the creation of Adam, and the place where the patriarch Abraham prepared to sacrifice his son Isaac at the command of God. In 691–92, a shrine was built over the rock using artisans trained in the Byzantine tradition. By appropriating a site holy to the Jewish and Christian

To view this image, please go to page 265 of the *Art History*, Fourth Edition by Marilyn Stokstad ebook.

5-56 • AERIAL VIEW OF HARAM AL-SHARIF, JERUSALEM
The Dome of the Rock occupies a place of visual height and prominence in Jerusalem and, when first built, strikingly emphasized the arrival of Islam and its community of adherents in that ancient city.

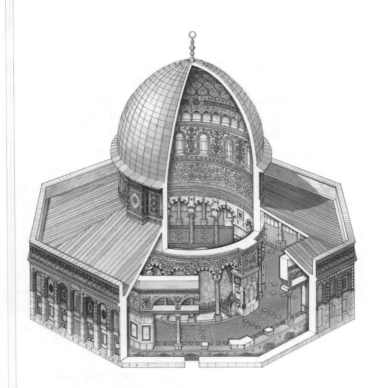

5-57 • CUTAWAY DRAWING OF THE DOME OF THE ROCK

faiths, the Dome of the Rock is the first architectural manifestation of Islam's view of itself as completing the prophecies of those faiths and superseding them.

Structurally, the Dome of the Rock imitates the centrally planned form of Early Christian and Byzantine martyria (SEE FIG. 5-30). However, unlike its models, with their plain exteriors, it is crowned by a golden dome that dominates the Jerusalem skyline. The ceramic tiles on the lower portion of the exterior were added later, but the opulent marble veneer and mosaics of the interior are original (see "Ornament," page 362). The dome, surmounting a circular drum pierced with windows and supported by arcades of alternating **piers** and **columns**, covers the central space containing the rock **(FIG. 5–57)**. These arcades create concentric **aisles** (**ambulatories**) that permit devout visitors to circumambulate the rock. Inscriptions from the Qur'an interspersed with passages from other texts, including information about the building itself, form a frieze around the inner and outer arcades. As the pilgrim walks around the central space to read the inscriptions in brilliant gold mosaic on turquoise green ground, the building communicates both as a text and as a dazzling visual display **(FIG. 5–58)**. These passages of text are especially notable because they are the oldest surviving written Qur'an verses and the first use of monumental Qur'anic inscriptions in architecture. Below are walls covered with pale marble, the veining of which creates abstract symmetrical patterns, and columns with shafts of gray marble and gilded capitals. Above the calligraphic frieze is another mosaic frieze depicting thick, symmetrical vine scrolls and trees in turquoise, blue, and green, embellished with imitation jewels, over a gold ground. The mosaics are variously

thought to represent the gardens of Paradise and trophies of Muslim victories offered to God. The decorative program is extraordinarily rich but, remarkably enough, the focus of the building is neither art nor architecture but the plain rock within it.

THE GREAT MOSQUE OF KAIROUAN. Muslim congregations gather on Fridays for regular worship in a mosque. The earliest mosque type was the hypostyle, following the model of the Prophet's own house. The Great Mosque of Kairouan, Tunisia **(FIG. 5–59)**, built in the ninth century, reflects the early form of the mosque but is elaborated with later additions. The large rectangular space is divided between a courtyard and a flat-roofed hypostyle prayer hall oriented toward Mecca. The system of repeated bays and aisles can easily be extended as the congregation grows in size—

To view this image, please go to page 266 of the *Art History*, Fourth Edition by Marilyn Stokstad ebook.

5-58 • DOME OF THE ROCK, JERUSALEM
691. Interior. The arches of the inner and outer face of the central arcade are encrusted with golden mosaics, a Byzantine technique adapted for Islamic use. The carpets and ceilings are modern but probably reflect the original patron's intention.

EXPLORE MORE: Click the Google Earth link for the Dome of the Rock **www.myartslab.com**

The Five Pillars of Islam

Islam emphasizes a direct, personal relationship with God. The Pillars of Islam, sometimes symbolized by an open hand with the five fingers extended, enumerate the duties required of Muslims by their faith.

- The first pillar (*shahadah*) is to proclaim that there is only one God and that Muhammad is his messenger. While monotheism is common to Judaism, Christianity, and Islam, and Muslims worship the god of Abraham, and also acknowledge Hebrew and Christian prophets such as Musa (Moses) and Isa (Jesus), Muslims deem the Christian Trinity polytheistic and assert that God was not born and did not give birth.

- The second pillar requires prayer (*salat*) to be performed by turning to face the Kaaba in Mecca five times daily: at dawn, noon, late afternoon, sunset, and nightfall. Prayer can occur almost anywhere, although the prayer on Fridays takes place in the congregational mosque. Because ritual ablutions are required for purity, mosque courtyards usually have fountains.

- The third pillar is the voluntary payment of annual tax or alms (*zakah*), equivalent to one-fortieth of one's assets. *Zakah* is used for charities such as feeding the poor, housing travelers, and paying the dowries of orphan girls. Among Shi'ites, an additional tithe is required to support the Shi'ite community specifically.

- The fourth pillar is the dawn-to-dusk fast (*sawm*) during Ramadan, the month when Muhammad received the revelations set down in the Qur'an. The fast of Ramadan is a communally shared sacrifice that imparts purification, self-control, and kinship with others. The end of Ramadan is celebrated with the feast day 'Id al-Fitr (Festival of the Breaking of the Fast).

- For those physically and financially able to do so, the fifth pillar is the pilgrimage to Mecca (*hajj*), which ideally is undertaken at least once in the life of each Muslim. Among the extensive pilgrimage rites are donning simple garments to remove distinctions of class and culture; collective circumambulations of the Kaaba; kissing the Black Stone inside the Kaaba (probably a meteorite that fell in pre-Islamic times); and the sacrificing of an animal, usually a sheep, in memory of Abraham's readiness to sacrifice his son at God's command. The end of the *hajj* is celebrated by the festival 'Id al-Adha (Festival of Sacrifice).

The directness and simplicity of Islam have made the Muslim religion readily adaptable to numerous varied cultural contexts throughout history. The Five Pillars instill not only faith and a sense of belonging, but also a commitment to Islam in the form of actual practice.

---

one of the hallmarks of the hypostyle plan. New is the large tower (the **minaret**, from which the faithful are called to prayer) that rises from one end of the courtyard and that stands as a powerful sign of Islam's presence in the city.

The **qibla** wall, marked by a centrally positioned *mihrab* niche, is the wall of the prayer hall that is closest to Mecca. Prayer is oriented towards this wall. In the Great Mosque of Kairouan, the *qibla* wall is given heightened importance by a raised roof, a dome over the *mihrab*, and a central aisle that marks the axis that extends from the minaret to the *mihrab* (for a fourteenth-century example of a *mihrab*, SEE FIG. 5–65). The *mihrab* belongs to the historical tradition of niches that signify a holy place—the shrine for the Torah scrolls in a synagogue, the frame for the sculpture of a god or ancestor in Roman architecture, the apse in a church.

To view this image, please go to page 267 of the *Art History*, Fourth Edition by Marilyn Stokstad ebook.

5-59 • THE GREAT MOSQUE, KAIROUAN, TUNISIA
836–875.

EXPLORE MORE: Click the Google Earth link for the Great Mosque of Kairouan **www.myartslab.com**

The Great Mosque of Cordoba

When the Umayyads were toppled in 750, a survivor of the dynasty, Abd al-Rahman I (r. 756–788), fled across north Africa into southern Spain (al-Andalus) where, with the support of Muslim settlers, he established himself as the provincial ruler, or emir. This newly transplanted Umayyad dynasty ruled in Spain from their capital in Cordoba (756–1031). The Hispano-Umayyads were noted patrons of the arts, and one of the finest surviving examples of Umayyad architecture is the Great Mosque of Cordoba.

In 785, the Umayyad conquerors began building the Cordoba mosque on the site of a Christian church built by the Visigoths, the pre-Islamic rulers of Spain. The choice of site was both practical—for the Muslims had already been renting space within the church—and symbolic, an appropriation of place (similar to the Dome of the Rock) that affirmed their presence. Later rulers expanded the building three times, and today the walls enclose an area of about 620 by 460 feet, about a third of which is the courtyard. This patio was planted with fruit trees, beginning in the early ninth century; today orange trees seasonally fill the space with color and sweet scent. Inside, the proliferation of pattern in the repeated columns and double flying arches is colorful and dramatic. The marble columns and capitals in the hypostyle prayer hall were recycled from the Christian church that had formerly occupied the site, as well as from classical buildings in the region, which had been a wealthy Roman province. The mosque's interior incorporates *spolia* (reused) columns of slightly varying heights. Two tiers of arches, one over the other, surmount these columns; the upper tier springs from rectangular posts that rise from the columns. This double-tiered design dramatically increases the height of the interior space, inspiring a sense of

monumentality and awe. The distinctively shaped **horseshoe arches**—a form known from Roman times and favored by the Visigoths—came to be closely associated with Islamic architecture in the West (see "Arches," page 369). Another distinctive feature of these arches, adopted from Roman and Byzantine precedents, is the alternation of white stone and red brick voussoirs forming the curved arch. This mixture of materials may have helped the building withstand earthquakes.

In the final century of Umayyad rule, Cordoba emerged as a major commercial and intellectual hub and a flourishing center for the arts, surpassing Christian European cities in science, literature, and philosophy. As a sign of this new wealth, prestige, and power, Abd al-Rahman III (r. 912–961) boldly reclaimed the title of caliph in 929. He and his son al-Hakam II (r. 961–976) made the Great Mosque a focus of patronage, commissioning costly and luxurious renovations such as a new *mihrab* with three bays in front of it. These capped the **maqsura**, an enclosure in front of the *mihrab* reserved for the ruler and other dignitaries, which became a feature of congregational

To view this image, please go to page 268 of the *Art History*, Fourth Edition by Marilyn Stokstad ebook.

PRAYER HALL, GREAT MOSQUE, CORDOBA, SPAIN
Begun 785/786.

mosques after an assassination attempt on one of the Umayyad rulers. A *minbar* formerly stood by the *mihrab* as the place for the prayer leader and as a symbol of authority. The melon-shaped, ribbed dome over the central bay may be a metaphor for the celestial canopy. It seems to float upon a web of crisscrossing arches, the complexity of the design reflecting the Islamic interest in mathematics and geometry, not purely as abstract concepts but as sources for artistic inspiration. Lushly patterned mosaics with inscriptions, geometric motifs, and stylized vegetation clothe both this dome and the *mihrab* below in brilliant color and gold. These were installed by a Byzantine master who was sent by the emperor in Constantinople, bearing boxes of small glazed ceramic and glass pieces (*tesserae*). Such artistic exchange is emblematic of the interconnectedness of the medieval Mediterranean—through trade, diplomacy, and competition.

To view this image, please go to page 269 of the *Art History*, Fourth Edition by Marilyn Stokstad ebook.

DOME IN FRONT OF THE MIHRAB, GREAT MOSQUE, CORDOBA
965.

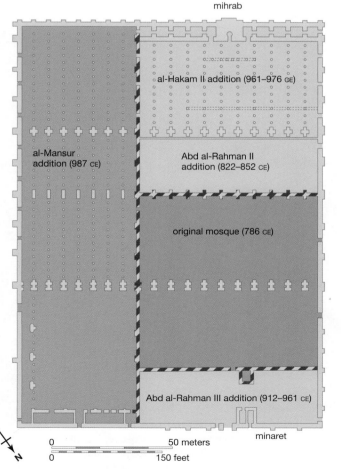

mihrab

al-Hakam II addition (961–976 CE)

al-Mansur addition (987 CE)

Abd al-Rahman II addition (822–852 CE)

original mosque (786 CE)

Abd al-Rahman III addition (912–961 CE)

minaret

0   50 meters
0   150 feet

PLAN, GREAT MOSQUE, CORDOBA

EXPLORE MORE: Click the Google Earth link for the Great Mosque at Cordoba **www.myartslab.com**

THE KUTUBIYA MOSQUE. In the Kutubiya Mosque, the principal mosque of Marrakesh, Morocco, an exceptionally exquisite wooden *minbar* survives from the twelfth century **(FIG. 5–60)**. It consists of a staircase from which the weekly sermon was delivered to the congregation (for example, SEE FIG. 5–54). The sides are paneled in wooden marquetry with strapwork in a geometric pattern of eight-pointed stars and elongated hexagons inlaid with ivory (see "Ornament," page 362). The body of each figure is filled with wood carved in swirling vines. The risers of the stairs represent **horseshoe arches** resting on columns with ivory capitals and bases: Thus the pulpit (which had been made originally for the Booksellers' Mosque in Marrakesh) reflected the arcades of its surrounding architectural context. This *minbar* resembled others across the Islamic world, but those at the Kutubiya Mosque and the Great Mosque of Cordoba were the finest, according to Ibn Marzuq (1311–1379), a distinguished preacher who had given sermons from 48 such *minbars*.

THE LATER PERIOD

The Abbasid caliphate began a slow disintegration in the ninth century, and thereafter power in the Islamic world became fragmented among more or less independent regional rulers. During the eleventh century, the Saljuqs, a Turkic people, swept from north of the Caspian Sea into Khurasan and took Baghdad in

To view this image, please go to page 270 of the *Art History*, Fourth Edition by Marilyn Stokstad ebook.

5-60 • *MINBAR*
From the Kutubiya Mosque, Marrakesh, Morocco. 1125–1130. Wood and ivory, 12′8″ × 11′4″ × 2′10″ (3.86 × 3.46 × 0.87 m). Badi Palace Museum, Marrakesh.

Islamic builders explored structure in innovative ways, using a variety of different arch types. The earliest is the simple semicircular arch, inherited from the Romans and Byzantines. It has a single center point that is level with the points from which the arch springs.

The horseshoe arch is a second type, which predates Islam but became the prevalent arch form in the Maghreb (see "The Great Mosque of Cordoba," page 366). The center point of this kind of arch is above the level of the arch's springing point, so that it pinches inward above the capital.

The pointed arch, introduced after the beginning of Islam, has two (sometimes four) center points, the points generating different circles that overlap (for a very slightly pointed arch, SEE FIG. 5–77).

A keel arch has flat sides, and slopes where other arches are curved. It culminates at a pointed apex (see "Ornament," cut tile, page 362).

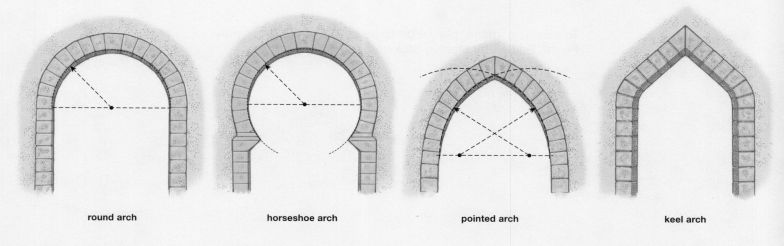

round arch   horseshoe arch   pointed arch   keel arch

SEE MORE: View a simulation about arches www.myartslab.com

1055, becoming the virtual rulers of the Abbasid Empire. The Saljuqs united most of Iran and Iraq, establishing a dynasty that endured from 1037/38 to 1194. A branch of the dynasty, the Saljuqs of Rum, ruled much of Anatolia (Turkey) from the late eleventh to the beginning of the fourteenth century. The central and eastern Islamic world suffered a dramatic rift in the early thirteenth century when the nomadic Mongols—non-Muslims led by Genghiz Khan (r. 1206–1227) and his successors—attacked northern China, Central Asia, and ultimately Iran. The Mongols captured Baghdad in 1258, encountering weak resistance until they reached Egypt, where they were firmly defeated by the new **Mamluk** ruler. The Maghreb (Morocco, Spain, and Portugal) was ruled by various Arab and Berber dynasties. In Spain the borders of Islamic territory were gradually pushed southward by Christian forces until the rule of the last Muslim dynasty, the Nasrids (1230–1492), was ended. Morocco was ruled by the Berber Marinids (from the mid thirteenth century until 1465).

Although the religion of Islam remained a dominant and unifying force throughout these developments, the history of later Islamic society and culture reflects largely regional phenomena. Only a few works have been selected here to characterize the art of Islam, and they by no means provide a comprehensive history of Islamic art.

ARCHITECTURE OF THE MEDITERRANEAN

The new dynasties built on a grand scale, expanding their patronage from mosques and palaces to include new functional buildings, such as tombs, **madrasas** (colleges for religious and legal studies), public fountains, urban hostels, and remote caravanserais (inns) for traveling merchants in order to encourage long-distance trade. A distinguishing characteristic of architecture in the later period is its complexity. Multiple building types were now combined in large and diverse complexes, supported by perpetual endowments (called *waqf*) that funded not only the building, but its administration and maintenance. Increasingly, these complexes included the patron's own tomb, thus giving visual prominence to the act of individual patronage and the expression of personal identity through commemoration. A new plan emerged, organized around a central courtyard framed by four large **iwans** (large vaulted halls with rectangular plans and monumental arched openings); this **four-iwan** plan was used for schools, palaces, and especially mosques.

THE *MADRASA*-MAUSOLEUM-MOSQUE IN CAIRO. Beginning in the eleventh century, Muslim rulers and wealthy individuals endowed hundreds of charitable complexes that displayed piety as well as personal wealth and status. The combined *madrasa*-mausoleum-mosque complex established in mid-fourteenth-century Cairo by

To view this image, please go to page 272 of the *Art History*,
Fourth Edition by Marilyn Stokstad ebook.

5–61 • *QIBLA* WALL WITH *MIHRAB* AND *MINBAR*, SULTAN HASAN *MADRASA*-MAUSOLEUM-MOSQUE COMPLEX
Main *iwan* (vaulted chamber) in the mosque, Cairo. 1356–1363.

EXPLORE MORE: Click the Google Earth link for the *Qibla* wall with *mihrab* and *minbar*,
Sultan Hasan *Madrasa*-Mausoleum-Mosque **www.myartslab.com**

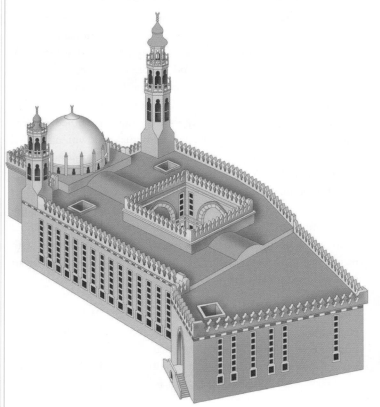

the Mamluk Sultan Hasan **(FIGS. 5–61 and 5–62)** is such an
example. A dark corridor—a deflected entrance that is askew from
the building's orientation—leads from the street into a central,
well-lit courtyard of majestic proportions. The complex has a classic four-*iwan* plan, each *iwan* serving as a classroom for a different
branch of study, the students housed in a multi-storied cluster of
tiny rooms around each one. The sumptuous *qibla iwan* served as
the prayer hall for the complex. Its walls are ornamented with typically Mamluk panels of sharply contrasting marbles (*ablaq* masonry,
see "Ornament," page 362) that culminate in a doubly recessed
mihrab framed by slightly pointed arches on columns. The marble
blocks of the arches are ingeniously joined in interlocking pieces
called **joggled voussoirs**. The paneling is surmounted by a wide
band of **Kufic** (an angular Arabic script) inscription in stucco set
against a background of scrolling vines, both the text and the orna-

**5–62 • THE SULTAN HASAN *MADRASA*-
MAUSOLEUM-MOSQUE COMPLEX**
The *qibla iwan* is visible in the top left face of the courtyard, and the
domed tomb looms behind it.

A Mamluk Glass Oil Lamp ▸ from Cairo, Egypt. c. 1350–1355. Glass, polychrome enamel, and gold. Diameter of the top 10⅝″ (26 cm), height 13⅝″ (35 cm). British Museum, London.

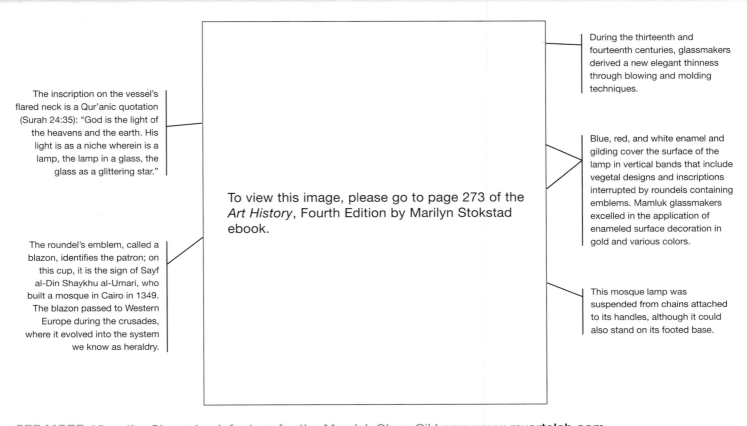

The inscription on the vessel's flared neck is a Qur'anic quotation (Surah 24:35): "God is the light of the heavens and the earth. His light is as a niche wherein is a lamp, the lamp in a glass, the glass as a glittering star."

The roundel's emblem, called a blazon, identifies the patron; on this cup, it is the sign of Sayf al-Din Shaykhu al-Umari, who built a mosque in Cairo in 1349. The blazon passed to Western Europe during the crusades, where it evolved into the system we know as heraldry.

To view this image, please go to page 273 of the *Art History*, Fourth Edition by Marilyn Stokstad ebook.

During the thirteenth and fourteenth centuries, glassmakers derived a new elegant thinness through blowing and molding techniques.

Blue, red, and white enamel and gilding cover the surface of the lamp in vertical bands that include vegetal designs and inscriptions interrupted by roundels containing emblems. Mamluk glassmakers excelled in the application of enameled surface decoration in gold and various colors.

This mosque lamp was suspended from chains attached to its handles, although it could also stand on its footed base.

SEE MORE: View the Closer Look feature for the Mamluk Glass Oil Lamp **www.myartslab.com**

ment referring to the paradise that is promised to the faithful. Next to the *mihrab* stands an elaborate, thronelike *minbar*. A platform for reading the Qur'an is in the foreground. Standing just beyond the *qibla iwan*, the patron's monumental domed tomb attached his identity ostentatiously to the architectural complex. The Sultan Hasan complex is excessive in its vast scale and opulent decoration, but money was not an object: The project was financed by the estates of victims of the bubonic plague that had raged in Cairo from 1348 to 1350.

The mosque in the Sultan Hasan complex—and many smaller establishments—required hundreds of lamps, and glassmaking was a booming industry in Egypt and Syria. Made of ordinary sand and ash, glass is the most ethereal of materials. The Egyptians produced the first glassware during the second millennium BCE, yet the tools and techniques for making it have changed little since then. Exqui-

site glass was also used for beakers and vases, but lamps, lit from within by oil and wick, glowed with special brilliance (see "A Closer Look," above).

THE ALHAMBRA. Muslim patrons also spent lavishly on luxurious palaces set in gardens. The Alhambra in Granada, in southeastern Spain, is an outstanding example of beautiful and refined Islamic palace architecture. Built on the hilltop site of an early Islamic fortress, this palace complex was the seat of the Nasrids (1232–1492), the last Spanish Muslim dynasty, by which time Islamic territory had shrunk from covering most of the Iberian Peninsula to the region around Granada. To the conquering Christians at the end of the fifteenth century, the Alhambra represented the epitome of luxury. Thereafter, they preserved the complex as much to commemorate the defeat of Islam as for its beauty. Essentially a

To view this image, please go to page 274 of the *Art History*, Fourth Edition by Marilyn Stokstad ebook.

EXPLORE MORE: Click the Google Earth link for the Court of the Lions, Alhambra **www.myartslab.com**

small town extending for about half a mile along the crest of a high hill overlooking Granada, it included government buildings, royal residences, gates, mosques, baths, servants' quarters, barracks, stables, a mint, workshops, and gardens. Much of what one sees at the site today was built in the fourteenth century or by Christian patrons in later centuries.

To view this image, please go to page 274 of the *Art History*, Fourth Edition by Marilyn Stokstad ebook.

5-64 • *MUQARNAS* DOME, HALL OF THE ABENCERRAJES, PALACE OF THE LIONS, ALHAMBRA
1354–1391.

The stucco *muqarnas* (stalactite) ornament does not support the dome but is actually suspended from it, composed of some 5,000 individual plaster pieces. Of mesmerizing complexity, the vault's effect can be perceived but its structure cannot be fully comprehended.

SEE MORE: View a video about the Alhambra **www.myartslab.com**

The Alhambra offered dramatic views to the settled valley and snow-capped mountains around it, while enclosing gardens within its courtyards. One of these is the Court of the Lions which stood at the heart of the so-called Palace of the Lions, the private retreat of Sultan Muhammad V (r. 1354–1359 and 1362–1391). The Court of the Lions is divided into quadrants by cross-axial walkways—a garden form called a *chahar bagh*. The walkways carry channels that meet at a central marble fountain held aloft on the backs of 12 stone lions (**FIG. 5–63**). Water animates the fountain, filling the courtyard with the sound of its life-giving abundance. In an adjacent court-yard, the Court of the Myrtles, a basin's round shape responds to the naturally concentric ripples of the water that spouts from a central jet (see "Ornament," page 362). Water has a practical role in the irrigation of gardens, but here it is raised to the level of an art form.

The Court of the Lions is encircled by an arcade of stucco arches embellished with **muqarnas** (see "Ornament," page 362) and supported on single columns or clusters of two and three. Second-floor **miradors**—windows that frame specifically intentioned views—look over the courtyard, which was originally either gardened or more likely paved, with aromatic citrus confined to corner plantings. From these windows, protected by latticework screens, the women of the court, who did not appear in public, would watch the activities of the men below. At one end of the Palace of the Lions, a particularly magnificent *mirador* looks out onto a large, lower garden and the plain below. From here, the sultan literally oversaw the fertile valley that was his kingdom.

On the south side of the Court of the Lions, the lofty Hall of the Abencerrajes was designed as a winter reception hall and music room. In addition to having excellent acoustics, its ceiling exhibits dazzling geometrical complexity and exquisitely carved stucco (**FIG. 5–64**). The star-shaped vault is formed by a honeycomb of clustered *muqarnas* arches that alternate with corner **squinches** that are filled with more *muqarnas*. The square room thus rises to an eight-pointed star, pierced by 16 windows, that culminates in a burst of *muqarnas* floating high overhead, perceived and yet ultimately unknowable, like the heavens themselves.

ARCHITECTURE OF THE EAST

The Mongol invasions brought devastation and political instability but also renewal and artistic exchange that provided the foundation for successor dynasties with a decidedly eastern identity. One of the empires to emerge after the Mongols was the vast Timurid Empire (1370–1506), which conquered Iran, Central Asia, and the northern part of South Asia. Its founder, Timur (known in the West as Tamerlane), was a Mongol descendant, a lineage strengthened through marriage to a descendant of Genghiz Khan. Timur made his capital at Samarkand, which he embellished by means of the forcible relocation of expert artisans from the areas he subdued. Because the empire's compass was vast, Timurid art could integrate Chinese, Persian, Turkic, and Mediterranean artistic ideas into a Mongol base. Its architecture is characterized by axial symmetry, tall double-shelled domes (an inner dome capped by an outer shell

of much larger proportions), modular planning with rhythmically repeated elements, and brilliant cobalt blue, turquoise, and white glazed ceramics. Although the empire itself lasted only 100 years after the death of Timur, its legacy endured in the art of the later Safavid dynasty in Iran and the Mughals of South Asia.

A TILE MIHRAB. Made during a period of uncertainty as Iran shifted from Mongol to Timurid rule, this *mihrab* (1354), originally from a *madrasa* in Isfahan, is one of the finest examples of architec-tural ceramic decoration from this era (**FIG. 5–65**). More than 11 feet tall, it was made by painstakingly cutting each individual piece of tile, including the pieces making up the letters on the curving

To view this image, please go to page 275 of the *Art History*, Fourth Edition by Marilyn Stokstad ebook.

5–65 • TILE MOSAIC *MIHRAB*
From the Madrasa Imami, Isfahan, Iran. Founded 1354. Glazed and cut tiles, 11′3″ × 7′6″ (3.43 × 2.29 m). Metropolitan Museum of Art, New York. Harris Brisbane Dick Fund (39.20)

This *mihrab* has three inscriptions: the outer inscription, in cursive, contains Qur'anic verses (Surah 9) that describe the duties of believers and the Five Pillars of Islam. Framing the niche's pointed arch, a Kufic inscription contains sayings of the Prophet. In the center, a panel with a line in Kufic and another in cursive states: "The mosque is the house of every pious person."

To view this image, please go to page 276 of the *Art History*, Fourth Edition by Marilyn Stokstad ebook.

5-66 • SHAH-I ZINDA FUNERARY COMPLEX, SAMARKAND
Late 14th–15th century.

Timurid princesses were buried here and built many of the tombs. The lively experimentation in varied artistic motifs indicates that women were well versed in the arts and empowered to exercise personal taste.

(a cousin of the Prophet and a saint). The women sought burial in the vicinity of the holy man in order to gain *baraka* (blessing) from his presence. Like all Timurid architecture, the tombs reflect modular planning—noticeable in the repeated dome-on-square unit—and a preference for blue glazed tiles. The domes of the individual structures were double-shelled and, for exaggerated effect, stood on high drums inscribed with Qur'anic verses. The ornament adorning the exterior façades consists of an unusually exuberant array of patterns and techniques, from geometry to chinoiserie, and both painted and cut tiles (see "Ornament," page 362). The tombs reflect a range of individual taste and artistic experimentation that was possible precisely because they were private commissions that served the patrons themselves, rather than the city or state (as in a congregational mosque).

PORTABLE ARTS

Islamic society was cosmopolitan, with pilgrimage, trade, and a well-defined road network fostering the circulation of marketable goods. In addition to the import and export of basic foodstuffs and goods, luxury arts brought particular pleasure and status to their owners and were visible signs of cultural refinement. On objects made of ceramics, ivory, and metal, as well as textiles, calligraphy was prominently displayed. These art objects were eagerly exchanged and collected from one end of the Islamic world to the other, and despite their Arabic lettering—or perhaps precisely because of its artistic cachet—they were sought by European patrons as well.

surface of the keel-profiled niche. The color scheme—white against turquoise and cobalt blue with accents of dark yellow and green—was typical of this type of decoration, as were the harmonious, dense, contrasting patterns of organic and geometric forms. The cursive inscription of the outer frame is rendered in elegant white lettering on a blue ground, while the Kufic inscription bordering the pointed arch reverses these colors for a pleasing contrast.

THE SHAH-I ZINDA.   Near Samarkand, the preexisting Shah-i Zinda (Living King) funerary complex was adopted for the tombs of Timurid family members, especially princesses, in the late fourteenth and fifteenth centuries **(FIG. 5–66)**. The mausolea are arrayed along a central avenue that descends from the tomb of Qutham b. Abbas

CERAMICS.   Script was the sole decoration on a type of white pottery made from the tenth century onward in and around the region of Nishapur (in Khurasan, in present-day Iran) and Samarkand (in present-day Uzbekistan). These elegant pieces are characterized by the use of a clear lead glaze applied over a black inscription on a white slip-painted ground. In **FIGURE 5–67** the script's horizontals and verticals have been elongated to fill the bowl's rim. The fine quality of the lettering indicates that a calligrapher furnished the model. The inscription translates: "Knowledge [or magnanimity]: the beginning of it is bitter to taste, but the end is sweeter than honey," an apt choice for tableware and appealing to an educated patron. The inscriptions on Islamic ceramics provide a storehouse of such popular sayings.

To view this image, please go to page 277 of the *Art History*, Fourth Edition by Marilyn Stokstad ebook.

5-67 • BOWL WITH KUFIC BORDER
Khurasan, 11th–12th century. Earthenware with slip, pigment, and lead glaze, diameter 14½″ (33.8 cm). Musée du Louvre, Paris.

The white ground of this piece imitated prized Chinese porcelains made of fine white kaolin clay. Khurasan was connected to the Silk Road, the great caravan route to China (Chapter 10), and was influenced by Chinese culture.

To view this image, please go to page 277 of the *Art History*, Fourth Edition by Marilyn Stokstad ebook.

5-68 • THE MACY JUG
Iran. 1215/1216. Composite body glazed, painted fritware and incised (glaze partially stained with cobalt), with pierced outer shell, 6⅝ × 7¾″ (16.8 × 19.7 cm). Metropolitan Museum of Art, New York. Fletcher Fund, 1932 (32.52.1)

Fritware was used to make beads in ancient Egypt and may have been rediscovered there by Islamic potters searching for a substitute for Chinese porcelain. Its components were one part white clay, ten parts quartz, and one part quartz fused with soda, which produced a brittle white ware when fired. The colors on this double-walled ewer and others like it were produced by applying mineral glazes over black painted detailing. The deep blue comes from cobalt and the turquoise from copper. Luster—a thin, transparent glaze with a metallic sheen—was applied over the colored glazes.

In the ninth century, potters developed a technique to produce a lustrous metallic surface on their ceramics. They may have learned the technique from Islamic glassmakers who had produced luster-painted vessels a century earlier. First the potters applied a paint laced with silver, copper, or gold oxides to the surface of already fired and glazed tiles or vessels. In a second firing with relatively low heat and less oxygen, these oxides burned away to produce a reflective sheen. The finished **lusterware** resembled precious metal. At first the potters covered the entire surface with luster, but soon they began to use luster to paint dense, elaborate patterns using geometric design, foliage, and animals in golden brown, red, purple, and green. Lusterware tiles, dated 862/863, decorated the *mihrab* of the Great Mosque at Kairouan.

The most spectacular lusterware pieces are the double-shell fritware, in which an inner solid body is hidden beneath a densely decorated and perforated outer shell. A jar in the Metropolitan Museum known as the *Macy Jug* (after a previous owner) exemplifies this style **(FIG. 5–68)**. The black underglaze-painted decoration represents animals and pairs of harpies and sphinxes set into an elaborate "water-weed" pattern. The outer shell is covered with a turquoise glaze, enhanced by a deep cobalt-blue glaze on parts of the floral decoration and finally an overglaze that gives the entire surface its metallic luster. An inscription includes the date AH 612 (1215/1216 CE).

METAL. Islamic metalsmiths enlivened the surface of vessels with scrolls, interlacing designs, human and animal figures, and calligraphic inscriptions. A shortage of silver in the mid twelfth century prompted the development of inlaid brasswork that used the more precious metal sparingly, as in **FIGURE 5–69**. This basin, made in Mamluk Egypt in the late thirteenth or early fourteenth century, may be the finest work of metal produced by a Muslim artisan. Its dynamic surface is adorned with three bands, the upper and lower depicting running animals, and the center showing chivalric scenes of horsemen flanked by attendants, soldiers, and falcons. The surface is crowded with overlapping figures, in vigorous poses, that nevertheless remain distinct by means of hatching, modeling, and the framing device of the four roundels. The piece was made and signed (six times) by Muhammad Ibn al-Zain. The narrative band displays scenes of the princely art of

5–69 • Muhammad Ibn al-Zain
BAPTISTERY OF ST. LOUIS
Syria or Egypt. c. 1300. Brass inlaid with silver and gold, 8⅝ × 19⅝″ (22.2 × 50.2 cm). Musée du Louvre, Paris.

This beautifully crafted basin, with its princely themes of hunting and horsemanship, was made for an unknown Mamluk patron, judging by its emblems and coats of arms. However, it became known as the *Baptistery of St. Louis*, because it was acquired by the French sometime before the end of the fourteenth century (long after the era of St. Louis) and used for royal baptisms.

horsemanship and hunting, but in later metalwork such pictorial cycles were replaced by large-scale inscriptions.

TEXTILES. A Kufic inscription appears on a tenth-century piece of silk from Khurasan (FIG. 5–70): "Glory and happiness to the Commander Abu Mansur Bukhtakin. May God prolong his prosperity." Such good wishes were common in Islamic art, appearing as generic blessings on ordinary goods sold in the marketplace or, as here, personalized for the patron. The woven bands of script are known as *tiraz* ("embroidered"), and they appear in textiles as well as illustrated manuscripts, such as the *Maqamat*, where the robes of figures have *tiraz* on their sleeves (SEE FIG. 5–54). Texts can sometimes help determine where and when a work was made, but they can be frustratingly uninformative when little is known about the patron, and they are not always truthful. Stylistic comparisons—in this case with other textiles, with the way similar subjects appear in other media, and with other inscriptions—sometimes reveal more than the inscription alone.

This silk must have been brought from the Near East to France by knights at the time of the First Crusade. Known as the Shroud of St. Josse, it was preserved in the church of Saint-Josse-sur-Mer, near Caen in Normandy. Rich Islamic textiles of brilliantly hued silk, gold thread, brocade, and especially *tiraz* were prized by Christians and were often preserved in Christian burial chambers and church treasuries. Textiles were one of the most actively traded commodities in the medieval Mediterranean region and formed a significant portion of dowries and inheritances. For these reasons, they were an important means of disseminating

5–70 • TEXTILE WITH ELEPHANTS AND CAMELS
Known today as the Shroud of St. Josse. From Khurasan or Central Asia. Before 961. Dyed silk, largest fragment 20½ × 37″ (52 × 94 cm). Musée du Louvre, Paris.

Silk textiles were both sought-after luxury items and a medium of economic exchange. Government-controlled factories, known as *dar al-tiraz*, produced cloth for the court as well as for official gifts and payments. A number of Islamic fabrics have been preserved in the treasuries of medieval European churches, where they were used for priests' ceremonial robes and as altar cloths, and to wrap the relics of Christian saints.

artistic styles and techniques. This fragment shows two elephants, themselves bearing highly ornamental coverings with Sasanian straps, facing each other on a dark red ground, each with a mythical griffin (a Chinese motif) between its feet. A caravan of two-humped Bactrian camels linked with rope moves up the elaborately patterned border along the left side. The inscription at the bottom is upside down, suggesting that the missing portion of the textile was a fragment from a larger and more complex composition. The technique and design derive from the sumptuous pattern-woven silks of Sasanian Iran (Persia). The Persian weavers had, in turn, adapted Chinese silk technology to the Sasanian taste for paired heraldic beasts and other Near Eastern imagery. The eclecticism of Islamic culture is demonstrated by the blending of Sasanian and Chinese sources in a textile made for a Turkic patron.

THE ARTS OF THE BOOK

The art of book production flourished from the first century of Islam because Islam's emphasis on the study of the Qur'an promoted a high level of literacy among both men and women. With the availability of paper, books on a wide range of religious as well as secular subjects were available, although hand-copied books always remained fairly costly. (Muslims did not adopt the printing press until the eighteenth and nineteenth centuries.) Libraries, often associated with *madrasas*, were endowed by members of the educated elite. Books made for royal patrons had luxurious bindings and highly embellished pages, the result of workshop collaboration between noted calligraphers and illustrators.

CALLIGRAPHY. Muslim society holds **calligraphy** (the art of fine hand lettering) in the highest esteem. Since the Qur'an is believed to reveal the word of God, its words must be written accurately, with devotion and embellishment. Writing was not limited to books and documents but—as we have seen—was displayed on the walls of buildings and on artwork. Since pictorial imagery developed relatively late in Islamic art (and there was no figural imagery at all in the religious context), text became a principal vehicle for visual communication. The written word thus played two roles: It could convey information about a building or object, describing its beauty or naming its patron, and it could delight the eye in an entirely aesthetic sense. Arabic script is written from right to left, and a letter's form varies depending on its position in a word. With its rhythmic interplay between verticals and horizontals, Arabic lends itself to many variations. Formal Kufic script (after Kufa, a city in Iraq) is blocky and angular, with strong upright strokes and long horizontals. It may have developed first for carved or woven inscriptions where clarity and practicality of execution were important.

Most early Qur'ans had large Kufic letters and only three to five lines per page, which had a horizontal orientation. The visual clarity was necessary because one book was often shared by multiple readers simultaneously. A page from a ninth-century Syrian Qur'an exemplifies the style common from the eighth to the tenth century (**FIG. 5–71**). Red diacritical marks (pronunciation guides) accent the dark brown ink; the *surah* ("chapter") title is embedded in the burnished ornament at the bottom of the sheet. Instead of

To view this image, please go to page 279 of the *Art History*, Fourth Edition by Marilyn Stokstad ebook.

5-71 • PAGE FROM THE QUR'AN
Surah 2:286 and title of Surah 3 in Kufic script. Syria. 9th century. Black ink pigments, and gold on vellum, 8⅜ × 11⅛″ (21.8 × 29.2 cm). Metropolitan Museum of Art, New York. Rogers Fund, 1937 (37.99.2)

EXPLORE MORE: Gain insight from a primary source, the Qur'an
www.myartslab.com

To view this image, please go to page 280 of the *Art History*, Fourth Edition by Marilyn Stokstad ebook.

5-72 • Attributed to Galinus ARABIC MANUSCRIPT PAGE
Iraq. 1199. Bibliothèque Nationale, Paris.

Headings are in ornamental Kufic script with a background of scrolling vines, while the text—a medical treatise—is written horizontally and vertically in *naskhi* script.

skin) and **vellum** (calfskin or a fine parchment). Paper was first manufactured in Central Asia during the mid eighth century, having been introduced earlier by Buddhist monks. Muslims learned how to make high-quality, rag-based paper, and eventually established their own paper mills. By about 1000, paper had largely replaced the more costly parchment for everything but Qur'an manuscripts, which adopted the new medium much later. It was a change as momentous as that brought about by movable type or the internet, affecting not only the appearance of manuscripts but also their content. The inexpensive new medium sparked a surge in book production and the proliferation of increasingly elaborate and decorative cursive scripts which generally superseded Kufic by the thirteenth century. Of the major styles, one extraordinarily beautiful form, known as *naskhi*, was said to have been revealed and taught to scribes in a vision. In **FIGURE 5–72**, its beautifully flowing lines alternate with an eastern variety of Kufic set against a field of swirling vine scrolls.

MANUSCRIPT PAINTING

The manuscript illustrators of Mamluk Egypt (1250–1517) executed intricate nonfigural geometric designs for the Qur'ans they

page numbers, the brilliant gold of the framed words and the knoblike projection in the left-hand margin are a distinctive means of marking chapter breaks.

Calligraphers enjoyed the highest status of all artists in Islamic society. Included in their number were princes and women. Apprentice scribes had to learn secret formulas for inks and paints; become skilled in the proper ways to sit, breathe, and manipulate their tools; and develop their individual specialties. They also had to absorb the complex literary traditions and number symbolism that had developed in Islamic culture. Their training was long and arduous, but unlike other artisans who were generally anonymous in the early centuries of Islam, outstanding calligraphers received public recognition.

By the tenth century, more than 20 cursive scripts had come into use. They were standardized by Ibn Muqla (d. 940), an Abbasid official who fixed the proportions of the letters in each script and devised a method for teaching calligraphy that is still in use today. The Qur'an was usually written on **parchment** (treated animal

To view this image, please go to page 280 of the *Art History*, Fourth Edition by Marilyn Stokstad ebook.

5-73 • QUR'AN FRONTISPIECE (RIGHT HALF OF TWO-PAGE SPREAD)
Cairo. c. 1368. Ink, pigments, and gold on paper, 24 × 18″ (61 × 45.7 cm). National Library, Cairo. MS. 7

The Qur'an to which this page belonged was donated in 1369 by Sultan Shaban to the *madrasa* established by his mother. A close collaboration between illuminator and scribe can be seen here and throughout the manuscript.

produced. Geometric and botanical ornamentation contributed to unprecedented sumptuousness and complexity. As in architectural decoration, the exuberant ornament was underlaid by strict geometric organization. In an impressive frontispiece originally paired with its mirror image on the facing left page, the design radiates from a 16-pointed starburst, filling the central square (FIG. 5–73). The surrounding frames are filled with interlacing foliage and stylized flowers that embellish the holy scripture. The page's resemblance to court carpets was not coincidental. Designers worked in more than one medium, leaving the execution of their efforts to specialized artisans. In addition to religious works, scribes copied and recopied famous secular texts—scientific treatises, manuals of all kinds, stories, and especially poetry. Painters supplied illustrations for these books and also created individual small-scale paintings—miniatures—that were collected by the wealthy and placed in albums.

THE HERAT SCHOOL. One of the great royal centers of miniature painting was at Herat in western Afghanistan. A **school** of painting and calligraphy was founded there in the early fifteenth century under the highly cultured patronage of the Timurid dynasty (1370–1507). In the second half of the fifteenth century, the leader of the Herat School was Kamal al-Din Bihzad (c. 1450–1514). When the Safavids supplanted the Timurids in 1506/07 and established their capital at Tabriz in northwestern Iran, Bihzad moved to Tabriz and briefly resumed his career there. Bihzad's paintings, done around 1494 to illustrate the *Khamsa* (*Five Poems*), written by Nizami, demonstrate his ability to render human activity convincingly. He set his scenes within complex, stagelike architectural spaces that are stylized according to Timurid conventions, creating a visual balance between activity and architecture. In a scene depicting the caliph Harun al-Rashid's visit to a bath (FIG. 5–74), the bathhouse, its tiled entrance leading to a high-ceiling dressing room with brick walls, provides the structuring element. Attendants wash long, blue towels and hang them to dry on overhead clotheslines. A worker reaches for one of the towels with a long pole, and a client prepares to wrap himself discreetly in a towel before removing his outer garments. The blue door on the left leads to a room where a barber grooms the caliph while attendants bring water for his bath. The asymmetrical composition depends on a balanced placement of colors and architectural ornaments within each section.

To view this image, please go to page 281 of the *Art History*, Fourth Edition by Marilyn Stokstad ebook.

5-74 • Attributed to Kamal al-Din Bihzad **THE CALIPH HARUN AL-RASHID VISITS THE TURKISH BATH**
From a copy of the 12th-century *Khamsa* (*Five Poems*) of Nizami. From Herat, Afghanistan. c. 1494. Ink and pigments on paper, approx. 7 × 6″ (17.8 × 15.3 cm). The British Library, London. Oriental and India Office Collections MS. Or. 6810, fol. 27v

Despite early warnings against it as a place for the dangerous indulgence of the pleasures of the flesh, the bathhouse (*hammam*), adapted from Roman and Hellenistic predecessors, became an important social center in much of the Islamic world. The remains of an eighth-century *hammam* still stand in Jordan, and a twelfth-century *hammam* is still in use in Damascus. *Hammam*s had a small entrance to keep in the heat, which was supplied by steam ducts running under the floors. The main room had pipes in the wall with steam vents. Unlike the Romans, who bathed and swam in pools of water, Muslims preferred to splash themselves from basins, and the floors were slanted for drainage. A *hammam* was frequently located near a mosque, part of the commercial complex provided by the patron to generate income for the mosque's upkeep.

ART AND ARCHITECTURE OF THE THREE EMPIRES

In the pre-modern era, three great powers emerged in the Islamic world. The introduction of gunpowder for use in cannons and guns caused a shift in military strategy because isolated lords in lone castles could not withstand gunpowder sieges. Power lay not in thick walls but in strong centralized governments that had the wherewithal to invest in fire power and train armies in its use. To the west was the Ottoman Empire (1342–1918), which grew from a small principality in Asia Minor. In spite of setbacks inflicted by the Mongols, the Ottomans ultimately created an empire that extended over Anatolia, western Iran, Iraq, Syria, Palestine, western Arabia (including Mecca and Medina), northern Africa (excepting Morocco), and part of eastern Europe. In 1453, their stunning capture of Constantinople (ultimately renamed Istanbul) brought the Byzantine Empire to an end. To the east of the Ottomans, Iran was ruled by the Safavid dynasty (1501–1732), distinguished for their Shi'ite branch of Islam. Their patronage of art and architecture favored the refinement of artistic ideas and techniques drawn from the Timurid period. The other heirs to the Timurids were the Mughals of South Asia (1526–1858). The first Mughal emperor, Babur, invaded Hindustan (India and Pakistan) from Afghanistan, bringing with him a taste for Timurid gardens, architectural symmetry, and modular planning.

THE OTTOMAN EMPIRE

Imperial Ottoman mosques were strongly influenced by Byzantine church plans and reflect a drive toward ever larger domes. The prayer hall interiors are dominated by a large domed space uninterrupted by structural supports. Worship is directed, as in other mosques, toward a *qibla* wall and *mihrab* opposite the entrance.

Upon conquering Constantinople, the rulers of the Ottoman Empire converted the great Byzantine church of Hagia Sophia into a mosque, framing it with two graceful Turkish-style minarets in the fifteenth century and two more in the sixteenth century (SEE FIG. 5–27). In conformance with Islamic aniconism, the church's mosaics were destroyed or whitewashed. Huge calligraphic disks with the names of God (Allah), Muhammad, and the early caliphs were added to the interior in the mid nineteenth century (SEE FIG. 5–29). At present, Hagia Sophia is neither a church nor a mosque but a state museum.

THE ARCHITECT SINAN.   Ottoman architects had already developed the domed, centrally planned mosque, but the vast open interior and structural clarity of Hagia Sophia inspired them to strive for a more ambitious scale. For the architect Sinan (c. 1489–1588) the development of a monumental centrally planned mosque was a personal quest. Sinan began his career in the army and served as engineer in the Ottoman campaigns at Belgrade, Vienna, and Baghdad. He rose through the ranks to become, in 1528, chief architect for Suleyman "the Magnificent," the tenth Ottoman sultan (r. 1520–1566). Suleyman's reign marked the height of Ottoman power, and the sultan sponsored an ambitious building program on a scale not seen since the days of the Roman Empire. Serving Suleyman and his successor, Sinan is credited with more than 300 imperial commissions, including palaces, *madrasas* and Qur'an schools, tombs, public kitchens, hospitals, caravanserais, treasure houses, baths, bridges, viaducts, and 124 large and small mosques.

To view this image, please go to page 282 of the *Art History*, Fourth Edition by Marilyn Stokstad ebook.

5–75 • Sinan MOSQUE OF SULTAN SELIM
Edirne, Turkey. 1568–1575.

The minarets that pierce the sky around the prayer hall of this mosque, their sleek, fluted walls and needle-nosed spires soaring to more than 295 feet, are only 12½ feet in diameter at the base, an impressive feat of engineering. Only royal Ottoman mosques were permitted multiple minarets, and having more than two was unusual.

EXPLORE MORE: Click the Google Earth link for the Mosque of Sultan Selim
www.myartslab.com

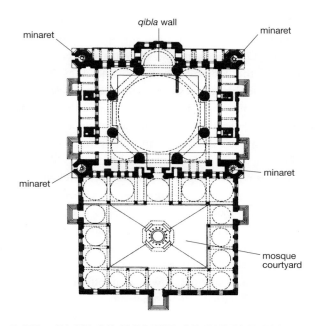

minaret   *qibla* wall   minaret

minaret   minaret

mosque courtyard

5-76 • PLAN OF MOSQUE OF SULTAN SELIM

To view this image, please go to page 283 of the *Art History*, Fourth Edition by Marilyn Stokstad ebook.

5-77 • INTERIOR, MOSQUE OF SULTAN SELIM

Sinan's crowning accomplishment, completed about 1579, when he was over 80, was a mosque he designed in the provincial capital of Edirne for Suleyman's son Selim II (r. 1566–1574) **(FIGS. 5–75, 5–76)**. The gigantic hemispheric dome that tops this structure is more than 102 feet in diameter, larger than the dome of Hagia Sophia, as Sinan proudly pointed out. It crowns a building of extraordinary architectural coherence. The transition from square base to the central dome is accomplished by corner half-domes that enhance the spatial plasticity and openness of the prayer hall's airy interior **(FIG. 5–77)**. The eight massive piers that bear the dome's weight are visible both within and without—on the exterior they resolve in pointed towers that encircle the main dome—revealing the structural logic of the building and clarifying its form. In the arches that support the dome and span from one pier to the next—and indeed at every level—light pours from windows into the interior, a space at once soaring and serene.

The interior was clearly influenced by Hagia Sophia—an open expanse under a vast dome floating on a ring of light—but it rejects Hagia Sophia's longitudinal pull from entrance to sanctuary. The Selimiye Mosque is truly a centrally planned structure. In addition to the mosque, the complex housed a *madrasa* and other educational buildings, a cemetery, a hospital, and charity kitchens, as well as the income-producing covered market and baths. Framed by the vertical lines of four minarets and raised on a platform at the city's edge, the Selimiye Mosque dominates the skyline.

The Topkapi, the Ottomans' enormous palace in Istanbul, was a city unto itself. Built and inhabited from 1473 to 1853, it consisted of enclosures within walled enclosures that mirrored the

immense political bureaucracy of the state. Inside, the sultan was removed from virtually all contact with the public. At the end of the inner palace, a free-standing pavilion, the Baghdad Kiosk (1638), provided him with a sumptuous retreat **(FIG. 5–78)**. The kiosk consists of a low dome set above a cruciform hall with four alcoves. Each recess contains a low sofa (a Turkish word) laid with cushions and flanked by cabinets of wood inlaid with ivory and shell. Alternating with the cabinets are niches with ornate profiles: When stacked in profusion such niches—called *chini khana*— form decorative panels. On the walls, the blue and turquoise glazed tiles contain an inscription of the Throne Verse (2:255) which proclaims God's dominion "over the heavens and the earth," a reference to divine power that appears in many throne rooms and places associated with Muslim sovereigns. Light sparkles through the stained glass above.

To view this image, please go to page 284 of the *Art History*, Fourth Edition by Marilyn Stokstad ebook.

5-78 • BAGHDAD KIOSK
Topkapi Palace, Istanbul. 1638.

To view this image, please go to page 284 of the *Art History*, Fourth Edition by Marilyn Stokstad ebook.

ILLUMINATED MANUSCRIPTS AND *TUGRAS*. A combination of abstract setting with realism in figures and details characterizes Ottoman painting. Ottoman painters adopted the style of the Herat School (influenced by Timurid conventions) for their miniatures, enhancing its decorative aspects with an intensity of religious feeling. At the Ottoman court of Sultan Suleyman in Istanbul, the imperial workshops produced remarkable illuminated manuscripts.

Following a practice begun by the Saljuqs and Mamluks, the Ottomans put calligraphy to political use, developing the design of imperial ciphers—**tugras**—into a specialized art form. Ottoman *tugras* combined the ruler's name and title with the motto "Eternally Victorious" into a monogram denoting the authority of the sultan and of those select officials who were also granted an emblem. *Tugras* appeared on seals, coins, and buildings, as well as on official documents called *firmans*, imperial edicts supplementing Muslim law. Suleyman issued hundreds of edicts, and a high court official supervised specialist calligraphers and illuminators who produced the documents with fancy *tugras* (FIG. 5–79).

Tugras were drawn in black or blue with three long, vertical strokes to the right of two concentric horizontal teardrops. Decorative foliage patterns fill the space. Fill decoration became more naturalistic by the 1550s and in later centuries spilled outside the emblems' boundary lines. The rare, oversized *tugra* below has a sweeping, fluid line drawn with perfect control according to set proportions. The color scheme of delicate floral interlace enclosed in the body of the *tugra* may have been inspired by Chinese blue-and-white ceramics; similar designs appear on Ottoman ceramics and textiles.

5-79 • ILLUMINATED *TUGRA* OF SULTAN SULEYMAN
From Istanbul, Turkey. c. 1555–1560. Ink, paint, and gold on paper, removed from a *firman* and trimmed to 20½ × 25⅜″ (52 × 64.5 cm). Metropolitan Museum of Art, New York. Rogers Fund, 1938 (38.149.1)

The *tugra* shown here is from a document endowing an institution in Jerusalem that had been established by Suleyman's powerful wife, Hurrem.

THE SAFAVID DYNASTY

Whereas the Ottomans took their inspiration from regional cultures such as that of the Byzantine Empire, the Safavids looked to the Timurid architecture of tall, double-shell domes, sheathed in blue tiles. In the Safavid capital of Isfahan, the typically Timurid taste for modular construction re-emerged on a grand scale that extended well beyond works of architecture to include avenues, bridges, public spaces, and gardens. To the preexisting city of Isfahan, the Safavid Shah Abbas I (1588–1629) added an entirely new extension, planned around an immense central plaza (*maydan*) and a broad avenue, called the Chahar Bagh, that ran through a zone of imperial palace pavilions and gardens down to the river. The city's prosperity and beauty so amazed visitors who flocked from around the world to conduct trade and diplomacy that it led to the popular saying, "Isfahan is half the world."

With the Masjid-i Shah (1611–1638) in Isfahan, the four-*iwan* plan mosque reached its apogee **(FIGS. 5–80, 5–81)**. Stately and huge, it anchors the south end of the city's *maydan*. Its 90-foot portal is aligned with the *maydan*, which is oriented astrologically,

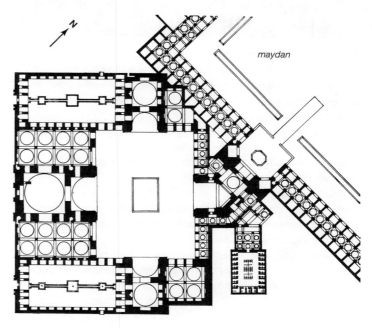

maydan

5–80 • PLAN OF THE MASJID-I SHAH

To view this image, please go to page 285 of the *Art History*, Fourth Edition by Marilyn Stokstad ebook.

5–81 • MASJID-I SHAH, ISFAHAN
1611–1638.

Four *iwan*s with *pishtaq* frames face onto the courtyard, and a fifth faces the *maydan*. The tall bulbous dome behind the *qibla iwan* and the large *pishtaq*s are pronounced vertical elements that made royal patronage visible not only from the far end of the *maydan* but throughout the city and beyond.

SEE MORE: View a video about Masjid-i Shah **www.myartslab.com**

Because textiles are made of organic materials that are destroyed through use, very few carpets from before the sixteenth century have survived. There are two basic types of carpet: flat-weave carpets and pile, or knotted, carpets. Both can be made on either vertical or horizontal looms.

The best-known flat-weaves today are kilims, which are typically woven in wool with bold, geometric patterns and sometimes with brocaded details. Kilim weaving is done with a **tapestry** technique called slit tapestry (see a).

Knotted carpets are an ancient invention. The oldest known example, excavated in Siberia and dating to the fourth or fifth century BCE, has designs evocative of Achaemenid art, suggesting that the technique may have originated in Central Asia. In knotted carpets, the pile—the plush, thickly tufted surface—is made by tying colored strands of yarn, usually wool but occasionally silk for deluxe carpets, onto the vertical elements (the **warp**) of a yarn grid (see b and c).

These knotted loops are later trimmed and sheared to form the plush pile surface of the carpet. The **weft** strands (crosswise threads) are shot horizontally, usually twice, after each row of knots is tied, to hold the knots in place and to form the horizontal element common to all woven structures. The weft is usually an undyed yarn and is hidden by the colored knots of the warp. Two common knot tying techniques are the asymmetrical knot, used in many carpets from Iran, Egypt, and Central Asia (formerly termed the Sehna knot), and the symmetrical knot (formerly called the Gördes knot) more commonly used in Anatolian Turkish carpet weaving. The greater the number of knots, the shorter the pile. The finest carpets can have as many as 2,400 knots per square inch, each one tied separately by hand.

Although royal workshops produced luxurious carpets (SEE FIG. 5–82), most knotted rugs have traditionally been made in tents and homes. Depending on local custom, either women or men wove carpets.

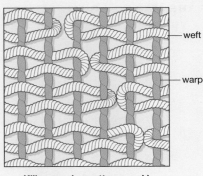

a. Kilim weaving pattern used in flat-weaving

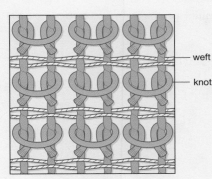

b. Symmetrical knot, used extensively in Turkey

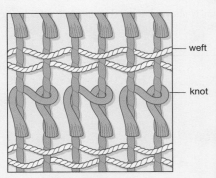

c. Asymmetrical knot, used extensively in Iran

but then turns to conform to the prayer hall, which is oriented to Mecca. The portal's great *iwan* is framed by a *pishtaq* (a rectangular panel framing an *iwan*) that rises above the surrounding walls, slender minarets enhancing its soaring verticality. The hood is filled with *muqarnas* and covered with glazed tiles with vine and flower motifs. The *iwan*'s profile is imitated and repeated by the double-tiered *iwan*s that parade across the façade of the mosque courtyard and the *maydan* as a whole. Achieving unity through the regular replication of a single element—the arch—is a hallmark of Safavid architecture. The Masjid-i Shah represents the culmination of Timurid aesthetics, but achieved on an unprecedented scale and integrated within a well-planned urban setting.

The Safavid period was also a golden age of carpet making (see "Carpet Making," above). Shah Abbas built workshops in Isfahan and Kashan that produced large, costly carpets that were often signed—indicating the weaver's growing prestige. Among the types produced were the medallion, centered around a sun or star, and the garden carpet, which represents Paradise as a shady garden with four rivers. Laid out on the floor of an open-air hall, and per-

haps set with bowls of ripe fruit and other delicacies, such carpets brought the beauty of nature indoors. Written accounts indicate that elaborate patterns appeared on Persian carpets as early as the seventh century. In one fabled royal carpet, garden paths were rendered in real gold, leaves were modeled with emeralds, and highlights on flowers, fruits, and birds were created from pearls and jewels. There were close parallels between carpet making and other arts: Many works of Islamic art represent flowers to evoke both garden and paradisiac associations.

The seventeenth-century *Wagner Carpet* is an extraordinarily sumptuous garden carpet made of wool pile (**FIG. 5–82**). It represents a dense field of trees (including cypresses) and flowers, populated with birds, animals, and even fish, and traversed by three large water channels that form an H with a central pool at the center. The carpet fascinates not only for the fact that so simple a technique as a knotted yarn can produce such complex, layered designs, but also for the combination of perspectives: From above, the carpet resembles a plan, but the trees are shown in profile, as if from ground level.

To view this image, please go to page 287 of the *Art History*, Fourth Edition by Marilyn Stokstad ebook.

5-82 • WAGNER CARPET

From Iran. 17th century. Wool pile, cotton warp, cotton and wool weft, 17′5″ × 13′11″ (5.31 × 4.25 m). Burrell Collection, Glasgow.

When this extraordinarily detailed large carpet was laid on the floor of a palace or wealthy home, it gave the illusion of a garden underfoot. Natural motifs in carpets, textiles, and tiled walls, together with large windows and porches offering delightful vistas, invited the outdoors inside and blurred any distinction between them.

Rugs have long been used for Muslim prayer, which involves repeatedly kneeling and touching the forehead to the floor before God. While individuals often had their own small prayer rugs, with representations of niches to orient the faithful in prayer, many mosques were furnished with wool-pile rugs received as pious donations (the floor of the Selimiye Mosque would have had such rugs). In Islamic houses, people sat and slept on cushions, carpets, and thick mats laid directly on the floor, so cushions took the place of the fixed furnishings of Western domestic environments. From the late Middle Ages to today, carpets and textiles are one of the predominant Islamic arts and the Islamic art form best known in the West. Historically, rugs from Iran, Turkey, and elsewhere were highly valued by Westerners, who often displayed them on tables rather than floors.

MUGHAL DYNASTY

Like the Safavids in Iran, the Mughals brought Timurid models with them from Central Asia into Hindustan. Although Islam had flourished in the Delhi region from the early thirteenth century onward, the Mughals unified the Muslim- and Hindu-ruled states of north India into an empire (see Chapter 7). The illustrations of the emperor Babur's memoirs, the *Baburnama*, show his active patronage of forms such as the *chahar bagh* four-part garden plan. In FIGURE 5–83, Babur—in an orange robe and turban—oversees the construction of a walled garden in Kabul, teeming with fruit trees and flowers. Babur had been raised in an environment thoroughly saturated with the Timurid artistic legacy of *iwan*s with *pishtaq* frames, tall bulbous domes, modular planning, axial symmetry, and the *chahar bagh*. His introduction of such forms into South Asia culminated several generations later in the Taj Mahal.

To view this image, please go to page 288 of the *Art History*, Fourth Edition by Marilyn Stokstad ebook.

To view this image, please go to page 288 of the *Art History*, Fourth Edition by Marilyn Stokstad ebook.

5-83 • Bishnadas "BABUR BUILDS THE BAGH-I WAFA," FROM THE *BABURNAMA*
India. c. 1590. Gouache and gold on paper, 8⅝ × 5⅝" (21.9 × 14.4 cm). Victoria & Albert Museum, London. IM.276-1913, f. 276

The Mughal emperor Babur, on the right, gestures to his architect who holds a red board with grid lines—reflecting the legacy of Timurid modular planning—while workmen measure and shovel, their leggings rolled up to their knees.

To view this image, please go to page 289 of the *Art History*, Fourth Edition by Marilyn Stokstad ebook.

5-84 • Paolo Portoghesi, Vittorio Gigliotti, and Sami Mousawi ISLAMIC MOSQUE AND CULTURAL CENTRE, ROME 1984–1992.

The prayer hall (197 × 13 feet/ 60 × 40 meters), which has an ablution area on the floor below, can accommodate a congregation of 2,500 on its main floor and balconies. The large central dome (65½ feet/ 20 meters in diameter) is surrounded by 16 smaller domes, all similarly articulated with concrete ribs.

THE MODERN ERA

The twentieth century saw the dissolution of the great Islamic empires and the formation of smaller nation-states in their place. The question of identity and its expression in art changed significantly as Muslim artists and architects sought training abroad and participated in an international movement that swept away many of the visible signs that formerly expressed their cultural character and difference. The abstract work of the architect Zaha Hadid, who was born in Baghdad and studied and practiced in London, is exemplary of the new internationalism. Other architects sought to reconcile modernity with an Islamic cultural identity that was distinct from the West. Thus the Iraqi architect Sami Mousawi and the Italian firm of Portoghesi-Gigliotti designed the Islamic Centre in Rome (completed 1992) with clean modern lines, exposing the structure while at the same time taking full advantage of opportunities for ornament **(FIG. 5–84)**. The structural logic appears in the prayer hall's columns, made of concrete with an aggregate of crushed Carrara marble. These rise to meet abstract capitals in the form of plain rings, then spring upward to make a geometrically dazzling eight-pointed star supporting a dome of concentric circles. There are references here to the interlacing ribs of the *mihrab* dome in the Great Mosque of Cordoba, to the great domed spans of Sinan's prayer halls, and to the simple palm-tree trunks that supported the roof of the Mosque of the Prophet in Medina.

THINK ABOUT IT

5.10 The Islamic Empire rapidly spread east to India and west to Spain. Explain how the form of the mosque varies among the far-flung lands of the empire with reference to three examples. Despite the contrasts, what features do mosques typically have in common?

5.11 Select an Islamic structure discussed in this chapter that is influenced by Rome and/or Byzantium, and note which forms are borrowed and how, in their new Islamic context, they are transformed.

5.12 What is a *tugra*? Although it is a secular art form, how is it linked to Islamic religious art traditions?

5.13 Islamic art has no images of people in religious contexts. Instead, what decorative motifs and techniques are used?

5.14 Discuss the spread of carpet making within the rapidly growing Islamic Empire. Can you discern any geographical features that would have expedited the sharing of carpet-making techniques and specific styles? Use the map on page 263.

PRACTICE MORE: Compose answers to these questions, get flashcards for images and terms, and review chapter material with quizzes **www.myartslab.com**

ADDITIONAL READINGS
SPREADING THE WORD
ILLUMINATED MANUSCRIPTS, C.350—C.1500

'In the beginning was the Word.' These are the first words of the last of the four Gospels, the Gospel according to Saint John. If the number of surviving manuscripts is anything to go by, more manuscripts were made of the Gospels than of any other text during the Middle Ages. Such 'glad tidings' (*godspel* in Old English means 'good news') were central to the success of the early Christian missionaries in converting large sections of the old Roman Empire to the new religion. The Gospels' words were preached out loud and written down in the form of a book, and the stories they told were all the more affecting for being available in a visible form. A gospel manuscript was looked on as much more than the documentary evidence of a revered historical figure, Jesus of Nazareth. It was the word of God himself made manifest within a uniquely divine artefact, and thus richly deserving of all the skill, attention and expense their makers could bring to bear. The brilliance of the burnished gold and silver leaf that illuminates the pages of the most precious manuscripts cannot be simulated in today's most sophisticated facsimiles. While few of us would consider such manuscripts to be truly holy in quite the same way, many of us would consider the best of them to be among the greatest glories of Western art.

The unique book art displayed within their pages has a special place in graphic design's pre-history. The beginnings of almost all current typographic conventions can be found there. Our word spacing, punctuation, use of headings, margins, borders and annotations all became established during the making of the medieval manuscript. The conventions that surrounded their use have provided ample ammunition for the subsequent battles of graphic style.

The word 'manu-script' (from the Latin *manus* meaning 'hand', and *scriptum*, 'written') does not only refer to something that is handwritten, it almost invariably refers to writing presented in the form of a book—as pages that have been bound together along a common edge. This format has sustained western literary culture for almost 2000 years, yet its very success has stopped it from receiving the credit it deserves. The book must rank as one of man's greatest inventions, but seldom does it appear in any list of such things. (Nor does the alphabet.) Recently, however, the book has begun to receive more attention and respect. A degree of flattery has come through imitation as various attempts have been made to create digital books. In fact these are more like digital wax tablets in that their single screens of text can be 'refreshed'. A closer approximation of the book would be an electronic device that used digital or electronic 'paper', but such a device has yet to appear. Explorations in digitization have combined with the newest mass-reading medium, the computer and the internet, to encourage talk of 'the paperless office' and 'the end of print'. Such warnings have turned out to be premature, coinciding as they do with year-on-year increases in paper use and rising quantities of production of nearly every kind of print medium—books, magazines, catalogues and so on. As a way of carrying substantial amounts of the same text in a portable and durable format, pages in book form have yet to be surpassed. This antique invention remains a standard method of storing and transmitting text-based information.

The impact of the manuscript on fourth-century Rome and subsequently throughout Europe increased the number of readers, and changed how and why people read. For a physician or lawyer or priest, the ability to refer to a portion of text easily and quickly, and then cross-reference it with other bits of text in the same volume, was becoming increasingly necessary. Such needs had been ill-served by the rolled scroll. When receiving information on separate bound pages, each of the kinds of readers mentioned above was able to compare the medical prescriptions, laws or biblical verses that concerned them. Furthermore, the book was eminently more portable than the scroll. A book could be easily carried and read in one hand, rather than two, and the amount of text it could hold easily exceeded its nearest rival in portability, the wax tablet.

The Romans' book or codex, as they called it (its plural is 'codices'), was an amalgam of two pre-existing Roman practices: first, the folding of papyrus sheets to form separate, portable pages (in the first century BC Julius Caesar is known to have used this device on the battlefield); and second, the binding of wooden wax tablets to make a kind of reusable notebook. It is these bound tablets that were first given the name *codex*, meaning literally 'block of wood'. (The English word 'book' has a similar derivation. It comes from the German word *boka* meaning 'beech', after the type of wood on which the Germanic indigenous runic script was written.) The earliest mention of the Romans' sheet-made codex appears at the end of the first century AD in the lines of the Roman poet Martial: 'The Iliad and all the adventures / of Ulysses, foe of Priam's kingdom, / all locked within a piece of skin / folded into several little sheets!'. The word 'skin' here is important. Animal skin is known to have been used by the Egyptians as a surface for writing on as far back as the middle of the third millennium BC, but it was only when the eastern Greeks had learnt how to stretch skin thin enough and had passed this knowledge on to the Romans that animal skin began to rival papyrus as the dominant writing material. Sheep, lamb, cow, calf or goat skins were processed—soaked, scraped, stretched, dried and cleaned—to form a smooth writing surface known as parchment or vellum (the strict definition distinguishes vellum as being the skin of young animals—from a calf or kid—rather than mature ones). Though never cheap, parchment was less expensive than papyrus, and it was also more durable. The fact that it could withstand being used on both sides made it especially suitable for the book format. As the use of parchment in books increased, so the number of papyrus scrolls declined. The early adoption of the parchment codex by the burgeoning Christian religion is thought

5-85 • CODEX SINAITICUS, EASTERN MEDITERRANEAN, Mid-Fourth Century AD
Courtesy of the British Library.

to have been decisive in the near-extinction of papyrus by the fourth century AD.

The pages of the earliest codices were based on the more-or-less square visible segment of an opened Roman scroll, the height of which was generally a little greater than that of a sheet of A4. In this fourth-century Greek codex of the Bible **(FIG. 5–85)**, the text is written out in sparse lines of letters, with none of the variety of letter forms or colourful illumination that came to distinguish later manuscripts. Its aesthetic cue was taken from the scroll, which apart from the expression of prestige in the choice of script had been a functional object rather than a decorative one. The scroll's main purpose had been to record speech, a task that writing remained wedded to throughout the life of the Roman Empire. Indeed, to some extent, the Romans held the human voice in even higher regard than the Greeks did. The great Roman orator Cicero (106–40 BC), who first articulated the doctrines of decorum and artistic style during the first century BC, became an idealized figure to later Romans on account of his speeches. They were copied down and circulated, and may still be read today. In order to serve the demands of speech, the text of a Roman scroll was laid out in an unbroken sequence of columns, usually running from left to right, so that by rolling and unrolling with his hands side by side the speaker could work his way through the text. This method contrasted with the Greek speaker, who usually held his scroll with one hand above the other in order to read from a continuous block of text that ran down the length of the scroll, in much the same way as we 'scroll' the text on a computer screen. Each of the columns in a Roman scroll had between 30 and 40 lines of roughly 20 to 30 letters, and, with the whole scroll being 6 to 10m (20 to 33ft) long when fully unrolled, the amount of text it contained was equivalent to that of a small novel.

By faithfully following the example of the Roman scroll, the early codex did as many new inventions have done. The history of

5-86 • CODEX SINAITICUS (DETAIL)
Courtesy of the British Library.

innovation in design, as elsewhere, is littered with examples of the straightforward mimicry of an established way of doing something: the first railway carriages looked like their horse-drawn predecessors; the subjects of early photographs, in portraits especially, were posed according to the established conventions of painted pictures; and, in the field of graphic design proper, the first printed books looked like manuscripts, as though they had been written out by hand. In each case their creators had been intent on improving a particular aspect of the technology, rather than all of it. Had they considered the problem more broadly and been able to see the potential for creating wholly new forms, they might have chosen to do so. Yet, there are advantages in making something new look like something old. By retaining an element of continuity, the new thing can appear less threatening and/or confusing. Familiarity does not always breed contempt.

The invention of the codex went some way towards satisfying the appetite of the expanding mass of readers in Rome's empire. In the city of Rome itself, where this appetite was greatest, there was never a popular literature as such, not, at least, as we understand the term. Roman readers learnt the writings ascribed to the Greek author Homer and the only Roman author to rival him, Virgil, through dictation and recitation. Nevertheless, the demand for books was greater than it had ever been under the Greeks. Roman literature reached its peak in the first century BC with the writings of Caesar, the historian Livy, the orator Cicero and the poets Virgil and Horace. From the end of the first century AD, the literate classes had begun to depend on writing, as had, indeed, the empire itself. Letters, contracts, laws and votes—civil administration was firmly founded on the ability to read and write. While most Roman writing was still set down on the reusable wax tablet, manuscript books became commodified, and their ownership a status symbol.

The main period of manuscript making followed the fall of the empire in the fifth century and continued throughout the Middle Ages, ceasing only in the fifteenth century, during the late Renaissance. Thus, as things stand, the history of the handwritten book is twice as long as the currently 500-year history of the printed book.

The long life enjoyed by the manuscript did not just coincide with the Middle Ages; it helped to define the age. During the middle centuries of the first millennium, the so-called Dark Ages, the relative order and security in Europe that had been established under Roman rule was swept away by successive waves of marauding Germanic and Norse tribes. Yet by the fourteenth century, at the start of the Renaissance, Europeans had inherited an extraordinarily integrated civilization with bustling cities, towering cathedrals and thriving universities. Each was the fruit of a thoroughgoing Christian culture maintained from its centre, in Rome, by a powerful and wealthy pope; and via a 'civic' clergy, with its parish churches and bishoprics, as well as more marginal monasteries of monks and nuns. Much of the Church's power, like that of the Romans before it, was forged by the command and control of the written word, and it was in the monasteries that the word was first made flesh in the form of manuscripts.

The manuscript's development within the cloistered walls of the Church was linked to its role as an aid to learning. The Christian religion was founded on a thorough knowledge of its sacred texts. Divine reading combined with manual labour and public worship to form the tripartite basis of monastic life. Studying the scriptures was facilitated by two distinct methods of reading: reading out loud in a group and reading to oneself in silence or a low murmur. The most well-known description of the second kind of reading was given by one of the founding fathers of the early Church, Saint Augustine of Hippo, who in AD384 wrote a short but revealing description of his teacher Saint Ambrose thus: '… when he read, his eyes would travel across the pages, and his mind would explore the sense, but his voice and tongue were silent. … who would have the heart to interrupt such a man … guessing that in the brief time he had seized for the refreshment of this mind, he was resting from the din of other people's affairs … another and perhaps more cogent reason for his habit of reading silently was his need to conserve his voice, which was very prone to hoarseness. But whatever his reason, that man undoubtedly had a good one.' This passage has often been interpreted as signalling a sudden change from reading aloud to reading in silence. But Saint Ambrose was certainly not the first silent reader. It was practised throughout antiquity. What the description does emphasize is the importance of silent reading as a way of 'exploring the sense' of a text. This was not merely a matter of learning a story, but of taking it in fully so that it and all its implications become thoroughly familiar and personal. Saint Ambrose was one of a growing number of literates who had begun to use texts autodidactically, for their own edification, rather than for sharing within a group.

This move away from public performance to private perusal had, in part, been influenced by the changed status of the language they were reading, an ecclesiastical form of Latin, which towards the end of the fourth century had become the language of literature and learning rather than a language of everyday speech. At one time, the same kind of Latin could be heard in any part of the Roman Empire, but after the fall of the empire classical Latin had fragmented into various regional dialects, the precursors of modern Italian, French and Spanish. Only in the Church, which had adopted Latin as the official language in the fourth century AD, was it preserved. Since most writing and manuscript production occurred in monasteries, the written word became closely identified with reading and learning rather than speaking, and as the number of silent readers steadily rose, so the feeling of being intimately connected to a text became more widespread. Not only could ideas be acquired more directly without having to listen to an intermediary, they also seemed to enter at a higher level of consciousness. This much more personal act of silently reading was further aided by the greater freedom provided by the manuscript to choose a favoured piece of text. The effect was such that by the end of the Middle Ages most readers had fallen silent.

The emancipation of the written word from the spoken one allowed some of the conventions inherited from the orator's scroll to be set aside. By the beginning of the fifth century the codex had become taller and narrower, so as to be more easily held in the hand, with two or sometimes only one column of text per page (FIG. 5–93). In this it assumed the current literary format that now dominates the West: a rectangular page with horizontal lines of alphabetic text surrounded by four margins. Within these standard features a range of local styles of script and illumination were included, especially by monasteries on the fringes of the old empire. Some of the most distinct early examples of regional designs appear in the so-called 'insular' (Latin for 'island') manu-

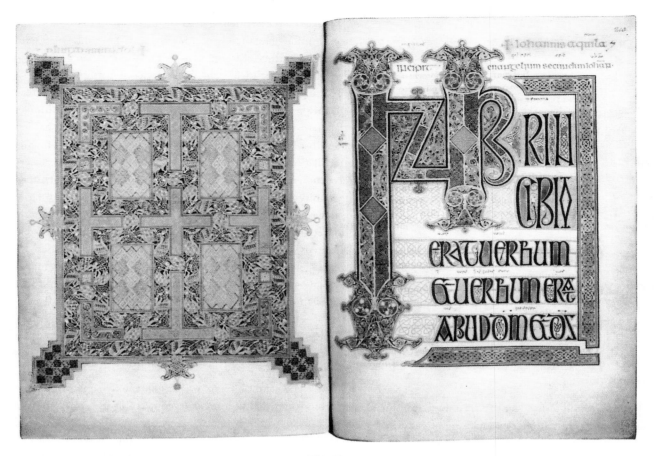

5-87 • LINDISFARNE GOSPELS, ENGLAND, c.710–721
Courtesy of the British Library.

scripts of the British Isles. From the middle of the fifth century, insular manuscripts began to be distinguished by two features that have since come to symbolize a Celtic style of design: a rounded script and an intricately woven style of decoration.

The three masterpieces of the insular manuscript are the Lindisfarne Gospels *c.*710–721, the Book of Durrow *c.*700 and the Book of Kells *c.*800. Each one is a gospel book, and their pages are filled with examples of elaborately and skilfully hand-rendered illuminations. An involved patterning or decoration dominates all three, but it is among the pages of the Lindisfarne Gospels that the decoration is at its most fevered and mesmeric **(FIG. 5–87)**. This large book of Gospels was made in a monastery founded by Irish missionaries on an island off the north-east coast of England, which was then known as Lindisfarne but is now called Holy Island. The book's size and splendour suggests it was intended as a showpiece, a manuscript for religious ceremony rather than private study, and was likely therefore to have been read only on special festival days. Its large pages (340 × 250 mm, 13⅜ × 9⅞ in) and ornateness are instantly impressive. The richness of the detail invites a contemplative awe, which fits the description that a twelfth-century historian made about a similarly decorative insular manuscript, 'You will make out intricacies so delicate and subtle, so exact and compact, so full of knots and links, with colours

so fresh and vivid, that you might say that all this was the work of an angel and not of a man'. The sense of wonder at the human endeavour is increased by the knowledge that the 259 pages of script and decoration are thought to have been the work of a single scribe.

This Lindisfarne scribe did not write with the standard Roman uncial script favoured in continental and other less geographically remote English scriptoria. He used an Irish half-uncial letter **(FIG. 5–88)**, in which nearly all the letters have developed our current small-letter or lowercase form (a clear exception being the letter 'R'). His steady and deliberate insular script is distinguished from the more common Roman half-uncial, by having especially thick and rounded letter shapes. They are shapes that have been written with a broad-nibbed pen held with the nib pointing straight up the page, and therefore with thin, almost hairline horizontal strokes and distinctive wedge-shaped serifs at the tops of the letters. Many of the horizontals are exaggeratedly extended, especially at the end of the lines of text. The text is written out *per cola et commata*, in lines of unbroken words the length of which is used to clarify the sense, although accompanying the classical method is a hint of word separation. Some of the text is written in red, or rubricated (from the Latin word *rubrica* meaning 'red earth').

5-88 • IRISH HALF-UNCIAL, LINDISFARNE GOSPELS
Courtesy of the British Library.

What most forcibly distinguishes these insular books from previous manuscripts is their illustration. The inclusion of patterns and pictures in medieval manuscripts was actively promoted by the Church. As well as wanting to impress the reader with exuberant colours and intricate decoration, Christian missionaries were aware of the power of pictures to communicate something of the Christian message to an audience who, even if more literate than had previously been thought, would still have struggled to read an entire text. The sixth-century pope, Gregory the Great, explicitly encouraged pictures to be used in this way: 'Let pictures be words for those who cannot read'.

For those who could read, pictures were important in a different way. They were used as an aid to memorizing the text. The use of pictures as a memory device is known to have taken place in ancient Greece. It was a process that continued in the Middle Ages, though it had a particular cast in monasteries. Pictures were used not as a form of representation, as we understand the term, to show what something looked like. They were visual hooks on which to hang a story. Their form referred to a narrative which needed to be inwardly digested and remembered. In this way they were similar to words.

As well as helping memory, the pictures can also be seen as an elaborate and extended form of punctuation. They were often used to mark the major divisions within the text of a book, its chapters and the sections within them. Among the most emphatic visual divisions in the Lindisfarne Gospels are the introductory double-page spreads from each of the four Gospels (FIG. 5–87). They are mostly ornamental—that is to say, non-figurative—and are filled with a dizzying array of intricately swirling lines and

bright, flat colours. Their particular patterns are made from a fusion of influences: the Celtic (the spiralling knot interlaces) and the Germanic (the birds and beasts). On the left-hand or 'verso' pages of each spread a rich, linear style of pattern making is applied to the shape of a cross set within a densely decorated rectangle. No part of the pattern is left unfilled; no space is too small to decorate. The appearance of such solid ornamentation has led these sorts of pages to be described as 'carpet pages'. It is a resemblance that may have been intentional since prayer mats were certainly known in that part of England, as they were in Eastern Christianity and Islam. The carpet pages of the Lindisfarne Gospels are densely packed with a number of tightly and precisely interlaced heads and limbs of birds and other indistinguishable quadrupeds (FIG. 5–89). The animals and abstract shapes are woven together in busy and fluid rhythms, yet they are tethered to a simple geometrical grid. The compass and divider marks that can be seen on the back of the pages show how an ordered symmetry of repeated rectangular units underpins the page's apparently free-form design. In this the illuminator had observed the rules of sacred geometry, which were then associated with God's design for Creation.

The right hand or 'recto' page is equally dynamic, though its dynamism is not tied to a regular geometry in the same way. It is linked, instead, to the irregular forms of several large ornamental letters. Each recto page is an 'initial page', one in which the first few words (incipits) of the Gospel are illuminated with grand decorated initials that lead into a sequence of ornamental letters of diminishing sizes. The more angular set of ornamental letters has forms that appear to have been inspired by the German runic alphabet (the runic M of three vertical strokes and a horizontal appears). The text on the initial page of Saint John's Gospel reads 'In principio erat verbum et verbum erat apud d(eu)m et d(eu)s [erat verbum]' ('In the beginning was the word and the word was with God and God [was the word]'), and each letter, as on the other incipit pages, is bordered by a buffer of tiny red drops of lead, carefully placed like a stippled kind of stitching. In other insular manuscripts they are only ever used as an adjunct to letters.

Almost a hundred years after the Lindisfarne Gospels was completed, the regional variety of scripts and decoration that had developed across western Europe was partially interrupted by a wholesale reform of the monasteries' scriptoria. The process of reform was part of a larger revival of classical learning, within the Church in particular, which historians refer to as the 'Carolingian Renaissance'. It was introduced by the devout Frankish king and emperor, Charlemagne (742–812)—whose family line came to be called the Carolingians—in an attempt to bring about a 'renewal of the Roman Empire' (as the legend on his personal seal put it) as well as a return to the standards of Christian worship achieved by the early Church Fathers. The territory under Charlemagne's rule was larger than any in the West since the Roman Empire (his successors, indeed, referred to their inherited dominions as 'the

5-89 • CARPET PAGE (DETAIL), LINDISFARNE GOSPELS
Courtesy of the British Library.

Holy Roman Empire'), and the effects of his reforms were wide ranging.

Central to the successful transmission of classical culture was the standardization of texts and the creation of a new, more legible script, the Carolingian (or Caroline) minuscule (FIG. 5–90). Though the form of this script was based on a Roman model, the half-uncial, and, to a lesser extent, on the insular half-uncial (FIG. 5–88), the clarity, efficiency and beauty of its letters were unprecedented. This very expert ninth-century example from France sets out the minuscule with a vibrant red ink. Its legibility is enhanced by its letter shapes, in particular the length of the strokes that rise above the main body of the letter, known as the 'ascenders' (as in the letters 'b', 'd' and 'h'), and then also the 'descenders' (those that fall below, as in 'g', 'p' and 'q'). The effect produces a much more consistent and recognizable word shape, which is also made more definite by the hint of word separation within the lines of text.

The shape of words is an important factor in legibility. When we read, our eyes pass over a line of text in a series of short jumps (called 'saccades', the fastest kind of movement in the human body), rather than an even sweep, and they absorb chunks of information at every pause. Within each chunk we register the overall shapes of the words (described by internal as well as external elements), rather than the shape of each letter separately. But clarity of word shape is not the only criterion. Legibility is not purely objective. We tend to read best the shapes we read most. Nor is legibility determined by word shape alone. There is always a degree of guesswork related to the context. It is spursinigly esay to raed wodrs taht hvae thier itneranl ltteres plcaed in the worng oredr bceuase tehy eixst in a cnotxet of maennig, of idoim and of smilair wrod sheaps. Nevertheless, the more distinct and consistent word shapes of the Carolingian minuscule do appear to be more

legible than earlier scripts, and we may suppose that many readers at that time will have thought so too.

Within the controlled and hierarchical environment of Charlemagne's reformed scriptoria, every aspect of manuscript manufacture was codified (the word itself is derived from *codex* via 'code'). Features such as initials, headings, word spacing and punctuation began to be used more regularly and consistently. Accompanying the Carolingian minuscule script were square capitals, which were considered the correct form for writing headings or names, though not yet the letter at the start of a sentence. By formalizing the use of capitals with small-letters, the Carolingian reforms required writers of the Latin alphabet to learn many more than 26 letter shapes. The strict and often complex division of labour that now exists between lowercase and capitals when writing English, for example, means that the total number of letter shapes for everyday writing is around 44 (some caps and lowercase are the same). If we go on and add the basic set of non-alphabetic symbols—such as punctuation marks, units of currency and the like—the number rises to around 89 separate shapes (FIG. 5–92).

The legibility of a Carolingian manuscript was further enhanced by a reduction in the number of abbreviations, suspensions (omitted letters) and ligatures (two letters combined in a single shape). Each of these acts of compression had been necessary when whole words were expected to fit the straitjacket of so-called 'justified' text; that is, a column aligned on the right as well as the left. Such columns had been a common feature of many Roman codices. But the Carolingian reforms promoted the 'unjustified' column (otherwise descriptively called 'ragged-right' or 'ranged-left'). When using this format, all the words within a text could be evenly spaced, and thus they contributed to a flowing and legible line of letters.

The effect of these reforms was to establish a common ground in many of the scriptoria in western Europe. Even when the Carolingian minuscule failed to dominate a particular region, due to the region's political independence or the existence of an established indigenous script, its influence was felt nevertheless. These lines (FIG. 5–91) of a small British psalter (a book of Old Testament songs or psalms—*psalamoi* in Greek means 'songs sung with a harp'), from the tenth century, have some of the characteristics of the earlier insular script—its roundness and its exaggerated thick and thin strokes—but in its more exaggerated ascenders and descenders and its more distinct letter and word shapes the influence of the Carolingian is clear.

By the twelfth century, texts such as the Worms Bible (FIG. 5–93) carry the essential features of a modern page. We feel we are in familiar territory just by the way the page is presented. The contents are arranged within an ordered hierarchy which guides the reader through the different parts of the page. Its elementary signage system allows us, for example, to check which book of the Bible we are looking at by glancing at the top of the page, above the central margin, to the 'running head' or 'header'

5-90 • CAROLINGIAN MINUSCULE, FRANCE,
Ninth Century
Courtesy of the British Library.

where the word 'Ezekiel' appears picked out in red. Our eye is then drawn down the page to the first line of the Book of Ezekiel by the large, decorated initial 'E' and the bearded figure of Ezekiel himself. As befits an important Old Testament prophet, he is crowned with a large, golden halo. In his left hand is an unrolled scroll revealing his prophecy ('Now it came to pass in the thirtieth year . . . that the heavens were opened, and I saw visions of God'). The swirling pattern that decorates the initial recalls the decoration of the earlier Lindisfarne Gospels, but the illuminator's inclusion of a figure from the text takes the decoration in a new direction. By using it to tell something of the story of the text, the illuminator is approaching the purpose of Pope Gregory's injunction, to provide pictures for the illiterate. But this approach is only one of several alternatives. Other manuscripts have no pictures at all, while some have illustrations that bear little relevance to the text. The subjects depicted might be chosen to display the illuminator's mastery (and enhance the owner's prestige) or they might be in response to a local fashion, or they may want to stand out by being comical or irreverent. Since pages were rarely numbered, part of the job of a picture was to provide a mental marker for the reader to pinpoint particular sections of text. The more irreverent the picture, the more likely a reader would remember it. Something of this nature occurs with the decorated initial 'I' in the left-hand column of text. At its base is the head of the prophet Ezekiel, whose words are being spoken with a grossly floriated tongue. Following the initial there is a gradual reduction in the size and complexity of the text's letters. The large black capital letters that come after the initial are themselves followed by a line of smaller capitals. Both kinds form a bridge between the initial and the main body of text. This hierarchical approach, which had been explicitly promoted by the Carolingian reforms, continues to be used at the start of many texts in books and magazines today.

An additional and more explicit way of separating sections of text was to have lines of rubricated capitals, beginning with the word *explicit* (meaning 'here ends', in reference to the preceding text), and towards the end of the capitals the word *incip* (an abbreviation of *incipit*, meaning 'here begins', in reference to the following text). A similar kind of 'incipit' text would sometimes appear at the beginning of each manuscript. It frequently bore the author's name and the title of the text, though what stopped it from being the equivalent to the modern-day title page was that it rarely appeared on a page of its own. Indeed, there was little need for a separate title page. Most books were made on commission so it was not necessary to display the contents so egregiously. Few owners would have had more than a handful of manuscripts on their shelves, so each would have been known intimately.

What makes the page most familiar is the main text. The words, clauses and sentences in the main body of text reveal themselves to be visually discrete units. A simple three-tiered hierarchy of word spaces, commas and full stops are used. Each is an emphatic confirmation of the changed role of writing away from being spoken and towards silent reading. The silent reader, being denied the vocal cues that came from reading out loud, would

5-91 • WINCHESTER MINUSCULE, ENGLAND, Tenth Century
Courtesy of the British Library.

capitals (x26)	A B C D E F G H I J K L M N O P Q R S T U V W X Y Z
lowercase (x18)	a b c d e f g h i j k l m n o p q r s t u v w x y z
numerals (x9)	0 1 2 3 4 5 6 7 8 9
punctuation (x21)	, . ; : … ' " ` " ' " ? ! ( ) [ ] - / * †
maths (x8)	+ - × ÷ = < > %
currency (x4)	£ $ € ¥
misc. (x5)	& # ° @ ©

5-92 • BASIC SET OF CHARACTER SHAPES FOR READING ENGLISH

5–93 • MANUSCRIPT PAGE, WORMS BIBLE, Twelfth Century
Courtesy of the British Library.

have welcomed the visual cues of word spaces and punctuation. The Church too would have welcomed the greater clarity that these elements brought to the sense of the text. An individual interpretation of the text was fundamental to good oratory, but it was anathema to the Church hierarchy. They wanted Christian readers to receive Christ's message clearly and unambiguously. Doctrinal differences could hang on the exact phrasing of a sentence. For example, the line from Matthew's Gospel, 'Judge not, that ye be not judged' ('Don't judge others, or they will judge you'), has an entirely different and more threatening meaning when the comma is removed: 'Judge not that ye be not judged' ('Don't think you won't be judged').

Punctuation, the text's most conspicuous sign system, was more limited and less uniform than it is today. Question, exclamation and quotation marks do not yet appear, partly because many of the parts of speech they signify are expressed within the Latin words themselves (suffixes added to the ends of words, or whole words placed at the beginning of a sentence—the clause *scriptum est*, for example, meaning 'as it is written', did the job of the modern quotation marks whenever it was placed in front of a quotation). The Carolingian reforms had also simplified the word order of Latin, bringing it closer to the native languages of its readers. By the thirteenth century, Latin had developed into a standardized tongue for scholars and theologians across western Europe (not that this changed the wording of the canonical texts). The galvanizing effect that these visual and linguistic reforms had on silent reading caused the voluble mutterings that had filled scriptoria during the early Middle Ages to gradually fade. By the late Middle Ages many monastic orders discouraged speaking entirely. For the new makers of the illuminated manuscript, silence was seen to be golden.

From around 1200, during the last 300 years of the Middle Ages, manuscripts were made increasingly outside the monasteries by professional book makers. The Church's long-standing monopoly was eroded by the rise of two new social groups: those within the new universities who began to make books for students; and the wealthy merchant class, who, for the purposes of trade as well as for their own edification, had become increasingly literate. Both groups wanted secular books as well as religious ones and each expected to be able to buy books just like any other commercial item. Running parallel with the fledgling book trade was a separate category of non-literary manuscripts used for businesses and civil administration. Accounts, correspondence, laws and charters were serviced by a growing band of professional scribes and clerks.

One of the most significant secular documents of the age is a charter contract (a charter is a legal document in which one party grants permission to another) sealed in 1215 by the English king John (1166–1216), at the insistence of a rebellious group of barons (**FIG. 5–94**). Apart from its size, Magna Carta (Latin for 'the Large Charter', a title bestowed some years later to distinguish it from a similar but smaller accompanying charter) looked like a typical legal document of the time. The script, a neat documentary cursive, was hurriedly written in a brownish ink with a typically thin-

5-94 • DOCUMENTARY CURSIVE, MAGNA CARTA, England, 1215
Courtesy of the British Library.

nibbed pen. Though not the grandest hand, there was some dressing up of the basic letters with various kinds of fancy looped ascenders. The document's importance has nothing to do with how it looks, nor much to do with the concessions contained in the text. What sets it apart is that it established, for the first time, that the power of the king could be limited by a written document; that he could be 'brought to book'. It is for this reason that some have claimed it to be the cornerstone of liberty in the English-speaking world.

Contrary to common parlance, 'the signing of Magna Carta' never happened. Neither party signed anything. The only authentication of the document was made with the king's principal royal seal, the Great Seal, which took on the standard design for English kings. On one side it showed an enthroned monarch dispensing justice, while on the other the monarch was mounted on his charger riding into battle. This wax seal might have been the only option available to this particular king, for there is no evidence that John was able to write at all. He, like other monarchs and members of the aristocracy of the time, may have thought it unbecoming to master this servile craft. It was an attitude that faded with the century. During the one that followed, the clerically influenced elite of western Europe were to claim reading and writing as their own.

The most popular secular literature of the late Middle Ages was a form of vernacular verse composed around episodic stories in rhyming couplets. The genre was supposed to be spoken out loud, and yet, popular performance literature of this kind was enjoyed as much by readers as by listeners. Two such works that continue to be read today are Dante's *The Divine Comedy* and Chaucer's *The Canterbury Tales*, but what was significant about them at the time they were written was that they appeared in their readers' native languages of Italian and English respectively, rather than in the ecclesiastical language of Latin. This made them immediately more accessible than any previous literature.

The enthusiasm for secular literature written in the vernacular did not at this stage threaten the existence of the ecclesiastical Latin manuscript. The importance placed on continuity within the traditional form of worship meant that it continued to remain popular. However, the situations in which it was read and the uses to which it was put became more varied. Both the formats and the layouts of this kind of manuscript reflected the greater variety of situations and uses. Pictures were added to various selections of biblical texts to create so-called Picture Bibles, among the most popular of which was the *Biblia Pauperum* (Bible of the Poor). It was one of the first to be made as a blockbook—with text and illustrations printed from carved blocks of wood—in the fifteenth century, at around the time that printing with type was invented.

New kinds of textual arrangements appeared during the first half of the twelfth century in Bibles whose pages were extensively annotated, or 'glossed' (from the Greek *glossa* meaning 'tongue' or 'language'). Glosses were explanatory texts written by established authorities who had fleshed out the allegorical meaning or

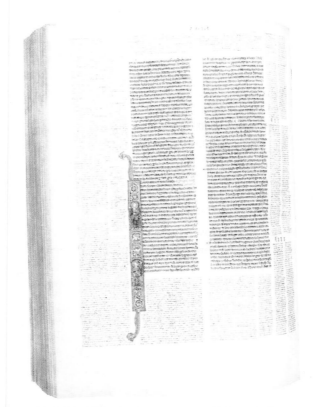

5-95 • GLOSSED BIBLE, FRANCE, Thirteenth Century
Courtesy of the British Library.

moral sense of the text (hence our word 'glossary'). Some attempts at laying out a formally glossed text had been made during the Carolingian period but more usually glosses were brief and informal often being confined to ad hoc translations of the text. Those that sit between the widely spaced lines of main text on the carpet page of the Lindisfarne Gospels (FIG. 5–87), for example, were added centuries after the manuscript had been completed. (They are Anglo-Saxon translations of the Latin text; the earliest surviving translation of the four Gospels into any form of English.) The columns of much more comprehensive glosses that surrounded the main text of a large French Bible from the thirteenth century **(FIG. 5–95, 5–96)** were written at the same time as the main text. Both its gloss and the main text were planned and spaced on a grid of lines that ran across the entire area of text. The ruling that guided the writing of the gloss has been harmonized with the text-ruling in such a way that six lines of the gloss could be written in the space taken by four lines of main text.

Like the modern study aids that English students use when studying Shakespeare, for example, a clear difference between the commentary and the main text was maintained not just by the position of the texts but also by their different sizes and styles of script. The main text in this French Bible is written in a compressed script that had been developed out of the Carolingian minuscule by northern European scribes. The woven-wicker texture of its text caused it to be called *littera textualis* or textura (from the Latin for 'weaving'), though its prominence in German manuscripts in particular led later Italian scribes and historians to refer to it as 'Gothic' (the terms 'Blackletter', after its dense appearance on the page, and 'Old English', after its popularity in England, are now also used). Between the twelfth and sixteenth centuries textura evolved into a complex hierarchy of formal and cursive scripts. A set of formal book scripts were devised and priced according to the effort involved in writing them. The chief determinant in this system was the effort involved in terminating each of the letter strokes. In the example here the main text is written in *textualis rotunda*, which has strokes whose feet are rounded off with a natural uplift of the pen. The gloss is in a smaller, modified version of this script, though its letters have become extended with the speed of writing. It is further distinguished from the main text by being written in a lighter, browner ink. At the beginning of each commentary red ink is used to make a paragraph mark followed by the relevant word from the main text that is referred to by the commentary. Such large quantities of text often required large pages. The pages here are nearly half a metre high (49.5 × 32 cm, 19½ × 12⅝ in) and when set out on display in a handsome binding, they would have bolstered the prestige of any church or private patron. The book would have been considered of equal standing to an altar painting or sculpted cross.

By contrast, the carefully illuminated late-fifteenth century prayer book with its decorated clasp (**FIG. 5–97**) is only 11cm (4⅚ in) high and 7.5 cm (2¹⁵⁄₁₆ in) wide. It was created for the private use of a wealthy individual and therefore needed to be small enough to carry or to hold in the hand for reading. It is a kind of manuscript known as a Book of Hours. The name refers to the practice of reading certain prayers and devotions during each of the eight periods or 'hours' of daily prayer required by monastic orders (in the Middle Ages 'hours' were periods devoted to religious duties rather than fixed units of time). They allowed ordinary people to take part in private prayer and meditation in their own home as well as in church.

Such books became popular in the early thirteenth century and by the fifteenth century they were bestsellers across Europe. As well as wealthy individuals acquiring their own personal copy, any household that could afford a book would have bought one (a whole Bible was too expensive). Because it was often the only book that people owned, many people first learnt to read from it (the word 'primer' comes from the office of Prime, the first set of morning prayers). Such books also allowed many people to engage directly with a religious text for the very first time, rather than having it mediated through a priest or parent. This change was especially significant for women. The role of women within early medieval literary culture was passive and peripheral. Some were involved as readers but very few as writers. As access to texts increased from the eleventh century, so a greater number of women became involved in making and writing books. For the first time in western European literature women were being celebrated both as authors (Julian [sic] of Norwich, 1342–c.1416, Christine de Pizan, 1363–c.1434) and theologians (Hildegard of Bingen, 1098–1179).

5-96 • GLOSSED BIBLE (DETAIL), SHOWING TEXTUAL ARRANGEMENT, Thirteenth Century
Courtesy of the British Library.

5-97 • BOOK OF HOURS, BRUGES, C.1490–1500

By allowing readers of both sexes to develop a close relationship with texts, manuscripts became cherished objects. The rich also used them as a means of displaying their wealth, status and taste and this demand for an overt demonstration of wealth created a series of more decorative and heavily illuminated manuscript pages. The large extended decorative initials that were already evident by the twelfth century were extended during the thirteenth into ever more elaborately foliated forms of decoration. They began to be painted around the main text and eventually came to envelop it completely. Whole figurative scenes were soon incorporated into the surround, especially on pages where a major division in the text needed to be marked. The subjects depicted in these illuminated miniatures included scenes from the life of the Virgin, Christ and the saints, as well as themes relating to death and judgment. The finest artists were commissioned to illustrate them with opulent colours and gilded decoration in the latest Gothic styles. Royal patronage encouraged artists to suffuse their subjects with the attitudes and conventions of the life of the court, which resulted in a special emphasis being placed on the depiction of elaborate folds in the elegant draperies worn by extenuated figures in swaying poses; such features defined a Gothic style of illustration.

The evident splendour of the Gothic illustrations, with their expensive pigments and touches of gold leaf, was joined during the fifteenth century by a new requirement, a demand for naturalism. Whereas splendour required wealth, naturalism depended on a more exclusive commodity, the skill of a master craftsman. In the Low Countries especially, naturalistic forms appeared in rich and colourful initials and borders. The border that appears in the manuscript of a popular French allegorical poem, the *Roman de la Rose* **(FIG. 5–98)**, shows how the desire for naturalism had led the artist to turn the whole border into a wooden panel and then decorate it with plants, flowers, birds and butterflies. In its detail and realism it reflected the new standards of artistic skill that were

being developed through the revolutionary techniques of oil painting and a more convincing illusion of space. Both developments made the studied charm of the Gothic style appear dated. The degree of naturalism in the border exceeds that contained in the more conventionalized Gothic illustration in the centre.

Accompanying the illustration is a style of Gothic script called *bâtarde*. It is a high grade cursive script that is particularly associated with manuscripts produced for the Burgundian court (which ruled over Belgium, the Netherlands and Luxembourg during the fifteenth century). It evolved out of a distinctively pointed cursive script called 'secretary', which had been developed in the French Chancery during the beginning of the fourteenth century. But instead of keeping the latter's hurried cursive form, *bâtarde* took on the upright letter shape of the textura to create a hybrid or bastard form of letter. During the fifteenth and sixteenth centuries the script rose in status to become the standard script for luxurious editions of romances and histories, and all but replaced the textura scripts except in the very grandest books. Scribes appeared to enjoy the greater calligraphic verve and freedom of expression allowed by its arched and pointed strokes.

Not all manuscripts of the late Middle Ages were illuminated. Few readers of educational books could have afforded the expense involved. Grammars, text books, literary works (epics and romances), as well as many Books of Hours and psalters, were made with modest materials and within an increasingly rationalized method of production. The need to meet the growing demand for manuscripts encouraged their makers to standardize the production process. The most time-consuming aspect of manuscript manufacture was the writing and illuminating, and even a practised scribe or illuminator could benefit from using a pattern book which provided templates for various standard book features, such as decorative initials **(FIG. 5–99)**.

As well as mastering the standard forms, manuscript makers also had to cater to local tastes. In Italy, where the influence of the Carolingian minuscule had remained strong, Italian scribes created a more rounded version of Gothic script, more so even than the northern *texturalis rotunda*. The large, less compressed and angular letters of this Italian *rotunda* **(FIG. 5–100)**, though eclipsed in the late fourteenth century by a revival of the Roman tradition of lettering, continued to be used until the seventeenth century in service and devotional books.

The revival of classical lettering in Italy was part of a wider 'renaissance' of classical learning initiated by a group of Florentine

5-98 • BÂTARDE SCRIPT, 'ROMAN DE LA ROSE', BRUGES, C.1500
Courtesy of the British Library.

5-99 • PATTERN BOOK, FRANCE, Fifteenth Century
Courtesy of the British Library.

5-100 • ROTUNDA SCRIPT, MILAN, 1490–1504
Courtesy of the British Library.

writers and artists during the final years of the fourteenth century. They called themselves *umanisti* or 'humanists' because of the human values, as opposed to religious beliefs, to which they had been drawn by recently discovered art and writing from pre-Christian Greece and Rome. By studying classical texts and artefacts, they had learnt that artists need not only relate their work to the ancient scriptures or historical myths; they could also hold a mirror up to their own world, to the here-and-now. Something

of this new attitude towards the potential of art and literature—the 'humanities' as they became known—spread to each of Europe's main cultural centres, though not all at the same time nor in the same way. Like all historical periods, the Middle Ages and its successor, the Renaissance, are blurred at the edges, and yet the dividing line was made a little less diffuse by a singular fact of history. That fact was the invention of printing with type in the West.

CATHEDRALS AND CRUSADES: EUROPE AND ITS NEIGHBORS IN THE MIDDLE AGES

THOUGHT PIECE

AN APPRECIATION OF THE FRANKISH CHARACTER

Their lack of sense.—Mysterious are the works of the Creator, the author of all things! When one comes to recount cases regarding the Franks, he cannot but glorify Allah (exalted is he!) and sanctify him, for he sees them as animals possessing the virtues of courage and fighting, but nothing else; just as animals have only the virtues of strength and carrying loads. I shall now give some instances of their doings and their curious mentality.

In the army of King Fulk, son of Fulk, was a Frankish reverend knight who had just arrived from their land in order to make the holy pilgrimage and then return home. He was of my intimate fellowship and kept such constant company with me that he began to call me "my brother." Between us were mutual bonds of amity and friendship. When he resolved to return by sea to his homeland, he said to me:

My brother, I am leaving for my country and I want thee to send with me thy son (my son,[1] who was then fourteen years old, was at that time in my company) to our country, where he can see the knights and learn wisdom and chivalry. When he returns, he will be like a wise man.

Thus there fell upon my ears words which would never come out of the head of a sensible man; for even if my son were to be taken captive, his captivity could not bring him a worse misfortune than carrying him into the lands of the Franks.

However, I said to the man:

By thy life, this has exactly been my idea. But the only thing that prevented me from carrying it out was the fact that his grandmother, my mother, is so fond of him and did not this time let him come out with me until she exacted an oath from me to the effect that I would return him to her.

Thereupon he asked, "Is thy mother still alive?" "Yes," I replied. "Well," said he, "disobey her not."

—From Usama ibn Munqidh, *An Arab-Syrian gentleman and warrior in the period of the Crusades.* Philip K. Hitti, tr. (New York: Columbia University Press, 1987), p. 161.

[1] Abu-al-Fawãris Murhaf.

THINGS TO CONSIDER

- What was the medieval understanding of beauty, and how was it manifest in the visual culture of this period?
- How were art and design used in this period to unify a culturally diverse empire?
- What can the names that historians have given to this period (Dark Ages, Middle Ages) tell us about the way we construct history? What happens to our picture of this period when we consider it alongside Islamic culture of the same time?

THE EARLY MIDDLE AGES

As Roman authority crumbled at the dissolution of the Western Empire in the fifth century, it was replaced by "barbarians," people from outside the Roman empire and cultural orbit who could only "barble" Greek or Latin **(MAP 6–1)**. Thus far we have seen these "barbarians" as adversaries viewed through Greek and Roman eyes—the defeated Gauls at Pergamon (SEE FIG. 4–33), the captives on the *Gemma Augustea* (SEE FIG. 3–60), or the enemy beyond the Danube River on Trajan's Column (SEE FIG. 3–83). But by the fourth century many Germanic tribes were allies of Rome. In fact, most of Constantine's troops in the decisive battle with Maxentius at the Milvian Bridge were Germanic.

A century later the situation was entirely different. The adventures of the Roman princess Galla Placidia, whom we have already met as a patron of the arts (SEE FIG. 5–24), bring the situation vividly to life. She had the misfortune to be in Rome when Alaric and the Visigoths sacked the city in 410 (the emperor and pope were living safely in Ravenna). Carried off as a prize of war by the Goths, Galla Placidia had to join their migrations through France and Spain and eventually married the Gothic king, who was soon murdered. Back in Italy, married and widowed yet again, Galla Placidia ruled the Western Empire as regent for her son from 425 to 437/38. She died in 450, thus escaping yet another sack of Rome, this time by the Vandals, in 455. The fall of Rome shocked the Christian world, although the wounds were more psychological than physical. Bishop Augustine of Hippo (St. Augustine, d. 430) was inspired to write *The City of God*, a cornerstone of Christian philosophy, as an answer to people who claimed that the Goths represented the vengeance of the pagan gods on people who had abandoned them for Christianity.

Who were these people living outside the Mediterranean orbit? Their wooden architecture is lost to fire and decay, but their metalwork and its animal and geometric ornament has survived.

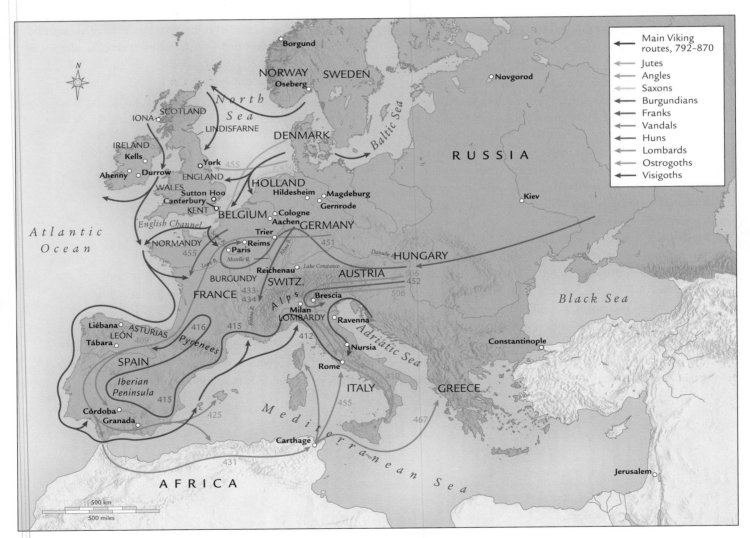

MAP 6–1 • EUROPE OF THE EARLY MIDDLE AGES

This map shows the routes taken by the groups of people who migrated into and through the western Roman world at the dawn of the Middle Ages. Modern country names have been used here for convenience, but at this time, these countries, as we know them, did not yet exist.

Defining the Middle Ages

The roughly 1,000 years of European history between the dissolution of the Western Roman Empire during the fifth century and the Florentine Renaissance in the fifteenth century are generally referred to as the Middle Ages, or the medieval period. These terms reflect the view of Renaissance humanists who regarded the period that preceded theirs as a "dark age" of ignorance, decline, and barbarism, standing in the middle and separating their own "golden age" from the golden ages of ancient Greece and Rome. Although scholars now acknowledge the ridiculousness of this self-serving formulation and recognize the millennium of the "Middle Ages" as a period of great richness, complexity, creativity, and innovation, the term has endured.

Art historians commonly divide the Middle Ages into three periods: early medieval (ending c. 1000), Romanesque (eleventh and twelfth centuries), and Gothic (beginning in the mid-twelfth and extending into the fifteenth century). In this chapter we can look at only a few of the many cultures that flourished during the early medieval period. For convenience, we will use modern geographic names as familiar points of reference (SEE MAP 6–1), but, in fact, European nations as we know them today did not yet exist.

They were hunters and fishermen, shepherds and farmers living in villages with a social organization based on extended families and tribal loyalties. They engaged in the practical crafts—pottery, weaving, woodwork—and they fashioned metals into weapons, tools, and jewelry.

The Celts controlled most of western Europe, and the Germanic people—Goths and others—lived around the Baltic Sea. Increasing population evidently forced the Goths to begin to move south, into better lands and climate around the Mediterranean and Black Seas, but the Romans had extended the borders of their empire across the Rhine and Danube rivers. Seeking the relative security and higher standard of living they saw in the Roman Empire, the Germanic people crossed the borders and settled within the Roman world.

The tempo of migration speeded up in the fifth century when the Huns from Central Asia swept down on western Europe; the Ostrogoths (Eastern Goths) moved into Italy and deposed the last Western Roman emperor in 476; the Visigoths (Western Goths) ended their wanderings in Spain; the Burgundians settled in Switzerland and eastern France; the Franks in Germany, France, and Belgium; and the Vandals crossed over into Africa, making Carthage their headquarters before circling back to Italy, sacking Rome in 455.

As these barbarian groups gradually converted to Christianity, the Church served to unify Europe's heterogeneous population. As early as 345, the Goths adopted Arian Christianity, beliefs considered heretical by the Church in Rome. (Arian Christians did not believe that Christ was divine or co-equal with God the Father.) Not until 589 did they accept Roman Christianity. But the Franks under Clovis (r. 481–511), influenced by his Burgundian wife Clotilda, converted to Roman Christianity in 496, beginning a fruitful alliance between French rulers and the popes. Kings and nobles defended the claims of the Roman Church, and the pope, in turn, validated their authority. As its wealth and influence increased throughout Europe, the Church emerged as the principal patron of the arts to fulfill growing needs for buildings and liturgical equipment, including altars, altar vessels, crosses, candlesticks, containers for the remains of saints (reliquaries), vestments (ritual garments), images of Christian figures and stories, and copies of sacred texts such as the Gospels. (See "Defining the Middle Ages," above.)

THE ART OF THE "BARBARIANS" IN EUROPE

Out of a tangled web of themes and styles originating from inside and out of the empire, from pagan and Christian beliefs, from urban and rural settlements, brilliant new artistic styles were born across Europe as barbarian people settled within the former Western Roman Empire. Many of the migratory groups were superb metalworkers and created magnificent colorful jewelry, both with precious metals and with inlays of gems. Most of the motifs were geometric or highly abstracted from natural forms.

THE MEROVINGIANS

One of the barbarian groups that moved into the Western Roman world during the fifth century was the Franks, who migrated westward from what is now Belgium and settled in the northern part of Roman Gaul (modern France). There they were soon ruled by a succession of leaders from a dynasty named "Merovingian" after its legendary founder, Merovech. The Merovingians established a powerful kingdom during the reigns of Childeric I (c. 457–481) and his son Clovis I (481–511), whose conversion to Christianity in 496 connected the Franks to the larger European world through an ecclesiastical network of communication and affiliation.

Though some early **illuminated** books (books that include not only text but pictures and decoration in color and gold) have

To view this image, please go to page 426 of the *Art History*, Fourth Edition by Marilyn Stokstad ebook.

6–1 • JEWELRY OF QUEEN ARNEGUNDE

Discovered in her tomb, excavated at the Abbey of Saint-Denis, Paris. Burial c. 580–590. Gold, silver, garnets, and glass beads; length of pin 10⅜″ (26.4 cm). Musée des Antiquités Nationales, Saint-Germain-en-Laye, France.

been associated with the dynasty, our knowledge of Merovingian art is based primarily on the jewelry that has been uncovered in the graves of kings, queens, and aristocrats, indicating that both men and women expressed their wealth (in death, as presumably in life) by wearing earrings, necklaces, finger rings, bracelets, and weighty leather belts, from which they suspended even more ornamental metalwork. One of the most spectacular royal tombs was that of Queen Arnegunde, unearthed during excavations in 1959 at the Abbey of Saint-Denis, near Paris, which was a significant center of Merovingian patronage.

Arnegunde was discovered within a stone sarcophagus—undisturbed since her burial in c. 580–590. From her bodily remains, archaeologists determined that she was slight and blond, 5 feet tall, and about 70 years old at the time of her death. The inscription of her name on a gold ring on her left thumb provided

the first clue to her identity, and her royal pedigree was confirmed by the sumptuousness of her clothing. She was outfitted in a short, purple silk tunic, cinched at the waist by a substantial leather belt from which was suspended ornamental metalwork. The stockings that covered her legs were supported by leather garters with silver strap tongues and dangling ornaments. Over this ensemble was a dark red gown embroidered in gold thread. This overgarment was opened up the front, but clasped at neck and waist by round brooches and a massive buckle **(FIG. 6–1)**. These impressive objects were made by casting their general shape in two-piece molds, refining and chasing them with tools, and inlaying within reserved and framed areas carefully cut garnets to provide color and sparkle. Not long after Arnegunde's interment, Merovingian royalty ceased the practice of burying such precious items with the dead—encouraged by the Church to donate them instead to religious institutions in honor of the saints—but we are fortunate to have a few early examples that presumably document the way these royal figures presented themselves on state occasions.

THE NORSE

In Scandinavia (present-day Denmark, Norway, and Sweden), which was never part of the Roman Empire, people spoke variants of the Norse language and shared a rich mythology with other Germanic peoples. Scandinavian artists had exhibited a fondness for abstract patterning from early prehistoric times. During the first millennium BCE, trade, warfare, and migration had brought a variety of jewelry, coins, textiles, and other portable objects into northern Europe. The artists incorporated the solar disks and stylized animals on these objects into their already rich artistic vocabulary.

By the fifth century CE, the so-called **animal style** dominated the arts, displaying an impressive array of serpents, four-legged beasts, and squat human figures, as can be seen in their metalwork. The **GUMMERSMARK BROOCH (FIG. 6–2)**, for example, is a large silver-gilt pin dating from the sixth century in Denmark. This elegant ornament consists of a large, rectangular panel and a medallionlike plate covering the safety pin's catch connected by an arched bow. The surface of the pin seethes with human, animal, and geometric forms. An eye-and-beak motif frames the rectangular panel, a man is compressed between dragons just below the bow, and a pair of monster heads and crouching dogs with spiraling tongues frame the covering of the catch.

Certain underlying principles govern works with animal style design: The compositions are generally symmetrical, and artists depict animals in their entirety either in profile or from above. Ribs and spinal columns are exposed as if they had been x-rayed; hip and shoulder joints are pear-shape; tongues and jaws extend and curl; and legs end in large claws.

The northern jewelers carefully crafted their molds to produce a glittering surface on the cast metal, turning a process intended to speed production into an art form of great refinement.

THE CELTS AND ANGLO-SAXONS IN BRITAIN

After the Romans departed Britain at the beginning of the fifth century, Angles and Saxons from Germany and the Low Lands, and Jutes from Denmark, crossed the sea to occupy southeastern Britain. Gradually they extended their control northwest across the island. Over the next 200 years, the arts experienced a spectacular efflorescence. A fusion of Celtic, Roman, Germanic, and Norse cultures generated a new style of art, sometimes known as Hiberno-Saxon (from the Roman name for Ireland, Hibernia). Anglo-Saxon literature is filled with references to sumptuous jewelry and weapons made of or decorated with gold and silver, and fortunately, some of it has survived to this day.

The Anglo-Saxon epic *Beowulf*, composed perhaps as early as the seventh century, describes its hero's burial with a hoard of treasure in a grave mound near the sea. Such a burial site was

To view this image, please go to page 427 of the *Art History*, Fourth Edition by Marilyn Stokstad ebook.

6-2 • GUMMERSMARK BROOCH
Denmark. 6th century. Silver gilt, height 5¾″ (14.6 cm). Nationalmuseet, Copenhagen.

discovered near the North Sea coast in Suffolk at a site called Sutton Hoo (*hoo* means "hill"). The grave's occupant had been buried in a ship—90 feet long and designed for rowing, not sailing—whose traces in the earth were recovered by careful excavators. The wood—and the hero's body—had disintegrated, and no inscriptions record his name. He has sometimes been identified with the ruler Raedwald, who died about 625. Whoever he was, the treasures buried with him prove that he was a wealthy and powerful man. They include weapons, armor, other equipment to provide for the ruler's afterlife, and many luxury items. The objects from Sutton Hoo represent the broad multicultural heritage characterizing Britain, Ireland, and Scotland at this time—Celtic, Scandinavian, and classical Roman, as well as Anglo-Saxon. There was even a Byzantine silver bowl at Sutton Hoo.

The story of the discovery of Sutton Hoo—unquestionably one of the most important archaeological discoveries in Britain—begins with Edith May Pretty, who decided late in her life to explore the burial mounds that were located on her estate in southeast Suffolk, securing the services of a local amateur archaeologist, Basil Brown. Excavations began in 1938 as a collaborative effort between the two of them, and in the following year they encountered the famous ship burial. As rumors spread of the importance of the find, its excavation was gradually taken over by renowned experts and archaeologists who moved from the remains of the ship to the treasures of the burial chamber for which Sutton Hoo is most famous. Police officers were posted to guard the site, and the treasures were sent for safekeeping to the British Museum in London, although, since Sutton Hoo was determined not to be "Treasure Trove" (buried objects meant to be retrieved by their original owners and now considered property of the Crown—see "The Mildenhall Treasure," page 214), it was the legal property of Mrs. Pretty. She, however, decided to donate the entire contents of the burial mound to the British Museum.

Excavation of Sutton Hoo was interrupted by World War II, but in 1945 Rupert Bruce-Mitford of the British Museum began a scholarly study of its treasures that would become his life work. He not only subjected each piece to detailed scrutiny; he proposed reconstructions of objects that were only partially preserved, such at the harp, helmet, and drinking horns. Using the evidence that had been gathered in a famous murder case, he proposed that Sutton Hoo was actually a burial, even though no evidence of human remains were ever found, since they could have disappeared completely in the notably acidic soil of the mound. Other scholars used radiocarbon dating of timber fragments and close analysis of coins to focus the dating of the burial to c. 625, which happened to coincide with the death date of King Raedwald of East Anglia, the most popular candidate for the identity of the person buried at Sutton Hoo.

After heated discussions and considerable controversy, new excavations were carried out in the area of Sutton Hoo during the 1980s and 1990s. These revealed a series of other discoveries in what emerged as an important early medieval burial ground and proved that the area had been inhabited since the Neolithic period, but they uncovered nothing to rival the collection of treasures that were preserved at Sutton Hoo.

One of the most exquisite finds was a clasp of pure gold that once secured over his shoulder the leather body armor of its distinguished owner (**FIG. 6–3**). The two sides of the clasp—essentially identical in design—were connected when a long gold pin, attached to one half by a delicate but strong gold chain, was inserted through a series of aligned channels on the back side of the inner edge of each. The superb decoration of this work is created by thin pieces of garnet and blue-checkered glass (known as **millefiori**, from the Italian for "a thousand flowers") cut into precisely stepped geometric shapes or to follow the sinuous contours of stylized animal forms. The cut shapes were then inserted into channels and supplemented by granulation (the use of minute granules of gold fused to the surface). Under the stepped geometric pieces that form a rectangular patterned field on each side, jewelers placed gold foil stamped with incised motifs that reflect light back up through the transparent garnet to spectacular effect. Around these carpetlike rectangles are borders of interlacing snakes, and in the curving compartments to the outside stand pairs of semi-transparent, overlapping boars stylized in ways that reflect the traditions of Scandinavian jewelry. Their curly pig's tails overlap their strong rumps at the outer edges on each side of the clasp, and following the visible vertebrae along the arched forms of their backs, we arrive at their heads, with floppy ears and extended tusks. Boars represented strength and bravery, important virtues in warlike Anglo-Saxon society.

To view this image, please go to page 428 of the *Art History*, Fourth Edition by Marilyn Stokstad ebook.

6-3 • HINGED CLASP, FROM THE SUTTON HOO BURIAL SHIP
Suffolk, England. First half of 7th century. Gold plaques with granulation and inlays of garnet and checked millefiori glass, length 5" (12.7 cm). British Museum, London.

ROMANESQUE ART

These three men seem to glide forward on tiptoe as their leader turns back, reversing their forward movement. Their bodies are sleek; legs cross in languid curves rather than vigorous strides; their shoulders, elbows, and finger joints seem to melt; draperies delicately delineate curving contours; bearded faces stare out with large, wide eyes under strong, arched brows. The figures interrelate and interlock, pushing against the limits of the architectural frame.

Medieval viewers would have quickly identified the leader as Christ, not only by his commanding size, but specifically by his cruciform halo. The sanctity of his companions is signified by their own haloes. The scene recalls to faithful Christians the story of the resurrected Christ and two of his disciples on the road from Jerusalem to Emmaus (Luke 24:13–35). Christ has the distinctive attributes of a medieval pilgrim—a hat, a satchel, and a walking stick. Even the scallop shell on his satchel is the badge worn by pilgrims to a specific site: the shrine of St. James at Santiago de Compostela. Early pilgrims reaching this destination in the far northwestern corner of the Iberian peninsula continued to the coast to pick up a shell as evidence of their journey. Soon shells were gathered (or fabricated from metal as brooches) and sold to the pilgrims—a lucrative business for both the sellers and the church. On the return journey home, the shell became the pilgrims' passport, a badge attesting to their piety and accomplishment. Other distinctive badges were adopted at other pilgrimage sites.

This relief was carved on a corner pier in the cloister of the Monastery of Santo Domingo in Silos, a major eleventh- and twelfth-century center of religious and artistic life south of the pilgrimage road across Spain (see "The Pilgrim's Journey," page 458). It engaged an audience of monks and religious pilgrims—who were well versed in the meaning of Christian images—through a new sculptural style that we call Romanesque. Not since the art of ancient Rome half a millennium earlier had sculptors carved monumental figures in stone within an architectural fabric. During the early Middle Ages, sculpture was small-scale, independent, and created from precious materials—a highlighted object within a sacred space rather than a part of its architectural envelope. But during the Romanesque period, narrative and iconic figural imagery in deeply carved ornamental frameworks would collect around the entrances to churches, focusing attention on their compelling portal complexes. These public displays of Christian doctrine and moral teaching would have been part of the cultural landscape surveyed by pilgrims journeying along the road to Santiago. Travel as a pilgrim opened the mind to a world beyond the familiar towns and agricultural villages of home, signaling a new era in the social, economic, and artistic life of Europe.

LEARN ABOUT IT

6.1 Explore the emergence of Romanesque architecture—with its emphasis on the aesthetic qualities of a sculptural wall—out of early masonry construction techniques.

6.2 Assess the impact of pilgrimage as a cultural phenomenon on the design and embellishment of church architecture.

6.3 Compare and contrast Romanesque architectural styles in different regions of Europe.

6.4 Investigate the integration of painting and sculpture within the Romanesque building, and consider the implications of placing art on the church exterior and what theological themes were emphasized.

6.5 Explore the eleventh- and twelfth-century interest in telling stories of human frailty and sanctity in sculpture, textiles, and manuscript painting—stories that were meant to appeal to the feelings as well as to the minds of the viewers.

HEAR MORE: Listen to an audio file of your chapter **www.myartslab.com**

EUROPE IN THE ROMANESQUE PERIOD

At the beginning of the eleventh century, Europe was still divided into many small political and economic units ruled by powerful families, such as the Ottonians in Germany (MAP 6–2). The nations we know today did not exist, although for convenience we shall use present-day names of countries. The king of France ruled only a small area around Paris known as the Île-de-France. The southern part of modern France had close linguistic and cultural ties to northern Spain; in the north the duke of Normandy (heir of the Vikings) and in the east the duke of Burgundy paid the French king only token homage.

When in 1066 Duke William II of Normandy (r. 1035–1087) invaded England and, as William the Conqueror, became that country's new king, Norman nobles replaced the Anglo-Saxon nobility there, and England became politically and culturally allied with Normandy. As astute and skillful administrators, the Normans formed a close alliance with the Church, supporting it with grants of land and gaining in return the allegiance of abbots and bishops. Normandy became one of Europe's most powerful feudal domains. During this period, the Holy Roman Empire, re-established by the Ottonians, encompassed much of Germany and northern Italy, while the Iberian peninsula remained divided between Muslim rulers in the south and Christian rulers in the north. By 1085, Alfonso VI of Castile and León (r. 1065–1109) had conquered the Muslim stronghold of Toledo, a center of Islamic and Jewish culture in the kingdom of Castile. Catalunya (Catalonia) emerged as a power along the Mediterranean coast.

By the end of the twelfth century, however, a few exceptionally intelligent and aggressive rulers had begun to create national states. The Capetians in France and the Plantagenets in England were especially successful. In Germany and northern Italy, the power of local rulers and towns prevailed, and Germany and Italy remained politically fragmented until the nineteenth century.

POLITICAL AND ECONOMIC LIFE

Although towns and cities with artisans and merchants grew in importance, Europe remained an agricultural society, with land the primary source of wealth and power for a hereditary aristocracy. In France and England in particular, social, economic, and political relations were governed by a system commonly referred to as "feudalism." Arrangements varied considerably from place to place, but typically a landowning lord granted property and protection to a subordinate, called a vassal. In return, the vassal pledged allegiance and military service to the lord. Peasants worked the land in exchange for a place to live, military protection, and other services from the lord. Allegiances and obligations among lords, vassals, and peasants were largely inherited but constantly shifting.

THE CHURCH

In the early Middle Ages, Church and state had forged some fruitful alliances. Christian rulers helped ensure the spread of Christianity throughout Europe and supported monastic communities with grants of land. Bishops and abbots were often royal relatives, younger brothers and cousins, who supplied crucial social and spiritual support and a cadre of educated administrators. As a result, secular and religious authority became tightly intertwined, and this continued through the Romanesque period. Monasteries continued to sit at the center of European culture, but there were two new cultural forces fostered by the Church: pilgrimages and crusades.

MONASTICISM. Although the first universities were established in the eleventh and twelfth centuries in the growing cities of Bologna, Paris, Oxford, and Cambridge, monastic communities continued to play a major role in intellectual life. Monks and nuns also provided valuable social services, including caring for the sick and destitute, housing travelers, and educating the elite. Because monasteries were major landholders, abbots and priors were part of the feudal power structure. The children of aristocratic families joined religious orders, helping forge links between monastic communities and the ruling elite.

As life in Benedictine communities grew increasingly comfortable and intertwined with the secular world, reform movements arose. Reformers sought a return to earlier monastic austerity and spirituality. The most important groups of reformers for the arts were the Burgundian congregation of Cluny, established in the tenth century, and later the Cistercians, who sought reform of what they saw as Cluniac decadence and corruption of monastic values.

PILGRIMAGES. Pilgrimages to the holy places of Christendom—Jerusalem, Rome, and Santiago de Compostela—increased, despite the great physical hardships they entailed (see "The Pilgrim's Journey," page 414). As difficult and dangerous as these journeys were, rewards awaited courageous travelers along the routes. Pilgrims could venerate the relics of local saints during the journey, and artists and architects were commissioned to create spectacular and enticing new buildings and works of art to capture their attention.

CRUSADES. In the eleventh and twelfth centuries, Christian Europe, previously on the defensive against the expanding forces of Islam, became the aggressor. In Spain, Christian armies of the north were increasingly successful against the Islamic south. At the same time, the Byzantine emperor asked the pope for help in his war with the Muslims surrounding his domain. The Western Church responded in 1095 by launching a series of holy wars, military offensives against Islamic powers known collectively as the crusades (from the Latin crux, referring to the cross crusaders wore).

This First Crusade was preached by Pope Urban II (pontificate 1088–1099) and fought by the lesser nobility of France, who had economic and political as well as spiritual objectives. The crusaders

MAP 6-2 • EUROPE IN THE ROMANESQUE PERIOD

Although a few large political entities began to emerge in places like England and Normandy, Burgundy, and León/Castile, Europe remained a land of small economic entities. Pilgrimages and crusades acted as unifying international forces.

captured Jerusalem in 1099 and established a short-lived kingdom. The Second Crusade in 1147, preached by St. Bernard and led by France and Germany, accomplished nothing. The Muslim leader Saladin united the Muslim forces and captured Jerusalem in 1187, inspiring the Third Crusade, led by German, French, and English kings. The Christians recaptured some territory, but not Jerusalem, and in 1192 they concluded a truce with the Muslims, permitting the Christians access to the shrines in Jerusalem. Although the crusades were brutal military failures, the movement had far-reaching cultural and economic consequences, providing western Europeans with direct encounters with the more sophisticated material culture of the Islamic world and the Byzantine Empire. This in turn helped stimulate trade, and with trade came the development of an increasingly urban society during the eleventh and twelfth centuries.

ROMANESQUE ART

The word "Romanesque," meaning "in the Roman manner," was coined in the early nineteenth century to describe early medieval European church architecture, which often displayed the solid masonry walls and rounded arches and vaults characteristic of imperial Roman buildings. Soon the term was applied to all the arts of the period from roughly the mid–eleventh century to the second half of the twelfth century, even though that art derives from a variety of sources and reflects a multitude of influences, not just Roman.

This was a period of great building activity in Europe. New castles, manor houses, churches, and monasteries arose everywhere. As one eleventh-century monk put it, the Christian faithful were so relieved to have passed through the apocalyptic anxiety that had gripped their world at the millennial change around the year 1000, that, in gratitude, "Each people of Christendom rivaled with the other, to see which should worship in the finest buildings. The world shook herself, clothed everywhere in a white garment of churches" (Radulphus Glaber, cited in Holt, vol. I, p. 18) (SEE FIG. 6–4). The desire to glorify the house of the Lord and his saints (whose earthly remains in the form of relics kept their presence alive in the minds of the people) increased throughout Christendom. There was a veritable building boom.

ARCHITECTURE

Romanesque architecture and art is a trans-European phenomenon, but it is inflected regionally, and the style varies in character from place to place. Although timber remained common in construction, Romanesque builders used stone masonry whenever possible. Masonry vaults were stronger and more durable, and they enhanced the acoustical effect of the Gregorian chants (plainsong, named after

To view this image, please go to page 456 of the *Art History*, Fourth Edition by Marilyn Stokstad ebook.

6-4 • SAINT-MARTIN-DU-CANIGOU
French Pyrenees. 1001–1026.

Pope Gregory the Great, pontificate 590–604) sung inside. Tall stone towers, at times flanking the main entrance portal, marked the church as the most important building in the community. The portals themselves were often encrusted with sculpture that broadcast the moral and theological messages of the Church to a wide public audience.

"FIRST ROMANESQUE"

Soon after the year 1000—while Radulphus Glaber was commenting on the rise of church building across the land—patrons and builders in Catalunya (northeast Spain), southern France, and northern Italy were already constructing all-masonry churches, employing the methods of late Roman builders. The picturesque Benedictine monastery of **SAINT-MARTIN-DU-CANIGOU**, nestled into the Pyrenees on a building platform stabilized by strongly buttressed retaining walls, is a typical example **(FIG. 6–4)**. Patronized by the local Count Guifred, who took refuge in the monastery and died here in 1049, the complex is capped by a massive stone tower sitting next to the sanctuary of the two-story church. Art historians call such early stone-vaulted buildings "First Romanesque," employing the term that Catalan architect and theorist Josep Puig I Cadafalch first associated with them in 1928.

THE CHURCH OF SANT VINCENC, CARDONA. One of the finest examples of "First Romanesque" is the **CHURCH OF SANT VINCENC** (St. Vincent) in the Catalan castle of Cardona **(FIG. 6–5)**. Begun in the 1020s, it was consecrated in 1040. Castle residents entered the church through a two-story narthex into a nave with low narrow side aisles that permitted clerestory windows in the nave wall. The sanctuary was raised dramatically over an aisled crypt. The Catalan masons used local materials— small split stones, bricks, even river pebbles, and very strong mortar—to raise plain walls and round barrel or groin vaults. Today we can admire their skillful stonework both inside and out, but the builders originally covered their masonry with a facing of stucco.

To strengthen the walls and vaults, the masons added vertical bands of masonry (called strip buttresses) joined by arches and additional courses of masonry to counter the outward thrust of the vault and to enrich the sculptural quality of the wall. On the interior these masonry strips project from the piers and continue up and over the vault, creating a **transverse arch**. Additional projecting bands line the underside of the arches of the nave arcade. The result is a compound pier that works in concert with the transverse arches to divide the nave into a series of bays. This system of bay division became standard in Romanesque architecture. It is a marked contrast to the flat-wall continuity and undivided space within a pre-Romanesque church like Gernrode.

PILGRIMAGE CHURCHES

The growth of a cult of relics and the desire to visit shrines such as St. Peter's in Rome or St. James's in Spain increasingly inspired the Christians of western Europe to travel on pilgrimages (see

To view this image, please go to page 457 of the *Art History*, Fourth Edition by Marilyn Stokstad ebook.

6-5 • INTERIOR, CHURCH OF SANT VINCENC, CARDONA
1020s–1030s.

"The Pilgrim's Journey," page 414). To accommodate the faithful and proclaim church doctrine, many monasteries on the major pilgrimage routes built large new churches, filled them with sumptuous altars and reliquaries, and encrusted them with elaborate stone sculpture on the exterior around entrances.

The Pilgrim's Journey

Western Europe in the eleventh and twelfth centuries saw an explosive growth in the popularity of religious pilgrimage. The rough roads that led to the most popular destinations—the tomb of St. Peter and other martyrs in Rome, the church of the Holy Sepulcher in Jerusalem, and the Cathedral of St. James in Santiago de Compostela in the northwest corner of Spain—were often crowded with pilgrims. Their journeys could last a year or more; church officials going to Compostela were given 16 weeks' leave of absence. Along the way the pilgrims had to contend with bad food and poisoned water, as well as bandits and dishonest innkeepers and merchants.

In the twelfth century, the priest Aymery Picaud wrote a guidebook for pilgrims on their way to Santiago through what is now France. Like travel guides today, Picaud's book provided advice on local customs, comments on food and the safety of drinking water, and a list of useful words in the Basque language. In Picaud's time, four main pilgrimage routes crossed France, merging into a single road in Spain at Puente la Reina and leading on from there through Burgos and León to Compostela. Conveniently spaced monasteries and churches offered food and lodging, as well as relics to venerate. Roads and bridges were maintained by a guild of bridge builders and guarded by the Knights of Santiago.

Picaud described the best-traveled routes and most important shrines to visit along the way. Chartres, for example, housed the tunic that the Virgin was said to have worn when she gave birth to Jesus. The monks of Vézelay had the bones of St. Mary Magdalen, and at Conques, the skull of Sainte Foy was to be found. Churches associated with miraculous cures—Autun, for example, which claimed to house the relics of Lazarus, raised by Jesus from the dead—were filled with the sick and injured praying to be healed.

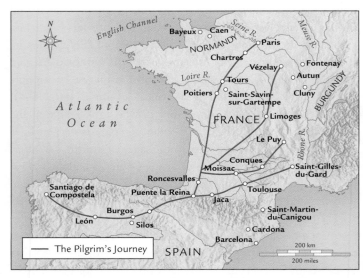

MAP 6–3 • THE PILGRIMAGE ROUTES TO SANTIAGO DE COMPOSTELA

THE CATHEDRAL OF ST. JAMES IN SANTIAGO DE COMPOSTELA. One major goal of pilgrimage was the **CATHEDRAL OF ST. JAMES IN SANTIAGO DE COMPOSTELA (FIG. 6–6)**, which held the body of St. James, the apostle to the Iberian peninsula. Builders of this and other major churches along the roads leading through France to the shrine developed a distinctive plan designed to accommodate the crowds of pilgrims and allow them to move easily from chapel to chapel in their desire to venerate relics (see "Relics and Reliquaries," page 418). This "pilgrimage plan" is a model of functional planning and traffic control. To the aisled nave the builders added aisled transepts with eastern chapels leading to an ambulatory (curving walkway) with additional radiating chapels around the apse **(FIGS. 6–7, 6–8)**. This expansion of the basilican plan allowed worshipers to circulate freely around the church's perimeter, visiting chapels and venerating relics without disrupting services within the main space.

At Santiago, pilgrims entered the church through the large double doors at the ends of the transepts rather than through the western portal, which served ceremonial processions. Pilgrims from France entered the north transept portal; the approach from the town was through the south portal. All found themselves in a transept in which the design exactly mirrored the nave in height and structure. Both nave and transept have two stories—an arcade and a gallery. Compound piers with attached half-columns on all four sides support the immense barrel vault and are projected over it vertically through a rhythmic series of transverse arches. They give sculptural form to the interior walls and also mark off individual vaulted bays in which the sequence is as clear and regular as the ambulatory chapels of the choir. Three different kinds of vaults are used here: barrel vaults with transverse arches cover the nave, groin vaults span the side aisles, and halfbarrel or quadrant vaults cover the galleries and strengthen the building by countering the outward thrust of the high nave vaults and transferring it to the outer walls and buttresses. Without a clerestory, light enters the nave only indirectly, through windows in the outer walls of the aisles and upper-level galleries that overlook the nave. Light from the choir clerestory and the large windows of an octagonal **lantern** tower (a structure built above the height of the main ceiling with windows that illuminate the space below) over the crossing would therefore spotlight the

6-6 • TRANSEPT, CATHEDRAL OF ST. JAMES, SANTIAGO DE COMPOSTELA

Galicia, Spain. 1078–1122. View toward the crossing.

SEE MORE: Click the Google Earth link for the Cathedral of Saint James, Santiago de Compostela **www.myartslab.com**

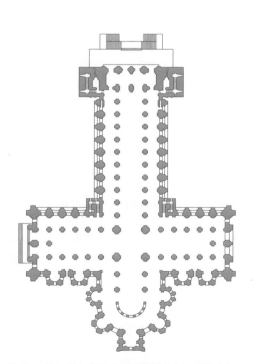

6-7 • PLAN OF CATHEDRAL OF ST. JAMES, SANTIAGO DE COMPOSTELA

SEE MORE: View a video about the Cathedral of Saint James, Santiago de Compostela **www.myartslab.com**

6-8 • RECONSTRUCTION DRAWING (AFTER CONANT) OF CATHEDRAL OF ST. JAMES, SANTIAGO DE COMPOSTELA

1078–1122; western portions later. View from the east.

EXPLORE MORE: Gain insight from primary sources related to the Cathedral of Saint James, Santiago de Compostela **www.myartslab.com**

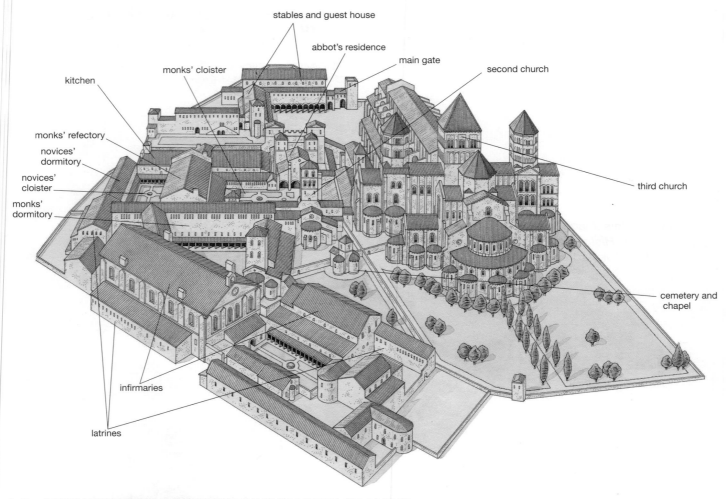

6-9 • RECONSTRUCTION DRAWING OF THE ABBEY AT CLUNY
Burgundy, France. 1088–1130. View from the east.

EXPLORE MORE: Gain insight from a primary source related to the abbey at Cluny www.myartslab.com

glittering gold and jeweled shrine of the principal relic at the high altar.

In its own time, Santiago was admired for the excellence of its construction—"not a single crack is to be found," according to the twelfth-century pilgrims' guide—"admirable and beautiful in execution…large, spacious, well-lighted, of fitting size, harmonious in width, length, and height…." Pilgrims arrived at Santiago de Compostela weary after weeks of difficult travel through dense woods and mountains. Grateful to St. James for his protection along the way, they entered a church that welcomed them with open portals, encrusted with the dynamic moralizing sculpture that characterized Romanesque churches. The cathedral had no doors to close—it was open day and night.

CLUNY

In 909, the duke of Burgundy gave land for a monastery to Benedictine monks intent on strict adherence to the original rules of St. Benedict. They established the reformed congregation of Cluny. From its foundation, Cluny had a special independent status; its abbot answered directly to the pope in Rome rather than to the local bishop or feudal lord. This unique freedom, jealously safeguarded by a series of long-lived and astute abbots, enabled Cluny to keep the profits from extensive gifts of land and treasure. Independent, wealthy, and a center of culture and learning, Cluny and its affiliates became important patrons of architecture and art.

The monastery of Cluny was a city unto itself. By the second half of the eleventh century, there were some 200 monks in residence, supplemented by troops of laymen on whom they depended for material support. As we have seen in the Saint Gall plan of the Carolingian period, the cloister lay at the center of the monastic community, joining the church with domestic buildings and workshops **(FIG. 6–9)**. In wealthy monasteries like this, the arcaded galleries of the cloister had elaborate carved capitals as well as relief sculpture on piers. The capitals may have served as memory devices or visualized theology to direct and inspire the monks' thoughts and prayers.

Cluniac monks observed the traditional eight Hours of the Divine Office (including prayers, scripture readings, psalms, and hymns) spread over the course of each day and night. Mass was celebrated after the third hour (terce), and the Cluniac liturgy was especially elaborate. During the height of its power, plainsong (or Gregorian chant) filled the church with music 24 hours a day.

The hallmark of Cluny—and the Cluniac churches of its host of dependent monasteries—was careful and elegant design that combined the needs of the monks with the desires of pilgrims to visit shrines and relics. They were also notable for their fine stone masonry with rich sculptured and painted decoration. In their homeland of Burgundy, the churches were distinguished by their use of classicizing elements from Roman art, such as fluted pilasters and Corinthian capitals. Cluniac monasteries elsewhere, however, were free—and perhaps even encouraged—to follow regional traditions and styles.

To view this image, please go to page 461 of the *Art History*, Fourth Edition by Marilyn Stokstad ebook.

THE THIRD CHURCH AT CLUNY.   The original church at Cluny, a small barnlike building, was soon replaced by a basilica with two towers and narthex at the west and a choir with tower and chapels at the east. Hugh de Semur, abbot of Cluny for 60 years (1049–1109), began rebuilding the abbey church for the third time in 1088 (FIGS. 6–9, 6–10). Money paid in tribute by Muslims to victorious Christians in Spain financed the building. When King Alfonso VI of León and Castile captured Toledo in 1085, he sent 10,000 pieces of gold to Cluny. The church (known to art historians as Cluny III because it was the third building at the site) was the largest in Europe when it was completed in 1130: 550 feet long, with five aisles like Old St. Peter's in Rome. Built with superbly cut masonry, and richly carved, painted, and furnished, Cluny III was a worthy home for the relics of St. Peter and St. Paul, which the monks had acquired from the church of St. Paul's Outside the Walls in Rome. It was also a fitting headquarters for a monastic order that had become so powerful within Europe that popes were chosen from its ranks.

In simple terms, the church was a basilica with five aisles, double transepts with chapels, and an ambulatory and radiating chapels around the high altar. The large number of chapels was necessary so that each monk-priest had an altar at which to perform the services of daily Mass. Octagonal towers over the two crossings and additional towers over the transept arms created a dramatic pyramidal design at the east end. The nave had a three-part elevation. A nave arcade with tall compound piers, faced by pilasters to the inside and engaged columns at the sides, supported pointed arches lined by Classical ornament. At the next level a blind arcade and pilasters created a continuous sculptural strip that could have been modeled on an imperial Roman triumphal monument. Finally, triple clerestory windows in each bay let sunlight directly into the church around its perimeter. The pointed barrel vault with transverse arches rose to a daring height of 98 feet with a span of about 40 feet, made possible by giving the vaults a steep profile, rather than the weaker round profile used at Santiago de Compostela.

The church was consecrated in 1130, but it no longer exists. The monastery was suppressed during the French Revolution, and this grandest of French Romanesque churches was sold stone by stone, transformed into a quarry for building materials. Today the site is an archaeological park, with only one transept arm from the original church still standing.

6-10 • RECONSTRUCTION DRAWING OF THE THIRD ABBEY CHURCH AT CLUNY LOOKING EAST
1088–1130.

ART AND ITS CONTEXTS

Relics and Reliquaries

Christians turned to the heroes of the Church, the martyrs who had died for their faith, to answer their prayers and to intercede with Christ on their behalf. In the Byzantine Church, the faithful venerated icons, that is, pictures of the saints, but Western Christians wanted to be close to the saints' actual earthly remains. Scholars in the Church assured the people that the veneration of icons or relics was not idol worship. Bodies of saints, parts of bodies, and things associated with the Holy Family or the saints were kept in richly decorated containers called reliquaries. Reliquaries could be simple boxes, but they might also be given the shape of the relic—the arm of St. John the Baptist, the rib of St. Peter, the sandal of St. Andrew. By the eleventh century, many different arrangements of crypts, chapels, and passageways gave people access to the relics kept in churches. When the Church decided that every altar required a relic, the saints' bodies and possessions were subdivided. In this way relics were multiplied; for example, hundreds of churches held relics of the true cross.

Owning and displaying these relics so enhanced the prestige and wealth of a community that people went to great lengths to acquire them, not only by purchase but also by theft. In the ninth century, for example, the monks of Conques stole the relics of the child martyr Sainte Foy (St. Faith) from her shrine at Agen. Such a theft was called "holy robbery," for the new owners insisted that it had been sanctioned by the saint who had communicated to them her desire to move. In the late ninth or tenth century, the monks of Conques encased their new relic—the skull of Sainte Foy—in a gold and jewel statue whose unusually large head was made from a reused late Roman work. During the eleventh century, they added the crown and more jeweled banding, and, over subsequent centuries, jewels, cameos, and other gifts added by pilgrims continued to enhance the splendor of the statue.

This type of reliquary—taking the form of a statue of the saint—was quite popular in the region around Conques, but not everyone was comfortable with the way these works functioned as cult images. Early in the eleventh century, the learned Bernard of Angers prefaces his tendentious account of miracles associated with the cult of Sainte Foy by confessing his initial misgivings about such reliquaries, specifically the way simple folks adored them. Bernard thought it smacked of idolatry: "To learned people this may seem to be full of superstition, if not unlawful, for it seems as if the rites of the gods of ancient cultures, or that the rites of demons, are being observed" (*Book of Sainte Foy*, p. 77). But when he witnessed firsthand the interaction of the reliquary statue with the faithful, he altered his position: "For the holy image is consulted not as an idol that requires sacrifices, but because it commemorates a martyr. Since reverence to her honors God on high, it was despicable of me to compare her statue to statues of Venus or Diana. Afterwards I was very sorry that I had acted so foolishly toward God's saint." (ibid., p. 78)

To view this image, please go to page 462 of the *Art History*, Fourth Edition by Marilyn Stokstad ebook.

RELIQUARY STATUE OF SAINTE FOY (ST. FAITH)
Abbey church of Conques, Conques, France. Late 9th or 10th century with later additions. Silver gilt over a wood core, with added gems and cameos of various dates. Height 33″ (85 cm). Church Treasury, Conques.

THE CISTERCIANS

New religious orders devoted to an austere spirituality arose in the late eleventh and early twelfth centuries. Among these were the Cistercians, who spurned Cluny's elaborate liturgical practices and emphasis on the arts, especially sculpture in cloisters (see "St. Bernard and Theophilus: The Monastic Controversy over the Visual Arts," page 420). The Cistercian reform began in 1098 with the founding of the abbey of Cîteaux (Cistercium in Latin, hence the order's name). Led in the twelfth century by the commanding figure of Abbot Bernard of Clairvaux, the Cistercians advocated strict mental and physical discipline and a life devoted to prayer and intellectual pursuits combined with shared manual labor. Like the Cluniacs, however, they did depend on the work of laypeople. To seclude themselves as much as possible from the outside world, the Cistercians settled and reclaimed swamps and forests in the wilderness, where they then farmed and raised sheep. In time, their monasteries could be found from Russia to Ireland.

FONTENAY. Cistercian architecture embodies the ideals of the order—simplicity, austerity, and purity. Always practical, the Cistercians made a significant change to the already very efficient monastery plan. They placed key buildings such as the refectory at right angles to the cloister walk so that the building could easily be extended should the community grow. The cloister fountain was relocated from the center of the cloister to the side, conveniently in front of the refectory, where the monks could wash when coming from their work in the fields for communal meals. For easy access to the sanctuary during their prayers at night, monks entered the church directly from the cloister into the south transept or from the dormitory by way of the "night stairs."

The **ABBEY OF FONTENAY** in Burgundy is among the best-preserved early Cistercian monasteries. The abbey church, begun in 1139, has a simple geometric plan (**FIGS. 6–11, 6–12**) with a long bay-divided nave, rectangular chapels off the square-ended transept arms, and a shallow choir with a straight east wall. One of its characteristic features is the use of pointed barrel vaults over the nave and pointed arches in the nave arcade and side-aisle bays. Although pointed arches are usually associated with Gothic architecture, they are actually common in the Romanesque buildings of some regions, including Burgundy (we have already seen them at Cluny). Pointed arches are structurally more stable than round ones, directing more weight down into the floor instead of outward to the walls. Consequently, they can span greater distances at greater heights without collapsing.

To view this image, please go to page 463 of the *Art History,* Fourth Edition by Marilyn Stokstad ebook.

6–11 • NAVE, ABBEY CHURCH OF NOTRE-DAME, FONTENAY
1139–1147.

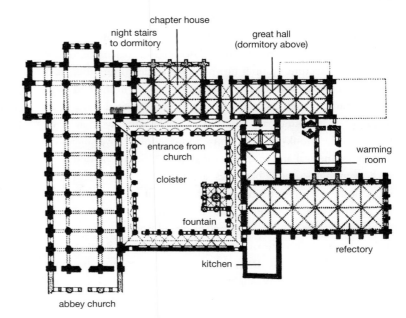

6–12 • PLAN OF THE ABBEY OF NOTRE-DAME, FONTENAY
Burgundy, France. 1139–1147.

St. Bernard and Theophilus: The Monastic Controversy over the Visual Arts

The twelfth century saw a heated controversy over the place and appropriateness of lavish art in monasteries. In a letter to William of Saint-Thierry, Bernard of Clairvaux wrote:

> What excuse can there be for these ridiculous monstrosities in the cloisters where the monks do their reading, extraordinary things at once beautiful and ugly? Here we find filthy monkeys and fierce lions, fearful centaurs, harpies, and striped tigers, soldiers at war, and hunters blowing their horns. Here is one head with many bodies, there is one body with many heads. Over there is a beast with a serpent for its tail, a fish with an animal's head, and a creature that is horse in front and goat behind, and a second beast with horns and the rear of a horse. All round there is such an amazing variety of shapes that one could easily prefer to take one's reading from the walls instead of a book. One could spend the whole day gazing fascinated at these things, one by one, instead of meditating on the law of God. Good Lord, even if the foolishness of it all occasion no shame, a least one might balk at the expense.
>
> (Bernard, "Apologia to Abbot William," p. 66)

"Theophilus" is the pseudonym used by a monk who wrote a book during the first half of the twelfth century on the practice of artistic craft, voiced as a defense of the place of the visual arts within the monastic traditions of work and prayer. The book gives detailed instructions for panel painting, **stained glass** (colored glass assembled into ornamental or pictorial windows), and goldsmithing. In contrast to the stern warnings of Bernard, perhaps even in response to them, "Theophilus" assured artists that "God delights in embellishments" and that artists worked "under the direction and authority of the Holy Spirit." He wrote:

> Therefore, most beloved son, you should not doubt but should believe in full faith that the Spirit of God has filled your heart when you have embellished His house with such great beauty and variety of workmanship ...
>
> ... do not hide away the talent given to you by God, but, working and teaching openly and with humility, you faithfully reveal it to those who desire to learn.
>
> ... if a faithful soul should see a representation of the Lord's crucifixion expressed in the strokes of an artist, it is itself pierced; if it sees how great are the tortures that the saints have endured in their bodies and how great the rewards of eternal life that they have received, it grasps at the observance of a better life; if it contemplates how great are the joys in heaven and how great are the torments in the flames of hell, it is inspired with hope because of its good deeds and shaken with fear on considering its sins.
>
> (Theophilus, *On Divers Arts*, pp. 78–79)

As we will see in the next chapter, Abbot Suger of Saint-Denis shared the position of Theophilus, rather than that of Bernard, and from this standpoint would sponsor a reconstruction of his abbey church that gave birth to the Gothic style.

Although Fontenay and other early Cistercian monasteries fully reflect the architectural developments of their time in masonry construction, vaulting, and planning, the Cistercians relied on harmonious proportions and superbly refined stonework, not elaborately carved and painted figural decoration, to achieve beauty in their architecture. Church furnishings included little other than altars with crosses and candles. The large windows in the end wall, rather than a clerestory, provided light, concentrated here as at Santiago, on the sanctuary. The sets of triple windows may have reminded the monks of the Trinity. Some scholars have suggested that the numerical and proportional systems guiding the design of such seemingly simple buildings are saturated with the sacred numerical systems outlined by such eminent early theologians as St. Augustine of Hippo. The streamlined but sophisticated architecture favored by the Cistercians spread from their homeland in Burgundy to become an international style. From Scotland and Poland to Spain and Italy, Cistercian designs and building techniques varied only slightly in relation to local building traditions. Cistercian experiments with masonry vaulting and harmonious proportions influenced the development of the French Gothic style in the middle of the twelfth century.

REGIONAL STYLES IN ROMANESQUE ARCHITECTURE

The Cathedral of Santiago de Compostela and the abbey church at Cluny reflect the cultural exchanges along the pilgrimage roads and the international connections fostered by powerful monastic orders, but Europe remained a land divided by competing kingdoms, regions, and factions. Romanesque architecture reflects this regionalism in the wide variety of its styles, traditions, and building techniques. Only a few examples can be examined here.

THE CATHEDRAL OF ST. MARY OF THE ASSUMPTION IN PISA. Throughout Italy artists looked to the still-standing remains of imperial Rome and Early Christianity. The influence remained especially strong in Pisa, on the west coast of Tuscany. Pisa became a maritime power, competing with Barcelona and Genoa as well as the Muslims for control of trade in the western Mediterranean. In 1063, after a decisive victory over the Muslims, the jubilant

To view this image, please go to page 465 of the *Art History*, Fourth Edition by Marilyn Stokstad ebook.

6–13 • CATHEDRAL COMPLEX, PISA

Tuscany, Italy. Cathedral, begun 1063; baptistery, begun 1153; campanile, begun 1174; Campo Santo, 13th century.

When finished in 1350, the Leaning Tower of Pisa stood 179 feet high. The campanile had begun to tilt while still under construction, and today it leans about 13 feet off the perpendicular. In the latest effort to keep it from toppling, engineers filled the base with tons of lead.

SEE MORE: Click the Google Earth link for the Cathedral complex, Pisa
www.myartslab.com

Pisans began an imposing new cathedral dedicated to the Virgin Mary **(FIG. 6–13)**. The cathedral was designed as a cruciform basilica by the master builder Busketos. A long nave with double side aisles (usually an homage to Old St. Peter's) is crossed by projecting transepts, designed like basilicas with their own aisles and apses. The builders added galleries above the side aisles, and a dome covers the crossing. Unlike Early Christian basilicas, the exteriors of Tuscan churches were richly decorated with marble—either panels of green and white marble or arcades. At Pisa, pilasters, applied arcades, and narrow galleries in white marble adorn the five-story façade.

In addition to the cathedral itself, the complex eventually included a baptistery, a campanile, and the later Gothic Campo Santo, a walled burial ground. The baptistery, begun in 1153, has arcading and galleries on the lower levels of its exterior that match those on the cathedral (the baptistery's present exterior dome and ornate upper levels were built later). The campanile (a free-standing bell tower—now known for obvious reasons as "the Leaning Tower of Pisa") was begun in 1174 by master builder Bonanno Pisano. Built on inadequate foundations, it began to lean almost immediately. The cylindrical tower is encased in tier upon tier of marble columns. This creative reuse of the Classical theme of

the colonnade, turning it into a decorative arcade, is characteristic of Tuscan Romanesque art.

THE BENEDICTINE CHURCH OF SAN CLEMENTE IN ROME. The Benedictine church of San Clemente in Rome was rebuilt beginning in the eleventh century (it was consecrated in 1128) on top of the previous church (which had itself been built over a Roman sanctuary of Mithras). The architecture and decoration reflect a conscious effort to reclaim the artistic and spiritual legacy of the early church **(FIG. 6–14)**. As with the columns of Santa Sabina (SEE FIG. 5–19), the columns in San Clemente are **spolia**: that is, they were reused from ancient Roman buildings. The church originally had a timber roof (now disguised by an ornate eighteenth-century ceiling). Even given the Romanesque emphasis on stone vaulting, the construction of timber-roofed buildings continued throughout the Middle Ages.

At San Clemente, the nave ends in a semicircular apse opening directly off the rectangular hall without a sanctuary extension or transept crossing. To accommodate the increased number of participants in the twelfth-century liturgy, the liturgical choir for the monks was extended into the nave itself, defined by a low barrier made up of ninth-century relief panels reused from the earlier

To view this image, please go to page 466 of the *Art History*, Fourth Edition by Marilyn Stokstad ebook.

6–14 • NAVE, CHURCH OF SAN CLEMENTE, ROME
Consecrated 1128.

San Clemente contains one of the finest surviving collections of early church furniture: choir stalls, pulpit, lectern, candlestick, and also the twelfth-century inlaid floor pavement. Ninth-century choir screen panels were reused from the earlier church on the site. The upper wall and ceiling decoration date from the eighteenth century.

church. In Early Christian basilicas, the area in front of the altar had been similarly enclosed by a low stone parapet (SEE FIG. 5–19), and the Romanesque builders may have wanted to revive what they considered a glorious Early Christian tradition. A **baldachin** (a canopy suspended over a sacred space, also called a ciborium), symbolizing the Holy Sepulcher, covers the main altar in the apse.

The apse of San Clemente is richly decorated with marble revetment on the curving walls and mosaic in the semidome, in a system familiar from the Early Christian and Byzantine world (SEE FIGS. 5–25, 5–31, 5–35). The mosaics attempt to recapture this past glory, portraying the trees and rivers of paradise, a lavish vine scroll inhabited by figures, in the midst of which emerges the crucified Christ flanked by Mary and St. John. Twelve doves on the cross and the 12 sheep that march in single file below represent the apostles. Stags drink from streams flowing from the base of the cross, evocation of the tree of life in paradise (FIG. 6–15). An inscription running along the base of the apse explains, "We liken the Church

of Christ to this vine that the law causes to wither and the Cross causes to bloom," a statement that recalls Jesus' reference to himself as the true vine and his followers as the branches (John 15:1–11), The learned monks of San Clemente would have been prepared to derive these and other meanings from the evocative symbols within this elaborate and arresting composition.

Although the subject of the mosaic recalls Early Christian art, the style and technique are clearly Romanesque. The artists have suppressed the sense of lifelike illusionism that characterized earlier mosaics in favor of ornamental patterns and schemas typical of the twelfth century. The doves silhouetted on the dark blue cross, the symmetrical repetition of circular vine scrolls, even the animals, birds, and humans among their leaves conform to an overriding formal design. By an irregular setting of mosaic tesserae in visibly rough plaster, the artists are able to heighten color and increase the glitter of the pervasive gold field, allowing the mosaic to sparkle.

To view this image, please go to page 467 of the *Art History*, Fourth Edition by Marilyn Stokstad ebook.

6-15 • STAGS DRINKING FROM STREAMS FLOWING UNDER THE CRUCIFIED CHRIST
Detail of mosaics in the apse of the church of San Clemente, Rome. Consecrated 1128.

The Paintings of San Climent in Taull: Mozarabic Meets Byzantine

As we see at San Clemente in Rome and at Saint-Savin-sur-Gartempe (SEE FIGS. 6–14, 6–16), Romanesque church interiors were not bare expanses of stone, but were often covered with images that glowed in flickering candlelight amid clouds of incense. Outside Rome during the Romanesque period, murals largely replaced mosaics on the walls of churches. Wall painting was subject to the same influences as the other visual arts: that is, the mural painters could be inspired by illuminated manuscripts, or ivories, or enamels in their treasuries or libraries. Some artists must have seen examples of Byzantine art; others had Carolingian or even Early Christian models.

Artists in Catalunya brilliantly combined the Byzantine style with their own Mozarabic and Classical heritage in the apse paintings of the church of San Climent in the mountain village of Taull (Tahull), consecrated in 1123, just a few years before the church of San Clemente in Rome. The curve of the semi-dome of the apse contains a magnificently expressive Christ in Majesty holding an open book inscribed *Ego sum lux mundi* ("I am the light of the world," John 8:12)—recalling in his commanding presence the imposing Byzantine depictions of Christ Pantocrator, ruler and judge of the world, in Middle Byzantine churches (SEE FIG. 5–44). The San Climent artist was one of the finest painters of the Romanesque period, but where he came from and where he learned his art is unknown. His use of elongated oval faces, large staring eyes, and long noses, as well as the placement of figures against flat bands of color and his use of heavy outlines, reflect the Mozarabic past. At the same time his work betrays the influence of Byzantine art in his painting technique of modeling from light to dark through repeated colored lines of varying width in three shades—dark, medium, and light. Instead of blending the colors, he delights in the striped effect, as he also does in the patterning potential in details of faces, hair, hands, and muscles.

To view this image, please go to page 468 of the *Art History*, Fourth Edition by Marilyn Stokstad ebook.

CHRIST IN MAJESTY
Detail of apse, church of San Climent, Taull, Catalunya, Spain. Consecrated 1123. Museu Nacional d'Art de Catalunya, Barcelona.

To view this image, please go to page 469 of the *Art History*, Fourth Edition by Marilyn Stokstad ebook.

THE ABBEY CHURCH OF SAINT-SAVIN-SUR-GARTEMPE.   At the Benedictine abbey church in Saint-Savin-sur-Gartempe in western France, a tunnel-like barrel vault runs the length of the nave and choir (FIG. 6–16). Without galleries or clerestory windows, the nave at Saint-Savin approaches the form of a "hall church," where the nave and aisles rise to an equal height. And unlike other churches we have seen (SEE, FOR EXAMPLE, FIG. 6–6), at Saint-Savin the barrel vault is unbroken by projecting transverse arches, making it ideally suited for paintings.

The paintings on the high vaults of Saint-Savin survive almost intact, presenting scenes from the Hebrew Bible and New Testament. The nave was built c. 1095–1115, and the painters seem to have followed the masons immediately, probably using the same scaffolding. Perhaps their intimate involvement with the building process accounts for the vividness with which they portrayed the biblical story of the TOWER OF BABEL (FIG. 6–17).

According to the account in Genesis (11:1–9), God (represented here by a striding figure of Christ on the left) punished the prideful people who had tried to reach heaven by means of their own architectural ingenuity by scattering them and making their languages mutually unintelligible. The tower in the painting is a medieval structure, reflecting the medieval practice of visualizing all stories in contemporary settings, thereby underlining their relevance for the contemporary audience. Workers haul heavy stone blocks toward the tower, presumably intending to lift them to masons on the top with the same hoist that has been used to haul up a bucket of mortar. The giant Nimrod, on the far right, simply hands over the blocks. These paintings embody the energy

To view this image, please go to page 469 of the *Art History*, Fourth Edition by Marilyn Stokstad ebook.

6-17 • TOWER OF BABEL
Detail of painting in nave vault, abbey church of Saint-Savin-sur-Gartempe, Poitou, France. c. 1115.

with smaller piers supporting the vaults of the aisle bays. This rhythmic, alternating pattern of heavy and light elements, first suggested for aesthetic reasons in Ottonian wooden-roofed architecture, became an important design element in Speyer. Since groin vaults concentrate the weight and thrust of the vault on the four corners of the bay, they relieve the stress on the side walls of the building. Windows can be safely inserted in each bay to flood the building with light.

The exterior of Speyer Cathedral emphasizes its Ottonian and Carolingian background. Soaring towers and wide transepts mark both ends of the building, although a narthex, not an apse, stands at the west. A large apse housing the high altar abuts the flat wall of the choir; transept arms project at each side; a large octagonal tower rises over the crossing; and a pair of tall slender towers flanks the choir (FIG. 6–19). A horizontal arcade forms an exterior gallery at the top of the apse and transept wall, recalling the Italian practice we saw at Pisa (SEE FIG. 6–13).

To view this image, please go to page 470 of the *Art History*, Fourth Edition by Marilyn Stokstad ebook.

6-18 • INTERIOR, SPEYER CATHEDRAL
Germany. As remodeled c. 1080–1106.

and narrative vigor that characterizes Romanesque art. A dynamic figure of God confronts the wayward people, stepping away from them even as he turns back, presumably to scold them. The dramatic movement, monumental figures, bold outlines, broad areas of color, and patterned drapery all promote the legibility of these pictures to viewers looking up in the dim light from far below. The team of painters working here did not use the *buon fresco* technique favored in Italy for its durability, but they did moisten the walls before painting, which allowed some absorption of pigments into the plaster, making them more permanent than paint applied to a dry surface.

THE CATHEDRAL OF THE VIRGIN AND ST. STEPHEN AT SPEYER. The imperial cathedral at Speyer in the Rhine River Valley was a colossal structure rivaled only by Cluny III. An Ottonian, wooden-roofed church built between 1030 and 1060 was given a masonry vault c. 1080–1106 (FIG. 6–18). Massive compound piers mark each nave bay and support the transverse ribs of a groin vault that rises to a height of over 100 feet. These compound piers alternate

To view this image, please go to page 470 of the *Art History*, Fourth Edition by Marilyn Stokstad ebook.

6-19 • EXTERIOR, SPEYER CATHEDRAL
c. 1080–1106 and second half of the 12th century.

6-20 • DURHAM CATHEDRAL
England. 1087–1133. Original east end replaced by a Gothic choir, 1242–c. 1280. Vault height about 73′ (22.2 m).

SEE MORE: View a panorama of Durham Cathedral
www.myartslab.com

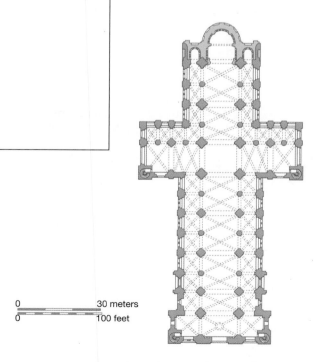

0 ———— 30 meters
0 ———— 100 feet

6-21 • PLAN OF DURHAM CATHEDRAL
Showing original east end.

DURHAM CATHEDRAL. In Durham, an English military outpost near the Scottish border, a prince-bishop held both secular and religious authority. For his headquarters he chose a natural defensive site where the bend in the River Wear formed a natural moat. Durham grew into a powerful fortified complex including a castle, a monastery, and a cathedral. The great tower of the castle defended against attack from the land, and an open space between buildings served as the courtyard of the castle and the cathedral green.

DURHAM CATHEDRAL, begun in 1087 and vaulting constructed from 1093, is an impressive example of Norman Romanesque, but like most buildings that have been in continuous use, it has been altered several times (FIGS. 6–20, 6–21). The nave retains its Norman character, but the huge circular window lighting the choir is a later Gothic addition. The cathedral's size and décor are ambitious. Enormous compound piers and robust columnar piers form the nave arcade and establish a rhythmic alternation. The columnar piers are carved with chevrons, spiral fluting, and diamond patterns, and some have scalloped, cushion-shape capitals. The richly carved arches that sit on them have multiple round moldings and chevron ornaments. All this carved ornamentation was originally painted.

Above the cathedral's massive piers and walls rises a new system of ribbed groin vaults. Romanesque masons in Santiago de Compostela, Cluny, Fontenay, Speyer, and Durham were all experimenting with stone vaulting—and reaching different conclusions. The Durham builders divided each bay with two pairs of diagonal crisscrossing rounded ribs and so kept the crowns of the vaults close in height to the keystones of the pointed transverse arches (SEE FIG. 6–20). Although this allows the eye to run smoothly down the length of the vault, and from vault to vault down the expanse of the nave, the richly carved zigzagging moldings on the ribs themselves invite us to linger over each bay, acknowledging traditional Romanesque bay division. This new system of ribbed groin vaulting will become a hallmark of Gothic architecture, though there it will create a very different aesthetic effect.

SECULAR ARCHITECTURE: DOVER CASTLE, ENGLAND

The need to provide for personal security in a time of periodic local warfare and political upheaval, as well as the desire to glorify the house of Christ and his saints, meant that communities used much of their resources to build castles and churches. Fully garrisoned, castles were sometimes as large as cities. In the twelfth century, **DOVER CASTLE**, safeguarding the coast of England from invasion, was a bold manifestation of military power **(FIG. 6–22)**. It illustrates the way in which a key defensive position developed over the centuries.

The Romans had built a lighthouse on the point where the English Channel separating England and France narrows. The Anglo-Saxons added a church (both lighthouse and church can be seen in FIG. 6–22 behind the tower, surrounded by the remains of

To view this image, please go to page 472 of the *Art History*, Fourth Edition by Marilyn Stokstad ebook.

6-22 • DOVER CASTLE
England

Aerial view overlooking the harbor and the English Channel. Center distance: Roman lighthouse tower, rebuilt Anglo-Saxon church, earthworks. Center: Norman Great Tower, surrounding earthworks and wall, twelfth century. Outer walls, thirteenth century. Modern buildings have red tile roofs. The castle was used in World War II and is now a museum.

The most important imagery on a Romanesque portal appears on the semicircular **tympanum** directly over the door—often a hieratically scaled image of abstract grandeur such as Christ in Majesty or Christ presiding over the Last Judgment—as well as on the **lintel** beneath it. **Archivolts**—curved moldings composed of the wedge-shape stone voussoirs of the arch—frame the tympanum. On both sides of the doors, the **jambs** (vertical elements) and occasionally a central pier (called the **trumeau**), support the lintel and archivolts, providing further fields for figures, columns, or narrative friezes. The jambs can extend forward to form a porch.

SEE MORE: View a simulation of a Romanesque church portal **www.myartslab.com**

earthen walls). In the early Middle Ages, earthworks topped by wooden walls provided a measure of security, and a wooden tower signified an important administrative building and residence. The advantage of fire-resistant walls was obvious, and in the twelfth and thirteenth centuries, military engineers replaced the timber tower and palisades with stone walls. They added the massive stone towers we see today.

The Great Tower, as it was called in the Middle Ages (but later known as a **keep** in England, and donjon in France), stood in a courtyard (called the **bailey**) surrounded by additional walls. Ditches outside the walls added to the height of the walls. In some castles, ditches were filled with water to form moats. A gate-house—perhaps with a drawbridge—controlled the entrance. In all castles, the bailey was filled with buildings, the most important of which was the lord's hall; it was used to hold court and for feasts and ceremonial occasions. Timber buildings housed troops, servants, and animals. Barns and workshops, ovens and wells were also needed since the castle had to be self-sufficient.

If enemies broke through the outer walls, the castle's defenders retreated to the Great Tower. In the thirteenth century, the builders at Dover doubled the walls and strengthened them with towers, even though the castle's position on cliffs overlooking the sea made scaling the walls nearly impossible. The garrison could be forced to surrender only by starving its occupants.

During Dover Castle's heyday, improvements in farming and growing prosperity provided the resources for increased building activity across Europe. Churches, castles, halls, houses, barns, and monasteries proliferated. The buildings that still stand—despite the ravages of weather, vandalism, neglect, and war—testify to the technical skills and creative ingenuity of the builders and the power, local pride, and faith of the patrons.

ARCHITECTURAL SCULPTURE

Architecture dominated the arts in the Romanesque period—not only because it required the material and human resources of entire communities, but because it provided the physical context for a revival of the art of monumental stone sculpture, an art that had been dormant in European art for 500 years. The "mute" façades used in early medieval buildings were transformed by Romanesque sculptors into "speaking" façades with richly carved portals projecting bold symbolic and didactic programs to the outside world (SEE FIG. 6–24). Christ Enthroned in Majesty might be carved over the entrance, and increasing importance is accorded to the Virgin Mary. The prophets, kings, and queens of the Hebrew Bible were seen by medieval Christians as precursors of people and events in the New Testament, so these were depicted, and we can also find representations of contemporary bishops, abbots, other noble patrons, and even ordinary folk. A profusion of monsters, animals, plants, geometric ornament, allegorical figures such as Lust and Greed, and depictions of real and imagined buildings surround the sculpture within its architectural setting. The elect rejoice in heaven with the angels; the damned suffer in hell, tormented by demons; biblical and historical tales come alive. All these events seem to take place in a contemporary medieval setting, and they are juxtaposed with scenes drawn from the viewer's everyday life.

These innovative portals are among the greatest artistic achievements of Romanesque art, taking the central messages of the Christian Church out of the sanctuary and into the public spaces of medieval towns. And figural sculpture appeared not only at entrances, but on the capitals of interior as well as exterior piers and columns, and occasionally spread all over the building in friezes, on corbels, even peeking around cornices or from behind

To view this image, please go to page 474 of the *Art History*, Fourth Edition by Marilyn Stokstad ebook.

6-23 • Wiligelmo CREATION AND FALL, WEST FAÇADE, MODENA CATHEDRAL
Emilia, Italy. Building begun 1099; sculpture c. 1099. Height approx. 3′ (92 cm).

moldings. There was plenty of work for stone sculptors on Romanesque building sites.

WILIGELMO AT THE CATHEDRAL OF MODENA

The spirit of ancient Rome pervades the sculpture of Romanesque Italy, and the sculptor Wiligelmo may have been inspired by Roman sarcophagi still visible in cemeteries when he carved horizontal reliefs across the west façade of Modena Cathedral, c. 1099. Wiligelmo took his subjects here from Genesis, focusing on events from the **CREATION AND FALL OF ADAM AND EVE (FIG. 6–23)**. On the far left, God, in a **mandorla** (body halo) supported by angels, appears in two persons as both Creator and Christ, identified by a cruciform halo. Following this iconic image, the narrative of creation unfolds in three scenes, from left to right: God brings Adam to life, then brings forth Eve from Adam's side, and finally Adam and Eve cover their genitals in shame as they greedily eat fruit from the forbidden tree, around which the wily serpent twists.

Wiligelmo's deft carving gives these figures a strong three-dimensionality. The framing arcade establishes a stagelike setting, with the rocks on which Adam lies and the tempting tree of paradise serving as stage props. Wiligelmo's figures exude life and personality. They convey an emotional connection with the narrative they enact, and bright paint, now almost all lost, must have increased their lifelike impact still further. An inscription at Modena proclaims, "Among sculptors, your work shines forth, Wiligelmo." This self-confidence turned out to be justified. Wiligelmo's influence can be traced throughout Italy and as far

away as Lincoln Cathedral in England.

THE PRIORY CHURCH OF SAINT-PIERRE AT MOISSAC

The Cluniac priory of Saint-Pierre at Moissac was a major stop on the pilgrimage route to Santiago de Compostela. The shrine at the site dates back to the Carolingian period, and after affiliating with Cluny in 1047, the monastery prospered from the donations of pilgrims and local nobility, as well as from its control of shipping on the nearby Garonne River. During the twelfth century, Moissac's monks launched an ambitious building campaign, and much of the sculpture from the cloister (c. 1100, under Abbot Ansquetil) and the church portal and porch (1100–1130, under Abbot Roger) has survived. The quantity and quality of the carving here are outstanding.

A flattened figure of **CHRIST IN MAJESTY** dominates the huge tympanum **(FIG. 6–24)**, visualizing a description of the Second Coming in Chapters 4 and 5 of Revelation. This gigantic Christ is an imposing, iconic image of enduring grandeur. He is enclosed by a mandorla; a cruciform halo rings his head. Although Christ is stable, even static, in this apocalyptic appearance, the four winged creatures symbolizing the evangelists—Matthew the man (upper left), Mark the lion (lower left), Luke the ox (lower right), and John the eagle (upper right)—who frame him on either side move with dynamic force, as if activated by the power of his unchanging majesty. Rippling bands extending across the tympanum at Christ's sides and under him—perhaps representing waves in the "sea of glass like crystal" (Revelation 4:6)—delineate three registers in which 24 elders with "gold crowns on their heads" and either a harp or a gold bowl of incense (Revelation 4:4 and 5:8) twist nervously to catch a glimpse of Christ's majestic arrival. Each of them takes an individually conceived pose and gesture, as if the sculptors were demonstrating their ability to represent three-dimensional human figures turning in space in a variety of postures, some quite challengingly contorted. Foliate and geometric ornament covers every surface surrounding this tableau. Monstrous heads in the lower corners of the tympanum spew ribbon scrolls, and other creatures appear at each end of the lintel, their tongues growing into ropes encircling acanthus rosettes.

Two side jambs and a trumeau (central portal pier) support the weight of the lintel and tympanum. These elements have scalloped profiles that playfully undermine the ability of the colonettes on the door jambs to perform their architectural function and give a sense of instability to the lower part of the portal, as if to underline the ability of the stable figure of Christ in Majesty to provide his own means of support. St. Peter and the prophet Isaiah flank the doorway on the jambs. Peter, a tall, thin saint, steps away from the door but twists back to look through it.

The **TRUMEAU** (**FIG. 6–25**) is faced by a crisscrossing pair of lions. On the side visible here, a prophet, usually identified as Jeremiah, twists toward the viewer, with legs crossed in a pose that

To view this image, please go to page 475 of the *Art History*, Fourth Edition by Marilyn Stokstad ebook.

6-24 • SOUTH PORTAL AND PORCH, SHOWING CHRIST IN MAJESTY, PRIORY CHURCH OF SAINT-PIERRE, MOISSAC
France. c. 1115.

SEE MORE: Click the Google Earth link for the priory church of Saint-Pierre www.myartslab.com

would challenge his ability to stand, much less move. The sculptors placed him in skillful conformity with the constraints of the scalloped trumeau; his head, pelvis, knees, and feet moving into the pointed cusps. This decorative scalloping, as well as the trumeau lions and lintel rosettes, may reveal influence from Islamic art. Moissac was under construction shortly after the First Crusade, when many Europeans first encountered the Islamic art and architecture of the Holy Land. People from the region around Moissac participated in the crusade; perhaps they brought Islamic objects and ideas home with them.

A porch covering the area in front of the portal at Moissac

To view this image, please go to page 476 of the *Art History*, Fourth Edition by Marilyn Stokstad ebook.

6-25 • TRUMEAU, SOUTH PORTAL, PRIORY CHURCH OF SAINT-PIERRE, MOISSAC
France. c. 1115.

provided a sheltered space for pilgrims to congregate and view the sculpture during their stopover along the way to Santiago. The side walls are filled with yet more figural sculptural (**FIG. 6–26**), but the style of presentation changes here with the nature of the subject matter and the response that was sought from the audience. Instead of the stylized and agitated figures on the tympanum and its supports, here sculptors have substituted more lifelike and approachable human beings. Rather than embodying unchanging theological notions or awe-inspiring apocalyptic appearances, these figures convey human frailties and torments in order to persuade viewers to follow the Church's moral teachings.

Behind the double arcade framework of the lower part of the wall are hair-raising portrayals of the torments of those who fall prey to the two sins that particularly preoccupied twelfth-century moralists: avarice (greed and the hoarding of money) and lust (sexual misconduct). At bottom left, a greedy man is attacked by demons while the money bags around his neck weigh him down, strangling him. On the other side of the column, his counterpart, the female personification of lust (*luxuria*), is confronted by a pot-bellied devil while snakes bite at her breasts and another predator attacks her pubic area. In the scene that extends behind the column and across the wall above them, *luxuria* reappears, kneeling beside the deathbed of the miser, as devils make off with his money and conspire to make his final moments miserable. These scenes are made as graphic as possible so that medieval viewers could identify with these situations, perhaps even feel the pain in their own bodies as a warning to avoid the behaviors that lead to such gruesome consequences.

In the strip of relief running across the top of the wall, the mood is calmer, but the moral message remains strong and clear, at least for those who know the story. The sculpture recounts the tale of Lazarus and Dives (Luke 16:19–31), the most popular parable of Jesus in Romanesque art. The broad scene to the right shows the greedy, rich Dives, relishing the feast that is being laid before him by his servants and refusing even to give his table scraps to the leprous beggar Lazarus, spread out at lower left. Under the table, dogs—unsatisfied by leftovers from Dives' feast—turn to lick the pus from Lazarus' sores as the poor man draws his last breath. The angel above Lazarus, however, transfers his soul (represented as a naked baby, now missing) to the lap of Abraham (a common image of paradise), where he is cuddled by the patriarch, the eternal reward for a pious life. The fate of Dives is not portrayed here, but it is certainly evoked on the lower section of this very wall in the torments of the greedy man, whom we can now identify with Dives himself. Clearly some knowledge is necessary to recognize the characters and story of this sculpture, and a "guide" may have been present to aid those viewers who did not readily understand. Nonetheless, the moral of sin and its consequences can be read easily and directly from the narrative presentation. This is not scripture for an ignorant illiterate population. It is a sermon sculpted in stone.

To view this image, please go to page 477 of the *Art History*, Fourth Edition by Marilyn Stokstad ebook.

6–26 • RELIEFS ON THE LEFT WALL OF THE PORCH, PRIORY CHURCH OF SAINT-PIERRE, MOISSAC
France. c. 1115.

The parable of Lazarus and Dives that runs across the top of this wall retains its moral power to our own day. This was the text of Martin Luther King's last Sunday sermon, preached only a few days before his assassination in Memphis, where he was supporting a strike by sanitation workers. Perhaps he saw the parable's image of the table scraps of the rich and greedy as particularly appropriate to his context. Just as in this portal, in Dr. King's sermon the story is juxtaposed with other stories and ideas to craft its interpretive message in a way that is clear and compelling for the audience addressed.

THE CHURCH OF SAINT-LAZARE AT AUTUN

A different sculptural style and another subject appear at Autun on the main portal of the abbey church (now cathedral) of Saint-Lazare (see "A Closer Look," page 434). This is the Last Judgment, in which Christ—enclosed in a mandorla held by two svelte angels—has returned at the end of time to judge the cowering, naked humans whose bodies rise from their sarcophagi along the lintel at his feet. The damned writhe in torment at Christ's left (our right), while on the opposite side the saved savor serene bliss. The inscribed message on the side of the damned reads: "Here

let fear strike those whom earthly error binds, for their fate is shown by the horror of these figures," and under the blessed: "Thus shall rise again everyone who does not lead an impious life, and endless light of day shall shine for him" (translations from Grivot and Zarnecki).

Another text, right under the feet of Christ, ascribes the Autun tympanum to a man named Gislebertus—*Gislebertus hoc fecit* ("Gislebertus made this"). Traditionally art historians have interpreted this inscription as a rare instance of a twelfth-century artist's signature, assigning this façade and related sculpture to an

The Last Judgment Tympanum at Autun

by Gislebertus (?), west portal, Cathedral (originally abbey church) of Saint-Lazare. Autun, Burgundy, France. c. 1120–1130 or 1130–1145.

In one of the most endearing vignettes, an angel pushes one of the saved up through an open archway and into the glorious architectural vision of heaven. Another figure at the angel's side reaches up, impatient for his turn to be hoisted up into paradise.

Christ's mother, Mary, is enthroned as queen of heaven. Below, St. Peter—identified by the large keys slung over his shoulder—performs his duties as heavenly gatekeeper, clasping the hands of someone waiting to gain entrance.

This inscription proclaims "I alone dispose of all things and crown the just. Those who follow crime I judge and punish." Clearly, some of the viewers could read Latin.

To view this image, please go to page 478 of the *Art History*, Fourth Edition by Marilyn Stokstad ebook.

The cross (a badge of Jerusalem) and scallop shell (a badge of Santiago de Compostela) identify these two figures as former pilgrims. The clear message is that participation in pilgrimage will be a factor in their favor at the Last Judgment.

The incised ornament on these sarcophagi is quite similar to that on ancient Roman sarcophagi, one of many indications that the Autun sculptors and masons knew the ancient art created when Autun was a Roman city.

Interestingly, hell is represented here as a basilica, with a devil emerging from the toothy maw that serves as a side entrance, capturing sinners for eternal torment. The devil uses a sharp hook to grab *luxuria*, the female personification of lust.

SEE MORE: View the Closer Look feature for the Last Judgment Tympanum at Autun **www.myartslab.com**

individual named Gislebertus, who was at the head of a large workshop of sculptors. Recently, however, art historian Linda Seidel has challenged this reading, arguing that Gislebertus was actually a late Carolingian count who had made significant donations to local churches. Like the names inscribed on many academic buildings of American universities, this legendary donor's name would have been evoked here as a reminder of the long and rich history of secular financial support in Autun, and perhaps also as a challenge to those currently in power to respect and continue that venerable tradition of patronage themselves.

Thinner and taller than their counterparts at Moissac, stretched out and bent at sharp angles, the stylized figures at Autun are powerfully expressive and hauntingly beautiful. As at Moissac, a huge, hieratic figure of Christ dominates the composition at the center of the tympanum, but the surrounding figures are not arranged here in regular compartmentalized tiers. Their posture and placement conform to their involvement in the story they enact. Since that story is filled with human interest and anecdotal narrative detail, viewers can easily project themselves into what is going on. On the lintel, angels physically assist the resurrected bodies rising from their tombs, guiding them to line up and await their turn at being judged. Ominously, a pair of giant, pincer-like hands descends aggressively to snatch one of the damned on the right side of the lintel. Above these hands, the archangel Michael competes with devils over the fate of someone whose judgment is being weighed on the scales of good and evil. The man himself perches on the top of the scale, hands cupped to his mouth to project his pleas for help toward the Savior. Another man hides nervously in the folds of Michael's robe, perhaps hoping to escape judgment or cowering from the loathsome prospect of possible damnation.

By far the most riveting players in this drama are the frenzied, grotesque, screaming demons who grab and torment the damned and even try, in vain, to cheat by yanking the scales to favor damnation. The fear they inspire, as well as the poignant portrayal of the psychological state of those whom they torment, would have been moving reminders to medieval viewers to examine the way they were leading their own lives, or perhaps to seek the benefits of entering the doors in front of them to participate in the community of the Church.

The creation of lively narrative scenes within the geometric confines of capitals (called **historiated capitals**) was an important Romanesque innovation in architectural sculpture. The same sculptors who worked on the Autun tympanum carved historiated capitals for pier pilasters inside the church. Two capitals (FIG. 6–27) depict scenes from the childhood of Jesus drawn from Matthew 2:1–18. In one capital, the Magi—who have previously adored and offered gifts to the child Jesus—are interrupted in their sleep by an angel who warns them not to inform King Herod of the location of the newborn king of the Jews. In an ingenious compositional device, the sculptor has shown the reclining Magi and the head of their bed as if viewed from above, whereas the angel and the foot of the bed are viewed from the side. This allows us to see clearly the angel—who is appearing to them in a dream—as he touches the hand of the upper Magus, whose eyes have suddenly popped open. As on the façade, the sculptor has conceived this scene in ways that emphasize the human qualities of its story, not its deep theological significance. With its charming, doll-like figures, the other capital shows an event that occurred just after the Magi's dream: Joseph, Mary, and Jesus are journeying toward Egypt to escape King Herod's order to murder all young boys so as to eliminate the newborn royal rival the Magi had journeyed to venerate.

To view this image, please go to page 479 of the *Art History*, Fourth Edition by Marilyn Stokstad ebook.

To view this image, please go to page 479 of the *Art History*, Fourth Edition by Marilyn Stokstad ebook.

6-27 • THE MAGI ASLEEP AND THE FLIGHT INTO EGYPT
Capitals from the choir, Cathedral of Saint-Lazare, Autun, Burgundy, France. c. 1125.

To view this image, please go to page 480 of the *Art History*, Fourth Edition by Marilyn Stokstad ebook.

6-28 • CRUCIFIX (MAJESTAT BATLLÓ)
Catalunya, Spain. Mid-12th century. Polychromed wood, height approx. 37¾″ (96 cm). Museu Nacional d'Art de Catalunya, Barcelona.

SCULPTURE IN WOOD AND BRONZE

Painted wood was commonly used when abbey and parish churches of limited means commissioned statues. Wood was not only cheap; it was lightweight, a significant consideration since these devotional images were frequently carried in processions. Whereas wood seems to have been a sculptural medium that spread across Europe, three geographic areas—the Rhineland, the Meuse River Valley, and German Saxony—were the principal metalworking centers. Bronze sculpture was produced only for wealthy aristocratic and ecclesiastical patrons. It drew on a variety of stylistic sources, including the work of contemporary Byzantine and Italian artists, as well as Classical precedents as reinterpreted by the sculptors' Carolingian and Ottonian forebears.

CHRIST ON THE CROSS (MAJESTAT BATLLÓ)

This mid-twelfth-century painted wooden crucifix from Catalunya, known as the **MAJESTAT BATLLÓ** (**FIG. 6–28**), presents a clothed, triumphant Christ, rather than the seminude figure we have seen at Byzantine Daphni (SEE FIG. 5–45) or on the Ottonian Gero Crucifix. This Christ's royal robes emphasize his kingship, although his bowed head, downturned mouth, and heavy-lidded eyes convey a quiet sense of sadness or introspection. The hem of his long, medallion-patterned tunic has pseudo-kufic inscriptions—designs meant to resemble Arabic script—a reminder that silks from Islamic Spain were highly prized in Europe at this time. Islamic textiles were widely used as cloths of honor hung behind thrones and around altars to designate royal and sacred places. They were used to wrap relics and to cover altars with apparently no concern for their Muslim source.

MARY AS THE THRONE OF WISDOM

Any Romanesque image of Mary seated on a throne and holding the Christ Child on her lap is known as "The Throne of Wisdom." In a well-preserved example in painted wood dating from the second half of the twelfth century (**FIG. 6–29**), Mother and Child are frontal and regal. Mary's thronelike bench symbolized the lion-throne of Solomon, the Hebrew Bible king who represented earthly wisdom in the Middle Ages. Mary, as Mother and "God-bearer" (the Byzantine *Theotokos*), gave Jesus his human nature. She forms a throne on which he sits in majesty, but she also represents the Church. Although the Child's hands are missing, we can assume that the young Jesus held a book—the Word of God—in his left hand and raised his right hand in blessing.

Such statues of the Virgin and Child served as cult objects on the altars of many churches during the twelfth century. They also sometimes took part in the liturgical dramas being added to church services at that time. At the feast of the Epiphany, celebrating the arrival of the Magi to pay homage to the young Jesus, townspeople representing the Magi acted out their journey by searching through the church for the newborn king. The roles of Mary and Jesus were "acted" by the sculpture, which the Magi discovered on the altar. On one of the capitals from Autun in FIG. 6–27, the Virgin and Child who sit on the donkey in the Flight to Egypt may record the theatrical use of a wooden statue, strapped to the back of a wooden donkey that would have been rolled into the church on wheels, possibly referenced by the round forms at the base of the capital.

To view this image, please go to page 481 of the *Art History*, Fourth Edition by Marilyn Stokstad ebook.

6-29 • VIRGIN AND CHILD
Auvergne region, France. Late 12th century. Oak with polychromy, height 31″ (78.7 cm). Metropolitan Museum of Art, New York.
Gift of J. Pierpont Morgan, 1916 (16.32.194)

TOMB OF RUDOLF OF SWABIA

The oldest known bronze tomb effigy (recumbent portraits of the deceased) is that of **KING RUDOLF OF SWABIA (FIG. 6–30)**, who died in battle in 1080. The spurs on his oversized feet identify him as a heroic warrior, and he holds a scepter and cross-surmounted orb, emblems of Christian kingship. Although the tomb is in the Cathedral of Merseburg, in Saxony, the effigy has been attributed to an artist originally from the Rhine Valley. Nearly life-size, it was cast in one piece and gilt, though few traces of the gilding survive. The inscription around the frame was incised after casting, and glass paste or semiprecious stones may have originally been set into the eyes and crown. We know that during the battle that ultimately led to Rudolph's death he lost a hand—which was mummified separately and kept in a leather case—but the sculptor of his effigy presents him idealized and whole.

To view this image, please go to page 481 of the *Art History*, Fourth Edition by Marilyn Stokstad ebook.

6-30 • TOMB COVER WITH EFFIGY OF KING RUDOLF OF SWABIA
Saxony, Germany. c. 1080. Bronze with niello, approx. 6′5½″ × 2′2½″ (1.97 × 0.68 m). Cathedral of Merseburg, Germany.

6-31 • Renier of Huy
BAPTISMAL FONT, NOTRE-DAME-AUX-FONTS
Liège, France. 1107–1118. Bronze, height 23⅝″ (60 cm); diameter 31¼″ (79 cm). Now in the church of St. Barthelemy, Liège.

RENIER OF HUY

Bronze sculptor Renier of Huy (Huy is near Liège in present-day Belgium) worked in the Mosan region under the profound influence of classicizing early medieval works of art, as well as the humanistic learning of church scholars. Hellinus of Notre-Dame-aux-Fonts in Liège (abbot 1107–1118) commissioned a bronze baptismal font from Renier **(FIG. 6–31)** that was inspired by the basin carried by 12 oxen in Solomon's Temple in Jerusalem (I Kings 7:23–24). Christian commentators identified the 12 oxen as the 12 apostles and the basin as the baptismal font, and their interpretive thought is given visual form in Renier's work. On the sides of the font are images of St. John the Baptist preaching and baptizing Christ, St. Peter baptizing Cornelius, and St. John the Evangelist baptizing the philosopher Crato. Renier models sturdy but idealized bodies—nude or with clinging drapery—that move and gesture with lifelike conviction, infused with dignity, simplicity, and harmony. His understanding of human anatomy

and movement must derive from his close observation of the people around him. He placed these figures within defined landscape settings, standing on an undulating ground line, and separated into scenes by miniature trees. Water rises in a mound of rippling waves (in Byzantine fashion) to cover nude figures discreetly.

TEXTILES AND BOOKS

Among the most admired arts during the Middle Ages are those that later critics patronized as the "minor" or "decorative" arts. Although small in scale, these works are often produced with very precious materials, and they were vital to the Christian mission and devotion of the institutions that housed them.

Artists in the eleventh and twelfth centuries were still often monks and nuns. They labored within monasteries as calligraphers and painters in the scriptorium to produce books and as metalworkers to craft the enamel- and jewel-encrusted works used in liturgical services. They also embroidered the vestments, altar coverings, and wall hangings that clothed both celebrants and settings in the Mass. Increasingly, however, secular urban workshops supplied the aristocratic and royal courts with textiles, tableware, books, and weapons, as well as occasional donations to religious institutions.

CHRONICLING HISTORY

Romanesque artists were commissioned not only to illlustrate engaging stories and embody important theological ideas within the context of sacred buildings and sacred books. They also created visual accounts of secular history, although here as well moralizing was one of the principal objectives of pictorial narrative.

THE BAYEUX EMBROIDERY. Elaborate textiles, including embroideries and tapestries, enhanced a noble's status and were thus necessary features in castles and palaces. The Bayeux Embroidery (see pages 440–441) is one of the earliest examples to have survived. This long narrative strip chronicles the events leading to Duke William of Normandy's conquest of England in 1066. The images depicted on this long embroidered band may have been drawn by a Norman designer since there is a clear Norman bias in the telling of the story, but style suggests that it may have been Anglo-Saxons who did the actual needlework. This represents the kind of secular art that must once have been part of most royal courts. It could be rolled up and transported from residence to residence as the noble Norman owner traveled throughout his domain, and some have speculated that it may have been the backdrop at banquets for stories sung by professional performers who could have received their cues from the identifying descriptions that accompany most scenes. Eventually the embroidery was given to Bayeux Cathedral, perhaps by Bishop Odo, William's brother; we know it was displayed around the walls of the cathedral on the feast of the relics.

THE WORCESTER CHRONICLE. Another Romanesque chronicle is the earliest known illustrated history book: the **WORCESTER CHRONICLE (FIG. 6–32)**, written in the twelfth century by a monk named John. The pages shown here concern Henry I (r. 1100–1135), the second of William the Conqueror's sons to sit on the English throne. The text relates a series of nightmares the

To view this image, please go to page 483 of the *Art History*, Fourth Edition by Marilyn Stokstad ebook.

6-32 • John of Worcester THOSE WHO WORK; THOSE WHO FIGHT; THOSE WHO PRAY— THE DREAM OF HENRY I, WORCESTER CHRONICLE
Worcester, England. c. 1140. Ink and tempera on vellum, each page 12¾ × 9⅜″ (32.5 × 23.7 cm). Corpus Christi College, Oxford. CCC MS. 157, pages 382–383

The Bayeux Embroidery

Rarely has art spoken more vividly than in the Bayeux Embroidery, a strip of embroidered linen that recounts the history of the Norman Conquest of England. Its designer was a skillful storyteller who used a staggering number of images to chronicle this history. In the 50 surviving scenes there are more than 600 human figures; 700 horses, dogs, and other creatures; and 2,000 inch-high letters.

On October 14, 1066, William, Duke of Normandy, after a hard day of fighting, became William the Conqueror, king of England. The story told in embroidery seeks to justify his action, with the intensity of an eyewitness account: The Anglo-Saxon nobleman Harold initially swears his feudal allegiance to William, but later betrays his feudal vows, accepting the crown of England for himself. Unworthy to be king, he dies in battle at the hands of William and the Normans.

Harold is a heroic figure at the beginning of the story, but then events overtake him. After his coronation, cheering crowds celebrate—until Halley's Comet crosses the sky (FIG. A). The Anglo-Saxons, seeing the comet as a portent of disaster, cringe and point at this brilliant ball of fire with a flaming

To view this image, please go to page 484 of the *Art History*, Fourth Edition by Marilyn Stokstad ebook.

A. MESSENGERS SIGNAL THE APPEARANCE OF A COMET (HALLEY'S COMET), THE BAYEUX EMBROIDERY

tail, and a man rushes to inform the new king. Harold slumps on his throne in the Palace of Westminster. He foresees what is to come: Below his feet is his vision of a ghostly fleet of Norman ships already riding the waves.

Duke William has assembled the last great Viking flotilla on the Normandy coast.

The tragedy of this drama has spoken movingly to audiences over the centuries. It is the story of a good man who, like

To view this image, please go to page 484 of the *Art History*, Fourth Edition by Marilyn Stokstad ebook.

B. BISHOP ODO BLESSING THE FEAST, THE BAYEUX EMBROIDERY
Norman–Anglo-Saxon embroidery from Canterbury, Kent, England, or Bayeux, Normandy, France. c. 1066–1082. Linen with wool, height 20″ (50.8 cm). Centre Guillaume le Conquérant, Bayeux, France.

Odo and William are feasting before the battle. Attendants bring in roasted birds on skewers, placing them on a makeshift table made of the knights' shields set on trestles. The diners, summoned by the blowing of a horn, gather at a curved table laden with food and drink. Bishop Odo—seated at the center, head and shoulders above William to his right—blesses the meal while others eat. The kneeling servant in the middle proffers a basin and towel so that the diners may wash their hands. The man on Odo's left points impatiently to the next event, a council of war between William (now the central and tallest figure), Odo, and a third man labeled "Rotbert," probably Robert of Mortain, another of William's halfbrothers. Translation of text: "and here the servants (*ministra*) perform their duty. / Here they prepare the meal (*prandium*) / and here the bishop blesses the food and drink (*cibu et potu*). Bishop Odo. William. Robert."

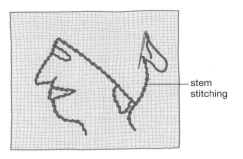
stem stitching

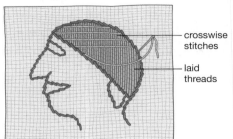
crosswise stitches
laid threads

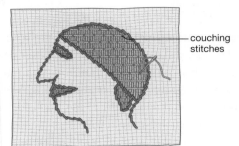
couching stitches

Shakespeare's Macbeth, is overcome by his lust for power and so betrays his lord. The images of this Norman invasion also spoke to people during the darkest days of World War II. When the Allies invaded Nazi-occupied Europe in June 1944, they took the same route in reverse from England to beaches on the coast of Normandy. The Bayeux Embroidery still speaks to us of the folly of human greed and ambition and of two battles that changed the course of history.

Although traditionally referred to as the "Bayeux Tapestry," this work is really an embroidery. In tapestry, colored threads that form the images or patterns are woven in during the process of making the fabric itself; **embroidery** consists of stitches applied on top of an already woven fabric ground. The embroiderers, probably Anglo-Saxon women, worked in tightly twisted wool that was dyed in eight colors. They used only two stitches: the quick, overlapping stem stitch that produced a slightly jagged line or outline, and the time-consuming laid-and-couched work used to form blocks of color. For the latter, the embroiderer first "laid" a series of long, parallel covering threads; then anchored them with a second layer of regularly spaced crosswise stitches; and finally tacked all the strands down with tiny "couching" stitches. Some of the laid-and-couched work was done in contrasting colors to achieve particular effects. The creative coloring is often fanciful: for example, some horses have legs in four different colors. Skin and other light-toned areas are represented by the bare linen cloth that formed the ground of the work.

To view this image, please go to page 485 of the *Art History*, Fourth Edition by Marilyn Stokstad ebook.

C. DETAIL OF BISHOP ODO BLESSING THE FEAST, THE BAYEUX EMBROIDERY

king had in 1130, in which his subjects demanded tax relief. The artist depicts the dreams with energetic directness. On the first night, angry farmers confront the sleeping king; on the second, armed knights surround his bed; and on the third, monks, abbots, and bishops present their case. In the fourth illustration, the king travels in a storm-tossed ship and saves himself by promising God that he will rescind the tax increase for seven years. The author of the Worcester Chronicle assured his readers that this story came from a reliable source, the royal physician Grimbald, who appears in the margins next to three of the scenes. The angry farmers capture our attention today because we seldom see working men with their equipment and simple clothing depicted in painting from this time.

SACRED BOOKS

Illustrated books played a key role in the transmission of artistic styles from one region to another. Monastic scriptoria continued to be the centers of production, which increased dramatically during the twelfth century. But the scriptoria sometimes employed lay scribes and artists who traveled from place to place. In addition to the books needed for the church services, scribes produced copies of sacred texts, scholarly commentaries, visionary devotional works, lives of saints, and collections of letters and sermons.

THE CODEX COLBERTINUS. The portrait of **ST. MATTHEW FROM THE CODEX COLBERTINUS (FIG. 6–33)** is an entirely Romanesque conception, quite different from Hiberno-Saxon and Carolingian author portraits. Like the sculptured pier figures of Silos, he stands within an architectural frame that completely surrounds him. He blesses and holds his book—rather than writing it—within the compact silhouette of his body. His dangling feet bear no weight, and his body has little sense of three-dimensionality, with solid blocks of color filling its strong outlines. The evangelist is almost part of the text—the opening lines of *Liber generationis*.

The text of Matthew's Gospel begins with a complementary block of ornament left of the evangelist. The "L" of *Liber generationis* ("The book of the generation") is a framed picture formed of plants and animals—called a historiated initial. Dogs or catlike creatures and long-necked birds twist, claw, and bite each other and themselves while, in the center, two humans—one dressed and one nude—

To view this image, please go to page 486 of the *Art History*, Fourth Edition by Marilyn Stokstad ebook.

6-33 • ST. MATTHEW, FROM THE CODEX COLBERTINUS
c. 1100. Tempera on vellum, 7½ × 4″ (19 × 10.16 cm). Bibliothèque Nationale, Paris.

clamber up the letter. This manuscript was made in the region of Moissac at about the same time that sculptors were working on the abbey church, and the stacking of intertwined animals here recalls the outer face of the Moissac trumeau (SEE FIG. 6–25).

Hildegard of Bingen

We might expect women to have a subordinate position in the hierarchical and militaristic society of the twelfth century. On the contrary, aristocratic women took responsibility for managing estates during their male relatives' frequent absences in wars or while serving at court. And women also achieved positions of authority and influence as the heads of religious communities. Notable among them was Hildegard of Bingen (1098–1179).

Born into an aristocratic German family, Hildegard transcended the barriers that limited most medieval women. She began serving as leader of her convent in 1136, and about 1147 she founded a new convent near Bingen. Hildegard also wrote important treatises on medicine and natural science, invented an alternate alphabet, and was one of the most gifted and innovative composers of her age, writing not only motets and liturgical settings, but also a musical drama that is considered by many to be the first opera. Clearly a major, multitalented figure in the intellectual and artistic life of her time—comparison with the later Leonardo da Vinci comes to mind—she also corresponded with emperors, popes, and the powerful abbots Bernard of Clairvaux and Suger of Saint-Denis.

Following a command she claimed to have received from God in 1141, and with the assistance of her nuns and the monk Volmar, Hildegard began to record the mystical visions she had been experiencing since she was 5 years old. The resulting book, called the *Scivias* (from the Latin *scite vias lucis*, "know the ways of the light"), is filled not only with words but with striking images of the strange and wonderful visions themselves (FIG. A). The opening page (FIG. B) shows Hildegard receiving a flash of divine insight, represented by the tongues of flame encircling her head—she said, "a fiery light, flashing intensely, came from the open vault of heaven and poured through my whole brain"—while her scribe Volmar writes to her dictation. But was she also responsible for the arresting pictures that accompany the text in this book? Art historian Madeline Caviness thinks so, both because of their unconventional

To view this image, please go to page 487 of the *Art History*, Fourth Edition by Marilyn Stokstad ebook.

To view this image, please go to page 487 of the *Art History*, Fourth Edition by Marilyn Stokstad ebook.

A. Hildegard of Bingen
THE UNIVERSE
1927–1933 facsimile of Part I, Vision 3 of the *Liber Scivias* of Hildegard of Bingen. Original, 1150–1175.

Hildegard begins her description of this vision with these words: "After this I saw a vast instrument, round and shadowed, in the shape of an egg, small at the top, large in the middle, and narrowed at the bottom; outside it, surrounding its circumference, there was a bright fire with, as it were, a shadowy zone under it. And in that fire there was a globe of sparkling flame so great that the whole instrument was illuminated by it."

nature and because they conform in several ways to the "visionary" effects experienced by many people during migraines, which plagued Hildegard throughout her life but especially during her forties while she was composing the *Scivias*. She said of her visions, "My outward eyes are open. So I have never fallen prey to ecstacy in the visions, but I see them wide awake, day and night. And I am constantly fettered by sickness, and often in the grip of pain so intense that it threatens to kill me." (Translated in Newman, p. 16.)

Perhaps in this miniature Hildegard is using the large stylus to sketch on the wax tablets in her lap the pictures of her visions that were meant to accompany the verbal descriptions she dictates to Volmar, who sits at the right with a book in his hand, ready to write them down.

B. HILDEGARD AND VOLMAR
From a 1927–1933 facsimile of the frontispiece of the *Liber Scivias* of Hildegard of Bingen. Original, 1150–1175.

This author portrait was once part of a manuscript of Hildegard's *Scivias* that many believe was made in her own lifetime, but it was lost in World War II. Today we can study its images only from prewar black-and-white photographs or from a full-color facsimile that was lovingly hand-painted by the nuns of the Abbey of St. Hildegard in Eigingen under the direction of Joesepha Krips between 1927 and 1933, the source of both pictures reproduced here.

To view this image, please go to page 488 of the *Art History*,
Fourth Edition by Marilyn Stokstad ebook.

6–34 • The Nun Guda
BOOK OF HOMILIES
Westphalia, Germany.
Early 12th century. Ink
on parchment. Stadtund
Universitäts-Bibliothek,
Frankfurt, Germany. MS.
Barth. 42, fol. 110v

THE GERMAN NUN GUDA.   In another historiated initial, this one
from Westphalia in Germany, the nun Guda has a more modest
presentation. In a **BOOK OF HOMILIES** (sermons), she inserted her
self-portrait into the letter *D* and signed it as scribe and painter,
"Guda, the sinful woman, wrote and illuminated this book" **(FIG.
6–34)**. This is a simple colored drawing with darker blocks of color
in the background, but Guda and her monastic sisters played an
important role in the production of books in the twelfth
century, and not all of them remain anonymous. Guda's image is
the earliest signed self-portrait by a woman in western Europe.
Throughout the Middle Ages, women were involved in the
production of books as authors, scribes, painters, and patrons (see
"Hildegard of Bingen," page 443).

A CISTERCIAN TREE OF JESSE.   The Cistercians were particularly
devoted to the Virgin Mary and are also credited with popularizing
themes such as the Tree of Jesse as a device for showing her
position as the last link in the genealogy connecting Jesus to King
David. (Jesse, the father of King David, was an ancestor of
Mary and, through her, of Jesus.) A manuscript of St. Jerome's
Commentary on Isaiah, made in the scriptorium of the Cistercian
mother house of Cîteaux in Burgundy about 1125, contains an
image of an abbreviated **TREE OF JESSE (FIG. 6–35)**.

A monumental Mary, with the Christ Child sitting on her
veiled arm, stands over the forking branches of the tree, dwarfing
the sleeping patriarch, Jesse, from whose body a small tree trunk
grows. The long, vertical folds of Mary's voluminous drapery—
especially the flourish at lower right, where a piece of her garment
billows up, as if caught in an updraft—recall the treatment of
drapery in the portal at Autun (see "A Closer Look," page 434),
also from Burgundy. The manuscript artist has drawn, rather than
painted, with soft colors, using subtle tints that seem somehow in
keeping with Cistercian restraint. Christ embraces his mother's
neck, pressing his cheek against hers in a display of tender affection
that recalls Byzantine icons of the period, like the Virgin of
Vladimir (SEE FIG. 5–47). The foliate form Mary holds in her hands

To view this image, please go to page 489 of the *Art History*, Fourth Edition by Marilyn Stokstad ebook.

6-35 • PAGE WITH THE TREE OF JESSE, EXPLANATIO IN ISAIAM (ST. JEROME'S COMMENTARY ON ISAIAH)

Abbey of Cîteaux, Burgundy, France. c. 1125. Ink and tempera on vellum, 15 × 4¾″ (38 × 12 cm). Bibliothèque Municipale, Dijon, France. MS. 129, fol. 4v

could be a flowering sprig from the Jesse Tree, or it could be a lily symbolizing her purity.

The building held by the angel on the left equates Mary with the Church, and the crown held by the angel on the right is hers as queen of heaven. The dove above her halo represents the Holy Spirit; Jesse Trees often have doves sitting in the uppermost branches. In the early decades of the twelfth century, church doctrine came increasingly to stress the role of the Virgin Mary and the saints as intercessors who could plead for mercy on behalf of repentant sinners, and devotional images of Mary became increasingly popular during the later Romanesque period. As we will see, this popularity would continue into the Gothic period.

THINK ABOUT IT

6.1 Discuss what is meant by the term "Romanesque" and distinguish some of the key stylistic features associated with architecture in this style.

6.2 What is a pilgrimage site? How did pilgrimage sites function for medieval Christians? Ground your answer in a discussion of Santiago de Compostela (FIGS. 6–6, 6–7, 6–8), focusing on specific features that were geared towards pilgrims.

6.3 Compare and contrast two Romanesque churches from different regions of Europe. Explain the key aspects of each regional style.

6.4 Discuss the sculpture that was integrated into the exteriors of Romanesque churches. Why was it there? Whom did it address? What were the prominent messages? Make reference to at least one church discussed in this chapter.

6.5 Analyze one example of a Romanesque work of art in this chapter that tells a story of human frailty and a second work that focuses on an exemplary, holy life. Compare and contrast their styles and messages.

PRACTICE MORE: Compose answers to these questions, get flashcards for images and terms, and review chapter material with quizzes www.myartslab.com

ADDITIONAL READINGS
A VISION OF LOVE (from *The Book of Divine Works* I, 1)

This excerpt from The Book of Divine Works, *written in the period 1163–73/4, sees Hildegard's visionary gifts at their height. Beginning with a vision reminiscent of the prophet Ezekiel, Hildegard moves to a paean of divine immanence as embodied in a figure who is at once Love, Wisdom and Power. Its nearest equivalents are the sapiential tradition of the Old Testament Apocrypha, notably Wisdom of Solomon 7–8, and its theme is summed up in Ecclesiasticus 24:1, which states that 'Wisdom shall praise herself, and shall glory in the midst of her people'.*

FROM *THE BOOK OF DIVINE WORKS* I, 1

1. And I saw as amid the airs of the South in the mystery of God a beautiful and marvellous image of a human figure; her face was of such beauty and brightness that I could more easily have stared at the sun. On her head she had a broad band of gold. And in that golden band above her head there appeared a second face, like an old man, whose chin and beard touched the top of the first head. Wings protruded from behind the neck of the figure on either side, and rising up clear of the golden band their tips met and joined overhead. On the right, above the sweep of the wing, was an image of an eagle's head, and I saw it had eyes of fire in which there appeared the brilliance of angels as in a mirror. On the left, above the sweep of the wing, was the image of a human face, which shone like the brightness of the stars. These faces were turned towards the East.

But from each of her shoulders, a wing extended down to the knee. And she wore a tunic like the glory of the sun and in her hands she carried a lamb like the bright light of day. But beneath her feet she trampled a monster of dreadful appearance, black and venomous, and also a serpent, which had fixed its teeth into the right ear of the monster and wound the rest of its body across its own head, and had stretched its tail on the left side.

2. The figure spoke: I am the supreme fire and energy. I have kindled all the sparks of the living, and I have breathed out no mortal things, for I judge them as they are. I have properly ordained the cosmos, flying about the circling circle with my upper wings, that is with wisdom. I am the fiery life of divine substance, I blaze above the beauty of the fields, I shine in the waters, I burn in sun, moon, and stars. And I awaken all to life with every wind of the air, as with invisible life that sustains everything. For the air lives in greenness and fecundity. The waters flow as though they are alive. The sun also lives in its own light, and when the moon has waned it is rekindled by the light of the sun and thus lives again; and the stars shine out in their own light as though they are alive.

I established the pillars that support the whole circle of the earth. I made the winds, and, subject to them, the wings of the winds, which are lesser winds. Through their gentle force, these contain the stronger winds and prevent them from showing their full strength with great danger; in the same way the body covers the soul and contains it lest it breathe out and expire. And conversely also, just as the breath of the soul strengthens and sustains the body so that it does not weaken, in the same way the stronger winds energize the subsidiary winds to carry out their appropriate tasks.

Thus I am concealed in things as fiery energy. They are ablaze through me, like the breath that ceaselessly enlivens the human being, or like the wind-tossed flame in a fire. All these things live in their essence, and there is no death in them, for I am life. I also am rationality, who holds the breath of the resonant word by which the whole of creation was created; and I have breathed life into everything, so that nothing by its nature may be mortal, for I am life.

And I am life: not the life struck from stone, or blossoming from branches, or rooted in a man's fertility, but life in its fullness, for all living things have their roots in me. Reason is the root, through which the resonant word flourishes.

Therefore as God is rational, how could it be that he did not act, since he allows all of his works to flourish through the human being whom he created in his own image and likeness and in whom he marked out all creatures according to their measure? But it was in eternity that God wished to create his great work—the human being—and when he had completed that work he entrusted human beings with all creation so that they could create with it in the same way that God created his work, that is, humanity.

So I am the helper, for all living things burn through me; and I am steady life in eternity, without beginning or end, the same life which is God in motion and activity; and yet this one life has three powers: eternity is the Father, the word the Son, and the breath connecting the two the Holy Spirit, and similarly God signified the same in human beings in whom there is body, soul and rationality.

The fact that I 'blaze above the beauty of the fields' means this: the earth is the matter from which God makes man and woman. The fact that 'I shine in the waters' signifies the soul, for—just as water flows through all the earth—the soul permeates all of the body. 'I burn in sun and moon'; this refers to rationality, and the 'stars' are the innumerable words of rationality. 'And I awaken all to life with every wind of the air, as with invisible life that sustains everything.' This signifies that whatever grows and matures is animated and preserved through air and wind, and it deviates in no way from the power within.

3. And again I heard a voice from heaven, which spoke to me:

God, who created all, made humanity in his own image and likeness, and in them he marked out both the higher and lower creatures. He had such love for humanity that he destined them to take the place from which the falling angel had been ejected, and he ordained them for the glory and honour which the angel in his bliss had lost. This is shown by the vision you see. For when you see 'as amid the airs of the South in the mystery of God a beautiful and marvellous image of a human figure', this signifies the

Love of the heavenly Father in the strength of his unceasing divinity, beautiful in its selectivity, and marvellous in its gifts of mysteries, appearing in the human figure because, when the son of God assumed human flesh, he redeemed lost humanity through the service of Love. This is why the face was 'of such beauty and brightness' that you 'could more easily have stared at the sun', because the abundance of Love emanates in such brightness of gifts that it far surpasses all exercise of human understanding (by which it can discern diverse ideas in the soul)—so far, in fact, that no person can grasp such abundance with their senses. This signifies symbolically that things may be perceived through faith that cannot be seen visibly with the eyes.

4. 'On her head the human figure had a broad band of gold', because only universal faith, diffused round the whole ambit of the earth and originating in the bright splendour of the first dawn, can encompass in all devotion the great abundance of true Love, namely that God in the humanity of his son redeemed human beings and confirmed them with the downpouring of the Holy Spirit, so that one God is acknowledged in the Trinity who without temporal beginning before eternity was God in the Godhead.

'And in that golden band above her head there appeared a second face, like an old man'; this signifies the all-surpassing goodness of the deity, without beginning or end, who succours the faithful, because his 'chin and beard touched the top of the first head', and so by his disposition and protection of all, God touches the height of utmost Charity, in which the Son through his humanity leads lost men and women back to the heavens.

5. 'Wings protruded from behind the neck of the figure on either side, and rising up clear of the golden band their tips met and joined overhead.' This means that the love of God cannot be separated from the love of neighbour, since they proceed from the virtue of Charity in the unity of faith, and through great longing they encompass that faith. And the holy Godhead covers the immeasurable splendour of his glory from human beings for as long as they remain in the shadow of death, deprived of the heavenly tunic which they lost with Adam.

6. 'On the right, above the sweep of the wing, was an image of an eagle's head', and you saw it had 'eyes of fire in which there appeared the brilliance of angels as in a mirror'. At the heights of triumphant subjection, then, when a person submits to God and conquers the devil, she is carried aloft in the joy of divine protection. And, fired by the Holy Spirit, when she raises up her mind and fixes her gaze upon God, then the blessed spirits appear in her in plain sight and offer to God the devotion of her heart. The eagle thus symbolizes the spiritual men and women who in full devotion of mind and in contemplation frequently gaze upon God like the angels. Therefore the blessed spirits, who ceaselessly contemplate God, rejoice in the good works of just people, and

they show these works to God with their own natures, and so they continue their praise of God and never come to an end, for they will never exhaust his fullness. Could anyone ever count all the innumerable wonders which God brings about through his power and might? Indeed for the angels there is a brightness as of many mirrors, and through this brightness they see, but no one is as active or as powerful as God, since no one is like him, and he is not subject to time.

7. Before the beginning of time, God held in his foreknowledge everything that he has since made. Outside of any moment or passing of time before eternity, all things visible and invisible appeared in the pure and sacred godhead, as trees and other created things when close to water are reflected in it; and though they are not actually in the water physically, nevertheless an accurate shape appears there. When God said 'Fiat, let there be . . .', at once all those things that did not have bodies assumed a physical shape—all those things which he had seen in his foreknowledge before the beginning of time. Just as in a mirror all things are reflected that stand before it, so all his created works appeared in holy divinity outside the passage of time. And how could God be empty of the foreknowledge of his works, since each of his creatures—once it has assumed physical form—is whole and perfect in its designated function; for the holy Divinity knew in advance how he would be present as thought, knowledge and function. A beam of light reveals the form of a created thing through its shadow, and likewise God's pure foreknowledge perceives the form of every creature before it is embodied. Each thing that God intended to create in his foreknowledge, before it was bodied forth, shone out according to his likeness; and in the same way a man or woman will catch sight of the sun's splendour before they actually see its substance. And just as the splendour of the sun indicates the sun itself, so also the praise of the angels reveals God, for it cannot ever be that the sun is without its light, and in the same way neither can the deity be without the praise of the angels. So the foreknowledge of God came first, and his work of creation followed; and if his foreknowledge had not preceded, then his work would not have appeared, for you can tell nothing by looking at a person's body until you see their face: but when you see the person's face, then you can praise their body. In this way a human being contains within him or her both the foreknowledge of God and the activity of God.

THE MEDIEVAL AESTHETIC SENSIBILITY

1. Most of the aesthetic issues that were discussed in the Middle Ages were inherited from Classical Antiquity. Christianity, however, conferred upon these issues a quite distinctive character. Some medieval ideas derived also from the Bible and from the Fathers; but again, these were absorbed into a new and systematic

philosophical world. Medieval thinking on aesthetic matters was therefore original. But all the same, there is a sense in which its thinking might be said to involve no more than the manipulation of an inherited terminology, one sanctified by tradition and by a love of system but devoid of any real significance. It has been said that, where aesthetics and artistic production are concerned, the Classical world turned its gaze on nature but the Medievals turned their gaze on the Classical world; that medieval culture was based, not on a phenomenology of reality, but on a phenomenology of a cultural tradition.

This, however, is not an adequate picture of the medieval critical viewpoint. To be sure, the Medievals respected the concepts which they had inherited and which appeared to them a deposit of truth and wisdom. To be sure, they tended to look upon nature as a reflection of the transcendent world, even as a barrier in front of it. But along with this they possessed a sensibility capable of fresh and vivid responses to the natural world, including its aesthetic qualities.

Once we acknowledge this spontaneity in the face of both natural and artistic beauty—a response which was also elicited by doctrine and theory, but which expanded far beyond the intellectual and the bookish—we begin to see that beauty for the Medievals did not refer first to something abstract and conceptual. It referred also to everyday feelings, to lived experience.

The Medievals did in fact conceive of a beauty that was purely intelligible, the beauty of moral harmony and of metaphysical splendour. This is something which only the most profound and sympathetic understanding of their mentality and sensibility can restore to us nowadays.

> When the Scholastics spoke about beauty they meant by this an attribute of God. The metaphysics of beauty (in Plotinus, for instance) and the theory of art were in no way related. 'Contemporary' man places an exaggerated value on art because he has lost the feeling for intelligible beauty which the neo-Platonists and the Medievals possessed. . . . Here we are dealing with a type of beauty of which Aesthetics knows nothing.[1]

Still, we do not have to limit ourselves to this type of beauty in medieval thought. In the first place, intelligible beauty was in medieval experience a moral and psychological *reality*; if it is not treated in this light we fail to do justice to their culture. Secondly, medieval discussions of non-sensible beauty gave rise to theories of sensible beauty as well. They established analogies and parallels between them or made deductions about one from premises supplied by the other. And finally, the realm of the aesthetic was much larger than it is nowadays, so that beauty in a purely metaphysical sense often stimulated an interest in the beauty of objects. In any case, alongside all the theories there existed also the everyday sensuous tastes of the ordinary man, of artists, and of lovers of art. There is overwhelming evidence of this love of the sensible world. In fact, the doctrinal systems were concerned to become its justification and guide, fearful lest such a love might lead to a neglect of the spiritual realm.[2]

The view that the Middle Ages were puritanical, in the sense of rejecting the sensuous world, ignores the documentation of the period and shows a basic misunderstanding of the medieval mentality. This mentality is well illustrated in the attitude which the mystics and ascetics adopted towards beauty. Ascetics, in all ages, are not unaware of the seductiveness of worldly pleasures; if anything, they feel it more keenly than most. The drama of the ascetic discipline lies precisely in a tension between the call of earthbound pleasure and a striving after the supernatural. But when the discipline proves victorious, and brings the peace which accompanies control of the senses, then it becomes possible to gaze serenely upon the things of this earth, and to see their value, something that the hectic struggle of asceticism had hitherto prevented. Medieval asceticism and mysticism provide us with many examples of these two psychological states, and also with some extremely interesting documentation concerning the aesthetic sensibility of the time.

2. In the twelfth century there was a noteworthy campaign, conducted by both the Cistercians and the Carthusians, against superfluous and overluxuriant art in church decoration. A Cistercian Statute denounced the misuse of silk, gold, silver, stained glass, sculpture, paintings, and carpets.[3] Similar denunciations were made by St. Bernard, Alexander Neckham, and Hugh of Fouilloi: these 'superfluities', as they put it, merely distracted the faithful from their prayers and devotions. But no one suggested that ornamentation was not beautiful or did not give pleasure. It was attacked just because of its powerful attraction, which was felt to be out of keeping with the sacred nature of its environment. Hugh of Fouilloi described it as a wondrous though perverse delight. The 'perversity' here is pregnant with moral and social implications, a constant concern of the ascetics; for them, the question was whether the churches should be decorated sumptuously if the children of God were living in poverty. On the other hand, to describe the pleasure as wondrous (*mira delectatio*) is to reveal an awareness of aesthetic quality.

In his *Apologia ad Guillelmum*, St. Bernard writes about what it is that monks renounce when they turn their backs upon the world. Here he reveals a similar viewpoint, though broadened to include worldly beauty of all kinds:

[1] E. R. Curtius, *European Literature and the Latin Middle Ages*, translated by Willard R. Trask (London, 1953), p. 224, n. 20.

[2] Alcuin admitted that it was easier to love beautiful creatures, sweet scents, and lovely sounds (*species pulchras, dulces sapores, sonos suaves*) than to love God (C. Halm, *Rhetores Latini Minores* [Leipzig, 1863], p. 550). But he added that if we admire these things in their proper place—that is, using them as an aid to the greater love of God—then such admiration, *amor ornamenti*, is quite licit.
[3] *Consuetudines Carthusienses*, chap. 40 (PL, 153, col. 717).

We who have turned aside from society, relinquishing for Christ's sake all the precious and beautiful things in the world, its wondrous light and colour, its sweet sounds and odours, the pleasures of taste and touch, for us all bodily delights are nothing but dung . . .[4]

The passage is full of anger and invective. Yet it is clear that St. Bernard has a lively appreciation of the very things that he denounces. There is even a note of regret, all the more vigorous because of the energy of his asceticism.

Another passage in the same work gives even more explicit evidence of his aesthetic sensitivity. Bernard is criticising churches that are too big and cluttered up with sculpture, and in so doing he gives an account of the Cluny style of Romanesque which is a model of critical description. He is contemptuous, yet paradoxically so, for his analysis of what he rejects is extraordinarily fine. The passage begins with a polemic against the immoderate size of churches: 'Not to speak of their enormous height, their immoderate length, their vacant immensity, their sumptuous finish, the astonishing paintings that confuse the eye during prayer and are an obstacle to devotion—to me they call to mind some ancient Jewish ritual.' Can it be, he goes on to ask, that these riches are meant to draw riches after them, to stimulate financial donations to the Church? 'Everything else is covered with gold, gorging the eyes and opening the purse-strings. Some saint or other is depicted as a figure of beauty, as if in the belief that the more highly coloured something is, the holier it is . . .' It is clear enough what he is denouncing here, and on the whole one is disposed to agree with him. It is not aesthetic qualities that are under question, but the use of the aesthetic for a purpose foreign to the nature of religion, for monetary profit. 'People run to kiss them, and are invited to give donations; it amounts to a greater admiration for beauty than veneration for what is sacred.' This is his point: ornament distracts from prayer. And if it does this, what use are the sculptures, the decorated capitals?

In the cloisters meanwhile, why do the studious monks have to face such ridiculous monstrosities? What is the point of this deformed beauty, this elegant deformity? Those loutish apes? The savage lions? The monstrous centaurs? The half-men? The spotted tigers? The soldiers fighting? The hunters sounding their horns? You can see a head with many bodies, or a body with many heads. Here we espy an animal with a serpent's tail, there a fish with an animal's head. There we have a beast which is a horse in front and a she-goat behind; and here a horned animal follows with hind-quarters like a horse. In short there is such a wondrous diversity of figures, such ubiquitous variety, that there is more reading matter available in marble than in books, and one could spend the whole day marveling at one such representation rather than in meditating on the law of God. In the name of God! If we are not ashamed at its foolishness, why at least are we not angry at the expense?

A noteworthy feature of these passages is their style, which is exceptionally well-wrought by the standard of the time. In fact this is typical of the mystics (St. Peter Damien is another who comes to mind): their denunciations of poetry and the plastic arts are models of style. This need not be particularly surprising, for nearly all of the medieval thinkers, whether mystics or not, went through a poetic stage in their youth. Abelard did, and so did St. Bernard, the Victorines, St. Thomas Aquinas, St. Bonaventure. In some cases they produced mere stylistic exercises, but in others they wrote some of the most exalted poetry in medieval Latin. We need only mention Aquinas's Office of the Blessed Sacrament.

The ascetics, however, had views whose extremity makes them all the more suitable for the present argument. For they campaigned against something whose fascination they were well able to understand, and felt to be dangerous as well as praiseworthy. In feeling this they had a precedent in the passionate sincerity of St. Augustine, writing in his *Confessions* about the man of faith, perturbed by the fear that he may be seduced from his prayers by the beauty of the sacred music.[5]

St. Thomas Aquinas, in similar though more amiable tones, advised against the use of sacramental music in the Liturgy. It should be avoided, he said, precisely because it stimulates a pleasure so acute that it diverts the faithful from the path appropriate to sacred music. The end of religious music is best achieved by song. Song provokes the soul to greater devotion, but instrumental music, he wrote, 'moves the soul rather to delight than to a good interior disposition'.[6] This clearly involves recognition of an aesthetic reality, valid in itself but dangerous in the wrong place.

When the medieval mystic turned away from earthly beauty he took refuge in the Scriptures and in the contemplative enjoyment of the inner rhythms of a soul in the state of grace. Some authorities speak of a 'Socratic' aesthetics of the Cistercians, one founded upon the contemplation of the beauty of the soul. 'Interior beauty', wrote St. Bernard, 'is more comely than external ornament, more even than the pomp of kings'.[7] The bodies of martyrs were repulsive to look upon after their tortures, yet they shone with a brilliant interior beauty.

The contrast between internal and external beauty was a recurrent theme in medieval thought. There was also a sense of melancholy, because of the transience of earthly beauty. Boethius is a moving example, lamenting on the very threshold of death, 'The beauty of things is fleet and swift, more fugitive than the

---

[4] This, and the quotations from St. Bernard immediately following, are in his *Apologia ad Guillelmum*, chap. 12 (PL, 182, cols. 914–16).

[5] St. Augustine, *Confessions*, X, 33.
[6] S.T., II–II, 91, 2.
[7] St. Bernard, *Sermones in Cantica*, XXV, 6 (PL, 183, col. 901).

passing of flowers in Spring . . .'[8] This is an aesthetic variation on the moralistic theme of *ubi sunt*, a constant theme in medieval culture: where are the great of yesteryear, where are the magnificent cities, the riches of the proud, the works of the mighty? In the background of the *danse macabre*, the triumph of death, we find in various forms a melancholy sense of the beauty that passes. The man of steadfast faith may look on at the dance of death with sincerity and hope, but suffer a pang of sorrow none the less. We think of Villon's most poignant refrain: *mais ou sont les neiges d'antan?*

Confronted with the beauty that perishes, security could be found in that interior beauty which does not perish. The Medievals, in fleeing to this kind of beauty, restored the aesthetic in the face of death. If men possessed the eyes of Lynceus, Boethius wrote, they would see how vile was the soul of Alcibiades the fair, he whose beauty seemed so worthy of love.[9] But this was a somewhat cantankerous kind of sentiment, and Boethius's study of the mathematics of music was quite different in spirit. So too were a number of texts that dealt with the beauty of an upright soul in an upright body, a Christian ideal of the soul externally revealed. Gilbert of Hoyt writes, 'And have regard also for the bodily countenance whose grace can be seen in its abundant beauty; for the exterior face can refresh the spirit of those who look upon it, and nourish us with the grace of the interior to which it witnesses.'[10] And here is St. Bernard:

> When the brightness of beauty has replenished to overflowing the recesses of the heart, it is necessary that it should emerge into the open, just like the light hidden under a bushel: a light shining in the dark is not trying to conceal itself. The body is an image of the mind, which, like an effulgent light scattering forth its rays, is diffused through its members and senses, shining through in action, discourse, appearance, movement—even in laughter, if it is completely sincere and tinged with gravity.[11]

Thus, at the very heart of ascetical polemics we discover a sense of human and natural beauty. And in Victorine mysticism, where discipline and rigour became subsumed in the serenity of knowledge and love, natural beauty was finally recovered in all its positive value. For Hugh of St. Victor, contemplation requires the use of intelligence; and it is not confined to specifically mystical experience but can arise also when attending to the sensible world. Contemplation, he writes, is 'an easy and clearsighted penetration of the soul into that which is seen';[12] and this then merges into a delighted attachment to the objects of love. An aesthetic pleasure arises when the soul finds its own inner harmony duplicated in its object. But there is also an aesthetic element when the intellect freely contemplates the wonder and beauty of earthbound form. 'Look upon the world and all that is in it: you will find much that is beautiful and desirable . . . Gold . . . has its brilliance, the flesh has its comeliness, clothes and ornaments their colour . . .'[13]

We see, therefore, that the aesthetic writings of the period do not consist merely of theoretical discussions of the beautiful, but are full of expressions of spontaneous critical pleasure. It is these which demonstrate how closely the sensibility of the time was interwoven with its theoretical discourses. The fact that they are found in the writings of the mystics gives them, if anything, an added demonstrative value.

One last example involves a subject very common in medieval times: female beauty. It is not perhaps too surprising that Matthew of Vendôme should formulate rules for describing women in his *Ars Versificatoria*;[14] in fact he was only half serious, indulging in a kind of erudite joke in imitation of the ancients. Also, it seems reasonable that laymen should possess greater sensitivity to the natural world. But we also find Ecclesiastics, writing on the *Canticle of Canticles*, discoursing on the beauty of the Spouse. Even though their aim was to discover allegorical meanings in the text, supernatural analogues of the physical attributes of the dark but shapely maid—still, every so often we find them pontificating on the proper ideal of female beauty, and revealing in the process a quite spontaneous appreciation of women which is earthy enough for all its chastity. Baldwin of Canterbury bestowed his praises upon plaits. He was allegorising, but this fails to conceal his sensitive taste in manners of fashion, for he described the beauty of plaits persuasively and with exactitude, and referred explicitly to their wholly aesthetic appeal.[15] Or there is the singular passage of Gilbert of Hoyt where he defines the correct dimensions of the female breasts, if they are to be truly pleasing. Only nowadays, perhaps, we can see that his gravity is infused with a certain malice. His ideal reminds us of the ladies of medieval miniaturists, their tight corsets binding and raising the bosom. 'The breasts are most pleasing when they are of moderate size and eminence. . . . They should be bound but not flattened, restrained with gentleness but not given too much licence'.[16]

---

[8]Boethius, *The Consolation of Philosophy*, III, 8.

[9]Boethius, *The Consolation of Philosophy*, III, 8.

[10]Gilbert of Hoyt, *Sermones in Canticum Salomonis*, XXV, 1 (PL, 184, col. 129).

[11]*Sermones in Cantica*, LXXV, 11, (PL, 183, col. 1193).

[12]Hugh of St. Victor (Hugh of Paris), *De Modo Dicendi et Meditandi*, 8 (PL, 176, col. 879).

[13]Hugh of St. Victor, *Soliloquium de Arrha Animae* (PL, 176, col. 951).

[14]Matthew of Vendôme, *The Art of Versification*, translated by Aubrey E. Galyon (Ames, Iowa, 1968).

[15]Baldwin of Canterbury, *Tractatus de Vulnere Charitatis* (PL, 204, col. 481).

[16]*Sermones in Canticum Salomonis*, XXXI, 4 (PL, 184, col. 163).

EMPIRES IN ASIA: FROM MUGHALS TO MONGOLS

THOUGHT PIECE

When Temujin had moved his camp to Kirmurgha Stream
Sacha Beki and Taichu, the eldest descendents of Khabul Khan,
left Jamugha and brought with them the Jurkin clan to join
Temujin.
Then Khuchar Beki, son of Temujin's uncle Nekun Taisi, joined
as well.
Finally Altan, the eldest descendent of Khutula Khan, arrived.
All these men left Jamugha to join Temujin's camp at Kirmurgha
Stream.

Then they moved the whole camp
to the shores of Blue Lake in the Gurelgu Mountains.
Altan, Khuchar, and Sacha Beki conferred with each other
there,
and then said to Temujin:
"We want you to be our Khan.
Temujin, if you'll be our Khan
we'll search through the spoils
for the beautiful women and virgins,
for the great palace tents,
for the young virgins and loveliest women,
for the finest geldings and mares.
We'll gather all of these and bring them to you.
When we go off to hunt for wild game
we'll go out first to drive them together for you to kill.
We'll drive the wild animals of the steppe together
so that their bellies are touching.
We'll drive the wild game of the mountains together so that
they stand leg to leg.
If we disobey your command during battle
take away our possessions, our children, and wives.
Leave us behind in the dust,
cutting off our heads where we stand and letting them fall to the
ground.
If we disobey your counsel in peacetime
take away our tents and our goods, our wives, and our children.

Leave us behind when you move,
abandoned in the desert without a protector."
Having given their word,
having taken this oath,
they proclaimed Temujin Khan of the Mongol
and gave him the name Chingis Khan.
[…]
[later] Chingis Khan set out to attack the Jurkin
and found them camped on the Kodoge Island in the Keleuren.
His army routed them and took all they had.
Sacha Beki and Taichu tried to escape
with a few followers and the clothes on their backs
but they were captured at Teletu Pass
and brought before Chingis Khan.
Chingis spoke to them, saying,
"What did you promise me long ago?"
And Sacha Beki and Taichu answered him:
"We have not kept our promise.
Make us honor our oath to you."
Remembering the oath that they'd sworn when they'd elected
him Khan,
they stretched out their necks to him.
And Chingis made them honor their oath,
executing them on the spot where they stood.

—From *The Secret History of the Mongols: The Origin of Chingis Khan*.
An adaptation by Paul Kahn from the translation by Francis Woodman
Cleaves (Boston: Cheng & Tsui, 1998), pp. 44–45, 51–52.

THINGS TO CONSIDER

- What is the role of art and material culture in the context of
  the Asian empires studied in these chapters? How does this
  compare with the European example from last week?

- Empire is destructive, but can also produce new hybrids, syn-
  theses, and influences. How might these earlier examples
  provide insight into our understanding of contemporary
  'global' culture?

To view this image, please go to page 778 of the *Art History*, Fourth Edition by Marilyn Stokstad ebook.

7–1 • GROUP OF VIETNAMESE CERAMICS FROM THE HOI AN HOARD
Late 15th to early 16th century, porcelain with underglaze blue decoration; barbed-rim dishes: (left) diameter 14″ (35.1 cm); (right) diameter 13¼″ (34.7 cm). Phoenix Art Museum. (2000.105–109)

More than 150,000 blue-and-white ceramic items were found in the hold of a sunken ship excavated in the late 1990s under commission from the Vietnamese government, which later sent many of the retrieved items for public auction. The 23 small cups among the works shown here were found packed inside the jar.

VIETNAMESE CERAMICS

Both the Burmese and Thai kingdoms produced ceramics, often inspired by stonewares and porcelains from China. Sukhothai potters, for example, made green-glazed and brown-glazed wares, called Sawankhalok wares. Even more widespread were the wares of Vietnamese potters. For example, excavation of the Hoi An "hoard" (FIG. 7–1), actually the contents of a sunken ship laden with ceramics for export, brought to light an impressive variety of ceramic forms made by Vietnamese potters of the late fifteenth to early sixteenth century. Painted in underglaze cobalt blue and further embellished with overglaze enamels, these wares were shipped throughout Southeast Asia and beyond, as far east as Japan and as far west as England and the Netherlands.

INDONESIAN TRADITIONS

Indonesia, now the world's most populous Muslim country, experienced a Hindu revival in the centuries following its Buddhist period, which came to a close in the eighth or ninth century. As a consequence, it has maintained unique traditions that build upon the Hindu epics, especially the *Ramayana*. Islamic monuments in Indonesia, like the Hindu and Buddhist ones, draw from a rich and diverse repertoire of styles and motifs. The **MINARET MOSQUE** of Kudus in central Java (FIG. 7–2) was built in 1549. The minaret serves as the tower from which Muslims are called to worship five times daily, but the minaret's red brick, general shape, and the niches that adorn its façade all recall Hindu temples built in east Java about two centuries earlier. As in India, Javanese artists worked in a consistent style, independent of the religion of the patron. Their architecture did, of course, accommodate the specific ritual functions of the building.

MUGHAL PERIOD

Islam first touched the South Asian subcontinent in the eighth century, when Arab armies captured a small territory near the Indus River. Later, beginning around 1000, Turkic factions from central Asia, relatively recent converts to Islam, began military campaigns into north India, at first purely for plunder, then seeking territorial control. From 1193, various Turkic and Afghan dynasties ruled portions of the subcontinent from the northern city of Delhi. These sultanates, as they are known, constructed forts, mausoleums, monuments, and mosques. Although these early dynasties left their mark, it was the Mughal dynasty that made the most inspired and lasting contribution to the art of India.

The Mughals, too, came from central Asia. Muhammad Zahir-ud-Din, known as Babur ("Lion" or "Panther"), was the first Mughal emperor of India (r. 1526–30). He emphasized his Turkic

To view this image, please go to page 779 of the *Art History*, Fourth Edition by Marilyn Stokstad ebook.

7-2 • MINARET MOSQUE
1549. Kudus, Java.

heritage, though he had equally impressive Mongol ancestry. After some initial conquests in central Asia, he amassed an empire stretching from Afghanistan to Delhi, which he conquered in 1526. Akbar (r. 1556–1605), the third ruler, extended Mughal control over most of north India, and under his two successors, Jahangir and Shah Jahan, northern India was generally unified by 1658. The Mughal Empire lasted until 1858, when the last Mughal emperor was deposed and exiled to Burma by the British.

MUGHAL ARCHITECTURE

Mughal architects were heir to a 300-year-old tradition of Islamic building in India. The Delhi sultans who preceded them had great forts housing government and court buildings. Their architects had introduced two fundamental Islamic structures, the mosque and the tomb, along with construction based on the arch and the dome. (Earlier Indian architecture had been based primarily on post-and-lintel construction.) They had also drawn freely on Indian architecture, borrowing both decorative and structural elements to create a variety of hybrid styles, and had especially benefited from the centuries-old Indian virtuosity in stonecarving and masonry. The Mughals followed in this tradition, synthesizing Indian, Persian, and central Asian elements for their forts, palaces, mosques, tombs, and cenotaphs (tombs or monuments to someone whose remains are actually somewhere else).

Akbar, an ambitious patron of architecture and city planning, constructed a new capital at a place he named Fatehpur Sikri ("City of Victory at Sikri"), celebrating his military conquests and the birth of his son Salim, who subsequently took on the throne name of Jahangir. The palatial and civic buildings, built primarily during Akbar's residence there from about 1572 to 1585, have drawn much admiration. There are two major components to Fatehpur Sikri: a religious section including the Jami Mosque and the administrative and residential section. Among the most extraordinary buildings in the administrative and residential section is the private audience hall (Diwan-i Khas) (see "A Closer Look," page 454). In the center of the hall is a tall pillar supporting a circular platform on which Akbar could sit as he received his nobles and dispensed justice. The structure recalls, perhaps consciously, the pillars erected by Ashoka to promulgate his law.

THE TAJ MAHAL.   Perhaps the most famous of all Indian Islamic structures, the Taj Mahal is sited on the bank of the Jamuna River at Agra, in northern India. Built between 1631 and 1648, it was commissioned as a mausoleum for his wife by the emperor Shah Jahan (r. 1628–58), who is believed to have taken a major part in overseeing its design and construction.

Visually, the Taj Mahal never fails to impress. As visitors enter through a monumental, hall-like gate, the tomb rises before them across a spacious garden set with long reflecting pools. Measuring some 1,000 by 1,900 feet, the enclosure is unobtrusively divided into quadrants planted with trees and flowers, and framed by broad walkways and stone inlaid in geometric patterns. In Shah Jahan's time, fruit trees and cypresses—symbolic of life and death, respectively—lined the walkways, and fountains played in the shallow pools. Truly, the senses were beguiled in this earthly evocation of paradise.

The garden in which the mausoleum is set is comprised of two parts divided by the Jamuna River. Thus while the structure appears to visitors to be set at the end of a garden, it is in fact in the center of a four-part garden, a traditional Mughal tomb setting used for earlier Mughal tombs. The tomb is flanked by two smaller structures not visible here, one a mosque and the other a hall designed in mirror image. They share a broad base with the tomb and serve visually as stabilizing elements. Like the entrance hall, they are made mostly of red sandstone, rendering even more startling the full glory of the tomb's white marble, a material previously reserved for the tombs of saints and so here implying an elevated religious stature for Shah Jahan and Mumtaz Mahal. The tomb is raised higher than these structures on its own marble platform. At each corner of the platform, a minaret defines the surrounding space. The minarets' three levels correspond to those of the tomb, creating a bond between them. Crowning each minaret is a **chattri** (pavilion). Traditional embellishments of Indian palaces, *chattris* quickly passed into the vocabulary of Indian Islamic architecture, where they appear prominently. Minarets occur in architecture throughout the Islamic world; from their heights, the faithful are called to prayer.

Private Audience Hall, Fatehpur Sikri › c.1570, north-central India.

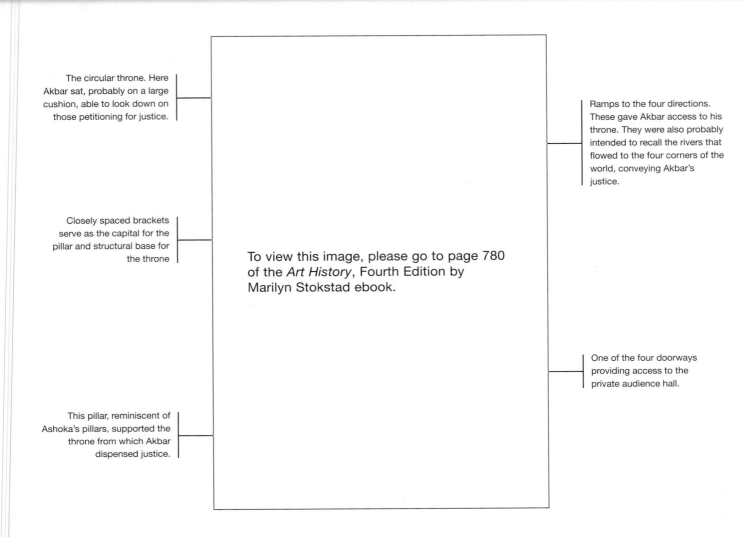

The circular throne. Here Akbar sat, probably on a large cushion, able to look down on those petitioning for justice.

Closely spaced brackets serve as the capital for the pillar and structural base for the throne

This pillar, reminiscent of Ashoka's pillars, supported the throne from which Akbar dispensed justice.

To view this image, please go to page 780 of the *Art History*, Fourth Edition by Marilyn Stokstad ebook.

Ramps to the four directions. These gave Akbar access to his throne. They were also probably intended to recall the rivers that flowed to the four corners of the world, conveying Akbar's justice.

One of the four doorways providing access to the private audience hall.

SEE MORE: View the Closer Look feature for the Private Audience Hall at Fatehpur Sikri **www.myartslab.com**

A lucid geometric symmetry pervades the tomb. It is basically square, but its **chamfered** (sliced-off) corners create a subtle octagon. Measured to the base of the **finial** (the spire at the top), the tomb is almost exactly as tall as it is wide. Each façade is identical, with a central *iwan* flanked by two stories of smaller *iwans*. By creating voids in the façades, these *iwans* contribute markedly to the building's sense of weightlessness. On the roof, four octagonal *chattris*, one at each corner, create a visual transition to the lofty, bulbous dome, the crowning element that lends special power to this structure. Framed but not obscured by the *chattris*, the dome rises more gracefully and is lifted higher by its drum than in earlier Mughal tombs, allowing the swelling curves and elegant lines of its beautifully proportioned, surprisingly large form to emerge with perfect clarity.

By the seventeenth century, India was well known for exquisite craftsmanship and luxurious decorative arts (see "Luxury Arts," page 456). The pristine surfaces of the Taj Mahal are embellished with utmost subtlety (**FIG. 7–3**). Even the sides of the platform on which the Taj Mahal stands are carved in relief with a **blind arcade** (decorative arches set into a wall) motif and carved relief panels of flowers. The portals are framed with verses from the Qur'an and inlaid in black marble, while the spandrels are decorated

7-3 • TAJ MAHAL, DETAIL
Agra, India. Mughal period, reign of Shah Jahan, c. 1631–1648.

7-4 • AKBAR INSPECTING THE CONSTRUCTION OF FATEHPUR SIKRI
Akbarnama. c. 1590. Opaque watercolor on paper, 14¾ × 10″ (37.5 × 25 cm). Victoria & Albert Museum, London. (I.S.2-1896 91/117)

Many of the painters in the Mughal imperial workshops are recorded in texts of the period. Based on those records and on signatures that occur on some paintings, the design of this work has been attributed to Tulsi Kalan (Tulsi the Elder), the painting to Bandi, and the portraits to Madhu Kalan (Madhu the Elder) or Madhu Khurd (Madhu the Younger).

with floral arabesques inlaid in colored semiprecious stones, a technique known by its Italian name **pietra dura**. Not strong enough to detract from the overall purity of the white marble, the embellishments enliven the surfaces of this impressive yet delicate masterpiece.

MUGHAL PAINTING

Probably no one had more control over the solidification of the Mughal Empire and the creation of Mughal art than the emperor Akbar. A dynamic, humane, and just leader, Akbar enjoyed religious discourse and loved the arts, especially painting. He created an imperial atelier (workshop) of painters, which he placed under the direction of two artists from the Persian court. Learning from these two masters, the Indian painters of the atelier soon transformed Persian styles into the more vigorous, naturalistic styles that mark Mughal painting (see "Indian Painting on Paper," page 458). At Akbar's cosmopolitan court, pictorial sources from Europe also became inspiration for Mughal artists.

PAINTING AT THE COURT OF AKBAR. Akbar's court artists also produced paintings documenting Akbar's own life and accomplishments recorded in the *Akbarnama*, a text written by Akbar's court biographer, Abul Fazl. Among the most fascinating in this imperial manuscript are those that record Akbar's supervision of the construction of Fatehpur Sikri. One painting **(FIG. 7–4)** documents his inspection of the stonemasons and other craftsmen.

PAINTING IN THE COURTS OF JAHANGIR AND SHAH JAHAN. Jahangir (r. 1605–1627), Akbar's son and successor, was a connoisseur of painting; he had his own workshop, which he

Luxury Arts

The decorative arts of India have been widely appreciated since the first century CE. An Indian ivory carving was found at Pompeii, while other Indian works of the time have been found along the Silk Route connecting China with Rome. For centuries Indian textiles have been made for export and copied in Europe for domestic consumption. Technically superb and crafted from precious materials, tableware, jewelry, furniture, and containers enhance the prestige of their owners and give visual pleasure as well. Metalwork and work in rock crystal, agate, and jade, carving in ivory, and intricate jewelry are all characteristic Indian arts. Because of the intrinsic value of their materials, however, pieces have been disassembled, melted down, and reworked, making the study of Indian luxury arts very difficult. Many pieces, like the carved ivory panel illustrated here, have no date or records of manufacture or ownership. And, like it, many such panels have been removed from a larger container or piece of furniture.

Carved in ivory against a golden ground, where openwork, stylized vines with spiky leaves weave an elegant arabesque, loving couples dally under the arcades of a palace courtyard, whose thin columns and cusped arches resemble the arcades of the palace of Tirumala Nayak (r. 1623–1659) in Madurai (present-day Tamil Nadu). Their huge eyes under heavy brows suggest the intensity of their gaze, and the artist's choice of the profile view shows off their long noses and sensuously thick lips. Their hair is tightly controlled; the men have huge buns, and the women long braids hanging down their backs. Are they divine lovers? After all, Krishna lived and loved on earth among the cowherd maidens. Or are we observing scenes of courtly romance?

The rich jewelry and well-fed look of the couples indicate a high station in life. Men as well as women have voluptuous figures—rounded buttocks and thighs, abdomens hanging over jeweled belts, and sharply indented slim waists that emphasize seductive breasts. Their smooth flesh contrasts with the diaphanous fabrics that swath their plump legs, and their long arms and elegant gestures seem designed to show off their rich jewelry—bracelets, armbands, necklaces, huge earrings, and ribbons. Such amorous couples symbolize harmony as well as fertility.

The erotic imagery suggests that the panel illustrated here might have adorned a container for personal belongings such as jewelry, perfume, or cosmetics. In any event, the ivory relief is a brilliant example of south Indian secular arts.

To view this image, please go to page 782 of the *Art History*, Fourth Edition by Marilyn Stokstad ebook.

PANEL FROM A BOX
From Tamil Nadu, south India. Nayak dynasty, late 17th–18th century. Ivory backed with gilded paper, 6 × 12⅜ × ⅛″ (15.2 × 31.4 × 0.3 cm). Virginia Museum of Fine Arts.
The Arthur and Margaret Glasgow Fund. 80.171

established even before he became emperor. His focus on detail was much greater than that of his father. In his memoirs, he claimed:

> My liking for painting and my practice in judging it have arrived at such a point that when any work is brought before me, either of deceased artists or of those of the present day, without their names being told me I say on the spur of the moment that it is the work of such and such a man, and if there be a picture containing many portraits, and each face be the work of a different master, I can discover which face is the work of each of them. And if any other person has put in the eye and eyebrow of a face, I can perceive whose work the original face is and who has painted the eye and eyebrows.

Portraits become a major art under Jahangir. The portrait Jahangir commissioned of himself with the Safavid-dynasty Persian emperor Shah Abbas (FIG. 7–5) demonstrates his sense of his superiority: Jahangir is depicted much larger than Shah Abbas, who appears to bow deferentially to the Mughal emperor; Jahangir's head is centered in the halo; and he stands on the lion, whose body

To view this image, please go to page 783 of the *Art History*, Fourth Edition by Marilyn Stokstad ebook.

7–6 • Nadir al-Zaman (Abu'l Hasan) PRINCE KHURRAM, THE FUTURE SHAH JAHAN AT AGE 25
From the Minto Album. Mughal period, c. 1616–1617. Opaque watercolor, gold and ink on paper, 18⅛ × 4½″ (20.6 × 11.5 cm); page 15¼ × 10½″ (39 × 26.7 cm). Victoria & Albert Museum, London

To view this image, please go to page 783 of the *Art History*, Fourth Edition by Marilyn Stokstad ebook.

7–5 • Nadir al-Zaman (Abu'l Hasan) JAHANGIR AND SHAH ABBAS
From the St. Petersburg Album. Mughal period, c. 1618. Opaque watercolor, gold and ink on paper, 9⅜ × 6″ (23.8 × 15.4 cm). Freer Museum of Art, Smithsonian Institution, Washington, DC. Purchase, F1945.9. Freer Gallery, Washington

spans a vast territory, including Shah Abbas's own Persia. We can only speculate on the target audience for this painting. Because it is small, it certainly would not be intended for Jahangir's subjects; a painting of this size could not be publicly displayed. But because we know that paintings were commonly sent by embassies from one kingdom to another, it may have been intended as a gift for Shah Abbas, one with a message of clear strength and superiority cloaked in the diplomatic language of cordiality.

Jahangir was succeeded by his son, Prince Khurram, who took the title Shah Jahan. Although Shah Jahan's greatest artistic achievements were in architecture, painting continued to flourish during his reign. A portrait of Prince Khurram bears an inscription indicating that he considered it "a very good likeness of me at age 25" (FIG. 7–6). Like all portraits of Shah Jahan, this one depicts him in profile, the view that has least likelihood of distortion. Holding an exquisite turban ornament, the prince stands quite

Before the fourteenth century most painting in India had been on walls or palm leaves. With the introduction of paper, about the same time in India as in Europe, Indian artists adapted painting techniques from Persia and over the ensuing centuries produced jewel-toned works on paper.

Painters usually began their training early. As young apprentices, they learned to make brushes and grind pigments. Brushes were made from the curved hairs of a squirrel's tail, arranged to taper from a thick base to a single hair at the tip. Paint came from pigments of vegetables and minerals—lapis lazuli to make blue, malachite for pale green—that were ground to a paste with water, then bound with a solution of gum from the acacia plant. Paper was made by crushing fibers of cotton and jute to a pulp, pouring the mixture onto a woven mat, drying it, and then burnishing with a smooth piece of agate, often achieving a glossy finish.

Artists frequently worked from a collection of sketches belonging to a master painter's atelier. Sometimes, to transfer the drawing to a blank sheet beneath, sketches were pricked with small, closely spaced holes that were then daubed with wet color. The resulting dots were connected into outlines, and the process of painting began.

First, the painter applied a thin wash of a chalk-based white, which sealed the surface of the paper while allowing the underlying sketch to show through. Next, outlines were filled with thick washes of brilliant, opaque, unmodulated color. When the colors were dry, the painting was laid face down on a smooth marble surface and burnished with a rounded agate stone, rubbing first up and down, then side to side. The indirect pressure against the marble polished the pigments to a high luster. Then outlines, details, and modeling—depending on the style—were added with a fine brush.

Sometimes certain details were purposely left for last, such as the eyes, which were said to bring the painting to life. Gold and raised details were applied when the painting was nearly finished. Gold paint, made from pulverized, 24-carat gold leaf bound with acacia gum, was applied with a brush and burnished to a high shine. Raised details such as the pearls of a necklace were made with thick, white, chalk-based paint, with each pearl a single droplet hardened into a tiny raised mound.

---

formally against a dark background, allowing nothing in the painting to compete for the viewer's attention.

RAJPUT PAINTING

Outside of the Mughal strongholds at Delhi and Agra, much of northern India was governed regionally by local Hindu princes, descendants of the so-called Rajput warrior clans, who were allowed to keep their lands in return for allegiance to the Mughals. Like the Mughals, Rajput princes frequently supported painters at their courts, and in these settings a variety of strong, indigenous Indian painting styles were perpetuated. Rajput painting, more abstract than the Mughal style, included subjects like those treated by Mughal painters, royal portraits and court scenes, as well as indigenous subjects such as Hindu myths, love poetry, and Ragamala illustrations (illustrations of musical modes).

The Hindu devotional movement known as *bhakti*, which had done much to spread the faith in the south from around the seventh century, now experienced a revival in the north. As it had earlier in the south, *bhakti* inspired an outpouring of poetic literature, this time devoted especially to Krishna, the popular human incarnation of the god Vishnu. Most renowned is the *Gita Govinda*, a cycle of rhapsodic poems about the love between God and humans expressed metaphorically through the love between the young Krishna and the cowherd Radha.

The illustration here (FIG. 7–7) is from a manuscript of the *Gita Govinda* probably produced in present-day Rajasthan about 1525–50. The blue god Krishna sits in dalliance with a group of cowherd women. Standing with her maid and consumed with love for Krishna, Radha peers through the trees, overcome by jealousy. Her feelings are indicated by the cool blue color behind her, while the crimson red behind the Krishna grouping suggests passion. The curving stalks and bold patterns of the flowering vines and trees express not only the exuberance of springtime, when the story unfolds, but also the heightened emotional tensions of the scene. Birds, trees, and flowers are as brilliant as fireworks against the black, hilly landscape edged in an undulating white line. As in the Jain manuscript earlier, all the figures are of a single type, with plump faces in profile and oversized eyes. Yet the resilient line of the drawing gives them life, and the variety of textile patterns provides some individuality. The intensity and resolute flatness of the scene seem to thrust all of its energy outward, irrevocably engaging the viewer in the drama.

Quite a different mood pervades **HOUR OF COWDUST**, a work from the Kangra School in the Punjab Hills, foothills of the Himalayas north of Delhi (FIG. 7–8). Painted around 1790, some 250 years later than the *Gita Govinda* illustration, it shows the influence of Mughal naturalism on the later schools of Indian painting. The theme is again Krishna. Wearing his peacock crown, garland of flowers, and yellow garment—all traditional iconography of Krishna-Vishnu—he returns to the village with his fellow cowherds and their cattle. All eyes are upon him as he plays his flute, said to enchant all who hear it. Women with water jugs on their heads turn to look; others lean from windows to watch and call out to him. We are drawn into this charming village scene by the diagonal movements of the cows as they surge through the gate and into the courtyard beyond. Pastel houses and walls create a sense of space, and in the distance we glimpse other villagers going about their work or peacefully sitting in their houses. A rim of dark trees softens the horizon, and an atmospheric sky completes the aura of enchanted naturalism. Again, all the figures are similar in

To view this image, please go to page 785 of the *Art History*, Fourth Edition by Marilyn Stokstad ebook.

7-7 • KRISHNA AND THE *GOPIS*

From the *Gita Govinda*, Rajasthan, India. Mughal period, c. 1525–1550. Gouache on paper, 4⅞ × 7½″ (12.3 × 19 cm). Prince of Wales Museum, Bombay.

The lyrical poem *Gita Govinda*, by the poet-saint Jayadeva, was probably written in eastern India during the latter half of the twelfth century. The episode illustrated here occurs early in the relationship of Radha and Krishna, which in the poem is a metaphor for the connection between humans and God. The poem traces the progress of their love through separation, reconciliation, and fulfillment. Intensely sensuous imagery characterizes the entire poem, as in the final song, when Krishna welcomes Radha to his bed. (Narayana is the name of Vishnu in his role as cosmic creator.)

> Leave lotus footprints on my bed of tender shoots, loving Radha!
> Let my place be ravaged by your tender feet!
> Narayana is faithful now. Love me Radhika!
> I stroke your feet with my lotus hand—you have come far.
> Set your golden anklet on my bed like the sun.
> Narayana is faithful now. Love me Radhika!
> Consent to my love. Let elixir pour from your face!
> To end our separation I bare my chest of the silk that bars your breast.
> Narayana is faithful now. Love me Radhika!

> (Translated by Barbara Stoler Miller)

7-8 • HOUR OF COWDUST

From Punjab Hills, India. Mughal period, Kangra School, c. 1790. Gouache on paper, 14¹⁵⁄₁₆ × 12⁹⁄₁₆″ (36 × 31.9 cm). Museum of Fine Arts, Boston. Denman W. Ross Collection (22.683)

To view this image, please go to page 785 of the *Art History*, Fourth Edition by Marilyn Stokstad ebook.

type, this time with a perfection of proportion and a gentle, lyrical movement that complement the idealism of the setting. The scene embodies the sublime purity and grace of the divine, which, as in so much Indian art, is evoked into our human world to coexist with us as one.

INDIA'S ENGAGEMENT WITH THE WEST

By the time *Hour of Cowdust* was painted, India's regional rulers, both Hindu and Muslim, had reasserted themselves, and the vast Mughal Empire had shrunk to a small area around Delhi. At the same time, however, a new power, Britain, was making itself felt, inaugurating a markedly different period in Indian history.

To view this image, please go to page 786 of the *Art History*, Fourth Edition by Marilyn Stokstad ebook.

7-9 • Sir Edwin Lutyens INDIA GATE
Originally the All India War Memorial. New Delhi. British colonial period, 20th century.

BRITISH COLONIAL PERIOD

First under the mercantile interests of the British East India Company in the seventeenth and eighteenth centuries, and then under the direct control of the British government as a part of the British Empire in the nineteenth century, India was brought forcefully into contact with the West and its culture, a very different situation from its long-standing role in a world system that had included trade in both commodities and culture. The political concerns of the British Empire extended even to the arts, especially architecture. Over the course of the nineteenth century, the great cities of India, such as Calcutta (present-day Kolkata), Madras (Chennai), and Bombay (Mumbai), took on a European aspect as British architects built in the revivalist styles favored in England.

NEW DELHI. In 1911, the British announced its intention to move the seat of government from Calcutta to a newly constructed Western-style capital city to be built at New Delhi, a move intended to capitalize on the long-standing association of Delhi with powerful rulers such as the Mughals. Two years later, Sir Edwin Lutyens (1869–1944) was appointed joint architect for New Delhi (with Herbert Baker), and was charged with laying out the new city and designing the Viceroy's House, the present-day Rashtrapati Bhavan (President's House). Drawing inspiration from Classical antiquity—as well as from more recent urban models, such as Paris and Washington, D.C.—Lutyens sited the Viceroy's House as a focal point along with the triumphal arch that he designed as the All India War Memorial, now called the **INDIA GATE (FIG. 7–9)**. In these works Lutyens sought to maintain the tradition of Classical architecture—he developed a "Delhi order" based on the Roman Doric—while incorporating massing, detail, and ornamentation derived from Indian architecture as well. The new capital was inaugurated in 1931.

MOTHER INDIA. Far prior to Britain's consolidation of imperial power in New Delhi a new spirit asserting Indian independence and pan-Asiatic solidarity was awakening. For example, working near Calcutta, the painter Abanindranath Tagore (1871–1951)—nephew of the poet Rabindranath Tagore (1861–1941), who went on to win the Nobel Prize for Literature in 1913—deliberately rejected the medium of oil painting and the academic realism of Western art. Like the Nihonga artists of Japan with whom he was in contact, Tagore strove to create a style that reflected his ethnic origins. In **BHARAT MATA** (Mother India) he invents a nationalistic icon by using Hindu symbols while also

To view this image, please go to page 787 of the *Art History*, Fourth Edition by Marilyn Stokstad ebook.

7-10 • Abanindranath Tagore
BHARAT MATA (MOTHER INDIA)
1905. Watercolor on paper, 10½ × 6"
(26.7 × 15.3 cm). Rabindra Bharati Society,
Calcutta.

drawing upon the format and techniques of Mughal and Rajput painting **(FIG. 7–10)**.

THE MODERN PERIOD

In the wake of World War II, the imperial powers of Europe began to shed their colonial domains. The attainment of self-rule had been five long decades in the making, when finally—chastened by the nonviolent example of Mahatma Gandhi (1869–1948)—the British Empire relinquished its "Jewel in the Crown," which was partitioned to form two modern nations: India and Pakistan. After independence in 1947, the exuberant young nation welcomed a modern, internationalist approach to art and architecture.

JAWAHAR KALA KENDRA.   Architect Charles Correa often draws on traditional Indian architectural forms. One example is his impressive **JAWAHAR KALA KENDRA**, a center for the visual and performing arts in Jaipur that was completed in 1992 **(FIG. 7–11)**. Like the original design of Jaipur, the building's design is based on a nine-square plan, and its elevation makes visual reference to the city's historic buildings. Correa's work is not confined to India, but

To view this image, please go to page 788 of the *Art History*, Fourth Edition by Marilyn Stokstad ebook.

7–11 • Charles Correa JAWAHAR KALA KENDRA
1992. Jaipur. Like many of Correa's buildings, this arts center draws upon traditional Indian motifs and forms. Its many open spaces provide a feeling of connected space rather than individual rooms.

includes buildings in Europe and the United States, for example the Cognitive Sciences Complex at MIT completed in 2005.

TWO MODERN ARTISTS. Artists working after Indian independence have continued to study and work abroad, but often draw upon India's distinctive literary and religious traditions as well as regional and folk art traditions. One example is Manjit Bawa (b. 1941), who worked in Britain as a silkscreen artist before returning to India to settle in New Delhi. His distinctive canvases, painted meticulously in oil, juxtapose illusionistically modeled figures and animals against brilliantly colored backgrounds of flat, unmodulated color. The composite result, for example in **DHARMA AND THE GOD (FIG. 7–12)**, brings a strikingly new interpretation to the heroic figures of Indian tradition.

With Anish Kapoor (b. 1954), as with so many artists living abroad, we must consider issues of identity. Although some of his work draws inspiration from his Indian origins, for example, his 1981 composition **AS IF TO CELEBRATE, I DISCOVERED A MOUNTAIN BLOOMING WITH RED FLOWERS (7–13)**, whose red and ocher mounds recall the vermilion and other pigments beautifully piled for sale outside Indian temples, other works make no reference to India. Kapoor represented Britain, where he now lives and works, at the Venice Biennale in 1990, further complicating the issue of his identity.

To view this image, please go to page 788 of the *Art History*, Fourth Edition by Marilyn Stokstad ebook.

7–12 • Manjit Bawa DHARMA AND THE GOD
1984. Oil on canvas, 85 × 72^{15}⁄$_{16}$″ (216 × 185.4 cm). Peabody Essex Museum, Salem, Massachusetts. The Davida and Chester Herwitz Collection

To view this image, please go to page 789 of the *Art History*, Fourth Edition by Marilyn Stokstad ebook.

7-13 • Anish Kapoor AS IF TO CELEBRATE, I DISCOVERED A MOUNTAIN BLOOMING WITH RED FLOWERS
1981. Wood, cement, polystyrene and pigment, 3 elements, 38¼ (highest point) × 30 (widest point) × 63″ (97 × 76.2 × 160 cm); 13 × 28 × 32″ (33 × 71.1 × 81.3 cm); 8¼ × 6 × 18½″ (21 × 15.3 × 47 cm), overall dimensions variable. Arts Council Collection, South Bank Centre, London.

THINK ABOUT IT

7.1   Explain some of the ways that Islamic art and culture impacted that of the Indian subcontinent. Explain how the Taj Mahal demonstrates influence from building styles studied in Chapter 5, and indicate how it departs from prior styles on the Indian subcontinent.

7.2   Analyze the Shwe-Dagon Stupa (Pagoda) in Yangon, and determine how the structure incorporates influence from Indian buildings. In your answer, compare the stupa to at least one Indian building.

7.3   Analyze the form of the India Gate (SEE FIG. 7–9) and explain how the ancient Roman form of the triumphal arch (see, for example, the Arch of Titus (SEE FIG. 3–73) is used within a new Indian context.

7.4   Explain how the artist Anish Kapoor utilizes Indian themes in his work *As if to Celebrate, I Discovered a Mountain Blooming with Red Flowers* (SEE FIG. 7–13). What other ideas can you infer from this work?

7.5   From the works discussed in this chapter, select a two-dimensional religious artwork from each of two religions practiced in India. Compare and contrast both directly, determining similarities in regional style and technique as well as differences due to their varying religious contexts.

PRACTICE MORE: Compose answers to these questions, get flashcards for images and terms, and review chapter material with quizzes
www.myartslab.com

THE MONGOL INVASIONS

At the beginning of the thirteenth century the Mongols, a nomadic people from the steppes north of China, began to amass an empire. Led first by Genghiz Khan (c. 1162–1227), then by his sons and grandsons, they swept westward into central Europe and overran Islamic lands from Central Asia through present-day Iraq. To the east, they quickly captured northern China, and in 1279, led by Kublai Khan, they conquered southern China as well. Grandson of the mighty Genghiz, Kublai proclaimed himself emperor of China and founder of the Yuan dynasty (1279–1368).

The Mongol invasions were traumatic, and their effect on China was long-lasting. During the Song dynasty, China had grown increasingly introspective. Rejecting foreign ideas and influences, intellectuals had focused on defining the qualities that constituted true "Chinese-ness." They drew a clear distinction between their own people, whom they characterized as gentle, erudite, and sophisticated, and the "barbarians" outside China's borders, whom they regarded as crude, wild, and uncivilized. Now, faced with the reality of barbarian occupation, China's inward gaze intensified in spiritual resistance. For centuries to come, long after the Mongols had gone, leading scholars continued to seek intellectually more challenging, philosophically more profound, and artistically more subtle expressions of all that could be identified as authentically Chinese (see "Foundations of Chinese Culture," opposite).

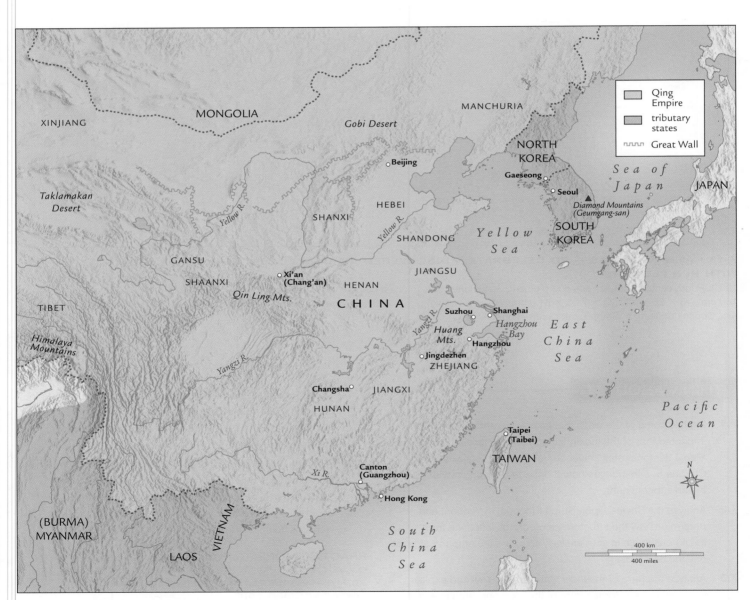

MAP 7–1 • CHINA AND KOREA

The map shows the borders of both contemporary China and Korea. The colored areas indicate the historical extent of the Qing dynasty empire (1644–1911) including its tributary states.

Foundations of Chinese Culture

Chinese culture is distinguished by its long and continuous development. Between 6000 and 2000 BCE a variety of Neolithic cultures flourished across China. Through long interaction these cultures became increasingly similar and they eventually gave rise to the three Bronze Age dynastic states with which Chinese history traditionally begins: the Xia, the Shang (c. 1700–1100 BCE), and the Zhou (1100–221 BCE).

The Shang developed traditions of casting ritual vessels in bronze, working jade in ceremonial shapes, and writing consistently in scripts that directly evolved into the modern Chinese written language. Society was stratified, and the ruling group maintained its authority in part by claiming power as intermediaries between the human and spirit worlds. Under the Zhou a feudal society developed, with nobles related to the king ruling over numerous small states.

During the latter part of the Zhou dynasty, states began to vie for supremacy through intrigue and increasingly ruthless warfare. The collapse of social order profoundly influenced China's first philosophers, who largely concerned themselves with the pragmatic question of how to bring about a stable society.

In 221 BCE, rulers of the state of Qin triumphed over the remaining states, unifying China as an empire for the first time. The Qin created the mechanisms of China's centralized bureaucracy, but their rule was harsh and the dynasty was quickly overthrown. During the ensuing Han dynasty (206 BCE–220 CE), China at last knew peace and prosperity. Confucianism was made the official state ideology, in the process assuming the form and force of a religion. Developed from the thought of Confucius (551–479 BCE), one of the many philosophers of the Zhou, Confucianism is an ethical system for the management of society based on establishing correct relationships among people. Providing a counterweight was Daoism, which also came into its own during the Han dynasty. Based on the thought of Laozi, a possibly legendary contemporary of Confucius, and the philosopher Zhuangzi (369–286 BCE), Daoism is a view of life that seeks to harmonize the individual with the Dao, or Way, the process of the universe. Confucianism and Daoism have remained central to Chinese thought— the one addressing the public realm of duty and conformity, the other the private world of individualism and creativity.

Following the collapse of the Han dynasty, China experienced a centuries-long period of disunity (220–589 CE). Invaders from the north and west established numerous kingdoms and dynasties, while a series of six precarious Chinese dynasties held sway in the south. Buddhism, which had begun to spread over trade routes from India during the Han era, now flourished. The period also witnessed the economic and cultural development of the south (previous dynasties had ruled from the north).

China was reunited under the Sui dynasty (581–618 CE), which quickly fell to the Tang (618–907), one of the most successful dynasties in Chinese history. Strong and confident, Tang China fascinated and, in turn, was fascinated by the cultures around it. Caravans streamed across central Asia to the capital, Chang'an, then the largest city in the world. Japan and Korea sent thousands of students to study Chinese culture, and Buddhism reached the height of its influence before a period of persecution signaled the start of its decline.

The mood of the Song dynasty (960–1279) was quite different. The martial vigor of the Tang gave way to a culture of increasing refinement and sophistication, and Tang openness to foreign influences was replaced by a conscious cultivation of China's own traditions. In art, landscape painting emerged as the most esteemed genre, capable of expressing both philosophical and personal concerns. With the fall of the north to invaders in 1126, the Song court set up a new capital in the south, which became the cultural and economic center of the country.

YUAN DYNASTY

The Mongols established their capital in the northern city now known as Beijing (MAP 7–1). The cultural centers of China, however, remained the great cities of the south, where the Song court had been located for the previous 150 years. Combined with the tensions of Yuan rule, this separation of China's political and cultural centers created a new dynamic in the arts.

Throughout most of Chinese history, the imperial court had set the tone for artistic taste: Artisans attached to the court produced architecture, paintings, gardens, and objects of jade, lacquer, ceramics, and silk especially for imperial use. Over the centuries, painters and calligraphers gradually moved higher up the social scale, for these "arts of the brush" were often practiced by scholars and even emperors, whose high status reflected positively on whatever interested them. With the establishment of an imperial painting academy during the Song dynasty, painters finally achieved a status equal to that of court officials. For the literati, painting came to be grouped with calligraphy and poetry as the trio of accomplishments suited to members of the cultural elite.

But while the literati elevated the status of painting by virtue of practicing it, they also began to develop their own ideas of what painting should be. Not needing to earn an income from their art, they cultivated an amateur ideal in which personal expression counted for more than "mere" professional skill. They created for themselves a status as artists totally separate from and superior to professional painters, whose art they felt was inherently compromised, since it was done to please others, and impure, since it was tainted by money.

The conditions of Yuan rule now encouraged a clear distinction between court taste, ministered to by professional

Marco Polo

China under Kublai Khan was one of four Mongol khanates that together extended west into present-day Iraq and through Russia to the borders of Poland and Hungary. For roughly a century, travelers moved freely across this vast expanse, making the era one of unprecedented cross-cultural exchange. Diplomats, missionaries, merchants, and adventurers flocked to the Yuan court, and Chinese envoys were dispatched to the West. The most celebrated European traveler of the time was a Venetian named Marco Polo (c. 1254–1324), whose descriptions of his travels were for several centuries the only firsthand account of China available in Europe.

Marco Polo was still in his teens when he set out for China in 1271. He traveled with his uncle and father, both merchants, bearing letters for Kublai Khan from Pope Gregory X. After a four-year journey the Polos arrived at last in Beijing. Marco became a favorite of the emperor and spent the next 17 years in his service, during which time he traveled extensively throughout China. He eventually returned home in 1295.

Imprisoned later during a war between Venice and Genoa, rival Italian city-states, Marco Polo passed the time by dictating an account of his experiences to a fellow prisoner. The resulting book, *A Description of the World*, has fascinated generations of readers with its depiction of prosperous and sophisticated lands in the East. Translated into many European languages, it was an important influence in stimulating further exploration. When Columbus set sail across the Atlantic in 1492, one of the places he hoped to find was a country Marco Polo called Zipangu—Japan.

---

artists and artisans, and literati taste. The Yuan dynasty continued the imperial role as patron of the arts, commissioning buildings, murals, gardens, paintings, and decorative arts. Western visitors such as the Italian Marco Polo were impressed by the magnificence of the Yuan court (see "Marco Polo," above). But scholars, profoundly alienated from the new government, took little notice of these accomplishments. Nor did Yuan rulers have much use for scholars, especially those from the south. The civil service examinations were abolished, and the highest government positions were bestowed, instead, on Mongols and their foreign allies. Scholars now tended to turn inward, to search for solutions of their own and to try to express themselves in personal and symbolic terms.

ZHAO MENGFU. Zhao Mengfu (1254–1322) was a descendant of the imperial line of Song. Unlike many scholars of his time, he eventually chose to serve the Yuan government and was made a high official. A painter, calligrapher, and poet, all of the first rank,

Zhao was especially known for his carefully rendered paintings of horses. But he also cultivated another manner, most famous in his landmark painting **AUTUMN COLORS ON THE QIAO AND HUA MOUNTAINS (FIG. 7–14)**.

Zhao painted this work for a friend whose ancestors came from Jinan, the present-day capital of Shandong Province, and the painting supposedly depicts the landscape there. Yet the mountains and trees are not painted in the accomplished naturalism of Zhao's own time but rather in the archaic yet oddly elegant manner of the earlier Tang dynasty (618–907). The Tang dynasty was a great era in Chinese history, when the country was both militarily strong and culturally vibrant. Through his painting Zhao evoked a nostalgia not only for his friend's distant homeland but also for China's past.

This educated taste for the "spirit of antiquity" became an important aspect of literati painting in later periods. Also typical of literati taste are the unassuming brushwork, the subtle colors sparingly used (many literati paintings forgo color altogether), the use of landscape to convey personal meaning, and even the

To view this image, please go to page 794 of the *Art History*, Fourth Edition by Marilyn Stokstad ebook.

7-14 • Zhao Mengfu AUTUMN COLORS ON THE QIAO AND HUA MOUNTAINS
Yuan dynasty, 1296. Handscroll, ink and color on paper, 11¼ × 36¾″ (28.6 × 9.3 cm). National Palace Museum, Taibei, Taiwan, Republic of China.

intended audience—a close friend. The literati did not paint for public display but for each other. They favored small formats such as **handscrolls**, **hanging scrolls**, or **album leaves** (book pages), which could easily be shown to friends or shared at small gatherings (see "Formats of Chinese Painting," page 469).

NI ZAN.   Of the considerable number of Yuan painters who took up Zhao's ideas, several became models for later generations. One such was Ni Zan (1301–74), whose most famous surviving painting is **THE RONGXI STUDIO (FIG. 7–15)**. Done entirely in ink, the painting depicts the lake region in Ni's home district. Mountains, rocks, trees, and a pavilion are sketched with a minimum of detail using a dry brush technique—a technique in which the brush is not fully loaded with ink but rather is about to run out, so that white paper "breathes" through the ragged strokes. The result is a painting with a light touch and a sense of simplicity and purity. Literati styles were believed to reflect the painter's personality. Ni's spare, dry style became associated with a noble spirit, and many later painters adopted it or paid homage to it.

Ni Zan was one of those eccentrics whose behavior has become legendary in the history of Chinese art. In his early years he was one of the richest men in the region, the owner of a large estate. His pride and his aloofness from daily affairs often got him into trouble with the authorities. His cleanliness was notorious. In addition to washing himself several times daily, he also ordered his servants to wash the trees in his garden and to clean the furniture after his guests had left. He was said to be so unworldly that late in life he gave away most of his possessions and lived as a hermit in a boat, wandering on rivers and lakes.

Whether these stories are true or not, they were important elements of Ni's legacy to later painters, for Ni's life as well as his art served as a model. The painting of the literati was bound up with certain views about what constituted an appropriate life. The ideal, as embodied by Ni Zan and others, was of a brilliantly gifted scholar whose spirit was too refined for the dusty world of government service and who thus preferred to live as a recluse, or as one who had retired after having become frustrated by a brief stint as an official.

MING DYNASTY

The founder of the next dynasty, the Ming (1368–1644), came from a family of poor uneducated peasants. As he rose through the ranks in the army, he enlisted the help of scholars to gain power and solidify his following. Once he had driven the Mongols from Beijing and firmly established himself as emperor, however, he grew to distrust intellectuals. His rule was despotic, even ruthless. Throughout the nearly 300 years of Ming rule most emperors shared his attitude, so although the civil service examinations were reinstated, scholars remained alienated from the government they were trained to serve.

To view this image, please go to page 795 of the *Art History*, Fourth Edition by Marilyn Stokstad ebook.

7-15 • Ni Zan THE RONGXI STUDIO
Yuan dynasty, 1372. Hanging scroll, ink on paper, height 29⅜″ (74.6 cm). National Palace Museum, Taibei, Taiwan, Republic of China.

The idea that a painting is not done to capture a likeness or to satisfy others but is executed freely and carelessly for the artist's own amusement is at the heart of the literati aesthetic. Ni Zan once wrote this comment on a painting: "What I call painting does not exceed the joy of careless sketching with a brush. I do not seek formal likeness but do it simply for my own amusement. Recently I was rambling about and came to a town. The people asked for my pictures, but wanted them exactly according to their own desires and to represent a specific occasion. [When I could not satisfy them,] they went away insulting, scolding, and cursing in every possible way. What a shame! But how can one scold a eunuch for not growing a beard?" (translated in Bush and Shih, p. 266).

To view this image, please go to page 796 of the *Art History*, Fourth Edition by Marilyn Stokstad ebook.

To view this image, please go to page 796 of the *Art History*, Fourth Edition by Marilyn Stokstad ebook.

7–16 • Yin Hong HUNDREDS OF BIRDS ADMIRING THE PEACOCKS
Ming dynasty, late 15th–early 16th century. Hanging scroll, ink and color on silk, 7′10½″ × 6′5″ (2.4 × 1.96 m). Cleveland Museum of Art. Purchase from the J. H. Wade Fund, 74.31

7–17 • Dai Jin RETURNING HOME LATE FROM A SPRING OUTING
Ming dynasty. Hanging scroll, ink on silk, 5½′ × 2′8¾″ (1.68 × 0.83 m). National Palace Museum, Taibei, Taiwan, Republic of China.

COURT AND PROFESSIONAL PAINTING

The contrast between the luxurious world of the court and the austere ideals of the literati continued through the Ming dynasty.

A typical example of Ming court taste is **HUNDREDS OF BIRDS ADMIRING THE PEACOCKS**, a large painting on silk by Yin Hong, an artist active during the late fifteenth and early sixteenth centuries **(FIG. 7–16)**. A pupil of well-known courtiers, Yin most probably served in the court at Beijing. The painting is an example of the birds–and–flowers genre, which had been popular with artists

of the Song academy. Here the subject takes on symbolic meaning, with the homage of the birds to the peacocks representing the homage of court officials to the imperial state. The style goes back to Song academy models, although the large format and multiplication of details are traits of the Ming.

A related, yet bolder and less constrained, landscape style was also popular during this period. Sometimes called the Zhe style since its roots were in Hangzhou, Zhejiang Province, where the Southern Song court had been located, this manner especially influenced

7–18 • Qiu Ying SECTION OF SPRING DAWN IN THE HAN PALACE
Ming dynasty, 1500–1550. Handscroll, ink and color on silk, 1′ × 18′13⁄16″ (0.30 × 5.7 m). National Palace Museum, Taibei, Taiwan, Republic of China.

With the exception of large wall paintings that typically decorated palaces, temples, and tombs, most Chinese paintings were done in ink and water-based colors on silk or paper. Finished works were generally mounted as **handscrolls**, **hanging scrolls**, or leaves in an album.

An album comprises a set of paintings of identical size mounted in a book. (A single painting from an album is called an **album leaf**.) The paintings in an album are usually related in subject, such as various views of a famous site or a series of scenes glimpsed on one trip.

Album-sized paintings might also be mounted as a handscroll, a horizontal format generally about 12 inches high and anywhere from a few feet to dozens of feet long. More typically, however, a handscroll would be a single continuous painting. Handscrolls were not meant to be displayed all at once, the way they are commonly presented today in museums. Rather, they were unrolled only occasionally, to be savored in much the same spirit as we might view a favorite film. Placing the scroll on a flat surface such as a table, a viewer would unroll it a foot or two at a time, moving gradually through the entire scroll from right to left, lingering over favorite details. The scroll was then rolled up and returned to its box until the next viewing.

Like handscrolls, hanging scrolls were not displayed permanently but were taken out for a limited time: a day, a week, a season. Unlike a handscroll, however, the painting on a hanging scroll was viewed as a whole—unrolled and put up on a wall, with the roller at the lower end acting as a weight to help the scroll hang flat. Although some hanging scrolls are quite large, they are still fundamentally intimate works, not intended for display in a public place.

Creating a scroll was a time-consuming and exacting process accomplished by a professional mounter. The painting was first backed with paper to strengthen it. Next, strips of paper-backed silk were pasted to the top, bottom, and sides, framing the painting on all four sides. Additional silk pieces were added to extend the scroll horizontally or vertically, depending on the format. The assembled scroll was then backed again with paper and fitted with a half-round dowel, or wooden rod, at the top of a hanging scroll or on the right end of a handscroll, with ribbons for hanging and tying, and with a wooden roller at the other end. Hanging scrolls were often fashioned from several patterns of silk, and a variety of piecing formats were developed and codified. On a handscroll, a painting was generally preceded by a panel giving the work's title and often followed by a long panel bearing **colophons**—inscriptions related to the work, such as poems in its praise or comments by its owners over the centuries. A scroll would be remounted periodically to better preserve it, and colophons and inscriptions would be preserved in each remounting. **Seals** added another layer of interest. A treasured scroll often bears not only the seal of its maker but also those of collectors and admirers through the centuries.

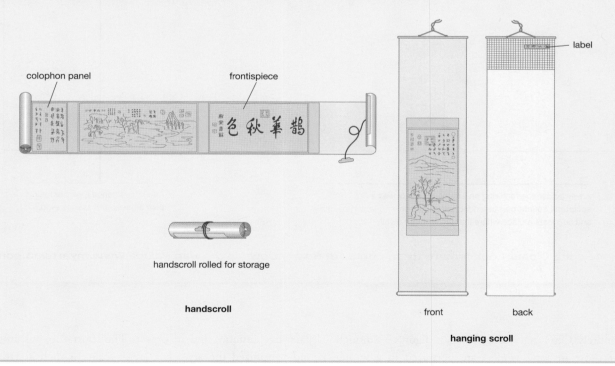

colophon panel

frontispiece

鵲華秋色

label

handscroll rolled for storage

handscroll

front

back

hanging scroll

painters in Korea and Japan. A major example is **RETURNING HOME LATE FROM A SPRING OUTING (FIG. 7–17)**, unsigned but attributed to Dai Jin (1388–1462). This work reflects the Chinese sources for such artists as An Gyeon (SEE FIG. 7–29) and Sesshu.

QIU YING.　A preeminent professional painter in the Ming period was Qiu Ying (1494–1552), who lived in Suzhou, a prosperous southern city. He inspired generations of imitators with exceptional works, such as a long handscroll known as **SPRING DAWN IN THE HAN PALACE (FIG. 7–18)**. The painting is based on Tang-dynasty depictions of women in the court of the Han dynasty (206 BCE–220 CE). While in the service of a well-known collector, Qiu Ying had the opportunity to study many Tang paintings, whose artists usually concentrated on the figures, leaving out the

Spring Dawn in the Han Palace ➤

Ming dynasty, 1500–1550. Section of a handscroll, ink and color on silk, 1′ × 18′13⁄16″ (0.30 × 5.7 m). National Palace Museum, Taibei, Taiwan, Republic of China.

Two ladies unwrap a *qin*, the zither or lute that was the most respected of musical instruments.

A seated lady plays the *pipa*, an instrument introduced from Central Asia during the Tang dynasty.

Antique vessels of bronze, lacquer, and porcelain adorn the room and suggest the ladies' refined taste.

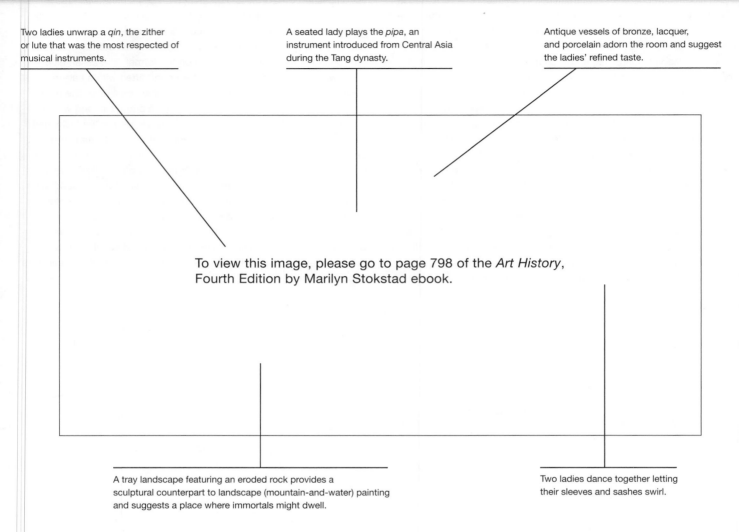

To view this image, please go to page 798 of the *Art History*, Fourth Edition by Marilyn Stokstad ebook.

A tray landscape featuring an eroded rock provides a sculptural counterpart to landscape (mountain-and-water) painting and suggests a place where immortals might dwell.

Two ladies dance together letting their sleeves and sashes swirl.

SEE MORE: View the Closer Look feature for the detail of *Spring Dawn in the Han Palace* **www.myartslab.com**

background entirely. Qiu's graceful and elegant figures—although modeled after those in Tang works—are portrayed in a setting of palace buildings, engaging in such pastimes as chess, music, calligraphy, and painting. With its antique subject matter, refined technique, and flawless taste in color and composition, *Spring Dawn in the Han Palace* brought professional painting to a new high point (see "A Closer Look," above).

DECORATIVE ARTS

Qiu Ying painted to satisfy his patrons in Suzhou. The cities of the south were becoming wealthy, and newly rich merchants collected paintings, antiques, and art objects. The court, too, was prosperous and patronized the arts on a lavish scale. In such a setting, the decorative arts thrived.

MING BLUE-AND-WHITE WARES. The Ming became famous the world over for its exquisite ceramics, especially **porcelain** (see "The Secret of Porcelain," opposite). The imperial kilns in Jingdezhen, in Jiangxi Province, became the most renowned center for porcelain not only in all of China, but in all the world. Particularly noteworthy are the blue-and-white wares produced there during the ten-year reign of the ruler known as the Xuande

Marco Polo, it is said, was the one who named a new type of ceramic he found in China. Its translucent purity reminded him of the smooth whiteness of the cowry shell, *porcellana* in Italian. **Porcelain** is made from kaolin, an extremely refined white clay, and petuntse, a variety of the mineral feldspar. When properly combined and fired at a sufficiently high temperature, the two materials fuse into a glasslike, translucent ceramic that is far stronger than it looks.

Porcelaneous stoneware, fired at lower temperatures, was known in China by the seventh century, but true porcelain was perfected during the Song dynasty. To create blue-and-white porcelain such as the flask in FIGURE 7–19, blue pigment was made from cobalt oxide, finely

ground and mixed with water. The decoration was painted directly onto the unfired porcelain vessel, then a layer of clear glaze was applied over it. (In this technique, known as **underglaze** painting, the pattern is painted beneath the glaze.) After firing, the piece emerged from the kiln with a clear blue design set sharply against a snowy white background.

Entranced with the exquisite properties of porcelain, European potters tried for centuries to duplicate it. The technique was finally discovered in 1709 by Johann Friedrich Böttger in Dresden, Germany, who tried—but failed—to keep it a secret.

To view this image, please go to page 799 of the *Art History*, Fourth Edition by Marilyn Stokstad ebook.

7-19 • FLASK
Ming dynasty, 1426–1435. Porcelain with decoration painted in underglaze cobalt blue. Collection of the Palace Museum, Beijing.

Dragons have featured prominently in Chinese folklore from earliest times—Neolithic examples have been found painted on pottery and carved in jade. In Bronze Age China, dragons came to be associated with powerful and sudden manifestations of nature, such as wind, thunder, and lightning. At the same time, dragons became associated with superior beings such as virtuous rulers and sages. With the emergence of China's first firmly established empire during the Han dynasty, the dragon was appropriated as an imperial symbol, and it remained so throughout Chinese history. Dragon sightings were duly recorded and considered auspicious. Yet even the Son of Heaven could not monopolize the dragon. During the Tang and Song dynasties the practice arose of painting pictures of dragons to pray for rain, and for Chan (Zen) Buddhists, the dragon was a symbol of sudden enlightenment.

Emperor (ruled 1426–1435), such as the **FLASK** in **FIGURE 7–19**. The subtle shape, the refined yet vigorous decoration of dragons posturing above the sea, and the flawless glazing embody the high achievement of Ming artisans.

ARCHITECTURE AND CITY PLANNING

Centuries of warfare and destruction have left very few Chinese architectural monuments intact. The most important remaining example of traditional Chinese architecture is **THE FORBIDDEN CITY**, the imperial palace compound in Beijing, whose principal buildings were constructed during the Ming dynasty (**FIG. 7–20**).

THE FORBIDDEN CITY. The basic plan of Beijing was the work of the Mongols, who laid out their capital city according to traditional Chinese principles. City planning began early in China—in the seventh century, in the case of Chang'an (present-day Xi'an), the capital of the Sui and Tang emperors. The walled city of Chang'an was laid out on a rectangular grid, with evenly spaced streets that ran north–south and east–west. At the northern end stood a walled imperial complex.

Beijing, too, was developed as a walled, rectangular city with streets laid out in a grid. The palace enclosure occupied the center of the northern part of the city, which was reserved for the Mongols. Chinese lived in the southern third of the city. Later, Ming and Qing emperors preserved this division, with officials living in the northern or Inner City and commoners living in the southern or Outer City. Under the third Ming emperor, Yongle (ruled 1403–1424), the Forbidden City was rebuilt as we see it today.

The approach to the Forbidden City was impressive. Visitors entered through the Meridian Gate, a monumental gate with side wings (SEE FIG. 7–20). Inside the Meridian Gate a broad courtyard is crossed by a bow-shaped waterway that is spanned by five arched marble bridges. At the opposite end of the courtyard is the Gate of Supreme Harmony, opening onto an even larger courtyard that houses three ceremonial halls raised on a broad platform. First is the Hall of Supreme Harmony, where, on the most important state occasions, the emperor was seated on his throne,

To view this image, please go to page 800 of the *Art History*, Fourth Edition by Marilyn Stokstad ebook.

7-20 • THE FORBIDDEN CITY
Now the Palace Museum, Beijing. Mostly Ming dynasty.
View from the southwest.

SEE MORE: View a simulation about the Forbidden City
www.myartslab.com

facing south. Beyond is the smaller Hall of Central Harmony, then the Hall of Protecting Harmony. Behind these vast ceremonial spaces, still on the central axis, is the inner court, again with a progression of three buildings, this time more intimate in scale. In its balance and symmetry the plan of the Forbidden City reflects ancient Chinese beliefs about the harmony of the universe, and it emphasizes the emperor's role as the Son of Heaven, whose duty was to maintain the cosmic order from his throne in the middle of the world.

THE LITERATI AESTHETIC

In the south, particularly in the district of Suzhou, literati painting, associated with the educated men who served the court as government officials, remained the dominant trend. One of the major literati figures from the Ming period is Shen Zhou (1427–1509), who had no desire to enter government service and spent most of his life in Suzhou. He studied the Yuan painters avidly and tried to recapture their spirit in such works as *Poet on a Mountaintop* (see "*Poet on a Mountaintop*," page 474). Although the style of the painting recalls the freedom and simplicity of Ni Zan (SEE FIG. 7–15), the motif of a poet surveying the landscape from a mountain plateau is Shen's creation.

To view this image, please go to page 800 of the *Art History*, Fourth Edition by Marilyn Stokstad ebook.

7-21 • ARMCHAIR
Ming dynasty, 16th–17th century. Huanghuali wood (hardwood), 39⅜ × 27¼ × 20″ (100 × 69.2 × 50.8 cm). The Nelson-Atkins Museum of Art, Kansas City, Missouri. Purchase, Nelson Trust (46-78/1)

To view this image, please go to page 801 of the *Art History*,
Fourth Edition by Marilyn Stokstad ebook.

7–22 • GARDEN OF THE CESSATION OF OFFICIAL LIFE (ALSO KNOWN AS THE HUMBLE ADMINISTRATOR'S GARDEN)
Suzhou, Jiangsu. Ming dynasty, early 16th century.

Early in the sixteenth century, an official in Beijing, frustrated after serving in the capital for many years without promotion, returned home. Taking an ancient poem, "The Song of Leisurely Living," for his model, he began to build a garden. He called his retreat the Garden of the Cessation of Official Life to indicate that he had exchanged his career as a bureaucrat for a life of leisure. By leisure, he meant that he could now dedicate himself to calligraphy, poetry, and painting, the three arts dear to scholars in China.

LITERATI INFLUENCE ON FURNITURE, ARCHITECTURE, AND GARDEN DESIGN. The taste of the literati came to influence furniture and architecture, and especially the design of gardens. Chinese furniture made for domestic use reached the height of its development in the sixteenth and seventeenth centuries. Characteristic of Chinese furniture, the chair in FIGURE 7–21 is constructed without the use of glue or nails. Instead, pieces fit together based on the principle of the **mortise-and-tenon** joint, in which a projecting element (tenon) on one piece fits snugly into a cavity (mortise) on another. Each piece of the chair is carved, as opposed to being bent or twisted, and the joints are crafted with great precision. The patterns of the wood grain provide subtle interest unmarred by any painting or other embellishment. The style, like that of Chinese architecture, is one of simplicity, clarity, symmetry, and balance. The effect is formal and dignified but natural and simple—virtues central to the Chinese view of proper human conduct as well.

The art of landscape gardening also reached a high point during the Ming dynasty, as many literati surrounded their homes with gardens. The most famous gardens were created in the southern cities of the Yangzi Delta, especially in Suzhou. The largest surviving garden of the era is the **GARDEN OF THE CESSATION OF OFFICIAL LIFE (FIG. 7–22)**. Although modified and reconstructed many times through the centuries, it still reflects many of the basic ideas of the original Ming owner. About a third of the garden is

Poet on a Mountaintop

In earlier landscape paintings, human figures were typically shown dwarfed by the grandeur of nature. Travelers might be seen scuttling along a narrow path by a stream, while overhead towered mountains whose peaks conversed with the clouds and whose heights were inaccessible. Here, the poet has climbed the mountain and dominates the landscape. Even the clouds are beneath him. Before his gaze, a poem hangs in the air, as though he were projecting his thoughts.

The poem, composed by Shen Zhou himself, and written in his distinctive hand, reads:

White clouds like a scarf enfold the mountain's waist;
Stone steps hang in space—a long, narrow path.
Alone, leaning on my cane, I gaze intently at the scene,
And feel like answering the murmuring brook with the music of my flute.

(Translation by Jonathan Chaves, *The Chinese Painter as Poet*, New York, 2000, p. 46.)

Shen Zhou composed the poem and wrote the inscription at the time he painted the album. The style of the calligraphy, like the style of the painting, is informal, relaxed, and straightforward—qualities that were believed to reflect the artist's character and personality.

The painting reflects Ming philosophy, which held that the mind, not the physical world, was the basis for reality. With its perfect synthesis of poetry, calligraphy, and painting, and with its harmony of mind and landscape, *Poet on a Mountaintop* represents the essence of Ming literati painting.

To view this image, please go to page 802 of the *Art History*, Fourth Edition by Marilyn Stokstad ebook.

Shen Zhou **POET ON A MOUNTAINTOP**
Leaf from an album of landscapes; painting mounted as part of a handscroll. Ming dynasty, c. 1500.
Ink and color on paper, 15¼ × 23¾" (40 × 60.2 cm). Nelson-Atkins Museum of Art, Kansas City, Missouri.
Purchase, Nelson Trust (46-51/2)

devoted to water through artificially created brooks and ponds. The landscape is dotted with pavilions, kiosks, libraries, studios, and corridors. Many of the buildings have poetic names, such as Rain Listening Pavilion and Bridge of the Small Flying Rainbow.

DONG QICHANG, LITERATI THEORIST.   The ideas underlying literati painting found their most influential expression in the writings of Dong Qichang (1555–1636). A high official in the late Ming period, Dong Qichang embodied the literati tradition as poet, calligrapher, and painter. He developed a view of Chinese art history that divided painters into two opposing schools, northern and southern. The names have nothing to do with geography— a painter from the south might well be classed as northern—but reflect a parallel Dong drew with the northern and southern schools of Chan (Zen) Buddhism in China. The southern school of Chan, founded by the eccentric monk Huineng (638–713), was unorthodox, radical, and innovative; the northern school was traditional and conservative. Similarly, Dong's two schools of painters represented progressive and conservative traditions. In Dong's view the conservative northern school was dominated by professional painters whose academic, often decorative, style emphasized technical skill. In contrast, the progressive southern school preferred ink to color and free brushwork to meticulous detail. Its painters aimed for poetry and personal expression. In promoting this theory, Dong gave his unlimited sanction to literati painting, which he positioned as the culmination of the southern school, and he fundamentally influenced the way the Chinese viewed their own tradition.

Dong Qichang summarized his views on the proper training for literati painters in the famous statement "Read ten thousand books and walk ten thousand miles." By this he meant that one must first study the works of the great masters, then follow "heaven and earth," the world of nature. These studies prepared the way for greater self-expression through brush and ink, the goal of literati painting. Dong's views rested on an awareness that a painting of scenery and the actual scenery are two very different things. The excellence of a painting does not lie in its degree of resemblance to reality—that gap can never be bridged—but in its expressive power. The expressive language of painting is inherently abstract and lies in its nature as a construction of brushstrokes. For example, in a painting of a rock, the rock itself is not expressive; rather, the brushstrokes that suggest a rock are expressive.

With such thinking Dong brought painting close to the realm of calligraphy, which had long been considered the highest form of artistic expression in China. More than a thousand years before Dong's time, a body of critical terms and theories had evolved to discuss calligraphy in light of the formal and expressive properties of brushwork and composition. Dong introduced some of these terms—ideas such as opening and closing, rising and falling, and void and solid—to the criticism of painting.

Dong's theories are fully embodied in his painting **THE QING- BIAN MOUNTAINS (FIG. 7–23)**. According to his own inscription,

To view this image, please go to page 803 of the *Art History*, Fourth Edition by Marilyn Stokstad ebook.

7-23 • Dong Qichang THE QINGBIAN MOUNTAINS
Ming dynasty, 1617. Hanging scroll, ink on paper, 21′8″ × 7′4⅜″ (6.72 × 2.25 m). Cleveland Museum of Art. Leonard C. Hanna, Jr., Fund

the painting was based on a work by the tenth-century artist Dong Yuan. Dong Qichang's style, however, is quite different from the styles of the masters he admired. Although there is some indication of foreground, middle ground, and distant mountains, the space is ambiguous, as if all the elements were compressed to the surface of the picture. With this flattening of space, the trees, rocks, and mountains become more readily legible in a second way, as semi-abstract forms made of brushstrokes.

Six trees arranged diagonally define the extreme foreground and announce themes that the rest of the painting repeats, varies, and develops. The tree on the left, with its outstretched branches and full foliage, is echoed first in the shape of another tree just across the river and again in a tree farther up and toward the left. The tallest tree of the foreground grouping anticipates the high peak that towers in the distance almost directly above it. The forms of the smaller foreground trees, especially the one with dark leaves,

are repeated in numerous variations across the painting. At the same time, the simple and ordinary-looking boulder in the foreground is transformed in the conglomeration of rocks, ridges, hills, and mountains above. This double reading, both abstract and representational, parallels the work's double nature as a painting of a landscape and an interpretation of a traditional landscape painting.

The influence of Dong Qichang on the development of Chinese painting of later periods cannot be overstated. Indeed, nearly all Chinese painters since the early seventeenth century have reflected his ideas in one way or another.

QING DYNASTY

In 1644, when the armies of the Manchu people to the northeast of China marched into Beijing, many Chinese reacted as though their civilization had come to an end. Yet, the Manchus had already

To view this image, please go to page 804 of the *Art History*, Fourth Edition by Marilyn Stokstad ebook.

7-24 • Yun Shouping AMARANTH
Leaf from an album of flowers, bamboo, fruits, and vegetables. 1633–1690. Album of 10 leaves; ink and color on paper; each leaf 10 × 13″ (25.3 × 33.5 cm). Collection of Phoenix Art Museum. Gift of Marilyn and Roy Papp

The leaf is inscribed by the artist: "Autumn garden abounds in beauty, playfully painted by Ouxiangguan (Yun Shouping)." Translation by Momoko Soma Welch.

To view this image, please go to page 805 of the *Art History*, Fourth Edition by Marilyn Stokstad ebook.

7–25 • Shitao
LANDSCAPE
Leaf from *An Album of Landscapes*. Qing dynasty, c. 1700. Ink and color on paper, 9½ × 11″ (24.1 × 28 cm). Collection C. C. Wang family

adopted many Chinese customs and institutions before their conquest. After gaining control of all of China, a process that took decades, they showed great respect for Chinese tradition. In art, all the major trends of the late Ming dynasty eventually continued into the Manchu, or Qing, dynasty (1644–1911).

ORTHODOX PAINTING

Literati painting had been established as the dominant tradition; it now became orthodox. Scholars followed Dong Qichang's recommendation and based their approach on the study of past masters, and they painted large numbers of works in the manner of Song and Yuan artists as a way of expressing their learning, technique, and taste.

The Qing emperors of the late seventeenth and eighteenth centuries were painters themselves. They collected literati painting, and their taste was shaped mainly by artists such as Wang Hui. Thus literati painting, long associated with reclusive scholars, ultimately became an academic style practiced at court. Imbued with values associated with scholarship and virtue, these paintings constituted the highest art form of the Qing court. The emperors also esteemed a style of bird-and-flower painting developed by Yun Shouping (1633–1690). Like the orthodox style of landscape painting, it was embraced by literati painters—many of them court officials themselves. The style, most often seen in albums or fans,

recalled aspects of Song- and Yuan-dynasty bird-and-flower painting, and artists cited their ancient models as a way to enrich both the meaning and the beauty of these small-format works. In a leaf from an album of flowers, bamboo, fruits and vegetables, which employs a variety of brush techniques (**FIG. 7–24**), Yun Shouping represents flowers of the autumn season.

INDIVIDUALIST PAINTING

The first few decades of Qing rule had been both traumatic and dangerous for those who were loyal—or worse, related—to the Ming. Some committed suicide, while others sought refuge in monasteries or wandered the countryside. Among them were several painters who expressed their anger, defiance, frustration, and melancholy in their art. They took Dong Qichang's idea of painting as an expression of the artist's personal feelings very seriously and cultivated highly original styles. These painters have become known as the individualists.

SHITAO. One of the individualists was Shitao (1642–1707), who was descended from the first Ming emperor and who took refuge in Buddhist temples when the dynasty fell. In his later life he brought his painting to the brink of abstraction in such works as **LANDSCAPE** (**FIG. 7–25**). A monk sits in a small hut, looking out onto mountains that seem to be in turmoil. Dots, used for centuries to indicate vegetation on rocks, here seem to have taken on a life of their own. The rocks also seem alive—about to swallow up the monk and his hut. Throughout his life Shitao continued to identify himself with the fallen Ming, and he felt that his secure world had turned to chaos with the Manchu conquest.

THE MODERN PERIOD

In the mid and late nineteenth century, China was shaken from centuries of complacency by a series of humiliating military defeats at the hands of Western powers and Japan. Only then did the government finally realize that these new rivals were not like the Mongols of the thirteenth century. China was no longer at the center of the world, a civilized country surrounded by "barbarians." Spiritual resistance was no longer sufficient to solve the problems brought on by change. New ideas from Japan and the West began to filter in, and the demand arose for political and cultural reforms. In 1911 the Qing dynasty was overthrown, ending 2,000 years of imperial rule, and China was reconceived as a republic.

During the first decades of the twentieth century Chinese artists traveled to Japan and Europe to study Western art. Returning to China, many sought to introduce the ideas and techniques they had learned, and they explored ways to synthesize the Chinese and the Western traditions. After the establishment of the present-day Communist government in 1949, individual artistic freedom was curtailed as the arts were pressed into the service of the state and its vision of a new social order. After 1979, however, cultural attitudes began to relax, and Chinese painters again pursued their own paths.

WU GUANZHONG. One artist who emerged during the 1980s as a leader in Chinese painting is Wu Guanzhong (b. 1919). Combining his French artistic training and Chinese background, Wu Guanzhong developed a semiabstract style to depict scenes from the Chinese landscape. He made preliminary sketches on site, then, back in his studio, he developed these sketches into free interpretations based on his feeling and vision. An example of his work, **PINE SPIRIT**, depicts a scene in the Huang (Yellow) Mountains **(FIG. 7–26)**. The technique, with its sweeping gestures of paint, is clearly linked to Abstract Expressionism, an influential Western movement of the post–World War II years; yet the painting also claims a place in the long tradition of Chinese landscape as exemplified by such masters as Shitao.

Like all aspects of Chinese society, Chinese art has felt the strong impact of Western influence, and the question remains whether Chinese artists will absorb Western ideas without losing their traditional identity. Interestingly, landscape remains an important subject, as it has been for more than a thousand years, and calligraphy continues to play a vital role. Using the techniques and methods of the West, some of China's artists have joined an international avant-garde, while other painters still seek communion with nature through their ink brushstrokes as a means to come to terms with human life and the world.

To view this image, please go to page 806 of the *Art History*, Fourth Edition by Marilyn Stokstad ebook.

7–26 • Wu Guanzhong PINE SPIRIT
1984. Ink and color on paper, 2′3⅝″ × 5′3½″ (0.70 × 1.61 m). Spencer Museum of Art, The University of Kansas, Lawrence. Gift of the E. Rhodes and Leonard B. Carpenter Foundation

ARTS OF KOREA: THE JOSEON DYNASTY TO THE MODERN ERA

In 1392, General Yi Seonggye (1335–1408) overthrew the Goryeo dynasty (918–1392), establishing the Joseon dynasty (1392–1910), sometimes called the Yi dynasty. He first maintained his capital at Gaeseong, the old Goryeo capital, but moved it to Seoul in 1394, where it remained through the end of the dynasty. The Joseon regime rejected Buddhism, espousing Neo-Confucianism as the state philosophy. Taking Ming-dynasty China as its model, the new government patterned its bureaucracy on that of the Ming emperors, even adopting as its own such outward symbols of Ming imperial authority as blue-and-white porcelain. The early Joseon era was a period of cultural refinement and scientific achievement, during which Koreans invented Han'geul (the Korean alphabet) and movable type, not to mention the rain gauge, astrolabe, celestial globe, sundial, and water clock.

JOSEON CERAMICS

Like their Silla and Goryeo forebears, Joseon potters excelled in the manufacture of ceramics, taking their cue from contemporaneous Chinese wares, but seldom copying them directly.

BUNCHEONG CERAMICS. Descended from Goryeo celadons, Joseon-dynasty stonewares, known as *buncheong* wares, enjoyed widespread usage throughout the peninsula. Their decorative effect relies on the use of white slip that makes the humble stoneware resemble more expensive white porcelain. In fifteenth-century examples, the slip is often seen inlaid into repeating design elements stamped into the body.

Sixteenth-century *buncheong* wares are characteristically embellished with wonderfully fluid, calligraphic brushwork painted in iron-brown slip on a white slip ground. Most painted *buncheong* wares have stylized floral décor, but rare pieces, such as the charming wine bottle in **FIGURE 7–27**, feature pictorial decoration. In fresh, lively brushstrokes, a bird with outstretched wings grasps a fish that it has just caught in its talons; waves roll below, while two giant lotus blossoms frame the scene.

Japanese armies repeatedly invaded the Korean peninsula between 1592 and 1597, destroying many of the *buncheong* kilns, and essentially bringing the ware's production to a halt. Tradition holds that the Japanese took many *buncheong* potters home with them to produce *buncheong*-style wares, which were greatly admired by connoisseurs of the tea ceremony. In fact, the spontaneity of Korean *buncheong* pottery has inspired Japanese ceramics to this day.

PAINTED PORCELAIN. Korean potters produced porcelains with designs painted in underglaze cobalt blue as early as the fifteenth century, inspired by Chinese porcelains of the early Ming period (SEE FIG. 7–19). The Korean court dispatched artists from the royal painting academy to the porcelain kilns—located some 30 miles southeast of Seoul—to train porcelain decorators. As a result, from the fifteenth century onward, the painting on the best Korean porcelains closely approximated that on paper and silk, unlike in China, where ceramic decoration followed a path of its own with but scant reference to painting traditions.

In another unique development, Korean porcelains from the sixteenth and seventeenth centuries often feature designs painted in underglaze iron-brown rather than the cobalt blue customary in Ming porcelain. Also uniquely Korean are porcelain jars with bulging shoulders, slender bases, and short, vertical necks, which

To view this image, please go to page 807 of the *Art History*, Fourth Edition by Marilyn Stokstad ebook.

7-27 • HORIZONTAL WINE BOTTLE WITH DECORATION OF A BIRD CARRYING A NEWLY CAUGHT FISH
Korea. Joseon dynasty, 16th century. *Buncheong* ware: light gray stoneware with decoration painted in iron-brown slip on a white slip ground, 6¹⁄₁₀ × 9½" (15.5 × 24.1 cm). Museum of Oriental Ceramics, Osaka, Japan. Gift of the Sumitomo Group (20773)

appeared by the seventeenth century and came to be the most characteristic ceramic shapes in the later Joseon period. Painted in underglaze iron-brown, the seventeenth-century jar shown in **FIGURE 7–28** depicts a fruiting grape branch around its shoulder. In typical Korean fashion, the design spreads over a surface unconstrained by borders, resulting in a balanced but asymmetrical design that incorporates the Korean taste for unornamented spaces.

JOSEON PAINTING

Korean secular painting came into its own during the Joseon dynasty. Continuing Goryeo traditions, early Joseon examples employ Chinese styles and formats, their range of subjects expanding from botanical motifs to include landscapes, figures, and a variety of animals.

Painted in 1447 by An Gyeon (b. 1418), **DREAM JOURNEY TO THE PEACH BLOSSOM LAND (FIG. 7–29)** is the earliest extant and dated Joseon secular painting. It illustrates a fanciful tale by China's revered nature poet Tao Qian (365–427), and recounts a dream about chancing upon a utopia secluded from the world for centuries while meandering among the peach blossoms of spring.

As with their Goryeo forebears, the monumental mountains and vast, panoramic vistas of such fifteenth-century Korean paintings, echo Northern Song painting styles. Chinese paintings of the Southern Song (1127–1279) and Ming periods (1368–1644) also influenced Korean painting of the fifteenth, sixteenth, and seventeenth centuries, though these styles never completely supplanted the imprint of the Northern Song masters.

THE SILHAK MOVEMENT. In the eighteenth century, a truly Korean style emerged, inspired by the *silhak* ("practical learning") movement, which emphasized the study of things Korean in addition to the Chinese classics. The impact of the movement is

To view this image, please go to page 808 of the *Art History*, Fourth Edition by Marilyn Stokstad ebook.

7-28 • BROAD-SHOULDERED JAR WITH DECORATION OF A FRUITING GRAPEVINE
Korea. Joseon dynasty, 17th century. Porcelain with decoration painted in underglaze iron-brown slip, height 22⅕″ (53.8 cm). Ewha Women's University Museum, Seoul, Republic of Korea.

Chinese potters invented porcelain during the Tang dynasty, probably in the eighth century. Generally fired in the range of 1300° to 1400° C, porcelain is a high-fired, white-bodied ceramic ware. Its unique feature is its translucency. Korean potters learned to make porcelain during the Goryeo dynasty, probably as early as the eleventh or twelfth century, though few Goryeo examples remain today. For many centuries, only the Chinese and Koreans were able to produce porcelains.

To view this image, please go to page 808 of the *Art History*, Fourth Edition by Marilyn Stokstad ebook.

7-29 • An Gyeon DREAM JOURNEY TO THE PEACH BLOSSOM LAND
Korea. Joseon dynasty, 1447. Handscroll, ink and light colors on silk, 15¼ × 41¾″ (38.7 × 106.1 cm). Central Library, Tenri University, Tenri (near Nara), Japan.

To view this image, please go to page 809 of the *Art History*, Fourth Edition by Marilyn Stokstad ebook.

7–30 • Jeong Seon
PANORAMIC VIEW OF THE DIAMOND MOUNTAINS (GEUMGANG-SAN)
Korean. Joseon Dynasty, 1734. Hanging scroll, ink and colors on paper, 40⅝ × 37″ (130.1 × 94 cm). Lee'um, Samsung Museum, Seoul, Republic of Korea.

exemplified by the painter Jeong Seon (1676–1759), who chose well-known Korean vistas as the subjects of his paintings, rather than the Chinese themes favored by earlier artists. Among Jeong Seon's paintings are numerous representations of the Diamond Mountains (Geumgang-san), a celebrated range of craggy peaks along Korea's east coast. Painted in 1734, the scroll reproduced in **FIGURE 7–30** aptly captures the Diamond Mountains' needlelike peaks. The subject is Korean, and so is the energetic spirit and the intensely personal style, with its crystalline mountains, distant clouds of delicate ink wash, and individualistic brushwork.

Among figure painters, Sin Yunbok (b. 1758) is an important exemplar of the *silhak* attitude. Active in the late eighteenth and early nineteenth centuries, Sin typically depicted aristocratic figures in native Korean garb. The album leaf entitled **PICNIC AT THE LOTUS POND (FIG. 7–31)** represents a group of Korean gentlemen enjoying themselves in the countryside on an autumn day in the company of several *gisaeng* (female entertainers). The figures are recognizably Korean—the women with their full coiffures, short jackets, and generous skirts, and the men with their beards, white robes, and wide-brimmed hats woven of horsehair and coated with black lacquer. The stringed instrument played by

To view this image, please go to page 810 of the *Art History*, Fourth Edition by Marilyn Stokstad ebook.

7-31 • Sin Yunbok PICNIC AT THE LOTUS POND
Leaf from an album of genre scenes. Korea. Joseon dynasty, late 18th century. Album of 30 leaves;
ink and colors on paper, 11⅛ × 13⅞″ (28.3 × 35.2 cm). Kansong Museum of Art, Seoul, Republic of Korea.

the gentleman seated at lower right is a *gayageum* (Korean zither), the most hallowed of all Korean musical instruments.

MODERN KOREA

Long known as "the Hermit Kingdom," the Joseon dynasty pursued a policy of isolationism, closing its borders to most of the world, except China, until 1876. Japan's annexation of Korea in 1910 brought the Joseon dynasty to a close, but effectively prolonged the country's seclusion from the outside world. The legacy of self-imposed isolation compounded by colonial occupation (1910–1945)—not to mention the harsh circumstances imposed by World War II (1939–1945), followed by the even worse conditions of the Korean War (1950–1953)—impeded Korea's artistic and cultural development during the first half of the twentieth century.

A MODERNIST PAINTER FROM KOREA. Despite these privations, some modern influences did reach Korea indirectly via China and Japan, and beginning in the 1920s and 1930s a few Korean artists experimented with contemporary Western styles, typically painting in the manner of Cézanne or Gauguin, but sometimes trying abstract, nonrepresentational styles. Among these, Gim Hwangi (1913–1974) was influenced by Constructivism and geometric abstraction and would become one of twentieth-century Korea's influential painters. Like many Korean artists after the Korean War, Gim wanted to examine Western modernism at its source. He visited Paris in 1956 and then, from 1964 to 1974, lived and worked in New York, where he produced his best-known works. His painting **5-IV-71** presents a large pair of circular radiating patterns composed of small dots and squares in tones of blue, black, and gray **(FIG. 7–32)**. While appearing wholly Western in style, medium, concept, and even title—Gim Hwangi typically adopted the date of a work's creation as its title—*5-IV-71* also seems related to Asia's venerable tradition of monochrome **ink painting**, while suggesting a transcendence that seems Daoist or

7-32 • Gim Hwangi 5-IV-71
Korea. 1971. Oil on canvas, 39½ × 39½″ (100 × 100 cm). Whanki Museum, Seoul, Republic of Korea.

Buddhist in feeling. Given that the artist was Korean, that he learned the Chinese classics in his youth, that he studied art in Paris, and that he then worked in New York, it is possible that his painting embodies all of the above. Gim's painting illustrates the paradox that the modern artist faces while finding a distinctive, personal style: whether to paint in an updated version of a traditional style, in a wholly international style, in an international style with a distinctive local twist, or in an eclectic, hybrid style that incorporates both native and naturalized elements from diverse traditions. By addressing these questions, Gim Hwangi blazed a trail for subsequent Korean-born artists, such as the renowned video artist Nam June Paik (1932–2006).

THINK ABOUT IT

7.1 Explain the role played by one of the following three ways of thought prevalent in Chinese society—Daoism, Confucianism, and Buddhism—and discuss the implications that it had for the visual arts. Make specific reference to works from this chapter.

7.2 Examine a work commissioned by the court at Beijing and distinguish which of its features are typical of court art.

7.3 Discuss the place that calligraphy held within Chinese society and in relation to other arts. Then, explain why Dong Qichang's *The Qingbian Mountains* (SEE FIG. 7–23) has elicited comparison with the art of calligraphy.

7.4 Discuss the culture of the literati, including their values and their system of art patronage, and distinguish the formats of painting that they used.

7.5 Theorize reasons for the emergence of individualist painting in China, using works such as Shitao's *Landscape* (SEE FIG. 7–25) to support your argument.

PRACTICE MORE: Compose answers to these questions, get flashcards for images and terms, and review chapter material with quizzes
www.myartslab.com

THE AMERICAS

THOUGHT PIECE

HISTORIES OF THE AMERICAS

PIERRE LANDRY

For several centuries, history painting topped the hierarchy of painting genres established by the French Academy. An instrument of authority, this painting of "history" came eventually to reflect the subordination of the artistic profession to those in power. As for America, its so-called "discovery" in the late fifteenth century would give birth to one of the principal "master narratives" of the Renaissance, generating a vast iconography that includes numerous allegories. One of these executed in the seventeenth century by Jan Van der Straet, has been described in particularly eloquent terms by Michel de Certeau: "Amerigo Vespucci the voyager arrives from the sea. A crusader standing erect, his body in armour, he bears the European weapons of meaning. Behind him are the vessels that will bring back to the European West the spoils of a paradise. Before him is the Indian 'America,' a nude woman reclining in her hammock, an unnamed presence of difference, a body which awakens within a space of exotic flora and fauna. An inaugural scene, after a moment of stupor, on this threshold dotted with colonnades of trees, the conqueror will write the body of the other and trace there his own history. From her he will make a historied body—a blazon—of his labours and phantasms. She will be 'Latin' America." In just a few words, this description identifies the "weightiest" features of this first contact between Europeans and Native Americans: its status as an inaugural event; the inception of an essentially Eurocentric history; a relationship to the other based on a manifestly racist and sexist power dynamic.

—Pierre Landry, "Histories of the Americas," in Pierre Landry, Johanne Lamoureux, and José Roca, eds, *Nous venons en paix—: Histoires des Amériques* (Montréal: Musée d'art contemporain de Montréal, 2004), p. 128.

THINGS TO CONSIDER

- What were the visual and material practices of the indigenous peoples in the Americas prior to European contact?
- What was the impact of the European conquest of the Americas on both the colonizers and the colonized?
- What role did different conceptions of land, territory and ownership play in this clash of cultures?

ART OF THE AMERICAS AFTER 1300

According to Navajo mythology, the universe itself is a weaving, its fibers spun by Spider Woman out of sacred cosmic materials. Spider Woman taught the art of weaving to Changing Woman (a Mother Earth figure), and she in turn taught it to Navajo women, who continue to keep this art vital, seeing its continuation as a sacred responsibility. Early Navajo blankets were composed of simple horizontal stripes, but over time weavers have introduced more intricate patterns, and today Navajo rugs are woven in numerous distinctive styles.

The Two Grey Hills style of weaving developed during the early twentieth century around a trading post of that name in northwest New Mexico. Weavers who work in this style use the natural colors of undyed sheep's wool (only the black wool is sometimes dyed) to create dazzling geometric patterns. The artist Julia Jumbo (1928–2007), who learned to weave as a child, used her weavings to support her family. She raised her own sheep, and carded and spun her wool by hand before incorporating it into painstakingly made textiles. Jumbo is renowned for the clarity of her designs and the technical perfection of her fine weave. This outstanding work, created in 2003, attests to the vital and dynamic nature of Native American arts today.

When the first Europeans arrived, the Western Hemisphere was already inhabited from the Arctic Circle to Tierra del Fuego by peoples with long histories and rich cultural traditions (MAP 8–1). After 1492, when Christopher Columbus and his companions first sailed to the New World, the arrival of Europeans completely altered the destiny of the Americas. In Mesoamerica and South America the break with the past was sudden and violent: two great empires—the Aztec in Mexico and the Inca in South America—that had risen to prominence in the fifteenth century were rapidly destroyed. In North America the change took place more gradually, but the outcome was much the same. In both North and South America, natives succumbed to European diseases to which they had no immunity, especially smallpox, leading to massive population loss and social disruption. Over the next 400 years, many Native Americans were displaced from their ancestral home-lands, and many present-day Native American ethnic groupings were formed by combinations of various survivor groups.

Despite all the disruption, during the past century the indigenous arts of the Americas have undergone a re-evaluation that has renewed the conception of what constitutes "American art." Native artists like Julia Jumbo continue to revive and reimagine indigenous traditions, revisit traditional outlooks, and restate their ancient customs and ideas in new ways. After being pushed to the brink of extinction, Native American cultures are experiencing a revival in both North and South America, as Native Americans assert themselves politically and insist on the connections between their history and the land.

THE AZTEC EMPIRE

In November 1519, the army of the Spanish soldier Hernán Cortés beheld for the first time the great Aztec capital of Tenochtitlan. The shimmering city, which seemed to be floating on the water, was built on an island in the middle of Lake Texcoco in the Valley of Mexico, and linked by broad causeways to the mainland. One of Cortés's companions later recalled the wonder the Spanish felt at that moment: "When we saw so many cities and villages built on the water and other great towns on dry land and that straight and level causeway going towards [Tenochtitlan], we were amazed … on account of the great towers and temples and buildings rising from the water, and all built of masonry. And some of our soldiers even asked whether the things that we saw were not a dream." (Bernal Díaz del Castillo, cited in Coe and Koontz 2005, p. 190.)

The Mexica people who lived in the remarkable city that Cortés found were then rulers of much of the land that later took their name, Mexico. Their rise to power had been recent and swift. Only 400 years earlier, according to their own legends, they had been a nomadic people living far north of the Valley of Mexico in a distant place called Aztlan. The term Aztec derives from the word Aztlan, and refers to all those living in Central Mexico who came from this mythical homeland, not just to the Mexica of Tenochtitlan.

The Mexica arrived in the Valley of Mexico in the thirteenth century. They eventually settled on an island in Lake Texcoco where they had seen an eagle perching on a prickly pear cactus (*nochtli*) growing out of a stone (*tetl*), a sign that their god Huitzilopochtli told them would mark the end of their wandering. They called the place Tenochtitlan. The city on the island was gradually expanded by reclaiming land from the lake, and serviced by a grid of artificial canals. In the fifteenth century, the Mexica—joined by allies in a triple alliance—began an aggressive campaign of expansion. The tribute they exacted from all over Mexico transformed Tenochtitlan into a glittering capital.

Aztec religion was based on a complex pantheon that combined Aztec deities with more ancient ones that had long been worshiped in central Mexico. According to Aztec belief, the gods had created the current era, or sun, at the ancient city of Teotihuacan in the Valley of Mexico (see Chapter 2). The continued existence of the world depended on human actions, including rituals of bloodletting and human sacrifice. Many Mesoamerican peoples believed that the world had been created multiple times before the present era. But while most Mesoamericans believed that they were living in the fourth era, or sun, the Mexica asserted that they lived in the fifth sun, a new era that coincided with the Aztec Empire. The Calendar Stone (see "A Closer Look," page 490) boldly makes this claim, using the dates of the destructions of the four previous eras to form the glyph that names the fifth sun, 4 Motion. The end of each period of 52 years in the Mesoamerican calendar was a particularly dangerous time that required a special fire-lighting ritual.

TENOCHTITLAN

An Aztec scribe drew an idealized representation of the city of Tenochtitlan and its sacred ceremonial precinct (FIG. 8–1) for the Spanish viceroy in 1545. It forms the first page of the *Codex Mendoza*. An eagle perched on a prickly pear cactus growing out of a stone—the symbol of the city—fills the center of the page. Waterways divide the city into four quarters, and indicate the lake surrounding the city. Early leaders of Tenochtitlan are shown sitting in the four quadrants. The victorious warriors at the bottom of the page represent Aztec conquests, and a count of years surrounds the entire scene. This image combines historical narration with idealized cartography, showing the city in the middle of the lake at the moment of its founding.

At the center of Tenochtitlan was the sacred precinct, a walled enclosure that contained dozens of temples and other buildings. The focal point of the sacred precinct was the Great Pyramid, a twin pyramid with paired temples on top: the one on the north dedicated to Tlaloc, an ancient rain god with a history extending

To view this image, please go to page 836 of the *Art History*, Fourth Edition by Marilyn Stokstad ebook.

8–1 • THE FOUNDING OF TENOCHTITLAN
Page from *Codex Mendoza*. Mexico. Aztec, 1545. Ink and color on paper, 12⅜ × 8⁷⁄₁₆" (21.5 × 31.5 cm). Bodleian Library, University of Oxford, England. MS. Arch Selden. A.1.fol. 2r

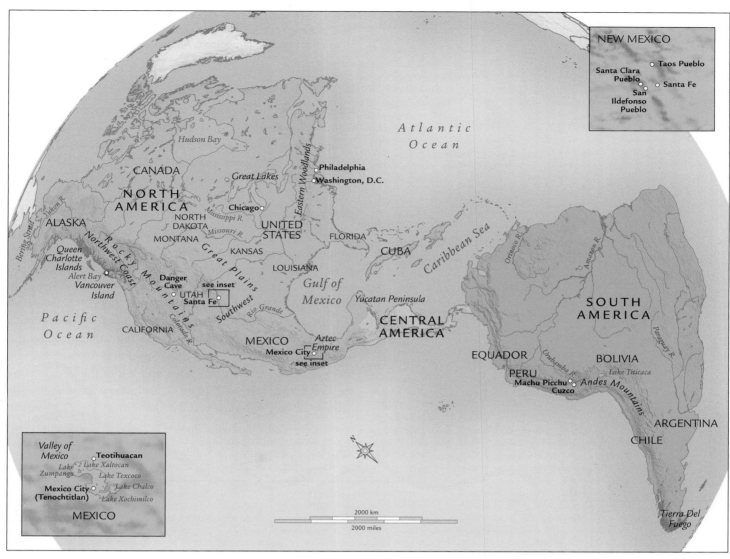

MAP 8–1 • THE AMERICAS AFTER 1300

Diverse cultures inhabited the Americas, each shaping a distinct artistic tradition.

back to Teotihuacan, and the one on the south dedicated to Huitzilopochtli, the solar god of the newly arrived Mexica tribe. Two steep staircases led up the west face of the pyramid from the plaza in front. Sacrificial victims climbed these stairs to the Temple of Huitzilopochtli, where priests threw them over a stone, quickly cut open their chests, and pulled out their still-throbbing hearts, a sacrifice that ensured the survival of the sun, the gods, and the Aztecs. The bodies were then rolled down the stairs and dismembered. Thousands of severed heads were said to have been kept on a skull rack in the plaza, represented in FIGURE 8–1 by the rack with a single skull to the right of the eagle.

During the winter rainy season the sun rose behind the Temple of Tlaloc, and during the dry season it rose behind the Temple of Huitzilopochtli. The double temple thus united two natural forces, sun and rain, or fire and water. During the spring and autumn equinoxes, the sun rose between the two temples.

SCULPTURE

Aztec sculpture was monumental, powerful, and often unsettling (see "A Closer Look," page 490). A particularly striking example is an imposing statue of Coatlicue, mother of the Mexica god Huitzilopochtli (FIG. 8–2). Coatlicue means "she of the serpent skirt," and this broad-shouldered figure with clawed feet has a skirt of twisted snakes. The statue may allude to the moment of Huitzilopochtli's birth: when Coatlicue conceived Huitzilopochtli from a ball of down, her other children—the stars and the moon—jealously conspired to kill her. As they attacked, Huitzilopochtli emerged from his mother's body fully grown and armed, drove off his half-brothers, and destroyed his half-sister, the moon goddess Coyolxauhqui. Coatlicue, however, did not survive the encounter. In this sculpture, she has been decapitated and a pair of serpents, symbols of gushing blood, rise from her neck to form her head. Their eyes are her eyes; their fangs, her tusks. Around her stump of

8-2 • THE GODDESS COATLICUE

Mexico. Aztec, c. 1500. Basalt, height 8′6″ (2.65 m).
Museo Nacional de Antropología, Mexico City.

To view this image, please go to page 838 of the *Art History*, Fourth Edition by Marilyn Stokstad ebook.

a neck hangs a necklace of human hands, hearts, and a dangling skull. Despite the surface intricacy, the statue's massive form creates an impression of solidity, and the entire sculpture leans forward, looming over the viewer. The colors with which it was originally painted would have heightened its dramatic impact.

FEATHERWORK

Indeed Aztec art was colorful. An idea of its iridescent splendor is captured in the feather headdress (**FIG. 8–3**) said to have been given by the Aztec emperor Moctezuma to Cortés, and thought to be the one listed in the inventory of treasures Cortés shipped to Charles V, the Habsburg emperor in Spain, in 1519. Featherwork was one of the glories of Mesoamerican art but very few of these extremely fragile artworks survive. The tropical feathers in this headdress exemplify the exotic tribute paid to the Aztecs; the long iridescent green feathers that make up most of the headdress are the exceedingly rare tail feathers of the quetzal bird—each male quetzal has only two such plumes. The feathers were gathered in small bunches, their quills reinforced with reed tubes, and then

8-3 • FEATHER HEADDRESS OF MOCTEZUMA

Mexico. Aztec, before 1519.
Quetzal, blue cotinga, and other feathers and gold on a fiber frame, 45⅝ × 68⅞″
(116 × 175 cm). Museum für Völkerkunde, Vienna.

To view this image, please go to page 838 of the *Art History*, Fourth Edition by Marilyn Stokstad ebook.

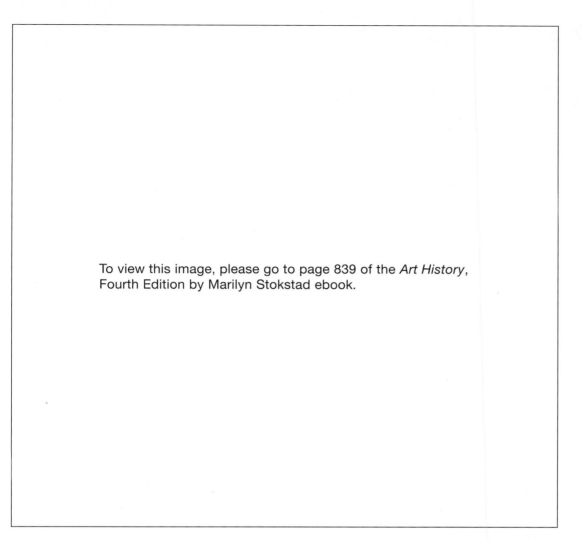

To view this image, please go to page 839 of the *Art History*, Fourth Edition by Marilyn Stokstad ebook.

8-4 • A VIEW OF THE WORLD
Page from *Codex Fejervary-Mayer*. Mexico. Aztec or Mixtec, c. 1400–1519. Paint on animal hide, each page 6⅞ × 6⅞" (17.5 × 17.5 cm), total length 13'3" (4.04 m). The National Museums and Galleries on Merseyside, Liverpool, England.

sewn to the frame in overlapping layers, the joins concealed by small gold plaques. Featherworkers were esteemed craftspeople. After the Spanish invasion, they turned their exacting skills to "feather paintings" of Christian subjects.

MANUSCRIPTS

Aztec scribes also created brilliantly colored books: histories, maps, and divinatory almanacs. Instead of being bound on one side like European books, Mesoamerican books took the form of a screenfold, accordion-pleated so that each page was connected only to the two adjacent pages. This format allowed great flexibility: a book could be opened to show two pages, or unfolded to show six or eight pages simultaneously; different sections of the book could also be juxtaposed. A rare manuscript that survived the Spanish conquest provides a concise summary of Mesoamerican cosmology **(FIG. 8–4)**. Mesoamerican peoples recognized five key directions: north, south, east, west, and center. At the center of the image is Xiuhtecutli, god of fire, time, and the calendar. Radiating from him are the four cardinal directions—each associated with a specific color, a deity, and a tree with a bird in its branches. Two hundred and sixty dots trace the eight-lobed path around the

central figure, referring to the 260-day Mesoamerican divinatory calendar; the 20 day signs of this calendar are also distributed throughout the image. By linking the 260-day calendar to the four directions, this image speaks eloquently of the unity of space and time in the Mesoamerican worldview.

The Aztec Empire was short-lived. Within two years of their arrival in Mexico, the Spanish conquistadors and their indigenous allies overran Tenochtitlan. They built their own capital, Mexico City, over its ruins and established their own cathedral on the site of Tenochtitlan's sacred precinct.

THE INCA EMPIRE

At the beginning of the sixteenth century the Inca Empire was one of the largest states in the world. It extended more than 2,600 miles along western South America, encompassing most of modern Peru, Ecuador, Bolivia, and northern Chile and reaching into present-day Argentina. Like the Aztec Empire, its rise was rapid and its destruction sudden.

The Incas called their empire the "Land of the Four Quarters." At its center was their capital, Cuzco, "the navel of

Calendar Stone ➤ Mexico. Aztec, c. 1500. Diameter 11′6¾″ (3.6 m).
Museo Nacional de Antropología, Mexico City.

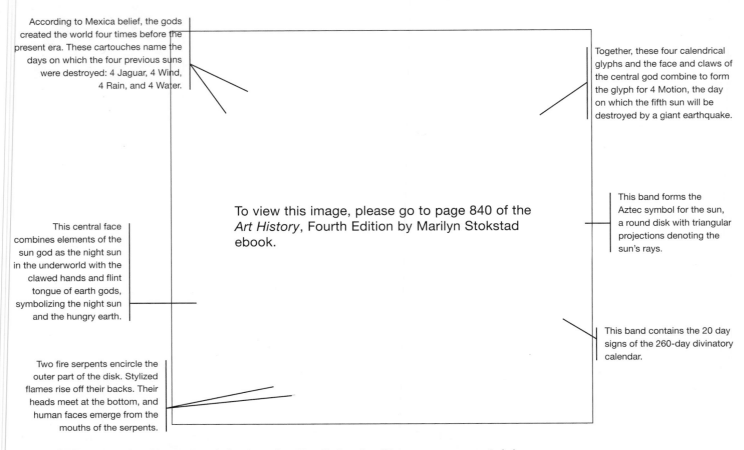

According to Mexica belief, the gods created the world four times before the present era. These cartouches name the days on which the four previous suns were destroyed: 4 Jaguar, 4 Wind, 4 Rain, and 4 Water.

Together, these four calendrical glyphs and the face and claws of the central god combine to form the glyph for 4 Motion, the day on which the fifth sun will be destroyed by a giant earthquake.

This central face combines elements of the sun god as the night sun in the underworld with the clawed hands and flint tongue of earth gods, symbolizing the night sun and the hungry earth.

This band forms the Aztec symbol for the sun, a round disk with triangular projections denoting the sun's rays.

This band contains the 20 day signs of the 260-day divinatory calendar.

Two fire serpents encircle the outer part of the disk. Stylized flames rise off their backs. Their heads meet at the bottom, and human faces emerge from the mouths of the serpents.

To view this image, please go to page 840 of the *Art History*, Fourth Edition by Marilyn Stokstad ebook.

SEE MORE: View the Closer Look feature for the Calendar Stone **www.myartslab.com**

the world," located high in the Andes Mountains. The Inca state began as one of many small competing kingdoms that emerged in the highlands. In the fifteenth century the Incas began to expand, suddenly and rapidly, and had subdued most of their vast domain—through conquest, alliance, and intimidation—by 1500.

To hold this linguistically and ethnically diverse empire together, the Inca ("Inca" refers to both the ruler and the people) relied on religion, an efficient bureaucracy, and various forms of labor taxation, in which the payment was a set amount of time spent performing tasks for the state. In return the state provided gifts through local leaders and sponsored lavish ritual entertainments. Men might cultivate state lands, serve in the army, or work periodically on public works projects—building roads and terracing hillsides, for example—while women wove cloth as

tribute. No Andean civilization ever developed writing, but the Inca kept detailed accounts and historical records on knotted and colored cords (*quipu*).

To move their armies and speed transport and communication within the empire, the Incas built more than 23,000 miles of roads. These varied from 50-foot-wide thoroughfares to 3-foot-wide paths. Two main north–south roads, one along the coast and the other through the highlands, were linked by east–west roads. Travelers journeyed on foot, using llamas as pack animals. Stairways helped them negotiate steep mountain slopes, and rope suspension bridges allowed river gorge crossings. All along the roads, storehouses and lodgings—more than a thousand have been found—were spaced a day's journey apart. A relay system of runners could carry messages between Cuzco and the farthest reaches of the empire in about a week.

CUZCO

Cuzco, a capital of great splendor, was home to the Inca, ruler of the empire. Its urban plan was said to have been designed by the Inca Pachacuti (r. 1438–1471) in the shape of a puma, its head the fortress of Sacsahuaman, and its belly the giant plaza at the center of town. The city was divided into upper and lower parts, reflecting the dual organization of Inca society. Cuzco was the symbolic as well as the political center of the Inca Empire: everyone had to carry a burden when entering the city, and gold, silver, or textiles brought into the city could not afterward be removed from it.

Cuzco was a showcase of the finest Inca masonry, some of which can still be seen in the present-day city (see "Inca Masonry," page 492). Architecture was a major expressive form for the Inca, the very shape of individually worked stones conveying a powerful aesthetic impact (FIG. 8–5). In contrast to the massive walls, Inca buildings had gabled, thatched roofs. Doors, windows, and niches were trapezoid-shaped, narrower at the top than the bottom.

MACHU PICCHU

MACHU PICCHU, one of the most spectacular archaeological sites in the world, provides an excellent example of Inca architectural planning (FIG. 8–6). At 9,000 feet above sea level, it straddles a

To view this image, please go to page 841 of the *Art History*, Fourth Edition by Marilyn Stokstad ebook.

8-5 • INCA MASONRY, DETAIL OF A WALL AT MACHU PICCHU
Peru. Inca, 1450–1530.

8-6 • MACHU PICCHU
Peru. Inca, 1450–1530.

SEE MORE: View a video about Machu Picchu
www.myartslab.com

To view this image, please go to page 841 of the *Art History*, Fourth Edition by Marilyn Stokstad ebook.

Working with the simplest of tools—mainly heavy stone hammers—and using no mortar, Inca builders created stonework of great refinement and durability: roads and bridges that linked the entire empire, terraces for growing crops, and structures both simple and elaborate. The effort expended on stone construction by the Inca was prodigious. Fine Inca masonry consisted of either rectangular blocks or irregular polygonal blocks (SEE FIG. 8–5). In both types, adjoining blocks were painstakingly shaped to fit tightly together without mortar. Their stone faces might be slightly beveled along their edges so that each block presented a "pillowed" shape expressing its identity, or walls might be smoothed into a continuous flowing surface in which the individual

blocks form a seamless whole. At a few Inca sites, the stones used in construction were boulder-size: up to 27 feet tall. In Cuzco, and elsewhere in the Inca empire, Inca masonry has survived earthquakes that have destroyed later structures.

At Machu Picchu (SEE FIGS. 8–5, 8–6), all buildings and terraces within its 3-square-mile extent were made of granite, the hard stone occurring at the site. Commoners' houses and some walls were constructed of irregular stones that were carefully fitted together, while fine polygonal or smoothed masonry distinguished palaces and temples.

polygonal-stone wall

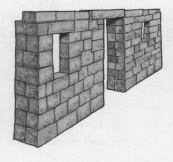

smooth-surfaced wall

SEE MORE: View a simulation about Inca masonry www.myartslab.com

ridge between two high peaks in the eastern slopes of the Andes and looks down on the Urubamba River. Stone buildings, today lacking only their thatched roofs, occupy terraces around central plazas, and narrow agricultural terraces descend into the valley. The site, near the eastern limits of the empire, was the royal estate of the Inca ruler Pachacuti. The court might retire to this warmer, lower-altitude palace when the Cuzco winter became too harsh to enjoy. Important diplomatic negotiations and ceremonial feasts may also have taken place at this country retreat. The entire complex is designed with great sensitivity to its surroundings, with walls and plazas framing stupendous vistas of the surrounding landscape, and carefully selected stones echoing the shapes of the mountains beyond.

TEXTILES

The production of fine textiles was already an important art in the Andes by the third millennium BCE (see Chapter 2). Among the

To view this image, please go to page 842 of the *Art History*, Fourth Edition by Marilyn Stokstad ebook.

8–7 • TUNIC
Peru. Inca, c. 1500. Camelid fiber and cotton, 35⅞ × 30″ (91 × 76.5 cm). Dumbarton Oaks Research Library and Collections, Pre-Columbian Collection, Washington, D.C.

Incas, textiles of cotton and camelid fibers (from llama, vicuña, and alpaca) were a primary form of wealth. One form of labor taxation required the manufacture of fibers and cloth, and textiles as well as agricultural products filled Inca storehouses. Cloth was deemed a fitting gift for the gods, so fine garments were draped around statues, and even burned as sacrificial offerings.

The patterns and designs on garments were not simply decorative but also carried symbolic messages, including indications of a person's ethnic identity and social rank. In the elaborate **TUNIC** in **FIGURE 8–7**, each square represents a miniature tunic. For example, tunics with checkerboard patterns were worn by military officers and royal escorts, and the four-part motifs may refer to the empire as the Land of the Four Quarters. The diagonal key motif is often found on tunics with horizontal border stripes but its meaning is not known. While we may not be sure what was meant in every case, patterns and colors appear to have been standardized like uniforms in order to convey information at a glance. Encompassing all these patterns associated with different ranks and statuses, this exquisitely woven tunic may have been a royal garment.

METALWORK

When they arrived in Peru in 1532, the Spanish were far less interested in Inca cloth than in their vast quantities of gold and silver. The Inca valued objects made of gold and silver not for their precious metal, but because they saw in them symbols of the sun and the moon. They are said to have called gold the "sweat of the sun" and silver the "tears of the moon." On the other hand, the Spanish exploration of the New World was propelled by feverish tales of native treasure. Whatever gold and silver objects the Spanish could obtain were melted down to enrich their royal coffers. Only a few small figures buried as offerings, like the little **LLAMA** shown in **FIGURE 8–8**, escaped the conquerors. The llama was thought to have a special connection with the sun, with rain, and with fertility, and a llama was sacrificed to the sun every morning in Cuzco. In this small silver figurine, the essential character of a llama is rendered with a few well-chosen details, but in keeping with the value that Andeans placed on textiles the blanket on its back is carefully described.

THE AFTERMATH OF THE SPANISH CONQUEST

Native American populations in Mexico and Peru declined sharply after the conquest because of the exploitative policies of the conquerors and the ravages of smallpox and other diseases that spread from Europe and against which the indigenous people had no immunity. This demographic collapse meant that the population of the Americas declined by as much as 90 percent in the century after contact with Europe. European missionaries suppressed local beliefs and practices and worked to spread Christianity throughout the Americas. Although increasing numbers of Europeans began to settle and dominate the land, native arts did not end with the Spanish conquest. Traditional arts,

To view this image, please go to page 843 of the *Art History*, Fourth Edition by Marilyn Stokstad ebook.

8-8 • LLAMA
From Bolivia or Peru, found near Lake Titicaca, Bolivia. Inca, 15th century. Cast silver with gold and cinnabar, 9 × 8½ × 1¾″ (22.9 × 21.6 × 4.4 cm). American Museum of Natural History, New York.

including fine weaving, continue to this day, transforming and remaining vital as indigenous peoples adjust to a changing world.

NORTH AMERICA

In America north of Mexico, from the upper reaches of Canada and Alaska to the southern tip of Florida, many different peoples with widely varying cultures coexisted. Here, the Europeans came less as military men seeking riches to plunder than as families seeking land to farm. Unlike the Spaniards, they found no large cities with urban populations to resist them. However, although they imagined that the lands they settled were an untended wilderness, in fact nearly all of North America was populated and possessed by indigenous peoples. Over the next 400 years, by means of violence, bribery, and treaties, the English colonies and, in turn, the United States displaced nearly all Native Americans from their ancestral homelands. What indigenous art Euro-Americans encountered they viewed as a curiosity, not art.

Much Native American artwork was small, portable, fragile, and impermanent. In previous times these artworks were not

MAP 8-2 • NORTH AMERICAN CULTURAL AREAS

The varied geographic regions of North America supported diverse cultures adapted to their distinct environments.

appreciated for their aesthetic qualities, but were collected as anthropological artifacts or souvenirs, often under coercive conditions. Today, many Native peoples have begun to reclaim sacred objects and human remains that were forcibly taken from them, and museums are beginning to work with Native communities to present their art in respectful and culturally sensitive ways. We will look at art from only four North American cultural areas: the Eastern Woodlands, the Great Plains, the Northwest Coast, and the Southwest (MAP 8–2).

THE EASTERN WOODLANDS

In the Eastern Woodlands, after the decline of the great Mississippian centers, most tribes lived in stable villages, and they combined hunting, gathering, and agriculture for their livelihood. In the sixteenth century, the Iroquois formed a powerful confederation of five northeastern Native American nations, which played a prominent military and political role until after the American Revolution. The Huron and Illinois also formed sizable confederacies.

The arrival in the seventeenth century on the Atlantic coast of a few boatloads of Europeans seeking religious freedom, land

to farm, and a new life for themselves brought major changes. Trade with these settlers gave the Woodlands peoples access to things they valued, while on their part the colonists learned native forms of agriculture, hunting, and fishing—skills they needed in order to survive. In turn, Native Americans traded furs for such useful items as metal tools, cookware, needles, and cloth, and they especially prized European glass beads and silver. These trade items largely replaced older materials, such as crystal, copper, and shell.

WAMPUM. Woodlands peoples made belts and strings of cylindrical purple and white shell beads called wampum. The Iroquois and Delaware peoples used wampum to keep records (the purple and white patterns served as memory devices) and exchanged belts of wampum to conclude treaties (FIG. 8–9). Few actual wampum treaty belts have survived, so this one, said to commemorate an unwritten treaty when the land now comprising the state of Pennsylvania was ceded by the Delawares in 1682, is especially prized. The belt, with two figures of equal size holding hands, suggests the mutual respect enjoyed by the Delaware and

Basketry is the weaving of reeds, grasses, and other plant materials to form containers. In North America the earliest evidence of basketwork, found in Danger Cave, Utah, dates to as early as 8400 BCE. Over the subsequent centuries, Native American women, notably in California and the American Southwest, developed basketry into an art form that combined utility with great beauty.

There are three principal basket-making techniques: coiling, twining, and plaiting. **Coiling** involves sewing together a spiraling foundation of rods with some other material. **Twining** twists multiple elements around a vertical warp of rods. Plaiting weaves strips over and under each other.

The coiled basket shown here was made by a Pomo woman in California. According to Pomo legend, the Earth was dark until their ancestral hero stole the sun and brought it to Earth in a basket. He hung the basket first just over the horizon, but, dissatisfied with the light it gave, he kept suspending it in different places across the dome of the sky. He repeats this process every day, which is why the sun moves across the sky from east to west. In the Pomo basket, the structure of coiled willow and bracken fern root produces a spiral surface into which the artist worked sparkling pieces of clam shell, trade beads, and soft tufts of woodpecker and quail feathers. The underlying basket, the glittering shells, and the soft, moving feathers make this an exquisite container. Such baskets were treasured possessions, cremated with their owners at death.

To view this image, please go to page 845 of the *Art History*, Fourth Edition by Marilyn Stokstad ebook.

FEATHERED BOWL
c. 1877. Willow, bulrush, fern, feather, shells, glass beads. Height 5½″ (14 cm), diameter 12″ (36.5 cm). Philbrook Museum, Tulsa, Oklahoma. Gift of Clark Field (1948.39.37)

Penn's Society of Friends (Quakers), a respect that later collapsed into land fraud and violence. In general, wampum strings and belts had the authority of legal agreement and also symbolized a moral and political order.

QUILLWORK. Woodlands art focused on personal adornment—tattoos, body paint, elaborate dress—and fragile arts such as **quillwork**. Quillwork involved dyeing porcupine and bird quills with a variety of natural dyes, soaking the quills to soften them,

To view this image, please go to page 845 of the *Art History*, Fourth Edition by Marilyn Stokstad ebook.

8-9 • WAMPUM BELT, TRADITIONALLY CALLED WILLIAM PENN'S TREATY WITH THE DELAWARE
1680s. Shell beads, 17⅜ × 6⅛″ (44 × 15.5 cm). Royal Ontario Museum, Canada. HD6364

To view this image, please go to page 846 of the *Art History*, Fourth Edition by Marilyn Stokstad ebook.

8–10 • BABY CARRIER
Upper Missouri River area. Eastern Sioux, 19th century. Wooden board, buckskin, porcupine quill, length 31″ (78.8 cm). Department of Anthropology, Smithsonian Institution Libraries, Washington, D.C. Catalogue No. 7311

and then working them into rectilinear, ornamental surface patterns on deerskin clothing and on birch-bark items like baskets and boxes. A Sioux legend recounts how a mythical ancestor, Doublewoman ("double" because she was both beautiful and ugly, benign and dangerous), appeared to a woman in a dream and taught her the art of quillwork. As the legend suggests, quillwork was a woman's art form, as was basketry (see "Basketry," page 495). The Sioux **BABY CARRIER** in **FIGURE 8–10** is richly decorated with symbols of protection and well-being, including bands of antelopes in profile and thunderbirds flying with their heads turned and tails outspread. The thunderbird was an especially beneficent symbol, thought to be capable of protecting against both human and supernatural adversaries.

BEADWORK. In spite of the use of shell beads in wampum, decorative beadwork did not become commonplace until after European contact. In the late eighteenth century, Native American artists began to acquire European colored-glass beads, and in the nineteenth century they favored the tiny seed beads from Venice

and Bohemia. Early beadwork mimicked the patterns and colors of quillwork. In the nineteenth century it largely replaced quillwork and incorporated European designs. Among other sources of inspiration, Canadian nuns introduced the young women in their schools to embroidered European floral motifs, and Native embroiderers began to adapt these designs, as well as European needlework techniques and patterns from European garments, into their own work. Functional aspects of garments might be transformed into purely decorative motifs; for example, a pocket would be replaced by an area of beadwork shaped like a pocket. A **SHOULDER BAG** from Kansas, made by a Delaware woman (**FIG. 8–11**), is covered with curvilinear plant motifs in contrast to the rectilinear patterns of traditional quillwork. White lines outline brilliant pink and blue leaf-shaped forms, heightening the intensity of the colors, which alternate within repeated patterns. This Delaware bag exemplifies the evolution of beadwork design and its adaptation to a changing world. The very shape of this bandolier bag is adapted from European military uniforms.

THE GREAT PLAINS

Between the Eastern Woodlands region and the Rocky Mountains to the west lay an area of prairie grasslands called the Great Plains. On the Great Plains, two differing ways of life developed, one a relatively recent and short-lived (1700–1870) nomadic lifestyle—dependent on the region's great migrating herds of buffalo for food, clothing, and shelter—and the other, a much older sedentary and agricultural lifestyle. Horses, from wild herds descended from feral horses brought to America by Spanish explorers in the sixteenth and seventeenth centuries, made travel and a nomadic life easier for the dispossessed eastern groups that moved to the plains.

European settlers on the eastern seaboard put increasing pressure on the Eastern Woodlands peoples, seizing their farmlands and forcing them westward. Both Native Americans and back-country settlers were living in loosely village-based, farming societies and thus were competing for the same resources. The resulting interaction of Eastern Woodlands artists with one another and with Plains artists led in some cases to the emergence of a new hybrid style, while other artists consciously fought to maintain their own cultures.

PORTABLE ARCHITECTURE. The nomadic Plains peoples hunted buffalo for food and hides from which they created clothing and a light, portable dwelling known as a tipi (formerly spelled teepee) (**FIG. 8–12**). The tipi was well adapted to withstand the strong and constant wind, the dust, and the violent storms of the prairies. The framework of a tipi consisted of a stable pyramidal frame of three or four long poles, filled out with about 20 additional poles, in a roughly oval plan. The framework was covered with hides (or, later, with canvas) to form a conical structure. The hides were specially prepared to make them flexible and waterproof. Between 20 and 40 hides were used to make a tipi, depending on its size. An opening at the top served as the smoke hole for a central hearth.

To view this image, please go to page 847 of the *Art History*, Fourth Edition by Marilyn Stokstad ebook.

8-11 • SHOULDER BAG
Kansas. Delaware people, c. 1860. Wool fabric, cotton fabric and thread, silk ribbon, and glass beads, 23 × 7¾″ (58.5 × 19.8 cm). The Detroit Institute of Arts. Founders Society Purchase (81.216)

8-12 • BLACKFOOT WOMEN RAISING A TIPI
Photographed c. 1900. Montana Historical Society, Helena, Montana.

To view this image, please go to page 848 of the *Art History*, Fourth Edition by Marilyn Stokstad ebook.

8-13 • BATTLE SCENE, HIDE PAINTING
North Dakota. Mandan, 1797–1800. Tanned buffalo hide, dyed porcupine quills, and black, red, green, yellow, and brown pigment, 7′10″ × 8′6″ (2.44 × 2.65 m). Peabody Museum of Archaeology, Harvard University, Cambridge, Massachusetts. 99-12-10/53121

This robe, collected in 1804 by Meriwether Lewis and William Clark on their expedition into western lands acquired by the United States in the Louisiana Purchase, is the earliest documented example of Plains painting. It was one of a number of Native American artworks that Lewis and Clark sent to President Thomas Jefferson. Jefferson displayed the robe in the entrance hall of his home at Monticello, Virginia.

The tipi leaned slightly into the prevailing west wind while the flap-covered door and smoke hole faced east, away from the wind. An inner lining covered the lower part of the walls and the perimeter of the floor to protect the occupants from drafts.

Tipis were the property and responsibility of women, who set them up at new encampments and lowered them when the group moved on. Blackfoot women could set up their huge tipis in less than an hour. Women quilled, beaded, and embroidered tipi linings, as well as backrests, clothing, and equipment. The patterns with which tipis were decorated, like their proportions and colors, varied from nation to nation, family to family, and individual to individual. In general, the bottom was covered with traditional motifs and the center section held personal images. When disassembled and packed to be dragged by a horse to another location, the tipi served as a platform for transporting other possessions. The Sioux arranged their tipis in two half-circles—one for the sky people and one for the earth people—divided along an east–west axis. When the Blackfoot people gathered in the summer for their ceremonial Sun Dance, their encampment contained hundreds of tipis in a circle a mile in circumference.

PLAINS INDIAN PAINTING.   Plains men recorded their exploits in paintings on tipis and on buffalo-hide robes. The earliest documented painted buffalo-hide robe, presented to Lewis and

Clark during their transcontinental expedition, illustrates a battle fought in 1797 by the Mandan (of what is now North Dakota) and their allies against the Sioux (FIG. 8–13). The painter, trying to capture the full extent of a conflict in which five nations took part, shows a party of warriors in 22 separate episodes. The party is led by a man with a pipe and an elaborate eagle-feather headdress, and the warriors are armed with bows and arrows, lances, clubs, and flintlock rifles. Details of equipment and emblems of rank—headdresses, sashes, shields, feathered lances, powder horns for the rifles—are depicted carefully. Horses are shown in profile with stick legs, C-shaped hooves, and either clipped or flowing manes.

The figures stand out clearly against the light-colored background of the buffalo hide. The painter pressed lines into the hide, then filled in the forms with black, red, green, yellow, and brown pigments. A strip of colored porcupine quills runs down the spine of the buffalo hide. The robe would have been worn draped over the shoulders of the powerful warrior whose deeds it commemorates. As the wearer moved, the painted horses and warriors would seem to come alive, transforming the warrior into a living representation of his exploits.

Life on the Great Plains changed abruptly in 1869, when the transcontinental railway linking the east and west coasts of the United States was completed, providing easy access to Native American lands. Between 1871 and 1890, Euro-American hunters killed off most of the buffalo, and soon ranchers and then farmers moved into the Great Plains. The U.S. government forcibly moved the outnumbered and outgunned Native Americans to reservations, land considered worthless until the later discovery of oil and, in the case of the Black Hills, gold.

THE NORTHWEST COAST

From southern Alaska to northern California, the Pacific coast of North America is a region of unusually abundant resources. Its many rivers fill each year with salmon returning to spawn. Harvested and dried, the fish could sustain large populations throughout the year. The peoples of the Northwest Coast—among them the Tlingit, the Haida, and the Kwakwaka'wakw (formerly spelled Kwakiutl)—exploited this abundance to develop a complex and distinctive way of life in which the arts played a central role.

ANIMAL IMAGERY. Animals feature prominently in Northwest Coast art because each extended family group (clan) claimed descent from a mythic animal or animal-human ancestor, from whom the family derived its name and the right to use certain animals and spirits as totemic emblems, or crests. These emblems appear frequently in Northwest Coast art, notably in carved cedar house poles and the tall, free-standing poles (mortuary poles) erected to memorialize dead chiefs. Chiefs, who were males in the most direct line of

descent from the mythic ancestor, validated their status and garnered prestige for themselves and their families by holding ritual feasts known as potlatches, during which they gave valuable gifts to the invited guests. Shamans, who were sometimes also chiefs, mediated between the human and spirit worlds. Some shamans were female, giving them unique access to certain aspects of the spiritual world.

Northwest Coast peoples lived in large, elaborately decorated communal houses made of massive timbers and thick planks. Carved and painted partition screens separated the chief's quarters from the rest of the house. The Tlingit screen illustrated in FIGURE 8–14 came from the house of Chief Shakes of Wrangell (d. 1916), whose family crest was the grizzly bear. The image of a rearing

To view this image, please go to page 849 of the *Art History*, Fourth Edition by Marilyn Stokstad ebook.

8-14 • GRIZZLY BEAR HOUSE-PARTITION SCREEN
The house of Chief Shakes of Wrangell, Canada. Tlingit people, c. 1840. Cedar, paint, and human hair, 15 × 8′ (4.57 × 2.74 m). Denver Art Museum, Denver, Colorado.

Hamatsa Masks

During the harsh winter season, when spirits are thought to be most powerful, many Northwest Coast peoples seek spiritual renewal through their ancient rituals—including the potlatch, or ceremonial gift giving, and the initiation of new members into the prestigious Hamatsa society. With snapping beaks and cries of "Hap! Hap! Hap!" ("Eat! Eat! Eat!"), Hamatsa, the people-eating spirit of the north, and his three assistants—horrible masked monster birds—begin their wild, ritual dance. The dancing birds threaten and even attack the Kwakwaka'wakw people who gather for the Winter Ceremony.

In the Winter Ceremony, youths are captured, taught the Hamatsa lore and rituals, and then in a spectacular theater-dance performance are "tamed" and brought back into civilized life. All the members of the community, including singers, gather in the main room of the great house, which is divided by a painted screen (SEE FIG. 8–14). The audience members fully participate in the performance; in early times, they brought containers of blood so that when

the bird-dancers attacked them, they could appear to bleed and have flesh torn away.

Whistles from behind the screen announce the arrival of the Hamatsa (danced by an initiate), who enters through the central hole in the screen in a flesh-craving frenzy. Wearing hemlock, a symbol of the spirit world, he crouches and dances wildly with outstretched arms as attendants try to control him. He disappears but returns again, now wearing red cedar and dancing upright. Finally tamed, a full member of society, he even dances with the women.

Then the masked bird-dancers appear—first Raven-of-the-North-End-of-the-World, then Crooked-Beak-of-the-End-of-the-World, and finally the untranslatable Huxshukw, who cracks open skulls with his beak and eats the brains of his victims. Snapping their beaks, these masters of illusion enter the room backward, their masks pointed up as though the birds are looking skyward. They move slowly counterclockwise around the floor. At each change in the music they crouch, snap their beaks, and let out their wild cries of "Hap!

Hap! Hap!" Essential to the ritual dances are the huge carved and painted wooden masks, articulated and operated by strings worked by the dancers. Among the finest masks are those by Willie Seaweed (1873–1967), a Kwakwaka'wakw chief, whose brilliant colors and exuberantly decorative carving style determined the direction of twentieth-century Kwakwaka'wakw sculpture.

The Canadian government, abetted by missionaries, outlawed the Winter Ceremony and potlatches in 1885, claiming the event was injurious to health, encouraged prostitution, endangered children's education, damaged the economy, and was cannibalistic. But the Kwakwaka'wakw refused to give up their "oldest and best" festival—one that spoke powerfully to them in many ways, establishing social rank and playing an important role in arranging marriages. By 1936, the government and the missionaries, who called the Kwakwaka'wakw "incorrigible," gave up. But not until 1951 could the Kwakwaka'wakw people gather openly for winter ceremonies, including the initiation rites of the Hamatsa society.

To view this image, please go to page 850 of the *Art History*, Fourth Edition by Marilyn Stokstad ebook.

To view this image, please go to page 850 of the *Art History*, Fourth Edition by Marilyn Stokstad ebook.

Edward S. Curtis **HAMATSA DANCERS, KWAKWAKA'WAKW**
Canada. Photographed 1914. Smithsonian Institution Libraries, Washington, D.C.

The photographer Edward S. Curtis (1868–1952) devoted 30 years to documenting the lives of Native Americans. This photograph shows participants in a film he made about the Kwakwaka'wakw. For the film, his Native American assistant, Richard Hunt, borrowed family heirlooms and commissioned many new pieces from the finest Kwakwaka'wakw artists. Most of the pieces are now in museum collections. The photograph shows carved and painted posts, masked dancers (including those representing people-eating birds), a chief at the left (holding a speaker's staff and wearing a cedar neck ring), and spectators at the right.

Attributed to Willie Seaweed **KWAKWAKA'WAKW BIRD MASK**
Alert Bay, Vancouver Island, Canada. Prior to 1951. Cedar wood, cedar bark, feathers, and fiber, 10 × 72 × 15" (25.4 × 183 × 38.1 cm). Collection of the Museum of Anthropology, Vancouver, Canada. (A6120)

The name "Seaweed" is an anglicization of the Kwakwaka'wakw name *Siwid*, meaning "Paddling Canoe," "Recipient of Paddling," or "Paddled To"—referring to a great chief to whose potlatches guests paddled from afar. Willie Seaweed was not only the chief of his clan, but a great orator, singer, and tribal historian who kept the tradition of the potlatch alive during years of government repression.

grizzly painted on the screen is itself made up of smaller bears and bear heads that appear in its ears, eyes, nostrils, joints, paws, and body. The oval door opening is a symbolic vagina; passing through it re-enacts the birth of the family from its ancestral spirit.

TEXTILES. Blankets and other textiles produced by the Chilkat Tlingit had great prestige among Northwest Coast peoples (FIG. 8–15). Both men and women worked on the blankets. Men drew the patterns on boards, and women wove the patterns into the blankets, using shredded cedar bark and mountain-goat wool. The weavers did not use looms; instead, they hung cedar warp threads from a rod and twined colored goat wool back and forth through them to make the pattern. The ends of the warp form the fringe at the bottom of the blanket.

The small face in the center of the blanket shown here represents the body of a large stylized creature, perhaps a sea bear (a fur seal) or a standing eagle. Above the body are the creature's large eyes; below it and to the sides are its legs and claws. Characteristic of Northwest painting and weaving, the images are composed of two basic elements: the ovoid, a slightly bent rectangle with rounded corners, and the formline, a continuous, shape-defining line. Here, subtly swelling black formlines define shapes with gentle curves, ovoids, and rectangular C shapes. When the blanket was worn, its two-dimensional shapes would have become three-dimensional, with the dramatic central figure curving over the wearer's back and the intricate side panels crossing over his shoulders and chest.

MASKS. Many Native American cultures stage ritual dance ceremonies to call upon guardian spirits. The participants in Northwest Coast dance ceremonies wore elaborate costumes and striking carved and painted wooden masks. Among the most elaborate masks were those used by the Kwakwaka'wakw in their Winter Ceremony, in which they initiated members into the shamanistic Hamatsa society (see "Hamatsa Masks," opposite). The dance re-enacted the taming of Hamatsa, a cannibal spirit, and his three attendant bird spirits. Magnificent carved and painted masks transformed the dancers into Hamatsa and the bird attendants, who searched for victims to eat. Strings allowed the dancers to manipulate the masks so that the beaks opened and snapped shut with spectacular effect. Isolated in museums as "art," the masks doubtless lose some of the shocking vivacity they have in performance; nevertheless their bold forms and color schemes retain power and meaning that can be activated by the viewer's imagination.

To view this image, please go to page 851 of the *Art History*, Fourth Edition by Marilyn Stokstad ebook.

8–15 • CHILKAT BLANKET
Tlingit people, before 1928. Mountain-goat wool and shredded cedar bark, 55⅛ × 63¾″ (140 × 162 cm). American Museum of Natural History, New York.

THE SOUTHWEST

The Native American peoples of the southwestern United States include, among others, the Pueblo (sedentary village-dwelling groups) and the Navajo. The Pueblo groups are heirs of the Ancestral Puebloans (Anasazi) and Hohokam cultures (see Chapter 2). The Ancestral Puebloans built apartmentlike villages and cliff dwellings whose ruins are found throughout the Four Corners region of New Mexico, Colorado, Arizona, and Utah in the American Southwest. The Navajo, who arrived in the region sometime between 1100 and 1500 CE, developed a semisedentary way of life based on agriculture and (after the introduction of sheep by the Spaniards) shepherding. Being among the very few Native American tribal groups whose reservations are located on their actual ancestral homelands, both groups have succeeded in maintaining the continuity of their traditions despite Euro-American pressure. Today, their arts reflect the adaptation of traditional forms to new technologies, new mediums, and the influences of the dominant American culture that surrounds them.

THE PUEBLOS. Some Pueblo villages, like those of their ancient ancestors, consist of multi-storied dwellings made of adobe. One of these, **TAOS PUEBLO**, shown in **FIGURE 8–16** in a photograph taken in 1947 by the American photographer of the Southwest, Laura Gilpin (1891–1979), is located in north-central New Mexico. Continually occupied and modified for over 500 years, the up to five-story house blocks of Taos Pueblo provide flexible, communal dwellings. Ladders provide access to the upper stories and to insulated inner rooms, entered through holes in the ceiling. Two large house blocks are arrayed around a central plaza that opens toward the neighboring mountains, rising in a stepped fashion to provide a series of roof terraces that can serve as viewing platforms. The plaza and roof terraces are centers of communal life and ceremony, as can be seen in Pablita Velarde's painting of the winter solstice celebrations (SEE FIG. 8–18).

CERAMICS. Pottery traditionally was a woman's art among Pueblo peoples. Wares were made by coiling and other hand-building techniques, and then fired at low temperature in wood bonfires. The best-known twentieth-century Pueblo potter was

To view this image, please go to page 852 of the *Art History*, Fourth Edition by Marilyn Stokstad ebook.

8-16 • Laura Gilpin TAOS PUEBLO
Taos, New Mexico. Photographed 1947. Amon Carter Museum, Fort Worth, Texas.

Laura Gilpin, photographer of the landscape, architecture, and people of the American Southwest, began her series on the Pueblos and Navajos in the 1930s. She published her work in four volumes of photographs between 1941 and 1968.

To view this image, please go to page 852 of the *Art History*, Fourth Edition by Marilyn Stokstad ebook.

8-17 • Maria Montoya Martinez and Julian Martinez BLACKWARE STORAGE JAR
New Mexico. c. 1942. Ceramic, height 18¾″ (47.6 cm), diameter 22½″ (57.1 cm). Museum of Indian Arts and Culture/Laboratory of Anthropology, Museum of New Mexico, Santa Fe.

Maria Montoya Martinez (1887–1980) of San Ildefonso Pueblo in New Mexico. Inspired by prehistoric pottery that was unearthed at nearby archaeological excavations and by the then fashionable Art Deco style, she and her husband, Julian Martinez (1885–1943), developed a distinctive **blackware** ceramic style notable for its elegant forms and subtle textures (FIG. 8–17). Maria Martinez made pots covered with a slip that was then burnished. Using additional slip, Julian Martinez painted the pots with designs that interpreted traditional Pueblo and Ancestral Puebloan imagery. After firing, the burnished ground became a lustrous black and the slip painting retained a matte surface. By the 1930s, production of blackware in San Ildefonso had become a communal enterprise. Family members and friends all worked making pots, and Maria Martinez signed all the pieces so that, in typical Pueblo communal solidarity, everyone profited from the art market.

THE SANTA FE INDIAN SCHOOL.   In the 1930s Anglo-American art teachers and dealers worked with Native Americans of the Southwest to create a distinctive, stereotypical "Indian" style in several mediums—including jewelry, pottery, weaving, and painting—to appeal to tourists and collectors. A leader in this effort was Dorothy Dunn (1903–1991), who taught painting in the Santa Fe Indian School, an off-reservation government boarding school in New Mexico, from 1932 to 1937. Dunn inspired her students to create a painting style that combined the outline drawing and flat colors of folk art, the decorative qualities of Art Deco, and "Indian" subject matter. She and her students formed the Studio School. Restrictive as the school was, Dunn's success made painting a viable occupation for young Native American artists.

Pablita Velarde (1918–2006), from Santa Clara Pueblo in New Mexico and a 1936 graduate of Dorothy Dunn's school, was only a teenager when one of her paintings was selected for exhibition at the Chicago World's Fair in 1933. Thereafter, Velarde documented Pueblo ways of life in a large series of murals for Bandelier National Monument, launching a long and successful career. In smaller works on paper, such as the one illustrated here, she continued this focus on Pueblo life. KOSHARES OF TAOS (FIG. 8–18) illustrates a moment during a ceremony celebrating the winter solstice when koshares, or clowns, take over the plaza from the Katsinas. Katsinas—the supernatural counterparts of animals, natural phenomena like clouds, and geological features like mountains—are central to traditional Pueblo religion. They manifest themselves in the human dancers who impersonate them during the winter solstice ceremony, as well as in the small figures known as Katsina dolls that are given to children as educational aids in learning to identify the masks. Velarde's painting combines bold, flat colors and a simplified decorative line with European perspective. Her paintings, with their Art Deco abstraction, influenced the popular idea of the "Indian" style in art.

To view this image, please go to page 853 of the *Art History*, Fourth Edition by Marilyn Stokstad ebook.

8–18 • Pablita Velarde KOSHARES OF TAOS
New Mexico. 1940s. Watercolor on paper, 13⅞ × 22⅜″ (35.3 × 56.9 cm). Philbrook Museum of Art, Tulsa, Oklahoma.
Museum Purchase (1947.37)

Navajo Night Chant

This chant accompanies the creation of a sand painting during a Navajo curing ceremony. It is sung toward the end of the ceremony and indicates the restoration of inner harmony and balance.

In beauty (happily) I walk.
With beauty before me I walk.
With beauty behind me I walk.
With beauty below me I walk.
With beauty above me I walk.
With beauty all around me I walk.
It is finished (again) in beauty.
It is finished in beauty.

(Cited in Washington Matthews, "The Night Chant: A Navaho Ceremony," in *Memoirs of the American Museum of Natural History*, Vol. 6. New York, 1902, p. 145.)

THE NAVAJOS. While some Navajo arts, like sand painting, have deep traditional roots, others have developed over the centuries of European contact. Navajo weaving depends on the wool of sheep introduced by the Spaniards, and the designs and colors of Navajo blankets continue to evolve today in response to tourism and changing aesthetics. Similarly, jewelry made of turquoise and silver did not become an important Navajo art form until the mid nineteenth century. Traditionally, Navajo arts had strict gender divisions: women wove cloth, and men worked metal.

Sand painting, a traditional Navajo art, is the exclusive province of men. Sand paintings are made to the accompaniment of chants by shaman-singers in the course of healing and blessing ceremonies, and they have great sacred significance (see "Navajo Night Chant," above). The paintings depict mythic heroes and events; and as ritual art, they follow prescribed rules and patterns that ensure their power. To make them, the singer dribbles pulverized colored stones, pollen, flowers, and other natural colors over a hide or sand ground. The rituals are intended to cure by restoring harmony to the world. The paintings are not meant to be seen by the public and certainly not to be displayed in museums. They are meant to be destroyed by nightfall of the day on which they are made.

In 1919 a respected shaman-singer named Hosteen Klah (1867–1937) began to incorporate sand-painting images into weaving, breaking with the traditional prohibitions. Many Navajos took offense at Klah both for recording the sacred images and for doing so in what was traditionally a woman's art form. Klah had learned to weave from his mother and sister. The Navajo traditionally recognize at least three genders; Hosteen Klah was a *nadle*, or Navajo third-gender. Hence, he could learn both female and male arts; that is, he was trained both to weave and to heal. Hosteen Klah was not breaking artistic barriers in a conventional sense, but rather exemplifying the complexities of the traditional

Navajo gender system. Klah's work was ultimately accepted because of his great skill and prestige.

The **WHIRLING LOG CEREMONY** sand painting, woven into tapestry (**FIG. 8–19**), depicts part of the Navajo creation myth. The Holy People create the earth's surface and divide it into four parts. They create humans, and bring forth corn, beans, squash, and tobacco—the four sacred plants. A male-female pair of humans and one of the sacred plants stand in each of the four quarters, defined by the central cross. The four Holy People (the elongated figures)

To view this image, please go to page 854 of the *Art History*, Fourth Edition by Marilyn Stokstad ebook.

8-19 • Hosteen Klah WHIRLING LOG CEREMONY
Sand painting; tapestry by Mrs. Sam Manuelito. Navajo, c. 1925. Wool, 5′5″ × 5′10″ (1.69 × 1.82 m). Heard Museum, Phoenix, Arizona.

surround the image, and the guardian figure of Rainbow Maiden frames the scene on three sides. Like all Navajo artists, Hosteen Klah hoped that the excellence of the work would make it pleasing to the spirits. Recently, shaman-singers have made permanent sand paintings on boards for sale, but they usually introduce slight errors in them to render the paintings ceremonially harmless.

ADDITIONAL READINGS

WIDER HORIZONS

European knowledge of the rest of the world was dramatically and vastly expanded around the year 1500. Vasco da Gama opened up the sea-route round Africa to India in 1497–9 and in 1492–1504 Christopher Columbus's attempts to reach the spice islands of the Far East by sailing westwards led, totally unexpectedly, to the discovery and subsequent exploration of America. Finally, in 1519–22, came the first circumnavigation of the globe. The boundaries of Classical geography were shattered by all this—and there were also some disconcerting implications which could not be ignored. As the Florentine historian Francesco Guicciardini wrote in the 1530s, 'not only has this navigation confounded the affirmations of former writers about terrestrial things, but it has also given some anxiety to the interpreters of Holy Scripture.' A reluctance to take in or an inability to assimilate the new knowledge persisted until late in the sixteenth century, nowhere more obviously than in European reactions to non-European art.

Both Near Eastern and Far Eastern arts had been known in the West since ancient Roman times at least, as we have seen, and if not fully understood were often greatly prized. Motifs from Chinese and Islamic art had long been acclimatized in Europe. But American artifacts, when they first reached Europe, were regarded in quite a different light. Mexican gold, silver and featherwork, sent by Hernando Cortés to the Emperor Charles V, were displayed at Brussels in 1520 and seen by Dürer, who wrote in his diary of these 'wonderful works of art', but neither he nor anyone else seems to have made a visual record of them. Such visual imagery was, perhaps, too strange to be digested. Further examples of Mexican art were imported after the conquest in 1521— illustrated codices, masks encrusted with turquoise and ingenious pieces of featherwork. Some were preserved as 'curiosities', but the majority were destroyed—and so, too, was the civilization that had produced them. Still more ruthless was the destruction of work in gold or silver sent to Europe from Peru in 1534. Not a single piece survives.

The ease with which small forces of Spaniards conquered Mexico and Peru fostered the belief, summed up by an Italian shortly before the end of the sixteenth century, that Europe 'was born to rule over Africa, Asia and America'. This preposterous notion is implicit in numerous European paintings and other images of the four parts of the world. While it prevailed, as it did until well into the nineteenth century, few Europeans were able to see more than a piquant exoticism in works of art from distant, alien traditions. So it is hardly a paradox that the great sixteenth-century expansion in knowledge of the world should have coincided with a resurgence of the Classical tradition in European art.

The visual arts	Historical landmarks
	c.200 BC Emergence of Maya civilization in Yucatan
c.100–650 Teotihuacán (12,1)	c.AD 100 Foundation of Teotihuacán
766 Quiriguá megalith (12,3)	
800–1000 Igbo-Ukwu bronze (12,19)	c.800 Foundation of Ife (Nigeria).
	1022 Murasaki completes *The Tale of Genji*
1100–1300 Ife head of queen (12,17)	c.1100 Foundation of kingdom of Benin. Islam spreads south of Sahara in West Africa
	1191 Zen Buddhism introduced into Japan
1200–1400 *Tales of Heiji Insurrection* (12,68)	c.1200 Incas found capital city of Cuzco (Peru)
	1210 Mongols invade China
c.1300 Li Kan, *Bamboo* (12,52)	
1354–91 Alhambra (12,28)	1354 Turks cross Dardanelles into Europe
	1364 First Ming dynasty emperor ends Mongol rule in China
	1370 Aztecs settle at Tenochtitlan (Mexico)
1403–5 Gur-i-Mir, Samarkand (12,30)	1453 Constantinople falls to Turks
c.1500 Machu Picchu (12,16)	1499 Vasco da Gama reaches India, opens sea-route from Europe to Far East
1500–1600 Benin bronze head (12,24). Katsura palace. Kyoto (12,79)	1502 Safavid dynasty begins rule in Iran, Iraq and Afghanistan
	1519–22 Cortés conquers Mexico
c.1525–35 Sultan Muhammad(?), *The Court of Gayumarth* (12,37)	1522 First circumnavigation of the world completed
	1526 Foundation of Mughal empire in India
1532 Wen Zhengming. *Seven Juniper Trees* (12,65)	1532–4 Pizarro conquers Peru
1567–74 Sinan. Selimiye Mosque, Edirne (12.32)	1571 Turks take Cyprus and Tunis, but their fleet destroyed at Lepanto
	1615 Edo (Tokyo) becomes capital of Japan
c.1618 *Imayat Khan Dying* (12.41)	1620 African slaves imported into N. America
1632–48 Taj Mahal (12,42)	1638 Christianity suppressed in Japan, foreigners expelled
	1644 Ming succeeded by Qing dynasty in China
	1658 Aurangzeb seizes Mughal throne in India

FIRST IMPRESSIONS

When a European sets out on his first journey to America he knows, or thinks he knows, not only where he is going but what he will find when he arrives. So did Columbus. When he sailed from Palos on Friday, August 3, 1492, he was bound for Cathay, the land of fabulous wealth described by Marco Polo and Mandeville. He took with him a letter from the King and Queen of Spain addressed to the Great Khan and enrolled among his few companions a man learned in Arabic to act as interpreter. Many Europeans had traveled to China in previous years and his voyage differed from theirs in only one, all important, respect: he took a westerly course. As he wrote in the dedication of his logbook to Ferdinand and Isabella:

> Your highnesses ordained that I should not go eastward by land in the usual manner but by the western way which no one about whom we have positive information has ever followed.

To reconcile what he found with his expectations became his main preoccupation on arrival and on his three subsequent voyages.

In his wake thousands upon thousands of Europeans have crossed the Atlantic equally laden with preconceptions which they have often been forced to modify but rarely persuaded to jettison. For the relationship between Europe and America has always been a "special" one. From a very early period America seemed almost a creation or extension of Europe—in a way which Asia and Africa could never be. And with time this relationship became ever more involved as Europeans increasingly tended to see in America an idealized or distorted image of their own countries, onto which they could project their own aspirations and fears, their self-confidence and sometimes their guilty despair.

In a celebrated sentence Francisco López de Gómara described the discovery of the Indies as "the greatest event since the creation of the world, excepting the Incarnation and Death of Him who created it"—but that was not until sixty years after Columbus made his landfall. At the time of Columbus's death at Valladolid in 1506—an event, incidentally, which went unmentioned by the official chronicler of that city—no one knew quite what he had discovered. But a few Europeans had already begun to form a mental picture of the Indies which was in due course to dominate that of the whole American continent. It seems to have been composed, initially, of two superimposed images which took their form from European art and literature and only their coloring from the newly discovered lands. One was classical and related to the West; the other medieval and related to the East.

Before these are described, however, something should be said about the myths and traditions concerning the Western Straits and what lay beyond them, especially the legendary islands. One of them was Atlantis which, according to Plato who recounted the story as no more than an instructive fable in the *Timaeus*, was inhabited by a warlike people who invaded Africa and Europe, were defeated by the Athenians and their allies, driven back, and went into a decline. As the tale culminates with Atlantis being swallowed up by the ocean in a single day and night, it hardly encouraged exploration beyond the Mediterranean. Nor did the fable of the Isles of the Blest or Hesperides, also set in the Western Ocean, for they were by definition inaccessible to the living. But accounts of them were, as we shall see, to have some influence on writers who described the Caribbean. A Christianized version of the Hesperides figures in the tenth-century account of the voyages of an Irish abbot, St. Brendan, who died in about 577, a very popular piece of medieval hagiography of which more than 120 manuscript copies are recorded. Its author seems to have had some knowledge of Iceland, perhaps Newfoundland, and some more southerly islands, probably the Azores. But the promised land of the Saints which Brendan and his monks visit after calling at many other Atlantic islands—and which Irish writers have attempted to identify with the Bahamas—is simply an idealized Ireland with a milder climate, abundant fruit, and precious stones. Whether or not St. Brendan crossed the Atlantic, his biographer was unable to provide an image of a distinctly new world. An appealing air of medieval fantasy pervades the book, which includes the story of the Irishman landing and lighting a fire on a floating island which proved to be a whale.

We are on firmer ground with the Norsemen. Icelandic sagas tell of an attempt made early in the eleventh century to colonize the district called "Vinland" on account of its wild "grapes" (probably red currants). It was given up partly because of the hostility of the local population (there was as yet no superiority in European weapons over those of Eskimos or Indians) and partly because it was insufficiently profitable. Vinland has been convincingly identified as the northern tip of Newfoundland. But the story of its brief colonization remained locked in sagas which were inaccessible to most Europeans until long after the area had been rediscovered. And even if it were to prove that Columbus was not, strictly speaking, the first European to set foot on American soil, that would be of little, if any, import to either the European vision of America or the late fifteenth- and early sixteenth-century exploration of the continent.

The twelfth-century cosmographer Vincent de Beauvais—followed by several other learned clerics including a fifteenth-century Florentine, Lorenzo Bonincontri—argued that Africa must be balanced on the other side of the Atlantic by a land mass of equal size, the Antipodes. This theory was probably known to Columbus, but he was seeking neither such a continent nor the Atlantic islands when he sailed westward.

> Your highnesses decided to send me, Christopher Columbus, to see these parts of India and the princes and the peoples of those lands . . .

he wrote in the dedication of his logbook. It was for Asia that he was bound in 1492. And in any case, his miscalculation of both the circumference of the world and the extent of Asia—he believed "Quinsay" (Hangchow) to be only some 3,550 nautical miles west of the Canary Islands whereas the real distance is 11,766—left no room in his view of the world for a separate Antipodean continent.

Europeans had long been aware of the strangeness as well as the riches of the Far East. It had been described by Marco Polo and still more vividly by "Sir John Mandeville," whose enormously popular mid-fourteenth century geographical fantasy abounded in islands in the Indian Ocean inhabited by men with no heads but eyes in their shoulders, people with ears so long that they hung down to their knees, with the heads of dogs or the feet of horses, and so on. As his logbook reveals, Columbus kept a weather-eye open for similarities between the islands he discovered and those which had previously been described; and in his letter which was printed in 1493 and spread the news of his voyage throughout Europe, he remarked: "I have not found the human monstrosities which many people expected." But he found much to confirm him in his belief that he had reached the Indian Ocean. Mandeville's Amazonia was peopled with women "who will not suffer men amongst them, to be their sovereigns," and Columbus reported that on the island of Matremonio there were no men but only women "who do not follow feminine occupations but use cane bows and arrows like those of the men." On "the great and fair isle called Nacumera," according to Mandeville, "the men go all naked except a little clout and are large men and warlike . . . and if they take any man in battle they eat him." Columbus was soon to find man-eaters—to be called cannibals, a corruption of the word Caribbean—

> people who are regarded in all the islands as very ferocious and who eat human flesh; they have canoes with which they range all the islands of India and pillage and take as much as they can; they are no more malformed than the others except that they have the custom of wearing their hair long like women.

No less striking affinities were to be found between the more docile inhabitants as well. "A good and true people" dwelt on Mandeville's Isle of Bragman: "and of good living after their belief, and of good faith, and although they are not christened, yet by natural law they are full of virtue and eschew all vice," caring "not for possessions or riches." Columbus noted that the Indians knew "neither sect nor idolatory, with the exception that all believe that the source of all power and goodness is in the sky." And although he had "been unable to learn whether they hold private property," it appeared to him that "all took a share in anything that one had, especially victuals."

But Columbus looked in vain for many of the more prominent elements in the traditional picture of the Indies. There were no very great riches, no great cities whatsoever, and no Great Khan. He went on searching, however, during his subsequent voyages. And when, in 1498, he finally set foot on the American mainland, he recognized at once that he had found "a very great continent, until today unknown," even possibly, he thought, the terrestial paradise which had always been located in the East. For by this time (his third voyage) he had begun to view his discoveries apocalyptically—as offering the possibility of converting all the races of the world, of global Christianity. He was dazzled by the vision of Christianity becoming not only dogmatically but geographically world-wide. And it was in a strain of Messianic, almost mystical, exaltation that he identified the Orinoco with one of the four rivers which went out of the Garden of Eden, perhaps the Pison, "which compasseth the whole land of Havilah, where there is gold; and the gold of that land is good: there is bedellium and the onyx stone."

It was not, however, of the Biblical so much as the classical landscape that readers of Columbus's first letter must have been reminded. Of Cuba he wrote:

> Its lands are lofty and in it there are many sierras and high mountains. . . . All are most beautiful, of a thousand shapes, and all accessible and filled with trees of a thousand kinds and tall, and they seem to touch the sky; and I am told that they never lose their leaves, which I can believe, for I saw them as green and beautiful as they are in Spain in May, for some of them were flowering, some with fruit and some in another condition, according to their nature. And there were singing the nightingale and other little birds of a thousand kinds in the month of November, there where I went. There are palm trees of six or eight kinds, which are a wonder to behold on account of their beautiful variety, and so are the other trees and fruits and herbs; there are marvellous pine groves, and broad fertile plains, and there is honey. There are many kinds of birds and varieties of fruit.

Mixed woods, a varied terrain, spontaneous fertility and bird-song, are the essential elements in the ideal poetic landscape from Homer onward. In the gardens of Alcinous there were trees that bore

> Fruit in his proper season all the year.
> Sweet Zephyr breathed upon them blasts that were
> Of varied tempers. These he made to bear
> Ripe fruits, these blossoms. Pear grew after pear,
> Apple succeeded apple, grape the grape,
> Fig after fig came, . . .
> And all th'adorned grounds their appearance made
> In flower and fruit. . . .

The translation is by George Chapman, who was later to write a description of British Guiana (*De Guiana. Carmen Epicum*, 1596) in very similar phrases. This fecund land also provided the background to life in the happy springtime of the human race, the Golden Age, when, according to Horace and Ovid, men had no need of iron to fight or to plough, when the untilled land yielded corn, the unpruned vine and fig tree were always in fruit, and honey flowed from the hollow oak. That the inhabitants of the newly found lands had "no iron or steel or arms, nor are they capable of using them," would not therefore have greatly surprised educated Europeans. They may indeed have read a good deal of Columbus's letter with a faint sense of *déjà vu*, visualizing the Bahamas and Cuba as being not unlike the background to Botticelli's *Primavera* or Jan van Eyck's vision of a Mediterranean paradise in which the palm, the pine, and fragrant orange flourish side by side while the ground is eternally bright with spring flowers.

This classical vision of the Indies was given its definitive form by Peter Martyr, an Italian humanist at the court of Ferdinand and Isabella and a friend of Columbus, in his *Decades de Orbe Novo* (of which the first part appeared in pirated editions in 1505 and 1511, before its official publication in 1515). Their inhabitants, he wrote, "seem to live in that golden world of which old writers speak so much, wherein men lived simply and innocently without enforcement of laws, without quarrelling, judges and libels, content only to satisfy nature." He pictured naked girls dancing "all so beautiful that one might think he beheld those splendid naiads or nymphs of the fountains, so much celebrated by the ancients." More than a century later Michael Drayton was to write of Virginia, where the "golden Age/Still Natures lawes doth give," and Andrew Marvell of the Bahamas with its "eternal Spring" in phrases which hark back to Horace and Ovid.

Sixteen editions of Columbus's letter were printed in the fifteenth century, and as none of these is known by more than one or two copies which have by chance survived, there may have been others. The first, a simple broadsheet in Spanish, was published in Barcelona in late April 1493 very shortly after Columbus went there with his cargo of parrots and Indians and gold and specimens of plants, to pay homage to Ferdinand and Isabella. Later that year a translation into Latin was printed in Rome, providing the text for further Latin editions issued in Paris, Basel, and Antwerp. A translation into Italian verse by Giuliano Dati also appeared before the end of 1493 in Florence and was reprinted four times in the next two years. So far as the vision of the new golden land is concerned, this is the most significant of all, for Dati incorporated Columbus's letter into a sixty-eight-stanza poem written in the newly fashionable *ottava rima*, which Boiardo had used for his chivalrous epic *Orlando Innamorato*, and thus set the Indies in the context of Romance.

To illustrate the Latin version of the letter the Basel publisher used, with slight modifications, woodcuts which had previously been issued with accounts of Mediterranean voyages—one inscribed *Insula hyspana* shows figures going ashore from a forty-oared galley wholly unsuitable for transatlantic travel (**FIG. 8–20**). Dati's poem was provided with a frontispiece which seems to have

8-20 • FRONTISPIECE TO THE FIRST ILLUS-TRATED EDITION OF COLUMBUS'S LETTER
Basel 1493
Courtesy of the British Library.

been specially commissioned: a king (presumably Ferdinand) is seated in the foreground watching ships approach an island on which a palm tree grows and naked figures are dancing (**FIG. 8–21**). Reminiscent of contemporary Florentine *cassone* paintings, such as *The Story of Paris* (**FIG. 8–22**), it might equally well have served to embellish a Renaissance version of the Troy legend or some tale of love and adventure like *Orlando Innamorato*.

8-21 • *COLUMBUS LANDING IN THE INDIES*
Frontispiece to Giuliano Dati's Lettera, 1493
Courtesy of the British Library.

While the letter in which Columbus had proclaimed the news of his discovery was gradually being diffused across Europe, the men who accompanied him on his second voyage were checking the realities they found against the expectations he had aroused. Columbus himself was distressed to find, on his return to the Indies, that the natives were less docile than they had at first seemed. Cannibalism was much more prevalent than he had supposed. And an Italian, better versed in natural history than he, noted that the flora not only differed from that of the Mediterranean but included plants with tempting fruits which proved to be virulently poisonous. But larger supplies of gold were found and sent back early the next year to Spain together with parrots and twenty-six Indians. Spices, the main object of trade with the Indies at this date, were also sent back but met with a less than enthusiastic reception from members of the Spanish court who sampled them—one complained that they included "so-called cinnamon, only it tasted like bad ginger; strong pepper but not with the flavour of Malayan pepper; wood said to be sandal-wood only it wasn't." At the same time reports revealed that life on Hispaniola was anything but idyllic: the explorers were in need of drugs, clothes, firearms, and even food. This was not widely publicized, however. Only one brief account of the second voyage seems to have been printed before the end of the century, by N. Scillacio in a book which also described eastward voyages, *De insulis meridiani atque indici maris nuper inventis* (Pavia, 1496).

In 1500 Pedro Álvares Cabral, in command of a Portuguese fleet bound for India by the Cape route, accidentally discovered Monte Pascoal on the Brazilian coast, decided that it was another island, stayed only long enough to find that the natives were

8-22 • DETAIL OF *THE STORY OF PARIS*
Late fifteenth century. Florentine
Courtesy of the Metropolitan Museum of Art.

friendly, and set his course for Calicut. But other navigators had already begun to exploit Columbus's discovery. Seeking another western route to the Indies, John Cabot sailed from Bristol in 1497 and Gaspare Corte Real from Lisbon in 1500, and both reached Newfoundland. No reports of these discoveries were printed for a few years (a brief letter about Corte Real is in Fracanzio da Montalboddo's *Paesi novamente retrovati*, Vicenza, 1507) but contemporary manuscript accounts, describing what they found, provide a striking contrast to Columbus's letter. They had found waters abounding in codfish, a land heavily forested with tall pine trees, and many animals and birds similar to those of Northern Europe. The inhabitants, some of whom were brought back to Lisbon in 1500 and (by Bristol merchants) to London in 1501, aroused some curiosity. They were "clothid in beastys skinnys," an English chronicler reported, "ete Rawe Flesh," and had the manners of "bruyt bestis." Alberto Cantino, ambassador of the Duke of Ferrara in Lisbon, not only saw but "touched and examined these people" and found them well formed, but noted the strange tattooing on their faces and remarked that their speech though unintelligible "was not harsh but almost human." However, they had "the most bestial manners and habits, like wild men." Clearly, the land they came from, though useful for stockfish and timber, would never nourish a vision like that of the Indies.

Cantino had a map made to record the new discoveries and mark the line which, by the Treaty of Tordesillas, determined the Portuguese and Spanish zones (**FIG. 8–23**). Here Newfoundland appears as an island with tall trees set in mid-Atlantic just to the east of the dividing line. To the south lies Brazil, an exotic country of mixed forests and swampy lagoons animated with brilliantly colored parrots (already clearly and correctly distinguished from those of Africa). Another map of 1502 (in the Staatsbibliothek, Munich) depicts a Brazilian cooking a human being—the first of many visual images of American cannibals. A distinct picture of South America was beginning to emerge and was soon given definitive literary expression in Vespucci's *Mundus Novus*, first published in Latin in Paris in 1503, translated into five modern languages, and reissued in some thirty editions before 1515, in England, Italy, Germany, the Netherlands, and Portugal.

Vespucci was not strictly truthful about himself. He antedated by two significant years his first voyage of 1499 and claimed to have been in command of it. And much of what he says of Brazil and its inhabitants seems to be the product of a fertile imagination, though perhaps as much that of his translator as his own, for the original text of the letter from which the *Mundus Novus* is derived is unfortunately lost. But he gave European readers the kind of information they wanted. Whereas Columbus had been cautious, vague, and on the sexual mores of the Indians, reticent, Vespucci was emphatic, explicit, and salacious. But like Columbus, he also set the New World (as he called it) in the context of the

European classical tradition. Of the region he named Venezuela (because the villages built on piles in the water reminded him of Venice), he declared the climate to be so temperate that there were neither cold winters nor hot summers. The inhabitants lived without private possessions, laws, kings, or lords; they had no churches and were not idolaters.

What more can I say? They live according to nature, rather as Epicureans so far as they can, than Stoics.

But despite all this, it is the exotic element that predominates in his account of the Indians. He revealed to a wondering Europe that they were not merely naked and wholly unashamed but had no hair on their bodies. The women were sexually attractive, even after childbirth, and also extremely libidinous. To satisfy their excessive lasciviousness they enlarged the penises of their lovers by the application of venomous insects—sometimes with fatal consequences. On the subject of cannibalism, to which Columbus had merely alluded in his published letter, Vespucci provided gruesomely circumstantial details.

I met a man who told me that he had eaten more than three hundred human bodies. And I spent twenty seven days in a town where I saw cured human flesh hung up in the houses as we hang up hams in ours. They are amazed that we do not eat our enemies and use their flesh for food which, they say, is very tasty.

Another longer publication, *Lettera di Amerigo Vespucci delle Isole Nuovamente Trovate*—known as the "Soderini letter" from the name of its recipient—first printed in Florence in 1505 and promptly translated into German, provided a still more vivid account of life among the Indians (and may depart still further than the *Mundus Novus* from Vespucci's original text). Here they were said to have no riches apart from brightly colored feathers and necklaces of fish bones and small stones. They did not trade and neither cultivated the land nor kept domesticated animals for food. Without regular mealtimes, they ate when they pleased from the floor. They obeyed no one, had no system of justice, and did not even chastise their children. Although they had no inhibitions about urinating publicly—in the course of a conversation if need be—they were pleasantly reticent about defecating and washed frequently (rather more, one suspects, than Europeans of the day). At night they slept in nets, soon to be known in Europe by their Carib name: hammocks. The strange wildlife of South America was described—the brilliance of the flowers, the diversity of the birds, and a reptile called *basilisco* or dragon, which is recognizably an iguana. This publication also gave an account of Vespucci's hair-raising adventures on his "four" (in fact, only three) expeditions.

To illustrate the Soderini letter, the Florentine printer copied the frontispiece to Dati's poetic version of Columbus's letter,

8-23 • AMERICAN SECTION OF THE CANTINO WORLD MAP, 1502

8-24 • FRONTISPIECE TO VESPUCCI'S *DE ORA ANTARCTICA (MUNDUS NOVUS)*
Strassburg, 1505

while a Milanese reprinted a woodcut previously used for an edition of Mandeville. But in Germany, where Vespucci seems to have been particularly popular, much more elaborate illustrations were provided for it and for the *Mundus Novus.* Curious naked figures apparently playing some childlike game appear on the title page of the *Mundus Novus* printed in Strassburg **(FIG. 8–24)**. And an early German edition of the Soderini letter, published in the same city in 1509, has woodcuts depicting several incidents described in it. A group of savages is shown conversing while one of them urinates and in the background a butcher chops up human limbs. In another, a wild naked woman swings a club to kill a European who is chatting with other members of her tribe **(FIG. 8–25)**. The combination of nudity and a light-colored skin, together with their outlandish behavior, characterize these figures as natives of the New World. In some editions, however, the natives are merely naked Europeans—occasionally even with long, curly Düreresque beards and hair **(FIG. 8–26)**.

From these descriptions and the more vivid prints a single dominant image of America began to emerge and soon found further visual expression. On a broadsheet printed by Jan van Doesborch in Antwerp, describing the many discoveries made on behalf of the King of Portugal, the people of America are represented by a group of naked cannibals. Another sheet, published in Germany (probably Augsburg or Nuremberg) in about 1505, consists of a large woodcut **(FIG. 8–27)** and several lines of text neatly summarizing the European conception of the New World at this date.

> The people are thus naked, handsome, brown, well-formed in body, their heads, necks, arms, privy parts, feet of women and men are slightly covered with feathers. The men also have many precious stones in their faces and breasts. No one owns anything but all things are in common. And the men have as wives those that please them, be they mothers, sisters or friends, therein they make no difference. They also fight with each other. They also eat each other even those who are slain, and hang the flesh of them in smoke. They live one hundred and fifty years. And have no government.

Though based almost word for word on Vespucci, this shows how much the New World still formed part of the Orient of Mandeville, in whose island of Lamary it was

> the custom for men and women to go all naked. . . . And they marry there no wives, for all the women are common. . . . And all land and property also is common, nothing being shut up, or kept under lock, one man being as rich as another. But in that country there is a cursed custom for they eat more gladly of man's flesh than any other flesh.

The newly found territories were still called islands, but Vespucci had discovered "what we may rightly call a New World . . . a continent more densely peopled and abounding in animals than our Europe or Asia or Africa." Very soon afterward, in 1507, Martin Waldseemüller, a young professor of geography at the college of Saint-Dié in Lorraine, delineated the New World as a vast continent in his edition of Ptolemy. Making what can have been no more than a guess—but a very intelligent guess—he created a single geographical entity by joining up the discoveries of Columbus with those of Vespucci in the south and of Cabot and Corte Real in the north. Since this fourth part of the world had "been discovered by Americus Vesputius," he wrote, "I do not see why there should be any objection to its being called after Americus the discoverer, a man of natural wisdom, Land of Americus or America, since both Europe and Asia have derived their names from women." On his map he placed the name *America* far down in the south—below a parrot symbolizing its natural products—and within half a century *America* was being used to designate the whole continent by most Europeans—apart, that is, from Spaniards who obstinately persisted in calling it *Las Indias.*

Yet despite Waldseemüller, who separated the new continent from China by a fairly wide stretch of water, most Europeans

8-25 • ILLUSTRATIONS TO VESPUCCI'S LETTER TO SODERINI
Strassburg, 1509

8-26A • ILLUSTRATION TO VESPUCCI'S *MUNDUS NOVUS*
Probably Rostock, 1505
Courtesy of the British Library.

8-26B • ILLUSTRATIONS TO VESPUCCI'S *MUNDUS NOVUS*
Dutch translation, c.1506–10
Courtesy of the British Library.

(including the cartographers) continued for many years to see America as the farthest extension of Asia. Similarly, no distinctions were as yet generally drawn between the West and East Indies. (Vasco da Gama had opened up the sea route to Calcutta in 1497–99, attracting rather more contemporary attention than Columbus.) Thus, in the early sixteenth century, the Portuguese painter of an Epiphany represented one of the Wise Men from the East as a Brazilian. Still more significantly, the artists who depicted the "people of Calicut" in the pictorial triumphal procession devised by the Emperor Maximilian I in 1512 showed them in the guise of American Indians. A German artist, perhaps Albrecht Altdorfer, in his gilded and exquisitely colored paintings on vellum gave them headdresses, skirts, and leg bands of feathers (**FIG. 8–28**).

Brazilians had been brought back to Europe from at least as early as 1505—when Binot Palmier de Gonneville returned with the son of a Tupinamba chief, Essomericq—and one of them or specimens of their accouterment must have reached Germany by 1515, for in that year no less an artist than Albrecht Dürer drew

8-27 • *THE PEOPLE OF THE ISLANDS RECENTLY DISCOVERED . . .*,
c.1505. German, probably Augsburg or Nuremberg
Courtesy of the Bayerisches National Museum.

8-28 • THE TRIUMPH OF MAXIMILIAN I
1512–16. Attributed to Albrecht Altdorfer
Courtesy of The Trustees of the British Museum.

8-29 • PAGE FROM THE PRAYER BOOK OF MAXIMILIAN I
1515. Albrecht Dürer
John R. Freeman & Co./Bayerisches Staatsbibliothek

an Indian with an accurately depicted Tupinamba feather cap and scepter in the margin of a Book of Hours he decorated for Maximilian I (FIG. 8–29). Together with an Oriental leading a camel on the next page, he illustrates the Twenty-fourth Psalm: "The earth is the Lord's and all that therein is: the compass of the world and they that dwell therein." Drawn with Dürer's exquisite linear sensitivity, this is incomparably the most beautiful sixteenth-century depiction of an Indian, although he looks more like a snub-nosed German youth dressed up for a Nuremberg pageant than a genuine Tupinamba.

That such figures were still associated indiscriminately with the East or the West is shown by Jorg Breu's illustrations to the 1515 Augsburg edition of Lodovico de Varthema's book of Eastern travels, *Die ritterliche Reise*, in which he depicted the inhabitants of Sumatra clad in feather caps and skirts. Similarly in Burgkmair's *The Triumph of Maximilian I* (drawn in about 1516 but not printed until 1526) the "people of Calicut" include feather-clad figures mingling with women and children, some totally naked apart from a few bangles, others carrying parrots, monkeys,

baskets of tropical fruit, and heads of Indian corn (the first in European art) and accompanied by the garlanded cows and fat-tailed sheep of Asia (FIG. 8–30A). Another German artist in the same circle, or perhaps Burgkmair, made two drawings of similar figures, one of whom carries a Mexican shield which could not, of course, have been seen or known in Europe until after 1519 (FIG. 8–30B).

Between 1519 and 1522 two events which were to transform the idea of the newly discovered lands took place contemporaneously: the circumnavigation of the world and the conquest of Mexico. Both helped to dissociate America from Asia, but in different ways. For while the one demonstrated the vast extent of the Pacific Ocean, the other revealed the potentialities of the New World, its barely credible riches and the existence in it of a civilization totally dissimilar from those of Asia with which Europeans had for centuries been familiar. It is perhaps significant that the Mexicans sent over to Europe by Cortés aroused far greater curiosity than Columbus's Indians, for they could be recognized as the denizens of a wholly New World rather than just as savages or members of some very remote Asiatic tribe. Nevertheless, it was the circumnavigation that seems to have had the more immediate influence.

The aim of Ferdinand Magellan, admiral in charge of this first journey around the world on which he lost his life, was to find a westerly route to the Spice Islands, believing them to be "no great distance from Panama and the Gulf of San Miguel" sighted by Balboa in 1513. After discovering the straits which were to be named after him and sailing up the southwest coast of America, Magellan was completely unprepared for a journey of eighty-eight days before reaching the Philippines—more than twice as long as Columbus's first crossing of the Atlantic. The narrative of the voyage by one of the few survivors, Antonio Pigafetta, first published in 1525 and frequently reprinted in the following years, left readers in no doubt about the width of the Pacific and thus the magnitude of Columbus's error. It also added some details to the picture of America—notably the giants of Patagonia, who performed a strange trick of swallowing arrows and pulling them out again without hurting themselves (as they were to be shown doing on many maps and prints). South America, however, became simply a hazard encountered on the way to the fabulously rich East Indian islands which Pigafetta described with far greater enthusiasm. The cargo of spices picked up there and brought home on the *Victoria* yielded more than enough money to pay for the equipment of the five ships which had set off in 1519. (The coat of arms which the Castilian heralds prepared for its captain, Elcano, bore two crossed cinnamon sticks, three nutmegs, and twelve cloves with Malay kings—not Patagonians—as supporters).

"America was discovered accidentally," Admiral Morison has recently remarked: "when discovered it was not wanted; and most of the exploration for the next fifty years was done in the hope of getting through or around it." The northern coast was investigated mainly in the hope of finding a passage less roundabout and per-

8-30A • DETAIL FROM *THE TRIUMPH OF MAXIMILIAN I*
1526. Hans Burgkmair
Courtesy of The Trustees of the British Museum.

ilous than that through the Straits of Magellan to what Giovanni da Verrazzano called "the happy shores of Cathay." With this as his objective he explored the coast from Cape Fear (in what is now North Carolina) to Maine on behalf of the King of France in 1524. "I did not expect to find such an obstacle of new land as I have found," he wrote; "and if for some reason I did expect to find it, I estimated there would be some strait to get through to the Eastern Ocean." Between 1534 and 1545 Jacques Cartier pursued the search further north, finding the St. Lawrence in the process. As the size and impenetrability of the continent was revealed a still more northern passage was sought, especially by the English who convinced themselves of its existence. In 1566 Sir Humphrey

8-30B • *INDIAN HOLDING A MEXICAN SHIELD*
Post 1519. Attributed to Hans Burgkmair
Courtesy of The Trustees of the British Museum.

Gilbert confidently declared that "any man of our country that will give the attempt, may with small danger passe in Cataia" by this route and reach "all other places in the East, in much shorter time than either the Spaniard or the Portingale doth."

The picture of North America which emerged from accounts of these voyages was hardly enticing. "I am inclined to regard this land as the one God gave to Cain," Jacques Cartier wrote of the barren coast of Labrador in 1534. And a member of Frobisher's expedition to the Northwest in 1577 remarked:

> In place of odiferous and fragrant smells of sweet gums, and pleasant notes of musical birds, which other countries in more temperate zones do yield, we tasted the most boisterous Boreal blasts mixed with snow and hail in the months of June and July, nothing inferior to our intemperate winter.

And this is fully borne out by a contemporary drawing of one of their encounters with the Eskimos in those icy solitudes (FIG. 8–31), perhaps that at Bloody Point on August 1, 1577, when Frobisher observed a "number of small things fleeting in the sea afarre off" which he supposed to be porpoises or seals until coming nearer he "discovered them to be men in small boats made of leather." The terrain in what was later to become the southern United States was much more attractive. Verrazzano named part of the coast "Archadia" because of the beauty of the trees which seems to have reminded him of Arcady as described by Virgil or, more recently, Jacopo Sannazaro. Just such a landscape is delicately delineated on a Portuguese map, probably drawn in 1525 by Lopo Homem, where it is labeled *Terra Bimene*, the fabulous island of the fountain of youth which Ponce de León was seeking when he discovered Florida (FIG. 8–32). But its wildlife is distinctly northern—birds like those of Europe, bears, deer, and a fox—in striking contrast with the balancing vignette of the South American scene where naked savages dig for gold.

"It is to the South, not to the icy North, that everyone in search of fortune should turn," wrote Peter Martyr in 1525; "below the equator everything is rich." Some explorers persisted, however, in hoping to find in the north another empire as rich as those of the Aztecs and the Incas. Cartier sought the mythical Kingdom of Saguenay of which Indians had told him. An English sailor David Ingram boasted of finding near the Penobscot estuary the city of Norumbega with streets larger than any of those in London and inhabitants who wore hoops of gold and silver "garnished with pearls, divers of them as big as one's thumb." Expeditions were dispatched to this wholly imaginary place which was even marked on maps. Martin Frobisher claimed to have discovered gold in the far north in 1576, though it turned out to be only iron pyrites.

The story of Norumbega and the hope of finding gold mines in the North were, of course, inspired by the accounts of Mexico and Peru which gradually focused attention on America for its own sake and not merely as an obstacle in the passage to the Orient. "How much the richest empire in the world is that of these Indies," wrote Fernández de Oviedo in 1535, and many other similar comments could be quoted. Gold was the magnet which drew men to explore the new continent. Yet the interest which sixteenth-century Europeans took in America, even with its promise of gold, should not be exaggerated. In an age when travel literature flourished, with such compendia of voyages as those edited by Fracanzio da Montalboddo in Vincenza and by Ramusio in Venice and Hakluyt in England, the discovery of America played by no means the most prominent part. Many more books were written about other parts of the world. In France between 1480 and 1609 twice as many books and ten times as many pamphlets were devoted to the Islamic lands.

That Charles V should have made no allusion to his American empire in his memoirs (even though the book is a political apologia rather than an autobiography) is also very striking. No less so is the fact that whereas a great series of tapestries was woven to commemorate his conquest of Tunis in 1535, which seems a relatively trivial incident in retrospect, no official works of art were commissioned to record the conquest of Peru the previous year. The main reason for this neglect seems to have been economic. Not until after the chance discovery of the silver mines of Potosí in 1545 and the settlement of the wars between the colonists in Peru a decade later did Hispanic America begin to yield substantial profits to the Spanish Crown (FIG. 8–33). In 1554 America was producing no more than 11 percent of the Spanish Crown's total income, and this did not swell to as much as 25 percent until the 1590s, partly because of a decline in other sources of wealth. At the same time increased production in Peru, made possible by a new technique of treating the ore introduced in 1571, substantially reduced the relative value of silver itself. These sobering facts were known only to the Crown officials, of course. Tales of vast fortunes made by individual conquistadors and exaggerated contemporary estimates of the amount of gold and silver shipped to Spain (some of which was captured en route and diverted to England) were, however, on everyone's lips and played a major part in the formation of the late sixteenth-century American image. Describing the supposed wealth of Guiana in 1595, Sir Walter Raleigh wrote:

> Although these reports may seem strange, yet if we consider the many millions which are daily brought out of Peru into Spain, we may easily believe the same: for we find that by the abundant treasure of that country the Spanish King vexeth all the princes of Europe, and is become, in a few years, from a poor King of Castille, the greatest monarch of the World.

Other imports from the New World—mainly beaver pelts, dried cod, and dyewood—could not as yet compete with the spices of the East Indies.

Of course, gold had glittered in the vision of America from the very beginning, in the accounts of Columbus and Vespucci, but it became much more prominent after the conquest of Mexico and Peru. Almost simultaneously, however, a new image

8-31 • *ENGLISH SAILORS IN A SKIRMISH WITH ESKIMO*
1577. By or after John White
Courtesy of The Trustees of the British Museum.

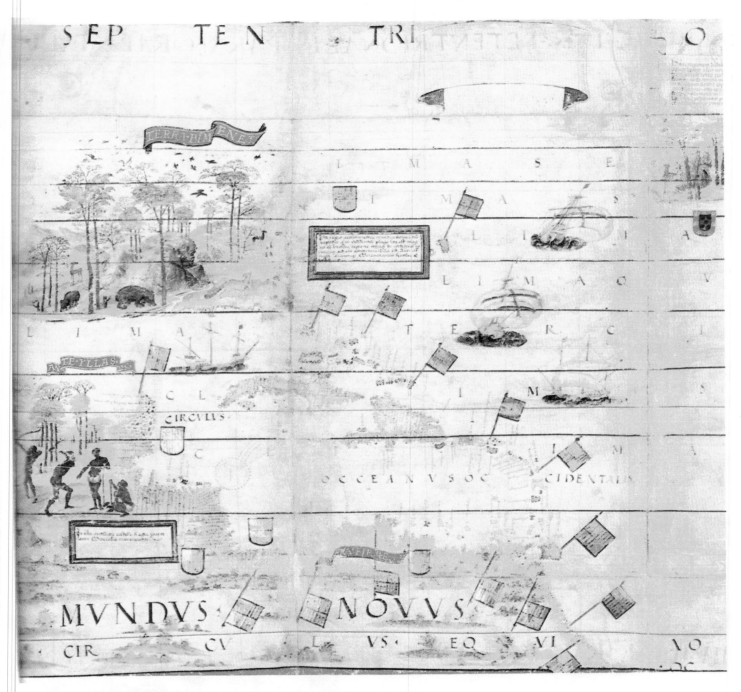

8-32 • WESTERN HEMISPHERE OF THE "MILLER" WORLD MAP, 1525. Attributed to Lopo Homem
Courtesy of The Bibliotheque Nationale de France.

was superimposed on those of the classical Golden Age and fabulous East. Once again it took its form from a long established European literary tradition—that of the *chansons de geste*, especially those which recounted the deeds of Christian knights humbling the proud paynims. This transposition was due perhaps, in the first place, to the coincidence that the centuries-long war to drive the Moors out of Spain had ended, as Columbus himself pointed out in the dedication of his logbook, on the very eve of

the discovery of America. And some of the energy previously expended on it was diverted to the conquest of the New World. Cortés referred to the Aztec temples as "mosques" and there can be little doubt that he saw himself as a champion of Christendom waging a holy war against the infidel. His accounts of combats between his men, shouting the time-honored battle cry *Señor Santiago*, and vast hordes of Mexicans seem almost to have been modeled on descriptions of those between the Spaniards and

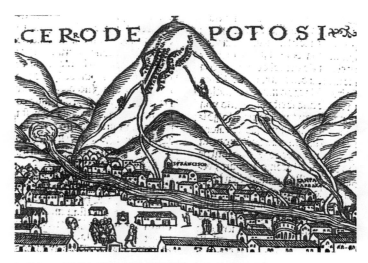

8-33 • THE SILVER MINES OF POTOSÍ
from Cieza de León, *Chronica del Peru*, 1553
Courtesy of Lilly Library, Indiana University Bloomington.

Moors. After one of them he knighted a converted Indian ally on the field. And Bernal Diaz, a soldier who served under Cortés, invoked the famous romance of *Amadis de Gaul* to describe his first sight of Tenochtitlán. The riches and luxury of this city, with its teeming markets, its handsome palaces and gardens, were very much of the kind previously associated with Islam; as were the manners and tastes of Montezuma and his courtiers, so reminiscent of the caliphs. (Polygamy and paederasty were common to both societies.) On the map of Tenochtitlán, illustrating a Nuremberg edition of the letters of Cortés published in 1524 (and copied elsewhere), a bold inscription marks Montezuma's *domus ad voluptate*, presumably his seraglio, the only explicitly Aztec features on the map being the central square with temples inscribed "where they sacrifice." In this way the conquest of Mexico was readily absorbed into the late medieval view of the world, and it is very tempting to see an allusion to it in a peculiar battle scene between Europeans in armor and naked, dark-skinned savages in the background of a votive picture of the *Virgin of the Palm* (or Victory) painted for Amiens Cathedral in 1520, the year in which news of Cortés's exploits first reached Europe **(FIG. 8–34)**.

The conquest of Mexico was also interpreted apocalyptically, almost as a confirmation of Columbus's mystical interpretation of his discovery. For the speedy conversion of the Mexicans could be seen as the fulfilment of one of the prophecies of the Apocalypse, as one of the events which were to precede the millennial kingdom of Christ. In his farewell sermon to the first twelve friars sent there, the minister-general of the Franciscans quoted the parable of the laborers in the vineyard, adding: "The day of the world is already reaching the eleventh hour; you of the Father of the family are called to go to the vineyard." Later in the century another Franciscan, Gerónimo de Mendieta, was to prophesy the imminent creation of an ideal theocratic state—a true City of God—

in the New World, more than compensating for the Church's losses to Protestantism in the Old, which he dismissed as the City of Man. He and others believed in the westward spread of Christianity, initiating the idea that was to be extended by Bishop Berkeley in the eighteenth century ("Westward the course of Empire . . .") and, as we shall see, completely transformed by Karl Marx in the nineteenth.

A very different view of the *Conquista* is presented in a picture probably dating from the 1540s and certainly from before 1555–56 when the artist, Jan Mostaert, died **(FIG. 8–35)**. This remarkable work depicts an imaginary scene of the conquest, not any specific incident. (Several scholars have tried to find evidence to the contrary but none is convincing.) The pastoral landscape, similar to that which Mostaert provided for Adam and Eve in another painting, is such as European readers of Columbus might well have imagined to exist in the Indies. And the stark naked figures with the lithe, athletic, well-proportioned bodies of Greek and Roman warriors drawn by Mantegna, Pollaiuolo, and others accord perfectly with the Indians as seen through the spectacles of a Renaissance humanist. Only the strange straw huts and a monkey squatting on a tree stump are manifestly exotic. It is a vision of the Golden Age of the Indies glimpsed at the moment when it is shattered by Spanish steel. While sheep and cows browse impassively on this fresh, green breast of the New World, the naked inhabitants, clutching primitive weapons, streak across the panel to encounter a posse of Europeans with pikes and halberds and cannon remorselessly advancing from the shore where they have beached their boats. Mostaert no doubt had personal experience of the behavior of Spanish soldiers and the picture may well allude, if only obliquely, to their activities in his native Low Countries. But more generally, it is a visual parable on the innocence and peace of unspoilt nature and the destructive urge of civilized man—a parallel to his painting of Eve banished from the pastoral dream of Eden, with Cain killing Abel nearby. It is a theme which was to echo down the ages in America.

The Black Legend of Spanish cruelty, which has a long medieval history, acquired still darker tones after the conquest of America. The man mainly responsible for adding them was himself a Spaniard. Bartolomé de las Casas, who had gone to the Indies as an adventurer, acquired an *encomienda* (a feudal grant of land with Indians to work it), but took holy orders, was suddenly struck with revulsion at the treatment of the native population by his fellow *encomienderos*, and devoted the rest of his life to its protection. In the early 1540s he wrote his *Brévissima relación de las destrucción de las Indias*, a bitter denunciation of the principles and practice of Spanish imperialism which was intended only for the eyes of officials but seems to have circulated widely in manuscript. (Mostaert may well have known of it.) The work was seized on by Europeans who were generally less concerned with the plight of the Indians in the New World than with the pretensions of Spain in the Old. And the fact that its author was a member of the Dominican Order, which staffed the hated and feared Inquisition,

8-34 • DETAIL OF *THE VIRGIN OF THE PALM*
1520. School of Amiens
Courtesy of Musee di Picardie, France.

gave it a special significance for Protestants in the Hapsburg lands. It was translated into Flemish in 1578, French in 1579 (as *Tyrannies et cruautés des Espagnols*), English in 1583, and German in 1597.

The cruelties of the Spaniards were also described in lurid detail by Girolamo Benzoni, a native of Milan (under Spanish rule from 1535), in his *Historia del mondo nuovo*, which was first published in 1565 and enjoyed success both widespread and enduring (outside Italy thirty-two editions were printed before the end of the eighteenth century). Providing a pocket history of America from the arrival of Columbus to the conquest of Peru, interspersed with lively anecdotes of Benzoni's own experiences in the Spanish colonies, this book denounced the treatment meted out not only to Indians but also (and for the first time in print) to the black slaves imported from Africa. But if the Spaniards are the villains of this piece, the Indians and Africans are no more than hapless victims. The same could be said of the accounts of American voyages published by Richard Hakluyt from 1582, though they also are provided with white Anglo-Saxon Protestant heroes who here make their bow on the American scene.

Benzoni's history fills three of the ten fully illustrated volumes in the collection of books on America issued by a Frankfurt publisher and engraver, Theodor de Bry, from 1590 to 1618. In them we can watch the gradual superimposition of one American image over another unfold before our eyes. It begins serenely in the pastoral paradise of Thomas Hariot's *Briefe and true report of the new found land of Virginia* (1590), illustrated by engravings after John White's watercolors made on the expedition, and it proceeds to an account of the brief golden age of happy relations between the French and Indians in Florida. Menacing clouds appear over the horizon in the third volume, which reprints Hans Staden's narrative of his adventures among the cannibals of Brazil. Then come the three Benzoni volumes vividly illustrating the atrocities committed by the gold-obsessed Spaniards **(FIG. 8–36)** and also the gangsterism among themselves **(FIG. 8–37)**. A later volume, taken over from Hakluyt, is devoted to the predominantly anti-Spanish activities of Drake and Raleigh. The Indians are thus gradually reduced to the role of "extras" in the great drama of European expansion. And when they reappear more prominently in illustrations to a digest of John Smith's *General History of Virginia, New England and the Summer Isles*, they figure as little more than an inconvenient hindrance to the establishment of a Protestant colony.

In such ways, despite the steadily increasing interest they held for philosophers and missionaries, and the fear they continued to inspire in settlers, the Indians were steadily pushed to the back of the European picture of America. Sometimes they were almost pushed out of it altogether. When the first large-scale works of art on American subjects were finally commissioned in Spain in the early 1630s—as part of a series celebrating recent victories, notable mainly because it includes Velázquez's *Surrender of Breda*—Eugenio Caxés painted *The Recovery of San Juan de Puerto Rico* (from the Dutch) and *The Recovery of the Island of San Cristobal* (from the English) and Juan Bautista Maino, *The Recovery of Bahia in Brazil* (from the Dutch) **(FIG. 8–38)**. The figures in these enormous canvases are all Europeans except in the third where two diminutive Indians may be dimly discerned on the beach in the background.

Thus, little more than a century after its discovery, America had already become, in fact and not just in a literary sense, an extension of Europe. In 1516 Thomas More had described Utopia as an island near those recently discovered by Vespucci, and its wise inhabitants were indigenous. But later dreams of an ideal state were usually located in a New World populated exclusively by Europeans. Nor were they merely fantasies. Sir Humphrey Gilbert—a reader of *Utopia*—drew up plans for a colony which he hoped to establish, ruled by a governor with an elected council, free housing provided for poor immigrants, land set apart for the support of a hospital, "learning, lectures, scholars and other good and godely uses," with all the colonists enjoying the rights of free-born Englishmen. And the chronicler of his voyages complacently remarked that it seemed "as if God has prescribed limits unto their Spanish nation which they might not exceed," apparently reserving North America for the English!—a land fit for English settlers!—"Earth's onely Paradise," as in Michael Drayton's Virginia of 1606:

> Where Nature hath in store
> Fowle, Venison and Fish,
> And the Fruitfull'st Soyle,
> Without your Toyle,
> Three Harvests more,
> All greater than your Wish.

8-35 • A WEST INDIAN SCENE

c.1540–50. Jan Mostaert

Courtesy of Frans Hals Museum.

8-36 • *THE SPANISH TREATMENT OF FUGITIVE BLACK SLAVES*
From T. de Bry, *America*, Part V, 1595
Courtesy of the British Library.

8-37 • *THE ASSASSINATION OF PIZARRO*
From T. de Bry, *America*, Part VI, 1596
Courtesy of the British Library.

8-38 • *THE RECOVERY OF BAHIA IN BRAZIL* 1635. Juan Bautista Maino *Courtesy of Museo Nationale del Prado.*

INTRODUCTION

Gerald McMaster and Lee-Ann Martin

To be an Aboriginal★ person, to identify with an indigenous heritage in these late colonial times, requires a life of reflection, critique, persistence and struggle.

> Our histories show that whenever new people came to this land, they had to follow its laws if they wished to stay. The Chiefs who were already here had the responsibility to teach the law to the newcomers. If it was not, the newcomers had to pay compensation and leave. The Gitksan and Wet'suwet'en have waited and observed the Europeans for a hundred years. The Chiefs have suggested that the newcomers may want to stay on their farms and in their towns and villages, but beyond the farm fences the land belongs to the Chiefs. Once this has been recognized, the Court can get on with its main task which is to establish a process for the Chiefs' and the newcomers' interests to be settled.

★ Note that the terms "Native," "Aboriginal," "First Nations," and "indigenous" are used interchangeably to refer to Canada's original inhabitants of Indian, Inuit and Metis ancestry.

Do not make the commonly made error that it is a people that we abhor, be clear that it is systems and processors which we must attack. Be clear that change to those systems will be promoted by people who can perceive intelligent and non-threatening alternatives.

This year, in Western time, marks the convergence of innumerable anniversaries, high among them the 1492 landfall of an Italian sailor, Christopher Columbus (Cristóbal Colón), in the Americas (Turtle Island).

Indigenous time, on the other hand, will mark this year as any other since time immemorial, giving thanks to the Creator in various festivals celebrating humankind's survival.

This time period, 1492–1992, has a five-hundred-year parallel history, Native and non-Native. The non-Native version tells of Columbus's "discovery" of the "New World." Not only have indigenous people disputed this claim since 1492, but numerous, highly respected writers of "official" History have also begun to see the facts differently. Those who were planning celebrations of "discovery" hastily revised their proposals to read "meeting of two worlds," or "encounters."

The subtext to all the rhetoric is that colonization began in 1492. Columbus's insistence that a number of indigenous people be taken back to Spain, obviously against their will, was the beginning of a five-hundred-year legacy of religious, cultural, social, economic and political intolerance that is still at every level of modern society.

In the Native version of history, figuratively and mythically, perhaps, indigenous people may have been floating on the Turtle's back, as the Iroquois believe. More meaningful to contemporary indigenous peoples are the developments and achievements of the previous thousands of years—linguistically, culturally, socially, philosophically, politically and economically. That moment of convergence and subsequent merger with the newcomer was the beginning of a mere five-hundred-year moment in Native history!

From that time on, however, indigenous peoples have been subordinate in official History, and the denial and erosion of indigenous history by the newcomers has effected lasting damage, rendering indigenous peoples all but invisible. Without a place in History, they've become objects for study, seen as "the mythic image of a 'natural man' who lived before history and civilisation," who was pure, free and simple, resembling the flora and the fauna.

In this quincentennial year of written historical contact, significant international attention will be paid to the themes of discovery, exploration and encounter. While the rest of the world revels in its accomplishments, indigenous peoples will reflect on this "meeting of cultures," addressing such issues as historicity, cultural conquest, Aboriginal title, identity and sovereignty. Perhaps there will be something to celebrate—aside from a nautical error—if 1992 can be a date when consciousness about indigenous histories and continued existence begins to be presented to a substantial audience throughout the world.

THE CONTEXT

In 1492, Europe was a world in decay. Death and pessimism dominated everyday life. Judicial, political and church-sanctioned violence rivalled that of the common criminal. Epidemic diseases periodically reduced the population of some cities by fifty percent. In addition, without the staple crops of potatoes and corn that the Americas would contribute, famine was frequent.

Certain social and intellectual tenets began to affect the world view of fifteenth-century Europe. Humanism elevated the human being above all species, supported the imperative of human domination and justified the new age of imperialism. Rationalism's pragmatic approach created a milieu of curiosity, restlessness and the need to explain and explore. This culture of science effectively reduced nature to a secular, rather than sacred, realm, and had long-lasting results in both technology and philosophy. For example, technological superiority enabled Europe to develop a seafaring power far beyond what its size or population suggested, and new technologies, especially the printing press and the gun, had an enormous impact. Finally, materialism, the celebration and possession of material goods, dominated the ethical and religious frameworks of European society.

The above conditions, in conjunction with the rise of nations, preceded the age of exploration. Beleaguered by a sense of doom at home, Europeans looked for a new frame of reference in both time and space as the key to their survival. Are things so much different today?

Ironically, the significance of Columbus's voyages was not immediately recognized in Europe. Only later did Columbus come to symbolize the complex of ideas and myths and dreams that characterized European expansion. Furthermore, he personified qualities of risk-taking and adventurism which were held in high esteem by a society based on individualism, materialism and rationalism.

While the myth of the "New World" as the land of innocence and abundance grew, so did the symbolic significance of Columbus's "discovery." The American continent came to be viewed as a land of regeneration and salvation in which to escape the horrors of European society, and accumulate wealth and status.

Paradoxically—and significantly for future relations of peoples on the American continent—the "discovery of the New World" glorified the European ethic and world view of the time while denying that the continent was fully explored and inhabited by many peoples. The process of bestowing European place names and denying Aboriginal title and ownership exemplifies the appropriation and possession that was central to the European approach. Why would colonists assume these lands were unclaimed and unnamed?

In fact, they overlooked the opportunity to learn about the peoples and the land. In their ignorance of the cultural practices that had enabled Aboriginal peoples to flourish for centuries, the colonists introduced to the continent a legacy of conquest, conversion, cumulation and control.

TECHNIQUE, TEXTILES, AND TEXT

THOUGHT PIECE

INTRODUCTION

A comparison between prehistoric and present-day textiles demonstrates the lack of logic in a linear history, which takes us from simple to complex, or from plain to patterned. Many of the materials, techniques and forms used in ancient times remain in use today, both as essential aspects of production in many regions of the world and as ingredients in textile arts. Such continuity makes textiles unique among all artifacts. The fact that their making often involves the creation of the 'ingredients'—unlike working with wood or stone—makes them extremely complex and particularly revealing of human ingenuity. It can be argued that as indicators of cultural mechanisms, textiles offer insights into the greatest range of developments, embracing not only technology, agriculture and trade, but also ritual, tribute, language, art and personal identity.

The relationship of textiles to writing is especially significant, not only for the cuneiform-like qualities of many patterns, but also for the parallels between ink on papyrus and pigment on bark cloth. There is, in fact, little difference between the two. Such connections are implied in many textile terms. For example, the Indian full-colour painted and printed 'kalamkari' are so named from the Persian for pen, *kalam*; the wax for Indonesian batiks is delivered by a copper-bowled *tulis*, also meaning pen. The European term for hand-colouring of details on cloth is 'pencilling'. And the Islamic term *tiraz*, originally denoting embroideries, came to encompass all textiles within this culture that carried inscriptions. With or without inscriptions, textiles convey all kinds of 'texts': allegiances are expressed, promises are made (as in today's bank notes, whose value is purely conceptual), memories are preserved, new ideas are proposed. Many anthropological and ethnographical studies of textiles aim at teaching us how to read these cloth languages anew. The 'plot' is provided by the socially meaningful elements; the 'syntax' is the construction, often only revealed by the application of archaeological and conservation analyses. Equally, the most creative textiles of today exploit a vocabulary of fibres, dyes and techniques. Textiles can be prose or poetry, instructive or the most demanding of texts. The ways in which they are used—and reused—add more layers of meaning, all significant indicators of sensitivities that can be traced back at least ten thousand years.

—Mary Schoeser, "Introduction," *World Textiles, A Concise History* (Thames & Hudson Inc., London and New York, 2003), pp. 7–8.

THINGS TO CONSIDER

- How do practices in textiles compare across cultures? How do textiles serve as texts?
- What is the role of the decorative arts and decoration in early modern Europe?
- How does the study of technique help us understand the art and culture of a particular place and time?

EUROPEAN MANUSCRIPT ILLUMINATION

By the late thirteenth century, private prayer books became popular among wealthy patrons. Because they contained special prayers to be recited at the eight canonical devotional "hours" between morning and night, an individual copy of one of these books came to be called a **Book of Hours**. Such a book included everything the lay person needed for pious practice—psalms, prayers to and offices of the Virgin and other saints (like the owner's patron or the patron of their home church), a calendar of feast days, and sometimes prayers for the dead. During the fourteenth century, a richly decorated Book of Hours was worn or carried like jewelry, counting among a noble person's most important portable possessions.

THE BOOK OF HOURS OF JEANNE D'ÉVREUX. Perhaps at their marriage in 1324, King Charles IV gave his 14-year-old queen, Jeanne d'Évreux, a tiny Book of Hours—it fits easily when open within one hand—illuminated by Parisian painter Jean Pucelle (see "A Closer Look," page 532). This book was so precious to the queen that she mentioned it and its illuminator specifically in her will, leaving this royal treasure to King Charles V. Pucelle painted the book's pictures in *grisaille*—monochromatic painting in shades of gray with only delicate touches of color. His style clearly derives from the courtly mode established in Paris at the time of St. Louis, with its softly modeled, voluminous draperies gathered loosely and falling in projecting diagonal folds around tall, elegantly posed figures with carefully coiffed curly hair, broad foreheads, and delicate features. But his conception of space, with figures placed within coherent, discrete architectural settings, suggests a firsthand knowledge of contemporary Sienese art.

Jeanne appears in the initial *D* below the Annunciation, kneeling in prayer before a lectern, perhaps using this Book of Hours to guide her meditations, beginning with the words written on this page: *Domine labia mea aperies* (Psalm 51:15: "O Lord, open thou my lips"). The juxtaposition of the praying Jeanne's portrait with a scene from the life of the Virgin Mary suggests that the sacred scene is actually a vision inspired by Jeanne's meditations. The young queen might have identified with and sought to feel within herself Mary's joy at Gabriel's message. Given what we know of Jeanne's own life story and her royal husband's predicament, it might also have directed the queen's prayers toward the fulfillment of his wish for a male heir.

In the Annunciation, Mary is shown receiving the archangel Gabriel in a Gothic building that seems to project outward from the page toward the viewer, while rejoicing angels look on from windows under the eaves. The group of romping children at the bottom of the page at first glance seems to echo the angelic jubilation. Folklorists have suggested, however, that the children are playing "froggy in the middle" or "hot cockles," games in which one child was tagged by the others. To the medieval viewer, if the game symbolized the mocking of Christ or the betrayal of Judas, who "tags" his friend, it would have evoked a darker mood by referring to the picture on the other page of this opening, foreshadowing Jesus' imminent death even as his life is beginning.

METALWORK AND IVORY

Fourteenth-century French sculpture is intimate in character. Religious subjects became more emotionally expressive; objects became smaller and demanded closer scrutiny from the viewer. In the secular realm, tales of love and valor were carved on luxury items to delight the rich (see "An Ivory Chest with Scenes of Romance," pages 534–535). Precious materials—gold, silver, and ivory—were preferred.

THE VIRGIN AND CHILD FROM SAINT-DENIS. A silver-gilt image of a standing **VIRGIN AND CHILD** (FIG. 9–1) is a rare survivor that verifies the acclaim that was accorded Parisian fourteenth-century

To view this image, please go to page 549 of the *Art History*, Fourth Edition by Marilyn Stokstad ebook.

9–1 • VIRGIN AND CHILD
c. 1324–1339. Silver gilt and enamel, height 27⅛" (69 cm). Musée du Louvre, Paris.

The Black Death

A deadly outbreak of the bubonic plague, known as the Black Death after the dark sores that developed on the bodies of its victims, spread to Europe from Asia, both by land and by sea, in the middle of the fourteenth century. At least half the urban population of Florence and Siena—some estimate 80 percent—died during the summer of 1348, probably including the artists Andrea Pisano and Ambrogio Lorenzetti. Death was so quick and widespread that basic social structures crumbled in the resulting chaos; people did not know where the disease came from, what caused it, or how long the pandemic would last.

Mid-twentieth-century art historian Millard Meiss proposed that the Black Death had a significant impact on the development of Italian art in the middle of the fourteenth century. Pointing to what he saw as a reactionary return to hieratic linearity in religious art, Meiss theorized that artists had retreated from the rounded forms that had characterized the work of Giotto to old-fashioned styles, and that this artistic change reflected a growing reliance on traditional religious values in the wake of a disaster that some interpreted as God's punishment of a world in moral decline.

An altarpiece painted in 1354–1357 by Andrea di Cione, nicknamed Orcagna ("Archangel"), under the patronage of Tommasso Strozzi—the so-called *Strozzi Altarpiece*—is an example of the sort of paintings that led Meiss to his interpretation. The painting's otherworldly vision is dominated by a central figure of Christ, presumably enthroned, but without any hint of an actual seat, evoking the image of the judge at the Last Judgment, outside time and space. The silhouetted outlines of the standing and kneeling saints emphasize surface over depth; the gold expanse of floor beneath them does not offer any reassuring sense of spatial recession to contain them and their activity. Throughout, line and color are more prominent than form.

Recent art historians have stepped back from Meiss's theory of stylistic change in mid-fourteenth-century Italy. Some have pointed out logical relationships between style and subject in the works Meiss cites; others have seen in them a mannered outgrowth of current style rather than a reversion to an earlier style; still others have discounted the underlying notion that stylistic change is connected with social situations. But there is no denying the relationship of works such as the *Strozzi Altarpiece* with death and judgment, sanctity and the promise of salvation. These themes are suggested in the narrative scenes on the **predella** (the lower zone of the altarpiece): Thomas Aquinas's ecstasy during Mass, Christ's miraculous walk on water to rescue Peter, and the salvation of Emperor Henry II because of his donation of a chalice to a religious institution. While these are not uncommon scenes in sacred art, it is difficult not see a relationship between their choice as subject matter here and the specter cast by the Black Death over a world that had just imagined its prosperity in path-breaking works of visual art firmly rooted in references to everyday life.

To view this image, please go to page 548 of the *Art History*, Fourth Edition by Marilyn Stokstad ebook.

Andrea di Cione (nicknamed Orcagna) **ENTHRONED CHRIST WITH SAINTS, FROM THE STROZZI ALTARPIECE** Strozzi Chapel, Santa Maria Novella, Florence. 1354–1357. Tempera and gold on wood, 9′ × 9′8″ (2.74 × 2.95 m).

EXPLORE MORE: Gain insight from a primary source related to the Black Death **www.myartslab.com**

The Hours of Jeanne d'Évreux

by Jean Pucelle, Two-Page Opening with the Kiss of Judas and the Annunciation. Paris. c. 1325–1328. *Grisaille* and color on vellum, each page 3½ × 2¼″ (8.9 × 6.2 cm). Metropolitan Museum of Art, New York. The Cloisters Collection (54.1.2), fols. 15v–16r.

In this opening Pucelle juxtaposes complementary scenes drawn from the Infancy and Passion of Christ, placed on opposing pages, in a scheme known as the Joys and Sorrows of the Virgin. The "joy" of the Annunciation on the right is paired with the "sorrow" of the betrayal and arrest of Christ on the left.

Christ sways back gracefully as Judas betrays him with a kiss. The S-curve of his body mirrors the Virgin's pose on the opposite page, as both accept their fate with courtly decorum.

The prominent lamp held aloft by a member of the arresting battalion informs the viewer that this scene takes place at night, in the dark.

The angel who holds up the boxlike enclosure where the Annunciation takes place is an allusion to the legend of the miraculous transportation of this building from Nazareth to Loreto in 1294.

To view this image, please go to page 550 of the *Art History*, Fourth Edition by Marilyn Stokstad ebook.

Christ reaches casually down to heal Malchus, the assistant of the high priest whose ear Peter had just cut off in angry retaliation for his participation in the arrest of Jesus.

Scenes of secular amusements from everyday life, visual puns, and off-color jokes appear at the bottom of many pages of this book. Sometimes they relate to the themes of the sacred scenes above them. These comic knights riding goats may be a commentary on the lack of valor shown by the soldiers assaulting Jesus, especially if this wine barrel conjured up for Jeanne an association with the Eucharist.

The candle held by the cleric who guards the "door" to Jeanne's devotional retreat, as well as the rabbit emerging from its burrow in the marginal scene, are sexually charged symbols of fertility that seem directly related to the focused prayers of a child bride required to produce a male heir.

SEE MORE: View the Closer Look feature for The Hours of Jeanne d'Évreux **www.myartslab.com**

goldsmiths. An inscription on the base documents the statue's donation to the abbey church of Saint-Denis in 1339 and the donor's name, the same Queen Jeanne d'Évreux whose Book of Hours we have just examined. In a style that recalls the work of artist Jean Pucelle in that Book of Hours, the Virgin holds Jesus in her left arm with her weight on her left leg, standing in a graceful, characteristically Gothic S-curve pose. Mary originally wore a crown, and she still holds a large enameled and jeweled *fleur-de-lis*—the heraldic symbol of royal France—which served as a reliquary container for strands of Mary's hair. The Christ Child, reaching out tenderly to caress his mother's face, is babylike in both form and posture. On the base, minuscule statues of prophets stand on projecting piers to separate 14 enameled scenes from Christ's Infancy and Passion, reminding us of the suffering to come. The apple in the baby's hand carries the theme further with its reference to Christ's role as the new Adam, whose sacrifice on the cross—medieval Christians believed—redeemed humanity from the first couple's fall into sin when Eve bit into the forbidden fruit.

ENGLAND

Fourteenth-century England prospered in spite of the ravages of the Black Death and the Hundred Years' War with France. English life at this time is described in the brilliant social commentary of Geoffrey Chaucer in the *Canterbury Tales*. The royal family, especially Edward I (r. 1272–1307)—the castle builder—and many of the nobles and bishops were generous patrons of the arts.

EMBROIDERY: OPUS ANGLICANUM

Since the thirteenth century, the English had been renowned for pictorial needlework, using colored silk and gold thread to create images as detailed as contemporary painters produced in manuscripts. Popular throughout Europe, the art came to be called *opus anglicanum* ("English work"). The popes had more than 100 pieces in the Vatican treasury. The names of several prominent embroiderers are known, but in the thirteenth century no one surpassed Mabel of Bury St. Edmunds, who created both religious and secular articles for King Henry III (r. 1216–1272).

THE CHICHESTER-CONSTABLE CHASUBLE. This *opus angicanum* liturgical vestment worn by a priest during Mass **(FIG. 9–2)** was embroidered c. 1330–1350 with images formed by subtle gradations of colored silk. Where gold threads were laid and couched (tacked down with colored silk), the effect resembles the burnished gold-leaf backgrounds of manuscript illuminations. The Annunciation, the Adoration of the Magi, and the Coronation of the Virgin are set in cusped, crocketed **ogee** (S-shape) arches, supported on animal-head corbels and twisting branches sprouting oak leaves with seed-pearl acorns. Because the star and crescent moon in the Coronation of the Virgin scene are heraldic emblems of Edward III (r. 1327–1377), perhaps he or a family member commissioned this luxurious vestment.

During the celebration of the Mass, especially as the priest moved, *opus anglicanum* would have glinted in the candlelight amid treasures on the altar. Court dress was just as rich and colorful, and at court such embroidered garments proclaimed the rank and status of the wearer. So heavy did such gold and bejeweled garments become that their wearers often needed help to move.

To view this image, please go to page 551 of the *Art History*, Fourth Edition by Marilyn Stokstad ebook.

9-2 • LIFE OF THE VIRGIN, BACK OF THE CHICHESTER-CONSTABLE CHASUBLE
From a set of vestments embroidered in *opus anglicanum* from southern England. c. 1330–1350. Red velvet with silk and metallic thread and seed pearls, length 4′3″ (129.5 cm), width 30″ (76 cm). Metropolitan Museum of Art, New York. Fletcher Fund, 1927 (27 162.1)

An Ivory Chest with Scenes of Romance

Fourteenth-century Paris was renowned for more than its goldsmiths (SEE FIG. 9–1). Among the most sumptuous and sought-after Parisian luxury products were small chests assembled from carved ivory plaques that were used by wealthy women to store jewelry or other personal treasures. The entirely secular subject matter of these chests was romantic love. Indeed, they seem to have been courtship gifts from smitten men to desired women, or wedding presents offered by grooms to their brides.

A chest from around 1330–1350, now in the Walters Museum (SEE FIG. A), is one of seven that have survived intact; there are fragments of a dozen more. It is a delightful and typical example. Figural relief covers five exterior sides of the box: around the perimeter and on the hinged top. The assembled panels were joined by metal hardware—strips, brackets, hinges, handles, and locks—originally wrought in silver. Although some chests tell a single romantic story in sequential episodes, most, like this one, anthologize scenes drawn from a group of stories, combining courtly romance, secular allegory, and ancient fables.

On the lid of the Walters casket (SEE FIG. B), jousting is the theme. Spread over the central two panels, a single scene catches two charging knights in the heat of a tournament, while trumpeting heralds call the attention of spectators, lined up above in a gallery to observe this public display of virility. The panel at right mocks the very ritual showcased in the middle panels by pitting a woman against a knight, battling not with lances but with a long-stemmed rose (symbolizing sexual surrender) and an oak bough (symbolizing fertility). Instead of observing these silly goings-on, however, the spectators tucked into the upper architecture pursue their own amorous flirtations. Finally, in the scene on the left, knights use crossbows and a catapult to hurl roses at the Castle of Love, while Cupid returns fire with his seductive arrows.

On the front of the chest (SEE FIG. A), generalized romantic allegory gives way to vignettes from a specific story. At left, the long-bearded Aristotle teaches the young Alexander the Great, using exaggerated gestures and an authoritative text to emphasize his point. Today's lesson is a stern warning not to allow the seductive power of women to distract the young prince from his studies. The subsequent scene, however, pokes fun at his eminent teacher, who has become so smitten by the wiles of a young beauty named Phyllis that he lets

To view this image, please go to page 552 of the *Art History*, Fourth Edition by Marilyn Stokstad ebook.

A. SMALL IVORY CHEST WITH SCENES FROM COURTLY ROMANCES
Made in Paris. c. 1330–1350. Elephant ivory with modern iron mounts, height 4½″ (11.5 cm), width 9¹¹⁄₁₆″ (24.6 cm), depth 4⅞″ (12.4 cm). The Walters Art Museum, Baltimore.

her ride him around like a horse, while his student observes this farce, peering out of the castle in the background. The two scenes at right relate to an eastern legend of the fountain of youth, popular in medieval Europe. A line of bearded elders approaches the fountain from the left, steadied by their canes. But after having partaken of its transforming effects, two newly rejuvenated couples, now nude, bathe and flirt within the fountain's basin. The man first in line for treatment, stepping up to climb into the fountain, looks suspiciously like the figure of the aging Aristotle, forming a link between the two stories on the casket front.

Unlike royal marriages of the time, which were essentially business contracts based on political or financial exigencies, the romantic love of the aristocratic wealthy involved passionate devotion. Images of gallant knights and their coy paramours, who could bring intoxicating bliss or cruelly withhold their love on a whim, captured the popular Gothic imagination. They formed the principal subject matter on personal luxury objects, not only chests like this, but mirror backs, combs, writing tablets, even ceremonial saddles. And these stories evoke themes that still captivate us since they reflect notions of desire and betrayal, cruel rejection and blissful folly, at play in our own romantic conquests and relationships to this day. In this way they allow us some access to the lives of the people who commissioned and owned these precious objects, even if we ourselves are unable to afford them.

To view this image, please go to page 553 of the *Art History*, Fourth Edition by Marilyn Stokstad ebook.

B. ATTACK ON THE CASTLE OF LOVE
Top of the chest.

To view this image, please go to page 553 of the *Art History*, Fourth Edition by Marilyn Stokstad ebook.

C. TRISTAN AND ISEULT AT THE FOUNTAIN; CAPTURE OF THE UNICORN
Left short side of the chest.

Two other well-known medieval themes are juxtaposed on this plaque from the short side of the ivory chest. At left, Tristan and Iseult have met secretly for an illicit romantic tryst, while Iseult's husband, King Mark, tipped off by an informant, observes them from a tree. But when they see his reflection in a fountain between them, they alter their behavior accordingly, and the king believes them innocent of the adultery he had (rightly) suspected. The medieval bestiary ("book of beasts") claimed that only a virgin could capture the mythical unicorn, which at right lays his head, with its aggressively phallic horn, into the lap of just such a pure maiden so that the hunter can take advantage of her alluring powers over the animal to kill it with his phallic counterpart of its horn, a large spear.

A Goldsmith in His Shop

by Petrus Christus. 1449. Oil on oak panel, 38⅝ × 33½″ (98 × 85 cm).
Metropolitan Museum of Art, New York, Robert Lehman Collection, 1975. 1975.1.110

The coat of arms of the dukes of Guelders hangs from a chain around this man's neck, leading some to speculate that the woman, who is the more active of the pair, is Mary of Guelders, niece of Duke Philip the Good, who married King James II of the Scots the same year this picture was painted.

Goldsmiths were expected to perform all their transactions, including the weighing of gold, in public view to safeguard against dishonesty. Here the scales tip toward the couple, perhaps an allusion to the scales of the Last Judgment, which always tip to the side of the righteous.

Three types of coins rest on the shop counter: "florins" from Mainz, "angels" from English King Henry VI's French territories, and "riders" minted under Philip the Good. Such diversity of currency could show the goldsmith's cosmopolitanism, or they could indicate his participation in money changing, since members of that profession belonged to the same guild as goldsmiths.

To view this image, please go to page 581 of the *Art History*, Fourth Edition by Marilyn Stokstad ebook.

This coconut cup was supposed to neutralize poison. The slabs of porphyry and rock crystal were "touchstones," used to test gold and precious stones.

The red coral and serpents' tongues (actually fossilized sharks' teeth) were intended to ward off the evil eye.

Two men, one with a falcon on his arm, are reflected in the obliquely placed mirror as they stand in front of the shop. The edges of the reflection catch the red sleeve of the goldsmith and the door frame, uniting the interior and exterior spaces and drawing the viewer into the painting.

The artist signed and dated his work in a bold inscription that appears just under the tabletop at the bottom of the painting: "Master Petrus Christus made me in the year 1449."

SEE MORE: View the Closer Look feature for *A Goldsmith in his Shop* www.myartslab.com

ADDITIONAL READINGS

CHURCH AND STATE AD 600–1500

From the rise of Islam to the European awareness of the Americas, this is a period of extensive ideological and cultural change. In AD 600 China had been riven by four centuries of internal strife, reunited only under the Tang Dynasty (618–906). Much of the Mediterranean and Middle East was in disarray, the latter changing in ethnic composition as Turkic tribes moved southwards from northeastern Siberia. Originating in Arabia, Islam spread rapidly through conquest after the death of its founder, the prophet and merchant Muhammad, in 632. By 651 Islamic caliphs ruled Syria, Palestine, Sasanian Iraq, Egypt and finally Sasanian Iran. Composed of decentralized states aligned (after 661) to Shi'i or

Sunni sects, some hundred years later Sunni Islam extended into the borders of China, deep into the northern African coast and across southern Iberia. Of these conquests, Syria and Egypt had been wrested from the Byzantine empire, which remained ideologically linked to the western Christian states until 1054, when a liturgical dispute led to the division between the Byzantine (Orthodox) and Roman (Catholic) churches. This schism marked the end of the early Middle Ages in Europe and the emergence of an increasingly powerful 'Latin' alliance in western Europe. It also coincided with the Turkic Seljuk conquest of Anatolia, which further threatened the Byzantine empire.

Textiles in this period were in many respects conservative. The Egyptians continued to weave linens and tapestry, and every-

9-3 • Said to have been found in the tomb of the Ming Dynasty emperor Hsi-ian-tê (Xuande), this fragment of silk and gilt thread *kesi* (tapestry) of 1426–35 depicts a frontal dragon above a flaming pearl. The surrounding cloud motifs were already long established within Chinese iconography and epitomize the conservatism of this period. The use of such cosmological emblems spread and continued into the 20th century.

where creativity was limited mainly to subtle improvements in technology or variations in cloth structure as seen in Chinese Song damasks (960–1279), which include the first extant example of a satin weave. The Silk Route was disrupted (but restored) by the rise of the Mongols in the early 13th century and their conquests in China, where they eventually established the Yuan Dynasty (1279–1368). By the 1450s Mongolian rulers held almost all the territory bounded by Korea, Vietnam, Syria and Poland. Entire cities were destroyed during the devastation wreaked by the Mongol Timur (or Tamerlane, *c.* 1336–1405) as he swept from Samarkand across Russia, Mongolia, Persia, Anatolia and India. Artisans were spared, treated as booty and relocated, and these enforced migrations hastened the dispersal of techniques. Weavers from Herat (in Afghanistan), who were known for their gold-woven

9-4 • Incorporating a weft of flat gilt membrane on a satin ground, this silk epitomizes Mongolian rulers' taste for gold thread-laden cloths, or *nāsij*. It was made in Turkestan or China between about 1280 and 1370, most probably by Muslim weavers.
Courtesy of Philadelphia Museum of Art.

9-6 • Probably made for King Roger (1130–54) and used by later German kings and Habsburg emperors, this red silk twill coronation mantle was embroidered in 1133–34 in Palermo, Sicily, facts recorded in the *tiraz*-like Kufic inscription. Worked in coloured silks, couched gold threads, and ornaments, pearls, enamels and jewels, the lion and camel represent Christianity triumphant over Islam.
Courtesy of Kunt Historishes Museum.

9-5 • Although this 8th-century eastern Mediterranean silk *samitum* depicts the Annunciation, with a few alterations its enthroned figure could represent 'State' rather than 'Church'. Closely entwined in this period, both were essentially conservative; one result was the longevity throughout Eurasia of the roundel arrangement and floral motifs seen here.
Courtesy of Biblioteca Apostolica Vaticana.

9-7 • Undoubtedly dispersed by Muslim artisans, decorative quilting was one of the 'cotton techniques' adopted throughout Europe by the 14th century (although protective linen doublets wadded with raw wool or cotton were made much earlier). This quilt, which depicts the Tristram legend in back-stitched trapunto and running stitches, was worked in 1392 for Sicilian aristocrats.
Courtesy of V & A Images.

silks and silver brocading, were removed to the Chinese Uighur region in 1222 and returned fifteen years later when their city was rebuilt. By 1260, Chinese craftsmen were at work in Tabriz, also famed for its golden cloths or *nāsij*. The Mongolian preference for these—as tributes, taxes or in trade—ensured the maintenance of conquered cities' imperial workshops (such as those in Baghdad) and the introduction of such techniques as far west as Armenia. Figured velvet weaving now appears in Yuan China and, by 1350, in India. In about 1400 *kesi* was introduced from China to Japan, where it was called *tsuzure-ori*, or 'fingernail weave'. Such diffusion is typical of this era of 'Church' and 'State'.

During the 11th and 12th centuries sericulture and silk weaving were established by Middle Eastern peoples in southern Italy and Sicily, where under Frederick II (1194–1250) dyeing was a Jewish monopoly, just as were silk processing and weaving. To mitigate the rising strength of Islamic states, the Pope formed an alliance with the Chinese Mongols, the Pax Mongolica (1260–1368), and this contributed greatly to the development of brocaded silk and velvet weaving in Italy. The Angevin conquest of Sicily in 1266 consolidated the position of Lucca, with the largest Jewish population north of Rome, as the first important Italian silk-weaving centre. Nevertheless, Byzantine weavers pro-

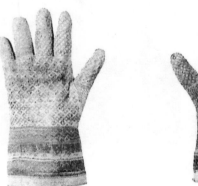

9-8, 9-9 • This silk pattern-knitted glove (seen from both sides) belonged to the Archbishop of Toledo, Rodrigo Ximénez de Rada who died in 1247. Like other contemporary Spanish examples of fine multi-needle silk knitting, its quality indicates a well-established skill.

vided the West's most sumptuous silks, even after the fall of Constantinople to the Latins in 1204. Together with Persian and Middle Eastern Islamic weavers and embroiderers—many in formerly Byzantine Syrian workshops—they supplied and inspired the silken splendour characteristic of courts and ceremonies throughout Eurasia until the Byzantine empire itself was overrun by the Ottomans in 1453.

To the west, life was even more uncertain. The 'barbarian' Franks from the Rhineland had captured Gaul during the 5th and 6th centuries, but had neither Roman law, with its strong administration, nor great cities as centres of trade and sources of labour. Roman Britons had been overrun by various tribes from modern-day Germany, Denmark and the Netherlands, and from 601 were focused on converting these invaders to Christianity. Expanses of Italy came first under the control of Byzantine governors (584–751) and then the new so-called 'Latin' world, an amalgam of Frankish and Italian Christian cultures solidified by Charlemagne (742–814), who also added large areas of Germany to his domain. Crowned emperor by Pope Leo III in 800, Charlemagne established the pattern of Christian courts, complete with lavish silks and embroideries, that defined ever larger areas of Europe. Between around 772 and his death, Charlemagne's extensive conquests included the pagan Saxons of the Elbe valley, who were forced to convert to Christianity and were scattered over his lands. At his death, power passed into the hands of large landholders who exercised power in their own regions, much like the caliphs of Islam. At the same time arose the

Nordic Viking sea warriors, whose vibrant textile culture—including complex tablet-woven braids and hangings in wrapped and woven tapestry—spread with them to settlements in the northern British Isles, Normandy, Greenland, Vinland (probably Newfoundland) and the eastern Baltic. From here exchange for silks and other luxuries took Viking textiles all the way to Constantinople and the mouth of the Volga river.

The treadle loom, documented in Syria and Egypt prior to the 6th century, reached Europe in the early Middle Ages. With the decline of the Vikings and the relative calm of the ensuing High Middle Ages (1050–1300) it began to displace the warp-weighted loom, except in northern Scandinavia and Iceland. Three times

9-11 • Religious buildings around the world often contained large iconographic panels; many were painted or stamped textiles such as this Chimu *manta* of 800–1200, with its centuries-old Peruvian symbols on a palm-leaf fibre cloth. Collection David Bernstein, New York. *Courtesy of David Bernstein Pre-Columbian Art.*

9-10 • Embroidery flourished between 600 and 1500, being the most expedient method of creating detailed imagery (particularly for items whose motifs did not repeat). This Chinese or Tibetan silk damask of 1375–1475 is embellished with needle-loop and flat stitches in gilded paper and silk threads. *Courtesy of Philadelphia Museum of Art.*

9-12 • Housed in the Shosoin temple treasury, Japan, this Tang Chinese silk of 620–700 imitates a Sasanian *samitum*. The details of the winged creature and roundel became more fluid in the translation, but the weave structure was copied precisely. *Courtesy of Shosoin Temple Treasury, Japan.*

more productive than the loom it replaced, it was an essential part of the revival of trade and the emergence of prosperous cities with a middle class. However, disruptive forces were never far away. The seven crusades between 1095 and 1291 led to cross-cultural encounters that disseminated ideas and stimulated East–West trade, but also ensured continued upheaval. In Iberia and southern Italy, friendly and hostile exchanges alike aided the introduction of Muslim textile techniques, some of which quite possibly had origins in India. Chief among these were cotton carding, wheel spinning of weft yarns and pattern knitting (known in Arabia and India from the 9th century), which were introduced in the 11th, 12th and 13th centuries respectively. These newly found skills were then gradually transferred to woollen manufacture across Europe, resulting in many new variations on existing cloth 'themes'. This prosperous interlude was brought to an end by the widespread famine of the early 14th century, followed by the Black Death plague epidemic (1347–50), which swept through Egypt and Europe from Syria, killing some thirty percent of these populations.

Such destructive events had profound consequences for textiles, causing an acute shortage of skilled workers and destroying knowledge as well as people. Particularly vulnerable to backlash from these and other calamities were the Jews, who had been highly regarded for their textile skills (especially in dyeing) since the days of the Roman Empire. Thus, labour shortages at the beginning and the end of the period covered by this chapter, and the resumption of extensive trade in the middle, accelerated the tendency towards less time-consuming textile techniques. Fulling mills were in use in Italy in the 10th century and spread northwards, marking a critical step towards industrialization with the subsequent gradual incorporation of waterpower, which was fairly widespread by 1500. Across Europe there emerged an increased division of labour, a trend that became associated with the introduction of the treadle loom, woollen weft preparation and, in the 13th century, the adoption of broad looms, which could make woollen cloth up to 2.5 metres (8 feet) wide. From the 13th century onwards, elaborate in-working of designs was increasingly aided by loom mechanisms or by pattern knitting. The latter required two or more needles and, for plain knitting, was also much faster than cross-loop knitting, which it replaced in Egypt. (Plain multi-needle knitting had been worked in Syria from at least the 3rd century.) Tapestry decorations, rather than being worked simultaneously with a plain cloth surround, were more typically applied as separate decorative bands or blazons. The tapestry technique itself was often replaced by embroidery which, as a quicker alternative to loom-patterned silks, provided some of the most resplendent textiles of this age. The exceptions were knotted carpets and textiles produced in *tiraz* and similar state workshops (see p. 543). Textiles made within tribal and peasant communities everywhere appear to demonstrate similar economics but were relatively untouched by the process of proto-industrialization and thus continued to elaborate upon established techniques, particularly embroidery.

In either case, this is the first period thoroughly covered by illustrated volumes and academic essays detailing textile structures, techniques and designs, and examining, over ever wider regions, the development and use of textiles and their points of inter-cultural exchange. Aside from Andean textiles, those surviving from the Americas now include substantial numbers from the Prehistoric Southwest and, between about 1250 and 1519, some examples from Precolumbian Mesoamerica. Sub-Saharan textiles enter the picture in the 9th century. Many of these were painted

9-13 • In this Byzantine silk *samitum* from an Italian reliquary of about 750, the arrangement echoes Sasanian patterns, as do some individual motifs, such as the 'tree of life' and the tunics worn by the hunters. Such arrangement of motifs had a long life, and similar roundels can still be found in textiles produced in the 1800s. Their scale, typically about 25 centimetres (10 inches) in diameter, was also maintained.
Courtesy of Biblioteca Apostolica Vaticana.

9-14 • The drawloom has had many forms but this 18th-century French engraving shows its essential elements: the leashes rising high above the loom, and the draw cords (here dropping down at the side). The upper X-like arms were standard in treadle looms and controlled the heddle-filled shafts or harnesses, which created the background weave.

9-15 • Perhaps the most ubiquitous Eurasian motifs between 600 and 1500 were the griffin and the large-winged bird, both of which appear in this 12th-century Syrian silk found in an Egyptian grave.
Courtesy of Museum of Fine Arts, Boston.

or pattern dyed. Despite individual differences, there seems to be a worldwide need—in autocratic feudal confederacies and tribal societies alike—to emphasize cultural certainties, expressed most commonly through textiles and associated regulations.

The most visible evidence of the importance of the *status quo* was the longevity of certain designs. Among these were Sasanian Persian patterns with a symmetrical arrangement of figures or animals, often confronted, set within a roundel itself filled with decorative devices. The adoption of local conventions by Islamic authorities preserved existing state workshops and the Sasanian patterns (which were also made in Constantinople) produced in them. This style rapidly dispersed even further, by way of Persia and Islamic Soghdia (western Turkestan)—where silks also bore hunting scenes, confronted animals and Sasanian-style 'tree of life' designs and roundels—to Tang China (618–906). Relationships between the Japanese and Tang cultures, via Korea (where seri-

culture had been introduced in around 200), can account for similar designs in Japan. Hundreds of examples across Eurasia attest to their popularity. Many that survive in Christian churches were, in the first instance, 'payment' for military support provided to the Byzantines by Italians, Bulgars, Russians and Austro-Germans. (The latter succeeded in 962 to Charlemagne's dynasty and as Holy Roman Emperors vied with the Papacy for control of Europe.) In Spain, where sericulture had been introduced by the Moors in 712, the caliphate capital of Cordoba was established by the Sunni survivors of the first Syrian Umayyad dynasty (755–1031), bringing *tiraz* workshops to it and other Andalusian cities. In the 9th century, weavers from Baghdad—which between 750 and 940 was the seat of the Abbasid Caliphate of Syria and Egypt—set up additional workshops in Spain that for another three hundred or so years produced designs based on Sasanian/Byzantine prototypes. These were made on drawlooms, as they were elsewhere.

The drawloom circumvented the need for numerous hand-inserted patterning rods or foot treadles by inserting each warp through a rising cord (leash) which, when drawn up, lifted that warp. The leashes were raised according to the desired pattern by assistants often known as draw-boys or draw-girls. The superstructure supporting the cords (which might be pulled from a platform at the top or by way of pulleys from the side) could be added to any type of horizontal loom, weaver-tensioned, warp-weighted or framed. The ground weave (for much of this period typically a weft-faced twill) continued to be controlled by harnesses whose actions were overridden by the leashes. Although still labour intensive, leashes controlling comparable points in any symmetrical pattern could be raised simultaneously by tying them together. The result was that by pulling a sequence for one motif it appeared from selvedge to selvedge half as many times as the number of leashes in each bundle. This had two consequences. Small patterns were especially time-saving and so those based on 'powderings' of motifs and lozenge-like structures became common. Once the leashes were bunched and harnesses threaded it was economical to keep these arrangements, so looms soon became dedicated to particular ground weaves and repeat sizes, a feature contributing to the longevity of structural and design elements. Until the 1400s, patterns seldom exceeded 75 centimetres (30 inches) in height.

Especially prevalent among roundel designs were those with charioteer and hunting themes, represented by horseriders, lions, eagles, elephants and bulls. These continued to be woven in Byzantine workshops even after the two periods of iconoclasm (726–87 and 815–43) banned narrative Christian themes. Hunting themes had an obvious appeal to feudal lords, who were essentially military leaders. Indeed, powerful and swift beasts, especially lions and leopards, were frequently adopted as royal and civic insignia in feudal societies around the world; Peruvian textiles throughout this period exhibit but one of many expressions of the awe of the hunter-cat. It is telling of the intimate connections

9-16 • Illustrating both the type of geometric patterns preferred by Sunni Muslims and *tiraz* production, this silk fabric was woven with Arabic inscriptions in a Nasrid caliphate workshop in 15th-century Spain.
Courtesy of Philadelphia Museum of Art.

9-17 • Known as the Shroud of St-Josse and kept for many centuries in a Parisian church, the Shi'i *tiraz* of about 950 contains recognizable camels and elephants. Such motifs are appropriate to its origins in Khorasan, situated in the ancient West Caspian corridor between the steppes and northern Iran, through which a near-constant stream of invaders and traders travelled.
Courtesy of Musee du Louvre.

9-18 • Within Latin American cultures cotton was a prestigious fibre; here it has been tapestry-woven into a Pachacamac sample of 1000–1350. The sample retains its own small loom (not illustrated), which reflects the Peruvian custom of burying weavers with tools of their trade. Collection David Bernstein, New York.
Courtesy of David Bernstein Pre-Columbian Art.

between Church and State that the same beasts and birds frequently occurred as symbols of the spiritual realm. In the Orthodox church of the 10th to 12th centuries, for example, the eagle and griffin represented heavenly flight. Similar concepts are widely recorded. Winged creatures and confronted motifs, particularly birds, were already meaningful symbols, the former long familiar within Persia and dominant among both Tiahuanaco and Huari Peruvian textile imagery of 500–700, the latter already established in Chinese iconography. During the mid-6th and early 7th centuries, the Japanese had embraced Buddhism and Chinese cosmology respectively and the resulting emblems—called *yūsoku* in Japan—now became standardized around twenty-seven basic groups. In a still largely illiterate world, many of these anthropomorphized motifs tapped so deeply into the universal desire to understand existence that they became fossilized and for centuries thereafter remained potent emblems of particular world views. For example, as the Iranian mystical sect of Islamic Sufi coalesced in the 8th and 9th centuries, it adopted the confronted or two-headed bird—often the peacock—as a symbol of its reciprocal mirrored view of the universe.

The use of such emblems among Muslims highlights the deepest theoretical divide between the Shi'i, who allowed representations of nature, and the Sunni, who did not. In practice, however, the division was never rigid. Persian caliphs were often Sunni in persuasion, but nevertheless maintained local textile designs, even if in simplified form. The entirely abstract, complex geometric patterns approved by the Sunni are best represented by those found in Iberia under the Nasrid caliphs (1230–1492). Even here, however, the influence already noted of the Moors and Baghdad weavers was followed by influences from Cairo, the seat of the Shi'i Fatimid dynasty, who held the allegiance of Egypt and Syria from 969 to 1171. The rise of the Sunni Seljuk Turks in 11th- and 12th-century Persia and Anatolia increased

9-19 • In Madagascar, the highland Merina preserve ties to southeast Asia through both their language and their weaving practice. Since 1500 they have woven narrow silk cloths using traditional motifs and techniques for special events from sacred offerings to diplomatic presents. The patterns, picked out by hand from individual leashes, come from Indonesia. The Malagasy terms for writing and preparing the loom are interchangable.
David Bernstein Pre-Columbian Art.

both the abstraction and elaboration of patterns, but throughout the entire period even the most decorative Islamic textiles had no overtly religious motifs, a feature that readily facilitated their use and imitation in other cultures. Thus, two-headed birds, particularly eagles, became emblematic of Christian Orthodox and Roman Catholic sovereignties.

This was true even of *tiraz*, literally meaning embroidery but also denoting any Islamic textile carrying an embroidered or inlaid tapestry-woven inscription and, more generally, the caliphate workshops, whether *khassa* (exclusive to the court) or *amma* (available for purchase). These workshops produced the finest embroidered and woven silks and, like the Sasanian and Byzantine royal workshops before them, were state controlled and carefully guarded due to the bullion embroidery produced within. The earliest known *khassa* dates from 724 to 743, though they are thought to have emerged in the late 7th century. Inscribed textiles were particularly associated with Fatimid Egypt, where the Copts had previously interwoven Greek inscriptions. The thousands of surviving *tiraz* demonstrate a change in the mid-11th century to shorter inscriptions or entirely decorative ones thus suitable only for non-Islamic or illiterate Islamic populations. The use of *tiraz* was only widespread throughout Islam until 1293, when the Mongols banned them except for court use. Thereafter they are well documented in Yuan China, and Mongolian conquests to the west coincided with the introduction of script borders in Orthodox embroidery in the early 15th century. Here and elsewhere *tiraz* influence lingered, and inscribed textiles were still sold in Cairo even after the closure of the Egyptian caliphate workshops in about 1341.

Islamic *tiraz* functioned as a 'contract' between the caliph and his people. Distributed as a sign of patronage and accepted as acknowledgment of his authority, they were also purchased and given to the caliph in lieu of taxes and as tribute. The long-established and more general tribute system also remained in place and the many gifts from wealthy donors to temples, churches and

monasteries were an extension of this practice. As a means of embodying the mutual obligations within a society, it has many parallels elsewhere. Mesoamerican pictographic codices include notations of the Aztec empire's tribute tallies illustrating both the designs and quantities of *mantas* or mantles—in the thousands—that were expected to arrive from the provinces every eighty days. Their Precolumbian contemporaries, the Andean Inkas (1438–1532), preserved from their preceding cultures a very similar system. Expressed as 'offerings', they constituted a well-defined exchange between the right to farm 'Crown' or 'Church' lands and use communal supplies of wool and cotton, and the obligation to work the land and weave cloth for the authorities in return.

Such pacts also summarize the position of Old World serfs. For those tied to monastic lands, this 'gift' of an often large proportion of their output in exchange for protection, subsistence and prayer survives in the less burdensome present-day meaning of tithing. Not surprisingly, the emerging independent weaver-drapers in Europe (*drapiers, lanaiuoli*, or clothiers) structured their businesses along the same lines. The materials belonged to the clothier and were distributed among workers who were obliged to return rovings, slivers, spun yarns or prepared warps—all made with their own tools—in exchange for the right to that work and payment in cash or in kind. Weaving was typically done on looms owned by the clothier but was otherwise also piecework. This concept became known as 'putting-out' and still exists today. In the absence of contractual laws, allegiances such as these extended from the clothiers to their customers, the merchants and finishers. The latter undertook fulling, tentering (stretching back into shape) and shearing, all important stages in woollen and some serge production, while others specialized in different categories of piece dyeing, including the over-dyeing of woad fibre-dyed wools or the carefully guarded process of scarlet dyeing. Merchant-drapers were clothiers who also finished and dyed cloths and many became wealthy in the process, thus entering the brotherhood of the urban elite.

In hierarchical societies the significance of textiles was more than a matter of the best to the richest (although that was also true). While it is easy to understand the awe inspired by the sumptuous woven, embroidered and jewel- or metal thread-encrusted silks exclusive to nobility in this period, rank and fealty were also denoted in many other ways. The Sufi were literally 'wearers of woollen cloth', eschewing the silks of the court, as did many monastics elsewhere. The earliest Burmans of Myanmar, the Pyu (500–900), were described by Tang chroniclers as weavers of fine cotton cloth, used in preference to silk because, as devout Buddhists (a religion otherwise closely associated with silk), they refused to kill the silkworms. Similar restrictions applied to some followers of Hinduism, an ancient amalgam of religious beliefs and institutions that had evolved in India. As Buddhism, Hinduism and Islam were dispersed, so too was knowledge of cotton preparation and cultivation. One result of this was the introduction of cotton crops in the 8th century to the Tarim Basin.

9-20 • The romantic notion of 'magnificent warfare' owes much to the richly wrought textiles associated with military campaigns, whether directly (as epitomized by this English knight of 1335–40) or indirectly (in the form of luxurious tributes and booty). Here, Sir Geoffrey Luttrell's brilliant blue and gold insignia have been stamped, painted or embroidered across his and his horse's trappings.
Courtesy of the British Library.

9-21 • Prized 'tartar cloths' containing wefts of flat gilt membrane were highly influential on southern European weavers. Their patterns had even wider impact, and the contrapuntal arrangement seen in this late 13th- or 14th-century Sino-Mongolian design remained fashionable in Europe for another 300 years.
Courtesy of Alte kapella, Regensburg.

Among Prehistoric Southwestern tribes, cotton (whose cultivation had been introduced from Mexico to the southern Arizonan Hohokam by 500 and passed by them to the Mogollon and Anasazi after about 1100) had several ritual and spiritual meanings, including symbolizing clouds. In the bast-based Mesoamerican textile culture, cotton was *the* luxury fibre, enhanced by embroidery using silken yarns of rabbit underbelly fur or, occasionally, wild silk, plumage, shells, stones and precious metals. Although for the Inkas the most valued object was weft-faced tapestry, in Peru as late as the 18th century one cotton cloth *manta* (blanket) given in tribute was worth two made of wool. (The tribute system continued to be used, and sometimes abused, by Spanish colonialists throughout the Americas.)

That few cotton cloths survive in Eurasia from this period may be due not to their lack of use or regard, but rather to the introduction of rag-paper-making from the East in the 8th century (although there it was made of hempen rags and mulberry bark). Nevertheless, in Europe at this time cotton appears to have been mainly used for candlewicks, while luxury cloths were instead being made of the finest wool fibres obtained from central England. A 30-metre (32-yard) piece of such broadcloth took about thirty people one month to make. Of these, only two would have been weavers. Yarn preparation accounted for close to half of the unfinished cloth's cost and ensured supple draping qualities, with the most sought-after being those dyed scarlet.

Colours alone could denote rank. A 10th-century Byzantine code reiterated the ban on purple dyes for private manufacture. Islamic and Eastern rulers similarly took particular colours as symbols of their dynasties. In 9th-century Islam, non-Muslims were required to wear a honey colour, and as a result the Byzantines were known in Arabic as the 'safflower people'. Yellow for 'outsiders' was long maintained in the West, and this meaning may also have been intended when it was adopted by the warrior Mamluk sultans (who ruled Egypt, Syria and much of Libya and the Sudan between 1250 and 1517). Elsewhere the colour yellow was used to signify 'insiders'. For example, in hierarchical Oceanic societies it was reserved, together with red, for the *tiputas* of chieftains and others of high status. The Japanese had a complex system of rank colours that only gradually declined under the

shoguns (from 1192), who adopted aspects of commoners' dress and, as in the West, developed armour initially based entirely on textile techniques. This was the age of pennants, heraldry and magnificent tents and horse trappings, all of which used colour as their primary distinguishing feature, underscoring the way it so readily identifies 'us' from 'them'. Only at close quarters were motifs important; a Byzantine silk woven with the monogram of the Emperor Heraclius (610–641) is an early surviving example of this practice, which could also be achieved by stamping, painting and embroidery. In Islam the wearing of amiral blazons ('rank badges' in the Far East) was associated with the Mamluks.

Much that is known about textile attributes comes from sumptuary laws. These attempts to prevent excess of finery prohibited or regulated the use of many elements of dress: colours, fibres, designs, metal embroidery and furs. In Byzantine, Islamic and Eastern cultures these seem principally to apply to men. However, such legislation was difficult to enforce because of the constant circulation of second-hand textiles, including some of the finest quality. Those made for the 1327 coronation of the English king Edward III were afterwards given away as gratuities and alms, the poor receiving most of the fifteen pieces of 'candlewickstreet' carpet, a term evoking the looped or tufted cottons known later. Hundreds of cloth names and technical nuances can be gleaned from the many royal accounts, statutes and guild regulations of this period but, as is the case here, it is often not possible to associate terms with surviving textiles. The attribution of surviving examples is only further complicated by the Norman conquest of Sicily and their establishment in 1147 of workshops in Palermo using native Islamic embroiderers and Byzantine weavers captured in the Peloponnese. This began the expansion of silk weaving into southern Italy (also under Norman control by this time). There and elsewhere in the Mediterranean many new textile centres emerged during the 12th and 13th centuries as the Islamic and Byzantine empires weakened. And the simultaneous influence of 'tartar' cloths available as a result of the Pax Mongolica introduced Sino-Mongolian designs and techniques to Europe, especially gold brocading. By 1500 several Italian city-states had become significant centres for silk production.

Faced with the incursion of new textiles and processes, many of those involved in textile manufacture at this time sought security and order, and this anxiety is reflected in many contemporary documents. Guild regulations and statutes everywhere demonstrate the desire to prevent adulteration of materials or techniques—particularly important for those catering for export markets—and reveal the attempts made by trades to both attain and maintain status. This is particularly the case in Europe, where weaver-drapers fought to gain supremacy over dyers and finishers, and manufacturing centres vied for supremacy. After around 1240 strife was widespread, with both economic gain and political power at stake. In this increasingly secular and market-driven world, the production and role of textiles began to change. While still esteemed as insights into the eternal world—and, for the finest cloths, as assurances in life—Western textiles were moving inexorably towards industrialization and the separation from art that this implies.

FRACTALS IN CROSS-CULTURAL COMPARISON

The fractal settlement patterns of Africa stand in sharp contrast to the Cartesian grids of Euro-American settlements. Why the difference? One explanation could be the difference in social structure. Euro-American cultures are organized by what anthropologists would call a "state society." This includes not just the modern nation-state, but refers more generally to any society with a large political hierarchy, labor specialization, and cohesive, formal controls—what is sometimes called "top-down" organization. Precolonial African cultures included many state societies, as well as an enormous number of smaller, decentralized social groups, with little political hierarchy—that is, societies that are organized "bottom-up" rather than "top-down." But if fractal architecture is simply the automatic result of a nonstate social organization, then we should see fractal settlement patterns in the indigenous societies of many parts of the world. In this chapter we will examine the settlement patterns found in the indigenous societies of the Americas and the South Pacific, but our search will turn up very few fractals. Rather than dividing the world between a Euclidean West and fractal non-West, we will find that each society makes use of its particular design themes in organizing its built environment. African architecture tends to be fractal because that is a prominent design theme in African culture. In fact, this cultural specificity of design themes is true not only for architecture, but for many other types of material design and cultural practices as well. We will begin our survey with a brief look at the design themes in Native American societies, which included both hierarchical state empires as well as smaller, decentralized tribal cultures.

NATIVE AMERICAN DESIGN

The Ancestral Pueblo society dwelled in what is now the southwestern United States around 1100 C.E. Aerial photos of these sites (FIG. 9–22) are some of the most famous examples of Native American settlements. But as we can see from this vantage point,

the architecture is primarily characterized by an enormous *circular* form created from smaller *rectangular* components—certainly not the same shape at two different scales. This juxtaposition of the circle and the quadrilateral (rectangle or cross-shaped) form is not a coincidence; the two forms are the most important design themes in the material culture of many Native American societies, including both North and South continents.

As far as architecture is concerned, there are no examples of the nonlinear scaling we saw in Africa. The only Native American architectures that come close are a few instances of linear concentric figures (FIG. 9–23). Shapes approximating concentric circles can be seen in the Poverty Point complex in northern Louisiana, for example, and there were concentric circles of tepees in the Cheyenne camps. The step-pyramids of Mesoamerica look like concentric squares when viewed from above. But linear concentric figures are not fractals. First, these are linear layers: the distance between lines is always the same, and thus the number of concentric circles within the largest circle is finite. The nonlinear scaling of fractals requires an ever-changing distance between lines, which means there can be an infinite number in a finite space (FIG. 9–23B). Second, even nonlinear concentric circles are only self-similar with respect to a single locus (the center point), rather than having the global self-similarity of fractals (FIG. 9–23C).

The importance of the circle is detailed in a famous passage by Black Elk (1961), in which he explains that "everything an Indian does is in a circle, and that is because the Power of the World always works in circles, and everything tries to be round." But he goes on to note that his people thought of their world as "the circle of the four quarters." A similar combination of the circle and quadrilateral form can be seen many Native American myths and artifacts; it is not their only design theme, but it can be found in a surprising number of different societies. Burland (1965), for example, shows a ceremonial rattle consisting of a wooden hoop with a cross inside from southern Alaska, a Navajo sand painting showing four equidistant stalks of corn growing from a circular lake, and a Pawnee buffalo-hide drum with four arrows emanating from its circular center. Nabokov and Easton (1989) describe the cultural symbolism of the tepee in terms of its

9-22 • EUCLIDEAN GEOMETRY IN NATIVE AMERICAN ARCHITECTURE
(a) Aerial photo of Bandelier, one of the Ancestral Pueblo settlements (starting around 1100 C.E.) in northwestern New Mexico. **(b)** Aerial photo of Pueblo Bonito, another Ancestral Pueblo settlement (starting around 950 C.E.). Note that they are mostly rectangular at the smallest scale and circular at the largest scale.
a, Photo coutesy of Tom Baker; b, Photo courtesy of Georg Gerster.

a

b

9-23 • LINEAR CONCENTRIC FORMS IN NATIVE AMERICAN ARCHITECTURE

(a) Native American architecture is typically based on quadrilateral grids or a combination of circular and grid forms. The only examples of scaling shapes are these linear concentric forms. In the Poverty Point complex, for example, concentric circles were used, and concentric squares can be seen if we look at the Mexican step pyramids from above. These forms are better characterized as Euclidean than fractal for two reasons: **(b)** First, they are linear. Here is an example of a nonlinear concentric circle. While the linear version must have a finite number of circles, this figure could have an infinite number and still fit in the same boundary. **(c)** Second, they only scale with respect to one point (the center). Here is an example of circles with more global scaling symmetry.

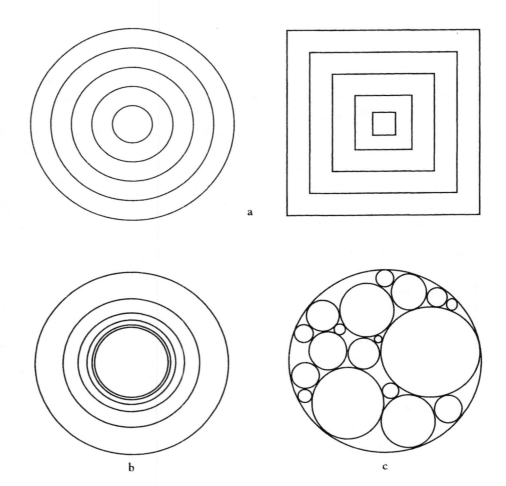

a

b

c

combination of circular hide exterior and the four main struts of the interior wood supports. Waters (1963) provides an extensive illustration of the cultural significance of combining the circular and cross form in his commentary on the Hopi creation myth.

The fourfold symmetry of the quadrilateral form has lead to some sophisticated conceptual structures in Native American knowledge systems. In Navajo sand painting, for example, the cruciform shape represents the "four directions" concept, similar to the Cartesian coordinate system. While orderly and consistent, it is by no means simple (see Witherspoon and Peterson 1995). The four Navajo directions are also associated with corresponding sun positions (dawn, day, evening, night), yearly seasons (spring, summer, fall, winter), principal colors (white, blue, yellow, black), and other quadrilateral divisions (botanical categories, partitions of the life cycle, etc.). These are further broken into intersecting bipolarities (e.g., the east/west sun path is broken by the north/south directions). Combined with circular curves (usually representing organic shapes and processes), the resulting schema are rich cultural resources for indigenous mathematics (see Moore 1994). But, except for minor repetitions (like the small circular kivas in the Chaco canyon site of FIG. 9–22) there is nothing particularly fractal about these quadrilateral designs.

Many Mesoamerican cities, such as the Mayans' Teotihuacán, the Aztec's Tenochtitlán, and the Toltec's Tula, embedded a wealth of astronomical knowledge in their rectangular layouts, aligning their streets and buildings with heavenly objects and events (Aveni 1980). J. Thompson (1970) and Klein (1982) describe the quadrilateral figure as an underlying theme in Mesoamerican geometric thinking, from small-scale material construction techniques such as weaving, to the heavenly cosmology of the four serpents. Rogelio Díaz, of the Mathematics Museum at the University of Querétaro, points out that the skin patterns of the diamondback rattlesnake were used by the Mayans to symbolize this concept **(FIG. 9–24A)**.

Comparing the Mayan snake pattern with an African weaving based on the cobra skin pattern **(FIG. 9–24B)**, we can see how geometric modeling of similar natural phenomena in these two cultures results in very different representations. The Native American example emphasizes the Euclidean symmetry *within one size frame* ("size frame" because the term "scale" is confusing in the context of snake skin). This Mayan pattern is composed of four shapes of the same size, a fourfold symmetry. But the African example emphasizes fractal symmetry, which is not about similarity between right/left or up/down, but rather similarity *between*

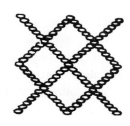

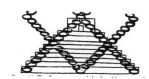

9-24 • SNAKESKIN MODELS IN NATIVE AMERICAN AND AFRICAN CULTURES
(a) Rogelio Díaz of the Mathematics Museum at the University of Querétaro shows how the skin patterns of the diamondback rattlesnake were used by the Mayans to symbolize a cosmology based on quadrilateral structure. **(b)** The Mandiack weavers of Guinea-Bissau have also created an abstract design based on a snakeskin pattern, but chose to emphasize the fractal characteristics.

a

b

different size frames. The African snake pattern shows diamonds within diamonds within diamonds. Neither design is necessarily more accurate: cobra skin does indeed exhibit a fractal pattern—the snake's "hood," its twin white patches, and the individual scales themselves are all diamond shaped—and yet snake skin patterns (thanks to the arrangement of the scales) are also characteristically in diagonal rows, so they are accurately modeled as Euclidean structures as well. Each culture chooses to emphasize the characteristics that best fit its design theme.

There are a few cases in which Native Americans have used scaling geometries in artistic designs. Several of these were not, however, part of the traditional repertoire. Navajo blankets, for example, were originally quite linear; it was only on examining Persian rugs that Navajo weavers began to use more scaling styles of design (and even then the designs were much more Euclidean than the Persian originals; see Kent 1985). The Pueblo "storyteller" figures have some scaling properties, but they are of recent (1960s) origin. Pottery and calabash (carved gourd) artisans in Africa often create scaling by allowing the design adaptively to change proportion according to the three-dimensional form on which it is inscribed, but this was quite rare in Native American pottery until the 1960s.

Finally, there are three Native American designs that are both indigenous and fractal. The best case is the abstract figurative art of the Haida, Kwakiutl, Tlingut, and others in the Pacific Northwest (Holm 1965). The figures, primarily carvings, have the kind of global, nonlinear self-similarity necessary to qualify as fractals and clearly exhibit recursive scaling of up to three or four iterations. They also make use of adaptive scaling, as illustrated by the shrinking series of figures on the diminishing handles of soup ladles. Researchers since Adams (1936) have pointed to the similarity with early Chinese art, which also has some beautiful examples of scaling form, and its style of curvature and bilateral symmetry could indeed be culturally tied to these New World designs through an ancient common origin. However, I doubt that is the case for the scaling characteristics. The Pacific Northwest art appears to have developed its scaling structure as the result of competition between artisans for increasingly elaborate carvings (Faris 1983). Although some researchers have attributed the competition pressure to European trading influences, the development of the scaling designs was clearly an internal invention.

The other two traditional Native American designs do not qualify as fractals quite as well. One involves the saw-tooth pattern found in several basket and weaving designs. When two sawtooth rows intersect at an angle, they create a triangle made from triangular edges. But these typically have only two iterations of scale, and there is no indication in the ethnographic literature that they are semantically tied to ideas of recursion or scaling (see Thomas and Slockish 1982, 18). The other is an arrangement of spiral arms often found on coiled baskets. Again, this is self-similar only with respect to the center point, but there are some nonlinear scaling versions (that is, designs that rapidly get smaller as you move from basket edge to center). However, these designs generally appear to be a fusion between the circular form of the basket and the cruciform shape of the arms: again more a combination of two Euclidean shapes than a fractal.

One of the most common examples of this fusion between the circle and the cross is the "bifold rotation" pattern in which the arms curve in opposite directions, as shown in FIG. 9–25A. FIG. 9–25B shows the figure of a bat from Mimbres pottery with a more complex version of the bifold rotation. Euclidean symmetry has been emphasized in this figure; for example, the ears and mouth of the bat have been made to look similar to increase the bilateral symmetry, and the belly is drawn as a rectangle. FIG. 9–25C shows the figure of a bat from an African design; it is a zigzag shape that expands in width from top to bottom, representing the wing of the bat. Here we see neglect of the bilateral symmetry of the bat, and an emphasis on the scaling folds of a single wing. Again, the Native American representation makes use of its quadrilateral/circular design theme, just as the African representation of the bat emphasizes scaling design.

There is plenty of complexity and sophistication in the indigenous geometry and numeric systems of the Americas (see Ascher 1991, 87–94; Closs 1986; Eglash 1998b), but with the impressive exception of the Pacific Northwest carvings, fractals are almost entirely absent in Native American designs.

DESIGNS OF ASIA AND THE SOUTH PACIFIC
Several of the South Pacific cultures share a tradition of decorative curved and spiral forms, which in certain Maori versions—

particularly their rafter and tattoo patterns—would certainly count as fractal (see Hamilton 1977). These are strongly suggestive of the curvature of waves and swirling water. Classic Japanese paintings of water waves were also presented as fractal patterns in Mandelbrot's (1982) seminal text (plate C16). These may have some historic relation to scaling patterns in Chinese art (see Washburn and Crowe 1988, fig. 6.9), which are based on swirling forms of water and clouds, abstracted as spiral scaling structures. While both the Japanese and Chinese patterns are explicitly associated with an effort to imitate nature, these Maori designs are reported to be more about culture—in particular, they emphasize mirror-image symmetries, which are associated with their cultural themes of complimentarity in social relations (Hanson 1983).

In almost all other indigenous examples, however, the Pacific Islander patterns are quite Euclidean. Settlement layout, for instance, is typically in one or two rows of rectangular buildings near the coasts, with circular arrangements of rectangles also occurring inland (see Fraser 1968). The building construction is generally based on a combination of rectangular grids with triangular or curved arch roofs. Occasionally these triangular faces are decorated with triangles, but otherwise nonscaling designs dominate both structural and decorative patterns.

Again, it is important to note that this lack of fractals does not imply a lack of sophistication in their mathematical thinking. For example, Ascher (1991) has analyzed some of the algorithmic properties of Warlpiri (Pacific Islander) sand drawings. Similar structures are also found in Africa, where they are called *lusona*. But while the lusona tend to use similar patterns at different scales, the Warlpiri drawings tend to use different patterns at different scales. Ascher concludes that the Warlpiri method of combining different graph movements is analogous to algebraic combinations, but the African lusona are best described as fractals.

Complicating my characterization of the South Pacific as dominated by Euclidean patterns is the extensive influence of India. It is perhaps no coincidence that the triangle of triangles mentioned above is most common in Indonesia. In architecture, a famous exception to the generally Euclidean form is that of Borobudur, a temple of Indian religious origin in Java. Although northern India tends toward Euclidean architecture, explicit recursive design is seen in several temples in southern India—the Kandarya Mahadeo in Khajuraho is one of the clearest examples—and is related to recursive concepts in religious cosmology. These same areas in southern India also have a version of the lusona drawings, and many other examples of fractal design. Interestingly, these examples from southern India are the products of Dravidian culture, which is suspected to have significant historical roots in Africa.

EUROPEAN DESIGNS
Most traditional European fractal designs, like those of Japan and China, are due to imitation of nature. There are at least two stellar exceptions, however, that are worth noting. One is the scaling

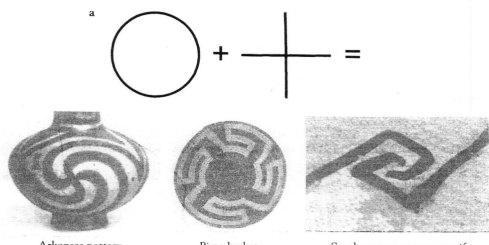

Arkansas pottery   Pima basket   Southwestern pottery motif

(a) The circular and quadrilateral forms were often combined in Native American designs as a fourfold or bifold rotation.

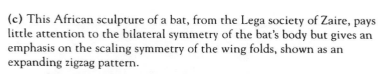

(b) This image of a bat, from a Mimbres pottery in Southwestern Native American tradition, shows an emphasis on circular and quadrilateral form. The ear and the mouth, for example, are made to look similar to emphasize bilateral symmetry, and the belly is drawn as a rectangle. It also shows the wing bones as a bifold rotation pattern.

(c) This African sculpture of a bat, from the Lega society of Zaire, pays little attention to the bilateral symmetry of the bat's body but gives an emphasis on the scaling symmetry of the wing folds, shown as an expanding zigzag pattern.

9-25 • THE BIFOLD ROTATION IN NATIVE AMERICAN DESIGN
a: Left, from Miles 1963. Courtesy of University of Arizona Press. Center, from Southwest Indian Craft Arts *by Clara Lee Tanner. Copyright 1968 by the Arizona Board of Regents. Courtesy of University of Arizona Press. Right, photo courtesy Don Crowe. b, from Zaslow 1977, courtesy of Ron Eglash. c, courtesy of Daniel Biebuyck.*

iterations of triangles in the floor tiles of the Church of Santa Maria in Cosmedin Rome. I have not been able to determine anything about their cultural origins, but they are clearly artistic invention rather than imitation of some natural form. The other can be found in certain varieties of Celtic interlace designs. Nordenfalk (1977) suggests that these are historically related to the spiral designs of pre-Christian Celtic religion, where they

trace the flow of a vital life force. They are geometrically classified as an Eulerian path, which is closely associated with mathematical knot theory (cf. Jones 1990, 99).

CONCLUSION
Fractal structure is by no means universal in the material patterns of indigenous societies. In Native American designs, only the

Pacific Northwest patterns show a strong fractal characteristic; Euclidean shapes otherwise dominate the art and architecture. Except for the Maori spiral designs, fractal geometry does not appear to be an important aspect of indigenous South Pacific patterns either. That is not to say that fractal designs appear nowhere but Africa—southern India is full of fractals, and Chinese fluid swirl designs and Celtic knot patterns are almost certainly of independent origin. The important point here is that the fractal designs of Africa should not be mistaken for a universal or pan-cultural phenomenon; they are culturally specific.

INTENTION AND INVENTION IN DESIGN

Before we can discuss the fractal shapes in African settlement architectures as geometric knowledge, we need to think carefully about the relation between material designs and mathematical understanding. Designs are best seen as positioned on a range or spectrum of intention. At the bottom of the range are unintentional patterns, created accidentally as the by-product of some other activity. In the middle of the range are designs that are intentional but purely intuitive, with no rules or guidelines to explain its creation. At the upper end of the range, we have the intentional application of explicit rules that we are accustomed to associating with mathematics. The following sections will examine the fractal designs that occur in various positions along this intentionality spectrum.

FRACTALS FROM UNCONSCIOUS ACTIVITY

An excellent example of unintentional fractals can be found in the work of Michael Batty and Paul Longley (1989), who examined the shape of large-scale urban sprawl surrounding European and American cities **(FIG. 9–26)**. While the blocks of these cities are typically laid out in rectangular grids, at very large scales—around 100 square miles—we can see that the process of population growth has created an irregular pattern. This type of fractal, a "diffusion limited aggregation," also occurs in chemical systems when particles in a solution are attracted to an electrode. Fractal urban sprawl is clearly the result of unconscious social dynamics, not conscious design. At the smaller scales in which there is conscious planning, European and American settlement architectures are typically Euclidean.

FRACTALS FROM NATURE: MIMESIS VERSUS MODELING

It might be tempting to think that the contrast between the Euclidean designs of Europe and the fractal designs of Africa can be explained by the important role of the natural environment in African societies. But this assumption turns out to be wrong; if anything, there is a tendency for indigenous societies to favor Euclidean shapes. Physicist Kh. S. Mamedov observed such a contrast in his reflections on his youth in a nomadic culture:

> My parents and countrymen . . . up to the second world war had been nomads. . . . Outside our nomad tents we were liv-

ing in a wonderful kingdom of various curved lines and forms. So why were the aesthetic signs not formed from them, having instead preserved geometric patterns . . .? [I]n the cities where the straight-line geometry was predominant the aesthetic signs were formed … with nature playing the dominating role. . . . [T]he nomad did not need the "portrait" of an oak to be carried with him elsewhere because he could view all sorts of oaks every day and every hour . . . while for the townsfolk their inclination to nature was more a result of nostalgia. (Mamedov 1986, 512–513)

Contrary to romantic portraits of the "noble savage" living as one with nature, most indigenous societies seem quite interested in differentiating themselves from their surroundings. It is the inhabitants of large state societies, such as those of modern Europe, who yearn to mimic the natural. When European designs are fractal, it is usually due to an effort to mimic nature. African fractals based on mimicry of natural form are relatively rare; their inspiration tends to come from the realm of culture.

How should we place such nature-based designs in our intentionality spectrum? That depends on the difference between mimesis and modeling. Mimesis is an attempt to mirror the image of a particular object, a goal explicitly stated by Plato and Aristotle as the essence of art, one that was subsequently followed in Europe for many centuries (see Auerbach 1953). A photograph is

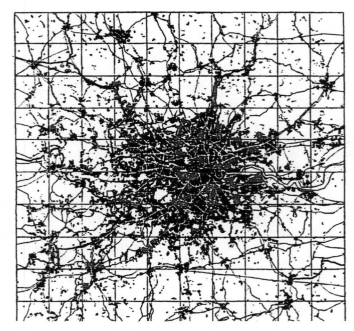

9-26 • URBAN SPRAWL IN LONDON
Large-scale urban sprawl generally has a fractal structure. The urban sprawl fractals only exist at very large scales—about 100 sq. miles—and result from the unconscious accumulation of urban population dynamics. At levels of conscious intent (e.g., the grid of city blocks), European cities are typically Euclidean. Area is 10 × 10 kilometers. *Courtesy of Batty et al.*

a good example of mimesis. A photo might capture the fractal image of a tree, but it would be foolish to conclude that the photographer knows fractal geometry. If artisans are simply trying to copy a particular natural object, then the scaling is an unintended by-product.

The most important attributes that separate mimesis from modeling are abstraction and generalization. Abstraction is an attempt to leave out many of the concrete details of the subject by creating a simpler figure whose structure is still roughly analogous to the original—often called a "stylized" representation in the arts. Generalization means selecting an analogous structure that is common to all examples of the subject; what is often referred to as an "underlying" form or law. For example, Mandelbrot (1981) points to the European Beaux Arts style as an attempt not merely to imitate nature, but to "guess its laws." He notes that the interior of the Paris opera house makes use of scaling arches-within-arches, a pattern that generalizes some of the scaling characteristics of nature, but is not a copy of any one particular natural object.

Since the ultimate generalization is a mathematical model, why didn't design practices such as the Beaux Arts style result in an early development of fractal geometry? For Europeans, such lush ornamentation was presented—and generally accepted—as embodying the *opposite* of mathematics; it was an effort to create designs that could only be understood in irrational, emotional, or intuitive terms. Even some movements against this attempt, such as the use of distinctly Euclidean forms in the high modern arts style, simply reinforced the association because it only offered a reversal, suggesting that "mathematical" shapes (cubes, spheres, etc.) could be esthetically appreciated. With rare exceptions (e.g., Thompson 1917), mimesis of nature in pre-WW II European art traditions merely furthered the assumption that Euclidean geometry was the only true geometry.

The difference between mimesis and modeling provides two different positions along the intentionality spectrum. The least intentional would be merely holding a mirror to nature—for example, if someone was just shooting a camera or painting a realistic picture outdoors and happened to include a fractal object (cloud, tree, etc.). This mimesis does not count as mathematical thinking. More intentional is a stylized representation of nature. If the artist has reduced the natural image to a structurally analogous collection of more simple elements, she has created an abstract model. Whether or not such abstractions move toward more mathematical models is a matter of local preference.

The two examples of African representations of nature we observed in the previous chapter certainly show that the artisans have gone beyond mere mimesis. The Mandiack cobra pattern we saw in FIGURE 9–23 shows a strictly systematic scaling pattern. This textile design conveys the scaling property of the natural cobra skin pattern—diamonds at many scales—in a stylized or abstract way. We can take this idea a step further by examining another Bwami bat sculpture (FIG. 9–27). This spiral pattern is also a stylized representation of the natural scaling of the bat's wing, but it is a different geometric design than the expanding zigzag pattern we saw in FIGURE 9–25C. It is more stylized in the sense of being further abstracted from the original natural bat's wing. This provides further evidence that the sculptors were focused on the scaling properties—the generalized underlying feature—and not particular concrete details.

The greatest danger of this book is that readers might misinterpret its meaning in terms of primitivism. The fact that African fractals are rarely the result of imitating natural forms helps remind us that they are *not* due to "primitives living close to nature." But even for those rare cases in which African fractals are representations of nature, it is clearly a self-conscious abstraction, not a mimetic reflection. The geometric thinking that goes into these examples may be simple, but it is quite intentional.

THE FRACTAL ESTHETIC

Just as we saw how designs based on nature range from unconscious to intentional, artificial designs also vary along a range of intention, with some simply the result of an intuitive inspiration, and others a more self-conscious application of rules or principles. The examples of African fractals in **FIGURE 9–28** did not appear to be related to anything other than the artisan's esthetic intuition or sense of beauty. As far as I could determine from descriptions in the literature and my own fieldwork, there were no explicit rules about how to construct these designs, and no meaning was attached to the particular geometric structure of the figures other than looking good. In particular, I spent several weeks in Dakar wandering the streets asking about certain fractal fabric patterns and jewelry designs, and the insistence that these patterns were "just for looks" was so adamant that if someone finally had offered an explanation, I would have viewed it with suspicion.

Since some professional mathematicians report that their ideas were pure intuition—a sudden flash of insight, or "Aha!" as Martin Gardner puts it—we shouldn't discount the geometric thinking of an artisan who reports "I can't tell you how I created that, it just came to me." Esthetic patterns clearly qualify as intentional designs. On the other hand, there isn't much we can say about the mathematical ideas behind these patterns; they will have to remain a mystery unless something more is revealed about their meaning or the artisan's construction techniques. It is worth noting, however, that they do contribute to the fractal design theme in Africa. Esthetic patterns help inspire practical designs, and vice versa. Since ancient trade networks were well established, the diffusion of esthetic patterns is probably one part of the explanation for how fractals came to be so widespread across the African continent.

Of course, there are plenty of African designs that are strictly Euclidean, but even these can occur in "fractalized" versions. One particularly interesting example is the *quincunx* (FIG. 9–29). The

9-27 • STYLIZED SCULPTURE OF A BAT

Another Lega bat sculpture, but unlike the zigzag design we saw in FIGURE 9–25C, here the scaling of the wing folds is represented by a spiral. *Courtesy of Museum of African Art, New York.*

basic quincunx is a pattern of five squares, with one at the center and one at each corner. The design is common in Senegal, where it is said to represent the "light of Allah." The quincunx is historically important because the image was recorded as being of religious significance to the early African American "man of science" Benjamin Banneker. Since evidence shows that Banneker's grandfather (Bannaka) came from Senegal, the quincunx is a fascinating possibility for geometry in the African diaspora (see Eglash 1997c for details). Because of the fractal esthetic, this religious symbol is often arranged in a recursive pattern—five squares of five squares—as shown in FIGURE 9–29 in the design for a leather neck bag.

Finally, there are also examples of the fractal esthetic in common household furnishings. Euro-American furniture is differentiated by form and function—stools are structured differently from chairs, which are structured differently from couches. But in African homes one often sees different sizes of the same shape (FIG. 9–30). A similar difference has been noted in cross-cultural comparisons of housing. Whereas Euro-Americans would never think to have a governor's mansion shaped like a peasant's shack (or vice versa), precolonial African architecture typically used the same form at different sizes. It is unfortunate that this African structural characteristic is typically described in terms of a lack—

9-28 • ESTHETIC FRACTALS

(a) Meurant (quoted in Reif 1996) reports that the Mbuti women who created this fractal design, a bark-cloth painting, told him the design was not "telling stories," nor was it "representing any particular object." (b) Scaling patterns can be found in many African decorative designs that are reported to be "just for beauty." Upper left, Shoowa Raffia cloth; lower left, Senegalese tie dye; right, Senegalese pendant.
a, Courtesy of Georges Meruant. b: Upper left, Courtesy of The Trustees of the British Museum; lower left, Courtesy of Musee Royal de l'Afrique Centrale. Copyright © by RMCA Tervuren; right, photo courtesy IFAN, Dakar.

b

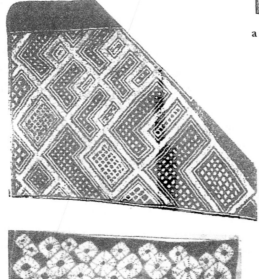

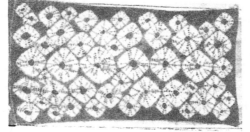

a

as the absence of shape distinctions rather than as the presence of a scaling design theme.

Conclusion

We now have some guidelines to help determine which fractal designs should count as mathematics, which should not, and which are in between. **FIGURE 9–31** summarizes this spectrum. Fractals produced by unconscious activity, or as the unintentional by-product from some other purpose, cannot be attributed to indigenous concepts. But some artistic activities, such as the creation of stylized representations of nature or purely esthetic designs, do show intentional activity focused on fractals. Such examples may be restricted in terms of geometric thinking—the artisans may only report that the design suddenly came to them in a flash of intuition—but these are clearly distinguished from those which are unconscious or accidental.

THE FIBERS OF NATIVE AMERICAN WEAVING:

A HISTORICAL BACKGROUND

The use of animal skins or hides to provide coverings for the body, protection from the weather, and containers for various personal possessions, must have developed very shortly after the first hunter captured his animal quarry. Taking the carcass, peeling off the hide, and wrapping it around one's body was an initial step; crudely sewing two hides together to form a tube or envelope was the second. This simple process eventually became more sophisticated, and subsequently, with the refinement of tanning techniques, these hide garments were given a slightly tailored cut—or at least, a more refined form, allowing the wearer comfortable clothing. As these merged into defined clothing styles, the human need for esthetics led to embellishment: this was achieved by various means, most notably by rubbing pigments onto the surface of the garment, or the application of color in specific designs by means of a brush.

9-30 • THE FRACTAL ESTHETIC IN HOUSEHOLD OBJECTS
African stools, chairs, and benches are often created in a scaling series.
Courtesy of Africa Place, Inc.

Unintentional	*Intentional but implicit*	*Intentional and explicit*
Unconscious activity • urban sprawl	*Conscious use of natural scaling* • stylistic abstraction of natural scaling	*Construction techniques*
Accidental fractals • "mirror" portrait of nature (*mimesis*; e.g., photography)	*Esthetic design* • intuitive fractal design theme	*Knowledge systems*

9-32 • Reconstructed kiva mural. Ceremonial figures in woven kilt and dress with brocaded or embroidered decorations. Anasazi; Awátovi Pueblo, Arizona. ca. 1600.
Courtesy of Watson Smith.

9-33 • Loose finger-woven wool *ceinture flèche* with beaded trim. Osage; Pawhuska, Oklahoma. ca. 1890–1910.
Courtesy of National Museum of the American Indian, Smithsonian Institution, #39986.

And shortly after the introduction of this very basic garment form, the ability to interlace fibers opened up the world of basketry, undoubtedly followed almost immediately by various forms of finger weaving—another form of non-loomed weaving. Although perhaps directed initially towards the limited production of belting, strips, and similar long, narrow objects, technical skill and experience slowly expanded to allow the creation of a wide variety of accessories. This form of interlacing probably progressed in complexity to the point where the true loom became inevitable; the finger weaver can go only so far in the production of textiles. **(FIG. 9–33)**

The earliest weaving was simply one-ply finger-woven netting, plaiting and braiding, and seems to have been known in North America at least as early as 1000 B.C. (Plaiting is the simplest, over and under cross-weave technique.) It was practiced for well over a thousand years before the introduction of the backstrap (or belt) loom, sometime between 500–750 A.D. This early loom created a warp tension by attaching one end of the warp to a tree, wall, or other stationary object, and the opposing end to a rod which was fastened to the weaver's waist. By leaning backward or forward, she can increase or decrease the tension.

This technique, however, is limited to the production of narrow-gauge textiles, and the need for wider cloth led in time to the invention of the more useful true loom, incorporating a rigid frame and heddle, which seems to have become widespread throughout the Southwest by no later than 1000 A.D. This time period was one of general transition rather than the abrupt and radical introduction of other techniques; the evidence certainly suggests that finger weaving yielded slowly to the more efficient belt loom, and that this in turn gave way to the true loom and its greater benefits. (see FIG. 9–48)

This was not an overnight development, even in any one area. Crafts traditions change slowly, and this is particularly true of weaving. There must have been a period of experimentation following the introduction into any village of the new apparatus, with the passing of several years—perhaps even a generation—before it replaced earlier techniques. And even so, the older practice never completely died out; certainly almost all regions in which the true loom is primarily used today still continue to produce occasionally some textiles on either the belt loom or by finger weaving techniques.

The true loom offers three major benefits: much faster and more efficient production, the creation of wider sections of weave, and a greater regularity in the finished textile. Various in-between steps may have preceeded it, but with the development of a frame for stretching the warp (vertical) threads, and a heddle to keep them separate, the true loom became an actuality.

Once this had been accomplished, ancient man was off to the creation of a tremendous variety of textiles. The many raw materials supplied by nature—plant fibers, including cotton, yucca, hemp, milkweed; the shredded inner bark of trees; animal hair and fur, even human hair; to mention only the most commonly seen—were all widely used for the purpose. Some materials were more effective than others; it is much easier to weave mountain sheep wool into garments than twisted corn husk, but each enjoyed a range, period, and style of human utilization, though not all were equally effectively loomed. It can be said, however, that every fibrous material available to ancient man was used somewhere, sometime, in the creation or embellishment of textiles.

Initially, these woven textiles were in all probability undecorated simple plain-weave squares intented for basic wrap-around purposes. But with increased experience and technical skill, these developed into a far more sophisticated design style, in which greater attention was given to the visual appearance, and eventually they became lavishly decorated as the demand required. The development of decorative technique seems to have paralleled that of the hide garments: color was rubbed onto the surface, then subsequently painted on, before it was finally achieved by means of skillfully weaving various pre-dyed fibers into fabric patterns. While this latter technique was a slow development, the ability to accomplish such elaborately woven designs was early in the history of man in North America, and can be demonstrated by some of the surviving fragments which have been recovered from excavations in the Southwestern United States. (**FIG. 9–35**)

Once body covering was comfortably achieved, it would seem that the weaver's attention next turned to coverings for beds, dwellings, floors, and walls. This must in all probability have been achieved through the production of matting which used various fibers, subsequently emerging into the manufacture of full-fledged blankets and rugs. These were probably plain at first, eventually taking on decorative qualities which in turn became more elaborate—indeed, as a source of color in prehistoric life, the weaver held an important place. Few other crafts provided as much color in as controllable a form, with perhaps only pottery or painted wood offering an equal palette. Along with body painting and tattooing, and a wide variety of shell, stone, clay, and related jewelry, textiles therefore provided an outlet for the human need for personal decoration.

Since early garments lacked pockets, containers were an indispensable product of these weavers, and they were created in a wide variety of forms, sizes, and styles. Carrying bags, pouches, and similar objects were required for the storage and transportation of personal possessions and for everyday use. Some of these containers were of critical importance to the survival of the family group: they kept the hunter's equipment together, or the warrior's weapons immediately at hand; they protected the religious paraphernalia of the priest; and they held the woman's cooking, sewing, and craft tools. Others were valued as holders for creature

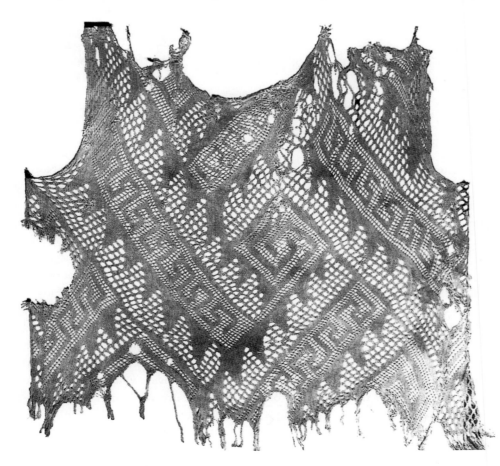

9-34 • Twine-plaited cotton shirt. The sleeveless feature is similar to the modern vest. Anasazi: Tonto National Monument, Arizona. ca. 1250–1400. 26x46 inches. *Courtesy of Arizona State Museum, E.B. Sayles photo, #1420.*

9-35 • Weft-float pattern weave pouch; black and white cotton. *Photo courtesy Glen E. Henderson: National Park Service.*

9-36 • Detail. Anasazi; Montezuma Castle National Monument. *ca.* 1300–1600. 5x12½ inches. *Photo courtesy Glen E. Henderson: National Park Service.*

comforts, game apparatus, or similar needs; most foodstuffs were carried in rawhide containers.

There is no way at this late date to accurately determine who was the weaver in ancient times; one can only assume on the basis of contemporary practice. Since this is an art deeply rooted in tradition, such a basis of postulation seems fair. Thus it would seem most likely that prehistoric weaving was the woman's domain, since the process could be easily undertaken while taking care of the home, supervising the children, and pursuing her daily program. The man, charged with constant travel in search of game, trade needs, or other more mobile demands, could not as readily follow a confining craft activity. It is true that throughout the Pueblo region of the Southwest men are the weavers, alternating the work with agricultural duties; however, this is a very sedentary culture with a cyclical calendar, and it is possible to divide one's time comfortably into such a variety of activities.

Just when man first produced woven articles in North America is still an unsettled debate between scholars. The fragile nature of both baskets and textiles has caused all but a very few fragments to disappear into oblivion, and even many of these remaining bits of evidence have been recovered under circumstances which make them impossible to date with any accuracy. However, the present cumulated information suggests that twined and plaited basketry was a widely practiced art at least as early as 7500 B.C. in the Southwest. (Twining is the wrapping of outer strands around inner foundations.) Weaving undoubtedly followed fairly shortly after, although no prehistoric examples have been found dating much earlier than *circa* 1000 B.C.

It is the dry climate of the Southwest which contributes to the preservation of such early evidence. While any sizeable quantity of surviving examples is not found elsewhere in North America, due largely to climatic conditions, certainly the art itself

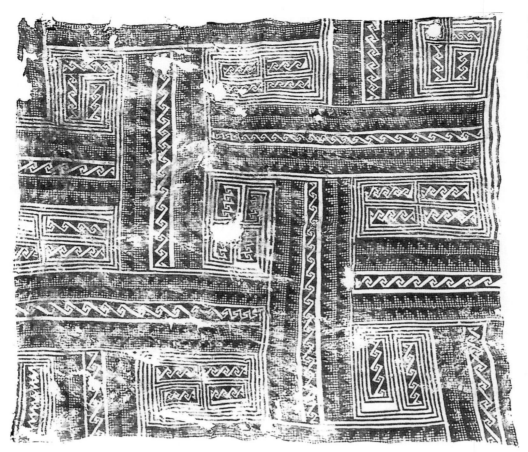

9-37 • Painted black-on-white cotton *manta* (shawl). Anasazi: Hidden House, Arizona. *ca.* 1200–1300. 64x64 inches. *Courtesy of Arizona State Museum, E. B. Sayles photo, #1415.*

existed in many areas. There are many scattered specimens recovered from caves, rock-shelters, and other dry repositories which testify to the ability of the local weavers to use various fibers in the production of textiles—and some fragments of cotton which have been found suggest that there was a wide trade in this raw material.

The ability to introduce and control color in prehistoric times must have been well developed, although evidence is very limited in this area. Certainly those few specimens which have survived—perhaps a thousand sizeable examples are known, and of these only a handful are of more than eight to ten inches in size—offer striking evidence of the strong color range available to and incorporated by these people in the preparation of their textiles.

In a brief survey of the continent in prehistoric times, one may conveniently start with the Northwest Coast, following the pattern of the early migrants into the New World. Here, the damp climate has resulted in the disintegration of almost all organic evidence, although recently a few well-preserved specimens have been recovered in Washington state, dating from the very early historic period. These follow much the same pattern as contemporary Northwest Coast weaving in both style and design. An abundance of bones from grave sites also suggests

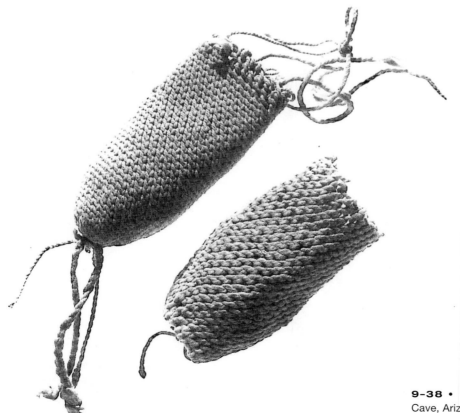

9-38 • Closed-loop weave cotton pouches. Anasazi: Gourd Cave, Arizona. *ca.* 1300–1500. L: 21½x23½ inches. *Arizona State Museum, Helga Tiewes photo, #39196.*

9-39 • Closed-loop weave pouch of human hair.
Courtesy of Anasazi: Arizona State Museum, Helga Tiewes photo, #39196.

that the use of dog hair for weaving is not an invention of modern times.

The antiquity of the famed "Chilkat blanket," as it is most commonly known, is not clearly established. Certainly the form and technical style indicate long ancestry, and the designs have undergone considerable changes, suggesting a fluidity in art fashion which would support the argument that this is not a newly introduced textile concept. But no truly prehistoric examples are known; one of the earliest to have been preserved is in the Peabody Museum, Salem, Massachusetts; it was collected sometime before 1832. While this is early for museum-collected specimens, it is not particularly so in the history of weaving; yet the technique, design, and style indicate that this was an art already long known to the Tlingit people.

The Plains region manifests very little evidence of a major weaving tradition; buffalo hair was the most common substance, but the cultural pattern of the prehistoric and early historic Indian seems not to have been one in which weaving was as important as the use of hides. It should be kept in mind, however, that the Plains Indian culture as we think of it today was of very recent dating in that area, and at best was of only a short duration, as world history goes—indeed, it was roughly equal to that of the United States itself. Therefore, the opportunity to develop a great

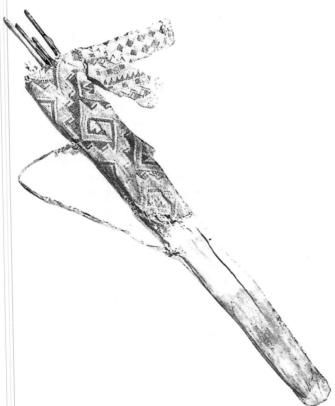

9-40 • Left. Tapestry-weave cotton quiver constructed in five sections: blue, brown, and white weft.
Courtesy of Anasazi: Hidden House, Arizona. ca. 1200 E. B. Sayles photo, #1410.

9-41 • Right. Yucca fiber carrying band, or tumpline, with geometrical designs. Basketmaker Utah. *ca.* 500–700.
Courtesy of The Field Museum of Natural History Chicago, #165170.

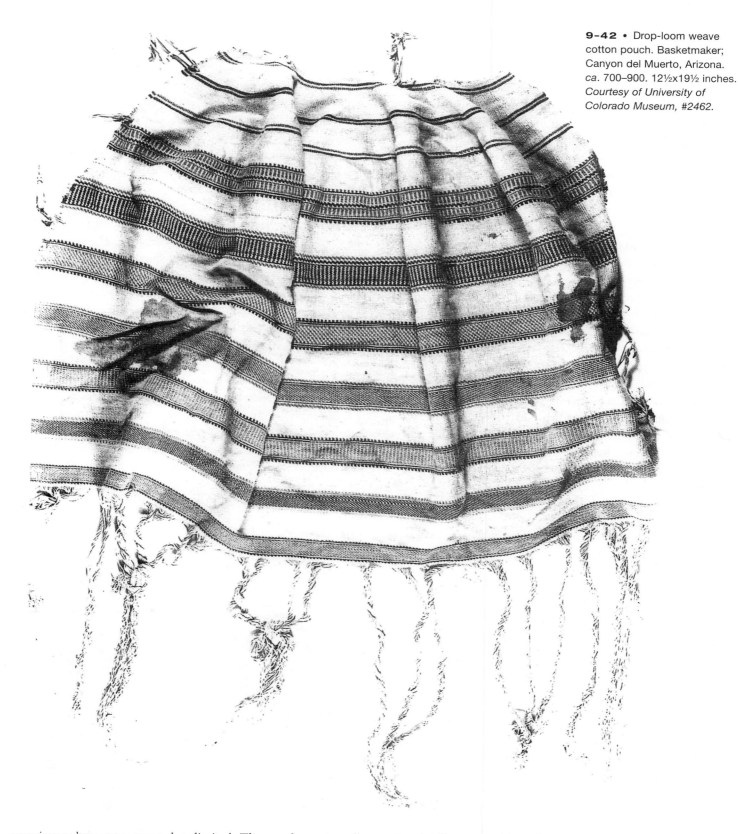

9–42 • Drop-loom weave cotton pouch. Basketmaker; Canyon del Muerto, Arizona. *ca.* 700–900. 12½x19½ inches. *Courtesy of University of Colorado Museum, #2462.*

weaving culture was somewhat limited. The needs were well served by the use of hides obtained from the tremendous herds of bison which roamed the prairies, and this served as an effective barrier against further technological experimentation.

The Midwest and Great Lakes region (from which many Plains people originally separated to form their new free-roaming culture) reflects something of a similar short–lived pattern, but this did not produce an individualistic textile exemplar of any measureable significance. Perhaps the best-known indicator of weaving activity from the Great Lakes tribes is to be found in the colorful "yarn bags" commonly used for storing personal possessions and sacred ritual paraphernalia. The use of bast for medicine or storage pouches certainly would seem to date from early times, but the technique of their manufacture is an early weaving form; the absence of any true loom work and the limited range of textile products from such weaving facilities as are now familiar in the region all support the impression of limited activity.

In the greater Southeast, there is ample evidence of one of the strong weaving traditions of North America. Although much of this is in fragmentary form, it removes any question as to the proficiency of the artists from this part of the continent. Any examination of the collections recovered from the great Spiro Mound (also known as the Temple, or Craig Mound) in LeFlore County, Oklahoma, will clearly establish this point. Additional examples attesting to this high level of weaving have been recovered from some of the so-called "Mound Builder" sites in Ohio, Georgia, and Tennessee, as well as dry cave or rock-shelter locations in Arkansas. All of these date to *circa* 1200–1600 A.D. Color is rich and certainly was easily incorporated into the fibers used, which included essentially all of the local animal and plant materials common to the region. Weaves are intricate, although the type of loom, if any, is not clear. **(FIG. 9–43)**

And, finally, any preservation of textile remains from the Eastern and Northeastern United States also suffers equally from an adverse climate. Some fragments have been found in late archeological excavations—but most of these date only to the early Colonial period. There are sufficient examples of cloth (even if in badly deteriorated form) in New York and adjoining areas to confirm the belief that sophisticated and competent weaving was a familiar art. One of the most important proofs of this is to be found in the thousands and thousands of fragments of pottery which have been collected from prehistoric sites. A large proportion of these bear textile markings. Some show the effects of vessels which were formed by wooden paddles which in turn were wrapped by woven cordage; others have textile impressions all over the surface, suggesting that they may have been formed with a textile wrapping which was burned off in the subsequent firing. From whatever origin or manufacturing technique, these provide clearly distinguishable varieties of weaves. This was one of the early Indian areas to be influenced by European trade, and the contact was so intense that almost all native craftwork was rapidly supplanted by introduced goods. Although some activities managed to survive in diluted form, pottery almost entirely vanished and the sole weaving still continuing was in the occasional manufacture of belting, sashes, and similar narrow-loomed products.

With the entry of the White man, the whole panorama changed rapidly; some of the change was dramatic and sudden, some was subtle or indirect. The presence of European traders brought a significant increase in textile production, encouraged by the introduction to the Indian weaver of new raw materials, fibers and dyestuffs, and with these new objects came an exposure to new design motifs—most particularly *via* mission schools conducted by Spanish and French Catholic nuns for their converts. European-tailored costumes and textiles also provided models and affected new design styles, influenced changes, and even raw materials, as yardage was acquired by the native weaver and unraveled to supply re-spun fibers for specific needs.

But without question the most significant European influence on weaving was the introduction of sheep by the Spanish settlers and missionaries in the sixteenth and seventeenth centuries. Earlier, native cotton had been the weaver's basic material;

9-43 • Fragments of woven textile: rabbit fur and canebrake fiber. Colors: black, red, and dull yellow; canebrake warp undyed. Spiro Mound; Le Flore County, Oklahoma. *ca.* 1400–1600. L: largest fragment: 12½ inches. *Courtesy of National Museum of the American Indian, Smithsonian Institution, #21080.*

planted the use of vegetal dyes. Painted textiles died out almost completely; those which did survive were largely the result of individual idiosyncracy. And the decoration of textiles by such means as moose hair, bird and porcupine quill, and other appliqué techniques more and more were replaced by silk or wool embroidery, brocading, and glass bead decoration. These latter were not only applied to the surfaces in decorative patterns, but were frequently interwoven into the fabric as the weaving proceeded, to give a more pleasing design or visual contrast.

with the acquisition of wool, cotton lost its popularity, since the heavier pelts of the sheep provided a greater yield of raw material. It was more effective for weaving, since it was ideal for the native loom; moreover, sheep were far easier to care for than cotton plants and they also provided food as well as wool. It should not be overlooked that even though cotton was known throughout the Southwest in particular, its cultivation had spread into many neighboring areas, and had come to be an important part of early trade. Therefore, this transfer of attention from cotton to wool was felt throughout the entire continent.

The introduction of chemical dyestuffs increased the color palette of the weaver, and in time, these almost completely sup-

With the increase in availability of materials and decorative resources, an inevitable result was elaboration of design. Fascination with technical skill also played its part, as well as the dictates of social status and political position. This in time became an important part of costume emerging from economic and social realities: one's clothing came to indicate one's position in society, precisely the same way as do the vestments of the Catholic prelate, or the policeman's uniform. Ritual costumes were woven for local use, and some tribes, *viz.* the Hopi, became specialists in their production.

The impressive costumes of the military had their influence upon men's clothing styles, and many of the "traditional" forms of

9–45 • Diagonal-weave bead choker and shell gorget incised with Underwater Panther design. Woven on a tension loom, as shown in Fig. 9–46. Potawatomi: Wisconsin. *ca.* 1880–1900. L: 14 inches.
Courtesy of National Museum of the American Indian, Smithsonian Institution.

9-46 • Woman using a tension loom. Note the yarn bag in front of her. Chippewa; Wisconsin. ca. 1900.
Courtesy of The Field Museum of Natural History, Chicago.

American Indian dress and accessory designs seen in textiles of the seventeenth to eighteenth centuries can be directly traced to such origins. Ornamentation, most particularly the frills and fancywork of the French and British colonial garments of the period became dominant in the decorative vocabulary of the native weaver. A certain degree of government control emerged from the introduction of the Federal Trading Post system active from 1783–1822, in which government monopoly was intended to guarantee Indian access to supplies. This in time gave way to "free enterprise" as private traders replaced the federal system; but both groups were responsible for the introduction of a wide range of new materials, ideas, needs, and designs.

One of these new major influences of course was the simple fact of White domination. This had a tremendous impact, since any subordinate people are inevitably affected deeply by the customs, practices, and demands of the controlling agency. And in this, the Indian was no different. While some individuals tended resolutely to avoid contact with White people, preferring their

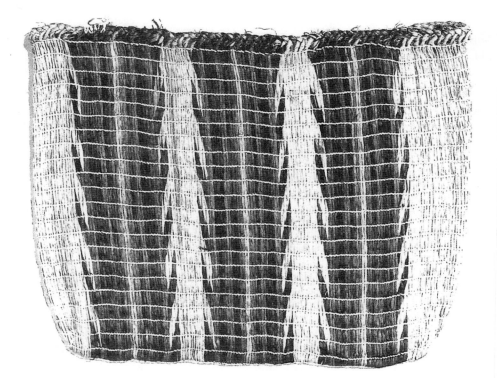

9-47 • Bast fiber bag. Fox; Tama, Iowa. *ca.* 1900. 15x18 inches. *Courtesy of Denver Art Museum.*

a certain aura of relationship, if not power, to the wearer.

Mention should be made of one other important factor in garment adaptation. Social censure became more and more impressed upon the native over the years of contact. In hot climates, native people wisely tended not to burden themselves with clothing, often dressing with minimal cover. Missionaries were adamant in their opposition, and introduced garments which, while they fulfilled European demands of Victorian modesty, were also ill-suited to the comfort and health of the wearers. And, although the Indian tended to continue to wear native-woven textiles in much the same manner, changes were introduced, not only for the purposes of modesty enforced by the outsiders, but more subtlety through the copying of decorative motifs, tailoring, and the use of pockets and buttons.

As a result, Indian weaving as such slowly disappeared from the frontier, as the trading posts pressed further into the interior. And, just as weaving had replaced animal hides for garments, new machine-made cloth supplanted the hand-woven textile; the ubiquitous Stroudcloth (named from its source in Stroud, England), became familiar to almost all of the Indian tribes

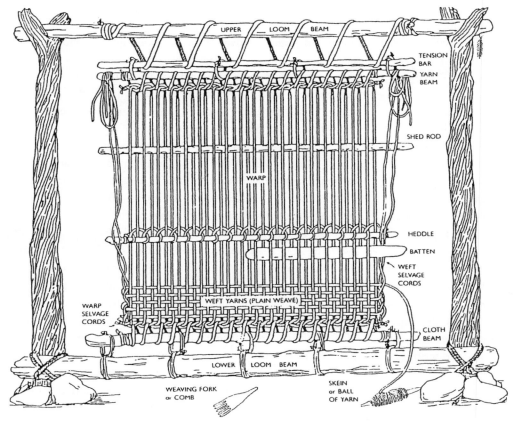

9-48 • A Navajo loom setup. Adapted from Kent, 1975.

own way of life, many willingly—even happily—accepted the manufactures and garments of the European, not only because they were plentiful, but even more because they represented the sum and substance of the dominant culture, and thereby bestowed

of North America. This close-weave woolen cloth, also known as "trade cloth," was introduced in the early seventeenth century and rapidly spread throughout the continent. The rich, solid color and firm quality of the material was popular for both its appearance and its warmth. In time it became the standard fabric of most Indian peoples, although it was less commonly seen in the Southwest than elsewhere. Woven in rich red, black, navy blue, green, and occasionally olive green or purple, it was traded by the yard or by the bolt. It came with a loose-weave rainbow-colored selvedge which added to its attractiveness in Indian eyes.

This cloth was made into shawls, blankets, and various garments and accessories, further ornamented with beadwork, ribbon appliqué, silver, or quillwork. So widespread and popular was the material, that shortly after its appearance it had replaced three-fourths or more of the native weaving in the Midwest and eastern areas of the continent. By the middle of the eighteenth century, it is safe to say that ninety-nine percent of the native weaving of North America, outside of the Southwest, had become outmoded, due largely to the introduction of Stroudcloth. While it is true that European cotton cloth was an important trade introduction, primarily gingham, calico and cotton plainweaves, the proportion of substitution was apparently never as great as that of the huge quantities of Stroudcloth used by the Indian.

Subsequently those same outside forces which had been so directly responsible for the encouragement of weaving, and then its disappearance, made another about-face. The Santa Fe Railroad had completed its route through the Southwest, and began conducting its celebrated "Indian Country Tours" allied with the Fred Harvey Company, whose curio outlets made contracts with traders to guarantee tremendous numbers of Navajo blankets and rugs for their tourist and Eastern markets. The quantities produced as a result caused a deterioration in quality, and by the late 1890s traders realized the need to promote a better grade textile. Among the most influential were Lorenzo Hubbell, Clinton N. Cotton, John B. Moore, and Hermann Schweizer; the latter, as a buyer for the Harvey firm, held a key position in this upgrading effort, since he refused to buy poor quality weaving.

These men all urged increased attention to fineness of weave, fast color, and strong design improvements. That many, if not most, of the designs were originally devised by the White traders (notably Cotton and Moore), prescribing what they felt were more saleable "Indian designs," was irrelevant. In fact, from this influence emerged many of the popular concepts of Indian art today, forming what are now regarded as "traditional Indian weaving designs." Furthermore, new socio-economic pressures were increasingly evident in this revival of Indian arts: the writings of such persons as Helen Hunt Jackson to secure fair treatment for the Indian did not go unnoticed, and this concern transmitted itself in turn to an interest in native art. (FIG. 9–50)

The entry of large numbers of tourists from the East meant large-scale demand, even though in numerically small dollar amounts. Although there were some individual connoisseurs responsible for the buying and selling of high-quality products, they were relatively few. The bulk of the sales involved mediocre quality, produced in tremendous quantity; indeed, most of the pottery was purchased in the Pueblos by the wagonload, and weaving was simply bought by the pound, regardless of the quality of the weave. This tourist aspect of the market was a force which continues to be dominant in the Southwest today, unbroken save for a brief period during the two World Wars and the Depression.

By the turn of the century, the tourist market, which had been a force in the Indian market since the arrival of the first Europeans—and even earlier, when the customer was another Indian from a distant tribe—began to take on a quite different aspect insofar as weaving is concerned. On the positive side came an emphasis on quality and attention to design, improvement in textiles, better prices to the weaver, and an increase in recognition of the work of the Navajo artist. But a less happy result was introduced design dictation, the imposition of so-called "traditional symbols" many of which were taken from Oriental rugs of the Victorian era, and the demand for huge quantities of more-or-less identical textiles whose exact duplication was avoided only by the fact of individual difference, temperament, and technical skill. (FIG. 9–49)

Preoccupation with World War I brought this phase of weaving activity to a temporary halt; it did not recover until new economic and social forces surfaced with the "New Deal" of the mid-1930s. In one of those periodic abrupt reversals of policy which has plagued Indian-White relationship throughout United States history, the Government encouraged a return to traditional values and introduced major programs to revive the old crafts, among them weaving. Federal monies flowed into craft programs, in part through the WPA projects, guild programs were established to try to develop greater cooperative activity among crafts people, and standards were drawn up to insure the quality of the product. This, combined with a newly awakened realization that here was an important indigenous art form in which there remained a vitality, esthetic brilliance, and a cultural integrity, inspired a recognition and ever-widening enthusiasm.

The establishment by Congress of the Indian Arts and Crafts Board in 1935 as a branch of the Department of the Interior further supported these efforts. The Board introduced better wool for weaving, a more effective marketing system, more permanent and less garish dyestuffs, and gave increased attention to the needs of the White market. The reservations were scoured to find those older craftsmen who had retained their knowledge and could teach their skills to the younger people. Non-Indians interested in Navajo weaving used their relationships to the weavers to stimulate better quality, improved designs, and fostered a return to the use of vegetal dyes. These healthy activities combined to make an impact upon the Indian art world and its friends which still continues. Quality of weave and attention to design, as well as an increased sense of self-worth on the part of the artist were all part of this movement, together with greatly increased economic income. The weaving guilds tended to draw people together in a craft community, frequently resulting in greater exchange of ideas, awareness of changes in the market, and improved access to raw

9-49 • A J. B. Moore rug, showing the "airplane" design, which was influenced by Bergamo, Turkey, weavings. Navajo; Crystal, New Mexico. *ca.* 1900–1910. 70x80 inches.
Courtesy of Gene Belzer photo Museum of Northern Arizona. #E7001.

materials, thereby promoting good weaving and allowing the weaver more time to concentrate upon production.

Museum exhibits offered the weaver an opportunity to visit and examine some of the older works or examples from other areas, thus widening the horizons of the visitors; and this greater prominence given to the textile arts increased the understanding of the White patron as well as to what constituted good weaving. Three of the most influential exhibits of the period included the *Exposition of Indian Tribal Art* in 1931, arranged by John Sloan, Amelia E. White, and Oliver LaFarge; held in New York City, it was one of the earliest to make a major impact upon the East. In 1938–1939, the show organized by Frederic H. Douglas for the Golden Gate Exposition in San Francisco opened the eyes of

Westerners to the beauty of Indian artistry; two years later, Douglas collaborated with René d'Harnoncourt to assemble an ambitious *Exhibition of Indian Arts of the United States* at the Museum of Modern Art in New York City, with outstanding success.

Cultural czars were heard from, of course, as fashion made its own appraisal, and markets far from the weaving centers set their requirements. Some of these demands were excellent: top quality, tight weaving, fast color, and sound design. But others were less helpful: the dictates of romantic, White-fancied designs, whimsical patterns, or new, less-functional creations—usually combined with an almost mirror-like duplication to meet set standards merchandised in tremendous quantities. With these came another

9-50 • Standard wool blanket, period 1910–1920. Navajo, New Mexico. *Courtesy of Museum of Northern Arizona. #E5454.*

problem which has always haunted the native art world: the influence of the ephemeral nature of fashion. Once established, a traditional weaver tends to produce along much the same pre-set line. It is difficult, if not impossible, to make changes quickly, in spite of the fact that this is a hand operation. The unstable fashion world, mercurial by nature, mindless in practice, and with but fickle interests, often changes direction abruptly in pursuit of another fancy. This can, and frequently does, leave the native craftsman with an oversupply of a product directed towards a totally alien market. The frustration, bewilderment, and economic loss suffered by the artist whose creations are suddenly no longer wanted (by native and non-native alike), can readily be understood.

By the mid-twentieth century, textiles slowly began to emerge as an important art force, and received a marked degree of attention; exhibits solely devoted to the art of hand weaving were held in museums and galleries, and weaving enjoyed a boom market, bringing many times the former selling prices for rugs and blankets — together with an increased recognition of the weavers as individual artists. Books were written about weaving, museums focussed even greater attention upon contemporary crafts, and prices ascended ever higher in the market. This was a new situation, and it levied a tremendous impact upon the Indian art world.

The results have been both good and bad. To the undiscriminating, any Navajo rug is a superior product, worth a large sum. This stems primarily from the common equation of native weaving as synonymous with high quality. "If it is Navajo, it is well woven and will last forever," came to be an accepted cliché,

totally ignoring the many important considerations which have a bearing upon any evaluation of craft work. On the other hand, the continual upgrading, close inspections, and general judgments through exhibition, coupled with the higher prices and intelligent selection by knowledgeable buyers did result in a product which today—at its best—is as fine a weave as has been produced by Navajo or Pueblo weavers at any time in Indian history.

In the Northwest Coast the so-called Chilkat weave had essentially died out; only a few elderly women retained their

9-51 • Contemporary textiles at the "Hopi Craftsman" fair. *ca.* 1960.
Courtesy of Museum of Northern Arizona.

knowledge of the technique. Some efforts have been made to teach this art to younger women, but the results are still tentative. A similar revival program was instituted in the Salish country, due largely to the initial efforts of White friends, which seems to have greater promise, although it is not yet certain how successful it will prove in the years to come. The Eastern weavers have shown far less interest in reviving their old skills; some individual practitioners of finger weaving and yarn bag work are active, but in the main this does not promise an equivalent reawakening as yet.

Actually, the major change has been in the market, not in the product. In older times, when textiles were produced for a knowledgeable native consumer, the market was relatively closed to outside influences. Today, ninety-five percent of the textiles woven on Indian looms are intended for the far less knowledgeable White purchaser. There are exceptions to this, of course: those experienced collectors who have made a study of the art, dealers who seek the best available textiles for their customers, and museum

curators requiring specific examples for their permanent collections. Furthermore, the actual function of these weaves changed dramatically, and by much the same proportion. Earlier, blankets were to be worn or slept on; floor coverings (when used as such) were to be walked on, and so on. Most of the textiles purchased today will never be subjected to such use; rather, they will be displayed on the wall, in exhibition vitrines, or carefully stored away for occasional showing. But rarely are they used for the purpose originally intended.

And these concentrated concerns of revival, study, social status, pricing, and esthetics are often accompanied by psychological upgrading of sorts: collectors, dealers—and even museum personnel—frequently sensationalize the interpretations of given forms and designs in an effort to romanticise the specimen and add in some indirect way to the value of the object. The obsession to classify results in the attachment of names to these designs, forms, and styles which have little, if any, relationship to weaving

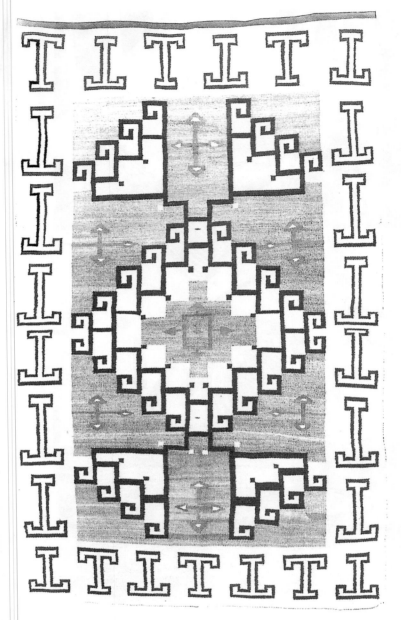

9-52 • A J. B. Moore blanket, period 1900–1910. Navajo; Crystal, New Mexico. *ca.* 1900–1910. 48x64 inches.
Courtesy of and Copyright © by Maxwell Museum of Anthropology.

realities. It should not be felt that this is all bad; it does add a degree of interest to the textile, perhaps a certain dignity to the artist, and often results in an atmosphere which greatly strengthens the role of weaving in human life. But when such pseudo-esoterica becomes an end in itself, it adds little luster to a noble art.

With the passing of Native American weaving from a product intended initially for the weaver's immediate family, to the demands of the limited native market, to the non-Indian trader, and finally to the White consumer, the journey is almost finished. Where will the native weaver go next? The New Indian has not yet taken his rightful place as a primary consumer; at the moment he seems relatively content with the product of the commercial

loom. But it seems certain that the time is not far off when contemporary Native American needs will return to major significance, as pride of self and personal values make their requirements felt. And then the cycle will be complete.

NATIVE AMERICAN ART

It is likely that the first type of decoration used by native Americans was colorful paint of some sort, applied either by rubbing colored powder into the skin or by applying moist, paintlike mixtures. At some point, native peoples began to attach various types of intricate and attractive materials to their clothing, for example, bones of small animals, or various types of sea shells or seeds. These materials may have been dyed various colors.

One very recognizable early style used porcupine quills. These sharp quills, resembling toothpicks, come in various sizes, the best of which, from the sides of the animal, are long and thin. Over the ages Indian artists have perfected many techniques of applying the quills, mainly by attaching them with strands of animal sinew.

Later, when white men came, bringing mixed blessings, Indian artists adapted new materials into their art styles. Glass beads, for example, became a popular medium for several reasons: they were easy to obtain, provided a wide array of color, and could be used to render many traditional patterns, especially geometric ones.

The first glass beads in the northern plains area were "pony" beads, which were about one-eighth of an inch in diameter, colored black, white, blue, and red, and roughly finished. In the mid 1800s, "seed" beads began to appear, and they soon replaced pony beads. These smaller beads came in a greater assortment of colors, permitting artisans to create intricate and nuanced patterns on all sorts of surfaces. Seed beads were also notable for their variety of shapes, sizes, and even surfaces; some were oblong, others were tubular, metal, faceted or took other forms. American Indian artists experimented with every type.

Designs ranged from the abstract and symbolic to the realistic and often expressed beliefs that reflected fundamental religious and philosophical views. Quillwork or beadwork fashioned in parallel lines on moccasins, for example, is said to express the artist's desire that the wearer meet with good luck on the road of life. Pyramids, both stepped and smooth, could mean *tepees*, that is, mountains representing Mother Earth. Square crosses, circles, and crescents portrayed the celestial heavens. Often, a symbol that represented something very specific at one time was reinterpreted later to mean something else, only to reappear later still, symbolizing something quite similar to its initial meaning. This is an ancient cycle.

Both men and women produced art, and the types of designs they created reflected their very different roles in society. The fundamental duty of the men, as warriors, was to pro-

DETAIL OF HIDE #21
Dancers wearing buffalo masks
Courtesy of Musée de l'Homme.

DETAIL OF HIDE #21
A she-bear and her cubs
Courtesy of Musée de l'Homme.

tect the tribe. Male art, then—much of it painted *tepees*, war para-phernalia, and robes—tended to be pictorial, proclaiming prowess on the battlefield, recording activities of daily life, or depicting aspects of supernatural visions. Heroic male art encouraged young warriors to follow their elders' path, thus ensuring the tribe's survival.

Women, on the other hand, were responsible for keeping the home, and ultimately the society, in order. The task of processing hides and making clothing and other items fell to the females. The majority of art was produced by women. Creatively using abstract forms in quillwork, beadwork, or other media, women incorporated pictures and symbols on moccasins, clothing, household materials, and some robes.

Although the actual construction of a *tepee* was done by women, often in a "quilting bee" arrangement, men were responsible for painting the exterior. Not all *tepees* were painted, though, since such endeavors were far from casual. *Tepee* painting was a declaration of one's religious or philosophical beliefs, and all the figures, colors, and images have special meaning.

Among the most spectacular of the traditional arts was the painted buffalo robe. Depending on the desired pattern, whether abstract or pictorial, men or women could contribute. To more fully appreciate this practice and the materials used, it is helpful to follow the steps involved in producing such a masterpiece.

EXPLOIT ROBES

Freed from everyday household duties, young men concentrated on military and spiritual responsibilities, excelling in battle by performing heroic deeds, or fasting, praying, and receiving powerful spiritual visions. These activities were often recorded

DETAIL OF HIDE #21
Hunter aiming at a stag and a doe
Courtesy of Musée de l'Homme.

DETAIL OF HIDE #15
Hunter firing on wounded buffalo
Courtesy of Musée de l'Homme.

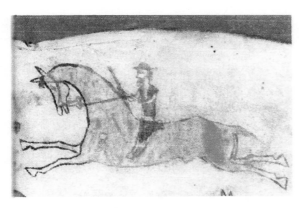

DETAIL OF HIDE #7
European hunting buffalo
Courtesy of Musée de l'Homme.

pictographically. *Tepees* and shields bore spiritual symbols, while exploit robes depicted heroic deeds.

Male artists recorded these visions and exploits through the economical use of symbols; thus, when presenting a herd of horses, rather than realistically draw every horse, the artist would arrange solid U-shaped hoofprints to convey the same meaning (split hoofprints represented buffalo). A number of horseheads could also depict a herd. The number of fingers shown on human hands varied as well. One finger could mean a man had no hand. Because two fingers might be mistaken for a cloven hoof, it was necessary to draw at least three to show that the figure had a normal human hand.

Although one occasionally sees one horse behind another, perspective was not a conventional way of depicting distance or dimension in native American painting; the placement of the figures on the robe told the story. Bodies are often "transparent": even when a rider is astride his mount, both of his legs can be seen.

Facial features are never detailed, because such specificity could never be accomplished on hide. Individuals are sometimes identified by their image-names, which were placed above their heads and connected by lines to the figures. Thus, a warrior may be known by a drawing of a small buffalo sitting down, as was Sitting Bull.

The tribal membership of the figures depicted was an important factor. There were "good" guys and "bad" guys; obviously, these values depended upon the tribal affiliation of the artist. Careful study of the details of the representations reveals tribal values with respect to weaponry, worldview, alliances, and styles of art—all in graphic form. Hairstyles or headpieces also can determine tribal identity. The clearest example of this involves the Crow Indians of Montana, whose "pompadour" hairstyles in their drawings always separate them from their antagonists. Painting on shields can also provide tribal or even individual identity, but one must have very specific knowledge to make the proper connection.

For me, the exploit robe is the most important type of painted hide because it is visual history—but it must be read correctly to tell its true story. In these hides, we see our warriors, holy men, and patriots struggling to survive and to protect their land against outside people, both Indian and non-Indian. We see them at their finest, at the peak of their glory. Their proud and fierce carriage bespeaks an indomitable dignity. The strong yet graceful flow of the horses reminds us, the present generation of Indian people, that this dignity lives on. We need this assurance today.

DETAIL OF HIDE #5
Combat scene.
The warrior on the black horse
is brandishing his shield;
he bleeds from a musket wound.
The horse's jaw is decorated
with a scalp;
two warriors face him,
wearing powder horns
around their necks.
Courtesy of Musée de l'Homme.

DETAIL OF HIDE #4
Combat scene
Courtesy of Musée de l'Homme.

DETAIL OF HIDE #4
Combat scene
Courtesy of Musée de l'Homme.

HIGH ART IN EUROPE

THOUGHT PIECE

PHILOSOPHY AND HISTORY OF THE ART OF PAINTING

What is fair in men, passes away, but not so in art.

He who despises painting loves neither philosophy nor nature. If you condemn painting, which is the only imitator of all visible works of nature, you will certainly despise a subtle invention which brings philosophy and subtle speculation to the consideration of the nature of all forms—seas and plains, trees, animals, plants, and flowers—which are surrounded by shade and light. And this is true knowledge and the legitimate issue of nature; for painting is born of nature—or, to speak more correctly, we will say it is the grandchild of nature; for all visible things are produced by nature, and these her children have given birth to painting. Hence we may justly call it the grandchild of nature and related to God.

That painting surpasses all human works by the subtle considerations belonging to it. The eye, which is called the window of the soul, is the principal means by which the central sense can most completely and abundantly appreciate the infinite works of nature; and the ear is the second, which acquires dignity by hearing of the things the eye has seen. If you, historians, or poets, or mathematicians, had not seen things with your eyes you could not report of them in writing. And if you, O poet, tell a story with your pen, the painter with his brush can tell it more easily, with simpler completeness and less tedious to be understood. And if you call painting dumb poetry, the painter may call poetry blind painting. Now which is the worse defect? to be blind or dumb? Though the poet is as free as the painter in the invention of his fictions they are not so satisfactory to men as paintings; for, though poetry is able to describe forms, actions, and places in words, the painter deals with the actual similitude of the forms, in order to represent them. Now tell me which is the nearer to the actual man: the name of the man or the image of the man. The name of the man differs in different countries, but his form is never changed but by death.

—"Philosophy and History of the Art of Painting," *The Notebooks of Leonardo da Vinci,* Pamela Taylor, ed. (New York: New American Library Plume Books, 1971), p. 73.

THINGS TO CONSIDER

- How did writers and artists of Renaissance Europe construct the notion of high art?
- What was Humanism?
- How did the creation of a hierarchy of artistic production in this period provide the basis for the distinctions between liberal arts and mechanical crafts, high and low art, fine and applied art, vernacular and academic art, etc.?

To view this image, please go to page 592 of the *Art History*,
Fourth Edition by Marilyn Stokstad ebook.

10-1 • Paolo Uccello NICCOLÒ DA TOLENTINO LEADING THE CHARGE
Detail from *The Battle of San Romano* (FIG. 10–21), 1438–1440. Tempera on wood panel. National Gallery, London.

RENAISSANCE ART IN FIFTEENTH-CENTURY ITALY

This ferocious but bloodless battle seems to take place only in a dream (**FIG. 10–1**). Under an elegantly fluttering banner, the Florentine general Niccolò da Tolentino leads his men against the Sienese at the Battle of San Romano, which took place on June 1, 1432. The battle rages across a shallow stage defined by the debris of warfare arranged in a neat pattern on a pink ground and backed by blooming hedges. In the center foreground, Niccolò holds aloft a baton of command, the sign of his authority. His bold gesture—together with his white horse and outlandish, though quite fashionable, crimson and gold damask hat—ensures that he dominates the scene. His knights charge into the fray, and when they fall, like the soldier at the lower left, they join the many broken lances on the ground—all arranged in conformity with the new mathematical depiction of receding space called **linear perspective**, posed to align with the implied lines that would converge at a single point on the horizon.

An eccentric Florentine painter nicknamed Paolo Uccello ("Paul Bird") created the panel painting (SEE FIG. 10–21) from which the detail in FIG. 10–1 is taken. It is one of three related panels now separated, hanging in major museums in Florence, London, and Paris. The complete history of these paintings has only recently come to light.

Lionardo Bartolini Salimbeni (1404–1479), who led the Florentine governing Council of Ten during the war against Lucca and Siena, probably commissioned the paintings. Uccello's remarkable accuracy when depicting armor from the 1430s, heraldic banners, and even fashionable fabrics and crests surely would have appealed to Lionardo's civic pride. The hedges of oranges, roses, and pomegranates—all ancient fertility symbols—suggest that Lionardo might have commissioned the paintings at the time of his wedding in 1438. Lionardo and his wife, Maddalena, had six sons, two of whom inherited the paintings. According to a complaint brought by Damiano, one of the heirs, Lorenzo de' Medici, the powerful *de facto* ruler of Florence, "forcibly removed" the paintings from Damiano's house. They were never returned, and Uccello's masterpieces are recorded in a 1492 inventory as hanging in the Medici palace. Perhaps Lorenzo, who was called "the Magnificent," saw Uccello's heroic pageant as a trophy more worthy of a Medici merchant prince. We will certainly discover that princely patronage was a major factor in the genesis of the Italian Renaissance as it developed in Florence during the early years of the fifteenth century.

LEARN ABOUT IT

10.1 Explore the development and use of linear perspective in fifteenth-century Florentine painting.

10.2 Examine how sculptors were instrumental in the early development of the Italian Renaissance by increasing the lifelike qualities of human figures and drawing inspiration from ancient Roman sculpture.

10.3 Assess the role of wealthy merchants and *condottieri* in driving the development of Renaissance art and architecture.

10.4 Consider how the new focus on artistic competition and individual achievement created a climate for innovative and ambitious works.

10.5 Evaluate the importance of the Classical past to the development of early Renaissance architecture.

HEAR MORE: Listen to an audio file of your chapter **www.myartslab.com**

HUMANISM AND THE ITALIAN RENAISSANCE

By the end of the Middle Ages, the most important Italian cultural centers lay north of Rome in the cities of Florence, Milan, and Venice, and in the smaller duchies of Mantua, Ferrara, and Urbino. Much of the power and influential art patronage was in the hands of wealthy families: the Medici in Florence, the Montefeltro in Urbino, the Gonzaga in Mantua, the Visconti and Sforza in Milan, and the Este in Ferrara (MAP 10–1). Cities grew in wealth and independence as people moved to them from the countryside in unprecedented numbers. As in northern Europe, commerce became increasingly important. Money conferred status, and a shrewd business or political leader could become very powerful. The period saw the rise of mercenary armies led by entrepreneurial (and sometimes brilliant) military commanders called *condottieri*. Unlike the knights of the Middle Ages, they owed allegiance only to those who paid them well; their employer might be a city-state, a lord, or even the pope. Some *condottieri*, like Niccolò da Tolentino (SEE FIG. 10–1), became rich and famous. Others, like Federico da Montefeltro, were lords or dukes themselves, with their own territories in need of protection. Patronage of the arts was an important public activity with political overtones. As one Florentine merchant, Giovanni Rucellai, succinctly noted, he supported the arts "because they serve the glory of God, the honour of the city, and the commemoration of myself" (cited in Baxandall, p. 2).

The term Renaissance (French for "rebirth") was only applied to this period by later historians. However, its origins lie in the thought of Petrarch and other fourteenth-century Italian writers, who emphasized the power and potential of human beings for great individual accomplishment. These Italian humanists also looked back at the thousand years extending from the disintegration of the Western Roman Empire to their own day and determined that the achievements of the Classical world were followed by what they perceived as a period of decline—a "middle" or "dark" age. They proudly saw their own era as a third age characterized by a revival, rebirth, or renaissance, when humanity began to emerge from what they erroneously saw as intellectual and cultural stagnation to appreciate once more the achievement of the ancients and the value of rational, scientific investigation. They looked to the accomplishments of the Classical past for inspiration and instruction, and in Italy this centered on the heritage of ancient Rome. They sought the physical and literary records of the ancient world—assembling libraries, collecting sculpture and fragments of architecture, and beginning archaeological investigations. Their aim was to live a rich, noble, and productive life—usually within the framework of Christianity, but always adhering to a school of philosophy as a moral basis.

Artists, like the humanists, turned to Classical antiquity for inspiration, emulating what they saw in ancient Roman sculpture and architecture, even as they continued to fulfill commissions for predominantly Christian subjects and buildings. But from the secular world a number of home furnishings such as birth trays and marriage chests have survived, richly painted with allegorical and mythological themes. Patrons began to collect art for their personal enjoyment.

Like the Flemish artists, Italian painters and sculptors increasingly focused their attention on rendering the illusion of physical reality. They did so in a more analytical way than the northerners. Rather than seeking to describe the detailed visual appearance of nature through luminosity and textural differentiation, Italian artists aimed at achieving lifelike but idealized weighty figures set within a rationally configured space organized through strict adherence to a mathematical system called linear perspective, which achieved the illusion of a measured and continuously receding space (see "Renaissance Perspective," page 592).

FLORENCE

In seizing Uccello's battle painting (SEE FIG. 10–1), Lorenzo de' Medici was asserting the role his family had come to expect to play in the history of Florence. The fifteenth century witnessed the rise of the Medici from among the most successful of a newly rich middle class (comprising primarily merchants and bankers) to become the city's virtual rulers. Unlike the hereditary aristocracy, the Medici emerged from obscure roots to make their fortune in banking. And from their money came their power.

The competitive Florentine atmosphere that had fostered mercantile success and civic pride also cultivated competition in the arts and encouraged an interest in ancient literary texts. This has led many to consider Florence the cradle of the Italian Renaissance. Under Cosimo the Elder (1389–1464), the Medici became leaders in intellectual and artistic patronage. They sponsored philosophers and other scholars who wanted to study the Classics, especially the works of Plato and his followers, the Neoplatonists. Neoplatonism distinguished between the spiritual (the ideal or Idea) and the physical (Matter) and encouraged artists to represent ideal figures. But it was writers, philosophers, and musicians—and not artists—who dominated the Medici Neoplatonic circle. Architects, sculptors, and painters learned their craft in apprenticeships and were therefore considered manual laborers. Nevertheless, interest in the ancient world rapidly spread from the Medici circle to visual artists, who gradually began to see themselves as more than laborers. Florentine society soon recognized their best works as achievements of a very high order.

Although the Medici were the *de facto* rulers, Florence was considered to be a republic. The Council of Ten (headed for a time by Salimbeni, who commissioned Uccello's *Battle of San Romano*) was a kind of constitutional oligarchy where wealthy men formed the government. At the same time, the various guilds wielded tremendous power; evidence of this is provided by the fact that guild membership was a prerequisite for holding government office. Consequently, artists could look to the Church and the

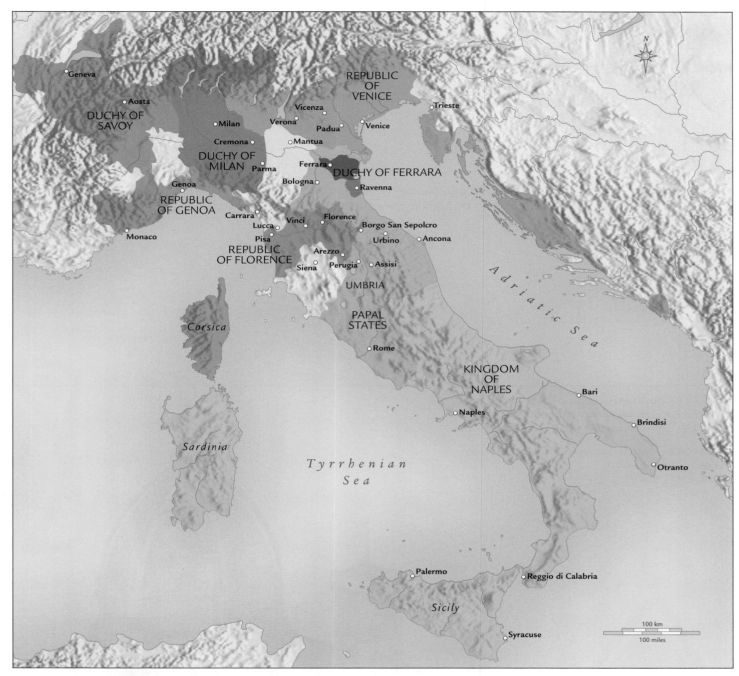

MAP 10–1 • FIFTEENTH-CENTURY ITALY

Powerful families divided the Italian peninsula into city-states—the Medici in Florence, the Visconti and Sforza in Milan, the Montefeltro in Urbino, the Gonzaga in Mantua, and the Este in Ferrara. After 1420, the popes ruled Rome, while in the south Naples and Sicily were French and then Spanish (Aragonese) territories. Venice maintained its independence as a republic.

state—the city government and the guilds—as well as private individuals for patronage, and these patrons expected the artists to re-affirm and glorify their achievements with works that were not only beautiful but intellectually powerful.

ARCHITECTURE

The defining civic project of the early years of the fifteenth century was the completion of Florence Cathedral with a magnificent dome over the high altar. The construction of the cathedral had begun in the late thirteenth century and had continued intermittently during the fourteenth century. As early as 1367, builders had envisioned a very tall dome to span the huge interior space of the crossing, but they lacked the engineering know-how to construct it. When interest in completing the cathedral revived, around 1407, the technical solution was proposed by a young sculptor-turned-architect, Filippo Brunelleschi.

To view this image, please go to page 596 of the *Art History*,
Fourth Edition by Marilyn Stokstad ebook.

10-2 • Filippo Brunelleschi **DOME OF FLORENCE
CATHEDRAL (SANTA MARIA DEL FIORE)**
1420–1436; lantern completed 1471.

SEE MORE: View a simulation about doming
www.myartslab.com

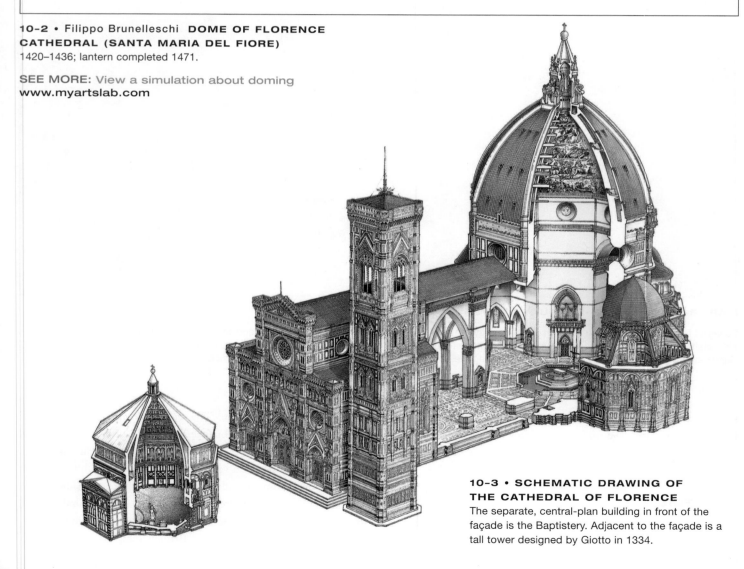

**10-3 • SCHEMATIC DRAWING OF
THE CATHEDRAL OF FLORENCE**
The separate, central-plan building in front of the
façade is the Baptistery. Adjacent to the façade is a
tall tower designed by Giotto in 1334.

FILIPPO BRUNELLESCHI. Filippo Brunelleschi (1377–1446), whose father had been involved in the original plans for the cathedral dome in 1367, achieved what many considered impossible: He solved the problem of the dome. Brunelleschi had originally trained as a goldsmith (see "The Competition Reliefs," page 585). To further his education, he traveled to Rome to study ancient Roman sculpture and architecture, and it was on his return to Florence that he tackled the dome. After the completion of a tall octagonal drum in 1412, Brunelleschi designed the dome itself in 1417, and it was built between 1420 and 1436 (FIGS. 10–2, 10–3). A revolutionary feat of engineering, the dome is a double shell of masonry 138 feet across. The octagonal outer shell is supported on eight large and 16 lighter ribs. Instead of using a costly and even dangerous scaffold and centering, Brunelleschi devised a system in which temporary wooden supports were cantilevered out from the drum. He moved these supports up as building progressed. As the dome was built up course by course, each portion of the structure reinforced the next one. Vertical marble ribs interlocked with horizontal sandstone rings, connected and reinforced with iron rods and oak beams. The inner and outer shells were linked internally by a system of arches. When completed, this self-buttressed unit required no external support to keep it standing.

An oculus (round opening) in the center of the dome was surmounted by a lantern designed in 1436. After Brunelleschi's death, this crowning structure, made up of Roman architectural forms, was completed by another Florentine architect, Michelozzo di Bartolomeo (1396–1472). The final touch—a gilt bronzed ball—was added in 1468–1471.

Other commissions came quickly after the cathedral dome project established Brunelleschi's fame. From about 1418 until his death in 1446, Brunelleschi was involved in a series of influential projects. In 1419, he designed a foundling hospital for the city (see "The Foundling Hospital," pages 582–583). Between 1419 and 1423, he built the elegant Capponi Chapel in the church of Santa Felicità. For the Medicis' parish church of San Lorenzo, he designed and built a centrally planned sacristy (a room where ritual attire and vessels are kept), from 1421 to 1428, and also conceived plans for a new church.

Brunelleschi's **SAN LORENZO** has a basilican plan with a long nave flanked by side aisles that open into shallow lateral chapels (FIG. 10–4). A short transept and square crossing lead to a square sanctuary flanked by additional chapels opening off the transept. Projecting from the left transept, as one faces the altar, are Brunelleschi's sacristy and the older Medici tomb. Brunelleschi based his mathematically regular plan on a square **module**—a basic unit of measure that could be multiplied or divided and

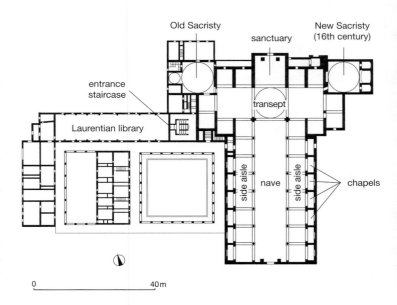

10–4 • Filippo Brunelleschi; continued by Michelozzo di Bartolomeo **INTERIOR AND PLAN OF CHURCH OF SAN LORENZO, FLORENCE**
c. 1421–1428; nave (designed 1434?) 1442–1470.

To view this image, please go to page 597 of the *Art History*, Fourth Edition by Marilyn Stokstad ebook.

The Foundling Hospital

In 1419, the guild of silk manufacturers and goldsmiths (Arte della Seta) in Florence undertook a significant public service: It established a large public orphanage and commissioned the brilliant young architect Filippo Brunelleschi to build it next to the church of the Santissima Annunziata (Most Holy Annunciation), which housed a miracle-working painting of the Annunciation, making it a popular pilgrimage site. Completed in 1444, the Foundling Hospital— *Ospedale degli Innocenti* —was unprecedented in terms of scale and design (FIG. A).

Brunelleschi created a building that paid homage to traditional forms while introducing features that we associate with the Italian Renaissance style. Traditionally, a charitable foundation's building had a portico open to the street to provide shelter, and Brunelleschi built an arcade of unprecedented lightness and elegance, using smooth round columns and richly carved capitals—his own interpretation of the Classical Corinthian order. Although we might initially assume that the sources for this arcade lay in the Roman architecture of Classical antiquity, columns were not actually used in antiquity to support free-standing arcades, only to support straight architraves. In fact, it was local Romanesque architecture that was the source for Brunelleschi's graceful design. It is the details of capitals and moldings that bring an air of the antique to this influential building.

The underlying mathematical basis for Brunelleschi's design—traced to the same Pythagorean proportional systems that were believed to create musical harmony—creates a distinct sense of harmony in this graceful arcade. Each bay encloses a cube of space defined by the 10-*braccia* (20-foot) height of the columns and the diameter of the arches. Hemispherical pendentive domes, half again as high as the columns, cover the cubes. The bays at the end of the arcade are slightly larger than the rest, creating a subtle frame for the composition. Brunelleschi defined the perfect squares and semicircles of his building with dark gray stone (*pietra serena*) against plain white walls. His training as a goldsmith and sculptor (see "The

To view this image, please go to page 598 of the *Art History*, Fourth Edition by Marilyn Stokstad ebook.

Competition Reliefs," page 585) served him well as he led his artisans to carve crisp, elegantly detailed capitals and moldings for the covered gallery.

A later addition to the building seems eminently suitable: About 1487, Andrea della Robbia, who had inherited the family firm and its secret glazing formulas from his uncle Luca, created for the interstices between the arches glazed terra-cotta medallions (FIG. B) that signified the building's function. Molds were used in the ceramic workshop to facilitate the production of the series of identical babies in swaddling clothes that float at the center of each medallion. The molded terra-cotta forms were covered with a tin glaze to make the sculptures both weatherproof and decorative, and the baby-blue ceramic backgrounds—a signature color for the della Robbia family workshop—makes

them seem to float as celestial apparitions. This is not altogether inappropriate: They are meant to evoke the "innocent" baby boys martyred by King Herod in his attempt to rid his realm of the potential rival the Magi had journeyed to venerate (Matthew 2:16).

Andrea della Robbia's adorable ceramic babies—which remain among the most beloved images of the city of Florence—seem to lay claim to the human side of Renaissance humanism, reminding viewers that the city's wealthiest guild cared for the most helpless members of society. Perhaps the Foundling Hospital spoke to fifteenth-century Florentines of an increased sense of social responsibility. Or perhaps, by so publicly demonstrating social concerns, the wealthy guild that sponsored it solicited the approval and support of the lower classes in the cut-throat power politics of the day.

B. Andrea della Robbia **INFANT IN SWADDLING CLOTHES (ONE OF THE HOLY INNOCENTS MASSACRED BY HEROD)**
Ospedale degli Innocenti (Foundling Hospital), Florence. 1487. Glazed terra cotta.

A. Filippo Brunelleschi **OSPEDALE DEGLI INNOCENTI (FOUNDLING HOSPITAL), FLORENCE**
Designed 1419; built 1421–1444.

To view this image, please go to page 599 of the *Art History*, Fourth Edition by Marilyn Stokstad ebook.

THE MEDICI PALACE. Brunelleschi may have been involved in designing the nearby Medici Palace (now known as the Palazzo Medici-Riccardi) in 1446. According to Giorgio Vasari, the sixteenth-century artist and theorist who wrote what some consider the first history of art, Cosimo de' Medici the Elder rejected Brunelleschi's model for the **palazzo** as too grand (any large house was called a *palazzo*—"palace"). Many now attribute the design of the building to Michelozzo. The austere exterior **(FIG. 10–5)** was in keeping with the Florentine political climate and concurrent religious attitudes, imbued with the Franciscan ideals of poverty and charity. Like many other European cities, Florence had sumptuary laws, which forbade ostentatious displays of wealth—but they were often ignored. For example, private homes were supposed to be limited to a dozen rooms, but Cosimo acquired and demolished 20 small houses to provide the site for his new residence. His house was more than a dwelling place; it was his place of business, his company headquarters. The palazzo symbolized the family and established its proper place in the Florentine social hierarchy.

Huge in scale—each story is more than 20 feet high—the building is marked by harmonious proportions and elegant, Classically inspired details. On one side, the ground floor originally opened through large, round arches onto the street, creating in effect a loggia that provided space for the family business. These arches were walled up in the sixteenth century and given windows designed by Michelangelo. The large, **rusticated** stone blocks—that is, blocks with their outer faces left rough—facing the lower story clearly set it off from the upper two levels. In fact, all three stories are distinguished by stone surfaces that vary from sculptural at the ground level to almost smooth on the third floor.

The builders followed the time-honored tradition of placing rooms around a central courtyard. Unlike the plan of the house of Jacques Coeur, however, the **PALAZZO MEDICI-RICCARDI COURTYARD** is square in plan with rooms arranged symmetrically **(FIG. 10–6)**. Round arches on slender columns form a continuous arcade under an enclosed second story. Tall windows in the second story

---

To view this image, please go to page 600 of the *Art History*, Fourth Edition by Marilyn Stokstad ebook.

10–5 • Attributed to Michelozzo di Bartolomeo FAÇADE, PALAZZO MEDICI-RICCARDI, FLORENCE
Begun 1446.

For the palace site, Cosimo de' Medici the Elder chose the Via de' Gori at the corner of the Via Larga, the widest city street at that time. Despite his practical reasons for constructing a large residence and the fact that he chose simplicity and austerity over grandeur in the exterior design, his detractors commented and gossiped. As one exaggerated: "[Cosimo] has begun a palace which throws even the Colosseum at Rome into the shade."

SEE MORE: Click the Google Earth link for the Palazzo Medici-Riccardi **www.myartslab.com**

---

applied to every element of the design, creating a series of clear, harmonious spaces. Architectural details, all in a Classical style, were carved in **pietra serena**, a gray Tuscan sandstone that became synonymous with Brunelleschi's interiors. Below the plain clerestory with its unobtrusive openings, the arches of the nave arcade are carried on tall, slender Corinthian columns made even taller by the insertion of an **impost block** between the column capital and the springing of the round arches—one of Brunelleschi's favorite details. Flattened architectural moldings in *pietra serena* repeat the arcade in the outer walls of the side aisles, and each bay is covered by its own shallow domical vault. Brunelleschi's rational approach, clear sense of order, and innovative incorporation of Classical motifs inspired later Renaissance architects, many of whom learned from his work firsthand by completing his unfinished projects.

10–6 • COURTYARD WITH SGRAFFITO DECORATION, PALAZZO MEDICI-RICCARDI, FLORENCE
Begun 1446.

The Competition Reliefs

In 1401, the building supervisors of the Baptistery of Florence Cathedral decided to commission a new pair of bronze doors, funded by the powerful wool merchants' guild. Instead of choosing a well-established sculptor with a strong reputation, a competition was announced for the commission. This prestigious project would be awarded to the artist who demonstrated the greatest talent and skill in executing a trial piece: a bronze relief representing Abraham's sacrifice of Isaac (Genesis 22:1–13) composed within the same Gothic quatrefoil framework used in Andrea Pisano's first set of bronze doors for the Baptistery, made in the 1330s. The narrative subject was full of dramatic potential. Abraham, commanded by God to slay his beloved son Isaac as a burnt offering, has traveled to the mountains for the sacrifice. Just as he is about to slaughter Isaac, an angel appears, commanding him to save his son and substitute a ram tangled in the bushes behind him.

Two competition panels have survived, those submitted by the presumed finalists—Filippo Brunelleschi and Lorenzo Ghiberti, both young artists in their early twenties. Brunelleschi's composition (FIG. A) is rugged and explosive, marked by raw dramatic intensity. Abraham lunges in from the left, grabbing his son by the neck, while the angel swoops energetically to stay his hand just as the knife is about to strike. Isaac's awkward pose embodies his fear and struggle. Ghiberti's version (FIG. B) is quite different, suave and graceful rather than powerful and dramatic. Poses are controlled and choreographed; the harmonious pairing of son and father contrasts sharply with the wrenching struggle in Brunelleschi's rendering. And Ghiberti's Isaac is not a stretched, scrawny youth, but a fully idealized Classical figure exuding calm composure.

The cloth merchants chose Ghiberti to make the doors. Perhaps they preferred the suave elegance of his figural composition. Perhaps they liked the prominence of elegantly disposed swags of cloth, reminders of the source of their patronage and prosperity. But they also may have been swayed by the technical superiority of Ghiberti's relief. Unlike Brunelleschi, Ghiberti cast background and figures mostly as a single piece, making his bronze stronger, lighter, and less expensive to produce. The finished doors—installed in the Baptistery in 1424—were so successful that Ghiberti was commissioned to create another set (SEE FIG. 10–12), his most famous work, hailed by Michelangelo as the "Gates of Paradise." Brunelleschi would refocus his career on buildings rather than bronzes, becoming one of the most important architects of the Italian Renaissance (SEE FIGS. 10–2 TO 10–4).

To view this image, please go to page 601 of the *Art History*, Fourth Edition by Marilyn Stokstad ebook.

A. Filippo Brunelleschi SACRIFICE OF ISAAC
1401–1402. Bronze with gilding, 21 × 17½″ (53 × 44 cm) inside molding. Museo Nazionale del Bargello, Florence.

To view this image, please go to page 601 of the *Art History*, Fourth Edition by Marilyn Stokstad ebook.

B. Lorenzo Ghiberti SACRIFICE OF ISAAC
1401–1402. Bronze with gilding, 21 × 17½″ (53 × 44 cm) inside molding. Museo Nazionale del Bargello, Florence.

match the exterior windows on this same level. Disks bearing the Medici arms surmount each arch in a frieze decorated with swags in **sgraffito** work (decoration produced by scratching through a darker layer of plaster or glaze). Such classicizing elements, inspired by the study of Roman ruins, gave the great house an aura of dignity and stability that enhanced the status of its owners. The Medici Palace inaugurated a new fashion for monumentality and regularity in residential Florentine architecture. Wealthy Florentine families soon emulated it in their own houses.

To view this image, please go to page 602 of the *Art History*, Fourth Edition by Marilyn Stokstad ebook.

10-7 • EXTERIOR VIEW OF ORSANMICHELE SHOWING SCULPTURE IN NICHES
Florence, begun in 1337.

At street level, Orsanmichele was constructed originally as an open loggia (similar to the Loggia dei Lanzi); in 1380 the spaces under the arches were filled in. In this view of the southeast corner, appearing on the receding wall to the left is first (in the foreground on the corner pier) Donatello's *St. George*, then, Nanni di Banco's *Four Crowned Martyrs*. However, the sculptures seen in this photograph are modern replicas; the originals have been removed to museums for safekeeping.

SEE MORE: Click the Google Earth link for Orsanmichele
www.myartslab.com

SCULPTURE

The new architectural language inspired by ancient Classical forms was accompanied by a similar impetus in sculpture. By 1400, Florence had enjoyed internal stability and economic prosperity for over two decades. However, until 1428, the city and its independence were challenged by two great antirepublican powers: the duchy of Milan and the kingdom of Naples. In an atmosphere of wealth and civic patriotism, Florentines turned to commissions that would express their self-esteem and magnify the importance of their city. A new attitude toward realism, space, and the Classical past set the stage for more than a century of creativity. Sculptors led the way.

ORSANMICHELE. In 1339, 14 of Florence's most powerful guilds had been assigned to fill the ground-floor niches that decorated the exterior of **ORSANMICHELE**—a newly completed loggia that served as a grain market—with sculpted images of their patron saints (FIG. 10–7). By 1400, only three had fulfilled this responsibility. In the new climate of republicanism and civic pride, the government pressured the guilds to furnish their niches with statuary. In the wake of this directive, Florence witnessed a dazzling display of sculpture produced by the most impressive local practitioners, including Nanni di Banco, Lorenzo Ghiberti, and Donatello, each of whom took responsibility for filling three niches.

In about 1409, Nanni di Banco (c. 1385–1421), son of a sculptor in the Florence Cathedral workshop, was commissioned by the stonecarvers and woodworkers' guild (to which he himself belonged) to produce **THE FOUR CROWNED MARTYRS** (FIG. 10–8). According to tradition, these third-century Christian martyrs were sculptors, executed for refusing to make an image of a pagan Roman god for Emperor Diocletian. Although the architectural setting is Gothic in style, Nanni's figures—with their solid bodies, heavy, form-revealing togas, noble hair and beards, and portraitlike features—reveal his interest in ancient Roman sculpture, particularly portraiture. They stand as a testimony to this sculptor's role in the Florentine revival of interest in antiquity.

To view this image, please go to page 603 of the *Art History*, Fourth Edition by Marilyn Stokstad ebook.

10-8 • Nanni di Banco THE FOUR CROWNED MARTYRS
c. 1409–1417. Marble, height of figures 6′ (1.83 m). Orsanmichele, Florence (photographed before removal of figures to a museum).

To view this image, please go to page 603 of the *Art History*, Fourth Edition by Marilyn Stokstad ebook.

10-9 • Donatello ST. GEORGE
1417–1420. Marble, height 6′5″ (1.95 m). Bargello, Florence. Formerly Orsanmichele, Florence.

The saints convey a new spatial relationship to the building and to the viewer. They stand in a semicircle, with feet and drapery protruding beyond the floor of the niche and into the viewer's space. The saints appear to be four individuals interacting within their own world, but a world that opens to engage with pedestrians (SEE FIG. 10–7). The relief panel below the niche shows the four sculptors at work, embodied with a similar solid vigor. Nanni deeply undercut both figures and objects to cast shadows that enhance the illusion of three-dimensionality.

Donatello (Donato di Niccolò di Betto Bardi, c. 1386/1387–1466) also received three commissions for the niches at Orsanmichele during the first quarter of the century. A member of

the guild of stonecarvers and woodworkers, he worked in both media, as well as in bronze. During a long and productive career, he developed into one of the most influential and distinguished figures in the history of Italian sculpture, approaching each commission as if it were the opportunity for a new experiment. One of Florence's lesser guilds—the armorers and sword-makers—called on Donatello to carve a majestic and self-assured St. George for their niche (FIG. 10–9). As originally conceived, the saint would have been a standing advertisement for their trade, carrying a metal sword in his right hand and probably wearing a metal helmet and sporting a scabbard, all now lost. The figure has remarkable presence, even without his accessories. St. George stands in solid contrapposto, legs braced to support his armor-heavy torso, the embodiment of alertness and determination. He seems to be staring out into our world, perhaps surveying his most famous adversary—a dragon that was holding a princess captive—lurking unsettlingly in the space behind us. With his wrinkled brow and fierce expression, he is tense, alert, focused, if perhaps also somewhat worried. Donatello's complex psychological characterization of this warrior-saint particularly impressed Donatello's contemporaries, not least among them his potential patrons.

For the base of the niche, Donatello carved a remarkable shallow relief showing St. George slaying the dragon and saving the princess, the next scene in his story. The contours of the foreground figures are slightly undercut to emphasize their mass, while the landscape and architecture are in progressively lower relief until they are barely incised rather than carved, an ingenious emulation of the painters' technique of atmospheric perspective. This is also a pioneering example of linear perspective (see "Renaissance Perspective," page 592), in which the orthogonals converge on the figure of the saint himself, using this burgeoning representational system not only to simulate spatial recession but also to provide narrative focus.

DONATELLO. Donatello's long career as a sculptor in a broad variety of media established him as one of the most successful and admired sculptors of the Italian Renaissance. He excelled in part because of his attentive exploration of human emotions and expression, as well as his ability to solve the technical problems posed by various media—from lost-wax casting in bronze and carved marble to polychromed wood. In a bronze **DAVID**, he produced the first life-size male nude since antiquity (**FIG. 10–10**), and in his portrait of the soldier Erasmo da Narni, one of the first life-size bronze equestrian portraits of the Renaissance (SEE FIG. 10–11).

Since nothing is known about the circumstances of its creation, the *David* has been the subject of continuing inquiry and speculation. Although the statue clearly draws on the Classical tradition of heroic nudity, the meaning of this sensuous, adolescent boy in a jaunty laurel-trimmed shepherd's hat and boots has long piqued interest. Some art historians have stressed an overt homoeroticism, especially in the openly effeminate conception of David and the way a wing from the helmet on Goliath's severed head caresses the young hero's inner thigh. Others have seen in David's angular pose and boyish torso a sense that he is poised between childish interests and adult responsibility, an image of improbable heroism. David was a potent political image in Florence, a symbol of the citizens' resolve to oppose tyrants regardless of their superior power, since virtue brings divine support and preternatural strength. Indeed, an inscription engraved into the base where the sculpture once stood suggests that it could have celebrated the

To view this image, please go to page 604 of the *Art History*, Fourth Edition by Marilyn Stokstad ebook.

10-10 • Donatello DAVID
c. 1446–1460(?). Bronze, height 5′2¼″ (1.58 m). Museo Nazionale del Bargello, Florence.

This sculpture is first recorded as being in the courtyard of the Medici Palace in 1469, where it stood on a base inscribed with these lines:

The victor is whoever defends the fatherland.
All-powerful God crushes the angry enemy.
Behold, a boy overcomes the great tyrant.
Conquer, O citizens!

SEE MORE: View a video about the process of lost-wax casting www.myartslab.com

Florentine triumph over the Milanese in 1425, a victory that brought resolution to a quarter-century struggle with despots and helped give Florence a vision of itself as a strong, virtuous republic.

In 1443, Donatello was probably called to Padua to execute an **EQUESTRIAN STATUE (FIG. 10–11)** to commemorate the Paduan general of the Venetian army, Erasmo da Narni, nicknamed "Gattamelata" (meaning "Honeyed Cat"—a reference to his mother, Melania Gattelli). If any image could be said to characterize the self-made men of the Italian Renaissance, surely it would be those of the *condottieri*—the brilliant generals such as Gattamelata and Niccolò da Tolentino (SEE FIG. 10–1) who organized the armies and fought for any city-state willing to pay for their services. As guardians for hire, they were tough, opportunistic mercenaries. But they also subscribed to an ideal of military and civic virtue. Horsemanship was more than a necessary skill for the *condottieri*.

The horse, a beast of enormous brute strength, symbolized animal passions, and skilled horsemanship demonstrated physical and intellectual control—self-control, as well as control of the animal—the triumph of the intellect, of "mind over matter."

Donatello's sources for this statue were surviving Roman bronze equestrian portraits, notably the famous image of Marcus Aurelius (SEE FIG. 3–91), which the sculptor certainly knew from his stay in Rome. Viewed from a distance, Donatello's man–animal juggernaut, installed on a high marble base in front of the church of Sant'Antonio in Padua, seems capable of thrusting forward at the first threat. Seen up close, however, the man's sunken cheeks, sagging jaw, ropy neck, and stern but sad expression suggest a warrior grown old and tired from the constant need for military vigilance and rapid response.

THE GATES OF PARADISE. The bronze doors that Lorenzo Ghiberti (1381?–1455) produced for the Florentine Baptistery after winning his famous competition with Brunelleschi in 1401 (see "The Competition Reliefs," page 585) were such a success that in 1425 he was awarded the commission for yet another set of bronze doors for the east side of the Baptistery, and his first set was moved to the north side. The new door panels, funded by the wool manufacturers' guild, were a significant conceptual leap from the older schemes of 28 small scenes employed for Ghiberti's earlier doors and those of Andrea Pisano in the fourteenth century. Ghiberti departed entirely from the old arrangement, producing a set of ten scenes from the Hebrew Bible—from the Creation to the reign of Solomon—composed in rectangular fields, like a set of framed paintings. Michelangelo reportedly said that the results, installed in 1452, were worthy of the **"GATES OF PARADISE"**—the name by which they are now commonly known **(FIG. 10–12)**.

Ghiberti organized the space in the ten square reliefs either by a system of linear perspective with obvious orthogonal lines (see "Renaissance Perspective," page 592)

To view this image, please go to page 605 of the *Art History*, Fourth Edition by Marilyn Stokstad ebook.

10–11 • Donatello EQUESTRIAN STATUE OF ERASMO DA NARNI (GATTAMELATA)
Piazza del Santo, Padua. 1443–1453. Bronze, height approx. 12'2" (3.71 m).

To view this image, please go to page 606 of the *Art History*,
Fourth Edition by Marilyn Stokstad ebook.

10-12 • Lorenzo Ghiberti **"GATES OF PARADISE" (EAST DOORS), BAPTISTERY OF
SAN GIOVANNI, FLORENCE**
1425–1452. Gilt bronze, height 15′ (4.57 m). Museo dell'Opera del Duomo, Florence.

The door panels, commissioned by the wool manufacturers' guild, depict ten scenes from the Hebrew Bible
beginning with the Creation in the upper left panel. The murder of Abel by his brother, Cain, follows in the
upper right panel, succeeded in the same left–right paired order by the Flood and the drunkenness of Noah,
Abraham sacrificing Isaac, the story of Jacob and Esau, Joseph sold into slavery by his brothers, Moses
receiving the Tablets of the Law, Joshua and the fall of Jericho, David and Goliath, and finally Solomon and the
queen of Sheba. Ghiberti placed his own portrait as a signature in the frame at the lower right corner of the
Jacob and Esau panel. He wrote in his *Commentaries* (c. 1450–1455): "I strove to imitate nature as clearly as
I could, and with all the perspective I could produce, to have excellent compositions with many figures."

To view this image, please go to page 607 of the *Art History*, Fourth Edition by Marilyn Stokstad ebook.

10-13 • Lorenzo Ghiberti JACOB AND ESAU, PANEL OF THE "GATES OF PARADISE" (EAST DOORS)
Formerly on the Baptistery of San Giovanni, Florence. c. 1435. Gilded bronze, 31¼″ (79 cm) square. Museo dell'Opera del Duomo, Florence.

POLLAIUOLO. Sculptors in the fifteenth century not only worked on a monumental scale in the public sphere; they also created small works, each designed to inspire the mind and delight the eye of its private owner. The ambitious and multi-talented Antonio del Pollaiuolo—goldsmith, embroiderer, printmaker, sculptor, and painter—who came to work for the Medici family in Florence about 1460, mostly created small bronze sculptures. His **HERCULES AND ANTAEUS** of about 1475 is one of the largest (**FIG. 10–14**). This study of complex interlocking figures has an explosive energy that can best be appreciated by viewing it from every angle.

Statuettes of religious subjects were still popular, but humanist patrons began to collect bronzes of Classical subjects. Many sculptors, especially those trained as goldsmiths, started to cast small copies after well-known ancient works. Some artists also executed

or more intuitively by a series of arches or rocks or trees charting the path into the distance. Foreground figures are grouped in the lower third of each panel, while the other figures decrease gradually in size to map their positioning in deep space. The use of a system of perspective, with clearly differentiated background and foreground, also helped Ghiberti combine a series of related events, separated by narrative time, within a single pictorial frame.

The story of Jacob and Esau (Genesis 25 and 27) fills the center panel of the left door. Ghiberti creates a coherent and measurable space peopled by graceful, idealized figures (**FIG. 10–13**). He pays careful attention to one-point perspective in laying out the architectural setting. Squares in the pavement establish the receding lines of the orthogonals that converge to a central vanishing point under the loggia, while towering arches overlap and gradually diminish in size from foreground to background to define the receding space above the figures. The story unfolds in a series of individual episodes and begins in the background. On the rooftop (upper right) Rebecca stands, listening as God warns of her unborn sons' future conflict; under the left-hand arch she gives birth to the twins. The adult Esau sells his rights as oldest son to his brother Jacob, and when he goes hunting (center right), Rebecca and Jacob plot against him. Finally, in the right foreground, Jacob receives Isaac's blessing, while in the center, Esau faces his father. Ghiberti's portrayal of the scene relates more closely to developments in painting than to contemporary sculpture. Ghiberti not only signed his work, but also included his self-portrait in the medallion beside the lower right-hand corner of this panel.

To view this image, please go to page 607 of the *Art History*, Fourth Edition by Marilyn Stokstad ebook.

10-14 • Antonio del Pollaiuolo HERCULES AND ANTAEUS
c. 1475. Bronze, height with base 18″ (45.7 cm). Museo Nazionale del Bargello, Florence.

Fifteenth-century Italian artists developed a system known as linear, or mathematical perspective that enabled them to represent three dimensions on a two-dimensional surface, simulating the recession of space in the visible world pictorially in a way they found convincing. The sculptor and architect Filippo Brunelleschi first demonstrated the system about 1420, and the theorist and architect Leon Battista Alberti codified it in 1436 in his treatise *Della Pittura* (*On Painting*).

For Alberti, in one-point linear perspective a picture's surface was conceived as a flat plane that intersected the viewer's field of vision at right angles. This highly artificial concept presumed a viewer standing dead center at a prescribed distance from a work of art. From this single fixed vantage point, everything would appear to recede into the distance at the same rate, following imaginary lines called

orthogonals that met at a single **vanishing point** on the horizon. By using orthogonals in concert with controlled diminution of scale as forms move back toward the vanishing point, artists could replicate the optical illusion that things appear to grow smaller, rise higher, and come closer together as they get farther away from us. Linear perspective makes pictorial spaces seem almost like extensions of the viewer's real space, creating a compelling, even exaggerated sense of depth.

Linear perspective is not the only way to simulate spatial recession in two-dimensional painting. In atmospheric perspective, variations in color and clarity convey the feeling of distance when objects and landscape are portrayed less clearly, and colors become grayer, in the background, imitating the natural effects of a loss of clarity and color when viewing things in the distance through an atmospheric haze.

To view this image, please go to page 608 of the *Art History*, Fourth Edition by Marilyn Stokstad ebook.

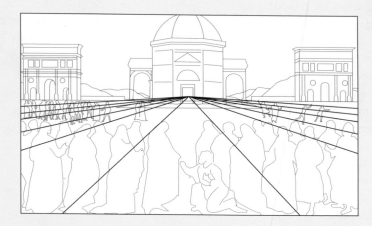

Perugino THE DELIVERY OF THE KEYS TO ST. PETER, WITH A SCHEMATIC DRAWING SHOWING THE ORTHOGONALS AND VANISHING POINT
Fresco on the right wall of the Sistine Chapel, Vatican, Rome. 1481. 11′5½″ × 18′8½″ (3.48 × 5.70 m).

The Delivery of the Keys to St. Peter is a remarkable study in linear perspective. The clear demarcation of the paving stones of the piazza provides a network of orthogonal and horizontal lines for the measured placement of the figures. People and buildings become increasingly, and logically, smaller as the space recedes. Horizontally, the composition is divided between the foreground frieze of figures and the widely spaced background buildings, vertically by the open space at the center between Christ and Peter and by the symmetrical architectural forms on either side of this central axis. Perugino's painting is, among other things, a representation of Alberti's ideal city, described in *De re aedificatoria* as having a "temple" (that is, a church) at the very center of a great open space raised on a dais and separate from any other buildings that might obstruct its view.

original designs *all'antica* ("in the antique style") to appeal to a cultivated humanist taste. Hercules was always a popular figure; as a patron of Florence, he was on the city seal. Among the many courageous acts by which Hercules gained immortality was the slaying of the evil Antaeus in a wrestling match by lifting him off the earth, the source of the giant's great physical power.

An engraving by Pollaiuolo, **THE BATTLE OF THE NUDES (FIG. 10–15)**, reflects two interests of Renaissance scholars—the study of Classical sculpture and anatomical research. Pollaiuolo may have intended this, his only known—but highly influential—print, as a study in composition involving the human figure in action. The naked men, fighting each other ferociously against a tapestrylike

To view this image, please go to page 609 of the *Art History*, Fourth Edition by Marilyn Stokstad ebook.

10–15 • Antonio del Pollaiuolo **THE BATTLE OF THE NUDES**
c. 1465–1470. Engraving, 15⅛ × 23¼″ (38.3 × 59 cm). Cincinnati Art Museum, Ohio. Bequest of Herbert Greer French. 1943.118

background of foliage, seem to have been drawn from a single model in a variety of poses, many of which were taken from Classical sources. Like the artist's *Hercules and Antaeus*, much of the engraving's fascination lies in how it depicts muscles of the male body reacting under tension.

PAINTING

Italian patrons commissioned murals and large altarpieces for their local churches and smaller panel paintings for their houses and private chapels. Artists experienced in fresco were in great demand and traveled widely to execute wall and ceiling decorations. At first the Italians showed little interest in oil painting, for the most part using tempera even for their largest works. But, in the last decades of the century, oil painting became popular in Venice.

MASACCIO. Even though his brief career lasted less than a decade, Tommaso di Ser Giovanni di Mone Cassai (1401–1428/1429?), nicknamed "Masaccio" (meaning "Big Tom"), established a new direction in Florentine painting, much as Giotto had a century earlier. He did this by integrating monumental and consistently scaled figures into rational architectural and natural settings using linear perspective. The chronology of Massaccio's works is uncertain, but his fresco of the **TRINITY** in the church of Santa Maria Novella in Florence must have been painted around 1426, the date on the Lenzi family tombstone that once stood in front of it (**FIGS. 10–16, 10–17**).

Masaccio's fresco was meant to give the illusion of a stone funerary monument and altar table set below a deep **aedicula** (framed niche) in the wall. The effect of looking up into a barrel-vaulted niche was made plausible through precisely rendered linear perspective. The eye level of an adult viewer standing within the church determined the horizon line on which the vanishing point was centered, just below the kneeling figures above the altar. And the painting demonstrates not only Masaccio's intimate knowledge of Brunelleschi's perspective experiments (see "Renaissance Perspective," opposite), but also his architectural style (SEE FIG. 10–4). The painted architecture is an unusual combination of Classical orders. On the wall surface, Corinthian pilasters support a plain architrave below a cornice, while inside the niche Renaissance variations on Ionic columns support arches on all four sides. The "source" of the consistent illumination of the architecture lies in front of the picture, casting reflections on the coffers, or sunken panels, of the ceiling.

The figures are organized in a measured progression through space. At the near end of the recessed, barrel-vaulted space is the Trinity—Jesus on the cross, the dove of the Holy Spirit poised in downward flight above his tilted halo, and God the Father, who stands behind to support the cross from his elevated perch on a high platform, apparently supported on the rear columns. As in many scenes of the Crucifixion, Jesus is flanked by the Virgin Mary and John the Evangelist, who contemplate the scene on either side of the cross. Mary gazes calmly out at us, her raised hand drawing our attention to the Trinity. Members of the Lenzi family kneel in front of the pilasters—thus closer to us than the Crucifixion; the red robes of the male donor signify that he was a member of the governing council of Florence. Below these donors, in an open sarcophagus, is a skeleton, a grim reminder of the Christian belief that since death awaits us all, our only hope is redemption and the promise of life in the hereafter, rooted in Christ's sacrifice on the cross. The inscription above the skeleton reads: "I was once that which you are, and what I am you also will be."

10–16 • Masaccio TRINITY WITH THE VIRGIN, ST. JOHN THE EVANGELIST, AND DONORS
Church of Santa Maria Novella, Florence. c. 1425–1427/1428.
Fresco, 21′ × 10′5″ (6.4 × 3.2 m).

To view this image, please go to page 610 of the *Art History*, Fourth Edition by Marilyn Stokstad ebook.

10–17 • SECTION DIAGRAM OF THE ILLUSIONISTIC SPATIAL WORLD PORTRAYED IN MASACCIO'S TRINITY
After Gene Brucker, *Florence: The Golden Age*, Berkeley, 1998.

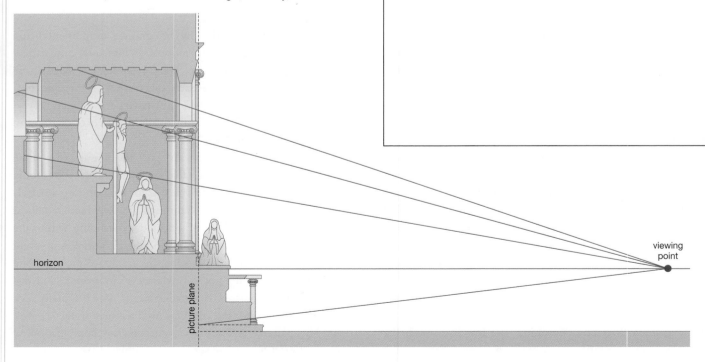

horizon

picture plane

viewing point

THE BRANCACCI CHAPEL. Masaccio's brief career culminated in the frescos he painted on the walls of the Brancacci Chapel in the church of Santa Maria del Carmine in Florence. Reproduced here are two of the best-known scenes: **THE EXPULSION OF ADAM AND EVE FROM PARADISE** (FIG. 10–18) and **THE TRIBUTE MONEY** (FIG. 10–19). In *The Expulsion*, he presented Adam and Eve as monumental nude figures, combining his studies of the human figure with an intimate knowledge of ancient Roman sculpture. In contrast to Flemish painters, who sought to record every visible detail of a figure's surface, Masaccio focused on the mass of bodies formed by the underlying bone and muscle structure, and a single light source emphasizes their tangibility with modeled forms and cast shadows. Departing from earlier interpretations of the event that emphasized wrongdoing and the fall from grace, Masaccio concerns himself with the psychological impact of shame on these first humans, who have been cast out of paradise mourning and protesting, thrown naked into the world.

In *The Tribute Money* (SEE FIG. 10–19), Masaccio portrays an incident from the life of Jesus that highlights St. Peter (Matthew 17: 24–27), to whom this chapel was dedicated. In the central scene a tax collector (dressed in a short red tunic and seen from behind) asks Peter (in the left foreground with the short gray beard) if Jesus pays the Jewish temple tax (the "tribute money" of the title). Set against the stable backdrop of a semicircular block of apostolic observers, a masterful series of dynamic diagonals in the postures and gestures of the three main figures interlocks them in a compositional system that imbues their interaction with a sense of tension calling out for resolution. Jesus instructs Peter to "go to the sea, drop in a hook, and take the first fish that comes up," which Peter does at the far left. In the fish's mouth is a coin worth twice the tax demanded, which Peter gives to the tax collector at the far right. The tribute story was especially significant for Florentines because in 1427, to raise money for defense against military aggression, the city enacted a graduated tax, based on the value of people's personal property.

The Tribute Money is particularly remarkable for its early use of both linear and atmospheric perspective to integrate figures, architecture, and landscape into a consistent whole. The group of disciples around Jesus and his disciples forms a clear central focus, from which the landscape seems to recede naturally into the far distance. To foster this illusion, Masaccio used linear perspective in the depiction of the house, and then reinforced it by diminishing the sizes of the barren trees and reducing the size of the crouching Peter at far left. At the central vanishing point established by the orthogonals of the house is the head of Jesus. A second vanishing point determines the position of the steps and stone rail at the right.

The cleaning of the painting in the 1980s revealed that it was painted in 32 *giornate* (a *giornata* is a section of fresh plaster that could be prepared and painted in a single day; see "Buon Fresco," page 530). The cleaning also uncovered Masaccio's subtle use of

To view this image, please go to page 611 of the *Art History*, Fourth Edition by Marilyn Stokstad ebook.

10–18 • Masaccio THE EXPULSION OF ADAM AND EVE FROM PARADISE
Brancacci Chapel, church of Santa Maria del Carmine, Florence. c. 1427. Fresco, 7′ × 2′11″ (214 × 90 cm).

Cleaning and restoration of the Brancacci Chapel paintings revealed the remarkable speed and skill with which Masaccio worked. He painted Adam and Eve in four *giornate* (each *giornata* of fresh plaster representing a day's work). Working from the top down and left to right, he painted the angel on the first day; on the second day, the portal; Adam on the third day; and Eve on the fourth.

To view this image, please go to page 612 of the *Art History*, Fourth Edition by Marilyn Stokstad ebook.

10-19 • Masaccio **THE TRIBUTE MONEY**
Brancacci Chapel, church of Santa Maria del Carmine, Florence. c. 1427. Fresco, 8′1″ × 19′7″ (2.46 × 6 m).

color to create atmospheric perspective in the distant landscape, where mountains fade from grayish-green to grayish-white and the houses and trees on their slopes are loosely sketched to simulate the lack of clear definition when viewing things in the distance through a haze. Green leaves were painted on the branches *al secco* (meaning "on the dry plastered wall").

As in *The Expulsion*, Masaccio modeled the foreground figures here with bold highlights and long shadows on the ground toward the left, giving a strong sense of volumetric solidity and implying a light source at the far right, as if the scene were lit by the actual window in the rear wall of the Brancacci Chapel. Not only does the lighting give the forms sculptural definition, but the colors vary in tone according to the strength of the illumination. Masaccio used a wide range of hues—pale pink, mauve, gold, blue-green, seafoam-green, apple-green, peach—and a sophisticated shading technique using contrasting colors, as in Andrew's green robe which is shaded with red instead of darker green. The figures of Jesus and the apostles originally had gold-leaf haloes, several of which have flaked off. Rather than silhouette the heads against consistently flat gold circles in the medieval manner, however, Masaccio conceived of haloes as gold disks hovering in space above each head that moved with the heads as they moved, and he foreshortened them depending on the angle from which each head is seen.

Some stylistic innovations take time to be fully accepted, and Masaccio's innovative depictions of volumetric solidity, consistent lighting, and spatial integration were best appreciated by a later generation of painters. Many important sixteenth-century Italian artists, including Michelangelo, studied and sketched Masaccio's Brancacci Chapel frescos, as they did Giotto's work in the Scrovegni Chapel. In the meantime, painting in Florence after Masaccio's death developed along somewhat different lines.

PAINTING IN FLORENCE AFTER MASACCIO

The tradition of covering walls with paintings in fresco continued uninterrupted through the fifteenth century. Between 1438 and 1445, the decoration of the Dominican monastery of San Marco in Florence, where Fra Angelico lived, was one of the most extensive projects.

FRA ANGELICO. Guido di Piero da Mugello (c. 1395/1400–1455), earned his nickname "Fra Angelico" ("Angelic Brother") through his piety as well as his painting: in 1984, he was beatified, the first step toward sainthood. Fra Angelico is first documented painting in Florence in 1417–1418, and he remained an active painter after taking vows as a Dominican monk in nearby Fiesole between 1418 and 1421.

Between 1438 and 1445, in the monastery of San Marco, Fra Angelico and his assistants—probably working under the patronage of Cosimo de' Medici—created paintings to inspire meditation in each monk's cell (44 in all), in the chapter house (meeting room), and even in the corridors (hallways). At the top of the stairs in the north corridor, where the monks would pass frequently on their way to their individual cells, Fra Angelico painted a serene picture of the **ANNUNCIATION (FIG. 10–20)**. To describe the quiet, measured space where the demure archangel greets the unassuming,

To view this image, please go to page 613 of the *Art History*, Fourth Edition by Marilyn Stokstad ebook.

10-20 • Fra Angelico ANNUNCIATION
North dormitory corridor, monastery of San Marco, Florence. c. 1438–1445. Fresco, 7'1" × 10'6" (2.2 × 3.2 m).

The shadowed vault of the portico is supported by a wall on one side and by slender Ionic and Corinthian columns on the other, a new building technique being used by Brunelleschi in the very years when the painting was being created.

youthful Mary, Fra Angelico used linear perspective with unusual skill, extending the monks' stairway and corridor outward into an imagined portico and garden beside the Virgin's home. The slender, graceful figures, wearing quietly flowing draperies, assume modest poses. Natural light falling from the left models their forms gently, casting an almost supernatural radiance over their faces and hands. The scene is a sacred vision rendered in a contemporary setting, welcoming the monks to the most intimate areas of the monastery and preparing them for their private meditations.

UCCELLO. At mid century, when Fra Angelico was still painting his radiant visions of Mary and Jesus in the monastery of San Marco, a new generation of artists began to emerge. Thoroughly conversant with the theories of Brunelleschi and Alberti, they had mastered the techniques (and tricks) of depicting figures in a constructed architectural space. Some artists became specialists, among them Paolo Uccello, who devoted his life to the study of linear perspective (**FIG. 10–21**; SEE ALSO FIG. 10–1). Vasari devoted a chapter in his biographies

of Italian artists to Uccello, whom he described as a man so obsessed with the science of perspective that he neglected his painting, his family, and even his pet birds (his *uccelli*). According to Vasari, Uccello's wife complained that he sat up drawing all night and when she called to him to come to bed he would say, "Oh, what a sweet thing this perspective is!" (Vasari, trans. Bondanella and Bondanella, p. 83).

To view this image, please go to page 613 of the *Art History*, Fourth Edition by Marilyn Stokstad ebook.

10-21 • Paolo Uccello THE BATTLE OF SAN ROMANO
1438–1440. Tempera on wood panel, approx. 6' × 10'7" (1.83 × 3.23 m). National Gallery, London.

To view this image, please go to page 614 of the *Art History*,
Fourth Edition by Marilyn Stokstad ebook.

10–22 • Andrea del Castagno THE LAST SUPPER
Refectory, convent of Sant'Apollonia, Florence. 1447. Fresco, width approx. 16 × 32' (4.6 × 9.8 m).

CASTAGNO. Notable Florentine painter Andrea del Castagno (c. 1417/19–1457) painted a fresco of **THE LAST SUPPER** for a convent of Benedictine nuns in 1447 **(FIG. 10–22)**. The Last Supper was often painted in monastic refectories (dining halls) to remind the monks or nuns of Christ's Last Supper with his first followers and encourage them to see their daily gatherings for meals almost as a sacramental act rooted in this biblical tradition. Here Castagno has not portrayed the scene in the biblical setting of an "upper room." Rather, the humble house of the original account has become a great palace with sumptuous marble revetment. The most brilliantly colored and wildly patterned marble panel frames the heads of Christ and Judas to focus viewers on the most important part of the picture. Judas sits on the viewer's side of the table, separated from the other apostles, and St. John sleeps, head collapsed onto the tabletop. The strong perspective lines of floor tiles, ceiling rafters,

To view this image, please go to page 614 of the *Art History*, Fourth Edition by Marilyn Stokstad ebook.

10–23 • Fra Filippo Lippi PORTRAIT OF A WOMAN AND MAN (ANGIOLA DI BERNARDO SAPITI AND LORENZO DI RANIERI SCOLARI?)
c. 1435–1445. Tempera on wood panel, 25¼ × 16½" (64.1 × 41.9 cm). Metropolitan Museum of Art, New York

Some art historians have seen in the sumptuousness of this woman's costume an indication that she is a newlywed, especially since the pearls sewn with gold threads into the embroidery on her sleeve spell out the word *lealtà*, meaning "loyalty." But since technical evidence shows that the face of the man was added after the portrait of the woman, and since he is unable to meet her gaze, others speculate that this was transformed into a memorial portrait after her death.

and paneled walls draw viewers into the scene, especially the nuns who would have seen the painting as an extension of their own dining hall. At first, the lines of the orthogonals seem perfectly logical, but close examination reveals that only the lines of the ceiling converge to a single point, below the hands of St. John. Two windows light the painting's room from the direction of the actual refectory windows, further unifying the two spaces. Castagno worked quickly, completing this huge mural in at most 32 days.

FRA FILIPPO LIPPI. Not all Florentine paintings of the mid fifteenth century were sacred scenes on the walls of religious buildings. It is during this period that portraiture comes into its own as a major artistic form in Italy, and among the most extraordinary—if enigmatic—examples is this **PORTRAIT OF A WOMAN AND MAN (FIG. 10–23)**, an early work of Fra Filippo Lippi (c. 1406–1469). This painting is also the earliest surviving double portrait of the Italian Renaissance. Lippi grew up as an orphan in the Carmelite church where Masaccio had painted frescos in the Brancacci Chapel, and art historians have stressed the impact this work had on Lippi's development as an artist. But although he may have absorbed Massacio's predilection for softly rounded forms situated in carefully mapped spaces, in Lippi's hands these artistic tools became the basis for pictures that often ask more questions than they answer, by stressing outline at the same time as form, and by creating complex and often confusing spatial systems.

The emphasis in this double portrait is squarely on the woman. She is spotlighted in the foreground, sharply profiled against a window that serves as an unsettling internal frame, not big enough to contain her. This window opens onto a vista, clearly a fragment of a larger world, but one that highlights an orthogonal to emphasize a spatial recession only partially revealed. The woman blocks most of this vista with her shining visage and sumptuous costume—notably its embroidered velvet, fur lining, and luminous pearls. There is no engagement with the viewer and little sense of likeness. And it is not at all clear where or to what she directs her attention, especially since the gaze of the man in the background does not meet hers. He is even more of a mystery. We see only a masklike sliver of his profile, although the substantiality of his face is reinforced by the strong shadow it casts against the window casement through which he looks. Unlike the woman, who clasps her inert hands in front of her as if to highlight her rings, this man fidgets with his fingers, perhaps to draw our attention to the heraldic device below him that may identify him as a member of the Scolari family. This could be a double portrait of Lorenzo di Ranieri Scolari and Angiola di Bernardo Sapiti, who married in 1436. But what does the painting say about them? Does it commemorate their marriage, celebrate the birth of their child, or memorialize one of their deaths? All have been proposed by art historians as an explanation for this innovative double portrait, but it remains a puzzle to be pondered. Could that pondering be the point of the picture?

To view this image, please go to page 630 of the *Art History*, Fourth Edition by Marilyn Stokstad ebook.

10-24 • Raphael **STANZA DELLA SEGNATURA**   Vatican, Rome. Fresco in the left lunette, *Parnassus*; in the right lunette, *The School of Athens*. 1510–1511.

SIXTEENTH-CENTURY ART IN ITALY

Two young artists—Raphael and Michelangelo—although rivals in almost every sense, were linked in service to Pope Julius II (pontificate 1503–1513) in the early years of the sixteenth century. Raphael was painting the pope's private library (1509–1511) while, nearby, Michelangelo painted the ceiling of his Sistine Chapel (1508–1512). The pope demanded an art that reflected his imperial vision of a new, worldwide Church based on humanistic ideas, which he would lead as a new St. Peter, founding a second great age of papal dominion. In fulfilling this proud demand, Raphael and Michelangelo united Renaissance principles of harmony and balance with a new monumentality based on Classical ideals, and they knit these elements into a dynamic and synthetic whole, rich in color and controlled by cohesive design. Working alongside the architect Donato Bramante and the multifaceted genius Leonardo da Vinci, they created a style we call the High Renaissance.

Julius II intended the **STANZA DELLA SEGNATURA**, or Room of the Signature, to be his personal study (FIG. 10–24). Raphael sought to create an ideal setting for papal activities, with murals proclaiming that all human knowledge exists under the power of divine wisdom. He organized the mural program itself like a library, separated into divisions of theology, philosophy, the arts, and justice. He created pictorial allegories to illustrate each theme. On one wall, churchmen discussing the sacraments represent theology, while across the room ancient philosophers led by Plato and Aristotle debate in the School of Athens. Plato holds his book *Timaeus*, in which creation is seen in terms of geometry, and in which humanity encompasses and explains the universe. Aristotle holds his *Nicomachean Ethics*, a decidedly human-centered book concerned with relations among people. Ancient representatives of the academic curriculum—Grammar, Rhetoric, Dialectic, Arithmetic, Music, Geometry, and Astronomy—surround them. On a window wall, Justice, holding a sword and scales, assigns each his due. Across the room, Poetry and the Arts are represented by Apollo and the Muses, and the poet Sappho reclines against the fictive frame of an actual window. Raphael included his own portrait among the onlookers on the extreme lower right in the *School of Athens* fresco and signed the painting with his initials—a signal that both artists and patrons were becoming increasingly aware of their individual significance.

Raphael achieved a lofty style in keeping with papal ambition—using ideals of Classical grandeur, professing faith in human rationality and perfectibility, and celebrating the power of the pope as God's earthly administrator. But when Raphael died at age 37 on April 6, 1520, the grand moment was already passing: Luther and the Protestant Reformation were challenging papal authority, and the world would never be the same again.

LEARN ABOUT IT

10.6 Trace the shift in the artistic center of Italy from Florence to Rome, and recognize the efforts of Pope Julius II to create a new "golden age."

10.7 Understand the Vatican as a site for the creative energies of the most important artists of the Italian Renaissance.

10.8 Explore the intentional subversion of Classical style and decorum in the work of Mannerist artists.

10.9 Compare and contrast the emphasis on drawing and clearly structured compositions in the work of Roman and Florentine painters with the expressive potential of color that characterizes the work of their Venetian counterparts.

10.10 Examine the architectural creativity lavished on the design of both grand churches and pleasurable retreats for the wealthy in sixteenth-century Italy.

HEAR MORE: Listen to an audio file of your chapter **www.myartslab.com**

EUROPE IN THE SIXTEENTH CENTURY

The sixteenth century was an age of social, intellectual, and religious ferment that transformed European culture. It was marked by continual warfare triggered by the expansionist ambitions of warring rulers. The humanism of the fourteenth and fifteenth centuries, with its medieval roots and its often uncritical acceptance of the authority of Classical texts, slowly developed into a critical exploration of new ideas, the natural world, and distant lands. Cartographers began to acknowledge the Earth's curvature and the degrees of distance, giving Europeans a more accurate understanding of their place within the world. The printing press sparked an explosion in book production, spreading new ideas through the translation and publication of ancient and contemporary texts, broadening the horizons of educated Europeans and encouraging the development of literacy. Since travel was growing more common, artists and their work became mobile, and the world of art was transformed into a more international community.

At the start of the sixteenth century, England, France, and Portugal were nation-states under strong monarchs. German-speaking central Europe was divided into dozens of principalities, counties, free cities, and small territories. But even states as powerful as Saxony and Bavaria acknowledged the supremacy of the Habsburg Holy Roman Empire—in theory the greatest power in Europe. Charles V, elected emperor in 1519, also inherited Spain, the Netherlands, and vast territories in the Americas. Italy, which was divided into numerous small states, was a diplomatic and military battlefield where, for much of the century, the Italian city-states, Habsburg Spain, France, and the papacy fought each other in shifting alliances. Popes behaved like secular princes, using diplomacy and military force to regain control over central Italy and in some cases to establish family members as hereditary rulers.

The popes' incessant demands for money, to finance the rebuilding of St. Peter's as well as their self-aggrandizing art projects and luxurious lifestyles, aggravated the religious dissent that had long been developing, especially north of the Alps. Early in the century, religious reformers within the established Church challenged beliefs and practices, especially Julius II's sale of indulgences promising forgiveness of sins and assurance of salvation in exchange for a financial contribution to the Church. Because they protested, these northern European reformers came to be called Protestants; their demand for reform gave rise to a movement called the Reformation.

The political maneuvering of Pope Clement VII (pontificate 1523–1534) led to a direct clash with Holy Roman Emperor Charles V. In May 1527, Charles's German mercenary troops attacked Rome, beginning a six-month orgy of killing, looting, and burning. The Sack of Rome, as it is called, shook the sense of stability and humanistic confidence that until then had characterized the Renaissance, and it sent many artists fleeing from the ruined city. Nevertheless, Charles saw himself as the leader of the Catholic forces—and he was the sole Catholic ally Clement had at the time. In 1530, Clement VII crowned Charles emperor in Bologna.

Sixteenth-century patrons valued artists highly and rewarded them well, not only with generous commissions but sometimes even with high social status. Charles V, for example, knighted the painter Titian. Some painters and sculptors became entrepreneurs and celebrities, selling prints of their works on the side and creating international reputations for themselves. Many artists recorded their activities—professional and private—in diaries, notebooks, and letters that have come down to us. In addition, contemporary writers began to report on the lives of artists, documenting their physical appearance and assessing their individual reputations. In 1550, Giorgio Vasari wrote the first survey of Italian art history—*Lives of the Best Architects, Painters, and Sculptors*—organized as a series of critical biographies but at its core a work of critical judgment. Vasari also commented on the role of patrons, and argued that art had become more realistic and more beautiful over time, reaching its apex of perfection in his own age. From his characterization developed our notion of this period as the High Renaissance—that is, as a high point in art since the early experiments of Cimabue and Giotto, marked by a balanced synthesis of Classical ideals and a lifelike rendering of the natural world.

During this period, the fifteenth-century humanists' notion of painting, sculpture, and architecture not as manual arts but as liberal (intellectual) arts, requiring education in the Classics and mathematics as well as in the techniques of the craft, became a topic of intense interest. And from these discussions arose the Renaissance formulation—still with us today—of artists as divinely inspired creative geniuses, a step above most of us in their gifts of hand and mind. This idea weaves its way through Vasari's work like an organizing principle. And this newly elevated status to which artists aspired favored men. Although few artists of either sex had access to the humanist education required by the sophisticated, often esoteric, subject matter used in paintings (usually devised by someone other than the artist), women were denied even the studio practice necessary to draw lifelike nude figures in foreshortened poses. Furthermore, it was almost impossible for an artist to achieve international status without traveling extensively and frequently relocating to follow commissions—something most women could not do. Still, some European women managed to follow their gifts and establish careers as artists during this period despite the obstacles that blocked their entrance into the profession.

ITALY IN THE EARLY SIXTEENTH CENTURY: THE HIGH RENAISSANCE

Italian art from the 1490s to about the time of the Sack of Rome in 1527 has been called the "High Renaissance." As we have already seen with the "High Classical" period in ancient Athens, the term "High Renaissance" encapsulates an art-historical

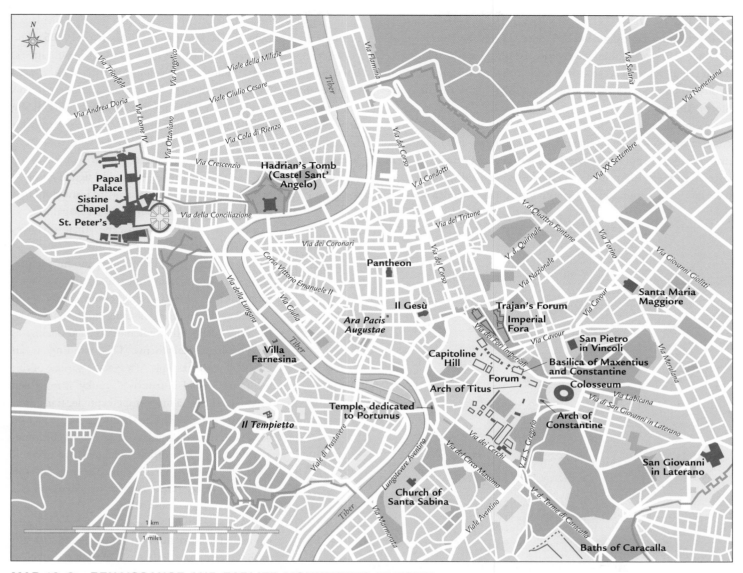

MAP 10-2 • RENAISSANCE AND EARLIER MONUMENTS IN ROME

In addition to situating the principal works of the Roman Renaissance that emerged from Julius II's campaign to revitalize the papal city, this map also locates the surviving works of Roman antiquity that would have been available to the Renaissance artists and architects who masterminded the Classical revival.

judgment, claiming that what happened in Rome at this time represents a pinnacle of achievement within a longer artistic movement, and that it set standards for the future **(MAP 10–2)**. High Renaissance art is characterized by a sense of gravity and decorum, a complex but ordered relationship of individual parts to the whole, and an emulation of the principles artists saw in ancient Classical art. Art historian Sydney Freedberg has stressed the way High Renaissance art fuses the real and the ideal, characterizing Leonardo's *Mona Lisa*, for example, as "a rare perfection between art and reality; an image in which a breathing instant and a composure for all time are held in suspension" (Freedberg, p. 28).

Two important practical developments at the turn of the sixteenth century affected the arts in Italy. Technically, the use of tempera gave way to the more flexible oil painting medium; and economically, commissions from private sources increased so that artists no longer depended so exclusively on the patronage of the Church, the court, or civic associations.

THREE GREAT ARTISTS OF THE EARLY SIXTEENTH CENTURY

Florence's renowned artistic tradition attracted a stream of young artists to that city, traveling there to study Masaccio's solid, monumental figures, with their eloquent facial features, poses, and gestures, in the Brancacci Chapel paintings. The young Michelangelo's sketches of the chapel frescos document the importance of Masaccio to his developing style. In fact, Michelangelo, Leonardo, and Raphael—the three leading artists of the High Renaissance— all began their careers in Florence, although they soon moved to other centers of patronage and their influence spread well beyond that city, even beyond Italy.

LEONARDO DA VINCI. Leonardo da Vinci (1452–1519) was 12 or 13 when his family moved to Florence from the Tuscan village of Vinci. After an apprenticeship in the shop of the Florentine painter and sculptor Verrocchio, and a few years on his own, Leonardo traveled to Milan in 1481 or 1482 to work for the ruling Sforza family.

Leonardo spent much of his time in Milan on military and civil engineering projects, including both urban-renewal and fortification plans for the city, but he also created a few key monuments of Renaissance painting. In April 1483, Leonardo contracted with the Confraternity of the Immaculate Conception to paint an altarpiece for their chapel in the church of San Francesco Grande in Milan, a painting now known as *The Virgin of the Rocks* (**FIG. 10–25**). The contract stipulated a painting of the Virgin and Child with angels, but Leonardo added a figure of the young John the Baptist, who balances the composition at the left, pulled into dialogue with his younger cousin Jesus by the long, protective arm of the Virgin. She draws attention to her child by extending her other hand over his head, while the enigmatic figure of the angel—who looks out without actually making eye contact with the viewer—points to the center of interaction. The stable, balanced, pyramidal figural group—a compositional formula that will become a standard feature of High Renaissance Classicism—is set against an exquisitely detailed landscape that dissolves mysteriously into the misty distance.

To ensure their dominance in the picture, Leonardo picks out the four figures with spotlights, creating a strong **chiaroscuro** (from the Italian words *chiaro*, meaning "light," and *oscuro*, meaning "dark") that enhances their modeling as three-dimensional forms. This painting is an excellent early example of a specific variant of this technique, called **sfumato** ("smoky"), in which there are subtle, almost imperceptible, transitions between light and dark in shading, as if the picture were seen through smoke or fog. *Sfumato* becomes a hallmark of Leonardo's style, and the effect is artificially enhanced in this painting by the yellowing of its thick varnish, which masks the original vibrancy of its color.

At Duke Ludovico Sforza's request, Leonardo painted **THE LAST SUPPER** (**FIGS. 10–26, 10–27**) in the refectory, or dining hall, of the monastery of Santa Maria delle Grazie in Milan between 1495 and 1498. In fictive space defined by a coffered ceiling and four pairs of tapestries that seem to extend the refectory itself into another room, Jesus and his disciples are seated at a long table placed parallel to the picture plane and to the monastic diners who would have been seated in the hall below. In a sense, Jesus' meal with his disciples prefigures the daily gathering of this local monastic community at mealtimes. The stagelike space recedes from the table to three windows on the back wall, where the vanishing point of the one-point linear perspective lies behind Jesus' head. A stable, pyramidal Jesus at the center is

To view this image, please go to page 634 of the *Art History*, Fourth Edition by Marilyn Stokstad ebook.

10–25 • Leonardo da Vinci THE VIRGIN OF THE ROCKS
c. 1485. Oil on wood panel (now transferred to canvas), 6′6″ × 4′ (1.9 × 1.2 m). Musée du Louvre, Paris.

To view this image, please go to page 635 of the *Art History*,
Fourth Edition by Marilyn Stokstad ebook.

10-26 • Leonardo da Vinci **THE LAST SUPPER**
Refectory of the monastery of Santa Maria delle Grazie, Milan, Italy. 1495–1498. Tempera and oil on plaster, 15′2″ × 28′10″ (4.6 × 8.8 m).

SEE MORE: View a video about Leonardo da Vinci's *The Last Supper* **www.myartslab.com**

**10-27 • REFECTORY OF THE
MONASTERY OF SANTA MARIA
DELLE GRAZIE, SHOWING
LEONARDO'S LAST SUPPER**
Milan, Italy.

Instead of painting in fresco, Leonardo devised an experimental technique for this mural. Hoping to achieve the freedom and flexibility of painting on wood panel, he worked directly on dry *intonaco*— a thin layer of smooth plaster—with an oil-and-tempera paint for which the formula is unknown. The result was disastrous. Within a short time, the painting began to deteriorate, and by the middle of the sixteenth century its figures could be seen only with difficulty. In the seventeenth century, the monks saw no harm in cutting a doorway through the lower center of the composition. The work has barely survived the intervening period, despite many attempts to halt its deterioration and restore its original appearance. The painting narrowly escaped complete destruction in World War II, when the refectory was bombed to rubble. The coats of arms at the top are those of patron Ludovico Sforza, the duke of Milan (r. 1494–1499), and his wife, Beatrice.

To view this image, please go to page 635 of the *Art History*,
Fourth Edition by Marilyn Stokstad ebook.

To view this image, please go to page 636 of the *Art History*, Fourth Edition by Marilyn Stokstad ebook.

10-28 • Leonardo da Vinci **MONA LISA**
c. 1503–1506. Oil on wood panel, 30¼ × 21″ (77 × 53 cm).
Musée du Louvre, Paris. (INV. 779)

EXPLORE MORE: Gain insight from a primary source by Leonardo **www.myartslab.com**

flanked by his 12 disciples, grouped in four interlocking sets of three.

On one level, Leonardo has painted a scene from a story—one that captures the individual reactions of the apostles to Jesus' announcement that one of them will betray him. Leonardo was an acute observer of human behavior, and his art captures human emotions with compelling immediacy. On another level, *The Last Supper* is a symbolic evocation of Jesus' coming sacrifice for the salvation of humankind, the foundation of the institution of the Mass. Breaking with traditional representations of the subject (SEE FIG. 10–22), Leonardo placed the traitor Judas—clutching his money bags in the shadows—within the first triad to the left of Jesus, along with the young John the Evangelist and the elderly Peter, rather than isolating him on the opposite side of the table. Judas, Peter, and John were each to play an essential role in Jesus' mission: Judas set in motion the events leading to Jesus' sacrifice; Peter led the Church after Jesus' death; and John, the visionary, foretold the Second Coming and the Last Judgment in the book of Revelation.

The painting's careful geometry, the convergence of its perspective lines, the stability of its pyramidal forms, and Jesus' calm demeanor at the mathematical center of all the commotion together reinforce the sense of gravity, balance, and order. The clarity and stability of this painting epitomize High Renaissance style.

Leonardo returned to Florence in 1500, after the French, who had invaded Italy in 1494, claimed Milan by defeating Leonardo's Milanese patron, Ludovico Sforza. Perhaps the most famous of his Florentine works is the portrait he painted between about 1503 and 1506 known as the **MONA LISA** (FIG. **10–28**). The subject may have been 24-year-old Lisa Gherardini del Giocondo, the wife of a prominent Florentine merchant. Leonardo never delivered the painting and kept it with him for the rest of his life. In a departure from tradition, the young woman is portrayed without jewelry, not even a ring. The solid pyramidal form of her halflength figure—another departure from traditional portraiture, which was limited to the upper torso—is silhouetted against distant hazy mountains, giving the painting a sense of mystery reminiscent of *The Virgin of the Rocks* (SEE FIG. 10–25). Mona Lisa's facial expression has been called "enigmatic" because her gentle smile is not accompanied by the warmth one would expect to see in her eyes, which have boldly—perhaps flirtatiously—shifted to the side to look straight out at the viewer. It is this expressive complexity, and the sense of psychological presence it gives the human face—especially in the context of the masklike detachment that was more characteristic of Renaissance portraiture (compare FIG. 10–31)—that makes the innovative *Mona Lisa* so arresting and haunting, even today.

A fiercely debated topic in Renaissance Italy was the question of the relative merits of painting and sculpture. Leonardo insisted on the supremacy of painting as the best and most complete means of creating an illusion of the natural world, while Michelangelo argued for sculpture. Yet in creating a painted illusion, Leonardo considered color to be secondary to the depiction of sculptural volume, which he achieved through his virtuosity in *sfumato*. He also unified his compositions by covering them with a thin, lightly tinted varnish, which enhanced the overall smoky haze. Because early evening light tends to produce a similar effect naturally, Leonardo considered dusk the finest time of day and recommended that painters set up their studios in a courtyard with black walls and a linen sheet stretched overhead to reproduce twilight.

Leonardo's fame as an artist is based on only a few works, for his many interests took him away from painting. Unlike his humanist contemporaries, he was not particularly interested in Classical literature or archaeology. Instead, his passions were mathematics, engineering, and the natural world. He compiled volumes of detailed drawings and notes on anatomy, botany, geology, meteorology, architectural design, and mechanics. In his drawings of human figures, he sought not only the precise details of anatomy but also the geometric basis of perfect proportions (see "The Vitruvian Man," opposite). Leonardo's searching mind is

The Vitruvian Man

Artists throughout history have turned to geometric shapes and mathematical proportions to seek the ideal representation of the human form. Leonardo, and before him the first-century BCE Roman architect and engineer Vitruvius, equated the ideal man with both circle and square. Ancient Egyptian artists laid out square grids as aids to design (see "Egyptian Pictorial Relief," page 167). Medieval artists adapted a variety of figures, from triangles to pentagrams.

Vitruvius, in his ten-volume *De architectura* (*On Architecture*), wrote: "For if a man be placed flat on his back, with his hands and feet extended, and a pair of compasses centered at his navel, the fingers and toes of his two hands and feet will touch the circumference of a circle described therefrom. And just as the human body yields a circular outline, so too a square figure may be found from it. For if we measure the distance from the soles of the feet to the top of the head, and then apply that measure to the outstretched arms, the breadth will be found to be the same as the height" (Book III, Chapter 1, Section 3). Vitruvius determined that the ideal body should be eight heads high. Leonardo added his own observations in the reversed writing he always used in his notebooks when he created his well-known diagram for the ideal male figure, called the Vitruvian Man.

To view this image, please go to page 637 of the *Art History*, Fourth Edition by Marilyn Stokstad ebook.

Leonardo da Vinci
VITRUVIAN MAN
c. 1490. Ink, 13½ × 9⅝″ (34.3 × 24.5 cm).
Galleria dell'Accademia, Venice.

To view this image, please go to page 638 of the *Art History*, Fourth Edition by Marilyn Stokstad ebook.

10-29 • Raphael THE SMALL COWPER MADONNA
c. 1505. Oil on wood panel, 23⅜ × 17⅜″ (59.5 × 44.1 cm).
National Gallery of Art, Washington, D.C.
Widener Collection (1942.9.57)

In the distance on a hilltop, Raphael has painted a scene he knew well from his childhood, the domed church of San Bernardino, two miles outside Urbino. The church contains the tombs of dukes of Urbino, Federico and Guidobaldo da Montefeltro, and their wives. Donato Bramante, whose architecture was key in establishing the High Renaissance style, may have designed the church.

cis I's invitation to relocate to France as an advisor on architecture, taking the *Mona Lisa* with him. He remained at Francis's court until his death in 1519.

RAPHAEL. About 1505—while Leonardo was working on the *Mona Lisa*—Raphael (Raffaello Santi or Sanzio, 1483–1520) arrived in Florence from his native Urbino after studying in Perugia with the city's leading artist, Perugino. Raphael quickly became successful in Florence, especially with small, polished paintings of the Virgin and Child, such as **THE SMALL COWPER MADONNA** (named for a modern owner) of about 1505 (**FIG. 10–29**). Already a superb painter technically, the youthful Raphael shows his indebtedness to his teacher in the delicate tilt of the figures' heads, the brilliant tonalities, and the pervasive sense of serenity. But Leonardo's impact is also evident here in the simple grandeur of these monumental shapes, the pyramidal composition activated by the spiraling movement of the child, and the draperies that cling to the Virgin's substantial form. In other Madonnas from this period, Raphael included the young John the Baptist (SEE FIG. 1–3), experimenting with the multiple figure interactions pioneered by Leonardo in *The Virgin of the Rocks* (SEE FIG. 10–25).

At the same time as he was producing engaging images of elegant Madonnas, Raphael was also painting portraits of prosperous Florentine patrons. To commemorate the marriage in 1504 of 30-year-old cloth merchant Agnelo Doni to Maddalena Strozzi, the 15-year-old daughter of a powerful banking family, Doni commissioned from Raphael pendent portraits of the newlyweds (**FIGS. 10–30, 10–31**). They are flawlessly executed by the mature painter at the peak of his illusionistic virtuosity. Like Piero della Francesca in his portraits of Battista Sforza and Federico da Montefeltro, Raphael silhouettes Maddalena and Agnelo against a meticulously described panoramic landscape. But unlike their predecessors, they turn to address the viewer. Agnelo is commanding but casual, leaning his arm on a balustrade to add three-dimensionality to his posture. Maddalena's pose imitates Leonardo's innovative presentation of his subject in the *Mona Lisa* (SEE FIG. 10–28), which Raphael had obviously seen in progress, but with Maddalena there is no sense of mystery, indeed little psychological presence, and Raphael follows tradition in emphasizing the sumptuousness of her clothing and making ostentatious display of her jewelry. Only the wisps of hair that escape from her sculpted coiffure offer a hint of human vulnerability in her haughty demeanor.

Raphael left Florence about 1508 for Rome, where Pope Julius II put him to work almost immediately decorating rooms (*stanze*, singular *stanza*) in the papal apartments. In the Stanza della Segnatura (SEE FIG. 10–24)—the papal library—Raphael painted the four branches of knowledge as conceived in the sixteenth century: Religion (the *Disputà*, depicting discussions concerning the true presence of Christ in the Eucharistic Host), Philosophy (the School of Athens), Poetry (Parnassus, home of the Muses), and Law (the Cardinal Virtues under Justice).

evident in his drawings, not only of natural objects and human beings, but also of machines, so clearly and completely worked out that modern engineers have used them to construct working models. He designed flying machines, a kind of automobile, a parachute, and all sorts of military equipment, including a mobile fortress. His imagination outran his means to bring his creations into being. For one thing, he lacked a source of power other than men and horses. For another, he may have lacked focus and follow-through. His contemporaries complained that he never finished anything and that his inventions distracted him from his painting.

Leonardo returned to Milan in 1508 and lived there until 1513. He also lived for a time in the Vatican at the invitation of Pope Leo X, but there is no evidence that he produced any works of art during his stay. In 1516, he accepted the French king Fran-

To view this image, please go to page 639 of the *Art History*, Fourth Edition by Marilyn Stokstad ebook.

10-30 • Raphael AGNELO DONI
c. 1506. Oil on wood panel, 24½ × 17¼″ (63 × 45 cm). Palazzo Pitti, Florence.

These portraits were not the only paintings commissioned by Agnelo Doni to commemorate his upwardly mobile marriage alliance with Maddalena Strozzi. He ordered a *tondo* portraying the holy family from rival artist Michelangelo. Tradition holds that Doni tried to haggle with Michelangelo over the cost of the painting, but ultimately had to pay the price demanded by the artist.

To view this image, please go to page 639 of the *Art History*, Fourth Edition by Marilyn Stokstad ebook.

10-31 • Raphael MADDALENA STROZZI
c. 1506. Oil on wood panel, 24½ × 17¼″ (63 × 45 cm). Palazzo Pitti, Florence.

Raphael's most influential achievement in the papal rooms was *The School of Athens*, painted about 1510–1511 (see "A Closer Look," page 610). Here, the painter seems to summarize the ideals of the Renaissance papacy in a grand conception of harmoniously arranged forms in a rational space, as well as in the calm dignity of the figures that occupy it. If the learned Julius II did not actually devise the subjects, he certainly must have approved them. Greek philosophers Plato and Aristotle take center stage—placed to the right and left of the vanishing point—silhouetted against the sky and framed under three successive barrel vaults. Surrounding Plato and Aristotle are mathematicians, naturalists, astronomers, geographers, and other philosophers, debating and demonstrating their theories with and to onlookers and each other. The scene takes place in an immense barrel-vaulted interior, flooded with a clear, even light from a single source, and seemingly inspired by the

new design for St. Peter's, under construction at the time. The grandeur of the building is matched by the monumental dignity of the philosophers themselves, each of whom has a distinct physical and intellectual presence. The sweeping arcs of the composition are activated by the variety and energy of their poses and gestures, creating a dynamic unity that is a prime characteristic of High Renaissance art.

In 1515, Raphael was commissioned by Pope Leo X (pontificate 1513–1521) to provide designs on themes from the Acts of the Apostles to be woven into tapestries for the strip of blank wall below the fifteenth-century wall paintings of the Sistine Chapel. For the production of the tapestries, woven in Brussels, Raphael and his large workshop of assistants made full-scale charcoal drawings, then painted over them with color for the weavers to match. Pictorial weaving was the most prestigious and expensive kind of wall decoration. With murals by the leading painters of the fifteenth century above and Michelangelo's work circling over all, Raphael must have felt both honored and challenged. The pope had given him the place of honor among the artists in the papal chapel.

The School of Athens ➤ by Raphael, fresco in the Stanza della Segnatura, Vatican, Rome. c. 1510–1511. 19 × 27′ (5.79 × 8.24 m).

Looking down from niches in the walls are sculptures of Apollo, the god of sunlight, rationality, poetry, music, and the fine arts; and of Minerva, the goddess of wisdom and the mechanical arts.

Plato points upward to the realm of ideas and pure forms that were at the center of his philosophy. His pupil Aristotle gestures toward his surroundings, signifying the empirical world that for him served as the basis for understanding.

The figure bent over a slate with a compass is Euclid, the father of geometry. Vasari claimed that Raphael gave this mathematician the portrait likeness of Bramante, the architect whose redesigned St. Peter's was under construction not far from this room.

Raphael placed his own portrait in a group that includes the geographer Ptolemy, who holds a terrestrial globe, and the astronomer Zoroaster, who holds a celestial globe.

To view this image, please go to page 640 of the *Art History*, Fourth Edition by Marilyn Stokstad ebook.

The brooding figure of Heraclitus, a late addition to the composition, is a portrait of Michelangelo, who was working next door on the ceiling of the Sistine Chapel, and whose monumental figural style is here appropriated (or is it mimicked?) by Raphael. The stonecutter's boots on his feet refer to Michelangelo's self-identification—or Raphael's insistence that he be seen—as a sculptor rather than a painter.

This figure is usually identified as Diogenes the Cynic following Vasari's account of the painting. It is more likely that he is Socrates, however. The cup next to him could refer to his deadly draught of hemlock, and his recumbent position recalls his teaching from his prison bed.

The group of figures gathered around Euclid illustrate the various stages of understanding: literal learning, dawning comprehension, anticipation of the outcome, and assisting the teacher. Raphael received acclaim for his ability to communicate so clearly through the poses and expressions of his figures.

SEE MORE: View the Closer Look feature for *The School of Athens* www.myartslab.com

MICHELANGELO'S EARLY WORK. Michelangelo Buonarroti (1475–1564) was born in the Tuscan town of Caprese into an impoverished Florentine family that laid a claim to nobility—a claim the artist carefully advanced throughout his life. He grew up in Florence, where at age 13 he was apprenticed to Ghirlandaio, in whose workshop he learned the technique of fresco painting and studied drawings of Classical monuments. Soon the talented youth joined the household of Lorenzo the Magnificent, head of the ruling Medici family, where he came into contact with Neoplatonic philosophy and studied sculpture with Bertoldo di Giovanni, a pupil of Donatello. After Lorenzo died in 1492, Michelangelo traveled to Venice and Bologna, then returned to Florence.

Michelangelo's major early work at the turn of the century was a marble sculpture of the **PIETÀ**, commissioned by a French cardinal and installed as a tomb monument in Old St. Peter's **(FIG. 10–32)**. The theme of the *pietà* (in which the Virgin supports and mourns the dead Jesus in her lap), long popular in northern Europe, was an unusual theme in Italy at the time. Michelangelo traveled to the marble quarries at Carrara in central Italy to select the block from which to make this large work, a practice he was to continue for nearly all of his sculpture. The choice of stone was important to him because he envisioned his sculpture as already existing within the marble, needing only his tools to set it free. Michelangelo was a poet as well as an artist, and later wrote in his Sonnet 15: "The greatest artist has no conception which a single block of marble does not potentially contain within its mass, but only a hand obedient to the mind can penetrate to this image."

To view this image, please go to page 641 of the *Art History*, Fourth Edition by Marilyn Stokstad ebook.

10–32 • Michelangelo PIETÀ
c. 1500. Marble, height 5′8½″ (1.74 m). St. Peter's, Vatican, Rome.

EXPLORE MORE: Gain insight from a primary source by Michelangelo on his *Pietà*
www.myartslab.com

To view this image, please go to page 642 of the *Art History*, Fourth Edition by Marilyn Stokstad ebook.

Michelangelo's Virgin is a young woman of heroic stature holding the unnaturally smaller, lifeless body of her grown son. Inconsistencies of scale and age are forgotten, however, when contemplating the sweetness of expression, technical virtuosity of the carving, and smooth modeling of the luscious forms. Michelangelo's compelling vision of beauty was meant to be seen up close so that the viewer can look directly into Jesus' face. The 25-year-old artist is said to have slipped into the church at night to sign the statue on a strap across the Virgin's breast after it was finished, answering directly questions that had come up about the identity of its creator.

In 1501, Michelangelo accepted a Florentine commission for a statue of the biblical hero **DAVID** (FIG. 10–33), to be placed high atop a buttress of the cathedral. But when it was finished in 1504, the *David* was so admired that the city council instead placed it in the principal city square, next to the Palazzo della Signoria, the seat of Florence's government. There it stood as a reminder of Florence's republican status, which was briefly reinstated after the expulsion of the powerful Medici oligarchy in 1494. Although in its muscular nudity Michelangelo's *David* embodies the antique ideal of the athletic male nude, the emotional power of its expression and its concentrated gaze are entirely new. Unlike Donatello's bronze *David* (SEE FIG. 10–10), this is not a triumphant hero with the trophy head of the giant Goliath already under his feet. Slingshot over his shoulder and a rock in his right hand, Michelangelo's *David* knits his brow and stares into space, seemingly preparing himself psychologically for the danger ahead, a mere youth confronting a gigantic experienced warrior. No match for his opponent in experience, weaponry, or physical strength, Michelangelo's powerful *David* stands for the supremacy of right over might—a perfect emblem for the Florentines, who had recently fought the forces of Milan, Siena, and Pisa, and still faced political and military pressure.

THE SISTINE CHAPEL. Despite Michelangelo's contractual commitment to Florence Cathedral for additional statues, in 1505, Pope Julius II, who saw Michelangelo as an ideal collaborator in

10-33 • Michelangelo DAVID
1501–1504. Marble, height 17′ (5.18 m) without pedestal. Galleria dell'Accademia, Florence.

Michelangelo's most famous sculpture was cut from an 18-foot-tall marble block. The sculptor began with a small model in wax, then sketched the contours of the figure as they would appear from the front on one face of the marble. Then, according to his friend and biographer Vasari, he chiseled in from the drawn-on surface, as if making a figure in very high relief. The completed statue took four days to move on tree-trunk rollers down the narrow streets of Florence from the premises of the cathedral shop where he worked to its location outside the Palazzo della Signoria. In 1504, the Florentines gilded the tree stump and added a gilded wreath to the head and a belt of 28 gilt-bronze leaves, since removed. In 1873, the statue was replaced by a copy, and the original was moved into the museum of the Florence Academy.

To view this image, please go to page 643 of the *Art History*, Fourth Edition by Marilyn Stokstad ebook.

10-34 • INTERIOR, SISTINE CHAPEL

Vatican, Rome. Built 1475–1481; ceiling painted 1508–1512; end wall, 1536–1541. The ceiling measures 45 × 128′ (13.75 × 39 m).

the artistic aggrandizement of the papacy, arranged for him to come to Rome to work on the spectacular tomb Julius planned for himself. Michelangelo began the tomb project, but two years later the pope ordered him to begin painting the ceiling of the **SISTINE CHAPEL** instead **(FIG. 10–34)**.

Michelangelo considered himself a sculptor, but the strong-minded pope wanted paintings; work began in 1508. Michelangelo complained bitterly in a sonnet to a friend: "This miserable job has given me a goiter….The force of it has jammed my belly up beneath my chin. Beard to the sky….Brush splatterings make a pavement of my face…. I'm not a painter." Despite his physical misery as he stood on a scaffold, painting the ceiling just above him, the results were extraordinary, and Michelangelo established a new and remarkably powerful style in Renaissance painting.

To view this image, please go to page 644 of the *Art History*, Fourth Edition by Marilyn Stokstad ebook.

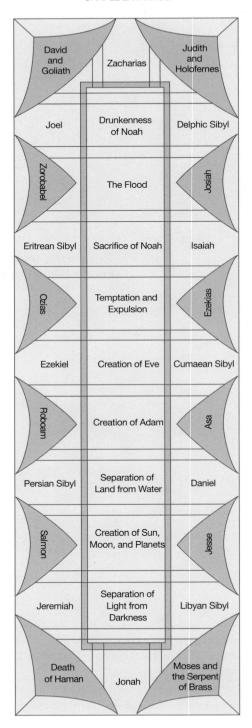

CHAPEL ENTRANCE

David and Goliath	Zacharias	Judith and Holofernes
Joel	Drunkenness of Noah	Delphic Sibyl
Zorobabel	The Flood	Josiah
Eritrean Sibyl	Sacrifice of Noah	Isaiah
Ozias	Temptation and Expulsion	Ezekias
Ezekiel	Creation of Eve	Cumaean Sibyl
Roboam	Creation of Adam	Asa
Persian Sibyl	Separation of Land from Water	Daniel
Salmon	Creation of Sun, Moon, and Planets	Jesse
Jeremiah	Separation of Light from Darkness	Libyan Sibyl
Death of Haman	Jonah	Moses and the Serpent of Brass

ALTAR

10-35 • Michelangelo SISTINE CHAPEL CEILING WITH DIAGRAM IDENTIFYING SCENES
1508–1512. Fresco.

Julius's initial order for the ceiling was simple: *trompe-l'oeil* coffers to replace the original star-spangled blue decoration. Later he wanted the 12 apostles seated on thrones on the triangular spandrels between the lunettes framing the windows. According to Michelangelo, when he objected to the limitations of Julius's plan, the pope told him to paint whatever he liked. This Michelangelo presumably did, although he was certainly guided by a theological advisor and his plan no doubt required the pope's approval. Then, as master painter, Michelangelo assembled a team of expert assistants to work with him.

In Michelangelo's design, an illusionistic marble architecture establishes a framework for the figures and narrative scenes on the vault of the chapel **(FIG. 10–35)**. Running completely around the ceiling is a painted cornice with projections supported by pilasters decorated with "sculptured" *putti*. Between the pilasters are figures of prophets and sibyls (female seers from the Classical world) who were believed to have foretold Jesus' birth. Seated on the fictive cornice are heroic figures of nude young men (called **ignudi**, singular, *ignudo*), holding sashes attached to large gold medallions. Rising behind the *ignudi*, shallow bands of fictive stone span the center of the ceiling and divide it into nine compartments containing successive scenes from Genesis—the Creation, the Fall, and the Flood—beginning over the altar and ending near the chapel entrance. God's earliest acts of creation are therefore closest to the altar, the Creation of Eve at the center of the ceiling, followed by the imperfect actions of humanity: Temptation, Fall, Expulsion from Paradise, and God's eventual destruction of all people except Noah and his family by the Flood. The eight triangular spandrels over the windows contain paintings of the ancestors of Jesus.

Perhaps the most familiar scene on the ceiling is the **CREATION OF ADAM (FIG. 10–36)**, where Michelangelo captures the moment when God charges the languorous Adam with the spark of life. As if to echo the biblical text, Adam's heroic body, outstretched arm, and profile almost mirror those of God, in whose image he has been created. Emerging under God's other arm, and looking across him in the direction of her future mate, is the robust and energetic figure of Eve before her creation. Directly below Adam, an *ignudo* grasps a bundle of oak leaves and giant acorns, which refer to Pope Julius's family name (della Rovere, or "of the oak") and possibly also to a passage in the prophecy of Isaiah (61:3): "They will be called oaks of justice, planted by the Lord to show his glory."

To view this image, please go to page 645 of the *Art History*, Fourth Edition by Marilyn Stokstad ebook.

10-36 • Michelangelo CREATION OF ADAM, SISTINE CHAPEL CEILING
1511–1512. Fresco. 9′2″ × 18′8″ (2.8 × 5.7 m).

ART AND THE COUNTER-REFORMATION

Pope Clement VII, whose miscalculations had spurred Emperor Charles V to attack and destroy Rome in 1527, also misjudged the threat to the Church and to papal authority posed by the Protestant Reformation. His failure to address the issues raised by the reformers enabled the movement to spread. His successor, Paul III (pontificate 1534–1549), the rich and worldly Roman noble Alessandro Farnese, was the first pope to pursue church reform in response to the rise of Protestantism. In 1536, he appointed a commission to investigate charges of church corruption and convened the Council of Trent (1545–1563) to define Catholic dogma, initiate disciplinary reforms, and regulate the training of clerics.

Pope Paul III also addressed Protestantism through repression and censorship. In 1542, he instituted the Inquisition, a papal office that sought out heretics for interrogation, trial, and sentencing. The enforcement of religious unity extended to the arts. Traditional images of Christ and the saints were sanctioned, but art was scrutinized for traces of heresy and profanity. Guidelines issued by the Council of Trent limited what could be represented in Christian art and led to the destruction of some works. At the same time, art became a powerful weapon of propaganda, especially in the hands of members of the Society of Jesus, a new religious order founded by the Spanish nobleman Ignatius of Loyola (1491–1556) and confirmed by Paul III in 1540. Dedicated to piety, education, and missionary work, the Jesuits, as they are known, spread worldwide and became important leaders of the Counter-Reformation movement and the revival of the Catholic Church.

ART AND ARCHITECTURE IN ROME AND THE VATICAN

To restore the heart of the city of Rome, Paul III began rebuilding the Capitoline Hill as well as continuing work on St. Peter's. His commissions include some of the finest art and architecture of the late Italian Renaissance. His first major commission brought Michelangelo, after a quarter of a century, back to the Sistine Chapel.

MICHELANGELO'S LATE WORK.   In his early sixties, Michelangelo complained bitterly of feeling old, but he nonetheless undertook the important and demanding task of painting the **LAST JUDGMENT** on the 48-foot-high end wall above the Sistine Chapel altar between 1536 and 1541 (FIG. 10–37).

Abandoning the clearly organized medieval conception of the Last Judgment, in which the saved are neatly separated from the damned, Michelangelo painted a writhing swarm of resurrected humanity. At left (on Christ's right side), the dead are dragged from their graves and pushed up into a vortex of figures around Christ, who wields his arm like a sword of justice. The shrinking Virgin under Christ's raised right arm represents a change from Gothic tradition, where she had sat enthroned beside, and equal in size to, her son. To the right of Christ's feet is St. Bartholomew, who in legend was martyred by being skinned alive. He holds his flayed skin, and Michelangelo seems to have painted his own distorted features on the skin's face. Despite the efforts of several saints to save them at the last minute, the damned are plunged toward hell on the right, leaving the elect and still-unjudged in a dazed, almost uncomprehending state. On the lowest level of the mural, right above the altar, is the gaping, fiery entrance to hell, toward which Charon, the ferryman of the dead to the underworld, propels his craft. The painting was long interpreted as a grim and constant reminder to celebrants of the Mass—the pope and his cardinals—that ultimately they too would face stern judgment at the end of time. Conservative clergy criticized the painting for its frank nudity, and after Michelangelo's death they ordered bits of drapery to be added by artist Daniele da Volterra to conceal the offending areas, earning Daniele the unfortunate nickname *Il Braghettone* ("breeches painter").

Another of Paul III's ambitions was to complete the new St. Peter's, a project that had been under way for 40 years. Michelangelo was well aware of the work done by his predecessors—from Bramante to Raphael to Antonio da Sangallo the Younger. The 71-year-old sculptor, confident of his architectural expertise, demanded the right to deal directly with the pope, rather than through a committee of construction deputies. Michelangelo further shocked the deputies—but not the pope—by tearing down or canceling parts of Sangallo's design and returning to Bramante's central plan, long associated with shrines of Christian martyrs. Although seventeenth-century additions and renovations dramatically changed the original plan of the church and the appearance of its interior, Michelangelo's **ST. PETER'S (FIG. 10–38)** still can be seen in the contrasting forms of the flat and angled exterior walls and the three surviving hemicycles (semicircular structures). Colossal pilasters, blind windows (frames without openings), and niches surround the sanctuary of the church. The current dome, erected by Giacomo della Porta in 1588–1590, retains Michelangelo's basic design: segmented with regularly spaced ribs, seated on a high drum with pedimented windows between paired columns, and surmounted by a tall lantern reminiscent of Bramante's *Il Tempietto*.

Michelangelo—often described by his contemporaries as difficult and even arrogant—alternated between periods of depression and frenzied activity. Yet he was devoted to his friends and helpful to young artists. He believed that his art was divinely inspired; later in life, he became deeply absorbed in religion and dedicated himself to religious works—many left unfinished—that subverted Renaissance ideals of human perfectibility and denied his own youthful idealism. In the process he pioneered new stylistic directions that would inspire succeeding generations of artists.

VIGNOLA.   A young artist who worked to meet the need for new Roman churches was Giacomo Barozzi (1507–1573), known as Vignola after his native town. He worked in Rome during the late 1530s, surveying ancient Roman monuments and providing

To view this image, please go to page 667 of the *Art History*,
Fourth Edition by Marilyn Stokstad ebook.

10-37 • Michelangelo **LAST JUDGMENT, SISTINE CHAPEL**
1536–1541. Fresco, 48 × 44′ (14.6 × 13.4 m).

Dark, rectangular patches left by recent restorers (visible, for example, in the upper left and right corners) contrast with the vibrant colors of the chapel's frescos. These dark areas show just how dirty the walls had become over the centuries before their recent cleaning.

EXPLORE MORE: Gain insight from a primary source of Michelangelo's poetry **www.myartslab.com**

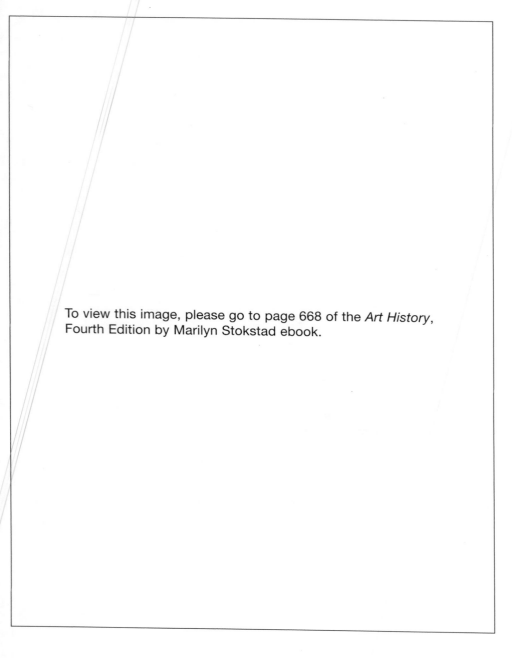

10–38 • Michelangelo ST. PETER'S BASILICA, VATICAN
c. 1546–1564; dome completed 1590 by Giacomo della Porta; lantern 1590–1593. View from the west.

illustrations for an edition of Vitruvius. From 1541 to 1543, he was in France with Francesco Primaticcio at the château of Fontainebleau. After returning to Rome, he secured the patronage of the Farnese family and profited from the Counter-Reformation program of church building.

Catholicism's new emphasis on individual, emotional participation brought a focus on sermons and music, requiring churches with wide naves and unobstructed views of the altar, instead of the complex interiors of medieval and earlier Renaissance churches. Ignatius of Loyola was determined to build **IL GESÙ**, the Jesuit headquarters church in Rome, according to these precepts, although he did not live to see it finished **(FIG. 10–39)**. The cornerstone was laid in 1540, but construction of *Il Gesù* did not begin until 1568; the Jesuits had considerable funds to raise first. Cardinal Alessandro Farnese (Paul III's namesake and grandson)

donated to the project in 1561 and selected Vignola as architect. After Vignola died in 1573, Giacomo della Porta finished the dome and façade.

Il Gesù was admirably suited for congregational worship. Vignola designed a wide, barrel-vaulted nave with shallow connected side chapels; there are no aisles and only truncated transepts contained within the line of the outer walls—enabling all worshipers to gather in the central space. A single huge apse and dome over the crossing directed attention to the altar. The design also allows the building to fit compactly into a city block—a requirement that now often overrode the desire to orient a church along an east–west axis. The symmetrical façade emphasized the central portal with Classical pilasters, engaged columns and pediments, and volutes scrolling out laterally to hide the buttresses of the central vault and to link the tall central section with the lower sides.

To view this image, please go to page 669 of the *Art History*, Fourth Edition by Marilyn Stokstad ebook.

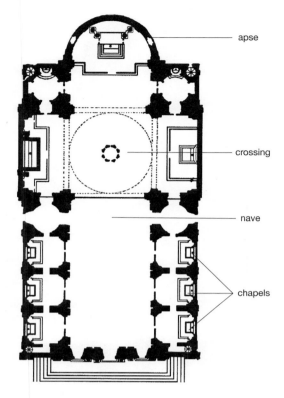

10-39 • Giacomo della Porta and Vignola
FAÇADE AND PLAN OF THE CHURCH OF IL GESÙ, ROME
c. 1573–1584.

As finally built by Giacomo della Porta, the façade design would have significant influence well into the next century. The early Renaissance grid of Classical pilasters and entablatures is abandoned for a two-story design that coordinates paired columns or pilasters, aligned vertically to tie together the two stories of the central block which corresponds with the nave elevation. The main entrance, with its central portal aligned with a tall upper-story window, became the focus of the composition. Centrally aligned pediments break into the level above, leading the eye upward to the cartouches with coats of arms—here of both Cardinal Farnese, the patron, and the Jesuits (whose arms display the initials IHS, the monogram of Christ).

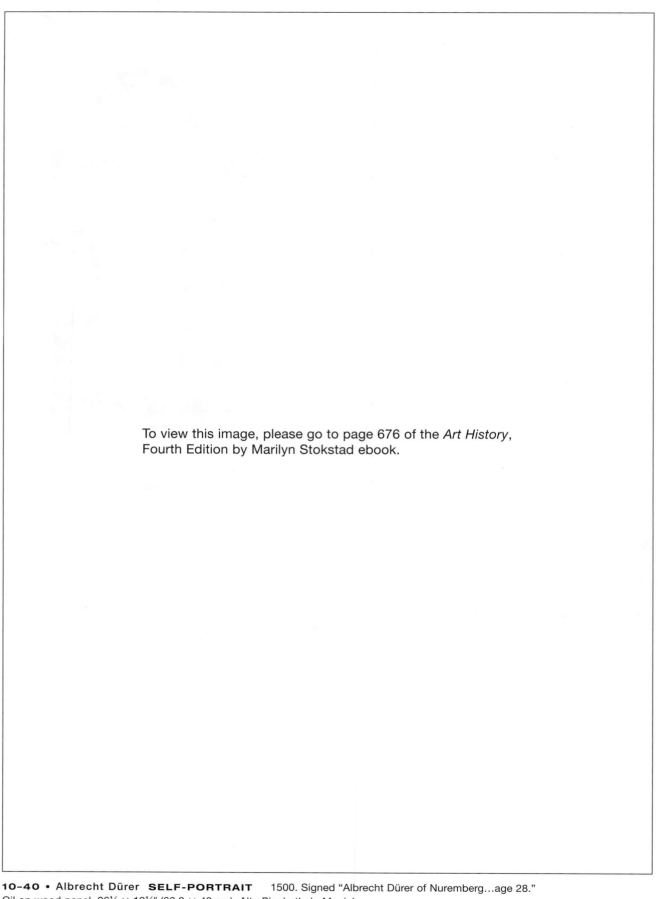

To view this image, please go to page 676 of the *Art History*, Fourth Edition by Marilyn Stokstad ebook.

10–40 • Albrecht Dürer **SELF-PORTRAIT**   1500. Signed "Albrecht Dürer of Nuremberg…age 28."
Oil on wood panel, 26¼ × 19¼″ (66.3 × 49 cm). Alte Pinakothek, Munich.

EXPLORE MORE: Gain insight from a primary source by Albrecht Dürer **www.myartslab.com**

SIXTEENTH-CENTURY ART IN NORTHERN EUROPE AND THE IBERIAN PENINSULA

This striking image (FIG. 10–40), dated 1500, seems to depict a blessing Christ, meant to rivet our attention and focus our devotion. But an inscription to the right of the iconic visage identifies this as a **SELF-PORTRAIT** by Albrecht Dürer, painted when he was 28 years old. We are already familiar with the practice of artists painting their own image. Self-portraits appear with some frequency during the Middle Ages (SEE FIG. 6–34); they truly blossom during the Renaissance. But this image is still peculiar, marked by an artistic hubris that may embarrass us. The picture becomes less puzzling, however, seen in context.

Dürer strikes an odd pose for a self-portrait—frontal and hieratic, intentionally recalling iconic images of Christ as *salvator mundi* (savior of the world) that were very popular in northern Europe. Dürer even alters the natural color of his own hair to align the image more closely with contemporary notions of Christ's physical appearance. But there is no reason to see this as blasphemous. Since a principal component of contemporary Christian devotion was the attempt to imitate Christ in the believer's own life, Dürer could be visualizing a popular spiritual practice. He could also be literalizing the biblical statement that humans are created in the image of God. But he is also claiming that artists are learned and creative geniuses—perhaps God-like—not laboring craftsmen. He wrote, "The more we know, the more we resemble the likeness of Christ who truly knows all things" (Snyder, p. 314).

Dürer had traveled to Italy in 1494–1495, where he encountered a new conception of artists as noble intellectuals, participants in humanistic discourse, purveyors of ideas as well as pictures. In 1498, back in Nuremberg, he published a woodcut series on the Apocalypse (SEE FIG. 10–45) that brought him a kind of international notice that was new to the German art world. He certainly had reason to feel pride. This stable, triangular composition—so consistent with High Renaissance norms of harmony and balance—could reflect Dürer's Italian adventure. But at its core, this picture fits into a long-standing northern European interest in the meticulous description of surface texture—the soft sheen of human flesh, the reflective wetness of eyes, the matte softness of cloth, and the tactile quality of hair, emphasized here by the way Dürer's hand fingers the fur collar of his outfit, encouraging viewers also to feel it as they see it. Ultimately what is showcased here are Dürer's awesome artistic gifts of hand as much as his intellectual gifts of mind, two aspects perhaps emblemized by the brightly illuminated body parts that align on a vertical axis to dominate this arresting self-portrait.

LEARN ABOUT IT

10.11 Investigate the broadening of regional interaction in the art of European courts as artists traveled across Europe to work for wealthy patrons and study with acclaimed masters.

10.12 Evaluate the impact of Italian ideas on the traditions of northern art and architecture, including the developing notion of artists as uniquely gifted individuals.

10.13 Analyze the developments that led to the creation of an art market in the Netherlands.

10.14 Assess the relationship between the religious conflicts in northern Europe and the growing interest in new secular subjects in works of art.

10.15 Recognize the continuing interest among northern European artists and patrons in the virtuosity of works in media such as wood and gold.

HEAR MORE: Listen to an audio file of your chapter **www.myartslab.com**

MAP 10-3 • WESTERN EUROPE DURING THE REFORMATION, C. 1560

Sixteenth-century Europe remained largely Roman Catholic, except in Switzerland and the far north, where the impact of the Protestant Reformation was strongest.

THE REFORMATION AND THE ARTS

In spite of the dissident movements and heresies that had challenged the Roman Catholic Church through the centuries, its authority and that of the pope always prevailed—until the sixteenth century (**MAP 10–3**). Then, against a backdrop of broad dissatisfaction with financial abuses and decadent lifestyles among the clergy, religious reformers from within the Church itself challenged first its practices and then its beliefs.

Two of the most important reformers in the early sixteenth century were themselves Catholic priests and trained theologians: Desiderius Erasmus (1466?–1536) of Rotterdam in Holland, who worked to reform the Roman Catholic Church from within, and Martin Luther (1483–1546) in Germany, who eventually broke with it. Indeed, many locate the beginning of the Reformation in 1517, when Luther issued his "95 Theses" calling for church reform. Among Luther's concerns were the practice of selling indulgences

(guarantees of relief from the punishment required after death for forgiven sins) and the excessive veneration of saints and their relics, which he considered superstitious. Luther and others emphasized individual faith and regarded the Bible as the ultimate religious authority. As they challenged the pope's supremacy, it became clear that the Protestants had to break away from Rome. The Roman Catholic Church condemned Luther in 1521.

Increased literacy and the widespread use of the printing press aided the reformers and allowed scholars throughout Europe to enter the religious debate. In Germany, the wide circulation of Luther's writings—especially his German translation of the Bible and his works maintaining that salvation comes through faith alone—eventually led to the establishment of the Protestant (Lutheran) Church there. In Switzerland, John Calvin (1509–1564) led an even more austere Protestant revolt; and in England, King Henry VIII (r. 1509–1547) also broke with Rome in

1534, for reasons of his own. By the end of the sixteenth century, Protestantism in some form prevailed throughout northern Europe.

Leading the Catholic cause was Holy Roman Emperor Charles V. Europe was wracked by religious war from 1546 to 1555 as Charles battled Protestant forces in Germany, until a meeting of the provincial legislature of Augsburg in 1555 determined that the emperor must accommodate the Protestant Reformation in his lands. By the terms of the peace, local rulers could select the religion of their subjects—Catholic or Protestant. Tired of the strain of government and prematurely aged, Charles abdicated in 1556 and retired to a monastery in Spain, where he died in 1558. His son Philip II inherited Habsburg Spain and the Spanish colonies, while his brother Ferdinand led the Austrian branch of the dynasty.

The years of political and religious strife had a grave impact on artists and art. Some artists found their careers at an end because of their reformist religious sympathies. Then as Protestantism gained ascendancy, Catholic artists had to leave their homes to seek patronage abroad. There was also widespread destruction of religious art. In some places, Protestant zealots smashed sculpture and stained-glass windows and destroyed or whitewashed religious paintings to rid the churches of what they considered idols—though Luther himself never directly supported **iconoclasm** (the smashing of religious images). With the sudden loss of patronage for religious art in the newly Protestant lands, many artists turned to portraiture and other secular subjects, including moralizing depictions of human folly and weaknesses, still lifes (paintings of inanimate objects), and landscapes. The popularity of these themes stimulated the burgeoning of a free art market, centered in Antwerp.

GERMANY

In German-speaking regions, the arts flourished until religious upheavals and iconoclastic purges took their toll at mid century. German cities had strong business and trade interests, and their merchants and bankers accumulated self-made, rather than inherited, wealth. They ordered portraits of themselves and fine furnishings for their large, comfortable houses. Entrepreneurial artists, like Albrecht Dürer, became major commercial successes.

SCULPTURE

Although, like the Italians, German Renaissance sculptors worked in stone and bronze, they produced their most original work in wood, especially fine-grained limewood. Most of these wooded images were gilded and painted, continuing an interest in heightening naturalism, until Tilman Riemenschneider began to favor natural wood finishes.

TILMAN RIEMENSCHNEIDER. Tilman Riemenschneider (c. 1460–1531) became a master in 1485 and soon had the largest workshop in Würzburg, which included specialists in both wood and stone sculpture. Riemenschneider attracted patrons from other cities, and

in 1501 he signed a contract with the church of St. James in Rothenburg, where a relic said to be a drop of Jesus' blood was preserved. The **ALTARPIECE OF THE HOLY BLOOD** (FIG. 10–41) is a spectacular limewood construction standing nearly 30 feet high.

To view this image, please go to page 679 of the *Art History*, Fourth Edition by Marilyn Stokstad ebook.

10–41 • Tilman Riemenschneider ALTARPIECE OF THE HOLY BLOOD (WINGS OPEN)
Center, *Last Supper*. c. 1499–1505. Limewood, glass, height of tallest figure 39″ (99.1 cm), height of altar 29′6″ (9 m). Sankt Jakobskirche (Church of St. James), Rothenburg ob der Tauber, Germany.

In Nuremberg, a city known for its master metalworkers, Hans Krug (d. 1519) and his sons Hans the Younger and Ludwig were among the finest. They created marvelous display pieces for the wealthy, such as this silver-gilt apple cup. Made about 1510, a gleaming apple, in which the stem forms the handle of the lid, balances on a leafy branch that forms its base.

The Krug family was responsible for the highly refined casting and finishing of the final product, but several artists worked together to produce such pieces—one drawing designs, another making the models, and others creating the final piece in metal. A drawing by Dürer may have been the basis for the apple cup. Though we know of no piece of goldwork by the artist himself, Dürer was a major catalyst in the growth of Nuremberg as a key center of German goldsmithing. He accomplished this by producing designs for metalwork throughout his career. Designers played an essential role in the metalwork process. With design in hand, the modelmaker created a wooden form for the goldsmith to follow. The result of this artistic collaboration was a technical *tour de force*, an intellectual conceit, and an exquisite object.

To view this image, please go to page 680 of the *Art History*, Fourth Edition by Marilyn Stokstad ebook.

Workshop of Hans Krug (?) APPLE CUP
c. 1510–1515. Gilt silver, height 8½″ (21.5 cm). Germanisches Nationalmuseum, Nuremberg.

Erhart Harschner, a specialist in architectural shrines, had begun work on the elaborate Gothic frame in 1499, and was paid 50 florins for his work. Riemenschneider was commissioned to provide the figures and scenes to be placed within this frame. He was paid 60 florins for the sculpture, giving us a sense of the relative value patrons placed on their contributions.

The main panel of the altarpiece portrays the moment at the Last Supper when Christ revealed that one of his followers would betray him. Unlike Leonardo da Vinci, who chose the same moment (SEE FIG. 10–26), Riemenschneider puts Judas at center stage and Jesus off-center at the left. The disciples sit around the table. As the event is described in the Gospel of John (13:21–30), Jesus extends a morsel of food to Judas, signifying that he will be the traitor who sets in motion the events leading to the Crucifixion. One apostle points down, a strange gesture until we realize that he is pointing to the crucifix in the predella, to the relic of Christ's blood, and to the altar table, the symbolic representation of the table of the Last Supper and the tomb of Christ.

Rather than creating individual portraits of the apostles, Riemenschneider repeated a limited number of facial types. His figures have large heads, prominent features, sharp cheekbones, sagging jowls, baggy eyes, and elaborate hair with thick wavy locks and deeply drilled curls. The muscles, tendons, and raised veins of hands and feet are also especially lifelike. His assistants and apprentices copied these faces and figures, either from drawings or from three-dimensional models made by the master. In the altarpiece, deeply hollowed folds create active patterns in the voluminous draperies whose strong highlights and dark shadows harmonize the figural composition with the intricate carving of the framework. The Last Supper is set in a "real" room containing actual benches for the figures. Windows in the back wall are glazed with bull's-eye glass so that natural light shines in from two directions to illuminate the scene, producing changing effects depending on the time of day and the weather. Although earlier sculpture had been painted and gilded, Riemenschneider introduced the use of a natural wood finish toned with varnish. This meant that details of both figures and environment had to be carved into the wood itself, not quickly added later with paint. Since this required more skillful carvers and more time for them to carve, this new look was a matter of aesthetics, not cost-saving.

In addition to producing an enormous number of religious images for churches, Riemenschneider was politically active in the city's government, and he even served as mayor in 1520. His career ended during the Peasants' War (1524–1526), an early manifestation of the Protestant movement. His support for the peasants led to a fine and imprisonment in 1525, and although he survived, Riemenschneider produced no more sculpture and died in 1531.

NIKOLAUS HAGENAUER. Prayer was the principal source of solace and relief to the ill before the advent of modern medicine. About 1505, the Strasbourg sculptor Nikolaus Hagenauer (active

To view this image, please go to page 681 of the *Art History*, Fourth Edition by Marilyn Stokstad ebook.

10–42 • Nikolaus Hagenauer ST. ANTHONY ENTHRONED BETWEEN SS. AUGUSTINE AND JEROME, SHRINE OF THE ISENHEIM ALTARPIECE (OPEN, SHOWING GRÜNEWALD WINGS)
From the Community of St. Anthony, Isenheim, Alsace, France. c. 1500. Painted and gilt limewood, center panel 9′9½″ × 10′9″ (2.98 × 3.28 m), predella 2′5½″ × 11′2″ (0.75 × 3.4 m), wings 8′2½″ × 3′½″ (2.49 × 0.93 m). Predella: *Christ and the Apostles*. Wings: *SS. Anthony and Paul the Hermit* (left); *The Temptation of St. Anthony* (right). 1510–1515. Musée d'Unterlinden, Colmar, France.

1493–1530s) carved an altarpiece for the abbey of St. Anthony in Isenheim near Colmar **(FIG. 10–42)** where a hospital specialized in the care of patients with skin diseases, including the plague, leprosy, and St. Anthony's Fire (caused by eating rye and other grains infected with the ergot fungus). The shrine includes images of SS. Anthony, Jerome, and Augustine. Three tiny men—their size befitting their subordinate status—kneel at the feet of the saints: the donor, Jean d'Orliac, and two men offering a rooster and a piglet.

In the predella below, Jesus and the apostles bless the altar, Host, and assembled patients in the hospital. This limewood sculpture was painted in lifelike colors, and the shrine itself was gilded to enhance its resemblance to a precious reliquary. A decade later, Matthias Grünewald painted wooden shutters to cover the shrine (SEE FIGS. 10–43, 10–44).

PAINTING

The work of two very different German artists has come down to us from the first decades of the sixteenth century. Matthias Grünewald continued currents of medieval mysticism and emotional spirituality to create extraordinarily moving paintings. Albrecht Dürer, on the other hand, used intense observation of the world to render lifelike representations of nature, mathematical perspective to create convincing illusions of space, and a reasoned canon of proportions to standardize depictions of the human figure.

MATTHIAS GRÜNEWALD. As a court artist to the archbishop of Mainz, Matthias Grünewald (Matthias Gothart Neithart, c. 1470/1475–1528) was a man of many talents, who worked as an architect and hydraulic engineer as well as a painter. He is best known today for painting the shutters or wings attached to Nikolaus Hagenauer's carved Isenheim Altarpiece (SEE FIG. 10–42). The completed altarpiece is impressive in size and complexity. Grünewald painted one set of fixed wings and two sets of movable ones, plus one set of sliding panels to cover the predella. The altarpiece could be exhibited in different configurations depending upon the church calendar. The wings and carved wooden shrine

To view this image, please go to page 682 of the *Art History*, Fourth Edition by Marilyn Stokstad ebook.

10-43 • Matthias Grünewald ISENHEIM ALTARPIECE (CLOSED)
From the Community of St. Anthony, Isenheim, Alsace, France. Center panels: *Crucifixion*; predella: *Lamentation*; side panels: *SS. Sebastian* (left) and Anthony Abbot (right). c. 1510–1515. Date 1515 on ointment jar. Oil on wood panel, center panels 9′9½″ × 10′9″ (2.97 × 3.28 m) overall; each wing 8′2½″ × 3′½″ (2.49 × 0.93 m); predella 2′5½″ × 11′2″ (0.75 × 3.4 m). Musée d'Unterlinden, Colmar, France.

To view this image, please go to page 682 of the *Art History*, Fourth Edition by Marilyn Stokstad ebook.

10-44 • Matthias Grünewald ISENHEIM ALTARPIECE (FIRST OPENING)
Left to right: *Annunciation, Virgin and Child with Angels, Resurrection*. c. 1510–1515. Oil on wood panel, center panel 9′9½″ × 10′9″ (2.97 × 3.28 m), each wing 8′2½″ × 3′½″ (2.49 × 0.92 m). Musée d'Unterlinden, Colmar, France.

complemented one another, the inner sculpture seeming to bring the surrounding paintings to life, and the painted wings protecting the precious carvings.

On weekdays, when the altarpiece was closed, viewers saw a grisly image of the Crucifixion in a darkened landscape, a *Lamentation* below it on the predella, and life-size figures of SS. Sebastian and Anthony Abbot—both associated with the plague— standing on *trompe l'oeil* pedestals on the fixed wings **(FIG. 10–43)**. The intensity of feeling here has suggested that Grünewald may have been inspired by the visions of St. Bridget of Sweden, a fourteenth-century mystic whose works—including morbidly detailed descriptions of the Crucifixion—were published in Germany beginning in 1492. Grünewald has scrupulously described the horrific character of the tortured body of Jesus, covered with gashes from his beating and pierced by the thorns used to form a crown for his head. His ashen body, clotted blood, open mouth, and blue lips signal his death. In fact, he appears already to be decaying, an effect enhanced by the palette of putrescent green, yellow, and purplish-red—all described by St. Bridget. She wrote, "The color of death spread through his flesh…." An immaculately garbed Virgin Mary has collapsed in the arms of a ghostlike John the Evangelist, and Mary Magdalen has fallen in anguish to her knees; her clasped hands with outstretched fingers seem to echo Jesus' fingers, cramped in rigor mortis. At the right, John the Baptist points to Jesus and repeats his prophecy, "He shall increase." The Baptist and the lamb, holding a cross and bleeding from its breast into a golden chalice, allude to baptism, the Eucharist, and to Christ as the sacrificial Lamb of God. In the predella below, Jesus' bereaved mother and friends prepare his racked body for burial—an activity that must have been a common sight in the abbey's hospital.

In contrast to these grim scenes, the first opening displays events of great joy—the Annunciation, the Nativity, and the Resurrection—appropriate for Sundays and feast days **(FIG. 10–44)**. Praying in front of these pictures, the patients must have hoped for miraculous recovery and taken comfort in these visions of divine rapture and orgiastic color. Unlike the awful darkness of the Crucifixion, the inner scenes are brilliantly illuminated, in part by phosphorescent auras and haloes, and stars glitter in the night sky of the Resurrection. The technical virtuosity of Grünewald's painting alone is enough to inspire euphoria.

The *Annunciation* on the left wing may be related to a special liturgy called the Golden Mass, which celebrated the divine motherhood of the Virgin. The Mass included a staged reenactment of the angel's visit to Mary, as well as readings from the story of the Annunciation (Luke 1:26–38) and the Hebrew Bible prophecy of the Savior's birth (Isaiah 7:14–15), which is inscribed in Latin on the pages of the Virgin's open book.

The central panels show the heavenly and earthly realms joined in one space. In a variation on the northern European visionary tradition, the new mother adores her miraculous Christ Child while envisioning her own future as queen of heaven amid angels and cherubims. Grünewald portrayed three distinct types of angels in the foreground—young, mature, and a feathered hybrid with a birdlike crest on its human head. The range of ethnic types in the heavenly realm may have emphasized the global dominion of the Church, whose missionary efforts were expanding as a result of European exploration. St. Bridget describes the jubilation of the angels as "the glowing flame of love."

The second opening of the altarpiece (SEE FIG. 10–42) reveals Hagenauer's sculpture and was reserved for the special festivals of St. Anthony. The wings in this second opening show to the left the meeting of St. Anthony with the hermit St. Paul, and to the right St. Anthony attacked by horrible demons, perhaps inspired by the horrors of the diseased patients, but also modeled in part on Schongauer's well-known print of the same subject. The meeting of the two hermits in the desert glorifies the monastic life, and in the wilderness Grünewald depicts medicinal plants used in the hospital's therapy. Grünewald painted the face of St. Paul with his own self-portrait, while St. Anthony is a portrait of the donor and administrator of the hospital, the Italian Guido Guersi, whose coat of arms Grünewald painted on the rock next to him.

Like Riemenschneider, Grünewald's involvement with the Peasants' War may have damaged his artistic career. He left Mainz and spent his last years in Halle, whose ruler was the chief protector of Martin Luther and a long-time patron of Grünewald's contemporary Albrecht Dürer.

ALBRECHT DÜRER. Studious, analytical, observant, and meticulous —and as self-confident as Michelangelo—Albrecht Dürer (1471–1528) was the foremost artist of the German Renaissance. He made his home in Nuremberg, where he became a prominent citizen. Nuremberg was a center of culture as well as of business, with an active group of humanists and internationally renowned artists. It was also a leading publishing center. Dürer's father was a goldsmith and must have expected his son to follow in his trade (see "German Metalwork: A Collaborative Venture," page 624). Dürer did complete an apprenticeship in gold-working, as well as in stained-glass design, painting, and the making of woodcuts—which he learned from Michael Wolgemut, illustrator of the *Nuremberg Chronicle*. But ultimately it was as a painter and graphic artist that he built his artistic fame.

In 1490, Dürer began traveling to extend his education. He went to Basel, Switzerland, hoping to meet Martin Schongauer, but arrived after the master's death. By 1494, Dürer had moved from Basel to Strasbourg. His first trip to Italy (1494–1495) introduced him to Italian Renaissance ideas and attitudes and, as we considered at the beginning of this chapter, to the concept of the artist as an independent creative genius. In his self-portrait of 1500 (SEE FIG. 10–40), Dürer represents himself as an idealized, Christ-like figure in a severely frontal pose, staring directly at the viewer.

On his return to Nuremberg, Dürer began to publish his own prints to bolster his income, and ultimately it was prints, not paintings, that made his fortune. His first major publication, *The*

decorative cloud and drapery patterns. Following the tradition established by his late fifteenth-century predecessors, he fills the foreground with large, active figures.

Perhaps as early as the summer of 1494, Dürer began to experiment with engravings, cutting the metal plates himself with an artistry rivaling Schongauer's. His growing interest in Italian art and his theoretical investigations are reflected in his 1504 engraving **ADAM AND EVE (FIG. 10–46)**, which represents his first documented use of ideal human proportions based on Roman copies of ancient Greek sculpture. He may have seen figures of Apollo and Venus in Italy, and he would have known ancient sculpture from contemporary prints and drawings. But around these idealized human figures he represents plants and animals with typically northern attention to descriptive detail.

Dürer filled the landscape with symbolic content reflecting the medieval theory that after Adam and Eve disobeyed God, they and their descendants became vulnerable to imbalances in the body fluids that controlled human temperament. An excess of black bile from the liver would produce melancholy, despair, and greed. Yellow bile caused anger, pride, and impatience; phlegm in the lungs resulted in lethargy and disinterest; and an

To view this image, please go to page 684 of the *Art History*, Fourth Edition by Marilyn Stokstad ebook.

10-45 • Albrecht Dürer **THE FOUR HORSEMEN OF THE APOCALYPSE**
From *The Apocalypse*. 1497–1498. Woodcut, 15½ × 11⅛″ (39.4 × 28.3 cm). Metropolitan Museum of Art, New York.
Gift of Junius S. Morgan, 1919 (19.73.209)

Apocalypse, appeared simultaneously in German and Latin editions in 1497–1498. It consisted of a woodcut title page and 14 full-page illustrations with the text printed on the back of each. Perhaps best known is **THE FOUR HORSEMEN OF THE APOCALYPSE (FIG. 10–45)**, based on figures described in Revelation 6:1–8: a crowned rider, armed with a bow, on a white horse (Conquest); a rider with a sword, on a red horse (War); a rider with a set of scales, on a black horse (Plague and Famine); and a rider on a sickly pale horse (Death). Earlier artists had simply lined up the horsemen in the landscape, but Dürer created a compact, overlapping group of wild riders charging across the world and trampling its cowering inhabitants, men and women, clerical and lay.

Dürer probably did not cut his own woodblocks but employed a skilled carver who followed his drawings faithfully. Dürer's dynamic figures show affinities with Schongauer's *Temptation of St. Anthony*. He adapted Schongauer's metal-engraving technique to the woodcut medium, using a complex pattern of lines to model the forms. Dürer's early training as a goldsmith is evident in his meticulous attention to detail, and in his

To view this image, please go to page 684 of the *Art History*, Fourth Edition by Marilyn Stokstad ebook.

10-46 • Albrecht Dürer **ADAM AND EVE**
1504. Engraving, 9⅞ × 7⅝″ (25.1 × 19.4 cm).
Philadelphia Museum of Art.
Purchased: Lisa Nora Elkins Fund

To view this image, please go to page 685 of the *Art History*, Fourth Edition by Marilyn Stokstad ebook.

10–47 • Albrecht Dürer
FOUR APOSTLES
1526. Oil on wood panel, each panel 7′½″ × 2′6″ (2.15 × 0.76 m). Alte Pinakothek, Munich.

excess of blood made a person unusually optimistic but also compulsively interested in the pleasures of the flesh. These four human temperaments, or personalities, are symbolized here by the melancholy elk, the choleric cat, the phlegmatic ox, and the sanguine (or sensual) rabbit. The mouse is a symbol of Satan, whose earthly power, already manifest in the Garden of Eden, was capable of bringing human beings to a life of woe through their own bad choices. Adam seems to be releasing the mouse into the world of his paradise as he contemplates eating the forbidden fruit that Eve receives from the snake. Dürer placed his signature prominently on a placard hung on a tree branch in Adam's grasp and on which perches a parrot—possibly symbolizing false wisdom, since it can only repeat mindlessly what it hears.

Dürer's familiarity with Italian art was greatly enhanced by a second, leisurely trip over the Alps in 1505–1506. Thereafter, he seems to have resolved to reform the art of his own country by publishing theoretical writings and manuals that discussed Renaissance problems of perspective, ideal human proportions, and the techniques of painting.

Dürer admired Martin Luther, but they never met. In 1526, the artist openly professed his Lutheranism in a pair of inscribed panels, the **FOUR APOSTLES (FIG. 10–47)**. On the left panel, the elderly Peter, who normally has a central position as the first pope, has been displaced with his keys to the background by Luther's favorite evangelist, John, who holds an open Gospel that reads "In the beginning was the Word," reinforcing the Protestant emphasis on the Bible. On the right panel, Mark stands behind Paul, whose epistles were particularly admired by the Protestants. A long inscription on the frame warns the viewer not to be led astray by "false prophets" but to heed the words of the New Testament as recorded by these "four excellent men." Below each figure are excerpts from their letters and from the Gospel of Mark—drawn from Luther's German translation of the New Testament—warning

To view this image, please go to page 686 of the *Art History*,
Fourth Edition by Marilyn Stokstad ebook.

10–48 • Lucas Cranach the Elder NYMPH OF THE SPRING
c. 1537. Oil on panel, 19 × 28½″ (48.5 × 72.9 cm). National Gallery of Art, Washington, D.C.

against those who do not understand the true Word of God. These paintings were surely meant to chart the possibility of a Protestant visual art.

Dürer presented the panels to the city of Nuremberg, which had already adopted Lutheranism as its official religion. Dürer wrote, "For a Christian would no more be led to superstition by a picture or effigy than an honest man to commit murder because he carries a weapon by his side. He must indeed be an unthinking man who would worship picture, wood, or stone. A picture therefore brings more good than harm, when it is honourably, artistically, and well made" (Snyder, p. 333).

LUCAS CRANACH THE ELDER. Martin Luther's favorite painter, Lucas Cranach the Elder (1472–1553), moved his workshop to Wittenberg in 1504, after a number of years in Vienna. In addition to the humanist milieu of its university and library, Wittenberg offered the patronage of the Saxon court. Appointed court painter to Elector Frederick the Wise, Cranach created woodcuts, altarpieces, and many portraits.

Just how far German artists' style and conception of the figure could differ from Italian Renaissance idealism is easily seen in Cranach's **NYMPH OF THE SPRING (FIG. 10–48)**, especially when compared with Titian's *"Venus" of Urbino*. The sleeping nymph was a Renaissance theme, not an ancient one. Cranach was inspired by a fifteenth-century inscription on a fountain beside the Danube, cited in the upper left corner of the painting: "I am the nymph of the sacred font. Do not interrupt my sleep for I am at peace." Cranach records the Danube landscape with characteristic northern attention to detail and turns his nymph into a rather provocative young woman, who glances slyly out at the viewer through half-closed eyes. She has cast aside a fashionable red velvet gown, but still wears her jewelry, which together with her transparent veil enhances rather than conceals her nudity—especially those coral beads that fall between her breasts, outlining their contours. Unlike other artists working for Protestant patrons, many of whom looked on earthly beauty as a sinful vanity, Cranach seems delighted by earthly things—the lush foliage that provides the nymph's couch, the pair of partridges (symbols of Venus and married love), and Cupid's bow and quiver of arrows hanging on the tree. Could this nymph be a living beauty from the Wittenburg court? She is certainly not an embodiment of an idealized, Classical Venus.

To view this image, please go to page 710 of the *Art History*,
Fourth Edition by Marilyn Stokstad ebook.

10-49 • Gianlorenzo Bernini **ST. TERESA OF ÁVILA IN ECSTASY**
1645–1652. Marble, height of the group 11′6″ (3.5 m). Cornaro Chapel, church of Santa Maria della Vittoria, Rome.

SEVENTEENTH-CENTURY ART IN EUROPE

In the Church of Santa Maria della Vittoria in Rome, the sixteenth-century Spanish mystic St. Teresa of Ávila (1515–1582, canonized 1622) swoons in ecstasy on a bank of billowing marble clouds (FIG. 10–49). A puckish angel tugs open her robe, aiming a gilded arrow at her breast. Gilded bronze rays of supernatural light descend, even as actual light illuminates the figures from a hidden window above. This dramatic scene, created by Gianlorenzo Bernini (1598–1680) between 1645 and 1652, represents a famous vision described with startling physical clarity by Teresa, in which an angel pierced her body repeatedly with an arrow, transporting her to a state of ecstatic oneness with God, charged with erotic associations.

The sculpture is an exquisite example of the emotional, theatrical style perfected by Bernini in response to the religious and political climate in Rome during the period of spiritual renewal known as the Counter-Reformation. Many had seen the Protestant Reformation of the previous century as an outgrowth of Renaissance Humanism with its emphasis on rationality and independent thinking. In response, the Catholic Church took a reactionary, authoritarian position, supported by the new Society of Jesus founded by Ignatius Loyola (d. 1556, canonized 1622). In the "spiritual exercises"

(1522–1523) initiated by St. Ignatius, Christians were enjoined to use all their senses to transport themselves emotionally as they imagined the events on which they were meditating. They were to feel the burning fires of hell or the bliss of heaven, the lashing of the whips and the flesh-piercing crown of thorns. Art became an instrument of propaganda and also a means of leading the spectator to a reinvigorated Christian practice and belief.

Of course, the arts had long been used to convince or inspire, but nowhere more effectively than by the Catholic Church in the seventeenth century. To serve the educational and evangelical mission of the revitalized and conservative Church, paintings and sculpture had to depict events and people accurately and clearly, following guidelines established by religious leaders. Throughout Catholic Europe, painters such as Rubens and Caravaggio created brilliant religious art under official Church sponsorship. And although today some viewers find this sculpture of St. Teresa uncomfortably charged with sexuality, the Church approved of the depictions of such sensational and supernatural mystical visions. They helped worshipers achieve the emotional state of religious ecstasy that was a goal of the Counter-Reformation.

LEARN ABOUT IT

10.16 Assess the impact of the Council of Trent's guidelines for the Counter-Reformation art of the Roman Catholic Church.

10.17 Explore how the work of Bernini and Caravaggio established a new dramatic intensity, technical virtuosity, and unvarnished naturalism that blossomed into the Baroque.

10.18 Trace the broad influence of Caravaggio's style on art across Europe during the seventeenth century.

10.19 Assess the resurgence of Classicism, especially in the work of seventeenth-century French artists and architects.

10.20 Analyze the way that seventeenth-century artists created works that embodied the power and prestige of the monarchy.

10.21 Examine the development of portraiture, still life, landscape, and genre scenes as major subjects for painting, especially within the prosperous art market of the Netherlands.

HEAR MORE: Listen to an audio file of your chapter **www.myartslab.com**

"BAROQUE"

The intellectual and political forces set in motion by the Renaissance and Reformation of the fifteenth and sixteenth centuries intensified during the seventeenth century. Religious wars continued, although gradually the Protestant forces gained control in the north, where Spain recognized the independence of the Dutch Republic in 1648. Catholicism maintained its primacy in southern Europe, the Holy Roman Empire, and France through the efforts of an energized papacy, aided by the new Society of Jesus, also known as the Jesuit Order (MAP 10–4). At the same time, scientific advances compelled people to question their worldview. Of great importance was the growing understanding that the Earth was not the center of the universe but rather was a planet revolving around the sun. As rulers' economic strength began to slip away, artists found patrons in the Church and the secular state, as well as in the newly confident and prosperous urban middle class. What evolved was a style that art historians have called "the Baroque." The label may be related to the Italian word *barocco*, a jeweler's term for an irregularly shaped pearl—something beautiful, fascinating, and strange.

Baroque art deliberately evokes intense emotional responses from viewers. Dramatically lit, theatrical compositions often combine several media within a single work as artists highlight their technical virtuosity. But the seventeenth century also saw its own version of Classicism, a more moving and dramatic variant of Renaissance ideals and principles featuring idealization based on observation of the material world; balanced (though often asymmetrical) compositions; diagonal movement in space; rich, harmonious colors; and the inclusion of visual references to ancient Greece and Rome. Many seventeenth-century artists sought lifelike depiction of their world in portraiture, **genre paintings** (scenes from everyday life), still life (paintings of inanimate objects such as food, fruit, or flowers), and religious scenes enacted by ordinary people in ordinary settings. Intense emotional involvement, lifelike renderings, and Classical references may exist in the same work, and are all part of the stylistic complexion of the seventeenth century.

The role of viewers also changed. Italian Renaissance painters and patrons had been fascinated with the visual possibilities of perspective and treasured idealism of form and subject which kept viewers at a distance, reflecting intellectually on what they were seeing. Seventeenth-century masters, on the other hand, sought to engage viewers as participants in the work of art, and often reached out to incorporate or activate the world beyond the frame into the nature and meaning of the work itself. In Catholic countries, representations of horrifying scenes of martyrdom or the passionate spiritual life of a mystic in religious ecstasy were intended to inspire viewers to a renewed faith by making them feel what was going on, not simply by causing them to think about it. In Protestant countries, images of communal parades and city views sought to inspire pride in civic accomplishments. Viewers participated in works of art like audiences in a theater—vicariously but completely—as the work of art drew them visually and emotionally

into its orbit. The seventeenth-century French critic Roger de Piles (1635–1709) described this exchange when he wrote: "True painting … calls to us; and has so powerful an effect, that we cannot help coming near it, as if it had something to tell us" (Puttfarken, p. 55).

ITALY

Italy in the seventeenth century remained a divided land in spite of a common history, language, and geography, with borders defined by the seas. The Kingdom of Naples and Sicily was Spanish; the Papal States crossed the center; Venice maintained its independence as a republic; and the north remained divided among small principalities. Churchmen and their families remained powerful patrons of the arts, especially as they recognized the visual arts' role in revitalizing the Roman Catholic Church. The Council of Trent (1563) had set guidelines for Church art that went against the arcane, worldly, and often lascivious trends exploited by Mannerism. The clergy's call for clarity, simplicity, chaste subject matter, and the ability to rouse a very Catholic piety in the face of Protestant revolt found a response in the fresh approaches to subject matter and style offered by a new generation of artists.

ARCHITECTURE AND SCULPTURE IN ROME

A major goal of the Counter-Reformation was to embellish churches properly, and Pope Sixtus V (pontificate 1585–1590) had begun the renewal in Rome by cutting long, straight avenues through the city to link the major pilgrimage churches with one another and with the main gates of Rome. Sixtus also ordered open spaces—piazzas—to be cleared in front of major churches, marking each site with an Egyptian obelisk. In a practical vein, he also reopened one of the ancient aqueducts to stabilize the city's water supply. Unchallengeable power and vast financial resources were required to carry out such an extensive plan of urban renewal and to refashion Rome—parts of which had been the victim of rapacity and neglect since the Middle Ages—once more into the center of spiritual and worldly power.

The Counter-Reformation popes had great wealth, although they eventually nearly bankrupted the Church with their building programs. Sixtus began to renovate the Vatican and its library; he completed the dome of St. Peter's and built splendid palaces. The Renaissance ideal of the central-plan church continued to be used for the shrines of saints, but Counter-Reformation thinking called for churches with long, wide naves to accommodate large congregations assembled to hear inspiring sermons as well as to participate in the Mass. In the sixteenth century, the decoration of new churches had been relatively austere, but seventeenth- and eighteenth-century Catholic taste favored opulent and spectacular visual effects to heighten the emotional involvement of worshipers.

ST. PETER'S BASILICA IN THE VATICAN. Half a century after Michelangelo had returned St. Peter's Basilica to Bramante's original

MAP 10-4 • SEVENTEENTH-CENTURY EUROPE

Protestantism still dominated northern Europe, while in the south Roman Catholicism remained strong after the Counter-Reformation. The Habsburg Empire was now divided into two parts, under separate rulers.

vision of a central-plan building, Pope Paul V Borghese (pontificate 1605–21) commissioned Carlo Maderno (1556–1629) to provide the church with a longer nave and a new façade **(FIG. 10–50)**. Construction began in 1607, and everything but the façade bell towers was completed by 1615. In essence, Maderno took the concept of *Il Gesù*'s façade (SEE FIG. 10–39) and enlarged it for the most important church of the Catholic world. Maderno's façade for St. Peter's "steps out" in three progressively projecting planes: from the corners to the doorways flanking the central entrance area, then the entrance area, then the central doorway itself. Similarly, the colossal orders connecting the first and second stories are flat pilasters at the corners but fully round columns where they flank the doorways. These columns support a continuous entablature that also steps out—following the columns—as it moves toward the central door.

When Maderno died in 1629, he was succeeded as Vatican architect by his collaborator of five years, Gianlorenzo Bernini (1598–1680). The latter was taught by his father, and part of his training involved sketching the Vatican collection of ancient sculpture, such as *Laocoön and His Sons* and the *Farnese Hercules*, as well as the many examples of Renaissance painting in the papal palace. Throughout his life, Bernini admired antique art and, like other artists of this period, considered himself a Classicist. Today, we not only appreciate his strong debt to the Renaissance tradition but also acknowledge the way he broke through that tradition to take us into a new, Baroque style.

When Urban VIII was elected pope in 1623, he unhesitatingly gave the young Bernini the daunting task of designing an enormous bronze baldachin, or canopy, over the high altar of St. Peter's. The church was so large that a dramatic focus on the altar

To view this image, please go to page 714 of the *Art History*, Fourth Edition by Marilyn Stokstad ebook.

10–50 • ST. PETER'S BASILICA AND PIAZZA, VATICAN, ROME
Carlo Maderno, façade, 1607–1626; Gianlorenzo Bernini, piazza design, c. 1656–1657.

Perhaps only a Baroque artist of Bernini's talents could have unified the many artistic periods and styles that come together in St. Peter's Basilica (starting with Bramante's original design for the building in the sixteenth century). The basilica in no way suggests a piecing together of parts made by different builders at different times but rather presents itself as a triumphal unity of all the parts in one coherent whole.

SEE MORE: Click the Google Earth link for an aerial view of St. Peter's, Vatican City
www.myartslab.com

was essential. The resulting *baldacchino* (**FIG. 10–51**), completed in 1633, stands almost 100 feet high and exemplifies the Baroque objective to create multimedia works, combining architecture and sculpture—and sometimes painting as well—that defy simple categorization. The gigantic corner columns symbolize the union of Christianity and its Jewish tradition—the vine of the Eucharist climbing the twisted columns associated with the Temple of Solomon. They support an entablature with a crowning element topped with an orb (a sphere representing the universe) and a cross (symbolizing the reign of Christ). Figures of angels and *putti* decorate the entablature, which is hung with tasseled panels in imitation of a cloth canopy. This imposing work not only marks the site of the tomb of St. Peter, but also serves as a tribute to Urban VIII and his family, the Barberini, whose emblems—honeybees and suns on the tasseled panels, and laurel leaves on the climbing vines—are prominently displayed.

Between 1627 and 1641, Bernini and several other sculptors, again in multimedia extravaganzas, rebuilt Bramante's crossing piers as giant reliquaries. Statues of SS. Helena, Veronica, Andrew, and Longinus stand in niches below alcoves containing their relics, to the left and right of the *baldacchino*. Visible through the *baldacchino*'s columns in the apse of the church is another reliquary: the gilded-stone, bronze, and stucco shrine made by Bernini between 1657 and 1666 for the ancient wooden throne thought to have belonged to St. Peter as the first bishop of Rome. The Chair of Peter symbolized the direct descent of Christian authority from Peter to the current pope, a belief rejected by Protestants and therefore deliberately emphasized in Counter-Reformation Catholicism. Above the shrine, a brilliant stained-glass window portrays the Holy Spirit as a dove surrounded by an oval of golden rays. Adoring gilded angels and gilt-bronze rays fan out around the window and seem to extend the penetration of the natural light—

To view this image, please go to page 715 of the *Art History*, Fourth Edition by Marilyn Stokstad ebook.

10–51 • Gianlorenzo Bernini BALDACCHINO
1624–1633. Gilt bronze, height approx. 100′ (30.48 m). Chair of Peter shrine, 1657–1666. Gilt bronze, marble, stucco, and glass. Pier decorations, 1627–1641. Gilt bronze and marble. Crossing, St. Peter's Basilica, Vatican, Rome.

made the basilica and its setting an even more awe-inspiring vision. The approach today—along the grand avenue of the Via della Conciliazione running from the Tiber to the Basilica—was conceived by Mussolini in 1936 as part of his masterplan to transform Rome into a grand fascist capital.

BERNINI AS SCULPTOR. Even after Bernini's appointment as Vatican architect in 1629, he was still able to accept outside commissions by virtue of his large workshop. In fact, he first became famous as a sculptor, and he continued to work as one throughout his career, for both the papacy and private clients. A man of many talents, he was also a painter and even a playwright—an interest that dovetailed with his genius for theatrical and dramatic presentation.

Bernini's *David* (FIG. 10–52), made for a nephew of Pope Paul V in 1623, introduced a new type of three-dimensional composition that intrudes forcefully into the viewer's space. The young hero bends at the waist and twists far to one side, ready to launch the lethal rock at Goliath. Unlike Donatello's already victorious

and the Holy Spirit—into the apse of the church. The gilding also reflects the light back to the window, creating a dazzling, ethereal effect that the seventeenth century, with its interest in mystics and visions, would equate with the activation of divinity.

At approximately the same time that he was at work on the Chair of Peter, Bernini designed and supervised the building of a colonnade to form a huge double piazza in front of the entrance to St. Peter's (SEE FIG. 10–50). The open space that he had to work with was irregular, and an Egyptian obelisk and a fountain previously installed by Sixtus V had to be incorporated into the overall plan. Bernini's remarkable design frames the oval piazza with two enormous curved porticos, or covered walkways, supported by Doric columns. These curved porticos are connected to two straight porticos, which lead up a slight incline to the two ends of the church façade. Bernini characterized his design as the "motherly arms of the Church" reaching out to the world. He had intended to build a third section of the colonnade closing the side of the piazza facing the church so that only after pilgrims had crossed the Tiber River bridge and made their way through narrow streets, would they encounter the enormous open space before the imposing church. This element of surprise would have

To view this image, please go to page 715 of the *Art History*, Fourth Edition by Marilyn Stokstad ebook.

10–52 • Gianlorenzo Bernini DAVID
1623. Marble, height 5′7″ (1.7 m). Galleria Borghese, Rome.

To view this image, please go to page 716 of the *Art History*, Fourth Edition by Marilyn Stokstad ebook.

10–53 • Gianlorenzo Bernini
CORNARO CHAPEL, CHURCH OF SANTA MARIA DELLA VITTORIA, ROME
1642–1652.

EXPLORE MORE: Gain insight from a primary source on Gianlorenzo Bernini www.myartslab.com

SEE MORE: View a simulation related to the Cornaro Chapel www.myartslab.com

was dedicated to the Spanish saint Teresa of Ávila, canonized only 20 years earlier. Bernini designed it as a rich and theatrical setting for the portrayal of a central event in Teresa's life. He covered the walls with multicolored marble panels and crowned them with a projecting cornice supported by marble pilasters.

In the center of the chapel and framed by columns in the huge oval niche above the altar, Bernini's marble group *St. Teresa of Ávila in Ecstasy* (SEE FIG. 10–49) represents a vision described by the Spanish mystic in which an angel pierced her body repeatedly with an arrow, transporting her to a state of indescribable pain, religious ecstasy, and a sense of oneness with God. St. Teresa and the angel, who seem to float upward on clouds of stucco (a moistened mixture of lime and marble dust that can be molded), are cut from a heavy mass of solid marble supported on a seemingly drifting pedestal that was fastened by hidden metal bars to the chapel wall. Bernini's skill at capturing the movements and emotions of these figures is matched by his virtuosity in simulating different textures and colors in the pure white medium of marble; the angel's gauzy, clinging draperies seem silken in contrast with Teresa's heavy woolen monastic robe. Bernini effectively used the configuration of the garment's folds to convey the saint's swooning, sensuous body beneath, even though only Teresa's face, hands, and bare feet are actually visible.

Kneeling against what appear to be balconies on both sides of the chapel are marble portrait sculptures of Federigo, his deceased father (a Venetian doge), and six cardinals of the Cornaro family.

sassy adolescent (SEE FIG. 10–10), or Michelangelo's pensive young man contemplating the task ahead (SEE FIG. 10–33), Bernini's more mature David, with his lean, sinewy body, tightly clenched mouth, and straining muscles, is all tension, action and determination. By creating a twisting figure caught in movement, Bernini incorporates the surrounding space within his composition, implying the presence of an unseen adversary somewhere behind the viewer. Thus, the viewer becomes part of the action, rather than its displaced and dispassionate observer.

From 1642 until 1652, Bernini worked on the decoration of the funerary chapel of Venetian cardinal Federigo Cornaro **(FIG. 10–53)** in the Church of Santa Maria della Vittoria, designed by Carlo Maderno earlier in the century. The Cornaro family chapel

The figures are informally posed and naturalistically portrayed. Two read from their prayer books, others exclaim at the miracle taking place in the light-infused realm above the altar, and one leans out from his seat, apparently to look at someone entering the chapel—perhaps the viewer, whose space these figures share. Bernini's intent was not to produce a spectacle for its own sake, but to capture a critical, dramatic moment at its emotional and sensual height, and by doing so guide viewers to identify totally with the event—and perhaps be transformed in the process.

BORROMINI'S CHURCH OF SAN CARLO. The intersection of two of the wide, straight avenues created by Pope Sixtus V inspired city planners to add a special emphasis, with fountains marking each of the four corners of the crossing. In 1634, Trinitarian monks

decided to build a new church at the site and awarded the commission for **SAN CARLO ALLE QUATTRO FONTANE** (St. Charles at the Four Fountains) to Francesco Borromini (1599–1667). Borromini, a nephew of architect Carlo Maderno, had arrived in Rome in 1619 from northern Italy to enter his uncle's workshop. Later, he worked under Bernini's supervision on the decoration of St. Peter's, and some details of the Baldacchino, as well as its structural engineering, are now attributed to him, but San Carlo was his first independent commission. Unfinished at Borromini's death, the church was nevertheless completed according to his design.

San Carlo stands on a narrow piece of land, with one corner cut off to accommodate one of the four fountains that give the church its name **(FIG. 10–54)**. To fit the irregular site, Borromini created an elongated central-plan interior space with undulating walls **(FIG. 10–55)**. Robust pairs of columns support a massive entablature, over which an oval dome, supported on pendentives, seems to float **(FIG. 10–56)**. The coffers (inset panels in geometric shapes) filling the interior of the oval-shaped dome form an eccentric honeycomb of crosses, elongated hexagons, and octagons. These coffers decrease sharply in size as they approach the apex, or highest point, where the dove of the Holy Spirit hovers in a climax that brings together the geometry used in the chapel: oval, octagon, circle, and—very important—a triangle, symbol of the Trinity as well as of the church's patrons. The dome appears to be shimmering and inflating—almost floating up and away—thanks to light sources placed in the lower coffers and the lantern.

It is difficult today to appreciate how audacious Borromini's design for this small church was. In it he abandoned the modular,

To view this image, please go to page 717 of the *Art History*, Fourth Edition by Marilyn Stokstad ebook.

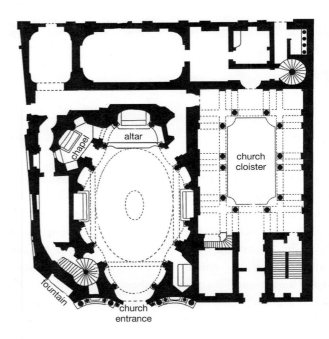

10-54 • Francesco Borromini **FAÇADE, CHURCH OF SAN CARLO ALLE QUATTRO FONTANE, ROME** 1638–1667.

10-55 • Francesco Borromini **PLAN OF THE CHURCH OF SAN CARLO ALLE QUATTRO FONTANE, ROME** 1638–1667.

additive system of planning taken for granted by every architect since Brunelleschi. He worked instead from an overriding geometrical scheme, as a Gothic architect might, subdividing modular units to obtain more complex, rational shapes. For example, the elongated, octagonal plan of San Carlo is composed of two triangles set base to base along the short axis of the plan (SEE FIG. 10–55). This diamond shape is then subdivided into secondary triangular units made by calculating the distances between what will become the concave centers of the four major and five minor niches. Yet Borromini's conception of the whole is not medieval. The chapel is dominated horizontally by a Classical entablature that breaks any surge upward toward the dome. Borromini's treatment of the architectural elements as if they were malleable was also unprecedented. His contemporaries understood immediately what an extraordinary innovation the church represented; the Trinitarian monks who had commissioned it received requests for plans from visitors from all over Europe. Although Borromini's innovative work had little impact on the architecture of Classically minded Rome, it was widely imitated in northern Italy and beyond the Alps.

To view this image, please go to page 718 of the *Art History*, Fourth Edition by Marilyn Stokstad ebook.

10-56 • Francesco Borromini VIEW INTO THE DOME OF THE CHURCH OF SAN CARLO ALLE QUATTRO FONTANE, ROME
1638–1667.

Borromini's design for San Carlo's façade (SEE FIG. 10–54), executed more than two decades later, was as innovative as his planning of the interior. He turned the building's front into an undulating, sculpture-filled screen punctuated with large columns and deep concave and convex niches that create dramatic effects of light and shadow. Borromini also gave his façade a strong vertical thrust in the center by placing over the tall doorway a statue-filled niche, then a windowed niche covered with a canopy, then a giant, forward-leaning cartouche held up by angels carved in such high relief that they appear to hover in front of the wall. The entire composition is crowned with a balustrade broken by the sharply pointed frame of the cartouche. As with the design of the building itself, Borromini's façade was enthusiastically imitated in northern Italy and especially in northern and eastern Europe.

PAINTING

Painting in seventeenth-century Italy followed one of two principal paths: the ordered Classicism of the Carracci or the dramatic naturalism of Caravaggio. Although the leading exponents of these paths were northern Italians—the Carracci family was from Bologna, and Caravaggio was born in or near Milan—they were all eventually drawn to Rome, the center of power and patronage. The Carracci family, like Caravaggio, were schooled in northern Italian Renaissance traditions, with its emphasis on *chiaroscuro*, as well as in Venetian color and *sfumato*. The Carracci quite consciously rejected the artifice of the Mannerist style and fused their northern roots with the central Italian Renaissance insistence on line (*disegno*), compositional structure, and figural solidity. They looked to Raphael, Michelangelo, and antique Classical sculpture for their ideal figural types and their expressive but decorous compositions. Caravaggio, on the other hand, satisfied the Baroque demand for drama and clarity by developing realism in a powerful new direction. He painted people he saw in the world around him—even the lowlife of Rome—and worked directly from models without elaborate drawings and compositional notes. Unlike the Carracci, he claimed to ignore the influence of the great masters so as to focus steadfastly on a sense of immediacy and invention.

THE CARRACCI.   The brothers Agostino (1557–1602) and Annibale Carracci (1560–1609) and their cousin Ludovico (1555–1619) shared a studio in Bologna. As their re-evaluation of the High Renaissance masters attracted interest among their peers, they opened their doors to friends and students and then, in 1582, founded an art academy, where students drew from live models and studied art theory, Renaissance painting, and antique Classical sculpture. The Carracci placed a high value on accurate drawing, complex figure compositions, complicated narratives, and technical expertise in both oil and fresco painting. During its short life, the academy had an impact on

To view this image, please go to page 719 of the *Art History*,
Fourth Edition by Marilyn Stokstad ebook.

10–57 • Annibale Carracci **CEILING OF GALLERY, PALAZZO FARNESE, ROME**
1597–1601. Fresco, approx. 68 × 21′ (20.7 × 6.4 m).

the development of the arts—and art education—through its insistence on both life drawing (to achieve naturalism) and aesthetic theory (to achieve artistic harmony).

In 1595, Annibale was hired by Cardinal Odoardo Farnese to decorate the principal rooms of his family's immense Roman palace. In the long *galleria* (gallery), to celebrate the wedding of Duke Ranuccio Farnese of Parma to the niece of the pope, the artist was requested to paint scenes of love based on Ovid's *Metamorphoses* (**FIG. 10–57**). Undoubtedly, Annibale and Agostino, who assisted him, felt both inspiration and competition from the important Farnese collection of antique sculpture exhibited throughout the palace.

The primary image, set in the center of the vault, is *The Triumph of Bacchus and Ariadne*, a joyous procession celebrating the wine god Bacchus's love for Ariadne, whom he rescued after her lover, Theseus, abandoned her on the island of Naxos. Annibale combines the great northern Italian tradition of ceiling painting—seen in the work of Mantegna and Correggio—with his study of central Italian Renaissance painters and the Classical heritage of Rome. Annibale organized his complex theme by using illusionistic devices to create multiple levels of reality. Painted imitations of gold-framed easel paintings called *quadri riportati* ("transported paintings") appear to "rest" on the actual

To view this image, please go to page 720 of the *Art History*, Fourth Edition by Marilyn Stokstad ebook.

10-58 • Annibale Carracci LANDSCAPE WITH THE FLIGHT INTO EGYPT
1603–1604. Oil on canvas, 48 × 90½″ (1.22 × 2.29 m). Galleria Doria Pamphili, Rome.

cornice of the vault and overlap "bronze" medallions that are flanked, in turn, by realistically colored *ignudi*, dramatically lit from below. The viewer is invited to compare the warm flesh tones of these youths, and their lifelike poses, with the more idealized "painted" bodies in the framed scenes next to them. Above, paintings of stucco-colored sculptures of herms (plain shafts topped by human torsos) twist and turn as they support the painted framework of the vault, exposing a variety of feelings with their expressions and seemingly communicating with one another. Many of Annibale's ideas are inspired by motifs in Michelangelo's Sistine Chapel ceiling (FIG. 10–35). The figure types, true to their source, are heroic, muscular, and drawn with precise anatomical accuracy. But instead of Michelangelo's cool illumination and intellectual detachment, the Carracci ceiling glows with a warm light that recalls the work of the Venetian painters Titian and Veronese, and seems buoyant with optimism and lively engagement.

The ceiling was highly admired, famous from the moment it was finished. The proud Farnese family generously allowed young artists to sketch the figures there, so that Carracci's masterpiece influenced Italian art well into the following century. Among those impressed at the initial viewing of the *galleria* was the nephew of Pope Clement VIII, Pietro Aldobrandini, who subsequently commissioned the artist to decorate the six lunettes of his private chapel with scenes from the life of the Virgin, sometime between 1603 and 1604. **LANDSCAPE WITH THE FLIGHT INTO EGYPT (FIG. 10–58)**, the largest of the six—one of only two that show painting

from Annibale's own hand—was probably above the altar. In contrast to the dramatic figural compositions in the Farnese gallery, the escape of the Holy Family is conceived within a contemplative pastoral landscape filled with golden light in the Venetian tradition of Giorgione. The design of the work and its affective spirit of melancholy derive, however, from a fundamental aspect of Baroque Classicism that would influence artists for generations to come. Here nature is ordered by humans. Trees in the left foreground and right middle ground gracefully frame the scene; and the collection of ancient buildings in the center of the composition forms a stable and protective canopy for the flight of the Holy Family. Space progresses gradually from foreground to background in diagonal movements that are indicated by people, animals, and architecture. Nothing is accidental, yet the whole appears unforced and entirely natural.

CARAVAGGIO. Michelangelo Merisi (1571–1610), known as "Caravaggio" after his family's home town in Lombardy, introduced a powerfully frank realism and dramatic, theatrical lighting and gesture to Italian Baroque art. The young painter brought an interest, perhaps a specialization, in still-life painting with him when he arrived in Rome from Milan late in 1592 and found studio work as a specialist painter of fruit and vegetables. When he began to work on his own, he continued to paint still lifes but also began to include half-length figures with them. By this time, his reputation had grown to the extent that an agent offered to market his pictures.

image about the transitory nature of sensual pleasure, either admonishing viewers to avoid sins of the flesh or encouraging them to enjoy life's pleasures while they can? The ambiguity seems to make the painting even more provocative.

Most of Caravaggio's commissions after 1600 were religious, and reactions to them were mixed. On occasion, patrons rejected his powerful, sometimes brutal, naturalism as unsuitable to the subject's dignity. Critics differed as well. An early critic, the Spaniard Vincente Carducho, wrote in his *Dialogue on Painting* (Madrid, 1633) that Caravaggio was an "omen of the ruin and demise of painting" because he painted "with nothing but nature before him, which he simply copied in his amazing way" (Enggass and Brown, pp. 173–174). Others recognized him as a great innovator who reintroduced realism into art and developed new, dramatic lighting effects. The art historian Giovanni Bellori, in his *Lives of the Painters* (1672), described Caravaggio's painting as

… reinforced throughout with bold shadows and a great deal of black to give relief to the forms. He went so far in this manner of working that he never brought his figures out into the daylight, but placed them in the dark brown atmosphere of a closed room, using a high light that descended vertically over the principal parts of the bodies while leaving the remainder in shadow in order to give force through a strong contrast of light and dark…. (Bellori, *Lives of the Painters*, Rome, 1672, in Enggass and Brown, p. 79)

Caravaggio's approach has been likened to the preaching of Filippo Neri (1515–1595), the Counter-Reformation priest and mystic who founded a Roman religious group called the Congregation of the Oratory. Neri, called the Apostle of Rome and later canonized, focused his missionary efforts on ordinary people for whom he strove to make Christian history and doctrine understandable and meaningful. Caravaggio, too, interpreted his

Caravaggio painted for a small, sophisticated circle associated with the household of art patron Cardinal del Monte, where the artist was invited to reside. His subjects from this early period of the 1590s include not only still lifes but also genre scenes featuring fortune-tellers, cardsharps, and glamorous young men dressed as musicians or mythological figures. The **BACCHUS** of 1595–1596 **(FIG. 10–59)** is among the most polished of these early works. Caravaggio seems to have painted exactly what he saw, reproducing the "farmer's tan" of those parts of this partially dressed youth's skin—hand and face—that have been exposed to the sun, as well as the dirt under his fingernails. The figure himself is strikingly androgynous. Made up with painted lips and smoothly arching eyebrows, he seems to offer the viewer the gorgeous goblet of wine held delicately in his left hand, while fingering the black bow that holds his loose clothing together at the waist. Is this a provocative invitation to an erotic encounter or a young actor outfitted for the role of Bacchus, god of wine? Does the juxtaposition of the youth's invitation with a still life of rotting fruit transform this into an

To view this image, please go to page 724 of the *Art History*, Fourth Edition by Marilyn Stokstad ebook.

10-60 • Caravaggio THE CONVERSION OF ST. PAUL
Cerasi Chapel, Santa Maria del Popolo, Rome. c. 1601. Oil on canvas, 7'6" × 5'8" (2.3 × 1.75 m).

EXPLORE MORE: Gain insight from a primary source on Caravaggio
www.myartslab.com

religious subjects directly and dramatically, combining intensely observed figures, poses, and expressions with strongly contrasting effects of light and color. His knowledge of Lombard painting, where the influence of Leonardo was strong, must have aided him in his development of the technique now known as **tenebrism**, in which forms emerge from a dark background into a strong light that often falls from a single source outside the painting. The effect is that of a theatrical spotlight.

One of Caravaggio's first religious commissions, paintings for the Contarelli Chapel in the French community's church of St. Louis (San Luigi dei Francesi), included *The Calling of St. Matthew*, painted about 1599–1600 (see "Caravaggio in the Contarelli Chapel," pages 644–645). The subject is conversion, a common Counter-Reformation theme. Jesus calls Levi, the tax collector, to join his apostles (Matthew 9:9; Mark 2:14). Levi—who will become St. Matthew—sits at a table, counting or collecting money, surrounded by elegant young men in plumed hats, velvet doublets, and satin shirts. Nearly hidden behind the back of the beckoning apostle—probably St. Peter—at the right, the gaunt-faced Jesus points dramatically at Levi with a gesture that is repeated in the presumed (other than Jesus, identities are not certain here) tax collector's own surprised response of pointing to himself, as if to say, "Who, me?" An intense raking light enters the painting from upper right, as if it were coming from the chapel's actual window above the altar to spotlight the important features of this darkened scene. Viewers encountering the painting obliquely across the empty space of the chapel interior seem to be witnessing the scene as it is occurring, elevated on a recessed stage opening through the wall before them.

The emotional power of Caravaggio's theatrical approach to sacred narrative is nowhere more evident than in his rendering of **THE CONVERSION OF ST. PAUL** for the Cerasi Chapel of Santa

Caravaggio in the Contarelli Chapel

As soon as he had established himself as an up-and-coming artist during the 1590s, Caravaggio turned to a series of important commissions for religious paintings in the chapels of Roman churches. Unlike in the Renaissance, where frescos were applied directly to the walls, Caravaggio produced large oil paintings on canvas in his studio, only later installing them within the chapels to form coordinated ensembles. Several such installations survive, giving us the precious opportunity to experience the paintings as Caravaggio and his patrons intended. One of these intact programs, in the Contarelli Chapel of San Luigi dei Francesi, was Caravaggio's earliest religious commission in Rome, perhaps obtained through the efforts of Cardinal del Monte, who had supported the artist through the 1590s.

This church served the French community in Rome, and the building itself was constructed between 1518 and 1589, begun under the patronage of Catherine de' Medici, Queen of France. The chapel Caravaggio decorated was founded in 1565 by Mathieu Cointrel—Matteo Contarelli—a French noble at the papal court who would serve as a financial administrator under Gregory XIII (pontificate 1572–1585). Although earlier artists had been called on to provide paintings for the chapel, it was only after Contarelli's death in 1585 that the executors of his will brought the decoration to completion, hiring Giuseppe Cesare in 1591 to paint the ceiling frescos, and Caravaggio in 1599 to provide paintings of scenes from the life of the patron's patron saint: *The Calling of St. Matthew* on the left wall and *The Martyrdom of St. Matthew* on the right (not visible in FIG. A), both installed in July 1600.

The commissioning document was explicit, requiring the artist to show, in *The Calling of St. Matthew* (fig. B), the saint rising from his seat to follow Christ in ministry. But Caravaggio was never very good at following the rules. Among the group of smartly dressed Romans who form Matthew's circle of cohorts seated at the left, no one rises to leave. Art historians have not even been able to agree on which figure is Matthew. Most identify him with a bearded man in the center, interpreting his pointing gesture as a self-referential, questioning response to Jesus' call. But some see Matthew in the figure hunched over the scattered coins at far left, seemingly unmoved by Jesus' presence. In this case, the bearded figure's pointing would question whether this bent-over colleague was the one Jesus

To view this image, please go to page 722 of the *Art History*, Fourth Edition by Marilyn Stokstad ebook.

A. CONTARELLI CHAPEL, SAN LUIGI DEI FRANCESI
Rome. Paintings by Caravaggio 1599–1602.

sought. The painting is marked by mystery, not by the clarity sought by Counter-Reformation guidelines.

In February 1602, Caravaggio received a second commission for the Contarelli Chapel, this time for a painting over the altar showing St. Matthew, accompanied by his angelic symbol and writing his Gospel. It was to be completed within three months, but Caravaggio did not receive payment for the picture until September of that year, and the painting he delivered was rejected. The clergy considered Caravaggio's rendering of the saint unacceptably crude and common, his cross-legged pose uncouth and unnecessarily revealing. The fleshiness of the angel, who sidles cozily up to Matthew, was judged inappropriately risqué. In short, the painting was inconsistent with guidelines for saintly decorum set for artists by the Council of Trent. Caravaggio had to paint a second, more decorous altarpiece for the chapel (seen in FIG. A), with a nobler Matthew and a more distant angel. The rejected version was snapped up by Roman collector Vincenzo Giustiniani, who actually paid for the replacement in order to acquire the more sensational original. Unfortunately, this first painting was destroyed in the 1945 bombing of Berlin during World War II.

To view this image, please go to page 723 of the *Art History*, Fourth Edition by Marilyn Stokstad ebook.

B. Caravaggio **THE CALLING OF ST. MATTHEW**
Contarelli Chapel, Church of San Luigi dei Francesi, Rome. 1599–1600.
Oil on canvas, 10′7½″ × 11′2″ (3.24 × 3.4 m).

Maria del Popolo (FIG. 10–60). This is one of two paintings commissioned for this chapel in 1600; the other portrayed the Crucifixion of St. Peter. The first pair was rejected when Caravaggio delivered them, and they were acquired by a private collector (see also "Caravaggio in the Contarelli Chapel," pages 644–645). This second version of Paul's conversion is direct and simple. Caravaggio focuses on Paul's internal involvement with a pivotal moment, not its external cause. There is no indication of a heavenly apparition, only Paul's response to it. There is no clear physical setting, only mysterious darkness. And Paul's experience is personal. Whereas he has been flung from his horse and threatens to tumble into the viewers' own space—arms outstretched and legs akimbo, bathed in a strong spotlight—the horse and groom behind him seem oblivious to Paul's experience. The horse actually takes up more space in the painting than the saint, and the unsettling position of its lifted foreleg, precariously poised over the sprawled body of Paul, adds further tension to an already charged presentation.

Despite the great esteem in which Caravaggio was held by some, especially the younger generation of artists, his violent temper repeatedly got him into trouble. During the last decade of his life, he was frequently arrested, initially for minor offenses such as carrying arms illegally or street brawling. But in May of 1606 he killed a man in a duel fought over a disputed tennis match and had to flee Rome as a fugitive under a death sentence. He supported himself on the run by painting in Naples, Malta, and Sicily. The Knights of Malta awarded him the cross of their religious and military order in July 1608, but in October he was imprisoned for insulting one of their number, and again he escaped and fled. Caravaggio died on July 18, 1610, just short of his 39th birthday, of a fever contracted during a journey back to Rome where he expected to be pardoned of his capital offense. Caravaggio's unvarnished realism and tenebrism influenced nearly every important European artist of the seventeenth century.

ARTEMISIA GENTILESCHI. One of Caravaggio's most brilliant Italian followers was Artemisia Gentileschi (1593–c. 1652/1653), whose international reputation helped spread the Caravaggesque style beyond Rome. Artemisia first studied and worked under her father, Orazio, one of the earliest followers of Caravaggio. In 1616, she moved from Rome to Florence, where she worked for the grand duke of Tuscany and was elected, at the age of 23, to

the Florentine Academy of Design. But like many great artists, her promise as a painter was already evident in her early work. At the age of 17, while she was still part of her father's studio, she painted a stunning rendering of the popular subject of *Susannah and the Elders* (FIG. 10–61), perhaps an intentional "masterpiece," meant to showcase her talent and secure her reputation as one of the preeminent painters of the age.

The subject is biblical, drawn from a part of the Book of Daniel that was excluded from the Protestant Bible, but—perhaps consequently—especially popular as a subject in Roman Catholic art. While bathing alone in her garden, the beautiful young Susannah is observed by two lecherous elders—Peeping Toms—who threaten to claim they saw her engaged in a lovers' tryst unless

To view this image, please go to page 725 of the *Art History*, Fourth Edition by Marilyn Stokstad ebook.

10–61 • Artemisia Gentileschi SUSANNAH AND THE ELDERS
1610. Oil on canvas, 67 × 47⅝″ (1.7 × 1.21 m). Count Schönborn Kunstsammlungen, Pommersfelden.

To view this image, please go to page 726 of the *Art History*, Fourth Edition by Marilyn Stokstad ebook.

10-62 • Artemisia Gentileschi SELF-PORTRAIT AS THE ALLEGORY OF PAINTING
1630. Oil on canvas, 38 × 29″ (96.5 × 73.7 cm). The Royal Collection, Windsor Castle, England.

EXPLORE MORE: Gain insight from a primary source on Artemisia Gentileschi **www.myartslab.com**

she agrees to have sex with them. Susannah refuses to surrender her chastity, and they make good on their threat. Initially sentenced to death for her supposed sexual transgression, through the intervention of Daniel, she is proven innocent, and the two dishonest voyeurs are executed instead.

Most male artists who painted this scene emphasized Susannah's sexual allure and the elders' lustful stares, but Artemesia shifts the narrative focus to the powerless young woman's vulnerability—and this Susannah actually looks like a woman. Although female artists were excluded from using male models, Artemesia has clearly studied the appearance and anatomy of unclothed women, creating one of the first truly lifelike female nudes in the European tradition. Her interest in unvarnished naturalism is probably derived from Caravaggio. His revolutionary art is also behind the theatricality of the heroine's rhetorical gesture (recalling that of Adam when expelled from paradise in the Sistine Ceiling), the complex interlocking of the figures' postures (note the

patterned relationship between the hands), and the crowding of figures up against the picture plane. But Artemisia has blended her sources and influences into a personal rendering of a traditional subject that moves viewers to empathize with the heroine's condition, and will perhaps inspire them to emulate her righteousness in a world still dominated by overpowering men.

Twenty years after this painting, Artemisia painted a **SELF-PORTRAIT AS THE ALLEGORY OF PAINTING (FIG. 10–62)**. A richly dressed woman, with palette and brushes in hand, is totally immersed in her work. Aspects of the image are derived from Cesare Ripa's sourcebook *Iconologia* (1593), which became an essential tool for creating and deciphering seventeenth- and eighteenth-century art. For instance, *Iconologia* is the source for the woman's gold necklace with its mask pendant: Ripa writes that the mask imitates the human face, as painting imitates nature, and the gold chain symbolizes "the continuity and interlocking nature of painting, each man [*sic*] learning from his master and continuing his master's achievements in the next generation" (Maser, trans. no. 197). By painting her own features on a personification of Painting, Artemisia not only commemorates her profession but also claims her own place within it.

FRANCE

Early seventeenth-century France was marked by almost continuous foreign and civil wars. The assassination of King Henry IV in 1610 left France in the hands of the queen, Marie de' Medici (regency 1610–1617), as regent for her 9-year-old son, Louis XIII (r. 1610–1643). When Louis came of age, the brilliant and unscrupulous Cardinal Richelieu became chief minister and set about increasing the power of the Crown at the expense of the French nobility. The death of Louis XIII again left France with a child king, the 5-year-old Louis XIV (r. 1643–1715). His mother, Anne of Austria, became regent, with the assistance of another powerful minister, Cardinal Mazarin. At Mazarin's death in 1661, Louis XIV began his long personal reign, assisted by yet another able minister, Jean-Baptiste Colbert.

An absolute monarch whose reign was the longest in European history, Louis XIV made the French court the envy of every ruler in Europe. He became known as *le Roi Soleil* ("the Sun King") and was sometimes glorified in art through identification with the Classical sun god, Apollo. In a 1701 portrait by court painter Hyacinthe Rigaud (1659–1743), the richly costumed **LOUIS XIV** is framed by a lavish, billowing curtain (**FIG. 10–63**). Proudly showing off his elegant legs, the 63-year-old monarch poses in a blue robe of state, trimmed with gold *fleurs-de-lis* and lined with white ermine. He wears the high-heeled shoes he devised to compensate for his shortness. Despite his pompous pose and magnificent surroundings, the directness of the king's gaze and the frankness of his aging face make him appear surprisingly human.

The arts, like everything else, came under royal control. In 1635, Cardinal Richelieu had founded the French Royal Academy,

Science and the Changing Worldview

From the mid-sixteenth through the seventeenth centuries, new discoveries about the natural world brought a sense of both the grand scale and the microscopic detail of the universe. To publish their theories and research, early scientists learned to draw or depended on artists to draw what they discovered in the world around them. This practice would continue until the invention of photography in the nineteenth century.

Artist and scientist were seldom the same person, but Anna Maria Sibylla Merian (1647–1717) contributed to botany and entomology both as a researcher and as an artist. German by birth and Dutch by training, Merian was once described by a Dutch contemporary as a painter of worms, flies, mosquitoes, spiders, "and other filth." In 1699, the city of Amsterdam subsidized Merian's research on plants and insects in the Dutch colony of Surinam in South America, where she spent two years exploring the jungle and recording insects. On her return to the Dutch Republic, she published the results of her research as *The Metamorphosis of the Insects of Surinam*, illustrated with 72 large plates engraved after her watercolors. For all her meticulous scientific accuracy, Merian carefully arranged her depictions of exotic insects and elegant fruits and flowers into skillful and harmonious compositions.

But interest in scientific exploration was not limited to the Netherlands. The writings of philosophers Francis Bacon (1561–1626) in England and René Descartes (1596–1650) in France helped establish a new scientific method of studying the world by insisting on scrupulous objectivity and logical reasoning. Bacon argued that the facts be established from observation and tested by controlled experiments. Descartes, who was also a mathematician, argued for the deductive method of reasoning, in which conclusions were arrived at logically from basic premises.

In 1543, the Polish scholar Nicolaus Copernicus (1473–1543) published *On the Revolutions of the Heavenly Spheres*, which contradicted the long-held view that the Earth is the center of the universe (the Ptolemaic theory) by arguing instead that it and the other planets revolve around the sun. The Church put Copernicus's work on its *Index of Prohibited Books* in 1616, but Johannes Kepler (1571–1630) continued demonstrating that the planets revolve around the sun in elliptical orbits. Galileo Galilei (1564–1642), an astronomer, mathematician, and physicist, developed the telescope as a tool for observing the heavens and provided further confirmation of Copernican theory but since the Church prohibited its teaching, Galileo was tried for heresy by the Inquisition and forced to recant his views.

The new seventeenth-century science turned to the study of the very small as well as to the vast reaches of space. This included the development of the microscope by the Dutch lens-maker and amateur scientist Anton van Leeuwenhoek (1632–1723). Leeuwenhoek perfected grinding techniques and increased the power of his lenses far beyond what was required for a simple magnifying glass. Ultimately, he was able to study the inner workings of plants and animals and even see micro-organisms.

To view this image, please go to page 756 of the *Art History*, Fourth Edition by Marilyn Stokstad ebook.

Anna Maria Sibylla Merian **PLATE 9 FROM THE METAMORPHOSIS OF THE INSECTS OF SURINAM** 1719. Hand-colored engraving, 18⅞ × 13″ (47.9 × 33 cm). National Museum of Women in the Arts, Washington, D.C. Gift of Wallace and Wilhelmina Holladay Collection, funds contributed by Mr. and Mrs. George G. Anderman and an anonymous donor 1976.56

directing the members to compile a definitive dictionary and grammar of the French language. In 1648, the Royal Academy of Painting and Sculpture was founded, which, as reorganized by Colbert in 1663, maintained strict control over the arts. Although it was not the first European arts academy, none before it had exerted such dictatorial authority—an authority that lasted in

To view this image, please go to page 757 of the *Art History*, Fourth Edition by Marilyn Stokstad ebook.

10–63 • Hyacinthe Rigaud
LOUIS XIV
1701. Oil on canvas, 9'2" × 7'10¾" (2.19 × 2.4 m). Musée du Louvre, Paris.

Louis XIV had ordered this portrait as a gift for his grandson, the future Philip V of Spain (r. 1700–1746), but when Rigaud finished the painting, Louis liked it too much to give it away and only three years later ordered a copy from Rigaud to give to his grandson. The request for copies of royal portraits was not unusual since the aristocratic families of Europe were linked through marriage. Paintings made appropriate gifts and at the same time memorialized important political alliances by recording them in visual form.

France until the late nineteenth century. Membership of the academy assured an artist of royal and civic commissions and financial success, but many talented artists did well outside it.

ARCHITECTURE AND ITS DECORATION AT VERSAILLES

French architecture developed along Classical lines in the second half of the seventeenth century under the influence of François Mansart (1598–1666) and Louis Le Vau (1612–1670). When the Royal Academy of Architecture was founded in 1671, its members developed guidelines for architectural design based on the belief that mathematics was the true basis of beauty. Their chief sources for ideal models were the books of Vitruvius and Palladio.

In 1668, Louis XIV began to enlarge the small château built by Louis XIII at Versailles, not far from Paris. Louis moved to the palace in 1682 and eventually required his court to live in Versailles; 5,000 aristocrats lived in the palace itself, together with 14,000 servants and military staff members. The town had another

To view this image, please go to page 758 of the *Art History*, Fourth Edition by Marilyn Stokstad ebook.

10–64 • Louis Le Vau and Jules Hardouin-Mansart **GARDEN FAÇADE OF THE PALACE OF VERSAILLES** with (foreground) Jean-Baptiste Tuby **NEPTUNE.** 1678–1685.

SEE MORE: View a video about Versailles **www.myartslab.com**

30,000 residents, most of whom were employed by the palace. The designers of the palace and park complex at Versailles were Le Vau, Charles Le Brun (1619–1690), who oversaw the interior decoration, and André Le Nôtre (1613–1700), who planned the gardens. For both political and sentimental reasons, the old château was left standing, and the new building went up around it. This project consisted of two phases: the first additions by Le Vau, begun in 1668; and an enlargement completed after Le Vau's death by his successor, Jules Hardouin-Mansart (1646–1708), from 1670 to 1685.

Hardouin-Mansart was responsible for the addition of the long lateral wings and the renovation of Le Vau's central block on the garden side to match these wings **(FIG. 10–64)**. The three-story façade has a lightly rusticated ground floor, a main floor lined with enormous arched windows separated by Ionic columns or pilasters, an attic level whose rectangular windows are also flanked by pilasters, and a flat, terraced roof. The overall design is a sensitive balance of horizontals and verticals relieved by a restrained overlay of regularly spaced projecting blocks with open, colonnaded porches.

In his renovation of Le Vau's center-block façade, Hardouin-Mansart enclosed the previously open gallery on the main level,

creating the famed **HALL OF MIRRORS (FIG. 10–65)**, which is about 240 feet (73 meters) long and 47 feet (13 meters) high. He achieved architectural symmetry and extraordinary effects by lining the interior wall opposite the windows with Venetian glass mirrors the same size and shape as the arched windows. Mirrors were small and extremely expensive in the seventeenth century, and these huge walls of reflective glass were created by fitting 18-inch panels together. The mirrors reflect the natural light from the windows and give the impression of an even larger space; at night, the reflections of flickering candles must have turned the mirrored gallery into a veritable painting in which the king and courtiers saw themselves as they promenaded.

Inspired by Carracci's Farnese ceiling (SEE FIG. 10–57), Le Brun decorated the vaulted ceiling with paintings (on canvas, which is more stable in the damp northern climate) glorifying the reign of Louis XIV and Louis's military triumphs, assisted by the Classical gods. In 1642, Le Brun had studied in Italy, where he came under the influence of the Classical style of his compatriot Nicolas Poussin. As "first painter to the king" and director of the Royal Academy of Painting and Sculpture, Le Brun controlled art education and patronage from 1661/63 until his death in 1690. He tempered the warmly exuberant Baroque ceilings he had seen in

To view this image, please go to page 759 of the *Art History*, Fourth Edition by Marilyn Stokstad ebook.

Rome with Poussin's cool Classicism to produce spectacular decorations for the king. The underlying theme for the design and decoration of the palace was the glorification of the king as Apollo the sun god, with whom Louis identified. Louis XIV thought of the duties of kingship, including its pageantry, as a solemn performance, so it is most appropriate that Rigaud's portrait presents him on a raised, stagelike platform, with a theatrical curtain (SEE FIG. 10–63). Versailles was the splendid stage on which the king played the principal role in the grandiose drama of state.

Academies and Academy Exhibitions

During the seventeenth century, the French government founded a number of **academies** for the support and instruction of students in literature, painting and sculpture, music and dance, and architecture. In 1664, the Royal Academy of Painting and Sculpture in Paris began to mount occasional exhibitions of members' recent work. This exhibition came to be known as the Salon because it was held in the Salon Carré in the Palace of the Louvre. As of 1737, the Salon was held every other year, with a jury of members selecting the works to be shown.

History paintings (based on historical, mythological, or biblical narratives and generally conveying a high moral or intellectual idea) were accorded highest place in the Academy's hierarchy of genres, followed by historical portraiture, landscape painting, various other forms of portraiture, genre painting, and still life. The Salon shows were the only public art exhibitions of importance in Paris, so they were highly influential in establishing officially approved styles and in molding public taste; they also consolidated the Academy's control over the production of art.

In recognition of Rome's importance as a training ground for aspiring history painters, the Royal Academy of Painting and Sculpture opened a French Academy in Rome in 1666. A competitive "Prix de Rome," or Rome Prize, enabled the winners to study in Rome for three to five years. A similar prize was established by the French Royal Academy of Architecture in 1720. Many Western cultural capitals emulated the French academic model: Academies were established in Berlin in 1696, Dresden in 1705, London in 1768, Boston in 1780, Mexico City in 1785, and New York in 1802. Members of London's Royal Academy of Arts are depicted in Johann Zoffany's portrait of 1771–1772.

Although there were several women members of the European academies of art before the eighteenth century, their inclusion amounted to little more than an honorary recognition of their achievements. In France, Louis XIV proclaimed in his founding address to the Royal Academy that its purpose was to reward all worthy artists "without regard to the difference of sex," but this resolve was not put into practice. Only seven women gained the title of "Academician" between 1648 and 1706, after which the Royal Academy was closed

to women. Nevertheless, four more women were admitted by 1770; however, the men, worried that women would become "too numerous," limited the total number of female members to four. Young women were neither admitted to the Academy School nor allowed to compete for Academy prizes, both of which were required for professional success. They fared even worse at London's Royal Academy. The Swiss painters Mary Moser and Angelica Kauffmann were both founding members in 1768, but no other women were elected until 1922, and then only as associates.

To view this image, please go to page 924 of the *Art History*, Fourth Edition by Marilyn Stokstad ebook.

Johann Zoffany **ACADEMICIANS OF THE ROYAL ACADEMY**
1771–1772. Oil on canvas, 47½ × 59½" (120.6 × 151.2 cm).
The Royal Collection, Windsor Castle, England.

Zoffany's group portrait of members of the London Royal Academy reveals how mainstream artists were taught in the 1770s. The painting shows artists, all men, setting up a life-drawing class and engaging in lively conversation. The studio is decorated with the Academy's study collection of Classical statues and plaster copies. Propriety prohibited the presence of women in life-drawing studios, so Zoffany includes Royal Academicians Mary Moser and Angelica Kauffmann in portraits on the wall on the right.

REVOLUTIONS IN PRINTING

THOUGHT PIECE

Of the quality and amusements of the renowned Don Quixote de la Mancha.

In a certain corner of la Mancha, the name of which I do not choose to remember, there lately lived one of those country gentlemen, who adorn their halls with a rusty lance and worm-eaten target, and ride forth on the skeleton of a horse, to course with a sort of a starved greyhound.

Three fourths of his income were scarce sufficient to afford a dish of hodge-podge, in which the mutton bore no proportion to the beef, for dinner; a plate of salmagundi, commonly at supper; gripes and grumblings on Saturdays, lentils on Fridays, and the addition of a pigeon or some such thing on the Lord's-day. The remaining part of his revenue was consumed in the purchase of a fine black suit, with velvet breeches and slippers of the same, for holy-days; and a coat of home-spun, which he wore in honour of his country, during the rest of the week.

He maintained a female house keeper turned of forty, a niece of about half that age, and a trusty young fellow, fit for field and market, who could turn his hand to anything, either to saddle the horse or handle the plough.

Our squire, who bordered upon fifty, was of a tough constitution, extremely meager, and hard-featured, an early riser, and in point of exercise, another Nimrod. He is said to have gone by the name of Quixada, or Quesada, (for in this particular, the authors who mention that circumstance, disagree) though from the most probable conjectures, we may conclude, that he was called by the significant name of Quixada; but this is of small importance to the history, in the course of which it will be sufficient if we swerve not farther from the truth.

—Miguel de Cervantes, *Don Quixote* (Modern Library, 2004), Book one, Chapter one.

THINGS TO CONSIDER

- What influence did the availability of printed books have on political and social life in Europe?
- How have world cultures used "books" to communicate knowledge?

- How do different graphic approaches to printing and mark-making express cultural values?

THE GRAPHIC ARTS

Printmaking emerged in Europe at the end of the fourteenth century with the development of printing presses and the increased local manufacture and wider availability of paper. The techniques used by printmakers during the fifteenth century were woodcut and engraving. **Woodblocks** cut in relief had long been used to print designs on cloth, but only in the fifteenth century did the printing of images and texts on paper and the production of books in multiple copies of a single edition, or version, begin to replace the copying of each book by hand. Both hand-written and printed books were often illustrated, and printed images were sometimes hand-colored.

SINGLE SHEETS

Large quantities of single-sheet prints were made using woodcut and engraving techniques in the early decades of the fifteenth century. Often artists drew the images for professional wood-workers to cut from the block.

THE BUXHEIM ST. CHRISTOPHER. Devotional images were sold as souvenirs to pilgrims at holy sites. The **BUXHEIM ST. CHRISTOPHER** was found in the Carthusian Monastery of Bux-heim, in southern Germany, glued to the inside of the back cover of a manuscript **(FIG. 11–1)**. St. Christopher, patron saint of travelers and protector from the plague, carries the Christ Child across the river. His efforts are witnessed by a monk holding out a light to guide him to the monastery door, but ignored by the hardworking millers on the opposite bank. Both the cutting of the block and the quality of the printing are very high. Lines vary in width to strengthen major forms. Delicate lines are used for inner modeling (facial features) and short parallel lines to indicate shadows (the inner side of draperies). The date 1423, which is cut into the block, was once thought to identify this print as among the earliest to survive. Recent studies have determined that the date refers to some event, and the print is now dated at mid century.

To view this image, please go to page 589 of the *Art History*, Fourth Edition by Marilyn Stokstad ebook.

11–1 • THE BUXHEIM ST. CHRISTOPHER
Mid 15th century. Hand-colored woodcut, 11⅜ × 8⅛" (28.85 × 20.7 cm). Courtesy of the Director and Librarian, the John Rylands University Library, the University of Manchester, England

The Latin text reads, "Whenever you look at the face of St. Christopher, you will not die a terrible death that day."

To view this image, please go to page 590 of the *Art History*, Fourth Edition by Marilyn Stokstad ebook.

11–2 • Martin Schongauer DEMONS TORMENTING ST. ANTHONY
c. 1480–1490. Engraving, 12¼ × 9" (31.1 × 22.9 cm). Metropolitan Museum of Art, New York. Rogers Fund, 1920 (20.5.2)

MARTIN SCHONGAUER. Engraving may have originated with goldsmiths and armorers, who recorded their work by rubbing lampblack into the engraved lines and pressing paper over the plate. German artist Martin Schongauer (c. 1435–1491), who learned engraving from his goldsmith father, was an immensely skillful printmaker who excelled both in drawing and in the difficult technique of shading from deep blacks to faintest grays using only line. In **DEMONS TORMENTING ST. ANTHONY**, engraved about 1470–1475 **(FIG. 11–2)**, Schongauer illustrated the original biblical meaning of temptation as a physical assault rather than a subtle inducement. Wildly acrobatic, slithery, spiky demons lift Anthony up off the ground to torment and terrify him in midair. The engraver intensified the horror of the moment by condensing the action into a swirling vortex of figures beating, scratching, poking, tugging, and no doubt shrieking at the stoical saint, who remains impervious to all, perhaps because of his power to focus inwardly on his private meditations.

PRINTED BOOKS

The explosion of learning in Europe in the fifteenth century encouraged experiments in faster and cheaper ways of producing books than by hand-copying them. The earliest printed books were block books, for which each page of text, with or without illustrations, was cut in relief on a single block of wood. Movable-type printing, in which individual letters could be arranged and locked together, inked, and then printed onto paper, was first achieved in Europe in the workshop of Johann Gutenberg in Mainz, Germany. More than 40 copies of Gutenberg's Bible, printed around 1455, still exist. As early as 1465, two German printers were working in Italy, and by the 1470s there were presses in France, Flanders, Holland, and Spain. With the invention of this fast way to make a number of identical books, the intellectual and spiritual life of Europe—and with it the arts—changed forever.

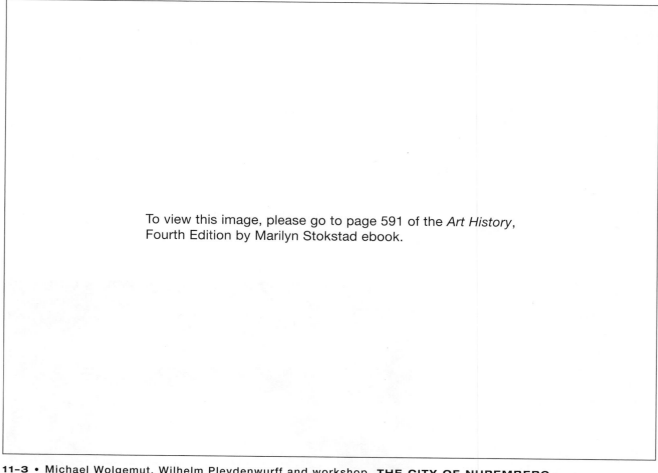

To view this image, please go to page 591 of the *Art History*, Fourth Edition by Marilyn Stokstad ebook.

11–3 • Michael Wolgemut, Wilhelm Pleydenwurff and workshop THE CITY OF NUREMBERG
Nuremberg Chronicle, published by Anton Koberger in 1493. Woodcut within a printed book, hand-colored after printing, each page 18½ × 12¾″ (47 × 32.4 cm). Bibliothèque Mazarine, Paris.

THE NUREMBERG CHRONICLE. The publication of the *Nuremberg Chronicle* by prosperous Nuremberg printer Anton Koburger was the culmination of his complicated collaboration with scholars, artists, and investors, in an early capitalist enterprise that is a landmark in the history of printed books. The text of this history of the world was compiled by physician and scholar Hartmann Schedel, drawing from the work of colleagues and the extensive holdings of his private library. When Koburger set out to publish Schedel's compilation, he sought financial support from Sebald Schregel and his brother-in-law Sebastian Kammermaister, who had a proven record of patronage in book publishing. He also contracted in the 1480s with artists Michael Wolgemut and Wilhelm Pleydenwurff to produce the woodcut illustrations and in 1491 to work on the layout.

The *Nuremberg Chronicle* was published in 1493 in an edition of 2,500. Woodcut illustrations—1,809 in total—were dispersed throughout the book, spreading across the width of whole pages or tucked into the text along either margin. Those interested in purchasing the book could obtain it in Latin or German, on parchment or on paper, bound or unbound, as it came from the press or tinted with color. It seems fitting that the only instance of a double-page picture—filling the entire expanse of an opening with text restricted to headings and labels—is a panoramic view of the city of Nuremberg where this collaborative enterprise was centered **(FIG. 11–3)**. Illustrated here is a view of this expansive cityscape in a copy of the book that was originally owned by a bibliophile who could afford to have the woodcuts painted by hand with color to enhance the appearance of this proud Renaissance city's portrait. As we will see, it was the site of significant artistic developments in the sixteenth century as well.

BACK TO THE FUTURE

Renaissance Italy & France, c.1460–c.1600

The first hundred years after Gutenberg's invention, from roughly 1455 to 1555, have been called the 'golden age' of printing. It is a title which recognizes both the large number of beautiful books that were printed during this period and the new kinds of beauty that sprang from their pages. Gothic type, which had so dominated the first printed books in Germany, was not the automatic choice of letterform for all printers elsewhere. In Italy a more rounded and open style of type was developed soon after printing first arrived there in 1465. The shape of these letters and the way they were placed on the page were linked to the 're-birth'—or renaissance, as later generations referred to it—of learning from ancient Greece and Rome. Books of Latin classics as well as some contemporary texts were set in a less angular, 'roman' style of type based on a script wrongly believed to have been written by the ancient Romans. The new roman types were set alongside exquisitely refined and, for the most part, unilluminated woodcuts of decorative initials and borders. The precision with which both type and decoration could be positioned on the page, and the uniformity with which ink could be impressed onto paper allowed the printed Renaissance page to look lighter and more refined than its manuscript equivalent. The very best Renaissance pages achieved a simplicity and grandeur not seen before and rarely matched since. The achievement is all the more remarkable since many of them were among the very first pages to pass through a printing press.

The revival of learning in Italy was largely based on books. Unlocking the ancient past required books in manuscript form to be studiously translated and annotated. From around the last quarter of the fifteenth century onwards, this newly recovered knowledge was transmitted by printed books. This critical mass of classical scholarship set off a series of chain reactions in almost every field of inquiry. Books on law, philosophy, art, mathematics, science, education and military warfare, among others seemed to find appropriate models or novel stimuli in classical texts. The production of indulgences, devotional prints and other forms of ephemera might have made up the bulk of printing during this time (so little exists its extent is difficult to gauge), but books were certainly the most prestigious form of print. The esteem in which the format and its often classical subject matter were held was reflected in the quality of the design. Buyers were willing to complement their elegant pages with solid bindings and handsome leather-clad protective covers. This emphasis on the book's appearance made it the dominant format for exercises in the evolution of graphic style.

What is striking about the Renaissance printed book compared with the medieval manuscript is the almost complete loss of colour. Where once varied hues of illuminated initials and brightly painted borders had suffused book pages with a sense of depth and richness, there was now a resolutely two-dimensional surface of black and white. The loss of the polychrome page was not immediate, however, nor was it quite total. Many religious books in particular retained the rubricator's distinctive red and some illustrations continued to be coloured by hand. In Italy especially, printing underwent a significant period of transition during which some books were both printed and illuminated (**FIG. 11–4**), just as copies of Gutenberg's Bible had been. But whereas many of the hand-painted decorations in that edition of

11–4 • Printed and illuminated book, Milan, 1490
Courtesy of the British Library.

the Bible had looked almost tokenistic in their sparseness, the illuminations in many of the early printed Italian books continued to be extremely highly wrought. The richness of the illuminator's palette was combined with a new mastery of the depiction of light and the new discovery of perspective to make ever more convincing *trompe l'oeil* effects. It was as though the Italian illuminators had been provoked into proving what skill and variety lay within the human hand as compared to a block of type or a woodcut illustration.

For all its apparent attractions, the illuminated printed page did not fit with the process of mass production that so defined the printing press. Painted pages took too long to make. And yet, paradoxically, their old-fashioned traits of slowness and unrepeatability helped to preserve the art of illumination for a period. Wealthy patrons who wished to commemorate a special occasion or own a unique artefact would commission an illuminated manuscript specifically because it was not mass-produced. Those who could not afford such extravagances might also turn to a scribe when in need of a simple one-off document, a certificate of marriage say. It is likely that in these sorts of instances a scribe could write it more quickly than the printer could set, ink and print it. But examples of this kind were few. By 1500 the scribe had been pushed from his thousand-year-old position at the heart of the book to the very fringes of the book world.

Being devoid of hand-painted decoration and colour, the Renaissance book saw a new emphasis placed on the form of the text. Italy was the first country to receive the German invention of printing (two German printers set up a press in the town of Subiaco, outside Rome, in 1464), and the first to reject the Gothic types preferred by their northerly neighbours. Though the first printers in Italy were German, their customers were Italian, and many of them had firm ideas about the right kind of lettering for the books they wanted. The kind of lettering commonly wished for was a script known as humanist bookhand, or as the humanists themselves called it, *littera antiqua* ('letter of the ancients'), in contrast with the then current *littera moderna* or rotunda script.

Humanist scribes had developed their bookhand at the beginning of the century for new editions of classical texts. They had based it on a model which they believed to be ancient Roman. In fact, it was a Carolingian minuscule from the ninth century (which indeed had been influenced by the Roman half-uncial). Being a 'minuscule', the model was without a fully developed set of capitals, so the humanist scribes combined it with a set of classical capital letters. The provenance of the capital form was beyond doubt. Roman inscriptional square capitals could be seen carved on a number of ancient buildings, monuments and tombstones.

Just as humanist scholars had scoured monastery libraries for neglected classical manuscripts, so ancient monuments had been studied for examples of Roman lettering. The proportion of the letters were copied and imitated by calligraphers, painters and architects throughout the century. One of the first to make a thor-

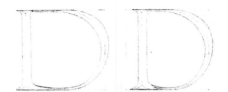

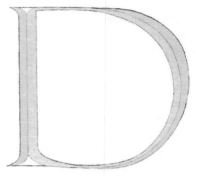

La soprascripta littera si fa a bene placito in duj modi: o vero che la pigli tutta la circonferentia o vero che 'l suo quadro si crea doue si taglia [la] linia .×. con la circonferentia, e sta bene ad ogni modo. Nota non te domenticare far tutte le littere grosse la parte . x^.

11–5 • 'Alphabetum Romanum', Felice Feliciano, Verona, 1460–3 *Courtesy of the British Library.*

ough study of Roman inscriptional lettering was the calligrapher and *antiquarius*—a student of antiquity—Felice Feliciano (1433–79) of Verona. By going back to the principles of geometrical construction that had guided Roman stonecutters during the early years of the empire, Feliciano designed an alphabet of capitals using squares and circles, which he set down in manuscript form *c.*1460–3 **(FIG. 11–5)**. Each letter of his *Alphabetum Romanum* was made in outline with an interline shading indicating the 'v'-shaped cut of inscribed Roman letters. The proportion of the letters was guided by a square, and the width of the main stem of each letter was loosely a tenth of its height, in accordance with early Roman practice. Feliciano intended his letters to serve as models for stonecutters, but his treatise also encouraged scribes and printers, during the next century especially, to investigate the effect of geometrical rules on the shape of capital letters. The influence of his treatise and others like it on printers and punch-cutters did not lead them to make shapes that were strictly proportional. The different requirements of type at different sizes didn't allow that. It was more a general sense of order that they picked up on, and perhaps too the germ of an idea that letters could be guided by criteria, geometrical or otherwise, that came from outside the physical act of carving or writing.

One of the first most complete transpositions of the humanist bookhand into roman type was a set of type made by the first non-German printer we know of, a Frenchman called Nicolas Jenson (1420–80). After learning how to print in Mainz, Jenson moved to Venice in 1467 to start his own printing workshop. He diligently sought out the best examples of incised capitals and *littera antiqua* and then adapted them so expertly that, despite his type being one of the earliest roman types, it is still regarded as one of the finest **(FIG. 11–6)**. His metal punches captured more of the sharpness of the incised capitals than the humanist scribes' had with their pen-and-ink letters. From 1470 onwards, his 'Venetian'

11-6 • Venetian type, Nicolas Jenson, Venice, 1470
Courtesy of the British Library.

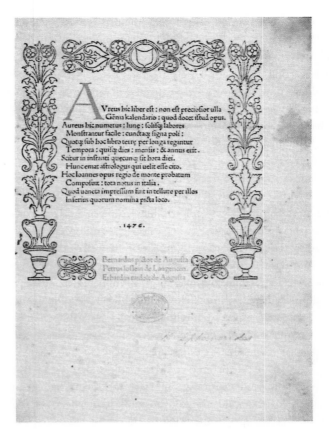

11-7 • Title page, 'Calendarium', Erhard Ratdolt, Venice, 1476
Courtesy of the British Library.

type (as all roman fonts made in Venice during this early period are known) set the standard for subsequent Venetian faces. Straight and strong, with only a slight contrast between the thick and thin strokes, the letters cohered into beautifully spaced words, which themselves combined to form soft and evenly textured lines of text. The uniformly light and spacious impression of one of Jenson's pages contrasted with the dark and dense pages of Gothic type. Within the lines of evenly spaced letters there were pleasant idiosyncrasies: the 'e' had a calligraphic diagonal slant (a defining characteristic of Venetian type), and the serifs on top of the 'M' pointed inwards as well as outwards. Jenson did not disguise the different origins of his capital and lowercase letters by melding them into a harmonious union. Relative to the lowercase letters, the capitals are wider and larger than we are used to seeing today. It appears as though the two cases are just good friends rather than husband and wife.

Despite the close proximity of Italy's first printing press to Rome, it was in Venice that the concentration of printers was greatest prior to the turn of the century. It was there too that early Italian printing was most innovative and dynamic. The first decorated title page (FIG. 11–7) was printed there in 1476 by the German printer Erhard Ratdolt (1442–1528), who had set up a press with two partners earlier in the year. The book it appeared in was a 'Calendar' written by a German author and printer referred to as Regiomontanus (a Latinized term for his home town of Königsberg, or 'Kingsmountain'). The page's distinctive woodcut decoration is of a kind more usually found on a page of text rather than a title page, which was itself a rarity at this time. The stylized outline of foliage and flowers, which extend upwards from two vases on either side of the text, is a typical Renaissance motif, as was the shield, though it was placed somewhat unconventionally at the head of the border rather than the foot. The visual tone of the outline decoration is matched by Ratdolt's roman type, and the dominance of the large initial 'A' is softened by being printed in red.

Another 'first' for this page was the content of the text. Unlike the label title page, Ratdolt's decorated version corresponded more closely to the modern title page in that it contained not only the title of the book, 'kalendario' (line 2), and the author's name, 'Ioannes opus regio de monte' (line 9), but also the year (centred below the verse), and then, in three lines along the bottom, the names of the three printers. In other ways, though, Ratdolt's design was different from a modern title page. As well as its unusual decoration, most of its text is set as a poem, some of which praises the book, much like a contemporary publisher's 'blurb'. The design also differed from those that came after it. No other decorated title page appeared before the 1490s and even after then they were rare. Ratdolt never produced another like it, but in other ways he continued to be innovative. He was the first to print mathematical figures, which appeared in 1482 in a book on Euclid's geometry, and was the first to print with gold ink, which he used in the same edition. Further innovations saw him print a type specimen sheet in 1486, the first piece of print dedicated to expounding the range of 14 type styles and sizes on offer. He was also the first to use Arabic numerals to date a book, and the first to list errata.

Ratdolt may have been the most experimental of the early Venetian printers and Jenson the first to master roman type, but the most celebrated and successful was the Italian scholar and publisher Aldus Manutius (1449/50–1515). His contribution to the Renaissance book was made through his skilful layouts, his introduction of 'italic' type and his making small-format books popular for non-religious texts. All Aldus's books were printed with types cut by a master punchcutter, Francesco Griffo of Bologna (1450–1518). Griffo's first 'Aldine' type was a roman based on Jenson's type, but with some of the calligraphic qualities removed. The letters were designed more on their own printerly terms, rather than being faithful transpositions of calligraphic and incised letters into type. It has been called the first real printed type, a so-called 'Old Style' (or 'Old Face') type (i.e. 'post-Venetian', despite its being made in Venice). The cross-stroke of the 'e' is horizontal, not slanted. The capitals are less wide and less high, smaller than the ascenders even, and consequently they blend better with the lowercase letters. The lowercase is more condensed, but in no way mean or cramped. The straighter and thinner strokes and their neater serifs emphasize the common horizontal baseline along which the letters sit, giving the whole text a more settled and orderly feel. This supreme roman became the archetypal roman form for the next 250 years.

The type first appeared in 1495 in a book called *De Aetna* ('From Etna'—the mountain in Sicily) which had been written by the Italian scholar and cardinal Pietro Bembo. In what later became one of several loose conventions that guided the naming of type and typefaces, this type was given the name Bembo, in reference to its first use. Griffo recut it soon after and used this new and many consider to be better 'Bembo' in one of Aldus's most celebrated books, *Hypnerotomachia Poliphili* ('Poliphilo's Struggle for Love in a Dream') of 1499 (FIG. 11–8). The book is not without mistakes, misprints and haphazard corrections, but the new type is set within a highly distinguished and varied typographic layout. Sections of the text are set in lines of continuous capitals which evoke some of the grandeur of ancient stone inscriptions. What they lose in legibility, by being set in such tightly leaded lines, is made up for by the beauty of the letters' shapes. Dramatic outlines of wedge-shaped blocks of text, so arranged perhaps in an effort to fill the page when the amount of text was small, sit alongside well-balanced woodcut initials. Being neither too heavy nor too light, though often astonishingly intricate, the initials could stand on their own as objects worthy of close scrutiny. The

POLIPHILO INCOMINCIA IL SECONDO LIBRO DI LA SVA HYPNEROTOMACHIA. NEL QVALE PO-LIA ET LVI DISERTABONDI, IN QVALE MODO ET VARIO CASO NARRANO INTERCALARIAMEN-TE IL SVO INAMORAMENTO.

NARRA QVIVI LA DIVA POLIA LA NOBILE ET ANTIQVA ORIGINE SVA. ET COMO PER LI PRE DE CESSORI SVI TRIVISIO FVE EDIFICATO. ET DI QVEL LA GENTE LELIA ORIVNDA. ET PER QVALE MO-DO DISAVEDVTA ET INSCIA DISCONCIAMENTE SE INAMOROE DI LEI IL SVO DILECTO POLIPHILO.

11–8 • "Hypnerotomachia Poliphili," Aldus Manutius, Venice, 1499
Courtesy of the British Library.

illustrations are made from a delicate line of an almost uniform width and then anchored within a simple but weighty double-line border. The quality of the printing—its evenness and crispness—and the quality of the paper and binding are the best available. It is said that during the first quarter of the sixteenth century this book alone was responsible for making French printers change from using Gothic types to roman ones. Though with this masterpiece completed, Aldus never again produced a fully illustrated book. Instead his attention turned to scholarly printing, an area of publishing on which his influence was to be equally profound.

Aldus's greatest commercial success came with a series of classical texts published between 1501 and 1505. A scholar and businessman as well as a printer, Aldus understood that the expanding group of reading professionals—doctors, lawyers, scientists and teachers—wanted books that not only related to their work, but which could also be carried and used easily. Whereas previous printers had issued secular books such as the Latin classics in grand folio or quarto sizes, Aldus made them in the smaller octavo size, the size of a small modern paperback, and sold them at a price that even the moderately wealthy could afford. In this way, he made it possible for readers to carry secular books alongside their Books of Hours or breviaries. They became the 'prayer books of a lay culture'. By leaving out the commentaries that usually accompanied such texts, he established a sparse but intimate style of design (just you and the text). This attribute combined with their novel and uniform size to make the series highly collectable.

The standard book sizes available to Aldus were those inherited from centuries of manuscript production. A manuscript's size was determined largely by the size of the unfolded and uncut sheets supplied by the paper maker. The largest of the three most common manuscript sizes was called 'folio' (from *folium*, the Latin for 'leaf', sometimes abbreviated to 'fo'), which was made by folding a sheet once to give four pages equivalent in size to a modern, large coffee-table book or broadsheet newspaper. The middle book size was called 'quarto' (abbreviated to 'Qto' or '4to'), which was a quarter of the sheet size. This was made by folding the sheet twice, with the second fold at right angles to the first, to give eight pages, which were each roughly the size of a sheet of A4 paper. The smallest common book size, 'octavo' ('8vo'), an eighth the size of the sheet, was made by folding three times to give 16 pages of a size that was equivalent to a standard hardback novel. Some miniature books went down to a twelfth ('12mo' from 'duodecimo'), a sixteenth ('16mo' from 'sextodecimo'), a thirty-second ('32mo' from 'tricesimo-secundo'), or even a sixty-fourth size ('64mo' from 'sexagesimo-quarto'). Beyond this they rarely went. There appears to be a physical limit as to how many times a piece of paper can be folded. More than five times ('32mo') is very difficult, and beyond seven is apparently impossible, irrespective of how large and thin the paper is.

What had not become standardized was the size of the initial sheet. Thus one octavo book might be somewhat smaller or larger than another, depending on who had made the paper. Sheets supplied by Italian paper makers generally came in two sizes, one referred to as Royal (70 × 50cm or 28 × 20in) and the other as Median (50 × 30cm or 20 × 12in), but paper makers in Venice, for example, tended to supply a slightly larger sheet referred to as Super-Royal or Super-Median. Confusing matters further was that most pages needed to be trimmed after the sheet had been folded, so as to remove the folds (or 'bolts' as they are known) along one of the edges, which otherwise prevented the pages from being turned. Not all binders trimmed the pages by the same amount, so the conventional way of describing a book's size, by stating the sheet size (i.e. 'Royal' or 'Median') and then the number of times the sheet was folded (i.e. 'folio', 'quarto', etc.) could only ever be suggestive of a book's size. Aldus's scholarly series, for example, was 'Median octavo', that is to say roughly the size of an adult's hand, but clearly that's not the same as saying they were 15.4 × 8.7cm (6⅛ × 3⅜in), which is their precise size. (In printing, unlike Cartesian co-ordinates and map references, the vertical measurement usually precedes the horizontal.)

The appeal of Aldus's portable octavos was added to by their new style of type. They were set with one of the very first italic types: a set of sloping calligraphic letters whose shapes were based on a popular cursive script which an earlier generation of humanists had developed for copying out classical texts. It has been thought that Aldus adopted this cursive humanist script as a space-saving device, but not only is there no quote or comment that supports this supposition, when the text is set in the same size of his roman type it does not increase in length. What is more certain is that his books benefited from the popularity of the humanist script, which was held as a model for handwriting among educated and literate Italians.

Aldus's use of italic type was not restricted to marking emphases or titles of books or paintings, as italic is today. Nor was it applied to both upper and lowercase letters. In accordance with the humanist model, his capitals remained upright. A page from the first Aldine octavo, an edition of verse by the classical Roman poet Virgil **(FIG. 11–9)**, shows how the letters were not always evenly sloped—the 'c' slopes forward while the 'g' almost leans backward—and thus the lines of text were rather unevenly spaced. This unevenness was added to by the large number of combined letters or 'ligatures' that Aldus included in his range of type. This one spread alone has something like 130 of them (today, the same text set in a standard typeface would have no more than a handful: the odd combination of 'ff', 'fi' or 'fl'). To the modern reader, whose eyes are used to a more regular array of letters, the Aldine italic is not an easy read, but it bears close scrutiny—some of the ligatures, 'ct' for example, are beautifully combined. On publication Aldus's type was seen to have taken typographic elegance to a new height. In Italy it quickly gained an equal status with roman. During the first quarter of the sixteenth century, as many Italian books were printed in italic type (though still with more or less upright capitals) as in roman. As other parts of the Continent came to know of Aldus's new type, so italic ('of Italy') type came to replace roman as the type associated with classicism. Decades later books across Europe were being set in imitations of the Aldine italic.

The impact of printing on the livelihood of the scribe was not wholly negative. The production of cheaper reading material led to an increase in the number of readers, which in turn increased the demand for lessons in writing. Not just learning how to write, but also to develop a beautiful and mature handwriting. In the higher echelons of the expanding class of literates, good handwriting was seen as an important accomplishment. It was a marker of one's social standing. So as well as serving the traditional need for handwritten text in chanceries and in business and legal offices, scribes found work as writing masters. To advertise their expertise as well as provide models for readers to emulate, they published writing books showing samples of their scripts. Three well-known and influential Italian examples are the books by Ludovico Arrighi (1475–1527), Giovanni Palatino (c.1515–c.1575) and Giovantonio Tagliente (1465/70–after 1527). Each was a master, figuratively as well as literally (though Arrighi is often referred to as a writing master, it is not certain that he ever did teach).

The earliest of the three manuals was written by Arrighi and published in about 1522. His *La Operina da Imparare di scriuere littera Cancellarescha* ('A Learning Guide to Writing the Chancery Letter', **FIG. 11–10**) was only a little book of 32 pages, though like

PHARMACEVTRIA.

T erna tibi hæc primum triplici diuersa colore
L icia circundo, terq; hæc altaria circum'
E ffigiem duco, numero Deus impare gaudet·
   Ducite ab urbe domū mea carmia, ducite Daphnim·
N ecte tribus nodis ternos Amarylli colores,
N ecte Amarylli modo, et Veneris dic uincula necto.
   Ducite ab urbe domū mea carmia, ducite Daphnim·
L inus ut hic durescit, et hæc ut cæra liquescit,
V no, eodemq; igni, sic nostro Daphnis amore.
S parge mola, et fragiles incende bitumine lauros·
D aphnis me malus urit, ego hanc i Daphnide laurū·
   Ducite ab urbe domū mea carmia, ducite Daphnim·
T alis amor Daphnin, qualis cum fessa iuuencam
P er nemora, atq; altos quærendo bucula lucos
P ropter aquæ riuum uiridi procumbit in herba
P erdita, nec seræ meminit decedere nocti,
T alis amor teneat, nec sit mihi cura mederi.
   Ducite ab urbe domū mea carmia, ducite Daphnim·
H as olim exuuias mihi perfidus ille reliquit
P ignora cara sui, quæ nunc ego limine in ipso
T erra tibi mando, debent hæc pignora Daphnin·
   Ducite ab urbe domū mea carmia, ducite Daphnim·
H as herbas, atq; hæc ponto mihi lecta uenena,
I pse dedit Mœris, nascuntur plurima ponto.
H is ego sæpe lupum fieri, et se condere syluis
M œrim, sæpe animas imis excire sepulchris,
A tq; satas alio uidi traducere messes.
   Ducite ab urbe domū mea carmia, ducite Daphnim·
F er cineres Amarylli foras, riuoq; fluenti
T ransq; caput iace, ne respexeris, his ego Daphnim.

OCTAVA·

A ggrediar, nihil ille deos, nil carmina curat·
   Ducite ab urbe domū mea carmina, ducite Daphnim.
A spice, corripuit tremulis altaria flammis
S ponte sua, dum ferre moror, cinis ipse, bonum sit.
M escio quid certe est, et Hylas in limine latrat.
C redimus, an qui amant, ipsi sibi somnia fingunt?
   Parcite, ab urbe uenit, ia parcite carmina Daphnis.

ECLOGA·IX. MOERIS.

   Lycidas.   Mœris.

Q Vo te Mœri pedes? an quo uia ducit in urbem?
O Lycida uiui peruenimus, aduena nostri   M.
Q uod nūquā ueriti sumus, ut possessor agelli
D iceret, hæc mea sunt, ueteres migrate coloni.
N unc uicti tristes, quoniam sors omnia uersat.
H os illi (quod nec bene uertat) mittimus hædos.
C erte equidem audierā, qua se subducere colles Ly·
I ncipiunt, molliq; iugum demittere cliuo,
V sque ad aquam, et ueteris iam fracta cacumina fagi
O mnia carminibus uestrum seruasse Menalcam·
A udieras, et fama fuit, sed carmina tantum   Mœ.
N ostra ualent Lycida tela inter Martia, quantum
C haonias dicunt aquila ueniente columbas.
Q uod nisi me quacunq; nouas incidere lites ·
A nte sinistra caua monuisset ab ilice cornix,
N ec tuus hic Mœris, nec uiueret ipse Menalcas.
H eu cadit in quenquā tantū scelus? heu tua nobis Ly·
P ene simul tecum solatia rapta Menalca·
Q uis caneret nymphas, quis humū florentibus herbis

11–9 • 'Opera' of Virgil, Aldus Manutius, Venice, 1501
Courtesy of the British Library.

the other two, it is not quite what it seems. His flowing calligraphic scripts were actually printed letters which had been cut into a woodblock by an engraver with a gouging tool. Despite this different method of shape making and the fact that the letters had had to be cut in reverse, they carry something of the calligraphic verve of the original pen and ink forms. As the title indicates, the model put forward by Arrighi was the script used in the papal office, or chancery, at the Vatican, where he worked as a scribe. This *cancellarescha corsiva* or 'Chancery cursive' was a stately, more decorative version of the humanist cursive that had guided Aldus's italics. Arrighi's upright roman capitals are distinguished by a set of variant 'swash' forms with exuberantly flourishing tails, and although these carved flourishes look a little static, they indicate the potential for expression that exists within a practised pen hand. The shape of Arrighi's cursive small-letters, at the bottom of

11–10 • Writing manual, Ludovico Arrighi, Rome, 1522
Courtesy of the British Library.

11–11 • Writing manual, Giovanni Palatino, Rome 1561
Courtesy of the British Library.

11–12 • Ornate Gothic letter, Paulus Franck, Germany, 1601
Courtesy of the Getty Research Institute.

the page, are only slightly inclined, yet they make a stark contrast with the upright capitals. Most of the ascenders and descenders have rounded billowing tails, which tip backwards on the down stroke and forwards on the up.

Where Arrighi's manual is a model of concentrated utility, with its clear and intimate instruction ('dear reader' was his mode of address), Palatino's is an exhibition in variety (**FIG. 11–11**). Vastly more wide-ranging, it comes closer to the modern type-specimen book in that it contains not only Palatino's version of the Chancery script, but a plethora of letter styles of the Latin alphabet and, indeed, 'every sort of ancient and modern letters of all nations': Arabic, Cyrillic and others. More influential than either Palatino's or Arrighi's though was Tagliente's writing manual. First published in 1524, it was reprinted in various editions until 1678. His own Chancery cursive is less expert than those of his compatriots, but the range of commercial scripts he provided and the more detailed instruction he gave contributed to the book's success. Many of his manual's historical and regional scripts have an angular bias, which might explain why his version of Chancery found favour in northern Europe, where the more angular Gothic letter was common.

The display of mastery between rival scribes created an inflationary pressure to outdo what had gone before. In northern Europe this pressure was directed towards an extreme form of decoration that rendered the letter all but illegible (**FIG. 11–12**). The initial spur to this superabundance of decoration was a frac-

tured form of Gothic letter or 'Fraktur', made with a number of individual letter strokes rather than a few joined-up ones. In some instances the separate nature of the strokes was visible. Some barely touched their adjacent strokes (a sense of this is given in Tagliente's page of Gothic letters). The extent to which an elaborate decoration could be built onto the separate strokes of a letter is shown in this late example of the letter 'F' (FIG. 11–12) from a series of capital initials that were penned by the German scribe Paulus Franck (*c.*1550–*c.*1610) in 1601. The rhythmical flourishes are organized into a series of contrasts: between thick and thin lines, parallel strokes and convergent ones, and between dense thickets of interlacing and light diaphanous swirls. The whole is suffused with an unbridled sense of exuberance, as though Franck was exulting in his mastery of the form. His extraordinary control and inventiveness were honed during his work as a chancery scribe, where a tradition of embellishing documents had been established. The skilful display of initial letters in particular was seen as proof of the document's prestige and authority.

In Italy the significance of classical models rather than recent home-grown traditions was demonstrated by the success of a treatise on architecture called *I Quattro Libri dell'Architettura* ('The Four Books of Architecture', **FIG. 11–13**). It was written by the Italian architect Andrea Palladio (1508–80) and first published in 1570, though its popularity led it to be reprinted frequently and,

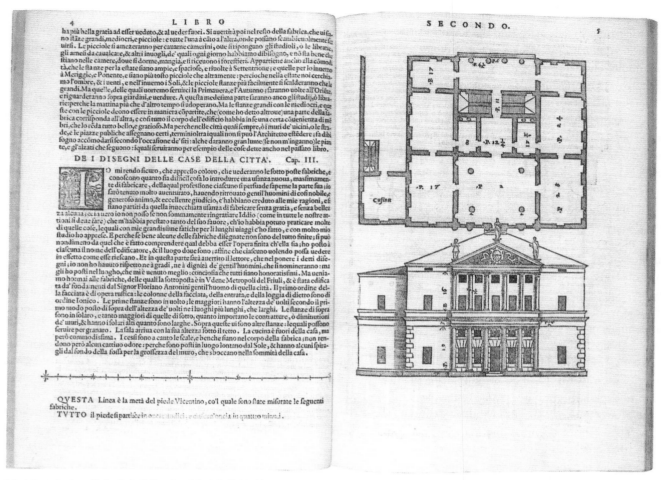

11–13 • Andrea Palladio's 'I Quattro Libri dell' Architettura', Venice, 1570
Courtesy of the British Library.

indeed, it remains in print today. The book made Palladio famous and helped to define a style of architecture that bore his name, 'Palladian'. The style went on to influence the development of architecture across northern Europe, and later in North America. In the early nineteenth century, Thomas Jefferson, a some-time architect as well as a statesman, referred to Palladio's 'Four Books' as 'the Bible'.

Palladio's book was both a visual display of classical Roman architecture and a practical guide to building in the classical style. It was illustrated with a series of large schematic woodcuts, made from his own drawings, which filled out at least a page on almost every spread. The woodcuts' simple lines showed plans and elevations of ancient buildings reconstructed as Palladio imagined they might have looked when first built. Also shown were new buildings that he had designed according to classical principles. Country houses, town houses, a monastery and even bridges were styled with pillars, capitals, arches, friezes and a panoply of attendant classical features.

The success of 'The Four Books' was founded on a combination of Palladio's clear and concise writing and the close correspondence of the writing with his illustrations. This clear and orderly fusion allowed readers to come away with a detailed understanding of the principles and methods of classical architecture. Palladio's own knowledge of classical forms had been guided by two important texts, one by the ancient Roman architect Vitruvius and the other by a fifteenth-century disciple of Vitruvius, Leon Battista Alberti. Both led Palladio to base his designs on mathematical proportions rather than the rich ornamental style that had characterized much early Renaissance architecture.

An important element in his explanation of the mathematical proportions behind his buildings was the printing of his unit of measure (which appears in the example above). Palladio was 'aware that units of measurement differ just as cities and regions do'—at that time the Venetian foot, for example, was different from the Vicentine foot (used in his home town of Vicenza)—but by actually printing his unit of measure readers were provided with a fixed point of reference. They could know the precise scale that Palladio was working on, and if they so wished, they could make the necessary adjustments when applying his designs to their own local unit of measure. (The text below the line says: 'This line, with which the following buildings have been measured, is half a Vicentine foot. The foot is divided into 12 inches, and each inch into four minutes.')

Most of the characteristics that defined this early period in graphic design were things made with ink: the formal clarity of the layout, the near monochrome palette and the rounded type. But there was another characteristic, equally visible though generally unnoticed. It was the unprinted, white parts of the page. Just as a sound is best heard against a background of silence, so the beauty of Renaissance printing relied on a neutral and uncluttered surround. The right amount of space between the lines of text, between the words in those lines, between the letters in the words, and even within the enclosed parts of the letters themselves, presented the reader with an inviting block of evenly textured lines. The printers of fine books had become more aware of the importance of the unprinted parts of the page when determining the best placement of printed matter. By making subtle differences in the widths of the margins they were able to hold the text within a balanced frame. Furthermore, their harmonious margins helped to express the pleasing proportions of their choice of format. In these ways, the unprinted parts of the Renaissance page were as eloquent of the book's style as any of the features that were made with ink.

In Italy, where an established craft tradition of paper making provided printers with some of the finest printing material, there was an incentive to exploit this resource. Some of the elegance of Aldus's series of octavo books comes from the large amount of unprinted paper. The effect of openness and lightness that could be created was further enhanced by the printers' restricted use of different sizes and styles of type. Cutting and casting a new style of type was expensive. Unlike today, where a single design can be scaled up or down automatically, printing with type required every character of every size of a particular style to be made piece by piece. The time and resources required to make a new size of type in the same style differed little from making a single size of a new style. In both cases a whole new set of types needed to be cut and cast. For this reason, the print in many Italian Renaissance books was restricted to just two sizes of a single style (usually one size for the heading and the other for the main text). Though this did not create any more white space, it did make the page look less cluttered.

The six so-called 'Italian' wars of the late fifteenth to mid-sixteenth centuries saw Rome sacked by an unpaid army of mercenaries, the collapse of Italy's system of city republics and eventually led to the Spanish domination of large parts of the peninsula. With Spanish support the Roman Church was able to centralize its power. It introduced a series of political and social reforms with a degree of control and devotional intensity that came to characterize the Counter-Reformation. The effect on printing was to make the publication of classical texts potentially heretical. An 'Index' or list of prohibited books was introduced in 1557 and regularly updated thereafter (it was only withdrawn in 1967). Italian publishers responded by selling cheap reprints of old best-sellers or traditional religious texts rather than fine editions of scholarly literature. The trend towards mass production that had

been established by printing and the concomitant demand for cheap books furthered the decline in the standards of book production in Italy. Types were poorly designed, words were crammed onto the page, and the quality of illustration deteriorated.

It was during this same period, the first half of the sixteenth century, that the influence of the Italian Renaissance book took hold in France. It was an influence that was encouraged by an unparalleled degree of royal patronage from a succession of monarchs whose fondness for classicism was matched by a desire to harness the power of the printed word. The greatest royal patron was Francis I, who, through his appointment of Geoffroy Tory (c.1480–1533) as *imprimeur du roi*, or 'printer to the king', in 1531, established a centralizing trend that was to dominate printing in France for the next 200 years. Tory, a scholar, teacher and illustrator as well as a printer, brought the Italian book to the attention of Parisian printers. They and others, in Lyon especially, introduced a lightness and orderliness to the French Renaissance book. Such books became admired throughout Europe.

From around 1540, roman types began to replace the Gothic ones that printers in France had relied on since the first press was established in that country in 1470. The style of these new types was dominated by a version created by the Parisian punch-cutter Claude Garamont, or Garamond (c.1510–61) (as a French spelling reform had led him to spell it). Unlike other cutters, Garamond was rarely side-tracked into other aspects of printing. He devoted most of his time to refining his types, and in particular the version of roman he first cut in 1530, which had been based on the heavier Aldine roman. A notable accompaniment to the roman was his new italic type. Unlike the pages of earlier Italian books, the two appear side by side **(FIG. 11–14)**. French printers had begun to mix italic and roman in this way during the 1540s. They had been encouraged to do so by the appearance of a more fluent and legible italic which broke from the Chancery tradition in that it had sloped rather than upright capitals. This new form is thought to have first come from the hand of Garamond in about 1539,

LE CINQIE
LIVRE DE THVC:
Comme les Atheniens
duyte de Cleon prindrent la cité d,
les Peloponefiens. Et d'vng voyage
ax Athenien en Italie & en Sicil,
Chapitre   I.

11-14 • Roman and italic type, Claude Garamond, 1545
Courtesy of the British Library.

11–15 • Geneva Bible, printed by Robert Estienne, 1553
Courtesy of the British Library.

though it was closely followed by a similar but more legible version cut by his compatriot Robert Granjon (1513–90). The evenness of slope in Granjon's letters set it apart. Yet its slope and the general form of its letters was still not of a kind that allowed the type to sit comfortably within a line of roman text. Italics designed to accompany a specific roman only began to appear after 1600.

Over a period of about 20 years, the brilliance of Garamond's types encouraged many imitators, so that by the time of his death in 1561 his style of type had appeared in all the main printing regions of Europe. Versions of it even ousted the Aldine roman from Italy. The fact that Latin was still the international language of scholarship is likely to have helped it become so popular. The pan-European trade of Latin books would have benefited from the existence of a universally accepted style of letter rather than a variety of regional styles.

The quality of these types was sometimes matched by the excellence of the printers who used them. Such printers created a graphic style that was more rigorously ordered and functional than any previous layout. A sign of this more ordered approach to text can be seen in a Bible produced by the Parisian printer Robert Estienne (1503–59) in 1553 **(FIG. 11–15)**. It was printed in Geneva, to where Estienne had had to move in order to escape

religious persecution. Though the design is undistinguished by the awkward spacing of the text, it is notable for being the first Bible to have its text divided into numbered verses. But the verses are not only numbered, they are also laid out as separate paragraphs with an exaggerated indent.

The functional nature of the book's typography gives an impression of stolid utility. The books of the Lyonnais scholar-printer Jean de Tournes (1504–64), though no less functional, demonstrate a light and polished harmony. In his edition of Jean Froissart's *Chroniques*, or 'Chronicles' **(FIG. 11–16)**, which he printed in 1559, the careful placement and weight of the printed forms makes them beautiful as well as useful. The large type at the top stands out as an introduction to the main text below. In doing so, it reveals the masterly shape of Garamond's letterforms. The thin column of Granjon's italic is a perfectly placed supplement to the block of roman text beside it. The column neither disrupts the block of main text by being too close to it, nor does it float in the margin. The italic's interline spacing, or 'leading' (so called because of the thin strips of lead that were used to separate the lines of type), is generous enough to allow the beauty of the vigorous flourishes to be expressed. In the floriated headband (the top bar of swirling floral patterns) and the wood-engraved decorative initial, cut in the *manière criblée* style (characterized by white dots on a black background), form and function are again united: both are exquisite decorations, but equally they serve as typographic signposts to aid the reader when he or she scans the pages in search of the beginning of the book.

It is no small achievement to make typographic elements that are beautiful and useful, but what really distinguishes the art of the French Renaissance book are the waves of harmonic rhythms that are set in motion by the judicious placement of the beautiful and useful within the workaday setting of a page. In de Tournes' page, there is a harmony that comes from the match between the height of the white initial 'A' and the height of the white space above, on which the largest type sits. There is the same feeling of unity between the sequence of forms running down the page—decoration (headband), large text, small text—and the sequence that runs across it—decoration (initial), large text (main text), small text (italic). And there is a similar accord between the height of the headband and the width of the column of italic. There are many other subtle harmonies besides.

The precision and detail available to a printed design, as opposed to one set down by hand in a manuscript, made it possible to create more firmly and finely graded hierarchies of type and image. The printerly combination of precision and subtlety applied not only to the pages of books but also to the less literary, more diagrammatic discipline of cartography. Printing made it possible to describe the earth's land-masses more faithfully. What it could not do is resolve the difficulty that all world maps had to contend with, the problem of turning the spherical surface of the earth into an image on a flat page. The same sort of problem had been encountered by printers of books on the important mathematical discipline of three-dimensional geometry. There was no easy way of depicting the sorts of geometrical objects that had been discussed by ancient mathematicians—spheres, cones, pyramids and cylinders—on the two-dimensional surface of a printed page. A laborious but otherwise effective solution to this problem appeared in the first English translation of Euclid's *Elements* (FIG. 11–17), printed in London in 1570 by the British printer John Day (1522–1584). He used geometric shapes made out of pasted flaps of paper that could be folded up into three-dimensional models, as in a 'pop-up' book. It is one of the earliest known books of this kind.

An accurate depiction of the world was not always the aim of map makers. The first, printed, world map was a copy of a T-O (or O-T) map (FIG. 11–18), which had been the common form in manuscripts of the Middle Ages. Its schematic arrangement was never meant to show the extent of geographical knowledge at that time and certainly not at the time the T-O map was first printed in 1475. Like the scribes who had devised it, the readers who read it knew it to be a symbolic representation rather than a faithful depiction of the topographical features of the Earth's surface. The symbolism was Christian. It reminded the reader that God had created a world around His chosen land Jerusalem at the junction of Europe, Africa and Asia. The shape formed by the 'T' recalled the Christian symbol of the crucifix, which signified the sacrifice that Christ had made for the salvation of

Cy commence le Prologue de messire Iehan Froissart, sur les Croniques de France & d'Angleterre, & autres lieux voisins.

✻

A FIN que les honnorables emprises & nobles auētures & faicts-d'armes, par les guerres de France & d'Angleterre, soyent notablement enregistrés & mis en memoire perpetuel, parquoy les preux ayent exemple d'eux encourager en bien faisant, ie vueil traicter & recorder Histoire de grand'louenge. Mais-auant que ie la commence, ie requier au Sauueur de tout le monde, qui de neant crea toutes choses, qu'il vueille creer & mettre en moy sens & entendement si vertueux, que ie puisse continuer & perseuerer en telle maniere que tous ceux & celles, qui le lirōt, verront, & orront, y puissent prendre ebatement & exemple, & moy encheoir en leur grâce.

On dit, & il est vray, que tous edifices sont massonnés & ouurés de plusieurs sortes de pierres, & toutes grosses riuieres sont faictes & rassemblees de plusieurs surgeons. Aussi les sciences sont extraictes & compilees de plusieurs Clercs : & ce, que l'un sçet, l'autre l'ignore. Non-pourtant rien n'est, qui ne soit sçeu, ou loing ou pres.

Donc, pour attaindre à la matiere que i'ay emprise, ie vueil commencer premierement par la grâce de Dieu & de la benoiste vierge Marie (dont tout confort & auancement viennent) & me vueil fonder & ordonner sur les vrayes Croniques, iadis faictes par reuerend homme, discret & sage, monseigneur maistre Iehan le Bel, Chanoine de Sainct-Lambert du Liege: qui grand'cure & toute bonne diligēce meit en ceste matiere, & la continua tout son viuant au plus iustement qu'il peut; & moule luy cousta à la querre & à l'auoir: mais, quelques fraiz qu'il y fist, riens ne les plaignit. car il estoit riche & puissant (si le pouuoit bien porter) & estoit de soy-mesme large, honorable, & courtois: & voulontiers voyoit le sien despendre. Aussi il fut en son viuant moult aimé & secret à monseigneur messire Iehan de Haynaut: qui bien est ramenteu, & de raison, en ce liure. car de moult belles & nobles aduenues fut il chef & cause, & des Roys moult prochain. parquoy le dessusdit messire Iehan le Bel peut delez luy veoir plusieurs nobles besongnes: lesquelles sont contenues cy-apres. Vray est que ie, qui ay empris ce liure à ordonner, ay par plaisance, qui à ce m'a tousiours encliné, frequenté plusieurs nobles & grans Seigneurs, tant en Frāce qu'en Angleterre, en Escoce, & en plusieurs autres païs: & en ay eu la congnoissance d'eux: & ay tousiours, à mon pouuoir, iustement enquis & demandé du faict des guerres & des auentures, & par especial depuis la grosse bataille de Poitiers, ou le noble Roy Iehan de France fut pris.† car deuāt iestoye encores moult ieune de sens & d'aage. Nonobstant si empris ie assez hardiment, moy issu de l'escole, à dicter & à ordonner les guerres dessusdites, & porter en Angleterre le liure tout compilé : si-comme ie fei, & le presentay adonc à Ma-dame Philippe de Haynaut, Royne d'Angleterre : qui liement & doucement le receut de moy, & m'en fit grand profit. Et peut estre que ce liure n'est

a   mie

De qui Froissart a pris la presente Histoire.

†De quel temps estoit Froissart, sur quoy faut noter qu'il ne porta que partie de ce premier Volume à la Royne Philippe. car vous verrez qu'il racomptera la mort d'icelle, selon l'ordre des temps, en cedit premier & present Volume.

11-16 • Jean Froissart's 'Chroniques', printed by Jean de Tournes, Lyons, 1559
Courtesy of the British Library.

all mankind, hence its placement on an encircling, globe-like 'O'. The three continents of Europe, Africa and Asia are usually shown with Europe on the left, Africa on the right and Asia uppermost (a scheme that led us to derive the word 'orientation' from 'Orient'). This print shows no fine grading within a complex visual hierarchy. That could only happen when maps had developed a more refined cartographic scheme. An important step in this direction was taken with the reintroduction into Europe of a

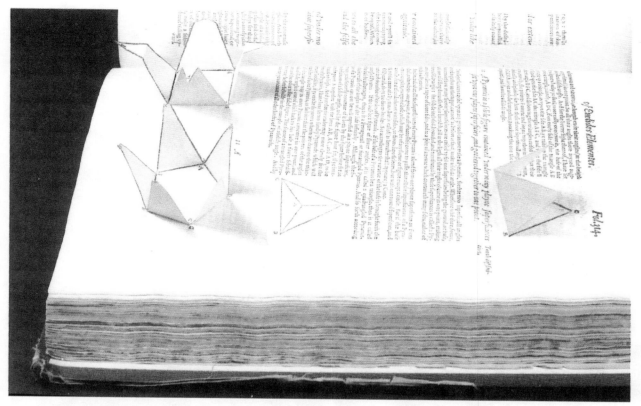

11–17 • Euclid's 'Elements' printed by John Day, London, 1570
Courtesy of the British Library.

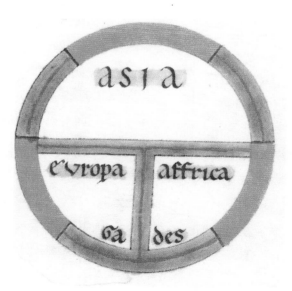

11–18 • T-O map, manuscript, early thirteenth century
Courtesy of the British Library.

second-century text called *Geographia* or 'Geography'. It had been written by the Greek astronomer and mathematician Ptolemy (AD 90–168), who had devised a method for preparing a world map using fixed co-ordinates plotted along lines of latitude and longitude. Though Ptolemy's text had been seen by some in the Near and Middle East, it was never widely known. In 1406, a Latin translation was made which allowed Europeans to follow his

instructions. The resultant map was printed in book form first in Italy in 1477—it was one of the first books to use engraved illustrations—and then subsequently, alongside the initial text, both in Italy (**FIG. 11–19**) and Germany. It was only through printing the map that the mathematical basis of Ptolemy's projection could be appreciated. While the extent of the knowledge of the world's land masses during the time of the Roman Empire was shown to be limited, Ptolemy's way of ordering space in two dimensions allowed others to start filling in the contours in ever greater detail.

Printing not only helped to make Ptolemy's projection more widely known, it also established a more mathematical approach to the whole field of cartography. The world map of 1507 by the German cartographer Martin Waldseemüller (*c.*1470–*c.*1518) (**FIG. 11–20**) shows the fruits of this new approach. Being the very first to extend Ptolemy's projection of longitude to 360° (though the north–south extent is incomplete), it presented a whole new vision of the world. It also has the distinction of being the first map to show the New World with its current name: 'America'. Waldseemüller added the name in honour of the Italian explorer Amerigo Vespucci, who had travelled across the Atlantic soon after Columbus. Whereas Columbus had not realized what he had discovered—he thought the islands he had arrived at were part of Asia, hence the name the West Indies—Vespucci recognized the continent as something new. (The contact made by Vikings and others had never brought it to the attention of Europeans as a whole.)

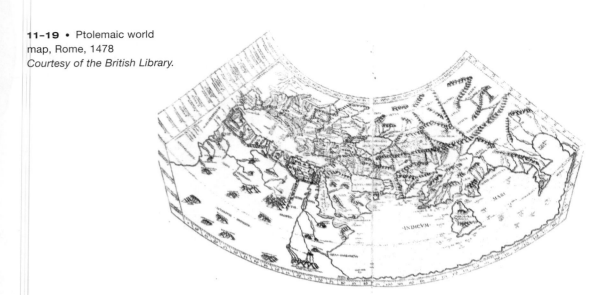

11–19 • Ptolemaic world
map, Rome, 1478
Courtesy of the British Library.

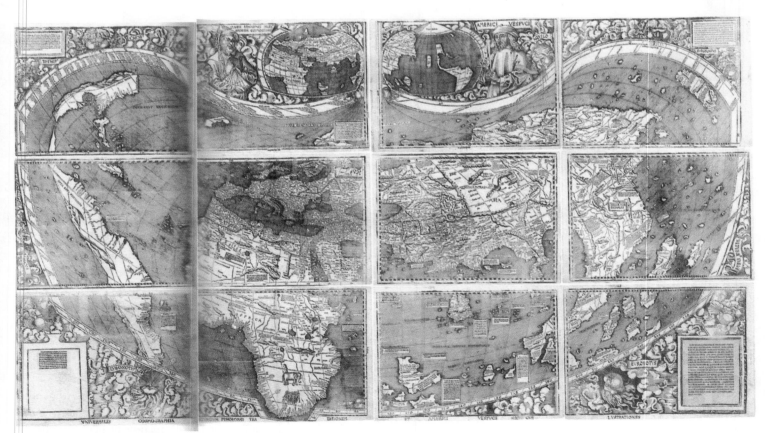

11–20 • World map, Martin Waldseemüller, Germany, 1507
Courtesy of the Library of Congress.

The quantity of detail in Waldseemüller's map was printed from 12 separate woodblocks which when printed amounted to an area almost 1.25m (4ft 1in) high and 2.5m (8ft 2in) wide. It was thus one of the first maps not to be bound in a book (no format could have contained a map so large without it being extensively folded). The detailed information in Waldseemüller's map adds depth to the large expanse of flat paper. There is a simple hierarchy between the important lines of latitude—the equator and the two tropics—and the lesser lines of latitude and longitude. There is a further hierarchy in the extensive labelling and the panels of descriptive text. Such descriptions of the topography, customs and history of various regions were a common feature of early printed maps. The map also contains a miscellany of places, objects and events: continents delineated by a fine shading, a legion of disparate place names, regional and colonial flags, mountain ranges, rivers, fish, an African elephant, and Vespucci sailing the Atlantic while being buffeted by the puff-cheeked Winds of classical mythology. In the top part of the map and towards the right, Waldseemüller showed Vespucci standing next to the New World, and had him looking across to Ptolemy, who stands next to the old one.

During the latter half of the sixteenth century, the centre of map publishing moved northwards to what is now the Netherlands. The seafaring prowess of this small north European republic, as it came to be in 1581, enabled the Dutch (for this time an inexact but convenient label) to seek out and successfully exploit new trading opportunities overseas. By establishing a vast trading empire in Asia, they were able to control the lucrative European spice trade. The unexpected levels of wealth that flowed into their young country throughout the seventeenth century resulted in a blossoming of culture known as the Dutch Golden Age. The republic became one of the world's most powerful nations and its coastal capital, Amsterdam, became the centre of international trade and finance. Untrammelled by monarchy or an established state church, Dutch society enjoyed a relative degree of intellectual freedom (from which the philosophers Descartes and Spinoza both benefited). This form of liberty combined with the country's newfound wealth to stimulate a huge growth in printing and publishing. By the end of the seventeenth century, the Dutch could claim to have published more books in the previous 100 years than all the other countries put together.

POPULAR PUBLISHING

Dutch Renaissance & Popular Prints, c.1530–c.1700

During the sixteenth century, the focus of the world's commercial power shifted northward from the Mediterranean towards the Atlantic. The coastal city of Antwerp, though only a relatively small regional capital, became both the centre of banking and trade as well as an important cultural hub. By the second half of the century, it had replaced Paris as the centre of the book trade. Among the foreigners who travelled to the city to find work in the burgeoning and, most importantly, more liberal publishing industry was the Frenchman, Christopher Plantin (c. 1520–89). In spite of the waves of religious and political conflict that swept through the region throughout the century, Plantin succeeded in founding a printing and publishing dynasty unrivalled in size and scope. By remaining at the forefront of the industry for 200 years, his successors became the wealthiest family in the whole of the southern Netherlands.

Though the 'Officina Plantiniana' was hardly a typical printing office of the late sixteenth century, its influence makes it important. Its size and completeness also provides u[...] of how involved print production had become by t[...] the facilities required to turn a block of lead into a [...] came to be located within the walls of its rambling R[...] buildings (now housing the Plantin-Moretus Muse....ii). The Officina housed a type foundry (installed post-Christopher Plantin), a type store in which 22 tonnes of roman, italic and Gothic type as well as Greek, Hebrew and musical lead type were kept, a printing workshop where the printing itself took place, a corrector's room where the proofs were edited, a library for proofreaders to use when checking the text, a bookshop where some of the books were sold, various sundry offices as well as the family's living quarters. At its height, it employed over 20 presses and a workforce some 70 strong. Plantin and his successors turned what had been, and for many still was, a handcraft into a complete industry.

Plantin himself published an average of 55 works each year, a huge number at that time. But because his books were aimed at an international elite of scholars and students the number of copies of any work was never large. His bestsellers, mostly classical texts published for schools, sold around 2500 copies, while the steady sellers sold half as many, and a then more select range of scientific books between 600 and 800. About a third of his output was religious texts, but it was the humanist and science books within the larger section of secular texts that cemented his reputation as a progressive publisher.

The range of types needed to service this varied output is indicated by Plantin's type specimen of 1585 (FIG. 11–21). Like other printers, or indeed typefounders, Plantin made a series of specimens to show potential clients the range of typefaces available. Though the example here was bound in book form, printers also produced specimens as leaflets or even on single sheets. Unlike many of his contemporaries, Plantin was keen to use the best types he could find. Rather than relying on those supplied by the handful of specialized type foundries throughout the southern Netherlands, he carefully sought out the finest punches and matrices from across Europe. In time, he was able to boast the largest collection of punches and matrices of any printer.

The sections of Latin text within his specimen are set in various kinds of roman type mostly based on the letterform made popular by Garamond. (Plantin had bought some of Garamond's punches, matrices and moulds from the sale of the deceased punch cutter's effects in 1563.) They are accompanied by some of Grandjean's italics, and both would have been used mainly in secular texts, while Gothic types would have mainly served religious texts.

Sometimes it was necessary for Plantin to combine a range of types within a single publication. One such was a large multi-language Bible known variously as the 'Antwerp Polyglot' (FIG. 11–22)—'polyglot' meaning 'many tongues'—or the *Biblia Regia* ('King's Bible') on account of its being issued under the auspices of the Spanish king, Philip II. Each of its eight volumes was

11-22 • Polyglot Bible, printed by Christopher Plantin, Antwerp, 1569–73
Courtesy of the British Library.

published in a large folio format and together they contained text set in five different languages. The spread from the Old Testament shown here has a left-hand page with Hebrew text alongside a standard Latin translation (Vulgate), while the right-hand page had a standard Greek version (Septuagint) of the same text accompanied by its Latin translation. Running across the bottom is the text paraphrased in an ancient form of Aramaic (Chaldean), which clarified certain portions of the Hebrew text, followed by its Latin translation. (The fifth language, Syriac, was used instead of the Aramaic in the New Testament.) The order of languages—the Hebraic followed by the Greek then Latin—possibly reflects the special emphasis then being placed on the earliest sources of scripture. Plantin completed his Polyglot Bible in quick time between 1569 (the year in which the typesetting was started) and 1572/3, and though the process nearly left him bankrupt the book secured his reputation as the grandest printer of his age.

The orderly arrangement of such a complex layout, with its different languages, scripts and styles of type, each divided by the appropriate verse numbers and separated by simple unadorned rules, shows the new level of sophistication in layout that had been reached by the best printers at this time (a comparison with the first printing of Bible verses, (FIG. 11–15, P. 665), makes this clear). Plantin's organized pages made it easier for scholars to make a detailed study of the text of the Bible. Such scrutiny went to the heart of the division between Protestants and Catholics, who each claimed to have a true understanding of the scriptures.

This kind of complex content and orderly layout gave an impetus to textual criticism and knowledge acquisition which extended far beyond the realm of biblical scholarship. Both activities were founded on an essential feature of the printed book: that of the edition. Because the printing process allowed texts to be duplicated identically—the same words appearing in the same order, size, style of lettering and position on a page—it conferred onto books a new authority. Readers were more inclined to look on a printed text as the unadulterated voice of the writer. The hand of the scribe had not been allowed to come between the writer's voice and the reader's eye. Readers could make judgements about the merit of a text and know that copies of the same edition would present others with an identical text. There was therefore a common basis for future discussion and thought. Where a certain text existed in different editions, each of the editions could be compared, and the best picked out as the standard work. Where improvements were made in a later edition, this would then become the new standard. Much of the text in Tyndale's Bible, for example, was used as the basis for the later Authorized or King James Bible, first published in 1611, which in turn, was used as the basis for many of the modern Revised versions that are common today.

Of course, like the scribe before him, the compositor, who set the type before it was printed, was not infallible. However, unlike a scribe's handwritten text, his printed text provided readers with a more reliable point of reference. In a 1631 edition of the Authorized Bible, the so-called 'wicked Bible', the compositor had left out the word 'not' from the seventh commandment. Thus 'Thou shalt commit adultery' was its injunction. The error was obvious because the passage was so well known, but with less familiar texts, printers were able to guard against similar errors becoming established by comparing their text with other editions. This process of standardization, comparison, revision and restandardization allowed knowledge to build up layer upon layer, and in this way the foundations of modern scholarship and science were laid. For a wide range of subjects, many of which were newly created, printing provided the means by which they could thrive and propagate.

The clarity that Plantin brought to a page of complex typography found an equivalent in many of his illustrations. His Polyglot Bible contained 22 illustrations, each of which were made from a process called copper engraving. This printing technique had been invented in Germany a few years before Gutenberg had first printed with movable type. It involved scratching lines with a sharp metal tool into a rectangular sheet of copperplate. After the engraved lines had been filled by rubbing a waxy ink into them, the surface of the plate, but not the engraved lines, was wiped clean. A sheet of dampened printing paper was then placed on top of the plate and both were put through a special rolling press that had two cylinders placed one above the other and a handle on the side, like an old-fashioned mangle (the English name given to such a press). As the paper and the plate passed through the rollers, the paper was forced into the engraved lines. The ink that it picked up tended to sit on top of the paper, rather than bleeding into it, leaving a darkly rich, raised imprint.

The arrival of copper engraving in Antwerp in the late 1540s led the city to become the printmaking centre of Europe throughout most of the next 100 years. The degree of detail, the range of textures and the size of print that could be produced with a copperplate surpassed anything that had been made with woodcuts at that time. A print made in Bruges during the early 1530s shows something of the appeal the medium must have held for artists and printers in Antwerp. The print shows the procession of Charles V into Bologna in 1529 prior to being crowned Holy Roman Emperor by Pope Clement VII. The king's extended retinue of noblemen, soldiers and servants was depicted with 40 large engravings which together appeared on a roll 18in high and 34ft long, before being bound in book form. Its greater detail and variety of textures were qualities that Plantin was keen to include in his Bible illustrations. They would allow him to show the skill of his artists and engravers, who had adopted the sophisticated late-Renaissance style of Mannerism/Baroque in which idealized forms of beauty rather than a truth to nature was emphasized. For them the overall effect of an image was more important than any particular subject within it.

Though fully engraved title pages had first appeared during the first decades of the century, they were still a rarity, especially in religious books, before the middle of the century. By including

11-23 • Title page from Polyglot Bible, printed by Christopher Plantin, Antwerp, 1569–73
Courtesy of the British Library.

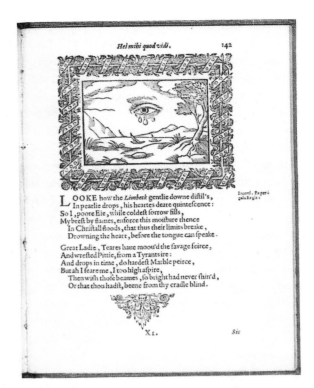

11-24 • Whitney's 'A Choice of Emblems,' printed by Christopher Plantin, Antwerp, 1586
Courtesy of the British Library.

an engraved title page in his Polyglot Bible (**FIG. 11–23**), as well as in other books, Plantin helped to popularize the medium for such pages. Other printers adopted a similar style of illustration and similar motifs. The use of a classical arch as a device for carrying the book's title, here *Biblia Sacra* ('The Holy Bible'), and the printer's device or logo—Plantin's compass logo appears on the base of the right-hand column while the picture of Achilles on the other represents the biblical scholar who helped Plantin prepare the book—can also be seen in later engraved title pages. The animals allude to the different languages used in the book and behind them is shown the lands governed by Christian rulers. Together they represent the breadth of God's dominion.

Copper engraving was not without its disadvantages. It was more expensive than woodcut printing. The plate took longer to engrave, longer to ink and de-ink, and longer to pass through the rollers of the press. The pressure applied by the engraving press was such that the copperplate yielded fewer prints than a woodblock before becoming worn. The greatest disadvantage

for publishers such as Plantin, who printed with type (as opposed to others who specialized in printing engravings), was that the copperplate and type could not be combined on the same press. Copper engravings belongs to a category of printing called intaglio (Italian for 'engravings') in which the printed image is formed by the recessed parts of the printing medium and not by the raised parts 'in relief,' as in a woodcut. So where an engraved illustration has to appear together with text, the printer either has to engrave both or to print each separately. For all the reasons mentioned above, when printing inexpensive books most printers still resorted to using woodcuts.

A popular and relatively cheap kind of picture book, which Plantin illustrated with woodcuts, was an emblem book. Such books could contain up to several hundred images, each one alluding cryptically to a moral contained in a motto and several lines of verse. The title page of *A Choice of Emblems* by Geffrey Whitney, which Plantin printed in 1586, describes the book as 'both fit for the vertuous, to their incoraging: and for the wicked, for their admonishing and amendment.' The example of one of its pages here (**FIG. 11–24**) shows a woodcut illustration of a crying eye floating within a thick decorative frame above 12 lines of English verse. Though Plantin printed most of his books in Latin, which then was still the language of scholarship, a few, such as his emblem books, used the language of everyday speech. The only piece of Latin on the page from Whitney's book is at the motto at the top (*Hei mihi quod vidi,* 'Woe is me because I can see'). As the title of the book suggests, the text was taken from a previous

published in two editions in 1613. The 'common' edition printed in black and white was intended as a reference book for herbalists, both medical and botanical, while the 'de luxe' edition was hand painted in a range of vivid and intricate colours. Its illustrations combined to form a catalogue of the different kinds of flowers contained in the garden at a Bishop's palace in the German diocese of Eichstätt in southern Germany. The garden boasted a series of eight terraces, each containing flowers from a different country, and a range of tulips in 500 colours. The garden's main designer, Basilius Besler (1561–1629) had over 1000 of the Bishop's favourite flowers and plants set down in detailed engravings based on drawings made from life and printed on the largest size of paper then available.

Besler's book predated the Linnean system of classification that was devised and adopted in the eighteenth century, but by showing many similar kinds of flowers it was necessary for him to distinguish them with a series of names in old German or Latin. By using a naming strategy based on the seasons Besler prompted others to adopt a more systematic approach later in the century.

However justified we might be in concentrating on some of the remarkable books that were printed during the first centuries after Gutenberg, we do so at the expense of a much larger group of printed items, one that was perhaps more representative of early printing as a whole. While books

11-25 • Engraving of flora from 'Hortus Eystettensis', Nuremberg, 1613 *Courtesy of the British Library.*

emblem book, but so too were most of the pictures. Plantin had made a double economy by using second-hand woodblocks.

As the range of secular books increased during the sixteenth century so illustrations came to be used in new ways. While textbooks, grammar books, dictionaries and other aids to textual scholarship remained mostly typographic, other books such as science books dealing with the anatomy of the human body, say, or the classification of flora or fauna, required text and pictures to be united more closely. Each element could not be fully understood without the other.

This close unity of text and illustration was exemplified by a grand book of flowers (known as a *florilegium*) called *Hortus Eystettensis*, or 'The Garden at Eichstätt' (**FIG. 11–25**), which was

were the most prestigious kind of printed item and the main drivers of developments in graphic style, they were not the most common kind. The bulk of all printed matter comprised the fleeting, workaday items known as 'job-printing' or, in reference to their short-lived day-to-day use, 'printed ephemera' (from Greek *epi* meaning 'on, about or round', and *hemera* meaning 'day'). Printed indulgences are an example, as are the printed copies of Luther's theses they provoked. Unlike each of these though, most ephemera, at least from the sixteenth century onwards, was secular in content. Among the many different kinds of popular street literature, such as handbills, proclamations, advertisements, calendars, almanacs and chapbooks, the most numerous were the printed ballads (**FIG. 11–26**) or folk-songs. Since few people had enough money for non-essential items during the sixteenth and

11–26 • Broadside ballad, England, 1634
Courtesy of the British Library.

seventeenth centuries, most would have read broadside ballads that were pinned to the walls of buildings. The ballads themselves recounted the traditional tales known and sung by ordinary people. One of the most popular subjects, which continues to have currency today, was a person of uncertain origins, the hero of English folklore, Robin Hood.

A Robin Hood ballad printed in England in 1634 (FIG. 11–26) tells of how he robbed the Sheriff of Nottingham by pretending to be a butcher. Below the ballad's title is a line of text giving the name of the tune to which the song should be sung. The woodcut corresponds to the story told in the song, though it may well have come, as in other ballads, from a previous edition. The style of type mixes italic and roman. Roman is used as a kind of emphasis: for the leading initial in the title, for subsequent mentions of Robin, for Nottingham and for the refrain of the chorus 'with a hey down down an a down', while Gothic is used for the rest of the text. A similar disregard for typographic purity and formal elegance was displayed in the way the text was positioned on the paper. It is bunched and cramped, with long broken lines having their remaining text placed either above or below the type line. But the very deliberate and consistent mixing of styles and positioning of broken lines show that the ballad's design was not wholly primitive. It was more that the printer had no need to create great art. Cheapness and speed trumped the need for quality.

Since few of the early printers were supported by wealthy patrons or established institutions, as many scribes had been, they had to rely on their own ability to create and exploit local markets. For many, this meant large runs of circulars (leaflets and broadsides) and short texts in cheap editions set almost exclusively in vernacular languages. The need to communicate through the language of everyday speech helped to standardize regional and national languages. Printing fixed not just the spelling of words but also their meaning. This, in turn, made reading easier and increased the demand for printed items.

One response to this demand was the publication of topical and often local information. Summaries of court, church or government events had appeared in print almost as soon as printing arrived in a region, but from around 1500 a more formal presentation of single events appeared on broadsides, leaflets and pamphlets. Towards the end of the century broadsides were being used to describe a number of separate events that had occurred within a given period of time. The names given to this form of publication were varied, but the word 'coranto' (derived from the French *courir* 'to run') and its linguistic variants were common terms. The important distinction between many corantos and other forms of news printing was that they established a continuing relationship with the reader. By the 1620s corantos were appearing weekly and reporting on events in many different countries. While most corantos were crudely illustrated a few used copper engraving to give a detailed visual description of what was being reported in the text. It was in the Netherlands and Germany that this form of reporting and publishing developed most rapidly. The Antwerp printer Abraham Verhoeven (1575–1652) used large engravings on the cover of his publication *Nieuwe Tydinghe* (FIG. 11–27) to show 'all recent news, victories, sieges and captures of cities' undertaken by the princes who had granted Verhoeven his licence to publish. The engraving showing the river battle in which Prince Maurice of Nassau captured Antwerp from the Spaniards in 1605 has numbers placed next to depictions of pivotal incidents in the battle, each of which are then described in the numbered text below.

The final stage in the development of the newspaper as we know it today was the appearance of news published in book form. Often named through the classical reference to the messenger of the gods Mercury, their bound and numbered pages included a title page and imprint. The more official looking versions took the name 'intelligencer' (FIG. 11–28) to impress on the reader the accurate and exclusive nature of the information or 'intelligence' contained in its pages. Weekly editions described the newsworthy events that had taken place during each day of the previous week and the range of subject-matter broadened and accounts became more detailed. Rival papers allied to competing political factions sought to persuade readers of their greater claim to truthful reporting. On the cover of *Londons Intelligencer* the

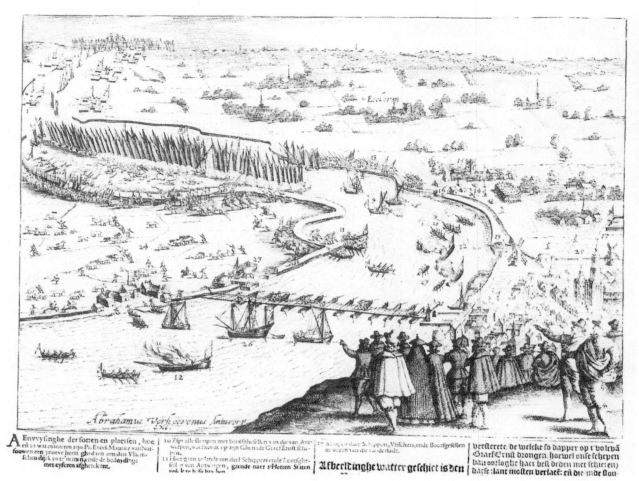

11-27 • 'Nieuwe Tydinghe', printed by Abraham Verhoeven, Antwerp, 1605

11-28 • 'Londons Intelligencer', 1643
Courtesy of the British Library.

descriptive subtitle declared 'Truth impartially related from thence to the whole Kingdome, to prevent mis-information'. Above the title, in the top left corner, appeared a primitive form of news headline, while below, precise dates for the period covered by the paper was given.

Despite the rapid development of form and content that took place throughout the seventeenth century, it was only well into the eighteenth century that newspapers became commonplace items. Until then most people continued to rely on the vast array of broadsides for information. While the majority imparted information through prose there were also instances when statistical information was shown. The broadside 'Londons Loud Cryes to the Lord by Prayer' **(FIG. 11–29)**, printed in 1665, shows columns of data listing the number of Londoners that had died since 1591 during successive plagues. The sheet also includes appropriate biblical texts and a recipe for a herbal remedy. The woodcut surround and central illustration made the broadside's grim theme clear.

Data collected by observation and set down in print combined with new forms of secular literature to loosen the hold that religion had exerted on European society throughout the last millenia. The truth of divine revelation manifested in the Bible was

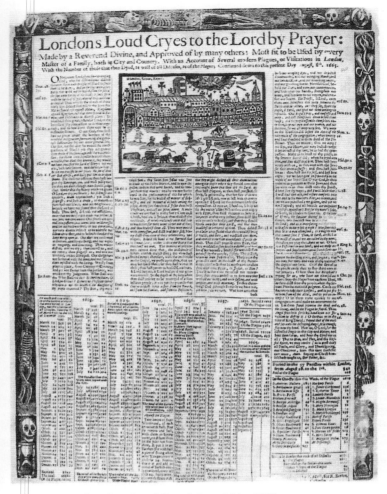

11-29 • 'Londons Loud Cryes', broadside, 1665
Courtesy of the British Library.

and most accessible form of print'.[2] In the case of political broadside ballads, however, the issue of accessibility is a good deal more complex than this simplistic connection with price suggests. Though certainly cheap, indeed sometimes free, much political ballad debate was not accessible to the less informed, traditional ballad consumers and, in further contradiction of orthodox scholarly opinion, probably intentionally so.[3] In this essay I will argue that typography, format and content are the key criteria by which accessibility must be judged.

A close analysis of the material nature and content of political broadside ballads, within the context of the whole genre and its market, reveals a spectrum of ballad products ranging from 'popular' to 'elite', or, since these terms have limited usefulness, from the accessible to the inaccessible.[4] As we shall see, political ballad broadsides were consciously and carefully adapted for different kinds of consumers. As contemporaries, such as Roger North, were well aware, some pamphlets were 'adapted to deceive Men of fortune and education, well penned, and, perhaps, in Heroic Verse; others for the Rabble, and drunken scottish clubs, in Ballad Doggerel, with witty pictures affixed'.[5] By understanding that product-range and its markets better, we can explore the multiple and sometimes overlapping political messages of the broadside ballad and identify a truly popular political *mentalité* or, at the very least, a market for it.

If we begin by looking at the format of print products in the seventeenth century we find that the broadside was ideally suited for group consumption. Printed on one side of a single sheet, it was designed to be pasted or pinned up on walls, or for folding up into a pocket ready to bring out at any time in any venue. Pepys records reading aloud a number of ballads that a friend had taken out of his pockets at a funeral![6] The broadside was also ideal for pasting into books by collectors, a growing breed from the seven-

forced to compete with the truth of nature as recorded and illustrated in an array of printed items. Through words and pictures Europeans became 'enlightened' to a new understanding of the natural world. It encouraged them to see the world more through their own eyes rather than the eyes of their priest or the text of the Bible.

TYPOGRAPHY MATTERS: BRANDING BALLADS AND GELDING CURATES IN STUART ENGLAND[1]

Angela McShane

It has long been a truism for historians and literary scholars that, as Tessa Watt expressed it, 'the printed broadside was the cheapest

---

[1]Ballads are anonymous and published in London unless stated otherwise. Full information on editions and extant sheets is not given, but citations offer finding information for one extant sheet. Bodleian ballads are freely accessible on http://www.bodley.ox.ac.uk/ballads/ballads.htm. This essay is based on a consideration of the 10,000 or so seventeenth-century broadside ballads still extant, about a third of which concern themselves with state affairs, which, for the purposes of this study, defines them as 'political'. For the full study see Angela McShane Jones, ' "Rime and Reason": The Political World of the Broadside Ballad, 1640–1689' (University of Warwick, PhD thesis, 2005).

[2]Tessa Watt, *Cheap Print and Popular Piety 1550–1640* (Cambridge, 1991), p. 1. See also Dagmar Freist, *Governed by Opinion: Politics, Religion and the Dynamics of Communication in Stuart London 1635–1645* (London, 1997), p. 147.

[3]Cf. Watt, *Cheap Print*, p. 37, who argues that cheap print was 'not expressly aimed at or written down to the understanding of … lower orders.' I use the term 'traditional' here to mean black-letter broadsides with illustrations.

[4]See Tim Harris, 'Problematising Popular Culture' in T. Harris, ed., *Popular Culture in England c. 1500–1850* (Basingstoke, 1995).

[5]Quoted in Mark Knights, *Politics and Opinion in Crisis 1678–1681* (Cambridge, 1994), p. 169. This difference has been noted by Charles C. Mish, 'Black-Letter as a Social Discriminant in the Seventeenth Century', *PMLA* Vol. 68: 3 (June, 1953); who, in line with the historiography of his period, sees the difference strictly in terms of class. See also Freist, *Governed by Opinion*, p. 151, who misreads the typical use of 'white-letter' for names as specifically intended in her discussion of a single 'black-letter' ballad. Her unsophisticated understanding of the form also leads her into misreading two satirical manuscript ballads as true opinion, p. 153.

[6]R. Latham, and W. Matthews, eds, *The Diary of Samuel Pepys* (10 vols, 1970—83), Vol. IX, 200: 15 May 1668.

teenth century, and it is thanks to this appeal that so many have survived.[7]

Ballad formats are usually divided into typographical groups. When categorizing his large collection of nearly 1,800 ballads Samuel Pepys used the term 'white-letter' to indicate any ballad broadside other than a 'black-letter' one.[8] He commented that by 1700 black-letter was 'for cheapnes sak … wholly laid aside', suggesting that the typographical difference between broadside ballads was entirely related to the cost of production and followed a clear line of development from 'black' to 'white' letter. But though widely accepted, Pepys's general categories and comments have blurred the fact that throughout the seventeenth century a wide range of typefaces, including italic and engraved script, were simultaneously used on all kinds of ballads.[9] Moreover, the production and marketing of political ballads were unlike those of other broadside ballads. They came in a very wide range of different formats and typefaces, directly linked to their content and style.

By the mid-seventeenth century the 'traditional' broadside ballad was usually printed on one side of a single folio sheet of cheap paper, largely, but never solely, in gothic type or 'black-letter', in three to four columns, in 'landscape' orientation and often divided into two parts, with woodcut illustrations.[10] By 1660 the majority of 'white-letter' ballads had only two columns in 'portrait' orientation, without illustration and on the same size and poor quality of paper as black-letter ballads.[11]

While black-letter ballads only occasionally deviated from their traditional norm, and then usually for a reason, the varieties of political 'white-letter' verse broadsides in the seventeenth century were considerable. Occasionally, for example, 'white-letter' ballads did carry illustrations, at the top of the page, always specially cut, specific to the ballad, and usually of reasonably good quality.[12] Some of the 'Rump' ballads in 1659–60 and a few ballad sheets in the 1680s were printed in high-quality roman type, on thicker, better-quality paper of larger size than the usual folio.[13] In the 1670s and 80s, a few political broadside ballads displayed many of the qualities of a 'white-letter' ballad but with a fine black-letter typeface and an engraved or finely worked woodcut illustration.[14] From the 1680s, as numbers of ballad broadsides along with all newsprint increased rapidly, some were printed on two sides of a folio or a half-size sheet.[15] Partly these changes reflected industrial experimentation and changing market needs, especially towards the end of the period, but largely they reflected a deliberate marketing and commissioning strategy, to separate the 'white-letter' ballad and its content from the traditional product and its consumer.

While black-letter ballad production was always considerable—their subject matter ranging broadly over all aspects of life, love and death as well as state affairs—up to 1680, 'white-letter' broadside ballads seem only to have become numerous at times of heightened political division. In the 1680s, political 'notation ballads', a brand-new 'white-letter' product carrying staves of music notation at the top, played a key part in campaigns against the Whigs, orchestrated by Tory publishers, especially Nathaniel Thompson and James Dean. At least it was a 'key part' if Thompson is to be believed.[16] Pepys mentioned his first sight of this novelty in 1667 but no examples survive before 1674.[17]

This was not an indication of increasing musical literacy, as in most cases the staves were nonsensical, merely a representation or

---

[7]The major seventeenth century collectors were John Selden, Anthony Wood, Narcissus Luttrell, Samuel Pepys, John Bagford and the Earl of Halifax. However, many other collections were broken up and rendered anonymous until their purchase in the nineteenth century by collectors, such as the Earl of Crawford.

[8]W. G. Day, ed., *Catalogue of the Pepys Library at Magdalene College, Cambridge. The Pepys Ballads* (5 Vols, Cambridge, 1987), vol. I, frontispiece: 'my collection of ballads … continued to the year 1700 when the form, till then peculiar thereto, viz.' of the Black Letter with Pictures seems (for cheapnes sak) wholly laid aside, for that of the White Letter without Pictures.'

[9]For an engraved ballad see *A TurnCoat of the Times* (n.d., publisher E. Barnet), Bodleian Douce Ballads.2(229b).

[10]See fig. 5. Bibliographers use the term 'oblong' to differentiate these formats. For a description of the materiality of the Pepys ballads see H. Weinstein, ed., *Catalogue of the Pepys Library at Magdalene College, Cambridge. II. i. Ballads Catalogue* (Cambridge, 1992), esp. pp. xxxi–xxxii.

[11]See fig. 4.

[12]Illustration of 'white-letter' verse, not broadside ballads, was well established as in *Mistris Turners Farewell to all Women* (1615); *The High and Mighty Prince Charles, Prince of Wales* (1623); William Hockham, *Prince Charles his Welcome to the Court* (1623), Society of Antiquaries. The woodcut on Hockham's poem was frequently reused on ballads. For illustrated white-letter ballads see e.g. *A New Ballad of the Protestant Joyner* (1681), Bute Broadsides, Harvard University Library.

[13]For example, *A New Ballade To An Old Tune, Tom of Bedlam* (1660) Bodleian Wood.416(31); *The Gang or the Nine Worthies and Champions* (1660), Bodleian Wood.416(34); *A Worthy Panegyrick Upon Monarchy* (1680), British Library.C40.M11(37).

[14]For example, *The Triumphing English Commanders* (1685), Bute Broadsides, Harvard University Library. Engraving was a technique usually reserved for more expensive products, such as royal print portraiture.

[15]For example, *An Answer To the Pamphlet Called The Loyal Feast* (1682), British Library.1876.f1(20) and *A Letany for St Omers* (1682), British Library.C20.f6(15).

[16]See Nathaniel Thompson, *Choice Collection of 180 Loyal Songs* (1684), 'To The Reader', sig. A2.

[17]Claude Simpson, *The British Broadside Ballad and its Music* (New Brunswick, 1966), p. 629. I know of only three pre-1680 notation ballads: a ballad (not extant) noted by Pepys in March 1667: Pepys, *Diary*, VIII, 99; Walter Pope, *The Catholic Ballad* (1674, 2nd edn, 1679), Euing 24 and *The Seekers Ballad* (1674) Bute Broadsides, Harvard University Library.

a 'picture' of music.[18] When they did depict a real tune it was often irrelevant to the tune cited on the broadside, or impossible to adapt to the metre of the ballad itself. Richard Luckett has suggested that this practice may have been a sop 'to flatter the musically illiterate', a kind of conspicuous consumption at a time when musical literacy was on the increase, marking a 'cleavage between the song-sheet and the ballad' so that the 'musically literate forgot the old mnemonic vehicles, the ancient tunes, and those who still relied on these were forced into a musical and social underground'.[19]

However, political broadside ballad tunes were rarely ancient, unless a satirical point was being made. For those that were intended for singing, the tunes they were sung to changed throughout the seventeenth century, influenced by the popular tunes emerging from the stage. It is possible that 'notation ballads' were simply mimicking the more sophisticated song sheets on the market. On the other hand, they may have been a publishing experiment. Such images may simply have operated as identifiers, necessary when many broadsides nestled together on a stall, or hung along with other sheets outside a shop. They were cheaper to print, using less ink than the old woodcuts, and may reflect competition from the growing and increasingly cheap printed images market.[20] But if it was an experiment it was abandoned. While there was certainly a developing market in musically accurate 'song sheets' by the end of the century, ballads continued to be printed, with images and without music. Of nearly 1,800 ballads in the Pepys collection fewer than ten percent (167) have staves, of which only one-third are really music.[21]

THE 'BRANDING' OF BALLADS

Why would the choice of typeface have radically influenced the market in political ballads? One argument is based on literacy. For much of the early seventeenth century, education in literacy tended to be in black letter. ABC hornbooks were combined with catechisms and printed in black letter right through the century.[22] It has been observed that in this period to read lower-case roman letter, a letter form based on Italian scribal practices, could have been as difficult as reading handwriting for the less educated.[23] The connection between print and scribal methods in this context was recognised by Samuel Pepys, who referred to a ballad broadside he was shown as being 'most incomparably writ in a printed hand'.[24] Adam Fox cites a number of examples of people who, though basically literate, had difficulties with reading handwriting, such as Richard Jerard (1611), who 'cannot reade written hand', and Thomas Mumby (1621), who tried to read a hand 'but could not, but here and there a part'. Equally, it was reported that a libel against a Gloucester alderman which had been 'framed in Romaino lettres' and another with letters in 'a large Romayne hand' had only reached 'even amongst the baser sort of the people' because of the pictures.[25]

While helpful, the literacy argument is not sufficient to explain the differences in ballad products. Readers of black- and 'white-letter' ballads had to be able to read all kinds of type. By the mid-seventeenth century even the most traditional 'black-letter' ballads invariably used roman type for titles, sometimes as long as a paragraph, and italic type to indicate names and places in the text.[26] 'White-letter' ballads sometimes used black-letter type in titles as a nod to the traditional form.[27] Readers of the pamphlet press were accustomed to authors using typeface as well as language and form for satirical effect and black letter was often used in texts to represent rustic or 'mobile' opinion.[28] In the same way, some 'white letter' ballads used gothic type for particular words in the text, to highlight the satirical effect of their attack.[29] Typography certainly matters, but we need a further explanation for why there was such a difference in the market.

[18]See Simpson, *British Broadside Ballad*, p. xii.

[19]Richard Luckett, 'The Collection: origins and history', in Robert Latham and Helen Weinstein, eds, *Catalogue of the Pepys Library at Magdalene College, Cambridge. II. ii. Ballads Indexes* (Cambridge, 1994), p. xv.

[20]Woodcuts were always the cheapest at only a few pence; the price for portraits in mezzotint and line engraving could be as little as 6*d* or as much as 2*s*. 6*d*. However, prices depended on the size, the artist and the age of the print, the price reducing after early impressions had been sold, or if secondhand.

[21]Latham and Weinstein, eds., *Catalogue. II. ii. Ballads Indexes*, p.xxv.

[22]See for example: Anon., *The A B C With The Catechism* (London, edns 1601, 1627, 1680, 1682, 1687, 1698).

[23]K. Thomas, 'The Meaning of Literacy in Early Modern England', in G. Baumann, ed., *The Written Word: Literacy in Transition* (Oxford, 1986), pp. 97–131; Joad Raymond, *Pamphlets and Pamphleteering* (Cambridge, 2003), pp. 74–75.

[24]Pepys, *Diary*, vol. I, p. 41.

[25]Adam Fox, *Oral and Literate Culture in England 1500—1700* (Oxford, 2000), pp. 312–314.

[26]On the changing use of the italic and the traditional 'value' of typeface and layout see Richard Wendorf, 'Abandoning the Capital in Eighteenth-century London' in Kevin Sharpe and Steven N. Zwicker, eds., *Reading Society and Politics in Early Modern England* (Cambridge, 2003), pp. 72–98.

[27]For example, *Young Jemmy. An Excellent New Ballad* (1681), Bodleian. Firth.b.20(84). This ballad was also published in black letter. Based on a song by Aphra Behn.

[28]For example, Anon., *Thirty and Two Extremes of These Times Discovered and Reduced to Sixteene Golden Meanes* (1647), British Library, Thomason.669.f.11(6); *A Free Parliament Letany* (1660), Thomason. 669.f.24(19); Anon., *Treason Made Manifest, or, A Discourse by Way of Dialogue between Richard and William* (1681).

[29]For example, *An Excellent New Ballad between Tom the Tory, and Toney the Whigg* (1678), Bodleian. Wood.417(1).

Black-letter type was chosen not because it was easier to read for the less well-educated, but because it had a 'brand' value. It conveyed tradition and guaranteed accessibility of content. It was the chosen typeface of official pronouncements of the government, the visual voice of the King to his people, while religious works intended for the least educated, including the young, especially the responses in the catechism, continued to be printed in black letter throughout the century. The Christian humanist content of the political messages that black-letter ballads conveyed enjoyed a secure place in the market. Publishers carefully maintained the 'brand' of the black-letter ballad through careful selection of material.

By the late seventeenth century the market was changing. Black letter may well have become less saleable as more people, especially the young, found it harder to read. Black-letter hornbooks and primers were slowly dying out from around 1660 in preference for roman-letter ones.[30] By the 1680s publishers began to print ballads of all kinds in white-letter formats, including romantic theatre songs.[31] Nevertheless, publishers were careful not to lose touch with the 'brand'. As we have seen, some moved to white letter format but retained black letter in titles for emphasis, or rather than abandon illustration altogether they introduced images of notation instead of expensive woodcuts. From 1688 publisher John Wallis printed broadside ballads that were traditional in almost all respects—woodcut illustrated, landscape orientation—but were printed entirely in 'white-letter' type.[32]

Everything changed for the ballad publishing trade when the liberalization of printing in 1695 led to presses being set up all over the country. The resulting proliferation of styles and products destroyed any 'branding' built up in the small world of London publishing. By 1700 many publishers had transferred the attributes of the accessible black-letter ballad, sung to the latest tune, to the 'slip' ballad. The songs were much shorter than old ballad forms and were often illustrated by a single poorly printed woodcut, while three ballads could be printed on a single sheet.[33] This did not herald a decline in the market, but it was a change in the product. Many new woodcuts and political songs, and some of the old ones, continued to appear on slips after 1700.[34]

Political, 'white-letter', verse broadsides depended on a very different kind of market appeal. They were unlike traditional black-letter ballads not only in typeface, format, quality of paper and printing, but also in the sophistication of their language, their political content and style. A close reading of these broadsides reveals a high level of allusion to relatively minor individuals, to Latin and legal terms, to pamphlets and the press. This suggests that both the authors and their target group were familiar with the political world of London and especially courtiers, lawyers and parliamentarians.

The detailed naming of MPs, or the use of initials only, and allusions to intimate, personal peccadilloes or unpublished speeches in parliament would be incomprehensible to any but those closest to parliamentary affairs and gossip.[35] In order to understand many of the jokes, readers needed to be versed in the newsprint of the present and the past.[36] Contemporary collectors, such as Narcissus Luttrell or Anthony Wood, sometimes filled in the gaps left by the use of initials and a line on a ballad sheet, but often they did not—perhaps because they could not—and sometimes they got it wrong.[37] If such informed observers were left in the dark, what hope for those who could not afford, or manage to read, the *London Gazette*, or for those at a geographical or social distance from Westminster and the street gossip around it?

It was an accepted practice for ballad verses to be commissioned from a writer and a printer for a whole range of purposes. Ballads were used as New Year gifts, as love letters, as jokes and pastimes, or as vehicles for political attack. They spoke for royalists, parliamentarians, Whigs and Tories; and for other groups such as brewers, soldiers, tailors and sailors' wives. The choice of format and typeface may have been at the behest of the commissioning client. However, judging from the clear difference in content of political ballads, unless they complied with the language, tone,

---

[30]See Charles Hoole, *The Petty-Schoole* (1659) pp. 9–10 but cf. Anon., *The Best And Plainest English Spelling-Book Containing All The Different Words, Syllables, & Letters In The Old English Character* (1700). As a grammar-school master, Hoole taught Latin so the reading of roman type was essential for his pupils.

[31]For example, *The Scotch Lasses Constancy* (1682) British Library, Roxburgh III.913, also published in black letter: see Bodleian. Don.b.13(79).

[32]For example, *Good Sport for Protestants* (1689–1691), Pepys.III.46; *The Jesuits Lamentation* (1689), Pepys.II.286; Richard Rigby, *A New Song* (1689), Pepys.II.293; Thomas Sibley, *The Royal Health* (1689), Pepys.II.343.

[33]Slips were not new. A number of royalist white-letter verse libels of the 1640s were slips, for example, *The Parliaments Knell* (1646), Crawford Ballads.389/3; *The Souldiers Sad Complaint* (1648), Crawford Ballads.703/4, National Library of Scotland. Black-letter ballads usually had two parts and sometimes two ballads on the same sheet.

[34]For example, *Freedom Triumphant, or the Whigs Downfall* (1784), Bodleian.G.A.Warw.b.1(723) and *The Lamenting Maid [with] The answer* (1700s), Bodleian.Firth.c.18(103).

[35]Alastair Bellany makes this point regarding early Stuart manuscript libels: 'Rayling Rymes and Vaunting Verse': Libellous Politics in Early Stuart England, 1603–1628' in K. Sharpe & P. Lake, eds., *Culture and Politics in Early Stuart England* (Basingstoke, 1994), pp. 288–290.

[36]For example see the contest of defamatory ballads between publisher Francis Smith, *The Protestant Cuckold A New Ballad Being a Full and Perfect Relation How B. H. the Protestant News Forger Caught his Beloved Wife Ruth in Ill Circumstances* (1681), BL.806.k.16.(113) and publisher Benjamin Harris, *The Leacherous Anabaptist or The Dipper Dipt* (1681), BL.1872.a.1.(91).

[37]See Elizabeth Herbert and John Gadbury, attrib., *A Ballad Upon the Popish Plot. Written by a Lady of Quality* (1679), BL.Lutt.III.143, which Luttrell wrongly attributed to 'ye strumpet the Dutchess of Portsmouth'.

content and accessibility that appealed to the broader black-letter market, publishers offered only a 'white-letter' service to commissioning clients. In particular, the existence of numerous 'cross-over' ballads, that is ballads that came onto the market at the same time in both white- and black-letter formats, strongly suggests that a publisher decided a commissioned product could be distributed in two separate markets.[38]

A black-letter ballad had to appeal across a wide section of the population and country. When, for example, *Perjury Punish'd* advertised the shame of Miles Prance in the pillory, it made very clear how far that song was expected to travel: 'I send my mournful ditty/ through every town and city/ Let me not fail, but now prevail/ to get the Nations pitty'.[39] *A New Ballad of Bold Robin Hood* described itself as being 'calculated for the meridian of Staffordshire, but may serve for Derbyshire or Kent'.[40]

Many ballads were bought by, or for, the young reader. Anthony Wood bought his first ballad—a political one—at the age of eight in 1640. Daniel Fleming and his wife, members of the gentry in Westmorland, often bought ballads for their children. John Bunyan famously regretted the time he had wasted on ballads as a young man. When the 'oppressed printer' William Jones complained in 1640 that he had been denied master status after being a printer for fifty-four years, he swore that he had 'refused to print ... scandalous pamphlets, Popish books, or ballads, or anything tending to poyson youth.'[41]

The market also provided for the older untutored reader who, though never very advanced in literacy skills, could still enjoy black-letter ballads. Ballads were freely available at the local tavern or alehouse where they might be pasted to the walls, sung by a balladeer or read during the evening. Some taverns kept their own instruments as part of a range of entertainment facilities and some may have encouraged ballad-singers to attract custom.[42]

Parish constables often complained that musicians had encouraged rowdy drinkers to overindulge. By the later part of the century 'Musick-houses' appear in the London court records, where all 'sorts' of men and women, men- and maid- servants, ladies and gentlemen, drank while listening and singing to music, performed as part of a variety show.[43]

Women were also important to the ballad market, a considerable cause of concern for the writers of conduct-books. In 1653, Thomas Hilder complained of 'locusts' who 'purposely do invent obscene, lascivious, scurrilous, and filthy songs and Ballads, on purpose to pollute and poyson young virgins and maids'.[44] In 1664, Robert Codrington's 'excellent directions for the education of young ladies' castigated the 'too much accostumed delight, which many young women have in reading vain pamphlets and singing vainer ballads'. He warned that, 'passion doth take fire with the Loves, which these ballads do decipher' and having 'made young maidens bold, it afterwards doth make them to practise what they read or sing'.[45]

Nevertheless, in 1689 *The Welsh Fortune-Teller*, a curious mixture between high politics and advice to young maids, claimed it 'was writ here in verses for lasses to sing'.[46] Ballads had to appeal to women as gifts, as reading exercises for their children, as potential decorations in their homes or as pastimes and expressions of emotion and for singing at work in fields, in dairies and while looking after children.[47] Ballads were often sung and sold by female hawkers on the streets, at fairs and markets.

The broad range of consumers, which must often have overlapped, does much to explain on one hand the sobriety, deference and morality of most broadside ballads, and on the other the riotous, yet still linguistically decorous, revelry in others. Even if intended for an adult reader it was not advisable to sully the 'brand' with inappropriate material that could ruin the market.

[38]For example, the black-letter *Rebellion Give Over Housekeeping: Or A General Sale Of Rebellious Househould Stuff* (1682), Bodleian. Wood.E25(21), and the white-letter *A General Sale Of Rebellious Houshold-Stuff* (1682), Bodleian. Ashm.G.16(195)

[39]*Perjury Punish'd with Equal Justice* (1686), Pepys.II.236.

[40]*A New Ballad Of Bold Robin Hood* (1689–1709), British Library. Roxburgh 1(360).

[41]Andrew Clark, ed., *The Life and Times of Anthony Wood, Antiquary of Oxford, 1632–1695, Described by Himself* (5 vols. Oxford, 1891–1900), Vol. I., 48–49; J. R. Magrath, ed., *The Flemings in Oxford being Documents Selected from the Rydall Papers* (2 vols, Oxford, 1904), Vol. I., 494 (16 April 1679) and Vol. II., 369 (16 May 1686); John Bunyan, *Sighs from Hell* (c. 1666), pp. 147–148, quoted in Margaret Spufford, *Small Books and Pleasant Histories* (Cambridge, 1985), p. 7; *Calendar of State Papers Domestic, 1640–41*, p. 327 (29 December 1640).

[42]See S. Overcome, *The Young Gallant's Academy* (1674), p. 48: 'I would further intreat our Poet to be in league with the mistress of the Ordinary; because from her, upon condition that he will but Rime knights and gentlemen to her House, he may easily make up his Mouth at her cost gratis'.

[43]Daniel Fleming attended a 'Musicke-House' in Oxford in August 1653 Magrath, *Flemings Papers*, vol. I., 62. See Rosemary Lane Musick-House *Proceedings Of The Old Bailey* STC t16840903-18, 3 September 1684; The Musick-House at the Hermitage, *Proceedings Of The Old Bailey* STC t16880425-31, 25 April 1688; The Gun Musick House at Salisbury Court, *Proceedings Of The Old Bailey* STC ti6910422-10, 22 April 1691; an unnamed music house, *Proceedings Of The Old Bailey* STC t16980720-30, 20 July 1698.

[44]Thomas Hilder, *Conjugall Counsell* (1653), p. 170.

[45]Robert Codrington, *The Second Part of Youths Behavior, or, Decency in Conversation Amongst Women* (1664), pp. 154–156.

[46]*The Welsh Fortune Teller* (1689), Pepys.IV.320.

[47]In the 1650s Dorothy Osborne described Chicksand Common: 'where a great many young wenches keep sheep and cows and sit in the shade singing of ballads', quoted in Anthony Fletcher, *Gender, Sex and Subordination in England 1500–1800* (New Haven, 1995), p. xx. See also Bruce R. Smith, *The Acoustic World of Early Modern England* (Chicago, 1999), p. 26.

Though there is little evidence of direct censorship of political black-letter ballads, it was important to a business to balance consumer demands for novelty and interest with the fear of stepping on important toes.[48] Though targeted at the lower end, black-letter ballads were more expensive to produce and, at one penny, to buy than most white-letter productions. 'White-letter' ballads cost a halfpenny, or when part of a deliberate campaign, were distributed free.[49]

To make the market pay, black-letter publishers depended on bulk buying from the warehouse by travelling pedlars, by hawkers on the streets around London, and by agents buying for regional shops and stalls. These products were then sold publicly in fairs, taverns, and streets all over the kingdom.[50] As far as possible, both seller and buyer needed to be free from the threat of prosecution. Any political messages carried by these ballads needed to be more or less legal but, above all, if they were to convince the public to part with their hard-earned, carefully husbanded cash, they had to be intelligible, acceptable and accessible to a broad range of people, geographically and socially.

To exemplify the way black- and 'white'-letter political ballads dealt with the same political stories in very different ways, using typeface as a deliberate marketing ploy to separate product and consumer, we turn to a case study.

THE 'GELDING OF CURATES'

In February 1663, as the recently restored king, his ministers, churchmen and Presbyterians were wrangling over issues of religious conformity and 'comprehension' within the re-established Church of England, a terrible murder was committed in Chelmsford, Essex.[51] A butcher, finding his wife and a local clergyman *in flagrante*, castrated the clergyman, who died almost instantly from his injuries. One black-letter and two large 'white-letter' ballads, one of them illustrated, were soon published concerning this politically sensitive event.

Making fun of the non-conformist clergy in ballad verse was nothing new in the 1660s. During the civil war and interregnum, cavalier poets had used the age-old, defamatory strategy of alleging sexual incontinence against all sectarians and Presbyterians and whenever they could they chose the 'white-letter' broadside ballad as the literary vehicle most suited to such shameful accusations.[52] From 1659 highly-placed, and supposedly high-minded, republican army officers, politicians and divines were constantly subjected to scandalous libels that spread rumours about their own or their wives' illicit sexual affairs. In particular Hugh Peters, republican preacher to the Council of State, was alleged to be having an affair with a butcher's wife.[53] A lasting framework for these verse satires was laid down in two much-cited broadsides, attributed to cavalier propagandists Sir John Denham and Sir John Birkenhead.[54]

The first was Birkenhead's *The Four Legged Elder* (1647), reprinted in anthologies in 1660 and on a broadside in 1677.[55] The ballad told the tale of Jane, maid to a Presbyterian elder, and Swash, the elder's dog. 'One evening late [Jane] stepp'd aside/ Pretending to fetch eggs/ And there she made herself a Bride/ To one that had four legges'. This joke was based on a deliberate misunderstanding of the Commonwealth's newly issued Directory of Worship, which had banned the rituals of marriage. The ballad claimed that simply by having intercourse 'according to the directory/ They two were man and wife.' The Elder, on discovering them, 'Not dreaming, without his consent/ His Dog would ever marry', laments that now 'They'll many graceless ballads sing/ Of a Presbyterian/ That a Lay-Elder is a thing/ Made up half dog, half man.' The outcome of this sorry tale was that Swash was executed for buggery, while Jane was taken to Newgate where she was 'naked stript' and 'whipt … till the cord did fail'. Nevertheless, the balladeer bitterly pointed out, 'had she been a cavalier/ Surely she had been hang'd'. The tune direction, 'The Lady's Fall' was purely satirical since, as Claude Simpson points out, the verses are not well adapted to this melody. The verses were intended for reading or reciting, rather than singing.[56]

The second scandalous story was based on Denham's *A Relation of a Quaker*. It had appeared in an anthology in 1659 but was amended, perhaps by Birkenhead, and reprinted as a white-letter broadside with an illustration a few years later as *The*

---

[48]One exception was the (ineffective) suppression of S. S., *The Parliament Routed or Here's a House to be Let* (1653), British Library, Thomason 669.f.17(12), discussed in McShane Jones, 'Rime and Reason', p. 277.

[49]Maureen Bell, 'Sturdy Rogues and Vagabonds: Restoration Control of Pedlars and Hawkers' in P. Isaac, and B. McKay, eds., *The Mighty Engine The Printing Press and its Impact* (Winchester, 2000), p. 92; Knights, *Politics and Opinion*, p.170.

[50]Watt, *Cheap Print*, pp. 14–30; Margaret Spufford, *The Great Reclothing of Rural England* (1984); John Feather, *History of British Publishing* (1988), p. 12: 'The basic mechanism of trade certainly existed through fairs and markets.'

[51]See John Spurr, *English Puritanism, 1603–1689* (Basingstoke, 1998), ch. 9.

[52]Similar accusations were made against Lollards in the fifteenth century: see Richard Rex, *The Lollards* (Basingstoke, 2002), p. 82. On civil war pamphlets of similar ilk see Bernard Capp, *When Gossips Meet* (Oxford, 2003), pp. 22–23.

[53]For example J.C., *Peter's Patern Newly Revived* (1659), p.13; Anon., *The Tales and Jests of Mr. Hugh Peters Collected into One Volume* (1660); Anon, *Hugh Peters Figaries* (1660).

[54]See for example citations in the satirical pamphlet Anon., *Manes Presbyteriani, or, The Monuments of the Kirk* (1661), p. 6 and the play-pamphlet, John Wilson, *The Cheats. A Comedy* (1664), p. 67.

[55]Sir John Birkenhead, *The Four-Legg'd Elder, Or, A True Relation Of A Dog And An Elder's Maid To The Tune Of The Lady's Fall*, (1647, repr.1677), British Library, Thomason.669.f.11(70).

[56]Simpson, *British Broadside Ballad*, p. 248.

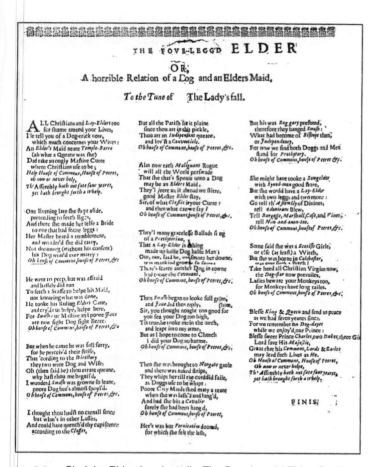

11–30 • Sir John Birkenhead, attrib. *The Four-Legg'd Elder, Or, A True Relation Of A Dog And An Elder's Maid To The Tune Of The Lady's Fall,* (1647), Thomason.669.f.11(70). *Courtesy of the British Library.*

11–31 • Sir John Denham and Sir John Birkenhead, *The Four-Legg'd Quaker To The Tune Of The Dog And Elder's Maid, Or, The Lady's Fall* (1662–1668), Bod.Wood.416(70). Wood added an ms note, 'Joh. Birkenhead the Author—Sr Joh. Denham hath such another Ballad in his poems & translations, printed at Lond. 1668'. *Courtesy of Bodleian Library.*

Four-legg'd Quaker to the Tune of the Dog and Elder's Maid, or, the Lady's Fall.[57] The broadside told the tale of George Mosse, a Quaker who had raped a young mare, an event that 'reveal'd why Quakers meet/ In Meadows Fields and Pastures'.

With this background in mind we now return to the mutilated minister of Chelmsford. A large 'white-letter' broadside appeared, which sought to make political capital from the tragedy. It was entitled, *The Fanaticks Barber or, A New Cut for Non-Conformists* to the (spurious) tune of, 'All the town shan't save thee' and sported a poor but graphic and specially made woodcut illustrating the moment of discovery by the cockolded butcher.[58] In a ridiculous 'ballad metre' with much repetition of lines, the balladeer tells us 'my song concerns a parson' and alleges 'they say he was a presbyter/ the which I do believe'.[59] It made two allusions to the Birkenhead ballad of the Quaker's mare: 'for Saints will crie/ Give me a mare behind/ If that a man must pay so dear/ for boaring woman kind', and (on the discovery of the couple): 'So Troy town after ten years was taken unaware/ And as the learned do recount/ So Mosse did catch his mare.'

The ballad is not altogether simple reading. Take for example the following lines, 'The Priest thought to have scar'd the

---

[57] In *A Relation of a Quaker* (1659), British Library, Thomason. 669.f.21(35) the Quaker's name was Green. He seeks to 'marry' the mare by having sex with her. Reprinted in *Ratts Rhimed To Death* (1660), pp. 69–72, and finally amended and reprinted as *The Four-Legg'd Quaker To The Tune Of The Dog And Elder's Maid. Or, The Lady's Fall* (1662–1668), Bodleian. Wood.416(70). Wood added in ms note, 'Joh. Birkenhead the Author—Sr Joh. Denham hath such another Ballad in his poems & translations, printed at Lond. 1668'.

[58] *The Fanaticks Barber or, A New Cut for Non-Conformists* (1662), Bodleian, Wood.416(94). This ballad is incorrectly dated 1655 on Early English Books Online.

[59] The 'ballad metre' used in this broadside satirises an oral ballad style, not a printed one.

11-32 • *The Fanaticks Barber or, A New Cut for Non-Conformists* (1662), Bod.Wood.416(94). This ballad is incorrectly dated 1655 on EEBO. *Courtesy of Bodleian Library.*

11-33 • The first (?) edition was printed on a large sheet, *Bloody News from Chelmsford* (Oxford, 1663), CB.425/3. *Courtesy of the Earl of Crawford.*

Butcher/ With a syllogism in Celarent', to which the Butcher replies, 'Priests were not made/ Ut Butchers wives amarent'. The *Fanaticks Barber* was directed against Presbyterians,

> All you that have long ears[60]
> Reach them unto my text
> For faith y'are all so given to't
> That God knows who'll be next …

But especially those at court;

> … If you ask
> Where all the sawcie trade is
> Why with players among Gentlemen
> And Parsons among ladies.

The following year *The Fanaticks Barber* was answered by another long ballad, printed in Oxford (and possibly written by a member of the University) in at least two editions. It was entitled, *Bloody News from Chelmsford*, and was set to the cliché tune of 'Chevy-Chase'.[61] *Bloody News* admonished the author of *Fanaticks Barber*, while making several allusions to white-letter ballad broadsides of the past:

> Give o'er, ye rhiming Cavaliers,
> That jeer'd at every turn;
> And sung how Jane towards Elders Cur
> In flames of love did burn.
> You too that writ how Peters Hugh,
> Was Butchers Cuckold maker,

Or penn'd the Courtship past between
She-Filly, and the Quaker.

It denied the parson concerned in this case was a Presbyterian,

> Where once was bred a Roundheaded Colt,
> And now a Cavalier Gelding
> Neer Chelmsford Town a certain grave
> Conforming Parson dwelt,
> Chast from the Navil to the Teeth;
> Yet this good man was Gelt.

Combining a witty tale with a concerted attack on the inadequacy and popish tendency of the newly restored ministry, in this version of events the 'Conforming Parson' is a 'reading rogue' who, rather than preaching extempore, the method preferred by Presbyterians, 'utter[s his] Sermon by retail/ which might be done by [a] dolt'. As he had nothing to occupy his mind during the service, he spies the butcher's wife from the pulpit and finds her 'purer text/ to handle than an Homily'. So as to pursue her after church, he rushes through the 'printed hurry' of his sermon 'with greater speed than a nun sings pater noster'. Full of learned allusions to Priapus, Rosamund, Trulla, the 'Cornelian tub', Dr Faustus, and an attack on Cambridge University, the ballad concludes with an address to its 'Courteous reader'.

A black letter version of this story, *The Careless Curate and The Bloudy Butcher*, was published in 1662, at the same time as *The Fanaticks Barbar*.[62] It was illustrated with woodcuts taken from

---

[60]'Long ears' was a frequently used insult against Presbyterians. As well as referring to an ass, it is also a satirical reference to the cutting off of prolific pamphleteer and Presbyterian MP William Prynne's ears as a punishment for sedition in the 1630s.

[61]The first edition was printed on a large sheet, *Bloody News from Chelmsford* (Oxford, 1663), Crawford Ballads.425/3, National Library of Scotland.

[62]*The Careless Curate and the Bloudy Butcher* (1662), Bodleian. Wood.401(187). A good example of the way woodcuts could be adapted to different uses, a woodcut on this ballad was adapted for use on *Romes Cruelty or, The Earl of Essex Barbarously Murthered in the Tower* [1688–1689], Pepys.II.177, where it indicated the examination of Essex's body by the authorities.

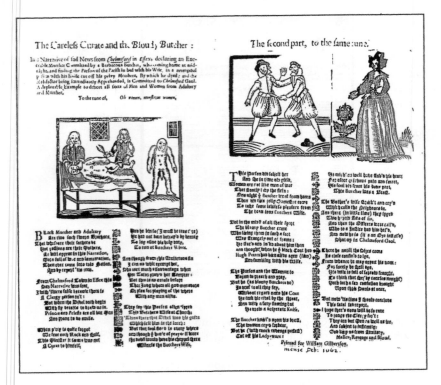

11-34 • *The Careless Curate and the Bloudy Butcher* (1662), Bodleian.Wood.401(187).
Courtesy of Bodleian Library.

store that were indicative of the action rather than descriptive of it. *The Careless Curate* sought to extract morals 'to dehort all sorts of men and women from adultery' and, allegedly, to prevent discredit to the clergy. It wished the story 'were false because there is / A Clergy person in it' and hoped 'none will be so rude/ To judge the clergy for't.' As it sadly observed, faced with the Devil, 'Princes and Priests are all but men'. Such democratic sentiments, pointing out the moral and mortal equivalence of greater and lesser men, were typical of black-letter balladry.

Less typical was an almost sympathetic approach towards the woman in the case. While in no way seeking to exonerate the butcher's wife from blame (the tune direction is 'o woman monstrous woman'), the ballad acknowledges that, 'she met much disadvantage when/ her tutor proves her temptor'.[63] Unlike the 'white-letter' broadsides, no explicit attempt was made to label this 'Careless Curate' and 'Parson of the Parish' as conforming or otherwise, but the *Careless Curate* did share one joke from the Puritan past. It told how, on finding the 'jolly gamester' Parson's black coat, the butcher thought 'Hugh Peters had been alive again/ and fumbling with his wife'.

Scholars have too frequently assumed that because a ballad was cheap and in a 'low' cultural form it was, by default, 'popular'

or accessible, and similarly that because a broadside specified a 'tune' it was necessarily intended to be sung in public and accessible by that means.[64] As we have seen, the 'white-letter' ballad was an ideal vehicle for satire, since it satirised the 'low' form of the ballad as part of its attack. It did not comment, explain, praise, blame, or moralise generally on state affairs, as black-letter ballads did. It had a role to play alongside the broader political pamphlet press, attacking and counter-attacking their intended targets, and each other. Tune tides and verses were dragooned into the task of mocking the victim, while a close reading shows that to be appreciated they depended upon considerable knowledge of past satirical literature, religious and legal texts. For much of the century, white-letter ballads were intended for the political cognoscenti, whoever they might be, while black-letter ballads, though equally interested in political events, were carefully manipulated by highly market-sensitive publishers market in order to appeal across the board of quotidian England. In dealing with broadside ballads, we need to be aware that typography matters and the variety of products on the market meant that there was a variety of political messages on offer.

BIRCHBARK, A PICTOGRAPHIC MEDIUM

A familiar sight almost anywhere in a mixed forest stand of the Shield country is the white trunk of a dead paper birch, still a seemingly solid vertical cylinder long after its branches and upper length have fallen to the ground **(FIG. 11–35)**. Given a gentle kick it will crumple and collapse, as allegorically eloquent as the biblical 'whited sepulchre.' The outer bark of the white birch is a tough flexible skin, equally resistant to moisture, fungi, and insects.

Left in water or buried in the ground this bark will remain intact for decades, even centuries. Pieces found in a cave on the Saguenay River in Quebec, in deposits believed to be four centuries old, still revealed clearly the awl holes where the pieces had been stitched together (Brassard 1961, 69, 74). A large piece of birchbark which I examined at the Royal Ontario Museum, from a digging of Walter Kenyon's in the Rainy River district, was associated with a 1000-year-old deposit. Both were well enough preserved that, had there been engravings on them, they would still have been distinguishable as such, despite a fair amount of rot on the older sample.

Around the world, wherever trees grew, the naturally smooth surface of the peeled bark has offered preliterate people a tempting surface on which to leave their marks, a medium so easily

[63]I can find no record of this tune; it may be intended as a joke.

[64]See, for example, Mark S.R. Jenner 'The Roasting of the Rump: Scatology and the Body Politic in Restoration England', *Past and Present*, 177 (2002), pp. 84–121 and debate in *Past and Present*, 196 (2007), pp. 253–286.

11–36 • Wooden panel with engraved totemic signs.
Courtesy of Minnesota Historical Society Museum.

11–35 • Trunk of paper birch (note deterioration of the exposed inner bark).
Courtesy of Ontario Ministry of Natural Resources.

obtained and so portable that it might have been used by Palae-olithic man long before he began painting and carving the walls of Franco-Cantabrian rock shelters and caves. To this day the Australian aborigines produce bark paintings, examples of which may be seen in every major museum. The bark, however, does not compare with that of the canoe birch for flexibility and lightness. In fact no other tree provides so ideal a bark for communication purposes as the paper birch.

Two words in the English language—'paper' and 'library'—offer clues as to the earliest kinds of materials used in the development of writing, apart from the marking of wet clay. Manuscripts written on *papyrus*, the leaf of a Mediterranean rush that was widely used for paper-making long before the Christian era, have survived to this day. The word 'library' derived from the Latin *liber*, whose root meaning is *bark*. In the Moscow Historical Museum I was shown a piece of birchbark on which were inscribed a few characters of an early Cyrillic alphabet. The fact that no specimens of preliterate pictography on birchbark have been preserved in northern Eurasia is probably due to the early diffusion of more sophisticated media from the south.

It is important to distinguish here between writing and pictography. The latter is not 'picture-writing' in the sense that a key enables one to read it. Gelb (1963, 24–50) prefers to use such phrases as 'primitive drawings,' 'descriptive-representational devices' and 'identifying-mnemonic devices,' accepting them only as 'forerunners' of writing. The term pictograph is so established in English usage, however, that to adopt an alternative merely adds

to the present confusion. In my own usage, on which I have elaborated elsewhere (Dewdney 1970b, 5–6), pictograph is the generic term for any form of preliterate art—executed on any available surface—that is known, or is assumed to have, a *communicative*, rather than a decorative or 'aesthetic' intent.

The European white or silver birch, *Betula alba*, is native to the whole of Eurasia north of latitude 45°, growing prolifically in Scandinavia, the Baltic states, and the Soviet Union from the Finnish border to the Pacific. *Betula papyrifera*, variously referred to as the white, paper, or canoe birch, is equally widespread in North America, native to all the Canadian woodlands south of the tundra and east of the Rockies, extending well into the upper Mississippi states and eastward to the Atlantic. These are the homelands of the two most widely ranging language groups on the continent: Athapascan-speakers from Alaska to the Churchill River; and Algonkian-speakers from the Churchill to the Atlantic seaboard. Both peoples used birchbark extensively in their daily life, but for the Algonkian hunter-fisherman of the northern woodlands it was basic.

It should not be assumed, however, that birchbark was the exclusive medium of Algonkian pictography. Frequently it appeared on the diaphragms of hide drums or carved in the wooden sides of the Midé water drums, whether as incised lines, in low relief, or intaglio. Wooden slabs were sometimes preferred over bark (see **FIG. 11–36**) in rendering song records, a striking instance being the *Walum Olum* of the Delaware (Beach 1967, 23–6). Ojibway communities in northern Minnesota carved census records in wood, using totemic signs to identify the family head and tally marks to indicate the number in his family. Grave markers and the headboards of bark canoes might be painted or cut with pictographic figures. The Naskapi of Labrador and eastern Quebec stamped abstractions in colour on their hide shirts (Podolinsky-Webber n.d., personal communication), with symbolic as well as decorative effect. And early treaties signed with the Europeans were signed on parchment with goose quill pens by native leaders using their pictographic identity marks (King's

Printer 1905, 15, 16, 20, etc.). Algonkian speakers on the plains and prairies painted or drew symbols of significant dreams as ownership marks, records of accomplishment, or for more obscure religious reasons. Thus a Cheyenne named Howling Wolf could identify himself graphically by drawing a wolf with undulating lines radiating from its open mouth (Petersen 1968, 45).

Preceding the census board was a more abstract record of genealogies in the male line, indicating each generation with a single stroke, sometimes adding symbols of a special event such as the coming of the European. Copway (1851b, 129–31) claimed that the Ojibway had three depositories near Lake Superior of 'records written on slate rock, copper, lead, and on the bark of birch trees.' Native copper could be hammered into sheets; but there is no other reference to the use of slate or lead, and the latter could not have come into use until the traders began to stock it. In the archives of the Minnesota Historical Society I went through a large collection of Midé pictography made with lead pencil on paper accounting forms of the lumber companies that were operating in northern Minnesota by the end of the last century. The Midé master appeared to have been oblivious of the content of the paper forms themselves, as often as not drawing on the printed side.

In spite of all the wide variety of media available and in actual use, the popularity of birchbark far outstripped that of all others combined. It was almost exclusively through this medium that the complex rituals and oral traditions of the southern Ojibway were transmitted by the Midé shamans to their disciples or candidates for initiation.

In the growing birch tree the bark is divided into two main layers: an outer *phloem* and an inner *sapwood*, with a thin *cambium* layer between (**FIG. 11–37**). The outer bark consists of finely laminated cork tissue scattered over with *lenticels*, the slim brownish 'breathing organs' that give the paper layers their distinctive appearance. The inner bark, roughly equal in thickness, turns a dark brown when stripped of the outer layer, drying out rapidly and then cracking to become easily vulnerable to insects and fungi and drastically reducing the age expectancy of the tree.

Only the outside layer was used for pictographic purposes. When removed in the spring, its inner surface—hereafter referred to as the cambium side—is found to be coated with a deposit, dull yellow to deep brick-red in colour. This may readily be scraped off to reveal a much lighter yellowish surface. Such scraping is the easiest way of creating a design, and the original contrast tends to deepen with age.

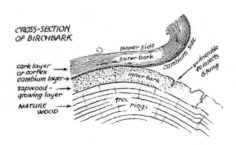

11–37 •
Schematic cross-section of the bark of the paper birch to show outer and inner layers.

This was one reason why most birchbark basketry was folded and stitched with the cambium side out; but it was also the natural way for the bark to curl. As the tree trunk swells with growth the tension on the outside paper layers increases, so that when the bark is removed it rolls itself up, so to speak, with the cambium side out. However, the spring bark is so flexible that even when rolled the 'wrong' way it will adjust its tensions and set with the paper side out.

For executing designs on birchbark a variety of techniques beyond the simple act of scraping was used. Porcupine quills, moose hair, spruce root and appliqué using bark cutouts were all employed by Algonkian-speakers. The full thickness of the outer bark was used, except for the unique *bitten* bark patterns (**FIG. 11–38**). To produce these the cork layers were separated into the thinnest possible sheets, which were folded, refolded, and frequently folded again, then bitten through with the eye teeth. When the bark is opened up and held against the light the full pattern is revealed. The Ob-Ugrians of westernmost Siberia also made birchbark bitings—of which an example is shown here (**FIG. 11–39**)—but instead of piercing the bark they textured it with the molar teeth.

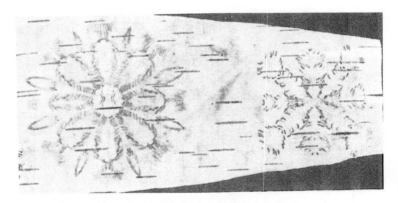

11–38 • Two patterns bitten into birchbark with eye teeth. *Courtesy of National Museum of Man.*

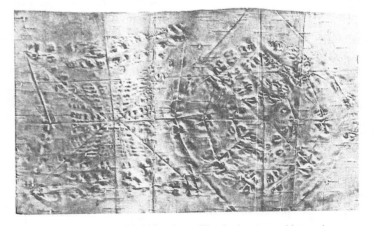

11–39 • Ob-Ugrian bark biting from Siberia, impressed by molar teeth.
Courtesy of Dr. Valery Chernetsov, Academy of Sciences, Moscow.

There is no problem in recognizing which side of the outer bark one is viewing. The outermost paper tissues readily bleach in the sun to produce the characteristic dead white of the tree. As natural pruning proceeds a dark, rough scar is left where each branch falls off. On the inside, however, as growth continues the scar is slowly filled in and finally sealed off, leaving only ripples on the cambium side to mark the healed wound. The cambium side is therefore always more consistently smooth than the paper side.

The difference between the two sides had a marked effect on the character of the drawings themselves. The paper layers are relatively hard and dry; the cambium side of the spring bark is quite soft and impressionable. Consequently a hardwood, bone, or steel stylus produces a line on the paper side which is more of a scratch than an engraving **(FIG. 11–40)**, while the same tool on the cambium side leaves a deep, soft-edged impression **(FIG. 11–41)**. So

11–40 • Midé ritual chart, engraved on the paper side. *Courtesy of Smithsonian Institution.*

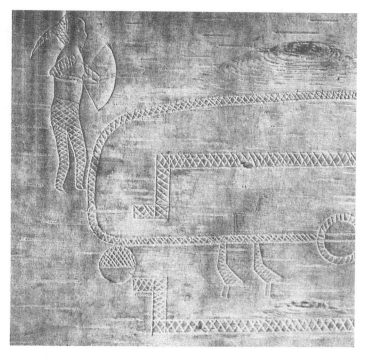

11–41 • Detail of Red Sky's Midéwegun scroll (gai-12) engraved on cambium side.

the stylus tends to cut through the outermost paper layers, while producing grooves on the cambium side. The latter was given overwhelming preference everywhere but in the Lake Winnipeg region where for some obscure reason the paper side was frequently used. Elsewhere, however, the paper side was sometimes used for overflow material.

Use of the paper side gave me some anxious moments in steaming open the older, drier specimens from Lake Winnipeg, for the paper layers separate more and more easily as they dry. Rolled inside, they dry shorter than the deeper layers, so that when the bark is flattened they will pull apart along the lines cut across the grain. Specimens where the cambium side is used, rolled in or out, never presented this problem, but they can fold and finally crack and split along the deeper cross-grain grooves unless steamed very thoroughly. The scroll makers were probably aware of all this but unconcerned, for they could always make new copies.

Whichever side was used the common practice was to make the lines more visible by doubling them and cross-hatching the space between (FIG. 11–41). Frequently the whole outlined figure was filled in with hatching or cross-hatching. Red ochre or trade vermilion was sometimes rubbed over the surface, perhaps partly to enhance the lines, but mainly— judging by the carelessness with which it was applied—to emphasize the sacredness of the scroll. Only in one specimen (from Crane Lake) was colour used to add definition to particular figures; it employed red, yellow, and blue trade colours. The sole instance where I have run across a scroll painted without any engraving is that published by Blessing (1963, 137) in which 'a dark purplish dye' was used. Red Sky's Midéwegun scroll was rubbed with yellow ochre.

Other style characteristics were due, directly or indirectly, to the nature of the birchbark medium. The grain probably accounts for the rectilinear tendencies that show up again and again. As the stylus moves along with the grain it is apt to become engaged, so that when the attempt is made to curve a line away from a straight path it too easily goes off the intended path to follow the grain again. Similarly a line that crosses the grain, as it curves toward it, may be pulled off its course. The solution for all lines of any length such as the outline of the Midé lodge is to eliminate the curves, allowing cross-grain and grainwise lines to meet at right angles. For shorter lines, where the stylus gets less deeply involved, the desired curve is easier to execute.

Another way of controlling a line so that neither the grain, pruning scars, nor larger lenticels would cause an unintended diversion was to use a template. With the availability of coins and cans in recent times curves were more easily produced, and a straight edge was often employed. According to Red Sky clay forms were used, but I have found no evidence of this. The use of bark cutouts from wornout scrolls for tracing some of the more repetitive forms was not unusual although never general. Note the

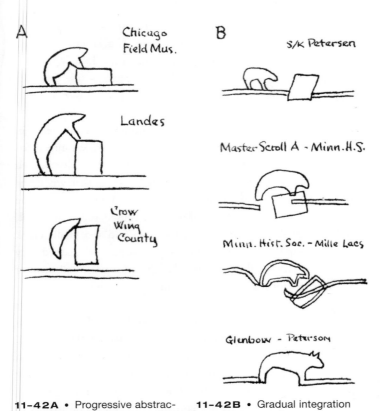

A Chicago Field Mus.

Landes

Crow Wing County

B S/K Petersen

Master Scroll A - Minn. H.S.

Minn. Hist. Soc. - Mille Lacs

Glenbow - Peterson

11-42A • Progressive abstraction of Bear and drum, the result of re-copying.

11-42B • Gradual integration of Bear, Bear's 'nest' and peripheral path, the result of re-copying.

gradual abstraction of the Bear in the sequences shown here (**FIGS. 11–42A** and **11–42B**), the result of tracing around cutouts of forms in earlier scrolls that had been traced around even earlier cutouts.

There are no descriptions in the literature of how a fresh copy was made from a wornout scroll, nor any means of judging how long an original might last. Some specimens in good condition showed evidence, in the patination of the outside of the rolled bark, of many handlings; others in very poor shape showed less. Copway (1851b, 130) recorded that the wornout scroll was 'divided equally among the wise men ... every fibre of it is considered sacred.' In a display in the National Museum of Man a few years ago I noticed a bark cutout of an animal form labelled as a 'charm,' which probably came from a scroll.

The nature of the bark and the re-copying of wornout scrolls had a number of effects on the style of Midé pictography. The *rectilinear* tendency has already been mentioned. Recopying encouraged *abstraction*, which led to *atrophy* in some instances, while in others, by losing a recognizable form, it might stimulate *elaboration* to become converted into a new form, a process I call *symbol conversion*. In recopying, too, anomalies might appear, as in Hoffman's Red Lake Master scroll where the unworn sections of the two older scrolls apparently were stitched together. Usually the outermost sections of the rolled bark wore out more rapidly than the more protected inner sections, except in cases where the scroll

was too tightly rolled, when flattening out the inner sections cracked them along the deeper cross-grain engravings. Another style effect was the result of copying a large scroll on a smaller piece of bark, cramping the design and demanding *condensation* of the figures. Copying from a smaller to a larger, the copyist was sometimes tempted to further elaboration, again leading to symbol conversion.

All of these style characteristics and others varied with the Midé master's personal teaching techniques. Should the secrecy of his information be uppermost in his mind he might employ condensation, abstraction, atrophy, or even *amputation*. Or he might go further, using symbolic conversion or the ultimate device for misleading the uninitiated: substitution of the significant form by another completely irrelevant one.

In order to convey to the apprentice the tremendous powers inherent in the higher degrees of initiation some instructors employed *power projection*, to represent the most prestigious figures by adding horns or other symbols to the head in particular (**FIG. 11–43**). At another level the master might be caught up in the decorative possibilities of the medium, producing, so to speak, variations on a theme by elaboration. In other instances a poetically inclined scroll engraver might employ a *zoomorphism*, where a river, for example, is represented as a snake.

Logically, as one Midé generation succeeded another the demand would grow for larger and larger scrolls to contain the increasing stock of lore. Since the grain of the bark runs around the circumference of the tree the length of pieces used rarely exceeded and seldom attained four feet. Bark from so large a tree, moreover, was thicker and less manageable than that from a smaller one so that lengths commonly used were less than twenty inches. Since Red Sky's and most of the other Migration charts

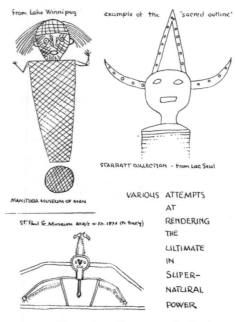

from Lake Winnipeg

example of the 'sacred outline'

STARRATT COLLECTION - from Lac Seul

MANITOBA MUSEUM OF MAN

St Paul Sc. Museum 80X/E + 50-1874 (Fr Tracy)

VARIOUS ATTEMPTS AT RENDERING THE ULTIMATE IN SUPER-NATURAL POWER

11-43 • Examples of 'power projection'

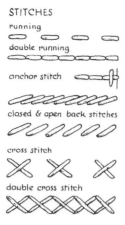

STITCHES

running

double running

anchor stitch

closed & open back stitches

cross stitch

double cross stitch

11-44 • Characteristic stitching

were close to nine feet long they had to be pieced together, a second, third, and even fourth section being stitched into a continuous roll of that length. In the south, where cedar and basswood were common, bast cord was made from the inner bark of either. In the north the split spruce root, known as *wautup*, was used. A few museum specimens were found stitched with linen thread, but it looked to me as if this had merely replaced the older, native material.

Prior to stitching, holes were punched through the overlapping edges of the two sections, using a bone or wooden awl, preferably before the bark was dry enough to create a splitting hazard. Several types of stitching were in use. Single and double running stitches and the back stitch were the commonest, sometimes finished off at the edge of the bark with an anchor stitch **(FIG. 11-44)**. Craftsmanship varied widely, from fine, tight even stitches to coarse, careless and even clumsy ones. Traditionally—but not always—this was women's work. Stitching in itself could be highly decorative as in the illustrated example **(FIG. 11-45)**.

It is not clear whether these pieced scrolls were used in earlier times. Although the 'genealogy' of some specimens appears to reach back into the early nineteenth century it is a curious fact that Kohl, sojourning at La Pointe in 1855 and taking a special interest in Ojibway pictography, makes no mention of *rolled* bark records (1957, 145).

'The Indians,' he writes, 'call a piece of birch bark to be employed for writing 'masinaigun'' (pronounced mazinah'igun). 'The word is derived from the verb *'nin masinaige'* (I make signs), and means something on which signs are made. They also give our paper and books the same name.

'The form of these masinaiguns varies greatly. At times I saw mere quadrangular plates, at others they made a species of pouch of it. Usually, however it is a long strip, which they fold in the middle, and looks like the cover of one of our books from which the contents have been removed **(FIG. 11-46)**. The writing is inside, and the rough bark outwards.'

Although most of the mazinah'iguns that Kohl saw were song or dream records, at least two were definitely Midé instruction charts. Yet neither was rolled. All the Museum specimens I have examined that could conceivably be of Midé origin, other than song records, were bound with endsticks and rolled **(FIGS. 11-47, 11-48)**. As the bark dries it tends to split. The ends of the song records were curved to minimize this, but the larger instruction scrolls were bound with endsticks **(FIG. 11-49)**, a pair of half-round pieces at each end of the scroll, between which the ends were doubled back, then securely bound to the sticks with bast or wautup. The edge folded back was sometimes trimmed close to the stick, sometimes—like the song records—finished off with a curve without endsticks.

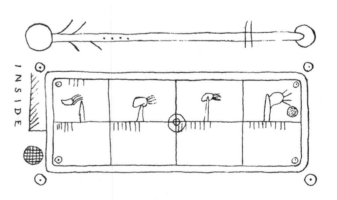

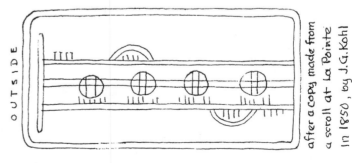

after a copy made from a scroll at La Pointe in 1850, by J.G. Kohl

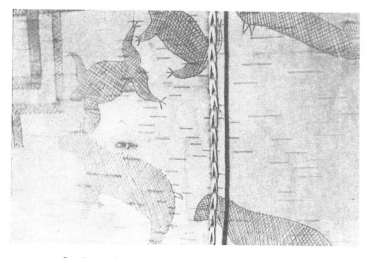

11-45 • Sections of bark scroll split-stitched together

11-46 • Early instruction chart, engraved on both sides of bark (Ko-1)

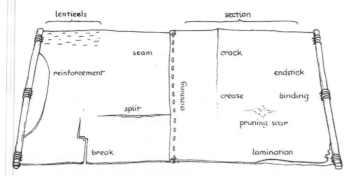

11-47 • Schematic rendering of birchbark prepared for engraving to show construction of, and flaws in a typical instruction scroll

11-48 • Cross-section of endstick

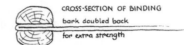

11-49 • A typical endstick, bound with wautup

The use or lack of endsticks, however, is not a reliable way of telling a song record from an instruction scroll. For example, the unique specimen from the Glenbow collection shown here is probably an elaborate song record, yet it is extraordinarily long and bound with endsticks (**FIG. 11–50**). Sixteen circles—twice the limit of eight degrees—further baffle identification.

It was my encounters with specimens such as this that frustrated earlier attempts at sorting my specimens into definable categories. Gradually, however, such rarities began to be pushed into the background, as variations on identifiable themes began increasingly to group themselves together. Finally, after frequent setbacks and revisions I arrived at the following categories.

1. *Origin scrolls* symbolizing the origin traditions of the Midéwewin.
2. *Migration charts* summarizing and charting the later accumulations of origin lore.
3. *Master scrolls and ritual charts* for instruction in the lore and rites preparatory to initiation.
4. *Ghost Lodge and Sky Degree scrolls* for instruction in specialized Midé rites.
5. *Deviant scrolls* suspected, as unorthodox Midé scrolls, of being used for destructive sorcery.
6. *Enigmatic scrolls* reflecting the results of the Midé diffusion and decline.

It cannot be overemphasized that the function of the birchbark scroll was mnemonic. It was not the written word, merely a means of recalling the oral tradition and the details of the Midé master's instruction. As we examine each group of scrolls in the sequence outlined above it will become clear that even the oral tradition was not transmitted in any rigid way from one generation to another.

Throughout the pages that follow it must be kept in mind that behind the instruction scrolls were individuals for whom the dream spoke with an authority equal to, and sometimes exceeding that of the oral tradition. Interaction between the dream, the sacred lore, and the mnemonic device of the scrolls produced, by a sort of cross-fertilization, a richer and richer body of rites, variations on the traditional themes, and birchbark pictography.

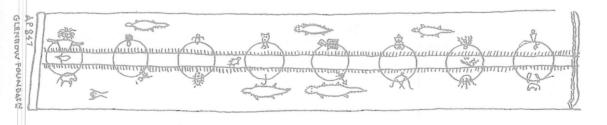

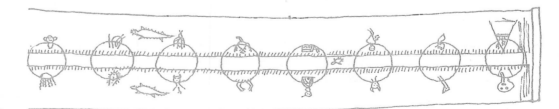

11-50 • Likely an unorthodox song record, with endsticks (GAI-1)

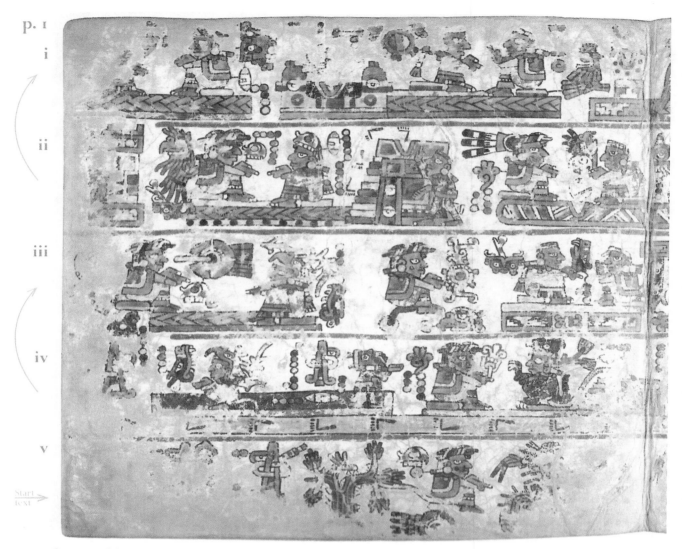

p. I

i

ii

iii

iv

v

Start
text

11-51 • *Courtesy of the Bodleian Library.*

p. 1/2–v Three dates, too damaged to reconstruct with certainty, refer to the sacred time of origin. The following scene contains a pochote, or thorny ceiba tree, clearly identified by its spines, while flames (ñuhu) painted above it express its sacredness (ñuhu). From this tree was born Lady 1 Death 'Sun Fan'. She was protected by two powerful spirits, Lord 4 Alligator 'Coyote Serpent' and Lord 11 Alligator 'Jaguar Serpent'. All went to an important shrine on the Mountain of Heaven, near the village of Yuta Tnoho (Apoala). The axe (caa) next to the sign for heaven helps to identify the place as Cavua ('rock') Caa ('which rises into' or 'where is stretched out') Andevui ('heaven'), a dominant peak east of the village. Here was the foundation of heaven and earth, symbolized by a column. Here two houses or families were to be united in an everlasting marital alliance.

Lord 4 Alligator 'Coyote Serpent' and Lord 11 Alligator 'Jaguar Serpent' offered precious gifts to a priest of Lord 4 Serpent—7 Serpent, the Patron Deity of Ñuu Tnoo, who in turn spoke to them and gave them tobacco, a priest's tunic, jade, and quetzal feathers.

p. 2/1–iv As a result of this interaction, in the year 5 Reed (939), on the day 6 Alligator, both lords instructed Lady 1 Death to leave the Place of Heaven. Before we hear where she went, a new lineage is introduced, associated with the sacred date year 5 Flint day 7 Flower, 'when the first day was born from earth', i.e. at the dawn of time. The date actually consists of a combination of calendar names of the founding couple: Lord 5 Flint 'Jaguar from the Tree' and Lady 7 Flower 'White Flower', ruling at Temple of Pearls, the Temple of Earthquakes. Their son was Lord 4 Alligator 'Blood Eagle', born in the Land of the Rain God, Ñuu Dzaui.

p. 1/2–iii It was with him that Lady 1 Death contracted matrimony on the day 6 Jaguar, eve of the ritually important day 7 Eagle, of the year 6 Flint (940). They had one daughter: Lady 1 Vulture 'Cloud Jewel'. Then the nine other leading couples of the region came together to found the village-state of Ñuu Tnoo. 1) Lord 5 Serpent 'Performer of Self-Sacrifice for the Earth' and Lady 8 Flower, 'Blood of the Town of Darkness', ruled the Place of Ceremonies in Ñuu Tnoo. 2) Lord 10 Dog 'War Foot' and Lady

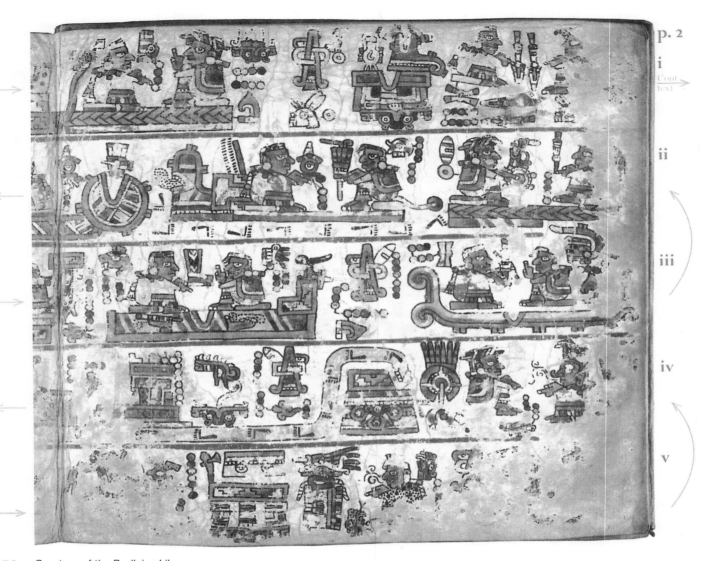

11–52 • *Courtesy of the Bodleian Library.*

8 Grass 'Cloud of Ñuu Dzaui' ruled the Place Where the Sacred Arrow Is Kept. 3) Lord 6 Movement 'Arrow' and Lady 9 House 'Sacred Seed of the Cave' were seated in the Cave of Clouds or the Cave of the Spring and the Tree. Its sacred date was year 7 Flint, day 9 House.

p. 2/1–ii 4) The son of Lord 6 Movement and Lady 9 House, Lord 5 Reed 'Born in War', married Lady 1 Flint 'Fire Serpent Jewel', the daughter of Lord 4 Rain 'Down-ball Quetzal' and Lady 7 Flower 'Eagle Wing', who ruled Stone of the Red and White Bundle. 5) The daughter of Lord 5 Reed and Lady 1 Flint was Lady 7 Death 'Fire Fan'. She married Lord 3 Rain 'Staff of Marks in the Ballcourt', ruler of Añute (Jaltepec). 6) Lord 10 Flint 'Skull' from the ancient Dark Altar married Lady 8 Death 'Quetzal, Performing Self-Sacrifice for the Earth'.

p. 1/2–i 7) In Temple of the Plant ruled Lord 7 Flower 'Jaguar, Mountain Bird' and Lady 5 Flint 'Cave Lady'. 8) Lord 10 Movement 'Flower Shield' and Lady 1 Movement 'Quetzal' ruled

Valley of Mud. 9) Lord 4 Lizard 'Serpent That Carries the Sky' and Lady 8 House 'Visible on Earth' ruled Town of the Drum. Apparently Lord 4 Alligator had succeeded in bringing their lineages together and so integrated the power base of what was to become the kingdom of Ñuu Tnoo. Another important political factor was the ancient Zapotec capital of Monte Albán, the ruins of which are situated on a huge mountain near the city of Oaxaca—today a major tourist attraction. Its main sign, the 'mountain that is opened or torn', is to be read as Yucu Cahnu, 'Big Mountain'. It was a place of altars and vessels, a place of origin. Here ruled Lord 10 Movement 'Arrow' and Lady 1 Rabbit 'Shield'. Its sacred date was year 1 Rabbit day 1 Rabbit.

Elsewhere this composite place-sign includes a mountain (*yucu*) with a moon or a field of reeds (both: *yoo*) and a mountain with an insect, either a fly or a louse (both: *tiyuqh*). These signs appear in a painting of Monte Albán on the colonial *Map of Xoxocotlan*, where they identify two major slopes of the site: Yucu Yoo (Acatepec in Nahuatl) and Tiyuqh (Sayultepec in Nahuatl).

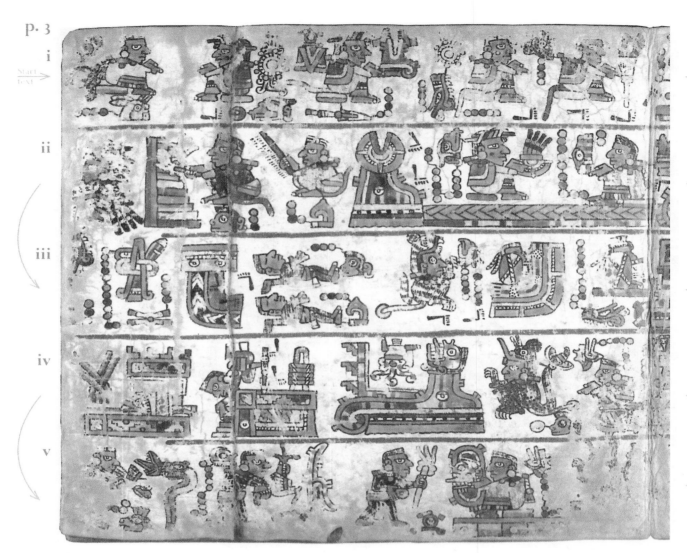

11-53 • *Courtesy of the Bodleian Library.*

p. 3/4–i Their son, Lord 4 Rabbit 'Jaguar That Carries One Alligator in his Breast', married Lady 1 Vulture 'Cloud Jewel', the daughter of Lady 1 Death and Lord 4 Alligator, whose birth was mentioned on p. 1–iii. Three daughters were born to this couple: Lady 5 Reed 'Rain Garment from Monte Albán', Lady 10 Alligator, 'War Jewel', and Lady 5 (here 4) Jaguar 'Quetzal Fan'. The second daughter, Lady 10 Alligator was sent to the Mountain of Pearls, probably Nuu Siya (Tezoatlan), where she married Lord 9 Deer 'Jade Bone, Flute', the son of Lord 7 Movement 'Face of the Earth' and Lady 12 Serpent 'Blood Knife', the rulers of Town of the Red and White Bundle. They had a son: Lord 12 Lizard 'Arrow Feet'.

p. 4/3–ii He was to marry his aunt, Lady 5 Jaguar 'Quetzal Fan', the above-mentioned third daughter of Lord 4 Rabbit and Lady 1 Vulture of Monte Albán. This new marital alliance would take the place of the former governmental structure of Monte Albán, the dynasty associated with the sacred date year 1 Rabbit day 1 Rabbit. Before, the site had been the seat of a dual rulership: Lord 12 Lizard 'Standing Firm on Big Mountain' and Lord 12 Vulture 'Quetzal Feather from Sun Mountain'. They are represented here as a couple, as 'father and mother of the people', seated on the mat of marriage and rulership. They had four 'sons', i.e. they were assisted by four governors. These were called: Lord 4 House 'Staff of Strokes', Lord 3 Monkey 'Burner of the Pyramids', Lord 10 Alligator 'Eagle' and Lord 10 Eagle 'Coyote'.

p. 3/4–iii They all died in an armed conflict, described as 'the war that came from Heaven', which marked the end of the last remains of the realm of Monte Albán and the political structure of the so-called 'Classic Period' (approximately 200–900 AD). Year 12 Flint day 4 Movement, the day of the 'new sun' or 'new era', was the date of the official funerary solemnity. Lord 4 House and Lord 3 Monkey, who had both been slain in battle, were buried in the Place of Heaven, the mountain near Yuta Tnoho (Apoala), which symbolizes the East. The mummy bundle of Lord 10 Eagle was deposited in the River of Ashes, Río Nejapa, the western boundary of Ñuu Dzaui. The mummy bundle of Lord 10

11-54 • *Courtesy of the Bodleian Library.*

Alligator was put to rest in the Split Dark Mountain, near Tepeji, the emblematic site of the North. The remains of Lord 12 Lizard and Lord 12 Vulture themselves were buried in the Temple of Death, a large and important funerary cave in the Mountain of Small Deer, in the region of Ñuu Ndaya (Chalcatongo), which symbolizes the South and stands under the supervision of the Death Goddess Lady 9 Grass, a deity of war. Until the day 12 Eagle of the year 6 Reed, commemorative rituals were celebrated in this Temple of Death.

p. 4/3–iv Year 10 House day 1 Grass was the sacred date of Lord 10 House 'Jaguar' and Lady 1 Grass 'Puma', divine patrons of the Yute Coo, 'Serpent River', near Ñuu Tnoo. From this Primordial Couple descended Lord 3 Eagle 'Eagle from the Serpent Place'. He married Lady 4 Rabbit 'Garment (Virtue) of Death Town'. Her name suggests that she came from the nearby Town of Death, Dzandaya (Mitlatongo). Lord 3 Eagle and Lady 4 Rabbit had two sons: Lord 9 Wind 'Stone Skull' and Lord 1 Monkey. The latter became the founding father of the Dzandaya

(Mitlatongo) dynasty. In front of him is the Skull Mountain, which appears to represent Dzandaya. Several other places follow.

p. 3/4–v Both brothers were recognized as local rulers: three priests—Lord 1 Rain, Lord 10 Death 'Cloud' and Lord 4 Dog 'Serpent-Maguey'—offered them fire, quails, and branches. Lord 9 Wind 'Stone Skull' then married Lady 5 Reed, one of the three princesses of Monte Albán, whose genealogical background is explained above (p. 3–i). Together they became rulers of Ñuu Tnoo. The year of the marriage was 4 Rabbit (990).

That date is given in Codex Yuta Tnoho (Vindobonensis) reverse, p. iii/iv–1, which also clarifies that Lord 9 Wind had been born in the year 8 Rabbit (940). The chronology of this early period has several problems, however.

p. 5/6–v Lord 9 Wind and Lady 5 Reed had three sons. In the year 6 Flint (992) was born Lord 10 Flower, 'Jaguar with Burnt Face'. Later followed Lord 13 Eagle 'Precious Jaguar' and Lord 3 Water 'White Arrow'. Lord 9 Wind and Lady 5 Reed arranged a

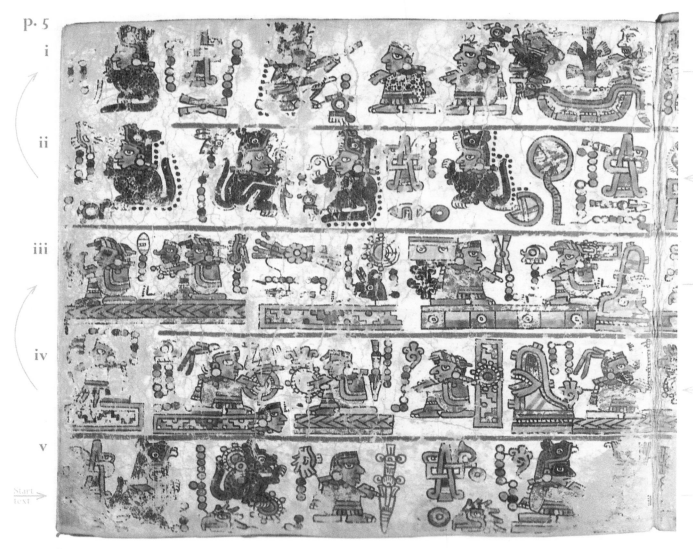

11-55 • *Courtesy of the Bodleian Library.*

marriage for their first-born son, establishing an alliance with the ruling couple of Chiyo Yuhu, known today by its Aztec name as Suchixtlan, near the important centre of Yanhuitlan.

Thus in the year 1 House (1013), on the day 1 Eagle, Lord 10 Flower, the son of Lord 9 Wind 'Stone Skull' and Lady 5 Reed, at the age of twenty or twenty-one, was engaged to be married to Lady 2 Serpent 'Plumed Serpent'. She was a princess of Chiyo Yuhu, daughter of Lord 8 Wind 'Twenty Eagles' and Lady 10 Deer. From this marriage seven children were born: 1) Lord 12 Lizard 'Arrow Feet', 2) Lord 10 Eagle 'Stone Jaguar', who married Lady 9 Wind 'Flint Garment' from neighbouring Añute.

p. 6/5–iv 3) Lady 12 Jaguar 'Jewelled Spiderweb', who married Lord 10 Reed from the Yahua (Tamazola) dynasty, and ruler of Staff Town (probably Yucu Tatnu/Topiltepec), 4) Lady 6 Grass 'Transparent Butterfly', who married Lord 10 Reed 'Precious Jaguar' from Torch Mountain (possibly Yucu Quesi/Tataltepec), 5) Lady 4 Rabbit 'Precious Quetzal', who married Lord 10 Flower 'Bow Tail' from Dark Specked Mountain, 6) Lady 7 Flower

'Jewel of the Town', who apparently did not marry, 7) Lady 7 Reed 'Jewel Flower', who married Lord 13 Death 'Setting Sun' from Head Town.

p. 5/6–iii The first-born, Lord 12 Lizard 'Arrow Feet', married his nieces, Lady 4 Flint 'Quetzal Feather Face' and Lady 4 Alligator 'Jewel Face', both daughters of his sister, Lady 12 Jaguar 'Jewelled Spiderweb', and her husband Lord 10 Reed, rulers of Staff Town. This family marriage was probably motivated by the wish to bring the divided heritage back together. The first of Lord 12 Lizard's children was Lord 5 Movement 'Smoke of Heaven'. He married first a princess of Añute, Lady 4 Death 'Jewel of the People'. She belonged to the Ñuu Tnoo royal family through her father, Lord 10 Eagle, who was the younger brother of the Ñuu Tnoo ruler Lord 10 Flower, and consequently an uncle of Lord 12 Lizard.

Lord 5 Movement's brother and sisters were: 1) Lord 12 Water 'Sky Jaguar', 2) Lady 3 Movement 'Fan of the Earth', who married Lord 8 Serpent 'Serpent in Flames' from River, 3) Lady 1

p. 6

i

Cont
text

ii

iii

iv

v

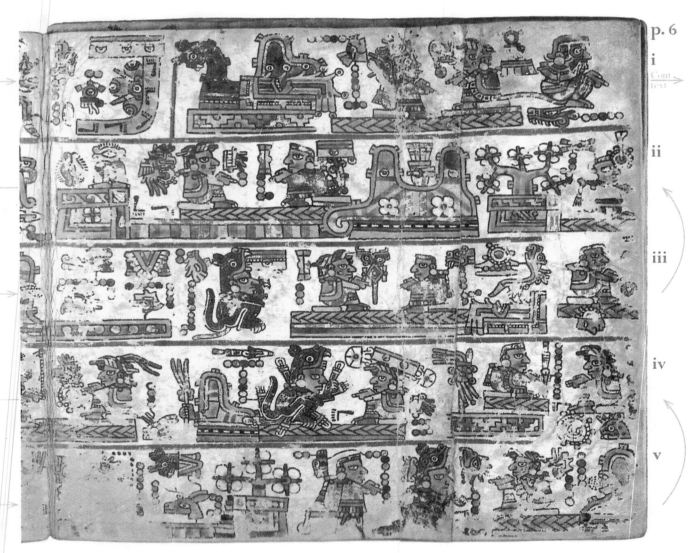

11–56 • *Courtesy of the Bodleian Library.*

Flint 'Jewel Face', who married Lord 6 Movement 'Precious Bone', a son of Lord 8 Wind of Chiyo Yuhu (Suchixtlan).

p. 6/5–ii Ñuu Tnoo's crown prince Lord 5 Movement 'Smoke of Heaven' remarried, this time to a princess from Lord 8 Wind's circle, Lady 2 Grass 'Precious Quetzal', who came from the community of Visible Stones, belonging to Chiyo Yuhu. Apparently he never ruled Ñuu Tnoo, but stood under the influence of the ruling family of Chiyo Yuhu. In the year 11 Reed (1075), Lady 2 Grass was close to giving birth to her first son. On the day 9 Reed a vision appeared in an obsidian mirror: a birth was announced, and an umbilical cord was seen, connected to 9 Reed. This was the day of the Goddess who was the Power of the Arrowhead of Volcanic Glass (obsidian). The vision stated that the child was going to be dedicated to that goddess, to be under her spell and supervision. This was not a pleasant announcement, because the Goddess 9 Reed could bring destruction. Her very name indicated the combination of fatality (symbolized by 9, the number of death) and war or conquest ('reed' being an arrow). Six days later

the child foreseen in the mirror was born: Lord 2 Rain 'Twenty Jaguars' (Ocoñaña). He was heir to the throne of Ñuu Tnoo, but another manuscript (Codex Tonindeye/Nuttall) shows that Lord 8 Wind of Chiyo Yuhu had him put under the watchful eyes of his warriors.

In the year 6 Flint (1096) Prince 2 Rain 'Twenty Jaguars' reached the age of twenty-one. On 1 Flint, the day before the day of his calendar name, he had an important conversation with Lord 10 Rabbit 'Blood Jaguar'. Other manuscripts show that this man was a grandson of the mighty Lord 8 Wind of Chiyo Yuhu (presumably deceased by now). As such he was a second cousin to Lord 2 Rain's father and would have been respected as an uncle by Lord 2 Rain himself. His relationship with Lord 2 Rain went back to 1076, when he had been present at the ceremony in which the young boy had been bestowed with the royal title (depicted in the map of Chiyo Cahnu/Teozacualco). The subject of the conversation between Lord 10 Rabbit and Lord 2 Rain is not made explicit, but in view of the age and family relationship of the two men, it is probable that the elder man gave counsel and instructions to the prince. They had a second conversation on the day 12 Water.

p. 5/6–i Then, on the day 7 Movement, the last day of the twenty-day period that had started on 1 Flint, Lord 2 Rain spoke with two priests: one in a white priestly tunic with black dots, the other an old man with a red tunic. The first was the priest in charge of the Sacred Arrow, and the second was the one with the title 'Smoke' or 'Cloud'. Both were members of the Supreme Council of Four that assisted the ruler of Ñuu Tnoo. Lord 2 Rain engaged in a ritual activity, probably aimed at claiming his rightful position as ruler of Ñuu Tnoo. His body is painted black with a hallucinogenic ointment and his eyes are closed; apparently he had entered the priestly trance. In one hand he holds a perforator for blood-letting; in the other he grasps an arrow, directing the point towards his chest. Probably this is the Sacred Arrow, the War-Spirit of Ñuu Tnoo. Still in a trance, the prince made a blood offering to the Divine Lord 7 Vulture in Serpent River, the place of a Sacred Tree. From here he went on a 'road of knife and star' to heaven, i.e. he died during his shamanic journey. This was the end of the first dynasty.

In order to understand the further political development, it is important to focus on another important person, necessitating a return in time. Lord 13 Dog 'White Eagle, Venus' and Lady 1 Vulture 'Rain Skirt' had founded a noble house at 'River, Black Mountain, Curved Jaguar Mountain', possibly nearby Ayuta, 'Place of the River'. Codex Tonindeye (Nuttall) reveals that Lady 1 Vulture belonged to the dynasty of another neighbouring settlement: Ñuu Ñañu, the old fortress of Yahua (Tamazola). This couple had one son: Lord 5 Alligator 'Rain Sun'.

Entries in italics indicate figures; those with an m following the entry indicate maps

A

Abacus, 190, 192
Abbey church, 337
Ablaq masonry, 362
Aboriginal Laws (Australia), 45
Aboriginals, essay on (McMaster and Martin), 527–528
Absolute dating, 21
Abstract art, 17
"Abstract Design in American Quilts," (exhibition at the Whitney Museum in New York), 4
Abstraction, 251
Abu Simbel, Egypt, Ramses II and, 176–178
Abu Simbel, Site of the Inscription, 240
Academicians of the Royal Academy (Zoffany) 1771–1772, 652
Academies and academy exhibitions, 652
Acanthus, 192
Acrophonic principle, 140
Acropolis, 197–198
Acropolis, model/reconstruction of, Athens c. 447–432 BCE, 197
Acroteria, 192
Adam and Eve (Dürer) 1504, 628
Adobe brick, 131
African art. *See* Early African art
Agnelo Doni (Raphael) c. 1506, 608–609
Agora (Marketplace), reconstruction drawing, Athens c. 400 BCE, 205
Aisles, 326, 364
Ajax and Achilles Playing a Game (Exekias) c. 540–530 BCE, 182–183
Akbar, 453, 455
Akbar Inspecting the Construction of Fatehpur Sikri, India c. 1590, 455
Akhenaten and His Family, Egypt, Eighteenth Dynasty c. 1353–1336 BCE, 173
Akhenaten, king of Egypt, Eighteenth Dynasty c. 1353–1336 BCE, 172–174
Akkad, Mesopotamia, 74, 77
  head of a ruler, 74, 77
  Stele of Naram–Sin, 67, 77
Album leaves, 467, 469
Alphabetic Letterforms, development of, Ninth to First century BCE, 141
Alphabetic script, 141–142
Alphabets, 135, 140–144, 238–241
Alphabetum Romanum (Feliciano) Verona 1460–1463, 657
Altamira cave paintings, 20, 136, 137
Altdorfer, Albrecht, *Triumph of Maximilian I,* The 1512–1516, 515
Al-Wasiti, Yahya Ibn, *The Maqamat by Al-Hariri* 1237, 358–359
Al-Zain, Muhammad Ibn, *Baptistery of St. Louis* c. 1300, 376
al-Zaman, Nadir (Abu'l Hasan)
  Jahangir and Shah Abbas, India c., 1618, 457
  Prince Khurram, The Future Shah Jahan at Age 25, India c. 1616–1617, 457
Amalaka, 254
Amalakas, 91
Amaranth (Yun), China 1633–1690, 476, 477
Amarna period (Egypt), 172–174
Ambulatory, 326, 364
American Section of the Cantino World Map 1502, 511m
Americas after 1300, 484–528
  Aztec empire, 486–489
    aftermath of the Spanish conquest, 493
    calendar stone, 490
    featherwork, 488–489
    manuscripts, 489
    sculpture, 487–488
    Tenochtitlan, 486–487

Inca empire, 489–493
  aftermath of the Spanish conquest, 493
  Cuzco, 491
  Machu Picchu, 491–492
  masonry, 492
  metalwork, 493
  textiles, 492–493
map, 487m
North America, 493–505
  Eastern woodlands, 494–496
  Great Plains, 496–499
  Northwest coast, 499–501
  Southwest, 502–505
Americas before 1300, 115–133
  Central America, 128–129
  map, 117m
  Mesoamerica, 116–128
    the Maya, 122–128
    the Olmec, 116–119
    Teotihuacán, 119–122
  the new world, 116
  South America: the Central Andes, 129–133
    Andean textiles, 132
    Chavin de Huantar, 129–130
    Moche culture, 131–133
    Nazca culture, 130, 131
    Paracas culture, 130
Amphora, 182–183
Anastasis, apse of funerary chapel in Church of Christ in Chora, 354
Anatolia, Hittites of, 305
Anavysos Kouros, Cemetery at Anavysos near Athens c. 530 BCE, 271, 272
Ancient Egypt, 150–181
  Early Dynastic Egypt c. 2950–2575 BCE, 152–157
    artistic conventions, 153–155
    funerary architecture, 155–157
    god-kings, 152–153
  Late Egyptian art c. 715–332 BCE, 181
  map, 152m
  Middle Kingdom c. 1975–1640 BCE, 164–166
    funerary stelae, 165–166, 167
    portraits of Sensusret III, 164
    rock-cut tombs, 164–165
    town planning, 166
  New Kingdom c. 1539–1075 BCE, 166–180
    Akhenaten and the art of the Amarna period, 172–174
    Books of the Dead, 149, 178–180
    great temple complexes, 167–169
    Hatshepsut, 169–171
    return to tradition: Tutankhamen and Ramses II, 174–178
    tomb of Ramose, 171–172
  the Nile Valley, 152
  Old Kingdom c. 2575–2150 BCE, 157–163
    great pyramids at Giza, 157–161
    pictorial relief in tombs, 163
    sculpture, 161–162
  pictorial relief technique, 167
  Third Intermediate Period c. 1075–715 BCE, 180
Ancient Greece 182–237
  Archaic period c. 600–480 BCE, 189–196
    ceramic painting, 196
    sanctuary at Delphi, 189–190
    temples, 190–195
  color in Greek sculpture, 195
  emergence of Greek civilization, 184
  Greek art c. 900–600 BCE, 184–188
    Geometric period c. 900–700 BCE, 184–187
    Orientalizing period c. 700–600 BCE, 187
  Greek orders of Classical Greek architecture, 192
  High Classical Period c. 450–400 BCE, 196–237
    the Acropolis, Athens c. 447–432 BCE, 197–198
    the Athenian agora c. 400 BCE, 204–205
    city plans, 204–206

Constantine the Great, 229–231
  the Flavians (Roman), 216–218
  imperial architecture (Roman), 219–227
  imperial portraits (Roman), 227–229
  the Julio-Claudians 14–68 CE, 207
  the Parthenon, Athens c. 447–432 BCE, 198–203
  Roman art after Constantine, 231–238
  Roman cities, 207–209
  Roman houses, 209–210
  Roman wall paintings, 210–216
  stele sculpture, 206
  Temple of Athena Nike, Athens c. 410–405 BCE, 204
  map of, 185m
Ancient Near East, 67–68, 70m
  See also Fertile Crescent and Mesopotamia
Ancient Rome. See Ancient Greece; High classical period
Andean civilization. See Inca empire; Americas after 1300
Andean textiles, 132
Andhra period
  early, 88–92
  later, 92–96
Angkor Vat, Cambodia, 12th century CE, 266, 268
An Gyeon, *Dream Journey to the Peach Blossom Land,* Korea 1447 CE, 480
Aniconism, 360–361
Animal style, 407
Annunciation (Fra Angelico) c. 1738–1445, 596–597
Anthemius of Tralles and Isidorus of Miletus, *Hagia Sophia Church* 532–537 CE, 332
Anthropological studies, 135
Apadana of Darius and Xerxes, Persepolis 518–c. 460 BCE, 311, 312, 313
Aphaia on Aegina temple c. 500 BCE, 190–191, 193–195
Aphrodite of Knidos (Praxiteles), copy of original of c. 350 BCE, 277, 278, 279
Aphrodite of Melos c. 150–100 BCE (also known as *Venus De Milo*), 286–287
Apollo's sanctuary (Sanctuary at Delphi) c. 6th–3rd century BCE, 188–190
Apple Cup (workshop of Hans Krug) c. 1510–1515, 624
Apses, 220, 328
Arabesques, 361
Arabic Manuscript (Galinus) 1199, 378
Ara Pacis Augustae, 295
Arcade, 192
Archaic period, Greece c. 600–480 BCE, 189–196
Archaic smile, 270
Archangel Michael, diptych, early 6th century, 340–341
Archer ("Paris"), reconstruction drawing, Temple of Aphaia, Aegina 2004 CE, 195
Archer ("Paris"), Temple of Aphaia, Aegina c. 500–490 BCE, 195
Arches, 369
Architecture
  concrete, 224
  early construction methods, 25
  funerary architecture, ancient Egypt, 155–157, 165–166
  Greek orders of Classical Greek architecture, 192
  Han dynasty, 105
  mastaba to pyramid, 157
  Neolithic period, 22–29
  Paleolithic period, 13–14
  portable tipi, 496–498
  stupas and temples, 91
Architrave, 190, 192
Archivolts, 429
Arch of Constantine, Rome 312–315 CE, 230, 231
Arch of Titus, Rome c. 81 CE, 215–217
Armchair, China, 16th–17th century, 472
Arnhem Land in the Northern Territory, Australia, 42–43
Arrighi, Ludovico, 660–662
  writing manual, Rome 1522, 661
Art
  architecture and, 3

defining, 2–4
as spoils of war, 73
Art history
analyzing formal structure, 7–8
assessing physical properties, 4–7
identifying subject matter, 8
Artifacts, 135
Ashoka, 81, 87–88
Ashokan Pillar, India c. 246 BCE, 80
Ashokan pillars, 80–81, 87
Asia and South Pacific designs, 548
Asian empires, 451–483
China's modern period, 478
foundations of Chinese culture, 465
India's engagement with the West, 460–463
Indonesian traditions, 452
Korea's Joseon dynasty (1392–1910), 479–482
Ceramics, 479–480
painting, 480–482
map of China and Korea, 464m
Marco Polo, 466
Ming dynasty (1368–1644), 467–476
architecture and city planning, 471–472
court and professional painting, 468–470
decorative arts, 470–471
literati aesthetic, 472–476
modern Korea, 482–483
Mongol invasions, 464
Mughal period, 452–460
architecture, 453–455
Indian painting on paper, 458
luxury arts, 456
painting, 455–457
Rajput painting, 458–460
Taj Mahal, 453–455
Qing dynasty (1644–1911), 476–478
individualist painting, 477–478
orthodox painting, 477
Vietnamese ceramics, 452
Yuan dynasty, 465–467
As If to Celebrate, I Discovered a Mountain Blooming with Red Flowers (Kapoor), India 1981, 462–463
Assassination of Pizarro, The (de Bry) 1596, 526
Asmat Ancestral Spirit Poles (Bisj), West Papua c. 1960, 49
Assurbanipal and His Queen in the Gardens, Nineveh c. 647 BCE, 308, 309
Assurnasirpal II Killing Lions, Kalhu c. 875–860 BCE, 306
Assyria, 305–309
Dur Sharrukin, 307–309
Kalhu, 305–307
Nineveh, 309
textiles, 309
Astragal, 192
Asuka period (Japan, 552–645 CE), 109–111
Athena Attacking the Giants, altar from Pergamon c. 175–150 BCE, 281, 283
Athena Nike, 204
Athenian Agora, 204
Athens, Greece, 184
Augustus of Primaporta, early 1st century CE, 294, 295
Aulus Metellus (The Orator), found near Peugia c. 80 BCE, 291
Australia, 45–46
Aboriginal Australians, 43, 45–46
Barunga statement, 42–43
Yirrkala Bark Petitions, 43
Autumn Colors on the Qiao and Hua Mountains (Zhao), China 1296, 466
Avenue of the Dead, Teotihuacán, Mexico, 120
Axis mundi, 87
Aztec pictographs, 691–697
Aztecs, 119–122, 486–489
See also Americas after 1300; Americas before 1300; Tenochtitlan; Teotihuacán
Aztlan, Mexico, 486

B

"Babur Builds the Bagh–I Wafa" from the Baburnama (Bishnadas) c. 1590, 386
Baby Carrier, Sioux, 19th century, 496
Babylon, 6th century BCE, reconstruction drawing of, 310

Babylon, Mesopotamia, 78–79
Code of Hammuarbi, 78–79
Bacchus (Caravaggio), 642
Bacon, Francis, 648
Baghdad Kiosk 1638, 382
Bailey, 429
Baldacchino (Bernini) 1624–1633, 635, 636
Baldachin, 423
Ballgames, Mesoamerican, 127
Baptismal Font, Notre-Dame-aux-Fonts (Renier of Huy) 1107–1118, 438
Baptistery of St. Louis (Al–Zain) c. 1300, 376
Barbarian, 281
Barberini Togatus, *Patrician Carrying Portrait Busts of Two Ancestors*, Pallazzo de Conservatori, Rome, 290
Bargeboards, 54
"Baroque," 633
Barozzi, Giacomo (Vignola), 616, 618, 619
Barrel vault, 217
Barunga statement (Australia, 1988), 42–43
Base, 192
Basic Set of Character Shapes for Reading English, 395, 396
Basilica Nova, 230, 233–234
Basilica of Maxentius and Constanine (Basilica Nova), reconstruction drawing, 234
Basilica of Maxentius and Constantine (Basilica Nova), Rome 306–313 CE, 233
Basilica or Maxentius and Constantine (Basilica Nova), Rome, floor plan 306–313 CE, 234
Basilicas, 219–221
Basilica Ulpia, Rome c. 112 CE, 219–220
Bath Advertisement, 244
Baths of Caracalla, Rome c. 211–217 CE, 299–301
Battle Between the Gods and the Giants (Titans), Sanctuary of Apollo, Delphi c. 530–525 BCE, 190
Battle of Centaurs and Wild Beasts from Hadrian's Villa, Tivoli c. 125 CE, 228
The Battle of San Romano (Uccello) 1438–1440, 577, 597
Battle of the Nudes (Dei Pollaiuoto) c. 1465–1470, 592–593
Battle Scene, Hide Painting, North Dakota 1797–1800, 498, 499
Bawa, Manjit, *Dharma and the God*, India 1984, 462
Bay, 191
Bayeux Embroidery, 439–441
Beadwork, Native American, 496, 497
Beauty, 251
Berlin Kore, CEmetery at Keratea, near Athens c. 570–560 BCE, 270, 271
Bernini, Gianlorenzo
Baldacchino 1624–1633, 635, 636
Cornaro Chapel, Church of Santa Maria Della Vittoria, Rome 1642–1652, 637
David 1623, 636
as sculptor, 636–638
St. Teresa of Avila in Ecstasy 1645–1652, 631, 632
Bhakti Movement in art, 264–265
Bharat Mata (Mother India) (Tagore), India 1905, 460–461
Bi, 103
Bilum (contemporary net bags of highland New Guinea), 47–48
Birchbark: a pictographic medium, 684–690
bitten bark patterns, 686
endsticks, 690
gradual integration of Bear, Bear's "nest" and peripheral path, the result of re-copying, 688
instruction charts, 689–690
Midés and, 687–690
power projection examples, 688
progressive abstraction of Bear and drum, the result of re-copying, 688
schematic cross-section of the bark of the paper birch to show outer and inner layers, 686
stitching, 689
trunk of paper birch, 685
wooden panel with engraved totemic signs, 685
Bird-Headed Man with Bison, Lascaux Cave, France, 20
Birkenhead, John, *Four-Legged Elder* 1647, 681, 682
Birkenhead, John and John Denham, *Four-legg'd Quaker to the Time of the Dog and Elder's Maid, or, the Lady's Fall, The* 1662–1668, 681–682

Bishnadas, "Babur Builds the Bagh–I Wafa" from the *Baburnama* c. 1590, 386
Bislebertus, Last Judgment Tympanum, Church of Saint-Lazare at Autunc 1120–1130 or 1130–1145, 433–434
Bison, Altamira cave, Spain, 20
Bison, Le Tuc d'Audoubert, France, 21
Black Death, influence on art, 531
Black-figure technique, 187
Blackfoot Women Raising a Tipi, Montana c. 1900, 497
Black-letter broadside ballads, 677–684
Blackware Storage Jar (Martinez and Martinez), New Mexico c. 1942, 502, 503
Blind arcade, 454
Blombos Cave, Southern Cape Coast, South Africa, 13
Bloodletting, 486
Bloodletting Ritual, Teotihuacán, Mexico c. 550–650 CE, 121–122
Bodhisattva, detail of wall painting in Cave 1, Ajanta, Maharashtra, India, Vakataka dynasty c. 475 CE, 252, 253
Bodhisattvas, 87, 252, 253
Body ideals, 251
Book of Homilies, the nun Guda, early 12th century, 444
Book of Hours, Bruges c. 1490–1500, 400, 401
Book of Hours of Jeanne d'Évereux, Kiss of Judas and Annunciation (Purcelle) c. 1325–1328, 530, 532
Books
Dutch Renaissance and popular prints 1530–1700, 669–673
illuminated, 656–657
printing in Renaissance Italy and France 1460–1600, 656–669
See also Illuminated books; Illuminated manuscripts; Printing, revolutions in
Books of the Dead, 149, 178–180
Borobudur, central Java, Indonesia c. 800 CE, 266, 267
Borromini, Francesco
Church of San Carlo Alle Quattro Fontane, Rome, Exterior and Plan 1638–1667, 638
Church of San Carlo Alle Quattro Fontane, Rome, View into the Dome 1638–1667, 638, 639
Boustrophedon format, 239
Bowl, China c. 5000–4000 BCE, 96
Bowl with Kufic Border 11th–12th century, 375
Boy Writing, Greece 5th century BCE, 241
Bracketing, 105
Brahma, 88
Brahmi script, 81
Brave Buffalo, wolf dream, 1
British colonial period, India, 460–461
Broad-Shouldered Jar with Decoration of a Fruiting Grapevine, Korea 17th century, 480
Broadside ballads, 673–684
branding of, 678–681
Gelding of Curates case study, 681, 682–684
Robin Hood, England 1634, 674
uses for, 679
white- and black-letter, 677–684
women and, 680
Bronze Age, 31–32, 31–34
in China, 98–101, 465
Bronze bells, 100–101
Bronze Foundry, Vulci, Italy 490–480 BCE, 274
Brotherhood of the Bent Billiard, The (Memmott), 63
Brunelleschi, Filippo, 579–583
Dome of Florence Cathedral 1420–1436, 580, 581
Ospedale Degli Innocenti (Foundling Hospital), Florence 1421–1444, 582–583
Sacrifice of Isaac 1401–1402, 585
Buddha
marks of, 112
Three Jewels, The, 147–148
Buddha and Attendants, India c. late 1st–early 2nd century CE, 95
Buddha Maitreya, Buriram Province, Thailand 8th century CE, 265
Buddha Shaka and Attendant Bodhisattvas in the Horyuji Kondo, Japan c. 623 CE, 111
Buddha, Shakyamuni, 87
Buddha Shakyamuni, Thailand, Mon Dvaravati period 9th century CE, 266

Buddhism, 81, 85–95, 465
  India, 265
  Japan and, 109–113
  rise of, 85–87
  types of, 87
Buddhist rock–cut halls, 92
Buddhist sculpture, 252
Buddhist symbols, 112
Buncheong ceramics (Korea), 479
Buonarroti, Michelangelo. See Michelangelo
Burgkmair, Hans
  Detail from The Triumph of Maximilian I 1526, 517
  Indian Holding a Mexican Shield post 1519, 517
Butcher, Egypt, Fifth Dynasty c. 2450–2325 BCE, 162
Buttressing, 292
Buxheim St. Christopher mid 15th century, 653
Byzantine art, early, 331–343
  architectural elements, 334
  Golden Age of Justinian, 331
  Hagia Sophia, 332–335
  icons and iconoclasm, 342
  objects of veneration and devotion, 340
Byzantine art, late, 352–357
  Constantinople: the Chora Church, 352–355
  Funerary Chapel of Theodore Metochites, 354
  Moscow: Rublyov, 356, 357
Byzantine art, middle, 344–352
  architecture and mosaics, 345
  objects of veneration and devotion, 350
  San Climent in Taull paintings, 424

C

Cairn, 26
"Calendarium" (Ratdolt), Venice 1476, 658
Calendar Stone, Mexico c. 1500, 486, 490
Calif Harun Al-Rashid Visits the Turkish Bath (Al-Din
  Bihzad) c. 1494, 379
Calligraphy, 377–378
The Calling of St. Matthew (Caravaggio) 1599–1600, 645
Cambodia, Angkor Vat, 266–269
Canal, The (Reflecting Pool), Hadrian's Villa, Tivoli
  125–135 CE, 228
Cannibalism, 510
"Canon of Polykleitos, The," 202
Cantino World Map 1502, 511m
Capital, 192
Caracalla early 3rd century CE, 299, 300
Caravaggio, 641–646
  Bacchus 1595–1596, 642
  The Calling of St. Matthew 1599–1600, 645
  Contarelli Chapel, San Luigi dei France 1599–1602,
    644–645
  The Conversion of St. Paul c. 1601, 643
Careless Curate and the Bloudy Butcher, The 1662, 683–684
Carolingian Minuscule, France 9th century, 394
Carpet making, 384–385
Carpet Page (from the Lindisfarne Gospels), 5
Carracci, Agostino, 639–641
Carracci, Annibale, 639–641
  Flight into Egypt Landscape 1603–1604, 639, 641
  Palazzo Farnese Gallery ceiling, Rome 1597–1601, 640
Carter, Howard, 151
Cartouches, 218
Carved Figure from Storehouse Doorway, New Zealand
  1500–1800, 55
Carved Spear Thrower, Mas-D-Azil, France 16,000–9000
  BCE, 136
Carved Vessel, Uruk c. 3300–3000 BCE, 71
Castagno, Andre del, *The Last Supper* 1447, 598
Catacombs, 317
Catalhöyük houses (Turkey), 23–25
Cathedral, 320
Cathedral of the Virgin and St. Stephen at Speyer, 426
Cathedrals and crusades: Europe and its neighbors in the
  Middle Ages, 403–450. *See also* Europe in the
  Middle Ages
Cave Painting, Altamira, Spain 16,000–9000 BCE, 137
Cave paintings, 17–21
  Altamira, 20
  Chauvet, 18
  Lascaux, 18–20

meaning of, 17–18
  technique, 19
Cave sculptures, 21–22
Cave-Temple of Shiva, Elephanta, Eternal Shiva,
  Maharashtra, India, Post-Gupta period,
    mid 6th century CE, 256, 257
Caxés, Eugenio
  Recovery of San Juan de Puerto Rico, The, 1630s, 523
  Recovery of the Island of San Cristobel, The, 1630s, 523
Cella, 190
Celts, 115, 282
Celts and Anglo–Saxons in Britain, 407–408
Cenote, 128
Centering, 292
Central America, Diquis culture 700–1500 CE, 128–129
Central-plan churches, 326
Ceramics
  defined, 31
  Neolithic, 29–31
  techniques, 31
Ceremonial Center of the City of Teotihuacán, Mexico
  c. 100–650 CE, 119
Ceremonial Complex, air view, Persepolis 518–c. 460 BCE,
  311, 312
Chacmools, 128
Chaitya Hall, Karle, India c. 1st century BCE–1st century
  CE, 92
Chaityas, 92
Chakra, 112
Chamered (sliced off) corners, 454
Changing Woman, 485
Character-based scripts, 135
Charioteer, Sanctuary of Apollo, Delphi c.470 BCE, 275
Chart of Greek and Roman Letters, 241
Chattri, 453
Chauvet cave paintings, 18
Chavin de Huantar culture, 129–130
Chiaroscuro, 604
Chichester-Constable Chasuble, Life of the Virgin
  c. 1330–1350, 533
Chilkat Blanket, North America before 1928, 501
Chimu *manta*, textiles painted or stamped for
  iconographic panels 800–1200, 539
China
  Bronze Age, 98–101
  Confucianism, 103–105
  Daoism, 103, 104
  Han dynasty (206 BCE–220 CE), 102–105
  map, 97m, 464m
  Middle Kingdom, 96
  Neolithic cultures, 96–98
  See also Asian empires; South and Southeast Asia
    before 1200
Chinese characters, 101
Chinese culture, foundations of, 465
Chinese painting, formats of, 469
Chinese Writing, Second Millennium BCE *to the Present*, 138
Chini khana, 362
Choice of Emblems, A (Whitney), Antwerp 1586, 672
Chora Church, 352–355
Christian art, early, 320–323
  catacomb paintings, 322–323
  Christian Bible, 329
  Dura-Europos excavation, 320, 321
  early church, 320–321
  narrative and iconic, 322
  sculpture, 323
  See also Imperial Christian architecture and art
Christian churches:
  naming/designation/dedication/location, 337
Christian Inscription 4th century CE, 247
Christ in Majesty, Priory Church of Saint-Pierre at Moissac
  c. 1115, 431–432
Christ in Majesty, San Climent Church, Taull, Spain,
  consecrated 1123, 424
Christ on the Cross (Majestat Batlló), 436
Christ Pantokrator at Crest of Central Dome, Church of the
  Dormition at Daphni, late 11th century, 348–349
Christus, Petrus, *Goldsmith in His Shop* 1449, 538
Churches
  in Europe in the Middle Ages, 410
  longitudinal-plan and Central-plan churches, 324, 326

Church portals, 429
Cione, Andrea di, *Enthroned Christ with Saints from the
  Strozzi Altarpiece* 1354–1357, 531
Cistercians, 419–420
Citadel and Palace Complex of Sargon II, reconstruction
  drawings, Dur Sharrukin c. 721–706 BCE, 306,
    307–308
City of Nuremberg (Wolgemut, Pleydenwurff, and
  workshop) 1493, 655
City plans, ancient Greece, 204–206
Cityscape, House of Publius Fannius Synistor, Boscoreale
  c. 50–30 BCE, 213
City-states, ancient Greece, 184
Classical literacy 2400 BCE–400 CE, 238–250
  function of graphic codes, 241–244
  models of writing: gestural and constructed, 245–247
  timeline for, 249–250
  tools of the trade, 250
  variations of literacy and the alphabet, 238–241
  writing at the end of the Classical Age, 247
Classic and classical, 274
Clay Tablet with Cuneiform Iraq 3000 BCE, 138
Clay Tokens Susa, Iran, Fourth Millennium BCE, 137
Clerestory, 326
Cluny, 416–417
Cluny Abbey, reconstruction drawing 1088–1130, 416
Cluny Third Abbey Church, reconstruction drawing
  1088–1130, 417
Code of Hammurabi, 78–79
Codes, 135
Codex, 248, 341
Codex Colbertinus, 442
Codex Fejervary-Mayer, Mexico c. 1400–1519, 489
Codex Mendoza, Mexico 1545, 486
Codex Sinaiticus, mid–fourth century, 389
Codifying law, 141
Coffers, 224
Colophons, 469
Color, 6
  in Greek sculpture, 195
Colossal Figure of Akhenaten, Egypt, 172
Colossal Head, San Lorenzo, Mexico, Olmec culture
  c. 1200–900 BCE, 117–118
Columbus, Christopher, 485, 505–510
Columbus Landing in the Indies, Frontispiece to Giuliano
  Dati's Lettera 1493, 509
Column of Trajan, Rome c. 113–117 CE, 221–223
Columns, 364
Columns with Papyriform and Bud Capitals, Hypostyle Hall,
  Great Temple of Amun at Karnak, Egypt, Nineteenth
    Dynasty c. 1292–1190 BCE, 169
Commocus as Hercules, Rome c. 191–192 CE, 297, 299
Communication, Cro–Magnon, 135
Competition reliefs, 581, 585
Complex of Nan Madol, The, Micronesia c. 1200/1300– c.
  1500/1600, 52
Complex, Temple of Aphaia, Aegina c. 500 BCE, 193
Composite order, 216
Composite pose, 18–19
Composition, 7, 136
Conches, 332
Concrete, 224
Confucianism, 103–105, 465
Confucius 551–479 BCE, 465
Cong, 96, 98
Cong, China c. 3200–2200 BCE, 98
Constantine the Great, 229–235
Constantine the Great, Rome c. 325–326 CE, 235
Constantinople: the Chora Church, 352
Constructed forms, 238
Constructed writing, 245
Contarelli Chapel, San Luigi dei Frances (Caravaggio)
  1599–1602, 644–645
Contrapposto, 273
Conventions, 135, 153–155
The Conversion of St. Paul (Caravaggio) c. 1601, 643
Cook, James, 43, 55
Copernicus, Nicolaus, 648
Corantos, 674
Cordoba Mosque, dome in front of the Mihrab 965,
  366–367
Corinth, Greece, 184

Corinthian order, 190, 192
Cornaro Chapel, Church of Santa Maia Della Vittoria, Rome (Bernini) 1642–1652, 637
Cornice, 192
Correa, Charles, *Jawahar Kala Kendra*, India 1992, 461–462
Cortés, Hernán, 486
Cotton tapestry, Latin America 1000–1350, 542
Counter-Reformation and art, 616–620
Court of the Lions, Alhambra, Granada, Spain 1354–1391, 372
Covered Ritual Wine-Pouring Vessel (Guang) with Tiger and Owl Décor, China c. 13th century BCE, 100
Coyolxauhqui, 487
Cranach, Lucas the Elder, *Nymph of the Spring* c. 1537, 630
Creation and Fall (Wiligelmo), Modena Cathedral 1099, 430
Crenellated, 310
Cro-Magnon culture, 135–136
Croniques (Froissart), Lyons 1559, 665, 666
Cross hatching (*rarrk*), 43
Crossing of the Red Sea, Syria 244–245 CE, 318
Crowned Head of a King (Ife, Yoruba, Nigeria), 35
Crucifix (Majestat Batlló), mid–12th century, 436
Crucifixion and Iconoclasts, Chludov Psalter, mid 9th century, 344
Crucifixion, Church of the Dormition at Daphni, late 11th century, 348–349
Cruciform, 330
Crusades, 410–411
Cubiculum of Leonis, Catacomb of Commodilla, near Rome, late 4th century, 322
Cultural values, 251
Cuneiform, development of 3100–600 BCE, 139
Cuneiform writing, 69, 71, 137–139
Cupids Making Perfume, Wall Painting in the House of the Vettii, Pompeii, rebuilt 62–79 CE, 211
Cursive script, 242
Cursive Script, early CE, 245
Cut tile, 362
Cuzco, Inca empire, 491
Cylinder Seal and Its Modern Impression, Ur c. 2600–2500 BCE, 74
Cylinder seals, 73–74
Cylindrical Vessel with Ballgame Scene, Maya c. 600–800 CE, 127

D

Dürer, Albrecht, *Page from the Prayer Book of Maximilian I* 1515, 516
Dado, 211
da Gama, Vasco, 505
Dancers in Ceremonial Attire, Algeria 5000–2000 BCE, 40
Dao, 104
Daodejing (The Way and Its Power) (Laozi), 104
Daoism, 103, 104, 465
Darius and Xerxes Receiving Tribute, Persepolis c. 491–486 BCE, 313
Dating, early art, 21
David (Bernini) 1623, 636
David (Donatello) c. 1446–1460, 588
David (Michelangelo) 1501–1504, 612
David Battling Goliath, one of the "David Plates," Constantinople 629–630 CE, 314, 315, 342
"David Plates," 314, 315, 342
David the Psalmist, Paris Psalter, second half of 10th century, 351
Da Vinci, Leonardo, 604–608
    The Last Supper 1495–1498, 604–605
    Mona Lisa c. 1503–1506, 606
    Virgin of the Rocks c. 1485, 604
    Vitruvian Man c. 1490, 607
Day, John, Euclid's *Elements*, London 1570, 666, 667
Dead, preserving in ancient Egypt, 158
de Bry, T., *Spanish Treatment of Fugitive Black Slaves, The* 1595, 526
de Certeau, Michel, 484
Decorative quilting by Muslim artisans 1392, 538
Decree on a Marble Stele Describing Procedures for Tribute 426 BCE, 240
Dei Pollaiuolo, Antonio
    Battle of the Nudes c. 1465–1470, 592–593
    Hercules and Antaeus c. 1475, 591

Deities, Greek and Roman, 186
de la Porte, Henri–Horace Roland, *Still Life* c., 1765, 61
de la Tour, Georges, *Education of the Virgin, The*, 5
del Castillo, Bernal Díaz, 486
de León, Cieza, *Silver Mines of Potosí* 1553, 518, 521
Delivery of the Keys to St. Peter with a schematic drawing (Perugino) 1481, 592
Demons Tormenting St. Anthony (Schongauer) c. 1480–1490, 654
Demotic hieroglyphs, 179
Denarius with Portrait of Julius Caesar 44 BCE, 293
Descartes, René, 648
"Descent of the Ganges" Relief, Mamallapuram, Tamil Nadu, India, Pallava period c. mid 7th century CE, 257–258, 259
Description of the World, A (Polo), 466
Detail from The Triumph of Maximilian I (Burgkmair) 1526, 517
Detail of Mask Decoration on a Jade Cong, China c. 3200–2200 BCE, 97
Detail of the Story of Paris, Florentine, late fifteenth century, 509
Devi, 88
Dharma, 86, 147–148
Dharma and the God (Bawa), India 1984, 462
Dharmaraja Ratha, Mamallapuram, Tamil Nadu, India, Pallava period c. mid 7th century CE, 258
Di Banco, Nanni, *Four Crowned Martyr* c. 1409–1417, 586–587
Diptych, 234
Dipylon Vase, inscription 730–720 BCE, 239
Diquis culture, Central America 700–1500 CE, 128–129
Djoser's complex at Saqqara, Egypt c. 2630–2575 BCE, 155–156
Djoser's Funerary Complex, Saqqara, reconstruction drawing, third dynasty, Egypt c. 2630–2575 BCE, 156
Dolmen, 26
Dome, 217
Dome of the Pantheon, Rome c. 125–128 CE, 226
Dome of the Rock, Haram Al-Sharif, Jerusalem
    aerial view, 363
    cutaway drawing, 364
    interior, 364
Donatello
    David c. 1446–1460, 588
    Equestrian Statue of Erasmo da Narni (Gattamelata) 1443–1453, 589
    St George 1417–1420, 587
Dong Qichang, *The Qingbian Mountains*, China 1617, 475–476
Doric frieze, 200, 201
Doric order, 192
Dover Castle, 428–429
Drawloom, 18th-century French engraving, 342
Dreaming stories (Indigenous Australian life), 45–46
Dream Journey to the Peach Blossom Land (An), Korea 1447 CE, 480
Dresden Codex, Yucatan 1200–1250 CE, 138
Drillwork, 296
Drums, 192
Dura–Europos excavation, 320, 321
Dürer, Albrecht, 627–630
    Adam and Eve, 1504, 628
    Four Apostles 1526, 629
    Four Horsemen of the Apocalypse 1497–1498, 628
    Self-Portrait 1500, 620–621
Durham Cathedral 1087–1133, 427–428
Durrington Walls, reconstruction drawing, near Stonehenge in England 2600 BCE, 28
Dur Sharrukin, 307–309
Dutch Renaissance and popular prints c. 1530–1700, 669–676
Dying Gallic Trumpeter (Epigonos), Roman copy of original bronze of c. 220 BCE, 280, 281
Dying Warrior, Temple of Aphaia, Aegina c. 500–490 BCE, 194, 195

E

Early African art, 35–41
    Africa—cradle of art and civilization, 37
    African rock art, 37–39, 41

    ancient Africa, 38m
    lure of ancient Africa, 37
    myth of "primitive" art, 39
    sub-Saharan civilizations, 39–41
Early dynastic Egypt c. 2950–2575 BCE, 152–157
Early Pottery: Franchthi Cave, Greece 6500 BCE, 30
Early Pottery: From Japan's Jomon Culture 12,000 BCE, 29
Early writing, 137–139
Earspools, Moche culture, Peru c. 300 CE, 132–133
Earth Drawing (Geoglyph) of a Hummingbird, Nazca Plain, Peru c. 0–700 CE, 131
Earthenware, 31
Easter Island. *See* Rapa Nui
Eastern woodlands Indians, North America, 494–496, 494m
    beadwork, 496
    quillwork, 495–496
    wampum, 494–495
Echinus, 192
Education of the Virgin, The (de la Tour), 5
Egypt. *See* Ancient Egypt; Early dynastic Egypt
Egyptian hieroglyphics, 139–140
Egyptian symbols, 153
Eighth through the fourteenth centuries, 258–265
    Bhakti Movement in art, 264–265
    monumental northern temple, 259–263
    monumental southern temple, 263–264
Electron spin resonance dating, 21
Elgin Marbles, 203
Emblemata, 298
Embroideries, 441, 529, 533
Enemies Crossing the Euphrates to Escape Assyrian Archers, Kalhu c. 875–860 BCE, 306–307
Engaged columns, 293
English Sailors in a Skirmish with Eskimo (White) 1577, 519
Enkidu, 64–66
Entablature, 190, 192
Entasis, 190
Enthroned Christ with Saints from the Strozzi Altarpiece (Cione) 1354–1357, 531
Epic of Gilgamesh, 69, 75
Epigonos, *Dying Gallic Trumpeter*, Roman copy of original bronze of c. 220 BCE, 280, 281
Equestrian Statue of Erasmo da Narni (Gattamelata) (Donatello) 1443–1453, 589
Equestrian Statute of Marcus Aurelius, Rome c. 176 CE, 229, 297
Erotic Couples on Wall, Kandariya Mahadeva Temple, Khajuraho, Madhya Pradesh, India, Chandella dynasty c. 1000 CE, 262, 263
Eskimos, 518, 519
Esthetic fractals, 552
Estienne, Robert, *Geneva Bible* 1553, 665
Euclid's *Elements* (printed by Day), London 1570, 666, 667
Euphronios Krater, 203
Eurocentric history, 484
Europe
    in Romanesque period, 410–411
    seventeenth-century, 634m
    seventeenth-century art, 632–652
    in the sixteenth century, 602
Europe in the Middle Ages, 403–450
    art of the "barbarians" in Europe, 405–408
        the Celts and Anglo-Saxons in Britain, 407–408
        the Merovingians, 405–407
        the Norse, 407
    the church, 410
    defining Middle Ages, 405
    early middle ages, 404
    map of early middle ages, 404
    politics and economic life, 410
    Sutton Hoo excavations, 408
    See also High art in Europe; Romanesque period
Exedrae, 225
Exekias, *Ajax and Achilles Playing a Game* c. 540–530 BCE, 182–183
Explorers/conquests of New World, 505–528
Expressionism, 281
Expulsion of Adam and Eve from Paradise (Masaccio) c. 1427, 595
Exterior of Korambo (Haus Tambaran), Papua New Guinea, 20th century, 47

F

Face of a Woman, Known As the Warka Head, Uruk c. 3300–3000 BCE, 73
Fanaticks Barber or, A New Cut for Non–Conformists 1662, 682–683
Fang ding, 98
Feather Cloak, Known As the Kearny Cloak, Hawaii. c. 1843, 56
Feather Headdress of Moctezuma, Mexico, before 1519, 488
Feliciano, Felice, *Alphabetum Romanum,* Verona 1460–1463, 657
Female Figure Holding a Fly-Whisk, India c. 250 BCE, 86
Fertile Crescent and Mesopotamia, 69–79
   Akkad, 74, 77
   Babylon, 78–79
   map, 70m
   Sumer, 69–74
   Ur and Lagash, 75–78
   writing in, 137–139
Figures of a Woman and a Man (Cernavoda, Romania), 33
Fillets, 192
Filocalus 4th century CE, 248
Finial, 254, 454
First Illustrated Edition of Columbus's Letter, frontispiece to, (Basel) 1493, 508
First Murder, The (Weegee/Arthur Felig) before 1945, 59
"First Romanesque," 413
5-IV-71 (Gim), Korea 1971 CE, 482–483
Five pillars of Islam, 365
Five-Stringed Lute (Biwa) with Design of a Central Asian Man Playing a Biwa Atop a Camel, Chinese, 8th century CE, 113
Flask, China 1426–1435 CE, 471
Flavian amphitheater, 217–218
Flavian Amphitheater (Colossuem), reconstruction drawing, Rome 70–80 CE, 217
Flavian Amphitheater, Outer Wall, Rome c. 70–80 CE, 218
Flavians, Rome, 216–218
Flavius Josephus, 289
Flight into Egypt Landscape (Carracci) 1603–1604, 639, 641
Florence Cathedral
   dome, (Brunelleschi) 1420–1436, 580, 581
   schematic drawing 1420–1436, 580
Florence, Italy. See Renaissance art in fifteenth-century Italy
Fluted shafts, 192
Fontenay Abbey, Church of Notre-Dame, nave and plan 1139–1147, 419, 420
Forbidden City, The (China), 471–472
Foreshortening, 6
Form, 6
Formal analysis, 7
Forum of Trajan, Rome, 219–221
Foundling Hospital, 581, 582–583
Four Crowned Martyrs (Di Banco) c. 1409–1417, 586–587
Four Horsemen of the Apocalypse (Dürer) 1497–1498, 628
Four-legg'd Quaker to the Time of the Dog and Elder's Maid, or, the Lady's Fall, The (Denham and Birkenhead) 1662–1668, 681–682
Four-Legged Elder (Birkenhead) 1647, 681, 682
Fourth through seventh centuries, 252–258
   Buddhist sculpture, 252
   early northern temple, 254–255
   early southern temple, 258
   Gupta period, 252–254
   Hindu temples and images, 256
   monumental narrative reliefs, 255–258
   painting, 252–253
Fra Angelico, *Annunciation* c. 1738–1445, 596–597
Fractal esthetic, 551–553
   in household objects, 553
Fractals
   in cross-cultural comparison, 545
   from nature, 550–551
   from unconscious activity, 550
Fragments of a Large Lapita Jar, Solomon Islands c. 1200–1100 BCE, 44
Frakturs, 662
Franck, Paulus, ornate Gothic letter, Germany 1601, 662
French seventeenth–century art, 647–652
Frieze, 190

Froissart, Jean, *Croniques,* Lyons 1559, 665, 666
Funeral Stone with Image of a Ten-Year-Old Girl 1st century BCE, 244
Funerary architecture, ancient Egypt, 155–157, 165–166
Funerary Chapel (Parekklesion), Church of Christ in Chora c. 1310–1321, Constantinople, 355
Funerary Krater, Athens c. 750–700 BCE, 185
Funerary Mask of Tutankhamen Eighteenth Dynasty 1332–1322 BCE, 150–151
Funerary Stele, Greece 459 BCE, 143
Funerary Temple of Hatshepsut, Deir el-Bahri, Egypt Eighteenth Dynasty c. 1473–1458 BCE, 170
Futhark alphabet, 144

G

Galilei, Galileo, 658
Galinus, *Arabic Manuscript* 1199, 378
Galleries, 334
Gandhara style, 93
Garamond, Claude, 664–665
   Roman and italic type 1545, 664
Garbhagriha, 254
Garbhagrihas, 91
Garden of the Cessation of Official Life (Also Known As the Hummingbird Administrator's Garden), China, early 16th century, 473, 475
"Gates of Paradise" (East Doors), Baptistery of San Giovanni, Florence (Ghiberti) 1425–1452, 589–590
Gelding of Curates broadside case study, 681, 682–684
Gemma Augustea, early 1st century CE, 207
Geneva Bible (printed by Estienne) 1553, 665
Genghis Khan c.1162–1227, 464
Genre paintings, 633
Gentileschi, Artemisia, 646–647
   Self–Portrait as the Allegory of Painting 1630, 647
   Susannah and the Elder, 1610, 646
Geoglyphs, 130, 131
Geometric period, Greece 900–700 BCE, 184–187
German art in the sixteenth century, 623–630
   metalwork, 624, 627
   painting, 625–630
   sculpture, 623–625
Gestural writing, 242, 245
Ghiberti, Lorenzo
   "Gates of Paradise" (East Doors) 1425–1452, 589–590
   Jacob and Esau, Panel of the "Gates of Paradise" (East Doors) c. 1435, 591
   Sacrifice of Isaac 1401–1402, 585
Gilgamesh legend, 64–66, 141
Gilpin, Laura, *Taos Pueblo,* New Mexico 1947, 502
Gim Hwangi, *5-IV-71,* Korea 1971 CE, 482–483
Gita Govinda, 458, 459
Giza Plateau, model of, 159
Glassmaking, in ancient Egypt, 174, 175
Glossed Bible thirteenth century, 398, 399
Glykon, 280
Glyphs, 135
Goddess Coatlicue, Mexico c. 1500, 487–488
God–Kings, early Egypt, 152–153
Gold Face Mask, Bulgaria 3800 BCE, 32
Gold leaf, 313
Gold Scepters, Bulgaria 3800 BCE, 32
Goldsmith art, 280
Goldsmith in His Shop (Christus) 1449, 536
Gold thread–laden cloths, between c. 1280–1369, probably by Muslim weavers, 538
Good Shepherd, sculpture, second half of 3rd century, 323
Good Shepherd Orants, and Story of Jonah, painted ceiling, late 3rd–early 4th century, 323
Good Shepherd, Oratory of Galla Placidia c. 425–426, 331
Good Shepherd with Adam and Eve after the Fall, Dura-Europos, 321
Gortyna Inscription, and Site of the Inscription 638 BCE, 239
Goryeo dynasty, Korea 918–1392, 479
Graphic codes, 241–244
Graphic principles, 137
Grave Stele of a Little Girl, Greek c. 450–440 BCE, 206
Great Lyre with Bull's Head, The, Ur c. 2600–2500 BCE, 76
Great Plains Indians, North America, 494m, 496–499
   painting, 498–499
   portable architecture (tipis), 496–498

Great Pyramid, Tenochtitlan, Mexico, 486–487
Great Pyramid and Plaza, La Venta, Mexico, Olmec culture c. 900–400 BCE, 117–118
Great Pyramids of Giza, Fourth Dynasty, Egypt c. 2575–2450 BCE, 157–161
Great Sphinx, Funerary Complex of Khafre, Giza, Old Kingdom c. 2520–2494 BCE, 160
Great Stupa, Sanchi, India, c. 150–50 BCE, 89–92
Great Temple of Amun at Karnak, reconstruction drawing, Egypt, New Kingdom c. 1579–1075 BCE, 168
Greece. See Ancient Greece
Greek and Roman deities, 186
Greek architectural orders, 192
Grids, 166
Grizzly Bear House–Partition Screen, North America c. 1840, 499
Groin vault, 217
Group of Vietnamese Ceramics from the Hoi An Hoard, late 15th to early 16th century, 452
Grünewald, Matthias, *Isenheim Alterpieces* c. 1510–1515, 625–626
Guardian Figures at Gate of the Citadel of Sargon II, during excavation, Dur Sharrukin c. 721–706 BCE, 308
Gudea, 77–78
Gummersmark Brooch, 6th century, 407
Gupta period, 252–254
Gutenberg, 656

H

Hadrian/Constantine Hunting Boar and Sacrificing to Apollo; Constantine Addressing the Roman People in the Roman Forum c. 130–138 CE, 232
Hadrian's Villa at Tivoli, 225, 227–228
Hadrian's Villa, Tivoli c. 125–135 CE, 227
Hagenauer, Nikolaus, *St Anthony Enthroned between SS. Augustine and Jerome* c. 1500, 625
Hagesandros, Polydoros, and Athenodoros of Rhodes, *Laocoön and His Sons,* 284
Hagia Sophia Church (Anthemius of Tralles and Isidorus of Miletus) 532–537 CE, 332–335
   interior of, 333
   plan and isometric drawing of, 332
Half–unical scripts, 245
"Hallelujah man," 136
Hall of Bulls, Lascaux Cave, France 15,000 BCE, 19
Hall of Mirrors, Palace of Versailles (Hardouin–Mansart and Le Brun) begun 678, 651
Hamatsa Dancers, Kwakwaka'wakw, Canada 1914, 500
Hamatsa masks, 500
Hammurabi, Code of, 78–79
Hammurabi's Code, Iraq, eighteenth century BCE, 143
Handscrolls, 467, 469
Han dynasty (China, 206 BCE– 221 CE), 97m, 102–105
Hanging scrolls, 467, 469
Haniwa, Japan c. 6th century CE, 108
Harappa, Indus Valley, 84–85
Harbaville Triptych mid 11th century, 350–351
Hardouin–Mansart, Jules and Le Brun, Charles, *Hall of Mirrors, Palace of Versailles* begun 678, 651
Harvesting of Grapes, Santa Costanza Church c. 350, 327
Hatshepsut (queen of Egypt, Eighteenth Dynasty, c. 1473–1458 BCE), 169–171
Hatshepsut Kneeling, Egypt, Eighteenth Dynasty c. 1473–1458 BCE, 170
Hawaii, 56–57
Hawke, Bob, 43
Head, Nok culture, Sudan c. 500 BCE–200 CE, 40
Head of a Man (Known As Akkadian Ruler), Nineveh c. 2300–2200 BCE, 74
Head of Senusret III, Egypt, Twelfth Dynasty c. 1836–1818 BCE, 164
Hellenistic sculpture, 280–287
Hellenistic Greece, 277m
Henge, 27
Hera I, Greece c. 550–540 BCE, 184, 190, 191
Herat School, 379
Hercules and Antaeus (Dei Pollaiuolo) c. 1475, 591
Hermes and the Infant Dionysos (Praxiteles), probably a copy of a Late Classical 4th century BCE original, 277, 278
Hieratic and Demotic Scripts 2900–100 BCE, 140

Hieratic scale, 68
Hieroglyphics, 139–140
  Rosetta Stone and, 179
Hieroglyphics, Lintel from the Reign of Sesostris III, Egypt
  1887–1850 BCE, 140
High art in Europe, 575–652
  academies and academy exhibitions, 652
  Renaissance art in fifteenth-century Italy, 577–599
  science and the changing worldview, 648
  seventeenth-century art in Europe, 632–652
  sixteenth-century art in Italy, 601
  sixteenth-century art in northern Europe and the
    Iberian Peninsula, 621–630
High Classical Period c. 450–400 BCE, 196–237
  See also Ancient Greece
High relief, 94
Hildegard of Bingen, 443
Hinduism, 88
  India, 265
Hindu temples and images, 256
Hinged Clasp from the Sutton Hoo Burial Ship, first half of
  7th century, 408
Hiragana, 107
Historiated capitals, 435
Histories of the Americas (Landry), 484
History paintings, 652
Hittites of Anatolia, 305
Holstein, Jonathan, 4
Holy Blood (Wings Open) Alterpiece (Riemenschneider) c.
  1499–1505, 623
Holy Family, The (Michelangelo) c. 1503, 6
Homem, Lopo, *Western Hemisphere of the "Miller" World
  Map* 1525, 520m
Homo sapiens, 11, 12
Homo sapiens sapiens, 11, 12
*Horizontal Wine Bottle with Decoration of a Bird Carrying a
  Newly Caught Fish*, Korea 16th century, 479
Horsemen, Parthenon c. 447–432 BCE, 201
Horseshoe arch, 366, 368, 369
Hortus Eystettensis, Nuremberg 1613, 673
Horyuji Compound, aerial view, Japan,
  7th century CE, 110
Horyuji temple, Japan c. 7th century CE, 110–111
Hosios Loukas. *See* Monastery Churches at Hosio Loukas,
  early 11th century
Hour of Cowdust, India c. 1790, 458, 459
House burning, in Neolithic period, 29
House of the Silver Wedding, Pompeii, 1st century CE, 209
House of the Vettii, Pompeii, 209–211
House of the Vettii, Pompeii, rebuilt 62–79 CE, 210
Huaca del Luna (Pyramid of the Moon), Moche Valley, 131
Huaca del Sol (Pyramid of the Sun), Moche Valley, 131
Huitzilopochtli, 486, 487
Human Figure, Jordan 6500 BCE, 30
Human-Fish Sculpture, Lepenski Vir, Serbia
  6300–5500 BCE, 23
Humanism and the Italian Renaissance, 578
Humans, modern, 11
Human sacrifice, 486
Humay and Humayun (Junayd), Iraq 1396, 6
Hundreds of Birds Admiring the Peacocks, China, late 15th to
  early 16th century, 468
Hungry Tigress Jataka, Japan c. 650 CE, 110–111
Hydria, 205
Hypnerotomachia Poliphili (Manutius), Venice 1499, 659
Hypostyle, 168, 362
Hypostyle Hall, Great Temple of Amun of Karnak,
  reconstruction drawing, Egypt, Nineteenth Dynasty
  c. 1292–1190 BCE, 169

I

Iconography, 8
Iconophiles, 344
Iconostasis, 343
Icons and iconoclasm, 342–344
Ife sculpture, Yoruba people, Nigeria, 12th–15th century
  CE, 35–36
Il Gesú Church, exterior and plan, (Giacomo della Porta
  and Vignola) c. 1573–1584, 518–519
Illuminated books, 656–657
Illuminated manuscripts, 34, 382, 388–402

Illuminated Tugra of Sultan Suleyman c. 1555–1560, 382
Illustrations to Vespucci's Letter to Soderini, Strassburg 1509, 513
Illustrations to Vespucci's Mundus Novus, Dutch translation
  c. 1506–1510, 514
Illustration to Vespucci's Mundus Novus, probably Rostock
  1505, 513
Imperial architecture, Roman, 219–227
Imperial Christian architecture and art, 324–331
  architecture, 324–327
  life of Jesus, 329
  longitudinal-plan and central-plan churches, 324, 326
  Ravenna, 328–331
  sculpture, 327–328
Imperial portraits, Rome, 227, 229
Imperial Rome, model of c. 324 CE, 219
Impost block, 584
Inca empire, 489–493
  See also Americas after 1300
Inca masonry, 492
Inca Masonry, Detail of a Wall at Machu Picchu, Peru
  1450–1530, 491
Incense Burner, China c. 113 BCE, 103
India, 452–463
  See also Asian empires; South and southeast Asia
    before 1200
India Gate (Lutyens), 20th century, 460
Indian painting on paper, 458
Indian subcontinent, 82, 83m
  See also Asian empires; South and Southeast Asia
    before 1200
Indian Triumph of Dionysus c. 190 CE, 297, 299, 303
Indus civilization, 82–85, 83m
  See also South and Southeast Asia before 1200
Indus Valley seals, 82, 84
Infant Virgin Mary Caressed by Her Parents, Church of
  Christ in Chora 1315–1321, mosaic, 353
*Initiation Rites of the Cult of Bacchus (?), Villa of the
  Mysteries*, Pompeii c. 60–50 BCE, 212
Ink painting, 482–483
Inlay, 71
Inner Coffin of Tutankhamen's Sarcophagus, Egypt,
  Eighteenth Dynasty c. 1332–1322 BCE, 175
Inner Shrine, Ise, main hall, Japan, 109
Intention and invention in design, 550–553
  the fractal esthetic, 551–553
  fractals from nature, 550–551
  fractals from unconscious activity, 550
  from unconscious accident to explicit design, 554
Interior of Old St. Peter's (Jacopo Grimaldi) 1619, 324
Intuitive perspective, 213
Ionic Inscription, late fifth century BCE, 240
Ionic order, 190, 192
"I Quattro Libri dell'Architettura" (Palladio), Venice
  1570, 662–663
Irish Half–Uncial, Lindisfarne Gospels, 391, 392
Iron technology, Nok culture and, 40
Isenheim Altarpieces (Grünewald) c. 1510–1515, 625–626
Ise Shrine, Japan, 108–109
Ishtar Gate and Throne Room Wall, Babylon c. 575 BCE,
  310, 311
Isis, 149
Islam, five pillars of, 365
Islam and early Islamic society, 360–362
Islam, Byzantium, Ancient Near East Monotheism:
  Religions of the Book, 304–402
Islamic art, 358–387
  arches, 369
  art and architecture through the 14th century,
    363–368
  carpet making, 384–385
  early architecture, 363–368
    Dome of the Rock, 363–364
    Great Mosque of Cordoba, 366–367
    Great Mosque of Kairquan, 364–365
    Kutubiya Mosque, 368
  five pillars of Islam, 365
  Islam and early Islamic society, 360–362
  later period, 368–379
    architecture of the East, 373–374
    architecture of the Mediterranean, 369–373
    arts of the book, 377–378

  Herat School, 379
    manuscript painting, 378–379
    portable arts, 374–377
  Mamluk glass oil lamp, 371
  map of Islamic world, 361
  modern era, 387
  Mughal Dynasty, 386
  ornamental techniques, 362
  Ottoman Empire, 380–382
    the architect Sinan, 380–381
    illuminated manuscripts and tugras, 382
  Safavid Dynasty, 383–386
  textiles in, 376–377
Islamic Mosque and Cultural Centre, Rome (Portoghesi,
  Gigliotti, and Mousaw 1984–1992, 387
Italian seventeenth-century art, 633–652
  architecture and sculpture in Rome, 633–639
    Bernini as sculptor, 636–638
    Borromini, Francesco, 238–239
    St. Peter's Basilica in the Vatican, 633–635
  Europe in seventeenth century, 634m
  painting, 639–647
    Caravaggio (Merisi, Michelangelo), 641–646
    the Carracci, 639–641
    Gentileschi, Artemisia, 646–647
Italian sixteenth–century art (the High Renaissance), 602–615
  the Counter-Reformation and art, 616–620
  map, 603
  Rome and the Vatican, 616–620
  three great artists, 603–615
    Leonardo da Vinci, 604–608
    Michelangelo, 611–620
    Raphael, 608–610
Ivory Chest with Scenes from Courtly Romances
  c. 1330–1350, 534–535
Iwans, 369

J

Jacob and Esau, Panel of the "Gates of Paradise" (East Doors)
  (Ghiberti) c. 1435, 591
Jade, 118
Jahangir, 455, 457
Jahangir and Shah Abbas (al–Zaman), India c., 1618, 457
Jambs, 429
Japan
  Asuka period (552–645 CE), 109–111
    map, 106m
  Nara period (645–794 CE), 111–113
  prehistoric, 106–109
    Jomon period (c. 11, 000–400 BCE), 106
    Kofun period (c. 300–552 CE), 106, 108–109
    Yayoi period (c. 400 BCE–300 CE), 106
  Shinto, 108–109
  writing, language, and culture, 107
Jataka tales, 90
Java, Borobudur, 266, 267
Jenson, Nicolas, Venetian type, Venice 1470, 658
Jeong Seon, *Panoramic View of the Diamond Mountains
  (Geumgang-San)*, Korea 1734 CE, 481
Jewelry of Queen Arnegunde c. 580–590, 406
Jewish art, early, 316–320
  catacomb art in Rome, 316, 317
  first temple in Jerusalem, 316–317
  synagogues, 318–320
Jewish, Early Christian, and Byzantine art, 315–357
Jews, Christians, and Muslims, 316–323
  Christian art, early, 320–323
  Jewish art, early, 316–320
Joggled voussoirs, 362, 370
John of Worcester, *Worchester Chronicle* c. 1140, 439, 442
Jomon culture, Japan, early pottery in, 29–30
Jomon period (Japan, c. 11, 000–400 BCE), 106
Joseon dynasty (Korea, 1392–1910), 479–482
  ceramics, 479–480
  painting, 480–482
Judgment of Hunefer before Osiris, Egypt, Nineteenth
  Dynasty c. 1285 BCE, 179
Julio-Claudians, 207
Junayd, D, *Humay and Humayun,* Iraq 1396, 6
Justinian, 331–340

K

The Kaaba, Mecca, 360
Kairquan Mosque, 364–365
Kalhu, 305–307
Kana, 107
Kandariya Mahadeva Temple, Khajuraho, Madhya
    Pradesh, India, Chandella dynasty c. 1000 CE,
    259, 261
Kanji, 107
Kapoor, Anish, *As If to Celebrate, I Discovered a Mountain
    Blooming with Red Flowers,* India 1981, 462–463
Karnak, Egypt, 168–169
Karomama, Egypt, Twenty–Second Dynasty
    c. 945–715 BCE, 180
*Katherine and Leonard Woolley Excavating at Ur in 1937,
    Beside Two Archaeological Assistants in One of the Royal
    Burials,* 75
Kearny, Lawrence, 56
Keel arch, 369
Keep, 420
Kepler, Johannes, 648
Kesi (tapestry) from Ming Dynasty (1426–1425), 537
Keystone, 292
Khafre, Giza, Fourth Dynasty c. 2520–2494 BCE, 161
Khafre's funerary complex (Giza, Old Kingdom),
    160–161
Kilns, 31
King Rudolf of Swabia, 437
King Rudolf of Swabia Effigy Tomb Cover c. 1080, 437
Kirouan, Tunisia 836–875, 365
Klah, Hosteen, 504–505
    Whirling Log Ceremony, Navajo c. 1925, 504–505
Knowles, Martha and Henrietta Thomas, *My Sweet Sister
    Emma,* 3, 4
Koburger, Anton, *Nuremberg Chronicle* 1493, 654–655
Kofun period, Japan c. 300–552 CE, 106, 108–109
Kondo, 110
Korambo (ceremonial house) of the Abelam of Papua
    New Guinea, 47
Kore, 270
Korea, 97m, 464m
    Joseon dynasty (1392–1910), 479–482
    modern, 482–483
    See also Asian empires
Koros, 270
Koru pattern, 54–55
Koshares of Taos (Velarde), New Mexico 1940s, 502, 503
Kowhaiwhai patterns, 54
Krishna and the Gopis, India c. 1525–1550, 459
Kritios Boy, Acropolis, Athens c. 480 BCE, 273
Krug, Hans, *Apple Cup* (workshop of Hans Krug)
    c. 1510–1515, 624
Kublai Khan, 464, 466
Kufic, 370
Kushan period, 92–96
Kutubiya Mosque, 368
Kwakwaka'wakw Bird Mask (Seaweed), Canada, prior to
    1951, 500
Kylix, 196, 274

L

Lady Xok's Vision (Accession Ceremony), Yaxchilan, Mexico
    726 CE, 126
Lagash, Mesopotamia. See Ur and Lagash, Mesopotamia
Lake Texcoco, Mexico, 486
Lakshanas, 93
Lamassus, 308
Lamp with Ibex Design (La Mouthe Cave, France), 22
"Land of the Four Quarters" (Inca empire), 489–490
Landry, Pierre, *Histories of the Americas,* 484
Landscape, China (Shitao) c. 1700 CE, 477–478
Lantern tower, 414
Lanzón, Chavín de Huantar, Peru, c. 900 BCE, 129–130
Laocoön and His Sons (Hagesandros, Polydoros, and
    Athenodoros of Rhodes, 1st century BCE), 284
Laozi, 465
    Daodejing (The Way and Its Power), 104
Lapis Niger, mid–sixth century BCE, 243
Lapith Fighting a Centaur, Parthenon c. 447–432 BCE,
    200, 202

Large Water Tank, Mohenjo-Daro, Indus Valley
    c. 2600–1900 BCE, 83
Lascaux cave paintings, France 15,000 BCE, 18–20, 136
Last Judgment, Sistine Chapel, (Michelangelo) 1536–1541,
    616–617
Last Judgment Tympanum (Gislebertus), Church of
    Saint–Lazare at Autun c. 1120–1130 or 1130–1145,
    433–434
The Last Supper (Castagno) 1447, 598
The Last Supper (Da Vinci) 1495–1498, 604–605
Late Egyptian art c. 715–332 BCE, 181
Later Andhra period, 92–96
La Venta (Olmec center), 114–115, 117–118
"Leaning Tower of Pisa," 421
Le Corbusier, *Notre-Dame-Du-Haut,* 3
Lepenski Vir House/Shrine, reconstruction drawing, Serbia
    6000 BCE, 22
Letters (symbols), 135
Le Vau, Louis and Hardouin-Mansart, Jules, *Versailles
    Palace Garden* 1678–1685, 650
Liangzhu culture (China), 96–98
Liber Scivias (Hildegard of Bingen) 1150–1175, 443
Lindisfarne Gospels, England 710–721, 391, 392–393
Line, 5
Linear perspective, 577, 592
Linga shrine, 256
Lion Capital, Sarnath c. 250 BCE, 86, 87–88
Lion Gate, Hattusha c. 1400 BCE, 305
Lion-Human, Hohlenstein–Stadel, Germany c.
    30,000–26,000 BCE, 14–15
Lippi, Fra Filippo, *Portrait of a Woman and Man*
    c. 1435–1445, 598–599
Literate cultures, vs. oral cultures, 135
Llama, Bolivia, 15th century, 493
Logosyllabic writing (Maya), 123
London Intelligencer 1642, 674–675
London Loud Cryes to the Lord by Prayer, broadside 1665,
    675, 676
Longitudinal-plan and central-plan churches, 324, 326
Lord Carnarvon, 151
Lotus flower, 112
Lotus throne, 112
Louis XIV (Regaud) 1701, 647, 649
Low relief, 306
Lunette, 321, 323
Lusterware, 375
Lutyens, Edwin, *India Gate,* 20th century, 460
Luxury arts, in India, 456
Lyre from a royal tomb in Ur, 75–76
Lysippos, 279–280
    Man Scraping Himself (Apoxyomenos), Roman copy of
        original of c. 350–325 BCE, 279
    Weary Herakles (Farnese Hercules), Roman copy by
        Glykon of 4th century BCE bronze original, 280

M

Machu Picchu, Peru 1450–1530, 491–492
Macy Jug 1215/1216, 375
Maddalena Strozzi (Raphael) c. 1506, 608–609
Maderno, Carlo, *St. Peter's Basilica and Piazza, Vatican*
    c. 1656–1657, 634, 635
Madonna of the Goldfinch (Madonna del Cardellino)
    (Raphael), 7
Madrasas, 369
Magellan, Ferdinand, 516–517
Magenta, Black and Green on Orange (Rothko), 2, 3
Magi Asleep and Flight into Egypt, Cathedral of Saint-
    Lazare at Autun c. 1125, 433–434
Magna Carta, documentary cursive 1215, 397
Magritte, René
    Treachery of Images, The 1928–1929, 61–62
    Two Mysteries, The, 1966, 62–63
Mahayana Buddhism, 87, 92–93
Mainardi, Patricia, "Quilts: The Great American Art," 4
Maino, Juan Bautista, *Recovery of Bahia in Brazil, The*
    1635, 523, 527
Majuscules, 238
Malagan Display, New Ireland, Papua New Guinea c.
    1930, 49–50
Mamluk Glass Oil Lamp c. 1350–1355, 371
Mamluk ruler, 369

Mammoth–bone houses, Ukraine
    c. 16,000–10,000 BCE, 13–14
Man and Centaur, Greece c. 750 BCE, 187
Mandalas, 89, 112
Mandapas, 91, 261
Mandorla, 430
Man Scraping Himself (Apoxyomenos) (Lysippos), Roman
    copy of original of c. 350–325 BCE, 279
Mantle with Bird Impersonators, Paracas, Peru
    c. 200 BCE–200 CE, 130
Manuscript illumination. See Illuminated manuscripts
    and books
Manuscript Page, Worms, twelfth century, 394, 396
Manuscript painting, 378–379. *See also* Illuminated
    manuscripts and books
Manuscripts, 341, 354. See also Illuminated manuscripts
    and books
Manutius, Aldus, 659–660
    Hypnerotomachia Poliphili, Venice 1499, 659
    Opera of Virgil, Venice 1501, 661
Maori, New Zealand, 43
Maori meeting house *(Te-Hau-Ki-Turanga),* 54–55
Maps
    American Section of the Cantino World Map 1502, 511m
    Americas after 1300, 487m
    Americas before 1300, 117m
    ancient Africa, 38m
    Ancient Egypt, 152m
    Ancient Greece, 185m
    Ancient Near East, 70m
    China, 97m
    China and Korea, 464m
    Europe in early Middle Ages, 404m
    Europe in seventeenth century, 634m
    Europe in the Romanesque Period, 411m
    fifteenth-century Italy, 579m
    Hellenistic Greece, 277m
    Japan, 106m
    Korea, 97m
    late Roman and Byzantine world, 317m
    Nile River Valley, 152m
    North American cultural areas, 494m
    pacific cultural-geographic regions, 45m
    prehistoric Europe, 12m
    Ptolemaic world, Rome 1478, 667m, 668m
    Qing dynasty, China, 464m
    Renaissance and earlier monuments in Rome, 603m
    Renaissance map publishing, 666–669m
    Santiago de Compostela pilgrimage routes, 414m
    South and Southeast Asia, 83m
    T-O map, manuscript, early thirteenth century,
        666m, 667m
    Western Europe during the Reformation, 622m
    Western Hemisphere of the "Miller" World Map (Homem)
        1525, 520m
    world map (Waldseemüller), Germany 1507,
        667m–669m
The Maqamat by Al-Hariri (Al-Wasiti, 1237), 358–359
Marianos and Hanina, *Mosaic Floor of the Beth Alpha
    Synagogue,* 6th century CE, 319, 320
Mark-making, 134, 135, 136
Marks of a buddha, 112
Marquesas Islands, 53, 56
    tattoo in the, 53, 56
Marshals and Young Women, Parthenon c. 447–432
    BCE, 203
Martinez, Maria Montoya and Julian, *Blackware Storage
    Jar,* New Mexico c. 1942, 502, 503
Martyrium, 335
Mary as the Throne of Wisdom, 436
Masaccio
    Expulsion of Adam and Eve from Paradise c. 1427, 595
    The Tribute Money c. 1427, 595–596
    Trinity with the Virgin, St. John the Evangelist, and Donors
        c. 1425–1427, 593–594
Masjid-I Shah, Isfahan 1611–1638, 383
Masqsura, 366
Mastaba, 155, 157
Mathew from the Codex Colbertinus c. 1100, 442
Mathura style, 93–95
Maurya period (c. 322–185 BCE), 85–88
Maximilian I, 514–517

Maya, 122–128
 ballgames, 127
 Maya stela, 125
 Maya writing, 123
 painting, 127
 Palenque, 124–126
 postclassic period (Chichen Itza), 128
 sculpture for Lady Xok, 126
 Tikal, 123–124
Maya Riding to Lumbini, 267
McMaster, Gerald and Lee-Ann Martin, aboriginals, essay on, 527–528
McShane, Angela, "Typography Matters: Branding Ballads and Gelding Curates in Stuart England," 676–684
Medallion, 323
Medici Palace, 584
Medieval aesthetic sensibility, 447–450
Megalithic architecture, 26
Meiss, Millard, 532
Melanesia, 46–50
 New Britain, 50, 51
 New Guinea, 47–49
 New Ireland, 49–50
Memmott, Talan, *Brotherhood of the Bent Billiard, The*, 63
Memory image, 17
Menkaure and a Queen, Egypt, Fourth Dynasty c. 2490–2472 BCE, 161
Menorahs and Ark of the Covenant, Jewish catacomb painting, Rome 3rd century, 316, 317
Merci, Michelangelo. *See* Caravaggio
Merian, Anna Maria Sibylla, *Metamorphosis of the Insects of Surinam, Plate 9* 1719, 648
Merovingians, 405–407
Mesoamerica. *See* Americas after 1300; Americas before 1300
Mesopotamia. *See* Fertile Crescent and Mesopotamia
Metal in Islamic art, 375–376
Metallurgy, 31–32
 See also Bronze Age
Metal work and ivory, 530, 534–535, 536
Metamorphosis of the Insects of Surinam, Plate 9 (Merian) 1719, 648
Metopes, 192
Metropolitan Kouros, Attica c. 600 BCE, 270
Michelangelo, 611–620
 Creation of Adam, Sistine Chapel ceiling 1511–1512, 615
 David 1501–1504, 612
 Holy Family, The c. 1503, 6
 Last Judgment, Sistine Chapel ceiling 1536–1541, 616–617
 Pieta c. 1500, 611
 Sistine Chapel ceiling with diagram identifying scenes 1508–1512, 614
 Sistine Chapel interior 1475–1481, 613
 St. Peter's Basilica, Vatican c. 1546–1564, 616, 618
Micronesia, 50–52
 Nan Madol, 51–52
 Wapepe Navigation Chart, Marshall Islands, 19th century, 51
Midés, birchbark pictographs and, 687–690
Middle Ages. See Europe in the Middle Ages
Middle Kingdom, China, 96
Middle Kingdom, Egypt c. 1975–1640 BCE, 164–166
Midjaw, Jimmy Midjaw, *Three Dancers and Two Musicians: Corroboree of Mimi, Spirits of the Rocks*, 46
Mihrab, 359, 373
Mildenhall Treasure, 233
Mimesis versus modeling, 550
Minaret Mosque, Java, 452, 453, 1549
Minbar, Kutubiya Mosque 1125–1130, 359, 368
Ming dynasty (China, 1368–1644 CE), 467–476
 architecture and city planning, 471–472
 blue-and-white porcelain, 470–471
 court and professional painting, 468–470
 decorative arts, 470–471
 literati aesthetic, 472–476
Miniatures, 341
Minuscules, 238
Miradors, 373
Mithuna couples, 92
Mme. Charpentier and Her Children (Renoir), 8

Moai Ancestor Figures, Rapa Nui (Easter Island) c. 1000–1500 CE, 57
Moche culture, 131–133
Moche Portrait Vessel, Peru c. 100–700 CE, 131
Moctezuma, 488
Modeling, 7, 21
Models, 238
Modern humans, 11
Modern period
 China, 478
 India, 461–463
 Korea, 482–483
Module, 581
Mohenjo-Daro, Indus Valley, 82–84
Moldings, 261
Mona Lisa (Da Vinci), c. 1503–1506, 606
Monastery Churches at Hosios Loukas, early 11th century, 345–347
 Central Domed Space and Apse (The Naos), Katholikon, 346
 plans of, 345
Monastic controversy over the visual arts, 420
Monasticism, 410
Mongol invasions, 464
Monoline, 239
Monumental narrative reliefs, 255–258
Monumental texts, 239
Mortise-and-tenon joints, 28
Mosaic, 362
Mosaic Floor of the Beth Alpha Synagogue (Marianos and Hanina), 6th century CE, 319, 320
Moscow: Rublyov, 357
Mosque, 159
Mostaert, Jan, *West Indian Scene* c. 1540–1550, 521, 524–525
Mudras Sanskrit for signs, 94
Mughal Dynasty, 386
Mughal period, India, 452–460
 See also Asian empires
Mummy Wrapping of a Young Boy, Egypt, Roman period c. 100–120 CE, 181
Mundus Novus (Vespucci), 510, 512–514
Muqarnas, 362, 373
Muqarnas Dome, Hall of the Abengerrajes, Palace of the Lions, Alhambra 1354–1391, 372
Muslims. *See* Jews, Christians, and Muslims
My Sweet Sister Emma (Knowles and Thomas), 3, 4

N

Nôtre-Dame-Du-Haut (Le Corbusier) 1950–1955, 3
Naming, power of, 15
Nan Madol, Micronesia, 51–52
Nanna Ziggurat, Ur c. 2100–2050 BCE, 77
Naram-Sin, 67–68, 73, 77
Nara period (Japan, 645–794 CE), 111–113
Narrative and iconic figure imagery, 322
Narrow silk cloths, since 1500, Madagascar, 542
Narthex, 320, 326
Native American art, 568–573
 details of hide designs, 569–573
 exploit robes, 569
Native American design, 545–548
 bifold rotation in, 548
 Euclidean geometry in architecture, 545
 linear concentric forms in architecture, 545
 snakeskin models, 546, 547
Native American weaving, 533–568
 closed-loop weave cotton pouches, 557
 closed-loop weave pouch of human hair, 558
 contemporary textiles at the "Hopi Craftsman" fair (1960), 567
 cotton weft-float pattern weave pouch, 556
 detail, Anasazi, Montezuma Castle National Monument, 556
 diagonal-weave bead choker, 561
 drop-loom weave cotton pouch, 559
 Exposition of Indian Tribal Art (1931), 565
 fiber bag, 563
 finger woven, 554
 fragments of textile-impressed pottery, 561
 fragments of woven textile of rabbit fur and cannebrake fiber, 560

J.B. Moore blanket, 568
J.B. Moore rug, 565
 kiva mural, 554
 Navajo loom setup, 563
 painted black-on-white cotton *manta* (shawl), 557
 standard wool blanket, 566
 tapestry-weave cotton quiver, 558
 twine-plaited cotton shirt, 555
 woman using a tension loom, 562
 yucca fiber carrying band or tumpline, 558
Naturalism, 251
Navajo mythology, 485
Navajo rugs, 485
Navajos, North American Indians, 504–505
Nave, 220
Nazca culture, 130, 131
Neanderthals, 12
Necking, 192
Necropolis, 155
Nefertiti, Egypt, Eighteenth Dynasty c. 1353–1336 BCE, 174
Neo-Babylonia, 309–310
Neolithic Building Methods (Thessaly, Greece), 25
Neolithic cultures (China), 96–98
 Liangzhu culture, 96–98
 painted pottery cultures, 96
Neolithic period, 22–31
 architecture, 22–29
 sculpture and ceramics, 29–31
 Stonehenge, 27–29
Neptune (Tuby) 1678–1685, 650
New Delhi, India, 460
New Guinea, Melanesia, 47–49
New Ireland, Melanesia, 49–50
New Kingdom, Egypt c. 1539–1075 BCE, 166–180
Newspapers, development of, 674–675
New Zealand, 53
 Maori meeting house *(Te-Hau-Ki-Turanga)*, 54–55
 Treaty of Waitangi (1840), 43
Niccoló da Tolentino Leading the Charge (Uccello) 1438–1440, 576–577, 578
Nieuwe Tydinghe (Verhoeven), Antwerp 1605, 674, 675
Nike (Victory) Adjusting Her Sandal, Acropolis, Athens c. 410–405 BCE, 204
Nike (Victory) of Samothrace, Sanctuary of the Great Gods, Samothrace c. 180 BCE, 284–286
Nile River Valley, 152, 152m
Nineveh, 309
Nirvana, 147
Ni Zan, *The Rongxi Studio*, China 1372, 467
Nok culture (Sudan), 40–41
Norse peoples, 407
North Acropolis (Left) and Temple I, Tikal, Guatemala, c. 4th century BCE–5th century CE, 122
North American cultural areas, 493–505, 494m
 Eastern woodlands, 494–496
 Great Plains, 496–499
 Northwest coast, 499–501
 Southwest, 502–505
Northwest coast Indians, North America, 494m, 499–501
 animal imagery, 499, 501
 Hamatsa masks, 500
 masks, 500, 501
 textiles, 501
Nuremberg Chronicle (Koburger) 1493, 654–655
Nymph of the Spring (Lucas Cranach the Elder) c. 1537, 630

O

Oculus, 217, 224
Offering 4, La Venta, Mexico c. 900–400 BCE, 114
Ogee, 533
Oinochoe, 196
Ojibway. *See* Birchbark: a pictographic medium
Old Kingdom, Egypt c. 2575–2150 BCE, 157–163
Old Testament Trinity (Rublyov) c. 1420–1425, 356–357
Old Woman, Roman copy, 1st century CE, 286
Olmec culture (Mesoamerica), 114–119
 colossal heads, 117–118
 Great Pyramid at La Venta, 117–118
Olpe (Pitcher), Corinth c. 650–625 BCE, 187
Olympic Games, ancient, 184

"Opera" of Virgil (Manutius), Venice, 1501, 661
Opus anglicanum (English work), 533
Oral cultures, vs. literate cultures, 135
Orant figures, 320
The Orator, Aulus Metellus, found near Peugia
c. 80 BCE, 291
Oratory, 330
Oratory of Galla Placidia, Ravenna c. 425–426, 330
Oratory of Galla Placidia, view from entrance, Ravenna
c. 425–426, 330
Ordinator, 244
Origins and Development of Alphabetic Scripts
3500 BCE–900 CE, 142
Orientalizing period, Greece c. 700–600 BCE, 187
Ornamental techniques, 362
Ornate Gothic letter (Franck), Germany 1601, 662
Orsanmichele Exterior View Showing Sculpture in Niches
begun in 1337, 586
Orthogonal (grid plan), 206
Orthogonals, 592
Osiris, 149, 153
Ospedale Degli Innocenti (Foundling Hospital), Florence
(Brunelleschi) 1421–1444, 582–583
Ottoman Empire, 380–382

P

Pacific cultural-geographic regions, 45m
Pacific cultures, 42–58
    Australia, 45–46
    Barunga statement (Australia), 42–43
    Melanesia, 46–50
    Micronesia, 50–52
    Pacific cultural-geographic regions, 45m
    peopling of the Pacific, 44–45
    Polynesia, 52–58
Page from the Prayer Book of Maximilian I (Dürer) 1515, 516
Painted Banner, Changsha, China c. 160 BCE, 102–103
Painted Stones, Mas-D'Azil, France 10,000 BCE, 136
Pakal the Great (Mayan), 124–126
Palace (Foreground) and Temple of the Inscriptions, Palenque,
    Mexico c. 5th–8th century CE, 124
Palatino, Giovanni, writing manual, Rome 1561, 662
Palazzo Farnese Gallery ceiling, Rome (Caracci)
    1597–1601, 640
Palenque (Maya), 124–126
Paleolithic hand-axe (Isimila Korongo, Tanzania), 12, 13
Paleolithic period, 11–22
    artifacts/works of art, 14–17
    female figures, 15–17
    Lion-Human, Hohlenstein-Stadel, Germany, 14–15
    shelters/architecture, 13–14
Palette of Narmer, Egypt c. 2950 BCE, 154, 155
Palladio, Andrea, "I Quattro Libri dell Architettura,"
    Venice 1570, 662–663
Pallazzo Medici-Riccardi, Florence, begun 1446, 584
Palmettes, 205
Panel from a Box, India, late 17th–18th century, 456
Panofsky, Irwin, 8
Panoramic View of the Diamond Mountains (Geumgang-San)
    (Jeong), Korea 1734 CE, 481
Pantheon, plan of, 225
Pantheon, reconstruction drawing, 225
Pantheon, Rome c. 118–128 CE, 222, 224–226
Papua New Guinea, Melanesia, 47
Paracas culture, 130
Parchment, 341
Parinirvana of the Buddha, Sri Lanka,
    11th–12th century CE, 269
Parish church, 337
Parthenon, 198–203
Passive grave, 26
Patrician Carrying Portrait Busts of Two Ancestors (Barberini
    Togatus, 1st century BCE), Pallazzo de Conservatori,
    Rome, 290
Pattern Book, France, fifteenth century, 400, 402
Peck, Marion, Still Life with Dralas 2003, 61–62
Pediments, 190, 199–201
Pendentives, 334
People of the Islands Recently Discovered, The, German
    c. 1505, 512, 514
"Peplos" Kore, Acropolis, Athens c. 530 BCE, 271, 272

Pergamon, 280–283
Pergamon, reconstructed west front of the altar, in modern
    Turkey c. 175–150 BCE, 281, 283
Perikles, 196–198
Peristyle, 168, 190
Peristyle Garden, House of the Vettii, Pompeii, rebuilt 62–79
    CE, 209
Persia, 310–313
Perugino, *Delivery of the Keys to St. Peter* with a schematic
    drawing 1481, 592
Pheidias, 198, 201
*Photographic Mock-Up of the East Pediment of the Parthenon
    (Using Photographs of the Extant Marble Sculpture)*
    c. 447–432 BCE, 00
Picking Figs, Egypt, Twelfth Dynasty c. 1890 BCE, 165
Picnic at the Lotus Pond (Sin), Korea, late 18th century,
    481–482
Pictographs, 101, 137
    Aztec, 691–697
    on birchbark, 684–690
Pictorial relief, Egyptian, 167
Piece-mold casting, 99
Piers, 364
Pieta (Michelangelo) c. 1500, 611
Pietra serena, 584
Pigments, 136
Pilgrimage churches, 337, 413–416
Pilgrimages, 410
Pilgrim's journey, 414m
Pillars, 317
Pine Spirit (Wu), China, 1984 CE, 478
Plains Indian painting, 498–499
Plantin, Christopher, 669–673
    Choice of Emblems, a (Whitney), Antwerp 1586, 672
    Polyglot Bible, Antwerp 1569–1573, 670
    Polyglot Bible, title page from, Antwerp 1569–1573, 672
    Type Specimen, facsimile of, Antwerp 1585, 670
Plan, Villa of the Mysteries, Pompeii, early 2nd century
    BCE, 212
Platter, mid 4th century CE, 231–232, 236
Pliny the Elder, 289
Poet on a Mountaintop (Shen), China c. 1500 CE, 472, 474
Pointed arch, 369
Polo, Marco, *A Description of the World*, 466
Polyglot Bible (Plantin), Antwerp 1569–1573, 670
Polyglot Bible (Plantin), title page from, Antwerp
    1569–1573, 672
Polynesia, 52–58
    Hawaii, 56–57
    Marquesas Islands, 53, 56
    Rapa Nui (Easter Island), 57–58
    Samoa, 58
Pompeii, 207–213
Pompeii, reconstruction drawing, 208
Pont du Gard, Nimes, France, late 1st century BCE, 292
Popular printing
    broadside ballads, 673–684
    Dutch Renaissance and popular prints c. 1530–1700,
        669–676
    newspapers, 674–675
Porcelain, 31
    Korean, 479–480
    Ming, 470–471
    technique for making, 471
Porches, 190
Porta, Giacomo della, and Vignola, *Il Gesù Church,
    Exterior and Plan* c. 1573–1584, 618–619
Portals, 306
Portoghesi, Paolo, Gigliotti, Vittorio, and Mousaw, Sami,
    Islamic Mosque and Cultural Centre, Rome
    1984–1992, 387
Portrait Head of an Elder c. 80 BCE, 291
Portrait of a Married Couple, Pompeii,
    mid 1st century CE, 214
Portrait of a Woman and Man (Lippi) c. 1435–1445,
    598–599
Portrait of Pakal the Great, Palenque, Mexico, mid 7th
    century CE, 126
Portrait vessels, 131
Poseidon, 190, 191
Potassium-argon dating, 21
Potsherds, 31

Pottery, techniques, 31
Poupou (house panel), 55
Prakrit, 81
Praxiteles, 277–279
    Aphrodite of Knidos, copy of original of c. 350 BCE, 277,
        278, 279
    Hermes and the Infant Dionysos, probably a copy of a
        Late Classical 4th century BCE original, 277, 278
Prayer Hall, Great Mosque of Cordoba, Spain, begun
    785/786, 366
Predella, 531
Prehistoric art, 10–34
    Bronze Age, 31–32
    cave paintings and sculptures, 17–22
    Neolithic period, 22–31
    Paleolithic period, 11–22
    prehistoric Europe, 12m
    rock carvings, 32, 34
    the Stone Age, 11–31
Prehistoric Europe, 12m
Prehistoric Japan. *See* Japan
Prehistoric writing, 135–136, 137
Prehistory to early writing (35,000 to 500 BCE), 134–146
    the alphabet, 140–144
    early writing, 137–139
    mark-making, 134–135
    prehistory, 135–136, 137
    protowriting, 136–137
    spread of writing as idea and script, 139–140
    timeline for, 145–146
    tools of the trade, 146
Priestess of Bacchus (?) c. 390–401 CE, 237
"Primitive" art, myth of, 39
*Prince Khurram, The Future Shah Jahan at Age (al-Zaman)
    25*, India c. 1616–1617, 457
Prinsep, James, 81
Printing, revolutions in, 653–684
    Aztec pictographs, 691–697
    birchbark pictographs, 684–690
    broadside ballads, 673–684
    emergence of printmaking, 653
    maps, 666–669
    popular publishing: Dutch Renaissance and popular
        prints c. 1530–1700, 669–676
    printed books, 654–666
    Renaissance Italy & France c. 1460–1600, 656–669
    single sheets, 653–654
Private Audience Hall, Fatehpur Sikri, India c. 1570, 454
Pronaos, 190
Proto-writing, 136–137
Psalter, 351
Ptolemaic world, Rome, 1478, 667m, 668m
Pueblos, 502–503
Purcelle, Jean, *Book of Hours* of Jeanne d'Évereux, *Kiss of
    Judas and Annunciation* c. 1325–1328, 530, 532
Pylons, 168
Pyramid ("El Castillo") with Chacmool in Foreground,
    Chichen Itza, Mexico, 9th–12th century CE, 128
Pyramid of the Feathered Serpent, Teotihuacán, Mexico c.
    200 CE, 120–121
Pyramid of the Sun, Teotihuacán, Mexico, 120

Q

Qibla wall, 365
*Qibla Wall with Mihrab and Minbar, Sultan Hasan Madrasa-
    Mausoleum-Mosque Complex* 1356–1363, 370
Qin Dynasty (China, 221–206 BCE), 102, 465
Qingbian Mountains, The (Dong), China 1617, 475–476
Qing dynasty (China, 644–1911), 464m, 476–478
    individualist painting, 477–478
    orthodox painting, 477
Qiu Ying, *Spring Dawn in the Han Palace*, China
    1500–1550 CE, 468–470
Queen Nefertari Making an Offering to Isis, Egypt,
    Nineteenth Dynasty c. 1290–1224 BCE, 178
Queen Tiy, Egypt, Eighteenth Dynasty c. 1352 BCE, 174
Quetzal bird, 488
Quillwork, 495–496
"Quilts: The Great American Art" (Mainardi), 4
Quilts, 3–4
Quincunx fractal, 553

Qur'an
  frontispiece c. 1368, 378
  page from, 377

R

Ra, 149, 153
Radiometric dating, 21
Raharaja I and His Teacher, Rajarajeshvara Temple of Shiva, Thanjavur, Tamil Nadu, India, Chola dynasty c. 1010 CE, 264–265
Rainbow Serpent Rock (Western Arnhem Land, Australia), 11
Rajarajeshvara Temple of Shiva, Thanjavur, Tamil Nadu, Indi, Chola dynasty 1003–1010 CE, 263–264
Rajput painting (India), 458–459
Ramose's Brother May and His Wife Werener, Thebes, Eighteenth Dynasty c. 1375–1365 BCE, 171–172
Ramses II (king of Egypt, Nineteenth Dynasty c. 1279–1213 BCE), 176–178
Rapa Nui (Easter Island), 57–58
Raphael, 608–610
  Agnelo Doni c. 1506, 608–609
  Maddalena Strozzi c. 1506, 608–609
  Madonna of the Goldfinch (Madonna del Cardellino), 7
  School of Athens c. 1510–1511, 609–610
  The Small Cowper Madonna c. 1505, 608
  Stanza Della Segnatura 1510–1511, 600–601
Ratdolt, Erhard, "Calendarium," Venice 1476, 658
Ravenna, 328–331
Rebecca at the Well, codex page, early 6th century, 341
Recovery of Bahia in Brazil, The (Maino) 1635, 523, 527
Recovery of San Juan de Puerto Rico, The (Caxés) 1630s, 523
Recovery of the Island of San Cristobel, The (Caxés) 1630s, 523
Recreation of Pheidias' Huge Gold and Ivory Figure, 198
Red Sky's Midéwegun scroll, 687
Reformation and the arts, 622–623, 622m
Registers, 71–72, 75–76
Relative dating, 21
Relics, 337
Relics and reliquaries, Romanesque period, 418
Relief from East Gateway of the Great Stupa, Sanchi, 1st century BCE, 90
Relief sculpture, 14
Reliquaries, 89
Reliquary Statue of Sainte Foy (St. Faith), late 9th or 10th century, 418
Removal of the Face of One of the Colossal Sculptures of Ramses II At Abu Simbel in the Mid 1960s, 177
Renaissance art in fifteenth-century Italy, 577–599
  Florence, 578–599
    architecture, 579–586
    Brunelleschi, Filippo, 579–583
    competition reliefs, 581, 585
    Foundling Hospital, 581, 582–583
    Medici Palace, 584
    painting, 593–596
    painting after Masaccio, 596–599
    sculpture, 586–593
  humanism and the Italian Renaissance, 578
  map of fifteenth-century Italy, 579
  Renaissance perspective, 592
Renaissance printing
  broadside ballads, 673–684
  Dutch Renaissance and popular prints 1530–1700, 669–676
  Italy and France c. 1460–1600, 656–669
  maps, 666–669
Renier of Huy, *Baptismal Font, Nôtre-Dame-aux-Fonts* 1107–1118, 438
Renoir, Auguste, *Mme. Charpentier and Her Children,* 8
Representation, 60–62
Republic of Rome (509–27 BCE), 289–294
  portrait sculpture, 289–293
  temples, 293–294
Restored Perspective View of the Central Hall, Basilica Ulpia, Rome c. 112 CE, 220
Returning Home Late from a Spring Outing (Dai), China, 468–469
Rhetorical skills, 240
Ridegepole, 25–26

Riemenschneider, Tilman, *Altarpiece of the Holy Blood (Wings Open)* c. 1499–1505, 623
Rigaud, Hyacintha, *Louis XIV* 1701, 647, 649
Ritual bronzes, 98–99
Robin Hood broadside ballad, England 1634, 674, 680
Rock Art: Boat and Sea Battle, Sweden c. 1500–500 BCE, 34
Rock art, early African, 37–39, 41
Rock carvings, Bronze Age, 32, 34
Rock-Cut Tombs, Beni Hasan, Egypt, Twelfth Dynasty c. 1938–1756 BCE, 164
Roman and Byzantine world, late, 317m
Roman and italic type (Garamond) 1545, 664
Roman arch, 292
Roman art, after Constantine, 231–238
  See also Ancient Greece
Roman cities, 207–209
Roman Cursive, 166 CE, 245
Roman deities, 186
Roman de la Rose, Bruges c. 1500, 400, 401
Roman Empire, early (27 BCE–19 CE)
  art in the age of Augustus, 294–296
  funerary sculpture, 297, 299, 303
  imperial portraits, 296–297
  mosaics, 298
Roman Empire, late (3rd and 4th centuries CE), 299–303
  Severan Dynasty (193–235 CE), 299–301, 478
  soldier emperors, 301
  Tetrarchic portraiture, 301–302
Romanesque period, 409–450
  architectural sculpture, 429–435
    the Church of Saint–Lazare at Autun, 433–435
    the Priory Church of Saint–Pierre at Moissac, 430–433
    Willgelmo at the Cathedral of Modena, 430
  architecture, 412–429
    church portals, 429
    the Cistercians, 419–420
    Cluny, 416–417
    "First Romanesque," 413
    pilgrimage churches, 413–416
    regional styles in, 420–429
    secular architecture: Dover Castle, England, 428–429
  art, 411–412
    Europe in, 410–411
      the church, 410–411
      political and economic life, 410
    map of Europe in, 411
    the medieval aesthetic sensibility, 447–450
    relics and reliquaries, 418
    San Climent in Taull paintings, 424
    sculpture in wood and bronze, 436–438
      Christ on the Cross (Majestat Batlló), 436
      Mary as the Throne of Wisdom, 436
      Renier of Huy, 438
      Tomb of Rudolf of Swabia, 437
    St. Bernard and Theophilus: monastic controversy over the visual arts, 420
    textiles and books, 438–445
      the Bayeux Embroidery, 439–441
      chronicling history, 439–442
      Codex Colbertinus, 442
      Hildegard of Bingen, 443
      sacred books, 442–445
      "A Vision of Love" from *The Book of Divine Works,* 446–447
  See also Europe in the Middle Ages; High art in Europe
Roman houses, 209–210
Romans, 288–303
  architecture elements, Roman arch, 292
  Early Empire (27 BCE–19 CE), 294–299
  Late Empire (3rd and 4th centuries CE), 299–303
  mosaics, 298
  origins of Rome, 288
  religion, 289
  Republic (509–27 BCE), 289–294
  writers on art, 289
  See also Ancient Greece; High classical period
Romans Crossing the Danube and Building a Fort 113–116 CE, 223
Roman vaulting, 217

Rome and the Vatican, 616–620
Rongxi Studio, The, China 1372, 467
Roof comb, 124
Rosetta Stone c. 196 BCE, 73, 179
Rosettes, 187
Rothko, Mark, *Magenta, Black and Green on Orange,* 2, 3
Rotunda, 224
Rotunda Script, Milan 1490–1504, 400, 402
Round arches, 292, 369
Rubbing of a stone relief, 105
Rubbing of a Stone Relief in the Wu Family Shrine, detail, China c. 151 CE, 105
Rublyov, Andrey, *Old Testament Trinity* c. 1410–1425, 356–357
Ruins and Plan of the Anu Ziggurat and White Temple, Uruk c. 3300–3000 BCE, 70
Ruins of Pompeii, aerial view, 208
Runes, CA. 600 CE, 144
Rustic Brushwork, Before 79 CE, 243
Rustic Letters, 194 CE, 244

S

Sacrifice of Isaac (Brunelleschi) 1401–1402, 585
Sacrifice of Isaac (Ghiberti) 1401–1402, 585
Safavid Dynasty, 383–386
Saharan rock art, 38–39
Saint-Lazare Church, at Autun, 433–435
Saint-Martin-Du-Canigoui 1001–1026, 412, 413
Saint-Pierre at Moissac Priory Church, reliefs on the left wall of the porch c. 1115, 432–433
Saint-Savin-Sur-Gartempe Abbey Church, Poitou c. 1060–1075, 425
Samoa, 58
San Carlo Alle Quattro Fontane Church, exterior and Plan (Borromini) 1638–1667, 638
San Carlo Alle Quattro Fontane Church, view into the dome (Borromini) 1638–1667, 638, 639
San Clemente Church, nave, Rome, consecrated 1128, 421–423
San Climent in Taull, Spain, paintings, 424
Sanctuaries, Greek, 184, 188
Sanctuary at Delphi (Apollo's sanctuary) c. 6th–3rd century BCE, 188–190
Sanctuary of Apollo, Delphi c. 6th–3rd century BCE, 188, 189
Sanctuary of Zeus, Olympia, 184
Sand paintings, Navajo, 504–505
Sangha, 147–148
San Lorenzo (Olmec center), 117–118
San Lorenzo Church, interior and plan (Brunelleschi and di Bartolomeo) c. 1421–1428, 581
Sanskrit, 81
Santa Costanza Church, interior view c. 350, 325
Santa Fe Indian School, 503
Santa Maria Delle Grazie, refectory showing *The Last Supper* (Da Vinci), 605
Sant' Apollinare in Classe, 339–340
Santa Sabina Church, exterior view c. 422–432, 324
Santa Sabina Church, interior view c. 422–432, 325
Santa Sophia Cathedral Interior, Kiev 1037–1046, apse mosaics, 347–348
Santiago de Compostela pilgrimage routes, 414m
Sant Vincenc Church, interior, Cardona 1020–1030s, 413
San Vitale Church, Ravenna, consecrated 547, 335–339
  Christ Enthroned, 337
  Emperor Justinian, 338
  Empress Theodora, 338
  plan and cutaway drawing, 335
Sarcophagus, 151
Sarcophagus of Constantina c. 350, 327
Sarcophagus of Junius Bassus c. 359, 328
Sarcophagus with the Indian Triumph of Dionysus c. 190 CE, 297, 299, 303
Scarification, 36
Schaden, Otto, 151
Schematic Drawing of the Funerary Temple of Hatshepsut (Deir el–Bahri), 171
Schematic Drawing of the Temple of Ramses II at Abu Simbel, 177
Schongauer, Martin, *Demons Tormenting St. Anthony* c. 1480–1490, 654
School of Athens (Raphael) c. 1510–1511, 609–610

Schools of painting, 379
Science and the changing worldview, 648
Scribes, 240, 340
Scriptoria, 340
Scripture: from Abstraction to Naturalism, Sacred to
    Secular, 251–303
Scrolls, 242, 341
Sculpture in the round, 14
Sculptures, Neolithic, 29–31
Seal Impressions, Indus Valley c. 2500–1500 BCE, 82
Seals, 469
Seated Scribe, Egypt, Fifth Dynasty c. 2450–2325 BCE, 162
Seaweed, Willie, *Kwakwaka'wakw Bird Mask*, Canada,
    prior to 1951, 500
Section of San Rock-Wall Painting (San peoples, South
    Africa), 41
Secular portrait sculpture, 251
Self-Portrait (Dürer) 1500, 620–621
Self-Portrait as the Allegory of Painting (Gentileschi)
    1630, 647
Serdab, 155
Sesklo Stone Foundation House (Greece), 24
Set of Bells, China c. 433 BCE, 101
Severan Dynasty (193–235 CE), 299–301
Sfumato, 504
Sgraffito, 586
Shaft, 192
Shah-i Zinda Funerary Complex, Samarkand,
    late 14th–15th century, 374
Shah Jahan, 457–458
Shaka Triad, Japan c. 623 CE, 111
Shaman with Drum and Snake, Costa Rica
    c. 13th–16th century CE, 129
Shang dynasty (China, 1700–1100 BCE), 98
Shen Zhou, *Poet on a Mountaintop*, China c. 1500 CE, 472,
    474
Shikhara, 254
Shikharas, 91
Shinto, 108–109
Shitao, *Landscape*, China c. 1700 CE, 477–478
Shiva, 88
Shiva Nataraja, Thanjavur, Tamil Nadu, Chola dynasty,
    12th century CE, 260
Shoulder Bag, Kansas c. 1860, 496, 497
Shroud of St. Josse, before 961, 376, 542
Shungas dynasty (185–72 BCE), 88–92
Siddhartha, 87
Siddhartha in the Palace, India c. 3rd century CE, 95
Silhak Movement (Korea, 18th century), 480–482
Silk damask embroidery, 1375–1475, Chinese or
    Tibetan, 541
Silk fabric woven with Arabic inscriptions, 15th-century
    Spain, 541
Silk pattern-knitted gloves, c. 1247, Spain, 538
Silk *samitum*, Byzantine, c. 650, 540
Silk *samitum*, eastern Mediterranean, 8th century, 538
Silk twill coronation mantle 1133–1334, Palermo,
    Sicily, 538
Silver Mines of Potosí (de León) 1553, 518, 521
Sinan, 380–381
    Mosque of Sultan Selim 1568–1575, 380
    Mosque of Sultan Selim, Interior 1568–1574, 381
Single sheets, 653–654
Sin Yunbok, *Picnic at the Lotus Pond*, Korea, late 18th
    century, 481–482
Sipán, Peru, 132–133
Siphnian Treasury, Sanctuary of Apollo, Delphi c.
    530–525 BCE, 189–190
Sistine Chapel
    ceiling with diagram identifying scenes,
        (Michelangelo) 1508–1512, 614
    Creation of Adam (Michelangelo) 1511–1512, 615
    interior, built 1475–1481, 613, 823
Sitting Bull, 572
The Small Cowper Madonna (Raphael) c. 1505, 608
"Soderini letter" (Vespucci), 510, 513
Song dynasty (China, 960–1279 CE), 464, 465
Sound Box of the Great Lyre, Ur, 76
South American cultures before 1300, 129–133
    Chavin de Huantar, 129–130
    Moche culture, 131–133
    Nazca culture, 130, 131

Paracas culture, 130
    See also Americas after 1300; Americas before 1300
South and Southeast Asia before 1200, 81–113
    Asuka period (552–645 CE), 109–111
    Bronze Age China, 98–101
        Qin dynasty (221–206 BCE), 102
        ritual bronzes, 98–99
        Shang dynasty (1700–1100 BCE), 98
        Zhou dynasty (1100–221 BCE), 99–101
    China and Korea, 97m
    daoism, 104
    Han dynasty (206 BCE–221 CE), 97m, 102–105
    Indian subcontinent, 82
    Indus civilization, 82–85
    Japan, 106m
    Kushan and Later Andhra periods, 92–96
        Gandhara style, 93
        Mathura style, 93–95
        Southeast Indian style, 95
    map, 82m
    Maurya period, 85–88
    Middle Kingdom, 96
    Nara period (645–794 CE), 111–113
    Neolithic cultures, 96–98
        Liangzhu culture, 96–98
        painted pottery cultures, 96
    prehistoric Japan, 106–109
        haniwa, 106, 108
        Jomon period, 106
        Kofun period, 106, 108–109
        Yayoi period, 106
    rise of Buddhism, 87
    rise of Hinduism, 88
    Shungas and Early Andhras periods, 88–92
    Shungas and Early Andrhas periods
        Buddhist rock-cut halls, 92
        stupas, 88–92
    Vedic period, 85
Southeast Asian art, 265–287
    bronze sculpture, 274–276
    Cambodia, Angkor Vat, 266–269
    classic and classical, 274
    free-standing sculpture, 270–272
    goldsmith art, 280
    Hellenistic sculpture, 280–287
    Java, Borobudur, 266, 267
    Lysippos, 279–280
    marble sculpture, 273
    Pergamon, 280–283
    Praxiteles, 277–279
    sculpture in fifth century BCE, 277–280
    sculpture in fourth century BCE, 277–280
    Sri Lanka, 269
    Thailand, Dvaravati style, 266
    Thailand, Prakhon Chai style, 265
Southeast Indian style, 95
Southern African rock art, 41
Southwest Indians, North America, 494m,
        502–505
    Navajos, 504–505
    Pueblos, 502–503
    Santa Fe Indian School, 503
Spandrels, 292
Spanish conquest, 484–487
    aftermath of, 493
Spanish Treatment of Fugitive Black Slaves, The (de Bry)
    1595, 526
Sparta, Greece, 184
Spear Bearer (Doryphoros) c. 450–440 BCE, 202
Speyer Cathedral c. 1080–1106, 426
Spider Woman, 485
Spirit poles of the Asmat of West Papua, 48–49
Spoils from the Temple of Solomon, 216
Spotted Horses and Human Hands, Pech–Merle Cave.
    Dordogne, France 25,000–15,000 BCE, 9–10
Spring Dawn in the Han Palace (Qiu), China
    1500–1550 CE, 468–470
Springings, 292
Squinches, 334, 373
Sri Lanka, 269
Stags Drinking, San Clemente Church, Rome,
    consecrated 1128, 423

Standing Buddha, Bamiyan, Afghanistan c. 5th century CE,
    252, 253
Standing Buddha, Pakistan c. 2nd–3rd century CE, 93
Standing Buddha, Uttar Pradesh, India, Gupta period,
    474 CE, 252
St Anthony Enthroned between SS. Augustine and Jerome
    (Hagenauer) c. 1500, 625
Stanza Della Segnatura (Raphael) 1510–1511, 600–601
St. Bernard and Theophilus: monastic controversy over
    the visual arts, 420
Stela, Maya, 125
Stelae, 118
Stele of Amenemhat, Egypt, Eleventh Dynasty
    c. 2000 BCE, 166
Stele of Hammurabi, Susa c. 1792–1750 BCE, 79
Stele of Naram-Sin, Mesopotamia 2254–2218 BCE, 67,
    73, 77
Stele of the Sculptor Userwer, Egypt, Twelfth Dynasty
    c. 1850 BCE, 165, 167
Stele sculpture, Greek, 206
Stenciled Hand, Pech Merle, France
    23,000–18,000 BCE, 134
*Step Pyramid and Sham Buildings, Funerary Complex of
    Djoser, Saqqara*, Egypt, 156
St George (Donatello) 1417–1420, 587
Still Life (de la Porte c. 1765), 61
Still Life, House of the Stags (Cervi), before 79 CE, 214
Still lifes, Roman, 214–216
Still Life with Dralas (Peck) 2003, 61–62
St. James Cathedral, transept, Santiago de Compostela
    1078–1122, 414–415
St. Mark's Cathedral, interior plan, begun 1063, Venice, 340
St. Mary of the Assumption Cathedral, in Pisa, 420–421
Stone Age, 11–31
    See also Neolithic period; Paleolithic period
Stonehenge (England), 27–29
Stoneware, 31
Story of Paris, Florentine, late fifteenth century, 509
St. Peter's Basilica and Piazza, Vatican (Maderno)
    c. 1656–1657, 634, 635
St. Peter's Basilica in the Vatican, 633–635
St. Peter's Basilica, Vatican (Michelangelo) c. 1546–1564, 618
St. Teresa of Avila in Ecstasy (Bernini) 1645–1652, 631, 632
Stupas, 88–92
Stylized sculpture of a bat, 552, 553
Stylobate, 192
Stylus, 69, 71
Sub-Saharan civilizations, 39–41
Sui dynasty (China, 581–618 CE), 465
Sultan Hasan Madrasa-Mausoleum-Mosque Complex, 370
Sultan Selim Mosque (Sinan) 1568–1575, 380, 381
Sumer, Mesopotamia, 69–74
    cuneiform writing, 69, 71
    cylinder seals, 73–74
    Uruk, 69, 71–72
    votive figures, 72–73
    ziggurats, 69, 70
Surrender of Breda (Velázquez) 1630s, 523
Susannah and the Elders (Gentileschi) 1610, 646
Sutton Hoo excavations, 408
Syllabaries, 140
Symbolic value, 135
Symbols, 135
    Buddhist, 112
    cuneiform writing and, 71
    Egyptian, 153
Syncretism, 320
Syrian silk, 12th-century, 541

T

Tagore, Abanindranath, *Bharat Mata (Mother India)*, India
    1905, 460–461
Taj Mahal, India c. 1631–1648, 453–455
Taliban of Afghanistan, destroying fifth-century Buddha
    statues in 2001, 344
Talud-tablero (slope-and-panel) construction, 120–121
Tang Chinese silk of 620–700, 541
Taos Pueblo (Gilpin), New Mexico 1947, 502
Tapa (Siapo Vala), Samoa 20th century, 58
Tapestry, 384
Tartar cloths, 14th-century, Sino-Mongolian design, 544

Technique, textile, and text, 529–573
    Asia and South Pacific designs, 548
    church and state AD 600–1500, 536–544
    England, 533
    European designs, 548
    fractals in cross–cultural comparison, 545
    intention and invention in design, 550
    manuscript illumination, 530
    metal work and ivory, 530, 534–535, 536
    Native American art, 568–573
    Native American design, 545–548
    Native American weaving, 553–568
    opus anglicanum (English work), 533
Temple of Aphaia, Aegina, Greece c. 500 BCE, 191, 193
Temple of Aphaia, Aegina, reconstruction drawing
    c. 500 BCE, 193
Temple of Hera I, Poseidonia (Roman Paestum), Italy
    c. 550–540 BCE, 190, 191
Temple of Minerva at Priene, inscription,
    third century BCE, 242
Temple of Ramses II, Egypt, Nineteenth Dynasty
    c. 1279–1213 BCE, 176
Temple, perhaps dedicated to Portunus, Forum Boarium
    (Cattle Market), Rome, late 2nd century BCE, 293
Tenochtitlan (Mesoamerican city), 486–487
Teotihuacán (Mesoamerican city), 119–122, 486
    Bloodletting Ritual, Teotihuacán, Mexico
      c. 550–650 BCE, 121–122
    ceremonial center, 119–120
    Pyramid of the Feathered Serpent, Teotihuacán, Mexico
      c. 200 CE, 120–121
Terra cotta, 270
Terra nullius (Australia), 43
Tetradrachma from Kymaea, second century BCE, 242
Tetrarchic portraiture, 301–302
Tetrarch Portrait, early 4th century CE, 301
Tetrarchs, The c. 300 CE, 302
Teve Tupuhia, Marquesan man tattooed in 1980 by
    Samoan Lese li'o, 53
Textiles, 529
    Andean, 132
    associated with military campaigns, 1335–1340, Sir
      Geoffrey Luttrell, 543
    Assyria, 309
    embroideries, 529, 533
    in Islamic art, 376–377
    See also Technique, textile, and text
Textiles and books, Romanesque period, 438–445
Textile with Elephants and Camels, before 961, 376
Thailand, Dvaravati style, 266
Thailand, Prakhon Chai style, 265
Thatched roof, 26
Theravada Buddhism, 87
Thermo–luminescence dating, 21
Third Intermediate Period, Egypt c. 1075–715 BCE, 180
Three Dancers and Two Musicians: Corroboree of Mimi, Spirits
    of the Rocks (Midjaw), 46
Three Jewels, The, 147–148
Thrust, 292
Tigris and Euphrates rivers, 69, 70m
    See also Fertile Crescent and Mesopotamia
Tikal (Maya), 122, 123–124
Tile Mosaic Miharab, 1354, 373
Till, Emmett, photo of, 60
Timelines
    Classical literacy 700 BCE–400 CE, 249–250
    comparing visual arts with historical landmarks, 505
    prehistory to early writing 35,000–500 BCE, 145–146
Tipis, 496–498
Ti Watching a Hippopotamus Hunt, Egypt, Fifth Dynasty
    c. 2450–2325 BCE, 163
Tlaloc, 486, 487
T-O map, manuscript, early 13th century, 666m, 667m
Tomb Interior with Corbeling and Engraved Stones,
    Newgrange, Ireland 3000–2500 BCE, 26
Tomb Model of a House, China c. 1st-mid
    2nd century CE, 104
Tomb of Rudolf of Swabia, 437
Tomb of the Warrior Priest, Moche culture, 132–133
Tondo, 196
Toranas, 90–91
Torc, Soucy, France, Celtic Gaul, 3rd–1st century BCE, 282

Torso, Indus Valley c. 2600–1900 BCE, 85
Torso of a "Priest–King," Indus Valley c. 2600–1900 BCE, 84
Tower of Babel in Abbey Church of Saint-Savin-Sur-
    Gartempe, Poitou c. 1060–1075, 425
Trajan, Rome, 219–222
Trajan's Column, Detail 114 CE, 246
Trajan's Forum and Market, Rome c. 110–113 CE, 220
Trajan's Market, main hall, Rome c. 110–112 CE, 221
Trajan's Market, reconstruction drawing, Rome
    c. 110–112 CE, 221
Transept, 326
Transfiguration of Christ with Sant' Apollinare, First Bishop of
    Ravenna, consecrated in 549, 339–340
Transverse arch, 413
Treachery of Images, The (Magritte) 1928–1929, 61–62
Treasury of the Siphnians, Sanctuary of Apollo, reconstruction
    drawing, Delphi c. 530–525 BCE, 189
Treaty of Waitangi, New Zealand 1840, 43
Tree of Jesse, page with Explanatio in Isaiam c. 1125,
    444–445
The Tribute Money (Masaccio) c. 1427, 595–596
Triglyphs, 192
Trinity with the Virgin, St. John the Evangelist, and Donors
    (Masaccio) c. 1425–1427, 593–595
Trinity with the Virgin, St. John the Evangelist, and Donors,
    diagram of spatial world (Masaccio) c. 1425–1427,
    593–595
Triumph of Maximilian I, The (Altdorfer) 1512–1516, 515
Trumeau, 420
Trumeau, Priory Church of Saint–Pierre at Moissa, c. 1115,
    431–432
Tubuan Mask Being Danced, Papua New Guinea c. 1990, 51
Tuby, Jean-Baptiste, *Neptune* 1678–1685, 650
Tugras, 382
Tunic, Peru c. 1500, 492, 493
Tutankhamun
    discovery of tomb, 151
    funeral mask of, 150
    tomb of, 174–175
Tympanum, 429
Two Mysteries, The (Magritte) 1966, 62–63
Type Specimen, facsimile of (Plantin), Antwerp 1585, 670
"Typography Matters: Branding Ballads and Gelding
    Curates in Stuart England" (McShane), 676–684

U

Uccello, Paolo, *The Battle of San Romano* 1438–1440,
    577, 597
Uccello, Paolo, *Niccoló da Tolentino Leading the Charge*
    1438–1440, 576–577, 578
Undercutting, 232
Unical scripts, 245
The Universe (Hildegard of Bingen) 1150–1175, 443
Unswept Floor, The, mosaic version of a 2nd century BCE
    painting by Sosos of Pergamon, 298
Ur and Lagash, Mesopotamia, 75–78
    lyre from a royal tomb at Ur (excavations), 75–76
Urban sprawl in London, 551
Urna, 93
Uruk, Sumer, 64–66, 69, 71–72
Ushnisha, 93

V

Vajrayana Buddhism, 87
Valley of Mexico, 486
Valley of the Kings, Egypt, 151
Valley Temple of Khafre, Giza, Old Kingdom
    c. 2520–2494 BCE, 160
van der Hoof, Gail, 4
Vanishing point, 592, 594
Van Leeuwenhoek, Anton, 648
Vasari, Giogio, *Lives of the Best Architects, Painters, and*
    Sculptors 1550, 602
Vault, 26
Vedas c. 1200–800 BCE, 88
Vedic period, 85
Velázquez, *Surrender of Breda* 1630s, 523
Velarde, Pablita, *Koshares of Taos,* New Mexico 1940s,
    502, 503
Vellum, 341, 378

Venetian type (Jenson), Venice 1470, 658
Venus De Milo (Aphrodite of Melos) c. 150–100 BCE,
    286–287
Verhoeven, Abraham, *Nieuwe Tydinghe,* Antwerp 1605,
    674, 675
Verism, 290
Versailles art and decoration, 649–652
Versailles Palace Garden (Le Vau and Hardouin-Mansart)
    1678–1685, 650
Vespucci, Amerigo, 484
    letter to Soderini, 510, 513
    Mundus Novus, 510, 512–514
Vespucci's De Ora Antarctica (Mundus Novus), frontispiece
    to (Strassburg) 1505, 512
Vietnamese ceramics, 452
View and Plan of the Parthenon, Acropolis, Athens
    c. 447–432 BCE, 199
View of the World, A, Mexico c. 1400–1519, 489
Vignola (Barozzi, Giacomo), 616, 618, 619
Vignola, *Il Gesú Church,* exterior and plan c. 1573–1584,
    618–619
Viharas, 91, 92
Villa at Boscoreale, Roman c. 50–30 BCE, 213
Villa of the Mysteries, Pompeii, 212–213
Virgin and Child from Saint-Denis c. 1324–1339, 530, 533
Virgin and Child, late 12th century, 436–437
Virgin and Child with Saints and Angels, icon, second half
    of 6th century, 343
Virgin of the Palm, detail from (School of Amiens) 1520,
    521, 522
Virgin of the Rocks (Da Vinci) c. 1485, 604
Virgin of Vladimir, icon, 11th–12th century, 350
Vishnu, 88
Vishnu Churning the Ocean of Milk, Angkor Vat, 268
Vishnu Temple on the Cosmic Waters, Deogarh, Uttar
    Pradesh, India, Gupta period c. 530 CE, 254, 255
"A Vision of Love" from *The Book of Divine Works,*
    446–447
Visual expression, elements of, 7
Vitruvian Man (Da Vinci) c. 1490, 607
Vitruvius, 289
Volute, 192
Votive figures, 72–73, 78
Votive Figures, Square Temple, Eshnunna c. 2900–2600
    BCE, 72
Votive Statue of Gudea, Girsu c. 2090 BCE, 78

W

Wagner Carpet, 17th century, 384–385
Waldseemüller, Martin, world map, Germany 1507,
    667m–669m
Wall Painting on the "Ixion Room," House of the Vettii,
    Pompeii, rebuilt 62–79 CE, 211
Wall paintings, ancient Rome, 210–216
Wall paintings, prehistoric technique, 19
Wall Painting with Horses, Rhinoceros, and Aurochs, Chauvet
    Cave, France 32,000–30,000 BCE, 18
Walls and Baptismal Font, Syria, model of, before
    256, 321
Wall with Torah Niche, Syria 244–245 CE, 318
Wampum Belt, Traditionally Called William Penn's Treaty with
    the Delaware, Eastern Woodlands 1680s, 494–495
Wapepe Navigation Chart, Marshall Islands, 19th century, 51
Warp, 384
Warrior, Italy c. 460–450 BCE, 275, 276
Water, 362
Wattle and daub, 26
Weary Herakles (Farnese Hercules) (Lysippos), Roman copy
    by Glykon of 4th century BCE bronze original, 280
Weegee, (Arthur Felig), 59–60
    First Murder, The, 59
Welt, 384
Western Europe during the Reformation, 622m
Western Hemisphere of the "Miller" World Map (Homem)
    1525, 520
West Indian Scene, A (Mostaert) c. 1540–1550, 521,
    524–525
West Papua, Melanesia, 47, 48–49
West Pediment of the Temple of Aphaia, Aegina
    c. 500–490 BCE, 194
Whirling Log Ceremony (Klah), Navajo c. 1925, 504–505

White, John, *English Sailors in a Skirmish with Eskimo* 1577, 519
White-letter broadside ballads, 677–684
Whitney, Geffrey, *A Choice of Emblems* (printed by Plantin), Antwerp 1586, 672
Wiligelmo, *Creation and Fall*, Modena Cathedral c. 1099, 430
William the Conqueror, 410
Winchester Minuscule, England 10th century, 395, 396
Wolgemut, Michael, Wilhelm Pleyenwurff, and workshop, *City of Nuremberg* 1493, 655
Woman from Brassempouy (Grotte de Pape, Brassempouy, Landes, France), 16–17
Woman from Dolní Věstonice (Moravia, Czech Republic), 16
Woman from Willendorf, Austria c. 24,000 BCE, 15
Woman Spinning, Susa c. 8th–7th century BCE, 309
Women at a Fountain House, Greece c. 520–510 BCE, 205
Women Wearing Net Bags (Bilum), Papua New Guinea 1990, 48
Woodblocks, 653
Wooden strapwork, 362

Woolley, Leonard and Katherine, 75
Worcester Chronicle (John of Worcester) c. 1140, 439, 442
World map (Waldseemüller), Germany 1507, 667m–669m
Writing. *See* Classical literacy (700 BCE–400 CE); Prehistory to early writing (35,000 to 500 BCE); Printing, revolutions in
Writing manual (Arrighi), Rome 1522, 661
Writing manual (Palatino) Rome 1561, 662
Wu Guanzhong, *Pine Spirit*, China 1984 CE, 478

X

Xia dynasty (China), 465

Y

Yakshi, 86, 91
Yakshi Bracket Figure, East torana of the Great Stupa at Sanchi, 90
Yayoi period (Japan c. 400 BCE–300 CE), 106

Yin Hong, *Hundreds of Birds Admiring the Peacocks*, China, late 15th to early 16th century, 468
Yirrkala Bark Petitions (Australia), 43
Youth Pouring Wine into the Kylix of a Companion, A, Greece c. 480 BCE, 196
Yuan dynasty (China, 1279–1368), 464, 465–467
Yun Shouping, *Amaranth*, China 1633–1690, 476, 477
Yunupingu, Galarrwuy, 43

Z

Zeus, 184, 190
Zhao Mengfu, *Autumn Colors on the Qiao and Hua Mountains*, China 1296, 466
Zhou dynasty (China, 1100–221 BCE), 99–101
Zhuangzi (369–286 BCE), 104, 465
Ziggurats, 69, 70, 77
Zoffany, Johann, *Academicians of the Royal Academy* 1771–1772, 652